1995

THE CANADIAN GLOBAL ALMANAC

1995

THE CANADIAN GLOBAL ALMANAC

John Robert Colombo
General Editor

Macmillan Canada
Toronto

Contents

1995 THE CANADIAN GLOBAL ALMANAC

General Editor	**JOHN ROBERT COLOMBO**
Publisher and Editor-in-Chief	**SUSAN GIRVAN**
Contributing Editors	**LIBA BERRY** *(Index)*
	KEVIN COURIER *(Arts & Entertainment)*
	MAGGIE DORNING *(Science)*
	MARTIN LEVIN *(Sports, Hall of Fame)*
	DAVID PHILLIPS *(Climate)*
Design/Typesetting	**JEFFREY STOLBERG DESIGN**
Researchers	**MATTHEW BEHRENS**
	MARIANNE MINNAKER
	SHANNON POTTS
	SONJA RUTHARD
	ELENA SIMONETTI
Cover Design	**BRANT COWIE, ARTPLUS**
Maps	**MAPPING SPECIALISTS**

Comments and Suggestions

Please feel free to send us your comments and any suggestions for subsequent editions. Many readers took the time to drop us notes and letters last year and the correspondence is most welcome, although it is not always possible to respond personally to each writer. Address all correspondence to the General Editor, *The Canadian Global Almanac*, c/o Macmillan Canada, 29 Birch Avenue, Toronto, Ontario M4V 1E2.

A portion of the information in this pub-lication is made available through the co-operation of Statistics Canada. Integral and/or adapted reproductions are published with permission of the Minister of Industry, Science and Technology. Readers wishing further information on any of the subjects credited "Statistics Canada" may obtain copies of related publications by contacting Publications Sales, Statistics Canada, Ottawa, Ontario, Canada K1A 0T6 or by calling (toll free in Canada) 1-800-267-6677; outside Canada, 1-613-951-7277. Readers may also facsimile orders by dialing 1-613-951-1584.

Canadian Cataloguing in Publication Data

The National Library of Canada has cata-logued this publication as follows:

Main entry under title:

The Canadian global almanac

1992-
Annual
"A book of facts".
ISSN 1187-4570
ISBN 0-7715-9015-6 (1995)

1. Almanacs, Canadian (English).*
2. Almanacs.

AY414.C38   031.02   C92-031173-3

Macmillan Canada wishes to thank the Canada Council, the Ontario Ministry of Culture and Communications and the Ontario Arts Council for supporting its publishing program.

Macmillan Canada
A Division of Canada Publishing
Corporation, Toronto

Printed in Canada

Preface

A NEW YEAR BRINGS A NEW ALMANAC. This is the 9th edition of *The Canadian Global Almanac* and we're quite proud of it!

We have spent the last twelve months updating facts, researching new developments, chasing sources, scrutinizing the news, thinking about trends, checking and correcting, and responding to readers' recommendations. As a matter of course, all the relevant statistical matter has been updated.

"The Nation," the political section, now reflects the results of the 1993 federal election (held after we last went to press), so we have taken a closer look at that election to give our readers some idea of what's involved in holding one, and taken a brief look at Elections Canada itself.

The section on the economy has been reorganized to present a more concise financial picture of the state of the nation. "Government Spending," a subsection, brings together formerly scattered facts and figures. Other new features include a capsule look at the General Agreement on Tariffs and Trade (GATT) and an examination of the present standing of the European Union (EU).

We are especially delighted to introduce with this issue full-colour maps of the countries of the world. We have always included information on the world's 232 countries, dependencies and protectorates, but many readers have written urging us to include colour maps of the countries. We are pleased to be able to satisfy that request.

It has taken us the last three editions to completely rebuild the Science section. It is now bigger and better than ever, and it gives a comprehensive, capsule look at the sciences. Especially interesting are two new subsections, Life Sciences and Information Technology.

Should we be awarded a medal for bravery for introducing a section called "Hall of Fame"? Over the years readers have asked us for a "who's who of famous Canadians." We accepted the challenge, but—who, after all, is famous? Our first effort contains over 900 names, but we know this feature is one that will grow from one edition to the next. Send us your list of candidates to add to next year's "Hall of Fame."

"Arts and Entertainment" and "Sports" are popular sections that offer hard-to-come-by information of national and international interest and importance. Not to be overlooked is the "News Events" section, which gives a summary of what has happened in this country and other countries over the last twelve months.

In short, this new edition of *The Canadian Global Almanac* offers something for everyone. Here are Canadian and world facts at your fingertips—whether you need to know them or want to know them!

John Robert Colombo
October 1994

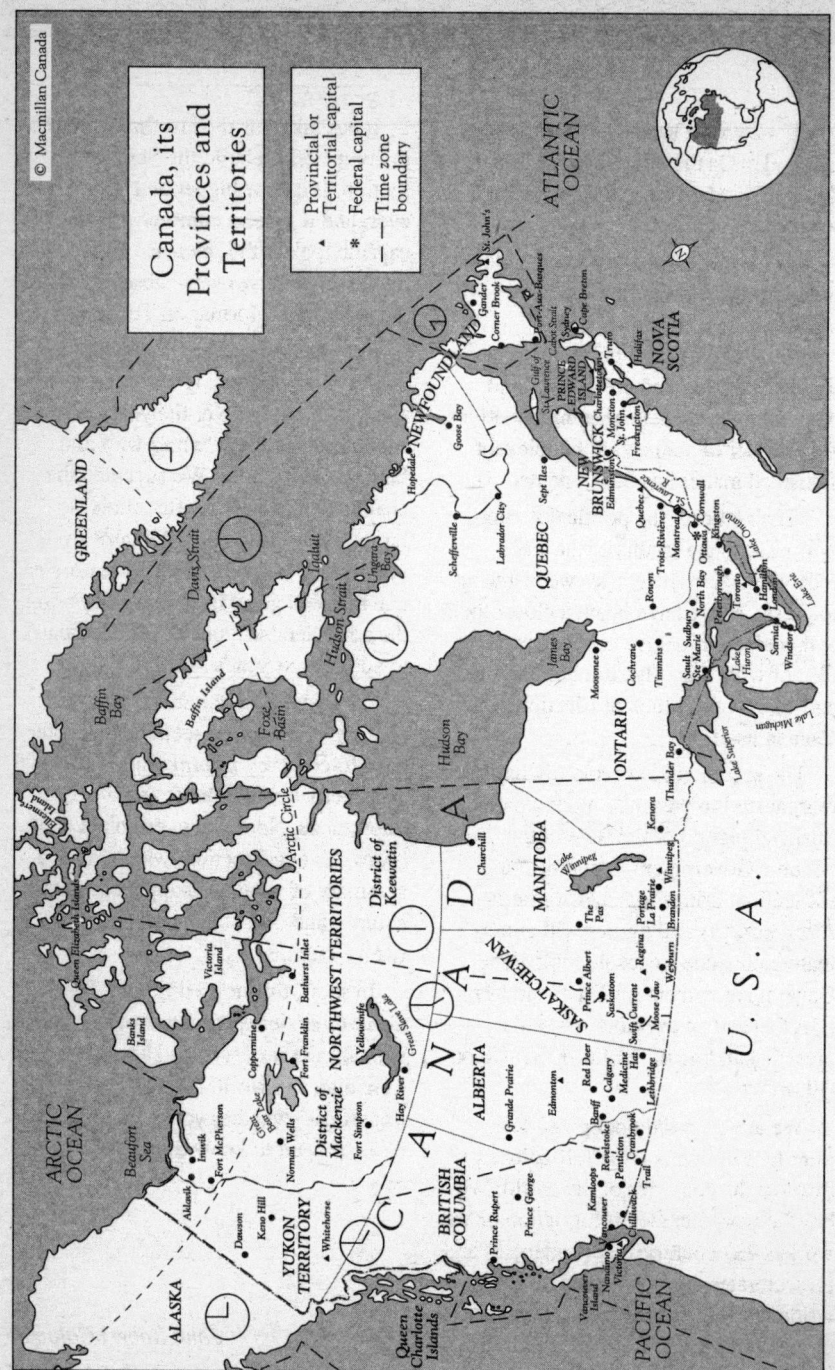

Canada, its Provinces and Territories

© Macmillan Canada

▲ Provincial or Territorial capital
✴ Federal capital
— — Time zone boundary

The Country at a Glance

(as of October 1, 1994)

■ GENERAL

Motto:	A Mari Usque ad Mare (From Sea to Sea)
National Symbols:	the Maple Leaf and the Beaver (both official)
National Game:	lacrosse (summer), hockey (winter)
Official Languages:	English and French
National Anthem:	O Canada
Royal Anthem:	God Save the Queen
Population:	27 296 000 (1991 Census)
Capital City:	Ottawa, Ontario
Provinces:	10
Territories:	2

■ GEOGRAPHY

Area:	9 970 610 sq. km
Length of coastline:	243 792 km (longest in the world)
Length of border with U.S. inc. Alaska:	8 890 km
Longitudinal centre of Canada:	97°W (close to Winnipeg)
Latitudinal centre of Canada:	62°N (close to Yellowknife, NWT)
Geographic centre of Canada:	Arviat, NWT (60°06'30"N, 94°03'30"W)
Greatest distance east to west:	5 514 km (Cape Spear, Nfld. to the Yukon/Alaska border)
Greatest distance north to south:	4 634 km (Cape Columbia, Ellesmere Is. to Middle Is., Lake Erie)

■ POLITICS

Confederation:	July 1, 1867
Governor General:	His Excellency, the Right Honourable Ramon Hnatyshn
Prime Minister:	The Right Honourable Jean Chrétien
Date of last general election:	October 25, 1993
No. of Seats in the House of Commons:	295
No. of Seats in the Senate:	104
House of Commons General Information Inquiry:	613-992-4793
Senate General Inquiry:	1-800-267-7362 (toll free)

■ ECONOMY

Rate of inflation:	2.1% (1992)
Rate of unemployment:	11.3% (1992)
Goods and services tax:	7%, payable on most goods and services

■ SOCIETY

Life expectancy:	**males:** 73.0; **females:** 79.7
Average family income:	$53 131 (1991)
Average family size:	3.1 (1991)
Education:	compulsory to age 16
Health care:	universal publicly-sponsored system

What time is it?

If it's 1:00 p.m. in the Pacific Standard time zone, it is 2 p.m. Mountain Standard Time, 3 p.m. Central Standard Time, 4 p.m. Eastern Standard Time, 5:00 p.m. Atlantic Standard time, and 5:30 p.m. in Newfoundland.

Superlative Canadian Facts

Largest province		Quebec	1 540 680 sq. km
Smallest province		Prince Edward Island	5 660 sq. km
Largest city[1]:	by area	Gagnon, Que.	5 970 sq. km
	by population	Montreal, Que.	1 017 700 people
	by density	Montreal-Nord, Que.	8 187 people/sq. km
Smallest city[1]:	by area	L'Ile-Dorval, Que.	0.18 sq. km
	by population	Gagnon, Que.	5 people
	by density	Gagnon, Que.	0.0008 people/sq. km
Largest island		Baffin Island, NWT	507 451 sq. km
Northernmost point		Cape Columbia, Ellesmere Island, NWT	83° 06'N.–69°57'W.
Southernmost point		Middle Island, Lake Erie, Ont.	41° 41'N.–82°40'W.
Easternmost point		Cape Spear, Nfld.	47° 31'N.–52° 37'W.
Westernmost point		Yukon-Alaska boundary	141° 00'W.
Northernmost community		Grise Fiord, Ellesmere Island, NWT	76° 25'N.–82°54'W.
Southernmost community		Pelee Island South, Ont.	41° 45'N.–82°38'W.
Easternmost community		Blackhead, Nfld.	47°32'N.–52° 39'W.
Westernmost community		Beaver Creek, YT	62°23'N.–140° 52'W.
Highest city		Kimberley, BC	1 128 m
Highest community		Lake Louise, Alta.	1 540 m
Northernmost ice-free port		Stewart, BC	55°56'N.
Longest river		Mackenzie River, NWT	4 241 km
Largest lake (partly) in Canada		Superior, Ont. Total area 84 100 sq. km: 28 700 in Canada; 53 400 in U.S.	
Largest lake (entirely) in Canada		Great Bear Lake, NWT	31 328 sq. km
Deepest lake		Great Slave Lake, NWT	614 m
Highest mountain		Mt. Logan, YT	5 959 m
Highest waterfall		Della Falls, BC	440 m (more than one leap)
Greatest waterfall by volume		Horseshoe Falls, Niagara River, Ont.	5 365 cubic metres/second
Longest bridge		Pierre-Laporte Suspension Bridge, Que.	668 m
Longest covered bridge		at Hartland, NB	391 m
Longest tunnel		Mt. Macdonald Railway Tunnel, Rogers Pass, BC	14.6 km

Source: *Natural Resources Canada; Statistics Canada*

(1) As of 1991 Census. The definition of city varies by province and, for Quebec, includes "ville."

Half an hour later in Newfoundland...

*D*uring *the 19th century (and as long as there were clocks before that), every community around the world set its clocks based on local conditions—when the sun was directly overhead, it was noon. The coming of railways and telegraphs made this system unworkable and railway officials in North America tried to establish a uniform system of time to solve the problem. While US railways prepared to adopt uniform time zones in the US, a Scottish-born Canadian railway surveyor and inventor, Sir Sandford Fleming, proposed an international system that established 24 time zones around the world, with a one hour difference between zones.*

In November of 1883, railway companies in North America adopted his system of standard time. At the International Prime Meridian Conference in Washington in 1884, 25 countries agreed to convert their timekeeping to "standard time." Greenwich Mean Time (GMT) officially became the meridian of the system on January 1, 1885 and during the years following, more and more countries conformed to standard time.

When first adopted, each time zone was exactly 15° wide, but the boundaries have been altered to make more convenient divisions. Time zones west of Greenwich (Canada) are successively one hour earlier than the time in Greenwich—until the 180th meridian where they meet the time zones east of Greenwich. Therefore 15°W is Greenwich Mean Time -1 hour; 30°W is -2 hours; 45°W is -3 hours and 60°W (Sydney, NS) is -4 hours. St. John's, Newfoundland is 52 1/2°W of the meridian, in the middle of a zone and thus the time there is -3 1/2 hours GMT.

LANDFORMS OF CANADA

Canada is the largest country in the Western Hemisphere and the second largest in the world, with a total area of 9,970,610 sq. km. It stretches north to south from Cape Columbia on Ellesmere Island to Middle Island in Lake Erie, a distance of 4,634 km. The greatest east-west distance is 5,514 km from Cape Spear, Nfld, to the Yukon-Alaska border. Within this vast expanse, Canada contains an extremely wide variety of geographical features: the towering peaks of the Rockies, the flat Prairies, the rugged north and the gently rolling landscape of the east. But within this seemingly wide range of features, five areas with common characteristics are found. These physiographic regions are generally used to describe Canada and form the basis of Canada's geographical landforms and geological regions.

■ The Canadian Shield

Also known as the Precambrian Shield, this area is located in the central part of the continent. Viewed from the air it is a vast, inhospitable land of rocks, lakes and trees. It makes up roughly half of Canada's surface area, sweeping around Hudson Bay like a giant horseshoe, but also is the foundation for the rest of the continent.

The Canadian Shield has not always looked as it does today. Early in the Earth's history this area was the site of towering mountains, deep valleys and mighty rivers. The mountains were thrust up by volcanic activity as long as 3.8 billion years ago, during the Precambrian era. Over time, the forces of erosion—wind, water, freezing temperatures, ice—wore down the rocks that formed the mountain peaks and carried the materials away. Now all that remains are the roots of the once-mighty mountains.

The processes of volcanism present at the time of mountain-building caused minerals to form in the cooling rock of the Precambrian mountains. Deep inside the mountains, minerals such as gold, silver, copper and nickel came together into veins of ore. These ore bodies make the Shield a rich storehouse of mineral wealth.

■ The Appalachian Region

To the east of the Shield, this region was also once the site of massive mountain peaks. The rock that forms these peaks is not as old as the rock of the Shield, and is of a type that is more easily eroded. The Appalachian Region runs in a northeasterly direction from the southern United States to Newfoundland.

The mineral deposits found in the region reflect the complexity of the geology, and include gypsum, barite, salt, copper, zinc, lead, gold and silver. Since the end of the mountain-building period, erosion has worn off the tops of the mountains and filled the valleys with sediments, which gives the area its present-day less rugged appearance.

■ The Interior Plains

West of the Shield, rock which formed at the bottom of ancient lakes and seas gives the Prairies their distinctive flatness.

The Interior Plains occupy the central portion of the continent. Minerals found in the Interior Plains include potash, a substance produced when lakes and shallow seas evaporate, leaving deposits. Potash deposits in Saskatchewan are among the largest in the world. Coal, oil and natural gas were formed from organic materials trapped by the sedimentary layers during Palaeozoic times. An extension of the Interior Plains thrusts up between the Canadian Shield and the Appalachian Region, forming the Great Lakes-St. Lawrence Lowlands landform area. Soils throughout the Interior Plains are fertile, since the sedimentary materials that are found in the Plains break down easily.

Other lowland areas were formed during the Palaeozoic era as a result of the deposit of sediment which created the Interior Plains. The Hudson Bay Lowlands on the southwestern edge of Hudson Bay are relatively thin layers of sedimentary rock on top of the Precambrian Shield. The Arctic Lowlands, between the Shield and the Innuition Mountains of the high Arctic, are similar in age and characteristics to the material of the Interior Plains.

■ The Western Cordillera

As the Precambrian mountains eroded, the sedimentary layers were deposited over a great distance and formed the Appalachian Region to the east. These deposits also provided the material from which future landforms would be built to the west. These landforms are now known as the Western Cordillera.

When the continent started its westward movement about 200 million years ago, its leading edge was forced against the adjacent oceanic plate and the land moved overtop the ocean. Geologists speculate that the tremendous pressure exerted during this process caused the sedimentary layers of the plate's edge to buckle into a massive dome. Magma, the hot fluid substance below the Earth's crust, flowed into the dome and formed a core which eventually collapsed between 65 and 160 million years ago, breaking the rock layers. This core stretches along the edge of the continental plate and absorbs the pressure of the two plates as they press upon each other.

The Western Cordillera is an area of great complexity; rocks composed of different materials and through different processes are thoroughly mixed. The Coast Ranges which form the leading western edge of the continent are composed of both igneous and metamorphic rock. The interior of the Cordillera is a jumble of plateaus, folded and broken rock layers and recent volcanoes. The sedimentary materials of the Rockies on the eastern edge of the Cordillera were folded and broken during a period of mountain-building in Eocene times, some 40-65 million years ago.

The Cordillera contains minerals associated with all the processes involved in its creation. The igneous rocks of the western part of the Cordillera are a major source of minerals including lead, zinc, silver, copper and gold. The sedimentary deposits of the eastern Cordillera are responsible for the coal and petroleum found there.

■ Innuitian Region

Mountain-building shaped the landforms of the high Arctic during the Devonian period (about 405 million years ago). The most recent activities appear to have occurred about 30 million years ago, which was long after the mountain-building period that thrust up the Rocky Mountains in the Cordillera.

Little detail is known about this region because research is so difficult in the inhospitable climate, but some geologists have suggested mountain-building is the result of the North American plate advancing on the Eurasian plate.

The topography of this region is characterized by low plateau mountains, with ridges as high as 3,000 m. The area is composed mainly of sedimentary rocks but includes some metamorphic and volcanic rocks.

For more information on geological time periods, see the chart in the Science and Nature Section.

The Rock Beneath Your Feet

T *here are three kinds of rock classified according to how they were formed. The most prevalent type of rock is sedimentary, so called because it is formed when sediment (material that settles at the bottom of a liquid) settles into the bottom of bodies of water (such as lakes or rivers) in layers. As the layers build up, the weight of the new layers compresses the matter at the bottom, squeezing it together and making it more solid; the process is helped along when the chemicals in the water form a kind of glue, but it still takes thousands of years to complete. Limestone, sandstone, coal and shale are common examples of sedimentary rock.*

Igneous rock is the second most common type, formed when molten magma from the earth's interior cools (the word igneous comes from the Latin word ignis or fire). This type of rock is often found where geological plates meet or diverge and material has seeped through the cracks; it is also found below the surface. Examples are granite, pumice, slate and obsidian.

The least common type of rock is metamorphic, named because it is a result of the material being changed by geological processes. For example, if a rock is buried, new pressures or chemical activity may cause it to change its nature; marble and gneiss are examples of metamorphic rock.

The Great Lakes

The Great Lakes form the largest body of fresh water in the world and with their connecting waterways are the largest inland water transportation unit. They enable shipping to reach the Atlantic via the St. Lawrence River; the Gulf of Mexico via the Illinois Waterway, from Lake Michigan to the Mississippi River; a third outlet connects with the Hudson River and thence the Atlantic via the New York State Barge Canal System.

	Superior	Michigan	Huron	Erie	Ontario
Length in km	563	494	332	388	311
Breadth in km	257	190	295	92	85
Deepest soundings in metres	405	281	229	64	244
Volume of water in cubic km	12 100	4 920	3 540	484	1 640
Area[1] (sq. km) in US	53 400	57 800	23 600	12 900	8 960
Area[1] (sq. km) in Canada	28 700	0	36 000	12 800	10 000
Total Area[1] (sq. km) US and Canada	82 100	57 800	59 600	25 700	18 960
National boundary line in km	430	0	446	404	281

Source: *Natural Resources Canada*   (1) Does not include islands larger than 0.052 sq. km.

Largest Lakes in Canada

Lake	Area[1] (sq. km)	Lake	Area[1] (sq. km)
Superior, Ont.[2]	82 100	Winnipegosis, Man.	5 374
Huron, Ont.[3]	59 600	Nipigon, Ont.	4 848
Great Bear, NWT	31 328	Manitoba, Man.	4 624
Great Slave, NWT	28 568	Dubawnt, NWT	3 833
Erie, Ont.[4]	25 700	Lake of the Woods, Ont./Man.[6]	4 472
Winnipeg, Man.	24 387	Amadjuak, NWT	3 115
Ontario, Ont.[5]	18 960	Melville, Nfld	3 069
Athabasca, Sask.	7 935	Wollaston, Sask.	2 681
Reindeer, Sask./Man.	6 650	Lac Mistassini, Que.	2 335
Smallwood Reservoir, Nfld	6 527	Nueltin, NWT/Man.	2 279
Nettilling, NWT	5 542	Southern Indian, Man.	2 247

Source: *Natural Resources Canada*

(1) Total area, including islands except for the Great Lakes, where area does not include islands larger than 0.052 sq. km. (2) Includes 53,400 sq. km in U.S. (3) Includes 23,600 sq. km in U.S. (4) Includes 12,900 sq. km in U.S. (5) Includes 8 960 sq. km in U.S. (6) Includes 1,322 sq. km in U.S.

Largest Islands in Canada

Island	Area (sq. km)	Island	Area (sq. km)
Baffin, NWT	507 451	Prince Patrick, NWT	15 848
Victoria, NWT	217 291	King William, NWT	13 111
Ellesmere, NWT	196 236	Ellef Ringnes, NWT	11 295
Newfoundland (main island)	108 860	Bylot, NWT	11 067
Banks, NWT	70 028	Cape Breton, N.S.	10 311
Devon, NWT	55 247	Prince Charles, NWT	9 521
Axel Heiberg, NWT	43 178	Anticosti Island, Que.	7 941
Melville, NWT	42 149	Cornwallis, NWT	6 995
Southampton, NWT	41 214	Graham, BC	6 361
Prince of Wales, NWT	33 339	Prince Edward Island (main island)	5 620
Vancouver, BC	31 285	Coats, NWT	5 498
Somerset, NWT	24 786	Amund Ringnes, NWT	5 255
Bathurst, NWT	16 042	Mackenzie King, NWT	5 048

Source: *Natural Resources Canada*

Canada's Highest Waterfalls

Name	Vertical drop (metres)	Location	Latitude	Longitude
Della Falls[1]	440	Della Lake, BC	49° 27'	125° 32'
Takakkaw Falls[1]	254	From the Daly Glacier, BC	51° 30'	116° 28'
Hunlen Falls	253	Atnarko River, BC	52° 17'	125° 46'
Panther Falls	183	Nigel Creek, Alta	52° 10'	117° 03'
Helmcken Falls	137	Murtle River, BC	51° 57'	120° 11'
Bridal Veil Falls	122	Bridal Creek, BC	49° 11'	121° 44'
Virginia Falls	90	South Nahanni River, NWT	61° 36'	125° 44'
Montmorency, Chute	84	Rivière Montmorency, Que.	46° 53'	71° 09'
Ouiatchouan, Chute	79	Rivière Ouiatchouaniche, Que.	48° 26'	72° 10'
Churchill Falls	75	Churchill River, Nfld	53° 36'	64° 19'
Brandywine Falls	61	Brandywine Creek, BC	50° 02'	123° 07'
Niagara Falls				
American Falls	59	Niagara River, US	43° 05'	79° 05'
Horseshoe Falls	57	Niagara River, Ont.	43° 05'	79° 04'
Wilberforce Falls	49	Hood River, NWT	67° 06'	108° 47'

Source: *Natural Resources Canada*

(1) Falls with more than one leap

Longest Rivers in Canada

River	Length (km)	Flows Into
Mackenzie	4 241	Arctic Ocean
Yukon	3 185	Bering Sea
St. Lawrence	3 058	Gulf of St. Lawrence
Nelson	2 575	Hudson Bay
Columbia	2 000	Pacific Ocean
Saskatchewan	1 939	Lake Winnipeg
Peace	1 923	Lake Athabasca
Churchill (Man.)	1 609	Hudson Bay
South Saskatchewan	1 392	Saskatchewan R.
Fraser	1 370	Pacific Ocean
North Saskatchewan	1 287	Saskatchewan R.
Ottawa	1 271	St Lawrence R.
Athabasca	1 231	Lake Athabasca
Liard	1 115	Mackenzie R.
Assiniboine	1 070	Red R.
Severn	982	Hudson Bay
Albany	982	James Bay
Back	974	Arctic Ocean
Thelon	904	Hudson Bay
La Grande Rivière	893	James Bay
Red	877	Lake Winnipeg

River	Length (km)	Flows Into
Rivière Koksoak	874	Ungava Bay
Churchill (Nfld)	856	Atlantic Ocean
Coppermine	845	Arctic Ocean
Dubawnt	842	Hudson Bay
Winnipeg	813	Hudson Bay
Kootenay	780	Columbia R.
Rivière Nottaway	776	James Bay
Rivière Rupert	763	James Bay
Rivière Eastmain	756	James Bay
Attawapiskat	748	James Bay
Kazan	732	Hudson Bay
Grande rivière de la Baleine	724	Hudson Bay
Red Deer	724	Saskatchewan R.
Porcupine	721	Pacific Ocean (via the Yukon)
Hay	702	Great Slave Lake
Rivière Saguenay	698	St. Lawrence R.
Anderson	692	Arctic Ocean
Peel	684	Arctic Ocean
Fairford	684	Hudson Bay
Saint John	673	Bay of Fundy

Source: *Natural Resources Canada*

Did You Know?

*T*he Earth's surface is mostly water—globally the ratio of land to water is 1:2.43, but it varies from north to south. The northern hemisphere is 60.7% water and 39.3% land; in the southern hemisphere, it's much more lopsided, with 80.9% water and only 19.1% land.

And the ratio is not fixed: warming climate trends could to raise coastal sea levels up to 1 metre during the next hundred years.

Highest Peaks in Canada

Mountain	Range	Prov./Terr.	Elev. (m)	Mountain	Range	Prov./Terr.	Elev. (m)
Mt. Logan	St. Elias Mtns	YT	5 959	Mt. Cook	St. Elias Mtns	YT/Alaska	4 194
Mt. St. Elias	St. Elias Mtns	YT/Alaska	5 489	Mt. Quincy Adams	St. Elias Mtns	BC/Alaska	4 133
Mt. Lucania	St. Elias Mtns	YT	5 226	Mt. Craig	St. Elias Mtns	YT	4 039
King Peak	St. Elias Mtns	YT	5 173	Mt. Waddington	Coast Mtns	BC	4 016
Mt. Steele	St. Elias Mtns	YT	5 067	Mt. Robson	Rocky Mtns	BC	3 954
Mt. Wood	St. Elias Mtns	YT	4 838	Mt. Root	St. Elias Mtns	BC/Alaska	3 901
Mt. Vancouver	St. Elias Mtns	YT/Alaska	4 785	Mt. Malaspina	St. Elias Mtns	YT	3 886
Mt. Macaulay	St. Elias Mtns	YT	4 663	Mt. Queen Mary	St. Elias Mtns	YT	3 886
Mt. Slaggard	St. Elias Mtns	YT	4 663	Mt. Badham	St. Elias Mtns	YT	3 848
Fairweather Mtn.	St. Elias Mtns	BC/Alaska	4 663	Mt. Tiedemann	Coast Mtns	BC	3 848
Mt. Hubbard	St. Elias Mtns	YT/Alaska	4 577	Combatant Mtn.	Coast Mtns	BC	3 756
Mt. Walsh	St. Elias Mtns	YT	4 505	Mt. Columbia	Rocky Mtns	Alta/BC	3 747
Mt. Alverstone	St. Elias Mtns	YT/Alaska	4 439	North Twin	Rocky Mtns	Alta	3 733
McArthur Peak	St. Elias Mtns	YT	4 344	Asperity Mtn.	Coast Mtns	BC	3 716
Mt. Augusta	St. Elias Mtns	YT/Alaska	4 289	Mt. Clemenceau	Rocky Mtns	BC	3 642
Mt. Kennedy	St. Elias Mtns	YT	4 235	Serra Peaks	Coast Mtns	BC	3 642
Avalanche Peak	St. Elias Mtns	YT	4 212	Mt. Alberta	Rocky Mtns	Alta	3 620
Mt. Strickland	St. Elias Mtns	YT	4 212	Mt. Assiniboine	Rocky Mtns	Alta/BC	3 618
Mt. Newton	St. Elias Mtns	YT	4 210				

Source: *Natural Resources Canada*

Highest Point in Each Province and Territory

Province/Territory	Highest Point	Elev. (m)
Newfoundland	Mt. Caubvick[1]	1 652
Prince Edward Island	46° 20'—63° 25' (Queen's County)	142
Nova Scotia	46° 42'—60° 36' (Cape Breton Highlands)	532
New Brunswick	Mt. Carleton	817
Quebec	Mont D'Iberville[2]	1 652
Ontario	Ishpatina Ridge	693
Manitoba	Baldy Mtn.	832
Saskatchewan	Cypress Hills	1 468
Alberta	Mt. Columbia	3 747
British Columbia	Fairweather Mtn.	4 663
Yukon Territory	Mt. Logan	5 959
Northwest Territories	61° 52'—127° 42' (unnamed peak, Mackenzie Mtns.)	2 773

Source: *Natural Resources Canada*

(1) On the Nfld/Que. border; also known as Mt. D'Iberville in Quebec; next highest point in Nfld is Cirque Mt. at 1,568 m. (2) On the Nfld/ Que. border; also known as Mt. Caubvick in Newfoundland; next highest point in Que. is Mont Jacques-Cartier at 1,268 m.

Defining Elevation

*E*levations in Canada are measured above Mean Sea Level—but what is Mean Sea Level? It is the average level of the sea at a particular location. Sea level varies from place to place along our coasts due to geographic conditions, and is also influenced by factors like the rotation of the earth, tides and gravity, which is why Mean Sea Level must be calculated at a particular site. It is most accurately determined by calculating the average water level based on 19 years of hourly readings at that site.

In Canada, readings for Mean Sea Level are taken at Halifax, Yarmouth, Pointe-au-Pere, Vancouver and Prince Rupert, and an average of each site's average readings defines the zero point. This zero point is then used to determine elevations throughout Canada.

VEGETATION

Coniferous forests dominated by spruce, fir and pine cover much of the Canadian landscape, sweeping across the continent in a broad band. Through the rest of the country there is a range of forest conditions. To the north, cold temperatures limit growth and the trees become small and fewer in number. At the tree line, trees grow only in sheltered river valleys. The tree line marks the northern extent of forests and the beginning of tundra conditions.

The massive spruce, fir and pine of the forests along the coast of British Columbia are encouraged by a friendly climate. The moisture-laden winds from the Pacific Ocean keep the land well-supplied with rain. Under these conditions tree growth is rapid: the soils are constantly being replenished with minerals by the rains, and plant decay is also rapid in the damp conditions, thereby releasing more minerals for tree growth. With average monthly temperatures seldom going below freezing, the growing season is long. Coniferous trees thrive under such conditions.

The Interior Plains is one region of Canada that is not covered by forests because there is not enough precipitation, or available moisture, to sustain tree growth. In Alberta, Saskatchewan and Manitoba, forests gradually give way from north to south through a transitional area called the park belt, which contains both trees and grassland, before yielding to grasslands. Within these provinces, there are areas where moisture levels are insufficient to support grasslands and even hardy grasses have difficulty growing. During the 1930s, the lack of rainfall in the Interior Plains led to "dust bowl" conditions because vegetation could not grow enough to anchor the soil.

The forests of southeastern Canada are mixed, containing both coniferous and deciduous trees. Adequate rainfall and warm temperatures allow the less hardy species such as oak, maple, hickory and walnut to flourish in southern Ontario and Quebec and the Maritime provinces.

The Arctic tundra is so very dry and cold that the growing season is very limited. The vegetation of the tundra consists of mosses, lichen, dwarf bushes and heather. These plants are able to grow because they have adapted to the difficult conditions through characteristics such as small size and slow growth. Some shrubs and lichen grow so slowly that their development must be measured in centimetres per century.

Spring and Fall Frost Dates in Canada

Frost occurs whenever temperatures fall to 0°C or lower. All dates and values are based on the available data during the period 1951-1980. Data reported from airport stations unless * designates city office station.

	1 in 10 Chance Last Spring Frost After Date	1 in 10 Chance First Fall Frost Before Date	Frost-free Period (days)	Growing Degree-Days Above 5°C[1]
Newfoundland				
Corner Brook*	June 10	Sept. 8	139	1 370
St. John's*	June 24	Sept. 19	131	1 196
Prince Edward Island				
Charlottetown	May 27	Oct. 6	151	1 626
Nova Scotia				
Halifax	May 28	Sept. 30	155	1 694
New Brunswick				
Fredericton	June 10	Sept. 13	126	1 770
Moncton	June 10	Sept. 14	124	1 650
Saint John	June 10	Sept. 18	139	1 499
Quebec				
Chicoutimi*	June 4	Sept. 18	135	1 655
Gaspé*	June 12	Sept. 11	123	1 428
Montreal	May 19	Sept. 26	157	2 113
Quebec	May 28	Sept. 14	137	1 690 ▶

	1 in 10 Chance Last Spring Frost After Date	1 in 10 Chance First Fall Frost Before Date	Frost-free Period (days)	Growing Degree-Days Above 5°C[1]
▶ Schefferville	June 27	Aug. 22	77	614
Ontario				
Kitchener*	May 25	Sept. 17	151	2 169
London	May 25	Sept. 23	147	2 139
Moosonee*	July 6	July 30	70	1 107
Ottawa	May 25	Sept. 21	147	2 043
St. Catharines*	May 18	Oct. 5	173	2 429
Sudbury	June 11	Sept. 11	128	1 664
Thunder Bay	June 13	Aug. 29	104	1 425
Timmins	June 23	Aug. 19	91	1 408
Toronto	May 25	Sept. 18	149	2 127
Windsor	May 10	Oct. 3	177	2 533
Manitoba				
Brandon	June 9	Aug. 31	108	1 643
Churchill	July 7	Aug. 20	76	555
Flin Flon	June 10	Sept. 2	115	1 340
Winnipeg	June 10	Sept. 11	121	1 785
Saskatchewan				
Prince Albert	June 21	Aug. 17	95	1 412
Regina	June 14	Aug. 27	109	1 677
Saskatoon	June 10	Sept. 1	117	1 620
Alberta				
Banff*	June 30	Aug. 6	89	1 081
Calgary	June 10	Aug. 27	112	1 387
Edmonton	June 14	Aug. 13	105	1 328
Fort McMurray	June 30	Aug. 2	84	1 290
Lethbridge	May 31	Sept. 2	124	1 776
Medicine Hat	May 27	Sept. 8	129	1 943
Peace River	June 23	Aug. 13	93	1 239
British Columbia				
Fort Nelson	June 7	Aug. 14	106	1 266
Kamloops	May 18	Sept. 19	149	2 216
Penticton	May 23	Sept. 14	148	2 136
Prince George	July 1	Aug. 11	85	1 199
Prince Rupert	May 25	Sept. 28	156	1 148
Vancouver	Apr. 21	Oct. 13	216	1 994
Victoria	Apr. 30	Oct. 17	201	1 864
Yukon				
Dawson*	June 16	Aug. 6	91	1 015
Whitehorse	June 24	Aug. 13	82	897
Northwest Territories				
Alert*	July 15	July 16	4	35
Iqaluit	July 12	July 26	59	179
Resolute	July 15	July 16	9	33
Yellowknife	June 9	Sept. 3	111	1 027

Source: *Environment Canada*
(1) Growing degree days represent the average total number of heat units (daily mean temp. -5°C) during the growing season

---

Measuring the Weather

An anemometer measures wind speed in km per hour. ▲ *A barometer measures atmospheric pressure in kilopascals.* ▲ *A Campbell Stokes recorder measures sunshine in hours.* ▲ *A rain gauge measures rainfall in millimetres.* ▲ *A ruler or a snow gauge measures snowfall in centimetres.* ▲ *A thermometer measures temperature in °C.* ▲ *A wet bulb thermometer measures humidity in °C/percent.* ▲ *A wind vane measures wind direction according to N E S W.*

AGRICULTURE

There are four main types of farms in Canada: livestock farms, grain farms producing such crops as wheat and oats, mixed farms producing both grain and livestock, and special crop farms producing vegetables, fruits, tobacco and other products. Both the type and amount of farming within Canada are affected by climate and location.

■ The Atlantic Region

The Atlantic region is an area of diverse agricultural activity. Newfoundland, because of poorly developed soils and a difficult climate, has a limited agricultural industry supplying only local markets. Encouraged by a moist climate and silty, stone-free soils, farming is the leading industry on Prince Edward Island; potatoes are the main crop. The land also supports mixed grains and dairy farms.

Nova Scotia's main agricultural areas surround the Bay of Fundy and Northumberland Strait where they are protected from Atlantic gales; dairy farming and poultry production are common. Nova Scotia's Annapolis Valley is famous for fruit, mainly apples. In New Brunswick, potatoes and livestock are produced in the Saint John River valley, and there is mixed farming in the northwest of the province.

■ The Central Region

In Canada's central region, the fertile soils and moist climate of southern Ontario and Quebec support a thriving agricultural industry. Although these growing conditions allow a variety of crops, the population concentration in this area encourages specialization in products with high transportation costs. Dairy farms are concentrated around Montreal and in southwestern Ontario, supplying milk, butter and cheese to the major centres such as London, Hamilton, Toronto, Kingston, Montreal and Quebec City. Vegetable crops are also grown near these centres. Farms specializing in poultry and egg production, sheep and hogs are also common.

The Niagara Peninsula, between Lakes Ontario and Erie, is a major fruit-growing centre. The moderating effects of the lakes delay the growth of the fruit trees in the spring until the danger of frost is past. Tender fruit crops—peaches, pears, plums and cherries—as well as grapes thrive in these conditions. Tobacco grows well on the glacially-created sand plains of southwestern Ontario.

■ The Prairie Provinces

Manitoba, Saskatchewan and Alberta contain 80 percent of Canada's farmland. Here, a combination of flat, easily-worked land, fertile soils, long sunny summer days and sufficient precipitation encourages the healthy growth of high-quality grains. This area grows most of Canada's wheat, about 90 percent of its barley and rye, and more than 75 percent of its oats.

Manitoba grows canola/rapeseed and flax in addition to wheat and other grains. Mixed farming in the province emphasizes beef cattle. Dairy farms are common around Winnipeg. Saskatchewan grows about 60 percent of Canada's wheat and large quantities of other grains. Mixed farming, poultry, egg and livestock production contribute to the provincial economy. Alberta, also a major grain producer, has more beef cattle ranches than any other province. They are located mainly in the south of the province and in the foothills of the Rocky Mountains where the steep slopes and dry land is unsuited to growing crops. ▶

*A*griculture Canada has designated ten plant hardiness zones for Canada, ranging from 0 (the coldest) to 9 (the mildest), and classified common Canadian shrubs and plants according to their ability to thrive (or not) in each zone's weather conditions.

Weather factors that affect a plant's survival include the lowest winter temperature, the length of frost-free growing time, the average amount of summer rainfall, the highest temperatures during the growing season and the average amount of snow cover and wind during the year. Other factors to consider are the age of the plants (young plants may need protection during their first winter), whether the growing area is much higher than the surrounding area, and how close the growing area is to the next zone boundary. These zones are not absolute, but they can tell you what should survive.

▶ ■ **The Pacific Region**

In the Pacific region, only 2 percent of British Columbia is agricultural land. But the pockets of farmland are extremely productive. The lower mainland and the southern tip of Vancouver Island comprise the Georgia Strait agricultural region, an area concentrating on dairy farming and poultry raising to supply the province's population centres. Other crops include raspberries, strawberries, peas, tomatoes and flowers.

The Okanagan Valley contains 90 percent of British Columbia's orchards, producing grapes, apples and tender fruit such as peaches, plums, apricots and cherries. Here, local climatic and physiographic characteristics have resulted in conditions suitable for the orchard industry, although irrigation is often necessary and frost damage is a hazard. Beef cattle and sheep are raised in the interior of the province, where growing conditions are not suitable for crops requiring cultivation, but grazing can be carried out.

■ **The North**

Canada's North generally has soil and climatic conditions unsuited to agriculture. A small number of farms produce some dairy products, beef cattle and vegetables for the local market.

CLIMATE

Within Canada, climate is primarily affected by surrounding landforms, proximity to large bodies of water and the degree of latitude.

Landforms Air masses are forced to rise over mountains which lie in their path. As this happens, the air cools and its ability to retain moisture is reduced. Condensation then occurs and precipitation falls in the form of snow or rain. For instance, Prince Rupert on the western side of the Coastal Mountains receives over 2,500 mm of precipitation annually.

On the leeward side of the mountains (the side away from the wind), the air mass descends, warms and is able to once again retain moisture. Moreover, there may be little moisture left in the air mass. Thus precipitation is light and a rain-shadow effect is created. In a rain-shadow area, such as near Kamloops, BC, desert-like conditions exist.

Water Parts of Canada near large bodies of water have more moderate climates due to the differing abilities of land and water to gain or lose heat. Whereas water can act like a heat bank, releasing accumulated heat through the fall and early winter and warming the land nearby, the reverse is also true. In the spring and early summer, the water is cooler than the land and can keep the land temperature lower.

Wind direction also determines the degree to which this influence is felt. On the Pacific coast the prevailing westerlies blow off the water onto the land and the influence of the Pacific Ocean is keenly felt. On the Atlantic coast, the westerlies blow off the land onto the water so the effect of the Atlantic Ocean is not as pronounced. Victoria has a monthly low of 4.1°C and a range of only 11.5°C while Halifax has a monthly low of -3.6°C and a range of 22.4°C.

Latitude Latitude is the distance north or south of the equator and is expressed in degrees. Its effects on climate are twofold. Firstly, the further north the location, the more the curvature of the earth results in the sunlight spreading over a greater surface area. This decreases the solar radiation per unit area of ground so that less warmth from the sun is felt. Secondly, solar radiation has to travel a greater distance through the atmosphere at higher latitudes which again reduces the amount of energy reaching the earth.

Other Factors Because the prevailing wind direction is from west to east, the air masses move eastward across the continent picking up moisture from lakes and rivers and releasing it further along. Therefore, generally, precipitation increases with greater distance eastward from the central continent: the average precipitation in Winnipeg is 526 mm, Toronto 762 mm, Montreal 946 mm and Halifax 1 282 mm.

Also, the Labrador Current affects climate on the Atlantic coast. This cold current within the Atlantic Ocean flows south along the coast of Newfoundland and Labrador and reduces the moderating effect of the ocean on the land. It also causes the thick Newfoundland fog when relatively warm air is cooled from below on contact with the cold waters.

A Glossary of Weather Terms

air mass: an extensive body of air with a fairly uniform distribution of moisture and temperature throughout

atmosphere: the envelope of air surrounding the earth. Most weather events are confined to the lower 10 km of the atmosphere.

atmospheric pressure: the force exerted on the earth by the weight of the atmosphere

blizzard: severe winter weather condition characterized by low temperatures, strong winds above 40 km/h, and visibility of less than 1 km due to blowing snow; condition lasts three hours or more

blowing snow: snow lifted from the earth's surface by the wind to a height of two metres or more. Blowing snow is higher than drifting snow.

bright sunshine: sunshine intense enough to burn a mark on recording paper mounted in the Campbell-Stokes sunshine recorder. The daily period of bright sunshine is less than that of visible sunshine because the sun's rays are not intense enough to burn the paper just after sunrise, near sunset and under cloudy conditions.

Chinook (also snow-eater): a dry, warm, strong wind that blows down the eastern slopes of the Rocky Mountains in North America. The warmth and dryness are due principally to heating by compression as the air descends the mountain slope.

cold wave: an occurrence of dangerous cold conditions, when temperatures often dip below -18°C, that usually lasts longer than a few days

deep low: used to describe the central barometric pressure of a low [usually when it is about 975 millibars (97.50 kPa or less)]. Often has winds of gale to storm force around the low.

developing low: a low in which the central pressure is decreasing with time. Winds would normally increase as the low deepens.

dew point temperature: the temperature at which air becomes saturated, allowing condensation of water vapour as frost, fog, dew, mist or precipitation.

drizzle: precipitation consisting of numerous minute water droplets which appear to float; the droplets are much smaller than in rain.

filling low: a low in which the central pressure is increasing with time., i.e. the low is gradually weakening

flash floods: a very rapid rise of water with little or no advance warning, most often when an intense thunderstorm drops a huge rainfall on a fairly small area in a very short space of time.

fog: a cloud based at the earth's surface consisting of tiny water droplets or, under very cold conditions, ice crystals or ice fog; generally found in calm or low wind conditions. Under foggy conditions, visibility is reduced to less than one km.

freezing precipitation: supercooled water drops of drizzle, or rain which freeze on impact to form a coating of ice upon the ground or any objects they strike

front: the boundary between two different air masses which have originated from widely separated regions. A cold front is the leading edge of an advancing cold air mass, while a warm front is the trailing edge of a retreating cold air mass.

frost: the deposit of ice crystals that occurs when the air temperature is at or below the freezing point of water. The term frost is also used to describe the icy deposits of water vapor that may form on the ground or on other surfaces like car windshields, which are colder than the surrounding air and which have a temperature below freezing.

gale: a strong wind. A gale warning is issued for expected winds of 65 to 100 km/h (34 to 47 knots).

gust: a sudden, brief increase in wind speed, for generally less than 20 seconds

heat wave: a period with more than three consecutive days of maximum temperatures at or above 32°C

high pressure: a term for an area of high (maximum) pressure with a closed, clockwise (in the Northern Hemisphere) circulation of air

humidex: a measure of what hot weather "feels like." Air of a given temperature and moisture content is equated in comfort to air with a higher temperature and that of negligible moisture content. At a humidex of 30°C some people begin to experience discomfort.

hurricane: a tropical storm with wind speeds of 120 km/h (65 knots) or more that can be many thousands of square kilometres in size. The storms originate over the warm tropical ocean as a small low-pressure system. They have a life span of several days and occur most frequently between August and October.

ice pellets: precipitation consisting of fragments of ice, 5 mm or less in diameter, that bounce when hitting a hard surface, making a sound upon impact

inversion: the term refers to a temperature increase with height, where the usual pattern is a decrease in temperature within increasing height.

isobar: a line on a weather map or chart connecting points of equal pressure. The large concentric lines on television or newspaper weather maps are isobars.

killing frost: a frost severe enough to end the growing season, usually when the air temperature falls below -2°C

land breeze: a small-scale wind set off when the air temperature over water is warmer than that over adjacent land. The land breeze develops at night and blows from the land out to the sea or onto the lake. Its counterpart is the sea or lake breeze.

low pressure: an area of low (minimum) atmospheric pressure that has a closed counter-clockwise circulation in the Northern Hemisphere

peak wind (gust): the highest instantaneous wind speed recorded for a specific time period

precipitation: any and all forms of water, whether liquid or solid, that fall from the atmosphere and reach the earth's surface. A day with measurable precipitation is a day when the water equivalent of the precipitation is equal to or greater than 0.2 mm.

probability of precipitation (POP): subjective numerical estimates of your chances of encountering measurable precipitation at some time during the forecast period. For example, a 40% probability of rain means there are four chances in 10 of getting wet. They cannot be used to predict when, where or how much precipitation will occur.

relative humidity: the ratio of water vapour in the air at a given temperature to the maximum which could exist at that temperature. It is usually expressed as a percentage.

ridge: an elongated area of high pressure extending from the centre of a high pressure region; the opposite of a trough.

sea breeze: a small-scale wind set off when the air temperature over land is greater than that over the adjacent sea. The sea breeze develops during the day and blows from the sea to the land. Its counterpart is the land breeze.

small craft warning: issued when winds over the coastal marine areas are expected to reach and maintain speeds of 20 to 33 knots

snow: precipitation consisting of white or translucent ice crystals and often agglomerated into snowflakes. A day with measurable snow is a day when the total snowfall is at least 0.2 cm.

squall: a strong, sudden wind which generally lasts a few minutes then quickly decreases in speed. Squalls are generally associated with severe thunderstorms.

storm track: the path taken by a low-pressure centre

storm warning: the wind warning that is issued to mariners when winds are expected to be 48 to 63 knots

thunderstorm: a local storm, usually produced by a cumulonimbus cloud, and always accompanied by thunder and lightning. A thunderstorm day is a day when thunder is heard or when lightning is seen (rain and snow need not have fallen).

tornado (also twister): a violently rotating column of air that is usually visible as a funnel cloud hanging from dark thunderstorm clouds. It is one of the least extensive of all storms, but in violence, it is the most destructive.

trough: an elongated area of low pressure extending from the centre of a low pressure region; the opposite of a ridge

typhoon: a severe tropical cyclone in the Pacific Ocean, counterpart of the Atlantic hurricane

waterspout: a small whirling storm over water which is spawned from the base of a thunderstorm. It is similar to but generally not as severe as a tornado.

weather advisory: issued when forecast conditions are expected to cause general inconvenience or concern, and do not pose a serious enough threat to require a weather warning. An advisory will often precede a warning.

weather warning: when severe local storms are expected, or have actually been sighted or detected by radar, eg. severe thunderstorm or tornado warnings.

Weatheradio: this is the name of Environment Canada's weather information broadcast network. The network has transmitters in every region and listeners need a receiver, which can be purchased from electronic equipment dealers, to pick up the broadcasts. Weatheradio signals warnings of severe weather automatically to receivers equipped with special alarm devices for that purpose.

westerlies (west-wind belt): the pronounced west-to-east motion of the atmosphere centred over middle latitudes from about 35 to 65° latitude.

wind chill: a simple measure of the chilling effect experienced by the human body when strong winds are combined with freezing temperatures. The larger the wind chill, the faster the rate of cooling. The wind chill factor is expressed in watts per square metre or in °C (an equivalent temperature).

wind direction: the direction from which the wind is blowing

Source: *Environment Canada*

Canadian Weather Highlights from July 1993 to June 1994

JULY 1993: Apart from southern Ontario and Quebec, July was cloudy, wet and cool across Canada. Sunshine was low across British Columbia, hovering near 60% of normal in the south. The dry areas were the western Maritimes, where only 50 to 70 percent of normal precipitation was recorded, and southern Ontario, where some locales experienced their driest July since the 70s.

Early in July very warm air prevailed across southern and central Ontario. In contrast to the cold summer of 1992, when the 30°C mark was not achieved until late August, daytime highs were in the 30s seven days in a row. Sunshine, warm temperatures and dry weekends helped diminish the memories of last July's miserable weather. For the Prairies, July '93 was one of the coldest on record—a re-run of the "non"-summer of 1992. The Maritimes had cool weather around mid-July when several new record lows were set.

On the 4th, heavy rain and hail caused $7 million in damage to fruit crops in the Okanagan Valley. During the same weekend 170 mm of rain caused flooding in several communities in northern Manitoba. Later in the month, 200 mm of rain fell in Winnipeg, flooding streets and inundating crops south of the city. At Victoria, an eight-hour rainfall of 50 mm on the 20th broke the record for the wettest day in July. Severe thunderstorms hit southwestern Quebec on the 29th, dropping more than 50 mm of rain, flooding downtown expressways in Montreal, and leaving more than 50 000 residents without power. Record rainfalls also occurred at Yellowknife and Iqaluit.

AUGUST 1993: Cool and wet weather again prevailed across most of western Canada in August. Near-freezing temperatures were more frequent than 30°C readings. In eastern Canada, the opposite was true as monthly mean temperatures were a degree or two above normal. At the end of the month, southern Ontario was in the grip of a heat wave with the humidex values at 44°C in Windsor. A smog advisory was issued for the 27th.

Most of the southern Prairies received measurable rainfall on two out of three days, but parts of the eastern Prairies received between 2 and 3 times their normal monthly rainfall. On the 16th, a 71 mm rainfall set a one-day record at Lethbridge. In the Red River Valley, August rains fell on ground soaked by July's near-record rainfalls. At Winnipeg, the summer precipitation total was well over 400 mm, a new record. Flood damages totalled more than $200 million.

On the 12th, 177 mm of rain fell at Beauceville, Quebec in just two hours. The storm washed out roads and flooded the town's water filtration plant. In the Maritimes, a heavy rainfall during the first week brought 60 mm to Nova Scotia, which set new daily records and damaged fruit and vegetable crops in the Annapolis Valley.

SEPTEMBER 1993: Cool, damp conditions characterized Canadian weather during September. Average temperatures for the month were as much as 3 degrees below the seasonal norm from Alberta to the Gulf of St Lawrence. In the Ontario Muskokas, it was the coolest since 1956, and in London the cloudiest since 1977.

The southern Prairie provinces received as much as twice the normal moisture. Totals of 50 to 60 mm were common. Farther east, precipitation amounts exceeded 100 mm from the Great Lakes to the Atlantic. Wettest of all was southern Newfoundland, where a combination of the end of Tropical Storm Floyd on the 9th and a very wet end of the month resulted in September totals of more than 200 mm.

September was more summer-like than July or August in British Columbia and the Yukon as a persistent ridge of high pressure produced dry, sunny and warm weather. But summer came to a dramatic end around the middle of September when eastward-moving cold air dropped temperatures 10 to 20 degrees in less than a day. On the 15th, frost warnings were in effect from the Rockies to southern Quebec. The day before daytime highs in southern Ontario and in New Brunswick had hit 31°C. With the cold came 20 cm of snow in higher elevations of southern Alberta, while lower elevations received more than 40 mm of rain.

OCTOBER 1993: Monthly average temperatures were below normal through most of the country in October. Only British Columbia and the Arctic saw above-normal averages. The dry weather was a concern in many sections of British Columbia. Logging operations were halted on Vancouver Island until cooler temperatures lowered the fire hazard. The lack of rain on the North Coast shut down the sport fishery on the Charlottes, as many streams were too low to allow spawning. Meanwhile all of eastern Canada received above-normal precipitation, with more than 100 mm in most locations. Few dry areas could be found through the rest of the country as most locales received at least 70 percent of their usual monthly amounts.

On the 5th, while southern Alberta basked in a high of 26°C, the northern portion of the province received a 15 cm snowfall. Southern Saskatchewan and Manitoba had a last fling at warm weather around the 22nd. A week later northern districts experienced new record-low minimums around -22°C.

In southern Ontario, the Thanksgiving Day weekend (October 9 to 11) was preceded by two days of record-breaking temperatures in the upper 20s. By the holiday, the arrival of arctic air brought below freezing temperatures and snow squalls to the lee of Lake Superior and Georgian Bay. October was generally cold and snowy in Ontario; only downtown Toronto escaped a measurable snowfall.

A vicious storm on the 27th brought 100 mm rainfalls to Nova Scotia and Newfoundland, 20 cm snowfalls to Labrador, and 150 to 200 km winds along the Atlantic coast.

NOVEMBER 1993: November weather ranged from warm, sunny days to frigid cold nights, including blizzards, flooding rains and fierce gales.

As the month began, heavy rains flooded roads and produced landslides in central and northern British Columbia. In northern BC, warm temperatures hindered the construction of ice roads, delaying logging operations. In the south, on Vancouver Island, warm dry weather aided the spread of brush fires. In Alberta, an Arctic cold front shifted back and forth during the middle of the month, giving scattered flurries and brief warm interludes to most areas. However by Grey Cup Day on the 28th, warm air covered all of southern Alberta. For the month as a whole, only the western Arctic and northern British Columbia and Alberta had above-normal temperature means. It was reasonably pleasant and mild in the Yukon. However, around the 20th, the temperature at Whitehorse plunged from 7°C to -10°C in just 15 minutes, ultimately dropping to -34°C on the 21st—a drop of 41 degrees in two days. In the far north, high winds brought blizzards to Alert, Eureka and Mould Bay.

In eastern Canada, November began three to five degrees cooler than normal, with significant snowfall from eastern Ontario to the Maritimes on the 1st. "Winter-coat" weather prevailed across Quebec. Most areas received 15 to 25 cm of snow; at Kuujjuarapik 98 cm of snow fell.

During the last 10 days of November, several storms brought rain and winds to the Atlantic provinces. On the 20th and 21st, ferry service between Cape Breton and Newfoundland was disrupted as a fierce storm brought heavy rain and winds. The next week cold air across the Gulf of St Lawrence triggered snow squalls from Prince Edward Island to Cape Breton.

DECEMBER 1993: Until the end of December, there was little significant winter weather across Canada. For the month, temperatures were generally above normal across southern Canada; as much as six degrees above in the western Prairies. Only the eastern Arctic was colder than usual. Not everyone benefited from the unseasonably warm weather. Petroleum and forest industries in northern British Columbia were hampered by the lack of ice roads, and southern Ontario's ice wine industry had warmth when it needed well-frozen grapes. Lack of snow also delayed the start of the skiing season.

Except for Vancouver Island and the Atlantic provinces, most of the country had only 50 to 75 percent of normal precipitation. Some parts of Ontario had the driest December in over 50 years. Flooding occurred on Vancouver Island when two storms, on the 9th and the 12th, produced one-day rainfalls of as much as 88 mm. West of Vancouver Island, on the 9th, wave heights topped 30m. Heavy rain and high winds also hit Atlantic Canada; single-day rainfalls approached 90 mm in Nova Scotia on the 5th and in southern New Brunswick on the 11th.

Winter finally hit a few days before Christmas. Wind-chill and intense cold warnings were issued in all provinces from Manitoba to the Atlantic coast as overnight lows dropped below -40°C in the north and below -20°C in the south. Only British

Columbia was spared the brunt of the cold air.

Two major storms struck the Maritimes: on Christmas Eve day, 30 to 45 cm of snow, whipped along by 140 km/h winds, severely disrupted transportation across Newfoundland and Cape Breton. A week later, heavy snowfall and blizzard conditions were reported for Nova Scotia, PEI and parts of Newfoundland.

JANUARY 1994: It was a January to remember. Average temperatures were 3 to 7°C above normal in southern British Columbia, with a few locations setting new marks for the month. Whereas cherry blossoms bloomed on southern Vancouver Island, from Ontario to the Atlantic coast this was the coldest January in more than a hundred years; in several places it was colder than any other month on record. In Quebec, only Sherbrooke (second coldest) and Sept-Iles (3rd coldest) failed to set new coldest January records. On the 19th Windsor, Ontario recorded its lowest temperature since 1885 as the mercury dropped to -29°C; the high on the same day was -21°C, the coldest ever for that location. In the Yukon temperatures dropped to near -50°C. For Saskatchewan and Manitoba, it was one of the coldest Januaries in the last 10 years.

Record-high snowfalls occurred in east-central British Columbia, central Alberta, southern Saskatchewan and New Brunswick. Regina's 47 cm of snow was the most in 110 years and Moose Jaw had a record 69 cm of snow. However, most areas in eastern Saskatchewan and Manitoba received less than 10 cm of snow. On the 5th, a major snow storm, including ice pellets and freezing rain, hit the St Lawrence Valley and the Atlantic provinces. The six-hour ferry from Cape Breton to Newfoundland took 40 hours.

Some dramatic swings in temperature also produced some chaotic travel. At Toronto, a rapid freeze produced sheets of ice that forced Pearson Airport to shut down for the first time in almost 60 years of operation.

January's extreme cold resulted in 50 percent more insurance claims than the year before, while the costs resulting from frozen pipes were double 1993's amount. Sales of cough and cold remedies increased by 10 percent.

FEBRUARY 1994: For most of Canada east of the Rockies, the first half of February saw a continuation of the bitter cold of January. At Edmonton, the overnight minimum on the 7th and 8th reached -44°C, the area's coldest temperature since 1977. Chinook winds provided some relief for residents of southern Alberta and Saskatchewan, pushing daytime highs up to 6°C in Alberta and 2°C in Saskatchewan on the 12th. The Yukon was the coldest region—temperatures bottomed at -48°C. In eastern Canada, the persistent cold spell that began shortly before Christmas finally broke around the 19th. Mild air in Quebec and the Maritimes reached near 20°C. A reading of 18°C at Halifax was the highest ever in 122 years of December to February records. Before the warmth came, sea ice conditions off Nova Scotia reached a record level.

The worst storm of the month blasted through the Maritimes at mid-month. With winds gusting to 170 km/h over the Gulf of St Lawrence, deep snowfalls, accumulating more than 34 cm and 70 cm respectively, fell across southwestern New Brunswick and Newfoundland. For the month, Gander received 125 cm, the most for any station in Canada. Snowfall was plentiful in southern Ontario and Quebec, thrilling skiers and snowmobilers, but taxing already exhausted snow removal budgets.

On the 8th, southwestern BC finally received its first snowfall of the season: a centimetre of snow fell at Victoria and almost 9 cm at Vancouver. The "dusting" forced schools to close and caused numerous traffic accidents. On the 9th, temperatures struggled to 4°C and the snow disappeared. And on the 24th-25th, 17 cm of snow covered the daffodils.

MARCH 1994: Almost the entire country was either mild or dry, or both during March. Only Newfoundland was cool and wet. The coldest temperature in Canada was -49.9°C at Eureka, and the warmest was 25.1°C at Hope, BC. In Alberta, many stations set a March record for least number of days with measurable precipitation and abundant sunshine. By the end of March southern Alberta was devoid of snow cover.

Precipitation was less than 50% of normal in many areas of southern Saskatchewan and Manitoba. At Kindersley, Saskatchewan it was the driest March in 50 years, but in the north, precipitation was more likely to be double the normal amount. In Ontario, total precipitation was generally below normal although snowfall was ample; Ottawa had 60 cm of snow, the rest of the south recorded 20 to 40 cm. By contrast, it was especially dry and sunny in the north.

From the 3rd to the 5th, the Gaspé received 55 cm of snow, and on the 31st Bagotville received 18 cm. It was wet across the Maritimes with new record totals at Moncton (131 mm), Charlottetown (95 mm) and Halifax (214 mm). The heavy rain combined with melting snow and ice-jams to cause several rivers in Nova Scotia to overflow. At St John's, a record 68 mm of rain fell on the 11th bringing the total monthly precipitation to 222 mm, a record for March.

APRIL 1994: The only significant departures from average normal temperatures came in British Columbia and in an area extending from northeastern Manitoba to northern Labrador, where they were as much as four degrees below normal. Precipitation values were well below the seasonal average across the Prairies, while parts of British Columbia, and most of the eastern third of the country had above-normal amounts. The Atlantic provinces had the wettest weather, with a few locations surpassing the 200 mm mark.

On the 6th and 7th, a general snowfall of 10 to 20 cm occurred from southern Ontario through southern Quebec and New Brunswick (more than 30 cm in the north) to Labrador. The same storm brought 70 mm of rain to Prince Edward Island, Nova Scotia, and Newfoundland.

By mid-month accelerated melting of snow and ice combined with 50 mm rainfalls to bring flooding to New Brunswick. A few communities along the Saint John River were briefly evacuated and the Trans-Canada Highway was closed.

Winter's last gasps brought 10 cm of snow to southwestern Alberta on the 25th, 23 cm to north of Lake Superior, and snow streamers east of the Gulf of St Lawrence. The first sign of severe summer weather appeared as heavy thunderstorms moved through the Ottawa Valley on the 27th, bringing damaging winds and a tornado.

MAY 1994: Storms moving across the Prairies resulted in precipitation totals that exceeded 50 mm in most areas, although in British Columbia, northern Ontario, and northern Quebec it was drier than normal. For many parts of the Atlantic provinces this was the third wet month in a row, resulting in spring precipitation totals that were as much as 200% of normal.

Mean temperatures were generally near normal across the country. Only in the northwestern Arctic (generally two to four degrees above normal), was there any significant departure from the long-term average. The cool spring weather left crop development in southern Ontario about two weeks behind schedule.

The most notable storm on the Prairies moved through central Saskatchewan on the 17th and 18th, bringing 48 mm of rain to Saskatoon, only 2 mm short of the May record. As the cold front associated with this storm moved through southern Manitoba, heavy thunderstorms produced rainfalls of 50 to 100 mm in and around Winnipeg. More severe weather occurred on the 26th in west central Alberta as thunderstorms spawned funnel clouds southeast of Edmonton and produced damaging winds and baseball-sized hail. On the 31st, thunderstorm activity generated three small tornadoes, one near Toronto, and two more southeast of Quebec City.

JUNE 1994: Average temperatures were generally within 1 degree of normal across Canada in June. With the exception of drier than normal conditions in the northern Prairies, and northwestern and eastern Ontario, precipitation across the country exceeded normal values. There were nine tornadoes in Saskatchewan in June, with five occurring on the 29th. A tornado touched down northeast of Brandon on the 10th.

In Ontario, a late frost on June 3 dipped well into part of southern Ontario. On the 16th, temperatures soared to 36°C at several localities, including Toronto. This was the warmest day at Pearson Airport since July 1988 and the earliest date on record that temperatures exceeded 35°C. In Quebec, many localities reported hail and severe thunderstorms with a tornado occurring between Montreal and Trois-Rivieres. In Newfoundland, despite a late spring storm that dumped 20 to 55 cm of snow on central and northeastern regions, June will be remembered as a good weather month, especially compared to the dismal weather of a year ago.

Weather Records

	Canada	United States	World
Highest maximum air temperature	45.0° Midale and Yellowgrass, Sask. July 5, 1937	56.7° Death Valley, CA July 10, 1913	58.0° Al'azizyah, Libya Sept. 13, 1922
Lowest minimum air temperature	-63.0° Snag, YT Feb. 3, 1947	-62.1° Prospect Creek Camp, AK Jan. 23, 1971	-89.6° Vostok, Antarctica July 21, 1983
Coldest month	-47.9° Eureka, NWT Feb. 1979		
Highest sea-level pressure	107.95 kPa Dawson, YT Feb. 2, 1989	107.86 kPa Northway, AK Jan. 31, 1989	108.38 kPa Agata, Siberia USSR Dec. 31, 1968
Lowest sea-level pressure	94.02 kPa St. Anthony, Nfld Jan. 20, 1977	89.23 kPa Matecumbe Key, FL Sept. 2, 1935	87.64 kPa in eye of Typhoon June (Pacific Ocean, 17°N, 138°E) Nov. 19, 1975
Greatest precipitation in 24hrs	489.2 mm Ucluelet Brynnor Mines, BC Oct. 6, 1967	1 090 mm Alvin, TX	1 869.9 mm Cilaos La Réunion Is. March 15, 1952
Greatest precipitation in one month	2 235.5 mm Swanson Bay, BC Nov. 1917	2 717.8 mm Kukui, HI March 1942	9 300 mm Cherrapunji, India July 1861
Greatest precipitation in one year	8 122.4 mm Henderson Lake, BC 1931	17 902.7 mm Kukui, HI 1982	26 461.2 mm Cherrapunji, India Aug. 1860-July 1861
Greatest average annual precipitation	6 655 mm Henderson Lake, BC	11 684 mm Mt. Waialeaie, Kauai, HI	11 684 mm Mt. Waialeaie, Kauai, HI
Least annual precipitation	12.7 mm Arctic Bay, NWT 1949	0.0 Bagdad, CA Oct. 3, 1912 to Nov. 8, 1914	0.0 Arica, Chile—no rain for 14 years
Greatest average annual snowfall	1 433 cm Glacier Mt. Fidelity, BC	1 460.8 cm Rainer Paradise Ranger Station, WA	
Greatest snowfall in one season	2 446.5 cm Revelstoke/Mt. Copeland, BC 1971–72	2 850 cm Rainer Paradise Ranger Station, WA 1971–72	
Greatest snowfall in one month	535.9 cm Haines Apps. No 2, BC Dec. 1959	990.6 cm Tamarack, CA Jan. 1911	
Greatest snowfall in one day	118.1 cm Lakelse Lake, BC Jan. 17, 1974	193.0 cm Silver Lake, CO April 14–15, 1921	
Highest average annual number of thunderstorm days	34 days London, Ont.	96 days Fort Meyers, FL	322 days Bogor, Indonesia
Heaviest hailstone	290 g Cedoux, Sask.	758 g Coffeyville, KS Sept. 3, 1970	5 000 g Guangxi region of China May 1, 1986
Highest average annual wind speed	36 km/h Cape Warwick, Resolution Island, NWT	56.3 km/h Mt. Washington, NH	
Highest wind speed for 1 hr	201.1 km/h Cape Hopes Advance (Quaqtaq), Que. Nov. 18, 1931	362.0 km/h Mt. Washington, NH April 12, 1934	
Highest average hours of fog	1 890 hrs Argentia, Nfld	2 552 hrs Cape Disappointment, WA	

Source: *Environment Canada*

Weather Here and There

	Temperature °C				Annual Total			
	Winter		Summer		Snowfall	Precipitation	Wet weather	Sunshine
Locations:	High	Low	High	Low	cm	mm	(days)	hours
Victoria	6.5	0.3	21.8	10.7	47	858	153	2 082
Vancouver	5.7	0.1	21.7	12.7	55	1 167	164	1 919
Calgary	-3.6	-15.7	23.2	9.5	135	399	111	2 395
Edmonton	-8.7	-19.8	22.5	9.4	127	466	122	2 303
Regina	-11.0	-22.1	26.3	11.9	107	364	109	2 365
Winnipeg	-13.2	-23.6	26.1	13.4	115	504	119	2 377
Toronto	-2.5	-11.1	26.8	14.2	124	781	141	2 038
Ottawa	-6.3	-15.5	26.4	15.1	222	911	159	2 054
Montreal	-5.8	-14.9	26.2	15.4	214	940	162	2 015
Quebec	-7.7	-17.3	24.9	13.2	337	1 208	178	1 910
Saint John	-2.8	-13.6	22.1	11.6	283	1 433	164	1 894
Halifax	-1.5	-10.3	23.4	13.2	261	1 474	170	1 949
Charlottetown	-3.4	-12.2	23.1	13.6	339	1 201	177	1 844
St. John's	-0.7	-7.9	20.2	10.5	322	1 482	217	1 527
Yellowknife	-23.9	-32.2	20.8	12.0	144	267	118	2 277
Whitehorse	-14.4	-23.2	20.3	7.6	145	269	122	1 852
Beijing	6.7	-16.1	36.3	15.9	30	623	66	2 706
Calcutta	33.4	7.0	34.8	23.4	—	1 592	102	2 528
London	6.0	2.0	22.0	14.0	—	594	107	1 514
Los Angeles	23.4	3.0	34.3	11.3	—	373	39	3 185
Mexico City	23.0	2.0	26.0	10.0	—	726	133	2 366
Miami	29.4	9.4	35.5	19.9	—	1 520	103	2 945
Moscow	-9.0	-16.0	23.0	13.0	161	575	181	1 597
New York	7.7	-6.3	34.4	15.4	77	1 076	121	2 564
Rome	12.3	3.4	30.9	17.7	—	749	76	2 491
Rio de Janeiro	26.7	13.7	30.9	19.3	—	1 093	131	2 351
Shanghai	11.6	-4.8	36.0	18.2	25	1 143	98	1 877
Sydney	19.7	3.9	29.3	14.7	—	1 205	152	2 440
Tokyo	13.8	-6.4	32.3	17.9	20	1 563	104	2 021

Source: *Environment Canada* (1) Canadian data based on 1961–90; international data based on 1951–80.

Name That Hurricane!

*A*t the turn of the century, an Australian meteorologist Clement Wragge (known affectionately as wet Wragge) assigned the names of people he had quarrelled with to violent storms. In the 1940s, the American media got into the hurricane name game, assigning Hurricane Harry (after Truman) to the first storm in 1949.

In the early 1950s other systems were used, such as naming hurricanes by letters of the phonetic alphabet used in radio code words (Able, Baker, Charlie). Then in 1953, the United States Weather Bureau started using female names for Atlantic hurricanes, despite thousands of letters of complaint. Weather sexism continued until 1979 when an international committee on hurricanes adopted a pre-selected, alphabetical list of male and female names. Short, distinctive English, French and Hispanic names are used and repeated every five years except for those retired because of infamy, such as Hazel, Andrew, and Gilbert. (If your name is Quentin, Ursala, Xavier, Yolanda or Zach, a hurricane will never bear your name—those letters are not used.)

A storm is named when its sustained winds reach 63 km/h—tropical storm strength; hurricane strength is 118 km/h. Here are some of the beauties and beasts you may see or hear about on the Northern Atlantic coast during 1995: Allison, Barry, Chantal, Dean, Erin, Felix, Gabrielle, Humberto, Iris, Jerry, Karen, Luis, Marilyn, Noel, Opal, Pablo, Roxanne, Sebastien, Tanya, Van and Wendy.

Average Number of Days Per Year With the Most...

Province	Frost			Smoke or Haze		
	Average # Days	Station		Average # Days	Station	
Newfoundland	259	Nain		25	St. John's A	
Prince Edward Island ...	175	O'Leary		34	Summerside A	
New Brunswick	215	Nine Mile Brk. (Camp 68)		42	Chatham A	
Nova Scotia	194	Northeast Margaree		29	Greenwood A	
Quebec	296	Cape Hopes Advance		118	St. Hubert A	
Ontario	254	Winisk A		228	Windsor A	
Manitoba	258	Churchill A		30	Winnipeg Int'l. A	
Saskatchewan	238	Stony Rapids		8	Saskatoon	
Alberta	269	Lake Louise		34	Edmonton Municipal A	
British Columbia	280	Alexis Creek Tautri Creek		187	Vancouver Int'l. A	
Yukon Territory	296	Komakuk Beach A		3	Dawson	
Northwest Territories ...	340	Isachsen		7	Fort Smith A	

Province	Fog			Hail		
	Average # Days	Station		Average # Days	Station	
Newfoundland	206	Argentia A		0	—	
Prince Edward Island ..	47	Charlottetown A		0	—	
New Brunswick	106	Saint John A		0	—	
Nova Scotia	127	Sable Island		0	—	
Quebec	85	Cape Hopes Advance		2	Matagami A	
Ontario	76	Mount Forest		1	Red Lake	
Manitoba	48	Churchill A		3	Winnipeg Int'l. A	
Saskatchewan	37	Collins Bay		2	Estevan A	
Alberta	39	Whitecourt		7	Edson A	
British Columbia	226	Old Glory Mountain		18	Cape Scott	
Yukon Territory	61	Komakuk Beach A		2	Dawson A	
Northwest Territories ...	196	Resolution Island		0	—	

Province	Thunderstorms			Blowing Snow		
	Average # Days	Station		Average # Days	Station	
Newfoundland	7	Daniels Harbour		45	Hopedale	
Prince Edward Island ..	11	Summerside A		26	Summerside A	
New Brunswick	13	Fredericton A		16	Chatham A	
Nova Scotia	12	Debert A		21	Greenwood A	
Quebec	27	St. Hubert		90	Border A	
Ontario	34	Windsor A		38	Winisk A	
Manitoba	26	Rivers A		64	Churchill A	
Saskatchewan	25	Wynyard		32	Regina A	
Alberta	26	Edmonton Int'l. A		15	Coronation A	
British Columbia	24	Prince George		25	Old Glory Mountain	
Yukon Territory	11	Snag		82	Komakuk Beach A	
Northwest Territories ..	12	Fort Smith A		91	Resolute A	

Source: *Environment Canada*

Provincial Weather Facts

Province	Warmest Temperature Ever Recorded °C	Date	Station	Coldest Temperature Ever Recorded °C	Date	Station
Newfoundland ...	41.7	Aug. 11, 1914	Northwest River	-51.1	Feb. 17, 1973	Esker 2
P.E.I.	36.7	Aug. 19, 1935	Charlottetown	-37.2	Jan. 26, 1884	Kilmahumaig
New Brunswick ..	39.4	Aug. 18, 1935	Nepisiguit Falls	-47.2	Feb. 2, 1955	Sisson Dam
Nova Scotia	38.3	Aug. 19, 1935	Collegeville	-41.1	Jan. 31, 1920	Upper Stewiacke
Quebec	40.0	July 6, 1921	Ville Marie	-54.4	Feb. 5, 1923	Doucet
Ontario	42.2	July 20, 1919	Biscotasing	-58.3	Jan. 23, 1935	Iroquois Falls
Manitoba	44.4	July 11, 1936	St. Albans	-52.8	Jan. 9, 1899	Norway House
Saskatchewan ...	45.0	July 5, 1937	Midale	-56.7	Feb. 1, 1893	Prince Albert
Alberta	43.3	July 21, 1931	Bassano Dam	-61.1	Jan. 11, 1911	Fort Vermilion
British Columbia .	44.4	July 16, 1941	Lillooet	-58.9	Jan. 31, 1947	Smith River
Yukon	36.1	June 14, 1969	Mayo	-63.0	Feb. 3, 1947	Snag
NWT	39.4	July 18, 1941	Fort Smith	-57.2	Dec. 26, 1917	Fort Smith

Source: *Environment Canada*

Province	Warmest Annual Temperature On Average °C	Station	Coldest Annual Temperature On Average °C	Station
Newfoundland	6.3	Holyrood Ultramar	-3.8	Wabush Lake A
Prince Edward Island	5.9	Charlottetown CDA	4.8	O'Leary
New Brunswick	6.2	St. Andrews	1.6	Upsalquitch Lake
Nova Scotia	7.6	Sable Island	4.9	Trafalgar
Quebec	7.6	Montreal Lafontaine	-7.2	Koartak
Ontario	9.7	Windsor University	-5.5	Winisk A
Manitoba	3.3	Morden CDA	-7.2	Churchill A
Saskatchewan	5.0	Maple Creek North	-4.6	Collins Bay
Alberta	5.9	Bow Island Rivers	-2.7	Fort Chipewyan A
British Columbia	10.7	Sumas Canal	-3.2	Cassiar Yukon
Territory	-1.0	Whitehorse Riverdale	-11.4	Komakuk Beach A
Northwest Territories	-2.2	Fort Liard	-19.7	Eureka

Source: *Environment Canada*

Average Annual Bright Sunshine

Province	Greatest hrs	Station	Least hrs	Station
Newfoundland	1 572	Churchill Falls A	1 303	St. Shotts
Prince Edward Island	1 967	Tignish	1 817	East Baltic
New Brunswick	2 010	Chatham A	1 373	Summit Depot
Nova Scotia	1 969	Shearwater A	1 449	Sable Island
Quebec	2 054	Montreal Int'l. A	1 158	Mont Logan
Ontario	2 203	Thunder Bay A	1 635	New Liskeard
Manitoba	2 460	Delta U	1 828	Churchill A
Saskatchewan	2 537	Estevan A	2 073	Cree Lake
Alberta	2 490	Coronation A	1 724	Banff
British Columbia	2 244	Cranbrook A	949	Stewart A
Yukon Territory	1 844	Whitehorse A	1 789	Watson Lake A
Northwest Territories	2 277	Yellowknife A	1 443	Mould Bay A

Source: *Environment Canada*

Average Annual Precipitation

Province	Greatest		Least	
	mm	Station	mm	Station
Newfoundland	1 699.7	Burgeo	739.8	Nain
Prince Edward Island	1 169.4	Charlottetown A	921.0	Montague
New Brunswick	1 444.4	Saint John A	909.6	Upsalquitch Lake
Nova Scotia	1 630.7	Ingonish Beach	973.7	Pugwash
Quebec	1 559.8	Mont Logan	295.9	Cape Hopes Advance
Ontario	1 191.1	West Guilford	569.0	Kenora TCPL
Manitoba	696.1	Peace Gardens	402.3	Churchill A
Saskatchewan	530.1	Brabant Lake	287.9	Nashlyn
Alberta	1 072.0	Waterton Park HQ	270.8	Empress
British Columbia	6 655.0	Henderson Lake	205.6	Ashcroft
Yukon Territory	590.6	Tuchitua	135.9	Komakuk Beach A
Northwest Territories	663.2	Cape Dyer A	61.0	Rea Point

Source: *Environment Canada*

Average Annual Snowfall

Province	Greatest		Least	
	mm	Station	mm	Station
Newfoundland	322.8	Woody Point	91.6	St. Shotts
Prince Edward Island	330.6	Charlottetown A	173.3	Montague
New Brunswick	448.8	Dawson Settlement	176.2	Southwest Head
Nova Scotia	406.7	Cheticamp	104.1	Baccaro
Quebec	648.2	Mont Logan	161.6	Havre aux Maisons
Ontario	430.0	Searchmount	74.0	Lakeview MOE
Manitoba	332.7	Island Lake	94.9	Lundar
Saskatchewan	348.6	Collins Bay	58.0	Aylesbury
Alberta	642.9	Columbia Icefield	59.9	Empress
British Columbia	1 433.0	Glacier NP Mt. Fidelity	20.4	Carnation Creek
Yukon Territory	365.7	Keno Hill	60.1	Komakuk Beach A
Northwest Territories	602.4	Cape Dyer A	28.6	Rea Point

Source: *Environment Canada*

Greatest Snow on the Ground Any Month

Province	Depth (cm)	Station	Province	Depth (cm)	Station
Newfoundland	313	Hopedale	Manitoba	175	Glenlea
Prince Edward Island	156	Charlottetown	Saskatchewan	224	Hudson Bay
New Brunswick	252	Harvey Station	Alberta	179	Parker Ridge
Nova Scotia	183	Nappan	British Columbia	450	Whistler Roundhouse
Quebec	259	Blanc-Sablon	Yukon Territory	149	Hour Lake
Ontario	219	Gravenhurst	Northwest Territories	241	Cape Dyer

Source: *Environment Canada*

Is It Ever Too Cold to Snow?

Warm air holds more moisture than cold air and the heaviest snowfalls usually occur when the temperature is near freezing. But even in the coldest regions of Canada, where there is little water vapour in the air, very fine snow can fall.

Nevertheless, some of the coldest weather occurs with clear blue skies and for some Prairie cities, March averages both the most snow and the mildest temperatures.

Wind

Province	Highest Wind Speed		Highest % of Calms	
	km/hr	Station	km/hr	Station
Newfoundland	28.0 (W)	Bonavista	17.1	Wabush Lake A
Prince Edward Island	22.4 (SSW)	Summerside A	4.4	Summerside A
New Brunswick	22.4 (W)	Miscou Island (AUT)	11.8	Fredericton A
Nova Scotia	25.7 (W)	Sable Island	16.9	Greenwood A
Quebec	32.0 (NW)	Grindstone Island	20.4	Gaspé A
Ontario	21.0 (SW)	Bruce Ontario Hydro	30.2	White River
Manitoba	22.7 (WNW)	Churchill A	21.0	Norway House A
Saskatchewan	22.9 (W)	Swift Current A	12.8	La Ronge A
Alberta	21.5 (W)	Pincher Creek	39.7	High Level A
British Columbia	33.7 (NW)	Cape St. James	48.5	Quesnel A
Yukon Territory	14.1 (SSE)	Whitehorse A	57.5	Dawson A
Northwest Territories	35.3 (NW)	Resolution Island	35.1	Eureka

Source: *Environment Canada*

"Coldest Days" (Wind Chill)

Province	ET/WCF[1]	Location	Date	Temp (°C)	Wind (km/hr)
Newfoundland	-71/2814	Wabush Lake	Jan. 20, 1975	-41	40
Prince Edward Island	-57/2450	Charlottetown	Jan. 18, 1982	-32	37
Nova Scotia	-53/2309	Sydney	Jan. 18, 1982	-25	59
New Brunswick	-61/2547	Charlo	Jan. 18, 1982	-31	54
Quebec	-77/3001	Nitchequon	Jan. 20, 1975	-42	56
Ontario	-70/2753	Thunder Bay	Jan. 10, 1982	-36	54
Manitoba	-76/2938	Churchill	Jan. 18, 1975	-41	56
Saskatchewan	-70/2757	Swift Current	Dec. 15, 1964	-34	89
Alberta	-68/2740	Red Deer	Dec. 15, 1964	-35	61
British Columbia	-69/2749	Old Glory Mtn.	Dec. 15, 1964	-36	58
Yukon Territory	-83/3152	Komakuk Beach	Feb. 12, 1975	-50	40
Northwest Territories	-92/3357	Pelly Bay	Jan. 13, 1975	-51	56

Source: *Environment Canada*

(1) ET is equivalent wind chill temperature in °C. WCF is wind chill factor in watts/square metre

---

Calculating Wind Chill

*Y*ou can calculate the wind chill equivalent temperature in degrees Celsius (°C) or the wind chill factor in watts per square metre for your own values of air temperature (°C) and wind speed in kilometres per hour, by using the following equations:

Wind Chill Equivalent Temperature [WET] in °C:
$$WET = 33 - ((12.1 + 6.12\sqrt{W} - 0.32 \times W)(33 - T)/27.8)$$

Wind Chill Factor [WCF] in watts per square metre:
$$WCF = (12.1 + 6.12\sqrt{W} - 0.32 \times W)(33 - T)$$

T = ambient air temperature in °C W = wind speed in kilometres per hour

This calculation gives meaningful values of WET and WCF for any air temperature lower than 5°C, and for any wind speed between 8 and 80 kilometres per hour.

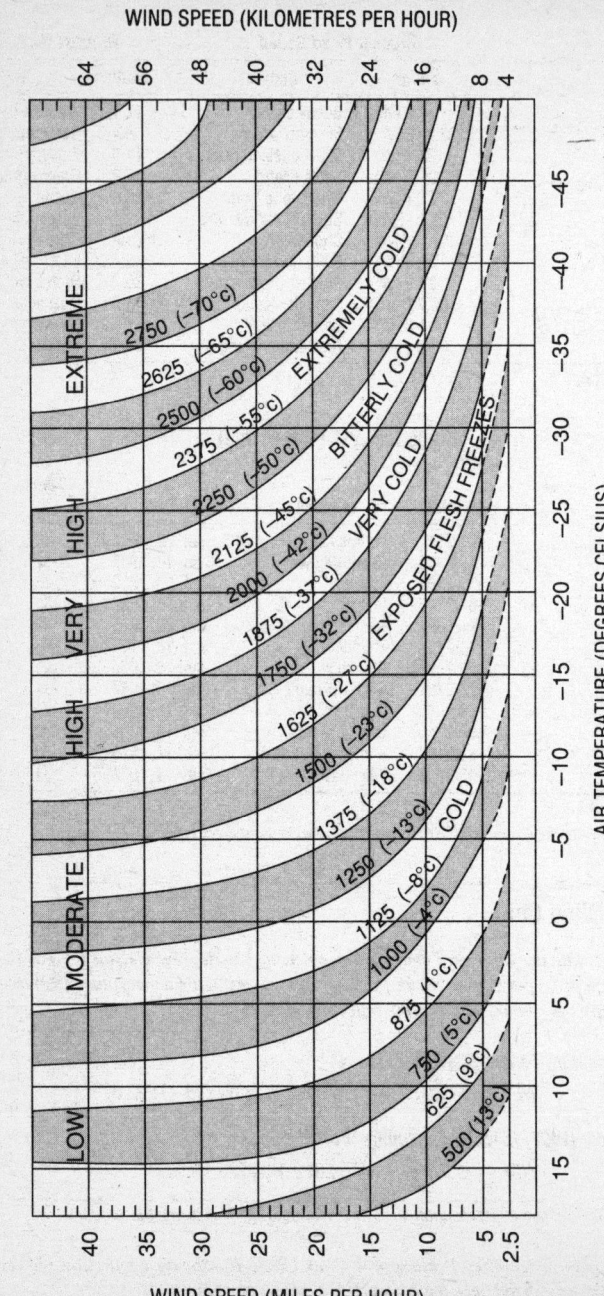

Wind Chill Factor

Watts Per Square Metre (equivalent temperature °C)

WIND SPEED (KILOMETRES PER HOUR)

64   56   48   40   32   24   16   8   4

EXTREME

HIGH

VERY HIGH

HIGH

MODERATE

LOW

2750 (-70°c)
2625 (-65°c)
2500 (-60°c)
2375 (-55°c)
2250 (-50°c)
2125 (-45°c)
2000 (-42°c)
1875 (-37°c)
1750 (-32°c)
1625 (-27°c)
1500 (-23°c)
1375 (-18°c)
1250 (-13°c)
1125 (-8°c)
1000 (-4°c)
875 (1°c)
750 (5°c)
625 (9°c)
500 (13°c)

EXTREMELY COLD
BITTERLY COLD
VERY COLD
EXPOSED FLESH FREEZES
COLD

AIR TEMPERATURE (DEGREES CELSIUS)

-45   -40   -35   -30   -25   -20   -15   -10   -5   0   5   10   15

40   35   30   25   20   15   10   5   2.5

WIND SPEED (MILES PER HOUR)

■ To determine the wind chill factor, follow the temperature across and the wind speed up until the two lines intersect. The value of the wind chill factor can be interpolated using the labelled wind chill factor curves. ■ For example, at -10°C with a wind speed of 20 miles per hour, the point of intersection lies between 1500 (-23°C) and 1625 (-27°C), or approximately 1570 (-25°C).

■ It is not recommended that wind chill factors be calculated for wind speeds below 8 km an hour and above 80 km an hour, since it is difficult to determine wind chill factors at these wind speeds.

Humidex

Relative Humidity (%)

Dry Bulb Temp (°C)	20	25	30	35	40	45	50	55	60	65	70	75	80	85	90	95	100
43	47	49	51	54	56												
42	46	48	50	52	54	56											
41	44	46	48	50	52	54	56										
40	43	44	47	49	51	52	54	57									
39	41	43	45	47	49	51	53	54	56	56							
38	40	42	43	46	47	49	51	52	54	53	57						
37		40	42	43	45	47	49	50	51	51	55	57	58				
36		38	40	42	43	45	47	48	50	49	53	54	56	57	58		
35		37	38	41	42	43	45	47	48	48	51	52	54	56	57	58	
34		36	37	39	41	42	43	45	47	46	49	51	52	53	55	57	58
33		34	36	37	38	40	42	43	44	43	47	48	50	51	52	54	55
32		33	34	36	37	38	39	41	42	41	45	46	47	49	50	51	52
31		31	33	34	35	36	38	39	40	40	43	44	45	46	48	49	50
30		31	31	33	34	35	36	37	38	38	41	42	43	44	46	47	48
29			30	31	32	33	34	36	37	36	39	41	42	43	44	45	46
28			28	29	31	32	33	34	35	34	37	38	39	41	41	42	43
27			28	28	29	30	31	32	33	32	35	36	37	38	39	40	41
26				27	28	28	29	31	31	31	33	34	35	36	37	38	39
25				26	27	27	28	29	30	29	32	33	33	34	35	36	37
24				25	26	26	27	28	28	27	31	31	32	33	33	34	35
23					23	24	25	26	27	26	30	29	30	31	32	32	33
22						23	23	24	24	24	28	27	28	28	29	29	31
21						22	23	23	24		26	26	27	27	28	29	29

DRY BULB TEMPERATURE (DEGREES CELSIUS)

Humidex (°C)	Degree of Comfort
20 - 29	Comfortable
30 - 39	Varying degrees of discomfort
40 - 45	Almost everyone uncomfortable
46 and over	Many types of labour must be restricted

■ In hot weather, our bodies regulate core temperature by using our sweat glands to shed water. Sweating doesn't cool the body, but the evaporation of sweat on your skin removes heat because it takes energy (heat) to change the liquid on your skin to vapour in the air. However, when it's humid, the air itself is already full of moisture and it can't absorb the moisture we are trying to shed, making us sticky and uncomfortable.

Monthly and Annual Temperature and Precipitation in Canada

All figures are based on the thirty-year period 1961 to 1990 inclusive.
*Airport station unless * designates city office station.*

Station	January Average Temperature (°C) Mid Afternoon	January Average Temperature (°C) Early Morning	January Total Precipitation (mm)	April Average Temperature (°C) Mid Afternoon	April Average Temperature (°C) Early Morning	April Total Precipitation (mm)
Calgary, Alta.	-3.6	-15.7	12.2	10.6	-2.4	25.1
Charlottetown, PEI	-3.4	-12.2	106.3	6.3	-1.8	81.6
Churchill, Man. ...	-22.9	-30.9	17.3	-5.2	-14.8	22.6
Dawson, Yukon* ..	-27.1	-34.2	16.5	5.9	-9.7	9.4
Edmonton, Alta.	-8.7	-19.8	22.9	9.9	-2.7	21.8
Fredericton, NB ...	-4.0	-15.4	93.3	9.4	-1.4	83.4
Iqaluit, NWT	-21.7	-30.0	21.8	-9.9	-19.6	28.4
Halifax, NS	-1.5	-10.3	146.9	8.0	-0.9	124.4
Hamilton, Ont.	-2.6	-10.0	61.3	11.3	1.2	74.3
Kitchener, Ont.* ..	-3.3	-11.4	54.3	11.2	0.4	72.6
London, Ont.	-2.8	-10.7	69.0	11.7	0.7	79.2
Moncton, NB	-3.7	-13.9	119.7	7.7	-2.0	100.9
Montreal, Que.	-5.8	-14.9	63.3	10.7	0.6	74.8
Ottawa, Ont.	-6.3	-15.5	58.0	10.8	0.3	69.0
Quebec, Que.	-7.7	-17.3	90.0	7.9	-1.5	75.5
Regina, Sask.	-11.0	-22.1	14.7	10.5	-2.4	20.4
Saint John, NB	-2.8	-13.6	128.3	7.9	-1.5	109.7
St. John's, Nfld ...	-0.7	-7.9	147.8	4.8	-2.2	110.4
Saskatoon, Sask. ..	-12.3	-22.9	15.9	10.0	-2.2	25.7
Sault Ste. Marie, Ont.	-5.5	-15.4	74.4	8.5	-2.0	65.2
Toronto, Ont.	-2.5	-11.1	45.6	11.5	0.6	64.0
Vancouver, BC	5.7	0.1	149.8	12.7	4.9	75.4
Victoria, BC	6.5	0.3	141.1	12.9	3.8	41.9
Whitehorse, Yukon	-14.4	-23.2	16.9	5.7	-5.1	8.3
Windsor, Ont.	-1.3	-8.8	50.3	13.4	2.7	80.3
Winnipeg, Man. ...	-13.2	-23.6	19.3	9.8	-2.3	35.9
Yellowknife, NWT .	-23.9	-32.2	14.9	-0.5	-12.0	10.3

Frosty Fridays

*F*rost is the frozen equivalent of dew. It forms when the temperature at ground level drops below freezing and the water vapour in the air condenses and freezes into ice crystals.

Not every cold night brings frost—the weather must be just right. The nights must be clear (or nearly so), and calm, and the air next to the ground must be relatively moist. Clouds make a blanket in the atmosphere that traps the remnants of daytime heat and prevents the cooling necessary for a frost. And a decent wind will mix the cold air at ground level with the warmer air higher up, raising the air temperature next to the ground and decreasing the likelihood of frost.

Gardeners trying to get the most out of Canada's growing season often gamble that their efforts will not be destroyed by a late spring or early fall frost. Some tips to prevent damage include covering plants with cloth, plastic or paper cups, straw or other mulches that will trap heat on nights when frost threatens. Another strategy involves planting on sloping or higher ground rather than in low-lying areas. Because cold air is denser and heavier than warm air, it settles to the ground, flowing downhill and filling every hollow, gulch and valley.

Station	July Average Temperature (°C) Mid Afternoon	July Average Temperature (°C) Early Morning	July Total Precipitation (mm)	October Average Temperature (°C) Mid Afternoon	October Average Temperature (°C) Early Morning	October Total Precipitation (mm)
Calgary, Alta.	23.2	9.5	69.9	12.6	-1.2	15.5
Charlottetown, PEI	23.1	13.6	81.6	12.1	4.0	111.7
Churchill, Man. . . .	16.9	6.8	50.7	1.4	-4.3	46.5
Dawson, Yukon* .	22.8	6.5	33.9	-0.5	-10.4	27.9
Edmonton, Alta. . .	22.5	9.4	101.0	11.3	-2.2	17.7
Fredericton, NB . . .	25.6	12.9	84.5	13.1	1.5	93.1
Iqaluit, NWT	11.6	3.7	58.2	-2.1	-7.8	42.4
Halifax, NS	23.4	13.2	96.8	13.0	4.0	128.9
Hamilton, Ont. . . .	26.4	15.1	81.0	13.9	4.7	66.3
Kitchener, Ont.* . .	26.1	13.6	90.4	13.2	2.9	70.4
London, Ont.	26.4	14.2	76.7	14.2	3.9	76.4
Moncton, NB	24.4	12.5	102.6	12.7	2.1	106.4
Montreal, Que. . . .	26.2	15.4	85.6	13.0	3.6	75.4
Ottawa, Ont.	26.4	15.1	88.1	12.8	3.0	74.8
Quebec, Que.	24.9	13.2	118.5	11.0	2.0	96.0
Regina, Sask.	26.3	11.9	58.9	11.9	-1.7	20.3
Saint John, NB . . .	22.1	11.6	103.7	12.1	2.9	122.5
St. John's, Nfld . . .	20.2	10.5	121.2	10.6	3.4	151.7
Saskatoon, Sask. . .	25.4	11.7	58.0	11.1	-1.5	16.9
Sault Ste. Marie, Ont.	24.3	11.2	65.6	11.8	2.9	83.2
Toronto, Ont.	26.8	14.2	76.6	14.1	3.6	63.0
Vancouver, BC . . .	21.7	12.7	36.1	13.5	6.4	115.3
Victoria, BC	21.8	10.7	17.6	14.1	5.3	74.4
Whitehorse, Yukon	20.3	7.6	39.3	4.3	-3.1	23.0
Windsor, Ont.	27.7	17.0	85.3	15.8	6.0	57.9
Winnipeg, Man. . . .	26.1	13.4	72.0	11.3	0.1	29.5
Yellowknife, NWT .	20.8	12.0	35.2	1.3	-4.2	34.8

Source: *Environment Canada*

Network of Weather Watchers

*E*nvironment Canada has a national network of more than 1,800 unpaid weather observers who record the temperature and precipitation every day of the year. Volunteers are of all ages and walks of life—farmers, housewives, teachers, dentists, bankers... even prisoners. Many weather stations are operated by an individual; others are operated by schools, power companies, industrial firms and municipalities.

The routine of a volunteer observer rarely varies. Twice a day, every day, the volunteer reads two thermometers—a maximum and a minimum—recording the extremes since the last observation. A rain gauge sits on the ground nearby. The observer measures any rain collected since the last observation, then empties the gauge. In winter, the depth of freshly fallen snow is measured. Notes regarding the character of the weather during the day are recorded. Some observers also measure elements such as bright sunshine and wind speed.

At the end of each month a report is mailed to a regional office of Environment Canada. There, after verification, the data is sent to the Atmospheric Environment Service in Downsview Ontario, where it is scrutinized again, processed and stored as a permanent record of Canada's climate.

Another corps of volunteers, severe weather watchers, maintain a sky watch for signs of hail, tornadoes, damaging winds or heavy rain, relaying sightings to the weather office. This simple task is vital for providing advance warning of dangerous conditions.

Environment Canada supplies and maintains the equipment for the observers and covers postage and other operating costs. In some parts of Canada, new observers and severe weather watchers are still needed. To join the volunteer program, contact the nearest Environment Canada weather office.

Annual Temperatures and Precipitation

(All figures are based on the thirty-year period 1961 to 1990 inclusive.)
*Airport station unless * designates city office station.*

Station	Average Temp (°C)	Total Precipitation (mm)	Total Snowfall (cm)	Station	Average Temp (°C)	Total Precipitation (mm)	Total Snowfall (cm)
Calgary, Alta.	3.9	399	135	Quebec, Que.	4.0	1 208	337
Charlottetown, PEI	5.2	1 201	339	Regina, Sask.	2.6	364	107
Churchill, Man. ...	-7.1	412	200	Saint John, NB	4.9	1 433	283
Dawson, Yukon*	-5.1	306	137	St. John's, Nfld	4.7	1 482	322
Edmonton, Alta. ..	2.1	466	127	Saskatoon, Sask. ...	2.0	347	105
Fredericton, NB ..	5.2	1 131	295	Sault Ste. Marie, Ont.	4.2	906	316
Iqaluit, NWT	-9.5	424	257	Toronto, Ont.	7.2	781	124
Halifax, NS	6.1	1 474	261	Vancouver, BC	9.9	1 167	55
Hamilton, Ont. ...	7.6	890	152	Victoria, BC	9.5	858	47
Kitchener, Ont.* ..	6.6	917	158	Whitehorse, Yukon ..	-1.0	269	145
London, Ont.	7.2	955	212	Windsor, Ont.	9.1	902	123
Moncton, NB	5.0	1 229	366	Winnipeg, Man.	2.4	504	115
Montreal, Que. ...	6.1	940	214	Yellowknife, NWT ...	-5.2	267	144
Ottawa, Ont.	5.8	911	222				

Source: *Environment Canada*

Greatest Number of Consecutive Days With Highest Temp Above 32°C

Province	# Days	Station	Starting Date
Newfoundland	3	Corner Brook	Aug. 10, 1936
Prince Edward Island	4	Charlottetown	Aug. 12, 1944
New Brunswick	8	Chipman	Aug. 11, 1944
Nova Scotia	7	Kentville	Aug. 11, 1944
Quebec	11	Nominingue	June 27, 1946
Ontario	22	Brantford	July 16, 1881
Manitoba	16	York Factory	June 27, 1878
Saskatchewan	22	Chaplin	July 4, 1894
Alberta	16	Peace River Crossing	July 17, 1925
British Columbia	31	Oliver/Hedley	July 14, 1971
Yukon Territory	4	Mayo	June 12, 1969
Northwest Territories	5	Hay River	July 31, 1984

Source: *Environment Canada*

Lightning Safety Tips

*E*ach year an average of 12 Canadians die as a result of lightning and many more are injured. The odds of being struck and killed are actually quite slim (one in 2 million), but you can ensure your safety by taking precautions:

- *If you're outside, avoid hilltops, open spaces and wire fences. You're safer in a low area like a ravine, a valley or even a roadside ditch.*
- *Only 1% of all lightning deaths occur indoors, so it's the safest place to be during a storm. Stay away from open doors and windows, and avoid metal objects and plug-in electrical appliances.*
- *Water is a conductor of electric current and even if the lightning strike is a good distance from a swimmer or boater, there can still be a serious shock, so stay out of the water.*
- *Cars are safe, but only if the windows are up and you don't touch metal parts; it's not the rubber tires but the frame that protects you.*

Average Weather Data for Selected Major Airports in Canada

	Temperature °C				Precipitation	
	Winter		Summer		Annual Snowfall cm	Total Precipitation mm
Airport	High	Low	High	Low		
Victoria	6.5	0.3	21.8	10.7	47	858
Vancouver	5.7	0.1	21.7	12.7	55	1 167
Calgary	-3.6	-15.7	23.2	9.5	135	399
Edmonton	-8.7	-19.8	22.5	9.4	127	466
Regina	-11.0	-22.1	26.3	11.9	107	364
Winnipeg	-13.2	-23.6	26.1	13.4	115	504
Toronto	-2.5	-11.1	26.8	14.2	124	781
Ottawa	-6.3	-15.5	26.4	15.1	222	911
Montreal	-5.8	-14.9	26.2	15.4	214	940
Quebec	-7.7	-17.3	24.9	13.2	337	1 208
Saint John	-2.8	-13.6	22.1	11.6	283	1 433
Halifax	-1.5	-10.3	23.4	13.2	261	1 474
Charlottetown	-3.4	-12.2	23.1	13.6	339	1 201
St. John's	-0.7	-7.9	20.2	10.5	322	1 482
Yellowknife	-23.9	-32.2	20.8	12.0	144	267
Whitehorse	-14.4	-23.2	20.3	7.6	145	269

	Wind			Sunshine		
Airport	Average Speed kn/hr	Prevailing Direction	Peak Wind km/hr	Bright Sunshine hours	sun	Possible Sunshine hours
Victoria	10	W	109	2 082		4 475
Vancouver	12	E	129	1 919		4 475
Calgary	16	N	127	2 395		4 483
Edmonton	13	S	146	2 303		4 488
Regina	20	SE	153	2 365		4 483
Winnipeg	18	S	129	2 377		4 482
Toronto	15	W	135	2 038		4 464
Ottawa	14	W	135	2 054		4 469
Montreal	15	W	161	2 015		4 465
Quebec	15	W	177	1 910		4 473
Saint John	18	S	146	1 894		4 452
Halifax	18	S	132	1 949		4 488
Charlottetown	19	W	177	1 844		4 467
St. John's	24	W	193	1 527		4 470
Yellowknife	15	E	113	2 277		4 644
Whitehorse	14	S	106	1 852		4 630

	Annual Number of Days						
Airport	Frost	Wet Weather	Thunder-storms	Freezing Precipitation	Smoke/ Haze	Blowing Snow	Fog
Victoria	60	153	3	—	29	—	24
Vancouver	55	164	6	1	120	—	34
Calgary	201	111	25	6	22	9	22
Edmonton	210	122	25	8	16	7	18
Regina	204	109	23	14	3	28	28
Winnipeg	195	119	28	13	20	24	17
Toronto	165	141	28	10	104	9	34
Ottawa	165	159	24	17	80	13	36
Montreal	156	162	26	13	75	12	18
Quebec	180	178	22	15	45	17	31
Saint John	173	164	11	12	22	13	102
Halifax	163	170	10	16	17	14	122
Charlottetown	169	177	9	17	20	26	47
St. John's	176	217	4	38	19	27	121
Yellowknife	226	118	6	11	6	9	19
Whitehorse	224	122	6	2	1	3	15

Source: *Environment Canada*

PROVINCES AND TERRITORIES

Latitude, Longitude, Elevation of Canadian Cities

City	Lat. N °	Lat. N '	Long.W °	Long.W '	Elev. (m)	City	Lat. N °	Lat. N '	Long.W °	Long.W '	Elev. (m)
Alert, NWT	82	30	62	22	31	Moose Jaw, Sask.	50	23	105	32	544
Brandon, Man.	49	51	99	57	409	Niagara Falls, Ont.	43	06	79	03	180
Brantford, Ont.	43	08	80	15	215	North Bay, Ont.	46	18	79	27	204
Burlington, Ont.	43	19	79	47	87	Ottawa, Ont.	45	26	75	41	56
Calgary, Alta.	51	02	114	03	1 045	Peterborough, Ont.	44	18	78	19	205
Charlottetown, PEI	46	14	63	07	9	Prince Rupert, BC	54	19	130	19	38
Churchill, Man.	58	45	94	10	29	Quebec, Que.	46	48	71	12	50
Dartmouth, NS	44	39	63	34	7	Regina, Sask.	50	27	104	36	577
Dawson, Yukon	64	03	139	26	369	Saint John, NB	45	16	66	03	8
Edmonton, Alta.	53	32	113	29	666	St. John's, Nfld	47	34	52	43	61
Fredericton, NB	45	57	66	38	9	Saskatoon, Sask.	52	07	106	39	484
Guelph, Ont.	43	32	80	14	325	Sault Ste. Marie, Ont.	46	30	84	20	180
Halifax, NS	44	38	63	34	18	Sherbrooke, Que.	45	24	71	53	191
Hamilton, Ont.	43	15	79	52	100	Sudbury, Ont.	46	29	80	59	347
Hull, Que.	45	25	75	42	56	Sydney, NS	46	08	60	11	62
Kingston, Ont.	44	13	76	28	80	Thunder Bay, Ont.	48	22	89	14	188
Kitchener, Ont.	43	26	80	29	335	Toronto, Ont.	43	39	79	23	91
LaSalle, Que.	45	25	73	39	34	Trois-Rivières, Que.	46	21	72	33	35
Laval, Que.	45	33	73	44	43	Vancouver, BC	49	18	123	04	43
Lethbridge, Alta.	49	41	112	49	910	Victoria, BC	48	25	123	21	17
London, Ont.	42	59	81	14	251	Whitehorse, Yukon	60	43	135	03	703
Moncton, NB	46	05	64	46	12	Winnipeg, Man.	49	53	97	08	232
Montreal, Que.	45	30	73	33	27	Yellowknife, NWT	62	28	114	22	205

Source: *Natural Resources Canada*

Area[1] of Canadian Provinces and Territories

(sq. km)

	Land	Fresh Water	Total	% of total area	Forested land	Area North of treeline
Newfoundland	371 690	34 030	405 720	4.1	142 000	30 040
Island of Newfoundland	105 700	5 690	111 390	1.1	n.a.	—
Prince Edward Island	5 660	...	5 660	0.1	3 000	—
Nova Scotia	52 840	2 650	55 490	0.6	41 000	—
New Brunswick	72 090	1 350	73 440	0.7	65 000	—
Quebec	1 356 790	183 890	1 540 680	15.5	940 000	268 320
Ontario	891 190	177 390	1 068 580	10.7	807 000	17 610
Manitoba	548 360	101 590	649 950	6.5	349 000	19 680
Saskatchewan	570 700	81 630	652 330	6.5	178 000	—
Alberta	644 390	16 800	661 190	6.6	349 000	—
British Columbia	929 730	18 070	947 800	9.5	633 000	—
Yukon Territory	478 970	4 480	483 450	4.8	242 000	34 190
Northwest Territories	3 293 020	133 300	3 426 320	34.4	615 000	2 358 960
District of: Franklin	1 423 560	19 430	1 442 990	14.5	n.a.	98 420
District of: Keewatin	575 470	25 120	600 590	6.0	n.a.	454 860
District of: Mackenzie	1 293 990	88 750	1 382 740	13.9	n.a.	440 300
Canada	**9 215 430**	**755 180**	**9 970 610**	**100.0**	**4 364 000**	**2 728 800**

Source: *Natural Resources Canada*

(1) Areas have been rounded to the nearest 10 sq. km; forested area has been rounded to nearest 1 000 sq. km; (—) = zero; ... = too small to be included; (n.a.) not available

Newfoundland

☐ **CAPITAL:** St. John's, CMA pop. (1991) 171 859. **Date entered Confederation:** Mar. 31, 1949.

☐ **POPULATION (1991):** 568 474; **Pop. density:** 1.5 per sq. km. **Pop. urban** (1991): 53.6%. **Official Languages** (1991): 97% English; 3% bilingual. **Religious distrib.** (1981): 63% Protestant; 36% Catholic.

☐ **VITAL STATISTICS:** Rates (per 1,000 pop., 1991): **Birth:** 12.5; **Death:** 6.6. **Life expectancy at birth** (1986): male 73; female 79.

☐ **MARITAL STATUS (1990):** 45% single; 49% married; 3% divorced and separated; 5% widowed. **Rates** (per 1,000 pop., 1991): **Marriage:** 6.6; **Divorce:** 1.8.

☐ **GEOGRAPHY:** Total area 405 720 sq. km; **Land area** 371 690 sq. km; **Forested land** 142 000 sq. km; **Length of coastline** 19 720 km. **Climate:** ranges from subarctic in Labrador and northern tip of island to humid continental with cool summers and heavy precipitation. **Topography:** Island of Newfoundland: highlands of the Long Range Mtns. (elev. 900 m) along w. coast; barren and rocky central plateau descends to lowlands towards the n. east; coast is deeply indented with bays and fjords. Labrador: mountainous in the n.; rugged coast and interior plateau.

☐ **ECONOMY:** **Gross Domestic Product** (1992): $9 232 million. **% change GDP** (1991–92): 0.2%. **Per capita GDP** (1992): $16 240. **Employment distrib.** (1992): services 35%; trade 19%; manu. 9%; primary ind. 7%; govt. 9%; transp., comm. and util. 8%; construc. 7%; finance 3%. **Unemployment rate** (1992): 20.2%. **Principal industries:** mining, manufacturing, fishing, logging and forestry, electricity production, tourism. **Metal production** (1991): $734 million: iron 97.4%. **Electricity production** (1991, mwh): 36 942 702: hydro 95.8%.

☐ **AGRICULTURE:** **Farm cash receipts** (1993): $60.2 million: crops 18.3%; livestock 81.7%. **No. of farms** (1991): 725.

☐ **EDUCATION (1991–92):** No. of schools: 515 elem. and sec.; 11 post-sec. **Enrolment:** 125 492 elem. and sec.; 17 273 post-sec.

☐ **INTERNATIONAL AIRPORTS:** Gander.

☐ **PROVINCIAL DATA:** **Motto:** *Quaerite Prime Regnum Dei:* "Seek Ye First the Kingdom of God." **Flower:** Pitcher plant. **Bird:** Atlantic Puffin (unofficial). **Anthem:** Ode to Newfoundland. **Tartan:** Newfoundland Tartan.

☐ **POLITICS:** **Premier:** Clyde Wells (Lib.). **Leaders, opposition parties:** Jack Harris (NDP), L. Simms (Prog. Cons.). **Date of last general election:** May 3, 1993. **Lt. Governor:** Frederick W. Russell.

Prince Edward Island

☐ **CAPITAL:** Charlottetown, metro pop. (1991) 33 153. **Date entered Confederation:** July 1, 1873.

☐ **POPULATION (1991):** 129 765; **Pop. density:** 22.9 per sq. km. **Pop. urban** (1991): 39.9%. **Official Languages** (1991): 10% English; 9% bilingual. **Religious distrib.** (1981): 50% Protestant; 47% Catholic.

☐ **VITAL STATISTICS:** Rates (per 1,000 pop., 1991): **Birth:** 14.5; **Death:** 9.1. **Life expectancy at birth** (1986): male 73; female 80.

☐ **MARITAL STATUS (1990):** 44% single; 49.1% married; 4% divorced and separated; 6% widowed. **Rates** (per 1,000 pop., 1988): **Marriage:** 7.6; **Divorce:** 2.1.

☐ **GEOGRAPHY:** Total area 5 660 sq. km; **Land area** 5 660 sq. km; **Forested land** 3 000 sq. km; **Length of coastline** 1 107 km. **Climate:** humid continental with temperatures moderated by maritime location. **Topography:** flat through gently rolling hills; sharply indented coastline; many streams but only small rivers and lakes.

☐ **ECONOMY:** **Gross Domestic Product** (1992): $2 151 million. **% change GDP** (1991–92): 1.5%. **Per capita GDP** (1992): $16 576. **Employment distrib.** (1992): services 37%; trade 16%; agr. 8%; govt. 10%; manu. 8%. **Unemployment rate** (1992): 17.7%. **Principal industries:** agriculture, tourism, fishing, manufacturing. **Electricity production** (1991, mwh): 71 384: steam 95.4%.

☐ **AGRICULTURE:** **Farm cash receipts** (1993): $226 million: 54.7% crops; 45.3% livestock. **No. of farms** (1991): 2 361.

☐ **EDUCATION (1991–92):** No. of schools: 72 elem. and sec.; 3 post-sec. **Enrolment:** 24 754 elem. and sec.; 3 711 post-sec.

☐ **INTERNATIONAL AIRPORTS:** none.

☐ **PROVINCIAL DATA:** **Motto:** *Parva Sub Ingenti:* "The small under the protection of the great." **Flower:** Lady's slipper. **Bird:** Blue Jay. **Tree:** Red Oak.

☐ **POLITICS:** **Premier:** Catherine Callbeck (Lib.). **Leaders, opposition parties:** P. Mella (Prog. Cons.), L. Duchesne (NDP). **Date of last general election:** March 29, 1989. **Lt. Governor:** Marion Reid.

Nova Scotia

☐ **CAPITAL:** Halifax, metro pop. (1991) 320 501. **Date entered Confederation:** July 1, 1867.

☐ **POPULATION (1991): 899 942;** Pop. density: 16.2 per sq. km. **Pop. urban** (1991): 53.5%. **Official Languages** (1986): 92% English; 8% bilingual. **Religious distrib.** (1981): 58% Protestant; 37% Catholic.

☐ **VITAL STATISTICS: Rates** (per 1,000 pop., 1991): **Birth:** 13.4; **Death:** 8.1. **Life expectancy at birth** (1986): male 72; female 79.

☐ **MARITAL STATUS (1986):** 44% single; 47% married; 4% divorced and separated; 6% widowed. **Rates** (per 1,000 pop., 1988): **Marriage:** 7.8; **Divorce:** 2.80.

☐ **GEOGRAPHY: Total area** 55 490 sq. km; **Land area** 52 840 sq. km; **Forested land** 41,000 sq. km; **Length of coastline** 5 934 km. **Climate:** humid continental with some moderating effects due to maritime location. **Topography:** Atlantic Uplands are segmented by river valleys; Cape Breton Is. rises from lowland in the s. to a high plateau; many rivers, lakes and jagged coastline.

☐ **ECONOMY: Gross Domestic Product** (1992): $17 987 million. **% change GDP** (1991–92): 2.4%. **Per capita GDP**(1992): $19 986. **Employment distrib.** (1992): services 34%; trade 20%; manu. 13%; govt. 8%; transp., comm. and util. 8%; construc. 6%; finance 4%; primary ind. 4%; agr. 2%. **Unemployment rate** (1992): 13.1%. **Principal industries:** manufacturing, fishing and trapping, mining, agriculture, pulp and paper. **Metal production** (1991): $32.4 million: tin 77.8%. **Electricity production** (1991, mwh): 9 393 515.

☐ **AGRICULTURE: Farm cash receipts** (1993): $302 million: crops 30.0%; livestock 70.0%. **No. of farms** (1991): 3 980.

☐ **EDUCATION (1991–92): No. of schools:** 524 elem. and sec.; 21 post-sec. **Enrolment:** 168 897 elem. and sec.; 31 254 post-sec.

☐ **INTERNATIONAL AIRPORTS:** Halifax

☐ **PROVINCIAL DATA: Motto:** *Munit Haec et Altera Vincit:* "One defends and the other conquers." **Flower:** Mayflower. **Bird:** none. **Tree:** Red Spruce. **Gem:** Agate.

☐ **POLITICS: Premier:** John Savage (Lib.). **Leaders, opposition parties:** T.R.B. Donahoe (Prog. Cons.), Alexa McDonough (NDP). **Date of last general election:** May 25, 1993. **Lt. Governor:** Lloyd R. Crouse.

New Brunswick

☐ **CAPITAL:** Fredericton, metro pop. (1991) 71 869. **Date entered Confederation:** July 1, 1867.

☐ **POPULATION (1991): 723 900;** Pop. density: 9.9 per sq. km. **Pop. urban** (1991): 47.7%. **Official Languages** (1986): 59% English; 12% French; 30% bilingual. **Religious distrib.** (1981): 54% Catholic; 43% Protestant.

☐ **VITAL STATISTICS: Rates** (per 1,000 pop., 1991): **Birth:** 13.1; **Death:** 7.5. **Life expectancy at birth** (1986): male 72; female 80.

☐ **MARITAL STATUS (1991):** 42% single; 49% married; 4% divorced and separated; 5% widowed. **Rates** (per 1,000 pop., 1990): **Marriage:** 7.0; **Divorce:** 2.34.

☐ **GEOGRAPHY: Total area** 73 440 sq. km; **Land area** 72 090 sq. km; **Forested land** 61,000 sq. km; **Length of coastline** 1 524 km. **Climate:** humid continental climate except along the shores where there is a marked maritime effect. **Topography:** northern upland; rolling central plateau; southern lowland plain with many rivers.

☐ **ECONOMY: Gross Domestic Product** (1992): $13 878 million. **% change GDP** (1991–92): 2.5%. **Per capita GDP**(1992): $19 171. **Employment distrib.** (1991): services 34%; trade 20%; manu. 13%; transp., comm. and util. 8%; govt. 8%; construc. 6%; primary ind. 4%; finance 4%; agr. 2%. **Unemployment rate** (1992): 12.8%. **Principal industries:** manufacturing, fishing, mining, forestry, pulp and paper, agriculture. **Metal production** (1991): $375 million: zinc 71.5%; silver 6.3%; lead 11.8%; cement 2%; copper 7.6%. **Electricity production** (1991, mwh): 15 807 472: steam 88.5%.

☐ **AGRICULTURE: Farm cash receipts** (1993): $268 million: crops 43.3%; livestock 56.7%. **No. of farms** (1991): 3 252.

☐ **EDUCATION (1991–92): No. of schools:** 453 elem. and sec.; 13 post-sec. **Enrolment:** 142 687 elem. and sec.; 21 084 post-sec.

☐ **INTERNATIONAL AIRPORTS:** none.

☐ **PROVINCIAL DATA: Motto:** *Spem Reduxit:* "Hope was restored." **Flower:** Purple Violet. **Bird:** Black-capped Chickadee. **Tree:** Balsam Fir.

☐ **POLITICS: Premier:** Frank McKenna (Lib.). **Leaders, opposition parties:** Danny Cameron (interim) (CoR), Dennis Cochrane (Prog. Cons.), Elizabeth Weir (NDP). **Date of last general election:** Sept. 23, 1991. **Lt. Governor:** Gilbert Finn.

Quebec

☐ **CAPITAL:** Quebec, metro pop. (1991) 645 550. **Date entered Confederation:** July 1, 1867.

☐ **POPULATION (1991): 6 895 963; Pop. density:** 4.5 per sq. km. **Pop. urban** (1991): 77.6%. **Official Languages** (1986): 59% French; 6% English; 35% bilingual. **Religious distrib.** (1981): 88% Catholic; 6% Protestant; 2% Jewish; 1% Eastern Orthodox; 1% Eastern non-Christian.

☐ **VITAL STATISTICS: Rates** (per 1,000 pop., 1991): **Birth:** 14.2; **Death:** 7.2. **Life expectancy at birth** (1986): male 72; female 79.

☐ **MARITAL STATUS (1986):** 43% single; 47% married; 5% divorced and separated; 5% widowed. **Rates** (per 1,000 pop., 1988): **Marriage:** 5.1; **Divorce:** 2.99.

☐ **GEOGRAPHY: Total area** 1 540 680 sq. km; **Land area** 1 356 790 sq. km; **Forested land** 940 000 sq. km; **Length of coastline** 10 839 km. **Climate:** varies from subarctic to continental. **Topography:** lowlands along the St. Lawrence R. valley separate the Laurentian Mtns. to the n. and the Appalachian Mtns. to the s.; Canadian Shield landscape dominates north.

☐ **ECONOMY: Gross Domestic Product** (1992): $157 067 million. **% change GDP** (1991–92): 1.2%. **Per capita GDP**(1992): $22 776. **Employment distrib.** (1992): services 36%; manu. 18%; trade 18%; transp., comm. and util. 7%; govt. 7%; finance 6%; construc. 5%; agr. 2%; primary ind. 1%; unclassified 1%. **Unemployment rate** (1992): 12.8%. **Principal industries:** manufacturing, electric power, mining, pulp and paper, transportation equipment. **Metal Production** (1991): $1.9 billion: gold 36.7%; copper 16.3%; zinc 8%. **Electricity production** (1991, mwh): 142 992 002: hydro 96.9%.

☐ **AGRICULTURE: Farm cash receipts** (1993): $2.6 billion: crops 23.2%; livestock 76.8%. **No. of farms** (1991): 38 076.

☐ **EDUCATION (1991–92): No. of schools:** 2 977 elem. and sec.; 97 post-sec. **Enrolment:** 1 145 066 elem. and sec.; 289 646 post-sec.

☐ **INTERNATIONAL AIRPORTS:** Dorval; Mirabel.

☐ **PROVINCIAL DATA: Motto:** *Je me souviens:* "I remember." **Flower:** Lys blanc de jardin (White Garden (Madonna) Lily). **Bird:** Harfang des neiges (Snowy Owl).

☐ **POLITICS: Premier:** Jacques Parizeau (Parti Québécois). **Leader, opposition parties:** Daniel Johnson (Lib.). **Date of last general election:** Sept. 12, 1994. **Lt. Governor:** Martial Asselin.

Ontario

☐ **CAPITAL:** Toronto, metro pop. (1991) 3 893 046. **Date entered Confederation:** July 1, 1867.

☐ **POPULATION (1991): 10 084 885; Pop. density:** 9.4 per sq. km. **Pop. urban** (1991): 81.8%. **Official Languages** (1986): 86% English; 1% French; 12% bilingual. **Religious distrib.** (1981): 52% Protestant; 36% Catholic; 2% Eastern Orthodox; 2% Jewish.

☐ **VITAL STATISTICS: Rates** (per 1,000 pop., 1991): **Birth:** 15.3; **Death:** 7.4. **Life expectancy at birth** (1986): male 73; female 80.

☐ **MARITAL STATUS (1986):** 42% single; 48% married; 5% divorced and separated; 5% widowed. **Rates** (per 1,000 pop., 1988): **Marriage:** 8.3; **Divorce:** 3.17.

☐ **GEOGRAPHY: Total area** 1 068 580 sq. km; **Land area** 891 190 sq. km; **Forested land** 807 000 sq. km; **Length of coastline** 1 210 km. **Climate:** ranges from humid continental in south to subarctic in far north; westerly winds bring winter storms; the Great Lakes moderate winter temperatures. **Topography:** Rugged, rocky Canadian Shield plateau is broken by lowlands around Great Lakes, St. Lawrence R. and Hudson Bay.

☐ **ECONOMY: Gross Domestic Product** (1992): $277 454 million. **% change GDP** (1991–92): 1.9%. **Per capita GDP** (1992): $27 511. **Employment distrib.** (1992): services 36%; manu. 18%; trade 16%; transp., comm. and util. 7%; govt. 6%; finance 7%; construc. 6%; agr. 2%; primary ind. .3%; unclassified .6%. **Unemployment rate** (1992): 10.8%. **Principal industries:** manufacturing, construction, agriculture, forestry, mining. **Metal production** (1991): $3.8 billion: nickel 32.2%; gold 27.2%; copper 18.7%; uranium 6.9%; zinc 7.2%. **Electricity production** (1991, mwh): 142 442 661: nuclear 49.7%; hydro 26.4%; steam 23%.

☐ **AGRICULTURE: Farm cash receipts** (1993): $5.5 billion: crops 39.1%; livestock 60.9%. **No. of farms** (1991): 68 633.

☐ **EDUCATION (1991–92): No. of schools:** 5 539 elem. and sec.; 53 post-sec. **Enrolment:** 2 035 618 elem. and sec.; 333 220 post-sec.

☐ **INTERNATIONAL AIRPORTS:** Pearson (Toronto); Ottawa.

☐ **PROVINCIAL DATA:** Motto: *Ut Incepit Fidelis Sic Permanet:* "Loyal she began, loyal she remains." **Flower:** White trillium. **Bird:** Common Loon. **Tree:** Eastern White Pine. **Gem:** Amethyst.

☐ **POLITICS: Premier:** Bob Rae (NDP). **Leaders, opposition parties:** Mike Harris (Prog. Cons.); Lyn McLeod (Lib.). **Date of last general election:** Sept. 6, 1990. **Lt. Governor:** Henry N. R. Jackman.

Manitoba

☐ **CAPITAL:** Winnipeg, metro pop. (1991) 652 354. **Date entered Confederation:** July 15, 1870.

☐ **POPULATION (1991):** 1 091 942; **Pop. density:** 1.7 per sq. km. **Pop. urban** (1991): 72.1%. **Official Languages** (1986): 90% English; 9% bilingual. **Religious distrib.** (1981): 57% Protestant; 31% Catholic; 2% Eastern Orthodox; 2% Jewish.

☐ **VITAL STATISTICS: Rates** (per 1,000 pop., 1991): **Birth:** 15.8; **Death:** 8.2. **Life expectancy at birth** (1986): male 73; female 80.

☐ **MARITAL STATUS (1986):** 44% single; 47% married; 4% divorced and separated; 6% widowed. **Rates** (per 1,000 pop., 1988): **Marriage:** 7.3; **Divorce:** 2.76.

☐ **GEOGRAPHY: Total area** 649 950 sq. km; **Land area** 548 360 sq. km; **Forested land** 349 000 sq. km; **Length of coastline** 917 km. **Climate:** continental with seasonal extremes. **Topography:** the land rises gradually south and west from Hudson Bay; flat plateau through south central region; countless lakes, streams and bogs.

☐ **ECONOMY: Gross Domestic Product** (1992): $23 969 million. **% change GDP** (1991–92): 1.9%. **Per capita GDP** (1992): $21 951. **Employment distrib.** (1992): services 36%; trade 18%; manu. 10%; transp., comm. and util. 9%; agr. 8%; govt. 7%; finance 5%; construc. 5%; primary ind. 2%. **Unemployment rate** (1992): 9.6%. **Principal industries:** manufacturing, agriculture, food industry, mining, construction. **Metal production** (1991): $948 million: nickel 62.1%; copper 15.7%; zinc 11.9%; gold 4%. **Electricity production** (1991, mwh): 22 891 405: hydro 98.5%.

☐ **AGRICULTURE: Farm cash receipts** (1993): $2.0 billion: crops 53.7%; livestock 46.3%. **No. of farms** (1991): 25 706.

☐ **EDUCATION (1991–92):** No. of schools: 831 elem. and sec.; 15 post-sec. **Enrolment:** 220 515 elem. and sec.; 24 484 post-sec.

☐ **INTERNATIONAL AIRPORTS:** Winnipeg.

☐ **PROVINCIAL DATA: Motto:** Glorious and Free. **Flower:** Prairie Crocus. **Bird:** Great Grey Owl. **Tartan:** Manitoba Tartan.

☐ **POLITICS: Premier:** Gary Filmon (Prog. Cons.). **Leaders, opposition parties:** Paul Edwards (Lib.), Gary Doer (NDP). **Date of last general election:** Sept. 11, 1990. **Lt. Governor:** W. Yvon Dumont.

Saskatchewan

☐ **CAPITAL:** Regina, metro pop. (1991) 191 692. **Date entered Confederation:** Sept. 1, 1905.

☐ **POPULATION (1991):** 988 928; **Pop. density:** 1.5 per sq. km. **Pop. urban** (1991): 63%. **Official Languages** (1986): 95% English; 5% bilingual. **Religious distrib.** (1981): 57% Protestant; 31% Catholic; 2% Eastern Orthodox; 2% Jewish.

☐ **VITAL STATISTICS: Rates** (per 1,000 pop., 1991): **Birth:** 15.4; **Death:** 8.1. **Life expectancy at birth** (1986): male 74; female 80.

☐ **MARITAL STATUS (1986):** 44% single; 47% married; 4% divorced and separated; 5% widowed. **Rates** (per 1,000 pop., 1988): **Marriage:** 6.7; **Divorce:** 2.44.

☐ **GEOGRAPHY: Total area** 652 330 sq. km; **Land area** 570 700 sq. km; **Forested land** 178 000 sq. km; **Climate:** continental, with cold winters and hot summers. **Topography:** gently rolling plains through south; higher, hilly plateaus in the s.w.; north is rugged Canadian Shield.

☐ **ECONOMY: Gross Domestic Product** (1992): $20 239 million. **% change GDP** (1991–92): -0.6%. **Per capita GDP** (1992): $20 466. **Employment distrib.** (1992): services 35%; trade 16%; govt. 7%; transp., comm. and util. 7%; manu. 5%; construc. 5%; finance 5%; primary ind. 3%; agri. 16%. **Unemployment rate** (1992): 8.2%. **Principal industries:** agriculture, mining, manufacturing, electric power, construction, chemical prod. **Metal production** (1991): $373 million: uranium 89.2%; gold 10.4%. **Electricity production** (1991, mwh): 13 598 251: steam 68.6%; hydro 31%.

☐ **AGRICULTURE: Farm cash receipts** (1993): $3.7 billion: crops 71.5%; livestock 28.5%. **No. of farms** (1991): 60 840.

☐ **EDUCATION (1991–92):** No. of schools: 978 elem. and sec.; 5 post-sec. **Enrolment:** 212 071 elem. and sec.; 25 901 post-sec.

☐ **INTERNATIONAL AIRPORTS:** none.

☐ **PROVINCIAL DATA: Motto:** *Multis E Gentibus Vires:* "from many peoples strength". **Flower:** Western Red Lily. **Bird:** Prairie sharp-tailed grouse. **Tree:** White Birch. **Tartan:** Saskatchewan Tartan.

☐ **POLITICS: Premier:** Roy Romanow (NDP). **Leaders, opposition parties:** Lynda Haverstock (Lib.), Rick Swenson (Prog. Cons.). **Date of last general election:** Oct. 21, 1991. **Lt. Governor:** Sylvia O. Fedoruk.

Alberta

☐ **CAPITAL:** Edmonton, metro pop. (1991) 839 924. **Date entered Confederation:** Sept. 1, 1905.

☐ **POPULATION (1991): 2 545 553; Pop. density:** 3.8 per sq. km. **Pop. urban** (1991): 79.8%. **Official Languages** (1986): 92% English; 6% bilingual. **Religious distrib.** (1981): 56% Protestant; 28% Catholic; 2% Eastern Orthodox; 2% Eastern non-Christian.

☐ **VITAL STATISTICS: Rates** (per 1,000 pop., 1991): **Birth:** 17.0; **Death:** 5.7. **Life expectancy at birth** (1986): male 74; female 80.

☐ **MARITAL STATUS (1986):** 44% single; 47% married; 5% divorced and separated; 4% widowed. **Rates** (per 1,000 pop., 1988): **Marriage:** 8.1; **Divorce:** 3.60.

☐ **GEOGRAPHY: Total area** 661 190 sq. km; **Land area** 644 390 sq. km; **Forested land** 349 000 sq. km. **Climate:** great variance in temperatures between regions and seasons; summer highs between 16°C and 32°C; winters as low as -45°C. **Topography:** Rocky Mtns. in s.w. to rolling prairie throughout southern region; far north is a forested plateau.

☐ **ECONOMY: Gross Domestic Product** (1992): $72 942 million. **% change GDP** (1991–92): 2.1%. **Per capita GDP** (1992): $28 655. **Employment distrib.** (1992): services 38%; trade 18%; transp., comm. and util. 7%; manu. 7%; agr. 7%; govt. 6%; primary ind. 6%; construc. 7%; finance 5%; 4 unclassified. **Unemployment rate** (1992): 9.5%. **Principal industries:** chemical products, mining, agriculture, food, manufacturing, construction, oil prod. and refinement. **Metal production** (1991): $3 billion: gold 15%. **Electricity production** (1991, mwh): 44 479 165: steam 90.6%.

☐ **AGRICULTURE: Farm cash receipts** (1993): $4.5 billion: crops 35.0%; livestock 65.0%. **No. of farms** (1991): 7 245.

☐ **EDUCATION (1991–92):** No. of schools: 1 727 elem. and sec.; 27 post-sec. **Enrolment:** 519 936 elem. and sec.; 74 681 post-sec.

☐ **INTERNATIONAL AIRPORTS:** Edmonton; Calgary.

☐ **PROVINCIAL DATA: Motto:** *Fortis et Liber:* "Strong and free." **Flower:** Wild Rose. **Bird:** Great horned owl. **Tree:** Lodge pole pine. **Tartan:** Alberta Tartan. **Stone:** Petrified wood.

☐ **POLITICS: Premier:** Ralph Klein (Prog. Cons.). **Leaders, opposition parties:** Betty Hughes (interim) (Lib.), Ross Harvey (NDP). **Date of last general election:** June 14, 1993. **Lt. Governor:** Gordon Towers.

British Columbia

☐ **CAPITAL:** Victoria, metro pop. (1991) 287 897. **Date entered Confederation:** July 20, 1871.

☐ **POPULATION (1991): 3 282 061; Pop. density:** 3.5 per sq. km. **Pop. urban** (1991): 80.4%. **Official Languages** (1986): 92% English; 6% bilingual. **Religious distrib.** (1981): 55% Protestant; 20% Catholic; 3% Eastern non-Christian; 1% Eastern Orthodox.

☐ **VITAL STATISTICS: Rates** (per 1,000 pop., 1991): **Birth:** 14.2; **Death:** 7.5. **Life expectancy at birth** (1986): male 74; female 80.

☐ **MARITAL STATUS (1986):** 41% single; 48% married; 6% divorced and separated; 5% widowed. **Rates** (per 1,000 pop., 1988): **Marriage:** 8.2; **Divorce:** 3.55.

☐ **GEOGRAPHY: Total area** 947 800 sq. km; **Land area** 929 730 sq. km; **Forested land** 633 000 sq. km; **Length of coastline** 17 856 km. **Climate:** maritime with mild temperatures and abundant rainfall in the coastal areas; continental climate with temperature extremes in the interior and northeast. **Topography:** mostly mountainous; deep river valleys and gorges, except for the n.e. area which is an extension of the Great Plains; indented coast with numerous bays and islands.

☐ **ECONOMY: Gross Domestic Product** (1992): $86 669 million. **% change GDP** (1991–92): 3.3%. **Per capita GDP** (1992): $26 407. **Employment distrib.** (1992): services 38%; trade 19%; manu. 10%; transp., comm. and util. 8%; govt. 5%; finance 6%; construc. 8%; primary ind. 3%; agr. 2%; .5 unclassified. **Unemployment rate** (1992): 10.4%. **Principal industries:** forestry, wood and paper, mining, tourism, agriculture, fishing, manufacturing. **Metal production** (1991): $1.5 billion: copper 60.2%; zinc 10.6%; gold 16.1%. **Electricity production** (1991, mwh): 63 373 895: hydro 95%.

☐ **AGRICULTURE: Farm cash receipts** (1993): $1.5 billion: crops 39.8%; livestock 60.2%. **No. of farms** (1991): 19 225.

☐ **EDUCATION (1991–92): No. of schools:** 1 952 elem. and sec.; 25 post-sec. **Enrolment:** 587 920 elem. and sec.; 73 752 post-sec.

☐ **INTERNATIONAL AIRPORTS:** Vancouver; Victoria.

☐ **PROVINCIAL DATA: Motto:** *Splendor Sine Occasu:* "Splendor without Diminishment." **Flower:** Dogwood. **Bird:** Stellar's Jay.

☐ **POLITICS: Premier:** Michael Harcourt (NDP). **Leader, opposition party:** Gordon Campbell (Lib.). **Date of last general election:** Oct. 17, 1991. **Lt. Governor:** David C. Lam.

Yukon Territory

☐ **CAPITAL:** Whitehorse, metro pop. (1994) 22 768. **Date entered Confederation:** June 13, 1898.

☐ **POPULATION (1994):** 31 197; **Pop. density:** .06 per sq. km. **Pop. urban** (1991): 58.8%. **Official Languages** (1986): 91% English; 9% bilingual.

☐ **VITAL STATISTICS: Rates** (per 1,000 pop., 1991): **Birth:** 21.1; **Death:** 4.2.

☐ **MARITAL STATUS (1986):** 48% single; 44% married; 6% divorced and separated; 2% widowed. **Rates** (per 1,000 pop., 1988): **Marriage:** 8.2; **Divorce:** 3.20.

☐ **GEOGRAPHY: Total area** 483 450 sq. km; **Land area** 478 970 sq. km; **Forested land** 242 000 sq. km; **Length of coastline** 343 km. **Climate:** great variance in temperatures; warm summers, very cold winters; low precipitation. **Topography:** main feature is the Yukon plateau with 21 peaks exceeding 3 300 m; open tundra in the far north.

☐ **ECONOMY: Gross Domestic Product** (1993): $904 million. **% change GDP** (1992–93): -7.1%. **Per capita GDP** (1993): $28 220. **Principal industries:** mining, tourism. **Metal production** (1993): $111.1 million: gold 45.4%; zinc 37.8%; lead 12.5%; silver 4.5%. **Electricity production** (1993, mwh): 334 879: hydro 85.6%; thermal 14.4%.

☐ **EDUCATION (1993–94): No. of schools:** 29 elem. and sec.; 1 post-sec. **Enrolment:** 5 623 elem. and sec.; 912 post-sec.

☐ **INTERNATIONAL AIRPORTS:** Whitehorse.

☐ **PROVINCIAL DATA: Flower:** Fireweed. **Bird:** Common Raven.

☐ **POLITICS: Commissioner:** Ken McKinnon; **Govt. Leader:** John Ostashek (Yukon Party). **Leader, opposition party:** Tony Penikett (NDP). **Date of last general election:** Oct. 19, 1992.

Northwest Territories

☐ **CAPITAL:** Yellowknife, metro pop. (1991) 15 179. **Date entered Confederation:** July 15, 1870.

☐ **POPULATION (1991):** 54 649; **Pop. density:** .02 per sq. km. **Pop. urban** (1991): 36.7%. **Official Languages** (1986): 81% English; 7% bilingual.

☐ **VITAL STATISTICS: Rates** (per 1,000 pop., 1991): **Birth:** 29.9; **Death:** 4.3.

☐ **MARITAL STATUS (1986):** 57% single; 38% married; 3% divorced and separated; 2% widowed. **Rates** (per 1,000 pop., 1988): **Marriage:** 4.2; **Divorce:** 2.12.

☐ **GEOGRAPHY: Total area** 3 426 320 sq. km; **Land area** 3 293 020 sq. km; **Forested land** 615 000 sq. km; **Length of coastline** 111 249 km. **Climate:** extreme temperatures and low precipitation; arctic and sub-arctic. **Topography:** mostly tundra plains formed on the rocks of the Canadian Shield; the Mackenzie Lowland is a continuation of the Great Plains; the Mackenzie River Valley is forested.

☐ **ECONOMY: Gross Domestic Product** (1992): $2 106 million. **% change GDP** (1991–92): 0.0%. **Per capita GDP** (1992): $38 536. **Principal industries:** construction, utilities, services, tourism. **Metal production** (1991): $477.6 million: zinc 46.4%; gold 46.8%. **Electricity production** (1991, mwh): 571 977: hydro 42.4%; steam 41.5%.

☐ **EDUCATION (1991–92): No. of schools:** 76 elem. and sec.; 1 post-sec. **Enrolment:** 15 515 elem. and sec.; 282 post-sec.

☐ **INTERNATIONAL AIRPORTS:** none.

☐ **PROVINCIAL DATA: Flower:** Mountain Avens. **Bird:** none.

☐ **POLITICS: Commissioner:** Dan L. Norris; **Govt. Leader:** Nellie Cournoyea. **Date of last general election:** Oct. 15, 1991.

CANADIAN CITIES

Calgary, Alta

☐ **YEAR INCORPORATED:** 1893. **Population** (1991): 754 033; 49.9% male, 50.1% female. **Area:** 5 086 sq. km. **Pop. density:** 148.3 per sq. km. **Pop. growth** (1986–1991): 12.3%. **Pop. over 65:** 24 200 males; 34 475 females. **Pop. under 35:** 219 585 males; 214 785 females.

☐ **OFFICIAL LANGUAGES (1991):** 91.2% English; 0.2% French; 7% bilingual; 1.5% neither. **Immigrant pop.** (1991): 151 745, 20.1%. **Religious breakdown** (1991): 46% Protestant; 25% Catholic; 22% no affiliation; 4% Eastern non-Christian; 1% Jewish; 1% other.

☐ **AVG. INCOME (1991):** $34 396 males; $19 391 females; $58 587 families. **Avg. family size** (1991): 3.1 persons. **Single parent families** (1991): 12.8% of families.

☐ **CLIMATE:** **Avg. day/night temps.** -3.6°/-15.7° (Jan.); 23.2°/9.5° (July). **Avg. annual precip.** 398.8 mm. **Avg. annual snowfall:** 135.4 cm.

Chicoutimi–Jonquière, Que.

☐ **YEAR INCORPORATED:** 1976. **Population** (1991): 160 930; 49.5% male, 50.5% female. **Area:** 1 723.31 sq. km. **Pop. density:** 93 per sq. km. **Pop. growth** (1986–1991): 1.6%. **Pop. over 65:** 6 090 males; 8 525 females. **Pop. under 35:** 43 880 males; 42 445 females.

☐ **OFFICIAL LANGUAGES (1991):** .93% English; 98.0% French; .34% neither. **Immigrant pop.** (1991): 1 170, .72%. **Religious breakdown** (1991): 97% Catholic; 1.5% no affiliation; 1% Protestant; .1% Eastern non-Christian; .03% other.

☐ **AVG. INCOME: (1991):** $29 873 males; $15 016 females; $45 475 families. **Avg. family size** (1991): 3.1 persons. **Single parent families** (1991): 13.4% of families.

☐ **CLIMATE:** **Avg. temps.** -15.8° (Jan.); 18° (July). **Avg. annual precip.** 641 mm. **Avg. annual snowfall:** 345 cm.

Edmonton, Alta

☐ **YEAR INCORPORATED:** 1904. **Population** (1991): 839 924; 49.8% male, 50.2% female. **Area:** 9 533 sq. km. **Pop. density:** 88.1 per sq. km. **Pop. growth** (1986–1991): 8.5%. **Pop. over 65:** 30 085 males; 41 125 females. **Pop. under 35:** 244 710 males; 238 700 females.

☐ **OFFICIAL LANGUAGES (1991):** 90.6% English; 0.1% French; 7.7% bilingual; 1.8% neither. **Immigrant pop.** (1991): 152 810, 18.2%. **Religious breakdown** (1991): 43% Protestant; 29% Catholic; 20% no affiliation; 4% Eastern non-Christian; 3% other; .5% Jewish.

☐ **AVG. INCOME (1991):** $30 952 males; $17 931 females; $52 967 families. **Avg. family size** (1991): 3.1 persons. **Single parent families** (1991): 14.2% of families.

☐ **CLIMATE:** **Avg. day/night temps.** -8.7°/-19.8° (Jan.); 22.5°/9.4° (July). **Avg. annual precip.** 465.8 mm. **Avg. annual snowfall:** 127.1 cm.

Halifax, NS

☐ **YEAR INCORPORATED:** 1841. **Population** (1991): 320 501; 48.7% male, 51.3% female. **Area:** 2 503 sq. km. **Pop. density:** 128 per sq. km. **Pop. growth** (1986–1991): 8.3%. **Pop. over 65:** 12 185 males; 18 185 females. **Pop. under 35:** 89 820 males; 89 910 females.

☐ **OFFICIAL LANGUAGES (1991):** 90.1% English; 0.1% French; 9.6% bilingual; 1.3% neither. **Immigrant pop.** (1991): 20 790, 6.5%. **Religious breakdown** (1991): 50% Protestant; 39% Catholic; 9% no affiliation; 1% Eastern non-Christian; .6% other; .5% Jewish.

☐ **AVG. INCOME (1991):** $30 821 males; $17 656 females; $51 877 families. **Avg. family size** (1991): 3.0 persons. **Single parent families** (1991): 14.0% of families.

☐ **CLIMATE:** **Avg. day/night temps.** -1.5°/-10.3° (Jan.); 23.4°/13.2° (July). **Avg. annual precip.** 1 473.5 mm. **Avg. annual snowfall:** 261.4 cm.

Hamilton, Ont.

☐ **YEAR INCORPORATED:** 1846. **Population** (1991): 599 760; 48.9% male, 51.1% female. **Area:** 1 359 sq. km. **Pop. density:** 441.5 per sq. km. **Pop. growth** (annual avg. 1986–1991): 7.7%. **Pop. over 65:** 32 085 males; 44 865 females. **Pop. under 35:** 154 415 males; 151 520 females.

☐ **OFFICIAL LANGUAGES (1991):** 91.9% English; 0.1% French; 6.6% bilingual; 3.4% neither. **Immigrant pop.** (1991): 139 560, 23.3%. **Religious breakdown** (1991): 47% Protestant; 35% Catholic; 13% no affiliation; 2% Eastern non-Christian; 2% other; .8% Jewish.

☐ **AVG. INCOME (1991):** $33 009 males; $18 180 females; $56 362 families. **Avg. family size (1991):** 3.1 persons. **Single parent families (1991):** 12.3% of families.

☐ **CLIMATE:** Avg. day/night temps. -2.6°/-10.0° (Jan.); 26.4°/15.1° (July). **Avg. annual precip.** 890.4 mm. **Avg. annual snowfall:** 152.4 cm.

Kitchener, Ont.

☐ **YEAR INCORPORATED:** 1912. **Population (1991):** 356 420; 49.3% male, 50.7% female. **Area:** 82 364 sq. km. **Pop. density:** 433 per sq. km. **Pop. growth (1986–1991):** 14.5%. **Pop. over 65:** 14 670 males; 21 790 females. **Pop. under 35:** 101 050 males; 98 255 females.

☐ **OFFICIAL LANGUAGES (1991):** 79.4% English; 1.3% French; 16.6% other. **Immigrant pop. (1991):** 75 980, 21.3%. **Religious breakdown (1991):** 50% Protestant; 33% Catholic; 11% no affiliation; 3% Eastern non-Christian; 1% other; .2% Jewish.

☐ **AVG. INCOME (1991):** $31 980 males; $17 900 females; $54 839 families. **Avg. family size (1991):** 3.1 persons. **Single parent families (1991):** 12.3% of families.

☐ **CLIMATE:** Avg. day/night temps. -3.3°/-11.4° (Jan.); 26.1°/13.6° (July). **Avg. annual precip.** 917.0 mm. **Avg. annual snowfall:** 158.0 cm.

London, Ont.

☐ **YEAR INCORPORATED:** 1855. **Population (1991):** 381 522; 48.3% male, 51.7% female. **Area:** 2 105 sq. km. **Pop. density:** 181.2 per sq. km. **Pop. growth (annual avg. 1986–1991):** 11.5%. **Pop. over 65:** 18 585 males; 27 565 females. **Pop. under 35:** 101 925 males; 102 195 females.

☐ **OFFICIAL LANGUAGES (1991):** 92.4% English; 0.2% French; 6.4% bilingual; 2.2% neither. **Immigrant pop. (1991):** 70 655, 19.3%. **Religious breakdown (1991):** 54% Protestant; 27% Catholic; 14% no affiliation; 2% Eastern non-Christian; 2% other; .6% Jewish.

☐ **AVG. INCOME (1991):** $31 696 males; $18 826 females; $54 945 families. **Avg. family size (1991):** 3.0 persons. **Single parent families (1991):** 13.4% of families.

☐ **CLIMATE:** Avg. day/night temps. -2.8°/-10.7° (Jan.); 26.4°/14.2° (July). **Avg. annual precip.** 955.1 mm. **Avg. annual snowfall:** 212.3 cm.

Montreal, Que.

☐ **YEAR INCORPORATED:** 1832. **Population (1991):** 3 127 242; 48.4% male, 51.6% female. **Area:** 3 509 sq. km. **Pop. density:** 891.2 per sq. km. **Pop. growth (1986–1991):** 7%. **Pop. over 65:** 136 735 males; 216 310 females. **Pop. under 35:** 805 070 males; 788 915 females.

☐ **OFFICIAL LANGUAGES (1991):** 9.6% English; 40.4% French; 48.3% bilingual; 1.7% neither. **Immigrant pop. (1991):** ˋ520 530, 16.6%. **Religious breakdown (1991):** 78% Catholic; 8% Protestant; 5% no affiliation; 3% Eastern non-Christian; 3% Jewish; 3% other.

☐ **AVG. INCOME (1991):** $29 865 males; $17 998 females; $50 496 families. **Avg. family size (1991):** 3.0 persons. **Single parent families (1991):** 15.6% of families.

☐ **CLIMATE:** Avg. day/night temps. -5.8°/-14.9° (Jan.); 26.2°/15.4° (July). **Avg. annual precip.** 939.7 mm. **Avg. annual snowfall:** 214.2 cm.

Oshawa, Ont.

☐ **YEAR INCORPORATED:** 1924. **Population (1991):** 240 104; 49.7% male, 50.3% female. **Area:** 894.19 sq. km. **Pop. density:** 269 per sq. km. **Pop. growth (1986–1991):** 18.0%. **Pop. over 65:** 9 085 males; 12 555 females. **Pop. under 35:** 68 165 males; 66 695 females.

☐ **OFFICIAL LANGUAGES (1991):** 87.3% English; 2.1% French; 8.9% neither. **Immigrant pop. (1991):** 40 845, 17.0%. **Religious breakdown (1991):** 54% Protestant; 29% Catholic; 14% no affiliation; 1% Eastern non-Christian; 1% other; .2% Jewish.

☐ **AVG. INCOME (1991):** $35 349 males; $19 090 females; $58 774 families. **Avg. family size (1991):** 3.1 persons. **Single parent families (1991):** 11.8% of families.

☐ **CLIMATE:** Avg. day/night temps. -1.7°/-9.9° (Jan.); 25.2°/15.3° (July). **Avg. annual precip.** 880.3 mm. **Avg. annual snowfall:** 125.7 cm.

Ottawa-Hull

☐ **YEAR INCORPORATED:** 1854 (Ottawa). **Population (1991):** 920 857; 48.9% male, 51.0% female. **Area:** 5 138 sq. km. **Pop. density:** 179.2 per sq. km. **Pop. growth (1986–1991):** 12.4%. **Pop. over 65:** 35 200 males; 53 440 females. **Pop. under 35:** 250 405 males; 247 030 females.

☐ **OFFICIAL LANGUAGES (1991):** 46.8% English; 9.6% French; 42.6% bilingual; 1.0% neither. **Immigrant pop. (1991):** 134 755, 14.6%. **Religious breakdown (1991):** 57% Catholic; 27% Protestant; 10% no affiliation; 3% Eastern non-Christian; 1% Jewish; 1% other.

☐ **AVG. INCOME (1991):** $35 046 males; $21 767 females; $61 538 families. **Avg. family size (1991):**

3.0 persons. **Single parent families** (1991): 14.0% of families.

☐ **CLIMATE:** Avg. day/night temps. -6.3°/-15.5° (Jan.); 26.4°/15.1° (July). **Avg. annual precip.** 910.5 mm. **Avg. annual snowfall:** 221.5 cm.

Quebec, Que.

☐ **YEAR INCORPORATED:** 1832. **Population** (1991): 645 550; 48.2% male, 51.8% female. **Area:** 3 150 sq. km. **Pop. density:** 204.9 per sq. km. **Pop. growth** (1986–1991): 7.0%. **Pop. over 65:** 25 550 males; 43 315 females. **Pop. under 35:** 165 900 males; 162 445 females.

☐ **OFFICIAL LANGUAGES (1991):** 0.3% English; 72.0% French; 27.7% bilingual. **Immigrant pop.** (1991): 14 020, 2.2%. **Religious breakdown** (1991): 94% Catholic; 3.4% no affiliation; 2% Protestant; .4% Eastern non-Christian; .15% other; .02% Jewish.

☐ **AVG. INCOME (1991):** $29 205 males; $17 272 females; $49 206 families. **Avg. family size** (1991): 3.0 persons. **Single parent families** (1991): 14.9% of families.

☐ **CLIMATE:** Avg. day/night temps. -7.7°/-17.3° (Jan.); 24.9°/13.2° (July). **Avg. annual precip.** 1 207.7 mm. **Avg. annual snowfall:** 337.0 cm.

Regina, Sask.

☐ **YEAR INCORPORATED:** 1903. **Population** (1991): 191 692; 48.8% male, 51.2% female. **Area:** 3 422 sq. km. **Pop. density:** 56 per sq. km. **Pop. growth** (1986–1991): 2.8%. **Pop. over 65:** 8 400 males; 12 525 females. **Pop. under 35:** 54 165 males; 54 090 females.

☐ **OFFICIAL LANGUAGES (1991):** 93.9% English; 0.1% French; 5.6% bilingual; 0.4% neither. **Immigrant pop.** (1991): 15 895, 8.3%. **Religious breakdown** (1991): 49% Protestant; 33% Catholic; 14% no affiliation; 2% other; 1.25% Eastern non-Christian; .25% Jewish.

☐ **AVG. INCOME (1991):** $30 765 males; $18 245 females; $52 550 families. **Avg. family size** (1991): 3.1 persons. **Single parent families** (1991): 14.4% of families.

☐ **CLIMATE:** Avg. day/night temps. -11.0°/-22.1° (Jan.); 26.3°/11.9° (July). **Avg. annual precip.** 364.0 mm. **Avg. annual snowfall:** 107.4 cm.

St. Catharines–Niagara, Ont.

☐ **YEAR INCORPORATED:** 1876. **Population** (1991): 364 550; 48.7% male, 51.3% female. **Area:** 1 399.8 sq. km. **Pop. density:** 260 per sq. km.

Pop. growth (1986–1991): 6.2%. **Pop. over 65:** 22 995 males; 31 595 females. **Pop. under 35:** 90 125 males; 88 205 females.

☐ **OFFICIAL LANGUAGES (1991):** 80.6% English; 3.7% French; 13.1% other. **Immigrant pop.** (1991): 67 875, 18.6%. **Religious breakdown** (1991): 51% Protestant; 37% Catholic; 10% no affiliation; 1.3% other; .7% Eastern non-Christian; .32% Jewish.

☐ **AVG. INCOME (1991):** $30 382 males; $15 864 females; $49 998 families. **Avg. family size** (1991): 3.0 persons. **Single parent families** (1991): 13.0% of families.

☐ **CLIMATE:** Avg. day/night temps. -1.3°/-8.4° (Jan.); 27.2°/15.8° (July). **Avg. annual precip.** 953.1 mm. **Avg. annual snowfall:** 163.7 cm.

Saint John, NB

☐ **YEAR INCORPORATED:** 1785. **Population** (1991): 124 981; 48.3% male, 51.7% female. **Area:** 2 905 sq. km. **Pop. density:** 43.0 per sq. km. **Pop. growth** (1986–1991): 3.1%. **Pop. over 65:** 6 095 males; 9 395 females. **Pop. under 35:** 33 290 males; 33 525 females.

☐ **OFFICIAL LANGUAGES (1991):** 89.1% English; 0.2% French; 10.6% bilingual; 0.1% neither. **Immigrant pop.** (1991): 5 295, 4.2%. **Religious breakdown** (1991): 54% Protestant; 40% Catholic; 6% no affiliation; .34% Eastern non-Christian; .31% other; .15% Jewish.

☐ **AVG. INCOME (1991):** $29 196 males; $15 261 females; $46 754 families. **Avg. family size** (1991): 3.1 persons. **Single parent families** (1991): 16.0% of families.

☐ **CLIMATE:** Avg. day/night temps. -2.8°/-13.6° (Jan.); 22.1°/11.6° (July). **Avg. annual precip.** 1 432.8 mm. **Avg. annual snowfall:** 283.2 cm.

St. John's, Nfld

☐ **YEAR INCORPORATED:** 1888. **Population** (1991): 171 859; 48.7% male, 51.3% female. **Area:** 1 130 sq. km. **Pop. density:** 152.1 per sq. km. **Pop. growth** (1986–1991): 6.2%. **Pop. over 65:** 6 375 males; 9 640 females. **Pop. under 35:** 49 250 males; 49 715 females.

☐ **OFFICIAL LANGUAGES (1991):** 95.2% English; 0% French; 4.3% bilingual; 0.2% neither. **Immigrant pop.** (1991): 4 770, 2.8%. **Religious breakdown** (1991): 49% Catholic; 47% Protestant; 2.9% no affiliation; .47% Eastern non-Christian; .19% other; .06% Jewish.

☐ **AVG. INCOME (1991):** $28 146 males; $16 639 females; $50 269 families. **Avg. family size** (1991):

3.3 persons. **Single parent families (1991):** 15.1 of families.

☐ **CLIMATE: Avg. day/night temps.** -0.7°/-7.9° (Jan.); 20.2°/10.5° (July). **Avg. annual precip.** 1 481.7 mm. **Avg. annual snowfall:** 322.1 cm.

Saskatoon, Sask.

☐ **YEAR INCORPORATED:** 1906. **Population (1991):** 210 023; 48.5% male, 51.5% female. **Area:** 4 749 sq. km. **Pop. density:** 44.2 per sq. km. **Pop. growth (1986–1991):** 4.7%. **Pop. over 65:** 8 920 males; 12 805 females. **Pop. under 35:** 60 425 males; 61 800 females.

☐ **OFFICIAL LANGUAGES (1991):** 93.1% English; 0.0% French; 6.3% bilingual; 0.6% neither. **Immigrant pop. (1991):** 17 120, 10.1%. **Religious breakdown (1991):** 51% Protestant; 31% Catholic; 14% no affiliation; 2% other; 1.25% Eastern non-Christian; .29% Jewish.

☐ **AVG. INCOME (1991):** $28 785 males; $16 602 females; $48 732 families. **Avg. family size (1991):** 3.1 persons. **Single parent families (1991):** 14.5% of families.

☐ **CLIMATE: Avg. day/night temps.** -12.3°/-22.9° (Jan.); 25.4°/11.7° (July). **Avg. annual precip.** 347.2 mm. **Avg. annual snowfall:** 105.4 cm.

Sherbrooke, Que.

☐ **YEAR INCORPORATED:** 1875. **Population (1991):** 139 194; 48.0% male, 52.0% female. **Area:** 916 sq. km. **Pop. density:** 152 per sq. km. **Pop. growth (1986–1991):** 7.1%. **Pop. over 65:** 5 990 males; 10 025 females. **Pop. under 35:** 36 705 males; 36 260 females.

☐ **OFFICIAL LANGUAGES (1991):** 2.3% English; 61.1% French; 21.1% bilingual; 0.1% neither. **Immigrant pop. (1991):** 5 165, 3.7%. **Religious breakdown (1991):** 89% Catholic; 5.6% Protestant; 4% no affiliation; .7% Eastern non-Christian; .23% other; .07% Jewish.

☐ **AVG. INCOME (1991):** $26 108 males; $15 683 females; $43 394 families. **Avg. family size (1991):** 3.0 persons. **Single parent families (1991):** 15.9% of families.

☐ **CLIMATE: Avg. day/night temps.** -5.6°/-17.7° (Jan.); 24.7°/11.2° (July). **Avg. annual precip.** 1 108.9 mm. **Avg. annual snowfall:** 288.2 cm.

Sudbury, Ont.

☐ **YEAR INCORPORATED:** 1930. **Population (1991):** 157 610; 49.2% male, 56.5% female. **Area:** 2 612.11 sq. km. **Pop. density:** 60 per sq. km. **Pop.**

growth (1986–1991): 5.9%. **Pop. over 65:** 7 105 males; 9 330 females. **Pop. under 35:** 41 715 males; 41 875 females.

☐ **OFFICIAL LANGUAGES (1991):** 59.8% English; 27.5% French; 8.2% other. **Immigrant pop. (1991):** 12 840, 8.1%. **Religious breakdown (1991):** 65% Catholic; 27% Protestant; 7.2% no affiliation; .81% other; .51% Eastern non-Christian; .15% Jewish.

☐ **AVG. INCOME (1991):** $32 790 males; $16 843 females; $54 532 families. **Avg. family size (1991):** 3.1 persons. **Single parent families (1991):** 13.9% of families.

☐ **CLIMATE: Avg. day/night temps.** -8.5°/-18.7° (Jan.); 24.8°/13.3° (July). **Avg. annual precip.** 871.8 mm. **Avg. annual snowfall:** 266.6 cm.

Thunder Bay, Ont.

☐ **YEAR INCORPORATED:** 1970. **Population (1991):** 124 427; 49.4% male, 50.6% female. **Area:** 2 202.55 sq. km. **Pop. density:** 56.5 per sq. km. **Pop. growth (1986–1991):** 1.8%. **Pop. over 65:** 7 050 males; 9 505 females. **Pop. under 35:** 32 330 males; 31 765 females.

☐ **OFFICIAL LANGUAGES (1991):** 91.2% English; .2% French; .7% other. **Immigrant pop. (1991):** 16 235, 22.1%. **Religious breakdown (1991):** 46% Protestant; 41% Catholic; 11% no affiliation; 1.7% other; .52% Eastern non-Christian; .17% Jewish.

☐ **AVG. INCOME (1991):** $31 886 males; $17 512 females; $55 056 families. **Avg. family size (1991):** 3.0 persons. **Single parent families (1991):** 14.8% of families.

☐ **CLIMATE: Avg. day/night temps.** -8.9°/-21.3° (Jan.); 24.4°/11.0° (July). **Avg. annual precip.** 703.5 mm. **Avg. annual snowfall:** 195.5 cm.

Toronto, Ont.

☐ **YEAR INCORPORATED:** 1834. **Population (1991):** 3 893 046; 49.0% male, 51.0% female. **Area:** 5 584 sq. km. **Pop. density:** 697.2 per sq. km. **Pop. growth (1986–1991):** 13.4%. **Pop. over 65:** 165 335 males; 237 250 females. **Pop. under 35:** 1 044 835 males; 1 026 680 females.

☐ **OFFICIAL LANGUAGES (1991):** 88.2% English; 0.1% French; 8.0% bilingual; 3.7% neither. **Immigrant pop. (1991):** 1 468 620, 37.7%. **Religious breakdown (1991):** 36% Catholic; 35% Protestant; 15% no affiliation; 8% Eastern non-Christian; 4% Jewish; 3.3% other.

☐ **AVG. INCOME (1991):** $35 779 males; $21 855 females; $63 736 families. **Avg. family size (1991):** 3.1 persons. **Single parent families (1991):** 13.5% of families.

□ **CLIMATE: Avg. day/night temps.** -2.5°/-11.1° (Jan.); 26.8°/14.2° (July). **Avg. annual precip.** 780.8 mm. **Avg. annual snowfall:** 124.2 cm.

Trois-Rivières, Que.

□ **YEAR INCORPORATED:** 1857. **Population** (1991): 136 300; 48.1% male, 51.9% female. **Area:** 871.91 sq. km. **Pop. density:** 156.32 per sq. km. **Pop. growth** (1986–1991): 5.8%. **Pop. over 65:** 6 100 males; 9 935 females. **Pop. under 35:** 33 820 males; 33 655 females.

□ **OFFICIAL LANGUAGES (1991):** 1.2% English; 97.3% French; .6% other. **Immigrant pop.** (1991): 1 725, 1.3%. **Religious breakdown** (1991): 96% Catholic; 2% no affiliation; 1.8% Protestant; .3% other; .22% Eastern non-Christian; .01% Jewish.

□ **AVG. INCOME (1991):** $28 111 males; $14 281 females; $43 696 families. **Avg. family size** (1991): 2.9 persons. **Single parent families** (1991): 15.2% of families.

□ **CLIMATE: Avg. day/night temps.** -7.5°/-17.7° (Jan.); 25.6°/14.1° (July). **Avg. annual precip.** 1 046.7 mm. **Avg. annual snowfall:** 242.0 cm.

Vancouver, BC

□ **YEAR INCORPORATED:** 1886. **Population** (1991): 1 602 502; 49.2% male, 50.8% female. **Area:** 2 786 sq. km. **Pop. density:** 575.1 per sq. km. **Pop. growth** (1986–1991): 16.1%. **Pop. over 65:** 80 525 males; 114 905 females. **Pop. under 35:** 411 385 males; 404 190 females.

□ **OFFICIAL LANGUAGES (1991):** 89.4% English; 0.0% French; 7.2% bilingual; 3.4% neither. **Immigrant pop.** (1991): 476 530, 29.7%. **Religious breakdown** (1991): 40% Protestant; 31% no affiliation; 19% Catholic; 8% Eastern non-Christian; 1.2% other; .9% Jewish.

□ **AVG. INCOME (1991):** $32 820 males; $19 499 females; $57 100 families. **Avg. family size** (1991): 3.0 persons. **Single parent families** (1991): 12.6% of families.

□ **CLIMATE: Avg. day/night temps.** 5.7°/0.1° (Jan.); 21.7°/12.7° (July). **Avg. annual precip.** 1 167.4 mm. **Avg. annual snowfall:** 54.9 cm.

Victoria, BC

□ **YEAR INCORPORATED:** 1862. **Population** (1991): 287 897; 47.9% male, 52.1% female. **Area:** 633 sq. km. **Pop. density:** 454.5 per sq. km. **Pop. growth** (1986–1991): 12.8%. **Pop. over 65:** 21 700 males; 31 785 females. **Pop. under 35:** 66 495 males; 65 660 females.

□ **OFFICIAL LANGUAGES (1991):** 91.7% English;

0.0% French; 7.7% bilingual; .6% neither. **Immigrant pop.** (1991): 55 410, 19.2%. **Religious breakdown** (1991): 51% Protestant; 30% no affiliation; 16% Catholic; 2% Eastern non-Christian; .92% other; .3% Jewish.

□ **AVG. INCOME (1991):** $30 971 males; $18 859 females; $52 907 families. **Avg. family size** (1991): 2.8 persons. **Single parent families** (1991): 12.5% of families.

□ **CLIMATE: Avg. day/night temps.** 6.5°/0.3° (Jan.); 21.8°/10.7° (July). **Avg. annual precip.** 857.9 mm. **Avg. annual snowfall:** 46.9 cm.

Windsor, Ont.

□ **YEAR INCORPORATED:** 1892. **Population** (1991): 262 075; 48.7% male, 51.3% female. **Area:** 861.66 sq. km.[2] **Pop. density:** 304 per sq. km. **Pop. growth** (1986–1991): 3.2%. **Pop. over 65:** 13 350 males; 20 075 females. **Pop. under 35:** 68 850 males; 67 555 females.

□ **OFFICIAL LANGUAGES (1991):** 76.0% English; 4.7% French; 15.3% other. **Immigrant pop.** (1991): 53 830, 20.5%. **Religious breakdown** (1991): 55% Catholic; 31% Protestant; 8% no affiliation; 3.3% other; 2.3% Eastern non-Christian; .6% Jewish.

□ **AVG. INCOME (1991):** $31 438 males; $17 645 females; $53 117 families. **Avg. family size** (1991): 3.1 persons. **Single parent families** (1991): 15.3% of families.

□ **CLIMATE: Avg. day/night temps.** -1.3°/-8.8° (Jan.); 27.7°/17.0° (July). **Avg. annual precip.** 901.6 mm. **Avg. annual snowfall:** 123.3 cm.

Winnipeg, Man.

□ **YEAR INCORPORATED:** 1873. **Population** (1991): 652 354; 48.6% male, 51.4% female. **Area:** 3 295 sq. km. **Pop. density:** 198 per sq. km. **Pop. growth** (1986–1991): 4.3%. **Pop. over 65:** 33 235 males; 50 765 females. **Pop. under 35:** 174 920 males; 170 730 females.

□ **OFFICIAL LANGUAGES (1991):** 88.0% English; 0.2% French; 10.5% bilingual; 1.3% neither. **Immigrant pop.** (1991): 113 165, 17.3%. **Religious breakdown** (1991): 43% Protestant; 34% Catholic; 16% no affiliation; 2.4% Eastern non-Christian; 2.3% other; 2.1% Jewish.

□ **AVG. INCOME (1991):** $28 287 males; $17 229 females; $49 619 families. **Avg. family size** (1991): 3.0 persons. **Single parent families** (1991): 14.8% of families.

□ **CLIMATE: Avg. day/night temps.** -13.2°/-23.6° (Jan.); 26.1°/13.4° (July). **Avg. annual precip.** 504.4 mm. **Avg. annual snowfall:** 114.8 cm.

NATIONAL PARKS

Park	Location	Size (sq. km)	Year est.	1993-4 Visitors	Description
Aulavik	northern portion of Banks Is., NWT	12 200	(1992)[1]	n.a.	Thomsen River forms core of park marked by deep river canyons and desert-like badlands. Area supports high concentration of muskoxen.
Auyuittuq[2]	Cumberland Peninsula, Baffin Is., NWT	21 469	1976	380	Located on the Arctic Circle; an isolated and very rugged wilderness area with mountains, fjords, tundra and permafrost.
Banff	Banff, Alta.	6 641	1885	4 340 000	The oldest national park; noted for ice-capped peaks, glaciers, hot springs, wildlife and skiing.
Bruce Peninsula	299 km northwest of Toronto, between Lake Huron and Georgian Bay	154	(1987)[1]	140 000	Niagara Escarpment, limestone cliffs on Georgian Bay. Includes Fathom Five National Marine Park: 19 islands, over 20 shipwrecks, clear water and distinctive under water geological features.
Cape Breton Highlands	across northern Cape Breton Is., NS	948	1936	590 000	The scenic Cabot Trail is characterized by a rugged shoreline with plunging cliffs.
Elk Island	45 km east of Edmonton, Alta.	194	1913	240 000	A large population of plains and wood bison, elk and moose inhabit the rolling woodlands and lakes.
Ellesmere Island[2]	northern tip of Canada	37 775	1988	450	Vast isolated high Arctic wilderness park. Mountains, glaciers, musk-oxen, Peary's caribou. Fragile permafrost environments.
Forillon	northeast tip of Gaspé Peninsula, Que.	240	1974	170 000	Rich variety of birds and animals; limestone cliffs, and the highest mountains in eastern Canada.
Fundy	southeastern shore on the Bay of Fundy, NB	206	1948	220 000	The giant tides of the Bay of Fundy, among the highest in the world, and a bold, irregular coastline.
Georgian Bay Islands	160 km northwest of Toronto, Ont.	25	1929	87 000	Endangered species, limestone cliffs, caves and archaeological sites are preserved on 77 islands.
Glacier	45 km east of Revelstoke, BC	1 349	1886	170 000	Glaciers, snowy peaks, avalanche slopes, turbulent rivers and grizzly bears are the main features.
Grasslands	100 km south of Swift Current, Sask.	906	(1975)[1]	2 500	Unique natural habitat of short-grass prairie; blacktailed prairie dogs, pronghorn antelope and the prairie falcon are found.
Gros Morne	west coast of Nfld	1 805	(1970)[1]	130 000	Gros Morne, spectacular fjords and the Long Range Mountains.
Ivvavik	northern tip of Yukon	10 168	1984	430	Migration route for Porcupine caribou herd; major North American waterfowl area; home to grizzly, black and polar bears
Jasper	340 km west of Edmonton, Alta.	10 878	1907	1 510 000	Contains the largest icefield in the Canadian Rockies—Columbia Icefield—and preserves the headwaters of major rivers, particularly the Athabasca.
Kejimkujik	central southwestern NS	404	1974	140 000	Gently rolling country with many lakes and rivers—provides good canoeing and camping
Kluane[2]	southwest corner of Yukon	22 013	1976	79 000	Features Mount Logan, Canada's highest peak, grizzly bears, dall sheep and whitewater rivers.
Kootenay	1 km east of Radium Hot Springs, BC	1 406	1920	1 260 000	Hot springs, alpine lakes, canyons, glaciers, 2 river valleys home to bighorn sheep, mountain goats.

Park	Location	Size (sq. km)	Year est.	1993-4 Visitors	Description
Kouchibouguac	eastern NB	239	1979	210 000	Swimming and sunbathing on the beaches and sand dunes; cycling, hiking trails; windsurfing.
La Mauricie	55 km north of Trois-Rivières, Que.	536	1977	250 000	Hilly terrain at the edge of the Canadian Shield; transitional forest vegetation from evergreens to deciduous.
Mingan Archipelago [2]	N of Anticosti Is. along the St. Lawrence shore, QC	151	1984	25 000	Interesting rock formations, plant species, nesting seabirds and whales, seals and porpoises.
Mount Revelstoke	Revelstoke, BC	260	1914	200 000	Dense rain forests, colorful alpine vegetation, lakes and deep snow.
Nahanni [2]	southwestern NWT	4 765	1976	3 800	Accessible only by air; site of Virginia Falls, whirlpools, hot springs, canyons and rapids.
North Baffin	eastern Arctic, northern Baffin Is. and Bylot Is.	22 252	(1992)[3]	n.a.	Spectacular fiords and glaciers, steep sea cliffs, huge colonies of seabirds and other wildlife.
Pacific Rim [2]	west coast of Vancouver Island	500	(1970)[1]	950 000	3 sections—Long Beach, Broken Group Islands and West Coast Trail; offers rain forest, beaches and scenic, rugged hiking.
Point Pelee	southernmost point of Ont.	15	1918	650 000	Extensive marshlands and beaches provide refuge for many migratory birds and butterflies.
Prince Albert	200 km north of Saskatoon, Sask.	3 874	1927	180 000	This mixture of forest land and lakes is home to woodland caribou, bison and a pelican nesting colony.
Prince Edward Island	north shore of PEI	22	1937	740 000	Saltwater beaches, sand dunes, high coastal cliffs, marshes, ponds and woodlands.
Pukaskwa	northeastern shore of Lake Superior	1 878	(1971)[1]	13 000	Impressive shoreline with 60 km of coastal hiking and white water canoe routes.
Riding Mountain	270 km northwest of Winnipeg, Man.	2 973	1929	290 000	Wildlife—wolf, elk, moose, black bear and beaver—abound.
St. Lawrence Islands	Thousand Islands	8	1914	44 000	Thousand Islands landscape and the St. Lawrence River.
South Moresby (Gwaii Haanas) [2]	southern part of Queen Charlotte Islands, BC	1 495	(1987)[1]	n.a.	Canada's "Galapagos," home to 39 unique plants and animals; rugged coastline, rain forests.
Terra Nova	east coast of Nfld on Bonavista Bay	400	1957	250 000	Rolling forested hills, spongy bogs and inland ponds are bordered by a rugged coastline.
Vuntut	Old Crow Flats, northern Yukon	4 345	(1993)[1]	n.a.	Wetland area is Yukon's most important waterfowl habitat and home to porcupine caribou, grizzly bear, moose, muskrat and several species of fish. Vertebrate fossils found at over 56 sites within park.
Waterton Lakes	southwest corner of Alta.	505	1895	350 000	Transition from prairie grasslands to Rocky Mountains; a rich variety of wildlife.
Wood Buffalo	straddles the Alta.-NWT border	44 802	1922	6 300	Home to the largest free-roaming herd of bison; only naturally nesting whooping cranes, peregrine falcons and red-sided garter snakes.
Yoho	25 km east of Golden, BC	1 313	1886	750 000	Contains several of the highest peaks in the Rocky Mountains, icefields, waterfalls and a varied plant and animal life.

Source: *Canadian Heritage, Parks Canada*

(1) Park created by federal/provincial/territorial agreement rather than federal enactment and administered by special legislation. (2) Park reserve, set aside for national park and under jurisdiction of National Parks Act, but lands, fish and wildlife are subject to future settlement of native land claims. (3) Agreement under negotiation; land has been designated for national park. (n.a.) not available.

THE PEOPLE

POPULATION

Population of Provinces and Territories
(thousands of persons)

	Canada	Nfld	PEI	NS	NB	Que	Ont	Man	Sask	Alta	BC	YT	NWT
1861	3 230	n.a.	81	331	252	1 112	1 396	*	n.a.	n.a.	52	*	7
1871	3 689	n.a.	94	388	286	1 192	1 621	25	n.a.	n.a.	36	*	48
1881	4 325	n.a.	109	441	321	1 360	1 927	62	n.a.	n.a.	49	*	56
1891	4 833	n.a.	109	450	321	1 489	2 114	153	*	*	98	*	99
1901	5 371	n.a.	103	460	331	1 649	2 183	255	91	73	179	27	20
1911	7 207	n.a.	94	492	352	2 006	2 527	461	492	374	393	9	7
1921	8 788	n.a.	89	524	388	2 361	2 934	610	758	588	525	4	8
1931	10 377	n.a.	88	513	408	2 875	3 432	700	922	732	694	4	9
1941	11 507	n.a.	95	578	457	3 332	3 788	730	896	796	818	5	12
1951	14 009	361	98	643	516	4 056	4 598	777	832	940	1 165	9	16
1961	18 238	458	105	737	598	5 259	6 236	922	925	1 332	1 629	15	23
1971	21 568	522	112	789	635	6 028	7 703	988	926	1 628	2 185	18	35
1976	22 993	558	118	829	677	6 235	8 264	1 022	921	1 838	2 467	22	43
1981	24 343	568	123	847	696	6 438	8 625	1 026	968	2 238	2 744	23	46
1986[1]	25 309	568	127	873	710	6 532	9 102	1 063	1 010	2 366	2 883	24	52
1991	27 297	568	130	900	724	6 896	10 085	1 092	989	2 546	3 282	28	58

Source: *Census of Canada*

(1) Includes estimates, rather than actual counts, for the population of some Indian reserves and settlements which were not completely enumerated. (*) Included with the Northwest Territories; n.a. not available.

Age Structure of the Population[1]

	Total (000s)	% Under 5 Years	% 5–19 Years	% 20–44 Years	% 45–64 Years	% 65+ Years
1851	2 436	18.51	37.81	31.65	9.40	2.67
1861	3 230	16.81	37.21	32.66	10.15	3.03
1871	3 689	14.67	38.03	32.58	11.14	3.66
1881	4 325	13.85	36.02	33.94	12.14	4.12
1891	4 833	12.64	34.49	35.40	12.91	4.55
1901	5 371	12.03	32.73	36.19	14.00	5.05
1911	7 207	12.35	30.15	38.81	14.06	4.66
1921	8 788	12.05	31.51	36.63	15.02	4.78
1931	10 377	10.36	31.29	36.07	16.74	5.55
1941	11 507	9.14	28.39	37.19	18.61	6.67
1951	14 009	12.29	25.60	36.63	17.74	7.75
1956	16 081	12.34	27.39	35.33	17.20	7.74
1961	18 238	12.37	29.44	33.19	17.37	7.63
1966	20 015	10.98	31.14	32.42	17.77	7.69
1971	21 568	8.42	30.97	33.87	18.66	8.09
1976	22 993	7.53	28.31	36.32	19.12	8.71
1981	24 343	7.32	24.70	39.14	19.13	9.70
1986	25 309	7.15	21.76	41.17	19.25	10.66
1991	27 297	6.99	20.42	41.33	19.66	11.61

Source: *Census of Canada*

(1) Total percentage for census year may not equal 100 due to rounding.

Male and Female Population by Age Group

(thousands of persons)

		Total Population	Under 5 Years	5–9 Years	10–14 Years	15–24 Years	25–34 Years	35–44 Years	45–54 Years	55–64 Years	65 Years and Over
1851	MALE	1 250	233	173	152	248	168	116	78	46	35
	FEMALE	1 186	218	173	146	252	161	103	67	38	30
1861	MALE	1 660	277	218	203	341	232	156	107	70	54
	FEMALE	1 570	266	211	196	337	222	141	92	59	44
1871	MALE	1 869	276	264	243	374	249	175	132	86	74
	FEMALE	1 820	265	255	233	385	256	171	120	73	61
1881	MALE	2 189	304	284	262	455	302	217	161	111	94
	FEMALE	2 136	295	278	251	464	301	212	153	100	84
1891	MALE	2 460	309	300	282	504	366	263	191	131	115
	FEMALE	2 373	302	292	272	499	354	246	180	122	105
1901	MALE	2 752	326	313	297	543	412	331	234	157	139
	FEMALE	2 620	320	306	285	530	386	299	214	148	133
1911	MALE	3 822	450	396	356	745	687	475	334	209	171
	FEMALE	3 385	440	389	346	653	535	388	286	184	165
1921	MALE	4 530	534	529	462	757	693	630	434	276	215
	FEMALE	4 258	525	521	452	761	650	532	366	246	206
1931	MALE	5 375	543	573	543	990	778	707	590	356	295
	FEMALE	5 002	531	560	531	962	717	627	485	306	281
1941	MALE	5 901	534	529	556	1 083	920	745	649	494	391
	FEMALE	5 606	518	517	545	1 069	891	691	579	421	377
1951	MALE	7 089	879	714	575	1 070	1 066	950	728	557	551
	FEMALE	6 921	843	684	556	1 077	1 108	919	679	520	535
1956	MALE	8 152	1 012	920	732	1 154	1 209	1 079	838	588	623
	FEMALE	7 929	972	887	703	1 138	1 206	1 062	774	566	622
1961	MALE	9 219	1 154	1 064	948	1 316	1 258	1 191	959	655	674
	FEMALE	9 019	1 102	1 016	908	1 301	1 222	1 199	920	635	717
1966	MALE	10 054	1 129	1 173	1 071	1 656	1 249	1 275	1 041	743	717
	FEMALE	9 961	1 069	1 128	1 022	1 643	1 233	1 268	1 037	736	823
1971	MALE	10 795	930	1 152	1 181	2 016	1 462	1 286	1 132	854	782
	FEMALE	10 773	887	1 102	1 129	1 988	1 428	1 241	1 160	877	963
1976	MALE	11 450	889	967	1 165	2 262	1 823	1 315	1 226	928	876
	FEMALE	11 543	843	921	1 112	2 217	1 798	1 282	1 246	997	1 127
1981	MALE	12 068	914	912	985	2 356	2 106	1 497	1 256	1 031	1 011
	FEMALE	12 275	869	865	936	2 303	2 110	1 471	1 242	1 128	1 350
1986[1]	MALE	12 486	928	920	917	2 117	2 249	1 822	1 276	1 124	1 133
	FEMALE	12 824	882	875	870	2 061	2 278	1 819	1 269	1 204	1 564
1991	MALE	13 455	976	978	963	1 944	2 420	2 176	1 487	1 180	1 330
	FEMALE	13 842	931	930	915	1 887	2 446	2 196	1 479	1 220	1 840

Source: *Census of Canada*

(1) Excludes incompletely enumerated Indian reserves and settlements.

Canadian Population Projections by Age Group

(thousands of persons)

		Total Population	Under 5 Years	5–9 Years	10–14 Years	15–24 Years	25–34 Years	35–44 Years	45–54 Years	55–64 Years	65 Years and Over
2011	MALE	16 486	997	1 011	1 060	2 277	2 240	2 299	2 534	2 047	2 021
	FEMALE	17 084	945	958	1 002	2 168	2 166	2 248	2 581	2 185	2 831
2036	MALE	18 875	1 057	1 089	1 134	2 332	2 381	2 573	2 486	2 211	3 613
	FEMALE	19 839	1 001	1 031	1 071	2 212	2 285	2 490	2 440	2 263	5 047

Source: *Statistics Canada, 1990 base*

Canadian Population by Country of Birth

	1911	1931	1951	1971	1991
Total Population	7 206 643	10 376 786	14 009 429	21 568 310	27 296 855
Total Foreign Born	1 586 961[11]	2 307 525[11]	2 059 911[11]	3 295 530[11]	4 335 185[11]
Africa - Other..............	—	—	—	—	42 245
Argentina[1]	—	—	—	—	11 110
Asia - Other	3 577	6 310	6 740	52 795	85 705
Australia..................	2 655	3 565	4 161	14 335	13 955
Austria[2]	121 430	37 391	37 598	40 450	26 680
Barbados[3]	—	—	—	—	14 820
Belgium	7 975	17 033	17 251	25 770	22 480
Brazil[1]	—	—	—	—	7 325
Caribbean - Other	—	—	—	—	25 990
Central America - Other.....	—	—	—	—	21 120
Chile[1]	—	—	—	—	22 870
China.....................	27 083	42 037	24 166	57 150	157 405
Czechoslovakia	—	22 835	29 546	43 100	42 615
Denmark...................	4 937	17 217	15 679	28 045	21 555
Ecuador[1]	—	—	—	—	8 015
Egypt[1]	—	—	—	—	28 015
El Salvador[1]	—	—	—	—	28 295
Ethiopia	—	—	—	—	11 060
Europe - Other[5]	12 394	10 657	10 858	87 255	9 215
Fiji[3]	—	—	—	—	16 000
Finland	10 987	30 354	22 035	24 930	16 830
France....................	17 619	16 756	15 650	51 655	55 160
Germany[6]	39 577	39 163	42 693	211 060	180 525
Greece	2 640	5 579	8 594	78 780	83 675
Guyana[3]	—	—	—	—	66 055
Haiti[1]	—	—	—	—	39 880
Hong Kong[3]	—	—	—	—	152 455
Hungary	—	28 523	32 929	68 495	57 010
India[3, 7]	4 491	4 672	3 934	43 645	173 670
Iran[1]	—	—	—	—	30 715
Ireland	—	—	24 110	38 490	28 405
Israel[1]	—	—	—	—	16 770
Italy......................	34 739	42 578	57 789	385 755	351 620
Jamaica[3]	—	—	—	—	102 440
Japan	8 425	12 261	6 239	9 485	12 280
Kenya[3]	—	—	—	—	16 585
Korea[4]	—	—	—	—	33 170
Laos[4]	—	—	—	—	14 445
Lebanon[1]	—	—	—	—	54 605
Malaysia[4]	—	—	—	—	16 100
Malta[3]	—	—	—	—	10 185
Mexico[1]	—	—	—	—	19 400
Morocco[1]	—	—	—	—	16 795
Netherlands...............	3 808	10 736	41 457	133 525	129 615
New Zealand[3]	903	—	—	—	7 480
North America - Other	—	—	—	—	455
Norway....................	20 968	32 679	22 969	16 350	8 260
Oceania - Other.............	—	—	—	—	545
Pakistan[1]	—	—	—	—	25 180
Philippines[4]	—	—	—	—	123 295

▶

	1911	1931	1951	1971	1991
Poland[8]	—	171 169	164 474	160 040	184 695
Portugal[8]	—	—	—	—	161 180
Romania[9]	9 657	40 322	19 733	24 405	33 790
Russia[10]	89 984	—	—	—	—
South America - Other	—	—	—	—	35 190
South Africa[3]	1 166	2 235	2 057	—	24 725
Spain[8]	—	—	—	—	11 175
Sri Lanka[4]	—	—	—	—	25 440
Sweden	28 226	34 415	22 635	14 110	7 805
Switzerland[8]	—	6 076	6 414	13 895	16 335
Taiwan[4]	—	—	—	—	17 770
Tanzania[1]	—	—	—	—	17 820
Trinidad/Tobago[3]	—	—	—	—	49 385
Turkey[8]	1 861	—	—	—	12 180
Uganda[1]	—	—	—	—	8 960
USSR	—	133 869	188 292	160 120	99 355
United Kingdom	784 526	1 138 942	912 482	933 040	717 745
UK possessions / dependencies[5]	40 699	35 416	10 415	112 120	—
United States	303 680	344 574	282 010	309 640	249 075
Vietnam[4]	—	—	—	—	113 595
Yugoslavia[8]		17 110	20 912	78 285	88 820

Source: *Statistics Canada*

(1) Included in "Other countries" until 1986 census. (2) Includes Hungary (Austria-Hungary) in 1911 census. (3) British possessions/dependencies (see UK possessions) during various census years could incl. African, Asian, Caribbean, Mediterranean, and Pacific possessions as well as any territory in British North America prior to confederation with Canada (in the case of Newfoundland, this was not until 1949); many not reported separately until 1986 census. (4) Included in "Asia - Other" until 1986 census. (5) More detailed breakdown given in subsequent census data. (6) Total for Germany includes both East and West Germany. (7) Totals for India before 1986 include Pakistan. (8) Where not reported, included in "Europe - Other." (9) For 1911 census, also includes Bulgaria. (10) For 1931, 1951, 1971 and 1991, see USSR. (11) Totals include those where country unknown or not noted: 1911–2 954; 1931–3 051; 1951–6 089;1971–78 805; 1991–65. (12) Includes Czech and Slovak Federal Republics. (13) Includes North and South Korea. (—) = not reported.

Population by Official Languages

(percentage distribution)

	1961			1981			1991		
	English[1]	French[1]	Bilingual[2]	English[1]	French[1]	Bilingual[2]	English[1]	French[1]	Bilingual[2]
Canada	**67.4**	**19.1**	**12.2**	**67.0**	**16.6**	**15.3**	**67.1**	**15.2**	**16.3**
Newfoundland	98.5	0.1	1.2	97.6	...	2.3	96.5	.04	3.3
Prince Edward Island	91.1	1.2	7.6	91.7	0.2	8.1	89.6	.2	10.1
Nova Scotia	92.9	0.8	6.1	92.3	0.2	7.4	91.1	.02	8.6
New Brunswick	62.0	18.7	19.0	60.5	13.0	26.5	57.9	12.5	29.5
Quebec	11.6	61.9	25.5	6.7	60.1	32.4	5.5	58.0	35.4
Ontario	89.0	1.5	7.9	86.7	0.7	10.8	86.1	.5	11.4
Manitoba	89.6	0.9	7.4	90.3	0.3	7.9	89.4	.2	9.2
Saskatchewan	93.6	0.4	4.5	94.6	0.1	4.6	94.2	.05	5.2
Alberta	94.1	0.4	4.3	92.4	0.2	6.4	92.1	.1	6.6
British Columbia	95.3	0.2	3.5	92.8	0.1	5.7	91.6	.04	6.4
Yukon	93.5	0.3	5.6	91.9	...	7.9	90.5	.09	9.3
Northwest Territories	58.9	0.5	7.0	79.9	0.1	6.0	85.1	.1	6.1

Source: *Census of Canada*

(1) Refers to persons who speak either English or French, but not both. (2) Refers to persons who speak both English and French. (...) = too small to be included.

Canadian Population by Mother Tongue[1]

(thousands of persons and percent of total population)

	1941	%	1951	%	1961	%	1971	%	1981	%	1991	%
English	6 448	56.0	8 281	59.1	10 661	58.5	12 974	60.2	14 918	61.3	16 170	60.0
French	3 355	29.2	4 069	29.0	5 123	28.1	5 794	26.9	6 249	25.7	6 503	24.1
Italian	80	0.7	92	0.7	340	1.9	538	2.5	529	2.2	511	1.9
German	322	2.8	329	2.3	564	3.1	561	2.6	523	2.2	466	1.7
Chinese	34	0.3	28	0.2	49	0.3	95	0.4	224	0.9	499	1.8
Ukrainian	313	2.7	352	2.5	361	2.0	310	1.4	292	1.2	187	.7
Portuguese	n.a.	n.a.	n.a.	n.a.	18	0.1	87	0.4	166	0.7	212	.8
Dutch	53	0.5	88	0.6	170	0.9	145	0.7	157	0.6	139	.5
Polish	129	1.1	129	0.9	162	0.9	135	0.6	128	0.5	190	.7
Greek	9	0.1	8	0.1	40	0.2	104	0.5	123	0.5	126	.5
Spanish	1		2	...	7	...	24	0.1	70	0.3	177	.7
Indo-Iranian	...	...	2	...	5	...	33	0.2	117	0.5	301	1.1
Aboriginal	131	1.1	166	1.2	167	0.9	180	0.9	146	0.6	173	.6
Hungarian	46	0.4	42	0.3	86	0.5	87	0.4	84	0.3	80	.3
Vietnamese	n.a.	n.a.	n.a.	n.a.	n.a.	n.a.	n.a.	n.a.	30	0.1	79	.3
Arabic	8	0.1	5	...	13	0.1	29	0.1	50	0.2	108	.4
Finnish	37	0.3	32	0.2	45	0.2	37	0.2	33	0.1	28	.1
Russian	52	0.5	39	0.3	43	0.2	32	0.1	31	0.1	35	.1
Yiddish	130	1.1	104	0.7	82	0.4	50	0.2	33	0.1	25	.09
Czech[2]	38	0.3	46	0.3	51	0.3	45	0.2	43	0.2	27	.09
Danish	19	0.2	16	0.1	35	0.2	27	0.1	26	0.1	22	.08
Japanese	22	0.2	18	0.1	18	0.1	17	0.1	20	0.1	30	.1
Armenian	n.a.	n.a.	n.a.	n.a.	n.a.	n.a.	n.a.	n.a.	17	0.1	26	.1
Norwegian	60	0.5	44	0.3	40	0.2	27	0.1	19	0.1	13	.05
Swedish	50	0.4	36	0.3	33	0.2	22	0.1	17	0.1	12	.04

Source: *Census of Canada*

(1) The language first spoken in childhood and still understood. (2) Includes Slovak.

(n.a.) not available. (...) = too small to be included.

Native Population of Canada

	1986				1991			
	Total Native Population[2]	Native Indian	Métis	Inuit	Total Population with Aboriginal Origins[1]	Native Indian	Métis	Inuit
Canada	711 725	548 945	151 605	36 460	1 002 675	783 980	212 650	49 255
Newfoundland	9 555	4 695	1 435	4 120	13 110	5 845	1 605	6 460
Prince Edward Island	1 290	1 115	160	30	1 880	1 665	185	75
Nova Scotia	14 225	13 060	1 110	315	21 885	19 950	1 590	770
New Brunswick	9 375	8 700	750	185	12 815	11 835	975	450
Quebec	80 945	68 585	11 435	7 360	137 615	112 590	19 480	8 480
Ontario	167 375	150 715	18 265	2 955	243 550	220 135	26 905	5 250
Manitoba	85 235	55 960	33 285	700	116 200	76 370	45 575	900
Saskatchewan	77 650	55 215	25 695	190	96 580	69 385	32 840	540
Alberta	103 925	68 965	40 125	1 125	148 220	99 650	56 310	2 825
British Columbia	126 625	112 790	15 295	1 035	169 035	149 570	22 295	1 990
Yukon	4 995	4775	220	65	6 390	5 870	565	170
Northwest Territories	30 530	9 380	3 825	18 360	35 390	11 100	4 310	21 355

Source: *Statistics Canada*

(1) The 1991 census question on ethnic or cultural origins gathered information on the number of people who reported North American Indian, Métis or Inuit origin as either a single response or in combination with other origins. (2) 1986 census excluded approximately 45 000 individuals living on incompletely enumerated native reserves and settlements; in 1991 census, 78 reserves were incompletely enumerated, representing approximately 37 000 individuals.

Status Indian Population[1], 1993

	Total Indian Population	On Reserve	Off Reserve	On Crown Land	Number of Bands
Canada	553 316	305 247	226 872	21 197	605
Atlantic Provinces	21 524	14 468	7 048	8	31
Quebec	54 273	37 169	15 970	1 134	39
Ontario	125 743	62 554	60 956	2 233	126
Manitoba	84 020	54 115	28 403	1 502	61
Saskatchewan	85 413	43 560	40 361	1 492	70
Alberta	68 639	42 816	23 658	2 165	43
British Columbia	94 006	49 756	43 916	334	196
Yukon	6 807	601	3 433	2 773	16
NWT	12 891	208	3 127	9 556	23

Source: *Dept. of Indian and Northern Affairs*

(1) Status Indians are those settled on reserves registered with the Department of Indian and Northern Affairs under the provisions of the Indian Act. (2) Total number of reserves is 2 284, but only 842 are inhabited.

Largest Native Bands in Canada, 1993

Band, Province	Population[1]	Band, Province	Population[1]
Six Nations of the Grand River, Ont.[2]	17 603	Fort Alexander, Man.	4 667
Kahnawake, Que.	7 878	Samson, Alta.	4 564
Mohawks of Akwesasne, Ont.	7 766	Norway House, Man.	4 377
Blood, Alta.	7 678	Cross Lake, Man.	4 362
Saddle Lake, Alta.	6 424	Siksika Nation, Alta.	4 348
Mohawks of the Bay of Quinte[3]	5 728	Bigstone Cree, Alta.	4 172
Lac La Ronge, Sask.	5 557	Montagnais du Lac St. Jean, Que.	3 979
Peguis, Man.	5 416	Onyota'a:ka, Ont.	3 970
Wikwemikong, Ont.	5 306	Sandy Bay, Man.	3 554
Peter Ballantyne, Sask.	5 216	Stoney Band, Alta.	3 251

Source: *Indian and Northern Affairs, Canada*

(1) As of Dec. 31. (2) This band consists of the following 13 groups: The Bay of Quinte Mohawks, Bearfoot Onondaga, Deleware, Konadaha Seneca, Lower Cayuga, Lower Mohawk, Niharondasa Seneca, Oneida, Onondaga Clear Sky, Tuscarora, Upper Cayuga, Upper Mohawk and Walker Mohawk. (3) This band is not part of the Six Nations of the Grand River. (4) Stoney Band consists of the following 3 groups: Stoney (Chiniki), Stoney (Goodstoney), Stoney Bearspaw.

Neither French nor English...

*A*ccording to the 1991 census, 308 500 people (out of 27.3 million) spoke neither French nor English. 62% of this group were women, and 40% lived in Toronto, with 15% in Vancouver and 14% in Montreal. The majority of these people were immigrants rather than non-permanent residents and 51% of them had been living in Canada for more than 10 years.

Although many recent arrivals had not yet had time to learn a new language, for those who had been in the country for a decade, it was clear that they could function in their daily lives without going outside of their linguistic community. They tended to live in large households and likely shouldered domestic responsibilities that did not require them to interact with other language groups. While 21% of the group spoke a variety of languages, 28% spoke Chinese, 15% Italian and 11% spoke Portuguese.

Canadian Urban and Rural Population

(thousands)

Year	Urban Total	Urban %	Rural Non-Farm	%	+	Rural Farm	%	=	Rural Total	%
1871	722	19.6	n.a.	n.a.		n.a.	n.a.		2 967	80.4
1881	1 110	25.7	n.a.	n.a.		n.a.	n.a.		3 215	74.3
1891	1 537	31.8	n.a.	n.a.		n.a.	n.a.		3 296	68.2
1901	2 014	37.5	n.a.	n.a.		n.a.	n.a.		3 357	62.5
1911	3 273	45.4	n.a.	n.a.		n.a.	n.a.		3 934	54.6
1921	4 352	49.5	n.a.	n.a.		n.a.	n.a.		4 436	50.5
1931	5 469	52.7	1 670	16.1		3 238	31.2		4 908	47.3
1941	6 271	54.5	2 123	18.4		3 113	27.1		5 236	45.5
1951	8 817	62.9	2 423	17.3		2 769	19.8		5 192	37.1
1956	10 715	66.6	2 734	17.0		2 632	16.4		5 366	33.4
1961	12 700	69.6	3 465	19.0		2 073	11.4		5 538	30.4
1966	14 727	73.6	3 374	16.9		1 914	9.6		5 288	26.4
1971	16 410	76.1	3 738	17.3		1 420	6.6		5 158	23.9
1976	17 367	75.5	4 591	20.0		1 035	4.5		5 626	24.5
1981	18 436	75.7	4 867	20.0		1 040	4.3		5 907	24.3
1986	19 352	76.5	5 067	20.0		890	3.5		5 957	23.5
1991	20 907	76.6	5 583	20.5		807	3.0		6 390	23.4

Source: *Census of Canada*

Definitions: Urban: persons living in a built-up area having a population of 1 000 or more and a population density of 400 or more per sq. km; **Rural:** persons living outside "urban areas"; **Rural Farm:** persons living in rural areas who are members of households of farm operators; **Rural Non-Farm:** persons living in rural areas who are not members of households of farm operators.

(n.a.) not available.

Urban and Rural Population by Province

Province	1911 Rural	1911 Urban	1951 Rural	1951 Urban	1991 Rural	1991 Urban
Canada	3 924 394	3 280 444	5 174 555	8 473 458	6 389 724	20 907 135
Newfoundland[1]	n.a.	n.a.	n.a.	n.a.	264 023	304 451
PEI	78 758	14 970	73 744	24 685	77 952	51 813
NS	306 210	186 128	297 753	344 831	418 434	481 508
NB	252 342	99 547	300 686	215 011	378 686	345 214
Quebec	1 032 618	970 094	1 358 363	2 697 318	1 544 752	5 351 211
Ontario	1 194 785	1 328 489	1 346 443	3 251 099	1 831 043	8 253 842
Manitoba	255 249	200 365	336 961	439 580	304 767	787 175
Saskatchewan	361 067	131 365	579 258	252 470	365 531	623 397
Alberta	232 726	141 937	489 826	449 675	514 660	2 030 893
BC	188 796	203 684	371 739	793 471	641 922	2 640 139
Yukon	4 647	3 865	6 502	2 594	11 462	16 335
NWT	17 196	—	13 280	2 724	36 492	21 157

Source: *Census of Canada*

(1) Newfoundland joined confederation in 1949 and urban/rural split in population was not included in 1951 census data.

Modern Farms

*F*arming today is less labour-intensive than it was years ago thanks to advances in machinery, chemicals and plant breeding. Although the last census reported fewer farms and farmers, both are much more efficient and the levels of agricultural output are at an all-time high.

Population of Canadian Towns and Cities

(5,000 to 50,000 inhabitants)

Town or city classification is made according to the official designations adopted by provincial or federal authority. *Indicates a city; all others are towns.

	POPULATION 1981	1991	AREA (sq. km)
■ **NEWFOUNDLAND**			
Bay Roberts	4 512	5 474	24.36
Carbonear	5 335	5 259	11.81
Channel-Port aux Basques . .	5 988	5 644	37.43
Conception Bay South	10 856	17 590	59.70
Corner Brook*	24 339	22 410	147.37
Gander	10 404	10 339	101.16
Goulds	4 242	6162	18.79
Grand Falls-Windsor	14 666	14 693	56.66
Happy Valley-Goose Bay	7 103	8 610	306.42
Labrador City	11 538	9 061	6.47
Marystown	6 299	6 739	62.99
Mount Pearl	11 543	23 689	25.29
St. John's*	83 770	95 770	101.59
Stephenville	8 876	7 621	34.81
■ **PRINCE EDWARD ISLAND**			
Charlottetown*	15 282	15 396	6.99
Summerside	7 828	7 474	4.31
■ **NOVA SCOTIA**			
Amherst	9 864	9 742	15.29
Bedford	6 777	11 618	39.79
Bridgewater	6 669	7 248	13.35
Glace Bay	21 466	19 501	23.15
Kentville	4 974	5 506	17.12
New Glasgow	10 464	9 905	10.36
New Waterford	8 808	7 695	5.26
North Sydney	7 820	7 260	5.38
Stellarton	5 435	5 237	8.55
Sydney*	29 444	26 063	23.49
Sydney Mines	8 501	7 551	10.91
Truro	12 552	11 683	38.09
Yarmouth	7 475	7 781	11.14
■ **NEW BRUNSWICK**			
Bathurst*	15 705	14 409	90.94
Campbellton*	9 818	8 699	17.30
Chatham	6 779	6 544	10.36
Dieppe	8 511	10 463	52.90
Edmunston*	12 044	10 835	34.58
Fairvale	3 960	5 041	7.85
Fredericton*	43 723	46 466	129.58
Grand Falls (Grand-Sault) . . .	6 203	6 083	17.73
Newcastle	6 284	5 711	14.09
Oromocto	9 064	9 325	22.26
Quispamsis	6 022	8 446	38.91
Riverview	14 907	16 270	34.26
Sackville	5 654	5 494	74.42

	POPULATION 1981	1991	AREA (sq. km)
■ **QUEBEC**			
Alma*	26 322	25 910	109.27
Amos*	9 421	13 783	108.05
Ancienne-Lorette*	12 935	15 242	7.87
Anjou*	37 346	37 210	13.65
Arthabaska*	6 827	7 584	8.94
Asbestos*	7 967	6 487	13.47
Aylmer*	26 695	32 244	91.21
Baie-Comeau*	12 866	26 012	352.27
Beaconsfield*	19 613	19 616	10.64
Beauharnois*	7 025	6 449	40.44
Bécancour*	10 247	10 911	434.29
Beloeil*	17 540	18 516	24.01
Blainville*	14 682	22 679	55.20
Boisbriand*	13 471	21 124	27.32
Bois-des-Filion	4 943	6 337	3.92
Boucherville*	29 704	33 796	69.33
Buckingham*	7 992	10 548	14.46
Candiac*	8 502	11 064	16.47
Cap-de-la-Madeleine*	32 626	33 716	17.30
Cap-Rouge*	8 492	14 105	6.39
Carignan	4 544	5 386	62.35
Chambly*	12 190	15 893	25.06
Charlemagne*	4 827	5 598	1.76
Charny*	8 240	10 239	8.76
Châteauguay*	36 928	39 833	35.40
Chibougamau*	10 732	8 855	754.08
Coaticook*	6 271	6 637	12.50
Côte-Saint-Luc*	27 531	28 700	7.21
Cowansville*	12 240	11 982	50.58
Delson	4 935	6 063	7.15
Deux-Montagnes*	9 944	13 035	6.05
Dolbeau*	8 766	8 181	46.36
Dollard-des-Ormeaux*	39 940	39 940	15.05
Donnacona*	5 731	5 659	20.12
Dorion*	5 749	5 920	3.70
Dorval*	17 722	17 249	20.64
Drummondville*	27 347	35 462	31.01
Farnham*	6 498	6 146	24.70
Gaspé*	17 261	16 402	1 105.11
Granby*	38 069	42 804	72.60
Grand-mère*	15 442	14 287	71.13
Greenfield Park*	18 527	17 652	4.58
Hampstead*	7 598	8 645	1.77
Iberville*	8 587	9 352	4.90
Ile-Perrot*	5 945	6 404	4.87
Joliette*	16 987	17 396	22.14
Kirkland*	10 476	17 495	10.34
L'Assomption*	3 457	5 706	2.07
La Baie*	20 935	20 995	261.69
La Prairie*	10 627	14 938	43.54
La Sarre*	8 861	8 513	148.30 ▶

	POPULATION		AREA
	1981	1991	(sq. km)
▶ La Tuque*	11 556	10 003	22.25
Lac-Mégantic*	6 119	5 838	20.21
Lachenaie*	8 631	15 074	42.79
Lachine*	37 521	35 266	17.38
Lachute*	11 729	11 730	96.24
Lauzon*	13 362	n.a.	16.40
Le Gardeur*	8 312	13 814	44.00
LeMoyne*	6 137	5 412	.96
Lévis*	17 895	39 452	16.70
Loretteville*	15 060	14 219	6.94
Lorraine*	6 881	8 410	5.46
Louiseville	3 735	8 000	62.57
Magog*	13 604	14 034	15.26
Marieville	4 877	5 164	3.57
Mascouche*	20 345	25 828	107.95
Masson	4 264	5 753	55.61
Matane*	13 612	12 756	24.35
Mercier*	6 352	8 227	45.89
Mirabel*	14 080	17 971	492.26
Mistassini*	6 682	6 842	248.38
Mont-Joli*	6 359	6 265	9.11
Mont-Laurier*	8 405	7 862	82.05
Mont-Royal*	19 247	18 212	7.43
Mont-Saint-Hilaire*	10 066	12 341	48.17
Montmagny*	12 405	11 861	125.77
Montréal-Nord*	94 914	85 516	11.03
Montréal-Ouest*	5 514	5 180	1.63
Otterburn Park	4 268	6 046	5.21
Outremont*	24 338	22 935	3.68
Pierrefonds*	38 390	48 735	24.40
Pincourt*	8 750	9 639	8.27
Plessisville*	7 249	6 952	4.34
Pointe-Claire*	24 571	27 647	19.19
Port-Cartier*	8 191	7 383	74.47
Repentigny*	34 419	49 630	24.42
Rimouski*	29 120	30 873	75.68
Rivière-du-Loup	13 459	14 017	16.94
Roberval*	11 429	11 628	147.05
Rock Forest*	12 283	14 551	51.41
Rosemère*	7 778	11 198	10.20
Rouyn-Noranda	25 991	26 448	63.27
Roxboro*	6 292	5 879	2.23
Saint-Antoine*	7 012	10 232	9.84
Saint-Basile-le-Grand*	7 658	10 127	34.83
Saint-Bruno-de-Montarville*	22 880	23 849	41.79
Saint-Constant*	9 938	18 423	57.02
Saint-David-de-L'Auberivière*	5 380	n.a.	10.90
Saint Emile	5 216	6 921	8.88
Saint-Eustache*	29 716	37 278	70.03
Saint-Félicien*	9 058	9 340	167.90
Saint-Georges*	16 720	19 583	19.01
Saint-Hyacinthe*	38 246	39 292	36.63
Saint-Jean-Chrysostome*	6 930	12 717	82.90
Saint-Jean-sur-Richelieu*	35 640	37 607	47.40
Saint-Jérôme*	25 123	23 384	15.79
Saint-Lambert*	20 557	20 976	6.42
Saint-Luc*	8 815	15 008	51.22
Saint-Nicolas*	5 074	7 600	36.93
Saint-Raphael de Ile Bizard	6 558	11 352	22.69
Saint-Rédempteur*	4 463	5 862	3.46

	POPULATION		AREA
	1981	1991	(sq. km)
Saint-Rémi*	5 146	5 768	79.67
Saint-Romuald*	9 849	9 830	18.34
Sainte-Agathe-des-Monts*	5 641	5 452	15.57
Sainte-Anne-des-Monts*	6 062	5 652	106.27
Sainte-Anne-des-Plaines	7 651	10 787	92.23
Sainte-Catherine*	6 372	9 805	9.06
Sainte-Julie*	14 243	20 632	47.91
Sainte-Marie*	8 937	10 542	105.49
Sainte-Marthe-sur-le-Lac*	5 586	7 410	9.01
Sainte-Thérèse*	18 750	24 158	10.09
Salaberry-de-Valleyfield*	29 574	27 598	35.74
Sept-Iles*	29 262	24 848	298.93
Shawinigan*	23 011	19 931	26.27
Shawinigan-Sud*	11 325	11 584	51.39
Sillery*	12 825	12 519	6.73
Sorel*	20 347	18 786	9.65
Terrebonne*	11 769	39 678	73.17
Thetford Mines*	19 965	17 273	23.15
Tracy*	12 843	13 181	19.11
Trois-Rivières*	50 466	49 426	77.86
Trois-Rivières-Ouest*	13 107	20 076	28.70
Val-Belair*	12 695	17 181	68.54
Val d'Or	21 371	23 842	1 217.16
Vanier*	10 725	10 833	4.66
Varennes*	8 764	14 758	93.96
Vaudreuil*	7 608	11 187	69.49
Victoriaville*	21 838	21 495	16.13
Westmount*	20 480	20 239	3.96

■ ONTARIO

	POPULATION		AREA
	1981	1991	(sq. km)
Alliston, Beeton, Tecumseth and Tottenham	16 191	20 239	269.55
Amherstburg	5 685	8 921	3.29
Ancaster	14 428	21 988	174.57
Arnprior	5 828	6 679	8.52
Aurora	16 267	29 454	49.16
Aylmer	5 254	6 244	4.78
Belleville*	34 881	37 243	29.13
Bracebridge	9 063	12 308	632.09
Bradford-West Gwillimbury	13 198	17 702	197.40
Brockville*	19 896	21 582	20.24
Caledon	26 645	34 965	686.84
Carleton Place	5 626	7 432	5.64
Chatham*	40 952	43 557	27.52
Cobourg	11 385	15 079	15.89
Colchester South	5 018	5 292	143.56
Collingwood	12 064	13 505	21.30
Cornwall*	46 144	47 137	63.49
Dryden	6 640	6 505	16.86
Dundas	19 586	21 868	24.42
Dunnville	11 353	12 131	302.92
East Gwillimbury	12 565	18 367	245.14
Elliot Lake	16 723	14 089	756.79
Espanola	5 836	5 527	17.66
Essex	6 295	6 759	6.48
Fergus	6 064	7 940	6.87
Flamborough	24 470	29 616	489.90
Fort Erie	24 096	26 006	168.30
Fort Frances	8 906	8 891	26.05
Gananoque	4 863	5 209	9.01 ▶

	POPULATION 1981	1991	AREA (sq. km)		POPULATION 1981	1991	AREA (sq. km)
▶ Georgina	20 111	29 746	286.27	Trenton*	15 085	16 908	11.69
Goderich	7 322	7 452	6.74	Valley East	20 433	21 939	518.03
Gravenhurst	8 532	9 988	524.01	Vanier*	18 792	18 150	2.93
Grimsby	15 797	18 520	68.12	Walden	10 139	9 805	718 62
Haldimand	16 866	20 573	638.15	Wallaceburg	11 506	11 846	10.71
Halton Hills	35 190	36 816	275.86	Wasaga Beach	4 705	6 224	52.10
Hanover	6 316	6 711	6.49	Welland*	45 448	47 914	81.23
Hawkesbury	9 877	9 706	8.16	Westminster	5 952	6 826	224.69
Hearst	5 533	6 079	28.85	Whitchurch-Stouffville	13 557	18 357	206.85
Huntsville	11 467	14 997	700.90	Woodstock*	26 603	30 075	24.53
Ingersoll	8 494	9 378	10.20	**■ MANITOBA**			
Iroquois Falls	6 339	5 999	689.94				
Kanata*	19 728	37 344	132.19	Brandon*	36 242	38 567	74.50
Kapuskasing	12 014	10 344	83.92	Dauphin	8 971	8 453	11.94
Kenora	9 817	9 782	15.33	Flin Flon* (part in Man. balance in Sask.)	7 894	7 119	11.55
Kincardine	5 778	6 585	7.65	Morden	4 579	5 273	10.53
Kingsville	5 134	5 716	4.27	Portage La Prairie*	13 086	13 186	24.03
Kirkland Lake	12 219	10 440	270.01	Selkirk	10 037	9 815	24.71
Leamington	12 528	14 182	8.75	Steinbach	6 676	8 213	25.24
Lincoln	14 196	17 149	163.43	The Pas	6 390	6 166	28.46
Lindsay	13 596	16 696	15.19	Thompson*	14 288	14 977	16.85
Listowel	5 026	5 404	6.19	Winkler	5 046	6 397	16.17
Marathon	2 277	5 064	162.39	**■ SASKATCHEWAN**			
Midland	12 132	13 865	16.01				
Milton	28 067	32 075	367.20	Estevan*	9 174	10 240	17.67
Nanticoke*	19 816	22 727	674.72	Humboldt	4 705	5 089	11.65
Napanee	4 803	5 179	4.02	Lloydminster*	15 031	7 241	39.38
New Liskeard	5 551	5 431	6.42	Melfort*	6 010	5 628	14.66
Newcastle	32 229	49 479	607.79	Melville*	5 092	5 123	15.41
Newmarket	29 753	45 474	35.91	Moose Jaw*	33 941	33 593	45.30
Niagara-on-the-Lake	12 186	12 945	131.11	North Battleford*	14 030	14 350	37.06
Nickel Centre	12 318	12 332	378.36	Prince Albert*	31 380	34 181	64.97
Onaping Falls	6 198	5 402	228.98	Swift Current*	14 747	14 815	20.50
Orangeville	13 740	17 921	13.39	Weyburn*	9 523	9 673	13.70
Orillia*	23 955	25 925	22.90	Yorkton*	15 339	15 315	23.16
Owen Sound*	19 883	21 674	20.29	**■ ALBERTA**			
Paris	7 485	8 600	10.67				
Parry Sound	6 124	6 125	14.98	Airdrie*	8 414	12 456	13.37
Pelham	11 104	13 328	124.52	Banff	5 768	5 688	4.86
Pembroke*	14 026	13 997	14.83	Beaumont	2 638	5 042	5.59
Penetanguishene	5 315	6 643	9.40	Bonnyville	4 454	5 132	14.39
Perth	5 655	5 574	8.92	Brooks	9 421	9 433	15.81
Port Colborne*	19 225	18 766	122.82	Camrose*	12 570	13 420	24.43
Port Elgin	6 131	6 857	5.92	Canmore	3 484	5 681	12.88
Port Hope	9 992	11 505	10.00	Coaldale	4 579	5 310	7.06
Rayside-Balfour	15 017	15 039	328.21	Cochrane	1 486	5 265	15.55
Renfrew	8 283	8 134	12.25	Crowsnest Pass	7 306	6 679	171.79
Rockland	3 961	6 771	8.49	Drayton Valley	5 042	5 983	7.95
Sault Ste. Marie*	82 697	81 476	221.52	Drumheller*	6 508	6 277	28.48
Simcoe	14 326	15 539	40.51	Edson	5 835	7 323	25.89
Smiths Falls	8 831	9 396	8.26	Fort McMurray*	31 000	34 706	56.61
St. Marys	4 883	5 496	12.14	Fort Saskatchewan*	12 169	12 078	32.94
St. Thomas*	28 165	29 990	18.10	Grande Prairie*	24 263	28 271	41.83
Stoney Creek*	36 762	49 968	98.65	High River	4 792	6 269	10.42
Stratford*	26 262	27 666	20.33	Hinton	8 342	9 046	22.52
Strathroy	8 748	10 566	13.89	Innisfail	5 247	5 700	9.82
Sturgeon Falls	6 045	5 837	5.79	Lacombe	5 591	6 934	11.40
Tecumseh	6 364	10 495	6.19	Leduc*	12 471	13 970	22.42
Thorold*	15 412	17 542	84.54	Lloydminster[3]*	15 031	10 042	39.38
Tillsonburg	10 487	12 019	20.58	Medicine Hat*	40 380	43 625	96.17 ▶
Timmins*	46 114	47 461	3 004.39				

	POPULATION 1981	1991	AREA (sq. km)
Morinville	4 657	6 104	12.32
Okotoks	3 847	6 720	11.67
Olds	4 813	5 542	9.79
Peace River	5 907	6 717	21.20
Ponoka	5 221	5 861	9.81
Rocky Mountain House	4 698	5 461	10.82
Slave Lake	4 506	5 607	7.43
Spruce Grove	10 326	12 884	19.56
St. Albert*	31 996	42 146	33.63
Stony Plain	4 839	7 226	26.51
Taber	5 988	6 660	15.62
Vegreville	5 251	5 138	13.99
Wetaskiwin*	9 597	10 634	13.27
Whitecourt	5 585	6 938	25.40

■ BRITISH COLUMBIA

	POPULATION 1981	1991	AREA (sq. km)
Castlegar*	6 902	6 579	16.16
Colwood	10 540	13 463	17.91
Comox	6 607	8 253	7.88
Courtenay*	8 992	11 652	11.00
Cranbrook*	15 915	16 447	16.29
Dawson Creek*	11 373	10 981	20.30
Fernie*	5 444	5 012	13.64
Fort St. John*	13 891	14 156	19.53
Kelowna*	59 196	75 950	212.56
Kimberley*	7 375	6 531	58.19
Langley*	15 124	19 765	10.18
Merritt*	6 110	6 253	8.34

	POPULATION 1981	1991	AREA (sq. km)
Nelson*	9 143	8 760	6.51
New Westminster*	38 550	43 585	15.38
North Vancouver*	33 952	38 436	10.77
Parksville	5 216	7 306	10.66
Penticton*	23 181	27 258	40.79
Port Alberni*	19 892	18 403	17.51
Port Coquitlam*	27 535	36 773	26.91
Port Moody*	14 917	17 712	13.72
Prince Rupert*	16 197	16 620	53.56
Quesnel*	8 240	8 179	20.56
Revelstoke*	5 544	7 729	29.99
Sidney	7 946	10 082	5.02
Smithers	4 570	5 029	13.17
Terrace	10 914	11 433	19.21
Trail*	9 599	7 919	13.79
Vernon*	19 987	23 514	22.67
Victoria*	64 379	71 228	18.78
White Rock*	13 550	16 314	5.05
Williams Lake	8 362	10 385	23.26

■ YUKON TERRITORY

	POPULATION 1981	1991	AREA (sq. km)
Whitehorse*	14 814	17 925	413.48

■ NORTHWEST TERRITORIES

	POPULATION 1981	1991	AREA (sq. km)
Yellowknife*	9 483	15 179	102.38

Source: *Census of Canada*

n.a. not available

Population of Canadian Cities

(with 50,000+ population in 1991)

City	Year incorporated[1]	Population (000s) 1966	1976	1981	1986	1991
Ajax, Ont.[4]	1955	9.4	20.8	25.5	36.6	57.4
Barrie, Ont.	1959	24.0	34.4	38.4	48.3	62.7
Beauport, Que.	1976	11.7	55.3	60.4	62.9	69.1
Brampton, Ont.	1974	36.3	103.5	149.0	188.5	234.4
Brantford, Ont.	1877	59.9	67.0	74.3	76.1	82.0
Brossard, Que.	1958	11.9	37.6	52.2	57.4	64.8
Burlington, Ont.	1974	65.9	104.3	114.9	116.7	129.6
Calgary, Alta.	1893	330.6	469.9	592.7	636.1	710.7
Cambridge, Ont.	1973	n.a.	72.4	77.2	79.9	92.8
Charlesbourg, Que.	1976	24.9	63.1	68.3	69.0	70.8
Chicoutimi, Que.	1976	32.5	57.7	60.1	61.0	62.7
Coquitlam, BC[2]	1891	40.9	55.5	61.1	69.3	84.0
Dartmouth, NS	1961	58.7	65.3	62.3	65.2	67.8
Delta, BC[2]	1879	20.7	64.5	74.7	79.6	89.0
East York, Ont.[3]	1967	74.2	107.0	102.0	101.1	102.7
Edmonton, Alta.	1904	376.9	461.4	532.2	574.0	616.7
Etobicoke, Ont.	1983	219.5	297.1	298.7	303.0	310.0
Gatineau, Que.	1975	17.7	73.5	75.0	81.2	92.3
Gloucester, Ont.	1981	23.2	56.5	72.9	89.8	101.7
Guelph, Ont.	1879	51.4	67.5	71.2	78.2	88.0
Halifax, NS	1841	86.8	117.9	114.6	113.6	114.5
Hamilton, Ont.	1846	298.1	312.0	306.4	306.7	318.5
Hull, Que.	1875	60.2	61.0	56.2	58.7	60.7
Jonquière, Que.	1976	29.7	60.7	60.4	58.5	57.9 ▶

City	Year incorporated[1]	Population (000s)				
		1966	1976	1981	1986	1991
▶ Kamloops, BC	1973	10.8	58.3	64.0	61.8	67.1
Kelowna, BC	1973	17.0	52.0	59.2	61.2	76.0
Kingston, Ont.	1846	59.0	56.0	52.6	55.0	56.6
Kitchener, Ont.	1912	93.3	131.9	139.7	150.6	168.3
LaSalle, Que.	1958	48.3	76.7	76.3	75.6	73.8
Laval, Que.	1965	196.1	246.2	268.3	284.1	314.4
Lethbridge, Alta.	1906	37.2	46.8	54.1	58.8	61.0
London, Ont.	1855	194.4	240.4	254.3	269.1	303.2
Longueuil, Que.	1920	25.6	122.4	124.3	125.4	129.9
Markham, Ont.[4]	1971	7.8	56.2	77.0	114.6	153.8
Matsqui, BC[2]	1892	16.2	31.2	42.0	51.4	68.1
Mississauga, Ont.	1974	93.5	250.0	315.1	374.0	463.4
Moncton, NB	1973	45.8	55.9	55.7	55.5	57.0
Montréal, Que.	1832	1 222.3	1 080.5	980.4	1 015.4	1 017.7
Montréal-Nord, Que.	1959	67.8	97.3	94.9	90.3	85.5
Nanaimo, BC	1874	15.2	40.3	47.1	49.0	60.1
Nepean, Ont.	1978	43.9	76.9	84.4	95.5	107.6
Niagara Falls, Ont.	1903	56.9	69.4	71.0	72.1	75.4
North Bay, Ont.	1925	23.6	51.6	51.3	50.6	55.4
North Vancouver, BC[2]	1891	48.1	63.5	65.4	68.2	75.2
North York, Ont.	1979	399.5	558.4	559.5	556.3	562.6
Oakville, Ont.[4]	1857	52.8	69.0	75.8	87.1	114.7
Oshawa, Ont.	1924	78.1	107.0	117.5	123.7	129.3
Ottawa, Ont.	1854	290.7	304.5	295.2	300.8	314.0
Peterborough, Ont.	1905	56.2	59.7	60.6	61.0	68.4
Pickering, Ont.	1956	20.0	27.9	37.8	48.9	68.6
Prince George, BC	1915	24.5	59.9	67.6	67.6	69.7
Québec, Que.	1832	167.0	177.1	166.5	164.6	167.5
Red Deer, Alta.	1913	26.2	32.2	46.4	54.4	58.1
Regina, Sask.	1903	131.1	149.6	162.6	175.0	179.2
Richmond, BC[2]	1879	50.5	80.0	96.1	108.5	126.6
Richmond Hill, Ont.	1957	19.8	34.7	37.8	46.8	80.1
Saanich, BC[2]	1906	58.8	73.4	78.7	82.9	95.6
Saint-Hubert, Que.	1958	17.2	49.7	60.6	66.2	74.0
Saint John, NB	1785	51.6	86.0	80.5	76.4	75.0
Saint-Laurent, Que.	1955	59.5	64.4	65.9	67.0	72.4
Saint-Leonard, Que.	1963	25.3	78.5	79.2	75.9	73.1
Sainte-Foy, Que.	1955	48.3	71.2	68.9	69.6	71.1
St. Catharines, Ont.	1876	97.1	123.4	124.0	123.5	129.3
St. John's, Nfld.	1888	79.9	86.6	83.8	96.2	95.7
Sarnia-Clearwater, Ont.	1914	54.6	55.6	50.9	49.0	74.4[5]
Saskatoon, Sask.	1906	115.9	133.8	154.2	177.6	186.1
Sault Ste. Marie, Ont.	1912	74.6	81.0	82.7	80.9	81.5
Scarborough, Ont.	1983	278.4	387.1	443.4	484.7	524.6
Sherbrooke, Que.	1875	75.7	76.8	74.1	74.3	76.4
Sudbury, Ont.	1930	84.9	97.6	91.8	88.7	92.9
Surrey, BC[2]	1879	81.8	116.5	147.1	181.4	245.2
Thunder Bay, Ont.	1970	104.5	111.5	112.5	112.3	113.9
Toronto, Ont.	1834	664.6	633.3	599.2	612.3	635.4
Vancouver, BC	1886	410.4	410.2	414.3	431.1	471.8
Vaughan, Ont.[4]	1971	n.a.	17.8	29.7	65.1	111.4
Verdun, Que.	1912	76.8	68.0	61.3	60.2	61.3
Victoria, BC	1862	57.5	62.6	64.4	66.3	71.2
Waterloo, Ont.	1948	29.9	46.6	49.4	58.7	71.2
Whitby, Ont.[4]	1855	17.3	28.1	36.7	45.8	61.3
Windsor, Ont.	1892	192.5	196.5	192.1	193.1	191.4
Winnipeg, Man.[6]	1873	257.0	560.9	564.5	594.6	616.8
York, Ont.	1983	134.7	141.4	134.6	135.4	140.5

Source: *Census of Canada*

(1) As a city, unless otherwise indicated by footnote. (2) District Municipality. (3) Borough. (4) Town. (5) 1991 includes Clearwater (6) Includes St. James-Assiniboia, Man.

Population of Census Metropolitan Areas in Canada

Statistics Canada defines a census metropolitan area (CMA) as a very large urban area, together with neighbouring urban and rural areas that have a high degree of economic and social integration with that large urban area. The urban area itself (or urbanized core) must have a population of at least 100,000 based on the previous census.

| CMA | Population[1] (000s) | | | | | Land Area |
	1951	1961	1971	1981	1991	1991
Calgary, Alta	142.3	279.1	403.3	592.6	754	5 085.8 sq. km
Chicoutimi-Jonquière, Que.	91.2	127.6	133.7	135.2	161	1 723.3 sq. km
Edmonton, Alta.	193.6	359.8	495.7	656.9	840	9 532.5 sq. km
Halifax, NS	138.4	193.4	222.6	277.7	321	2 503.1 sq. km
Hamilton, Ont.	281.9	401.1	498.5	542.1	600	1 358.5 sq. km
Kitchener, Ont.	107.5	154.9	226.8	287.8	356	823.6 sq. km
London, Ont.	167.7	226.7	286.0	283.7	382	2 105.1 sq. km
Montreal, Que.	1 539.3	2 215.6	2 743.2	2 828.3	3 127	3 508.9 sq. km
Oshawa, Ont.	n.a.	n.a.	120.3	154.2	240	894.2 sq. km
Ottawa-Hull, Ont.-Que.	311.6	457.0	602.5	718.0	921	5 138.3 sq. km
Quebec, Que.	289.3	379.1	480.5	576.0	646	3 150.3 sq. km
Regina, Sask.	72.7	113.7	140.7	164.3	192	3 421.6 sq. km
St. Catharines-Niagara, Ont.	189.0	257.8	303.4	304.4	365	1 399.8 sq. km
St. John's, Nfld.	80.9	106.7	131.8	154.8	172	1 130.0 sq. km
Saint John, NB	80.7	98.1	106.7	114.0	125	2 904.8 sq. km
Saskatoon, Sask.	55.7	95.6	126.4	154.2	210	4 749.4 sq. km
Sherbrooke, Que.	n.a.	n.a.	n.a.	125.2	139	915.8 sq. km
Sudbury, Ont.	80.5	127.4	155.4	149.9	158	2 612.1 sq. km
Thunder Bay, Ont.	73.7	102.1	112.1	121.4	124	2 202.6 sq. km
Toronto, Ont.	1 261.9	1 919.4	2 628.0	2 998.7	3 893	5 583.5 sq. km
Trois-Rivières, Que.	46.1	53.5	55.9	111.4	136	871.9 sq. km
Vancouver, B.C.	586.2	826.8	1 082.4	1 268.1	1 603	2 786.3 sq. km
Victoria, B.C.	114.9	155.8	195.8	233.5	288	633.4 sq. km
Windsor, Ont.	182.6	217.2	258.6	246.1	262	861.7 sq. km
Winnipeg, Man.	357.2	476.5	540.3	584.8	652	3 294.8 sq. km

Source: *Census of Canada*   (1) Population is based on a boundary CMA at time of that particular census. (n.a.) not available.

The Growth of a Census Metropolitan Area

*T*he 1991 census reported that "Toronto" was home to nearly 4 million people—14% of Canada's 1991 population. Toronto has been the country's largest census metropolitan area (CMA) since 1976 and in 1991 its residents outnumbered the population of all the Atlantic provinces put together, and were more numerous than the 1991 population of British Columbia. Where are all these people? What exactly is the Toronto census metropolitan area?

The simplest definition of Toronto is based on its political boundaries. The City of Toronto covers 97.15 sq. km and its population in 1991 was 635 395—this is the "urbanized core." Since cities are nearly always interacting with their neighbouring municipalities (workers living outside the core or residents working outside it), Statistics Canada devised a more flexible definition of this type of area to try to capture the population under a city's social and economic influence.

Since that process began in the 1940s, the definition has changed to include such things as commuting characteristics and the definition (noted above) now means that outlying municipalities are included if a minimum of 50% of the employed labour force living in that municipality work in the urban core, or if at least 25% of the employed labour force working in the outlying area live in the urban core. These changes in the CMA definition mean that the land area considered to be part of the Toronto CMA has expanded over the years: in 1966 the Toronto CMA included 2 071 sq. km., in 1976 the area was 3 743, and by 1991 it was 5 584.

Canadian Population by Religious Denominations

(thousands of persons)

	1941	%	1951	%	1961	%	1971	%	1981	%	1991	%
Total population	11 507	100.0	14 009	100.0	18 238	100.0	21 568	100.0	24 083	100.0	26 994	100.0
Adventist	18	0.2	21	0.1	26	0.1	29	0.1	42	0.2	52	.2
Anglican	1 754	15.2	2 061	14.7	2 409	13.2	2 543	11.8	2 436	10.1	2 188	8.1
Bahai	n.a.	n.a.	n.a.	n.a.	n.a.	n.a.	n.a.	n.a.	8	...	15	.1
Baptist	484	4.2	520	3.7	594	3.3	667	3.1	697	2.9	663	2.5
Buddhist	16	0.1	8	0.1	12	0.1	16	0.1	52	0.2	163	.6
Christian and Missionary Alliance	4	...	6	...	18	0.1	24	0.1	34	0.1	59	.2
Christian Reformed[1]	n.a.	n.a.	n.a.	n.a.	62	0.3	83	0.4	77	0.3	85	.3
Churches of Christ, Disciples	21	0.2	15	0.1	20	0.1	16	0.1	15	0.1	18	.1
Confucian	22	0.2	6	...	5	...	2	...	n.a.	n.a.	.4	...
Doukhobor	17	0.1	13	0.1	13	0.1	9	...	7	...	5	...
Free Methodist	9	0.1	9	0.1	14	0.1	19	0.1	12	0.1	15	.1
Greek Orthodox	140	1.2	172	1.2	240	1.3	317	1.5	315	1.3	232	.9
Hindu	n.a.	n.a.	n.a.	n.a.	n.a.	n.a.	n.a.	n.a	.70	0.3	157	.6
Hutterite[2]	n.a.	n.a.	n.a.	n.a.	n.a.	n.a.	14	0.1	17	0.1	22	.1
Islam	n.a.	n.a.	n.a.	n.a.	n.a.	n.a.	n.a.	n.a.	98	0	253	.9
Jehovah's Witnesses	7	0.1	35	0.2	68	0.4	175	0.8	143	0.6	168	.6
Jewish	169	1.5	205	1.5	254	1.4	276	1.3	296	1.2	318	1.2
Latter Day Saints	25	0.2	33	0.2	50	0.3	67	0.3	90	0.4	101	.4
Lutheran	402	3.5	445	3.2	663	3.6	716	3.3	703	2.9	636	2.4
Mennonite[3]	112	1.0	126	0.9	152	0.8	168	0.8	189	0.8	208	.8
Pentecostal	58	0.5	95	0.7	144	0.8	220	1.0	339	1.4	436	1.6
Presbyterian	831	7.2	782	5.6	819	4.5	872	4.0	812	3.4	636	2.4
Roman Catholic	4 806	41.8	6 069	43.3	8 343	45.7	9 975	46.2	11 210	46.5	12 204	45.2
Salvation Army	34	0.3	70	0.5	92	0.5	120	0.6	125	0.5	112	.4
Sikh	n.a.	n.a.	n.a.	n.a.	n.a.	n.a.	n.a.	n.a.	68	0.3	147	.5
Ukrainian Catholic[4]	186	1.6	191	1.4	190	1.0	228	1.1	191	0.8	128	.5
Unitarian	6	0.1	4	...	15	0.1	21	0.1	15	0.1	17	.1
United Church[5]	2 209	19.2	2 867	20.5	3 664	20.1	3 769	17.5	3 758	15.6	3 093	11.5
No religion	19	0.2	60	0.4	95	0.5	930	4.3	1 752	7.3	3 386	12.5

Source: *Census of Canada.*

(1) Included with United Church 1931–1951. (2) Included with Mennonite 1931–61. (3) Includes Hutterite 1931–1961. (4) Includes Greek Catholic 1931–71. (5) Includes Christian Reformed 1931–1951. (...) = too small to be included; n.a. not available.

Demographic Change

Canadian society in the 1990s is very different from that of early Canadians, and not just because we have televisions and VCRs—200 years ago people lived half as long and the average family had twice as many children.

In general, all Canadians are living longer, which means not only is our working life extended but we can expect to "retire" and live for another 15 to 20 years.

How big a change has there been? Canadians born in 1700 had an average life expectancy of 30 to 35 years thanks to poor diet, disease, and limited understanding of the importance of hygiene. By 1831 four generations had passed and there had been a slight improvement in life span, with the average male surviving to age 40 and the average female to age 42. During the next four generations there was a dramatic increase in our ability to protect ourselves from infectious diseases, cut down infant mortality and protect women in childbirth: by 1951, the average life span was nearly twice as long as it had been in 1831 and the gap between men's and women's life spans increased from two years to eight.

VITAL STATISTICS

Births in Canada, 1921–1993

	Live Births	Birth Rate[1]		Live Births	Birth Rate[1]
1921	264 879	29.3	1958	470 118	27.5
1922	259 825	28.3	1959	479 275	27.4
1923	247 404	26.7	1960	478 551	26.8
1924	251 351	26.7	1961	475 700	26.1
1925	249 365	26.1	1962	469 693	25.3
1926	240 015	24.7	1963	465 767	24.6
1927	241 149	24.3	1964	452 915	23.5
1928	243 616	24.1	1965	418 595	21.3
1929	242 226	23.5	1966	387 710	19.4
1930	250 335	23.9	1967	370 894	18.2
1931	247 205	23.2	1968	364 310	17.6
1932	242 698	22.5	1969	369 647	17.6
1933	229 791	21.0	1970	371 988	17.5
1934	228 296	20.7	1971	362 187	16.8
1935	228 396	20.5	1972	347 319	15.9
1936	227 980	20.3	1973	343 373	15.5
1937	227 869	20.1	1974	350 650	15.4
1938	237 091	20.7	1975	359 323	15.8
1939	237 991	20.6	1976	359 987	15.7
1940	252 577	21.6	1977	361 400	15.5
1941	263 993	22.4	1978	358 852	15.3
1942	281 569	23.5	1979	366 064	15.9
1943	292 943	24.2	1980	370 709	15.5
1944	293 967	24.0	1981	371 346	15.3
1945	300 587	24.3	1982	373 082	15.0
1946	343 504	27.2	1983	373 689	15.0
1947	372 589	28.9	1984	377 031	15.0
1948	359 860	27.3	1985	375 727	14.8
1949	367 092	27.3	1986	372 913	14.7
1950	372 009	27.1	1987	369 742	14.4
1951	381 092	27.2	1988	376 795	14.5
1952	403 559	27.9	1989	392 661	15.0
1953	417 884	28.1	1990	405 474	15.2
1954	436 198	28.5	1991	411 910	15.2
1955	442 937	28.2	1992	398 642	14.0
1956	450 739	28.0	1993[2]	397 110	n.a.
1957	469 093	28.2			

Source: *Statistics Canada*

(1) Per 1,000 population. (2) Based on preliminary figures.

Births by Province, 1992

	Live Births	Birth Rate[1]		Live Births	Birth Rate[1]
Canada	398 642	14.0	Manitoba	16 590	14.9
Newfoundland	6 918	11.9	Saskatchewan	15 004	14.9
Prince Edward Island	1 850	14.2	Alberta	42 039	16.0
Nova Scotia	11 874	12.9	British Columbia	46 156	13.4
New Brunswick	9 389	12.5	Yukon Territory	529	17.5
Quebec	96 146	13.4	Northwest Territories	1 554	24.9
Ontario	150 593	14.2			

Source: *Statistics Canada*

(1) Per 1,000 population.

Canadian Births by Age of Mother, 1991

Age of Mother	Total Births	Order of birth[1]									
		1st	2nd	3rd	4th	5th	6th	7th	8	9	10+
under 15 years.....	265	262	2	1							
15................	949	919	30								
16................		2 439	2 297	135	7						
17................	4 676	4 208	431	34	3						
18................	6 916	5 748	1 060	101	6						
19................	9 200	7 020	1 886	263	29	1					
20................	11 767	8 200	2 907	568	77	11	2				
21................	13 592	8 627	3 826	936	176	20	5	1			
22................	15 538	9 143	4 800	1 278	258	46	7				
23................	18 228	10 057	5 871	1 763	427	90	13	3			
24................	21 598	11 553	7 166	2 138	572	122	34	8			
25................	25 686	13 271	8 709	2 737	722	178	53	5	4	3	1
26................	29 545	14 250	10 520	3 535	901	241	64	17	9	1	
27................	31 882	14 269	11 815	4 270	1 121	270	88	33	9	1	1
28................	32 287	13 397	12 459	4 739	1 222	314	112	25	7	4	
29................	30 624	11 348	12 157	5 093	1 422	402	121	58	12	2	3
30................	29 063	9 945	11 482	5 449	1 534	407	160	49	16	7	7
31................	25 395	7 679	10 255	5 249	1 523	433	156	51	33	8	5
32................	21 393	6 031	8 382	4 691	1 537	452	172	75	30	13	5
33................	17 554	4 533	6 893	4 062	1 398	396	148	69	34	9	10
34................	14 155	3 630	5 329	3 416	1 147	361	145	58	38	13	17
35................	11 212	2 777	4 040	2 731	1 028	331	159	59	47	21	15
36................	8 641	2 110	2 990	2 085	906	270	134	51	44	21	29
37................	6 033	1 436	2 038	1 417	644	265	105	57	31	22	17
38................	4 282	1 025	1 396	980	509	179	85	39	19	26	22
39................	2 939	615	953	694	345	142	74	41	29	20	25
40................	1 858	427	582	414	215	92	38	19	25	14	31
41................	1 139	263	325	252	129	72	37	20	18	8	15
42................	604	138	152	132	72	37	21	17	6	11	17
43................	359	81	88	79	52	27	9	5	7	2	9
44................	164	25	37	35	21	17	6	7	4	4	8
45................	78	17	17	13	12	7	5	2		3	2
46................	41	6	8	6	5	9	1	2	2		2
47................	12	3	3	3		1	1	1			
48................	7	1	2		1	2					1
49................											
50+...............											
Not stated........	2 407	104	95	45	6	2	1	1	3		
Total births	**402 528**[2]	**175 415**	**138 841**	**59 216**	**18 020**	**5 197**	**1 956**	**773**	**427**	**213**	**242**

Source: *Statistics Canada*

(1) The order of birth takes into account all children born alive to the mother. (2) Includes 2 150 births where order of birth not stated.

Changing Families

*T*he last 30 years and, in particular the last decade, have seen an increase in births outside marriage, but it does not mean a corresponding increase of young, single mothers. The growth in common-law relationships has kept pace with the change, and the age of the unmarried mothers has risen: in 1961, 72% of non-marital births were to women under 25; in 1990, more than 50% were to women over 25. There were provincial differences within these changes—Quebec has the highest proportion of such births (41%), but also the highest proportion of common-law couples; as might be expected, Ontario, which has the lowest proportion of common-law relationships, had the lowest proportion of births to unmarried women (17%).

Age of Mother at Birth of First Child[1]

Age of mother	1931	1950	1971	1991
Under 15	14	15	292	262
15–19	9 639	14 251	33 258	20 192
20–24	25 224	41 018	65 618	47 580
25–29	13 826	24 330	32 918	66 535
30–34	4 802	8 558	7 236	31 818
35–39	1 580	3 086	1 830	7 963
40–44	342	677	380	934
45 and over	27	37	15	27
Total first borns[2]	55 486	92 018	142 008	175 415

Source: *Statistics Canada*

(1) Excludes Newfoundland. (2) Includes births for which age of mother not stated.

Most Popular Baby Names in Canada, 1950–1990 [in order of popularity]

1950 Boys	1950 Girls	1970 Boys	1970 Girls	1990 Boys	1990 Girls
Robert	Linda	Michael	Lisa	Michael	Jessica
David	Patricia	David	Michelle	Matthew	Amanda
John	Barbara	Robert	Jennifer	Christopher	Sarah
James	Susan	Jason	Tracy	Andrew	Stephanie
William	Sharon	James	Tammy	Kyle	Samantha
Richard	Margaret	Christopher	Karen	Ryan	Ashley
Kenneth	Donna	John	Nicole	Joshua	Brittany
Donald	Judith	Richard	Christine	Daniel	Jennifer
Ronald	Carol	Kevin	Shannon	Jordan	Nicole
Douglas	Sandra	Mark	Susan	Justin	Kayla
Michael	Wendy	Steven	Angel	David	Melissa
Brian	Karen	William	Laura	Tyler	Megan
Gordon	Shirley	Paul	Sandra	James	Michelle
Thomas	Elizabeth	Brian	Tanya	Nicholas	Rebecca
Gary	Kathleen	Scott	Heather	Robert	Emily
Wayne	Heather	Darren	Kimberly	Adam	Laura
Peter	Brenda	Daniel	Patricia	Alexander	Danielle
Dennis	Janet	Kenneth	Brenda	Kevin	Alexandra
Bruce	Catherine	Andrew	Lori	Steven	Lauren
Daniel	Janice	Sean	Tracey	Joseph	Courtney
Larry	Marilyn	Gregory	Julie	Jonathan	Cassandra
Edward	Diane	Stephen	Kelly	Brandon	Rachel
George	Maureen	Dean	Cheryl	Eric	Lindsay
Gerald	Gail	Peter	Tara	John	Victoria
Patrick	Joan	Jeffrey	Andrea	Thomas	Marie

Expected Years of Life Remaining, by Age, 1986

Age	Male % Dying[1]	Male Years of Life Remaining	Female % Dying[1]	Female Years of Life Remaining	Age	Male % Dying[1]	Male Years of Life Remaining	Female % Dying[1]	Female Years of Life Remaining
0	.86	73.04	.68	79.73	52	.66	24.75	.38	30.08
1	.07	72.67	.06	79.27	53	.74	23.92	.41	29.19
2	.05	71.72	.04	78.32	54	.82	23.09	.45	28.31
3	.04	70.76	.03	77.35	55	.91	22.28	.49	27.43
4	.04	69.79	.03	76.38	56	1.01	21.48	.53	26.56
5	.03	68.81	.02	75.40	57	1.11	20.69	.58	25.70
6	.02	67.83	.02	74.41	58	1.22	19.92	.63	24.85
7	.02	66.85	.02	73.43	59	1.34	19.16	.69	24.00
8	.02	65.86	.01	72.44	60	1.47	18.41	.75	23.17
9	.02	64.87	.01	71.45	61	1.61	17.68	.82	22.34
10	.02	63.88	.01	70.46	62	1.77	16.96	.90	21.52
11	.02	62.89	.02	69.47	63	1.95	16.25	.99	20.71
12	.03	61.91	.02	68.48	64	2.14	15.57	1.08	19.91
13	.04	60.92	.02	67.49	65	2.35	14.90	1.18	19.12
14	.06	59.95	.03	66.50	66	2.57	14.24	1.29	18.34
15	.07	58.98	.03	65.52	67	2.82	13.61	1.42	17.58
16	.09	58.02	.04	64.54	68	3.09	12.99	1.56	16.82
17	.11	57.08	.04	63.57	69	3.37	12.38	1.70	16.08
18	.12	56.13	.04	62.59	70	3.67	11.80	1.87	15.35
19	.12	55.20	.04	61.62	71	4.01	11.23	2.06	14.63
20	.13	54.27	.04	60.65	72	4.38	10.68	2.28	13.93
21	.14	53.34	.04	59.67	73	4.78	10.14	2.52	13.24
22	.14	52.41	.04	58.70	74	5.21	9.63	2.79	12.57
23	.14	51.48	.04	57.72	75	5.68	9.13	3.09	11.92
24	.14	50.55	.04	56.74	76	6.19	8.65	3.42	11.28
25	.13	49.62	.04	55.77	77	6.75	8.19	3.81	10.66
26	.13	48.68	.04	54.79	78	7.34	7.74	4.23	10.07
27	.13	47.75	.04	53.81	79	7.98	7.32	4.68	9.49
28	.13	46.81	.05	52.83	80	8.67	6.91	5.17	8.93
29	.13	45.87	.05	51.86	81	9.41	6.52	5.74	8.39
30	.13	44.92	.05	50.88	82	10.22	6.14	6.38	7.87
31	.13	43.98	.05	49.91	83	11.09	5.78	7.09	7.37
32	.14	43.04	.06	48.94	84	12.02	5.44	7.86	6.90
33	.14	42.10	.06	47.96	85	13.02	5.12	8.71	6.44
34	.14	41.16	.07	46.99	86	14.09	4.81	9.65	6.01
35	.15	40.21	.07	46.02	87	15.25	4.52	10.70	5.60
36	.15	39.27	.07	45.05	88	16.49	4.24	11.84	5.21
37	.16	38.33	.08	44.09	89	17.80	3.98	13.08	4.84
38	.17	37.39	.09	43.12	90	19.20	3.73	14.42	4.49
39	.18	36.45	.10	42.16	91	20.69	3.50	15.87	4.16
40	.20	35.52	.11	41.20	92	22.28	3.28	17.47	3.85
41	.22	34.59	.13	40.25	93	23.09	3.07	18.25	3.56
42	.24	33.66	.14	39.30	94	23.08	2.85	18.21	3.25
43	.26	32.74	.16	38.33	95	23.63	2.55	18.77	2.86
44	.28	31.82	.17	37.41	96	26.08	2.19	21.36	2.41
45	.31	30.91	.19	36.48	97	31.77	1.78	27.41	1.92
46	.35	30.01	.21	35.54	98	42.75	1.38	39.08	1.46
47	.38	29.11	.23	34.62	99	58.11	1.04	55.42	1.08
48	.43	28.22	.26	33.70	100	74.80	0.78	73.18	0.80
49	.48	27.34	.28	32.78	101	89.78	0.60	89.13	0.61
50	.53	26.47	.31	31.87	102	100.00	0.50	100.00	0.50
51	.59	25.61	.34	30.97					

Source: *Statistics Canada*

(1) Represents the percentage of the population that will die before reaching the next age; in some cases totals do not equal 100% due to rounding of percentages to two decimal places.

Leading Causes of Death Among Canadians

(total deaths: 155 961)

	1970									
	Circulatory and Heart Disease		Stroke		Cancer		Respiratory Diseases		AIDS/HIV Infection	
Age	Male	Female	Male	Female	Male	Female	Male	Female	Male	Female
less than 1	17	11	7	1	16	14	421	314	n.a.	n.a.
1-4	9	6	4	2	61	68	87	84	n.a.	n.a.
5-9	6	3	1	1	118	75	27	31	n.a.	n.a.
10-14	16	10	4	1	92	62	27	26	n.a.	n.a.
15-19	27	21	9	8	88	56	27	28	n.a.	n.a.
20-24	34	37	8	12	99	70	25	23	n.a.	n.a.
25-29	57	59	15	28	104	69	28	27	n.a.	n.a.
30-34	139	75	28	29	110	128	22	31	n.a.	n.a.
35-39	323	133	45	56	197	271	47	43	n.a.	n.a.
40-44	754	270	80	92	391	520	79	53	n.a.	n.a.
45-49	1 422	467	112	140	658	866	141	87	n.a.	n.a.
50-54	2 353	673	215	167	1 072	1 186	236	116	n.a.	n.a.
55-59	3 529	1 243	335	258	1 684	1 411	383	162	n.a.	n.a.
60-64	4 700	1 796	516	378	2 194	1 507	578	190	n.a.	n.a.
65-69	5 626	2 953	773	635	2 572	1 616	773	243	n.a.	n.a.
70-74	6 026	4 128	1 083	894	2 496	1 701	963	359	n.a.	n.a.
75-79	6 507	5 630	1 359	1 477	2 265	1 592	967	469	n.a.	n.a.
80-84	6 287	6 551	1 443	1 756	1 730	1 250	925	598	n.a.	n.a.
85+	6 534	8 944	1 500	2 266	1 245	1 099	1 094	964	n.a.	n.a.
TOTAL	44 368	33 011	7 557	8 201	17 192	13 570	6 850	3 848	n.a.	n.a.

	1970							
	Meningitis		Accidents		Suicide		Murder	
Age	Male	Female	Male	Female	Male	Female	Male	Female
less than 1	9	5	201	115	-	-	4	8
1-4	11	9	288	182	-	-	10	5
5-9	5	1	384	187	-	-	9	6
10-14	-	3	348	166	14	3	7	9
15-19	2	2	999	281	106	39	22	13
20-24	1	-	1 054	198	203	53	26	18
25-29	-	1	604	132	146	61	20	19
30-34	-	1	430	141	136	59	33	14
35-39	-	-	406	111	171	60	23	8
40-44	-	-	432	130	175	75	19	16
45-49	-	1	426	136	165	93	22	10
50-54	2	-	358	129	148	73	14	8
55-59	-	-	344	121	149	62	19	5
60-64	1	-	270	123	116	34	11	6
65-69	-	-	289	94	82	35	12	6
70-74	-	-	162	87	53	17	5	3
75-79	-	-	134	80	33	9	3	4
80-84	-	-	162	60	27	5	2	1
85+	-	-	81	51	8	3	-	2
TOTAL	31	23	7 226	2 528	1 732	681	261	160

Source: *Statistics Canada*

(1) Includes cases in which age was not specified. (—) = zero.

Leading Causes of Death Among Canadians

(total deaths: 196 050)

	1990									
	Circulatory and Heart Disease		Stroke		Cancer		Respiratory Diseases		AIDS/HIV Infection	
Age	Male	Female	Male	Female	Male	Female	Male	Female	Male	Female
less than 1	8	17	-	2	5	8	23	22	-	-
1-4	7	7	1	3	30	28	11	10	2	1
5-9	8	3	5	2	38	27	8	5	-	-
10-14	4	7	2	2	34	33	8	6	1	-
15-19	18	15	3	3	47	31	11	9	1	-
20-24	35	17	11	9	81	35	13	9	9	4
25-29	70	40	15	19	88	92	14	17	99	10
30-34	126	66	30	29	157	209	25	24	173	11
35-39	253	103	49	40	267	373	34	21	202	7
40-44	508	150	67	57	451	617	49	30	200	1
45-49	786	223	86	60	840	879	56	54	120	4
50-54	1 204	395	114	93	1 350	1 237	127	66	58	2
55-59	2 059	690	206	111	2 318	1 844	22 6	136	37	1
60-64	3 371	1 333	354	232	3 711	2 532	492	282	20	1
65-69	4 810	2 430	548	404	4 754	3 362	865	479	5	1
70-74	5 764	3 651	802	694	4 785	3 435	1 265	746	5	2
75-79	6 790	5 743	1 102	1 147	4 493	3 405	1 846	1 000	4	-
80-84	6 095	7 157	1 194	1 697	3 313	2 813	1 872	1 211	-	-
85+	6 907	14 219	1 481	3 347	2 415	2 964	2 406	2 794	1	-
TOTAL	38 823	36 266	6 070	7 951	29 178	23 924	9 351	6 921	937	45

	1990							
	Meningitis		Accidents		Suicide		Murder	
Age	Male	Female	Male	Female	Male	Female	Male	Female
less than 1	3	2	44	26	-	-	5	2
1-4	4	3	148	78	-	-	10	9
5-9	1	1	116	73	-	1	5	7
10-14	1	3	171	71	23	6	4	3
15-19	7	3	696	201	182	43	28	17
20-24	2	3	925	235	302	51	41	16
25-29	-	-	998	229	347	63	55	28
30-34	-	1	966	266	356	91	49	34
35-39	1	-	793	247	303	105	41	15
40-44	1	-	653	237	251	83	26	21
45-49	-	-	500	164	191	58	29	11
50-54	-	1	417	157	139	47	13	7
55-59	-	1	436	145	148	38	16	7
60-64	-	-	411	157	113	27	8	2
65-69	-	-	338	191	88	33	10	6
70-74	2	-	352	201	81	27	9	8
75-79	-	1	335	243	74	13	3	4
80-84	-	1	341	299	40	12	2	2
85+	-	-	424	773	35	7	1	-
TOTAL	22	20	9 065	3 995	2 673	706	355	199

Source: *Statistics Canada*

(1) Includes cases in which age was not specified. (—) = zero.

Expected Years of Life Remaining, 1921–86

| | At Birth | | At Age 20 | | At Age 40 | | At Age 60 | | At Age 80 | |
	Male	Female	Male	Female	Male	Female	Male	Female	Male	Female
1921[1]	n.a.	n.a.	49.1	49.2	32.2	33.0	16.6	17.1	6.0	6.1
1931	60.0	62.1	49.1	49.8	32.0	33.0	16.3	17.2	5.6	5.9
1941	63.0	66.3	49.6	51.8	31.9	34.0	16.1	17.6	5.5	6.0
1951	66.3	70.8	50.8	54.4	32.5	35.6	16.5	18.6	5.8	6.4
1956	67.6	72.9	51.2	55.8	32.7	36.7	16.5	19.3	5.9	6.8
1961	68.4	74.2	51.5	56.7	33.0	37.5	16.7	19.9	6.1	6.9
1966	68.8	75.2	51.5	57.4	33.0	38.2	16.8	20.6	6.4	7.3
1971	69.3	76.4	51.7	58.2	33.2	39.0	17.0	21.4	6.4	7.9
1976	70.2	77.5	52.1	59.0	33.6	39.7	17.2	22.0	6.4	8.2
1981	71.9	79.0	53.4	60.1	34.7	40.7	18.0	22.9	6.9	8.8
1986	73.0	79.7	54.3	60.7	35.5	41.2	18.4	23.2	6.9	8.9

Source: *Statistics Canada*

(1) Excludes Quebec. (n.a.) not available.

Deaths in Canada, 1925–1993

| | Deaths | Death Rates[1] | | | | Deaths | Death Rates[1] | | |
		Both Sexes	Males	Females			Both Sexes	Males	Females
1921	104 531	11.6	11.9	11.2	1977	167 498	7.2	8.4	6.0
1926	111 055	11.4	11.9	10.9	1978	168 179	7.2	8.3	6.0
1931	108 446	10.2	10.5	9.6	1979	168 183	7.1	8.2	6.0
1936	111 111	9.9	10.3	9.3	1980	171 473	7.2	8.2	6.1
1941	118 797	10.1	10.9	9.1	1981	171 029	7.0	8.0	6.0
1946	118 785	9.4	10.3	8.4	1982	174 413	7.1	8.0	6.1
1951	125 823	9.0	10.1	7.8	1983	174 484	7.0	7.9	6.1
1956	131 961	8.2	9.4	7.0	1984	175 727	7.0	7.9	6.1
1961	140 985	7.7	9.0	6.5	1985	181 323	7.2	8.0	6.3
1966	149 863	7.5	8.7	6.2	1986	184 224	7.3	8.1	6.5
					1987	184 953	7.2	8.0	6.4
1971	157 272	7.3	8.5	6.1	1988	190 011	7.3	8.1	6.5
1972	162 413	7.4	8.7	6.2	1989	190 965	7.3	8.0	6.6
1973	164 039	7.4	8.6	6.2	1990	191 973	7.2	7.9	6.5
1974	166 794	7.4	8.6	6.3	1991	195 568	7.2	7.9	6.6
1975	167 404	7.3	8.5	6.2	1992	198 980	7.3	n.a.	n.a.
1976	167 009	7.3	8.4	6.1	1993	201 020[4]	n.a.	n.a.	n.a.

Source: *Statistics Canada*

(1) Per 1,000 population. (2) Excludes Que., Nfld, Yukon and NWT. (3) Excludes Nfld, Yukon and NWT. (4) Based on preliminary figures

Deaths by Province, 1992

	Deaths	Death Rate[1]		Deaths	Death Rate[1]
Canada	198 980	7.3	Manitoba	9 190	8.4
Newfoundland	3 850	6.7	Saskatchewan	8 310	8.4
Prince Edward Island	1 220	9.3	Alberta	14 530	5.7
Nova Scotia	7 490	8.3	British Columbia	24 800	7.5
New Brunswick	5 580	7.7	Yukon Territory	120	4.3
Quebec	50 650	7.3	Northwest Territories	251	4.4
Ontario	72 990	7.2			

Source: *Statistics Canada*

(1) Rate per 1,000 population.

MIGRATION

Canadian Immigration Totals, 1852–1993

1852 .... 29 307	1888 .... 88 766	1924 .... 124 164	1960 .... 104 111
1853 .... 29 464	1889 .... 91 600	1925 .... 84 907	1961 .... 71 689
1854 .... 37 263	1890 .... 75 067	1926 .... 135 982	1962 .... 74 586
1855 .... 25 296	1891 .... 82 165	1927 .... 158 886	1963 .... 93 151
1856 .... 22 544	1892 .... 30 996	1928 .... 166 783	1964 .... 112 606
1857 .... 33 854	1893 .... 29 633	1929 .... 164 993	1965 .... 146 758
1858 .... 12 339	1894 .... 20 829	1930 .... 104 806	1966 .... 194 743
1859 .... 6 300	1895 .... 18 790	1931 .... 27 530	1967 .... 222 876
1860 .... 6 276	1896 .... 16 835	1932 .... 20 591	1968 .... 183 974
1861 .... 13 589	1897 .... 21 716	1933 .... 14 382	1969 .... 161 531
1862 .... 18 294	1898 .... 31 900	1934 .... 12 476	1970 .... 147 713
1863 .... 21 000	1899 .... 44 543	1935 .... 11 277	1971 .... 121 900
1864 .... 24 779	1900 .... 41 681	1936 .... 11 643	1972 .... 122 006
1865 .... 18 958	1901 .... 55 747	1937 .... 15 101	1973 .... 184 200
1866 .... 11 427	1902 .... 89 102	1938 .... 17 244	1974 .... 218 465
1867 .... 10 666	1903 .... 138 660	1939 .... 16 994	1975 .... 187 881
1868 .... 12 765	1904 .... 131 252	1940 .... 11 324	1976 .... 149 429
1869 .... 18 630	1905 .... 141 465	1941 .... 9 329	1977 .... 114 914
1870 .... 24 706	1906 .... 211 653	1942 .... 7 576	1978 .... 86 313
1871 .... 27 773	1907 .... 272 409	1943 .... 8 504	1979 .... 112 096
1872 .... 36 578	1908 .... 143 326	1944 .... 12 801	1980 .... 143 117
1873 .... 50 050	1909 .... 173 694	1945 .... 22 722	1981 .... 128 618
1874 .... 39 373	1910 .... 286 839	1946 .... 71 719	1982 .... 121 147
1875 .... 27 382	1911 .... 331 288	1947 .... 64 127	1983 .... 89 157
1876 .... 25 633	1912 .... 375 756	1948 .... 125 414	1984 .... 88 239
1877 .... 27 082	1913 .... 400 870	1949 .... 95 217	1985 .... 84 302
1878 .... 29 807	1914 .... 150 484	1950 .... 73 912	1986 .... 99 219
1879 .... 40 492	1915 .... 36 665	1951 .... 194 391	1987 .... 152 098
1880 .... 38 505	1916 .... 55 914	1952 .... 164 498	1988 .... 161 929
1881 .... 47 991	1917 .... 72 910	1953 .... 168 868	1989 .... 192 001
1882 .... 112 458	1918 .... 41 845	1954 .... 154 227	1990 .... 214 230
1883 .... 133 624	1919 .... 107 698	1955 .... 109 946	1991 .... 232 020
1884 .... 103 824	1920 .... 138 824	1956 .... 164 857	1992 .... 253 345
1885 .... 79 169	1921 .... 91 728	1957 .... 282 164	1993 .... 254 670
1886 .... 69 152	1922 .... 64 224	1958 .... 124 851	
1887 .... 84 526	1923 .... 133 729	1959 .... 106 928	

Source: *Citizenship and Immigration Canada*

Non-permanent Canadian Residents

*T*he 1991 census counted non-permanent residents for the first time and it was found that 1% of the Canadian population was considered to be in the country only temporarily.

Three-quarters of this population lived in Toronto (which accounted for 44%), Montreal (18%), and Vancouver (10%), and the group included those working with an employment authorization, overseas students, people admitted on compassionate, national interest or humanitarian grounds (such as refugees), visitors with visas and those without legal status.

The largest component was those with employment authorizations. Historically, this group was composed mostly of agricultural workers recruited to help in peak periods such as harvests, now such workers are more likely to be here for more than a season. Many with employment authorizations were given them in order to enable residents, such as refugee applicants, to work rather than be dependent on local social services.

Immigration[1] to Canada, 1956–93

	Total Immigrants	United States	Asia	Europe	Caribbean[3]	South America	Africa	Oceania
1956	164 857	9 777	3 537	145 554	1 351	1 551	1 079	1 924
1957	282 164	11 008	3 244	257 540	1 586	2 376	2 970	3 345
1958	124 851	10 846	4 223	102 279	1 519	2 168	1 355	2 344
1959	106 928	11 338	5 368	84 517	1 529	1 750	8 43	1 512
1960	104 111	11 247	4 002	82 922	1 542	1 823	8 33	1 657
1961	71 689	11 516	2 706	52 132	1 454	1 301	1 088	1 432
1962	74 586	11 643	2 593	53 790	1 842	1 103	2 171	1 384
1963	93 151	11 736	3 553	69 069	2 611	1 779	2 431	1 692
1964	112 606	12 565	6 121	82 798	2 467	2 257	3 874	2 303
1965	146 758	15 143	11 215	108 285	3 420	2 471	3 196	2 711
1966	194 743	17 514	13 835	148 410	4 357	2 604	3 661	4 057
1967	222 876	19 038	20 740	159 979	9 004	3 090	4 608	6 168
1968	183 974	20 422	21 686	120 702	8 129	2 693	5 204	4 815
1969	161 531	22 785	23 319	88 363	13 908	4 767	3 297	4 411
1970	147 713	24 424	21 170	75 609	13 371	4 943	2 863	4 385
1971	121 900	24 366	22 171	52 031	11 653	5 058	2 841	2 902
1972	122 006	22 618	23 325	51 293	9 218	4 309	8 308	2 143
1973	184 200	25 242	43 193	71 883	20 704	11 057	8 307	2 671
1974	218 465	26 541	50 566	88 694	25 276	12 528	10 450	2 594
1975	187 881	20 155	47 382	72 898	19 483	13 270	9 867	2 174
1976	149 429	17 315	44 328	49 903	16 198	10 628	7 752	1 886
1977	114 914	12 888	31 368	40 748	13 187	7 840	6 372	1 545
1978	86 313	9 945	24 007	30 075	9 240	6 782	4 261	1 233
1979	112 096	9 617	50 540	32 858	7 060	5 898	3 958	1 395
1980	143 117	9 926	71 602	41 168	8 141	5 433	4 330	2 497
1981	128 618	10 559	48 831	46 299	9 625	6 163	4 889	2 253
1982	121 147	9 360	41 686	46 156	10 317	6 871	4 513	2 119
1983	89 157	7 381	36 906	24 312	10 864	4 816	3 659	1 213
1984	88 239	6 922	41 920	20 901	9 706	4 085	3 552	1 151
1985	84 302	6 669	38 597	18 859	11 143	4 356	3 545	1 128
1986	99 219	7 275	41 600	22 709	14 947	6 686	4 770	1 227
1987	152 098	7 967	67 337	37 563	18 100	10 801	8 501	1 827
1988	161 929	6 537	81 136	40 689	15 108	7 255	9 380	1 822
1989	192 001	6 931	93 261	52 105	16 764	8 685	12 199	2 041
1990	213 334	6 057	111 195	51 667	19 459	8 888	13 426	2 642
1991	232 020	20 122[4]	120 736	48 232	12 978	10 632	16 175	3 145[5]
1992	253 345	20 123	139 546	44 933	14 993	10 415	19 669	3 666[5]
1993	254 670	15 718[4]	146 672	46 343	16 515	9 562	16 852	3 053[5]

Source: *Citizenship and Immigration Canada*

(1) By country of last permanent residence. (2) Includes China and Hong Kong. (3) Includes Central America, Greenland and St. Pierre & Miquelon for 1956–76. (4) Includes Central America. (5) Includes Australasia.

How Many Immigrants?

*T*he 1991 census counted 4.3 million immigrants in Canada. Nearly half of these people (48%) had been living here for over 20 years—they arrived before 1971. 24% came between 1971 and 1980, and 28% came in the last decade. In the period from 1981 to 1986 the immigrant population grew by 2%; between 1986 and 1991 it grew by 11%, reflecting the increase in annual target levels for immigrants set by the federal government during the same period.

As a percentage of the total Canadian population, the number of immigrants has remained roughly the same since the 1950s. In 1951, immigrants represented 14.7% of the Canadian people, in 1986 they were 15.6% and in 1991 the percentage was 16.1. New arrivals mainly settled in Canada's cities, and 94% of them headed for Ontario, British Columbia, Quebec or Alberta.

Immigration by Province of Intended Destination

	Total immigrants[1]	Nfld	PEI	NS	NB	Que	Ont	Man	Sask	Alta	BC	YK	NWT
1956 ...	164 857	426	112	1 639	852	31 396	90 662	5 796	2 202	9 959	17 812	n.a.	n.a.
1960 ...	104 111	306	83	1 210	634	23 774	54 491	4 337	2 087	6 949	10 120	n.a.	n.a.
1965 ...	146 758	604	137	1 612	1 074	30 346	79 702	3 948	2 649	8 049	18 502	n.a.	n.a.
1970 ...	147 713	630	185	2 007	1 070	23 261	80 732	5 826	1 709	10 405	21 683	n.a.	n.a.
1975 ...	187 881	1106	235	2 124	2 093	28 042	98 471	7 134	2 837	16 277	29 272	n.a.	n.a.
1980 ...	143 117	541	190	1 616	1 207	22 538	62 257	7 683	3 603	18 839	24 437	n.a.	n.a.
1981 ...	128 618	483	128	1 405	990	21 182	55 032	5 370	2 402	19 330	22 095	n.a.	n.a.
1982 ...	121147	406	165	1 256	751	21 336	53 049	4 931	2 125	17 949	18 999	n.a.	n.a.
1983 ...	89 157	275	105	833	554	16 374	40 036	3 978	1 735	10 688	14 447	n.a.	n.a.
1984 ...	88 239	299	109	1 034	600	14 641	41 527	3 903	2 150	10 670	13 190	n.a.	n.a.
1985 ...	84 302	325	113	974	609	14 884	40 730	3 415	1 905	9 001	12 239	n.a.	n.a.
1986 ...	99 219	274	168	1 097	641	19 459	49 630	3 749	1 860	9 673	12 552	49	67
1987 ...	152 098	458	159	1 227	642	26 822	84 807	4 799	2 119	11 975	18 913	80	72
1988 ...	161 929	408	153	1 299	679	25 789	88 996	5 009	2 223	14 025	23 204	68	76
1989 ...	192 001	468	159	1 473	905	34 171	104 799	6 138	2 142	16 211	25 335	100	100
1990 ...	214 230	546	176	1 563	842	40 842	113 438	6 637	2 361	18 994	28 723	83	75
1991 ...	232 020	641	150	1 504	685	52 155	119 257	5 659	2 455	17 043	32 263	84	124
1992 ...	253 345	787	151	2 359	754	48 597	138 453	5 084	2 511	17 696	36 709	133	111
1993 ...	254 670	805	170	3 001	705	44 737	133 665	4 882	2 391	18 487	45 546	104	170

Source: *Citizenship and Immigration Canada*

Persons Granted Canadian Citizenship, 1920–1993[1]

1920	3 004	**1945**	13 562	**1970**	57 556
1921	10 507	**1946**	9 047	**1971**	63 669
1922	10 360	**1947**	15 335	**1972**	80 866
1923	7 589	**1948**	11 410	**1973**	104 697
1924	7 659	**1949**	11 991[2]	**1974**	130 278
1925	13 288	**1950**	10 441	**1975**	137 507
1926	15 403	**1951**	10 301	**1976**	117 276
1927	16 917	**1952**	10 888	**1977**	123 655
1928	13 466	**1953**	13 562	**1978**	223 214
1929	13 099	**1954**	19 545	**1979**	156 699
1930	21 221	**1955**	58 711	**1980**	118 590
1931	21 392	**1956**	55 404	**1981**	94 457
1932	32 517	**1957**	95 462	**1982**	87 468
1933	23 613	**1958**	84 183	**1983**	90 328
1934	21 908	**1959**	71 280	**1984**	109 504
1935	20 903	**1960**	62 378	**1985**	126 466
1936	30 679	**1961**	56 476	**1986**	103 800
1937	31 744	**1962**	72 082	**1987**	73 638
1938	27 455	**1963**	69 468	**1988**	58 810
1939	21 418	**1964**	64 334	**1989**	87 478
1940	18 207	**1965**	63 844	**1990**	104 267
1941	15 594	**1966**	60 852	**1991**	118 630
1942	14 213	**1967**	59 968	**1992**	115 757
1943	12 533	**1968**	60 055	**1993**	149 579
1944	12 827	**1969**	59 900		

Source: *Citizenship and Immigration Canada*

(1) For fiscal year ending Mar 31 for 1920 to 1951; calendar years 1952 onwards. (2) Does not include approx 359,000 Newfoundlanders who became Canadian citizens when Newfoundland became Canada's 10th province in 1949.

Refugees[1] to Canada, 1959–93

1959	3 047	1968	820	1977	1 061	1986	18 625
1960	2 329	1969	799	1978	775	1987	20 673
1961	1 813	1970	1 387	1979	27 740	1988	25 716
1962	1 733	1971	626	1980	40 640	1989	34 349
1963	2 024	1972	365	1981	14 996	1990	40 190
1964	2 279	1973	405	1982	16 908	1991	53 760
1965	2 131	1974	537	1983	13 643	1992	52 054
1966	2 058	1975	748	1984	15 400	1993	30 170
1967	1 499	1976	1 014	1985	16 550		

Source: *Citizenship and Immigration Canada*

(1) Includes persons admitted from abroad as Convention Refugees or members of Designated Classes, as well as persons recognized in Canada as Convention Refugees or members of the special Backlog Clearance Designated Class. Does not include special humanitarian movements of other persons.

Refugees to Canada by Country[1]

	1980	1990	1991	1992	1993
Total Refugees	**40 640**	**40 190**	**53 760**	**52 054**	**30 170**
Afghanistan	7	979	1 153	896	491
Argentina	22	13	97	351	329
Bangladesh	0	77	693	567	239
Bosnia-Hercegovina	0	0	0	74	1 648
Bulgaria	51	142	430	521	168
Chile	355	675	948	447	182
China	16	152	835	1 122	398
Croatia	0	0	0	29	166
Czechoslovakia	1 015	1 156	312	146	15
El Salvador	1	3 821	5 694	4 029	1 563
Ethiopia	72	2 220	2 190	1 591	1 180
Ghana	0	145	665	1 263	1 025
Guatemala	2	771	1 624	1 202	778
Haiti	8	42	150	259	266
Honduras	0	190	496	464	213
Hungary	296	509	330	226	102
India	4	64	383	564	593
Iran	16	2 064	4 108	4 336	1 496
Iraq	5	532	531	1 527	2 434
Kampuchea	3 270	720	338	222	154
Laos	6 304	572	979	50	7
Lebanon	10	733	3 108	1 845	547
Nicaragua	3	552	1 034	690	433
Pakistan	1	206	663	878	608
Panama	0	33	568	423	253
Peru	1	44	197	374	300
Poland	477	11 951	10 155	4 878	851
Romania	307	1 022	531	610	207
Rwanda	0	28	28	37	60
Seychelles	0	62	208	311	120
Somalia	6	1 092	2 967	4 711	2 492
Sri Lanka	1	1 264	4 223	8 009	3 871
Sudan	9	188	272	512	416
United States	0	223	495	390	142
USSR	1 914	1 161	712	893	511
Vietnam	25 342	5 339	3 173	2 267	1 951
Yugoslavia	2	18	62	227	303

Source: *Citizenship and Immigration Canada*

(1) By country of last permanent residence. Represents total number of refugees admitted to Canada from abroad as Convention Refugees or members of Designated Classes. Excludes Special Humanitarian Movements. (2) Preliminary figures. (3) Includes the Caribbean and Mexico. (—) = zero.

Special Refugee and Humanitarian Movements, 1947–93

1947–52	Post-War European Movement	186 150
1956–57	Hungarian Movement	37 149
1968–69	Czechoslovakian Movement	11 943
1970	Tibetans	228
1972–73	Ugandan Asians	7 069
1973–79	Special South American Program	7 016
1975	Cypriots	700
1975–78	Special Vietnamese/Cambodian Program	9 060
1976	Kurds from Iraq	98
1976–79	Lebanese Movement	11 321
1978–84	Argentine Political Detainee Program	9
1982–85	Polish Special Movement	7 445[1]
1982—present	Iranian Special Movement	3 321[1]
1982—present	El Salvadoran Special Movement	2 506[1]
1983—present	Lebanese Special Movement	11 836[1]
1983—present	Sri Lankan Special Movement	3 079[1]
1984—present	Guatemalan Special Movement	1 218[1]
1992—present	Special Measures for Citizens of the Former Yugoslavia	4 252[1]

Source: *Citizenship and Immigration Canada*

(1) Figure represents preliminary total up to end of Dec. 1993. Does not include persons recognized as Convention Refugees or members of Designated Classes, as defined in the Immigration Act of 1976.

Where Canadians Move Within Canada

When Canadians move from one province to another, it tends to be directly related to economic conditions. This was most apparent from 1976–1981 when the resource boom in Alberta caused a large influx there from other provinces. But falling international oil prices in the early 1980s led to a reversal of this trend as Canadians moved east, especially to Ontario. In recent years, those moving to another province have tended to head to British Columbia.

The following table shows net interprovincial migration—the number of persons moving into a province minus the number of persons moving out of that province.

	Nfld	PEI	NS	NB	Que	Ont	Man	Sask	Alta	BC	YT	NWT
1956–61	-4 671	-1 099	-15 295	-5 270	-7 756	34 345	-15 957	-33 557	16 787	33 230	n.a.	n.a.
1961–66	-15 213	-2 969	-27 124	-25 680	-19 859	85 369	-23 471	-42 094	-1 983	77 747	n.a.	n.a.
1966–71	-19 344	-2 763	-16 396	-19 599	-122 736	150 712	-40 690	-81 399	32 005	114 964	n.a.	n.a.
1971–76	-1 857	3 754	11 307	16 801	-77 610	-38 560	-26 827	-40 752	186 364	122 625	988	1 900
1976–81	-18 983	-829	-7 140	-10 351	-156 496	-57 826	-42 218	-9 716	186 364	122 625	-933	-4 497
1981–86	-15 051	751	6 895	-65	-81 254	121 767	-2 634	-2 974	-31 676	7 382	-2 775	-366
1986–91	-15 971	-771	-2 117	-5 246	-40 382	72 318	-36 454	-66 079	-41 438	138 860	1 219	-3 999
1992	-3 626	504	-2 132	-1 890	-15 497	-2 956	-6 513	-8 472	-1 278	41 240	1 232	-612

Source: *Statistics Canada*

What is a Refugee?

*A*ccording to Article 1 of the United Nations Convention Relating to the Status of Refugees (1951), it is a person who "…owing to well founded fear of being persecuted for reasons of race, religion, nationality, membership of a particular social group or political opinion, is outside the country of his nationality and is unable, or owing to such fear, is unwilling to avail himself of the protection of that country…"

Canada has signed the UN convention and uses this definition of a refugee when assessing claimants. In addition, the Canadian Immigration Act (1976) and later amendments (1992), provided further criteria for claimants coming from "refugee like" situations that include internally displaced people (such as oppressed people, political prisoners and those displaced by civil war).

Canadian Emigration by Province

(number of persons moving from Canada)

	Canada[1]	Nfld	PEI	NS	NB	Que	Ont	Man	Sask	Alta	BC	YK	NWT
1961–66	432 100	10 971	2 436	17 172	13 972	124 877	147 896	21 595	21 378	31 972	38 934	n.a.	n.a.
1966–71	472 400	13 901	2 390	17 549	20 517	144 078	179 523	15 330	15 907	23 974	38 127	n.a.	n.a.
1971–76	357 200	3 501	393	4 857	3 358	82 085	163 312	12 501	9 073	26 254	51 866	n.a.	n.a.
1976–81	278 641	3 551	921	8 967	7 027	43 439	127 740	11 311	6 548	34 012	33 969	n.a.	n.a.
1981–82	45 338	261	48	432	874	6 963	21 184	1 570	780	6 769	6 374	n.a.	n.a.
1982–83	50 249	372	78	373	708	8 402	23 448	1 487	842	7 315	7 125	n.a.	n.a.
1983–84	48 826	253	87	398	665	8 146	22 319	1 745	954	7 200	6 981	n.a.	n.a.
1984–85	46 252	332	71	350	612	7 203	21 916	1 255	837	6 214	7 389	n.a.	n.a.
1985–86	44 816	245	66	371	710	6 141	22 385	1 299	936	5 677	6 893	n.a.	n.a.
1981–86	235 481	1 463	350	1 924	3 569	36 855	111 252	7 356	4 349	33 175	34 762	n.a.	n.a.
1986–87	51 040	496	62	541	867	6 408	24 849	1 833	805	7 434	7 640	n.a.	n.a.
1987–88	40 528	268	44	400	708	4 778	19 733	1 692	886	6 247	5 704	n.a.	n.a.
1988–89	37 437	178	32	404	749	4 542	18 224	2 027	810	5 324	5 006	n.a.	n.a.
1989–90	37 915	216	56	359	735	4 269	18 459	1 717	854	5 988	5 170	n.a.	n.a.
1990–91	39 236	174	57	440	748	4 760	19 101	2 107	844	5 619	5 296	n.a.	n.a.
1986–91	206 156	1 332	251	2 144	3 807	24 757	100 366	9 376	4 199	30 612	28 816	n.a.	n.a.
1991	43 125	280	94	873	768	5 902	18 451	1 945	775	7 682	6 231	69	51
1992	44 459	313	100	958	847	6 488	20 295	2 101	862	8 475	6 892	73	53
1993	44 745	303	92	910	778	5 992	19 204	1 984	792	8 038	6 533	67	52

Source: *Statistics Canada*

(n.a.) not available.

Canadian Population Growth Components

(thousands)

Census Period	Births	− Deaths	= Natural Increase	Immigration	− Emigration	= Net Migration	Population Growth	Total population[1]
1851–1861	1 281	670	611	352	170	182	793	3 230
1861–1871	1 370	760	610	260	410	-150	460	3 689
1871–1881	1 480	790	690	350	404	- 54	636	4 325
1881–1891	1 524	870	654	680	826	-146	508	4 833
1891–1901	1 548	880	668	250	380	-130	538	5 371
1901–1911	1 925	900	1 025	1 550	740	810	1 835	7 207
1911–1921	2 340	1 070	1 270	1 400	1 089	311	1 581	8 788
1921–1931	2 420	1 060	1 360	1 200	970	230	1 589	10 377
1931–1941	2 294	1 072	1 222	149	241	- 92	1 130	11 507
1941–1951	3 212	1 220	1 992	548	382	166	2 503	14 009
1951–1956	2 106	633	1 473	783	185	598	2 071	16 081
1956–1961	2 362	687	1 675	760	378	482	2 157	18 238
1961–1966	2 249	731	1 518	539	280	259	1 777	20 015
1966–1971	1 856	766	1 090	890	427	463	1 553	21 568
1971–1976	1 758	823	934	841	352	489	1 424	22 993
1976–1981	1 820	842	978	588	217	371	1 349	24 343
1981–1986	1 873	885	988	500	477	23	1 011	25 354
1986–1991	2 328	1 142	1 186	2 396	1 640	756	1 942[2]	27 297

Source: *Statistics Canada*

(1) At end of the census period. (2) Includes refugee claimants and non-permanent residents.

EDUCATION

Enrolment in Canadian Schools, 1993–94[1]

The number of students in Canadian schools increased for the 1993–94 school year, continuing a recent trend. The number of elementary and secondary students rose by approximately 75 500 Canada-wide, with the largest increase in British Columbia, showing a jump of 6.6%.

The gradual increase follows a sharp enrolment decline during the 1970s and early 1980s. Community college and university enrolment also increased in 1993-94.

	Elementary and Secondary[2]		Community Colleges		Universities	
	Enrolment[3]	Schools	Enrolment[3]	Schools	Enrolment[3]	Schools
Canada	5 363 245	16 249	365 065	203	585 200	69
Newfoundland	120 690	498	4 460	12	13 720	1
Prince Edward Island	24 420	69	1 400	2	2 830	1
Nova Scotia	170 480	521	2 830	10	30 260	12
New Brunswick	139 830	444	3 800	8	20 310	5
Quebec	1 149 460	3 341	174 510	89	141 350	8
Ontario	2 110 090	5 578	111 170	32	234 470	22
Manitoba	221 820	840	4 570	10	20 860	6
Saskatchewan	208 040	960	3 820	1	23 340	3
Alberta	547 955	1 832	27 030	18	51 650	5
British Columbia	646 780	2 050	30 620	19	46 410	6
Yukon	5 970	32	290	1	–	–
Northwest Territories	17 210	80	565	1	–	–

Source: *Statistics Canada*

(1) Estimates. (2) Includes public, private and federal schools and schools for the blind and deaf. (3) Full-time. (4) Includes 500 overseas students/4 schools (Dept. of National Defence). (—) = zero.

Educational Attainment[1] in Canada

(percentages)

	1971		1981		1991	
	Males	Females	Males	Females	Males	Females
Less than grade 9	33.2	31.4	20.8	20.6	14.3	14.3
High school	43.5	48.2	41.8	45.4	41.8	43.3
Some post-secondary	16.7	17.5	27.5	27.8	31.0	32.4
University degree	6.6	3.0	9.9	6.2	12.8	10.0
Bachelor	4.9	2.6	7.7	5.3	8.5	7.3
Master's or doctorate	1.7	0.4	2.2	0.8	4.3	2.7
Total Population[1] (000s)	7 474	7 579	9 152	9 458	10 422	10 883

Source: *Census of Canada*   (1) Population 15 years and over.

Higher Education–How We Compare

A ccording to comparisons with populations of other developed countries, Canada is close to the top when it comes to percentage of university-educated adults, high school enrolment and spending on education, however we rank much further down when it comes to the percentage of graduates with science or engineering degrees.

Education Spending[1] in Canada

(millions of dollars)

	1960	1965	1970	1975	1980	1985	1990	1994[2]
Canada[3]	1 706	3 400	6 624	11 061	19 975	32 116	44 170	55 495
Newfoundland	23	41	104	234	411	658	977	1 212
Prince Edward Island	6	11	26	53	85	127	178	225
Nova Scotia	57	103	230	363	629	1 027	1 389	1 616
New Brunswick	43	73	172	261	464	808	1 108	1 370
Quebec	448	981	1 700	3 222	6 114	8 863	10 757	13 648
Ontario	609	1 239	2 669	3 995	6 883	10 988	16 641	21 022
Manitoba	81	147	272	467	760	1 333	1 840	2 177
Saskatchewan	95	155	262	399	722	1 296	1 699	1 798
Alberta	157	285	535	875	1 712	3 370	4 439	5 236
British Columbia	166	313	561	1 042	1 931	3 140	4 497	6 310
Yukon	n.a.	n.a.	n.a.	n.a.	n.a.	n.a.	79	92
Northwest Territories	n.a.	n.a.	n.a.	n.a.	n.a.	n.a.	205	257

Source: *Statistics Canada*

(1) From all sources of funding for academic years ending in the spring. (2) Estimates. (3) Provinces may not add up to Canadian total due to overseas and undistributed funds.

French Immersion Enrolment in Canada

French Immersion programs, through which non-francophone students take most or all of their subjects in French, have become increasingly popular in Canadian schools over the past decade. Most school boards offer early immersion (beginning in kindergarten) or middle immersion (usually starting in Grade 4). The goal of the program is to make students bilingual.

	1980–81		1985–86		1991–92	
	No. of Fr. Imm. Students	% of Total Enrol-ment[2]	No. of Fr. Imm. Students	% of Total Enrol-ment[2]	No. of Fr. Imm. Students	% of Total Enrol-ment[2]
Canada[1]	64 761	1.9	162 339	4.3	267 486	6.5
Newfoundland	392	0.3	2 015	1.4	4 999	4.0
Prince Edward Island	1 280	4.7	2 492	9.9	3 511	14.3
Nova Scotia	590	0.3	1 859	1.1	7 548	4.5
New Brunswick	5 532	3.6	14 530	10.1	14 987	10.6
Ontario	46 638	2.4	87 819	4.7	150 023	7.3
Manitoba	4 286	1.9	12 581	5.7	19 669	8.9
Saskatchewan	1 603	0.7	5 965	2.8	10 851	5.1
Alberta	n.a.	n.a.	19 017	4.1	27 044	5.2
British Columbia	4 368	0.8	15 590	3.0	28 040	4.7
Yukon	35	0.7	247	5.4	391	7.2
Northwest Territories	37	0.3	224	1.7	423	2.9

Source: *Statistics Canada*

(1) Includes elementary and secondary. (2) Excludes Quebec and Dept. of National Defence Schools overseas. For 1980–81 only, also excludes Alberta for which data was not available. (n.a.) not available.

Education Spending Around the World

I n 1988 Canadian governments spent 14.4% of budget on education, 62.5% of that spending on primary and secondary schools. Compared to other developed countries only Finland (at 17.1%) and Switzerland (14.7%) spent more. The average OECD country spent 12.0% on education that year, with 73.0% on primary and secondary education and a smaller percentage devoted to post secondary.

Reading and Numeracy Skills of Canadians, 1989

(percentage of adult population)

A national survey of 9,500 Canadians aged 16 to 69 was conducted in October 1989 to assess literacy and numeracy skills. Both were defined as "the information processing skills necessary to use the printed material commonly encountered at work, at home and in the community." A series of tests designed to simulate real life tasks was used in the testing.

For literacy, tasks ranged from locating a word in a document (such as locating the expiry date on a driver's licence) to tasks such as reading a chart to determine eligibility for a benefit. Four levels of reading skills were classified. At Level 1, readers had difficulty dealing with printed materials. Level 2s could use materials for limited purposes such as finding a familiar word in a simple text. Level 3s could use materials in a variety of situations if the material and the required tasks were simple and clearly laid out; level 4 readers could meet everyday reading demands. The results showed that 62% of adult

Canadians had reading abilities sufficient to deal with everyday requirements and that their skills would enable them to use written material to find out more. But 16%, or 2.9 million adults, did not have sufficient reading skills to deal with the demands of everyday life.

Numeracy skills were also tested with common documents and forms—a swimming pool schedule, a bank deposit slip and a catalogue order form. Level 1 indicated very limited abilities; at most, numbers could be located and recognized in isolation or a short text. Level 2s could perform simple numerical operations such as addition and subtraction; level 3s could perform simple sequences of numerical operations and meet everyday demands. Again, 62% of adult Canadians had numeracy skills sufficient to handle everyday tasks; 14% were at level 1 and 24% functioned at level 2.

	Reading Skills				Numeracy Skills			
	Pop. (000s)	Level 1[1] (lowest)	Level 2	Level 3	Level 4 (highest)	Pop.[2] (000s)	Level 1 (lowest)	Level 2	Level 3 (highest)
Canada	**18 024**	**7%**	**9%**	**22%**	**62%**	**17 206**	**14%**	**24%**	**62%**
Atlantic Provinces	1 546	6	13	30	52	1 497	25	26	52
Newfoundland	384	7	17	36	39	369	29	26	45
Prince Edward Island	85	n.a.	n.a.	n.a.	n.a.	79	n.a.	n.a.	n.a.
Nova Scotia	594	5[3]	10	28	57	581	21	23	56
New Brunswick	483	6	12	26	56	468	22	24	54
Quebec	4 721	6	13	25	57	4 577	19	27	54
Ontario	6 689	9	8	21	62	6 228	11	25	64
Prairies	2 984	4	7	19	70	2 888	10	22	68
Manitoba	703	5[3]	73	23	65	678	13[3]	26	61
Saskatchewan	632	3[3]	53	19	72	620	9[3]	26	66
Alberta	1 649	4	73	17	71	1 589	8[3]	20	72
British Columbia	2 084	5	7	19	69	2 015	9	22	69

Sources: *Statistics Canada; National Literacy Secretariat*

(1) Includes persons who reported having no skills in either English or French. (2) Excludes persons who reported having no reading skills in either English or French and those whose reading skills were too limited to undertake the main test items. (3) Figure less reliable due to high sampling variability. (n.a.) not available.

Reading, Writing and Working

*T*he 1989 study found that in general, those working in the service sector—which includes information-oriented businesses—had higher literacy skills than their counterparts in other industries. Over 70% of those working in insurance, real estate, finance, community services or public administration had level 4 skills; those in manufacturing, personal services and construction had a lower percentage of level 4s and the figure dropped to 50% for those workers in agriculture and primary industries. The percentage of those with level 4 skills jumped to 85% for those in occupational groups such as management and administration; 86% in engineering, social sciences and natural sciences and 92% in teaching and related jobs in education.

University Degrees[1] Awarded in Canada: Male and Female

(percentage distribution)

	1970 Males	1970 Females	1980 Males	1980 Females	1990 Males	1990 Females	1991 Males	1991 Females
Total Degrees	61.7	38.3	50.4	49.6	44.3	55.7	43.5	56.5
Education	46.6	53.4	31.9	68.8	29.2	70.8	30.0	70.0
Fine Arts	40.6	59.4	35.3	64.7	34.3	65.7	32.3	67.7
Humanities	n.a.	n.a.	39.9	60.1	37.2	62.8	36.4	63.6
English	n.a.	n.a.	29.0	71.0	27.7	72.3	28.0	72.0
History	n.a.	n.a.	54.3	45.7	54.6	45.4	51.7	48.3
Journalism	43.2	56.8	33.5	66.5	37.1	62.9	37.9	62.1
Theology	74.3	25.7	64.7	35.3	55.1	44.9	54.9	45.1
Social Sciences	n.a.	n.a.	57.2	42.8	45.6	54.4	44.6	55.4
Commerce	93.5	6.5	72.1	27.9	54.1	45.9	53.3	46.7
Economics	n.a.	n.a.	75.4	24.6	67.5	32.5	65.9	34.1
Geography	n.a.	n.a.	63.2	36.8	62.3	37.7	60.9	39.1
Law	92.9	7.1	65.0	35.0	52.8	47.2	50.0	50.0
Political Science	n.a.	n.a.	65.0	35.0	56.3	43.7	55.7	44.3
Psychology	n.a.	n.a.	31.0	69.0	24.2	75.8	22.0	78.0
Social Work	55.9	44.1	25.5	74.5	17.3	82.7	17.7	82.3
Sociology	n.a.	n.a.	32.7	67.3	23.7	76.3	23.9	76.1
Biological Sciences	n.a.	n.a.	49.5	50.5	43.0	57.0	42.7	57.3
Agriculture	93.6	6.4	65.7	34.3	58.7	41.3	54.1	45.9
Biology	n.a.	n.a.	55.0	45.0	48.2	51.8	47.8	52.2
Veterinary Medicine	94.0	6.0	60.5	39.5	36.9	63.1	40.7	59.3
Applied Sciences	n.a.	n.a.	92.4	7.6	86.7	13.3	85.2	14.8
Architecture	92.6	7.4	59.6	20.4	69.2	30.8	65.0	35.0
Engineering	98.9	1.1	94.3	5.7	88.3	11.7	87.1	12.9
Chemical	n.a.	n.a.	86.9	13.1	73.4	26.6	69.3	30.7
Civil	n.a.	n.a.	93.4	6.6	87.6	12.4	82.6	17.4
Electrical	n.a.	n.a.	96.5	3.5	91.8	8.2	91.7	8.3
Mechanical	n.a.	n.a.	97.5	2.5	92.8	7.2	91.0	9.0
Forestry	97.8	2.2	87.4	12.6	83.5	16.5	86.2	13.8
Health Sciences	n.a.	n.a.	40.7	59.3	29.8	70.2	29.0	71.0
Dentistry	94.9	5.1	83.3	16.7	64.2	35.8	60.3	39.7
Medicine	89.7	10.3	66.4	33.6	54.1	45.9	54.3	45.7
Nursing	2.7	97.3	4.9	95.1	4.4	95.6	3.9	96.1
Rehabilitation	2.2	97.8	8.8	91.2	15.1	84.9	14.5	85.5
Pure Sciences	n.a.	n.a.	71.6	28.4	71.2	28.8	71.3	28.7
Chemistry	n.a.	n.a.	69.4	30.6	63.3	36.7	62.6	37.4
Computer Sciences	n.a.	n.a.	75.2	24.8	80.2	19.8	80.2	19.8
Geology	n.a.	n.a.	78.5	21.5	74.1	25.9	75.5	24.5
Mathematics	n.a.	n.a.	63.4	36.6	60.3	39.7	60.6	39.4
Physics	n.a.	n.a.	89.0	11.0	84.9	15.1	85.5	14.5

Source: *Statistics Canada*   (1) Bachelor's and first professional degrees. (n.a.) not available.

Educational Attainment–How We Compare

*I*n the developed world, the US led with 23% holding a university degree. Canada came second with 15%, then Japan (13%), and Sweden (12%). In a ranking of populations with any post-secondary education we came 4th with 30%, behind the US (35%), and Australia and New Zealand (tied with 31%). Those that followed were Switzerland (24%), Sweden (23%), Japan and Norway (21%), the Netherlands (19%), Finland (18%), Belgium, Germany and Denmark (17%), United Kingdom (15%), France and Ireland (14%), Spain (9%), Italy and Portugal (6%) and Austria (5%).

Canadian Universities

Acadia University: Wolfville, NS B0P 1X0

Athabasca University: Box 10 000, Athabasca, Alta T0G 2R0

Atlantic School of Theology: 640 Francklyn St, Halifax, NS B3H 3B5

Augustana University College: 4901-46 Ave, Camrose, Alta T4V 2R3

Banff Centre: Box 1020, Banff, Alta T0L 0C0

Bishop's University: Lennoxville, Qué. J1M 1Z7

Brandon University: 270-18th St, Brandon, Man. R7A 6A9

Brock University: 500 Glenridge Ave, St. Catharines, Ont. L2S 3A1

Carleton University: Ottawa, Ont. K1S 5B6

Collège Universitaire de Sainte-Boniface: 200, ave de la Cathédrale, Sainte-Boniface, Man. R2H 0H7

Concordia University: Campus Loyola, 7141 Sherbrooke St W, Montréal, Qué. H4B 1R6

Dalhousie University: Halifax, NS B3H 4H6

Lakehead University: Oliver Rd, Thunder Bay, Ont. P7B 5E1

Laurentian University: Sudbury, Ont. P3E 2C6

McGill University: 845 Sherbrooke St W, Montréal, Qué. H3A 2T5

McMaster University: Hamilton, Ont. L8S 4L8

Memorial University of Newfoundland: St John's, Nfld A1C 5C7

Mount Allison University: Sackville, NB E0A 3C0

Mount Saint Vincent University: 166 Bedford Hwy, Halifax, NS B3M 2J6

Nipissing University: 100 College Dr., North Bay, Ont. P1B 8L7

Queen's University: Kingston, Ont. K7L 3N6

Royal Military College of Canada: Kingston, Ont. K7K 5L0

Royal Roads Military College: Victoria, BC V0S 1B0

Ryerson Polytechnic University: 350 Victoria St, Toronto, Ont. M5B 2K3

Simon Fraser University: Burnaby, BC V5A 1S6

St Francis Xavier University: Antigonish, NS B2G 1C0

St Mary's University: 923 Robie Street, Halifax, NS B3H 3C3

St Thomas University: Fredericton, NB E3B 5G3

Technical University of Nova Scotia: Box 1000, Halifax, NS B3J 2X4

The King's College: 10766-97 St, Edmonton, Alta T5H 2M1

Trent University: Peterborough, Ont. K9J 7B8

Trinity Western University: 7600 Glover Rd, Langley, BC V3A 6H4

Université de Moncton: Moncton, NB E1A 3E9

Université de Montréal: Registrar's office, CP 6128, Succ. A., Montréal, Qué. H3C 3J7

Université de Sherbrooke: 2500 University Blvd, Sherbrooke, Qué. J1K 2R1

Université du Quebec: 2875, boul. Laurier, Sainte-Foy, Qué. G1V 2M3

Université Laval: Registrar's office, Pavillon Jean-Charles Bonenfant (2440), Sainte-Foy, Qué. G1K 7P4

Université Sainte-Anne: Church Point, Digby County, NS B0W 1M0

University College of Cape Breton: Box 5300, Sydney, NS B1P 6L2

University of Alberta: Edmonton, Alta T6G 2E8

University of British Columbia: 204-2075 Westbrook Mall, Vancouver, BC V6T 1W5

University of Calgary: 2500 University Dr. NW, Calgary, Alta T2N 1N4

University of Guelph: Gordon St, Guelph, Ont. N1G 2W1

University of King's College: Halifax, NS B3H 2A1

University of Lethbridge: 4401 University Dr., Lethbridge, Alta T1K 3M4

University of Manitoba: Winnipeg, Man. R3T 2N2

University of New Brunswick: Fredericton, NB E3B 5A3

University of Northern British Columbia: Bag 1950, Stn A, Prince George, BC V2L 5P2

University of Ottawa: 550 Cumberland St, Ottawa, Ont. K1N 6N5

University of Prince Edward Island: 550 University Ave, Charlottetown, PEI C1A 4P3

University of Regina: Regina, Sask. S4S 0A2

University of Saskatchewan: Saskatoon, Sask. S7N 0W0

University of Toronto: Toronto, Ont. M5S 1A1

University of Victoria: Box 3025, Victoria, BC V8W 3P2

University of Waterloo: 200 University Ave W, Waterloo, Ont. N2L 3G1

University of Western Ontario: London, Ont., N6A 3K7

University of Windsor: 401 Sunset Ave, Windsor, Ont. N9B 3P4

University of Winnipeg: 515 Portage Ave, Winnipeg, Man. R3B 2E9

Wilfrid Laurier University: Waterloo, Ont. N2L 3C5

York University: 4700 Keele Street, Downsview, Ont. M3J 1P3

Canadian Colleges

■ Atlantic Provinces

Avalon Community College: Box 800, Carbonear, Nfld A0A 1T0

Cabot Institute of Applied Arts & Technology: Box 1693, St John's, Nfld A1C 5P7

Central Newfoundland Community College: Box 745, Grand Falls, Nfld A2A 2M4

Cobatec Community College: 60 Lorne St, Truro, NS B2N 3K3

Eastern Community College: Box 400, Bruin, Nfld A0E 1E0

Fisher Institute of Applied Arts & Technology: Box 822, Corner Brook, Nfld A2H 6H6

Holland College: 140 Weymouth St, Charlottetown, PEI C1A 4Z1

Institute of Fisheries and Marine Technology: Bx 4920, St John's, Nfld A1C 5R3

Labrador Community College: Box 3013, Stn B, Happy Valley-Goose Bay, Nfld A0P 1E0

New Brunswick Community College:
Bathust: Box 1, Bathurst, NB E2A 3Z2
Campbellton: Box 309, Campbellton, NB E3N 3G3
Dieppe: 4519, Dieppe, NB E1A 6G1
Edmunston: Box 70, Edmunston, NB E3V 3K7
Grand-Sault: Box 1270, Grand Falls, NB E0J 1M0
Miramichi: Box 1053, Chatham, NB E1N 3W4
Moncton: Box 2100, Stn A, Moncton, NB E1C 8H9
St Andrews: Box 427, St Andrews, NB E0G 2X0
Saint John: Box 2270, Saint John, NB E2L 3V1

Woodstock: Box 1175, Woodstock, NB E0J 2B0

Nova Scotia Agricultural College: Box 550, Truro, NS B2N 5E2

Nova Scotia College of Art & Design: 5163 Duke St, Halifax, NS B3J 3J6

Nova Scotia Community College:
Annapolis Campus: Box 940, 295 Commercial St, Middleton, NS B0S 1P0
Burridge Campus: 372 Pleasant St, Yarmouth, NS B5A 2L2
Colchester Campus: 60 Lorne St, Truro, NS B2N 3K3
College of Geographic Sciences Campus: RR #1, Lawrencetown, Ann. Co., NS B0S 1M0
Cumberland Campus: 1 Main St, Box 550, Springhill, NS B0M 1X0
Dartmouth Adult Vocational Training Campus: 10 Acadia St, Dartmouth, NS B2Y 4H3
Halifax Campus: 1825 Bell Rd, Halifax, NS B3H 2Z4
Hants Campus: Wentworth Rd, Box 2079, Windsor, NS B0N 2T0
Institute of Technology Campus: 5685 Leeds St, Box 2210, Halifax, NS B3J 3C4
I.W. Akerley Campus: 21 Woodlawn Rd, Dartmouth, NS B2W 2R7
Kingstec Campus: Belcher St, Box 487, Kentville, NS B4N 3X3
Lunenburg Campus: 75 High St, Bridgewater, NS B4V 1V8
Nautical Institute Campus: Box 1225, Reeves St, Port Hawkesbury, NS B0E 2V0
Pictou Campus: 39 Acadia St, Box 820, Stellarton, NS B0K 1S0
Shelburne Campus: Sandy Point Rd, Box 760, Shelburne, NS B0T 1W0 ▶

▶ **Strait Campus:** Box 2000, Reeves St, Port Hawkesbury, NS B0E 2V0

Sydney Campus: 365 Prince St, Sydney, NS B1P 5L2

Nova Scotia Teachers College: Box 810, Truro, NS B2N 5G5

Sir Wilfred Grenfell College: University Dr., Corner Brook, Nfld A2H 6P9

Western Community College: Box 5400, Stephenville, Nfld A2N 2Z6

■ Quebec

Cégep Ahuntsic: 9155 Rue Saint-Hubert, Montréal, Qué. H2M 1Y8

Cégep André-Laurendeau: 1111 Rue Lapierre, LaSalle, Qué. H8N 2J4

Cégep Beauce-Appalaches: 1055-116 Rue E, Saint-Goerges, Qué. G5Y 3G1

Cégep d'Alma: 675 boul. Auger O, Alma, Qué. G8B 2B7

Cégep de Baie-Comeau: 537 boul. Blanche, Baie-Comeau, Qué. G5C 2B2

Cégep de Bois-de-Boulogne: 10555, ave de Bois-de-Boulogne, Montréal, Qué. H4N 1L4

Cégep de Chicoutimi: 534 Rue Jacques-Cartier E, Chicoutimi, Qué. G7H 1Z6

Cégep de Drummondville: 960 Rue Saint-Georges, Drummondville, Qué. J2C 6A2

Cégep de Granby-Haute-Yamaska: 50 Rue Saint-Joseph, CP 7000, Granby, Qué. J2G 9H7

Cégep de Jonquière: 2505 Rue Saint-Hubert, Jonquière, Qué. G7X 7W2

Cégep de l'Abitibi-Téminsacmingue: CP 1500, Rouyn-Noranda, Qué. J9X 5E5

Cégep de l'Outaouais: 333 boul. Cité des Jeunes, CP 5220, Succ.A, Hull, Qué. J8Y 6M5

Cégep de La Pocatière: 140-4th Ave, La Pocatière, Qué. G0R 1Z0

Cégep de la Gaspésie et des Îles: 96 Rue Jacques-Cartier, CP 590, Gaspé, Qué. G0C 1R0

Cégep de la Région de l'Amiante: 671 boul. Smith S, Thetford-Mines, Qué. G6G 1N1

Cégep de Lévis-Lauzon: 205 Rue Mgr-Ignace-Bourget, Lévis, Qué. G6V 6Z9

Cégep de Limoilou: 1300-8th Ave, CP 1400, Quebec, Qué. G1K 7H3

Cégep de Maisonneuve: 3800 Rue Sherbrooke E, Montréal, Qué. H1X 2A2

Cégep de Matane: 616 ave Saint-Rédempteur, Matane, Qué. G4W 1L1

Cégep de Rimouski: 60 Rue de l'Évêché O, Rimouski, Qué. G5L 4H6

Cégep de Rosemont: 6400-16th Ave, Montréal, Qué. H1X 2S9

Cégep de Saint-Félicien: 1105 boul. Hamel, CP 7300, Saint-Félicien, Qué. G8K 2R8

Cégep de Saint-Hyacinthe: 3000 Rue Boullé, Sainte-Hyacinthe, Qué. J2S 1H9

Cégep de Saint-Jérôme: 455 Rue Fournier, Saint-Jérôme, Qué. J7Z 4V2

Cégep de Saint-Laurent: 625 Ave Sainte-Croix, Saint-Laurent, Qué. H4L 3X7

Cégep de Sainte-Foy: 2410 chemin Sainte-Foy, Sainte-Foy, Qué. G1V 1T3

Cégep de Sept-Îles: 175 Rue De La Vérendrye, Sept-Îles, Qué. G4R 5B7

Cégep de Shawinigan: 2263 boul. du Collège, CP 610, Shawinigan, Qué. G9N 6V8

Cégep de Sherbrooke: 475 Rue Parc, Sherbrooke, Qué. J1H 5M7

Cégep de Sorel-Tracy: 3000 boul. de la Mairie, Tracy, Qué. J3R 5B9

Cégep de Trois-Rivières: 3500 Rue de Courval, CP 97 et 397, Trois Rivières, Qué. G9A 5E6

Cégep de Valleyfield: 169 Rue Champlain, Valleyfield, Qué. J6T 1X6

Cégep de Victoriaville: 475 Rue Notre-Dame E, Victoriaville, Qué. G6P 4B3

Cégep du Vieux Montréal: 255 Rue Ontario E, CP 144, Succ. C, Montréal, Qué. H2X 3M8

Cégep Édouard-Montpetit: 945 chemin de Cahmbly, Longueuil, Qué. J4H 3M6

Cégep François-Xavier-Garneau: 1660 boul. de L'Entente, Quebec, Qué. G1S 4S3

Cégep Joliette–De Lanaudière: 20 Rue Saint-Charles S, Joliette, Qué. J6E 4T1

Cégep Lionel-Groulx: 100 Rue Duquet, Sainte-Thérèse, Qué. J7E 3G6

Cégep Marie-Victorin: 7000 Rue Marie-Victorin, Montréal, Qué. H1G 2J6

Cégep Montmorency: 475 boul. de l'Avenir, Laval, Qué. H7N 5H9

Cégep Saint-Jean-suro-Richelieu: 30 boul. du Séminaire, CP 1018, Saint-Jean-sur-Richelieu, Qué. J3B 7B1

Cégepde Rivière-du-Loup: 80 Rue Frontenac, Rivière-du-Loup, Qué. G5R 1R1 ▶

▶ **Champlain Regional College:** 554 Rue Ontario, CP 5000, Sherbrooke, Qué. J1J 3R6

Dawson College: 3040, Rue Sherbrooke O, Westmount, Qué. H3Z 1A4

Heritage College: 205 Rue Laurier, CP 1757, Hull, Qué. J8X 3Y8

John Abbott College: 21275, chemin du Bord-du-Lac, CP 2000, Sainte-Anne-de-Bellevue, Qué. H9X 3L9

Vanier College: 821 Ave Sainte-Croix, Saint-Laurent, Qué. H4L 3X9

■ Ontario

Algonquin College of Applied Arts & Technology: 1385 Woodroffe Ave, Nepean, Ont. K2G 1V8

Cambrian College of Applied Arts & Technology: 1400 Barrydowne Road, Sudbury, Ont. P3A 3V8

Canadore College of Applied Arts & Technology: 100 College Drive, Box 5001, North Bay, Ont. P1B 8K9

Centennial College of Applied Arts & Technology: Box 631, Stn A, Scarborough, Ont. M1K 5E9

La Cité Collégiale: 2465, St Laurent Blvd, Ottawa, Ont. K1G 5H8

Conestoga College of Applied Arts & Technology: 299 Doon Valley Dr., Kitchener, Ont. N2G 4M4

Confederation College of Applied Arts & Technology: Box 398, Stn F, Thunder Bay, Ont. P7C 4W1

Durham College of Applied Arts & Technology: Box 385, 2000 Simcoe St N, Oshawa, Ont. L1H 7L7

Fanshawe College of Applied Arts & Technology: 1460 Oxford St E, London, Ont. N5W 5H1

George Brown College of Applied Arts & Technology: Box 1015, Stn B, Toronto, Ont. M5T 2T9

Georgian College of Applied Arts & Technology: 1 Georgian Dr., Barrie, Ont. L4M 3X9

Humber College of Applied Arts & Technology: Box 1900, 205 Humber College Blvd, Etobicoke, Ont. M9W 5L7

Lambton College of Applied Arts & Technology: Box 969, 1457 London Rd, Sarnia, Ont. N7T 7K4

Loyalist College of Applied Arts & Technology: Box 4200, Wallbridge Loyalist Rd, Belleville, Ont. K8N 5B9

Mohawk College of Applied Arts & Technology: Box 2034, Fennell Ave & West 5th, Hamilton, Ont. L8N 3T2

Niagara College of Applied Arts & Technology: Box 1005, Woodlawn Rd, Welland, Ont. L3B 5S2

Northern College of Applied Arts & Technology: Box 2002, South Porcupine, Ont. P0N 1H0

Ontario College of Art: 100 McCaul St, Toronto, Ont. M5T 1W1

St Clair College of Applied Arts & Technology: 2000 Talbot Rd W, Windsor, Ont. N9A 6S4

St Lawrence College of Applied Arts & Technology: King and Portsmouth, Kingston, Ont. K7L 5A6

Sault College of Applied Arts & Technology: Box 60, 443 Northern Ave, Sault Ste Marie, Ont. P6A 5L3

Seneca College of Applied Arts & Technology: 1750 Finch Ave E, North York, Ont. M2J 2X5

Sheridan College of Applied Arts & Technology: 1430 Trafalgar Rd, Oakville, Ont. L6H 2L1

Sir Sanford Fleming College of Applied Arts & Technology: Brealey Dr., Peterborough, Ont. K9H 7B1

■ Prairies

Alberta College of Art: 1407-14th Ave NW, Calgary, Alta T2N 4R3

Assiniboine Community College: 1430 Victoria Ave E, Brandon, Man. R7A 2A9

Carlton Trail Regional College: Box 720, Humboldt, Sask. S0K 2A0

Cumberland Regional College: Box 2225, Nipawin, Sask. S0E 1E0

Cypress Hills Regional College: 129-2nd Ave NE, Swift Current, Sask. S9H 2C6

Fairview College: Box 3000, Fairview, Alta T0L 1L0

Grande Prairie Regional College: 10726-106 Ave, Grande Prairie, Alta T8V 4C4

Grant Macewan Community College: Box 1796, Edmonton, Alta T5J 2P2

Keewatin Community College: 436-7th St E, The Pas, Man. R9A 1P7

Keyano College: 8115 Franklin Ave, Fort McMurray, Alta T9H 2H7

Lakeland College: Vermilion campus, Bag 5100, Vermilion, Alta T0B 4M0 ▶

▶ **Lakeland College:** Bag 6600, Lloydminster, Sask. S9V 1Z3

Lethbridge Community College: 3000 College Dr. S, Lethbridge, Alta T1K 1L6

Medicine Hat College: 299 College Dr. SE, Medicine Hat, Alta T1A 3Y6

Mount Royal College: 4825 Richard Rd SW, Calgary, Alta T3E 6K6

North West Regional College: 1381-101st St, North Battleford, Sask. S9A 0Z9

Northern Alberta Institute of Technology: 11762-106 St, Edmonton, Alta T5G 2R1

Northlands College: Box 1000, Air Ronge, Sask. S0J 3G0

Olds College: 4500-50 St, Olds, Alta T4H 1R6

Parkland Regional College: Box 790, Melville, Sask. S0A 2P0

Prairie West Regional College: Box 700, Biggar, Sask. S0K 0M0

Red Deer College: Box 5005, Red Deer, Alta T4N 5H5

Red River Community College: 2055 Notre Dame Ave, Winnipeg, Man. R3H 0J9

Saskatchewan Indian Community College: 401 Packham Place, Asimakaniseekan Askiy Reserve, Sask. S7N 2T7

Saskatchewan Institute of Applied Science & Technology:

> **Kelsey Campus:** Box 1520, Saskatoon, Sask. S7K 3R5

> **Palliser Campus:** Box 1420, Moose Jaw, Sask. S6H 4R4

> **Wascana Campus:** Box 556, Regina, Sask. S4P 3A3

> **Woodland Campus:** Box 3003, Prince Albert, Sask. S6V 6G1

Southeast Regional College: 22-3rd St NE, Weyburn, Sask. S4H 0V9

Southern Alberta Institute of Technology: 1301-16 Ave NW, Calgary, Alta T2M 0L4

St Joseph's College: University of Alberta, Edmonton, Alta T6G 2E8

St Stephen's College: 8810-112 St, University of Alberta Campus, Edmonton, Alta T6G 2J6

■ British Columbia and Territories

Arctic College: Box 1769, Yellowknife, NWT Y1A 2C6

BC Institute of Technology: 3700 Willingdon Ave, Burnaby, BC V5G 3H2

Camosun College: 3100 Foul Bay Rd, Victoria, BC V8P 5J2

Capilano College: 2055 Purcell Way, North Vancouver, BC V7J 3H5

College of New Caledonia: 330-22nd Ave, Prince George, BC V2N 1P8

Douglas College: Box 2503, New Westminster, BC V3L 5B2

East Kootenay Community College: 2700 College Way, Box 8500, Canbrook, BC V1C 5L7

Emily Carr College of Art & Design: 1399 Johnston St, Granville Island, Vancouver, BC V6H 3R9

Justice Institute of BC: 4180 West 4th Ave, Vancouver, BC V6R 4J5

Kwantlen College: Box 9030, Surrey, BC V3T 5H8

Malaspina College: 900-5th St, Nanaimo, BC V9R 5S5

North Island College: 2300 Ryan Rd, Courtenay, BC V9N 8N6

Northern Lights College: 11401-8th St, Dawson Creek, BC V1G 4G2

Northwest Community College: 5331 McConnell Ave, Terrace, BC V8G 4C2

Okanagan University College: 1000 K.L.O. Rd, Kelowna, BC V1Y 4X8

Open Learning Agency: 4355 Mathissi Place, Burnaby, BC V5G 4S8

Pacific Marine Training Institute: 265 West Esplanade, North Vancouver, BC V7M 1A5

Selkirk College: 301 Frank Beinder Way, Box 1200, Castlegar, BC V1N 3J1

University College of the Cariboo: Box 3010, Kamloops, BC V2C 5N3

University College of the Fraser Valley: 33844 King Rd, RR #2, Abbotsford, BC V2S 4N2

Vancouver Community College: 1155 East Broadway, Box 24700, Vancouver, BC V5N 5V1

Yukon College: Box 2799, Whitehorse, YT Y1A 5K4

FAMILIES AND INCOME

Marriages and Divorces in Canada

	Marriages				Divorces		
			Average Age at Marriage				**Average Length of Marriage[2]**
	Total	Rate[1]	Brides[3]	Grooms[3]	Total	Rate[1]	
1925	66 378	6.9	25.3	29.8	550	0.06	n.a.
1930	73 341	7.0	25.0	29.2	875	0.09	n.a.
1935	78 908	7.1	25.0	29.0	1 431	0.13	n.a.
1940	125 797	10.8	25.2	28.9	2 416	0.21	n.a.
1945	111 376	9.0	25.5	29.0	5 101	0.42	n.a.
1950	125 083	9.1	25.3	28.5	5 386	0.39	n.a.
1955	128 029	8.2	25.1	28.0	6 053	0.39	n.a.
1960	130 338	7.3	24.7	27.7	6 980	0.39	n.a.
1965	145 519	7.4	24.5	27.2	8 974	0.46	n.a.
1970	188 428	8.8	24.9	27.3	29 775	1.40	n.a.
1975	197 585	8.7	22.0	24.4	50 611	2.22	n.a.
1980	191 069	8.0	22.8	25.0	62 019	2.59	12.0
1981	190 082	7.8	23.0	25.2	67 671	2.78	12.1
1982	188 360	7.6	23.2	25.4	70 436	2.86	12.0
1983	184 675	7.4	23.5	25.7	68 567	2.76	12.0
1984	185 597	7.4	23.8	26.0	65 172	2.59	12.4
1985	184 096	7.3	24.1	26.2	61 980	2.44	12.5
1986	175 518	6.9	24.3	26.5	78 160	3.09	12.5
1987	182 151	7.1	24.7	26.9	90 985	3.55	12.4
1988	187 728	7.2	25.0	27.1	83 507	3.11	12.9
1989	190 640	7.3	25.2	27.3	80 998	2.96	13.0
1990	187 737	7.1	25.5	27.4	78 463	2.82	13.0
1991	172 251	6.4	25.7	27.7	77 020	2.74	12.9
1992	164 573	5.8	n.a.	n.a.	79 034	1.11	n.a.

Source: *Statistics Canada*

(1) Rate per 1 000 population. (2) Refers to the average length (in years) of those marriages ending in divorce during the year stated. (n.a.) not available. (3) Data after 1975 represents average age of bride and groom at first marriage.

Marriages and Divorces by Province

	Marriages				Divorces	
	1982		**1992**		**1991**	
	Total	Rate[1]	Total	Rate[1]	Total	Rate[1]
Canada	188 360	7.5	164 573	5.8	77 020	2.74
Newfoundland	3 764	6.5	3 254	5.6	912	1.57
Prince Edward Island	855	6.9	850	6.5	269	2.06
Nova Scotia	6 486	7.5	5 623	6.1	2 280	2.48
New Brunswick	4 923	6.9	4 313	5.8	1 652	2.21
Quebec	38 354	5.8	25 841	3.6	20 274	2.86
Ontario	71 595	8.0	70 079	6.6	27 694	2.65
Manitoba	8 264	7.9	6 899	6.2	2 790	2.51
Saskatchewan	7 491	7.6	5 664	5.6	2 240	2.22
Alberta	22 312	9.4	17 871	6.8	8 388	3.23
British Columbia	23 831	8.2	23 749	6.9	10 368	3.07
Yukon Territory	225	9.1	221	7.3	67	2.31
Northwest Territories	260	5.2	209	3.4	86	1.41

Source: *Statistics Canada*

(1) Rate per 1 000 population.

Marital Status of the Canadian Population, 1993

Age Group	Total Population Male (000s)	Female (000s)	Single Male (%)	Female (%)	Married Male (%)	Female (%)	Widowed Male (%)	Female (%)	Divorced Male (%)	Female (%)
15 and over	**11 200.2**	**11 610.3**	**22.78**	**19.6**	**67.9**	**55.5**	**5.6**	**19.8**	**3.9**	**4.8**
15-19 years	990.8	944.9	99.5	98.2	0.4	1.7	...	...	...	...
20-24 years	1 046.1	1 014.6	87.0	71.4	12.7	27.9	...	...	0.3	0.7
25-29 years	1 188.6	1 158.0	50.1	32.0	47.9	64.9	...	...	2.1	3.0
30-34 years	1 329.6	1 300.9	27.7	17.6	68.2	77.1	...	0.1	4.1	5.2
35-39 years	1 236.0	1 231.8	16.8	11.6	77.3	80.7	0.1	0.3	5.8	7.4
40-44 years	1 095.1	1 091.9	11.3	8.6	81.3	81.2	0.1	0.7	7.3	9.5
45-49 years	950.7	937.7	8.2	6.7	84.0	81.4	0.2	1.5	7.6	10.3
50-54 years	729.5	725.4	6.8	5.8	85.6	81.4	0.4	3.1	7.2	9.7
55-59 years	617.0	622.3	6.4	5.4	86.3	80.1	0.9	6.1	6.4	8.4
60-64 years	591.5	617.1	7.5	5.6	86.1	75.9	2.1	6.2	6.2	7.0
65-69 years	510.7	588.7	6.8	5.9	85.5	68.7	3.5	20.1	4.3	5.3
70-74 years	400.2	514.7	6.4	6.5	84.7	58.8	5.6	30.9	3.3	3.9
75-79 years	261.9	378.7	6.3	7.8	82.4	45.7	8.7	44.0	2.6	2.6
80-84 years	156.3	262.2	6.7	9.1	77.2	32.2	14.1	57.1	1.9	1.7
85-89 years	67.8	143.7	7.4	10.0	69.2	19.8	22.0	69.3	1.5	1.0
90 years and over	28.4	77.7	9.5	11.1	57.4	10.8	32.0	77.3	1.4	0.6

Source: *Statistics Canada*   (...) = too small to be included.

Lone-Parent Families by Province, 1991

Male Parent

Province	Total Lone-Parent Families	Total	Number of Children at Home 1	2 +	3 +
Canada	**954 710**	168 240	104 705	47 000	16 535
Newfoundland	**17 920**	3 390	1 970	950	470
Prince Edward Island	**4 375**	740	445	195	100
Nova Scotia	**33 120**	5 395	3 395	1 465	535
New Brunswick	**26 545**	4 580	2 855	1 285	440
Quebec	**268 880**	48 760	31 195	13 565	4 005
Ontario	**342 805**	59 000	36 215	16 800	5 985
Manitoba	**37 365**	6 485	3 930	1 795	760
Saskatchewan	**30 230**	5 335	3 230	1 420	685
Alberta	**83 005**	14 675	8 880	4 080	1 710
British Columbia	**107 375**	19 135	12 190	5 235	1 710
Yukon Territory	**1 040**	230	145	65	20
Northwest Territories	**2 045**	520	255	140	120

Female Parent

Province	Total	Number of Children at Home 1	2 +	3 +
Canada	786 470	455 170	239 745	91 560
Newfoundland	14 530	7 875	4 460	2 195
Prince Edward Island	3 635	2 115	1 015	500
Nova Scotia	27 725	16 105	8 250	3 365
New Brunswick	21 965	12 775	6 685	2 500
Quebec	220 120	135 840	64 395	19 885
Ontario	283 805	161 465	87 915	34 420
Manitoba	30 885	17 370	9 195	4 320
Saskatchewan	24 895	13 340	7 310	4 240
Alberta	68 335	36 765	21 910	9 660
British Columbia	88 245	50 295	27 935	10 010
Yukon Territory	810	470	250	90
Northwest Territories	1 530	745	415	375

Source: *1991 Census of Canada*

Composition of Canadian Families

(thousands)

	1961 No. of Families	1961 %	1971 No. of Families	1971 %	1981 No. of Families	1981 %	1991 No. of Families	1991 %
Total families[1]	4 147	100.0	5 071	100.0	6 325	100.0	7 356	100.0
Without children at home	1 217	29.3	1 545	30.5	2 013	31.8	2 580	35.1
With children at home	2 930	70.7	3 526	69.5	4 312	68.2	4 776	64.9
one child	839	20.2	1 045	20.6	1 580	25.0	1 945	26.4
two children	855	20.6	1 077	21.2	1 648	26.1	1 927	26.2
three children	557	13.4	677	13.4	730	11.5	691	9.4
four children	312	7.5	367	7.2	243	3.8	165	2.2
five children	162	3.9	186	3.7	70	1.1	33	0.4
six children[2]	206	5.0	84	1.7	25	0.4	10	0.1
seven children[2]	206	5.0	43	0.8	10	0.2	3	...
eight or more[2]	206	5.0	47	0.9	7	0.1	2	...
Lone parent families	385	9.3	471	9.3	653	10.3	955	13.0
lone female parent	305	7.4	371	7.3	541	8.6	786	10.7
lone male parent	80	1.9	100	2.0	112	1.8	168	2.3

Source: *Census of Canada*

(1) Based on the census family definition: a husband and wife (without children or with children who never married) or a parent with one or more children who never married, living together in the same home. (2) Includes six or more children.

Size of Families in Canada

(thousands of families)

	1951 No. of Families	1951 Avg. Size	1961 No. of Families	1961 Avg. Size	1971 No. of Families	1971 Avg. Size	1981 No. of Families	1981 Avg. Size	1991 No. of Families	1991 Avg. Size
Canada	3 287	3.7	4 147	3.9	5 071	3.7	6 325	3.3	7 356	3.1
Newfoundland	75	4.4	89	4.7	108	4.4	135	3.8	151	3.3
Prince Edward Island	21	4.0	22	4.2	24	4.0	30	3.5	34	3.2
Nova Scotia	145	3.9	162	4.0	181	3.8	216	3.3	245	3.1
New Brunswick	112	4.1	125	4.3	140	4.0	177	3.4	198	3.1
Quebec	856	4.2	1 104	4.2	1 357	3.9	1 672	3.3	1 883	3.0
Ontario	1 163	3.4	1 511	3.6	1 882	3.6	2 279	3.2	2 727	3.1
Manitoba	191	3.6	216	3.7	236	3.6	262	3.2	286	3.1
Saskatchewan	196	3.7	212	3.8	216	3.7	246	3.3	258	3.2
Alberta	223	3.7	306	3.8	382	3.7	566	3.3	668	3.1
British Columbia	300	3.3	394	3.6	534	3.5	728	3.1	888	3.0
Yukon	5[1]	3.9[1]	7[1]	4.3[1]	11[1]	4.3[1]	6	3.3	7	3.1
Northwest Territories	5[1]	3.9[1]	7[1]	4.3[1]	11[1]	4.3[1]	9	4.0	13	3.7

Source: *Census of Canada* (1) Includes both the Yukon and Northwest Territories.

The New "Traditional" Family

*I*n the old "traditional" family, there was only one income—the husband's. In 1951, just 11% of married women worked for wages, and although dual-earner families became more common, the husband was still the sole earner in 58% of 1967's husband-wife families.

By the mid-70s, 42% of married women were at work and by 1991, that number had climbed to 61%. The norm for 1951 is now the minority: 19% of familes rely on the husband's income; 61% of families have both partners working outside the home.

Average Family Income

The average Canadian family earned $53,131 in 1991, a real (after inflation) decrease of 2.6 percent from 1990. This continues a recent trend that is a departure from the previous decade—between 1984 and 1989, the standard of living of the average Canadian family improved, as real income rose 11 percent. This was partly due to a trend towards families with two or more wage earners. In 1989, less than a third of Canadian households relied on a single income.

Families in Ontario still tend to have the highest family income and those in the Maritimes the lowest. Families which include both a husband and wife tend to have higher than average incomes ($59 014) while those with single female parents earn, on average, far less ($22 186).

In the table below, family is defined as a husband and wife (with or without unmarried children), or a parent with one or more unmarried children, living in the same home.

	1971	1975	1980	1985	1991
Canada	$10 113	$16 368	$27 246	$37 981	$53 131
Newfoundland	6 855	12 359	20 374	29 022	41 654
Prince Edward Island	6 669	12 032	22 574	30 473	42 779
Nova Scotia	7 721	13 068	21 625	33 786	45 130
New Brunswick	7 882	13 283	21 021	31 196	44 323
Quebec	9 713	15 273	25 408	35 278	48 634
Ontario	11 154	17 772	28 313	41 291	58 634
Manitoba	9 083	14 869	25 029	35 576	46 621
Saskatchewan	7 762	15 784	26 315	35 453	45 930
Alberta	10 107	16 878	31 868	41 245	55 552
British Columbia	10 989	17 520	30 272	37 533	54 895

Source: *Statistics Canada*

Percentage Income Distribution in Canada by Gender[1]

(percent)

	1971		1981		1991	
	male	female	male	female	male	female
Under $1 000	12.3	15.3	3.3	8.2	—	—
$1 000 - 2 499	24.1	33.4	—	—	4.5	7.9
$2 500 - 4 999	20.4	24.4	11.4	26.3	3.8	7.5
$5 000 - 6 999	16.1	14.0	7.5	14.1	—	—
$7 000 - 9 999	15.9	8.5	8.9	13.2	10.2	18.2
$10 000 - 14 999	8.3	3.4	13.8	17.3	12.0	19.0
$15 000 - 17 499	2.9[2]	0.9[2]	—	—	5.1	7.0
$17 500 - 19 999	—	—	14.6	10.6	4.5	5.4
$20 000 - 22 499	—	—	—	—	4.9	4.9
$22 500 - 24 999	—	—	14.0	5.2	4.4	4.3
$25 000 - 29 999	—	—	10.2	2.7	9.1	8.4
$30 000 - 34 999	—	—	16.4[3]	2.4[3]	8.6	5.7
$35 000 - 39 999	—	—	—	—	7.2	3.7
$40 000 - 44 999	—	—	—	—	6.0	2.5
$45 000 - 49 999	—	—	—	—	4.6	1.8
$50 000+	—	—	—	—	15.1	3.6

Source: *Census of Canada*

[1] Data represents income of unattached individuals, i.e. not family income. (2) 1971 data reported as $15 000+ for final category. (3) 1981 data reported as $30 000+ for final category. (—) = not reported.

Personal Expenditure on Consumer Goods and Services

(per capita expenditure in dollars)

	1966	%	1975	%	1980	%	1990	%	1993	%
Total	$1 896	100.0	$4 299	100.0	$7 171	100.0	$14 988	100.0	$15 237	100.
Rent and fuel	337	17.8	773	18.0	1 452	20.2	3 371	22.5	3 659	24.
Food	331	17.5	641	14.9	970	13.5	2 344	15.6	1 582	10.
Recreation equipment and services	70	3.7	245	5.7	401	5.6	995	6.6	521	3.
Restaurants and hotels	110	5.8	294	6.8	500	7.0	951	6.4	929	6.
Clothing	157	8.3	307	7.2	485	6.8	806	5.4	773	5.
New and used cars	118	6.2	241	5.6	348	4.8	808	5.4	685	4.
Financial, legal and other services	81	4.3	193	4.5	318	4.4	828	5.5	902	5.
Household furnishings and supplies	82	4.3	213	5.0	358	5.0	694	4.6	1 295	8.
Car repairs, parts and services	48	2.5	116	2.7	202	2.8	480	3.2	302	2.
Gas and oil	51	2.7	130	3.0	244	3.4	466	3.1	442	2.
Education	44	2.3	124	2.9	209	2.9	417	2.8	462	3.
Alcohol	68	3.6	155	3.6	230	3.2	397	2.7	396	2.
Tobacco	53	2.8	90	2.1	134	1.9	327	2.2	347	2.
Purchased transportation	31	1.6	78	1.8	150	2.1	309	2.1	287	1.
Reading and entertainment supplies	31	1.6	74	1.7	127	1.8	243	1.6	253	1.
Communications	27	1.4	62	1.4	115	1.6	235	1.5	247	1.
Furniture	34	1.8	92	2.1	131	1.8	213	1.4	185	1.
Household appliances	30	1.6	77	1.8	112	1.6	207	1.4	188	1.
Domestic, childcare and other household services	23	1.2	41	1.0	73	1.0	229	1.5	178	1.
Drugs	22	1.2	47	1.1	77	1.1	221	1.5	249	1.
Toilet articles	18	0.9	36	0.8	62	0.9	137	0.9	154	1.
Personal care	19	1.0	33	0.8	55	0.8	136	0.9	144	0.
Jewellery, watches and repairs	11	0.6	36	0.8	63	0.9	88	0.6	77	0.
Laundry and dry cleaning	13	0.7	15	0.3	22	0.3	44	0.3	44	0.

Source: *Statistics Canada*

Historical Growth in Average Family Income[1]

	1951	1961	1972	1982
Atlantic Provinces	2 515	4 156	9 144	26 850
Quebec	3 523	5 294	10 834	30 509
Ontario	3 903	5 773	12 430	34 457
Prairie Provinces	3 261	4 836	10 471	33 725
British Columbia	3 669	5 491	11 447	35 172

Source: *Statistics Canada*   (1) Not adjusted for inflation.

Home Electronics and Appliances Owned by Canadians

(percentage of households owning item)

Many consumer products that started out as luxury items during the early 1980s have become standard fixtures in the average household as we approach the mid-1990s.

In 1981, only 8 percent of households owned microwave ovens; by 1993, they were a common kitchen appliance, with 79.1 percent of households owning them. Built-in dishwashers are also more popular, with 36.9 percent of dwellings having one; in Alberta and British Columbia the figure climbs to 45 percent. Gas barbecues are also present in the majority of households—as of 1993, they were present in 51.9 percent of homes.

On the entertainment scene, 46.1 percent of Canadian homes now have two or more colour televisions; 77.3 percent have VCRs (12.9 percent have more than one VCR, but there are no corresponding figures for the number of households able to program them.) Compact disk players are also gaining ground in Canadian households: in 1993, 33.2 percent of households had one; five years ago only 7.9 percent could claim one. (CD players are most popular in British Columbia (38.5 percent) and Alberta (36.7 percent).)

Home computers are also increasing in popularity with 23.3 percent of households having one on the premises; again British Columbia (26.9 percent) and Alberta (27.1 percent) led the way in ownership, with Ontario a close third (26.1 percent). Data was collected for the first time on ownership of satellite dishes: in 1993 2.7 percent of households across the country have one, with the highest ownership in Saskatchewan (6.4 percent).

	1960	1965	1970	1975	1980	1985	1990	1993
Air conditioners	n.a.	2.2	4.3	12.4	16.7	18.0	24.4	25.7
Automobiles	66.6	75.0	77.7	78.9	79.8	77.3	77.8	77.5
Camcorders	n.a.	n.a.	n.a.	n.a.	n.a.	n.a.	5.6	12.4
Clothes dryers	12.2	25.2	40.8	48.1	63.2	68.4	73.4	75.1
Compact disc players	n.a.	n.a.	n.a.	n.a.	n.a.	n.a.	15.4	33.2
Dishwashers	n.a.	2.7	7.5	15.2	28.6	37.1	42.0	45.2
Electric stoves	56.2	69.0	78.6	85.1	89.4	92.3	93.8	93.9
Electric washers	86.8	86.2	83.7	76.9	77.3	77.3	78.6	79.3
Freezers	11.5	22.6	33.2	41.8	51.0	57.0	57.6	58.7
Gas barbecues	n.a.	n.a.	n.a.	n.a.	n.a.	19.9[1]	45.9	51.9
Home computers	n.a.	n.a.	n.a.	n.a.	n.a.	n.a.	16.3	23.3
Microwave ovens	n.a.	n.a.	n.a.	0.8	8.0[2]	23.0	68.2	79.1
Radios	96.2	96.1	97.2	98.3	98.7	98.7	99.1	98.9
Refrigerators	90.3	95.8	98.4	99.3	99.6	99.2	99.5	99.8
Telephones	83.3	89.4	93.9	96.4	97.6	98.2	98.5	99.0
Television, cable	n.a.	n.a.	n.a.	40.4	54.8	62.5	71.4	72.4
Televisions	80.6	92.6	96.0	96.8	97.7	98.3	99.0	99.0
Televisions, color	n.a.	n.a.	12.1	53.4	81.1	91.4	96.9	97.7
Video recorders	n.a.	n.a.	n.a.	n.a.	n.a.	23.5	66.3	77.3
Number of households[3]	**4 404**	**5 000**	**5 784**	**6 721**	**7 787**	**8 762**	**9 624**	**10 247**

Source: *Statistics Canada*

(1) 1984 figure. (2) 1981 figure. (3) In thousands. (n.a.) not available.

Assessing Growth in Wages

W hile economic growth throughout the 1900s resulted in increases in wages for the average family, prices also rose—how much farther ahead are we?

Once inflation has been taken into account (by using the CPI) a meaningful comparison can be made; the conclusion is that the "real" average wage has gone from $6 800 in 1920 to $24 300 in 1990—3.6 times that of the average wages of a worker 70 years ago. This period has seen recession, depression and boom times, but it also saw a major shift from agricultural and resource-based industries to higher-paying professional, technical or managerial jobs.

Low Income in Canada, 1992

In 1992, some 4 227 000 Canadians had low incomes. This includes some 1 210 000 children under 18 years of age.

The low-income cut-off level is set by Statistics Canada, using a standard that families or individuals who spend 54.7% or more of their pre-tax income on food, clothing and shelter are in financial difficulty.

The table below shows the minimum income level necessary to avoid financial hardship. It varies according to changes in the cost of living, family size and place of residence. For instance, in 1991 the poverty line for a family of 4 living in Vancouver was $29 661; for a family of 4 living in a rural area it was $20 192.

| | Urban Areas | | | | |
Family size[1]	Pop. Under 30 000	Pop. 30 000 to 99 999	Pop. 100 000 to 499 999	Pop. 500 000 or more	Rural Areas
1 person	12 829	13 787	13 883	16 186	11 186
2 persons	16 036	17 234	17 354	20 233	13 982
3 persons	19 943	21 433	21 583	25 163	17 390
4 persons	24 142	25 945	26 126	30 460	21 050
5 persons	26 986	29 002	29 205	34 049	23 531
6 persons	29 830	32 059	32 284	37 638	26 012
7 or more persons	32 674	35 116	35 363	41 227	28 493

Source: *Statistics Canada*

(1) Does not distinguish between adults and children as family members.

Canadian Residents Living Below the Poverty Line

(thousands of persons)

	1981	1983	1985	1987	1989	1991
Total	**3 643**	**4 406**	**4 170**	**3 912**	**3 487**	**4 227**
Children under 18	998	1 221	1 165	1 057	934	1 210
Adults, 18 to 65	1 911	2 466	2 337	2 228	1 954	2 427
Adults, 65 and over	733	719	669	627	599	590
Family Members, total	**2 632**	**3 223**	**3 035**	**2 775**	**2 387**	**2 969**
Children under 18	998	1 221	1 165	1 057	934	1 210
Adults, 18 to 65	1 350	1 760	1 618	1 492	1 269	1 589
Adults, 65 and over	284	242	251	227	184	170
Single Individuals, total	**1 010**	**1 183**	**1 136**	**1 137**	**1 100**	**1 258**
Adults, 18 to 65	561	706	718	736	685	837
Adults, 65 and over	449	477	417	401	415	421

Source: *Statistics Canada*

THE NATION

The National Anthem: O Canada

The music of *O Canada* was composed by Calixa Lavallée and the lyrics were written in French by Adolphe-Basile Routhier in Quebec City. Originally called *Chant National* it was first performed at a banquet in Quebec City on June 24, 1880. The anthem grew in popularity in Quebec but was not heard in English until the early 1900s. There have been several English versions of the work, the most popular of which was written in 1908 by Robert Stanley Weir. In 1967 a Special Joint Committee of the Senate and the House of Commons was formed to recommend official versions of Canada's National and Royal Anthems. With a few minor changes, the official English version of *O Canada* is based on Weir's lyrics. On June 27, 1980 the House of Commons passed Bill C-36 designating both the music and lyrics of *O Canada* as Canada's national anthem. It was proclaimed July 1, 1980.

O Canada

O Canada! Terre de nos aïeux,

Ton front est ceint de fleurons glorieux!

Car ton bras sait porter l'épée,

Il sait porter la croix!

Ton histoire est une épopée

Des plus brillants exploits,

Et ta valeur, de foi trempée,

Protégera nos foyers et nos droits,

Protégera nos foyers et nos droits.

O Canada

O Canada! Our home and native land!

True patriot love in all thy sons command.

With glowing hearts we see thee rise,

The True North strong and free!

From far and wide, O Canada,

We stand on guard for thee.

God keep our land glorious and free!

O Canada, we stand on guard for thee.

O Canada, we stand on guard for thee!

The National Flag

The National Flag was adopted by Parliament Oct. 22, 1964 and proclaimed by Queen Elizabeth II. It was inaugurated on Feb. 15, 1965.

It is a red flag of the proportions two by length and one by width, containing in its centre a white square, the width of the flag, bearing a single, red, stylized maple leaf. The maple leaf has been looked upon as an emblem of Canada since the early 1700s. Red and white were declared Canada's official colours by King George V Nov. 21, 1921.

The National Flag is to be flown daily at all federal government buildings, airports and military bases and establishments within and outside Canada. When flown with other flags, it should be given a place of honour.

CANADIAN HISTORY

Exploration and First Settlements

The first people who came to North America arrived during the last Ice Age which began about 80 000 years ago and ended about 12 000 years ago. These Native People were hunters who crosssed from Asia via a land bridge that is now submerged beneath the Bering Sea. Although there is continuing debate among archeologists as to how early humans might have settled in what is now Canada, the earliest accepted occupation site is at the Bluefish Caves in the Yukon; artifacts at least 12 000 to 17 000 years old have been found there. As the glaciers of the Ice Age retreated, human settlements spread across Canada and gradually, these first Canadians developed lifestyles based on the environments in which they lived. They obtained their food by hunting, fishing, gathering, and in the case of Eastern Woodland tribes, by farming. By the time explorers from Europe reached Canada, the Native People had well developed trading patterns, arts and crafts, languages, writing, religious beliefs, laws and government.

There has been much conjecture as to who the first Europeans to come to Canada were. The claim that an Irish monk, St. Brendan, arrived about the year 550 has not been proven. However the theory that Vikings settled in Newfoundland was confirmed by archeological excavations at L'Anse aux Meadows during the 1960s and 1970s.

A burst of European exploration didn't take place until the Age of Discovery in the 15th and 16th centuries. Explorers found what they called a New World while in search of a route to the Far East. In 1497, Giovanni Caboto (John Cabot), an Italian sailing for England, landed on the Canadian coast, likely in Cape Breton or Newfoundland, and claimed the land for Henry VII. Although Cabot probably died on a second expedition in 1498, his voyages helped open up the rich fishing grounds of the Grand Banks.

European navigators and fishermen continued to visit the shores of Canada, but the first serious exploration of the area was undertaken by Jacques Cartier, who discovered the Gulf of St. Lawrence while searching for a passage to Asia, in 1534. The next year he travelled up the St. Lawrence River as far as the native settlements of Stadacona (Quebec) and Hochelaga (Montreal). On this voyage, Cartier picked up the Iroquoian word for village, Kanata (thought to be the origin of "Canada"), and used it to apply to the whole region he had discovered. Cartier's discoveries gave France a claim to Canada and led to the first French settlements.

In 1541–2, Cartier and the Sieur de Roberval established a short-lived settlement at Charlesbourg-Royal just above Quebec. In 1605, the Sieur de Monts and Samuel de Champlain established the colony of Port Royal in what is now Nova Scotia. Champlain went on to establish a settlement at Quebec in 1608, to explore the interior and to draw maps of New France. Champlain also started a fur-trading network (mostly in beaver pelts) with the Algonquins and the Hurons who inhabited the St. Lawrence and Great Lakes regions. This trade relationship became a military alliance as Champlain supported these groups against the Iroquois. This enmity between the French and the Iroquois prevailed throughout most of the history of New France.

The Growth of New France (1627-1660)

The economic foundation of New France was the fur trade. In fact, the French kings were content to let fur-trading companies run the colony. Although these companies expanded the territory's boundaries, they failed to encourage settlement. One of King Louis XIII's most able advisers, Cardinal Richelieu, tried to remedy this problem by granting a fur-trading monopoly to the Company of One Hundred Associates in 1627, on condition that it bring out several hundred settlers each year. However, war between England and France broke out and Quebec was captured in 1629. Even after peace was restored in 1633, the Company of One Hundred Associates failed to honor its commitment to bring out settlers.

Despite the lack of settlers, the colony was expanding in other ways. As governor, Champlain encouraged the expansion of the fur trade. The Jesuits had arrived in 1625 and were vigorously pursuing their missionary work among the Hurons.

Champlain died in 1635, just two years after the colony was restored to France. No leader possessing his vision or drive emerged to replace him. Next, despite their conviction, the French missionaries made few converts among the Native People. Even Ste. Marie Among the Hurons, their central mission-post, was abandoned in 1649 in the face of invasion by the Iroquois, who dispersed the Hurons and disrupted the French fur-trading network. Finally, the security of the centre of the fur trade, Montreal (founded in 1642), and the rest of the colony was threatened by the wars against the Iroquois. When the wars were renewed in 1659-1660, after a brief peace, there were still only about 3 000 French settlers in the colony. Clearly, the French King would have to act to secure France's foothold in North America.

Royal Government in New France (1663-1700)

In 1663 King Louis XIV made New France a crown colony. Regular troops were sent out and undertook a successful campaign against the Iroquois, which resulted in the signing of a peace treaty in 1667. Several hundred of these regulars stayed on as settlers, thereby adding to the security of the colony. A system of government headed by a governor, an intendant, and a bishop was instituted. The governor, who was the king's representative, was charged with defence. The intendant was responsible for industry, trade, and administrative affairs. The bishop looked after religious matters, which included education. In theory, this system provided for a clear separation of powers; but, in practice, there were frequent disputes among the three officials. Still, this system survived intact for the remainder of the colony's history, and it provided New France with some remarkably dynamic officials. Two of these arrived in the first years of the Royal Government.

The first intendant of New France, Jean Talon (1665 to 1672), introduced innovative measures, including awards for early marriage, to boost the population. As well, he tried to build a diversified economy on the St. Lawrence by promoting crafts, farming, and local industry. Few subsequent officials in New France shared Talon's concern for settlement or economic diversity. Most were more interested in profits from the fur trade. Count Frontenac, governor for all but seven years between 1672 and 1698, threw his support behind the fur trade, not only raising profits but also encouraging exploration. Under his rule, French adventurers explored the Mississippi River from its upper reaches to the Gulf of Mexico, greatly expanding the fur-trading boundaries of New France. Frontenac gained more fame when he withstood the attack of an English army which besieged Quebec in 1690.

But Frontenac had not only exceeded his powers in promoting territorial expansion, he had also undermined the security of the colony. With its limited population, New France now found itself competing for the fur trade with the more populous English colonies around them. In the north, there was rivalry with the Hudson's Bay Company, founded in 1670. To the south, there was border warfare between French fur traders and their Indian allies, and the English with their Iroquois allies. New France fared well in the limited warfare of the 1680s and 1690s; but in the 18th century there was a series of major wars which resulted in disaster for the colony.

The Collapse of New France (1701-1763)

In the early years of the 18th century, New France stretched from Hudson Bay to the Gulf of Mexico, and from Newfoundland to the Great Lakes. Its population was thinly scattered in the north, south and west but its fur-trading posts in these regions gave legitimacy to its territorial claims. In the Atlantic region, there were several hundred colonists in Newfoundland and another 1 500 in Acadia. The heartland of New France was the settlement of about 20 000 colonists in Montreal, Quebec and in the small communities along the St. Lawrence. The prosperity of the French settlements was to be hurt by long periods of war.

The first of these was the war of the Spanish Succession fought between France and Austria (and their allies) between 1701-1714). Although the British failed to capture their main objective in the North American campaign, the fortress city of Quebec, they made other gains at the bargaining table. In the Treaty of Utrecht, which ended the conflict, France gave up claims to the Hudson Bay territory, all of Acadia except for Cape Breton, and Newfoundland.

During a 30-year period of peace, New France enjoyed limited prosperity. The populaton grew, farm yields increased, some industry was established, and furs were still exported. But military expenditure necessary to protect the colony was turning it into a financial burden for France. Much of that expenditure went into the huge fortress of Louisbourg, built on Cape Breton Island to protect the offshore fisheries and guard the St. Lawrence.

Prussia, France, Spain, Naples, Bavaria and Saxony fought Austria and England when the war of Austrian Succession broke out in 1740 and Louisbourg was a natural target. The fortress fell to the British, although it was returned to France at the war's end in 1748. The British established their own military and naval base at Halifax in 1749.

The fragile peace was broken in 1754, when fighting broke out between the English and French colonists in the Ohio Valley. Within two years, Britain and France were officially at war again in what became known as the Seven Years' War. Despite some early victories, the French suffered the loss of Louisbourg in 1758. In the following year, General Wolfe defeated General Montcalm on the Plains of Abraham above the St. Lawrence at Quebec. Although Montreal did not fall until the next year, the loss of Quebec was an irreversible setback. The British army occupied New France, and in 1763 the treaty ending the Seven Years' War confirmed British sovereignty.

New France had fallen because of decisive military defeats at Louisbourg and Quebec, but more significant was the inability of France to supply its colony in the face of British naval supremacy. The British were now masters in North America.

The First Years of British Rule (1763-1812)

The British had been active on the continent during their search for a northwest passage to the far east, however their victory over the French encouraged a shift from exploration and fur trading to settlement and the strengthening of British customs in the new territory.

In 1763 a Royal Proclamation was imposed by the British government on the newly-acquired territories of New France. The intent of this proclamation was clear. By encouraging the establishment of Protestant schools, by promoting the Church of England, and by stipulating that an assembly be elected, the proclamation aimed at Anglicization. The intent was most visible in the matter of the assembly. Although the French inhabitants were in the majority, under British law no Roman Catholic could hold office. If an assembly were elected, a few hundred British settlers would control about 65 000 Canadiens.

Fortunately for the French in Canada, James Murray, the governor of Quebec from 1760 to 1768, felt that the loyalty of the French colonists could more likely be gained by fair treatment. Murray refused to call elections for the assembly, and allowed French legal practices to continue. Murray's sympathies provoked a storm of protest from the British colonists in Quebec and he was recalled. But his successor, Guy Carleton, also realized that the Royal Proclamation of 1763 would only alienate the recently-defeated colonists. Carleton saw that even if Anglicization were carried out, few colonists from the Thirteen Colonies in America or immigrants from Britain would be lured to the rugged colony of Quebec. Consequently, Carleton advised the Government in London to replace the proclamation with more liberal legislation.

The result was the Quebec Act of 1774, which dropped the assembly in favour of an appointed council on which Catholics might serve. As well, the French system of civil law and the seigneurial system of land tenure were both guaranteed. Finally, the Quebec Act expanded the borders of the colony to include the rich lands of the Ohio Valley. The British had acted to win the support of the Canadiens. In doing so, however, the British government angered the citizens of the Thirteen Colonies, who resented the special treatment given to their former enemies. These English colonists were especially upset over the loss of the Ohio Valley, a region into which they expected to expand.

The Quebec Act was not the only cause for complaint in the Thirteen Colonies. Protests over British taxation policies and trade restriction led to talk of revolution. That talk led to action, and in 1775 an invading American army took Montreal. Quebec held out against the American siege until relieved by British forces. Although there was some sympathy for the American cause in both Quebec and Nova Scotia, it was not a strong enough sentiment to cause these two colonies to join the revolution.

During and immediately after the American Revolution, some American colonists who wished to retain their British ties fled into the newly-created United States into the Maritimes and Quebec. The arrival of about 30 000 of these Loyalists in Nova Scotia resulted in the creation of a new colony, New Brunswick, in 1784. Similarly, the influx of 10 000 Loyalists into Quebec led to division of the colony, and in 1791, the western part of the colony became Upper Canada. The remainder of the old colony was known as Lower Canada.

Despite these changes fur trading remained an important economic activity in the interior of British North America. In fact, there was keen rivalry for furs between the Hudson's Bay Company and the newly-formed (1784) North West Company based in Montreal which led to a flurry of western exploration. Alexander Mackenzie, a partner in the North West Company, explored a river (now known as the Mackenzie) to its mouth on the Beaufort Sea in 1789, and found a route to the Pacific via the Fraser and Bella Coola Rivers in 1793. Two other North West Company employees, Simon Fraser and David Thompson, also carried out voyages of discovery. Fraser followed the river named after him to the Pacific in 1808, and Thompson travelled down the Columbia River to the coast in 1811. These voyages, along with the earlier coastal explorations of James Cook in 1778 and George Vancouver in 1792-1795, helped establish Britain's claim to the northwest part of the continent.

The War of 1812

Although the British and Americans signed a peace treaty in 1783 to end the American War of Independence, there was still friction between them. One source of conflict was the British fur-trading posts in the Ohio Valley which now belonged to the United States. Although Britain surrendered these posts in 1796 as stipulated by Jay's treaty (1794), there were still American complaints that the British were arming the local native people. At the same time there was growing American resentment over British interference with shipping. The British, who were at war with France, claimed the right to search American ships for cargoes bound for the enemy. In the process, the British often forced American sailors on these ships to join the British navy. Resentment grew among Americans until June 1812, when the United States declared war on Britain.

In the first year of the war, the Americans under General William Hull crossed the Detroit River to invade Upper Canada. Hull expected Canadian sympathizers to flock to his cause but he was disappointed. Without fighting a major battle, he retreated to Detroit. British General Isaac Brock and the Shawnees, under Chief Tecumseh, moved against Detroit and General Hull surrendered. This British and Canadian victory was followed by a victory at Queenston Heights on the Niagara River. Brock was killed in this battle which nevertheless gave confidence to the defenders of the British colonies.

In 1813, the Americans carried out a successful raid on York (now Toronto), and also gained a foothold in the Niagara district. But by the summer of that year the Americans had been pushed back across the Niagara River by British victories at Stoney Creek and Beaver Dam. Meanwhile, the Americans were building up a large fleet on the Great Lakes, and in Sept. 1813 the Americans won control of Lake Erie at the Battle of Put-in-Bay. This victory prompted the British under General Proctor to abandon Fort Malden on the Detroit River. However, the American General Harrison caught the retreating forces at Moraviantown on the Thames River and defeated Proctor. Tecumseh was killed in this battle. In the east, a two-pronged attack on Montreal was repulsed. The American invaders were defeated on the Chateauguay River and at Crysler's Farm near Cornwall in the fall of 1813.

In 1814, the Americans again invaded the Niagara district but were halted at the Battle of Lundy's Lane. From Halifax, British forces attacked targets in Maine, and occupied most of that state. Another attack from Halifax was launched on the American capital, Washington. The British raiders burned the government buildings there in retaliation for the destruction of York the previous year. Despite these successes, a major British offensive against Plattsburg on Lake Champlain failed. By now the war was in stalemate and both sides were tired. British and American negotiators signed the Treaty of Ghent in Dec. 1814, to end the war.

In the aftermath of the war, the two sides made an effort to settle outstanding differences. The Rush-Bagot Agreement of 1817 provided for naval disarmament on the Great Lakes. In the following year Britain and the United States agreed to accept the 49th parallel as the international boundary from the Lake of the Woods to the Rocky Mountains. In addition, they agreed to the joint occupation of the Oregon Territory for 10 years.

Rebellion and Reform (1814-1839)

In the years after the War of 1812, there was considerable growth in British North America. The population increased as immigrants from both the United States and Britain arrived to take up land that was free or inexpensive. The economy became more diversified as lumbering, farming, and shipbuilding developed in the Canadas and in the Maritimes. Finally, a sense of nationalism began to grow in parts of British North America. This feeling arose partly out of postwar patriotism and partly out of the shared experiences of a demanding colonial life.

As the colonies became more populous, political interest increased. In both the Canadas and the Maritimes friction between ruling elites and the ordinary colonists developed and was partially fueled by the form of government in each colony. British governors or lieutenant-governors picked their own officials, including the members of legislative or executive councils. There were elected assemblies in each colony, but their powers were limited. Legislation might pass in the assembly, but be turned down by the legislative council. The assemblies, the voice of the people, found themselves frustrated by the power of appointed officials.

By the mid-1830s, economic distress increased the discontent that had been building during the 1820s. In Lower Canada, where cultural prejudice against the Canadiens added to the tension, Louis Joseph Papineau emerged as leader of the radical Patriote Party. When the colonial authorities would not grant the reforms called for by Papineau and his followers, rebellion broke out in November 1837. But loyalist forces quickly defeated the badly-organized and poorly-led rebels. Papineau and other leaders fled to the United States.

In Upper Canada, the reform movement was able to gain a majority in the assembly in several elections. Still, the reformers could not turn their program into legislation because of Tory control of the Legislative Council. When an anti-reform lieutenant-governor, Sir Francis Bond Head, took over in 1836, some reformers became more radical. Their leader was William Lyon Mackenzie, a newspaper editor and member of the assembly. The Tories won the election of 1836, when Head directly intervened in the campaign. Mackenzie and his followers, spurred on by events in Lower Canada, took up arms in early December of 1837. Mackenzie's disorganization, and lack of widespread support among the colonists, doomed the rebellion. After a skirmish north of Toronto the main body of rebels fled. An uprising in the western districts of Upper Canada was equally unsuccessful. Throughout the following year some rebels and American sympathizers mounted raids on Upper Canada from the United States, but these received no popular support.

In the aftermath of the rebellions came political change. The British government sent out Lord Durham to act as Governor General of British North America and investigate the rebellion. The Durham Report of 1839 contained two main recommendations: the first called for the union of Upper and Lower Canada as a first step in the eventual assimilation of the French Canadians; the second recommended the granting of responsible government (in which the executive is responsible to the assembly), a key demand of reformers.

The Road to Confederation (1840-1867)

The middle years of the 19th century were both satisfying and disturbing for British North Americans. Immigrants from Europe streamed into the colonies, more land was cleared, and towns grew. Local industries were started, while lumbering and shipbuilding activities increased. Montreal and Toronto became commercial centres and the ports of the Maritimes were prosperous, fuelled by ship building and trade. Transportation improved as roads, canals, and, by the 1850s, railways were built. Some British North Americans looked beyond their borders and began to think of a federation of British colonies that included not only Canada and the Maritimes, but the Red River settlement and the colonies in British Columbia.

Despite the prosperity, there were reasons to consider such an alliance. Until the mid-1840s, the colonies had enjoyed a preferential trading relationship whereby Britain reduced tariffs on colonial products. This advantage was lost in 1846 when Britain adopted free trade. At first, the colonies found some advantage in entering into a limited free trade arrangement with the United States. But the Americans allowed this Reciprocity Treaty of 1854 to lapse in 1866. British North Americans would have to look to themselves as trading partners.

There was also concern in British North America about the United States. That country seemed intent on fulfilling its "Manifest Destiny" to take over North America. The threat was especially clear during and after the American Civil War (1861-5). During the war, the Northern States were angered by British support for the South, and after the war, there was a fear that the large Northern army might march into British territory.

As well, there was a serious political problem in the colony of Canada. The union of Upper and Lower Canada in 1841 had resulted in the creation of a single legislature for the new colony, Canada. By the 1860s, however, this legislature was barely functioning. No single party could gain enough support from both Francophones and Anglophones to gain a majority. There had been 12 different governments in 15 years, and Canadian politicians were desperate for a solution.

Three powerful figures in Canada's legislature, John A. Macdonald, George Brown and George-Étienne Cartier formed a coalition and proposed a larger union of British North America as a way to end the political deadlock. In addition, this proposal would solve the problem of trade, and provide security against the American threat. Meanwhile, on the east coast there was interest in a union too, a union of the Maritimes. A conference had been called for Charlottetown in September 1864 to discuss that topic. When the leaders of the new Canadian coalition heard of this meeting, they asked for an invitation. At Charlottetown the British North American delegates decided on a federation of all the colonies. A second conference at Quebec in October, 1864 resulted in a plan for federal union. A federal government would control defence, trade and other matters of national interest. Provincial governments would have power over local matters such as roads and education. The final details were hammered out at another conference in London, England, in 1866.

The British government, which supported this colonial initiative, passed the British North America Act in March of 1867. On July 1, 1867, the provinces of Nova Scotia, New Brunswick, Ontario (formerly Canada West) and Quebec (formerly Canada East), became the Dominion of Canada.

The Nation Expands (1867-1885)

Soon after the Confederation of Ontario, Quebec, New Brunswick and Nova Scotia in 1867, the new nation of Canada began to acquire more territory. In 1869, guided by the national vision of Prime Minister John A. Macdonald, the federal government bought Rupert's Land from the Hudson's Bay Company. This was a huge territory which included most of modern Manitoba, as well as parts of Saskatchewan, Alberta and the Northwest Territories. The few Ontario immigrants in the Red River Settlement there welcomed this move; but the far more numerous Métis (descendants of French fur traders and Indians) were suspicious, especially because they had not been consulted beforehand. When newly-appointed Lieutenant-Governor William McDougall tried to enter the settlement before the territory had officially been transferred to Canada, the Métis turned him back. In the absence of a legitimate government, the Métis, under their leader Louis Riel, seized Fort Garry on the Red River and proclaimed a provisional government. The Métis demanded the right to vote, land laws, the official use of both French and English, and the provision of both Roman Catholic and Protestant schools. The Métis list of rights became the terms for negotiating Manitoba's entry into Confederation in 1870.

In the same year, representatives from the colony of British Columbia arrived in Ottawa to discuss union. With the promise from Ottawa to build a transcontinental railway, British Columbia entered Confederation in 1871. Canada now stretched from sea to sea, but the work of nation building was still not complete.

In 1868 Nova Scotia elected an anti-Confederation provincial government and sent a delegation, led by veteran politician Joseph Howe, to London to seek a repeal of the union. But Britain was unsympathetic, and in 1869 Macdonald seized the opportunity to offer Nova Scotia better terms and Howe a cabinet position. With the Nova Scotia situation resolved, Macdonald turned his attention to Prince Edward Island. The Islanders were more attracted to the idea of union after an expensive railway project nearly bankrupted the colony. Macdonald agreed to assume the colony's debts, offered a cash subsidy, and promised a steamer service to the mainland. In 1873, Prince Edward Island agreed to the terms and became Canada's 7th province.

In the 1870s and 1880s railways were built to link the provinces of the new nation. The Intercolonial Railway, joining central Canada to the Maritimes, was completed in 1876, but construction of a rail link to British Columbia ran into several delays. First, Macdonald's government was defeated in 1873 over charges of corruption associated with the railway project. The new prime minister, Alexander Mackenzie, refused to fund railway projects because the country was the midst of a depression. However, after Macdonald's re-election in 1878, railway building began in earnest. In February 1881 the Canadian Pacific Railway Company (CPR) was incorporated, and in November 1885 the last spike was driven at Craigellachie in British Columbia to complete the link to the Pacific.

Even before it was fully completed, the CPR was used to carry troops to quell a rebellion in the spring of 1885. Trouble had started several years earlier when settlers in the North-West Territory (modern Alberta and Saskatchewan) complained to the government about land title, shipping rates, and their lack of an elected government. Among those who complained were the Métis, some of whom had moved farther west after the Red River troubles of 1870. When the federal government was slow to respond, the Métis, again under Louis Riel, rose up in March 1885 against the territorial council appointed by Ottawa. By late April, 5 000 Canadian soldiers, who had travelled by the new railway, were on the march against Riel and his Métis and Indian followers. At the Battle of Batoche in May, the forces of General Middleton defeated the rebels. Riel was found guilty of treason by an English-speaking jury and executed.

The Laurier Era (1896-1911)

Conservative Prime Minister John A. Macdonald died in 1891, soon after winning a federal election. The Conservatives could not find a suitable successor and by 1896 there had been four prime ministers—John Abbott, John Thompson, Mackenzie Bowell and Charles Tupper. During this period, the Conservatives had to deal with a crisis over school legislation introduced in Manitoba. The Manitoba legislature had replaced the dual school system (both Protestant and Catholic schools) which had been guaranteed in the terms of union, with a single Protestant system. Francophone Catholics across Canada were already bitter about Louis Riel's execution. Now the Manitoba schools legislation convinced them that English Protestant Canadians wanted to stamp out French Catholic rights. Extremists on both sides inflamed the issue, and the Conservatives' inability to settle the matter hurt them in the election of 1896. The Liberals, under Wilfrid Laurier, formed a government.

Laurier settled the Manitoba school question by adopting a compromise approach. Religious instruction would be allowed within the single system, and instruction in French could take place where numbers warranted. The issue died down, but Laurier remained sensitive to the tensions between Anglophone Protestants and Francophone Catholics. Many English Canadians were swept up in a great wave of pro-imperial sentiment associated with the Diamond Jubilee of Queen Victoria. In Britain the event was seen as an opportunity to strengthen ties within the British Empire. Laurier acknowledged Canada's support for the Empire, but resisted proposals for a closer relationship with Britain and the other colonies. The prime minister did not wish to yield Canadian autonomy, nor did he wish to lose support in French Canada. The issue of Canada's role in the Empire came to a head in 1899 during the Boer War (the South African Republic (Transvaal) and the Orange Free State fought against Britain). Once again steering a middle course, Laurier agreed to equip and transport Canadian volunteers to South Africa, but sent no official troops. Although this compromise did not satisfy all Canadians, it avoided a bitter dispute. For a time, imperial issues were forgotten, as Canadians enjoyed boom times after the turn of the century.

Laurier summed up the nation's mood when he declared that the "twentieth century is Canada's century." Impressive growth in both industrial and agricultural production provided support for his words. Canada's prospects appealed to immigrants who flocked to the industrial cities and to the farmland of the Prairies. Many of them were attracted by an extensive government advertising campaign and by the lure of free land in the west. As a result of this influx, two new provinces, Alberta and Saskatchewan, were created in 1905. The immigrant tide boosted Canada's population from 5 371 315 in 1901 to 7 206 643 in 1911. The mood of the country was so confident that two new transcontinental railway building projects got under way in the early years of the century.

The international scene, however, was not so bright. In 1903, the British sided with the Americans in the Alaska Boundary Dispute, a disagreement over the international boundary near the Klondike gold fields. Canadians were dismayed, but Britain was less concerned about the Canadian claim than for the need to maintain good relations with the United States. Tension in Europe was increasing and Britain found itself outside of complicated system of allegiances which had developed there. This same concern led both the British government and the Canadian pro-imperialists to pressure Laurier into providing money to build British warships. Again, Laurier staked out a middle position by introducing a Naval Service Act which created a Canadian navy that could help Britain where the need arose.

Laurier's compromise on naval policy satisfied neither side. Some French Canadians supported the views of Quebec nationalist Henri Bourassa who claimed Laurier had betrayed his people. Anglophone pro-imperialists complained that Laurier's "tin pot navy" was not enough. Canada's naval policy became an issue in the 1911 election, as did the Liberal plan for free trade with the United States. Conservative leader Robert Borden was able to use both to characterize Laurier as not only disloyal to Britain but favoring annexation to the United States. The Conservatives won the election. Borden became prime minister and Laurier stayed on as leader of the Opposition, continuing to advocate conciliatory policies when the interests of French and English Canadians clashed.

Canada and the First World War (1914-1918)

In August 1914, Britain declared war on Germany and Austro-Hungary. The declaration automatically applied to Canada, as part of the British Empire. At first, there was an enthusiastic response, especially among recent British immigrants. When the minister of militia, Sam Hughes, called for 25 000 volunteers, nearly 33 000 appeared. In 1915, when the government asked the Canadian public to buy $50 million in war bonds, they bought $100 million. But enthusiasm for war began to fade as the casualties mounted and the realities of trench warfare became known.

Canadian troops sailed for Europe in October 1914 and, after training in Britain, went into action at Ypres, Belgium in April 1915. There they gained a reputation for courage, holding their positions in the face of a poison gas attack, a new weapon at the time. Canadians took part in the costly battles at St. Eloi and Mont Sorrel in 1916. By the Battle of the Somme, in late summer of 1916, Canada had four army divisions in France; in the spring of 1917, all four were deployed in the attack on Vimy Ridge, which resulted in the first real Canadian victory of the war. But by now it was clear that every battle would result in terrible losses. At Passchendaele in October 1917, the Canadians sustained more than 15 000 casualties.

Voluntary recruitment could not keep pace with the high casualty rates. Prime Minister Borden was forced to consider conscription to draft soldiers into the army and took the question to the electorate in 1917, unleashing one of the most bitterly fought campaigns in Canadian history. In Quebec, Henri Bourassa rallied anti-conscription supporters and argued that Canada had done enough. In Ontario, Borden's supporters condemned French-Canadian anti-conscriptionists as traitors. For his part Borden introduced the Wartime Elections Act to help secure victory. This act removed the right to vote from enemy aliens, even though some were Canadian citizens. It also gave the right to vote to women relatives of soldiers. In the election Borden won in every province except Quebec where he was soundly rejected. Conscription had created a deep division between Quebec and the rest of Canada and once in practice, it had little impact on the course of the war. When the first 400 000 conscripts were called up, 90% of them appealed for exemption, and by the war's end only about 24 000 conscripts had reached the front.

While the conscription crisis raged at home, Canadian soldiers played a major role in the events leading to an Allied victory. They took part in the successful battle at Amiens in August 1918 and helped to roll the Germans back to Mons by November. The Canadians were still fighting at Mons when the armistice was signed November 11, 1918.

Canadians also served with distinction in other theatres of war. By 1918, Canadians made up almost 25% of the pilots in Britain's Royal Flying Corps. Other Canadians served in the Royal Navy or on coastal patrol in Canada's own small navy. Some served in forestry corps overseas and others operated the railways behind the British lines. Some, including women, served as ambulance drivers at the front. Many Canadian women also played key roles as nurses overseas, and in the munitions factories in Canada.

Canada's war effort won the country a place in the Imperial War Cabinet during the war, and a seat in the League of Nations afterwards. There were other benefits, too. Women's contributions to the war effort helped them win the right to vote in federal elections and in provincial elections in seven of the provinces by 1919. Yet these advances came at a terrible cost. Overseas, 68 300 Canadians had died. At home, bitterness over the conscription issue had created a division between French and English Canadians that would be remembered for decades.

Canada in the 1920s

As the soldiers returned home, many expected to find a Canada ready to reward them for their sacrifices. What they found was a nation in the midst of painful postwar readjustment. Industry had to convert to peacetime production, but interest rates were so high investment capital was scarce. Jobs were hard to find and wages were low, and tariffs on imported goods kept prices high. By 1921, 300 000 men and women—more than 15% of the work force—were unemployed. Farmers, especially on the Prairies, also suffered. During the war, the west had become the

world's breadbasket: wheat prices had soared and many farmers had borrowed heavily to expand their production. But with the war's end, world markets collapsed; wheat prices fell by almost half within two years.

These conditions, along with resentment over wartime profiteering by big business, created unrest. The One Big Union movement, centered in western Canada, attempted to create a single union to represent all workers. The Winnipeg General Strike of 1919 grew out of the organizers' efforts and the general discontent. Although the Winnipeg workers were striking over such issues as the right to collective bargaining, better wages and improved working conditions, the opponents of the general strike characterized it as a communist conspiracy by raising the spectre of a revolution similar to the one in Russia two years earlier. The federal government sided with the anti-strike forces. Immigration laws were amended to deport "alien" labor radicals, the strike leaders were arrested and the Royal North West Mounted Police fired into a rioting crowd on June 21, 1919—"Bloody Sunday"—killing 1 and wounding 30. The six-week strike was over and so was the growth of labor unions. In 1919 alone there were more than 400 strikes, but after the Winnipeg General Strike, the federal government and most governments at the provincial level opposed union activities. Throughout the 1920s there was a decline in union membership.

The reasons for unrest and discontent varied from region to region in the 1920s. The government takeover of five financially troubled railways had led to the creation of the Canadian National Railways in 1919 and railway rates in the Maritimes were raised 40% to bring them up to central Canadian levels. Angry over the rail rates and feeling that Ottawa was making decisions on the basis of central Canada's interests, many Maritimers protested by forming the Maritimes Rights movement, aimed at winning transportation concessions and federal subsidies. At the same time it promoted regional rights and pride.

Canadian farmers, resentful over low prices for farm products, high rail rates and high prices for manufactured goods, formed the United Farmers' movement. United Farmers' parties won provincial elections in Ontario in 1919, in Alberta in 1921, and in Manitoba in 1922. At the federal level, the Progressive

Party embraced some of the program of the United Farmers' movement. The Progressives called for free trade, nationalization (especially in the case of railways) and more direct democracy (such as the use of a referendum to decide a controversial issue). Although they were a new party, the Progressives were to play an important role in politics in the 1920s.

The election of 1921 marked new directions in Canadian politics. Both major parties had new leaders: Arthur Meighen had replaced Borden as prime minister; William Lyon Mackenzie King had taken over as Liberal leader after Laurier's death. Of even greater significance was that for the first time, Canadians could vote for one of three parties at the federal level: the Liberals, the Conservatives or the Progressives. The Liberals won the 1921 election, but the Progressives finished second and formed the opposition. Their position in the House of Commons was even more important after the 1925 election in which the Conservatives under Meighen won the most seats, but King remained in power by claiming the support of the Progressives. After 1925 the Progressives declined, and many of their supporters voted Liberal in King's 1926 election victory. But the influence of the Progressive movement was felt as King's government, anxious to keep their support, passed Canada's first Old Age Pension Act in 1927.

In foreign affairs, King made sure that Canada played a cautious role in the League of Nations, because he feared that Canada would be drawn into international disputes. In imperial matters, his insistence on autonomy contributed to a redefinition of the empire at the Imperial Conference of 1926. There it was acknowledged that Canada and the other British dominions were autonomous even in their external affairs. As a result, by 1929, Canada had diplomatic posts in Washington, Paris and Tokyo and Britain had a high commissioner in Ottawa. The Governor General became a symbolic representative of the Crown rather than a representative of the British government.

At home, there were many signs that good times had finally come to Canada. World markets for Canadian manufactured goods had revived, and wheat prices were soaring to new levels. New mining and lumbering areas were developed. By 1928, more than a billion dollars' worth of products were being extracted from the newly-developed primary industries of the Canadian Shield. Immigrants poured into Canada by the hundreds of thousands to provide labor in the growing industrial cities. Cars, radios, telephones, electrical appliances and other consumer goods were being bought, especially by middle-class Canadians, often using credit plans. Credit was also used to buy shares on the stock market, as the country became increasingly optimistic about its future. On both sides of the Canadian-American border, the Roaring Twenties were in full swing and there seemed no end in sight to the good times.

The Great Depression (1929-1939)

In 1929, Canadians looked with confidence toward the next decade and that confidence made the effects of the Great Depression of the 1930s even more bitter. The Depression was worldwide, but the effects were especially felt in Canada because about a third of the nation's gross national product was based on exports. The first signs of Canadian economic collapse appeared in October 1929 when wheat prices began to fall. In the same month the stock market collapsed, ruining thousands of shareholders, some of whom, on paper at least, had been millionaires. By 1930, the number of unemployed had doubled and the Conservatives, under R.B. Bennett, won the 1930 federal election decisively as voters hoped a change in government would bring a change in fortune. However by 1933, one in five Canadians was unemployed.

Western Canada was hardest hit in "The Dirty Thirties" because of its reliance on wheat. The Prairie provinces also suffered from a drought, which lead to crop failure, during these hard times. The combined results were devastating. In Saskatchewan, provincial income fell by 90% and two-thirds of the province's population had to go on welfare. In the 1930s, welfare, or "relief" as it was then known, became a burden for municipal and provincial governments across the country. By 1935, 10% of Canadians were on relief.

Bennett's government did not intervene to rebuild the economy. In the 1930s, politicians, economists and business leaders assumed that the Depression, like other downswings in the business cycle, would soon be followed by a recovery. Their experience, and most economic theory at the time, did not encourage them to consider major government spending as a way to stimulate a depressed economy.

One of the few federally financed programs created involved sending single unemployed men to camps where they did manual work in return for their keep and a small allowance. Working in isolated conditions, often at meaningless tasks, did nothing to satisfy the men and those in the British Columbia camps took action. In 1935 about 1 500 camp inmates decided to present their complaints directly to Bennett in Ottawa. They began the "On to Ottawa" trek by taking over freight trains heading east. By the time they reached Regina, there were about 2 000 protesters and the railway refused to provide further transportation. Representatives of the Trekkers met with Prime Minister Bennett in Ottawa, but the talks were inconclusive. When the delegation returned to Regina, Bennett decided to arrest the protest leaders. On July 1, there was a bloody riot in Regina involving the Trekkers, local police and the RCMP, which left one policeman dead and several dozen rioters, constables and local citizens injured. The Trek was over and the protesters returned home over the next few days; but Bennett's handling of the affair hurt his image. In the election of 1935, the people turned to King again, in the hope that this time he could deal with the Depression.

After 1935, economic conditions began to improve slowly, yet federal politicians did little to speed this recovery. The failure of the Liberals and the Conservatives to deal with the Depression led to the rise of reform parties. A socialist party, the Co-operative Commonwealth Federation (CCF) won seven seats in the 1935 election and elected members to several provincial legislatures. Other new parties appeared at the provincial level. In Alberta, the Social Credit Party promised $25 prosperity certificates to each resident; but the plan fell flat because the province did not have the power to issue currency. In Quebec, Maurice Duplessis established the Union Nationale and promised economic reform. But the Union Nationale, like the other parties, could not end the Depression, the effects of which faded only with the outbreak of World War II in 1939.

Canada in World War II (1939-1945)

While most Canadians focused attention on the effects of the Depression at home, events in Europe during the 1930s were moving the world closer to another global conflict. After taking over Austria and Czechoslovakia (present-day Czech and Slovak republics), Germany invaded Poland in 1939; Britain and France responded by declaring war. Following Britain's action, King quickly summoned Parliament. On September 10, one week after Britain had entered the conflict, the Canadian Parliament declared war on Germany and its allies.

Parliamentary support for the war declaration was based in part on King's known preference for a limited Canadian role and his assurance that there would be no conscription. Initially, only one Canadian division was sent to Britain. But by 1940, France had fallen and Britain faced invasion. King abandoned the concept of limited participation and decided to dispatch more troops. By late 1942, Canada had five divisions overseas. Canadian soldiers first saw action in December 1941 during the unsuccessful defence of Hong Kong. In August 1942, 5 000 Canadians took part in the disastrous raid on the French port of Dieppe, suffering casualties of 2 200 killed or captured. Despite these setbacks, the Canadian army played a major role in defeating enemy forces in Italy and took part in the Allied landings at Normandy in June of 1944. After taking key targets in France, Canadian soldiers moved northward to liberate Holland in 1945.

Canadians contributed to the war effort in other important ways. The Royal Canadian Navy grew from six destroyers and less than 2 000 personnel in 1939 to 471 warships, 99 688 men and 6 500 women by the war's end in 1945. The navy helped win the Battle of the Atlantic against German submarines by providing protection to the convoys carrying essential supplies from North America to Britain. Canadians also fought in the air as members of Britain's Royal Air Force, and, in increasing numbers throughout the war, in the Royal Canadian Air Force (RCAF). By 1945, there were 48 RCAF squadrons overseas. Other members of the RCAF were involved in the British Commonwealth Air Training Plan. Operating from Canadian airfields, this plan trained 131 000 aircrew from around the Commonwealth.

Canada also produced a wide variety of munitions, and provided important food supplies to the Allied war effort. Much of Canada's war production went directly to Britain, so did more than $3 billion in financial assistance.

While the contributions of Canadian men and women to the war effort were significant, the conflict raised disturbing issues at home. In reversing his earlier stand against conscription, Prime Minister King called for a national plebiscite on the issue in 1942. In all provinces except Quebec the electorate voted for conscription; relations between Quebec and the rest of Canada were strained, although not as severely as in World War I.

In a move that would later become controversial, Japanese Canadians were interned and their property was confiscated in the name of national security after the Japanese attack on Pearl Harbour in 1941. The interned included Japanese Canadians who had fought for Canada in World War I and more than 40 years later the Canadian government would officially apologize to the interned and their families.

By the war's end, more than a million Canadians had served in the armed forces and more than 42 000 had died. Canada's war effort enhanced its international image. At the same time, Canada had developed closer ties with the United States as the country's interests shifted away from Britain and Europe.

Postwar Canada: 1945-1968

In the years following World War II, Canadians enjoyed a standard of living that was in stark contrast to the Depression years. The economy had boomed during the war and the gross national product had doubled. The war had prompted development in new industries which continued to expand in peacetime. Consumer spending had increased dramatically during the war, and continued to rise with the postwar baby boom. This boom, along with large numbers of European immigrants, resulted in a 40% population increase between the war's end and 1958. In Canada's quickly growing cities and suburbs, home ownership was made easier by the National Housing Act, designed to make mortgages easier to obtain. This example of

government involvement in the economy was characteristic of the times. By 1945, unemployment insurance and family allowance legislation had been passed and other social welfare measures were being discussed.

Prime Minister King retired in 1948, and was followed as Liberal leader by Louis St. Laurent. One of St. Laurent's first achievements was the entry of Newfoundland into Confederation in 1949. In 1951, his government increased old age pensions and, in 1957, introduced a hospital insurance plan. St. Laurent negotiated with the United States to build the St. Lawrence Seaway, an impressive feat of engineering completed in 1959. In 1956, however, the government used closure (a limit on debate) to cut off the parliamentary debate concerning the building of the trans-Canada pipeline for oil and gas. In the election the following year, the Conservatives under John Diefenbaker won a minority victory. In 1958, Diefenbaker called another election to consolidate his position. This time the Conservatives swept the country, winning 208 of 265 seats.

Western agriculture found huge new markets when the government arranged wheat sales to China. In 1960, Diefenbaker's government introduced the Bill of Rights to protect the rights of all Canadians, and granted Native Canadians the right to vote in federal elections.

Despite continuing popular support for the British Commonwealth, the government of Canada signed the North American Air Defence Agreement (NORAD) with the United States in order to increase security during a time of international tension. But it could not deal with an economic recession that led to a devalued dollar and high unemployment. Also, the prime minister dealt Canada's fledging aircraft industry a serious blow when he cancelled production of the Canadian-made Avro Arrow fighter jet, and his refusal to allow nuclear warheads on the American missiles based in Canada earned him the emnity of the US government. In the election of 1962, his government was returned to power, but in a minority situation that forced another election in 1963. The 1963 election also resulted in a minority government situation, but this time, the Liberals, under Lester B. Pearson, were in power.

As prime minister, Pearson, a career diplomat, concentrated on domestic matters. His government relied on the support of the New Democratic Party (formerly the CCF) to hold a majority in the House of Commons and the partnership produced legislation that broadened social welfare by introducing Medicare, the Canada Pension Plan and the Canada Assistance Plan. Canadian nationalism was heightened with the adoption of the maple leaf flag in 1965, and in the same year another federal election produced a Liberal government one seat short of a clear majority. The opening of the world's fair, Expo in Montreal, in Canada's centennial year, 1967 marked a year of celebration across the country.

During the 1960s, Pearson was sensitive to growing nationalism in Quebec. His government established a Royal Commission on Bilingualism and Biculturalism in 1963, to demonstrate that Quebec's interests could be served by federalism, and he encouraged some of those closely associated with the Quiet Revolution to run for federal office. Quebec had been transformed from traditional to modern attitudes towards education, social reform and industrialization, a movement known as the Quiet Revolution, under premier Jean Lesage. The Quebec government was implementing the ideas of the Quiet Revolution, and championed provincial rights with its slogan *maîtres chez nous* (masters in our own house). This sentiment took centre stage during Centennial celebrations. Visiting French President Charles de Gaulle ended a Montreal speech with the cry *"Vive le Québec libre!"* ("Long live free Quebec") which set off a storm of diplomatic protest and delighted local nationalists. Despite growing nationalist sentiment, many Quebeckers, including Pierre Trudeau went to Ottawa. Trudeau was elected to the House of Commons in 1965, and was named minister of justice in 1967. In 1968, following Pearson's retirement, Trudeau became Liberal leader.

The Trudeau Years (1968-1984)

The Liberals won a majority victory in the election of 1968. Trudeau was an strong federalist, determined to show that Ottawa could promote the rights of French Canada. The Official Languages Act of 1969 recognized both English and French as official languages, and required federal institutions to provide services in both languages. Although the legislation was supported by all parties, it was not universally popular, even in Quebec.

In the October Crisis of 1970 separatist extremists belonging to the FLQ (Front de Libération du Québec) kidnapped British Trade Commissioner James Cross, and killed Quebec cabinet minister Pierre Laporte. Trudeau used the War Measures Act to apply emergency measures of arrest, detention and martial law. This move was generally accepted, but was criticized by advocates of civil rights, especially since the FLQ had little real support and the Act was in effect across the country.

In his early years in power, Trudeau attempted to concentrate decision-making in Ottawa, and his newly created Prime Minister's office led to western Canadian accusations of an eastern-dominated federal government. At the same time opposition parties charged that Trudeau was undermining both the power of the cabinet and of Parliament. The Liberals were almost defeated in the election of 1972, but retained office through a minority government that saw the New Democrats, under David Lewis, hold the balance of power. During this period the Foreign Investment Review Agency was set up (1973) to protect the Canadian economy against foreign domination; business critics claimed that it discouraged investment.

By 1974, the Liberals had regained a majority; their agenda was dominated by an economy battered by inflation. The government tried a variety of economic measures, including a three-year imposition of wage and price controls under the Anti-Inflation Act of 1975. Although the controls may have had some effect, world conditions, especially the international oil crisis, kept inflation high.

In 1976, the separatist Parti Québecois under René Lévesque defeated the provincial Liberals, led by Robert Bourassa in the Quebec election. This election fueled public uncertainty over the future of Quebec (and Canada), while continuing inflation and western alienation also undermined Liberal support. In the 1979 election, the Liberals lost, and Conservative leader Joe Clark took office as head of a minority government. Clark's government was short-lived as it suffered defeat in the House of Commons that same year.

The Liberals won the election of 1980, and Trudeau, lured out of planned retirement by the sudden election, embarked on an eventful term of office. He and members of his government actively campaigned on the victorious NO side in the 1980 Quebec referendum on sovereignty association. The Liberals brought in the National Energy Program in the same year, again attempting to regulate ownership and control in part of the economy, and again succeeding in alienating foreign and local business interests. Resistance to the NEP, particularly in the west, was deep and persistent.

Then, after a long (18 months) and difficult campaign waged in Parliament, at federal-provincial meetings and in the media, Trudeau succeeded in getting an agreement on patriating the Canadian constitution amongst all provinces except Quebec. Patriation officially took place when Queen Elizabeth II proclaimed the new Constitution Act in Ottawa on April 17, 1982. The Charter of Rights and Freedoms is also proclaimed, entrenching bilingualism in the federal jurisdiction and providing for minority language education rights across Canada.

By 1984 the country was mired in a recession and in no mood for the international interest Trudeau was pursuing; he retired and John Turner became Liberal leader and prime minister for a brief period. The Liberal government was at the end of its mandate and parliament was dissolved. After nearly 16 years of Liberal government, the voters were eager for a change.

Mulroney in Power (1984-1993)

In the 1984 general election, the Conservatives, under Brian Mulroney, won a decisive victory, taking 211 of 282 seats in the House of Commons, including 58 seats in Quebec, a former Liberal stronghold. In contrast to the previous government, the Conservatives sought to strengthen ties with the United States and took steps to attract more foreign investment to Canada. The recession of the early 80s was over and business and government were both ready to expand.

One of the goals of the Mulroney government was to amend the Constitution Act of 1982 to obtain the support of Quebec.

The prime minister and 10 provincial premiers reached an agreement, which became known as the Meech Lake Accord, on such an amendment in 1987; the agreement was to be taken to provincial legislatures and to parliament for approval by June 23, 1990. Also in 1987, the government negotiated a Canada-U.S. free trade agreement (FTA) which provided for the elimination of all cross-border tariffs over 10 years. But the deal was rejected by both opposition parties and Liberal leader John Turner announced that the Liberal-dominated senate would not approve free trade unless the Conservatives obtained public support in a general election. Mulroney called an election for November 1988. The campaign that followed was fractious; emotions ran high and there were wide fluctuations in public opinion. Anti-FTA sentiment was split between the opposition parties and the Conservatives won a second majority government. The FTA was approved in December and took effect January 1, 1989.

As the deadline for ratification of the Meech Lake Accord approached, its confirmation became increasingly uncertain. Provincial governments had changed in the interim and both Manitoba and Newfoundland indicated that they had reservations about the agreement. Despite a last-minute first ministers' conference and a great deal of political pressure, the Manitoba legislature failed to ratify the accord and Newfoundland withdrew its consent; the deal lapsed on June 23, 1990. The following years were marked by numerous federal-provincial conferences, a variety of proposals and pressure from Quebec to include recognition of its distinct society. In August 1992 a new federal-provincial agreement was reached (the Charlottetown Accord) in time to be considered in a referendum Quebec premier Robert Bourassa had pledged to hold on the future of Quebec. The other provinces also took part in a national referendum on the terms of the accord, which included not only recognition of Quebec as a distinct society, but also provisions to transfer mining, forestry, telecommunications and many other jurisdictions to the provinces. Canadians from all walks of life grappled with the issues raised by the terms of the Charlottetown Accord and the question dominated national media, (aside from the sports pages which were distracted by the prospect of a Canadian team, the Toronto Blue Jays, winning the

1992 world series). The referendum was held on October 26, 1992 and the deal was rejected by 54.8% of the voters.

The Conservatives' second term of office was also marked by the introduction of the Goods and Services Tax (GST), a tax designed to replace the manufacturers' tax and spread the tax burden more evenly across the economy. This tax was deeply unpopular and the Liberal-appointed members of the senate vowed to block its passage in the upper chamber. Mulroney responded by temporarily increasing the number of senators to 112, with new appointees who would support the measure. The tax was the subject of heated debate and much protest across the country as Canadians transferred their frustration over the endless constitutional discussion, the now faltering economy and disappointment over the results of FTA to the government.

The GST took effect on January 1, 1991 and the Conservative government continued to pursue wider trade agreements by joining the U.S. and Mexico in negotiations for a North American Free Trade Agreement that would supersede the FTA. Amid much controversy, the deal was signed in December and the government's popularity continued to plumb the depths of the popularity polls. In February, Mulroney announced his decision to step aside as leader; Kim Campbell became the new leader of the Conservatives and the country's first female prime minister after a June leadership convention. As the Conservative mandate drew to a close, Campbell attempted to present herself as a brand-new prime minister at the head of a brand-new government. In the election in October 1993, Canadian voters made it clear they did not accept this stance: the Liberals under Jean Chrétien won a lopsided victory in an election that changed the political map of the country. The new government took office with a record number of rookie MPs, the Loyal Opposition was made up of members of the separatist Bloc Québécois, with the Reform Party from western Canada nearly matching the BQ's number of seats. The Conservatives elected only 2 members and the NDP also fared poorly at the hands of an electorate.

A Chronology of Events in Canada

Circa 1000 **Leif Ericsson** and other **Vikings** visit Labrador and Newfoundland.

1497 **John Cabot** (Giovanni Caboto) claims Cape Breton Island (or possibly Newfoundland or Labrador) for Henry VII of England (June 24).

1498 **Cabot** makes his second voyage to North America.

1534 **Jacques Cartier** visits the Strait of Belle Isle (Newfoundland), and charts the Gulf of St Lawrence (landing in Gaspé July 14).

1535 **Cartier** sails up the St Lawrence River to **Quebec** and **Montreal**.

1541 Cartier and the Sieur de Roberval found Charlesbourg-Royal, the **first French settlement** in America.

1577 **Martin Frobisher** of England makes the first of his three attempts to find a north-west passage, sailing as far as Hudson Strait.

1600 King Henry IV of France grants a **fur-trading monopoly** in the Gulf of St Lawrence to a group of French merchants.

1605 **Samuel de Champlain** and the Sieur de Monts found Port Royal (Annapolis, NS).

1608 **Champlain** founds Quebec.

1609 Champlain supports the Algonquins against the Iroquois at Lake Champlain.

1610 **Étienne Brûlé** goes to live among the Huron and eventually becomes the first European to see Lakes Ontario, Huron and Superior. **Henry Hudson** explores Hudson Bay.

1617 Louis Hébert, the **first habitant (farmer),** arrives in Quebec.

1625 Jesuits arrive in Quèbec to begin missionary work among the Indians.

1627 The **Company of One Hundred Associates** is founded (Apr. 29) to establish a French empire in North America.

1629 **David Kirke** captures Quebec for Britain (July 19).

1632 The **Treaty of Saint-Germain-en-Laye** returns Quebec to France.

1634–40 The **Huron nation** is reduced by half from European diseases (smallpox epidemic, 1639).

1637 **Kirke** is named first governor of Newfoundland.

1642 **Montreal** is founded (May 18) by the Sieur **de Maisonneuve**.

1649 The Jesuit Father Jean **de Brébeuf** is martyred by the **Iroquois** at St-Ignace (Mar. 16). The Iroquois disperse the Huron nation (1648–49).

1659 François **de Laval,** later to become Canada's first bishop, arrives in Quebec (June).

1660 Adam **Dollard des Ormeaux** makes his last stand against the Iroquois at Long Sault (May). The small party of French fights so well that the Iroquois decide not to attack Montreal.

1663 Quebec becomes a **royal province.**

1665 The Carignan-Salières regiment is sent from France to Quebec to deal with the Iroquois. Jean **Talon** becomes Quebec's intendant.

1667 Canada's **first census** counts 3,215 non-native inhabitants in 668 families.

1670 The **Hudson's Bay Company** is formed and granted trade rights over all territory draining into Hudson Bay (May 2).

1672 Count **Frontenac** becomes Governor of Quebec.

1673 **Marquette** and **Jolliet** explore the Mississippi to its junction with the Arkansas.

1674 **Laval** becomes first Bishop of Quebec.

1678–79 **Dulhut** explores the headwaters of the Mississippi.

1682 **La Salle** explores the Mississippi to its mouth.

1686 **De Troyes** and **D'Iberville** capture the English posts of Moose Fort (June 20), Rupert House (July 3) and Fort Albany (July 26) on James Bay.

1689 The Iroquois kill many French settlers at Lachine.

1690 **Sir William Phips captures Port Royal** (May 11). Frontenac repels Phips's attack on Quebec (Oct.).

1697 The **Treaty of Ryswick** restores the status quo in the struggle between England and France. All captured territory is returned.

1701 The **War of the Spanish Succession** begins in Europe; the conflict spreads to North America the following year.

1710 Francis Nicholson captures Port Royal for England.

1713 The **Treaty of Utrecht** confirms British possession of Hudson Bay, Newfoundland and Acadia (except Cape Breton Island). France starts building Fort **Louisbourg.**

1739 **La Vérendrye** expedition explores Lake Winnipeg.

1740 The **War of the Austrian Succession** pits Britain against France; the European conflict spreads to North America (**King George's War**) in 1744.

1745 Massachusetts Governor William Shirley takes the French fortress of **Louisbourg.**

1748 Louisbourg is returned to France by the **Treaty of Aix-la-Chapelle.**

1749 Britain founds **Halifax** to counter the French presence at Louisbourg.

1752 Canada's **first newspaper,** the Halifax *Gazette,* appears (Mar. 25).

1753 George **Washington**'s military expedition to the Monogahela is defeated by the French.

1754 Beginning of **French and Indian War** in America. Although war is not officially declared for another two years, this marks the final phase in the struggle between France and Britain in North America.

1755 Britain expels the **Acadians** from Nova Scotia, scattering them throughout her other North American colonies.

1756 Beginning of the **Seven Years' War** in Europe pits Britain against France. The Marquis **de Montcalm** assumes command of French troops in North America.

1758 The British under Generals Amherst and Wolfe take Louisbourg.

1759 Wolfe takes Quebec, defeating Montcalm on the Plains of Abraham (Sept. 13). Both generals are killed.

1760 General **James Murray** is appointed military governor of Quebec; he becomes civil governor in **1764**.

1763 France cedes its North American possessions to Britain by the **Treaty of Paris**. A Royal Proclamation imposes British institutions on Quebec (Oct.). This proclamation also serves as the cornerstone for relations between Canadian aboriginal peoples and the Canadian government, preserving land for their use and giving the government exclusive right to negotiate treaties.

1768 Guy Carleton succeeds Murray as governor of Quebec.

1769 Frances Brooke publishes *The History of Emily Montague*, a novel with descriptions of geography, climate and social culture in the New World.

1774 The **Quebec Act** provides for British criminal law but restores French civil law and guarantees religious freedom for Roman Catholic colonists.

1775 Americans under Montgomery capture Montreal (Nov.) and attack Quebec (Dec. 31).

1776 Under Carleton, Quebec withstands American siege until the appearance of a British fleet (May 6).

1778 Captain **James Cook** anchors in Nootka Sound, Vancouver Island (Mar. 29–Apr. 26).

1783 The American Revolutionary War ends; the border between Canada and the US is accepted between the Atlantic Ocean and Lake of the Woods.

1784 United Empire Loyalists arrive in Canada. The province of **New Brunswick** is created. The **North West Company** is formed.

1789 Alexander Mackenzie journeys to the Beaufort Sea, following what would later be named the Mackenzie River.

1791 Constitutional Act divides Quebec into Upper and Lower Canada.

1792 George Vancouver begins his explorations of the Pacific coast.

1793 Alexander **Mackenzie reaches** the **Pacific**.

1794 Jay's Treaty (Nov. 19) between the US and Britain promises British evacuation of the Ohio Valley forts. The treaty's appointment of officials to settle boundary disputes marks the beginning of international arbitration through its provisions for boundary settlements.

1797 David Thompson joins the North West Company as a surveyor and mapmaker.

1806 *Le Canadien*, Quebec nationalist newspaper, is founded.

1808 Simon Fraser, a North West Company employee, travels the river named after him to the Pacific.

1811 David Thompson charts the Columbia River to the Pacific coast.

1812 The US declares war on Britain (June 18), beginning the **War of 1812**. Americans under General William Hull invade Canada from Detroit (July 11). The Red River settlement is begun in Canada's northwest (Aug.–Oct.). Battle of Queenston Heights (Oct. 13): Canadian victory. British **General Isaac Brock** is killed in this battle.

1813 Americans burn York (Apr. 27). Battle of Stoney Creek (June 5): Canadian victory. Battle of Beaver Dams (June 23): Canadian victory; **Laura Secord**, driving a cow, passes American sentries and walks 32 km through dense bush to warn of American attack. Battle of Put-in-Bay, Lake Erie (Sept. 10): American victory. Battle of Moraviantown (Oct. 5): American victory; the Indian Chief **Tecumseh** is killed. Battle of Chateauguay (Oct. 25): Canadian victory. Battle of Crysler's Farm (Nov. 11): Canadian victory.

1814 Battle of Chippewa (July 5): American victory. Battle of Lundy's Lane (July 25): Canadian victory. A British naval force takes Washington (Aug. 24). Battle of Lake Champlain (Sept. 6–11): American victory. The **Treaty of Ghent** ends the War of 1812 (Dec. 24).

1816 Agents of the North West Company kill Robert Semple, governor of the Hudson's Bay Company's Red River colony, and 20 others at White Oaks (June 19).

1817 The **Rush-Bagot** agreement limits the number of battleships on the Great Lakes.

1818   The **49th parallel** is accepted as **Canada's border** with the US from Lake of the Woods to the Rocky Mountains.

1821   The Hudson's Bay Company and the North West Company are amalgamated as the HBC.

1829   The **Lachine** and **Welland Canals** are completed.

1835   **William Lyon Mackenzie** becomes the first mayor of Toronto.

1836   Opening of Canada's **first railway line,** from St. Johns, Que., to La Prairie, Que.

1837   Unsuccessful **rebellions** in Upper and Lower Canada are led by Mackenzie and Louis-Joseph Papineau.

1839   **Lord Durham's Report** recommends union of Upper and Lower Canada and the establishment of responsible government.

1841   The **Act of Union** unites Upper and Lower Canada.

1842   The Ashburton-Webster Treaty settles the Maine-New Brunswick border dispute.

1843   **Fort Victoria** is built to bolster Britain's claim to Vancouver Island.

1846   Great Britain ends a preferential trading policy with the British North American colonies and enters into a **limited free trade agreement** with the United States.

1848   **Responsible government** is achieved in the Canadas and in the Maritimes, thanks to the work of **Robert Baldwin** and **Joseph Howe**.

1849   The boundary of the 49th parallel is extended to the Pacific Ocean. Canada begins its policy of **official bilingualism.** All bills of the United Canada Parliament, now Quebec and Ontario, are given assent in both English and French.

1851   Britain transfers control of the colonial postal system to Canada.

1854   The **Reciprocity Treaty** between Canada and the U.S. is signed (June 6).

1857   **Ottawa** is named **Canada's capital** by Queen Victoria.

1860   Cornerstone of the **Parliament buildings** is laid (Sept. 1).

1861   The **Grand Trunk Railway** through the length of the Province of Canada and as far as the City of Halifax is completed.

1864   The **Charlottetown Conference** (Sept. 1–9) takes the first steps toward **Confederation.** The **Quebec Conference** (Oct. 10–27) sets out the basis for union.

1866   The **London Conference** (Dec. 4) passes resolutions which are redrafted to become the **British North America Act.** First raid into Canada by the **Fenians,** a radical Irish-American, anti-British group, takes place (June 2). The American government allows the **Reciprocity Treaty of 1854** to lapse.

1867   **Confederation.** Britain's North American colonies are united by means of the **BNA Act** to become the **Dominion of Canada** (July 1). **Sir John A. Macdonald** is Canada's first prime minister. The BNA Act, now the **Constitution Act, 1867,** confirms the practice of **official bilingualism,** guaranteeing the use of French and English in the debates of the House of Commons and in the Senate, in federal courts and in publications of federal statutes. The provincial legislature, statutes and courts of Quebec are also made bilingual.

1868   Confederationist **Thomas D'Arcy McGee** is **assassinated** by a Fenian in Canada's first political assassination.

1869   Canada purchases Rupert's Land from the Hudson's Bay Company for £300,000.

1870   **Louis Riel** leads the Métis in resisting Canadian authority in Canada's northwest. The Métis negotiate with the Canadian government over the right to vote, land laws, the official use of both French and English and the provision of Roman Catholic and Protestant schools. The Manitoba Act creates the province of **Manitoba.**

1871   **British Columbia** joins Confederation upon the promise from Ottawa to build a **transcontinental railway.**

1872   Macdonald's Conservatives win federal re-election.

1873   **Prince Edward Island** joins Confederation. A period of economic depression begins. The North-West Mounted Police are formed. **Alexander Mackenzie** becomes Canada's second prime minister after **Macdonald resigns** over the **Pacific Scandal.**

1874   **Liberals** win federal election.

1875   The **Supreme Court of Canada** is established.

1876 The **Intercolonial Railway** linking central Canada and the Maritimes is completed (July 1). The **Indian Act of 1876** defines special status for aboriginal people living on land reserves and sets out land regulations. Status Indians have no vote in Canadian elections and are exempted from taxation.

1878 Conservatives under Macdonald win federal election.

1879 Macdonald introduces **protective tariffs** as part of his **National Policy**.

1880 **Emily Stowe** receives her medical licence after practising medicine in Toronto since her graduation from a New York medical school in 1867.

1881 The **Canadian Pacific Railway** is incorporated.

1884 **Riel returns** to Canada.

1885 Métis and the NWMP clash at Duck Lake (Mar. 26). The Métis are defeated at Batoche (May 9–12). The **last spike of the transcontinental railway** is driven at Craigellachie in Eagle Pass, BC, by Donald Smith (Nov. 7). Louis **Riel** is **hanged** in Regina (Nov. 16).

1887 Conservatives win federal election. Liberals choose **Wilfrid Laurier** as leader. The **first provincial premiers' conference** takes place in Quebec City.

1889 The **Dominion Women's Enfranchisement Association** is created to campaign for female voting rights in Canada.

1890 Manitoba Liberals under Thomas Greenway halt public funding of Catholic schools in Manitoba (Mar.).

1891 Conservatives win federal election. **Sir John A. Macdonald dies**. **Sir John Abbott** takes office as prime minister (June 16).

1892 Abbott resigns (Nov. 24). **Sir John Thompson** becomes prime minister (Dec. 5). He establishes the **Canadian Criminal Code**.

1894 Thompson dies (Dec. 12). **Sir Mackenzie Bowell** is asked by the governor general, the Earl of Aberdeen, to form the fourth Conservative government since 1891.

1896 The economic depression ends. Bowell resigns, calling his cabinet a "nest of traitors" (April 27). **Sir Charles Tupper** leads an interim government until the Liberals

under Laurier win federal election on **Manitoba Schools Question** (June 23). Canada's minister of the interior, **Clifford Sifton,** develops an immigration plan that will bring farmers from central and eastern Europe to settle on the Prairies. Gold is discovered in the Klondike (Aug. 16).

1897 **Gold Rush** begins in the Klondike. **Clara Brett Martin** is the first woman admitted to the bar of Ontario.

1898 **Yukon** becomes a separate entity from the Northwest Territories. **Kit Coleman**, the first female Canadian war correspondent, covers the Spanish-American War for a Toronto newspaper.

1899 The first **Canadian troops** ever sent overseas are dispatched to the **Boer War** (Oct. 30).

1901 Marconi receives the **first transatlantic radio message** at St. John's, Newfoundland.

1903 Canada loses the **Alaska Boundary Dispute** when British tribunal representative Lord Alverstone sides with the US (Oct. 20). In northern Ontario, Fred LaRose throws hammer at what he thinks are fox's eyes and hits world's richest silver vein.

1904 Liberals win federal election.

1905 The provinces of **Alberta** and **Saskatchewan** are formed.

1907 The **National Council of Women** calls for "equal pay for equal work."

1908 Liberals win federal election.

1909 The Department of External Affairs is formed. John McCurdy's Silver Dart is first heavier-than-air machine to achieve powered flight in Canada at Baddeck, NS. University of Toronto wins **first Grey Cup** football match.

1910 Laurier creates a Canadian navy via the Naval Service Bill.

1911 **Robert Borden** and the Conservatives win federal election, defeating Laurier on the Reciprocity issue.

1914 CP ship *Empress of Ireland* sinks in the St Lawrence in 14 minutes after being rammed in fog, with the loss of 1,014 lives (May 29). **Canada is automatically at war** with Germany when Britain declares war (Aug. 4). The first Canadian troops leave for England (Oct. 3). Parliament passes the **War**

Measures Act, allowing suspension of civil rights during periods of emergency. European immigration to Canada increases. Over one million settlers come between 1911 and 1913, bringing total immigration to three million since 1891.

1915 Canadians face German gas attack at **Ypres,** Belgium (Apr. 22). John McCrae writes "In Flanders Fields."

1916 **Nellie McClung** succeeds in persuading the Manitoba government to grant women the right to vote and to hold office (Jan.). The Parliament buildings are destroyed by fire (Feb. 3). Canadian troops fight in the Battle of the **Somme** (July to Nov.); 24,713 Canadians and Newfoundlanders are killed. The unreliable, Canadian-made Ross rifle is withdrawn from war service (Aug.). **Emily Gowan Murphy** is the first woman magistrate appointed within the British Empire.

1917 **Income tax** is **introduced** as a "temporary wartime measure." Prime Minister Sir Robert Borden sits as a member of the Imperial War Cabinet (Feb. 23), giving Canada a voice in war policy. The Military Service Bill is introduced (June 11), leading to the **Conscription Crisis** between Quebec and English Canada. Unionist government under Borden wins federal election, in which **women vote** for the first time. **Louise McKinney** is elected to the Alberta legislature, the first woman in the British Commonwealth to hold such office. Canadians capture **Vimy Ridge,** France (Apr. 9–12). Canadians take **Passchendaele,** Belgium, (Nov. 7) in one of the war's worst battles; of the 20,000 Canadian troops sent into the two-week battle, 15,654 are killed or wounded. Explosion of a munitions ship in **Halifax harbour** wipes out two square miles (5.2 sq km) of Halifax, killing almost 2,000 and injuring 9,000 (Dec. 6).

1918 Canadians break through German trenches at Amiens (Aug. 8), "the black day of the German army." The period from this date until the end of the war becomes known as "Canada's Hundred Days." Armistice ends war (Nov. 11).

1919 Alcock and Brown take off from St. John's, Nfld, (June 14) on the first successful flight across the Atlantic to Cliften, Ireland. A **general strike paralyzes Winnipeg** (May–June), where an armed charge by the RCMP kills one person and injures 30 (June 21).

1920 **Canada joins** the **League of Nations** at its inception (Jan. 10). The flow of emigrants from the British Isles and Europe resumes, many going to urban centres. Federal legislation makes **women eligible** to sit in the **House of Commons.** The Northwest Mounted Police became the Royal Canadian Mounted Police (RCMP).

1921 Liberals under **Mackenzie King** defeat Conservatives under Arthur Meighen in federal election; the Progressive Party comes in second. **Agnes Macphail** becomes the first woman elected to Parliament. The world's fastest fishing schooner, the *Bluenose,* is launched at Lunenburg, NS. (Mar. 26). **Postwar economic depression** puts 300,000 men and women out of work—more than 15% of the work force.

1922 Canada declines to rally to Britain's side during the Chanak Crisis. Sir Frederick **Banting,** Dr Charles **Best,** Dr J.J.R. MacLeod and J.B. Collip share Nobel Prize for the **discovery of insulin.**

1923 The Canadian Northern and Canadian Transcontinental are merged to form the **Canadian National Railways.** Canada signs the Halibut Treaty with the US without a corroborating British signature. Mackenzie King leads opposition to a common imperial policy ("one voice for the empire") at an Imperial Conference in London.

1924 The Saskatchewan Wheat Pool begins operations.

1925 Although Conservatives win more seats in federal election, Mackenzie King's Liberals remain in power with the support of the Progressives.

1926 King's Liberals win federal election. An Imperial Conference defines British dominions as autonomous (Balfour Report).

1927 Britain's Privy Council awards Labrador to Newfoundland instead of to Quebec (Mar. 1). The Diamond Jubilee of Confederation (July 1) is marked by Canada's first coast-to-coast radio network broadcast. King's government, with the support of the Progressive Party, passes Canada's first **Old Age Pension Act**.

1928 The Supreme Court of Canada rules that, according to the British North America Act, women are not "persons" who could hold public office. This decision is reversed by British Privy Council in 1929.

1929   The **Great Depression** begins.

1930   **Cairine Wilson** is appointed Canada's first woman senator (Feb. 20). The Canadian Federation of Business and Professional Women's Clubs is organized. Conservatives under **R.B. Bennett** win federal election (Aug. 7).

1931   The **Statute of Westminster** (Dec. 11) grants Canada full legislative authority domestically and in external affairs. The Governor General becomes a representative of the Crown.

1932   Ottawa Agreements provide for preferential trade between Canada and other Commonwealth nations. The **Co-operative Commonwealth Federation (CCF)** is founded at Calgary.

1933   One in five Canadians is unemployed.

1934   The Bank of Canada is formed. The **Dionne quintuplets** are born in Callander, Ont.

1935   Ten percent of Canadians rely on welfare or "relief." The **On to Ottawa Trek** by young men from government work camps ends in a riot at Regina (July 1). Liberals under Mackenzie King win federal election. The CCF win seven seats. Social Credit claims 17. **William Aberhart** leads Social Credit into office in Alberta. The Canadian Wheat Board is created.

1936   Union Nationale under **Maurice Duplessis** wins its first election in Quebec.

1937   The **Rowell-Sirois Commission** is appointed to investigate the financial relationship between the federal government and the provinces. First regular flight of **Trans Canada Air Lines** (Sept. 1).

1938   Franklin D. Roosevelt becomes first US President in office to visit Canada, meeting Mackenzie King at Kingston.

1939   **Canada declares war** on Germany (Sept. 10) after remaining neutral for a week following the British declaration. Quebec Premier Maurice Duplessis, who opposed Quebec participation in the war, is defeated by the Liberals on that issue (Oct. 26).

1940   **Unemployment insurance** is **introduced**. Liberals win federal election (Mar. 26). The Permanent Joint Board of Defence is formed between Canada and the US. **Thérèse Casgrain** wins women in Quebec the right to vote and to hold provincial office.

1941   Canadians are captured when Hong Kong falls to Japanese (Dec. 25); about 500 of the POWs subsequently die in Japanese camps. Immigration has changed Canadian demographic structure. Canadians of British ancestry now make up 49.7% of the population, of French descent 30.3% and of other ethnic backgrounds 20%.

1942   In Canada's first European war action, many Canadians are captured or killed in the disastrous **Dieppe** raid (Aug. 19). Canadians of Japanese descent are moved inland from the coast of British Columbia as "security risks"; their property is confiscated. A national plebiscite releases Mackenzie King from his pledge of no conscription but reveals deep divisions between Quebec and the rest of Canada.

1943   Canadians participate in the invasion of Sicily (July 10). Canadians win the Battle of Ortona (Dec. 20–28). **Ernest C. Manning** wins first of nine successive elections for the Social Credit in Alberta.

1944   Canadian troops push further inland than any other Allied unit on D-Day (June 6). Canadian forces fight as a separate army (July 23). Saskatchewan elects Tommy Douglas's CCF, the first socialist government in North America. Maurice Duplessis regains office for the Union Nationale in Quebec.

1945   War in Europe ends (May 5). One million Canadians fought in WW II; 42,042 were killed. Canadians killed while fighting for other Allied forces numbered 4,500. Liberals win federal election (June 11). First **family allowance payments** are **made** (June 20). Canada joins the **United Nations** (June 26). Igor Gouzenko defects from the Soviet Embassy in Ottawa (Sept. 5) and reveals the existence in Canada of a Soviet spy network. Canada's first nuclear reactor begins operations at Chalk River, Ont.

1947   Imperial Oil discovers the **Leduc oil field** (Feb. 13).

1948   **Louis St. Laurent** succeeds Mackenzie King as prime minister (Nov. 15).

1949   Under Premier **Joey Smallwood, Newfoundland** becomes Canada's 10th province (Mar. 31). Canada joins NATO. Canadian appeals to Britain's Judicial Committee of the Privy Council are abolished: Canada's Supreme Court becomes final court of appeal. Liberals under St Laurent defeat Conservatives under George Drew in federal election (June 3).

1950 The Korean War begins (June 25); Canadian troops participate in the conflict as part of a United Nations force.

1951 The midcentury census reports Canada's population as 14,009,429. **Postwar immigration** to Canada exceeds 100,000 annually during the 1950s, primarily moving from central and eastern Europe to hold manufacturing jobs in urban centres. The Massey Royal Commission reports that Canadian cultural life is dominated by American influences. Revisions to the **Indian Act**, beginning in 1951, limit its coverage of aboriginal people. Indian women married to non-Indian men are excluded from the act. This provision was removed in 1985 after much protest of discrimination. **Charlotte Whitton** the first woman to be elected mayor of a major Canadian city, is elected in Ottawa.

1952 Vincent Massey becomes the first native-born Governor General of Canada. Canada's **first television** stations begin broadcasting in Montreal (Sept. 6) and Toronto (Sept. 8). **W.A.C. Bennett** begins **Social Credit's** administration in British Columbia.

1953 Canada's National Library is established in Ottawa (Jan. 1). The Stratford Festival opens (July 13). The **Korean War ends** (July 27); total Canadian casualties are 314 killed and 1 211 wounded. Liberals under St Laurent defeat Conservatives under Drew in federal election (Aug. 10).

1954 An economic slump interrupts the postwar boom. Canada's **first subway** opens in Toronto (Mar. 30). Roger Bannister and John Landy run the "miracle mile" at the British Empire Games in Vancouver (Aug.), the first to run a mile in less than four-minutes. Sixteen-year-old Marilyn Bell becomes the first person to swim Lake Ontario (Sept. 9). **Hurricane Hazel** hits Toronto, killing 83 people (Oct. 15). The Geneva Conference on the Far East invites Canada to join India and Poland in **supervising peace in Indochina**. This peacekeeping commitment continues for nearly 20 years to 1973.

1955 The Canadian Labour Congress is formed. The suspension of Montreal Canadiens' hockey star Maurice (Rocket) Richard leads to rioting in Montreal (Mar. 17).

1956 The Liberals use closure to limit the **Pipeline Debate** (May 8–June 6), a manoeuvre that contributes to their electoral defeat the following year.

1957 Conservatives under **John Diefenbaker** win federal election (June 10) and form minority government. Ellen Fairclough becomes the first woman federal cabinet minister. The Canada Council is created to help foster Canadian cultural life. **Lester B. Pearson wins Nobel Prize** (Oct. 12) for his role in resolving the Suez Crisis. Canadian supply and services troops are sent to work with a multinational UN force around the **Gulf of Aqaba**. They stay until 1967 and return there in 1973.

1958 Conservatives under Diefenbaker win 208 seats in federal election (Mar. 31). Coal mine disaster at Springhill, NS, results in death of 74 miners.

1959 The **Avro Arrow** project is terminated, with a loss of almost 14,000 jobs (Feb. 20). The **St. Lawrence Seaway** is **opened** (June 26).

1960 Liberals under **Jean Lesage** win provincial election in Quebec (June 22), inaugurating the **Quiet Revolution. A Canadian Bill of Rights** is approved by Parliament. Native people get the right to vote in federal elections. During the 1960s French is recognized as a language of instruction in elementary and secondary schools in New Brunswick, Ontario and Manitoba. It is recognized subsequently in other provincial jurisdictions.

1961 The **New Democratic Party** replaces the CCF.

1962 Conservatives are reduced to minority status in federal election (June 18). Social Credit wins 30 seats and NDP take 19 to control the balance of power in the House of Commons. The Saskatchewan NDP introduces the first Canadian **Medicare** plan (July 1), and is opposed by a doctors' strike. **Trans-Canada Highway** officially opens (Sept. 3). Canadian-made satellite *Alouette* is launched (Sept. 29), making Canada the third nation in space. Canada's last execution, the double hanging of Ronald Turpin and Arthur Lucas, takes place (Dec. 11), at the Don Jail in Toronto.

1963 Liberals under Pearson win federal election (Apr. 8), and form a minority government. The Quebec separatist group **Front de Libération du Québec (FLQ)** sets off a series of bombs in Montreal (Apr.–May). A TCA flight crashes in Quebec, killing all 118 people aboard (Nov. 29). The **Royal Commission on Bilingualism and Biculturalism** begins its work.

1964 Canadians get social insurance cards (Apr.). Northern Dancer becomes the first Canadian horse to win the Kentucky Derby (May 2). Canada ends difficult peacekeeping duties in the Congo (Zaïre) after four years of service with heavy casualties. Canadian troops join UN forces in Cyprus, a posting which continues until 1993.

1965 Canada gets a new flag (Feb. 15). The **Autopact** between Canada and the US is signed. Canadian Roman Catholic Churches begin to celebrate mass in English (Mar. 7). Liberals win federal election (Nov. 8) to continue as a minority government. Failure of an Ontario Hydro relay device at Queenston plunges eastern North America into a power blackout (Nov. 9).

1966 The Munsinger Affair becomes Canada's first major parliamentary sex scandal (Mar. 4). The **Canada Pension Plan** is established. The CBC begins colour television broadcasting (Oct. 1).

1967 The Canadian army, navy and air forces are **unified** to become the Canadian **Armed Forces** (Apr. 25). Montreal hosts a world's fair, **Expo 67** (opened Apr. 27). Canada celebrates its **Centennial** (July 1). French President Charles **de Gaulle** delivers his "Vive Québec Libre" speech in Montreal (July 24). The federal Department of Manpower and Immigration establishes the **"points system"** for immigrants. Patterns shift in the 1960s from European to Third World immigration as humanitarian objectives and family reunification policies increase multicultural immigration.

1968 **Pierre Elliott Trudeau** succeeds Pearson as Prime Minister (Apr. 6), and leads Liberals to majority in federal election (June 25). A Royal Commission on the Status of Women is appointed. Canadian divorce law is reformed.

1969 Saturday postal deliveries end. Abortion law is liberalized (May). English and French become **official languages** of federal administration (July 9). New Brunswick declares official bilingualism. The breathalizer comes into use as a test for alcohol-impaired drivers (Dec. 1).

1970 The FLQ kidnaps British trade commissioner James Cross (Oct. 5), precipitating the **October Crisis**. Quebec labour and immigration minister Pierre Laporte is kidnapped (Oct. 10), and found murdered (Oct. 17). The federal government invokes the **War Measures Act** (Oct. 16), leading to the arrest of 465 people.

1971 A policy of **multiculturalism** is adopted by the federal government. Canadian Gerhard Herzberg wins the Nobel Prize in chemistry for his studies of chemical reactions that help produce smog.

1972 Canada defeats the USSR in the first hockey series between the Soviets and Canadian professionals (Aug.–Sept.). Liberals win federal election with 109 seats to the Conservatives 107, with the NDP holding the balance of power at 31 (Oct. 30).

1973 The House of Commons passes a resolution (Jan. 5) criticizing US bombing of North Vietnam. The separatist Parti Québécois becomes the official Opposition in Quebec. Canadian troops are sent to the Middle East and serve with the United Nations Emergency Task Force there until 1979. Canada continues to send observers for the UN to the Golan Heights and to provide truce supervision personnel in Israel, Egypt, Lebanon, Jordan and Syria.

1974 Liberals under Trudeau win federal election and form majority government (July 8). **Pauline McGibbon** becomes the first female lieutenant-governor (Ont.) in the British Commonwealth.

1975 The **CN Tower**, the world's tallest free-standing structure at 553.339 metres, is completed in Toronto (Apr. 2). Federal government announces (July 18) its intention to screen foreign investment in Canada, via the Foreign Investment Review Agency (FIRA). Television cameras are allowed inside the House of Commons for the first time. Federal government imposes **wage and price controls** in an effort to fight inflation (Oct. 14). **Grace Hartman** is elected president of the Canadian Union of Public Employees.

1976 Canada announces 200-nautical-mile coastal fishing zone (June 4). **Death penalty**

is **abolished** in a free vote (130–124) in Parliament (July 14). Montreal hosts **Olympic Games** (July 17–31). Team Canada wins the first **Canada Cup** hockey series (Sept. 15). The **Parti Québécois** under René Lévesque wins provincial election in Quebec (Nov. 15).

1977 Quebec government pases Bill 101, restricting English-language schooling to children whose mother or father had attended English elementary school in Quebec (Aug. 26). Highway signs in most of Canada become metric (Sept. 6).

1978 Soviet nuclear-powered satellite crashes in Canadian north (Jan. 24). Sun Life Assurance Co. announces a head office move from Montreal to Toronto because of language laws and political instability in Quebec.

1979 Conservatives under **Joe Clark** win federal election (May 22). Canada's first gold bullion coin, the Maple Leaf, goes on sale (Sept. 5). 220 000 people are evacuated from Mississauga, Ont., because of derailed tanker cars containing chlorine and other chemicals (Nov. 10). Supreme Court of Canada declares Manitoba and Quebec legislation creating unilingual courts and legislatures unconstitutional (Dec. 13). Federal Conservatives lose non-confidence vote on budget (Dec. 13), forcing the government's resignation. **Antonine Maillet** wins the prestigious French literary prize, the Prix Goncourt, for her novel *Pélagie-la-Charette*.

1980 Canada's ambassador to Iran, Ken Taylor, arranges the successful **escape of six American Embassy staff** from Tehran while their colleagues are held hostage (Jan. 28). Liberals win federal election (Feb. 18). Canada decides to boycott the Olympic Games in Moscow because of the Soviet invasion of Afghanistan. **Jeanne Sauvé** becomes the first female Speaker of the House of Commons (April 14). **Quebec votes "no"** to "sovereignty-association" (separatism) in a **referendum** (May 22). **O Canada** becomes Canada's national anthem (June 27). The Supreme Court awards Rosa Becker half the assets accumulated during a 19-year common-law relationship. **National Energy Program** is created to encourage oil self-sufficiency, increase Canadian ownership in the oil industry and obtain a larger share of Canadian energy revenues.

1981 Terry Fox dies of cancer at age 22 (June 29); his "Marathon of Hope," across Canada, running on one leg after having lost the other to cancer, raised $25 million for cancer research. Quebec bans public signs in English (Sept. 23). The federal government and every province except Quebec reach agreement on a method for patriating Canada's constitution (Nov. 5). The 1981 census indicates significant increases in the percentage of new Canadians from Asia, the Caribbean and Latin America.

1982 The *Ocean Ranger,* an oil platform off the coast of Newfoundland, sinks with the loss of 84 lives (Feb. 15). Bertha Wilson becomes Canada's first woman to be appointed a justice of the Supreme Court (Mar. 4). The Quebec Court of Appeal rejects the Quebec government's claim of veto power over constitutional change (Apr. 7). Canada gains a new **Constitution** and **Charter of Rights and Freedoms** (Apr. 17). Canada's GNP falls 4.8% in the worst recession since the Great Depression of the 1930s.

1983 Canadian pay-TV channels begin operation (Feb. 1). **Jeanne Sauvé** is Canada's first woman to be appointed Governor General (Dec. 23). Canada approves a US plan to test unarmed **cruise missiles** in western Canada beginning in 1984.

1984 Trudeau wins the 1984 Albert Einstein Peace Award for his globetrotting efforts to draw world leaders' attention to the disarmament talks. He is succeeded as prime minister by **John Turner** (June 30). Conservatives under **Brian Mulroney** win federal election with 211 seats, the largest majority in Canada's history (Sept. 4). The **Pope visits Canada** (Sept. 9–20). **Marc Garneau** becomes the first Canadian in space, aboard US space shuttle *Challenger* (Oct. 5). Council for the Northwest Territories recognizes the use of **aboriginal languages** as well as English and French.

1985 The voyage through the Northwest Passage of US icebreaker *Polar Sea* challenges Canada's **Arctic sovereignty**. Long-time premiers Bill Davis (Ont.), René Lévesque (Que.) and Peter Lougheed (Alta) retire. Prime Minister Mulroney and US President Reagan declare mutual support for **Star Wars research** and **free trade** between the two nations at "Shamrock Summit" (Mar. 18) in Quebec City. The Quebec provincial Liberals under Robert Bourassa defeat the Parti Québécois (Dec. 2). Ontario Liberals under David Peterson end four decades of Conservative rule.

1986 The Canadian dollar hits a then all-time low of 70.20 cents US (Jan. 31). The **Expo 86** world's fair is held in Vancouver (May 2–Oct. 13). The US imposes stiff tariffs (May 22) on imported Canadian shakes and shingles. Canada joins other Commonwealth nations (Aug. 5) in adopting **economic sanctions against South Africa** because of its apartheid policy. One hundred and fifteen **Tamil refugees** from Sri Lanka are found drifting in lifeboats off the coast of Newfoundland (Aug. 11). Canada receives a United Nations award (Oct. 6) for providing a haven for world refugees. Canadian John Polanyi shares the Nobel Prize for chemistry.

1987 The Bank of Canada rate drops to a 13-year low of 7.49% (Jan. 28); 6-month residential mortgages are as low as 7.5%. The **Meech Lake Accord**, proposing major constitutional amendments, is agreed to by Prime Minister Brian Mulroney and the 10 provincial premiers (Apr. 30). Ontario passes the first **pay equity legislation** for the private sector enacted in North America (June). A free vote in Parliament on restoration of **capital punishment** defeats the proposal 148–127 (June). A tornado kills 26 and injures 250 others in Edmonton (July 20). Team Canada wins the Canada Cup in a 6-5 victory over the Soviet Union (Sept. 15). A **free trade** agreement between Canada and the United States is reached (Oct. 3). **Stock prices tumble** (Oct. 19) in Canada and throughout the world. The founding assembly of the **Reform Party** of Canada is held (Nov.)

1988 Canada is left without an **abortion law** (Jan. 28) when the Supreme Court rules that existing legislation is unconstitutional. The XV **Winter Olympics** open in Calgary (Feb. 13). Canadian sprinter **Ben Johnson** sets a world record and wins a gold medal at the Summer Olympics in Seoul (Sept. 24) but is stripped of both (Sept. 26) after testing positive for steroids. Yukon Territory passes language legislation recognizing the use of aboriginal languages. Brian Mulroney's Progressive Conservatives win a second consecutive majority in the **federal election** (Nov. 21), a bitter campaign fought over the free trade agreement with the US. Quebec's **French-only sign law** is struck down by the Supreme Court (Dec. 15) but is re-instated by Quebec (Dec. 21) using the "notwithstanding"

clause in the Charter of Rights and Freedoms. Free trade legislation passes the House of Commons (Dec. 24) and the Senate (Dec. 30). The "Kamloops Amendment" to the Indian Act grants band councils jurisdiction over all reserve land, including the power to impose taxes.

1989 The Free Trade Agreement takes effect (Jan. 1). The federal government announces a new **goods and services tax** (GST) to take effect Jan. 1991. Audrey McLaughlin becomes Canada's **first female national party leader** as the NDP chooses a successor to Ed Broadbent (Dec. 2). Fourteen **female university students are killed** by an anti-feminist gunman in Montreal (Dec. 6).

1990 Revisions to the Criminal Code provide choice of language in criminal hearings (Jan.). Several Quebec Conservative MPs, led by cabinet minister Lucien Bouchard (May 21), leave the government to form the pro-independence **Bloc Québécois**. The **Meech Lake Accord dies** when both Newfoundland and Manitoba fail to ratify the constitutional agreement by the deadline (June 23). Manitoba MLA **Elijah Harper** refuses the unanimous consent required for debate and a vote on the Meech Lake Accord because the accord does not provide special status for aboriginal peoples as it does for Quebec. Jean Chrétien becomes leader of the federal Liberal party. A land dispute leads to a 78-day armed confrontation between Mohawk warriors and government forces at the Kanesatake reserve near **Oka**, Que. **Canada sends warships** to the Persian Gulf as part of the multinational force being assembled to force Iraq to withdraw from occupied Kuwait. Ontario elects its **first NDP government**, led by **Bob Rae** (Sept. 7). Brian Mulroney's Conservative government stacks the Senate (Sept. 27) with new appointees to ensure passage of the federal **goods and services tax (GST)**, which becomes law Dec. 17 to take effect Jan. 1.

1991 Canadian military personnel participate with the Allied forces in the assault against Iraq beginning Jan. 16. (the **Gulf War**). After the war 300 Canadian military engineers join the UN mission patrolling the demilitarized zone between Iraq and Kuwait. Former Chicago Cubs pitcher **Ferguson Jenkins** becomes the first Canadian to be voted into baseball's hall of fame. Prime Minister Brian Mulroney and US President George Bush sign an **acid rain accord** with the goal of ending acid rain within ten years. **Rita Johnston** succeeds BC Premier **William Vander Zalm** as premier, the first woman to enter the provincial premier's office in Canada. Mulroney's government announces a **new constitutional reform package** promising aboriginal self-government within 10 years and guaranteeing aboriginal representation in an elected Senate. Economists charge that Bank of Canada's fight against inflation stalls economy; cross-border shopping is reported up 57% in first six months of the year; Michael Harcourt and NDP defeat Socreds in BC; Roy Romanow and NDP oust Conservatives in Saskatchewan. **Gun control** bill passed, imposing tougher controls and banning imported military assault weapons; **Yukon First Nations** sign umbrella agreement on land claims and self-government; agreement reached on creation of Nunavut in Northwest Territories.

1992 A year-long crisis in the Atlantic **fisheries** results in a two-year shutdown of the cod fishery (July 2), a five-year ban on commercial salmon fishing in Nfld. (Mar. 6) and international negotiations to protect the fish stocks; **Gwich'in Indians** sign a deal with Ottawa, giving them title to nearly 24 000 sq. km of land in the NWT and Yukon (Apr. 22); details of North American Free Trade Agreement (**NAFTA**) are announced Aug. 12, Prime Min. Mulroney signs the deal on Dec. 17; negotiations on **constitutional reform** take place throughout the year and an agreement (the Charlottetown Accord) that has Quebec's approval is announced Aug. 19 (proposals include Senate reform, an enlarged House of Commons and self-government for native people); a national referendum on the accord is held Oct. 26 and No side claims victory, killing the deal. The Toronto Blue Jays win the World Series (Oct. 25).

1993 The Sahtu Tribe of the Great Bear Lake region in the NWT settled a land claim to 41 437 sq. km; the Cree in northern Quebec win compensation from Hydro-Quebec for damage done by the hydro projects around James Bay. The last fighter jets leave Baden-Soellingen, Germany on Jan. 19 as the Canadian troops begin the planned pull-out from NATO bases. On Feb. 24 Prim. Min. Mulroney announces his resignation, to take effect in June. Four members of the Canadian Airborne Regiment, in Somalia since Jan. on a peacekeeping mission, are charged in the death of a Somali civilian. NAFTA legislation passes in the House of Commons on May 27. Yukon's 14 First Nations signs the Umbrella Final Agreement in Whitehorse on May 29; the settlement includes 41 400 sq. km of land and C$280 million. On June 15, Canada officially ends its role in Cyprus after 29 years of peacekeeping duties on the island. Defence Min. Kim Campbell takes over the reigns of the Conservative government after a 2nd ballot victory at the leadership convention on June 25. The US and Canada have numerous trade disputes during the year, including battles over steel rods and durum wheat. On Sept. 8 a federal election is called for Oct. 25; on Sept. 14 Quebec Prem. Robert Bourassa announces he is stepping down in 1994; on Sept. 30 the Supreme Court rules against Sue Rodriguez in a controversial case over the right to a doctor-assisted suicide. On Oct. 23, the Toronto Blue Jays win their second consecutive World Series; on Oct. 25 the Liberal Party wins a decisive victory in a federal election that sees the emergence of two new parties—the Bloc Québécois and the Reform Party—and the near demise of the Progressive Conservatives, who are reduced to two seats in the House of Commons.

1994 See "News Events of the Year."

"On the beach behind us,

Canadians gave their lives so the

world would be a better place.

In death they were not anglophones or

francophones, not from the West

or the East, not Christians or Jews,

not aboriginal people or immigrants.

They were Canadians."

Jean Chrétien, Prime Minister, in his address to commemorate the fiftieth anniversary of the D-Day Invasion, delivered at Juno Beach, near Courseulles, France, June 6, 1994, as quoted by Allan Thompson in The Toronto Star *the next day. During the first twenty-four hours of the D-Day invasion on June 6, 1944, 359 Canadians died.*

Quotes of the Year

Selected by John Robert Colombo

It is the custom at *The Canadian Global Almanac* to reprint a selection of outstanding remarks made by public figures in Canada over the last year. For almanac-makers, the past year ran from Sept. 1993 to Sept. 1994. These twelve months marked a period of transition in Canadian public life—365 days of elevated hopes and worried fears, and here are a few things that were said or written that made the headlines and the footnotes.

1 "Give me back the Berlin Wall/ Give me Stalin and St Paul/ I've seen the future, brother:/ It is murder"

(Lines from the title song of the record album *The Future*, the text of which is included in Leonard Cohen's *Stranger Music: Selected Poems and Songs*, 1993)

2 "Canada is the only country in the world where being a nationalist automatically disqualifies someone—in media eyes—as a serious person."

(Michael Valpy, columnist, *The Globe and Mail*, Sept. 17, 1993.)

3 "There's more chance to do crazy things in Canada, because nobody pays any attention. In Europe, you're under surveillance as an artist all the time."

(R. Murray Schafer, innovative composer, interviewed by Robert Everett-Green in *The Globe and Mail*, Sept. 23, 1993.)

4 "Yes, I have a respect for Canada and even feel an emotional attachment to Canada, as most Quebecers do, even sovereignists. But my first loyalty is to Quebec."

(Lucien Bouchard, leader of the Bloc Québécois, addressing the editorial board of *The Toronto Star*, Sept. 22, 1993.)

5 "This is a $700 billion gross domestic product economy. If you believe you can kick start that with a $2 billion investment in sewers, then you believe you can start a 747 with a flashlight battery."

(Preston Manning, leader of the Reform Party of Canada, referring to the announced Liberal job plan, leadership debate, CBC-TV, Oct. 4, 1993, quoted by Rosemary Speirs and David Vienneau in *The Toronto Star* the following day.)

6 "I want to tell you, I know very well who I am... a proud Québécois and a proud Canadian. And I have said it's possible to have a happy Quebec in a united Canada."

(Jean Chrétien, Liberal leader, referring to Bloc Québécois leader Lucien Bouchard's criticism of his federalism during French-language leaders' debate, Radio-Canada, Oct. 3, 1993, published in *The Globe and Mail*, Oct. 5, 1993.)

7 "There's a little bit of a tendency to feel that we cannot do first-rate things in Canada because we're too small. This award says the science done here is as good as the science done anywhere, and you can do science in BC as well as anywhere in the world."

(Michael Smith, biochemist at the University of British Columbia, co-winner of the 1993 Nobel Prize for Chemistry (specifically for research involving site-directed mutagenesis in genes), quoted by Robert Matas in *The Globe and Mail*, Oct. 14, 1993.)

8 "I just wanted to make contact."

(Joe Carter, baseball player, after hitting a home run in the bottom of the ninth inning that gave the Toronto Blue Jays an 8-6 victory over the Philadelphia Phillies and their second straight World Series title, Toronto, Oct. 23, 1993, quoted by Rosie DiManno in *The Toronto Star* the following day.)

9 "Our day in the sun will come again, I promise you."

(Kim Campbell, Prime Minister, conceding electoral defeat, national television, Vancouver, BC, Oct. 25, 1993, quoted by Ross Howard in *The Globe and Mail* the following day. After a stunning defeat in the general election that day, in which she lost her own seat and the Conservative Party, which she led, lost all but two seats across the country, she added, "We have a responsibility to bind our wounds, perhaps snurf into a Kleenex, and then return to fight again.")

10 "We have to concentrate all our efforts on the economy, to create jobs. Together we will work hard and Canada will enter the 21st century as a proud, united, independent, generous nation."

(Jean Chrétien, Prime Minister designate, victory speech, national television, Shawinigan, Que., Oct. 25, 1993, quoted by Susan Delacourt in *The Globe and Mail* the following day.)

11 "We serve two million Canadians a day, but we serve them one at a time."

(George Cohon, President, McDonald's Restaurants of Canada Ltd., expounding his company's policy, interviewed in *The Canadian Jewish News*, Nov. 4, 1993.)

12 "We face a disaster of monumental proportions... In Newfoundland, the threat is greater than just to coastal communities; it is to the province and the society as a whole. Concerted action is needed. We need today's equivalent of a Marshall Plan."

(Richard Cashin, Chair, Task Force on Incomes and Adjustment in the Atlantic Fishery, report tabled Dec. 6, 1993, quoted in *The Globe and Mail*, Dec. 14, 1993.)

13 "Canada became the first country in the world to pass, unanimously, an all-party resolution condemning the Iranian government for its appalling human rights record and calling for the withdrawal of the fatwa and bounty. That was a remarkable thing."

(Salman Rushdie, Anglo-Indian novelist who has been living under a death-threat from the Iranian government, statement read to the 1993 PEN Benefit on the first anniversary of his appearance there, Dec. 7, 1992, reproduced in *The Toronto Star*, Dec. 16, 1993.)

14 "Maybe is my favourite word in the dictionary."

(Attributed to Quebec Premier Robert Bourassa at a press conference in Quebec City, Dec. 16, 1993, as noted by Rhéal Séguin in *The Globe and Mail* the following day.)

15 "The corporate system that is at the heart of the modern economy works on the principles of ever-expanding power and ever-diminishing responsibility."

(Walter Stewart, journalist, *Too Big to Fail: Olympia & York: The Story Behind the Headlines*, 1993.)

16 "I spent the first half of my life fighting the Right Wing and I fear that I may be spending my second half fighting the Left Wing."

(Alan Borovoy, General Counsel, Canadian Civil Liberties Association, referring to inroads made by proponents of "political correctness," Toronto, Jan. 1, 1994.)

17 "Despite the tough times, compared with just about any other land on earth, Canada is still blessed with the mandate of heaven."

(Peter C. Newman, columnist, "From Hope to Defiance," *Maclean's*, Jan. 3, 1994.)

18 "Think of a stretch limo in the potholed streets of New York City, where homeless beggars live. Inside the limo are the air-conditioned post-industrial regions of North America, Europe, the emerging Pacific Rim, and a few other isolated places, with their trade summitry and computer information highways. Outside is the rest of mankind, going in a completely different direction."

(Thomas Fraser Homer-Dixon, head of the Peace and Conflict Studies Program at the University of Toronto, quoted by Robert D. Kaplan in "The Coming Anarchy," *The Atlantic Monthly*, Feb. 1994.)

19 "I was a junk dealer, then I became a scrap dealer, then a secondary materials engineer, and now I'm in recycling. But the job hasn't changed."

(Chester Waxman, president of IWS Ltd., appearing at an Ontario Liberal Task Force on Jobs, Hamilton, Jan. 27, 1994, quoted in *The Hamilton Spectator*, Jan. 29, 1994.)

20 "Judging from the media coverage, Americans seem quite hung up on how health care is rationed in Canada. It's true, Canada does ration health care according to the severity of illness, compared to the US which rations according to the patient's bank balance."

(Lisa Priest, journalist, "Caught in the Middle of a US Debate," *The Toronto Star*, Feb. 15, 1994.)

21 "For years governments have been promising more than they can deliver, and delivering more than they can afford."

(Paul Martin Jr, Minister of Finance, budget speech, House of Commons, Feb. 22, 1994, quoted by Alan Freeman in *The Globe and Mail* the following day.)

22 "The highest duty of a member of Parliament is love... I really believe that. What that encompasses is love and respect for the environment, love and respect for those who are dispossessed and powerless, and those who have traditionally been voiceless."

(Svend Robinson, M.P., describing his feelings as he watched Sue Rodriguez die through an assisted suicide, quoted by Warren Caragata in *Maclean's*, Feb. 28, 1994.)

23 "Bouchard... has the habit of being 'serially sincere,' as one person who knows him well has put it. He believes totally in whatever it is he happens to believe in."

(Richard Gwyn, columnist, describing Bloc Québécois leader Lucien Bouchard, "Home and Away," *The Toronto Star*, Feb. 27, 1994.)

24 "Since Confederation seven generations of Canadians—French-speaking, English-speaking, and immigrants from around the world—have flourished, economically and culturally, under a regime of peace, order, and occasional good government. To throw this lightly away is a folly almost beyond belief."

(Michael Bliss, historian and columnist, *The Toronto Star*, May 20, 1994.)

25 "In my continuing education as a Canadian I have learned an important fact of political life in this country, namely that the personal convictions and strengths and weaknesses of the party leaders have more influence on the course of events than the principles of the parties they lead, principles that in any event are not well defined."

(Mitchell Sharp, former Minister of Finance and former Minister of External Affairs, *Which Reminds Me... A Memoir*, 1994.)

Fathers of Confederation

Union of the British North American colonies into the Dominion of Canada was discussed and its terms negotiated at three confederation conferences held at Charlottetown (C), Sept. 1, 1864; Quebec (Q), Oct. 10, 1864; and London (L), Dec. 4, 1866. The names of delegates are followed by the provinces they represented; Canada refers to what are now the provinces of Ontario and Quebec.

Adams G. Archibald, NS	C,Q,L
George Brown, Canada	C,Q
Alexander Campbell, Canada	C,Q
Frederick B.T. Carter, Nfld	Q
George-Étienne Cartier, Canada	C,Q,L
Edward B. Chandler, NB	C,Q
Jean-Charles Chapais, Canada	Q
James Cockburn, Canada	Q
George H. Coles, PEI	C,Q
Robert B. Dickey, NS	Q
Charles Fisher, NB	Q,L
Alexander T. Galt, Canada	C,Q,L
John Hamilton Gray, NB	C,Q
John Hamilton Gray, PEI	C,Q
Thomas Heath Haviland, PEI	Q
William A. Henry, NS	C,Q,L
William P. Howland, Canada	L
John M. Johnson, NB	C,Q,L
Hector L. Langevin, Canada	C,Q,L
Jonathan McCully, NS	C,Q,L
A.A. Macdonald, PEI	C,Q
John A. Macdonald, Canada	C,Q,L
William McDougall, Canada	C,Q,L
Thomas D'Arcy McGee, Canada	C,Q
Peter Mitchell, NB	Q,L
Oliver Mowat, Canada	Q
Edward Palmer, PEI	C,Q
William H. Pope, PEI	C,Q
John W. Ritchie, NS	L
J. Ambrose Shea, Nfld	Q
William H. Steeves, NB	C,Q
Sir Étienne-Paschal Taché, Canada	Q
Samuel Leonard Tilley, NB	C,Q,L
Charles Tupper, NS	C,Q,L
Edward Whelan, PEI	Q
R.D. Wilmot, NB	L

Canadian Disasters

Aug. 29, 1583: Canada's first recorded marine disaster took 85 lives when the *Delight* was wrecked on Sable Island.

Aug. 23, 1711: As many as 950 drowned when ships attached to the British fleet preparing to attack Quebec were grounded and sank on the rocks of Ile-aux-Oeufs.

Oct. 5, 1825: The Miramichi fire, north of New Brunswick's Miramichi River, destroyed the towns of Newcastle and Douglastown, and killed between 200–500 people.

May 17, 1841: On this date, several large boulders from Cap Diamant tumbled down the precipitous cliffs above the Lower Town of Quebec City and demolished eight houses, killing 32 people.

Oct. 27, 1854: In one of the earliest Canadian train disasters, a gravel train running near Baptiste Creek, 24 km west of Chatham, Ont., was hit by an express train on the same line. In the collision, 52 persons were killed and 48 seriously injured.

June 29, 1864: Near St-Hilaire, Que., a passenger train was unable to stop for an open drawbridge at the Beloeil bridge on the Richelieu River. The train plunged through the opening onto passing barges, killing 99 and injuring 100 people.

Apr. 1, 1873: Sailing from Liverpool to New York, the steamer *Atlantic* struck Meager's Rock off the coast of Nova Scotia and sank with the loss of 535 people.

May 13, 1873: Sixty men died when a fire and subsequent explosion in a coal mine at Westville, Pictou County, N.S., trapped firemen and workers. The mine was eventually sealed to starve the fire of oxygen and it was two years before all the bodies were recovered.

Aug. 25, 1873: The Great Nova Scotia Cyclone swept over Cape Breton Island. The hurricane destroyed 1,200 vessels and 900 buildings, demolished dykes, wharves and bridges and claimed 500 lives.

May 3, 1887: An explosion at the Number One mine in Nanaimo, BC owned by the Vancouver Coal Mining and Land Company, killed 148 miners.

Jan. 24, 1888: Seventy-seven men lost their lives in a fire in the Number Five Mine at Wellington, just outside of Nanaimo, BC.

Feb. 21, 1891: In the first of several major disasters in the coal mines of Springhill, N.S., 125 men were killed in an explosion.

May 26, 1896: Fifty-five people were killed when a bridge at Point Ellice in Victoria, B.C., collapsed while a streetcar was passing over it. The bridge was too weak to support the weight of a recently built tramline.

Sept. 19, 1899: A massive rockslide from the cliffs above Quebec City's Lower Town demolished most of Champlain St, killing 45 people.

Apr. 29, 1903: Parts of the town of Frank, Alta., were obliterated by a sudden landslide when over 50 million tonnes of limestone came crashing down Turtle Mountain, crossed the four-km-wide valley floor and rolled up the other side of the valley. Approximately 50 people were killed. The landslide also sealed a mine entrance at the foot of the mountain and trapped 17 miners inside. The men were able to escape by digging a new tunnel to the surface.

Aug. 29, 1907: The Quebec Bridge, 11 km north of Quebec City, was the largest cantilevered bridge in the world at the time. As the bridge was nearing completion, the southern cantilever span collapsed, killing 75 workmen.

Mar. 5, 1910: A CPR work crew clearing the tracks from a previous snow slide in Rogers Pass, B.C., was hit by an avalanche. Sixty-two men were killed; one survived.

June 30, 1912: The worst tornado in Canadian history swept through Regina, Sask., killing 28 residents, injuring hundreds and causing $75 million damage (est. 1990 dollars).

May 29, 1914: The Canadian Pacific liner *Empress of Ireland* collided with a Norwegian coal ship in the St Lawrence River near Rimouski, Que., and sank in only 14 minutes with the loss of 1,014 lives. This was one of the worst naval disasters in history, with the eighth largest loss of life for a naval accident.

June 19, 1914: The worst coal mine disaster in Canadian history occurred at Hillcrest, Alta., when dust explosions killed 189 men.

July 29, 1916: A forest fire in northern Ontario, thought to have been started by lightning and locomotive sparks, engulfed the towns of Cochrane and Matheson, killing at least 233 persons.

Sept. 11, 1916: The Quebec Bridge was the scene of further tragedy when a new centre span being hoisted into position fell into the river below. Thirteen men were killed, bringing the loss of life during construction of the bridge to 88.

Dec. 6, 1917: Halifax was the scene of Canada's worst single disaster when a French munitions ship filled with explosives collided with a freighter in Halifax harbour. The French ship, the *Mont Blanc*, was split to the waterline; fuel oil spilled over its explosive cargo and started a fire in the hold. The crew abandoned ship without attempting to extinguish the fire.

In the explosion that followed, the *Mont Blanc* was tossed more than 1,000 m into the air. The explosion levelled homes and businesses in a large part of the city and set off explosives stockpiled on shore. The blast, heard as far away as Prince Edward Island, is thought to be the largest-ever accidental explosion, and the largest non-nuclear blast in history. More than 1,600 people were killed, 9,000 injured, and 6,000 left homeless. Property damage was estimated at $35 million.

Oct. 23, 1918: The Canadian Pacific steamship *Princess Sophia* ran onto Vanderbilt Reef while sailing from Alaska to Vancouver. The ship sank two days later on Oct. 25. All 343 aboard were drowned.

Jan. 9, 1927: A small fire that broke out in Montreal's Laurier Palace Theatre was quickly extinguished, but in the panic that ensued 12 people were crushed to death and 64 were asphyxiated, including many children.

Apr. 14, 1928: The 18-gun sloop *Acorn* sank near Halifax with 115 men on board.

Nov. 18, 1929: Newfoundland's Burin Peninsula was struck by a 4.5 m tidal wave. Property damage was extensive and 27 were killed.

Dec. 12, 1942: An arsonist set fire to the Knights of Columbus hostel in St. John's. Because the hostel had no emergency lighting, the doors opened inwards and exits were restricted, 99 people died and another 100 were seriously injured.

Sept. 9, 1949: A Quebec Airways DC-3 was sabotaged with a bomb and the plane exploded and crashed near St. Joachim, Que., killing 32 people. J.A. Guay and two accomplices were convicted of the crime and hanged.

Sept. 17, 1949: Seven hundred people were aboard the Great Lakes excursion ship *Noronic* when it caught fire and burned at its pier in Toronto harbour. The ship's fire hydrants were dry and no alarm was sent to the city fire department until 15 minutes after the blaze was discovered. In the meantime, the single exit became blocked by fire and 118 lives were lost.

Oct. 15, 1954: During the worst inland storm in Canadian history, Hurricane Hazel, over 10 cm of rain fell in Toronto in 12 hours. At that time, many houses in Toronto were built on low-lying flood plains. The storm and resulting floods caused 83 deaths and widespread property damage.

Nov. 1, 1956: A second major tragedy struck the coal mines at Springhill, N.S., when an accident killed 39 men.

Dec. 9, 1956: A DC-4 North Star flown by Trans-Canada Airways (later Air Canada) crashed into the east face of Mount Slesse, killing all 62 on board.

June 17, 1958: Design errors in Vancouver's Second Narrows Bridge caused one section to collapse. The accident killed 18 men, including the two engineers that an investigation later determined were responsible for the errors.

Oct. 23, 1958: A third mining accident in Springhill, N.S,. killed 75 when a tunnel collapsed.

Nov. 19, 1963: A Trans Canada Airlines DC-8F crashed after takeoff from Dorval in Montreal, killing. 118.

July 5, 1970: At Toronto International Airport, an Air Canada DC-8 lost one starboard engine during a landing attempt. During the pilot's effort to take off and land again, the remaining starboard engine fell off. The aircraft crashed, killing all 109 persons aboard.

May 4, 1971: During a prolonged rainstorm in St-Jean-Vianney, Que., a giant sinkhole appeared in the ground. The hole swallowed 36 houses, several cars and a bus, and killed 31 people.

Sept. 1, 1972: The Blue Bird Bar in Montreal was set afire by three disgruntled patrons who had been ejected from the bar earlier in the evening. The blaze killed 37.

Nov. 10, 1975: The 218-m ore carrier *Edmund Fitzgerald*, based in Sault Ste Marie, broke apart during a storm on Lake Superior and sank in 156 m of water with all 29 members of the crew aboard. Two days later only two rubber rafts and some life preservers from the ship were found.

June 21, 1977: A fire that broke out in the cell block of the city police headquarters of St. John, N.B., was so hot that the locks on several cell doors were fused. Twenty prisoners were killed and 12 police officers who attempted to rescue the prisoners were injured.

Feb. 11, 1978: A Pacific Western Airlines aircraft crashed at Cranbrook, B.C., killing 43 people.

Aug. 4, 1978: The worst bus disaster in Canada occurred when the brakes on a chartered bus failed near Eastman, Que. The bus plunged into a lake, and 41 mentally and physically handicapped passengers were killed.

Dec. 31, 1979: Forty-four persons were killed during New Year's Eve celebrations at a social club in Chapais, Que., in a fire caused by a man playing with a lighter who set decorations ablaze.

Feb. 15, 1982: The ocean drilling rig *Ocean Ranger* overturned and sank during a storm while operating 265 km east of Newfoundland, killing 84 men. Inadequate safety procedures and equipment were later blamed for the accident.

May 31, 1985: A midafternoon tornado struck Barrie, Ont., killing 12, including four children. Property damage was in the hundreds of millions of dollars.

June 23, 1985: An Air India 747 flying from Toronto never reached its destination of London, England. Wreckage from the plane was found floating in the Atlantic, west of Ireland. The tragedy, thought to be caused by a bomb on board, killed 280 Canadians.

Dec. 12, 1985: In the worst air crash in Canada, an Arrow Airlines DC-8, after refueling in Gander en route to Hopkinsville, Ky., crashed seconds after takeoff, killing 256 passengers and crew.

Feb. 8, 1986: A 16-unit VIA Rail passenger train slammed head-on into a 118-unit CN freight train near Hinton, Alta. Twenty-six people were killed and dozens were seriously injured.

July 31, 1987: A tornado touched down in Edmonton, Alta., killing 26 people, injuring 250 others and causing an estimated $250 million damage.

Mar. 10, 1989: An Air Ontario jet crashed immediately after takeoff from Dryden, Ont., killing 24 people.

Dec. 6, 1989: Gunman Marc Lepine shot and killed 14 women and wounded 13 others at Montreal's l'École Polytechnique before killing himself. Lepine left a letter claiming he had attacked the female students because they were feminists.

Feb. 12, 1990: One of the worst tire fires in North America broke out near Hagersville, Ont., spewing oil and toxic smoke. The dump, which stored 14 million tires for recycling, burned for 16 days; the blaze was extinguished at a cost of $1.5 million.

May 9, 1992: Twenty-six miners died underground in the Westray coal mine near Plymouth, N.S., after a methane gas explosion. Fifteen bodies were recovered but the bodies of the remaining victims could not be reached in the debris.

July 16, 1993: Nineteen people died when a truck towing tanks of diesel fuel collided with a van carrying senior citizens near Lac-Bouchette, Que.

Prime Ministers of Canada

■ Sir John A. Macdonald

Canada's first prime minister, Sir John A. Macdonald, was born in Glasgow, Scotland, Jan. 11, 1815. At age 5 he came to Canada with his parents who settled at Kingston, Upper Canada.

Called to the bar in 1836, Macdonald practised law in Kingston, and then in Toronto. He established a reputation as a corporate lawyer, company director, and businessman.

He was elected to the Legislative Assembly of the Province of Canada in 1844, and was re-elected in 1848, 1851, 1854, 1857, 1861 and 1863. In 1864, he joined a coalition with George Brown, leader of the Upper Canadian reformers, dedicated to bringing about Confederation. That same year, Macdonald was a delegate to the Charlottetown and Quebec Conferences, and became the principal author of the Confederation resolutions agreed upon in Quebec. He was chairman of the London Conference (1866–67), and played a pivotal role in bringing about Confederation.

Macdonald became Canada's first prime minister when the Conservative party won a majority of seats in Parliament following the first post-Confederation general election in 1867. Though he was re-elected in 1872, Macdonald's second administration was marred by the "Pacific Scandal" in 1873, when the Liberal opposition charged that his government had awarded the C.P.R. contract to Sir Hugh Allan in return for political contributions. An investigation into these charges was held, and the government resigned on Nov. 5, 1873.

Macdonald's Liberal-Conservatives were re-elected Sept. 17, 1878, and Macdonald remained prime minister until his death in Ottawa on June 6, 1891.

During his first administration, the Dominion of Canada expanded to include the provinces of British Columbia, Prince Edward Island, and the newly created Manitoba.

The building of the transcontinental railway is the most memorable feature of his second administration, but other accomplishments include the establishment of the "National Policy"—a system of tariff protection to aid the development of Canadian industries (1879)—and the increased settlement of the Western provinces that followed the construction of the railway.

■ Alexander Mackenzie

Alexander Mackenzie was born on Jan. 28, 1822 near Dunkeld, Perthshire, Scotland. He left school and became a stonemason at the age of 14.

He emigrated to Canada in 1842 and became a contractor at Lambton, Ontario and then editor of the *Lambton Shield*. From 1866–74, he was a major in the 27th Lambton Battalion Volunteer Infantry.

In 1861, Mackenzie was elected to the Legislative Assembly of the Province of Canada, where he gave his support to the Confederation plan. When George Brown was defeated in the 1867 election, Mackenzie became *de facto* leader of the Opposition, though it was not until after the 1872 elections that he formally accepted this title.

It was Mackenzie who led the attack on the Macdonald administration over the "Pacific Scandal"; when Macdonald resigned on Nov. 5, 1873, Mackenzie became prime minister.

During his 5-year term of office, Mackenzie introduced changes to election laws that included the secret ballot and universal male suffrage. The Supreme Court of Canada was established under Mackenzie's rule, and Wilfrid Laurier was brought into Mackenzie's cabinet.

Severe economic depression plagued Canada during the Mackenzie years, and in 1878, his Liberal party was routed at the polls.

Mackenzie retained his own seat, however, and was still a member of Parliament when he died Apr. 17, 1892, in Toronto.

■ Sir John Abbott

Sir John Joseph Caldwell Abbott was born Mar. 12, 1821 at St. Andrews, Lower Canada—the first prime minister to be born on Canadian soil.

After taking his law degree from University of McGill College, he was admitted to the bar in 1847 and practised law in Montreal. From 1855–80 he was dean of the Faculty of Law, McGill University.

Abbott was elected to the Legislative Assembly of the Province of Canada in 1857, re-elected in 1861 and 1863, and sat until Confederation. He was then elected to the

House of Commons in 1867, 1872, and 1874. He was last elected in 1882, and appointed to the Senate on May 12, 1887.

When Sir John A. Macdonald died in 1891, Abbott—though a senator—inherited the Conservative leadership. The three other leading Conservatives—Langevin, Tupper and Thompson—were unwilling or unable to assume the post. Abbott held the office of prime minister from June 16, 1891 until his resignation on Nov. 24, 1892. He died in Montreal on Oct. 30, 1893.

■ Sir John Thompson

Sir John Sparrow David Thompson was born in Halifax, N.S., on Nov. 10, 1845.

Thompson was called to the Nova Scotia bar in 1865, and was instrumental in founding Dalhousie Law School in 1883, where he eventually became a lecturer.

In May 1882, Thompson became premier of Nova Scotia, but when his government was defeated 2 months later, he retired from politics and became a judge of the Supreme Court of Nova Scotia.

Prime Minister Macdonald coaxed Thompson back into politics, making him Minister of Justice in 1885. When Macdonald died in 1891, Thompson declined the leadership, fearing that his conversion to Roman Catholicism in 1870 would hinder his party's fortunes. However, the following year, Thompson changed his mind, and on Dec. 5, 1892, he became prime minister.

Though prime minister for just over 2 years, Thompson was largely responsible for the establishment of the Criminal Code and penetentiary reforms. He very nearly succeeded in bringing Newfoundland into Confederation in 1894, and successfully negotiated fisheries clauses in the Treaty of Washington.

He died while still in office on Dec. 12, 1894.

■ Sir Mackenzie Bowell

Mackenzie Bowell was born at Rickinghall, Suffolk, England, on Dec. 27, 1823, and came to Canada in 1832. In 1834, he became an apprentice printer at Belleville, Upper Canada, and was later editor and proprietor of the Belleville *Intelligencer*. He served in the Militia of the United Province of Canada during the American Civil War and the Fenian raids of 1866.

Bowell was elected to the House of Commons in 1867 for Hastings North, Ont., and was re-elected in 1872, 1874, 1878, 1887 and 1891.

As spokesman for the Orange Association of British America, Bowell was instrumental in having Louis Riel expelled from the Commons in 1874.

On Dec. 5, 1892, Bowell was appointed to the Senate and, after Thompson's death in 1894, was invited by the Governor General to form a government.

Perhaps the thorniest problem facing Prime Minister Bowell was the Manitoba Schools question. In 1890, Manitoba legislation had withdrawn school privileges from the Roman Catholic and primarily French minority in that province. By the time Bowell assumed office, attempts were being made to restore those lost school privileges by federal remedial legislation. Bowell was not equal to the political challenges facing him; he lost control of his cabinet ministers, several of whom eventually called for his resignation. Bowell denounced this cabinet rebellion as a "nest of traitors," but eventually he resigned on Apr. 27, 1896. He died in Belleville, Ont., on Dec. 10, 1917 at age 93.

■ Sir Charles Tupper

Charles Tupper was born at Amherst, N.S., July 2, 1821. He took a degree in medicine at Edinburgh University. At the age of 22, he began practising medicine in Amherst, and became the first president of the Canadian Medical Association (1867–70).

The 1855 election that brought him to the Legislative Assembly of Nova Scotia was declared void on Feb. 24, 1857. He was subsequently re-elected in a by-election that same year and was elected again in 1859 and 1863.

Tupper was active in the Confederation movement, and was a delegate to the Charlottetown, Quebec and London Conferences. He was elected to the House of Commons in 1867, and re-elected 1870, 1872, 1874, 1878 and 1882. He resigned in 1884, and served as High Commissioner for Canada in the United Kingdom from May 28 of that year to Jan. 26, 1887. In 1887, he was re-elected to the House of Commons, but resigned the following year and again served as High Commissioner from May 23, 1888 to Jan. 14, 1896.

In 1896, following the rebellion of Bowell's

cabinet, Tupper became *de facto* leader of the administration until Bowell formally resigned on Apr. 27, 1896. At that time, the Governor General invited Tupper to form the government. Parliament was dissolved shortly thereafter and in the election that followed on June 23, Tupper's Conservatives were defeated. Tupper stayed on as leader of the Opposition until Feb. 5, 1901, then retired from public life. He died Oct. 30, 1915 at Bexley Heath, Kent, England.

■ Sir Wilfrid Laurier

Wilfrid Laurier was born at St-Lin, Canada East, Nov. 20, 1841. He first attended College de l'Assomption, and then took his degree from McGill University.

He was called to the bar of Lower Canada in 1865. He practised law at Montreal and at Arthabaskaville, Que.

First elected to the Legislative Assembly of Quebec in 1871, Laurier resigned in Jan. 1874 and later that year was elected to the House of Commons. He became leader of the Liberal Opposition in June 1887. Then, following the 1896 election that gave his party a 23-seat majority, Laurier became Canada's first French-speaking prime minister on July 11, 1896. The Liberals retained power in 1900, and won a landslide election victory in 1904.

Immigration increased during his time in office as Clifford Sifton, Laurier's minister of the interior from 1896–1905, mounted a powerful campaign to attract immigrants from Britain, the United States and Europe. In 1905, Laurier created the provinces of Alberta and Saskatchewan and established the boundaries of Manitoba. During Laurier's years in power the Canadian West became a major world wheat producer. In 1909, Laurier established the External Affairs Department.

His government's controversial support for the creation of a Canadian navy, and his unpopular attempt to enter into a reciprocal trade agreement with the United States (an agreement that would have reduced or eliminated duties on many imported goods) spelled trouble for Laurier in 1911. His party was defeated in the Sept. 21 election. He remained an Opposition M.P. until his death on Feb. 17, 1919 in Ottawa.

■ Sir Robert Borden

Robert Laird Borden was born at Grand Pré, N.S., June 26, 1854. At age 14 he gave up formal schooling to become an assistant master in classical studies. He taught classics and mathematics in New Jersey in 1873, before returning to Nova Scotia to study law. He was admitted to the Nova Scotia bar in 1878, and practised first in Halifax, then in Kentville, N.S.

Borden was elected to the House of Commons in 1896 and 1900 and became leader of the Conservative party on Feb. 6, 1901. He served as leader of the Opposition until 1911, when he led his party to victory in the Sept. 21 election.

Borden was prime minister throughout World War I and during the war years his government was accused of scandal over British munitions contracts and its staunch support of the Ross Rifle—a weapon known to jam in battle. Borden's government introduced the first federal income tax, nationalized Canadian railways and introduced conscription in 1917.

In the election of Dec. 17, 1917, Borden led a re-organized Union Government made up of Conservatives and pro-conscription Liberals to victory. Borden headed the Canadian delegation at the Paris Peace Conference in 1919, where the autonomy of Canada and other dominions within the British Commonwealth was successfully established. He resigned on July 10, 1920 and died in Ottawa June 10, 1937.

■ Arthur Meighen

Arthur Meighen was born at Anderson, Ont., June 16, 1874. Following his graduation from university in 1896, Meighen taught high school for a year, then moved to Winnipeg in 1898 to study law. He was called to the Manitoba bar in 1902, and practised at Portage La Prairie.

He was first elected to the House of Commons in 1908, re-elected in 1911, 1913 and 1917, defeated in 1921, and re-elected in 1922 and 1925.

Meighen first achieved national prominence in 1913 when he helped devise a closure rule which permitted the government to end debate on a bill which was to effect a $35-million contribution to the British navy. Prior to closure, the bill had been obstructed by a fierce and protracted Opposition party blockade.

Prime Minister Borden appointed Meighen his solicitor general on Oct. 2, 1915, and

Meighen held this post for 2 years. A strong supporter of conscription, Meighen essentially drafted Canada's 1917 Conscription bill, and put it into operation. He was also the chief draughtsman of the *Wartime Elections Act*.

When Borden resigned on July 10, 1920, Meighen succeeded him as prime minister. In the general election of Dec. 6, 1921, Meighen's party was defeated. Though his Conservatives won the most seats in the election of Oct. 29, 1925, the Liberals were able to stay in power with the support of Progressive and Labour members.

Following the resignation of William Lyon Mackenzie King's government on June 28, 1926, the Governor General invited Meighen to form a new ministry. This government was less than 3 months old, however, when it was defeated in the House of Commons (by only one vote) and Canadians again went to the polls.

Following a Liberal victory in the election of Sept. 14, 1926, Meighen resigned as Conservative leader in the House of Commons. He was appointed to the Senate on Feb. 3, 1932 during Richard Bennett's ministry and became government leader in the Senate. Then, following King's victory in 1935, he became Senate Opposition leader.

On Nov. 12, 1941, he once again became leader of the Conservative party, but failed in his bid to win a seat in the Commons in a federal by-election on Feb. 2, 1942. Following this defeat, he retired from politics and resumed his law practice in Toronto where he died Aug. 5, 1960.

■ Mackenzie King

William Lyon Mackenzie King, grandson of William Lyon Mackenzie, was born in Kitchener (then called Berlin) on Dec. 17, 1874.

He took his B.A. and law degrees from the University of Toronto, and also studied at the University of Chicago and Harvard University.

He served as deputy minister of labour from 1900–08.

He was first elected to the House of Commons in 1908, and succeeded Laurier as leader of the Liberal party in 1919. King became prime minister when the Liberals won the general election of Dec. 6, 1921.

Though Meighen's Conservatives won a majority of seats in the general election of Oct. 29, 1925, King stayed in office with the help of Progressive and Labour members who supported his proposed tariff reductions and old-age pension legislation. King had lost his York North seat in the 1925 election but returned to the House of Commons as the member for Prince Albert, Sask., following a by-election on Feb. 15, 1926. King's government was shaken in 1926 by the revelation that the Customs department was tainted with corruption and incompetence. In the furor that followed, King lost the support of many members of Parliament and, although never technically defeated in the House of Commons, decided that he could no longer hold his minority government. He appealed to the Governor General, Lord Byng, to dissolve Parliament, even though the government had not been defeated. Byng refused. King subsequently resigned on June 28, 1926, and the Governor General invited Arthur Meighen to form a government which was subsequently defeated in the House of Commons.

In the general election of Sept. 14, 1926, King's Liberals regained power and held it until 1930. But the disastrous fall in the price of wheat and other Canadian exports in 1929 soured Canadians on their government, and King was defeated by R.B. Bennett's Conservatives in the election of July 28, 1930.

Five years later, King was back in the prime minister's office, following the Liberal victory in the general election of Oct. 14, 1935. In the coming years, King, an ardent supporter of Canada's autonomy within the British Commonwealth was faced with the issue of Canada's participation in an impending European war. To soothe French-Canadian concerns over Canadian support of Great Britain, King promised there would be no conscription; Canada declared war in Sept. 1939. Later, however, heavy casualties in France and Italy in 1944 prompted King to break his promise and send conscripts overseas.

King's government began introducing postwar recovery legislation even before peace was declared. These measures included reconstruction plans and social security schemes such as mother's allowances.

King resigned as prime minister on Nov. 15, 1948, supporting Louis St. Laurent as his successor. In poor health in his final years, King died July 22, 1950 at Kingsmere, his estate in Wright County, Que.

■ Richard Bennett

Richard Bedford Bennett was born at Hopewell, N.B., July 3, 1870. Bennett studied law at Dalhousie University. He read and practised law in Chatham, N.B., from 1893–97, before moving to Calgary where he entered a legal partnership with Senator James A. Lougheed.

Bennett was first elected to the House of Commons in 1911. He served as minister of justice in Arthur Meighen's 1921 cabinet, and minister of finance and minister of mines in Meighen's 1926 government.

Bennett was chosen to replace Meighen as Conservative leader at the party convention in Winnipeg in 1927. He became prime minister following the Conservative victory in the election of July 28, 1930.

Bennett had the task of governing Canada during the worst years of the Depression. Virtually every measure his government attempted ended in failure. High unemployment levels continued despite Bennett's efforts to reduce them. Negotiations for a reciprocity treaty with the United States did not succeed. A plan of preferential tariffs agreed to in 1930 at the Imperial Conference did little to ease Canada's economic woes.

Then, in 1935, near the end of his term, Bennett took an unexpected step to the political left. He proclaimed that "the old order is gone" and that it was time for a new economic system. That new system was to include a state-planned economy, and new unemployment and health insurance legislation and old-age pension laws.

In the election of Oct. 14, 1935, Bennett's Conservatives suffered a devastating defeat, winning just 39 seats. Bennett remained in Opposition until 1937, when he retired to England. There he was given the title Viscount Bennett of Mickelham, Hopewell and Calgary.

Despite the overwhelming problems of the Great Depression, Bennett's term saw the creation of the Canadian Radio Broadcasting Corporation (the predecessor to the CBC) and the Bank of Canada. As well, it was during Bennett's tenure that the Statute of Westminster gave Canada increased autonomy in 1931.

Bennett died June 27, 1947.

■ Louis St. Laurent

Louis Stephen St. Laurent was born at Compton, Que., Feb. 1, 1882. Called to the Quebec bar in 1905, he practised law in Quebec City, and became Professor of Law at Université Laval. He was elected president of the Canadian Bar Association in 1930.

St. Laurent became justice minister in Mackenzie King's cabinet on Dec. 10, 1941. On Feb. 9, 1942, he was elected to the House of Commons in a by-election for Quebec East.

Originally planning to hold his cabinet post only during the war, St. Laurent was persuaded to stay on. On Dec. 10, 1946, he became secretary of state for external affairs. A firm believer in collective security, St. Laurent was one of the architects of the North Atlantic Treaty Organization (NATO). On Aug. 7, 1948, he accepted his party's nomination to be King's successor, and on Nov. 15 became prime minister.

While in power St. Laurent ended the practice of appealing court cases to the Judicial Committee of the Privy Council in England, and made the Supreme Court of Canada the final Canadian court of appeal. He won the acceptance of a new apportionment of taxes in 1956 and, in negotiation with President Truman, laid the foundation for a U.S.-Canada agreement to develop the St. Lawrence Seaway.

In 1958, he retired and returned to Quebec City to practise law. He died July 25, 1973.

■ John Diefenbaker

John George Diefenbaker was born at Neustadt, Ont., Sept. 18, 1895. He received his B.A. from the University of Saskatchewan in 1915, and his M.A. one year later.

After the outbreak of World War I, he joined the Canadian Officers' Training Corps, and served overseas as a lieutenant with the 105th 'Saskatoon Fusiliers' Regiment from 1916 to 1917.

Returning to Saskatchewan, he took his law degree from the University of Saskatchewan in 1919 and established a law practice at Wakaw. He later moved to Prince Albert.

After several unsuccessful attempts to gain a seat, first in the federal, then in Saskatchewan's provincial parliament, Diefenbaker was finally elected to the House of Commons in 1940. He was a candidate for leadership of the Progressive Conservative Party at the 1942 and 1948 conventions, but did not win the nomination until Dec. 14, 1956.

The PCs won the election of June 10, 1957

by a slim margin, and on June 21, John Diefenbaker officially became prime minister. A year later, he called an election, hoping to turn his Conservative minority government into a clear majority. He was overwhelmingly successful, winning 208 of the 265 seats in the Mar. 31, 1958 election. He fared less well in the 1962 election, when only 116 PCs were elected, and in the general election of 1963, a Liberal victory relegated Diefenbaker to the role of Opposition leader. Diefenbaker remained Conservative leader until Sept. 1967, when he was replaced by Robert Stanfield.

The Diefenbaker years (1957–63) saw the passage of the Canadian Bill of Rights, a "roads-to- resources" program to encourage the development of northern resources, legislation providing support for agriculture, encouragement of technical training and improved health and welfare programs. Regional development was emphasized by significant public works such as construction of the South Saskatchewan Dam, and simultaneous translation was introduced in the House of Commons.

Diefenbaker died Aug. 16, 1979 at his home in Rockliffe Park, Ottawa.

■ Lester Pearson

Lester Bowles Pearson was born at Newtonbrook, Ont., on Apr. 23, 1897. He took his B.A. at the University of Toronto, and his M.A. at Oxford University.

After serving overseas in World War I, he became a history professor at the University of Toronto, where he taught from 1924–1928. He joined Canada's foreign service in 1928, became Canada's ambassador to the U.N. in 1945, was appointed under-secretary of state for external affairs in 1946, and accepted the invitations of King and St. Laurent to become minister of external affairs in Sept. 1948.

In 1956, following the Anglo-French-Israeli invasion of Egypt, Pearson's work at the United Nations helped establish a U.N. Emergency Force which kept peace on the Israeli/Egyptian border for the next decade. His settlement of the Suez crisis brought him the Nobel Peace Prize in 1957—the only time a Canadian has been so honored.

Pearson was chosen leader of the Liberal Party Jan. 15, 1958. In the general election of Apr. 8, 1963, the Liberals won 129 seats in the House of Commons, and Pearson became the leader of a minority government.

In the 1965 election, the Liberals made slight gains, but were still short of a majority. Pearson announced his resignation in Dec. 1967 and, in Apr. 1968, was succeeded by Pierre Trudeau.

Under Pearson, the old age pension was extended and a national health plan created. He secured the adoption of a national flag and established the Royal Commission on Bilingualism and Biculturalism.

Though he retired in 1968, his international reputation prompted the World Bank to commission him to prepare a report on international aid programs.

He died in Ottawa, Dec. 27, 1972.

■ Pierre Trudeau

Pierre Elliott Trudeau was born in Montreal on Oct. 18, 1919. He attended the University of Montreal, Harvard University, Université de Paris and the London School of Economics. He was called to the Quebec bar in 1943. From 1949–51, he was a member of the Privy Council staff in Ottawa. In 1950, he co-founded the magazine *Cité Libre*. From 1952–62, he practised law and was a journalist and broadcaster in Montreal. From 1962–65,. he was a law professor at the University of Montreal.

First elected to the House of Commons in 1965, Trudeau was named justice minister in Lester Pearson's cabinet in 1967. The following year, he won the Liberal leadership and became prime minister Apr. 19, 1968. In the general election of the same year, the Liberals won a solid majority.

During his first 4 years in power, Trudeau faced the "F.L.Q. Crisis"—the kidnapping of British diplomat James Cross and Quebec cabinet minister Pierre Laporte by the radical separatist organization Front de Libération du Québec. (Laporte was later murdered.) In response he invoked the War Measures Act, a statute giving the state broad powers of arrest and detention.

In the general election of 1972, Trudeau returned to power with a minority government. In 1974, he regained a majority.

In the general election of 1979, the Progressive Conservatives under Joe Clark won a narrow victory, and were able to form a minority government. Trudeau announced his intention to retire, but when the Clark government fell later that year, Trudeau led the-

Liberals in the election and won a majority on Feb. 18, 1980.

Trudeau's final term in office was devoted to constitutional reform which, for the first time, allowed Canada's Parliament to amend the constitution without appeal to the U.K. government. A constitutionally-entrenched Charter of Rights and Freedoms was also introduced.

Trudeau's introduction of a National Energy Program led to bitter disputes between the federal government and the energy-producing provinces, particularly Alberta. The NEP was aimed at increasing Canadian control of the oil industry, promoting energy self-sufficiency and generating more federal revenues in the energy sector.

During his final year as prime minister Trudeau launched a world peace initiative, visiting more than 40 world leaders to appeal for peace and an end to the nuclear arms race.

In June of 1984, Trudeau resigned. He was succeeded by John Turner and left politics, eventually joining a Montreal law firm.

■ Joe Clark

Charles Joseph "Joe" Clark was born at High River, Alta., on June 5, 1939. He was educated at the University of Alberta.

Clark was first elected to the House of Commons in 1972. In 1976 he became leader of the Progressive Conservative Party and, in the general election of 1979, won enough seats to form a minority government. At 39, Clark was Canada's youngest prime minister. But his minority government fell in Dec. of that year on a vote of non-confidence on its proposed budget. In the Feb. 1980 election that followed, the Liberals returned to power.

At a national general meeting of the Conservative party in Jan. 1983, Clark received the support of only two-thirds of the delegates and called for a national party leadership convention. In June 1983, Clark lost the leadership to Brian Mulroney on the 4th ballot. He remained an MP and, when Mulroney became prime minister in 1984, Clark joined the cabinet as secretary of state for external affairs.

In 1991, he was appointed as minister responsible for constitutional affairs, and given the task of succeeding where the Meech Lake Accord had failed. Late 1991 and the first half of 1992 were marked by weeks of cross-country constitutional negotiations under Clark's guidance. In August, 1992 the Charlottetown

Accord—an agreement to amend the Constitution Act of 1982—was agreed upon by all first ministers. The text of the agreement was presented to Canadians and a national referendum was held on Oct. 26, 1992 on the issue of whether or not to approve the deal. The agreement was rejected by the majority of voters across the country.

In the spring of 1993, Clark announced his retirement from Canadian political life, effective as of the fall 1993 election.

■ John Turner

John Napier Turner was born at Richmond, Surrey, England on June 7, 1929. He attended the University of British Columbia, Oxford University and Université de Paris. He was called to the bar in England in 1953 and the bar in Quebec in 1954. He lectured for a time in the Faculty of Commerce at Sir George Williams University.

First elected to the House of Commons in 1962, Turner entered Lester Pearson's cabinet in 1965. He became minister of consumer and corporate affairs in 1967. In 1968, he was a candidate for the Liberal leadership, finishing 3rd on the final ballot.

In 1968, Turner was appointed minister of justice in Pierre Trudeau's cabinet. In 1972, he became minister of finance, a post he held until his resignation in Sept. 1975. In Feb. 1976 he left politics and joined a Toronto law firm.

Turner remained in private practice until Trudeau's retirement in 1984, when he successfully ran for leader of the Liberal Party and became prime minister on June 30, though he did not have a seat in the House of Commons. He dissolved Parliament July 9, and in the ensuing general election the Liberals were overwhelmingly defeated by the Progressive Conservatives.

As leader of the Opposition, Turner used the Liberal majority in the Senate to block passage of the Conservatives' free trade legislation and force an election on the issue in 1988. The Conservatives won the election and were able to form another majority government.

Early in 1989, Turner announced plans to step down as leader; in June 1990, he was succeeded by Jean Chrétien.

■ Brian Mulroney

Martin Brian Mulroney was born at Baie Comeau, Que., Mar. 20, 1939. He attended St.

Francis Xavier University and Université Laval. Called to the bar of Quebec in 1965, Mulroney practised law in Montreal. In 1976, he joined the Iron Ore Company of Canada as executive vice-president, and was elected company president the following year.

Mulroney made an unsuccessful bid for the Progressive Conservative party leadership in 1976. In 1983 he ran again, defeating the incumbent leader, Joe Clark, on the 4th ballot.

A by-election for the Maritime riding of Central Nova brought Mulroney into Parliament as leader of the Opposition. In the general election of 1984, he led the Conservatives to victory, winning the largest number of seats (211) in Canadian history.

Mulroney's major initiatives between 1984 and 1988 were the Meech Lake Accord—a package of constitutional changes designed to end Quebec's boycott of the 1982 constitutional reform—and the negotiation of a free trade agreement with the United States.

In 1988, with free trade the central election issue, Mulroney won a second majority government. The free trade agreement subsequently received final approval and took effect in 1989.

His term from 1988 to 1993 was marked by intense negotiations to bring about a new constitutional agreement to replace the Meech Lake Accord which was not ratified by all provinces by the June 1990 deadline. Agreement was reached amongst federal and provincial officials in what became known as the Charlottetown Accord, but the proposals were rejected in a national referendum held on October 26, 1992.

The Conservatives under Mulroney continued their free trade initiative and finalized a North American free trade deal (NAFTA) with the US and Mexico.

Mulroney announced his intention to retire in February 1993 and on June 25, 1993 he was replaced by Kim Campbell, newly-elected leader of the Conservative party.

■ Kim Campbell

Avril Phaedra (Kim) Campbell was born March 10, 1947 in Port Alberni, BC. She attended the University of British Columbia, earning an honours degree in political science.

After an academic career in BC, she studied law at UBC. In Sept. 1985, she joined BC Premier William Bennett's office as a policy advisor. In May 1986, Campbell ran in the provincial election and won a seat in the legislature, representing the riding of Vancouver/Point Grey. She served in the provincial legislature until October 1988 when she resigned her seat to contest the federal riding of Vancouver Centre. An ardent defender of free trade, Campbell joined the junior ranks of Prime Min. Mulroney's cabinet with the Indian Affairs and Northern Development portfolio.

In 1990 Campbell was promoted to the Attorney General and Justice post; in January of 1993 she was named Minister of Defence and became a candidate in the Conservative leadership contest that year. On June 13, 1993, she was elected leader on the second ballot and on June 25, she was sworn in as Canada's 19th Prime Minister.

■ Jean Chrétien

Jean Chrétien was born in Shawinigan, Quebec, on January 11, 1934. He studied law at Laval University and was called to the bar of Quebec in 1958.

Chrétien was first elected to the House of Commons in 1963 and after re-election in 1965 served as parliamentary secretary to the Prime Minister (1965) and the Minister of Finance (1966). He was appointed Minister of National Revenue in 1968 and after the election in June of that year was sworn in as Minister of Indian Affairs and Northern Development. In 1974, he was appointed President of the Treasury Board; beginning in 1976, he served as Minister of Industry, Trade and Commerce. In 1977, he was named Minister of Finance; in 1980, he was appointed Minister of Justice and Attorney General of Canada and also served as Minister of State for Social Development and Minister Responsible for constitutional negotiations, playing a significant role in the repatriation of the Canadian constitution. In 1982 Chrétien was appointed Minister of Energy, Mines and Resources and in 1984 became Deputy Prime Minister and Secretary of State for External Affairs.

In 1986 Chrétien left public life, returning after his election as Liberal leader in 1990 and his re-election to the House in a December by-election in Beausejour, taking his seat as leader of the Official Opposition. In the federal election in October of 1993, Chrétien led his party to a majority victory.

GOVERNMENT OF CANADA

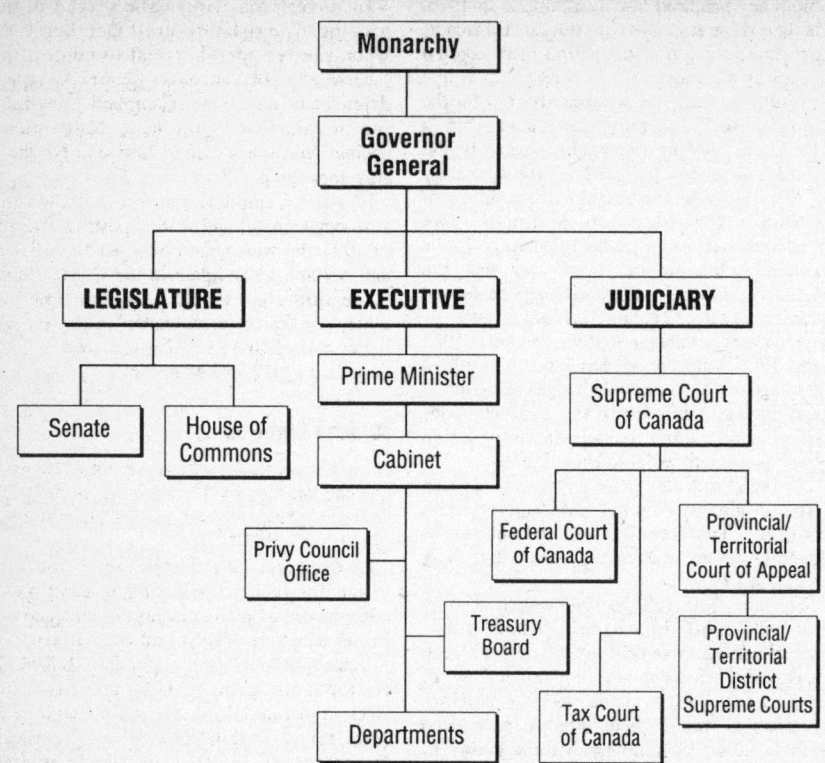

Canada is an independent, self-governing democracy whose form of government is a constitutional monarchy. There are three types of government power: legislative, executive and judicial. In Canada the legislative and executive powers are joined, while the judiciary remains separate. The executive proposes legislation, presents budgets and implements laws; the legislature adopts laws and votes on recommendations for taxes or other revenue; the judiciary interprets the laws.

■ The Monarchy

The British monarch (since June 2, 1953 Queen Elizabeth II) is Canada's official head of state through which the entire authority of the government is set in motion and in whose name laws are enacted. The Queen's role is set out in the *Constitution Act, 1867,* and that same act gives the monarch ultimate authority over Canada's armed forces.

In practice, however, the Queen has little or no part to play in Canadian government. She appoints the Governor General, but does so only on the prime minister's recommendation. Once appointed, it is the Governor General who performs the monarch's duties, and these duties have been mainly ceremonial for many years. Only during royal visits does the Queen carry out those functions normally performed in her name by the Governor General, such as the opening of Parliament.

■ The Governor General

The Governor General is selected by the prime minister and formally appointed by the Queen to act as her representative in Canada. The appointment is usually for five years but has sometimes been extended to seven.

Bills passed in the House of Commons and

Senate do not become law until the Governor General has given them royal assent. The Governor General executes all orders-in-council and other state documents, appoints all superior court judges (on the advice of Cabinet) and summons, prorogues and dissolves Parliament (on the advice of the prime minister). Also, the Governor General invites the leader of the political party with the most support in the House of Commons to form a government. Thus, that leader becomes prime minister.

The Imperial Conferences of 1926 and 1930 established that the Governor General was not the representative or agent of the British government and should act only on the advice of the Canadian prime minister and Cabinet. Therefore, the Governor General is obliged to respect the principle of responsible government and to follow the wishes of Canada's elected representatives. Because of this, the role of the Governor General has become largely symbolic, with duties that are chiefly ceremonial.

Two members of the Royal Family have held the post: the Duke of Connaught (1911–16) and the Earl of Athlone (1940–46). The first Canadian Governor General was Vincent Massey (1952–59).

The Legislature

Canada's legislature or Parliament consists of the Queen, an upper house, known as the Senate, and the House of Commons. Senators are appointed by the Governor General on the advice of the prime minister; the seats in the Senate are distributed on a regional basis; originally, there were 72 senators, but through the years the Senate has increased as the number of provinces and the population have grown. In 1975 the Senate was increased to 104 members; in 1990 Prime Minister Brian Mulroney employed a never-before-used section of the Constitution Act to increase the number to temporarily 112. The House of Commons is an elected assembly in which each member represents one of 295 electoral districts distributed according to population.

■ The Senate

The Senate is the Upper House of the Canadian Parliament through which all legislation must pass before it becomes law. Its members, appointed by the Governor General on the recommendation of the prime minister, hold office until age 75. (If appointed before June 1965 they hold office for life).

After 1975, there were 104 Senate seats apportioned on a regional basis: 24 from the Maritime provinces (Nova Scotia, 10; New Brunswick, 10; Prince Edward Island 4); 24 from Quebec; 24 from Ontario; 24 from the Western provinces (Manitoba, 6; Saskatchewan, 6; Alberta, 6; British Columbia, 6); 6 from Newfoundland; 1 each from the Northwest Territories and Yukon.

To be eligible for Senate appointment, a person must be a Canadian citizen, at least 30 years old, a resident of the province for which he or she is appointed, possess land in that province with an unencumbered value of $4 000 and have a net estate of $4 000. A Senator for Quebec must either be resident in the division for which he or she is appointed, or have property qualification there.

Technically, the Senate's legislative powers are equal to those of the House of Commons with two restrictions: first, on certain constitutional amendments, the Senate may delay resolutions of the House of Commons for up to 180 days, but cannot defeat them; second, the Senate cannot initiate money bills.

In practice, however, the Senate's chief role is to provide technical reviews of legislation proposed in the House of Commons rather than to initiate political action. These reviews are done by Senate committees, which inspect each bill clause-by-clause and hear evidence from groups or individuals who may be affected by the proposed legislation.

Historically, the Senate rarely used its powers to impede legislation originating from the elected House of Commons. From 1984 to 1990, however, the Liberal-dominated Senate attempted several times to stall or block legislation approved by the Conservative majority in the House of Commons. In 1990, when the Senate blocked his government's goods and services tax, Mulroney temporarily increased the size of the Senate and added eight new Conservatives, ensuring that the measure would be made law.

In recent years, there have been repeated calls, especially from the West, for constitutional reform which would include an elected Senate with more representation from the Western provinces and Newfoundland. Plans for discussions leading to a Senate overhaul are now part of other constitutional discussions.

■ The House of Commons

The House of Commons is Canada's 295-member elected federal assembly. Its members are chosen in general elections held at least once every five years. By-elections are held if a member dies or resigns between general elections.

All bills governing matters within federal jurisdiction must be passed by a majority of members of Parliament to become law.

Members of Parliament usually belong to a political party and will normally vote with that party on any proposed legislation. Occasionally, members will break with their party on a vote and will sometimes leave the party they were affiliated with when elected to sit as independents or to join another political party within the House. Members of Parliament can also be elected as independent candidates who do not belong to a political party.

The **prime minister** is the leader of the political party able to command the support of a majority of the members of the House of Commons. If no party holds a clear majority of seats, a "minority government" is formed, usually led by the party with the most seats in Parliament, provided it has enough support from the other parties to enable it to pass legislation.

When the House of Commons is in session it convenes at two o'clock daily and 11 o'clock on Fridays when the Speaker of the House takes the chair. After the mace is laid on the table in front of the Speaker and the daily prayer is read, business commences. Members of the government sit to the Speaker's right and the Opposition sits on the left. The leaders of other opposition parties sit on the left farther away from the Speaker's chair.

An important feature of Parliament is the daily question period at which time members question Cabinet ministers about their policies and actions. But most of Parliament's time is spent discussing proposed legislation introduced as "bills". Any member may introduce a bill, although this is usually done by a member of Cabinet. After readings in the House and detailed examination in committee, the bill will go for "third reading" in the House and if passed, will be forwarded to the Senate.

When a major piece of legislation introduced by the government is defeated in the House of Commons, the government is obliged to resign. The Governor General may then call on the leader of the Opposition to form a government but, in most cases, will call a general election so that the electorate can decide which party has the most public support for its policies.

The Executive

■ The Prime Minister

The prime minister is the pre-eminent figure in Canadian politics. The power and authority of the office come from the fact that the prime minister is the leader of the party (or group of parties) that has control of, if not a clear majority of seats in the House of Commons, at least more seats than any of the other parties. The prime minister is an elected member of parliament as well as national party leader and as such has a mandate to govern via programs and policies and to speak on behalf of Canada.

The prime minister has control over appointments, including appointing (and shifting) cabinet members, senior staff in the public service and parliamentary secretaries; and appointing senators, judges, lieutenant governors, privy councillors, provincial administrators, and speakers of the senate. In addition, the prime minister recommends to the monarchy the appointment of the governor general. The prime minister has the authority to dissolve parliament and can therefore control the timing of an election. The prime minister also controls the organization of government, including the power to: create or shut down crown corporations; create, modify or merge cabinet portfolios and bureaucratic agencies; and appoint royal commissions.

■ The Cabinet

The Cabinet is a group of government ministers who, chosen and led by the prime minister, determine executive policies and are responsible for them to the House of Commons. Cabinet members are usually given responsibility for heading specific areas of the government such as finance or foreign policy and will introduce legislation pertaining to them in the House of Commons. They will also explain or defend government actions when questioned in the House.

Cabinet ministers are generally chosen from members of the government's party in the House of Commons, although Senators are sometimes appointed to provide Cabinet representation from all parts of the country. When Senators join the Cabinet they do not usually head a government department because a Senator is constitutionally forbidden to introduce tax or "money bill" legislation.

There are five categories of cabinet ministers:

1. Department Ministers who assume responsibility for running one or more government departments.

2. Ministers with special parliamentary responsibilities.

3. Ministers without portfolios who do not have responsibility for running a department and are often appointed to balance regional representation in the Cabinet.

4. Ministers of state for designated purposes who formulate and develop new policies outside normal departmental responsibilities.

5. Other ministers of state who may assist departmental ministers, though the departmental minister remains legally responsible for the duties and functions performed by the minister of state.

■ **The Privy Council Office**

The Privy Council Office is directed by the senior member of the public service, the Clerk of the Privy Council, who also serves as the Secretary to the Cabinet. As part of the executive branch of government, the Office staffs the Cabinet secretariat and provides services to ensure the smooth functioning of the Cabinet and Cabinet meetings. In its advisory capacity, the Privy Council Office advises the Prime Minister on government appointments, relations with Parliament and the Monarchy, the roles and responsibilities of ministers and the organization of government. The Office assists in the co-ordination of policy, ensuring that new proposals are compatible both with existing policy and the government's objectives. During a transition period between governments, the Privy Council Office assists in the winding down of outgoing administrations and the startup of the newly-elected government.

The Privy Council Office's primary responsibilities are to ensure the smooth functioning of the machinery of government and the decision-making process, provide support to the Cabinet, monitor developments throughout the government, and act as a broker to resolve governmental problems.

■ **The Treasury Board**

The Treasury Board is a committee of the Privy Council that reviews planned expenditures and programs proposed by the various government departments, and assigns priorities to each. The Board is responsible for preparing a long-range and comprehensive fiscal plan that projects government income and expenses for up to four years; it also prepares operational plans for departmental programs. The Board's estimates of the costs of existing programs, major statutory payments (such as transfer payments) and public debt charges form the basis of the Main Estimates, which are tabled by the first of March each year for review by various House committees.

The Treasury Board is also responsible for administrative policy; organization of the public service; and financial, expenditure and personnel management. In 1988, the Board was also given responsibility for the policies and programs of the Official Languages Act. The Board's Secretariat negotiates collective agreements with the federal public service, acting as employer on the government's behalf.

■ **Departments**

Legislation and government policies are administered through departments, departmental branches and corporations, corporations owned or controlled by the government, special boards and various commissions and advisory bodies. Departments and departmental corporations are accountable to a Cabinet minister and ultimately to Parliament; they perform research, administrative, advisory, supervisory or regulatory roles. Crown corporations usually operate in a competitive or commercial environment and some are accountable to Parliament through a minister as well.

The Canadian Judiciary

■ The Supreme Court of Canada

The Supreme Court of Canada is Canada's highest court of law. It was created by federal statute in 1875. Originally, Supreme Court decisions could be appealed to a special tribunal in England, but such appeals were abolished for criminal cases in 1933 and for civil cases in 1949. Since then, the Supreme Court of Canada has been the court of last resort for every case—criminal or civil— commenced in a Canadian court.

The Supreme Court has jurisdiction to hear appeals from the courts of appeal of each province, as well as from the Federal Court of Canada. The Court is also empowered to consider questions referred to it by the federal cabinet, and to rule on the legality of bills submitted by the government.

The *Constitution Act, 1982,* with its new Canadian Charter of Rights and Freedoms, has expanded the role of the courts in general, and of the Supreme Court in particular. Though it has always been within the power of Canadian courts to declare laws or other government actions invalid, this power had narrow limits prior to 1982. Legislation could only be struck down if the government introducing it had exceeded its legislative authority as defined in the *Constitution Act, 1867* (the BNA Act). In other words, the federal government was not permitted to legislate on matters within provincial legislative authority, and the provincial governments were not permitted to legislate on matters within federal legislative authority. As long as the legislation satisfied that test, it was valid.

But since the *Constitution Act* became law in 1982, the courts have had the power to strike down legislation or invalidate other government actions if they infringe or deny any of the fundamental rights and freedoms recognized by the Charter of Rights and Freedoms. This new power has made Supreme Court judges the watchdogs of Parliament and, ultimately, the guardians of our constitutionally-guaranteed rights. As the highest court in the land, it is the Supreme Court of Canada that has the final word on whether laws violate the Constitution.

The Supreme Court consists of 9 judges, including the Chief Justice. Three of the judges must be appointed from Quebec. By convention (although it is not legall required) 3 have usually been appointed from Ontario, 2 from the West and one from Atlantic Canada. All judges are appointed and paid by the federal government, and may hol office until age 75.

■ Federal Court of Canada

This Court consists of a trial division and court of appeal and has jurisdiction over a small range of specialized areas such as admiralty law, income tax, patents and customs Once called the Exchequer Court, the Federal Court is administered by the federal government.

■ Appellate Courts

When a decision of the provincial superior courts is to be appealed, these courts hear the appeal and decide upon it. An appeal is not a new trial; there are rarely any witnesses called and the judges do not rehear the whole case Instead, they examine written transcripts of the trial and listen to legal arguments presented by the parties' lawyers. The appellate courts are provincial institutions and are called either the Court of Appeal, the Supreme Court Appeal Division or Appellate Division; the judges are appointed by the federal government.

■ Superior Court of Original Jurisdiction

This is the highest court at the provincial level, with jurisdiction to hear all civil and criminal cases, unless a statute specifically says otherwise. The name of the superior court differs among provinces. It can be called either the Court of Queen's Bench, the High Court of Justice or the Supreme Court Trial Division. The judges of these courts are appointed and paid by the federal government.

■ District or County Courts

These trial courts hear all but the most serious criminal matters and civil matters up to a certain dollar value. The judges of these courts are also appointed by the federal government.

■ Provincial Courts

This is the lowest rung of the judicial ladder. The jurisdiction of the provincial courts is limited by statute to the less serious criminal matters and civil cases involving relatively small sums of money. These judges are appointed and paid by the province in which they serve.

■ Federal and Provincial Legislative Authority

Because Canada is a federal state, legislative powers are divided between 2 levels of government: federal and provincial. (Municipal governments only exercise powers delegated to them by the provincial government).

Each level of government has a distinct sphere of authority. With a few exceptions, neither level is permitted to encroach on the legislative authority of the other.

The Constitution Act, 1867 (formerly called the British North America Act, 1867), lists the classes of subject over which the federal and provincial governments have exclusive authority. The federal government, in addition to a general power to make laws for the "peace, order and good government of Canada," has exclusive power in a number of areas including criminal law, unemployment insurance, postal service, regulation of trade, external relations, money and banking, transportation, citizenship, Indian affairs and defence. Matters exclusively within provincial legislative authority include property and civil rights, administration of justice, education, health and welfare, municipal institutions and matters of a merely local or private nature.

Many of the subject classes set out in the Constitution Act, 1867, are broadly worded, and considerable debate has arisen over which level of government has authority to pass certain laws. Confusion has also arisen over the proper distribution of powers to regulate matters that could not have been foreseen by the Fathers of Confederation, such as air travel, radio and television broadcasting, etc. These difficulties have led to long political debates and frequently to court challenges which arise when a person adversely affected by a particular law claims that the law is invalid because it is *ultra vires*—beyond the powers of the level of government that enacted it. Prior to the passing of the Constitution Act, 1982, only statutes found to be *ultra vires* could be declared inoperative by the Constitution. Now, there is an additional restraint on the federal parliament and the provincial legisla-

tures to comply with constitutional provisions, including the Canadian Charter of Rights and Freedoms.

■ The Provincial Governments

Canada's provinces have a system of government which parallels that of the federal government in several ways. A premier, like the prime minister, leads the government by virtue of being leader of the party with the most support in the provincial legislature and forms a Cabinet from the elected members of the governing party. Members of a provincial legislature, like members of the federal Parliament, represent constituencies and approve legislation within their constitutional jurisdiction. A lieutenant-governor, like the Governor General, gives royal assent to the laws passed by the legislature.

The major difference between the provincial and federal systems is that the provinces have no equivalent body to Canada's Senate.

■ Government in the Yukon and Northwest Territories

Both the Yukon and Northwest Territories are governed by elected representatives. Although the administration of each territory is technically in the hands of a commissioner appointed by the federal government, in practice, the commissioners' role has become much like that of the provincial lieutenant-governors' in that they follow the wishes of the territories' elected representatives when exercising their authority.

In the Northwest Territories, real executive power is in the hands of a 24-person elected assembly whose members run for office as independents rather than as members of political parties. This assembly then selects an 8-member executive council, one of whom is chosen to serve as Government Leader.

Yukon has a 16-member legislative assembly which operates on a political party system. As of Oct. 1989, the government leader (the leader of the political party supported by a majority of the assembly's elected representatives) is given the title premier. Executive power is in the hands of an executive council, which functions like a provincial Cabinet. Its members are appointed by Yukon's commissioner on the advice of the premier.

In both territories, the elected bodies have jurisdiction over such areas as education, housing, social services and renewable resources. A 1988 accord between the federal government and the Northwest Territories has opened the way for negotiation on the transfer of responsibility for oil and gas resource management and control of oil and gas revenues. Similar negotiations are underway between Yukon and the federal government.

In 1990, the Northwest Territories established six aboriginal languages (Dogrib, Chipewyan, Gwich'in, Cree, Slavey and Inuktitut) as Official Languages, in addition to English and French.

■ Mechanics of Government

Formation of Government General elections to choose House of Commons members occur at least every five years. But they may take place more often if the prime minister decides to call an election or if the governing party loses the support of the majority of members of the House.

Following an election, the Governor General calls upon the leader of the party with the greatest House of Commons support to become prime minister. This is almost always the leader of the party with the most seats in the House but, under unusual circumstances, it could be the leader of another party which is able to gain majority support in Parliament.

The prime minister selects the cabinet, usually from members of his party in the House of Commons. Formally, the prime minister and cabinet act as advisors to the Governor General. In practice, however, they wield executive power and the Governor General's role is mainly ceremonial.

Passage of Legislation To become law, proposed legislation (known as bills) must be passed by a majority of members in both the House of Commons and the Senate and must then be given royal assent by the Governor General. Most bills are introduced by members of the government in the House of Commons. Typically, a bill is given three "readings" in the House. The first reading is simply to introduce the bill. The second reading is accompanied by debate on the principle of the bill. The bill is then voted on and, if approved, is sent to a House committee composed of representatives of all parties to be considered clause-by-clause. The committee prepares a report and submits it to the House of Commons along with any proposed amendments. These amendments, plus any others

moved by any member of Parliament, are debated and usually voted on. A motion is then brought for the bill to be given third reading. If the vote is favorable, the bill is then introduced in the Senate where it undergoes a similar process. After a bill has been approved by both Houses, the Governor General gives it royal assent in a ceremony that takes place in the Senate chamber.

Defeat of a Government Between elections, a government can be forced to resign if it is defeated in a vote on a major government bill. When this happens the government is considered to have lost the support of the majority of Parliament's elected representatives. This typically occurs only when the party in power has formed a minority government—that is, if it holds more seats than any other single party but fewer seats than the combined Opposition parties. This last happened federally in 1979 when a minority Conservative government, elected earlier that year, introduced a budget which was defeated by the combined votes of the Liberal and New Democratic Party members in the House. Parliament was dissolved, an election was called and the Liberals regained power.

■ The Constitution of Canada

Canada's constitution consists of written documents and unwritten conventions. The written constitution is embodied in the Constitution Acts 1867–1982. The 1867 legislation (originally titled the British North America Act) was a British statute that established a federal state with a Parliament modelled on the British system. That Act assembled the colonies of Nova Scotia, New Brunswick and Canada (Ontario and Quebec) into the "Dominion of Canada," created a federal government in Ottawa, and divided the powers of government between Ottawa and the provinces.

The BNA Act gave Ottawa broad jurisdiction over internal matters, including unlimited powers of taxation, while allowing the provinces only a narrow field of local control. In general, the Canadian constitution of the late 19th century was a centralist document.

Under the BNA Act, Britain still had the power to veto Canadian laws or to enact statutes affecting Canada. But the British had no desire to raise revenue in Canada, for example, or to tax Canadians directly. This approach extended to trade and tariffs.

Gradually, the practice was established that where money was involved, even in trade treaties, Canada would determine its own policy.

The same was not true of political foreign policy. When Britain declared war on Germany in 1914, Canada, as part of the British Empire, was automatically at war, even though it had not been consulted on the matter. During this period, British courts also interpreted Canadian statutes, especially those involving the division of power between Ottawa and the provinces. As a result, the constitution's strong centralist thrust was altered to give more authority to the provinces.

The constitution was also adjusted more directly, through amendments. But because the BNA Act was a British statute, Canada could make formal changes to it only with the consent of the British Parliament. Ottawa tended to seek such amendments only when they did not affect provincial powers or when the provinces agreed with the changes. This process worked at least some of the time: 29 times, in fact, between 1870 and 1975. In 1940, for example, unemployment insurance became a federal responsibility through an amendment to the BNA Act.

In 1931, Britain attempted to tidy up relations with Canada and other self-governing dominions within the Commonwealth by passing the Statute of Westminster. The Statute conceded full powers over foreign affairs and trade to Canada. But because the federal and provincial governments could not agree on a method for amending the BNA Act at home, the British Parliament retained ultimate power over Canada's constitution. Until 1949, British courts continued to review Canadian constitutional cases.

From 1927 until 1982, a succession of federal governments attempted to resolve the problem by getting the provinces to agree to an amending formula. These negotiations failed as the provinces attempted to use them as a means of gaining concessions from Ottawa.

The catalyst in constitutional discussions during the late 20th century has been the province of Quebec, where successive provincial governments since 1960 have sought to expand the province's jurisdiction and limit that of the federal government. The rationale for the change has been Quebec's unique status as a French-speaking entity in North America—the only one with French speakers in the majority.

To protect French culture, the Quebec government requested more powers, over culture itself, but also over the economy and social institutions. Where a provincial power such as education had an international dimension, the Quebec government also asserted that it had the power to represent itself abroad without Ottawa's authority or intervention. Ottawa, alarmed that such representation could lead by stages to Quebec's complete independence, resisted the trend under prime ministers Lester Pearson and Pierre Trudeau.

Trudeau was determined to see the constitution patriated, but not at the cost of the federal government's basic jurisdiction. Without a strong central power, he argued, a country as sprawling and diverse as Canada would be fatally weakened and might disintegrate. In lengthy negotiations with the provinces, Trudeau was unable to gain agreement, even when he offered increased powers in return. In 1976, the election of the separatist Parti Québécois in Quebec made constitutional compromise even more unlikely. Instead, the government of Premier Réne Lévesque wanted "sovereignty-association" with Canada: political separation with economic union.

In 1980, the Quebec government risked a referendum on sovereignty-association and lost. Trudeau, who helped defeat sovereignty-association, promised constitutional renewal if Quebeckers chose to stay within Canada. Federal-provincial discussions became mired in disagreement through the summer of 1980. Then, in September, Trudeau announced that the federal government, with the support of only Ontario and New Brunswick, would ask the British parliament to amend the BNA Act so that the constitution could be patriated and a Charter of Rights and Freedoms established to protect individual liberties. Trudeau also sought to protect minority rights in education and the mobility rights of Canadian citizens. Finally, Trudeau changed the name of the constitution: the BNA Act became the Constitution Act, 1982.

It took 18 months to get the new amendments approved by the Canadian Parliament, work around the disagreement of eight provincial governments, and get the act through the British Parliament. But, in April 1982, the Constitution Act was proclaimed—although the consent of the Quebec government was never given. It was legal nevertheless, although some observers felt its credibility and acceptability were damaged by Quebec's abstention.

The Constitution Act, 1982, consolidated all the previous BNA Acts and added an amending formula and a Charter of Rights and Freedoms. The Charter, which provided for basic democratic rights, also contained a "notwithstanding" clause that allowed Parliament or any provincial legislature to over-ride its provisions.

The amending formula provided for two types of constitutional change: the division of powers between the federal and provincial governments could be modified with the consent of the federal Parliament and seven provincial legislatures in provinces totalling more than 50 percent of the Canadian population; matters such as the composition of the Supreme Court or the status of English or French, however, required unanimous consent. No amendment could take longer than three years to be ratified by Ottawa and all 10 provinces.

This last point proved to be a major obstacle when the Conservative government of Brian Mulroney sought further constitutional reform to obtain Quebec's consent to the 1982 constitution. Under the new Liberal government of Premier Robert Bourassa, Quebec was prepared to accept the 1982 settlement, thus legitimizing it in the eyes of many critics, only if Ottawa and the other provinces agreed to modify the division of powers and to include a reference to Quebec as a "distinct society" in the constitution. In June 1987, in the Meech Lake Accord, Mulroney and the 10 provincial premiers agreed to do just that. Ottawa conceded a provincial role in appointments to the Supreme Court and Senate, conceded Quebec a role in setting immigration policy, and partly weakened the federal government's ability to impose shared-cost programs on the provinces.

Because parts of the Meech Lake agreement involved an amendment to the constitution of the Canadian Senate and the Supreme Court, unanimous provincial consent was required. The Meech Lake agreement lapsed when Newfoundland withdrew its ratification and Manitoba failed to ratify it within the three-year time limit (June 23, 1990).

The failure of the Meech Lake accord plunged Canada into another constitutional crisis. Nationalism, sovereignty and total independence all acquired more support inside Quebec. The government of Quebec studied constitutional options during 1991, as did a number of federal commissions which travelled the country and consulted the population. Despite recommendations for sovereignty for Quebec, Quebec premier Robert Bourassa asked for further proposals from the federal government and scheduled a provincial referendum on those proposals to be held no later than October, 1992.

In September 1991, Prime Min. Mulroney tabled a new constitutional plan with 28 proposals, and meetings and discussions concerning the plan lasted well into 1992. On Aug. 28, 1992, federal-provincial agreement was reached on revised proposals in Charlottetown, PEI, and the resulting document became known as the Charlottetown Accord.

Proposals in the accord included provisions for: a smaller but elected Senate; an expanded House of Commons (337 seats instead of the present 295); annual First Ministers conferences; entrenchment of equalization payments to provinces to ensure each provincial government of sufficient revenues; recognition of the inherent right of Aboriginal peoples to self-government within Canada; recognition of Quebec as a distinct society; a transfer of responsibility for forestry, mining, telecommunications, regional development, municipal and urban affairs, culture within the province, tourism, housing and recreation to the provinces, with the federal government also committed to negotiating agreements with individual provinces concerning immigration.

The referendum in Quebec concerning the proposals was set for October 26, 1992 and the rest of the country followed suit with a national referendum on the same date on the question "Do you agree that the Constitution of Canada should be renewed on the basis of the agreement reached on August 28, 1992?"

Both the "yes" and the "no" sides waged a fierce campaign on the issue; the final, national verdict was 54.8% of votes cast for the "no" side and 44.9% for the "yes." Provincially, the Charlottetown Accord was approved by the Northwest Territories, Prince Edward Island, Newfoundland, New Brunswick and Ontario; the Yukon, Nova Scotia, Quebec, Manitoba, Saskatchewan, Alberta and British Columbia rejected it.

Text of the Canadian Charter of Rights and Freedoms

Whereas Canada is founded upon principles that recognize the supremacy of God and the rule of law:

■ Guarantee of Rights and Freedoms

1 The Canadian Charter of Rights and Freedoms guarantees the rights and freedoms set out in it subject only to such reasonable limits prescribed by law as can be demonstrably justified in a free and democratic society.

■ Fundamental Freedoms

2 Everyone has the following fundamental freedoms: (a) freedom of conscience and religion; (b) freedom of thought, belief, opinion and expression, including freedom of the press and other media of communication; (c) freedom of peaceful assembly; and (d) freedom of association.

■ Democratic Rights

3 Every citizen of Canada has the right to vote in an election of members of the House of Commons or of a legislative assembly and to be qualified for membership therein.

4 (1) No House of Commons and no legislative assembly shall continue for longer than five years from the date fixed for the return of the writs at a general election of its members. (2) In time of real or apprehended war, invasion or insurrection, a House of Commons may be continued by Parliament and a legislative assembly may be continued by the legislature beyond five years if such continuation is not opposed by the votes of more than one-third of the members of the House of Commons or the legislative assembly, as the case may be.

5 There shall be a sitting of Parliament and of each legislature at least once every twelve months.

■ Mobility Rights

6 (1) Every citizen of Canada has the right to enter, remain in and leave Canada. (2) Every citizen of Canada and every person who has the status of a permanent resident of Canada has the right (a) to move to and take up residence in any province; and (b) to pursue the gaining of a livelihood in any province. (3) The rights specified in subsection (2) are subject to (a) any laws or practices of general application in force in a province other than those that discriminate among persons primarily on the basis of province of present or previous residence; and (b) any laws providing for reasonable residency requirements as a qualification for the receipt of publicly provided social services. (4) Subsections (2) and (3) do not preclude any law, program or activity that has as its object the amelioration in a province of conditions of individuals in that province who are socially or economically disadvantaged if the rate of employment in that province is below the rate of employment in Canada.

■ Legal Rights

7 Everyone has the right to life, liberty and security of the person and the right not to be deprived thereof except in accordance with the principles of fundamental justice.

8 Everyone has the right to be secure against unreasonable search or seizure.

9 Everyone has the right not to be arbitrarily detained or imprisoned.

10 Everyone has the right on arrest or detention (a) to be informed promptly of the reasons therefor; (b) to retain and instruct counsel without delay and to be informed of that right; and (c) to have the validity of the detention determined by way of *habeas corpus* and to be released if the detention is not lawful.

11 Any person charged with an offence has the right (a) to be informed without unreasonable delay of the specific offence; (b) to be tried within a reasonable time; (c) not to be compelled to be a witness in proceedings against that person in respect of the offence; (d) to be presumed innocent until proven guilty according to law in a fair and public hearing by an independent and impartial tribunal; (e) not to be denied reasonable bail without just cause; (f) except in the case of an offence under military law tried before a military tribunal, to the benefit of trial by jury where the maximum punishment for the offence is imprisonment for five years or a more severe punishment; (g) not to be found guilty on account of any act or omission unless, at the time of the act or omission, it constituted an offence under Canadian or international law or was criminal according to the general principles of law recognized by the community of nations; (h) if finally acquitted of the offence, not to be tried for it again and, if finally found guilty and punished for the offence, not to be tried or punished for it again; and (i) if found guilty of the offence and if the punishment for the offence has been varied between the time of commission and the time of sentencing, to the benefit of the lesser punishment.

12 Everyone has the right not to be subjected to any cruel and unusual treatment or punishment.

13 A witness who testifies in any proceedings has the right not to have any incriminating evidence so given used to incriminate that witness in any other proceedings, except in a prosecution for perjury or for the giving of contradictory evidence.

14 A party or witness in any proceedings who does not understand or speak the language in which the proceedings are conducted or who is deaf has the right to the assistance of an interpreter.

■ Equality Rights

15 (1) Every individual is equal before and under the law and has the right to the equal protection and equal benefit of the law without discrimination and, in particular, without discrimination based on race, national or ethnic origin, colour, religion, sex, age or mental or physical disability. (2) Subsection (1) does not preclude any law, program or activity that has as its object the amelioration of conditions of disadvantaged individuals or groups including those that are disadvantaged because of race, national or ethnic origin,

colour, religion, sex, age or mental or physical disability.

■ Official Languages of Canada

16 (1) English and French are the official languages of Canada and have equality of status and equal rights and privileges as to their use in all institutions of the Parliament and government of Canada. (2) English and French are the official languages of New Brunswick and have equality of status and equal rights and privileges as to their use in all institutions of the legislature and government of New Brunswick. (3) Nothing in this Charter limits the authority of Parliament or a legislature to advance the equality of status or use of English and French.

17 (1) Everyone has the right to use English or French in any debates and other proceedings of Parliament. (2) Everyone has the right to use English or French in any debates and other proceedings of the legislature of New Brunswick.

18 (1) The statutes, records and journals of Parliament shall be printed and published in English and French and both language versions are equally authoritative. (2) The statutes, records and journals of the legislature of New Brunswick shall be printed and published in English and French and both language versions are equally authoritative.

19 (1) Either English or French may be used by any person in, or in any pleading in or process issuing from, any court established by Parliament. (2) Either English or French may be used by any person in, or in any pleading in or process issuing from, any court of New Brunswick.

20 (1) Any member of the public in Canada has the right to communicate with, and to receive available services from, any head or central office of an institution of the Parliament or government of Canada in English or French, and has the same right with respect to any other office of any such institution where (a) there is a significant demand for communications with and services from that office in such language; or (b) due to the nature of the office, it is reasonable that communications with and services from that office be available in both English and French. (2) Any member of the public in New Brunswick has the

right to communicate with, and to receive available services from, any office of an institution of the legislature or government of New Brunswick in English or French.

21 Nothing in sections 16 to 20 abrogates or derogates from any right, privilege or obligation with respect to the English and French languages, or either of them, that exists or is continued by virtue of any other provision of the Constitution of Canada.

22 Nothing in sections 16 to 20 abrogates or derogates from any legal or customary right or privilege acquired or enjoyed either before or after the coming into force of this Charter with respect to any language that is not English or French.

■ Minority Language Educational Rights

23 (1) Citizens of Canada (a) whose first language learned and still understood is that of the English or French linguistic minority population of the province in which they reside, or (b) who have received their primary school instruction in Canada in English or French and reside in a province where the language in which they received that instruction is the language of the English or French linguistic minority population of the province, have the right to have their children receive primary and secondary school instruction in that language in that province. (2) Citizens of Canada of whom any child has received or is receiving primary or secondary school instruction in English or French in Canada, have the right to have all their children receive primary and secondary school instruction in the same language. (3) The right of citizens of Canada under subsections (1) and (2) to have their children receive primary and secondary school instruction in the language of the English or French linguistic minority population of a province (a) applies wherever in the province the number of children of citizens who have such a right is sufficient to warrant the provision to them out of public funds of minority language instruction; and (b) includes, where the number of those children so warrants, the right to have them receive that instruction in minority language educational facilities provided out of public funds.

■ Enforcement

24 (1) Anyone whose rights or freedoms, as guaranteed by this Charter, have been infringed or denied may apply to a court of competent jurisdiction to obtain such remedy as the court considers appropriate and just in the circumstances. (2) Where, in proceedings under subsection (1), a court concludes that evidence was obtained in a manner that infringed or denied any rights or freedoms guaranteed by this Charter, the evidence shall be excluded if it is established that, having regard to all the circumstances, the admission of it in the proceedings would bring the administration of justice into disrepute.

■ General

25 The guarantee in this Charter of certain rights and freedoms shall not be construed so as to abrogate or derogate from any aboriginal, treaty or other rights or freedoms that pertain to the aboriginal peoples of Canada including (a) any rights or freedoms that have been recognized by the Royal Proclamation of October 7, 1763; and (b) any rights or freedoms that may be acquired by the aboriginal peoples of Canada by way of land claims settlement.

26 The guarantee in this Charter of certain rights and freedoms shall not be construed as denying the existence of any other rights or freedoms that exist in Canada.

27 This Charter shall be interpreted in a manner consistent with the preservation and enhancement of the multicultural heritage of Canadians.

28 Notwithstanding anything in this Charter, the rights and freedoms referred to in it are guaranteed equally to male and female persons.

29 Nothing in this Charter abrogates or derogates from any rights or privileges guaranteed by or under the Constitution of Canada in respect of denominational, separate or dissentient schools.

30 A reference in this Charter to a province or to the legislative assembly or legislature or a province shall be deemed to include a reference to the Yukon Territory and the Northwest Territories, or to the appropriate legislative authority thereof, as the case may be.

31 Nothing in this Charter extends the legislative powers of any body or authority.

■ Application of Charter

32. (1) This Charter applies (a) to the Parliament and government of Canada in respect of all matters within the authority of Parliament including all matters relating to the Yukon Territory and Northwest Territories; and (b) to the legislature and government of each province in respect of all matters within the authority of the legislature of each province. (2) Notwithstanding subsection (1), section 15 shall not have effect until three years after this section comes into force.

33 (1) Parliament or the legislature of a province may expressly declare in an Act of Parliament or of the legislature, as the case may be, that the Act or a provision thereof shall operate notwithstanding a provision included in section 2 or sections 7 to 15 of this Charter. (2) An Act or a provision of an Act in respect of which a declaration made under this section is in effect shall have such operation as it would have but for the provision of this Charter referred to in the declaration. (3) A declaration made under subsection (1) shall cease to have effect five years after it comes into force or on such earlier date as may be specified in the declaration. (4) Parliament or a legislature of a province may re-enact a declaration made under subsection (1). (5) Subsection (3) applies in respect of a re-enactment made under subsection (4).

■ Citation

34 This Part may be cited as the Canadian Charter of Rights and Freedoms.

Canadian Honours and Decorations

■ The Order of Canada

History Creation of the Order of Canada was announced by Prime Minister Lester B. Pearson in 1967. It was instituted on the centennial of Canadian Confederation, July 1, 1967.

Basis of Award To honour Canadians for outstanding achievement and service to their country or humanity at large. Appointments are announced twice annually, around July 1 and January 1. Investitures occur three times a year, in February, April and October when the awards are given by the Governor General.

Eligibility Every Canadian is eligible to become a member.

Membership There are three categories of membership: Companion of The Order of Canada (C.C.): no more than 15 may be appointed in any one year and the total number is not to exceed 150 living companions.

Officer of The Order of Canada (O.C.): not more than 50 appointments annually.

Member of The Order of Canada (C.M.): Designed to recognize service in a locality or a particular field of activity. Not more than 100 appointments annually.

Badge A stylized snowflake with a ribbon in the same proportions of white and red which appear on the Canadian flag. Bears the words "Desiderantes Meliorem Patriam" (They Desire for a Better Country). Worn at the neck by Companions and Officers and on the left breast by Members.

■ The Order of Military Merit

History The Order was instituted in 1972.

Basis of Award To recognize exceptional service and conspicuous merit by regular and reserve members of Canada's Armed Forces.

Appointments are made by the Governor General on the recommendation of the chief of Defence staff.

Eligibility Members of the Canadian Armed Forces, regular and reserve.

Membership Commander of the Order of Military Merit (C.M.M.): Commanders constitute 6% of the .1% of the Armed Forces who are annually eligible for an appointment.

Officer of the Order of Military Merit (O.M.M.): Of the .1%, 30% may be made Officers.

Member of the Order of Military Merit (M.M.M.): The balance of appointments are as Members.

Badge In the form of an enamelled blue cross having expanded arms, with a blue ribbon edged in gold. Bears the words "Merit Merite Canada". Worn at the neck by Commanders and on the left breast by Officers and Members.

■ Victoria Cross (V.C.) (Canadian)

History Approved by Queen Elizabeth II on February 2, 1993. The British Victoria Cross was created by Queen Victoria in 1856 and was awarded to Canadians in all wars until 1945. There have been 93 Canadian recipients of the British V.C. and none of the Canadian version.

Basis of Award In recognition of "the most conspicuous bravery, a daring or pre-eminent act of valour or self-sacrifice or extreme devotion to duty, in the presence of the enemy." The V.C. will be awarded by the Governor General on the advice of the Military Valour Advisory Committee. It is the highest in the order of precedence in Canadian honours.

Eligibility Members of the Canadian Forces or a member of an allied armed force that is serving with or in conjunction with the Canadian Forces on or after January 1, 1993. The V.C. may be awarded posthumously.

Badge The Cross is a bronze straight armed cross, suspended from a crimson ribbon. The face has, in the middle of the cross, a lion guardant standing on the Royal Crown, with the Latin inscription "Pro Valore." (For Valour) The date of the act for which the decoration is bestowed is engraved in a raised circle on the reverse.

■ The Star of Military Valour (S.M.V.)

History Approved by Queen Elizabeth II on February 2, 1993.

Basis of Award Awarded for distinguished and valiant service in the presence of the enemy.

Eligibility Members of the Canadian Forces or a member of an allied armed force that is serving with or in conjunction with the Canadian Forces on or after January 1, 1993. The S.M.V. may be awarded posthumously.

Badge A gold star with four points with a maple leaf in each of the angles, on the face of which a gold maple leaf is superimposed in the centre of a sanguine field surrounded by a silver wreath of laurel and on the reverse of which the Royal Cypher and Crown and the inscription "Pro Valore" shall appear. The Star shall be worn, suspended from a crimson ribbon with two white stripes, immediately after any order and before the Star of Courage.

■ The Medal of Military Valour (M.M.V.)

History Approved by Queen Elizabeth II on February 2, 1993.

Basis of Award Awarded for an act of valour or devotion to duty in the presence of the enemy.

Eligibility Members of the Canadian Forces or a member of an allied armed force that is serving with or in conjunction with the Canadian Forces on or after January 1, 1993. The M.M.V. may be awarded posthumously.

Badge A circular gold medal, on the face of which there shall be a maple leaf surrounded by a wreath of laurel and on the reverse of which the Royal Cypher and Crown and the inscription "Pro Valore" will appear. The medal shall be worn, from a crimson ribbon with three white stripes, immediately after the Meritorious Service Cross and before the Medal of Bravery.

■ The Cross of Valour (C.V.)

History Created in 1972, The Cross of Valour replaced all non-combattant common-wealth medals: the George Cross, the George Medal and the Queen's Gallantry Medal. The Cross of Valour takes precedence before all orders and other decorations except the Victoria Cross.

Basis of Award Awarded for instances of extraordinary heroism in circumstances of extreme peril.

Eligibility May be awarded to civilians or members of the Armed Forces. Only 17 have been awarded.

Badge A gold cross bearing the words "Valour Vaillance."

■ The Star of Courage (S.C.)

History Created in 1972.

Basis of Award Awarded for other outstandingly courageous actions and in cases where there is a greater degree of personal risk involved than to warrant a Medal of Bravery.

Eligibility May be awarded to civilians or members of the Armed Forces.

Badge A 4-pointed silver star with the word "Courage."

■ The Medal of Bravery (M.B.)

History Created in 1972.

Basis of Award Awarded for other outstandingly courageous actions.

Eligibility May be awarded to civilians or members of the Armed Forces.

Badge A circular silver medal with the words "Bravery Bravoure."

■ The Meritorious Service Cross (M.S.C.) (military and civilian)

History Military division created in 1984; civilian division created in 1991.

Basis of Award *Military division*: awarded in recognition of a military deed or activity that has been performed in an outstandingly professional manner, according to a rare high standard that brings considerable benefit or great honour to the Canadian Forces. *Civilian division*: awarded in recognition of the performance of a deed or activity performed in an outstandingly professional manner or according to an uncommonly high standard that brings considerable benefit or great honour to Canada.

Eligibility A member of the Canadian and allied forces, persons serving in conjunction with the Canadian Forces or other persons, Canadian and foreigners.

Badge A Greek cross of silver, ends splayed and convexed, ensigned with the Royal Crown. On the face appear a maple leaf within a circle and a laurel wreath between the arms. Recipients are entitled to use the letters "M.S.C." after their names.

■ The Meritorious Service Medal (M.S.M.) (military and civilian)

History Created in 1991.

Basis of Award *Military division*: awarded in recognition of a military deed or activity that has been performed in a highly professional manner or is of a very high standard that brings benefit or honour to the Canadian Forces. *Civilian division*: awarded in recognition of the performance of a deed or activity performed in a highly professional manner or of a very high standard that brings benefit or honour to Canada.

Eligibility A member of the Canadian and allied forces, persons serving in conjunction with the Canadian Forces or other persons, Canadian and foreigners.

Badge A circular medal of silver ensigned with the Royal Crown. On the face appears the design of the Cross. On the reverse appears the Royal Cypher and, within a double circle, the words "Meritorious Service Méritoire." Recipients are entitled to use the letters "M.S.M." after their names.

Awards for Bravery

Canadian recipients of awards for the Order of Canada, the Order of Military Merit, and the Bravery or Meritorious Service Decorations (and a guest) are invited to Rideau Hall for the formal ceremony. The ceremony is also attended by special guests and members of the Advisory Council or Committee that selected the candidates. The Governor General presents each award and reads the citation. After the presentations, the Governor General hosts a cocktail party and buffet at Government House.

The most recent recipients of the **Star of Courage** included Richard Alexander Archibald of Ontario (posthumous), Ted Greves (BC); Sergeant Lech Kwasiborski, C.D. (Que.); and David Andrew Talbot (Ont). **The Medal of Bravery** was awarded to Corporals Brent C. Ashton, Robert W. Farquhar, Dino L. Simone and Paul D. Sprenger for a rescue during their service in Somalia. Other recipients were Richard M. Brogan and Thomas R. Brogan, Jr. of Nova Scotia; Edward Brown (Ont.); Sergeant Stephen J. Carroll and Constables Gonzalo Couce and Thomas A. Doherty (Ont.); Corporal Joseph J.M. Charette for his work in Somalia; William G. Clifton, Jr. (BC); Danny Gagné (Que.); Norman W. Hales and Dave Hill of Sask.; Brian D. McLaughlin of NB; Donald A. McNeill and Richard A. Robinson of BC; James B. Murphy (Ont.); Quentin T. Riggs and Gregory J. Stewart of NS; Julius R. Rosenberg (Man.); Lyle R. Schweighardt (Sask.); Ralph J. Scully of Nova Scotia; and Russell Snudden and Jason D. Srigley of Ontario.

Governors General of Canada

Name	Date Appointed	Assumed Office	Term
Sir Charles Stanley, Viscount Monck	June 1, 1867	July 1, 1867	1867–69
Sir John Young, Baron Lisgar	Dec. 29, 1868	Feb. 2, 1869	1869–72
Frederick Temple Hamilton Blackwood, Earl of Dufferin	May 22, 1872	June 25, 1872	1872–78
John Douglas Sutherland Campbell, Marquess of Lorne	Oct. 5, 1878	Nov. 20, 1878	1878–83
Henry Charles Keith Petty-Fitzmaurice, Marquess of Lansdowne	Aug. 18, 1883	Oct. 23, 1883	1883–88
Frederick Arthur Stanley, Baron Stanley of Preston	May 1, 1888	June 11, 1888	1888–93
John Campbell Hamilton-Gordon, Earl of Aberdeen	May 22, 1893	Nov. 18, 1893	1893–98
Gilbert John Elliott Murray-Kynynmound, Earl of Minto	July 30, 1898	Nov. 12, 1898	1898–1904
Albert Henry George Grey, Earl Grey	Sept. 26, 1904	Dec. 10, 1904	1904–11
His Royal Highness The Prince Arthur, Field Marshall Duke of Connaught	Mar. 21, 1911	Oct. 13, 1911	1911–16
Victor Christian William Cavendish, Duke of Devonshire	Aug. 19, 19	Nov. 11, 1916	1916–21
Julian Byng, General Baron Byng of Vimy and of Thorpe	Aug. 2, 1921	Aug. 11, 1921	1921–26
Freeman Freeman-Thomas, Baron Willingdon of Ratton	Aug. 5, 1926	Nov. 2, 1926	1926–31
Vere Brabazon Ponsonby, Earl of Bessborough	Feb. 9, 1931	Apr. 4, 1931	1931–35
John Buchan, Baron Tweedsmuir	Aug. 10, 1935	Nov. 2, 935	1935–40
Alexander George Cambridge, Major General Earl of Athlone	Apr. 3, 1940	June 21, 1940	1940–46
Sir Harold George Alexander, Field Marshall Viscount Alexander of Tunis	Aug. 1, 1945	Apr. 18, 1946	1946–52
The Right Honourable Vincent Massey	Jan. 24, 1952	Feb. 22, 1952	1952–59
General the Right Honourable Georges P. Vanier	Aug. 1, 1959	Sept. 15, 1959	1959–67
The Right Honourable Daniel Roland Michener	Mar. 25, 1967	Apr. 15, 1967	1967–73
The Right Honourable Jules Léger	Oct. 5, 1973	Jan. 14, 1974	1973–79
The Right Honourable Edward Richard Schreyer	Dec. 7, 1978	Jan. 22, 1979	1979–83
The Right Honourable Jeanne Sauvé	Dec. 23, 1983	May 14, 1984	1984–90
The Right Honourable Ramon John Hnatyshyn	Oct. 6, 1989	Jan. 21, 1990	1990—

Prime Ministers of Canada

Prime Minister	Party	Term(s)	Born	P.M. at age	Died
Sir John A. Macdonald	Conservative	July 1, 1867–Nov. 5, 1873 Oct. 9, 1878–June 6, 1891	Jan. 11, 1815	52	June 6, 1891
Alexander Mackenzie	Liberal	Nov. 5, 1873–Oct. 9, 1878	Jan. 28, 1822	51	Apr. 17, 1892
Sir John Abbott	Conservative	June 15, 1891–Nov. 24, 1892	Mar. 12, 1821	70	Oct. 30, 1893
Sir John Thompson	Conservative	Nov. 25, 1892–Dec. 12, 1894	Nov. 10, 1845	48	Dec. 12, 1894
Sir Mackenzie Bowell	Conservative	Dec. 13, 1894–Apr. 27, 1896	Dec. 27, 1823	70	Dec. 10, 1917
Sir Charles Tupper	Conservative	Apr. 27, 1896–July 8, 1896	July 2, 1821	74	Oct. 30, 1915
Sir Wilfrid Laurier	Liberal	July 11, 1896–Oct. 6, 1911	Nov. 20, 1841	54	Feb. 17, 1919
Sir Robert Borden	Conservative/ Unionist	Oct. 12, 1917–July 10, 1920 Oct. 10, 1911–Oct. 12, 1917	June 26, 1854	57	June 10, 1937
Arthur Meighen	Unionist/ Conservative	June 29, 1926–Sept. 25, 1926 July 10, 1920–Dec. 29, 1921	June 16, 1874	46	Aug. 5, 1960
Mackenzie King	Liberal	Dec. 29, 1921–June 28, 1926 Sept. 25, 1926–Aug. 6, 1930 Oct. 23, 1935–Nov. 15, 1948	Dec. 17, 1874	47	July 22, 1950
Richard B. Bennett	Conservative	Aug. 7, 1930–Oct. 23, 1935	July 3, 1870	60	June 27, 1947
Louis St. Laurent	Liberal	Nov. 15, 1948–June 21, 1957	Feb. 1, 1882	66	July 25, 1973
John Diefenbaker	Prog. Cons.	June 21, 1957–Apr. 22, 1963	Sept. 18, 1895	61	Aug. 16, 1979
Lester Pearson	Liberal	Apr. 22, 1963–Apr. 20, 1968	Apr. 23, 1897	65	Dec. 27, 1972
Pierre Trudeau	Liberal	Apr. 20, 1968–June 4, 1979 Mar. 3, 1980–June 30, 1984	Oct. 18, 1919	48	
Joe Clark	Prog. Cons.	June 4, 1979–Mar. 3, 1980	June 5, 1939	39	
John Turner	Liberal	June 30, 1984–Sept. 17, 1984	June 7, 1929	55	
Brian Mulroney	Prog. Cons.	Sept. 17, 1984–June 25, 1993	Mar. 20, 1939	45	
Kim Campbell	Prog. Cons.	June 25, 1993–Nov. 4, 1993	Mar. 10, 1947	46	
Jean Chrétien	Liberal	Nov. 4, 1993–	Jan. 11, 1934	59	

The Canadian Cabinet

(as of Sept. 1994)

Jean Chrétien . . . . . . Prime Minister

Herb Gray . . . . Solicitor General of Canada; Leader of the Government in the House of Commons

André Ouellet . . . . . . Minister of Foreign Affairs

Lloyd Axworthy . . . . Minister of Human Resources Development; Minister of Western Economic Diversification

David Collenette . . . . Minister of National Defence; Minister of Veterans Affairs

Roy MacLaren . . . . . . Minister for International Trade

David Anderson . . . . Minister of National Revenue

Ralph Goodale . . . . . Minister of Agriculture and Agri-Food

David Dingwall . . . . Minister of Public Works and Government Services; Minister for the Atlantic Canada Opportunities Agency

Ron Irwin . . . . Minister of Indian Affairs and Northern Development

Brian Tobin . . . . Minister of Fisheries and Oceans

Joyce Fairbairn . . . . . Leader of the Government in the Senate; Minister with special responsibility for Literacy

Sheila Copps . . . . Deputy Prime Minister; Minister of the Environment

Sergio Marchi . . . . . . Minister of Citizenship and Immigration

John Manley . . . . Minister of Industry

Diane Marleau . . . . . Minister of Health

Paul Martin . . . . Minister of Finance; Minister responsible for the Federal Office of Regional Development - Quebec

Douglas Young . . . . . Minister of Transport

Michel Dupuy . . . . . . Minister of Canadian Heritage

Art Eggleton . . . . President of Treasury Board; Minister responsible for Infrastructure

Marcel Massé . . . . . . President of the Queen's Privy Council for Canada; Minister of Intergovernmental Affairs; Minister responsible for Public Service Renewal

Anne McLellan . . . . . Minister of Natural Resources

Allan Rock . . . . Minister of Justice; Attorney General of Canada

Sheila Finestone . . . Secretary of State: Multiculturalism, Status of Women

Fernand Robichaud . Secretary of State: Agriculture and Agri-Food, Fisheries and Oceans

Ethel Blondin-Andrew Secretary of State: Training and Youth

Lawrence MacAulay Secretary of State: Veterans

Christine Stewart . . . Secretary of State: Latin America and Africa

Raymond Chan . . . . . Secretary of State: Asia-Pacific

Jon Gerrard . . . . Secretary of State: Science, Research and Development

Douglas Peters . . . . . Secretary of State: International Financial Institutions

Alfonso Gagliano . . . Secretary of State: Parliamentary Affairs, and Deputy Leader of the Government in the House of Commons

Supreme Court Justices of Canada

(as of Sept. 1994)

Name	Date of Birth	Date Appointed	Appointed from
The Right Hon. Mr. Justice Antonio Lamer	July 8, 1933	Mar. 28, 1980[1]	Quebec Court of Appeal
The Hon. Mr. Justice Gérard V. La Forest	Apr. 1, 1926	Jan. 16, 1985	Court of Appeal of NB
The Hon. Madam Justice Claire L'Heureux-Dubé	Sept. 7, 1927	Apr. 15, 1987	Quebec Court of Appeal
The Hon. Mr. Justice John Sopinka	Mar. 19, 1933	May 24, 1988	private law practice
The Hon. Mr. Justice Charles Gonthier	Aug. 1, 1928	Feb. 1, 1989	Quebec Court of Appeal
The Hon. Mr. Justice Peter de Carteret Cory	Oct. 25, 1925	Feb. 1, 1989	Ontario Court of Appeal
The Hon. Madam Justice Beverley McLachlin	Sept. 7, 1943	Mar. 30, 1989	Supreme Court of BC
The Hon. Mr. Justice Frank Iacobucci	June 29, 1937	Jan. 7, 1991	Federal Court of Canada
The Hon. Mr. Justice John Charles Major	Feb. 20, 1931	Nov. 13, 1991	Alberta Court of Appeal

(1) Appointed Chief Justice July 1, 1990.

Members of Canada's Senate

(as of Sept. 30, 1994; 102 Senators, 2 vacancies)

Senator	Birthdate	Date Appointed	Appointed by	Province
Willie Adams	June 22, 1934	Apr. 5, 1977	Trudeau	NWT
Raynell Andreychuk	Aug. 14, 1944	Mar. 11, 1993	Mulroney	Sask.
W. David Angus	July 21, 1937	June 10, 1993	Mulroney	Que.
Norm Atkins	June 27, 1934	July 2, 1986	Mulroney	Ont.
Jack Austin	Mar. 2, 1932	Aug. 19, 1975	Trudeau	BC
Lise Bacon	Aug. 25, 1934	Sept. 15, 1994	Chrétien	Que.
James Balfour	May 22, 1928	Sept. 13, 1979	Clark	Sask.
Gérald Beaudoin	Apr. 15, 1929	Sept. 26, 1988	Mulroney	Que.
Eric Arthur Berntson	May 16, 1941	Sept. 27, 1990	Mulroney	Sask.
Roch Bolduc	Sept. 10, 1928	Sept. 26, 1988	Mulroney	Que.
M. Lorne Bonnell	Jan. 4, 1923	Nov. 4, 1971	Trudeau	PEI
Peter Bosa	May 2, 1927	Apr. 5, 1977	Trudeau	Ont.
John Buchanan	Apr. 22, 1931	Sept. 12, 1990	Mulroney	NS
Pat Carney	May 26, 1935	Aug. 30, 1990	Mulroney	BC
Sharon Carstairs	Apr. 26, 1942	Sept. 15, 1994	Chrétien	Man.
Guy Charbonneau	June 21, 1922	Sept. 27, 1979	Clark	Que.
Ethel Cochrane	Sept. 23, 1937	Nov. 17, 1986	Mulroney	Nfld
Michel Cogger	Mar. 21, 1939	May 2, 1986	Mulroney	Que.
Erminie J. Cohen	July 23, 1926	June 4, 1993	Mulroney	NB
Gérald J. Comeau	Feb. 1, 1946	Aug. 30, 1990	Mulroney	NS
Anne C. Cools	Aug. 12, 1943	Jan. 13, 1984	Trudeau	Ont.
Eymard Corbin	Aug. 2, 1934	July 9, 1984	Turner	NB
Keith Douglas Davey	Apr. 21, 1926	Feb. 24, 1966	Pearson	Ont.
Paul David	Dec. 25, 1919	Apr. 16, 1985	Mulroney	Que.
Pierre De Bané	Aug. 2, 1938	June 29, 1984	Trudeau	Que.
Jean Noël Desmarais	Apr. 11, 1924	June 4, 1993	Mulroney	Ont.
Mabel Margaret DeWare	Aug. 9, 1926	Sept. 23, 1990	Mulroney	NB
Consiglio Di Nino	Jan. 24, 1938	Aug. 30, 1990	Mulroney	Ont.
C. William Doody	Feb. 26, 1931	Oct. 3, 1979	Clark	Nfld
Richard J. Doyle	Mar. 10, 1923	Mar. 21, 1985	Mulroney	Ont.
John Trevor Eyton	July 12, 1934	Sept. 23, 1990	Mulroney	Ont.
Joyce Fairbairn	Nov. 6, 1939	June 29, 1984	Trudeau	Alta
John Michael Forrestall	Sept. 23, 1932	Sept. 27, 1990	Mulroney	Maritime[1]
Ronald D. Ghitter	Aug. 22, 1935	Mar. 25, 1993	Mulroney	Alta
Philippe D. Gigantès	Aug. 16, 1923	Jan. 13, 1984	Trudeau	Que.
Jerahmiel S. Grafstein	Jan. 2, 1935	Jan. 13, 1984	Trudeau	Ont.
B. Alasdair Graham	May 21, 1929	Apr. 27, 1972	Trudeau	NS
Normand Grimard	June 16, 1925	Sept. 27, 1990	Mulroney	Que.[1]
Leonard J. Gustafson	Nov. 10, 1933	May 26, 1993	Mulroney	Sask.
Stanley Haidasz	Mar. 4, 1923	Mar. 23, 1978	Trudeau	Ont.
Earl A. Hastings	Jan. 7, 1924	Feb. 24, 1966	Pearson	Alta
Daniel Hays	Apr. 24, 1939	June 29, 1984	Trudeau	Alta
Jacques Hébert	June 21, 1923	Apr. 20, 1983	Trudeau	Que.
Duncan J. Jessiman	June 5, 1923	May 26, 1993	Mulroney	Man.
Janis Johnson	Apr. 27, 1946	Sept. 27, 1990	Mulroney	Man.
James Francis Kelleher	Oct. 2, 1930	Sept. 23, 1990	Mulroney	Ont.
William M. Kelly	July 21, 1925	Dec. 23, 1982	Trudeau	Ont.
Colin Kenny	Dec. 10, 1943	June 29, 1984	Trudeau	Ont.
Wilbert Joseph Keon	May 17, 1935	Sept. 27, 1990	Mulroney	Ont.[1]
Noel A. Kinsella	Nov. 28, 1939	Sept. 12, 1990	Mulroney	NB
Michael Kirby	Aug. 5, 1941	Jan. 13, 1984	Trudeau	NS
E. Leo Kolber	Jan. 18, 1929	Dec. 23, 1983	Trudeau	Que.
Thérèse Lavoie-Roux	Mar. 12, 1928	Sept. 27, 1990	Mulroney	Que.[1]
Edward M. Lawson	Sept. 24. 1929	Oct. 7, 1970	Trudeau	BC
Roméo LeBlanc	Dec. 18. 1927	June 29, 1984	Trudeau	NB
Marjory LeBreton	July 4, 1940	June 18, 1993	Mulroney	Ont.
P. Derek Lewis	Nov. 28, 1924	Mar. 23, 1978	Trudeau	Nfld

▶

Senator	Birthdate	Date Appointed	Appointed by	Province
► Paul Lucier	July 29, 1930	Oct. 23, 1975	Trudeau	Yukon
John Lynch-Staunton	June 19, 1930	Sept. 23, 1990	Mulroney	Que.
Finlay MacDonald	Jan. 4, 1923	Dec. 21, 1984	Mulroney	NS
John M. Macdonald	May 3, 1906	June 24, 1960	Diefenbaker	NS
Allan J. MacEachen	July 6, 1921	June 29, 1984	Trudeau	NS
Len Marchand	Nov. 16, 1933	June 29, 1984	Trudeau	BC
Jack Marshall	Nov. 26, 1919	Mar. 23, 1978	Trudeau	Nfld
Michael Arthur Meighen	Mar. 25, 1939	Sept. 27, 1990	Mulroney	Ont.[1]
Gildas L. Molgat	Jan. 25, 1927	Oct. 7, 1970	Trudeau	Man.
Robert Muir	Nov. 10, 1919	Mar. 26, 1979	Trudeau	NS
Lowell Murray	Sept. 26, 1936	Sept. 13, 1979	Clark	Ont.
Pierre Claude Nolin	Oct. 30, 1950	June 18, 1993	Mulroney	Que.
Joan Neiman	Sept. 9, 1920	Sept. 1, 1972	Trudeau	Ont.
Donald H. Oliver	Nov. 16, 1938	Sept. 7, 1990	Mulroney	NS
H.A. (Bud) Olson	Oct. 6, 1925	Apr. 5. 1977	Trudeau	Alta
Gerald R. Ottenheimer	June 4, 1934	Dec. 30, 1987	Mulroney	Nfld
Landon Pearson	Nov. 16, 1930	Sept. 15, 1994	Chrétien	Ont.
Raymond J. Perrault	Feb. 6, 1926	Oct. 5, 1973	Trudeau	BC
William J. Petten	Jan. 28, 1923	Apr. 8, 1968	Pearson	Nfld
Orville H. Philips	Apr. 5, 1924	Feb. 5, 1963	Diefenbaker	PEI
P. Michael Pitfield	June 18, 1937	Dec. 22, 1982	Trudeau	Ont.
Marcel Prud'homme	Nov. 30, 1934	May 26, 1993	Mulroney	Que.
Maurice Riel	Apr. 3, 1992	Oct. 5, 1973	Trudeau	Que.
Jean-Claude Rivest	Jan. 27, 1943	Mar. 11, 1993	Mulroney	Que.
Pietro Rizzuto	Mar. 18, 1934	Dec. 23, 1976	Trudeau	Que.
Fernand Roberge	July 19, 1940	May 26, 1993	Mulroney	Que.
Brenda Mary Robertson	May 23, 1929	Dec. 21, 1984	Mulroney	NB
Louis J. Robichaud	Oct. 21, 1925	Dec. 21, 1973	Trudeau	NB
Eileen Rossiter	July 14, 1929	Nov. 17, 1986	Mulroney	PEI
Jean-Louis Roux	May 18, 1923	Aug. 31, 1994	Chrétien	Que.
Gerry St. Germain	Nov. 6, 1937	June 23, 1993	Mulroney	BC
Jean-Maurice Simard	June 21, 1931	June 26, 1985	Mulroney	NB
Herbert O. Sparrow	Jan. 4, 1930	Feb. 9, 1968	Pearson	Sask.
Mira Spivak	July 12, 1934	Nov. 17, 1986	Mulroney	Man.
Richard J. Stanbury	May 2, 1923	Feb. 13, 1968	Pearson	Ont.
John B. Stewart	Nov. 19, 1924	Jan. 13, 1984	Trudeau	NS
Peter A. Stollery	Nov. 29, 1935	July 2, 1981	Trudeau	Ont.
Terrance R. Stratton	Mar. 16, 1938	Mar. 25, 1993	Mulroney	Man.
John Sylvain	June 7, 1924	Sept. 7, 1990	Mulroney	Que.
L. Norbert Thériault	Feb. 16, 1921	Mar. 26, 1979	Trudeau	NB
Andrew E. Thompson	Dec. 14. 1924	Apr. 6, 1967	Pearson	Ont.
David Tkachuk	Feb. 18, 1945	June 8, 1993	Mulroney	Sask.
Walter Patrick Twinn	Mar. 29, 1934	Sept. 27, 1990	Mulroney	Alta
Charlie Watt	June 29, 1944	Jan. 16, 1984	Trudeau	Que.
Dalia Wood	Aug. 21, 1924	Mar. 26, 1979	Trudeau	Que.

(1) Represents region rather than a province

To Become a Senator...

*T*o be eligible for a Senate appointment a candidate must be a Canadian citizen, a minimum of 30 years old, a resident in the region the appointment represents, have land in that region or province with an unencumbered value of $4 000, and have a net estate of $4 000. Senators appointed after June 1965 may hold office until they reach the age of 75. (Those appointed before June 1965 hold office for life.)

Regional representation in the senate is as follows: Maritimes—24 (PEI—4; NS—10; NB—10); Que.—24; Ont.—24; West—24 (Man.—6; Sask.—6; Alta—6; BC—6). Newfoundland and the territories are separate: Nfld—6; YT—1; NWT—1, for a total of 104 members.

Members of Parliament

(as of Sept. 1994)

Correspondence to Members of Parliament should be addressed individually and may be sent postage free to the following address: (Name of M.P.), House of Commons, Ottawa, Ontario, K1A 0A6.

■ Newfoundland

Riding	Member	Party	Occupation	First Elected[1]
Bonavista-Trinity-Conception	Fred Mifflin	Lib.	Politician	1988
Burin-St. George's	Roger Simmons	Lib.	Politician	1988
Gander-Grand Falls	George S. Baker	Lib.	M.P.	1974
Humber-St. Barbe-Baie Verte	Brian Tobin	Lib.	Journalist	1980
Labrador	Bill Rompkey	Lib.	M.P.	1972
St. John's East	Bonnie Hickey	Lib.	Homemaker	1993
St. John's West	Jean Payne	Lib.	Businessperson	1993

■ Prince Edward Island

Riding	Member	Party	Occupation	First Elected[1]
Cardigan	Lawrence MacAulay	Lib.	M.P.	1988
Egmont	Joe McGuire	Lib.	M.P.	1988
Hillsborough	George Proud	Lib.	Property Sup.	1988
Malpeque	Wayne Easter	Lib.	Farmer	1993

■ Nova Scotia

Riding	Member	Party	Occupation	First Elected[1]
Annapolis Valley-Hants	John Murphy	Lib.	Social Worker	1993
Cape Breton Highlands-Canso	Francis G. LeBlanc	Lib.	Politician	1988
Cape Breton-East Richmond	Dave C. Dingwall	Lib.	Lawyer	1980
Cape Breton-The Sydneys	Russell MacLellan	Lib.	M.P.	1979
Central Nova	Roseanne Skoke	Lib.	Lawyer	1993
Cumberland-Colchester	Dianne Brushett	Lib.	Businesswoman	1993
Dartmouth	Ron MacDonald	Lib.	M.P.	1988
Halifax	Mary Clancy	Lib.	Politician	1988
Halifax West	Geoff Regan	Lib.	Lawyer	1993
South Shore	Derek Wells	Lib.	Lawyer	1993
South West Nova	Harry Verran	Lib.	Retired	1993

■ New Brunswick

Riding	Member	Party	Occupation	First Elected[1]
Acadie-Bathurst	Douglas Young	Lib.	Lawyer	1988
Beauséjour	Fernand Robichaud	Lib.	Assistant	1993
Carleton-Charlotte	Harold Culbert	Lib.	Insurance Agent	1993
Fredericton-York-Sunbury	Andy Scott	Lib.	Public Servant	1993
Fundy-Royal	Paul Zed	Lib.	Lawyer	1993
Madawaska-Victoria	Pierrette Ringuette-Maltais	Lib.	Politician	1993
Miramichi	Charles Hubbard	Lib.	School Principal	1993
Moncton	George S. Rideout	Lib.	Lawyer	1988
Restigouche–Chaleur	Guy H. Arseneault	Lib.	Teacher	1988
Saint John	Elsie Wayne	PC	Retired	1993

▶

▶ ■ **Quebec**

Riding	Member	Party	Occupation	First Elected[1]
Abitibi	Bernard Deshaies	BQ	Merchant	1993
Ahuntsic	Michel Daviault	BQ	Administrator	1993
Anjou-Rivière-des-Prairies	Roger Pomerleau	BQ	Carpenter	1993
Argenteuil-Papineau	Maurice Dumas	BQ	Professor	1993
Beauce	Gilles Bernier	Ind.	M.P.	1984
Beauharnois-Salaberry	Laurent Lavigne	BQ	Farmer	1993
Beauport-Montmorency-Orléans	Michel Guimond	BQ	Lawyer	1993
Bellechasse	François Langlois	BQ	Lawyer	1993
Berthier-Montcalm	Michel Bellehumeur	BQ	Lawyer	1993
Blainville-Deux-Montagnes	Paul Mercier	BQ	n.a.	1993
Bonaventure-Îles-de-la-Madeleine	Patrick Gagnon	Lib.	Consultant	1993
Bourassa	Osvaldo Nunez	BQ	Counsellor	1993
Brome-Missisquoi	vacant[2]			
Chambly	Ghislain Lebel	BQ	Notary Public	1993
Champlain	Réjean Lefebvre	BQ	Forestry	1993
Charlesbourg	Jean-Marc Jacob	BQ	Veterinarian	1993
Charlevoix	Gérard Asselin	BQ	Foreman	1993
Châteauguay	Maurice Godin	BQ	Retired	1993
Chicoutimi	Gilbert Fillion	BQ	Retired	1993
Drummond	Pauline Picard	BQ	Admin. Assistant	1993
Frontenac	Jean-Guy Chrétien	BQ	Professor	1993
Gaspé	Yvan Bernier	BQ	Administrator	1993
Gatineau-La Lièvre	Mark Assad	Lib.	Professor	1988
Hochelaga-Maisonneuve	Réal Ménard	BQ	Political Attaché	1993
Hull-Aylmer	Marcel Massé	Lib.	Economist	1993
Joliette	René Laurin	BQ	Director General	1993
Jonquière	André Caron	BQ	Guidance Couns.	1993
Kamouraska-Rivière-du-Loup	Paul Crête	BQ	Personnel Dir.	1993
La Prairie	Richard Bélisle	BQ	Rehab. Counsellor	1993
Lac-Saint-Jean	Lucien Bouchard	BQ	M.P.	1988*
Lachine-Lac-Saint-Louis	Clifford Lincoln	Lib.	Consultant	1993
LaSalle-Émard	Paul Martin	Lib.	M.P.	1988
Laurentides	Monique Guay	BQ	Businesswoman	1993
Laurier-Sainte-Marie	Gilles Duceppe	BQ	M.P.	1990*
Laval Centre	Madeleine Dalphond-Guiral	BQ	Professor	1993
Laval-Est	Maud Debien	BQ	Retired	1993
Laval-Ouest	Michel Dupuy	Lib.	Foreign Pol. Cons.	1993
Lévis	Antoine Dubé	BQ	Administrator	1993
Longueuil	Nic Leblanc	BQ	M.P.	1984
Lotbinière	Jean Landry	BQ	Photographer	1993
Louis-Hébert	Philippe Paré	BQ	Retired	1993
Manicouagan	Bernard St-Laurent	BQ	Cor. Services	1993
Matapédia-Matane	René Canuel	BQ	Teacher	1993
Mégantic-Compton-Stanstead	Maurice Bernier	BQ	Public Servant	1993
Mercier	Francine Lalonde	BQ	Lecturer	1993
Mont-Royal	Sheila Finestone	Lib.	M.P.	1984
Notre-Dame-de-Grâce	Warren Allmand	Lib.	M.P.	1965
Outremont	Martin Cauchon	Lib.	Lawyer	1993
Papineau-Saint-Michel	André Ouellet	Lib.	Lawyer	1967*
Pierrefonds-Dollard	Bernard Patry	Lib.	Doctor	1993
Pontiac-Gatineau-Labelle	Robert Bertrand	Lib.	Insurance Agent	1993
Portneuf	Pierre de Savoye	BQ	Professor	1993
Québec	Christiane Gagnon	BQ	Real Estate Agent	1993
Québec-Est	Jean-Paul Marchand	BQ	Writer	1993
Richelieu	Louis Plamondon	BQ	Businessman	1984
Richmond-Wolfe	Gaston Leroux	BQ	Communications	1993
Rimouski-Témiscouata	Suzanne Tremblay	BQ	Professor	1993
Roberval	Michael Gauthier	BQ	Administrator	1993 ▶

▶ Rosemont	Benoît Tremblay	BQ	Economist	1988
Saint-Denis	Eleni Bakopanos	Lib.	Vice President	1993
Saint-Henri-Westmount	David Berger	Lib.	Lawyer	1979
Saint-Hubert	Pierrette Venne	BQ	Notary Public	1988
Saint-Hyacinthe-Bagot	Yvan Loubier	BQ	n.a.	1993
Saint-Jean	Claude Bachand	BQ	Educator	1993
Saint-Laurent–Cartierville	Shirley Maheu	Lib.	Insurance Broker	1988
Saint-Léonard	Alfonso Gagliano	Lib.	CGA	1984
Saint-Maurice	Jean Chrétien	Lib.	Lawyer	1963
Shefford	Jean H. Leroux	BQ	Teacher	1993
Sherbrooke	Jean. J. Charest	PC	M.P.	1984
Témiscamingue	Pierre Brien	BQ	Economist	1993
Terrebonne	Benoît Sauvageau	BQ	Teacher	1993
Trois-Rivières	Yves Rocheleau	BQ	Dev. Consultant	1993
Vaudreuil	Nunzio Discepola	Lib.	Mayor	1993
Verchères	Stéphane Bergeron	BQ	Political Attaché	1993
Verdun-Saint-Paul	Raymond Lavigne	Lib.	Consultant	1993

■ **Ontario**

Riding	Member	Party	Occupation	First Elected[1]
Algoma	Brent St. Denis	Lib.	Parl. Assistant	1993
Beaches-Woodbine	Maria Minna	Lib.	Consultant	1993
Bramalea-Gore-Malton	Gurbax Singh Malhi	Lib.	Real Estate Agent	1993
Brampton	Colleen Beaumier	Lib.	Businesswoman	1993
Brant	Jane Stewart	Lib.	Human Resources	1993
Broadview-Greenwood	Dennis Mills	Lib.	Businessman	1988
Bruce-Grey	Ovid L. Jackson	Lib.	Teacher	1993
Burlington	Paddy Torsney	Lib.	Consultant	1993
Cambridge	Janko Peric	Lib.	Welder	1993
Carleton-Gloucester	Eugène Bellemare	Lib.	M.P.	1988
Cochrane-Superior	Réginald Bélair	Lib.	M.P.	1988
Davenport	Charles Caccia	Lib.	Economist	1968
Don Valley East	David Michael Collenette	Lib.	Mgmt. Consultant	1993
Don Valley North	Sarkis Assadourian	Lib.	Exec. Director	1993
Don Valley West	John Godfrey	Lib.	Journalist	1993
Durham	Alex Shepherd	Lib.	C.A.	1993
Eglinton-Lawrence	Joseph Volpe	Lib.	n.a.	1988
Elgin-Norfolk	Gar Knutson	Lib.	Manager	1993
Erie	John Maloney	Lib.	Lawyer	1993
Essex-Kent	Jerry Pickard	Lib.	Teacher	1988
Essex-Windsor	Susan Whelan	Lib.	Lawyer	1993
Etobicoke Centre	Allan Rock	Lib.	Lawyer	1993
Etobicoke North	Roy MacLaren	Lib.	Publisher	1988
Etobicoke-Lakeshore	Jean Augustine	Lib.	School Principal	1993
Glengarry-Prescott-Russell	Don Boudria	Lib.	Civil Servant	1984
Guelph-Wellington	Brenda Chamberlain	Lib.	Exec. Director	1993
Haldimand-Norfolk	Bob Speller	Lib.	M.P.	1988
Halton-Peel	Julian Reed	Lib.	Farmer	1993
Hamilton East	Sheila Copps	Lib.	M.P.	1984
Hamilton Mountain	Beth Phinney	Lib.	M.P.	1988
Hamilton-Wentworth	John Bryden	Lib.	Journalist	1993
Hamilton West	Stan Keyes	Lib.	M.P.	1988
Hastings-Frontenac-Lennox & Addington	Larry McCormick	Lib.	Consultant	1993
Huron-Bruce	Paul Steckle	Lib.	Businessman	1993
Kenora-Rainy River	Robert D. Nault	Lib.	M.P.	1988
Kent	Rex Crawford	Lib.	Farmer	1988
Kingston & the Islands	Peter Milliken	Lib.	Lawyer	1988
Kitchener	John English	Lib.	Teacher	1993
Lambton-Middlesex	Rose-Marie Ur	Lib.	Sr. Const. Asst.	1993 ▶

Lanark-Carleton	Ian Murray	Lib.	Govt. Relations	1993
Leeds-Grenville	Jim Jordan	Lib.	M.P.	1988
Lincoln	Tony Valeri	Lib.	Insurance Cons.	1993
London East	Joe Fontana	Lib.	Businessperson	1988
London-Middlesex	Pat O'Brien	Lib.	Teacher	1993
London West	Sue Barnes	Lib.	Lawyer	1993
Markham-Whitchurch-Stouffville	Jag Bhaduria	Ind.Lib	Mgmt. Cons.	1993
Mississauga East	Albina Guarnieri	Lib.	M.P.	1988
Mississauga South	Paul Szabo	Lib.	Chartered Acct.	1993
Mississauga-West	Carolyn Parrish	Lib.	Teacher	1993
Nepean	Beryl Gaffney	Lib.	Elected Official	1988
Niagara Falls	Gary Pillitteri	Lib.	Farmer	1993
Nickel Belt	Raymond Bonin	Lib.	Professor	1993
Nipissing	Bob Wood	Lib.	M.P.	1988
Northumberland	Christine Stewart	Lib.	M.P.	1988
Oakville-Milton	Bonnie Brown	Lib.	n.a.	1993
Ontario	Dan McTeague	Lib.	PR Officer	1993
Oshawa	Ivan Grose	Lib.	Businessman	1993
Ottawa Centre	Mac Harb	Lib.	M.P.	1988
Ottawa South	John Manley	Lib.	Lawyer	1988
Ottawa West	Marlene Catterall	Lib.	M.P.	1988
Ottawa-Vanier	Jean-Robert Gauthier	Lib.	M.P.	1972
Oxford	John Finlay	Lib.	Retired	1993
Parkdale-High Park	Jesse Flis	Lib.	M.P.	1988
Parry Sound-Muskoka	Andy Mitchell	Lib.	Bank Manager	1993
Perth-Wellington-Waterloo	John Richardson	Lib.	Self-employed	1993
Peterborough	Peter Adams	Lib.	Professor	1993
Prince Edward-Hastings	Lyle Vanclief	Lib.	Agrologist	1988
Renfrew-Nipissing-Pembroke	Leonard Hopkins	Lib.	Teacher	1965
Rosedale	Bill Graham	Lib.	Lawyer	1993
Sarnia-Lambton	Roger Gallaway	Lib.	Lawyer	1993
Sault Ste. Marie	Ron Irwin	Lib.	Lawyer	1993
Scarborough Centre	John Cannis	Lib.	HR Consultant	1993
Scarborough East	Doug Peters	Lib.	Economist	1993
Scarborough West	Tom Wappel	Lib.	M.P.	1988
Scarborough-Agincourt	Jim Karygiannis	Lib.	Ind. Engineer	1988
Scarborough-Rouge River	Derek Lee	Lib.	Lawyer	1988
Simcoe Centre	Ed Harper	Ref.	Businessman	1993
Simcoe North	Paul DeVillers	Lib.	Lawyer	1993
St. Catharines	Walt Lastewka	Lib.	Plant Manager	1993
St. Paul's	Barry Campbell	Lib.	Lawyer	1993
Stormont-Dundas	Bob Kilger	Lib.	Businessman	1988
Sudbury	Diane Marleau	Lib.	M.P.	1988
Thunder Bay-Atikokan	Stan Dromisky	Lib.	Retired	1993
Thunder Bay-Nipigon	Joe Comuzzi	Lib.	M.P.	1988
Timiskaming-French River	Ben Serré	Lib.	Businessman	1993
Timmins-Chapleau	Peter Thalheimer	Lib.	Lawyer	1993
Trinity-Spadina	Tony Ianno	Lib.	Businessman	1993
Victoria-Haliburton	John O'Reilly	Lib.	Real Estate Broker	1993
Waterloo	Andrew Telegdi	Lib.	n.a.	1993
Welland-St. Catharines-Thorold	Gilbert Parent	Lib.	M.P.	1988
Wellington-Grey-Dufferin-Simcoe	Murray Calder	Lib.	Poultry Producer	1993
Willowdale	Jim Peterson	Lib.	Lawyer	1988
Windsor West	Herb Gray	Lib.	Lawyer	1962
Windsor-St. Clair	Shaughnessy Cohen	Lib.	Lawyer	1993
York Centre	Arthur C. Eggleton	Lib.	Consultant	1993
York North	Maurizio Bevilacqua	Lib.	n.a.	1988
York South-Weston	John Nunziata	Lib.	Lawyer	1984
York-Simcoe	Karen Kraft Sloan	Lib.	Self-employed	1993
York West	Sergio Marchi	Lib.	M.P.	1984 ▶

▶ ■ **Manitoba**

Riding	Member	Party	Occupation	First Elected[1]
Brandon-Souris	Glen McKinnon	Lib.	Retired	1993
Churchill	Elijah Harper	Lib.	Consultant	1993
Dauphin-Swan River	Marlene Cowling	Lib.	Farmer	1993
Lisgar-Marquette	Jake E. Hoeppner	Ref.	Farmer	1993
Portage-Interlake	Jon Gerrard	Lib.	Physician	1993
Provencher	David Iftody	Lib.	Business Adv.	1993
Selkirk-Red River	Ron Fewchuk	Lib.	Self-employed	1993
St. Boniface	Ronald J. Duhamel	Lib.	M.P.	1988
Winnipeg North Centre	David Walker	Lib.	Professor	1988
Winnipeg North	Rey Pagtakhan	Lib.	Physician	1988
Winnipeg South	Reg Alcock	Lib.	Politician	1993
Winnipeg St. James	John Harvard	Lib.	n.a.	1988
Winnipeg-South Centre	Lloyd Axworthy	Lib.	M.P.	1979
Winnipeg-Transcona	Bill Blaikie	NDP	Clergyman	1979

■ **Saskatchewan**

Riding	Member	Party	Occupation	First Elected[1]
Kindersley-Lloydminster	Elwin Hermanson	Ref.	Farmer	1993
Mackenzie	Vic Althouse	NDP	Farmer	1980
Moose Jaw-Lake Centre	Allan Kerpan	Ref.	Farmer	1993
Prince Albert-Churchill River	Gordon Kirkby	Lib.	Mayor	1993
Regina-Lumsden	John Solomon	NDP	Businessman	1993
Regina-Qu'Appelle	Simon de Jong	NDP	Businessman	1979
Regina-Wascana	Ralph E. Goodale	Lib.	Business Exec.	1993
Saskatoon-Clark's Crossing	Chris Axworthy	NDP	Professor	1988
Saskatoon-Dundurn	Morris Bodnar	Lib.	Lawyer	1993
Saskatoon-Humboldt	Georgette Sheridan	Lib.	Lawyer	1993
Souris-Moose Mountain	Bernie Collins	Lib.	Retired	1993
Swift Current-Maple Creek-Assiniboia	Lee Morrison	Ref.	Farmer	1993
The Battlefords-Meadow Lake	Len Taylor	NDP	M.P.	1988
Yorkton-Melville	Garry Breitkreuz	Ref.	Teacher	1993

■ **Alberta**

Riding	Member	Party	Occupation	First Elected[1]
Athabasca	David Chatters	Ref.	Farmer	1993
Beaver River	Deborah Grey	Ref.	M.P.	1989*
Calgary Centre	Jim Silye	Ref.	Businessman	1993
Calgary North	Diane Ablonczy	Ref.	Lawyer	1993
Calgary Northeast	Art Hanger	Ref.	Police Officer	1993
Calgary Southeast	Jan Brown	Ref.	Business Mgmt.	1993
Calgary Southwest	Preston Manning	Ref.	Consultant	1993
Calgary West	Stephen Harper	Ref.	Economist	1993
Crowfoot	Jack Ramsay	Ref.	Bus. Consultant	1993
Edmonton East	Judy Bethel	Lib.	n.a.	1993
Edmonton North	John Loney	Lib.	Businessman	1993
Edmonton Northwest	Anne McLellan	Lib.	Professor	1993
Edmonton Southwest	Ian McClelland	Ref.	Businessman	1993
Edmonton-Southeast	David Kilgour	Lib.	M.P.	1979
Edmonton-Strathcona	Hugh Hanrahan	Ref.	Teacher	1993
Elk Island	Ken Epp	Ref.	Instructor	1993
Lethbridge	Ray Speaker	Ref.	Farmer	1993
Macleod	Grant Hill	Ref.	Physician	1993
Medicine Hat	Monte Solberg	Ref.	Businessman	1993
Peace River	Charlie Penson	Ref.	Farmer	1993 ▶

▶ Red Deer	Bob Mills	Ref.	Businessman	1993
St. Albert	John Williams	Ref.	Accountant	1993
Vegreville	Leon E. Benoit	Ref.	Farmer	1993
Wetaskiwin	Dale Johnston	Ref.	Farmer	1993
Wild Rose	Myron Thompson	Ref.	Retired	1993
Yellowhead	Cliff Breitkreuz	Ref.	Farmer	1993

■ British Columbia

Riding	Member	Party	Occupation	First Elected[1]
Burnaby-Kingsway	Svend J. Robinson	NDP	M.P.	1979
Capilano-Howe Sound	Herb Grubel	Ref.	Professor	1993
Cariboo-Chilcotin	Philip Mayfield	Ref.	Ord. Minister	1993
Comox-Alberni	Bill Gilmour	Ref.	Forester	1993
Delta	John Cummins	Ref.	Teacher	1993
Esquimalt-Juan de Fuca	Keith Martin	Ref.	Physician	1993
Fraser Valley East	Chuck Strahl	Ref.	Logging Cont.	1993
Fraser Valley West	Randy White	Ref.	CMA	1993
Kamloops	Nelson Riis	NDP	M.P.	1980
Kootenay East	Jim Abbott	Ref.	Businessman	1993
Kootenay West-Revelstoke	Jim Gouk	Ref.	Real Estate Agt.	1993
Mission-Coquitlam	Daphne Jennings	Ref.	Teacher	1993
Nanaimo-Cowichan	Bob Ringma	Ref.	Retired	1993
New Westminster-Burnaby	Paul E. Forseth	Ref.	Probation Officer	1993
North Island-Powell River	John Duncan	Ref.	Forester	1993
North Vancouver	Ted White	Ref.	Company Pres.	1993
Okanagan Centre	Werner Schmidt	Ref.	Businessman	1993
Okanagan-Shuswap	Darrel Stinson	Ref.	Mining	1993
Okanagan-Similkameen-Merritt	Jim Hart	Ref.	Account Exec.	1993
Port Moody-Coquitlam	Sharon Hayes	Ref.	Homemaker	1993
Prince George-Bulkley Valley	Richard M. Harris	Ref.	Retired	1993
Prince George-Peace River	Jay Hill	Ref.	Farmer	1993
Richmond	Raymond Chan	Lib.	Research Eng.	1993
Saanich-Gulf Islands	Jack Frazer	Ref.	Retired	1993
Skeena	Mike Scott	Ref.	Businessman	1993
Surrey North	Margaret Bridgman	Ref.	Nurse	1993
Surrey-White Rock-South Langley	Val Meredith	Ref.	Businesswoman	1993
Vancouver Centre	Hedy Fry	Lib.	Physician	1993
Vancouver East	Anna Terrana	Lib.	Exec. Director	1993
Vancouver Quadra	Ted McWhinney	Lib.	Professor	1993
Vancouver South	Harbance Singh Dhaliwal	Lib.	Businessman	1993
Victoria	David Anderson	Lib.	Env. Consultant	1993

■ Yukon Territory

Riding	Member	Party	Occupation	First Elected[1]
Yukon	Audrey McLaughlin	NDP	Businessperson	1987*

■ Northwest Territories

Riding	Member	Party	Occupation	First Elected[1]
Nunatsiaq	Jack I. Anawak	Lib.	Politician	1988
Western Arctic	Ethel Blondin-Andrew	Lib.	Politician	1988

(1) General election unless * indicating by-election. (2) Gaston Péloquin (BQ) elected Sept. 1993; died Sept. 1994. (n.a.) not available.
PC—Progressive Conservative; Lib.—Liberal; NDP—New Democratic Party; Ref.—Reform Party; Ind.—Independent; Ind. Lib.—Independent Liberal.

Salaries of Federal Political Figures

(as of Sept. 30, 1994)

The **GOVERNOR GENERAL** receives $97 000 per year.

SENATORS . . . . $64 400 plus $10 100 tax-free expense allowance and 64 travel points[2] per year.

The following senators receive as *extra* salary on top of their Senate salaries:

Leader of the Government . . . . $46 645 plus $2 000 car allowance.
Leader of the Opposition $23 800
Speaker of the Senate . . . . $31 000 plus $3 000 residence allowance and $1 000 car allowance.
Deputy Leader of the Government $14 900
Deputy Leader of the Opposition $9 400
Government Whip $7 500
Opposition Whip $4 800

MEMBERS OF PARLIAMENT—$64 400 plus $21 300 tax-free expense allowance[1], and 64 travel points[2] per year.[3]

The following members of Parliament receive as *extra* salary on top of their MP salaries:

Prime Minister $69 920
Cabinet Ministers $46 645
Speaker of the House $49 100
Deputy Speaker $25 700
Official Opposition Leader $49 100
Other Party Leaders $29 500
Opposition House Leader $23 800
Other House Leaders $10 100
Government and Opposition Whips $13 200
Other Party Whips $7 500
Government and Opposition Deputy Whips $7 500
Deputy Chairman, Committees of the Whole House $10 500
Assistant Deputy Chairman, Committees of the Whole House $10 500
Parliamentary Secretaries $10 500

(1) 24 MPs representing remote or distant ridings receive $26 200 tax-free expense allowance; 2 MPs representing NWT ridings receive $28 200 tax-free allowance. (2) One travel point represents a first-class return air trip anywhere in Canada and can be used by representatives or their spouses or a designated family member. (3) Members who travel in Canada on official business and are at least 100 km from their principal residences may claim $6 000 in food, accomodation, and incidental expenses.

■ OFFICE BUDGET

Each of the 295 elected Members has an office in both Ottawa and their riding, with staff to assist constituents with problems they may encounter when dealing with federal government departments and agencies. Each member's office budget covers staff salaries in Ottawa and constituency offices, as well as individuals or firms hired under contract. The budget is also intended to cover the costs of renting, equipping and maintaining constituency offices, as well as covering the costs of travel within the constituency and within the members' province.

A Member's office budget is set at $171,700; $174,700 or $177,600 according to the size of the constituency and its number of urban and/or rural polling divisions.

Geographic and Electoral Supplement: Members receive supplements to the main office budget if they represent large constituencies with over 70,000 voters (e.g. the riding of York North) and/or geographic boundaries over 8,000 sq. km (e.g. the riding of Nunatsiaq). These annual budgetary supplements cover the additional staff, operating and travel expenses required to serve the riding. Based on constituency characteristics, these supplements range from $5,380 to $32,220 and may change after each general election as the riding demographics change. A Member may have more than one constituency office should he or she so desire, and many do.

Furniture and equipment allowance: Re-elected Members receive an allowance of up to $3,000 (per Parliament) to assist in purchasing office furniture and equipment for the constituency office. Newly-elected Members are entitled to up to $5,000 for their first Parliament for this purpose.

Other Services: To help meet the needs and requests of their constituents, Members are also given access to printing, translation, mail and other support services that help them respond to the thousands of letters and requests they receive. (Canadians may write to Members of Parliament free of charge from anywhere in Canada.) The services also allow Members to keep the public up-to-date on the events in Ottawa through a parliamentary report generally known as a "householder." Finally, Members are provided with desks, computers, typewriters, photocopiers and other office supplies and equipment required to run an efficient office in Ottawa.

■ **PARLIAMENTARY PENSION PLAN**

Members' pensions are provided for by law under the "Members of Parliament Retiring Allowances Act" and, like many pension plans, Members must make a financial contribution. Specifically, Members must contribute 11% of their annual Sessional Allowance (salary) of $64,400. For Members who are receiving additional salaries for extra duties such as Ministers, Whips or Parliamentary Secretaries, they have the option to contribute up to 11% of these salaries as well. The Act also provides that, upon ceasing to be a Member of the House of Commons, a former Member is immediately entitled to an annual pension after a minimum of six years of service. This pension is payable at the rate of 5% per year of service (i.e. a minimum of 30%: 6 x 5%) up to a maximum of 75% (15 years of service) of the average of the best consecutive six years of earnings. Members who serve less than six years must withdraw their contributions.

Indexing of a former Member of the House of Commons' pension begins only when he or she reaches the age of 60, except for extraordinary situations such as disability. Survivors' benefits are payable to spouses and dependent children. If a former Member in receipt of a pension is re-elected to the House of Commons or becomes a Senator, the pension allowance is suspended for the period in office.

Source: *Public Information Office, House of Commons*

Per Capita Legislative Costs

The following table apportions the costs of the various legislatures according to the population count in the 1991 census.

Jurisdiction	Legislative Budget 1991/92	Population (1991)	Cost of Each Legislature	Per Capita Total Per Capita Cost[1]
Canada: House of Commons	$229 350 000	27 023 100	$ 8.49	$ 8.49
Canada: Senate	43 489 300	27 023 100	1.61	1.61
Newfoundland	6 752 700	571 700	11.81	21.91
Prince Edward Island	2 542 100	129 900	19.57	29.67
Nova Scotia	7 648 600	897 500	8.52	18.62
New Brunswick	6 602 000	725 600	9.10	19.20
Quebec	76 000 000	6 811 800	11.16	21.26
Ontario	129 131 700	9 840 300	13.12	23.22
Manitoba	9 749 800	1 092 600	8.92	19.02
Saskatchewan	14 435 700	995 300	14.50	24.60
Alberta	23 346 717	2 501 400	9.33	19.43
British Columbia	24 711 000	3 185 900	7.76	17.86
Yukon Territory	2 196 000	26 500	81.33	91.43
Northwest Territories	9 209 000	54 000	170.54	180.64

Source: *Canadian Legislatures 1992, Robert J. Fleming*

(1) Includes the per capita costs of the Senate, House of Commons and the respective legislature.

Lieutenant-Governors of the Provinces

(as of Sept. 1994)

Each of Canada's 10 provinces has a lieutenant-governor appointed by the Governor General on advice of the prime minister. The lieutenant-governor is the monarch's representative in the province and performs the same duties at the provincial level that the governor general performs at the federal level; the lieutenant-governor opens, prorogues and dissolves the provincial legislative assembly and gives royal assent to provincial legislation and provincial orders in council.

Lieutenant-governors are paid by the federal government and are usually appointed for a term of five years.

Province	Lieutenant-Governor	Birthdate	Date Sworn in
Newfoundland	Hon. Frederick W. Russell	Sept. 10, 1923	Nov. 5, 1991
Prince Edward Island	Hon. Marion Reid	Jan. 4, 1929	Aug. 16, 1990
Nova Scotia	Hon. John James Kinley	Sept. 23, 1925	June 23, 1994
New Brunswick	Hon. Margaret McCain	Oct. 1, 1934	June 21, 1994
Quebec	Hon. Martial Asselin	Feb. 3, 1924	Aug. 9, 1990
Ontario	Hon. Henry N.R. Jackman	June 10, 1932	Dec. 11, 1991
Manitoba	Hon. W. Yvon Dumont	Jan. 21, 1951	Mar. 5, 1993
Saskatchewan	Hon. John E.N. Wiebe	May 31, 1936	May 31, 1994
Alberta	Hon. Gordon Towers	July 5, 1919	Mar. 11, 1991
British Columbia	Hon. David C. Lam	Sept. 2, 1923	Sept. 9, 1988

n.a. not available

Provincial Premiers: An Historical Listing

(as of Sept. 1994)

■ Newfoundland

Premier	Term	Party	Elected or sworn in
Joseph R. Smallwood	1949–1972	Liberal	Apr. 1, 1949
Frank D. Moores	1972–1979	Conservative	Jan. 18, 1972
A. Brian Peckford	1979–1989	Conservative	Mar. 26, 1979
Tom Rideout	1989	Conservative	Mar. 22, 1989
Clyde Wells	1989—	Liberal	May 5, 1989

■ Prince Edward Island

Premier	Term	Party	Elected or sworn in
C. Pope	1873	Conservative	Apr., 1873
L. C. Owen	1873–76	Conservative	Sept., 1873
L. H. Davies	1876–79	Liberal (Coalition)	Aug.,1876
W. W. Sullivan	1879–89	Conservative	Apr. 25, 1879
N. McLeod	1889–91	Conservative	Nov., 1889
F. Peters	1891–97	Liberal	Apr. 27, 1891
A. B. Warburton	1897–98	Liberal	Oct., 1897
D. Farquharson	1898–1901	Liberal	Aug., 1898
A. Peters	1901–08	Liberal	Dec. 29, 1901
F. L. Haszard	1908–11	Liberal	Feb. 1, 1908
H. James Palmer	1911	Liberal	May 16, 1911
John A. Mathieson	1911–17	Conservative	Dec. 2, 1911
Aubin Arsenault	1917–19	Conservative	June, 21, 1917
J. H. Bell	1919–23	Liberal	Sept. 9, 1919
James D. Stewart	1923–27	Conservative	Sept. 5, 1923
Albert C. Saunders	1927–30	Liberal	Aug. 12, 1927
Walter M. Lea	1930–31	Liberal	May 20, 1930
James D. Stewart	1931–33	Conservative	Aug. 29, 1931
William J. P. MacMillan	1933–35	Conservative	Oct. 14, 1933

Walter M. Lea	1935–36	Liberal	Aug. 15, 1935
Thane A. Campbell	1936–43	Liberal	Jan. 14, 1936
J. Walter Jones	1943–53	Liberal	May 11, 1943
Alexander W. Matheson	1953–59	Liberal	May 25, 1953
Walter Shaw	1959–66	Prog. Conservative	Sept. 16, 1959
Alexander B. Campbell	1966–78	Liberal	July 28, 1966
William Bennett Campbell	1978–79	Liberal	Sept. 18, 1978
J. Angus MacLean	1979–81	Prog. Conservative	May 3, 1979
James M. Lee	1981–86	Prog. Conservative	Nov. 17, 1981
Joseph A. Ghiz	1986–93	Liberal	May 2, 1986
Catherine Callbeck	1993—	Liberal	Jan. 25, 1993

■ Nova Scotia

Premier	Term	Party	Elected or sworn in
H. Blanchard	1867	Conservative	July 4, 1867
William Annand	1867–75	Liberal	Nov. 7, 1867
P. C. Hill	1875–78	Liberal	May 11, 1875
S. H. Holmes	1878–82	Conservative	Oct. 22, 1878
John S. D. Thompson	1882	Conservative	May 25, 1882
W. T. Pipes	1882–84	Liberal	Aug. 3, 1882
W. S. Fielding	1884–96	Liberal	July 28, 1884
George H. Murray	1896–1923	Liberal	July 20, 1896
E. H. Armstrong	1923–25	Liberal	Jan. 24, 1923
E. N. Rhodes	1925–30	Conservative	July 16, 1925
Col. Gordon S. Harrington	1930–33	Conservative	Aug. 11, 1930
Angus L. Macdonald	1933–40	Liberal	Sept. 5, 1933
A. S. MacMillan	1940–45	Liberal	July 10, 1940
Angus L. Macdonald	1945–54	Liberal	Sept. 8, 1945
Harold Connolly	1954	Liberal	Apr. 13, 1954
Henry D. Hicks	1954–56	Liberal	Sept. 30, 1954
Robert L. Stanfield	1956–67	Prog. Conservative	Nov. 20, 1956
George Smith	1967–70	Prog. Conservative	Sept. 13, 1967
Gerald A. Regan	1970–78	Liberal	Oct. 28, 1970
John Buchanan	1978–90	Prog. Conservative	Oct. 5, 1978
Roger Bacon	1990–91	Prog. Conservative	Sept. 12, 1990
Donald Cameron	1991–93	Prog. Conservative	Feb. 9, 1991
John Savage	1993—	Liberal	June 11, 1993

■ New Brunswick

Premier	Term	Party	Elected or sworn in
Andrew Wetmore	1867–70	Confederation Party	1867
G.E. King	1870–71	Conservative	1870
George Hatheway	1871–72	Conservative	1871
G.E. King	1872–78	Conservative	1872
James Fraser	1878–82	Conservative	1878
D. L. Hanington	1882–83	Conservative	1882
Andrew Blair	1883–96	Liberal	1883
James Mitchell	1896–97	Liberal	July, 1896
Henry Emmerson	1897–1900	Liberal	Oct. 29, 1897
L. J. Tweedie	1900–07	Liberal	Aug. 31, 1900
William Pugsley	1907	Liberal	Mar. 6, 1907
Clifford Robinson	1907–08	Liberal	May 31, 1907
John Douglas Hazen	1908–11	Conservative	Mar. 24, 1908
James K. Flemming	1911–14	Conservative	Oct. 16, 1911
George J. Clark	1914–17	Conservative	Dec. 17, 1914
James Murray	1917	Conservative	Feb. 1, 1917
Walter E. Foster	1917–23	Liberal	Apr. 4, 1917
Peter Veniot	1923–25	Liberal	Feb. 28, 1923
John B. M. Baxter	1925–31	Conservative	Sept. 14, 1925
Charles D. Richards	1931–33	Conservative	May 19, 1931
Leonard Tilley	1933–35	Conservative	June 1, 1933
Allison Dysart	1935–40	Liberal	July 16, 1935

John McNair	1940–52	Liberal	Mar. 13, 1940
Hugh J. Flemming	1952–60	Prog. Conservative	Oct. 8, 1952
Louis J. Robichaud	1960–70	Liberal	July 12, 1960
Richard Hatfield	1970–87	Prog. Conservative	Nov. 12, 1970
Frank McKenna	1987—	Liberal	Oct. 27, 1987

■ Quebec

Premier	Term	Party	Sworn in
Pierre-Joseph-Olivier Chauveau	1867–73	Conservative	July 15, 1867
Gédéon Ouimet	1873–74	Conservative	Feb. 26, 1873
Charles E. Boucher deBoucherville	1874–78	Conservative	Sept. 22, 1874
Henri Joly	1878–79	Liberal	Mar. 8, 1878
J. Adolphe Chapleau	1879–82	Conservative	Oct. 31, 1879
J. Alfred Mousseau	1882–84	Conservative	July 31, 1882
John J. Ross	1884–87	Conservative	Jan. 23, 1884
L. Olivier Taillon	1887	Conservative	Jan. 25, 1887
Honoré Mercier	1887–91	Liberal	Jan. 27, 1887
Charles E. Boucher deBoucherville	1891–92	Conservative	Dec. 21, 1891
L. Olivier Taillon	1892–96	Conservative	Dec. 16, 1892
Edmund J. Flynn	1896–97	Conservative	May 11, 1896
F. Gabriel Marchand	1897–1900	Liberal	May 24, 1897
S. Napoléon Parent	1900–05	Liberal	Oct. 3, 1900
Lomer Gouin	1905–20	Liberal	Mar. 23, 1905
L. Alexandre Taschereau	1920–36	Liberal	July 9, 1920
Adélard Godbout	1936	Liberal	June 11, 1936
Maurice Duplessis	1936–39	Union Nationale	Aug. 26, 1936
Adélard Godbout	1939–44	Liberal	Nov. 8, 1939
Maurice Duplessis	1944–59	Union Nationale	Aug. 30, 1944
Paul Sauvé	1959–60	Union Nationale	Sept. 11, 1959
Antonio Barrette	1960	Union Nationale	Jan. 8, 1960
Jean Lesage	1960–66	Liberal	July 5, 1960
Daniel Johnson	1966–68	Union Nationale	June 16, 1966
Jean-Jacques Bertrand	1968–70	Union Nationale	Oct. 2, 1968
Robert Bourassa	1970–76	Liberal	May 12, 1970
René Lévesque	1976–85	Parti Québécois	Nov. 25, 1976
Pierre-Marc Johnson	1985	Parti Québécois	Oct. 3, 1985
Robert Bourassa	1985–94	Liberal	Dec. 12, 1985
Daniel Johnson	1994–94	Liberal	Jan. 11, 1994
Jacques Parizeau	1994—	Parti Québécois	Sept. 26, 1994

■ Ontario

Premier	Term	Party	Elected or sworn in
J.S. Macdonald	1867–71	Coalition	July 16, 1867
Edward Blake	1871–72	Liberal	Dec. 20, 1871
Oliver Mowat	1872–96	Liberal	Oct. 25, 1872
Arthur S. Hardy	1896–99	Liberal	July 25, 1896
George William Ross	1899–1905	Liberal	Oct. 21, 1899
Sir James P. Whitney	1905–14	Conservative	Feb. 8, 1905
Sir William Hearst	1914–19	Conservative	Oct. 2, 1914
Ernest C. Drury	1919–23	United Farmers of Ontario	Nov. 14, 1919
George Howard Ferguson	1923–30	Conservative	July 16, 1923
George Stewart Henry	1930–34	Conservative	Dec. 15, 1930
Mitchell F. Hepburn	1934–42	Liberal	July 10, 1934
George Daniel Conant	1942–43	Liberal	Oct. 21, 1942
Harry C. Nixon	1943	Liberal	May 18, 1943
George Drew	1943–48	Prog. Conservative	Aug. 17, 1943
Thomas L. Kennedy	1948–49	Prog. Conservative	Oct. 19, 1948
Leslie M. Frost	1949–61	Prog. Conservative	May 4, 1949
John P. Robarts	1961–71	Prog. Conservative	Nov. 8, 1961
William G. Davis	1971–85	Prog. Conservative	Mar. 1, 1971
Frank Miller	1985	Prog. Conservative	Feb. 8, 1985
David Peterson	1985–90	Liberal	June 26, 1985
Bob Rae	1990—	New Democratic	Oct. 1, 1990

■ Manitoba

Premier	Term	Party	Elected or sworn in
A. Boyd	1870–71	n.a.	Sept. 16, 1870
M. A. Girard	1871–72	Conservative	Dec. 14, 1871
H. H. Clarke	1872–74	n.a.	Mar. 14, 1872
M. A. Girard	1874	Conservative	July 8, 1874
R. A. Davis	1874–78	n.a.	Dec. 3, 1874
John Norquay	1878–87	Conservative	Oct. 16, 1878
D. H. Harrison	1887–88	Conservative	Dec. 26, 1887
T. Greenway	1888–1900	Liberal	Jan. 19, 1888
H. J. Macdonald	1900	Conservative	Jan. 8, 1900
Sir R. P. Roblin	1900–15	Conservative	Oct. 29, 1900
T. C. Norris	1915–22	Liberal	May 12, 1915
John Bracken	1922–43	Coalition[1]	Aug. 8, 1922
S. S. Garson	1943–48	Coalition	Jan. 8, 1943
D. L. Campbell	1948–58	Conservative	Nov. 11, 1948
Duff Roblin	1958–67	Prog. Conservative	June 16, 1958
Walter Weir	1967–69	Prog. Conservative	Nov. 25, 1967
Edward Schreyer	1969–77	New Democratic	July 15, 1969
Sterling Lyon	1977–81	Prog. Conservative	Nov. 24, 1977
Howard Pawley	1981–88	New Democratic	Nov. 30, 1981
Gary Filmon	1988—	Prog. Conservative	Apr. 26, 1988

■ Saskatchewan

Premier	Term	Party	Elected or sworn in
Walter Scott	1905–16	Liberal	Sept. 5, 1905
W. M. Martin	1916–22	Liberal	Oct. 20, 1916
C. A. Dunning	1922–26	Liberal	Apr. 5, 1922
J. G. Gardiner	1926–29	Liberal	Feb. 26, 1926
J. T. M. Anderson	1929–34	Conservative	Sept. 9, 1929
J. G. Gardiner	1934–35	Liberal	July 19, 1934
W. J. Patterson	1935–44	Liberal	Nov. 1, 1935
Tommy Douglas	1944–61	C.C.F.[2]	July 10, 1944
W. S. Lloyd	1961–64	C.C.F.—N.D.P.	Nov. 7, 1961
W. Ross Thatcher	1964–71	Liberal	May 22, 1964
Allan E. Blakeney	1971–82	New Democratic	June 30, 1971
Grant Devine	1982–91	Prog. Conservative	May 8, 1982
Roy Romanow	1991—	New Democratic	Nov. 1, 1991

■ Alberta

Premier	Term	Party	Elected or sworn in
Alex Rutherford	1905–10	Liberal	Sept. 2, 1905
A. L. Sifton	1910–17	Liberal	May 26, 1910
Charles Stewart	1917–21	Liberal	Oct. 30, 1917
Herbert Greenfield	1921–25	United Farmers of Alberta	Aug. 13, 1921
John E. Brownlee	1925–34	United Farmers of Alberta	Nov. 23, 1925
Richard G. Reid	1934–35	United Farmers of Alberta	July 10, 1934
William Aberhart	1935–43	Social Credit	Sept. 3, 1935
E. C. Manning	1943–68	Social Credit	May 31, 1943
Harry Strom	1968–71	Social Credit	Dec. 12, 1968
Peter Lougheed	1971–85	Prog. Conservative	Sept. 10, 1971
Don Getty	1985–92	Prog. Conservative	Nov. 1, 1985
Ralph P. Klein	1992—	Prog. Conservative	Dec. 14, 1992

■ British Columbia

Premier	Term	Party	Elected or sworn in
J. F. McCreight	1871–72	n.a.	Nov. 13, 1871
Amor De Cosmos	1872–74	n.a.	Dec. 23, 1872
G. A. Walkem	1874–76	n.a.	Feb. 11, 1874
A. C. Elliott	1876–78	n.a.	Feb. 1, 1876
G. A. Walkem	1878–82	n.a.	June 25, 1878
Robert Beaven	1882–83	n.a.	June 13, 1882
William Smithe	1883–87	n.a.	Jan. 29, 1883
A. E. B. Davie	1887–89	n.a.	May 1, 1887
John Robson	1889–92	n.a.	Aug. 2, 1889
Theodore Davie	1892–95	n.a.	July 2, 1892
J. H. Turner	1895–98	n.a.	Mar. 4, 1895
C. A. Semlin	1898–1900	n.a.	Aug. 15, 1898
Joseph Martin	1900	n.a.	Feb. 28, 1900
James Dunsmuir	1900–02	n.a.	June 15, 1900
E. G. Prior	1902–03	n.a.	Nov. 21, 1902
Richard McBride	1903–15	Conservative	June 1, 1903
William J. Bowser	1915–16	Conservative	Dec. 15, 1915
Harlan C. Brewster	1916–18	Liberal	Nov. 23, 1916
John Oliver	1918–27	Liberal	Mar. 6, 1918
John D. MacLean	1927–28	Liberal	Aug. 20, 1927
Simon F. Tolmie	1928–33	Conservative	Aug. 21, 1928
T. D. Pattullo	1933–41	Liberal	Nov. 15, 1933
John Hart	1941–47	Liberal[3]	Dec. 9, 1941
Byron Johnson	1947–52	Liberal[3]	Dec. 29, 1947
W. A. C. Bennett	1952–72	Social Credit	Aug. 1, 1952
David Barrett	1972–75	New Democratic Party	Sept. 15, 1972
William R. Bennett	1975–86	Social Credit	Dec. 22, 1975
Bill Vander Zalm	1986–91	Social Credit	Aug. 6, 1986
Rita Johnston	1991–91	Social Credit	Apr. 2, 1991
Michael Harcourt	1991—	New Democratic Party	Nov. 5, 1991

■ Yukon Territory

Government Leaders	Term	Party	Elected or sworn in
Chris Pearson	1978–85	Yukon Progressive Conservative	
Willard Phelps	1985	Yukon Progressive Conservative	
Tony Penikett	1985–92[4]	NDP	
John Ostashek	1992—	Yukon Party	

■ Northwest Territories

Government Leaders	Term	Party	Elected or sworn in
George Braden	1980–83	n.a.	July 25, 1980
Richard Nerysoo	1984–85	n.a.	Jan. 12, 1984
Nick Sibbeston	1985–87	n.a.	Nov. 5, 1985
Dennis Patterson	1987–91	n.a.	Nov. 12, 1987
Nellie Cournoyea	1991—	n.a.	Nov. 13, 1991

Source: *Historical Statistics of Canada; Provincial Archives*

(1) United Farmer/Progressive, 1922–27; Coalition, 1927–37; Liberal—Progressive, 1937–43. (2) Co-operative Commonwealth Federation. (3) Coalition. (4) From 1989–92, Government Leader was designated Premier. (n.a.) not available.

Cabinets of the Provinces and Territories

(as of Sept. 1994)

■ Newfoundland

Ministry or Portfolio	Minister
Premier	Clyde Wells
Treasury Board; Finance	Winston Baker
Fisheries, Food and Agriculture	Dr. Bud Hulan
Employment and Labour Relations	Tom Murphy
Health	Lloyd Matthews
Justice	Edward Roberts

▶

▶ Social Services	Kay Young
Tourism Culture and Recreation	Roger Grimes
Industry, Trade and Technology	Chuck Furey
Natural Resources	Dr. Rex Gibbons
Works, Services and Transportation	John Efford
Municipal and Provincial Affairs	Art Reid
Environment	Kevin Aylward
Education and Training	Chris Decker
Speaker of the House of Assembly	Paul Dicks

■ New Brunswick

Ministry or Portfolio	Minister
Premier; President of Executive Council	Frank McKenna
Advanced Education and Labour	Camille Thériault
Agriculture	Doug Tyler
Finance	Allan Maher
Economic Development and Tourism	Leo McAdam
Education	Vaughn Blaney
Environment; Status of Women	Marcelle Mersereau
Fisheries and Aquaculture	Bernard Thériault
Health and Community Services	Russell King, M.D.
Income Assistance, Minister of State for Literacy	Ann Breault
Intergovernmental Affairs	Roland Beaulieu
Justice, Attorney General	Edmond Blanchard
Municipal Affairs and Housing; Culture	Paul Duffie
Natural Resources and Energy	Alan Graham
Minister of State for Mines and Energy	Laureen Jarrett
NB Power	Raymond Frenette
Solicitor General	Jane Barry
Supply and Services	James Lockyer
Transportation	Sheldon Lee

■ Nova Scotia

Ministry or Portfolio	Minister
Premier; President of Executive Council; Intergovernmental Affairs	John P. Savage, M.D.
Deputy Premier; Justice and Attorney General	J. William Gillis
Finance	J. Bernard Boudreau, Q.C.
Economic Development; Tourism and Culture	Ross Bragg
Education	John MacEachern
Health	Ronald D. Stewart, M.D.
Community Services	James A. Smith, M.D.
Transportation and Communications	Richard W. Mann
Municipal Affairs	Sandra L. Jolly
Natural Resources	Donald R. Downe
Supply and Services	F. Wayne Adams
Agriculture and Marketing	Wayne J. Gaudet
Environment	Robert S. Harrison
Civil Service Act; Status of Women	Eleanor E. Norrie
Housing and Consumer Affairs	Guy A.C. Brown
Fisheries	James A. Barkhouse
Labour; Youth Secretariat	Jay F. Abbass

■ Prince Edward Island

Ministry or Portfolio	Minister
Premier; President of Executive Council	Catherine S. Callbeck
Economic Development and Tourism	Robert J. Morrissey
Provincial Treasurer	Wayne D. Cheverie
Transportation and Public Works	Keith Milligan
Education and Human Resources	Gordon MacInnis
Environmental Resources	Barry W. Hicken
Agriculture, Fisheries and Forestry	Walter Bradley

▶

▸ Health and Social Services . . . . Walter McEwen
Provincial Affairs and Attorney-General . . . . Alan Buchanan
Higher Education, Training and Adult Learning . . . . Jeannie Lea

■ Quebec

Ministry or Portfolio	Minister
Premier; Native, International, Francophone Affairs; Imm. and Cult. Communities,	Jacques Parizeau
Parl. Leader; Electoral Reform; Regional Dev.; Mun. Affairs	Guy Chevrette
Treasury Bd; Family Services; Public Admin.	Pauline Marois
Employment; Planning	Louise Harel
Canadian Intergovernmental Affairs.	Louise Beaudoin
Finance	Jean Campeau
Transport	Jacques Léonard
Education	Jean Garon
Natural Resources.	François Gendron
Environment and Wildlife.	Jacques Brassard
Revenue Security; Status of Women	Jeanne Blackburn
Public Security.	Serge Ménard
Agriculture, Fish and Food.	Marcel Landry
Justice; Application of Professional Laws.	Paul Bégin
Tourism, Olympic Installations Board	Rita Dionne-Marsolais
Culture and Communications; French Language Charter	Marie Malavoy
Industry, Commerce, Science and Technology	Daniel Paille
Health and Social Services	Jean Rochon

■ Ontario

Ministry or Portfolio	Minister
Premier; President of the Council; Intergovernmental Affairs	Bob Rae
Deputy Premier; Minister of Finance	Floyd Laughren
Labour	Bob Mackenzie
Municipal Affairs	Ed Philip
Environment and Energy; Native Affairs	C.J. (Bud) Wildman
Education and Training	Dave Cooke
Health	Ruth Grier
Transportation; Francophone Affairs	Gilles Pouliot
Natural Resources.	Howard Hampton
Northern Development and Mines	Shelley Martel
Housing.	Evelyn Gigantes
Attorney General; Women's Issues	Marion Boyd
Agriculture, Food and Rural Affairs	Elmer Buchanan
Economic Development and Trade.	Frances Lankin
Culture, Tourism and Recreation	Anne Swarbrick
Citizenship; Human Rights, Disabled, Seniors and Race Relations	Elaine Ziemba
Management Board of Cabinet; Government House Leader	Brian A. Charlton
Consumer and Commercial Relations	Marilyn M. Churley
Community and Social Services	Antonio V.G. Silipo
Solicitor General; Correctional Services	David Christopherson
Minister without Portfolio (Economic Development and Trade)	Richard Allen
Minister without Portfolio (Municipal Affairs)	Allan C. Pilkey
Minister without Portfolio (Health)	Shelley Wark-Martyn
Minister without Portfolio (Culture, Tourism and Recreation)	Shirley Coppen
Minister without Portfolio (Chief Government Whip)	Fred Wilson
Minister without Portfolio (Finance)	Brad Ward
Minister without Portfolio (Education and Training)	Mike Farnan

■ Manitoba

Ministry or Portfolio	Minister
Premier; President of Executive Council; Federal/Provincial Relations	Gary A. Filmon
Agriculture	Harry J. Enns
Deputy Premier; Industry, Trade and Tourism.	James E. Downey

▶

▶ Energy and Mines .... Donald W. Orchard
Natural Resources .... Albert Driedger
Education and Training .... Clayton S. Manness
Environment .... James G. Cummings
Health .... James C. McCrae
Consumer and Corporate Affairs .... James A. Ernst
Highways and Transportation .... Glen M. Findlay
Rural Development .... Leonard Derkach
Government Services; Seniors .... Gerald Ducharme
Family Services .... Bonnie E. Mitchelson
Culture, Heritage and Citizenship .... Harold Gilleshammer
Labour; Civil Service Act; French Language Services .... Darren T. Praznik
Finance .... Eric Stefanson
Urban Affairs .... Linda McIntosh
Justice and Attorney-General .... Rosemary Vodrey

■ Saskatchewan

Ministry or Portfolio	Minister
Premier; President of Executive Council	Roy Romanow, Q.C.
Deputy Premier; Provincial Secretary	Ed Tchorzewski
Economic Development	Dwain Lingenfelter
Health; Status of Women	Louise Simard
Environment and Resource Management	Bernhard Wiens
Municipal Government	Carol Carson
Justice and Attorney General	Robert Mitchell, Q.C.
Finance	Janice MacKinnon
Associate Minister of Finance; Crown Investments	John Penner
Agriculture and Food	Darrel Cunningham
Labour	Ned Shillington
Education, Training and Employment	Pat Atkinson
Associate Minister of Health	Lorne Calvert
Saskatchewan Property Management Corporation	Eldon Lautermilch
Associate Minister of Education, Training and Employment	Keith Goulet
Energy and Mines	Doug Anguish
Social Services; Seniors	Robert Pringle
Highways and Transportation	Andy Renaud

■ Alberta

Ministry or Portfolio	Minister
Premier; President of Executive Council; Intergovernmental Affairs	Ralph Klein
Advanced Education and Career Development	Jack Ady
Energy	Pat Black
Family and Social Services	Mike Cardinal
Labour; Government House Leader	Stockwell Day
Provincial Treasurer	Jim Dinning
Environmental Protection	Brian Evans
Education	Halvar Jonson
Deputy Premier; Economic Development and Tourism	Ken Kowalski
Community Development	Gary Mar
Health	Shirley McClellan
Minister without Portfolio	Dianne Mirosh
Agriculture, Food and Rural Development	Walter Paszkowski
Justice and Attorney General	Ken Rostad
Public Works, Supply and Services	Tom Thurber
Transportation and Utilities	Peter Trynchy
Municipal Affairs	Stephen West

▶

■ British Columbia

Ministry or Portfolio	Minister
Premier; President of Executive Council	Michael Harcourt
Deputy Premier; Finance and Corporate Relations	Elizabeth Cull
Attorney General	Colin Gabelmann
Forests	Andrew Petter
Environment, Lands and Parks; responsible for Multiculturalism and Human Rights	Moe Sihota
Education	Art Charbonneau
Agriculture, Fisheries and Food	David Zirnhelt
Energy, Mines and Petroleum Resources	Anne Edwards
Skills, Training and Labour	Dan Miller
Small Business, Tourism and Culture	Bill Barlee
Municipal Affairs	Darlene Marzari
Health; responsible for Seniors	Paul Ramsey
Social Services	Joy MacPhail
Transportation and Highways	Jackie Pement
Employment and Investment	Glen Clark
Housing, Recreation and Consumer Services	Joan Smallwood
Government Services; responsible for Sports	Robin Blencoe
Aboriginal Affairs	John Cashore
Women's Equality	Penny Priddy

■ Yukon Territory

Ministry or Portfolio	Minister
Government Leader; Executive Council Office; Finance; Land Claims; Economic Development	John Ostashek
Renewable Resources; Yukon Liquor Corporation	Bill Brewster
Health and Social Services; Justice; Yukon Development Corporation; Yukon Energy Corporation	Willard Phelps
Education; Tourism; Women's Directorate	Doug Phillips
Community and Transportation Services; Yukon Housing Corporation	Mickey Fisher
Government Services, Public Service Commission; Workers' Compensation and Health and Safety Board	Alan Nordling

■ Northwest Territories

Ministry or Portfolio	Minister
Premier; Health and Social Services; NWT Power Corporation; Special Advisor on Women	Nellie J. Cournoyea
Government House Leader; Finance	John Pollard
Intergovernmental and Aboriginal Affairs; Justice	Stephen Kakfwi
Renewable Resources	Silas Arngna'naaq
Public Works and Services; NWT Housing Corporation	Don Morin
Education, Culture and Employment; Safety and Public Services	Richard Nerysoo
Personnel; Municipal and Community Affairs	Rebecca Mike
Transportation; Economic Development and Tourism; Energy, Mines and Petroleum Resources; Public Utilities Board; Workers' Compensation Board	John Todd

POLITICS AND ELECTIONS

Winner of National Newspaper Award for Political Cartooning, 1993

Source: Bruce MacKinnon, *The Halifax Chronicle Herald* and *The Mail Star*

Registered Federal Political Parties

(as of Sept. 1994)

Abolitionist Party of Canada—7400 Woodbine Avenue, Markham, ON L3R 1A5; Tel: (905) 474-4324; Fax: (905) 474-4327; leader: John C. Turmel.

Bloc Québécois—Room 1475, 425 de Maisonneuve Street West, Montréal, QC H3A 3G5; Tel: (514) 499-3000; Fax: (514) 499-3638; leader: The Hon. Lucien Bouchard.

Canada Party—1216 12th Avenue East, Regina, SK S4N 0M5; Tel: (306) 757-0773; leader: Claire Foss.

Christian Heritage Party of Canada— 156 Walts Street, Welland, ON L3C 6G5; Tel: (905) 788-2238; Fax: (905) 788-2943; leader: Jean Blaquière.

Liberal Party of Canada—Suite 200, 200 Laurier Avenue West, Ottawa, ON K1P 6M8; Tel: (613) 237-0740; Fax: (613) 235-7208; leader: The Right Hon. Jean Chrétien.

Libertarian Party of Canada—Suite 301, 1 St. John's Road, Toronto, ON M6P 1T7; Tel: (416) 763-3688; Fax: (416) 763-5306; leader: Hilliard James Cox.

Marxist-Leninist Party of Canada—171 Dalhousie Street, Ottawa, ON K1N 7C7; Tel: (613) 241-7052; leader: Hardial Bains.

Natural Law Party of Canada— 500 Wilbrod Street, Ottawa, ON K1N 6N2; Tel: (613) 565-8517; Fax: (613) 565-6546; leader: Neil Paterson.

New Democratic Party—310 Somerset Street West, Ottawa, ON K2P 0J9; Tel: (613) 236-3613; Fax: (613) 230-9950; leader: The Hon. Audrey McLaughlin.

Party for the Commonwealth of Canada—Ste. 300, 8129 St. Denis Street, Montréal, QC H2P 2G7; Tel: (514) 385-5494; Fax: (514) 385-9130; leader: Gilles Gervais.

Progressive Conservative Party of Canada—6th Floor, 275 Slater Street, Ottawa, ON K1P 5H9; Tel: (613) 238-6111; Fax: (613) 238-7429; leader: The Hon. Jean Charest (interim).

Reform Party of Canada—Suite 600, 833 4th Avenue SW, Calgary, AB T2P 0K5; Tel: (403) 269-1990; Fax: (403) 269-4077; leader: E. Preston Manning.

The Green Party of Canada—Ste. 5, 3147 Kingsway, Vancouver, BC V5R 5K2; Tel: (604) 436-1437; Fax: (604) 436-1438; leader: Chris Lea.

Source: *Elections Canada*

Exporting Our Election Expertise

C anada plays a leading role in elections on the international scene. As a member of organizations such as the UN, the OAS, and the Commonwealth, Canada offers electoral assistance by taking part in international programs sponsored by such organizations or by responding to direct requests made to Foreign Affairs or CIDA by foreign governments.

Elections Canada keeps a list of 600 names of Canadians with expertise in all areas of the democratic process, including administration, voter registration, electoral and constitutional law, information systems and digital mapping, journalism, civic education and the training of election officials and staff.

Major shifts in the political climate since the mid-1980s have meant increased demand on that expertise: between 1984-9, the agency took part in or carried out 17 electoral missions; from 1990-3, there were 143 such missions in 58 countries on four continents. Staff included 320 election specialists from all parts of Canada as well as academics, retired diplomats and politicians.

Federal Election Results, 1867–1988

🍁1867–1904	1867	1872	1874	1878	1882	1887	1891	1896	1900	1904
Canada										
Conservative	101	103	73	137	139	123	123	89	80	75
Liberal	80	97	133	69	71	92	92	117	133	139
Other	—	—	—	—	—	—	—	7	—	—
Prince Edward Island[1]										
Conservative	—	—	—	5	4	—	2	3	2	3
Liberal	—	—	6	1	2	6	4	2	3	1
Nova Scotia										
Conservative	3	11	4	14	15	14	16	10	5	—
Liberal	16	10	17	7	6	7	5	10	15	18
New Brunswick										
Conservative	7	7	5	5	10	10	13	9	5	6
Liberal	8	9	11	11	6	6	3	5	9	7
Quebec										
Conservative	45	38	32	45	48	33	30	16	7	11
Liberal	20	27	33	20	17	32	35	49	58	54
Other	—	—	—	—	—	—	—	5	—	—
Ontario										
Conservative	46	38	24	59	54	52	48	44	55	48
Liberal	36	50	64	29	37	40	44	43	37	38
Other	—	—	—	—	—	—	—	5	—	—
Manitoba[2]										
Conservative	—	3	2	3	2	4	4	4	4	3
Liberal	—	1	2	1	3	1	1	2	3	7
Other	—	—	—	—	—	—	—	1	—	—
British Columbia[3]										
Conservative	—	6	6	6	6	6	6	2	2	—
Liberal	—	—	—	—	—	—	—	4	4	7
Yukon[4]										
Conservative	—	—	—	—	—	—	—	—	—	1
Northwest Territories[2]										
Conservative	—	—	—	—	—	4	4	1	—	3
Liberal	—	—	—	—	—	—	—	2	4	7
Other	—	—	—	—	—	—	—	1	—	—

(1) Entered Confederation July 1, 1873. (2) Entered Confederation July 15, 1870. (3) Entered Confederation July 20, 1871. (4) Entered Confederation June 13, 1898. (5) Entered Confederation Mar. 31, 1949. (6) Entered Confederation Sept. 1, 1905. (7) For the 1917 election, Conservative refers to "Unionists," a coalition of Conservatives and pro-conscription Liberals; Liberals, for the 1917 election, are sometimes called "Laurier Liberals" because of their support for Laurier's anti-conscription stand. (8) The New Democratic Party (NDP) replaced the Co-operative Commonwealth Federation (CCF) in Aug. 1961. (9) From 1908-1957 shared one representative.

♣1908–1940	1908	1911	1917[7]	1921	1925	1926	1930	1935	1940
Canada									
Conservative	85	133	153	50	116	91	137	39	39
Liberal	133	86	82	117	101	116	88	171	178
Progressive	—	—	—	64	25	—	2	—	—
CCF	—	—	—	—	—	—	—	7	8
Social Credit	—	—	—	—	—	—	—	17	10
Other	3	2	—	4	3	38	18	11	10
Newfoundland[5]									
Conservative	—	—	—	—	—	—	—	—	—
Liberal	—	—	—	—	—	—	—	—	—
Prince Edward Island									
Conservative	1	2	2	—	2	1	3	—	—
Liberal	3	2	2	4	2	3	1	4	4
Nova Scotia									
Conservative	6	9	12	—	11	12	10	—	1
Liberal	12	9	4	16	3	2	4	12	10
CCF	—	—	—	—	—	—	—	—	1
New Brunswick									
Conservative	2	5	7	5	10	7	10	1	5
Liberal	11	8	4	5	1	4	1	9	5
Other	—	—	—	1	—	—	—	—	—
Quebec									
Conservative	11	27	3	—	4	4	24	5	—
Liberal	53	37	62	65	60	60	40	55	61
Other	1	1	—	—	1	1	1	5	4
Ontario									
Conservative	48	72	74	37	68	53	59	25	25
Liberal	36	36	8	21	12	23	22	56	55
Progressive	—	—	—	24	2	4	—	—	—
Other	2	1	—	—	—	2	1	1	2
Manitoba									
Conservative	8	8	14	—	7	—	11	1	1
Liberal	2	2	1	2	1	4	1	12	14
CCF	—	—	—	—	—	—	—	2	1
Progressive	—	—	—	12	7	4	—	—	—
Other	—	—	—	1	2	9	5	2	1
Saskatchewan[6]									
Conservative	1	1	16	—	—	—	8	1	2
Liberal	9	9	—	1	15	16	11	16	12
CCF	—	—	—	—	—	—	—	2	5
Progressive	—	—	—	15	6	5	2	—	—
Social Credit	—	—	—	—	—	—	—	2	—
Other	—	—	—	—	—	—	—	—	2
Alberta[6]									
Conservative	3	1	11	—	3	1	4	1	—
Liberal	4	6	1	—	4	3	3	1	7
Progressive	—	—	—	10	9	—	—	—	—
Social Credit	—	—	—	—	—	—	—	15	10
United Farmers of Alta..	—	—	—	—	—	11	9	—	—
Other	—	—	—	2	—	1	—	—	—
British Columbia									
Conservative	5	7	13	7	10	12	7	5	4
Liberal	2	—	—	3	3	1	5	6	10
CCF	—	—	—	—	—	—	—	3	1
Progressive	—	—	—	2	1	—	—	—	—
Social Credit	—	—	—	—	—	—	—	—	—
Other	—	—	—	1	—	1	2	2	1
Yukon and Northwest Territories[9]									
Conservative	—	1	—	1	1	1	1	—	1
Liberal	1	—	—	—	—	—	—	—	—
Other	—	—	—	—	—	—	—	1	—

🍁 1945–1968	1945	1949	1953	1957	1958	1962	1963	1965	1968
Canada									
Conservative	67	41	51	112	208	116	95	97	72
Liberal	125	190	170	105	48	99	129	131	155
NDP (CCF)[8]	28	13	23	25	8	19	17	21	22
Social Credit	13	10	15	19	—	30	24	5	—
Other	12	8	6	4	1	1	—	11	15
Newfoundland									
Conservative	—	2	—	2	2	1	—	—	6
Liberal	—	5	7	5	5	6	7	7	1
NDP (CCF)	—	—	—	—	—	—			
Prince Edward Island									
Conservative	1	1	1	4	4	4	2	4	4
Liberal	3	3	3	—	—	—	2	—	—
Nova Scotia									
Conservative	3	2	1	10	12	9	7	10	10
Liberal	8	10	10	2	—	2	5	2	1
NDP (CCF)	1	1	1	—	—	1	—	—	—
New Brunswick									
Conservative	3	2	3	5	7	4	4	4	5
Liberal	7	7	7	5	3	6	6	6	5
Other	—	1	—	—	—	—	—	—	—
Quebec									
Conservative	1	2	4	9	50	14	8	8	4
Liberal	54	66	66	63	25	35	47	56	56
NDP (CCF)	—	—	—	—	—	—	—	—	—
Social Credit	—	—	—	—	—	26	20	—	—
Other	10	5	5	3	—	—	—	11	14
Ontario									
Conservative	48	25	33	61	67	35	27	25	17
Liberal	34	56	50	20	14	43	52	51	64
NDP (CCF)	—	—	—	3	3	6	6	9	6
Other	—	2	2	1	1	1	—	—	1
Manitoba									
Conservative	2	1	3	8	14	11	10	10	5
Liberal	10	12	8	1	—	1	2	1	5
NDP (CCF)	5	3	3	5	—	2	2	3	3
Saskatchewan									
Conservative	1	1	1	3	16	16	17	17	5
Liberal	2	14	5	4	—	1	—	—	2
NDP (CCF)	18	5	11	10	1	—	—	—	6
Alberta									
Conservative	2	2	2	3	17	15	14	15	15
Liberal	2	5	4	1	—	—	1	—	4
NDP (CCF)	—	—	—	—	—	—	—	—	—
Social Credit	13	10	11	13	—	2	2	2	—
British Columbia									
Conservative	5	3	3	7	18	6	4	3	—
Liberal	5	11	8	2	—	4	7	7	16
NDP (CCF)	4	3	7	7	4	10	9	9	7
Social Credit	—	—	4	6	—	2	2	3	—
Other	2	1	—						
Yukon[9]									
Conservative	1	—	—	—	1	1	1	1	1
Liberal	—	1	2	1	—	—	—	—	—
NDP (CCF)	—	—	—	—	—	—	—	—	—
Northwest Territories[9]									
Conservative	n.a.	n.a.	n.a.	—	—	—	1	—	—
Liberal	n.a.	n.a.	n.a.	1	1	1	—	1	1
NDP (CCF)	n.a.	n.a.	n.a.	—	—	—	—	—	—

☘ 1972–1993	1972	1974	1979	1980	1984	1988	1993
Canada							
Bloc Québécois.........	—	—	—	—	—	—	54
Conservative............	107	95	136	103	211	169	2
Liberal..................	109	141	114	147	40	83	177
NDP (CCF)[8]	31	16	26	32	30	43	9
Reform..................	—	—	—	—	—	—	52
Social Credit...........	15	11	6	—	—	—	—
Other	2	1	—	—	1	—	1
Newfoundland							
Conservative............	4	3	2	2	4	2	—
Liberal	3	4	4	5	3	5	7
NDP (CCF)	—	—	1	—	—	—	—
Prince Edward Island							
Conservative...........	3	3	4	2	3	—	—
Liberal	1	1	—	2	1	4	4
Nova Scotia							
Conservative...........	10	8	8	6	9	5	—
Liberal	1	2	2	5	2	6	11
NDP (CCF)	—	1	1	—	—	—	—
New Brunswick							
Conservative...........	5	3	4	3	9	5	1
Liberal	5	6	6	7	1	5	9
Other	—	1	—	—	—	—	—
Quebec							
Bloc Québécois.........	—	—	—	—	—	—	54
Conservative...........	2	3	2	1	58	63	1
Liberal	56	60	67	74	17	12	19
NDP (CCF)	—	—	—	—	—	—	—
Social Credit...........	15	11	6	—	—	—	—
Other	1	—	—	—	—	—	1
Ontario							
Conservative...........	40	25	57	38	67	46	—
Liberal	36	55	32	52	14	43	98
NDP (CCF)	11	8	6	5	13	10	—
Reform.................	—	—	—	—	—	—	1
Other	1	—	—	—	1	—	—
Manitoba							
Conservative...........	8	9	7	5	9	7	—
Liberal	2	2	2	2	1	5	12
NDP (CCF)	3	2	5	7	4	2	1
Reform.................	—	—	—	—	—	—	1
Saskatchewan							
Conservative............	7	8	10	7	9	4	—
Liberal	1	3	—	—	—	—	5
NDP (CCF)	5	2	4	7	5	10	5
Reform.................	—	—	—	—	—	—	4
Alberta							
Conservative...........	19	19	21	21	21	25	—
Liberal	—	—	—	—	—	—	4
NDP (CCF)	—	—	—	—	—	1	—
Reform	—	—	—	—	—	—	22
British Columbia							
Conservative...........	8	13	19	16	19	12	—
Liberal	4	8	1	—	1	1	6
NDP (CCF)	11	2	8	12	8	19	2
Reform.................	—	—	—	—	—	—	24
Yukon							
Conservative...........	1	1	1	1	1	—	—
Liberal	—	—	—	—	—	—	—
NDP (CCF)	—	—	—	—	—	1	1
Northwest Territories							
Conservative...........	—	—	1	1	2	—	—
Liberal	—	—	—	—	—	2	2
NDP (CCF)	1	1	1	1	—	—	—

Federal Election 1993—Total Votes by Province and Party

	Bloc Québécois	Conservative	Liberal	New Democrat	Reform	Other[1]
Newfoundland	0	61 488	155 237	8 080	2 392	3 393
Prince Edward Island ...	0	23 126	43 412	3 731	744	1 209
Nova Scotia	0	106 411	235 684	30 907	60 377	20 015
New Brunswick	0	107 583	215 769	18 694	32 628	10 425
Quebec	1 846 024	506 683	1 235 868	57 339	0	98 287
Ontario	0	859 596	2 583 065	291 658	982 691	163 206
Manitoba..............	0	64 515	243 214	90 091	120 934	22 302
Saskatchewan	0	55 197	156 216	129 649	132 587	13 223
Alberta...............	0	175 556	301 774	49 097	629 402	48 000
British Columbia	0	219 838	458 802	252 257	593 599	107 498
Yukon	0	2 566	3 359	6 252	1 891	357
Northwest Territories ...	0	3 863	15 552	1 820	2 000	538
Total votes............	1 846 024	2 186 422	5 647 952	939 575	2 559 245	488 453
Total seats............	54	2	177	9	52	1

Source: *Elections Canada*

(1) Other includes Abolitionist Party of Canada, Canada Party, Christian Heritage Party of Canada, Libertarian Party of Canada, Marxist-Leninist Party of Canada, National Party of Canada, Natural Law Party of Canada, Party for the Commonwealth of Canada, The Green Party of Canada, independents and those with no affiliation.

Voter Turnout at Canada's Federal Elections, 1867–1993

(percentage of eligible voters casting votes)

Year	Voter turnout[1]	Year	Voter turnout[1]	Year	Voter turnout[1]	Year	Voter turnout[1]
1867	73%	1904	84%	1940	71%	1968	76%
1872	70	1908	79	1945	76	1972	77
1874	75	1911	72	1949	75	1974	71
1878	71	1917	90	1953	68	1979	76
1882	72	1921	71	1957	75	1980	69
1887	70	1925	69	1958	81	1984	75
1891	65	1926	70	1962	80	1988	76
1896	61	1930	76	1963	80	1993	70
1900	79	1935	75	1965	76		

Source: *Elections Canada*

(1) Percentage of actual votes to eligible voters. In many early general elections, several electoral districts were won by acclamation; hence, no eligible voters nor actual votes were recorded. Furthermore, in some of the more remote districts, votes were cast but no voters' lists had been prepared.

Federal Election 1993 — Voter Turnout by Province

	Eligible voters	Actual votes cast[1]	Voter turnout[2]		Eligible voters	Actual votes cast[1]	Voter turnout[2]
Canada	19 906 796	13 863 135	69.6	Manitoba	791 374	543 339	68.7
Newfoundland	419 635	231 424	55.1	Saskatchewan	704 248	488 755	69.4
PEI	99 645	72 973	73.2	Alberta	1 851 822	1 206 871	65.2
Nova Scotia	707 202	457 610	64.7	British Columbia. .	2 420 709	1 640 614	67.8
New Brunswick ...	562 128	391 247	69.6	Yukon	38 108	23 962	62.9
Quebec	5 025 263	3 873 050	77.1	Northwest			
Ontario	7 266 097	4 918 819	67.7	Territories	20 565	14 471	70.4

Source: *Elections Canada*

(1) Valid and non-valid votes. (2) Percentage of actual votes to eligible voters.

Election 1993–Canada's 35th General Election

■ Calling an election

On the advice of Prime Min. Kim Campbell, Canada's 34th parliament was dissolved on Sept. 8, 1993 by the Governor General. He then directed that writs ordering a general election on Mon. Oct. 25 be issued immediately, to be made returnable on Nov. 15. Nomination day was Mon. Sept. 27 and the dates for advance polls were set as Oct. 15, 16 and 18.

The period for 35th federal election was 47 days long, the minimum specified in the Canada Elections Act. During that time Elections Canada had to ensure that all eligible Canadians were registered to vote, a list of electors was prepared and all candidates were registered. The agency is also responsible for instructing and assisting the 295 returning officers whose duties included establishing an office, hiring the necessary staff, registering all electors on the voters lists, locating sites for polling stations and ensuring that those sites were accessible to all voters, receiving the nominations of candidates, having the ballots printed, overseeing the casting and counting of ballots and declaring the official winner in their riding when the election writ was returned to Ottawa.

During the election the officers dealt with a total of 711 tonnes of election material, including pamphlets, ballot boxes, voter registration forms, computer equipment, signs and even a Canadian flag with a stand for each office.

■ Parties and Candidates

A record number of parties and candidates contested this election. The deadline for nominations was 2 p.m., Mon. Sept. 27, the 28th day before the vote, and in order for a party to be officially registered for the election, it had to have candidates nominated in at least 50 ridings. On Sept. 27 600 candidates (28% of total nominations) filed their nomination papers with their local returning officer, and of the 24 political parties either registered or approved for registration, only 14 met the statutory registration requirements. By the close of nominations there were 2 155 candidates, and 6 new parties.

As soon as nominations closed, Elections Canada employees set to work to produce a list of official candidates which was given to Canadian Press for publication the next day, and by noon on Sept. 28 printed copies were also in the hands of Foreign Affairs and National Defence departments for transmission to Canadian Forces bases and diplomatic missions and posts around the world. On the same day, each returning officer sent the names and political affiliation of candidates for their riding to the local supplier contracted to print the ballots.

■ Tracking Down the Voters

Each of the 295 returning officers and their staff prepared four lists of electors; the preliminary list was based on enumeration in Quebec and the 1992 voters' lists for the referendum held in other provinces and territories. A first revised list was prepared for the advance polls; a second revised list that included changes made during the revision period was prepared for use on voting day and the fourth list included all voters who registered on voting day, plus all those who registered when they applied to vote by special ballot from outside their ridings.

The preliminary list came to returning officers outside Quebec on computer diskettes, with a set of mailing labels for the information cards. Enumeration for Quebec and the mailing of revision cards elsewhere began on Sept. 20 and lasted for seven days. Revision cards went out to nearly 13.7 million voters and by Sept. 25, there had been 340 000 additions, 153 000 deletions, and over 61 000 corrections to the preliminary list. During the last few days of Sept. a pamphlet went out to 8.1 million households explaining the need to revise the voters lists and urging voters to make sure they were registered. In addition some returning officers held special registration drives in shopping malls, high schools and university residences to ensure that prospective voters got their names on the list by the Oct. 20 deadline.

■ **Casting a Special Ballot**

A new provision for a special ballot enabled eligible Canadians in nearly all circumstances to exercise their right to vote. Voters who couldn't go to the polls in their own riding, but could vote by special ballot included Canadians living abroad for less than five years, those in prison for a term of less than two years, patients in acute care or other facilities, crews aboard ship in various parts of the country, as well as Defence and diplomatic personnel overseas.

Voters could register by mail or fax and vote by mail, using the special ballot voting kit and sending their ballot to Elections Canada for inclusion in the count in their home riding. Special ballot registration forms and guides were sent to shipping companies, and qualified crew members were able to register and later vote when they arrived in port; three employees from the Elections Canada office in Iqaluit visited a coast guard icebreaker anchored in Frobisher Bay to collect ballots from registered voters on board ship; Canadian Forces members in Bosnia and Haiti cast their vote by special ballot, as did patients in several hundred acute care hospitals. More than 200 000 electors, inside and outside the country, voted by special ballot.

■ **Voting Day**

On Monday, Oct. 25, six and half weeks of preparation and campaigning came to an end. Over 54 000 polling stations opened at 9 a.m. local time across the country and stayed open for 11 hours. Over 98% of them were fully accessible to voters in wheelchairs or those with special needs and 651 of the polling stations were mobile.

There were 19 471 105 names on the voters lists at the beginning of the day, but for the first time voters could register at the polling station and several thousand took advantage of this new provision. The total number of eligible voters at the end of the day was 19 906 796. Voter turnout was just under 70%—13 835 018 ballots were cast. Despite all of the advances in modern technology, those ballots were counted the old-fashioned way—by hand.

■ **How much did it cost?**

The cost of the 1988 election, adjusted for inflation, was $153 million. For the 1993 election, it was estimated that the reuse of the voters lists from the federal referendum saved about $16 million, however extensive reform of the electoral system since the last election, including computerization, improving accessibility, administrative changes and the fact that there were 37% more candidates, increased costs. In April it was estimated that 1993 election costs in the 1993-4 fiscal year were approximately $162 million, with expected additional costs of $25 million in fiscal 1994-5.

Election Facts and Figures

Total number of electors: 19 906 796
Total number of candidates: 2 155
Total number of registered parties: 14
Total number of ballots cast: 13 835 018
Total number of ballots rejected: 195 464
Riding with the fewest voters: Nunatsiaq, Northwest Territories - 14 368
Riding with the most voters: York North, Ontario - 162 848
Riding with the lowest turnout: Gander-Grand Falls, Newfoundland - 52.4%
Riding with the highest turnout: Lachine-Lac-Saint-Louis, Quebec - 84.0%

Riding with the fewest rejected ballots: Yukon, Yukon Territory - 46
Riding with the most rejected ballots: Terrebonne, Quebec - 3 973
Tightest race: Anne McLellan, Lib. Edmonton Northwest, Alberta beat her closest rival, from the Reform Party, by 12 votes
Biggest win: Sheila Finestone, Lib., Mount Royal, Quebec had the widest margin - 82.9% of the votes cast for a lead of 36 274 votes, her closest rival was the BQ candidate with 3 324 (7%); not surprisingly, the winner in the riding with the most voters won by the most votes: Maurizio Bevilacqua, Lib., had 51 389 more votes than the second place finisher, taking 63.3% of votes cast.

Federal Political Party Leaders

■ Progressive Conservative[1] Party

Leader	Term
Sir John A. Macdonald	1854–July 6, 1891
Sir J.J.C. Abbott	June 16, 1891–Dec. 5, 1892
Sir John Thompson	Dec. 5, 1892–Dec. 12, 1894
Sir Mackenzie Bowell	Dec. 21, 1894–Apr. 27, 1896
Sir Charles Tupper	May 1, 1896–Feb. 5, 1901
Sir Robert Borden	Feb. 6, 1901–July 10, 1920
Arthur Meighen	July 10, 1920–Oct. 11, 1926
Hugh Guthrie[2]	Oct. 11, 1926–Oct. 12, 1927
R.B. Bennett	Oct. 12, 1927–July 7, 1938
R.J. Manion	July 7, 1938–May 13, 1940
R.B. Hanson[2]	May 13, 1940–Nov. 12, 1941
Arthur Meighen	Nov. 12, 1941–Dec. 11, 1942
John Bracken	Dec. 11, 1942–Oct. 2, 1948
George A. Drew	Oct. 2, 1948–Dec. 14, 1956
John G. Diefenbaker	Dec. 14, 1956–Sept. 9, 1967
Robert L. Stanfield	Sept. 9, 1967–Feb. 22, 1976
Joe Clark	Feb. 22, 1976–Feb. 8, 1983
Erik Nielsen[2]	Feb. 9, 1983–June 11, 1983
Brian Mulroney	June 11, 1983–June 13, 1993
Kim Campbell	June 13, 1993–Dec. 13, 1993
Jean Charest (interim)	Dec. 14, 1993–

■ Liberal Party

Leader	Term
Robert Baldwin	1804–1858
Louis-H. Lafontaine	1807–1864
George Brown	1867–1872
Alexander Mackenzie	Mar. 6, 1873–Apr. 27, 1880
Edward Blake	May 4, 1880–June 2, 1887
Sir Wilfrid Laurier	June 1887–Feb. 17, 1919
Daniel D. McKenzie[2]	Feb. 1919–Aug. 1919
W.L. Mackenzie King	Aug. 7, 1919–Aug. 7, 1948
Louis St. Laurent	Aug. 7, 1948–Jan. 16, 1958
Lester B. Pearson	Jan. 16, 1958–Apr. 2, 1968
Pierre E. Trudeau	Apr. 6, 1968–June 16, 1984
John N. Turner	June 16, 1984–June 23, 1990
Jean Chrétien	June 23, 1990–

■ New Democratic Party[3]

Leader	Term
James S. Woodsworth	Aug. 1932–July 1942
M.J. Coldwell	July 1942–Aug. 1960
Hazen Argue	Aug. 1960–Aug. 1961
Tommy Douglas	Aug. 1961–Apr. 1971
David Lewis	Apr. 24, 1971–July 7, 1975
Ed Broadbent	July 7, 1975–Dec. 2, 1989
Audrey McLaughlin	Dec. 2, 1989–

(1) Name changed from Conservative to Progressive Conservative Dec. 1942. (2) Interim leader appointed to fill a vacancy until a party leadership convention could be held. (3) Prior to Aug. 1961 was called the Co-operative Commonwealth Federation.

Federal Political Party Leadership Conventions

■ **Progressive Conservative Party, 1993**

Candidates	First ballot	Second ballot
Kim Campbell	**1 664**	**1 817**
Jean Charest	1 369	1 630
Jim Edwards	307	—
Garth Turner	76	—
Patrick Boyer	53	—

■ **Liberal Party, 1990**

Candidates	First ballot
Jean Chrétien	**2 662**
Paul Martin	1 176
Sheila Copps	499
Tom Wappel	267
John Nunziata	64

■ **New Democratic Party, 1989**

Candidates	First ballot	Second ballot	Third ballot	Fourth ballot
Audrey McLaughlin	**646**	**829**	**1 072**	**1 316**
Dave Barrett	566	780	947	1 072
Steven Langdon	351	519	393	—
Simon de Jong	315	289	—	—
Howard McCurdy	256	—	—	—
Ian Waddell	213	—	—	—
Roger Lagassé	53	—	—	—

Preparing a Voters List in the 90s

E lections Canada has noted a need for a better way to prepare voters lists than door-to-door enumeration. Given the demands of the various levels of government, the solution would be a continuous register—a voters list that is regularly maintained and updated—made available to all levels of government.

A 1991-2 project in BC proved the feasibility of a shared computer system to maintain and produce voters lists for federal, provincial and municipal jurisdictions. It specifically dealt with linking electoral and map data.

The first step in the larger process would be the creation of a national address register—an accurate, comprehensive collection of computerized civic address information that would cover all residents and their locations, and provide a reference to associated electoral entities such as polling divisions. The national address register would be the first in a series of three projects; the other two linking the addresses to a digitally mapped street network, and then to a register of voters.

The computerized address register and digitized map files would also be of interest to Canada Post and Statistics Canada, and the three organizations are studying ways to work together to implement such a system. Up-to-date data would be exchanged and the duplication of data gathering could then be eliminated. Before any such register can be used however, changes to election legislation must be made and issues relating to security and privacy must be considered in depth.

Provincial Election Results

■ Newfoundland

	1962	1966	1971	1972	1975	1979	1982	1985	1989	1993
Liberal	34	38	20	9	16	19	8	15	31	35
Progressive Conservative	7	4	21	33	30	33	44	36	21	16
New Democratic	—	—	—	—	—	—	—	1	—	1
Other	1	—	1	—	5	—	—	—	—	—
Size of legislature	42	42	42	42	51	52	52	52	52	52

■ Prince Edward Island

	1962	1966	1970	1974	1978	1979	1982	1985	1989	1993
Liberal	11	17	27	26	17	11	14	21	30	31
Progressive Conservative	19	15	5	6	15	21	18	11	2	1
Size of legislature	30	32	32	32	32	32	32	32	32	32

■ Nova Scotia

	1960	1963	1967	1970	1974	1978	1981	1984	1988	1993
Liberal	15	4	6	23	31	17	13	6	21	40
New Democratic[1]	1	—	—	2	3	4	1	3	2	3
Progressive Conservative[2]	27	39	40	21	12	31	37	42	28	9
Other	—	—	—	—	—	—	1	1	1	—
Size of legislature	43	43	46	46	46	52	52	52	52	52

■ New Brunswick

	1956	1960	1963	1967	1970	1974	1978	1982	1987	1991
Liberal	15	31	32	32	26	25	28	18	58	48
Progressive Conservative[3]	37	21	20	26	32	33	30	39	—	1
New Democratic	—	—	—	—	—	—	—	1	—	1
Confederation of Regions	—	—	—	—	—	—	—	—	—	8
Size of legislature	52	52	52	58	58	58	58	58	58	58

■ Quebec

	1960	1962	1966	1970	1973	1976	1981	1985	1989	1994
Crédit Social	—	—	—	12	2	1	—	—	—	—
Equality	—	—	—	—	—	—	—	—	4	—
Liberal	51	63	50	72	102	26	42	99	92	47
Parti Québécois[4]	—	—	—	7	6	71	80	23	29	77
Union Nationale	43	31	56	17	—	11	—	—	—	—
Other	1	1	2	—	—	1	—	—	—	1
Size of legislature	95	95	108	108	110	110	122	122	125	125

■ Ontario

	1959	1963	1967	1971	1975	1977	1981	1985	1987	1990
Liberal	22	24	28	20	36	34	34	48	95	36
New Democratic[5]	5	7	20	19	38	33	21	25	19	74
Progressive Conservative[3]	71	77	69	78	51	58	70	52	16	20
Size of legislature	98	108	117	117	125	125	125	125	130	130

■ Manitoba

	1959	1962	1966	1969	1973	1977	1981	1986	1988	1990
Liberal	—	13	14	4	5	1	—	1	20	7
Liberal and Liberal Progressive	11	—	—	—	—	—	—	—	—	—
New Democratic[5]	10	7	11	28	31	23	34	30	12	20
Progressive Conservative[6]	35	36	31	22	21	33	23	26	25	30
Other	1	1	1	3	—	—	—	—	—	—
Size of legislature	57	57	57	57	57	57	57	57	57	57

■ Saskatchewan

	1956	1960	1964	1967	1971	1975	1978	1982	1986	1991
Liberal	14	17	33	35	15	15	—	—	1	1
New Democratic[7]	36	38	25	24	45	39	44	8	25	55
Progressive Conservative[8]	—	—	1	—	—	7	17	56	38	10
Other	3	—	—	—	—	—	—	—	—	—
Size of legislature	53	55	59	59	60	61	61	64	64	66

■ Alberta

	1959	1963	1967	1971	1975	1979	1982	1986	1989	1993
Liberal	1	2	3	—	—	—	—	4	8	32[9]
New Democratic[1]	—	—	—	1	1	1	2	16	16	—
Progressive Conservative[6]	1	—	6	49	69	74	75	61	59	51
Social Credit	62	60	55	24	4	4	—	—	—	—
Other	1	1	1	1	1	—	2	2	—	—
Size of legislature	65	63	65	75	75	79	79	83	83	83

■ British Columbia

	1960	1963	1966	1969	1972	1975	1979	1983	1986	1991
Liberal	4	5	6	5	5	1	—	—	—	17
New Democratic[5]	16	14	16	12	38	18	26	21	22	51
Progressive Conservative[6]	—	—	—	—	2	1	—	—	—	—
Social Credit	32	33	33	38	10	35	31	35	47	7
Other	—	—	—	—	—	—	—	1	—	—
Size of legislature	52	52	55	55	55	55	57	57	69	75

(1) Known as the Co-operative Commonwealth Federation until 1962. (2) Known as the Conservative Party until 1946. (3) Known as the Conservative Party until 1943. (4) Formed in 1968. (5) Known as the Co-operative Commonwealth Federation until 1961. (6) Known as the Conservative Party until 1944. (7) Known as the Co-operative Commonwealth Federation until 1967. (8) Known as the Conservative Party until 1945. (9) One Alberta Liberal now sits as an independent.

Provincial Party Leaders[1]

(as of Sept. 1994)

■ Newfoundland

Progressive Conservative Party		Liberal Party		New Democratic Party	
G. R. Ottenheimer	1966–69	Donald Jamieson	1979–82	Peter Fenwick	1981–89
Frank D. Moores	1970–79	Len Sterling	1982–84	Cle Newhook	1989–92
A. Brian Peckford	1979–89	Stephen Neary	1984–85	Jack Harris	1992—
Tom Rideout	1989–91	Leo Barry	1985–87		
Len Simms	1991—	Clyde Wells	1987—		

■ Prince Edward Island

Progressive Conservative Party		Liberal Party		New Democratic Party	
Angus MacLean	1976–81	J. Walter Jones	1943–53	Aquinas Ryan	1974–77
James M. Lee	1981–87	Alexander W. Matheson	1953–65	Douglas Murray	1979–81
Leone Bagnall	1987–88	Alex Campbell	1965–78	David Burke	1982–83
Melbourne Gass	1988–90	Bennett Campbell	1978–81	Jim Mayne	1983–89
Pat Mella	1990—	Joseph Ghiz	1981–93	Larry Duchesne	1991—
		Catherine Callbeck	1993—		

■ Nova Scotia

Progressive Conservative Party[2]		Liberal Party		New Democratic Party[3]	
Leonard Wm. Fraser	1940–46	Gerald A. Regan	1965–80	Michael J. McDonald	1952–63
Robert Stanfield	1948–67	A.M. (Sandy) Cameron	1980–85	No member elected	1963–66
George I. Smith	1967–71	Vincent J. MacLean	1985	James Aitchison	1966–68
John M. Buchanan	1971–90	J. William Gillis	1985–86	Jeremy Akerman	1968–80
Donald Cameron	1991–93	Vincent J. MacLean	1986–92	Alexa McDonough	1980—
Terence R.B. Donahoe	1993—	John Savage	1992—		

■ New Brunswick

Progressive Conservative Party		Liberal Party		Confederation of Regions	
C. B. Sherwood	1960–66	Louis Robichaud	1958–71	Arch Pafford	1989–91
Charles Van Horne	1966–69	Robert Higgins	1971–78	Danny Cameron	1991—
Richard B. Hatfield	1969–87	Joe Daigle	1978–8	**New Democratic Party**	
Malcolm MacLeod	1987–89	Doug Young	1982–83	Elizabeth Weir	1988—
Barbara Baird Filliter	1989–91	Frank McKenna	1985—		
Dennis Cochrane	1991—				

■ Quebec

Parti Québécois		Parti Libéral		Equality Party	
René Lévesque	1968–85	Georges-Emile Lapalme	1950–58	Robert M. Libman	1989–93
Pierre-Marc Johnson	1985–88	Jean Lesage	1958–70	Keith Henderson	1993—
Jacques Parizeau	1988—	Robert Bourassa	1970–77		
		Claude Ryan	1978–82		
		Robert Bourassa	1983–94		
		Daniel Johnson	1994—		

■ Ontario

Progressive Conservative Party		Liberal Party		New Democratic Party[4]	
John Robarts	1961–71	Andrew E. J. Thompson	1964–66	Edward B. Joliffe	1942–53
William G. Davis	1971–85	Robert Nixon	1967–76	Donald C. MacDonald	1953–70
Frank Miller	1985	Stuart Smith	1977–81	Stephen H. Lewis	1970–78
Larry Grossman	1985–87	David Peterson	1982–90	Michael Cassidy	1978–82
Andrew Brandt	1987–90	Lyn McLeod	1992—	Bob Rae	1982—
Mike Harris	1990—				

■ Manitoba

Progressive Conservative Party		Liberal Party		New Democratic Party[4]	
Duff Roblin	1954–67	Robert Bend	1969–70	Lloyd Stinson	1952–60
Walter C. Weir	1967–70	Israel (Izzy) Asper	1970–75	A. Russell Paulley	1960–69
Sidney Spivak	1971–75	Charles Huband	1975–78	Edward R. Schreyer	1969–79
Sterling Lyon	1975–83	Doug Lauchlan	1980–82	Howard R. Pawley	1979–88
Gary Filmon	1983—	Sharon Carstairs	1984–93	Gary Doer	1988—
		Paul Edwards	1993—		

■ Saskatchewan

Progressive Conservative Party		Liberal Party		New Democratic Party[4]	
Alvin Hamilton	1949–57	Ross Thatcher	1961–71	John H. Brockelbank	1941–44
Martin Pederson	1958–68	Dave Steuart	1971–76	Tommy Douglas	1944–61
Ed Nasserden	1969–73	E.C. Ted Malone	1976–81	Woodrow Lloyd	1961–70
Dick Collver	1973–79	Ralph E. Goodale	1981–88	Allan Blakeney	1970–87
Grant Devine	1979–92	Lynda Haverstock	1989—	Roy Romanow	1987—
Rick Swenson	1992—				

■ Alberta

Progressive Conservative Party		Liberal Party		New Democratic Party[4]	
W. J. C. Cam Kirby	1958–60	J. Walter Grant McEwan	1959–62	Chester A. Ronning	1939–42
Ernest Watkins	1960–62	David Hunter	1962–65	Elmer Roper	1942–55
Milt Harradance	1962–64	Mike Maccagno	1967–68	Neil Reimer	1955–67
Peter Lougheed	1965–85	Nick Taylor	1974–88	W. Grant Notley	1968–82
Donald R. Getty	1985–92	Laurence Decore	1988–94	Ray Martin	1982–94
Ralph P. Klein	1992—	Betty Hughes (interim)	1994—	Ross Harvey	1994—

■ British Columbia

Social Credit[5]		New Democratic Party		Liberal	
W. A. C. Bennett	1952–73	Robert M. Strachan	1956–69	Jevington Blair Tothill	1979–81
Bill Bennett	1973–86	Thomas Berger	1969	Shirley McLoughlin	1981–83
Bill Vander Zalm	1986–91	Dave Barrett	1969–84	Arthur Lee	1984–87
Rita Johnston	1991–92	Bob Skelly	1984–87	Gordon Wilson	1987–93
Jack Weisgerber (interim)	1992–94	Michael Harcourt	1987—	Gordon Campbell	1993—

Reform Party of British Columbia

Ron Gamble	1993—

(1) Includes up to 5 most recent leaders of the major parties; for years no leader is listed, the leadership was vacant or there was an interim leader. (2) Known as the Conservative Party until 1946. (3) Known as the Co-operative Commonwealth Federation until 1962. (4) Known as the Co-operative Commonwealth Federation until 1961. (5) In 1994 the party was reduced to 2 members in the legislature and lost official party status.

DEFENCE

Canadian security policy is based on three elements: defence and collective security, arms control and disarmament, and the peaceful resolution of disputes. The Department of National Defence and the Canadian Forces support this policy by their contributions to strategic deterrence, conventional defence, sovereignty, peacekeeping and arms control.

In addition, the Department of National Defence provides special support to other government departments in areas such as search and rescue, fisheries patrols, enforcement of drug prohibitions, disaster relief, and aid to civil powers in law enforcement. These tasks are carried out both in emergencies and where it complements military surveillance and control responsibilities.

Canadian Regular Armed Forces Strength

Canada has an all-volunteer Armed Forces which, since 1968, has been a single body composed of what had been a separate army, navy and air force.

	Navy	Army	Air Force	Total Armed Forces		Navy	Army	Air Force	Total Armed Forces
1914	379	3 000	—	3 379	1945	92 529	494 258	174 254	761 041
1915	1 255	81 195	—	82 450	1950	9 259	20 652	17 274	47 185
1916	1 557	274 194	—	275 751	1951	11 082	34 986	22 359	68 427
1917	2 220	304 585	—	306 805	1952	13 505	49 278	32 611	95 394
1918	4 792	326 258	—	331 050	1953	15 546	48 458	40 423	104 427
1919	5 495	228 292	—	233 787	1955	19 207	49 409	49 461	118 077
1920	1 048	4 684	—	5 732	1960	20 675	47 185	51 737	119 597
1925	496	3 410	384	4 290	1965	19 756	46 264	48 144	114 164
1930	783	3 510	844	5 137	1970	—	—	—	93 353
1935	860	3 509	794	5 163	1975	—	—	—	79 817
1939	1 585	4 169	2 191	7 945	1980	—	—	—	80 166
1940	6 135	76 678	9 483	92 296	1985	—	—	—	83 740
1941	17 036	194 774	48 743	260 553	1990	—	—	—	87 976
1942	32 067	311 118	111 223	454 408	1991	—	—	—	87 319
1943	56 259	460 387	176 307	692 953	1992	—	—	—	84 792
1944	81 582	495 804	210 089	787 475	1993	—	—	—	78 376
					1994	—	—	—	75 256

Source: *Department of National Defence*

Senior Canadian Military Personnel

(as of Sept. 1994)

Chief of the Defence Staff . . . . General A.J.G.D. de Chastelain
Vice-Chief of the Defence Staff . . . . Lt.–Gen. P.J. O'Donnell
Deputy Chief of the Defence Staff . . . . Vice-Admiral L.G. Mason
Maritime Command . . . . Vice-Admiral L.E. Murray
Maritime Command Pacific . . . . Rear-Admiral B. Johnston
Maritime Command Atlantic . . . . Rear-Admiral G.L. Garnett
Land Force Command . . . . Lt.-Gen. Gordon Reay
Air Command . . . . Lt.-Gen. Scott Clements
Canadian Military Representative, North Atlantic Treaty Organization . . . . Vice-Admiral R.E. George
Deputy Commander-in-Chief, North American Aerospace Defence . . . . Lt.-Gen. J.D. O'Blenis
Commander, Canadian Defence Liaison Staff (London) . . . . Brig.-Gen. D.M. Dean
Commander, Canadian Defence Liaison Staff (Washington) . . . . Major-Gen. D.R. Williams
Chief of Staff to UN Secretary-General . . . . Maj.-Gen. J.M. Baril
Training Systems . . . . Brig.-Gen. R.D. Buck
Canadian Forces Northern Area . . . . Brig.-Gen. R. Dwayne Daly

Source: *Department of National Defence*

Canadian Military Ranks

Army/Air Force

General Officers: General, Lieutenant-General, Major-General, Brigadier-General
Senior Officers: Colonel, Lieutenant-Colonel, Major
Junior Officers: Captain, Lieutenant, Second-Lieutenant
Non-commissioned Members: Chief Warrant Officer, Master Warrant Officer, Warrant Officer, Sergeant, Master Corporal, Corporal, Private

Navy

General Officers: Admiral, Vice-Admiral, Rear-Admiral, Commodore
Senior Officers: Captain (N), Commander, Lieutenant-Commander
Junior Officers: Lieutenant (N), Sub-Lieutenant, Acting Sub-Lieutenant
Non-commissioned Members: Chief Petty Officer 1st class, Chief Petty Officer 2nd class, Petty Officer 1st class, Petty Officer 2nd class, Master Seaman, Leading Seaman, Able Seaman

Source: *Department of National Defence*

Canadian Participation in UN Peacekeeping Missions 1947-1994

Location	Year	Mission
Korea	1947-8	Supervision of elections
India-Pakistan	1949-79	Supervision of ceasefire between India and Pakistan
Korea	1953—	Supervision of Armistice Agreement
Egypt, Israel, Jordan, Lebanon, Syria	1954—	Supervision of General Armistice Agreements
Egypt (Sinai)	1956-67	Supervision of withdrawal of French, British and Israeli forces
Lebanon	1958	Ensure no infiltration across Lebanese borders
Congo	1960-4	Assist in maintaining law and order
West New Guinea (now West Irian)	1962-3	Maintain peace and security
Yemen	1963-4	Observe withdrawal of Egyptian troops
Cyprus	1964-93	Assist in maintaining law and order
Dominican Republic	1965-6	Observe withdrawal of OAS forces
India-Pakistan border	1965-6	Supervise ceasefire
Egypt (Sinai)	1973-9	Supervise redeployment of Israeli and Egyptian forces
Syria (Golan Heights)	1974—	Supervise redeployment of Israeli and Syrian forces
Southern Lebanon	1978	Confirm withdrawal of Israeli forces
Afghanistan	1988-90	Confirm withdrawal of Soviet forces
Iran/Iraq	1988-91	Supervise ceasefire and withdrawal of forces
Namibia	1989-90	Assist in transition to independence
Central America	1989-92	Verify compliance with Esquipulas Agreement
Afghanistan, Pakistan	1990-93	Military advisory unit
Haiti	1990-91	Observe 1990 elections
Iraq, Kuwait	1991—	Monitor demilitarized zone; inspection of biological and chemical weapons
Western Sahara	1991—	Monitor ceasefire
Angola	1991-93	Monitor ceasefire
El Salvador	1991—	Investigate human rights violations and monitor progress leading to military reform
Cambodia	1991-2	Monitor ceasefire and establish a mine awareness programme
Cambodia	1992-93	Facilitate communications, establish mine awareness and provide transportation and other logistic support
Yugoslavia	1992—	Observation patrols, mine clearance, construction and maintenance of shelters
Mozambique	1992—	Security, monitor de-mining operations, ceasefire verification
Somalia	1992—	Distribution of relief supplies; headquarters personnel
Uganda, Rwanda	1993—	Force commander and military observer
Haiti	1993—	Construction engineers, headquarters and support personnel

Source: *Department of National Defence*

Canadian Forces Bases (CFB) and Detachment Bases (BFC)

3 Wing Bagotville: .... Alouette, Quebec, GOV 1AO
CFB Borden: .... Borden, Ontario, LOM 1CO
CFB Calgary: .... Calgary, Alberta, T3E 1T8
.... Wainwright Detachment, Denwood, Alberta, TOB 1BO
CFB Chatham: .... Curtis Park, New Brunswick, EOC 2EO
CFB Chilliwack: .... Chilliwack, British Columbia, VOX 2EO
4 Wing Cold Lake: .... Medley, Alberta, TOA 2MO
19 Wing Comox: .... Lazo, British Columbia, VOR 2KO
CFB Cornwallis: .... Cornwallis, Nova Scotia, BOS 1HO
18 Wing Edmonton: .... P.O. Box 10500, Alberta, T5J 4J5
CFB Esquimalt: .... FMO Victoria, British Columbia, VOS 1BO
.... Nanaimo Detachment, Nanaimo, British Columbia, V9R 5J9
CFB Gagetown: .... Oromocto, New Brunswick, EOG 2PO.
9 Wing Gander: .... P.O. Box 6000, Gander, Newfoundland, A1V 1X1
5 Wing Goose Bay: .... Goose Airport—Station A, Goose Bay, Newfoundland, AOP 1SO
14 Wing Greenwood: .... Greenwood, Nova Scotia, BOP 1NO
CFB Halifax: .... FMO Halifax, Nova Scotia, B3K 2XO
CFB Kingston: .... Kingston, Ontario, KOK 5LO
CFB Moncton: .... Moncton, New Brunswick, E1C 8K4
BFC Montreal: .... St-Hubert, Quebec, J3Y 5T4
15 Wing Moose Jaw: .... P.O. Box 5000, Moose Jaw, Saskatchewan, S6H 7Z8
.... Dundurn Detachment, Dundurn, Saskatchewan, SOK 1KO
22 Wing North Bay: .... Hornell Heights, Ontario, POH 1PO
10 Wing Ottawa: .... Ottawa, Ontario, K1A OK5
CFB Petawawa: .... Petawawa, Ontario, K8H 2X3
CFB and 16 Wing Saint-Jean: .... Richelain, Quebec, JOJ 1RO
12 Wing Shearwater: .... Shearwater, Nova Scotia, BOJ 3AO
CFB Shilo: .... Shilo, Manitoba, ROK 2AO
CFB Suffield: .... Ralston, Alberta, TOJ 2NO
CFB Toronto : .... Downsview, Ontario, M3K 1Y6
8 Wing Trenton: .... Astra, Ontario, KOK 1BO
BFC Valcartier: .... Courcelette, Quebec, GOA 1RO
17 Wing Winnipeg: .... Westwin, Manitoba, R3J OTO

Source: *Department of National Defence*   as of Sept. 1994

Canadian Forces Stations (CFS)

CFS Aldergrove: .... P.O. Box 4000, Aldergrove, British Columbia, VOX 1A0
CFS Alert: .... Belleville, Ontario, KOK 3SO
CFS Carp: .... P.O. Box 48, Carp, Ontario, KOA 1LO
CFS Debert: .... Debert, Nova Scotia, BOM 1GO
CFS Flin Flon: .... P.O. Box 338, Flin Flon, Manitoba, R8A 1N1
CFS Leitrim: .... Ottawa, Ontario, K1A OK5
CFS Masset: .... P.O. Box 2000, Masset, British Columbia, VOT 1MO
CFS Mill Cove: .... Hubbards, Nova Scotia, BOJ 1TO
CFS St. John's: .... P.O. Box 2028, St. John's, Newfoundland, A1C 6B5
CFS Shelburne: .... Shelburne, Nova Scotia, BOT 1WO
Naval Radio Station: .... Newport Corner, Ellershouse Post Office, Hants County, Nova Scotia

Source: *Department of National Defence*   as of Sept. 1994

CRIME AND JUSTICE

Canadian Law Enforcement

Policing in most Canadian provinces is carried out by municipal police forces and the Royal Canadian Mounted Police (R.C.M.P.). In addition, Ontario, Quebec and New-foundland have their own provincial forces. The two territories are policed solely by the R.C.M.P. In 1991 there were 56 774 police officers in Canada.

■ Municipal Police Forces

Each city and town is required by provincial law to have enough police to maintain law and order. Municipalities will either operate their own police forces, or contract with the R.C.M.P. or the provincial police force to provide the necessary police. In 1991 there were 31 790 independent municipal police officers.

■ Royal Canadian Mounted Police

The R.C.M.P. was founded as the North-West Mounted Police in 1873. The force is maintained by the federal government, and is the responsibility of the federal solicitor general. The R.C.M.P. has contracts with every province except Ontario and Quebec to provide police services to communities that do not maintain their own police forces. In those communities, the R.C.M.P. enforces all laws—federal, provincial and municipal. In 1991 there were 15 555 R.C.M.P. officers.

■ Ontario Provincial Police

The Ontario Provincial Police force is operated by the provincial government, and is the responsibility of Ontario's solicitor general. The O.P.P. enforces the Criminal Code and provincial statutes in those parts of Ontario where provincial law does not require municipal police forces. The force also maintains a traffic patrol on many of the province's highways, and enforces the Liquor Licence Act. As well, the O.P.P. provides municipal policing under contract. In 1991 there were 4 630 O.P.P. officers.

■ Quebec Police Force

The Quebec Police Force is similar to the O.P.P. in that it is a provincial force, with jurisdiction throughout the province. The force is responsible to Quebec's attorney general, and has a mandate to maintain peace, order and public safety throughout Quebec. It enforces criminal and provincial laws. In 1991 there were 4 431 Quebec Police Force officers.

■ Royal Newfoundland Constabulary

The Royal Newfoundland Constabulary (R.N.C.) was created in 1872. Although technically a provincial police force, R.N.C. policing is confined to the urban centres of St. John's, Labrador City and Corner Brook. The remainder of the province is policed by the R.C.M.P. In 1991 there were 368 R.N.C. officers.

Youth Crime Update

A n examination of crime statistics since 1986 that looked at charges laid against young people aged 12-17 revealed that the number of youths charged under Canada's Criminal Code (for offences other than traffic offences) decreased from 135 313 to 126 932 (a drop of 7%).

Of the 126 932 youths charged under the Criminal Code in 1993, 17% of the charges involved violent crime. This proportion was a 2% increase over the 1992 total and 11% higher than in 1986. (By contrast, 28% of adults charged under the Criminal Code in 1993 were charged with violent crimes.) The study went on to indicate that the number of youths charged in violent incidents has increased at a faster rate than the number of adults charged with violent crimes: in 1993, 24 471 young people were charged with violent incidents, an average annual increase of 13% since 1986; during the same period, the average annual increase in violent crime by adults has been only 7%.

Number of Police[1], by Province

	1965		1975		1985		1991[5]	
	Police officers	Population per police officer	Police officers	Population per police officer	Police officers	Population per police officer	Police officers	Population per police officer
Canada[2]	32 010	620	50 663	452	53 464	477	56 774	476
Newfoundland	521	940	777	714	927	626	917	625
Prince Edward Is.	104	1 038	198	596	180	711	188	695
Nova Scotia	889	848	1 197	690	1 439	614	1 542	584
New Brunswick	582	1 058	1 105	610	1 175	613	1 298	560
Quebec	9 531	602	14 526	428	13 893	476	14 575	470
Ontario[3]	10 773	639	17 439	472	18 461	495	21 210	467
Manitoba	1 184	813	2 036	500	2 086	516	2 193	498
Saskatchewan[4]	1 114	855	1 846	497	1 964	519	1 996	498
Alberta	1 956	744	3 362	540	4 526	557	4 526	557
British Columbia	2 599	711	4 728	520	5 784	501	6 149	523
Yukon	56	268	83	263	116	196	117	230
Northwest Terr.	128	219	185	229	232	219	238	230

Source: *Statistics Canada*

(1) Full-time police officers as of Sept. 30, 1991. (2) Until 1987, this total included RCMP officers from HQ, N, and Depot Divisions, and police officers from CN Railways, CP Railways and Ports Canada. Beginning in 1987, officers from CN, CP, and Ports Canada were no longer included in this total. (3) Excludes police officers from RCMP HQ. (4) Excludes police officers from the RCMP Training Depot. (5) Preliminary figures.

Number of Inmates in Canadian Prisons[1]

Year	Federal prisons	Provincial prisons	Year	Federal prisons	Provincial prisons
1960	6 738	10 896	1986	11 106	15 787
1965	7 518	12 627	1987	10 557	16 077
1970	7 375	12 124	1988	11 030	16 436
1975	8 456	11 277	1989	11 415	18 116
1980	8 651	13 851	1990	11 289	17 944
1985	11 214	16 178	1991	11 783	18 944

Source: *Statistics Canada*   (1) Average number of offenders in custody daily during the fiscal year.

Homicides[1] in Canada, 1961–93

	Canada	Nfld	PEI	NS	NB	Que	Ont	Man	Sask	Alta	BC	Yukon	NWT
1961	233	1	1	6	2	52	89	15	14	18	34	1	—
1966	250	3	1	9	6	56	71	17	12	27	48	—	—
1971	473	2	—	16	10	124	151	33	29	45	61	—	2
1976	668	6	2	25	14	205	183	31	34	68	88	4	8
1981	648	4	1	11	17	186	170	41	29	73	110	1	5
1986	569	4	—	15	12	156	139	47	26	64	89	3	14
1987	644	5	—	14	20	174	204	44	30	73	78	—	2
1988	576	7	1	11	8	154	186	31	23	66	80	1	8
1989	657	5	1	16	18	215	175	43	22	67	86	2	7
1990	660	—	1	9	12	184	182	39	36	74	110	1	12
1991	756	11	2	21	17	181	245	43	21	84	128	—	3
1992	732	2	—	21	11	166	242	29	32	92	122	2	13
1993	630	7	2	19	11	159	193	31	30	49	122	—	7

Source: *Statistics Canada*

(1) Includes offences of murder, manslaughter and infanticide. One "offence" is counted for each victim. (—) = zero.

Canadian Criminal Offences and Crime Rate

There were more than 2.8 million Criminal Code non-traffic offences in 1991—an increase of eight percent over the previous year. The violent crime rate increased by eight percent over 1990, while the property crime rate increased nine percent.

Criminal Code offence rates increased in all provinces from 1990 to 1991. The rate for Narcotic Control Act offences decreased by five percent over the previous year.

	1971				
	No. of offences	Adults Charged male	female	Youth charged	Crime rate[1]
Total criminal code offences..................	**259 431**	**180 469**	**24 774**	**54 188**	**1 365.7**
Total crimes of violence.........................	*38 756*	*33 644*	*2 214*	*2 898*	*203.9*
Homicides	415	353	43	19	2.1
Attempted murder	278	235	33	10	1.5
Assault[2]	30 207	26 614	1 890	1 703	159
Other sexual offences	3 448	3 041	31	376	18.1
Robbery	4 408	3 401	217	790	23.2
Total Property Crimes	*147 833*	*88 897*	*15 692*	*43 244*	*778.3*
Breaking and entering	36 512	20 884	639	14 989	192.2
Theft-motor vehicle	13 905	8 496	231	5 178	73.2
Theft-over $50	17 888	11 702	1 523	4 663	94.2
Theft-$50 or under.....................	52 127	25 910	10 166	16 051	274.4
Possession of stolen goods	9 965	7 584	658	1 723	52.5
Fraud........	17 436	14 321	2 475	640	91.8
Total Other Crimes	*72 842*	*57 928*	*6 868*	*8 046*	*383.5*
Prostitution	2 011	401	1 595	15	10.6
Gaming and betting	3 137	2 885	231	21	16.5
Offensive weapons.....................	4 738	4 220	178	340	24.9
Other criminal code offences	62 974	50 422	4 864	7 688	331.5
Federal statutes[3]	**21 897**	**19 669**	**1 184**	**1 044**	**115.3**
Total Drug-related Offences	*16 397*	*13 499*	*1 630*	*1 268*	*86.2*
LSD........	2 134	1 751	162	221	11.2
Addicting drugs	1 168	903	237	28	6.1
Cannabis ...,.....................	12 453	10 314	1 143	996	65.5
Controlled drugs (trafficking)...................	642	531	88	23	3.4
Provincial statutes	236 024	211 955	15 209	8 860	1 242.3
Municipal by-laws.....................	43 152	36 521	5 286	1 345	227.1
All offences	**560 504**	**448 614**	**46 453**	**65 437**	**2 950.4**

Source: *Statistics Canada*

(1) Per 100 000 population. (2) Includes sexual assault. (3) Also includes Bankruptcy Act, Canada Shipping Act, Customs Act, Excise Act, Immigration Act and other federal statutes

	1991				
	No. of offences	Adults Charged male	female	Youth charged	Crime rate[1]
Total criminal code offences..................	**2 898 814**	**397 457**	**83 773**	**208 702**	**10 736**
Total crimes of violence.........................	*296 838*	*109 762*	*12 915*	*26 827*	*1 099*
Homicides	753	508	47	54	3
Attempted murder	1 044	714	69	67	4
Assault[2]	256 790	99 576	12 126	23 349	950
Other sexual offences	3 933	1160	34	283	15
Abduction........	1 093	176	73	10	4
Robbery	33 225	7 628	566	3 064	123
Total Property Crimes	*1 726 726*	*156 734*	*47 510*	*128 144*	*6 395*
Breaking and entering	434 600	37 479	1 732	34 495	1 610
Theft-motor vehicle	139 310	9 953	606	11 228	516 ▶

▶ Theft-over $1,000.................	117 554	6 177	1 345	2 732	435
Theft-$1,000 or under.......................	864 351	60 153	30 096	66 966	3 201
Possession of stolen goods..................	34 020	14 526	1 975	8 312	126
Fraud..................................	136 891	28 446	11 756	4 411	507
Total Other Crimes............................	*875 250*	*130 961*	*23 348*	*53 731*	*3 242*
Prostitution..............................	10 568	5 075	5 596	500	39
Gaming and betting........................	1 386	1 061	156	11	5
Offensive weapons........................	19 702	7 236	549	3 023	74
Other criminal code offences..................	843 594	117 589	17 047	50 197	3 124
Federal statutes[3].........................	**93 751**	**42 946**	**6 465**	**6 185**	**347**
Total Drug-related Offences....................	*57 123*	*35 549*	*5 321*	*3 249*	*212*
Heroin...................................	1 363	735	258	12	5
Cocaine..................................	16 135	10 026	1 802	336	60
Other drugs..............................	4 148	2 088	303	239	15
Cannabis................................	33 275	21 724	2 819	2 466	123
Controlled drugs (trafficking)................	630	141	48	15	2
Restricted drugs..........................	1 572	835	91	181	6
Provincial statutes........................	343 244	176 818	23 489	28 991	1 271
Municipal by-laws.........................	102 570	23 469	4 269	4 133	380
All offences.............................	**3 438 199**	**640 690**	**117 996**	**248 011**	**12 734**

Source: *Statistics Canada*

PUBLIC WORKS

Public Works Canada (PWC) provides "common" services through the federal government, that is, services that are used by many or all departments. It employs over 18 000 people to provide those services, which range from translation, payroll, pension administration and group insurance services to historic restorations, stone carving, ship procurement and architecture and engineering services for all government facilities.

Each year, Public Works buys an average of $10 billion worth of goods and services for every government department and operation, including overseas embassies.

Public Works is also the largest real estate agency in Canada, buying and selling land and buildings, managing shopping malls and office towers. The holdings amount to $6.5 billion in federal real estate that is managed by Public Works and Government Services Canada. On behalf of the Canadian government, PWC owns landmarks like the Parliament Buildings in Ottawa, and its property includes 4 000 other locations across the country. Construction contracts in relation to the properties amount to $500 million annually.

As the Receiver General for Canada, PWC deposits all money paid to the government, keeps the books and make all government payments—200 million per year—by cheque or direct deposit.

Communications services include not only translators and interpreters in dozens of languages, but also telephone and computer networks and the Canada Communications Group, which is responsible for printing, photography, exhibit design, government publishing and public relations.

The Canadian General Standards Board develops standards for consumer products and now has approved standards for 1 500 things, including hand tools, computer disks, life jackets and clothing for firefighters.

Public Works and Government Services Canada also oversees a number of crown corporations and agencies, including: **Atlantic Canada Opportunities Agency**, which works to improve the economy of that region; **Canada Lands Company**, a real property holding company with leasehold interests and shares in subsidiaries; **Canada Mortgage and Housing Corporation**, which is involved in residential mortgage loan insurance, housing and land development, rent supplements and rural and native housing; **Canada Post Corporation**, which handles over 10 billion pieces of mail annually; **Canadian Commercial Corporation**, which acts as prime contractor for sales by Canadian companies to foreign governments and international agencies; **Defence Construction Canada**, which provides construction and property maintenance for National Defence; **Queen's Quay West Land Corporation Inc.**, which implements agreements affecting the harbourfront Lands on the Toronto waterfront; and **Royal Canadian Mint**, which strikes all coinage for Canada and 40 nations worldwide.

SEARCH AND RESCUE

The National Search and Rescue Secretariat provides leadership and facilitates cooperation, communication and coordination among all search and rescue providers in the development of search and rescue policy, resource planning, research and development, analysis and review. A large number of organizations carry out search and rescue activities—they range from the federal jurisdiction to the provincial and municipal, and at the federal level include: **Canadian Heritage** through Parks Canada, is responsible for marine and land search and rescue within the parks; **Environment Canada** through Atmospheric Environment Service provides weather reports and forecasts to mariners, aviators and outdoor enthusiasts, and special briefings for on-site Search and Rescue (SAR) coordinators; **Fisheries and Oceans** provides search and rescue assistance to mariners in distress; **National Defence** delivers primary air search and rescue services for air and marine incidents, air services for marine medical evacuations and operates three rescue coordination centres with the assistance of Transport Canada; **Ports Canada** through its various police detachments, is mandated to provide enforcement and some marine SAR services in 15 Canadian ports; **Royal Canadian Mounted Police** provide ground and inland marine SAR services for lost or missing persons in provinces, territories and municipalities where it is responsible for police services; **Transport Canada** through the Canadian Coast Guard delivers primary marine SAR for air and marine incidents and for marine medical evacuations in coastal waters and the Great Lakes-St. Lawrence system.

The provincial and territorial, as well as local, authorities are responsible for land and inland water search and rescue. These groups can include police departments, fire departments and emergency services as well as the RCMP, which often plays a key role in coordinating SAR activities. Private organizations such as offshore resource companies also play a part by training employees in SAR work, and there are approximately 450 volunteer SAR organizations across the country. Volunteer groups provide cost-effective resources and have important knowledge of local geographic conditions. The volunteer SAR organizations are the **Civil Air Search and Rescue Association**, with approximately 6 500 members and 1 000 aircraft at its disposal; the **Canadian Marine Rescue Auxiliary**, 3 600 members and 1 400 vessels, and land SAR associations which include more than 400 groups involved either directly or indirectly in land search and rescue.

SAR Goes High-tech

SARSAT (Search And Rescue Satellite-Aided Tracking) is a satellite system operated by Canada, France and the United States. It works in conjunction with COSPAS, a similar system operated by Russia, and together they form a constellation of four satellites in low polar orbit. These satellites are able to receive signals from emergency radio beacons and relay them to ground stations. Canada has three of the operational ground stations in the world, in Edmonton, Churchill and Goose Bay. The centres process the signals to determine the location of the beacon and the information is relayed to the control centre at CFB Trenton, which, like other control centres around the world, alerts local search and rescue authorities.

Three types of beacons can send signals to the satellites: Emergency Locator Transmitters, usually found in aircraft; Emergency Position Indicating Radio Beacons, found at sea; and Personal Locator Beacons, used during land activities such as hiking or wilderness camping. The newer type of beacon can send codes that identify the beacon, its vehicle, country of registration, and its owner. The origin of the signal can be located within a two-kilometre radius worldwide, making it easier for SAR forces to respond quickly. Since its inception, the system has saved many lives in Canada alone, and nations around the world have joined the original partners in the program.

THE ECONOMY

Understanding the Economy: A Glossary of Terms

Appreciation: the increase in the value of a currency relative to other currencies under free market conditions.

Balanced budget: when a government's budget is balanced, all revenues equal expenditures in a budget year. Thus there is no surplus or deficit, but a national debt may still exist.

Balance of payments: a measure of all yearly business transactions between one country and the rest of the world. It is the difference between the value of exports and imports, as well as the difference between investment money coming into and leaving the country.

Bank of Canada: the sole money-issuing bank in Canada, acting as banker to all other financial institutions and the government. It is responsible for Canada's banking system, sets interest rates and regulates the money supply.

Bank rate: the interest rate at which the Bank of Canada is prepared to lend money to the chartered banks.

Cartel: a group of companies in a specific industry which band together to restrict output and increase prices in order to get higher profits. In Canada, cartels are illegal. The best known international cartel is the Organization of Petroleum Exporting Countries (OPEC).

Consumer price index: an indexed measure of the average prices of household goods to show inflationary trends; compiled monthly by Statistics Canada.

Cost of living: the cost of maintaining a particular standard of living measured in terms of purchased goods and services. The rise in the cost of living is the same as the rate of inflation.

Deficit spending: the practice whereby a government goes into debt to finance some of its expenditures.

Demand-side economics: a school of thinking which states that an economy can prosper through policies which tend to increase public and private spending on goods and services.

Depreciation: the decrease in the value of a currency relative to other currencies under free market conditions. This differs from a devaluation.

Depression: a long period of little business activity when prices are low, unemployment is high, and purchasing power decreases sharply.

Devaluation: the official lowering of the value of a nation's currency relative to foreign currencies.

Disposable income: income after taxes which is available to persons for spending and saving.

Equalization payments: transfers of tax revenues from the Canadian government to provinces with a higher proportion of lower income earners, to compensate them for their lower per capita tax revenues.

Exchange rate: the price of one country's currency relative to another country's currency.

Fiscal policy: the deliberate use of government budget measures (i.e., tax and spending policies) to alleviate economic problems such as low GNP, high unemployment and inflation.

Free trade: a system whereby the free movement of all goods and services, investment money and workers between countries is neither restricted nor encouraged by governments.

Gross domestic product (GDP): the value of all goods and services produced in a country.

Gross national product (GNP): the value of all goods and services produced by citizens of a country both inside and outside the country.

Inflation: a steady rise in the average level of prices in an economy.

Less developed countries (LDCs): also known as Third World countries, these are countries considered economically-underdeveloped relative to the western industrialized nations.

Minimum wage: a minimum hourly wage as set by federal or provincial legislation.

Monetary policy: the government's manipulation of interest rates and the money supply to achieve economic growth, employment and price stability.

Money supply: the amount of money in an economy, with money defined as all currency in circulation and chequing accounts.

National debt: the debt of the central government; in Canada's case, the federal government.

Per capita GNP: also known as per capita income, it is the nation's gross national product divided by its population.

Prime interest rate: the rate charged by chartered banks on short-term loans to large commercial customers with the highest credit rating.

Protectionism: government policies designed to restrict imports in order to protect domestic industries. These policies include customs duties (tariffs) and restrictions on the quantity of imports (quotas). ▶

Real GNP: gross national product adjusted for inflation.

Recession: not as severe or as long-lasting as a depression but with the same general characteristics: a decline in real GNP for two consecutive quarters, with consequent unemployment and widespread softening in many sectors of the economy.

Stagflation: a high inflation rate combined with a high unemployment rate.

Supply-side economics: a school of thinking which states that an economy can prosper through policies affecting costs of production—that is, by giving production incentives to labor and greater financial rewards to investors.

Trade balance: the difference between the value of exports and imports.

Transfer payments: government payments to the provinces where no productive return is provided, such as old age pensions, unemployment insurance and welfare.

Wage-price controls: legislation whereby the government sets wage, salary and price increases in order to curb inflation.

Wage-price spiral: inflation brought about by increased wages which increase costs to the producers, who in turn increase prices. The increase in prices would cause labor to bargain for higher wages, resulting in a spiralling inflation.

ECONOMIC INDICATORS

Canadian Gross Domestic Product

(millions of dollars)

The gross domestic product (GDP) measures the value of all goods and services produced in Canada. The real (adjusted for inflation) change in the GDP shows year-to-year changes in economic activity and is considered a prime indicator of how well the nation's economy is performing.

	Current Dollars		Constant (1986) Dollars	
	GDP	Annual % Change	Real GDP	Annual % Change
1926	5 354	n.a.	43 986	n.a.
1927	5 777	7.9	48 108	9.4
1928	6 279	8.7	52 527	9.2
1929	6 400	1.9	52 997	0.9
1930	6 009	-6.1	51 262	-3.3
1931	4 975	-17.2	45 521	-11.2
1932	4 079	-18.0	41 302	-9.3
1933	3 723	-8.7	38 331	-7.2
1934	4 186	12.4	42 318	10.4
1935	4 514	7.8	45 357	7.2
1936	4 879	8.1	47 437	4.6
1937	5 477	12.3	51 635	8.9
1938	5 523	0.8	52 354	1.4
1939	5 880	6.5	56 265	7.5
1940	6 987	18.8	63 722	13.3
1941	8 532	22.1	72 214	13.3
1942	10 497	23.0	84 925	17.6
1943	11 282	7.5	88 164	3.8
1944	12 068	7.0	91 385	3.7
1945	12 063	0.0	89 170	-2.4
1946	12 167	0.9	87 177	-2.2
1947	13 940	14.6	91 665	5.1
1948	15 969	14.6	93 056	1.5
1949	17 347	8.6	97 234	4.5
1950	19 125	10.3	104 821	7.8
1951	22 280	16.5	109 492	4.5
1952	25 170	13.0	118 627	8.3
1953	26 395	4.9	124 526	5.0
1954	26 531	0.5	123 163	-1.1
1955	29 250	10.2	134 889	9.5
1956	32 902	12.5	146 523	-8.6
1957	34 467	4.8	150 179	2.5
1958	35 689	3.5	153 439	2.2
1959 ...	37 877	6.1	159 484	3.9

	Current Dollars		Constant (1986) Dollars	
	GDP	Annual % Change	Real GDP	Annual % Change
1960 ...	39 448	4.1	164 126	2.9
1961 ...	40 886	3.6	169 271	3.1
1962 ...	44 408	8.6	181 264	7.1
1963 ...	47 678	7.4	190 672	5.2
1964 ...	52 191	9.5	203 382	6.7
1965 ...	57 523	10.2	216 802	6.6
1966 ...	64 388	11.9	231 519	6.8
1967 ...	69 064	7.3	238 306	2.9
1968 ...	75 418	9.2	251 064	5.4
1969 ...	83 026	10.1	264 508	5.4
1970 ...	89 116	7.3	271 372	2.6
1971 ...	97 290	9.2	286 998	5.8
1972 ...	108 629	11.7	303 447	5.7
1973 ...	127 372	17.3	326 848	7.7
1974 ...	152 111	19.4	341 235	4.4
1975 ...	171 540	12.8	350 113	2.6
1976 ...	197 924	15.4	371 688	6.2
1977 ...	217 879	10.1	385 122	3.6
1978 ...	241 604	10.9	402 737	4.6
1979 ...	276 096	14.3	418 328	3.9
1980 ...	309 891	12.2	424 537	1.5
1981 ...	355 994	14.9	440 127	3.7
1982 ...	374 442	5.2	425 970	-3.2
1983 ...	405 717	8.4	439 448	3.2
1984 ...	444 735	9.6	467 167	6.3
1985 ...	477 988	7.5	489 437	4.8
1986 ...	505 666	5.8	505 666	3.3
1987 ...	551 597	9.1	526 730	4.2
1988 ...	605 906	9.8	552 958	5.0
1989 ...	650 748	7.4	566 486	2.4
1990 ...	669 467	2.9	565 155	-0.2
1991 ...	674 766	0.8	554 735	-1.8
1992 ...	688 391	2.0	558 165	0.6
1993	711 658	3.4	570 541	2.2

Source: *Statistics Canada*

n.a. not available

Canadian Consumer Price Index by Year

1986 = 100

1915 .... 9.4	1956 .... 21.8	1969 .... 30.0	1982 .... 83.7
1920 .... 17.3	1957 .... 22.5	1970 .... 31.0	1983 .... 88.5
1925 .... 13.9	1958 .... 23.1	1971 .... 31.9	1984 .... 92.4
1930 .... 13.9	1959 .... 23.4	1972 .... 33.4	1985 .... 96.0
1935 .... 11.1	1960 .... 23.7	1973 .... 36.0	1986 .... 100.0
1940 .... 12.2	1961 .... 23.9	1974 .... 39.9	1987 .... 104.4
1945 .... 13.9	1962 .... 24.2	1975 .... 44.2	1988 .... 108.6
1950 .... 19.0	1963 .... 24.6	1976 .... 47.5	1989 .... 114.0
1951 .... 21.1	1964 .... 25.1	1977 .... 51.3	1990 .... 119.5
1952 .... 21.6	1965 .... 25.7	1978 .... 55.9	1991 .... 126.2
1953 .... 21.4	1966 .... 26.6	1979 .... 61.0	1992 .... 128.1
1954 .... 21.5	1967 .... 27.6	1980 .... 67.2	1993 .... 130.4
1955 .... 21.5	1968 .... 28.7	1981 .... 75.5	1994 .... 130.2

Source: *Statistics Canada*

(1) As of June 1994.

Canadian Consumer Price Index by Item

1986 = 100

This table shows the relative costs, as far back as 1950, of categories of purchases made by Canadian consumers. To compare today's (1994) costs with those of another year, divide the 1994 index by the index for the year you wish to compare it with; then multiply that by your actual cost in the year for which you are making the comparison.

Example: you spent $40 per week on family food purchases in 1960. To calculate what that would be in today's dollars, divide the 1994 food index (122.8) by the 1960 food index (20.4). Now multiply the result by $40. The answer, $240.78, is what you now must spend to buy the same package of groceries that cost $40 in 1960.

	All Items	Food	Housing	Clothing	Trans- portation	Health and Personal Care	Recreation and Education	Tobacco and Alcohol
1950	19.0	17.1	19.0	30.3	18.0	15.7	20.7	19.0
1955	21.5	18.7	22.3	32.7	20.2	19.5	24.9	20.0
1960	23.7	20.4	24.2	33.7	24.0	23.8	29.3	21.5
1965	25.7	22.6	25.7	36.9	25.2	27.1	31.3	22.7
1970	31.0	26.9	31.8	43.4	30.0	33.4	38.9	27.3
1975	44.2	44.0	44.3	55.0	40.3	45.4	51.7	34.8
1976	47.5	45.2	49.2	58.1	44.7	49.3	54.8	37.2
1977	51.3	48.9	53.8	62.0	47.8	52.9	57.3	39.9
1978	55.9	56.5	57.9	64.4	50.6	56.7	59.6	43.1
1979	61.0	63.9	61.9	70.3	55.5	61.9	63.7	46.2
1980	67.2	70.8	66.9	78.6	62.6	68.0	69.7	51.4
1981	75.5	78.9	75.3	84.2	74.1	75.4	76.8	58.0
1982	83.7	84.6	84.7	88.9	84.5	83.4	83.4	67.0
1983	88.5	87.7	90.4	92.5	88.7	89.2	88.8	75.5
1984	92.4	92.6	93.8	94.7	92.5	92.7	91.8	81.6
1985	96.0	95.2	97.1	97.3	96.9	95.9	95.6	89.4
1986	100.0	100.0	100.0	100.0	100.0	100.0	100.0	100.0
1987	104.4	104.4	104.0	104.2	103.6	105.0	105.4	106.7
1988	108.6	107.2	108.6	109.6	105.6	109.6	111.3	114.6
1989	114.0	111.1	114.3	114.1	111.1	114.4	116.2	125.2
1990	119.5	115.7	119.5	117.3	117.3	120.0	121.3	136.1
1991	126.2	121.2	124.7	128.4	119.4	128.4	130.2	159.5
1992	128.1	120.8	126.4	129.5	121.8	131.3	131.9	169.0
1993	130.4	122.8	128.0	130.8	125.7	134.8	135.3	171.7
1994	130.2	123.3	128.1	131.6	130.9	136.3	138.7	140.9

Source: *Statistics Canada*

(1) As of June 1994.

Canadian Inflation Rate by Year

This table shows annual inflation rates, as measured by the percentage change in the Consumer Price Index (CPI) from one year to the next. The CPI, determined monthly by Statistics Canada, is a "weighted" average of the cost of a package of goods and services—such as food, clothing, housing and health care—normally purchased by Canadian households. Weighted average means that some items are given more importance according to the proportion of household income spent on them.

Prices increase for several reasons: rising production costs, limited availability of the commodity, unfavourable exchange rates pushing up import prices, excessive consumer demand and too much currency in the economy.

Year	Rate	Year	Rate	Year	Rate	Year	Rate
1915	2.2	1956	1.4	1969	4.5	1982	10.9
1920	16.1	1957	3.2	1970	3.3	1983	5.7
1925	1.5	1958	2.7	1971	2.9	1984	4.4
1930	-0.7	1959	1.3	1972	4.7	1985	3.9
1935	0.9	1960	1.3	1973	7.8	1986	4.2
1940	4.3	1961	0.8	1974	10.8	1987	4.4
1945	0.7	1962	1.3	1975	10.8	1988	4.0
1950	2.7	1963	1.7	1976	7.5	1989	5.0
1951	11.1	1964	2.0	1977	8.0	1990	4.8
1952	2.4	1965	2.4	1978	9.0	1991	5.6
1953	-0.9	1966	3.5	1979	9.1	1992	1.5
1954	0.5	1967	3.8	1980	10.2	1993	1.8
1955	0.0	1968	4.0	1981	12.4		

Source: *Statistics Canada*

Canadian Interest Rates, 1981–93

(average annual)

	Bank Rate	Prime Rate	Savings Rate[1]	Conventional 5 Year Mortgage	Govt. of Canada Average Bond Yield (10 yrs. and over)
1981	17.93	19.29	15.42	18.15	15.22
1982	13.96	15.81	11.50	17.89	14.26
1983	9.55	11.17	6.85	13.29	11.79
1984	11.31	12.06	7.69	13.59	12.75
1985	9.65	10.58	6.08	12.13	11.04
1986	9.21	10.52	6.02	11.21	9.52
1987	8.40	9.52	4.81	11.17	9.95
1988	9.69	10.83	5.69	11.65	10.22
1989	12.29	13.33	8.08	12.06	9.92
1990	13.05	14.06	8.77	13.35	10.85
1991	9.03	9.94	4.48	11.13	9.76
1992	6.78	7.48	2.27	9.51	8.77
1993	5.09	6.10	0.77	8.78	7.85

Source: *Bank of Canada* (1) Non-chequable savings account.

Help Wanted

*A*nother economic indicator is the Help-wanted Index, based on the number of help-wanted ads in 22 metropolitan area newspapers. During expansion, an increase in demand for labour means more help-wanted ads; during a downturn, the opposite happens. Since the need to advertise job openings happens early in the business cycle, an index that measures the level of job ads is an early indicator of labour market conditions and general activity. Statistics Canada reported in August 1994 that the Help-wanted Index had gone up by 1% from July, for a gain of 9% over the first seven months of the year.

Foreign Currency Exchange Rates

	Canadian Dollars in US Dollars			Foreign Currency Units Per Canadian Dollar (annual averages)					
	High	Low	Average	British Pound	French Franc	German Mark	Swiss Franc	Japanese Yen	Italian Lira
1971	n.a.	n.a.	0.9903	0.4051	5.4555	3.4483	4.0717	343.4066	611.9951
1972	n.a.	n.a.	1.0096	0.4033	5.0891	3.2175	3.8551	305.8104	588.9282
1973	1.0127	0.9885	0.9999	0.4076	4.4307	2.6441	3.14 96	270.5628	581.3954
1974	1.0443	1.0044	1.0225	0.4370	4.9140	2.6420	3.03 49	298.1515	664.8936
1975	1.0095	0.9615	0.9830	0.4426	4.2070	2.4131	2.53 68	291.5452	641.0256
1976	1.0389	0.9588	1.0141	0.5615	4.8379	2.5510	2.53 36	300.5711	840.3361
1977	0.9985	0.8963	0.9403	0.5385	4.6189	2.1805	2.25 02	251.2563	829.8755
1978	0.9170	0.8363	0.8770	0.4568	3.9448	1.7572	1.55 47	182.4818	743.4944
1979	0.8778	0.8320	0.8536	0.4023	3.6311	1.5640	1.41 92	186.0465	709.2199
1980	0.8767	0.8249	0.8554	0.3677	3.6088	1.5518	1.43 14	192.9385	730.9942
1981	0.8506	0.8031	0.8340	0.4117	4.3346	1.8804	1.63 35	183.4862	942.5071
1982	0.8446	0.7680	0.8103	0.4634	5.3050	1.9662	1.64 18	201.3693	1 094.0919
1983	0.8208	0.7990	0.8114	0.5352	6.1576	2.0687	1.70 27	192.6782	1 228.5012
1984	0.8038	0.7486	0.7723	0.5780	6.7250	2.1911	1.80 93	183.2509	1 351.3514
1985	0.7587	0.7107	0.7325	0.5649	6.5232	2.1381	1.78 09	173.4004	1 392.7577
1986	0.7332	0.6913	0.7197	0.4905	4.9751	1.5564	1.28 72	120.5400	1 069.5187
1987	0.7721	0.7248	0.7541	0.4603	4.5290	1.3543	1.12 30	108.8376	997.5171
1988	0.8444	0.7688	0.8124	0.4560	4.8263	1.4229	1.18 44	104.0150	1 053.7407
1989	0.8652	0.8254	0.8445	0.5151	5.3821	1.5863	1.38 01	116.1980	1 157.4074
1990	0.8859	0.8275	0.8570	0.4806	4.6577	1.3824	1.18 62	123.6094	n.a.
1991	0.8934	0.8573	0.8728	0.4932	4.9044	1.4422	1.24 58	117.3709	1 078.7487
1992	0.8771	0.7729	0.8276	0.4694	4.3706	1.2892	1.1592	104.7120	1 016.2600
1993	0.8065	0.7416	0.7753	0.5162	4.3879	1.2814	1.1449	85.8369	1 216.5450

Source: *Bank of Canada*

n.a. not available.

Building Construction in Canada

(millions of dollars)

	1960 Value	1960 %	1970 Value	1970 %	1980 Value	1980 %	1990 Value	1990 %	1993 Value	1993 %
Total Construction ...	4 051	100.0	8 098	100.0	24 706	100.0	61 471	100.0	61 315	100.0
Residential	**1 913**	**47.2**	**4 009**	**49.5**	**14 267**	**57.7**	**38 337**	**62.4**	**38 432**	**62.7**
Single detached ...	n.a.	n.a.	1 367	16.9	5 533	22.4	15 405	25.1	12 802	20.9
Semi-detached	n.a.	n.a.	141	1.7	630	2.5	545	0.9	723	1.2
Apartments	n.a.	n.a.	1 250	15.4	2 395	9.7	5 869	9.5	4 795	7.8
Other	n.a.	n.a.	1 251	15.4	5 709	23.1	16 518	26.9	20 112	32.8
Industrial	**452**	**11.2**	**1 000**	**12.3**	**2 096**	**8.5**	**3 437**	**5.6**	**2 594**	**4.2**
Factories	366	9.0	848	10.5	1 774	7.2	3 131	5.1	2 380	3.9
Commercial	**738**	**18.2**	**1 287**	**15.9**	**5 098**	**20.6**	**13 827**	**22.5**	**11 146**	**18.2**
Hotels[1]	48	1.2	93	1.1	417	1.7	1 068	1.7	525	.6
Office buildings ...	310	7.7	617	7.6	1 989	8.1	6 710	10.9	6 344	10.3
Stores	188	4.6	273	3.4	1 370	5.5	3 658	6.0	1 868	3.0
Theatres[2]	32	0.8	86	1.1	399	1.6	964	1.6	957	1.6
Institutional	**615**	**15.2**	**1 330**	**16.4**	**1 831**	**7.4**	**3 837**	**6.2**	**6 205**	**10.1**
Schools	347	8.6	890	11.0	908	3.7	1 653	2.7	3 735	6.1
Churches	70	1.7	29	0.4	78	0.3	145	0.2	79	.1
Hospitals	154	3.8	263	3.2	544	2.2	1 085	1.8	1 372	2.2
Other	**333**	**8.2**	**473**	**5.8**	**1 414**	**5.7**	**2 033**	**3.3**	**2 937**	**4.8**
Farm buildings	168	4.1	208	2.6	749	3.0	752	1.2	921	1.5
Airports, bus and train stations	26	0.6	27	0.3	60	0.2	106	0.2	325	.5

Source: *Statistics Canada*

(1) Includes clubs, restaurants, cafeterias and tourist cabins. (2) Includes arenas, amusement and recreation buildings. (n.a.) not available.

Annual Bankruptcies in Canada 1966-93

	Personal	Business	Total		Personal	Business	Total
1966	1 903	2 774	4 677	1980	21 025	6 595	27 620
1967	1 549	2 474	4 023	1981	23 036	8 055	31 091
1968	1 308	2 481	3 789	1982	30 643	10 765	41 408
1969	1 725	2 354	4 079	1983	26 822	10 260	37 082
1970	2 732	2 927	5 659	1984	22 022	9 578	31 600
1971	3 107	3 045	6 152	1985	19 752	8 663	28 415
1972	3 647	3 081	6 728	1986	21 765	8 502	30 267
1973	6 271	2 934	9 205	1987	24 384	7 659	32 043
1974	6 992	2 790	9 782	1988	25 817	8 031	33 848
1975	8 335	2 958	11 293	1989	29 202	8 664	37 866
1976	10 049	3 136	13 185	1990	42 782	11 642	54 424
1977	12 772	3 905	16 677	1991	62 277	13 496	75 773
1978	15 938	5 546	21 484	1992	61 822	14 317	76 139
1979	17 876	5 694	23 570	1993	54 456	12 527	66 983

Source: *Bankruptcy Branch, Industry and Science Canada*

Business Bankruptcies by Province[1] 1993

	Total Bankruptcies	Total Assets	Total Liabilities	Total Deficiency
Canada	12 527	$1 862 531 981	$5 383 385 779	$3 520 853 798
Newfoundland	139	10 223 338	23 938 262	1 714 924
Prince Edward Island	36	1 933 986	7 336 943	5 402 957
Nova Scotia	534	65 900 963	161 443 749	95 542 786
New Brunswick	197	17 137 470	38 912 454	21 774 984
Quebec	4 623	819 678 650	2 012 013 495	1 192 334 845
Ontario	3 984	621 529 167	2 348 228 030	1 726 698 863
Manitoba	266	61 411 465	111 980 710	50 569 245
Saskatchewan	400	33 000 582	68 244 023	35 243 441
Alberta	1 476	170 748 105	355 559 255	184 811 149
British Columbia	862	59 796 154	248 456 667	188 660 513
Yukon	9	1 170 000	7 252 792	6 082 792
Northwest Territories	n.a.	n.a.	n.a.	n.a.

Source: *Bankruptcy Branch, Industry and Science Canada*   (1) totals include all reported bankruptcies

Checking the Indicators

*S*tatistics Canada reviews Canada's economic performance on a monthly basis and publishes the results in the Canadian Economic Observer. The review includes a look at the percentage change in employment, the unemployment rate, and the composite leading index. (The index is a combination of figures such as housing (both starts and sales), business and personal services employment, the TSE 300 price index, money supply, the US Composite Leading Index, and indices in manufacturing and retail trade.) Stats Canada also reports the percentage change in CPI, GDP, retail sales, and export and imports.

New Vehicle Sales in Canada 1953-93

(thousands of units)

	Total units sold	Total commercial vehicles	Total passenger cars	Passenger cars manufactured in North America	% of total passenger cars	Passenger cars manufactured overseas	% of total passenger cars
1953	466	103	363	337	.93	26	.07
1954	384	72	312	292	.94	20	.06
1955	463	78	385	363	.94	23	.06
1956	495	91	404	370	.92	34	.08
1957	460	76	384	333	.87	50	.13
1958	450	69	381	302	.79	78	.21
1959	500	78	423	310	.73	113	.27
1960	522	75	446	321	.72	126	.28
1961	515	75	440	339	.77	102	.23
1962	577	82	495	420	.85	74	.15
1963	648	98	550	499	.91	51	.09
1964	723	108	614	549	.89	65	.11
1965	828	122	706	631	.89	75	.11
1966	931	133	698	630	.90	68	.10
1967	812	136	677	603	.89	74	.11
1968	887	148	739	636	.86	104	.14
1969	920	157	763	641	.84	122	.16
1970	773	134	640	496	.78	144	.22
1971	935	159	776	588	.76	187	.24
1972	1 062	207	855	651	.76	204	.24
1973	1 230	256	973	784	.81	190	.19
1974	1 249	306	943	796	.84	147	.16
1975	1 328	328	1 000	844	.84	156	.16
1976	1 281	343	939	785	.84	153	.16
1977	1 349	355	994	802	.81	192	.19
1978	1 365	377	987	816	.83	171	.17
1979	1 396	393	1 003	862	.86	141	.14
1980	1 268	332	936	742	.79	194	.21
1981	1 191	286	906	649	.72	256	.28
1982	925	207	718	494	.69	224	.31
1983	1 079	238	841	623	.74	218	.26
1984	1 283	312	971	724	.75	247	.25
1985	1 528	393	1 135	795	.70	340	.30
1986	1 523	422	1 102	765	.69	337	.31
1987	1 530	469	1 061	698	.66	364	.34
1988	1 564	508	1 056	724	.69	332	.31
1989	1 481	496	985	671	.68	313	.32
1990	1 318	433	885	579	.65	306	.35
1991	1 281	411	869	570	.66	299	.34
1992	1 231	432	799	507	.63	293	.37
1993	1 194	453	741	497	.67	244	.33

Source: *Statistics Canada*

Trends in Car Sales

*I*n June 1994 Statistics Canada announced that new motor vehicle sales had returned to levels not seen since late 1991, with both passenger and truck sales contributing to the growth.

They also noted a continuing shift to vehicles built in North America, with North American-built products showing increased sales for 10 of the previous 12 months, while purchases of foreign-built vehicles decreased over the same period.

Canadian Unemployment Rates

	1970	1975	1980	1985	1987	1988	1989	1990	1991	1992	1993
Canada	**5.7**	**6.9**	**7.5**	**10.5**	**8.8**	**7.8**	**7.5**	**8.1**	**10 .3**	**11.3**	**11.2**
Nfld	7.3	14.0	13.3	20.8	17.9	16.4	15.8	17.1	18.4	20.2	20.2
PEI	n.a.	8.0	10.6	13.3	13.2	13.0	14.1	14.9	16.8	17.7	17.7
NS	5.3	7.7	9.7	13.6	12.3	10.2	9.9	10 .5	12.0	13.1	14.6
NB	6.3	9.8	11.0	15.1	13.1	12.0	12.5	12.1	12.7	12.8	12.6
Que	7.0	8.1	9.8	11.8	10.3	9.4	9.3	10 .1	11.9	12.8	13.1
Ont	4.4	6.3	6.8	8.0	6.1	5.0	5.1	6.3	9.6	10.8	10.6
Man	5.3	4.5	5.5	8.2	7.4	7.8	7.5	7.2	8.8	9.6	9.2
Sask	4.2	2.9	4.4	8.1	7.4	7.5	7.4	7.0	7.4	8.2	8.0
Alta	5.1	4.1	3.7	10.0	9.6	8.0	7.2	7.0	8.2	9.5	9.6
BC	7.7	8.5	6.8	14.1	11.9	10.3	9.1	8.3	9.9	10.4	9.7

Source: *Statistics Canada*

GOVERNMENT SPENDING

Federal Ministry Spending[1], 1971–93

(millions of dollars)

Department	1971–72	1981–82	1991–92	1992-93
Agriculture..........................	286.1	1 125.0	4 327.4	2 996.4
Atlantic Canada Opp. Agcy	—	—	293.5	278.4
Communications....................	21.7	1 134.0	1 997.1	2 263.9
Consumer and Corporate Affairs.........	23.9	95.0	180.3	179.3
Economic Development..............	—	13.0	—	—
Employment & Immigration.............	792.9	2 209.0	2 109.7	2 078.6
Energy, Mines & Resources.............	175.6	1 398.0	955.3	963.9
Environment........................	200.7	627.0	1 055.4	1 079.5
External Affairs.....................	314.5	1 285.0	3 803.8	4 178.8
Finance............................	3 542.1	19 824.0	49 986.4	47 876.7
Fisheries and Oceans.................	—	441.0	756.9	966.3
Forestry	—	—	196.6	234.1
Governor General	1.2	4.0	10.6	10.2
Indian Aff. & Northern Dev.	426.6	1 507.0	4 020.1	4 312.2
Industry, Science & Technology	—	—	2 668.1	2 634.9
Industry, Trade and Commerce	362.7	990.0	—	—
Justice	28.7	200.0	723.9	735.7
Labour	17.3	71.0	277.4	272.4
Multiculture and Citizenship............	—	—	—	119.9
National Defence....................	1 895.2	6 028.0	11 751.1	11 914.5
National Health and Welfare	2 706.1	17 818.0	36 034.3	38 464.5
National Revenue....................	185.3	816.0	2 166.1	2 283.0
Parliament	32.6	151.0	448.3	288.5
Post Office.........................	413.3	1 156.0	—	—
Privy Council.......................	15.5	64.0	207.5	310.8
Public Works.......................	336.8	2 188.0	3 305.0	3 697.9
Regional Economic Expansion..........	346.4	745.0	—	—
Science and Technology	—	486.0	—	—
Secretary of State...................	867.8	2 264.0	3 546.2	4 164.8
Social Development	—	3.0	—	—
Solicitor General....................	260.1	1 184.0	2 389.6	2 462.7
Supply & Services	83.7	394.0	415.1	587.9
Transport..........................	512.5	2 280.0	3 410.7	2 907.4
Treasury Board	438.4	318.0	483.6	839.1
Urban Affairs and Housing	129.9	—	—	—
Veterans Affairs....................	423.3	1 140.0	1 899.1	1 983.7
Western Economic Div	—	—	185.8	196.9
TOTAL...........................	**14 840.9**	**67 958.0**	**139 604.7**	**141 256.1**

Source: *Public Accounts of Canada*   (1) Includes transfer payments and program spending.

Federal Government Annual Surplus or Deficit[1]

(millions of dollars; fiscal year ending Mar. 31)

	Surplus or Deficit	% of GDP[2]		Surplus or Deficit	% of GDP[2]		Surplus or Deficit	% of GDP[2]
1957	-325	1.0[3]	1969	-400	0.5	1981	-13 522	4.4
1958	-196	0.6[3]	1970	332	0.4	1982	-14 872	4.2
1959	-877	2.5[3]	1971	-780	0.9	1983	-27 816	7.4
1960	-600	1.7[3]	1972	-1 542	1.6	1984	-32 399	8.0
1961	-529	1.4[3]	1973	-1 675	1.5	1985	-38 324	8.7
1962	-948	2.3	1974	-1 999	1.6	1986	-34 404	7.2
1963	-833	1.9	1975	-2 009	1.3	1987	-30 733	6.0
1964	-1 169	2.5	1976	-5 737	3.3	1988	-28 201	5.1
1965	-315	0.6	1977	-6 297	3.2	1989	-28 951	4.8
1966	-303	0.5	1978	-10 426	4.8	1990	-28 996	4.4
1967	-187	0.3	1979	-12 617	5.2	1991	-30 618	4.7
1968	-711	1.0	1980	-11 501	4.2	1992	-34 643	5.1
						1993	-40 500	5.9

Source: *Finance Canada*

(1) A minus (-) sign indicates a deficit. (2) GDP (Gross Domestic Product) represents the value of all goods and services produced in Canada. (3) Represents percentage of GNP.

Per Capita Accumulated Federal Debt, 1940–93

	(millions of dollars)		*(dollars)*	
Year[1]	Net Debt[2]	Interest on Debt	Net Debt Per Capita	Interest Per Capita
1940	3 271	139	288	12
1945	11 298	409	936	34
1950	11 645	440	849	32
1955	11 263	478	718	30
1960	12 089	736	677	41
1965	15 504	1 012	789	52
1970	16 943	1 676	796	79
1975	19 276	3 164	849	139
1980	72 159	8 494	2 853	353
1981	85 681	10 658	3 520	438
1982	100 553	15 114	4 090	615
1983	128 369	16 903	5 179	682
1984	160 768	18 077	6 436	724
1985	199 092	22 445	7 911	892
1986	233 496	25 441	9 210	1 003
1987	264 101	26 658	10 306	1 040
1988	292 184	29 028	11 276	1 120
1989	320 918	33 183	12 240	1 266
1990	357 811	38 820	13 484	1 472
1991	388 429	42 537	14 424	1 590
1992	423 072	41 020	15 469	1 499
1993	465 300	39 400	16 231	1 374

Source: *Finance Canada*

(1) As of Mar. 31, on a public accounts basis. (2) Accumulated budgetary deficit (net recorded assets minus gross liabilities) since Confederation.

Annual Federal Government Expenditure

(millions of dollars)

Year	Total Expenditure	Expenditure on Goods & Services	Transfer Payments[1]	Interest on Public Debt
1926	288	95	63	130
1930	313	105	87	121
1935	420	136	150	134
1940	998	668	193	137
1945	4 284	3 100	805	379
1950	2 291	923	941	427
1955	4 644	2 364	1 793	487
1960	6 518	2 426	3 339	753
1965	8 229	2 835	4 342	1 052
1970	14 826	4 530	8 434	1 862
1975	34 577	8 380	22 492	3 705
1980	60 324	13 901	36 526	9 897
1981	71 387	16 484	41 164	13 739
1982	85 130	18 858	49 597	16 675
1983	93 114	19 555	56 147	17 412
1984	104 016	21 130	61 989	20 897
1985	112 464	23 398	64 446	24 620
1986	113 309	23 845	63 357	26 107
1987	119 644	24 397	67 446	27 801
1988	127 774	25 728	70 358	31 688
1989	137 737	27 867	72 513	37 357
1990	150 838	30 548	78 482	41 808
1991	161 182	31 243	88 443	41 496
1992	163 373	32 114	92 452	38 807
1993	167 518	33 284	95 896	38 338

Source: *Statistics Canada*   (1) Includes payments to persons, businesses, non-residents, and provinces and local administrations.

Provincial Government Accumulated Surplus or Deficit

(millions of dollars; fiscal years ending Mar. 31)

Each year, most provincial governments spend more money than they receive in taxes and other income. This produces a debt (deficit) which continues to accumulate as this practice continues. In the table below, a minus sign represents an accumulated deficit; a plus sign represents an accumulated surplus.

	Nfld	PEI	NS	NB	Que	Ont	Man	Sask	Alta	BC	Yuk	NWT
1978	-1 094	-105	-566	-760	-5 662	-8 116	-657	+713	+4 841	+1 443	-20	-76
1979	-1 365	-114	-731	-815	-6 711	-9 658	-707	+837	+7 656	+1 648	-14	-77
1980	-1 541	-119	-812	-813	-8 209	-10 696	-652	+913	+9 418	+1 962	-26	-66
1981	-1 533	-135	-966	-925	-10 904	-11 926	-730	+1 050	+11 045	+2 144	+15	+52
1982	-1 699	-135	-1 439	-1 079	-9 097	-13 524	-970	+1 176	+13 547	+1 948	+25	+71
1983	-1 866	-165	-1 820	-1 476	-12 467	-16 586	-1 375	+884	+13 354	+817	+33	+68
1984	-2 143	-161	-2 148	-1 751	-15 214	-19 625	-1 916	+599	+13 918	-125	+50	+112
1985	-2 415	-164	-2 594	-1 983	-19 179	-21 872	-2 373	+131	+15 591	-730	+63	+115
1986	-2 616	-169	-3 010	-2 232	-24 699	-26 591	-3 497	-627	+15 674	-1 404	+87	+149
1987	-2 751	-183	-3 239	-2 409	-28 111	-28 840	-4 499	-1 859	+11 814	-2 051	+111	+153
1988	-2 889	-202	-3 438	-2 827	-31 225	-30 694	-5 205	-2 497	+10 676	-1 970	+127	+137
1989	-2 852	-229	-3 502	-2 834	-32 551	-31 551	-4 517	-2 803	+8 740	-1 016	+138	+166
1990	-3 012	-233	-4 500	-2 795	-33 854	-30 495	-4 508	-3 100	+6 625	-297	+150	+169
1991	-3 228	-268	-4 773	-2 959	-37 065	-32 524	-4 671	-3 328	+5 611	-630	+162	+172
1992	-3 561	-318	-5 307	-3 335	-42 842	-43 201	-5 295	-5 379	+3 312	-3 028	+159	+151

Source: *Statistics Canada 1993*

Social Security

Canada Assistance Plan

The Canada Assistance Plan (CAP), introduced in 1966, is a cost-shared program in which the federal government contributes to shareable costs incurred by provinces, territories, and municipalities in providing social assistance and welfare services. The provinces are responsible for the design and administration of social assistance programs. While all these programs have key features in common, each is governed by its own set of regulations and these vary from province to province.

The primary objectives of the CAP are: 1) to support the provision by provinces of adequate assistance and institutional care for persons in need; 2) to support the provinces' ability to provide welfare services which aim to lessen, remove or prevent the causes and effects of poverty, child neglect, or dependence on public assistance.

The principal eligibility criterion for all welfare programs throughout the country is that applicants must be in need of social assistance. "Need" is determined on the basis of a test to ensure that individuals have insufficient means to support themselves and their dependents. The needs test takes into account budgetary requirements as well as the resources available to meet those needs.

Persons who benefit from assistance and welfare services include: one-parent families; mentally and physically disabled persons; the aged; children who are in care or who are in need of protection because of abuse or neglect; the unemployed; families/individuals in crisis; low-income workers; and battered women.

The Plan also provides for the federal government to pay half the shareable costs of work activity projects. Such agreements have been signed with all the provinces but not with the territories. Work activity projects are designed to improve the employability of persons who have difficulty finding or retaining jobs or in undertaking job training.

Source: *Human Resources Development Canada; National Council of Welfare*

Canada Assistance Plan[1] Payments

	Recipients[2]				Expenditures[3] ($000)			
	1970	1980	1990	1993	1970	1980	1990	1993
Canada	1 346 009	1 505 481	1 930 100	2 975 000	456 473	1 894 869	5 502 554	7 382 653
Newfoundland	85 698	53 003	47 900	68 100	20 289	43 187	101 049	151 398
Prince Edward Island	9 404	10 070	8 600	12 600	3 293	10 268	23 881	35 491
Nova Scotia	51 814	56 125	78 400	98 700	15 246	53 670	157 211	248 611
New Brunswick ...	54 343	71 952	67 200	78 100	11 795	66 403	158 936	227 314
Quebec	477 440	562 960	555 900	741 400	162 213	738 583	1 723 610	2 486 218
Ontario	354 913	404 516	675 700	1 287 000	132 257	472 570	1 761 482	2 282 903
Manitoba	58 667	53 439	66 900	88 000	19 260	60 181	194 497	294 233
Saskatchewan	55 578	46 990	54 100	68 200	17 233	60 060	152 857	197 050
Alberta	84 386	94 585	148 800	196 000	31 441	127 388	513 187	618 960
British Columbia ..	113 766	144 454	216 000	323 300	43 086	255 602	693 783	803 204
Yukon Territory	n.a.	7 387[4]	1 000	2 500	360	1 093	5 202	10 953
Northwest Territories	n.a.	7 387[4]	9 600	11 100	n.a.	5 865	16 859	26 318

Source: *Health and Welfare Canada.*

(1) Expenditures shown are from the federal government only. (2) As of March. Because individuals may appear in more than one category, double counting may occur. (3) For fiscal years ending Mar. 31. Federal government payments are shown for the years in which they were made to the provinces. Some payments include reimbursements to the provinces for expenditures made during previous fiscal years. (4) Includes Yukon and Northwest Territories. (n.a.) not available or not applicable.

Unemployment Insurance

The Unemployment Insurance program covers most workers in Canada, major exclusions being the self-employed (except fishermen who are covered by special arrangement) and those who work less than 15 hours per week and earn less than 20 percent of the maximum insurable earnings ($156.00 per week in 1994).

To qualify for regular UI benefits, claimants must have suffered an interruption of earnings from employment and have accumulated 12 to 20 weeks of insurable employment. To receive benefits, a person must file a claim stating that they are willing to work and are looking for a job. Following a two-week waiting period, claimants are eligible to receive 55% of their average weekly insurable earnings up to a maximum of $429.00 per week in 1994. However, claimants can receive 60 per cent of their average weekly insurable earnings if: they earn at or below a certain level ($390 per week in 1994); and they (or their spouse) have a dependant. The period for which benefits can be claimed ranges from 14 to 50 weeks, depending on the length of previous employment as well as the regional unemployment rate in the area where they reside.

Maternity and sickness benefits are payable to persons who prove pregnancy or sickness with a medical certificate and who have 20 weeks of insurable employment. A maximum of 15 weeks of maternity benefits are payable as part of initial benefits. There are also 10 weeks of parental benefits which can be paid to the mother or the father of a natural or an adopted child. To qualify, 20 weeks of insurable employment are also required.

The Unemployment Insurance program is financed through contributions from employer and employee. The basic employee premium rate for 1994 was $3.07 for each $100 of weekly insurable earnings. The employer premium is 1.4 times the employee rate. The maximum weekly insurable earnings in 1994 was $780.00. This amount is adjusted in accordance with the rate of increase in wages and salaries averaged over the most recent eight-year period.

Source: *Employment and Immigration Canada*

Unemployment Insurance Program Payments

Year	Claims[1] (000s)	Benefit payments ($000)	Weeks paid (000s)	Maximum weekly payment	Average weekly payment
1943	36.7	941	85	$14.40	$ 11.12
1945	296.4	14 576	1 224	14.40	11.91
1950	1 150.2	98 994	6 980	21.00	14.18
1955	1 929.8	228 860	12 375	30.00	18.49
1960	2 700.4	481 836	21 592	36.00	22.32
1965	1 628.2	312 110	12 718	36.00	24.54
1970	2 260.8	695 222	19 817	53.00	35.08
1975	2 857.2	3 146 497	37 327	123.00	84.64
1980	2 762.2	4 393 308	36 333	174.00	120.92
1985	3 312.4	10 266 888	59 788	276.00	171.05
1986	3 353.1	10 513 557	58 063	297.00	181.07
1987	3 220.8	10 440 709	54 875	318.00	190.26
1988	3 230.8	10 852 400	53 527	339.00	202.75
1989	3 215.2	11 528 036	53 399	363.00	215.88
1990	3 259.0	13 189 000	57 052	384.00	231.18
1991	3 876.5	17 685 617	71 460	408.00	243.91
1992	3 805.7	19 308 233	73 795	426.00	254.78
1993	3 322.0	17 972 200	68 469	42 500	260.20

Source: *Human Resources Development Canada*

(1) Initial and renewal. (2) Prior to April 1, 1993, the maximum weekly payment for 1993 was $447.00. The figure listed above was the maximum weekly payment which came into effect as a result of an amendment to the Unemployment Insurance Act which took effect on that date.

Canada and Quebec Pension Plans

The Canada and Quebec Pension Plans were instituted in 1966 to provide benefits to Canadians who have contributed to the plan during their working lives. Both plans pay a monthly retirement benefit in addition to a one-time death benefit, survivor benefits for the spouse and dependent children of a deceased contributor and benefits to the severely disabled and their families.

Payments to the plan are made by all workers between the ages of 18 and the time they claim retirement (between the ages of 60 and 70). Payments are based on a contribution rate which in 1993 was 5.0 percent of "pensionable earnings." This payment is shared equally by employers and employees; self-employed persons must pay the entire amount themselves. The contribution rate is scheduled to increase steadily, reaching 9.1 percent in 2011. Contributions are not paid if income falls below an annual minimum ($3 400 in 1994) or on income above an annual maximum ($34 400 in 1994).

Retirement benefits from the plan are based on lifetime earnings and generally amount to 25 percent of average annual income, adjusted for inflation. The maximum monthly benefit at age 65 in 1994 was $694.44.

Spouses in a continuing marriage and partners in a common-law relationship may apply to receive an equal share of the retirement pension earned by both parties during their life together.

A provision that allows divorced couples to divide CPP credits earned during marriage was introduced in 1978. On Jan. 1, 1987, the provision was expanded to include legally-separated married spouses and those living in a common-law union. In March 1991 a further amendment allowed those previously denied a division due to a property waiver to have their situation remedied.

Since Jan. 1987, Canadians eligible for CPP benefits who retire before age 65 can receive partial pensions beginning as early as age 60. Those who begin collecting at 60 receive 70 percent of the amount they would be entitled to at age 65. For each month past age 60 that a person delays retirement, an additional half a percentage point is added—so that someone retiring at age 61 would receive 76 of their full (age 65) pension while someone postponing retirement to age 70 would receive 130 percent.

The Canada Pension Plan is administered by the federal government while the Quebec Pension Plan is administered by the Government of Quebec's Pension Board. Essentially the same rules and benefits apply to each.

Source: *Human Resources Development Canada*

Canada and Quebec Pension Plans Payments

	Canada Pension				Quebec Pension Plan			
	Benefi-ciaries[1]	Benefits paid[2] ($000)	Contrib-utors[4] (000s)	Avg. monthly retirement payments[1]	Benefi-ciaries[1]	Benefits paid[2] ($000)	Contrib-utors[4] (000s)	Avg. monthly retirement payments[1]
1971	251 853	$ 89 236	6 755	$ 23	79 649	$ 47 576	2 231	$ 25
1976	774 890	587 834	7 561	67	232 815	266 181	2 721	66
1981	1 274 306	2 010 924	8 626	144	406 069	704 798	2 902	148
1986	1 764 604	4 887 134	8 932	247	627 317	1 899 730	2 917	243
1987	1 974 417	5 721 315	9 269	270	666 847	2 132 658	3 033	258
1988	2 173 225	7 329 222	9 530	289	702 141	2 406 453	3 114	276
1989	2 335 711	8 445 044	9 600	306	736 176	2 663 521	3 152	292
1990	2 463 222	9 472 955	9 603	324	771 838	2 946 125	3 158	307
1991	2 584 986	10 541 912	9 630	342	809 409	3 182 379	3 167	323
1992	2 713 692	11 792 756	9 429	363	845 846	3 605 378	n.a.	341
1993	2 845 059	13 199 084	n.a.	370	883 610	3 860 717	n.a.	349
1994	2 988 911	14 402 175	n.a.	380	919 866	4 069 022	n.a.	357

Source: *Human Resources Development Canada; Régie des Rentes du Québec; Statistics Canada*

(1) As of March. (2) For fiscal years ending Mar. 31. (3) From 1971 to 1978, data is for calendar years; Jan. 1979 to Mar. 1980, data is for 15 months; from 1981 to 1988, data is for fiscal years ending Mar. 31. (4) Calendar years. (n.a.) not available.

Old Age Security, Guaranteed Income Supplement and Spouse's Allowance

The Old Age Security (OAS) program, introduced in 1952, provides pensions to persons 65 years and older who meet Canadian residence requirements. Full monthly pensions ($387.74 per month as of April 1, 1994) are given to persons who have lived in Canada for 40 years since the age of 18; some persons who have lived in Canada for 10 consecutive years are also eligible for full pensions. Partial pensions, introduced in 1977, are based on the number of years a pensioner has lived in Canada.

The Guaranteed Income Supplement (GIS) was introduced in 1966 to assist those with little or no income other than their OAS pension. The amount of income supplement depends upon the pensioner's income, marital status and spouse's income. Generally, the maximum GIS payment is reduced by $1 for every $2 of income a pensioner has above his/her old age security pension. For example, in April 1994 a single pensioner with no personal income received OAS benefits of $387.74 per month and an income supplement of $460.79 per month. If this person had a private pension of $400 per month, the GIS would be reduced $200 to $260.79 per month.

Spouse's Allowance (SPA) benefits are payable to persons aged 60 to 64 whose spouses have died or those with low income whose spouse receives an Old Age Security pension. Like Guaranteed Income Supplement benefits, the amount of the SPA benefit is dependent on income and marital status. The maximum SPA benefit payable in April 1994 was $759.42 for widows and widowers and $687.88 for spouses of OAS pensioners.

Source: *Human Resources Development Canada*

Old Age Security Program Payments

	Number of Recipients[1] (000s)			Net Payments[2] ($000 000)			Average Yearly[3] payment per pensioner		
	OAS	GIS	SPA	OAS	GIS	SPA	OAS	GIS	SPA
1952	$643	$n.a.	$n.a.	$76	$n.a.	$n.a.	$n.a.	$n.a.	$n.a.
1961	905	n.a.	n.a.	592	n.a.	n.a.	n.a.	n.a.	n.a.
1966	1 106	n.a.	n.a.	927	n.a.	n.a.	n.a.	n.a.	n.a.
1971	1 720	860	n.a.	1 627	280	n.a.	956	340	n.a.
1976	1 957	1 087	54	2 976	923	35	1 537	863	1 788
1981	2 303	1 245	85	5 322	1 918	178	2 338	1 592	2 168
1986	2 652	1 330	142	8 858	3 319	348	3 385	2 555	3 105
1987	2 749	1 345	144	9 520	3 451	473	3 517	2 615	3 375
1988	2 835	1 357	140	10 248	3 618	483	3 659	2 702	3 474
1989	2 919	1 364	134	10 963	3 766	473	3 803	2 803	3 538
1990	3 006	1 359	127	11 804	3 888	461	3 974	2 907	3 652
1991	3 099	1 346	121	12 705	3 976	450	4 153	3 009	3 759
1992	3 180	1 329	116	13 808	4 139	446	4 386	3 171	3 927
1993	3 264	1 331	113	14 421	4 250	435	4 464	3 268	3 964
1994	3 341	1 355	112	15 027	4 446	429	4 542	3 372	3 984

Source: *Human Resources Development Canada*

(1) As of March. (2) For fiscal years ending Mar. 31. (3) For fiscal years ending Mar. 31 using annual average number of recipients. (n.a.) not available or not applicable; OAS = Old Age Security; GIS = Guaranteed Income Supplement; SPA = Spouse's Allowance.

Veterans' Allowances and Disability Pensions

The War Veterans Allowances Act, approved in 1930, gives benefits to Canadian veterans who suffered disabilities or are unable to work as a result of injuries sustained in World War I, World War II or the Korean War. To qualify, the veteran must have lived in Canada for at least 10 years, be 60 years or older (younger if medical reasons warrant), and have little or no income. As of June 1994, the maximum monthly allowance was $926.83 for a single veteran and $1 407.22 for a married veteran.

Source: *Health and Welfare Canada*

Allowances are also paid to civilians who served alongside the armed forces during a war; these include firefighters and the merchant marine. Counselling services, treatment services and emergency funds are also available to veterans and their spouses and children.

The Pension Act, 1919, gives compensation to armed forces personnel for disability or death related to military service. Since 1962, benefits have also been paid to civilians working with the armed forces during wartime. In some cases, benefits are paid to veterans of Commonwealth forces. The amount of the monthly pension varies according to the disability.

Number of Veterans Receiving Benefits

Year[1]	Disability Pensions[2] (by period of service)					Veterans Allowances		
	World War I	World War II	Korean War	Peacetime service	Surviving dependants	Veterans	Veterans' surviving dependants	Civilians[3]
1946 ...	72 396	36 454	—	—	33 821	25 030	3 282	n.a.
1951 ...	66 001	95 650	—	—	34 009	30 608	7 992	n.a.
1961 ...	45 588	105 338	1 651	1 389	32 699	47 865	21 681	n.a.
1966 ...	33 688	106 191	1 843	2 133	30 712	55 947	29 888	1 318
1971 ...	22 298	102 666	2 010	3 344	28 808	48 384	32 749	2 822
1976 ...	12 404	96 776	2 084	4 106	26 884	47 999	37 297	4 075
1981 ...	6 581	90 840	2 139	5 793	25 141	51 175	38 897	4 446
1986 ...	2 669	84 237	2 204	8 883	42 969	47 455	31 852	4 519
1987 ...	2 123	83 153	2 125	9 842	43 691	47 101	30 891	4 408
1988 ...	1 672	81 705	2 225	10 848	44 573	40 385	28 093	4 180
1989 ...	1 319	80 295	2 251	11 870	45 467	34 226	26 153	3 903
1990 ...	981	78 657	2 275	13 038	49 772	28 990	24 102	3 655
1991 ...	732	77 203	2 271	14 314	52 515	23 852	22 039	3 293
1992 ...	549	75 563	2 251	15 516	54 074	19 809	20 189	2 978
1993 ...	387	73 573	2 245	16 754	54 805	16 591	18 544	2 808
1994 ...	272	71 608	2 232	18 055	55 626	15 017	16 927	2 635

Source: *Veterans Affairs Canada*

(1) As of March. (2) Includes recipients of Civilian War Disability pensions. (3) Includes surviving dependants. (—) = zero. (n.a.) not available.

Health Care Statistics

- *In 1993, Canada spent an estimated $72 billion on health, or $2,507 per person.*
- *Spending on drugs continued a decade-long trend of being of the fastest growing component of estimated health spending. Drug spending increased by 10.9% in 1991, 8.6% in 1992 and 8.2% in 1993.*
- *Estimated health spending in Canada has levelled off at about 10% of GDP.*

Health Care

Total Health Care Expenditures by Category

(millions of dollars)

	Hospitals	Other Institutions	Physicians	Other Professionals	Drugs	Capital	Other	Total
1975	5 443.0	1 194.1	1 927.3	731.1	1 091.2	612.4	1 265.5	12 264.6
1976	6 349.8	1 424.5	2 165.7	853.4	1 196.7	649.6	1 476.4	14 116.2
1977	6 786.3	1 628.7	2 390.3	1 006.9	1 289.3	672.6	1 721.6	15 495.8
1978	7 373.3	1 918.8	2 687.2	1 164.5	1 480.5	769.0	1 850.0	17 243.2
1979	8 107.7	2 235.4	3 021.5	1 353.1	1 749.6	831.0	2 108.4	19 406.6
1980	9 293.9	2 638.4	3 448.3	1 577.7	2 026.9	1 233.6	2 479.3	22 698.1
1981	10 983.0	3 031.0	3 986.2	1 822.8	2 407.0	1 409.4	3 003.9	26 643.3
1982	13 036.4	3 535.7	4 649.8	2 082.1	2 728.1	1 712.6	3 398.7	31 143.3
1983	14 385.5	3 868.1	5 317.0	2 265.6	3 127.7	1 783.6	3 756.6	34 504.2
1984	15 310.1	4 026.5	5 803.9	2 460.1	3 642.6	1 822.2	4 234.8	37 300.2
1985	16 227.7	4 259.0	6 333.3	2 744.6	4 229.6	1 862.5	4 742.3	40 399.0
1986	17 555.1	4 553.8	6 938.1	2 999.3	4 910.0	2 107.6	5 267.8	44 331.6
1987	19 202.9	4 902.5	7 608.3	3 347.2	5 768.7	2 240.9	5 571.6	48 642.1
1988	20 675.2	5 408.6	8 239.7	3 554.6	6 702.7	2 266.1	5 991.6	52 838.5
1989	22 579.4	5 809.2	8 828.5	3 860.8	7 587.8	2 515.9	6 599.2	57 780.9
1990	24 087.1	6 285.3	9 600.4	4 003.4	8 381.2	2 589.3	7 210.2	62 156.9
1991	25 960.4	6 842.5	10 445.5	4 111.9	9 292.9	2 559.6	7 755.3	66 968.2
1992	26 997.6	7 111.2	10 711.7	4 222.6	10 087.1	2 609.6	8 086.9	69 826.7
1993	27 392.9	7 375.1	10 904.8	4 329.2	10 911.0	2 690.1	8 468.3	72 071.5

Source: *Health and Welfare Canada*

Total Health Care Expenditures—Summary

	Expenditures in Current Dollars		Expenditures in Constant 1986 Dollars		Expenditures as a % of GDP	
	Total ($millions)	Per Capita ($)	Total ($millions)	Per Capita ($)	Canada	United States
1975	12 264.6	528.44	29 179.8	1 257.25	7.1	8.4
1976	14 116.2	600.24	29 946.4	1 273.37	7.1	8.6
1977	15 495.8	651.18	30 498.3	1 281.64	7.1	8.7
1978	17 243.2	717.38	31 678.1	1 317.93	7.1	8.7
1979	19 406.6	799.39	32 503.4	1 338.86	7.0	8.7
1980	22 698.1	922.94	34 535.7	1 404.27	7.3	9.2
1981	26 643.3	1 070.01	35 903.2	1 441.90	7.5	9.6
1982	31 143.3	1 235.75	37 546.7	1 489.83	8.3	10.4
1983	34 504.2	1 355.44	39 018.0	1 532.74	8.5	10.5
1984	37 300.2	1 451.27	40 375.0	1 570.90	8.4	10.3
1985	40 399.0	1 557.30	41 950.2	1 617.10	8.5	10.5
1986	44 331.6	1 691.80	44 331.6	1 691.80	8.8	10.7
1987	48 642.1	1 832.11	46 518.6	1 752.13	8.8	10.9
1988	52 838.5	1 964.64	48 360.7	1 798.14	8.7	11.1
1989	57 780.9	2 110.38	50 603.7	1 848.24	8.9	11.5
1990	62 156.9	2 236.62	51 613.8	1 857.24	9.3	12.2
1991	66 968.2	2 381.72	53 611.6	1 906.69	9.9	13.2
1992	69 826.7	2 455.61	53 931.5	1 896.62	10.1	13.9
1993	72 071.5	2 506.57	54 523.4	1 896.27	10.1	14.4

Source: *Health and Welfare Canada*

Total[1] Health Care Expenditures by Source

(%)

	Federal Direct	Provincial Expenditures		Municipal Expenditures	Workers' Compensation	Private Expenses
		Federal Transfer	Provincial Funds			
1975	3.2	27.5	43.5	1.1	1.0	23.6
1976	3.1	28.1	43.7	1.1	1.0	22.9
1977	3.1	29.9	41.8	1.1	1.0	23.2
1978	2.8	31.0	40.2	1.0	1.0	23.9
1979	2.6	31.3	39.3	1.4	1.0	24.3
1980	2.6	30.2	39.5	1.6	0.9	25.3
1981	2.6	28.9	41.2	1.8	1.1	24.4
1982	2.7	27.8	42.9	1.5	1.0	24.1
1983	2.9	27.8	43.2	1.3	0.9	24.0
1984	3.0	28.0	42.2	1.1	0.9	24.8
1985	2.9	27.9	41.8	1.1	1.0	25.3
1986	2.9	27.2	42.5	1.1	0.9	25.5
1987	2.8	26.2	42.2	1.4	0.8	26.6
1988	2.7	25.6	42.5	1.2	0.8	27.2
1989	2.5	25.0	43.5	1.1	0.8	27.2
1990	2.2	23.9	45.1	1.1	0.8	26.9
1991	2.0	22.7	46.8	1.1	0.9	26.6
1992	1.8	22.2	46.8	1.0	0.9	27.3
1993	1.8	21.7	46.5	1.0	0.9	28.1

Source: *Health and Welfare Canada*

(1) Total may not be 100% due to rounding.

Federal Direct Health Care Expenditures by Category

(millions of dollars)

	Hospitals	Other Institutions	Physicians	Other Professionals	Drugs	Capital	Other	Total
1975	143.9	0.2	10.6	5.3	13.5	21.3	203.7	398.4
1976	154.9	0.8	11.7	6.1	15.7	20.7	230.0	439.8
1977	163.5	0.8	11.9	7.0	17.8	25.4	249.0	475.4
1978	155.4	0.5	11.5	7.8	20.3	19.2	271.0	485.8
1979	163.6	0.8	13.3	9.7	21.1	21.3	283.3	513.0
1980	161.3	1.2	15.2	15.2	26.7	28.3	334.4	582.2
1981	180.5	1.6	17.2	18.7	30.4	32.1	412.4	692.9
1982	210.9	3.6	20.6	25.5	36.8	45.3	512.4	855.0
1983	233.4	6.1	22.6	32.6	43.8	58.0	598.6	995.1
1984	242.3	9.3	23.8	25.2	49.6	86.0	670.2	1 106.3
1985	241.6	13.5	25.1	24.7	58.0	81.0	714.0	1 157.9
1986	265.3	20.1	30.9	28.4	63.8	80.7	782.9	1 272.1
1987	291.2	34.2	31.6	30.5	68.7	78.3	814.3	1 348.8
1988	309.2	36.2	33.7	32.6	72.7	80.3	864.4	1 429.1
1989	308.2	36.2	33.7	32.6	72.7	79.2	862.4	1 425.0
1990	294.2	35.2	32.7	30.5	68.7	76.3	823.3	1 360.9
1991	284.2	33.2	31.6	29.4	66.7	74.6	795.3	1 315.0
1992	275.4	32.4	30.3	28.2	65.4	75.7	771.2	1 278.6
1993	277.2	32.7	30.6	28.4	64.0	74.6	760.5	1 267.9

Source: *Health and Welfare Canada*

Canadian Defence Spending

(millions of dollars; fiscal years ending Mar. 31)

	Spending	%of Govt. spending		Spending	%of Govt. spending		Spending	%of Govt. spending
1910	6	7.4	1942	1 268	67.3	1981	5 049	8.7
1914	14	7.6	1943	2 563	58.4	1982	5 907	9.2
1915	72	29.3	1944	4 242	79.7	1983	7 041	9.7
1916	173	51.2	1945	4 000	76.2	1984	7 840	9.2
1917	312	62.3	1950	387	15.8	1985	8 767	9.3
1918	344	59.9	1951	787	27.1	1986	9 383	9.2
1919	439	63.1	1952	1 447	38.5	1987	9 955	9.3
1920	347	46.9	1953	1 959	42.2	1988	10 340	9.4
1925	13	3.7	1955	1 762	37.8	1989	11 200	9.4
1930	22	5.4	1960	1 537	24.5	1990	11 340	8.7
1935	14	2.9	1965	1 582	19.5	1991	12 005	8.8
1939	35	6.3	1970	1 791	11.9	1992	11 751	8.4
1940	126	18.5	1975	2 361	10.7	1993	11 970	8.4
1941	730	58.4	1980	4 375	8.6			

Source: *Department of National Defence*

Government Expenditures on Culture

(thousands of dollars)

	Federal		Provincial		Municipal	
	1987-88	1991-92	1987-88	1991-92	1987	1991
Libraries	36 365	40 668	554 473	723 810	686 796	961 180
Museums	210 054	172 107	162 866	226 587	20 614	21 196
Public archives	47 858	62 388	18 769	25 234	1 302	4 576
Historic parks and sites	55 048	69 184	74 586	91 546	6 717	9 246
Nature/provincial parks	167 467	173 240	55 139	57 908	n.a.	n.a.
Other heritage resources	113 687	164 581	23 567	34 317	n.a.	n.a.
Arts education	3 564	3 622	62 094	75 045	n.a.	n.a.
Literary arts	285 993	217 219	16 994	21 264	n.a.	n.a.
Performing arts	93 057	121 324	112 104	148 537	22 925	35 056
Visual arts and crafts	14 469	16 382	27 105	40 080	n.a.	n.a.
Film and video	201 093	262 005	30 485	78 463	n.a.	n.a.
Broadcasting	1 234 972	1 463 887	158 457	219 425	n.a.	n.a.
Sound recording	4 453	6 640	2 252	1 543	n.a.	n.a.
Multiculturalism	25 669	7 174	35 030	35 577	n.a.	n.a.
Multidisciplinary activities	104 020	86 205	60 742	113 531	n.a.	n.a.
Other	11 041	13 490	52 030	40 271	163 013	231 655
Total expenditures	**2 608 810**	**2 880 114**	**1 446 693**	**1 933 140**	**901 367**	**1 262 909**

Source: *Statistics Canada*   (n.a.) – not available.

Provincial Government Expenditures on Culture, by Province or Territory

(in thousands of dollars)

Province or Territory	1986–87	1988–89	1990–91	1991-92
Newfoundland	20 061	22 004	23 529	25 743
Prince Edward Island	9 908	10 839	10 760	12 836
Nova Scotia	37 261	57 180	60 444	55 257
New Brunswick	22 660	27 276	27 631	29 354
Quebec	405 349	468 311	536 387	592 019
Ontario	465 524	516 715	597 833	641 526
Manitoba	67 055	67 439	79 198	80 444
Saskatchewan	59 615	59 764	62 385	57 365
Alberta	171 411	156 075	160 373	167 707
British Columbia	153 175	160 807	209 463	246 678
Yukon	6 284	6 918	7 744	12 264
Northwest Territories	4 643	6 302	12 700	11 947
Total	**1 422 946**	**1 559 630**	**1 788 447**	**1 933 140**

Source: *Statistics Canada*

Federal Government Expenditures on Culture, by Province or Territory

(in thousands of dollars)

Province or Territory	1986–87	1988–89	1990–91	1991-92
Newfoundland	47 768	48 772	54 899	45 198
Prince Edward Island	10 764	11 512	14 339	17 678
Nova Scotia	71 191	79 304	97 846	90 609
New Brunswick	43 069	43 524	50 732	50 174
Quebec	710 587	844 238	877 511	862 147
Ontario	889 907	953 504	1 056 530	1 116 566
Manitoba	67 090	75 432	86 098	80 712
Saskatchewan	47 903	47 322	55 974	48 660
Alberta	123 741	134 393	151 325	141 735
British Columbia	116 608	161 063	144 195	140 825
Yukon	8 724	13 537	12 800	15 601
Northwest Territories	28 760	30 505	32 757	36 153
Other (1)	285 757	303 199	254 222	234 056
Total	**2 450 869**	**2 746 305**	**2 889 228**	**2 880 114**

Source: *Statistics Canada*

(1) includes national organizations, foreign countries, and unallocated expenditures.

Foreign Aid

Canadian Official Development Assistance (ODA) totalled $2.9 billion in the 1992–93 fiscal year. About 74 percent of ODA is distributed through the Canadian International Development Agency (CIDA), whose primary goal is to help the poorest countries and people in the world to help themselves. CIDA places special priority on alleviating poverty, improving economic management, promoting the increased participation of women in development programs, encouraging environmentally sound development and ensuring secure food and energy supplies.

Canada's foreign aid projects started with contributions to the United Nations during the 1940s. In 1950, Canada supported the Colombo Plan, assistance aimed at the newly-independent Asian nations of India, Pakistan and Ceylon (now Sri Lanka). During the next 2 decades, Canadian aid expanded to include the Caribbean (1958), Commonwealth Africa (1959), Francophone Africa (1961) and Latin America (1964).

By the time CIDA was created in 1968, Canadian foreign aid had begun focussing on self-sufficiency rather than its earlier goal of encouraging rapid industrial development. During the 1970s, Canadian aid was aimed at improving social conditions in very poor countries by assisting in such areas as rural planning and public health.

Canadian Expenditure on Foreign Aid, 1950-1993

(millions of dollars)

	Foreign aid[1]	% of GNP		Foreign aid[1]	% of GNP		Foreign aid[1]	% of GNP
1950	13	.08	1965	101	.20	1980	1 291	.47
1951	13	.07	1966	123	.22	1981	1 307	.43
1952	27	.12	1967	214	.34	1982	1 489	.43
1953	8	.03	1968	193	.29	1983	1 670	.46
1954	14	.05	1969	212	.28	1984	1 812	.45
1955	16	.06	1970	279	.34	1985	2 097	.49
1956	29	.10	1971	346	.40	1986	2 174	.46
1957	30	.09	1972	398	.41	1987	2 522	.50
1958	62	.18	1973	525	.47	1988	2 624	.48
1959	72	.20	1974	591	.46	1989	2 947	.49
1960	70	.19	1975	750	.49	1990	2 850	.45
1961	76	.20	1976	910	.53	1991	3 021	.45
1962	61	.15	1977	972	.49	1992	3 184	.49
1963	58	.13	1978	1 050	.49	1993	2 957	.44
1964	65	.14	1979	1 166	.49			

Source: *Canadian International Development Agency*

(1) For fiscal year ending Mar. 31.

CIDA's Work

*D*uring the 1991-92 period there were major changes, including the collapse of communism and the rise of democracy in many countries in Asia, Africa and Latin America.

In 1991-92 CIDA's aid budget was used to launch 400 new country-to-country projects, fund Canadian organizations supporting thousands of overseas projects, give more than a million dollars a day for food aid, and provide thousands of training opportunities for people in developing countries, as well as provide assistance to refugees and victims of disaster. The aid budget also paid our share of the cost of international agencies, where Canada's voice is heard in shaping the global community's response to worldwide problems.

Canadian Foreign Aid, by Country

(millions of dollars; for fiscal year ending Mar. 31)

Country	1970[1]	1975[1]	1980[1]	1985[1]	1990[2]	1992[2]
Africa	37.39	208.01	285.67	548.28	1 064.41	1 072.55
Algeria	3.91	9.21	0.88	5.84	4.36	5.51
Angola	—	—	—	1.85	13.06	8.17
Botswana	—	7.20	3.56	7.56	16.29	9.71
Burkina Faso	—	4.02	18.09	11.21	22.52	26.67
Cameroon	2.29	4.58	15.29	33.36	44.92	29.90
Côte d'Ivoire	1.11	4.24	16.99	17.88	18.79	12.71
Egypt	—	—	27.78	10.73	37.72	41.42
Ethiopia	0.03	6.47	2.09	47.00	57.98	63.58
Gabon	n.a.	0.77	—	0.87	12.07	3.59
Ghana	4.44	13.17	17.97	45.97	63.53	58.01
Guinea	—	0.51	0.05	18.06	15.32	11.99
Kenya	1.99	5.20	12.78	38.71	35.74	48.15
Lesotho	—	0.62	7.02	4.67	12.49	10.11
Madagascar	0.25	0.48	3.86	1.03	16.40	14.46
Malawi	—	9.11	15.96	4.31	17.62	31.98
Mali	—	6.57	12.79	14.43	41.37	37.68
Morocco	0.50	4.86	2.58	8.58	39.73	19.38
Mozambique	—	—	0.06	13.14	41.86	58.12
Namibia	—	0.02	0.02	0.15	2.81	6.01
Niger	1.11	16.84	4.08	21.87	29.23	22.55
Nigeria	4.63	10.20	0.56	1.70	5.42	6.10
Rwanda	0.86	3.68	5.84	15.03	28.54	21.21
Senegal	1.98	5.69	8.76	20.35	79.66	50.23
Somalia	n.a.	n.a.	n.a.	n.a.	22.37	27.84
South Africa	n.a.	—	—	0.98	8.52	16.51
Sudan	—	—	2.40	22.19	30.95	36.70
Tanzania	2.24	38.34	27.64	44.93	46.53	51.24
Tunisia	7.24	11.72	10.87	6.53	10.97	7.11
Uganda	1.17	0.36	0.27	3.83	20.87	29.82
Zaire	0.96	6.33	8.18	24.33	48.73	18.78
Zambia	—	4.39	15.98	22.89	20.72	34.84
Zimbabwe	—	0.01	0.04	18.07	19.99	35.41
Asia	140.93	244.25	234.62	410.85	812.04	795.51
Afghanistan	0.02	1.78	7.02	n.a.	3.58	25.87
Bangladesh	—	69.13	65.18	105.76	201.03	164.25
China	—	—	—	13.51	94.87	115.30
India	88.61	96.40	42.60	90.08	93.15	106.12
Indonesia	2.33	19.52	11.75	37.05	73.77	52.85
Jordan	n.a.	—	—	0.66	22.95	6.77
Malaysia	1.57	1.61	1.75	3.17	8.28	12.36
Myanmar (Burma)	—	1.39	6.33	3.22	15.19	8.56
Nepal	—	0.07	6.74	10.08	28.13	32.52
Pakistan	32.76	32.23	67.17	66.30	99.07	67.06
Philippines	—	0.02	0.37	8.34	44.62	37.64
Sri Lanka	6.40	10.84	15.94	37.97	31.75	21.63
Thailand	2.26	0.41	6.79	22.02	36.19	25.90
Americas[3]	n.a.	n.a.	66.18	197.93	343.3	340.05
Argentina	n.a.	—	—	1.80	5.14	5.78
Bolivia	n.a.	0.99	1.01	3.28	19.17	23.72
Brazil	n.a.	1.44	2.39	8.38	14.31	15.97 ▶

Country	1970[1]	1975[1]	1980[1]	1985[1]	1990[2]	1992[2]
Chile	n.a.	0.30	—	4.67	6.00	6.46
Colombia	n.a.	1.74	7.11	7.97	20.10	16.08
Costa Rica	n.a.	0.15	0.17	8.07	16.17	7.94
Dominica	n.a.	0.56	1.95	9.57	7.17	2.58
Dominican Republic	n.a.	3.71	0.34	5.00	4.55	3.76
Ecuador	n.a.	3.33	0.30	1.58	6.95	10.69
El Salvador	n.a.	1.42	1.37	1.51	6.08	9.92
Guatemala	n.a.	0.02	2.94	2.39	7.65	10.26
Guyana	2.15	4.05	5.95	2.15	20.60	15.04
Haiti	n.a.	1.34	7.59	8.77	22.10	20.72
Honduras	n.a.	2.19	4.62	20.45	11.20	19.75
Jamaica	2.72	3.11	7.76	29.11	39.65	23.97
Mexico	n.a.	—	—	1.78	6.49	9.93
Nicaragua	n.a.	1.02	0.20	8.52	10.15	15.41
Peru	n.a.	1.61	4.02	16.90	30.59	39.46
Trinidad & Tobago	2.15	0.65	—	0.60	4.16	1.86
Oceania	**n.a.**	**n.a.**	**0.42**	**3.05**	**19.17**	**15.20**

Source: *Canadian International Development Agency*

(1) Includes only country-to-country aid—i.e., Canadian aid to specified countries. It does not include Canadian aid to international organizations such as the United Nations relief programs, international financial institutions dealing with foreign aid and the World Food Program. Country-to-country aid represents about 2/3 of all Canadian foreign aid. Includes only countries with $2.5 million or more in aid. (2) Includes country-to-country and multi-lateral aid to international organizations. (3) Includes Central America, the Caribbean and South America; — = zero; n.a. not available.

How We Compare – World Assistance to Developing Countries

(millions of U.S. dollars)

Donor Country	1965 Foreign aid	1965 % of GNP[1]	1975 Foreign aid	1975 % of GNP[1]	1980 Foreign aid	1980 % of GNP[1]	1985 Foreign aid	1985 % of GNP[1]	1990 Foreign aid	1990 % of GNP[1]
Algeria	n.a.	n.a.	41	0.28	81	0.20	54	0.10	7	0.03
Australia	119	0.53	552	0.65	667	0.48	749	0.48	955	0.34
Austria	10	0.11	79	0.21	178	0.23	248	0.38	394	0.25
Belgium	102	0.60	378	0.59	595	0.50	440	0.55	889	0.45
Canada	**96**	**0.19**	**880**	**0.54**	**1 075**	**0.43**	**1 631**	**0.49**	**2 470**	**0.44**
Denmark	13	0.13	205	0.58	481	0.74	440	0.80	1 171	0.93
France	752	0.76	2 093	0.62	4 162	0.63	3 995	0.78	9 380	0.79
Italy	60	0.10	182	0.11	683	0.15	1 098	0.26	3 395	0.32
Japan	244	0.27	1 148	0.23	3 353	0.32	3 797	0.29	9 069	0.31
Kuwait	n.a.	n.a.	946	7.18	1 140	3.52	771	3.17	1 666	...
Libya	n.a.	n.a.	259	2.29	376	1.16	57	0.24	4	0.01
Netherlands	70	0.36	608	0.75	1 630	0.97	1 136	0.91	2 529	0.94
New Zealand	n.a.	n.a.	66	0.52	72	0.33	54	0.25	95	0.23
Nigeria	n.a.	n.a.	14	0.04	35	0.04	45	0.06	13	0.06
Norway	11	0.16	184	0.66	486	0.87	574	1.01	1 205	1.17
Qatar	n.a.	n.a.	338	15.58	277	4.16	8	0.15	1	0.02
Saudi Arabia	n.a.	n.a.	2 756	7.76	5 682	4.87	2 630	2.98	3 692	3.90
Sweden	38	0.19	566	0.82	962	0.78	840	0.86	2 012	0.90
Switzerland	12	0.09	104	0.19	253	0.24	302	0.31	750	0.31
United Arab Emirates	n.a.	n.a.	1 046	11.68	1 118	4.21	122	0.45	888	2.65
United Kingdom	472	0.47	904	0.39	1 854	0.35	1 530	0.33	2 638	0.27
United States	4 023	0.58	4 161	0.27	7 138	0.27	9 403	0.24	11 394	0.21
Venezuela	n.a.	n.a.	31	0.11	135	0.23	32	...	15	0.03
West Germany	456	0.40	1 689	0.40	3 567	0.44	2 942	0.47	6 320	0.42

Source: *World Development Report 1991, World Bank*

(1) Gross National Product. (n.a.) not available. (...) = too small to be included.

FOREIGN TRADE

Canadian Balance of International Payments

(millions of dollars)

The Canadian balance of payments is a measure of all yearly business transactions between Canada and the world. These transactions are in 2 accounts: current account and capital account. The current account notes all Canadian payments for imported goods and services and all money received for Canadian exports of goods and services. The capital account records all investment transactions (stocks, bonds, real estate, new companies, loans, foreign currency trading, interest payments) between Canada and other countries.

The balance of payments, or sum of the two, shows if Canada has a surplus (more money flowing in than out) or the opposite.

Year	Balance of Payments[1]	Current Account			Capital Account		
		Receipts[2]	Payments	Balance[3]	Investment Inflow[4]	Investment Outflow[5]	Total Investment Balance[6]
1970	316	21907	20 874	1 033	1 860	-2 577	-717
1971	1 289	23 043	22 673	370	1 877	-958	919
1972	1 564	25 674	25 956	-283	2 619	-772	1 847
1973	850	32 061	31 749	312	2 686	-2 148	538
1974	1 032	40 610	41 909	-1 299	5 014	-2 683	2 331
1975	1 326	42 076	46 707	-4 631	7 202	-1 245	5 957
1976	3 780	47 440	51 536	-4 096	11 349	-3 473	7 876
1977	2 224	54 544	58 866	-4322	7 615	-1 068	6 546
1978	3 146	65 098	70 001	-4 903	13 493	-5 444	8 049
1979	2 508	79 725	84 590	-4 864	12 974	-5 602	7 372
1980	1 063	93 064	94 857	-1 793	9 861	-7 005	2 856
1981	8 280	103 024	109 908	-6 884	33 033	-17 869	15 164
1982	1 561	104 569	102 565	2 004	5 929	-6 372	-443
1983	4 918	110 824	112 602	-1 777	11 601	-4 906	6 695
1984	6 175	136 213	137 028	-815	18 012	-11 021	6 990
1985	6 300	145 702	151 894	-6 192	16 249	-3 756	12 492
1986	2 695	148 165	162 218	-14 053	27 013	-10 265	16 748
1987	3 150	158 218	173 860	-15 643	35 357	-16 565	18 793
1988	586	173 465	194 578	-21 114	39 065	-17 365	21 700
1989	-630	178 527	205 475	-26 948	37 275	-10 958	26 318
1990	1 641	184 154	209 378	-25 224	37 495	-10 630	26 865
1991	2 614	178 297	205 863	-27 566	40 951	-10 772	30 180
1992	-1 495	194 555	221 037	-26 483	27 853	-2 977	24 988
1993	6 688	222 063	252 767	-30 704	57 683	-20 291	37 392

Source: *Statistics Canada*

(1) Sum of the current and capital account balances. (2) Money received for Canadian exports of goods and services. (3) Receipts minus payments. (4) Represents net foreign investment to Canada. (5) Represents net Canadian investment to other countries. (6) Investment inflow minus investment outflow.

Canadian Trade Balance[1]

(millions of dollars)

	1960	1970	1980	1985	1990	1992	1993
All Countries	-97	2 868	6 885	15 119	12 249	5 891	7 297
United States[2]	-651	983	728	21 039	23 399	22 024	28 826
USSR[5]	5	93	1 468	1 577	940	994	—
Netherlands	32	202	1 211	365	794	827	637
Belgium[3]	29	140	764	204	688	644	395
Iran	-28	-26	17	-81	336	232	18
Algeria	...	19	352	9	229	53	6
Morocco	...	5	60	154	194	49	24
Egypt	1	38	101	162	64	40	-20
Libya	...	3	-7	57	53	80	88
India	8	91	253	317	89	232	-87
Spain	3	33	39	-292	-109	-1	-183
Turkey	2	21	28	182	73	67	68
Romania	1	-1	-18	-9	-63	-5	3
Colombia	4	-2	135	73	79	98	51
Australia	64	56	157	310	136	-120	-365
United Arab Emirates	-8	-7	-41	19	-28	51	75
Israel	4	1	53	45	20	-15	-13
Lebanon	3	4	40	9	5	21	30
Peru	6	32	-40	-19	-67	-7	20
China	3	123	692	858	263	-315	-1 563
Kenya	-2	-4	-4	2	43	11	-5
El Salvador	1	-1	-12	-26	-4	-1	3
South Africa	42	59	-183	-79	20	-9	14
Hungary	1	-2	-17	-20	-37	-10	-8
Philippines	15	27	-27	-80	5	-71	-193
Cuba	6	50	262	286	43	-143	-37
Poland	15	3	282	-27	-44	-5	24
Yugoslavia[6]	4	20	36	-3	-36	-33	-30
Chile	6	20	16	-48	17	-57	-15
Nicaragua	1	1	-16	-7	-52	-22	-6
Czechoslovakia[7]	...	-20	64	-48	-53	14	-7
Venezuela	-159	-227	-1 533	-761	-292	-9	-44
Argentina	16	51	192	-29	-92	-11	15
Switzerland	3	40	-101	-147	405	475	217
Jamaica	-20	21	15	-98	-48	-109	-98
Brazil	-5	44	605	-125	-290	-95	-38
New Zealand	14	1	-36	30	-55	-100	-133
Malaysia	-133	-20	-71	5	-125	-368	-664
Singapore	-133	-9	97	-66	-147	-325	-479
South Korea	...	19	80	-866	-688	-603	-498
Hong Kong	6	-57	-358	-507	-379	-377	-492
Saudi Arabia	-34	-17	-2 330	213	-357	-256	-48
Nigeria	-2	-37	42	-172	-531	-423	-640
Sweden	1	-57	-138	-491	-572	-587	-684
Italy	26	42	363	-869	-780	-660	-1 063
United Kingdom	336	763	1 275	-515	-1 329	-1 090	-1 632
Taiwan	2	18	-325	-945	-1 313	-1 517	-1 621
France	24	-1	210	-686	-1 132	-1 349	-1 039
West Germany[4]	41	18	175	-1 559	-1 532	-1 370	-1 147
Mexico	18	49	152	-928	-1 124	-1 981	-2 804
Japan	69	231	1 469	-994	-1 302	-3 345	-2 297
East Germany[4]	...	-4	...	94	—	n.a.	n.a.
Iraq	2	-10	-127	70	84	3.41	2
Russia	—	—	—	—	—	—	31

Source: *Statistics Canada*

(1) The trade balance is the value of merchandise exports minus the value of merchandise imports; it does not include services. Prior to 1980, imports were attributed to country of export/consignment. From 1980, imports are attributed to country of origin (the country in which the goods were grown, extracted or manufactured). (2) 1990 data not directly comparable to previous years due to improvements in data collection procedures which resulted in higher values for 1990. Also beginning in 1990, includes Puerto Rico and the U.S. Virgin Islands. (3) Includes Luxembourg. (4) From Oct. 1990 on, all data for reunified Germany is listed under West Germany. Figures for East Germany represent trade prior to Oct. 1990 only. (—) = zero; ... = too small to be included. (5) After 1992 refers to former USSR. (6) Denotes former Yugoslavia. (7) Denotes former Czechoslovakia.

Canadian Imports by Country[1]

(millions of dollars)

	1970	%	1980	%	1990	%	1992	%	1993	%
Total Imports	13 952	100.0	69 273	100.0	135 922	100.0	147 865	100.0	169 460	100.0
United States[2]	9 917	71.1	47 445	68.5	87 803	64.6	96 397	65.1	113 602	67.0
Japan	582	4.2	2 904	4.2	9 517	7.0	10 757	7.3	10 690	6.3
United Kingdom	738	5.3	1 969	2.8	4 840	3.6	4 102	2.8	4 429	2.6
West Germany[3]	370	2.7	1 492	2.2	3 832	2.8	3 531	2.4	3 504	2.1
France	158	1.1	807	1.2	2 434	1.8	2 688	1.8	2 260	1.3
Mexico	47	0.3	342	0.5	1 730	1.3	2 751	1.9	3 594	2.1
Taiwan	52	0.4	578	0.8	2 109	1.6	2 469	1.7	2 619	1.5
South Korea	15	0.1	432	0.6	2 252	1.7	2 008	1.4	2 196	1.3
China	19	0.1	181	0.3	1 392	1.0	2 447	1.7	3 088	1.8
Italy	145	1.0	641	0.9	1 953	1.4	1 744	1.2	1 934	1.1
Hong Kong	78	0.6	557	0.8	1 059	0.8	1 134	0.8	1 194	0.7
Sweden	106	0.8	423	0.6	899	0.7	791	0.5	858	0.5
Brazil	49	0.4	357	0.5	790	0.6	715	0.5	788	0.5
Australia	146	1.0	521	0.8	767	0.6	750	0.5	1 065	0.6
Switzerland	81	0.6	488	0.7	648	0.5	651	0.4	665	0.4
Netherlands	79	0.6	230	0.3	721	0.5	598	0.4	666	0.4
Singapore	20	0.1	104	0.2	552	0.4	644	0.4	797	0.5
Saudi Arabia	24	0.2	2 643	3.8	635	0.5	542	0.4	533	0.3
Nigeria	45	0.3	63	0.1	561	0.4	473	0.3	689	0.4
Russia	—	—	—	—	—	—	—	—	433	0.3
Venezuela	339	2.4	2 212	3.2	562	0.4	334	0.2	351	0.2
Spain	34	0.2	197	0.3	496	0.4	436	0.3	503	0.3
Belgium[4]	52	0.4	237	0.3	550	0.4	428	0.3	501	0.3
Malaysia	34	0.2	166	0.2	380	0.3	598	0.4	870	0.5
India	40	0.3	106	0.2	227	0.2	278	0.2	354	0.2
USSR[5]	9	0.1	72	0.1	185	0.1	269	0.2	271	0.2
Philippines	4	...	113	0.2	202	0.1	276	0.2	386	0.2
New Zealand	43	0.3	150	0.2	214	0.2	204	0.1	254	0.1
Chile	3	...	96	0.1	180	0.1	202	0.1	208	0.1
Jamaica	27	0.2	50	0.1	157	0.1	173	0.1	182	0.1
Cuba	9	0.1	163	0.2	130	0.1	256	0.2	171	0.1
Colombia	27	0.2	101	0.1	132	0.1	130	...	172	0.1
Argentina	9	0.1	40	0.1	140	0.1	112	...	116	0.1
Israel	14	0.1	62	0.1	125	0.1	131	...	154	0.1
South Africa	46	0.3	388	0.6	141	0.1	137	...	140	0.1
Morocco	...	...	10	...	40	...	76	...	68	...
Peru	4	...	96	0.1	126	0.1	95	...	63	...
Yugoslavia[6]	7	0.1	34	...	94	0.1	56	...	57	...
Iran	34	0.2	24	...	21	...	126	...	239	0.1
Turkey	1	...	13	...	84	0.1	67	...	81	...
Czechoslovakia[7]	27	0.2	64	0.1	70	0.1	60	...	54	...
Poland	12	0.1	75	0.1	79	0.1	57	...	62	...
Algeria	...	...	41	0.1	62	...	98	...	225	0.1
Nicaragua	1	...	31	...	63	...	31	...	17	...
Hungary	9	0.1	27	...	45	...	41	...	34	...
Romania	5	...	40	0.1	87	0.1	31	...	41	...
United Arab Emirates	7	0.1	86	0.1	58	...	3	...	6	...
El Salvador	4	...	27	...	19	...	12	...	17	...
Kenya	6	...	18	...	14	...	13	...	16	...
Egypt	...	...	29	...	9	...	58	...	93	...
Lebanon	1	...	...	...	3	...	4	...	4	...
Iraq	14	0.1	280	0.4	113	0.1	59	...	—	...
East Germany[3]	4	0.1	11	...	22	...	—		—	...
Libya	...	...	80	0.1	—	—	—	—		

Source: *Statistics Canada*

(1) Prior to 1980, imports were attributed to country of export/consignment. From 1980, imports are attributed to country of origin (the country in which the goods were grown, extracted or manufactured). (2) Beginning with 1990, includes Puerto Rico and the U.S. Virgin Islands. (3) From Oct. 1990 on, all data for reunified Germany is listed under West Germany. Figures for East Germany represent trade prior to Oct. 1990 only. (4) Includes Luxembourg. (5) After 1992 refers to former USSR. (6) Denotes former Yugoslavia. (7) Denotes former Czechoslovakia.

(—) = zero; ... = too small to be included.

Canadian Exports by Country[1]

(millions of dollars)

	1970	%	1980	%	1990	%	1992	%	1993	%
Total Exports[2]	**16 820**	**100.0**	**76 158**	**100.0**	**148 170**	**100.0**	**153 756**	**100.0**	**176 757**	**100.0**
United States[2]	10 900	64.8	48 173	63.3	111 202	75.0	118 421	77.0	142 428	80.6
Japan	813	4.8	4 373	5.7	8 215	5.5	7 412	4.8	8 393	4.7
United Kingdom	1 501	8.9	3 244	4.3	3 511	2.4	3 012	2.0	2 797	1.6
West Germany[3]	388	2.3	1 667	2.2	2 300	1.6	2 161	1.4	2 357	1.3
South Korea	19	0.1	512	0.7	1 563	1.1	1 405	1.0	1 698	1.0
China	142	0.8	873	1.1	1 654	1.1	2 132	1.3	1 525	0.9
Netherlands	281	1.7	1 441	1.9	1 515	1.0	1 425	1.0	1 303	0.7
USSR[5]	102	0.6	1 540	2.0	1 125	0.8	1 263	0.8	—	...
France	157	0.9	1 017	1.3	1 302	0.9	1 339	0.9	1 221	0.7
Belgium[4]	192	1.1	1 001	1.3	1 237	0.8	1 072	0.7	896	0.5
Italy	187	1.1	1 004	1.3	1 173	0.8	1 084	0.7	871	0.5
Taiwan	18	0.1	253	0.3	796	0.5	952	0.6	998	0.6
Hong Kong	21	0.1	199	0.3	680	0.5	757	0.5	602	0.3
Australia	202	1.2	678	0.9	903	0.6	630	0.4	700	0.4
Brazil	93	0.6	962	1.3	499	0.3	620	0.4	750	0.4
Switzerland	41	0.2	387	0.5	1 053	0.7	1 126	0.7	882	0.5
Spain	67	0.4	236	0.3	387	0.3	435	0.3	320	0.2
Mexico	96	0.6	494	0.6	606	0.4	770	0.5	790	0.4
Russia	—	—	—	—	—	—	—	—	464	0.3
Venezuela	112	0.7	679	0.9	270	0.2	325	0.2	307	0.2
Singapore	11	0.1	201	0.3	405	0.3	319	0.2	318	0.2
Iran	8	...	41	0.1	357	0.2	358	0.2	257	0.1
Malaysia	14	0.1	95	0.1	256	0.2	230	0.1	206	0.1
India	131	0.8	359	0.5	316	0.2	510	0.3	267	0.1
Saudi Arabia	7	...	313	0.4	278	0.2	286	0.2	485	0.3
Algeria	19	0.1	393	0.5	291	0.2	151	0.1	231	0.1
Sweden	49	0.3	285	0.4	328	0.2	204	0.1	174	0.1
Philippines	31	0.2	86	0.1	206	0.1	205	0.1	193	0.1
Morocco	5	...	70	0.1	234	0.2	125	0.1	92	...
Colombia	25	0.1	236	0.3	211	0.1	228	0.1	223	0.1
Chile	23	0.1	112	0.1	197	0.1	145	0.1	193	0.1
Israel	15	0.1	115	0.2	145	0.1	116	0.1	141	0.1
Cuba	59	0.4	425	0.6	173	0.1	113	0.1	134	0.1
South Africa	105	0.6	205	0.2	161	0.1	128	0.1	154	0.1
Egypt	38	0.2	130	0.2	74	...	98	0.1	73	...
New Zealand	44	0.3	114	0.2	158	0.1	104	0.1	121	0.1
Turkey	22	0.1	41	0.1	157	0.1	134	0.1	149	0.1
Jamaica	48	0.3	65	0.1	109	0.1	64	...	84	...
Peru	36	0.2	56	0.1	58	...	88	0.1	83	...
Argentina	60	0.4	232	0.3	48	...	101	0.1	135	0.1
Libya	3	...	73	0.1	53	...	80	0.1	88	...
Romania	4	...	22	...	25	...	26	...	44	...
Yugoslavia[6]	27	0.2	70	0.1	57	...	23	...	27	...
Poland	15	0.1	357	0.5	35	...	52	...	86	...
United Arab Emirates	...	...	45	0.1	30	...	54	...	81	...
Czechoslovakia[7]	7	...	128	0.2	17	...	74	...	47	...
Hungary	7	...	10	...	8	...	31	...	26	...
Lebanon	5	...	40	0.1	8	...	25	...	34	...
El Salvador	3	...	15	...	15	...	11	...	20	...
Nicaragua	2	...	15	...	12	...	9	...	11	...
Kenya	2	...	14	...	56	...	24	...	11	...
Nigeria	8	...	105	0.1	30	...	50	...	58	...
East Germany[3]	...	...	11	...	23	...	—	—	—	...
Iraq	4	...	153	0.2	197	0.1	4	...	2	...

Source: *Statistics Canada*

(1) 1990 data not directly comparable to previous years due to improvements in data collection procedures which resulted in higher values for 1990. (2) Also beginning in 1990, includes Puerto Rico and the U.S. Virgin Islands. (3) From Oct. 1990 on, all data for reunified Germany is listed under West Germany. Figures for East Germany represent trade prior to Oct. 1990 only. (4) Includes Luxembourg until 1993. (5) After 1992 refers to former USSR. (6) Denotes former Yugoslavia. (7) Denotes former Czechoslovakia. (—) = zero. (...) = too small to be included.

Foreign Investment in Canada

(millions of dollars)

	1960	1970	1980	1990	1992
All Countries	13 582	27 374	64 708	131 517	138 924
Africa[1]	23	180	139	7	5
Australia	7	12	74	790	749
Austria	—	3	18	247	435
Bahamas	14	74	131	148	155
Belgium/Luxembourg	194	260	681	670	774
Bermuda	3	29	658	1 278	1 313
Denmark	10	14	31	18	71
France	145	475	1 287	3 859	4 220
Germany	112	364	1 806	5 148	5 221
Greece	—	—	2	19	21
Hong Kong	—	20	51	1 370	2 524
India	—	5	1	8	7
Ireland	—	6	81	44	79
Israel	—	—	2	56	37
Italy	—	68	63	310	464
Japan	—	103	605	5 203	1 370
Malaysia	—	—	1	24	44
Mexico	—	5	1	-13	69
Middle East[2]	—	—	40	305	175
Netherlands	102	452	1 219	3 162	3 409
Netherlands Antilles	3	10	49	92	58
Norway	—	5	20	598	630
Pacific Rim[3]	31	7	5	455	934
Panama	9	17	99	117	148
Saudi Arabia	—	—	13	83	17
Singapore	—	—	—	141	145
South Korea	—	—	—	312	46
Spain	—	—	22	48	36
Sweden	33	126	322	598	1 075
Switzerland	129	353	960	3 139	3 142
Taiwan	—	—	—	33	97
United Kingdom	1 550	2 641	5 772	18 217	17 543
United States	11 210	22 054	50 368	84 311	88 468
Venezuela	2	3	3	3	22

Source: *Statistics Canada*

(1) Except South Africa. (2) Except for Saudi Arabia and Israel. (3) Other than countries specified.

Canadian Direct Investment Abroad

(millions of dollars)

	1960	1970	1980	1990	1992
All Countries...	2 468	6 188	26 967	91 541	106 534
Africa[1]	41	61	137	176	205
Australia	64	237	694	2 456	2 602
Austria	—	10	31	8	19
Bahamas	13	151	268	1 946	2 153
Belgium/.					
Luxembourg..	2	40	74	639	1 349
Bermuda	5	136	1 003	1 820	2 744
Brazil	35	648	691	1 699	1 889
Denmark	—	3	80	46	36
France	24	82	289	1 685	1 970
Germany	10	77	276	874	1 066
Greece	—	1	30	89	91
Hong Kong	2	—	39	572	805
India	10	34	61	92	96
Indonesia	1	24	590	866	779
Ireland	4	43	233	994	1 766
Italy	8	53	125	382	839
Japan	15	48	109	918	2 641
Malaysia	—	2	19	82	91

	1960	1970	1980	1990	1992
Mexico	12	45	165	232	357
Middle East	3	7	233	201	412
Netherlands	2	52	300	1 346	1 557
Netherlands					
Antilles	—	6	153	78	38
Norway	23	68	64	57	20
Pacific Rim[2]	7	34	156	339	815
Panama	7	2	15	24	19
Portugal	—	1	10	117	176
Singapore	—	2	8	1 804	2 035
South Africa	28	73	159	21	37
South Korea	—	—	—	59	89
Spain	3	34	168	542	401
Sweden	3	2	10	29	5
Switzerland	12	21	291	1 264	1 128
Taiwan	—	—	16	162	195
United Kingdom	257	586	2 860	11 810	11 360
United States	1 618	3 273	16 781	55 420	61 527
Venezuela	40	12	59	55	94

Source: *Statistics Canada*

(1) Except South Africa. (2) Other than countries specified.

Canadian Grain Exports

(millions of metric tonnes; millions of dollars)

	1980	1987	1988	1989	1990	1991	1992
Wheat							
Gross production	19.2	31.4	26.0	16.0	24.6	32.7	32.0
Gross exports	15.6	20.8	23.5	12.4	17.2	21.9	25.1
Gross value of exports	n.a.	$3 224.0	$4 439.5	$2 578.9	$3 340.9	$3 796.9	$4 690.7
Canola/Rapeseed							
Gross production	2.5	3.8	3.8	4.3	3.1	3.3	4.2
Gross exports	1.4	2.1	1.8	1.9	2.0	1.9	1.9
Gross value of exports[1]	n.a.	$490.6	$607.4	$623.9	$612.8	$507.4	$504.7
Barley							
Gross production	11.3	14.6	14.0	10.2	11.7	13.9	11.6
Gross exports	3.2	6.7	4.6	2.9	4.5	4.8	3.3
Gross value of exports	n.a.	$448.2	$282.7	$573.1	$506.1	$450.4	$325.5
Flax/Linseed							
Gross production	0.4	1.0	0.7	0.4	0.5	0.9	0.6
Gross exports	0.6	0.7	0.6	0.5	0.5	0.5	0.5
Gross value of exports	n.a.	$147.3	$168.5	$201.8	$174.2	$98.2	$89.5
Oats							
Gross production	3.0	3.3	3.0	3.0	3.5	2.9	1.8
Gross exports	0.05	0.3	0.3	0.7	0.7	0.4	.3
Gross value of exports	n.a.	$44.9	$63.1	$159.7	$75.4	$38.7	$68.3

Source: *Statistics Canada*

(1) Rape or colza seeds, whether broken or not.

Canada's Share of the World Wheat Market[1]

(thousands of metric tonnes)

	1976			1981			1993		
	World Imports	Canadian Exports Total	Share (%)	World Imports	Canadian Exports Total	Share (%)	World Imports	Canadian Exports Total	Share (%)
All Countries[2]	63 105	12 810	20.3	94 116	17 067	18.1	121 015	20 324	16.8
United States	n.a.	n.a.	n.a.	n.a.	n.a.	n.a.	1 905	1 471	77.2
Russia..............	n.a.	n.a.	n.a.	n.a.	n.a.	n.a.	14 000	1 306	9.3
Venezuela	740	43	5.8	800			1 125	282	25.1
USSR	4 600	1 166	25.3	16 000	4 459	27.9	n.a.	n.a.	n.a.
Iran	1 200	—		1 700	173	10.2	2 800	1 415	50.5
Cuba	922	814	88.3	1 030	1 014	98.4	865	223	25.8
United Kingdom	3 424	1 333	38.9	2 150	1 339	62.3	1 232	201	16.3
China	3 158	1 929	61.1	13 789	2 921	21.2	6 691	3 470	51.9
Japan	5 521	1 320	23.9	5 840	1 463	25.1	5 919	1 470	24.8
South Korea	1 993	55	2.8	1 998	17	0.9	3 895	2 014	51.7
India	3 804	148	3.9	50	40	80.0	2 500	847	33.9
Algeria	1 338	418	31.2	1 800	750	41.7	3 800	551	14.5
Belgium[3]	699	38	5.4	1 600	—		2 485	207	8.3
Brazil	2 911	975	33.5	3 893	1 426	33.2	5 825	1 136	19.5
Indonesia	1 155	151	13.1	1 500	—		2 600	801	30.8
Portugal	416	—		742	17	2.3	895	—	
Italy	2 431	499	20.5	3 300	858	26.0	4 862	299	6.1
Syria	316	24	7.6	511	—		732	9	1.2
Greece	2	1	5.0	2	1	50.0	228	1	0.4
Egypt	4 028	219	5.4	5 600	12	0.2	5 937	43	0.7
East Germany	1 700	292	17.2	500	67	13.4	n.a.	n.a.	n.a.
France	187	30	16.0	700	12	1.7	461	—	—
Iraq................	911	200	22.0	1 600	467	29.2	420	4	1.0
Mexico	1	—	—	1 240	38	3.1	1 349	551	40.8
Netherlands	1 373	167	12.2	1 400	28	2.0	2 458	68	2.8
Peru	718	94	13.1	813	—		1 060	57	5.4
Poland	2 225	804	36.1	3 962	1 165	29.4	961	118	12.3
Spain	107	—	—	303	25	8.3	1 144	—	—
Sri Lanka	750	77	10.3	650	—		900	—	—
West Germany[4]	1 480	346	23.4	1 500	1	0.1	1 473	—	—

Source: *Statistics Canada*

(1) For the crop year ending June 30. (2) May include countries not listed here. (3) Includes Luxembourg. (4) After 1992 refers to unified Germany.

(—) = zero; n.a. not available.

Agriculture is still Big Business

*I*n 1993, $2.6 billion worth of Canadian agricultural products contributed to our trade balance with rest of the world. Total agricultural exports were $13 billion, and shipments of wheat, barley, oats and corn made up 40% of that amount. Another 22% of the exports were live animals and red meat. The biggest markets for these exports were the United States, Europe and Mexico—38% of total cattle and beef production went to the US in 1993.

Agriculture and the food industry, which includes value-added stages such as processing and packaging, are among the top five Canadian industries, and agricultural production within the country contributed for more than $20 billion in our economy.

As we embrace high-tech new economic sectors such as information processing, it must be remembered that the resource-based sector is still a significant part of our GDP and provides jobs and underpins communities across the country.

BUSINESS

Agriculture in Canada

(millions of dollars)

	1950	1960	1970	1980	1990	1993
Total value of agricultural products	2 135.8	2 811.7	4 250.9	15 958.8	21 933.8	24 226.5
Barley	45.8	69.4	144.7	553.6	545.0	404.6
Canola	n.a	14.8	96.7	673.6	789.6	1 236.5
Cattle	421.8	469.7	858.9	3 221.4	3 590.3	4 481.2
Corn	7.2	10.1	49.4	467.5	516.9	417.1
Dairy products	328.2	486.5	678.9	2 015.5	3 154.8	3 130.5
Eggs	86.9	137.8	172.8	407.0	486.6	537.6
Forest Products	37.6	26.9	20.1	64.9	88.1	114.9
Fruits	33.6	52.1	91.8	137.3	188.5	173.7
Honey	n.a	n.a.	n.a.	44.8	45.9	53.6
Maple products..........	8.9	9.5	8.1	34.1	70.8	65.9
Nurseries	n.a.	n.a.	n.a.	276.2	913.6	942.6
Oats	42.6	23.9	20.9	53.5	81.1	137.3
Pigs.....................	286.9	266.8	484.5	1 404.2	2 030.1	2 035.9
Potatoes.................	29.9	67.4	90.1	211.9	399.2	445.9
Poultry	80.1	135.5	262.7	670.2	1 201.5	1 216.6
Sheep	1.3	.4	.3	2.9	3.2	4.4
Soybeans................	n.a.	10.0	23.7	183.3	256.2	438.2
Sugar Beets.............	13.5	12.8	15.1	73.5	42.9	31.7
Tobacco	56.7	96.4	154.8	212.5	281.1	290.4
Vegetables..............	43.8	68.1	125.1	360.1	697.4	740.0
Wheat...................	377.5	442.7	570.1	2 774.5	2 694.1	1 797.7

Source: *Statistics Canada*

Canadian Agriculture by Province, 1993

(millions of dollars)

	Nfld	PEI	NS	NB	Que	Ont	Man	Sask	Alta	BC
Cattle	1.6	33.7	27.8	22.7	205.3	874.9	290.7	638.3	2 142.7	243.5
Dairy Products	20.8	38.9	83.8	56.7	1 141.5	1 072.5	115.1	88.5	244.7	268.1
Wheat (excl durum).....	-	1.2	.6	.4	11.7	58.4	115.1	88.5	244.7	268.1
Pigs....................	2.9	21.6	26.4	16.0	610.8	563.0	276.7	155.3	322.5	40.7
Poultry	14.8	4.1	40.4	31.1	338.6	432.0	53.1	n.a.	103.7	161.1
Canola	-	-	-	-	-	8.8	252.4	532.2	434.6	8.5
Nurseries	4.3	1.1	24.7	15.2	140.9	438.2	20.6	13.6	212.2	71.7
Vegetables.............	3.5	6.5	16.0	6.8	182.4	362.5	19.5	1.2	36.3	105.2
Eggs	8.2	2.8	19.7	20.0	100.8	194.6	50.0	20.7	47.4	73.4
Barley	-	4.8	n.a.	2.2	19.6	11.5	53.8	143.3	166.6	2.5

Source: *Statistics Canada*

Mining in Canada

(millions of dollars)

	1950	1960	1970	1980	1990	1993
Total Value	1 045.5	2 492.5	5 722.1	31 841.8	40 778.4	36 062.2
METALS:						
Cadmium	1.9	3.3	15.3	7.6	11.6	1.6
Cobalt	1.0	6.7	10.2	134.7	49.6	89.8
Copper	123.2	264.8	779.2	1 859.6	2 428.9	1 759.7
Gold	168.9	157.2	88.1	1 165.4	2 407.6	2 258.0
Iron Ore	23.4	175.1	588.6	1 700.9	1 258.8	1 036.6
Lead	47.9	43.9	123.1	273.7	279.3	96.2
Nickel	112.1	295.6	830.2	1 497.4	2 027.9	1 216.0
Platinum metals	10.3	28.9	43.6	159.1	189.4	138.8
Silver	18.8	30.2	81.9	828.8	249.7	152.9
Uranium	n.a.	269.9	n.a.	702.0	887.9	509.0
Zinc	98.0	108.6	398.9	858.2	2 272.6	1 228.8
NON-METALS:						
Asbestos	65.9	121.4	208.1	618.5	272.1	215.1
Gypsum	6.7	9.5	14.2	39.5	80.1	83.1
Potash	—	178.7	108.7	1 020.7	964.9	901.5
Salt	7.1	19.4	36.1	122.8	240.9	279.8
Sulphur	2.2	4.3	28.4	444.1	368.9	2.4
STRUCTURAL MATERIALS:						
Cement	35.9	93.3	155.7	581.4	991.4	764.6
Sand and gravel	36.4	111.2	133.6	508.4	817.3	736.5
Stone	25.9	60.6	87.9	341.2	663.4	469.6

Source: *Statistics Canada*

Mining by Province, 1993

(millions of dollars)

	Nfld	PEI	NS	NB	Que	Ont	Man	Sask	Alta	BC	Yuk	NWT
METALS:												
Copper	9	—	—	26.5	196.3	677.2	155.2	—	—	703.6	—	—
Gold	—	—	—	7.3	619.9	1 065.0	45.1	—	.3	212.5	50.4	192.6
Iron Ore	637.0	—	—	—	—	—	—	—	—	1.3	—	—
Lead	—	—	—	37.5	—	—	1.1	—	—	28.9	13.9	14.8
Nickel	—	—	—	—	836.2	379.8	—	—	—	—	—	—
Zinc	—	—	—	379.9	157.6	225.1	117.5	—	—	127.2	41.7	179.8
NON-METALS:												
Asbestos	5.2	—	—	—	209.9	—	—	—	—	—	—	—
STRUCTURAL MATERIALS:												
Cement	—	—	—	—	146.5	301.8	—	—	—	133.4	—	—
Sand and gravel	17.5	1.7	19.9	14.0	105.0	265.3	31.9	17.8	118.4	127.1	6.3	11.6
Stone	9.5	—	26.5	14.6	176.8	193.8	9.9	—	4.1	32.1	—	2.2

Source: *Statistics Canada*

Fuel Production in Canada

(millions of dollars)

	1950	1960	1970	1980	1990	1993
Total Fuels	201.2	565.9	1 717.7	17 943.9	22 989.9	22 979.6
Coal	110.1	74.7	86.1	932.0	1 823.7	1 783.0
Natural gas	6.4	52.2	315.1	6 148.8	5 692.0	7 248.6
Natural gas by-products[1]	n.a.	16.1	160.1	1 825.1	2 370.8	2 793.0
Petroleum, crude	84.6	422.9	1 156.5	9 037.9	13 103.4	11 155.0

Source: *Statistics Canada*

(1) Incl. butane, propane and pentane plus.

Primary Energy Supply

(annual petajoules[1])

	Natural[2] Gas	Coal	Hydro-electricity	Nuclear Energy	Petroleum	Steam and Biomass	Total
1971	2 185	405	580	14	3 461	404	7 049
1972	2 491	461	648	24	4 006	329	7 959
1973	2 577	495	694	51	4 596	345	8 758
1974	2 552	526	760	50	4 361	345	8 594
1975	2 580	635	729	43	3 775	257	8 019
1976	2 593	620	766	59	3 478	263	7 779
1977	2 733	686	791	89	3 486	264	8 049
1978	2 530	744	842	106	3 438	305	7 965
1979	2 800	811	875	120	3 911	324	8 842
1980	2 560	891	902	130	3 760	348	8 590
1981	2 526	970	948	136	3 410	336	8 326
1982	2 580	1 028	919	130	3 360	351	8 368
1983	2 476	1 066	948	165	3 537	381	8 574
1984	2 695	1 396	1 022	177	3 757	378	9 426
1985	2 927	1 487	1 085	205	3 834	391	9 928
1986	2 716	1 382	1 111	242	3 837	413	9 702
1987	2 932	1 394	1 131	262	4 038	430	10 188
1988	3 445	1 614	1 097	281	4 249	416	11 101
1989	3 631	1 718	1 039	271	4 147	413	11 220
1990	3 732	1 669	1 058	248	4 140	388	11 234
1991	3 980	1 748	1 100	288	4 146	404	11 666

Source: *Statistics Canada*

(1) A petajoule is one quadrillion joules (10^{15}) (2) Incl. butane, propane and pentane plus.

Forestry and Forestry Product Manufacturing

(millions of dollars)

	1963	1971	1981	1990	1991
Logging[1]	1 355.7	2 315.3	6 286.7	11 291.0	10 598.8
Wood	1 472.7	3 349.8	11 820.5	20 454.2	18 065.1
Sawmill and planing mill products	869.4	1 967.1	6 800.4	11 285.0	10 497.8
Shakes and shingles	24.2	66.3	178.8	351.6	291.2
Veneer and plywood	204.0	450.8	1 192.0	1 472.7	1 216.8
Pulp and paper mills	2 473.4	4 104.9	17 025.5	26 326.1	21 255.5
Paper and allied industries	3 273.8	5 773.3	22 673.3	34 500.8	29 045.6

Source:*Statistics Canada*

(1) Including value of shipments and value added.

Forestry and Forestry Product Manufacturing by Province, 1991

(millions of dollars)

	Nfld	PEI	NS	NB	Que	Ont	Man	Sask	Alta	BC	Yuk/NWT
Logging[1]	187.7	5.6	275.4	669.7	2 145.2	1 477.7	82.4	101.4	391.1	5 261.8	1.0
Wood	53.0	15.0	160.2	579.8	4 340.0	3 166.5	265.5	143.4	1 217.4	8 124.2	—
Sawmill and planing mill products	20.8	6.5	86.9	327.0	2 087.9	905.1	46.3	61.3	630.1	6 125.9	—
Shakes and shingles	—	—	—	...	20.1	...	...	...	...	260.4	—
Veneer and plywood	—	—	—	...	181.9	...	—	...	...	726.7	—
Pulp and paper mills	118.7	-	588.4	1 559.3	7 250.1	4 828.5	...	...	933.7	5 218.9	—
Paper and allied industries	...	...	700.4	1 644.9	9 589.9	9 155.7	338.8	...	1 287.9	5 599.7	—

Source:*Statistics Canada*

(1) Including value of shipments and value added.

Communications—Telephones

	Revenue (millions of dollars)			Telephones in service (thousands)		
	Total	Local	Long Distance	Total	Residential	Business
1975	2 788	1 307	1 407	12 328	8 620	3 709
1976	3 296	1 537	1 664	12 975	9 067	3 908
1977	3 766	1 756	1 892	13 695	9 599	4 095
1978	4 391	2 010	2 239	14 337	10 053	4 284
1979	5 080	2 246	2 636	15 071	10 534	4 538
1980	5 775	2 512	3 053	15 844	11 054	4 790
1981	6 828	2 948	3 625	16 375	11 366	5 008
1982	7 708	3 360	4 058	16 503	11 499	5 004
1983	8 363	3 524	4 404	16 296	11 467	4 829
1984	9 099	3 666	4 842	16 174	11 480	4 693
1985	9 814	3 798	5 333	15 555	11 126	4 429
1986	10 455	3 896	5 817	15 524	11 086	4 438
1987	10 954	4 044	6 055	15 383	10 991	4 392
1988	11 704	4 237	6 319	15 392	10 915	4 476
1989	12 659	4 593	6 791	15 497	10 949	4 548
1990	13 251	4 906	7 143	15 472	10 888	4 585
1991	13 267	5 137	7 006	15 103	10 611	4 493
1992	13 536	5 430	6 915	14 690	10 314	4 376
1993	13 838	5.827	6 795	14 182	9 985	4 196

Source: *Statistics Canada*

Transportation—Railway

	Total Railway Operating Revenue ($millions)	Freight Revenues ($millions)	Passenger Revenues ($millions)	Passenger Miles (millions)		Total Railway Operating Revenue ($millions)	Freight Revenues ($millions)	Passenger Revenues ($millions)	Passenger Miles (millions)
1946 ..	711.3	527.1	99.4	n.a.	1972 ..	1 930.4	1 679.4	68.7	3 289
1947 ..	776.4	602.1	87.1	5 952	1973 ..	2 029.3	1 741.3	51.0	2 396
1948 ..	866.4	692.2	83.0	5 550	1974 ..	2 422.8	2 051.1	74.9	2 844
1949 ..	885.5	701.2	84.4	5 094	1975 ..	2 619.0	2 171.2	75.1	2 639
1950 ..	947.6	761.7	78.0	4 491	1976 ..	3 058.3	2 523.6	79.6	2 648
1951 ..	1 078.9	867.7	88.5	4 969	1977 ..	3 389.4	2 819.7	86.7	2 661
1952 ..	1 161.4	933.4	90.5	5 060	1978 ..	3 722.9	3 119.5	111.9	2 789
1953 ..	1 194.5	962.1	86.0	4 801	1979 ..	4 601.5	3 693.7	349.9	2 790
1954 ..	1 087.0	865.5	82.1	4 598	1980 ..	5 194.5	3 998.7	457.0	2 906
1955 ..	1 037.3	868.6	78.0	4 659	1981 ..	5 924.1	4 525.8	546.5	4 440
1956 ..	1 292.4	1 108.4	85.2	4 674	1982 ..	6 012.0	4 378.0	164.3	2 262
1957 ..	1 261.1	1 079.6	86.7	4 703	1983 ..	6 785.7	5 120.0	172.8	2 073
1958 ..	1 160.6	994.8	77.2	4 013	1984 ..	7 354.3	6 020.2	182.9	2 087
1959 ..	1 218.7	1 053.8	73.5	3 937	1985 ..	7 451.6	6 000.2	210.2	2 328
1960 ..	1 178.4	992.7	69.0	3 646	1986 ..	7 377.2	6 091.5	214.9	2 089
1961 ..	1155.3	1 012.5	61.2	3 152	1987 ..	7 715.9	6 449.7	204.8	1 849
1962 ..	1 163.8	1 018.5	60.6	3 243	1988 ..	7 777.2	6 445.2	228.8	2 139
1963 ..	1 202.5	1 060.0	59.6	3 367	1989 ..	7 233.6	5 940.4	249.0	2 227
1964 ..	1 322.2	1 168.1	63.7	4 218	1990 ..	6 875.8	5 845.6	146.0	1 186
1965 ..	1 369.8	1 208.2	66.0	4 389	1991 ..	7 015.1	6 034.0	153.2	1 379
1966 ..	1 476.5	1 278.0	62.7	4 189	1992 ..	6 748.9	5 785.8	152.9	1 389
1967 ..	1 514.1	1 216.8	79.3	5 174					
1968 ..	1 527.4	1 261.7	66.6	4 402					
1969 ..	1 581.2	1 324.7	65.8	4 065					
1970 ..	1 671.5	1 428.6	63.7	3 649					
1971 ..	1 795.2	1 570.7	63.9	3 579					

Source: *Statistics Canada*

Major Canadian Airlines

	Total Operating Revenues ($thousands)	Total Operating Expenses ($thousands)	Total Passengers (thousands)	Total Passenger Kilometres (thousands)	Total Goods Transported (thousands of kilograms)	Total Goods Tonne-kilometres (thousands)
1981	3 853 425	3 722 696	24 785	45 203 811	366 564	852 722
1982	3 892 339	3 943 533	22 694	43 295 779	358 073	860 535
1983	3 878 531	3 832 550	21 115	41 933 394	357 531	968 603
1984	4 169 498	4 089 755	22 628	44 665 698	396 632	1 120 391
1985	4 653 924	4 564 665	23 281	47 169 986	403 403	1 169 013
1986	4 889 763	4 599 049	23 188	49 124 261	379 238	1 155 488
1987	4 980 699	4 796 049	23 799	48 628 014	380 907	1 210 285
1988	5 453 507	5 262 624	24 097	54 279 293	403 806	1 323 315
1989	5 608 588	5 535 479	22 482	53 178 429	442 675	1 445 191
1990	5 660 477	5 765 017	21 236	50 091 785	435 224	1 487 833
1991	5 514 264	5 845 917	21 000	43 626 433	390 819	1 315 448
1992	5 498 189	5 820 218	21 261	45 414 285	392 514	1 331 586
1993	5 601 108	5 739 512	21 947	44 806 137	419 838	1 463 995

Source: *Statistics Canada*

Manufacturing in Canada

(millions of dollars)

	1983		1985	
	Value of Shipments of Goods Manufactured	Value Added	Value of Shipments of Goods Manufactured	Value Added
All Industries	203 255.9	76 936.0	248 492.6	95 875.3
Food	29 591.4	8 548.3	32 792.9	9 737.6
Beverage	4 290.7	2 511.4	4 863.7	2 735.9
Tobacco products	1 516.5	756.1	1 640.9	808.6
Rubber products	2 141.2	1 024.8	2 554.2	1 268.4
Plastic products	3 042.9	1 325.1	3 860.9	1 749.0
Leather and allied products	1 166.4	583.5	1 308.2	634.0
Primary textile	2 716.6	1 145.7	2 669.7	1 156.7
Textile products	2 394.8	1 058.5	2 650.1	1 145.8
Clothing	4 891.1	2 537.2	5 543.2	2 807.9
Wood	9 405.9	3 941.9	11 121.6	4 623.8
Furniture and fixtures	2 668.2	1 393.7	3 398.6	1 797.1
Paper and allied products	15 010.8	5 929.2	18 074.6	7 555.2
Printing, publishing and allied products	7 579.4	4 806.5	9 534.8	5 982.6
Primary metal	13 571.6	5 502.9	16 971.0	7 006.3
Fabricated metal products	11 098.8	5 280.8	13 971.0	6 638.1
Machinery	5 784.8	2 847.9	7 450.8	3 634.9
Transportation equipment	28 455.6	9 225.2	43 182.3	14 089.5
Electrical and electronic products	9 903.1	5 084.3	13 270.3	6 677.0
Non-metallic mineral products	4 779.1	2 447.5	5 879.1	3 047.1
Refined petroleum and coal products	23 324.4	2 630.3	24 420.8	2 614.2
Chemical and chemical products	15 750.3	6 288.7	18 268.6	7 625.3
Other manufacturing	4 172.5	2 066.7	5 065.4	2 540.6

	1987		1990	
	Value of Shipments of Goods Manufactured	Value Added	Value of Shipments of Goods Manufactured	Value Added
All Industries	314 049.5	118 289.6	298 918.5	122 972.5
Food	42 437.9	12 810.2	38 582.5	13 126.3
Beverage	6 159.9	3 167.5	5 620.6	3 331.0
Tobacco products	2 567.3	983.5	1 883.3	1 123.6
Rubber products	3 362.3	1 421.6	2 557.9	1 310.6
Plastic products	5 814.3	2 349.4	5 996.8	2 760.3
Leather and allied products	1 489.7	660.1	1 162.3	548.5
Primary textile	3 420.1	1 450.8	2 779.6	1 259.8
Textile products	3 498.3	1 417.6	3 363.6	1 418.6
Clothing	6 960.8	3 380.6	6 831.3	3 438.4
Wood	15 033.1	6 547.9	14 805.9	5 648.3
Furniture and fixtures	4 510.2	2 219.0	4 661.9	2 430.4
Paper and allied products	23 993.5	10 959.2	24 026.3	10 474.6
Printing, publishing and allied products	11 684.4	7 091.4	13 703.9	8 729.4
Primary metal	19 598.7	8 398.5	19 243.8	7 461.6
Fabricated metal products	17 951.0	8 133.0	17 876.9	8 678.1
Machinery	9 987.7	4 224.3	10 396.1	5 049.1
Transportation equipment	61 132.9	14 855.2	51 654.9	15 906.2
Electrical and electronic products	18 221.4	8 701.4	18 474.8	9 119.6
Non-metallic mineral products	8 375.4	4 163.0	7 391.6	3 836.1
Refined petroleum and coal products	17 682.3	2 066.5	18 569.5	2 703.9
Chemical and chemical products	23 583.7	10 153.3	23 117.9	11 330.3
Other manufacturing	6 584.7	3 135.8	6 217.2	3 287.8

Source: *Statistics Canada*

Manufacturing[1] by Province, 1993

(millions of dollars)

	Nfld	PEI	NS	NB	Que	Ont
All Industries..........................	1 551.8	396.4	5 150.5	5 865.5	73 973.6	155 995.2
Food	696.6	288.5	1 247.2	1 174.3	9 593.2	15 359.5
Beverage............................	n.a.	n.a.	139.3	137.8	1 579.3	2 507.6
Tobacco products.....................	... .	—	—	...	n.a.	n.a.
Rubber products......................	—	—	n.a.	n.a.	n.a.	1 352.3
Plastic products......................	7.5	—	63.0	49.7	1 452.5	3 454.8
Leather and allied products............	n.a.	—	n.a.	n.a.	527.0	520.9
Primary textile	—	n.a.	n.a.	n.a.	1 426.5	1 166.9
Textile products......................	1.6	n.a.	96.7	n.a.	1 641.6	1 376.3
Clothing	1.2	1.1	51.2	21.1	4 270.5	1 731.6
Wood................................	32.1	13.5	147.5	449.3	3 404.4	2 729.8
Furniture and fixtures.................	2.4	—	28.1	22.2	1 458.5	2 532.0
Paper and allied products	n.a.	n.a.	629.8	1 514.2	7 549.9	7 606.4
Printing, publishing and allied products ..	53.7	17.6	162.1	107.6	3 623.0	7 286.1
Primary metal	n.a.	—	n.a.	n.a.	6 236.1	10 139.7
Fabricated metal products.............	40.2	8.9	122.6	206.5	4 072.7	10 370.3
Machinery...........................	n.a.	n.a.	31.9	65.9	2 045.3	5 913.5
Transportation equipment.............	n.a.	5.5	n.a.	n.a.	6 319.0	41 825.0
Electrical and electronic products	n.a.	n.a.	136.0	25.7	4 837.1	11 576.8
Non-metallic mineral products..........	50.6	4.1	115.1	106.7	1 632.9	3 786.2
Refined petroleum and coal products	n.a.	—	n.a.	n.a.	3 514.8	7 198.0
Chemical and chemical products	15.4	24.6	65.1	95.8	5 630.6	12 813.1
Other manufacturing..................	9.2	7.6	n.a.	58.3	n.a.	n.a.

	Man	Sask	Alta	BC	Yuk	NWT
All Industries..........................	6 739.5	3 786.0	20 048.8	25 335.9	19.3	56.1
Food	1 488.7	1 076.7	4 490.5	3 167.3	1.2	2.1
Beverage............................	152.6	84.6	398.2	492.8	n.a.	n.a.
Tobacco products.....................	...	—	...	...	n.a.	n.a.
Rubber products......................	n.a.	n.a.	n.a.	38.1	n.a.	n.a.
Plastic products......................	203.1	31.3	299.6	435.3	n.a.	n.a.
Leather and allied products............	40.7	5.8	24.0	21.2	n.a.	n.a.
Primary textile	n.a.	n.a.	n.a.	22.2	n.a.	n.a.
Textile products......................	54.1	13.7	66.2	108.8	n.a.	n.a.
Clothing	323.8	16.8	157.3	256.8	n.a.	n.a.
Wood................................	209.5	124.8	933.4	6 761.7	n.a.	n.a.
Furniture and fixtures.................	149.1	8.1	240.9	220.6	n.a.	n.a.
Paper and allied products	305.8	n.a.	795.5	4 912.1	n.a.	n.a.
Printing, publishing and allied products ..	482.3	213.5	771.3	986.6	4.4	10.1
Primary metal	559.5	n.a.	873.8	909.6	n.a.	n.a.
Fabricated metal products.............	411.1	176.9	1 117.6	1 350.1	4.6	n.a.
Machinery...........................	523.9	221.2	798.3	782.1	n.a.	n.a.
Transportation equipment.............	763.8	95.4	296.2	922.4	n.a.	n.a.
Electrical and electronic products	562.8	236.2	608.6	472.2	n.a.	n.a.
Non-metallic mineral products..........	152.8	85.3	665.2	792.8	n.a.	n.a.
Refined petroleum and coal products	n.a.	n.a.	3 749.3	1 709.6	n.a.	n.a.
Chemical and chemical products	240.9	203.4	3 311.1	717.7	n.a.	n.a.
Other manufacturing..................	84.2	33.1	298.0	255.9	n.a.	n.a.

Source:*Statistics Canada*

(1) Value of shipments of goods of own manufacture only; i.e. does not include value added.

... too small to be counted n.a. indicates that the number of establishments is so small that confidentiality would be breached if statistics were published — not reported

Retail Merchandising in Canada

(millions of dollars[1])

	1981	1985	1990	1991	1992	1993
TOTAL	103 431	142 212	192 558	181 208	185 049	193 815
Total excl. motor vehicles	84 078	111 850	150 863	143 519	146 548	152 450
Supermarkets and grocery stores	25 267	33 006	42 475	43 512	45 445	47 696
All other food stores	1 822	2 570	3 946	3 579	3 112	3 386
General merchandise stores	15 011	18 002	21 354	20 683	20 860	20 495
Other semi-durable goods stores	3 123	4 267	6 951	5 977	6 416	6 658
Other durable goods stores	2 715	3 659	5 475	4 876	4 935	5 207
Recreational and motor vehicle dealers	19 353	30 362	41 695	37 689	38 501	41 365
Gasoline service stations	8 057	11 840	15 355	14 288	14 168	14 246
Automotive parts	6 505	8 277	12 321	10 610	10 288	10 871
Clothing stores - men's	1 242	1 529	2 076	1 713	1 666	1 739
Clothing stores - women's	2 121	3 238	4 000	3 691	3 672	3 819
Other clothing stores	2 036	2 871	4 017	3 756	3 904	4 264
Shoe stores	1 072	1 404	1 826	1 590	1 506	1 614
Furniture and appliance stores	4 108	6 097	8 597	7 412	7 661	8 386
Other household furnishings stores	1 095	1 456	2 612	2 033	2 172	2 247
Drugs and patent medicine stores	3 597	5 944	9 476	9 795	10 722	11 889
All other retail stores	6 310	7 693	10 384	10 003	10 022	9 934

Source: *Statistics Canada*

(1) Current dollars

Merchandising by Province, 1993

(millions of dollars)

	Nfld	PEI	NS	NB	Que	Ont
Supermarkets, grocery and other food stores	1 053.1	203.4	1 754.5	1 388.1	13 379.5	15 193.9
Drugs and patent medicine stores	256.2	66.6	448.6	324.5	2 926.5	4 520.1
Clothing stores	152.3	14.3	245.0	220.0	2 690.9	3 592.0
Shoe stores	21.4	3.1	32.2	26.9	541.5	601.6
Household goods	109.2	31.7	205.9	181.1	2 588.6	4 049.1
Motor vehicle, recreational vehicle, gas stations and automotive parts stores	1 020.4	306.8	2 221.8	1 790.1	15 782.9	25 420.4
General merchandise and all other stores	687.4	187.4	1 414.6	1 017.4	8 188.0	16 645.9

	Man	Sask	Alta	BC	Yuk	NWT
Supermarkets, grocery and other food stores	1 843.0	1 420.9	4 581.6	6 228.8	58.4	101.3
Drugs and patent medicine stores	267.3	363.3	1 139.9	1 453.8	...	n.a.
Clothing stores	328.1	253.2	1 035.4	1 173.1	n.a.	n.a.
Shoe stores	40.0	33.6	116.2	182.2	n.a.	n.a.
Household goods	282.1	217.1	1 289.1	1 606.8	4.2	9.3
Motor vehicle, recreational vehicle, gas stations and automotive parts stores	2 226.6	2 000.5	6 737.2	8 777.3	27.0	51.3
General merchandise and all other stores	1 574.8	1 377.5	5 220.8	6 461.6	9.4	21.1

Source: *Statistics Canada*

Canada's Largest Corporations, 1993[1]

(ranked by assets)

Company (Head office)	Assets (millions)	Revenues (millions)	Profit or Loss (−) (millions)	Employees	% Foreign Owned
Imasco Ltd. (Montreal)	50 407.0	7 972.0	409.0	71 500	41 (UK)
Hydro Québec (Montreal)	47 879.0	7 036.0	761.0	21 028	-
Ontario Hydro (Toronto)	44 706.0	8 363.0	10.0	22 590	-
BCE Inc. (Montreal)	36 708.0	19 827.0	-656.0	118 000	15 (widely held)
Power Corp. of Canada (Montreal)	29 574.5	6 087.2	150.2	9 800	-
Canadian Pacific Ltd. (Montreal)	17 134.3	6 579.4	-190.6	39 300	-
The Seagram Co. Ltd. (Montreal)	15 579.1	6 760.6	490.2	15 800	n.a.
Alcan Aluminium Ltd. (Montreal)	13 054.2	9 329.3	-134.2	44 000	41 (widely held)
Imperial Oil Ltd. (Toronto)	12 796.0	7 809.0	279.0	9 470	70 (US)
The Thomson Corp. (Toronto)	10 929.0	7 545.2	357.3	46 400	-
BC Hydro & Power Authority (Vancouver)	10 005.0	2 178.0	301.0	6 318	-
Noranda Inc. (Toronto)	9 756.0	5 255.0	-37.0	31 000	-
The Canadian Wheat Board (Winnipeg)	8 651.1	4 428.1	n/a	519	-
TransCanada Pipelines Ltd. (Calgary)	8 157.8	4 242.1	355.6	1 764	38 (widely held)
Canadian National Railway Co. (Montreal)	7 100.0	4 200.0	-79.0	34 707	-
Nova Corp. of Alberta (Calgary)	6 923.0	3 274.0	202.0	6 300	-
General Motors of Canada Ltd. (Oshawa)	6 570.2	21 777.2	327.7	40 572	100 (US)
Westcoast Energy Inc. (Vancouver)	6 562.0	3 627.0	158.0	6 043	16 (widely held)
Shell Canada Ltd. (Calgary)	5 979.0	4 701.0	18.0	4 876	78 (Nether-lands)
Amoco Canada Petroleum (Calgary)	5 875.0	4 086.0	309.0	2 400	100 (US)
Petro-Canada (Calgary)	5 532.0	4 507.0	162.0	7 319	-
Manitoba Hydro (Winnipeg)	5 455.0	823.0	-24.0	4 200	-
Inco Ltd. (Toronto)	5 176.8	2 748.3	36.4	16 087	33 (widely held)
Air Canada (Montreal)	5 039.0	3 598.0	-326.0	18 152	10 (widely held)
Laidlaw Inc. (Burlington)	4 722.0	2 523.1	-369.1	37 000	15 (widely held)

Source: *The Financial Post 500 Magazine, 1993*

(1) Figures represent fiscal year ending Dec. 1992 unless otherwise stated.

Tops in Their Fields, 1993

(thousands of dollars)

■ Agriculture

Company	Revenue
The Canadian Wheat Board	$4 428 107
Cargill Ltd.	2 103 000
Saskatchewan Wheat Pool	1 622 493
Coopérative fédérée de Québec	1 537 609
United Grain Growers Ltd.	1 049 301
Agropur, Coopérative agro-alimentaire	1 043 000
Alberta Wheat Pool	868 630
XCAN Grain Pool Ltd.	823 110
Manitoba Pool Elevators	545 469
Co-op Atlantic	452 141

■ Mining

Company	Revenue
Alcan Aluminium Ltd.	$9 329 280
Inco Ltd.	2 748 295
Noranda Minerals Inc.	1 922 900
Falconbridge Inc.	1 432 953
Placer Dome Inc.	1 182 930
Cominco Ltd.	982 504
Rio Algom Ltd.	955 427
American Barrick Resources Corp.	883 816
Canadian Reynolds Metals Ltd.	865 460
Lac Minerals Ltd.	567 166

▶ ■ **Forestry**

Company	Revenue
MacMillan Bloedel Ltd.	$3 762 000
Domtar Inc.	1 968 000
Abitibi-Price Inc.	1 869 000
Avenor Inc.	1 834 100
Cascades Inc.	1 608 985
Noranda Forest Inc.	1 570 000
Repap Enterprises Inc.	1 328 100
Fletcher Challenge Canada Ltd.	1 226 800
Canfor Corp.	1 166 575
Stone-Consolidated Corp.	927 986

■ **Energy**

Company	Revenue
Ontario Hydro	$8 363 000
Imperial Oil Ltd.	7 809 000
Hydro-Québec	7 036 000
Shell Canada ltd.	4 701 000
Petro-Canada.	4 507 000
TransCanada PipeLines Ltd.	4 242 100
Amoco Canada Petroleum Co. Ltd.	4 086 000
Westcoast Energy Inc.	3 627 000
NOVA Corp. of Alberta	3 274 000
Total Petroleum (North America) Ltd.)	3 004 038

■ **Transportation**

Company	Revenue
Canadian National Railway Co.	$4 200 000
Air Canada	3 598 000
PWA Corp.	2 973 100
Laidlaw Inc.	2 523 067
Trimac Ltd.	618 803
VIA Rail Canada Inc.	487 741
British Columbia Railway Co.	334 262
Newfoundland Capital Corp. Ltd.	214 754
Greyhound Lines of Canada Ltd.	205 698
CSL Group Inc.	176 660

■ **Media**

Company	Revenue
The Thomson Corp.	$7 545 210
Quebecor Inc.	3 076 946
Macleand Hunter Ltd.	1 740 400
Rogers Communications Inc.	1 336 478
Southham Inc.	1 176 158
Torstar Corp.	974 970
Hollinger Inc.	888 005
G.T.C. Transcontinental Group Ltd.	638 162
Le Groupe Vidéotron ltée.	583 696
Canadian Broadcasting Corp.	371 801

■ **General Manufacturing**

Company	Revenue
Bombardier Inc.	$4 448 000
Moore Corp. Ltd.	3 003 948
Stelco Inc.	2 490 784
Dofasco Inc.	2 102 900
DuPont Canada Inc.	1 570 188
General Electric Canada Inc.	1 467 155
Pratt & Whitney Canada Inc.	1 436 317
Dominion Textile Inc.	1 335 203
Ivaco Inc.	1 221 855
Unilever Canada Ltd.	1 180 953

■ **Auto & Parts**

Company	Revenue
General Motors of Canada Ltd.	$21 777 209
Ford Motor Co. Of Canada, Ltd.	15 918 400
Chrysler Canada Ltd.	13 594 800
Magna Intl. Inc.	2 606 700
Honda Canada Inc.	2 246 267
Hayes-Dana Inc.	572 512
Ford Electronics Manufacturing Corp.	427 154
Rockwell Intl. of Canada Ltd.	427 102
Volvo Canada Inc.	274 813
Budd Canada Inc.	233 289

■ **Food & Beverage**

Company	Revenue
The Seagram Co. Ltd.	$6 760 602
Maple Leaf Foods Inc.	3 034 917
McCain Foods Ltd.	3 001 750
John Labatt Ltd.	2 136 000
Pepsi-Cola Canada Ltd.	1 600 000
Ault Foods Ltd.	1 175 202
Nestlé Canada Inc.	983 545
Coca-Cola Beverages Ltd.	882 257
Beatrice Foods Inc.	822 700
Burns Foods (1985) Ltd.	789 876

■ **High-Tech**

Company	Revenue
IBM Canada Ltd.	$6 698 000
Digital Equipment of Canada Ltd.	1 212 688
SHL Systemhouse Inc.	912 861
Hewlett-Packard (Canada) Ltd.	820 230
Spar Aerospace Inc.	527 204
Newbridge Networks Corp.	488 868
Apple Canada Inc.	390 949
AT&T Global Information Solutions Canada	330 060
EDS Canada	260 000
Computing Devices Canada Ltd.	236 492 ▶

■ Merchandising

Company	Revenue
George Weston Ltd.	$11 931 00
Univa Ltd.	6 207 200
The Oshawa Group Ltd.	5 727 800
Hudson's Bay Co.	5 441 498
Canada Safeway Ltd.	4 456 700
Sears Canada Inc.	3 938 711
Canadian Tire Corp., Ltd.	3 479 919
Métro-Richelieu Inc.	2 772 692
Great Atlantic & Pacific Co. of Canada Ltd.	2 709 217
Mitsui & Co. (Canada) Ltd.	2 423 143

Source: *The Financial Post 500 Magazine, 1994*

■ Conglomerates

Company	Revenue
Imasco Ltd.	$7 972 000
Canadian Pacific Ltd.	6 579 400
Power Corp. of Canada	6 087 185
Noranda Inc.	5 255 000
Brascan Ltd.	5 130 000
Onex Corp.	4 025 000
The Horsham Corp.	2 906 873
The Molson Cos. Ltd.	2 716 368
United Dominion Industries Ltd.	2 356 547
James Richardson & Sons, Ltd.	1 990 566

Source: *The Financial Post 500 Magazine, 1994*

Largest Foreign-Owned Companies in Canada, 1993

(ranked by revenues/thousands of dollars)

Company	Revenues	Foreign Ownership	Parent
General Motors of Canada Ltd.	$21 777 209	100	General Motors (US)
Ford Motor Co. Of Canada., Ltd.	15 918 400	94	Ford Motor (US)
Chrysler Canada Ltd.	13 594 800	100	Chrysler (US)
Imperial Oil Ltd.	7 809 000	70	Exxon (US)
IBM Canada Ltd.	6 698 000	100	IBM (US)
Shell Canada Ltd.	4 701 000	78	Shell Petroleum (Netherlands)
Canada Safeway Ltd.	4 456 700	100	Safeway (US)
Amoco Canada Petroleum Co. Ltd.	4 086 000	100	Amoco (US)
Sears Canada Inc.	3 938 711	62	Sears Roebuck (US)
Maple Leaf Foods Inc.	3 034 917	55	Hillsdown Holdings (UK)

Source: *The Financial Post 500 Magazine, 1994*

Canadian Corporate Profits and Losses, 1993

(thousands of dollars)

Largest Profits

Hydro-Québec	761 000
The Seagram Co. Ltd.	490 199
Imasco Ltd.	409 000
The Thomson Corp.	357 330
TransCanada PipeLines Ltd.	355 600
General Motors of Canada Ltd.	327 730
Amoco Canada Petroleum Co. Ltd.	309 000
BC Hydro & Power Authority	301 000
American Barrick Resources Corp.	282 509
Imperial Oil Ltd.	279 000

Largest Losses

BCE Inc.	-656 000
Laidlaw Inc.	-369 072
Air Canada	-326 000
PWA Corp	-291 800
Rogers Communications Inc.	-287 049
Avenor Inc.	-285 600
Ford Motor Co. of Canada, Ltd.	-246 700
Repap Enterprises Inc.	-211 100
Canadian Pacific Ltd.	-190 600
SHL Systemhouse Inc.	-145 121

Source: *The Financial Post 500 Magazine, 1994*

Largest Canadian Financial Institutions[1], 1993

(millions of dollars)

Company (1992 rank)	Assets	Revenue	Net Income	Employees
Royal Bank of Canada (1)	164 941	11 676	300.0	52 745
Canadian Imperial Bank of Commerce (2)	141 299	10 934	730.3	45 000
Bank of Montreal (3)	116 869	8 706	709.0	32 067
Bank of Nova Scotia (4)	107 620	8 313	714.0	30 766
Toronto-Dominion Bank (5)	85 011	6 366	275.0	25 603
Movement des caisses populaires Desjardins (6)	58 537	6 147	288.7	38 677
Caisse de dépôt et placement du Québec (8)	48 022	3 989	n.a.	336
CT Financial Services Inc. (7)	46 132	3 703	166.0	13 404
National Bank of Canada (9)	42 734	3 419	174.6	11 528
Power Financial Corp. (10)	28 491	5 826	200.5	7 800

Source: *The Financial Post 500 Magazine*   (1) For the fiscal year ending Oct. 31, 1993.

Largest Canadian Subsidiaries,[1] 1993

(millions of dollars)

Company	Revenue	Assets	Major shareholder
Northern Telecom Ltd.	10 511	12 622	BCE 52%
Loblaw Cos. Ltd.	9 356	2 743	George Weston 70%
Bell Canada	7 957	18 945	BCE 100%
Zellers Inc.[2]	3 159	1 344	Hudson's Bay 100%
Westfair Foods Ltd.	2 584	741	George Weston 70%
Quebecor Printing Inc.	2 249	1 944	Quebecor 75%
Noranda Minerals Inc.	1 923	4 466	Noranda 100%
Hudon et Deaudelin Itée	1 703	n.a.	Oshawa Group 100%
Leob Inc.[2]	1 653	628	Univa 100%
Noranda Forest Inc.	1 570	2 356	Noranda 74%

Source: *The Financial Post 500 Magazine, 1994*

(1) For fiscal year ending Dec. 1991, unless otherwise stated. (2) For fiscal year ending Jan. 1993. (n.a.) not available.

Changes in Employment

*M*ost of Canada's top corporations experienced changes in employment levels as well as changes in financial performance. Of the top 10, only two companies reported an increase in the number of employees, one stayed the same and the rest collectively shed over 26 000 jobs.

Company	No. of Employees - 1992	No. of Employees - 1993
General Motors of Canada	41 318	40 572
BCE Inc.	124 000	118 000
Ford Motor Co. of Canada	21 800	21 800
Chrysler Canada	13 800	14 200
George Weston Ltd.	62 000	55 000
Alcan Aluminium Ltd.	46 000	44 000
Ontario Hydro	29 000	22 590
Imasco Ltd.	75 000	71 500
Imperial Oil Ltd.	10 152	9 470
The Thomson Corp.	45 700	46 400

Canadian Business Directory

The following is a list of the addresses for the corporate headquarters of the 40 largest Canadian companies, based on the 1994 *Financial Post 500* ranking. (Corporate rank by revenues is shown in brackets).

☐ **Air Canada** (34)
Air Canada Centre,
Box 14000, St. Laurent Stn,
Montréal, Que. H4Y 1H4
President & CEO: Hollis L. Harris [transportation]

☐ **Alcan Aluminum Ltd.** (6)
100-1188 Sherbroke St W,
Montréal, Que. H3A 3G2
Chairman & CEO: David Morton [resources]

☐ **Amoco Canada Petroleum Co. Ltd.** (28)
Amoco Centre,
240-4 Ave SW,
Calgary, Alta T2P 4H4
Chairman & CEO: T. Don Stacy [resources]

☐ **BCE Inc.** (2)
3700-1000 de la Gauchetière St W,
Montréal, Que. H3B 4Y7
Chairman, President & CEO: Lynton Ronald Wilson [communications]

☐ **Bombardier Inc.** (24)
1700-800 Réne-Lévesque Blvd W,
Montréal, Que. H3B 1Y8
Chairman & CEO: Laurent Beaudoin [mfg]

☐ **Brascan Ltd.** (20)
Box 762, BCE Place,
4400-181 Bay St,
Toronto, Ont. M5J 2T3
Chairman: Hon. J. Trevor Eyton [mgmt]

☐ **Canada Post Corp.** (31)
2701 Riverside Dr,
Ottawa, Ont. K1A 0B1
President & COO: Georges C. Clermont [services]

☐ **Canada Safeway Ltd.** (23)
47th floor, 150-6 Ave SW,
Calgary, Alta T2P 2J6
President & CEO: R.H. Kinnie [food/bev.]

☐ **Canadian National Railway Co.** (27)
935 de la Gauchetière St W,
Montréal, Que. H3B 2M9
Chairman: Brian R.D. Smith [transportation]

☐ **Canadian Pacific Ltd.** (14)
Canada Place, 800-1050 Gauchetière St W,
Montréal, Que. H3B 4C9
Chairman & CEO: William Wade Stinson [mgmt]

☐ **Canadian Tire Corp. Ltd.** (35)
Box 770 Stn K,
Toronto, Ont. M4P 2V8
Chairman: Hugh L. Macaulay [retail]

☐ **Canadian Wheat Board** (25)
423 Main St, Box 816,
Winnipeg, Man. R3C 2P5
Chief Commissioner: Lorne F. J. Hehn [food/bev.]

☐ **Chrysler Canada Ltd.** (4)
2450 Chrysler Centre,
Box 1621, Stn A,
Windsor, Ont. N9A 4H6
President & CEO: G. Yves Landry [mfg]

☐ **Ford Motor Co. of Canada, Ltd.** (3)
The Canadian Road
Oakville, Ont. L6J 5E4
President & CEO: G. O'Connor [mfg]

☐ **General Motors of Canada Ltd.** (1)
1901 Colonel Sam Dr.,
Oshawa, Ont. L1H 8P7
Pesident & General Manager: Maureen Kempston Darkes [mfg]

☐ **George Weston Ltd.** (5)
Suite 1901, 22 St Clair Ave E,
Toronto, Ont. M4T 2S7
Chairman, President & CEO: W. Galen Weston [food/bev.]

☐ **Hudson's Bay Co.** (18)
500-401 Bay St,
Toronto, Ont. M5H 2Y4
President & CEO: George J. Kosich [retail]

☐ **Hydro-Québec** (11)
101-75 René-Levesque Blvd W,
Montréal, Que. H2Z 1A4
Chairman & CEO: Richard Drouin [utility]

☐ **IBM Canada Ltd.** (13)
3600 Steeles Ave E,
Markham, Ont. L3R 9Z7
Chairman: John M. Thompson [tech.]

☐ **Imasco Ltd.** (8)
Flr 20, 1900-600 de Maisonneuve Blvd W,
Montréal, Que. H3A 3K7
Chairman & CEO: Purdy Crawford [mgmt]

▶ ☐ **Imperial Oil Ltd.** (9)
111 St Clair Ave W,
Box 4029, Stn A,
Toronto, Ont. M5W 1K3
Chairman & CEO: Robert Byron Peterson [resources]

☐ **Jim Pattison Group** (37)
1600-1055 Hastings St W,
Vancouver, BC V6E 2H2
Chairman: James A. Pattison [mgmt]

☐ **MacMillan Bloedel Ltd.** (32)
925 Georgia St W,
Vancouver, BC V6C 3L2
Chairman: Raymond V. Smith [resources]

☐ **Maple Leaf Foods Inc.** (39)
1500-30 St. Clair Ave. W,
Toronto, Ont M4V 3A2
Chairman: Sir John Nott [food/bev]

☐ **Noranda Inc.** (19)
Box 755, BCE Place,
4100-181 Bay St,
Toronto, Ont. M5J 2T3
President & CEO: David W. Kerr [resources]

☐ **NOVA Corp. of Alberta** (36)
801 7 Ave SW, Box 2535, Stn M
Calgary, Alta T2P 2N6
Chairman: Richard F. Haskayne [resources]

☐ **Onex Corp.** (29)
Box 700, BCE Place, 161 Bay St,
Toronto, Ont. M5J 2S1
Chairman, President & CEO: Gerald W. Schwartz [holdings]

☐ **Ontario Hydro** (7)
200-700 University Ave,
Toronto, Ont. M5G 1X6
Chairman & CEO: Maurice Strong [utility]

☐ **Oshawa Group Ltd.** (17)
200-302 The East Mall,
Etobicoke, Ont. M9B 6B8
Chairman & CEO: Allister P. Graham [food/bev.]

☐ **Petro-Canada** (22)
150-6 Ave SW,
Box 2844, Stn M,
Calgary, Alta T2P 3E3
President & CEO: James M. Stanford [resources]

☐ **Power Corp. of Canada** (16)
751 Victoria Square,
Montréal, Que. H2Y 2J3
Chairman & CEO: Hon. Paul G. Desmarais [mgmt]

☐ **Quebecor** (38)
900-612 rue Saint-Jacques
Montreal, Que. H3C 4M8
Chairman: Jean Neveu [pub/prtg]

☐ **Seagram Co. Ltd.** (12)
1430 Peel St,
Montréal, Que. H3A 1S9
Co-Chairman & CEO: Edgar M. Bronfman [food/bev.]

☐ **Sears Canada Inc.** (30)
222 Jarvis St,
Toronto, Ont. M5B 2B8
President & CEO: G. Joseph Reddington [retail]

☐ **Shell Canada Ltd.** (21)
400-4 Ave SW,
Box 100, Stn M,
Calgary, Alta T2P 2H5
President & CEO: Charles W. Wilson [resources]

☐ **The Thomson Corp.** (10)
2706 Toronto Dominion Bank Tower,
Toronto-Dominion Centre,
Toronto, Ont. M5K 1A1
Chairman: Kenneth R. Thomson [pub/prtg]

☐ **Total Petroleum (North America) Ltd.,**
3700-400 3 Ave SW
Calgary, Alta T2P 4H2
Chairman: Daniel L. Valot [resources]

☐ **TransCanada Pipelines Ltd.** (26)
TransCanada PipeLines Tower,
111-5 Ave SW,
Calgary, Alta T2P 3Y6
Chairman: Gerald James Maier [resources]

☐ **Univa Inc.** (15)
4100-1250 René-Lévesque Blvd W,
Montréal, Que. H3B 4X1
Chairman: Pierre Michaud [food/bev.]

☐ **Westcoast Energy Inc.** (33)
1100-1333 Georgia St W,
Vancouver, BC V6E 3K9
Chairman & CEO: Michael E.J. Phelps [resources]

Source: *Financial Post 500 Magazine, 1993. The Blue Book of Canadian Business*

LABOUR

Canadian Labour Force by Province, 1991

(thousands)

	Population 15 Years and Over	Labour Force[1]	Participation Rate[2]	Employed	% Employed[3]	Un-employed	% Un-employed[4]
Canada	20 882	13 757	66.3	12 340	59.5	1 417	10.3
Newfoundland	438	241	55.3	197	45.1	44	18.4
Prince Edward Island	97	64	65.1	53	54.2	11	16.8
Nova Scotia	692	422	61.3	371	53.9	51	12.0
New Brunswick	560	327	58.6	286	51.1	42	12.7
Quebec	5 382	3 392	63.4	2 987	55.8	405	11.9
Ontario	7 778	5 276	68.3	4 770	61.8	506	9.6
Manitoba	810	541	66.9	494	61.0	48	8.8
Saskatchewan	720	484	67.1	449	62.2	36	7.4
Alberta	1 889	1 357	72.5	1 246	66.5	111	8.2
British Columbia	2 516	1 652	66.4	1 489	59.9	163	9.9

Source: *Census, Statistics Canada*

(1) The labour force consists of employed workers and those who are unemployed but actively seeking work. (2) Participation rate is the percent of the total population aged 15 and over that makes up the labour force. (3) The percent of the total population aged 15 and over that is employed. (4) The percent of the labour force that is unemployed.

Labour Force by Industry

(thousands)

Industry	Total Labour Force			% Unemployed		
	1971	1981	1991	1971	1981	1991
All Industries	5 845	11 645	13 513	8.7	8.5	10.2
Agriculture	372	462	441	9.6	6.4	8.1
Other primary industries	226	329	299	10.0	12.7	16.2
Manufacturing	1 339	2 236	2 051	8.5	10.6	12.5
Construction	514	726	833	10.6	16.0	22.5
Transportation, communication, utilities	564	940	993	5.8	5.6	7.6
Trade	838	2 035	2 419	9.1	6.6	9.4
Finance, insurance, real estate	183	622	816	7.8	4.3	4.8
Community, business and personal services	925	3 452	4 709	11.4	6.5	8.3
Public administration	483	783	886	4.8	6.2	6.5
Unclassified	402	61	66	—	—	—

Source: *Census, Statistics Canada*

Good News on the Labour Front

A fter months of dismal prospects Statistics Canada reported steady growth in employment during the first half of 1994. Employment increased by 0.5% in July, continuing a pattern of monthly gains that began in March. In addition, job creation outstripped growth in both the labour force and the general population, which translated into a reduced the national unemployment rate of 10.2%, its lowest in level in three years.

The employment growth reported in August included all segments of the population, with full-time positions and manufacturing jobs enjoying a resurgence.

Labour Force by Age

(thousands)

	Population 1971	Population 1991	Labour Force[1] 1971	Labour Force[1] 1991	Employed 1971	Employed 1991	% Unemployed[2] 1971	% Unemployed[2] 1991
Both Sexes								
15 yrs. and over	14 870	20 740	8 639	13 757	8 104	12 340	6	10
15–24 yrs.	3 925	3 728	2 228	2 500	1 982	2 095	11	16
25 yrs. and over	10 950	17 020	6 410	11 257	6 121	10 246	5	9
Males								
15 yrs. and over	7 330	10 121	5 667	7 569	5 329	6 751	6	11
15–24 yrs.	1 966	1 896	1 232	1 308	1 083	1 062	12	19
25 yrs. and over	5 367	8 223	4 435	6 261	4 245	5 690	4	9
Females								
15 yrs. and over	7 541	10 626	2 972	6 188	2 775	5 589	7	10
15–24 yrs.	1 963	1 832	997	1 192	899	1 033	10	13
25 yrs. and over	5 583	8 795	1 975	4 996	1 876	4 556	5	9

Source: *Census, Statistics Canada*

(1) The labour force consists of employed workers and those who are unemployed but actively seeking work. (2) The percent of the labour force that is unemployed.

Employment in Canada's Industries by Province, 1993

(thousands)

	Canada	Nfld	PEI	NS	NB	Que	Ont	Man	Sask	Alta	BC
All Industries	12 383	186	53	357	291	2 960	4 793	490	440	1 252	1 561
Services[1]	4 554	68	21	139	105	1 081	1 760	179	152	459	590
Trade[2]	2 138	36	9	67	55	491	809	80	70	223	298
Manufacturing	1 800	17	4	38	36	521	837	52	25	96	174
Utilities[3]	909	16	4	26	25	223	321	44	33	90	127
Government[4]	855	18	5	31	23	223	316	37	30	77	95
Finance[5]	766	6	...	17	13	180	341	25	24	65	95
Construction	656	9	...	18	16	135	251	22	17	80	108
Agriculture	445	...	...	6	4	70	124	43	78	88	32
Primary[6]	248	16	...	16	13	36	34	7	11	73	42

Source: *Statistics Canada*

(1) Services refers to occupations in which a service is provided but no goods are produced—e.g. teaching, health care. (2) Trade is the sales and distribution network of merchandise. (3) Utilities comprise transportation, communications, electricity, gas and waterworks. (4) Government includes municipal, provincial and federal levels. (5) Finance includes insurance, real estate, banking and related activities. (6) Primary industries include fishing, trapping, forestry and mining.

Where the Jobs Increased

*E*mployment gains during the first half of 1994 included 31 000 jobs in manufacturing, and the construction and primary industries also maintained a generally upward trend, although the service sector was static.

The gains were mostly confined to central Canada, where most manufacturing jobs are held. Quebec led job creation and posted the largest drop in unemployment, going from a peak of over 13% in 1993 to 11.5% by July 1994. Ontario also had an increase in jobs, but growth in its labour force was greater. Atlantic and Western Canada reported little change after a flat performance in June.

Canadian Minimum Wages[1]

(hourly rate for experienced adult workers)

	1965	1970	1975	1980	1985	1990	1993[2]	1994
Federal[3]	$1.25	$1.65	$2.60	$3.25	$3.50	$4.00	$4.00	$4.00
Nfld	.70 (m)	1.25 (m)	2.20	3.15	4.00	4.25	4.75	4.75
	.50 (f)	1.00 (f)						
PEI	1.00	1.25 (m)	2.30	3.00	4.00	4.50	4.75	4.75
		.95 (f)						
NS	1.05 (m)	1.25 (m)	2.25	3.00	4.00	4.50	5.15	5.15
	.80 (f)	1.00 (f)						
NB	.80	1.15	2.30	3.35	3.80	4.50	5.00	5.00
Que	.85	1.40	2.80	3.65	4.00	5.30	5.70	6.00
Ont	1.00	1.50	2.40	3.00	4.00	5.40	6.35	6.70
Man	.85[4]	1.50	2.60	3.15	4.30	4.70	5.00	5.00
Sask	$38.00/wk	1.25	2.50	3.65	4.50	5.00	5.35	5.35
Alta	1.00	1.55	2.50	3.50	3.80	4.50	5.00	5.00
BC	1.00	1.50	2.75	3.65	3.65	5.00	6.00	6.00
Yukon	1.25	1.50	2.70	3.35	4.25	5.97	6.24	6.24
NWT	1.25	1.50	2.50	3.50	4.25	5.00	6.50	6.50

Minimum wage rates (1991)[2] for young workers and students: **PEI:** under 18, $4.35; **NS:** 14 to 18, $4.55; **Ont.:** students under 18, $6.25; **Alta.:** under 18, attending school, $4.50; **B.C.:** 17 and under, $5.50; **N.W.T.** under 16, $6.00; if distant from NWT highway system adult $7.00; under 16 $6.50. The federal jurisdiction, Nfld.,

N.B., Que., Man., Sask., and Yukon do not have special rates for young workers and students.

Some provinces have different minimum wage rates for special categories of workers such as domestics and farm workers.

Source: *Labour Canada*

(1) Represents highest minimum rate in effect during the year. (2) As of July 1993. (3) Applies to work under federal government jurisdiction as defined by the Constitution Act, 1867, Sections 91 and 92. (4) .85 urban, .80 rural. (m) male. (f) female.

Unions with Largest Membership

	1980	1990	1994
Canadian Union of Public Employees (CUPE)	257 180	376 975	409 810
National Union of Provincial Government Employees (NUPGE)	195 754	301 217	307 592
United Food and Commercial Workers' International Union (UFCW)	120 000	170 000	175 000
Public Service Alliance of Canada (PSAC)	155 731	162 772	171 091
National Automobile, Aerospace and Agricultural Implement Workers Union of Canada (CAW)	130 000	167 410	170 000
United Steel Workers of America (USWA)	203 000	160 000	161 232
Communications, Energy and Paperworkers Union of Canada (CEP)	n.a.	n.a.	149 000
International Brotherhood of Teamsters, Chauffeurs, Warehousemen and Helpers of America (IB of TCW&H of A)	91 000	100 000	95 000
Fédération des affaires sociales inc. (FAS)	70 000	94 675	94 675
Service Employees International Union (SEIU)	65 000	75 000	80 000
Fédération des enseignantes et enseignants des commissions scolaires (FCECS)	81 033	75 000	75 000

Source: *Labour Canada*

Union Membership in Canada, 1961–94

(thousands)

	1961	1971	1981	1991	1993	1994
Total civilian labor force	6 055	8 395	11 573	13 681	13 797	13 946
Total union membership	1 447	2 231	3 487	4 068	4 071	4 078
% of civilian labor force	22.6	26.6	30.1	29.7	29.5	29.2
% in national unions	28.1	38.0	55.3	64.4[1]	65.8	66.1
%in international unions	71.9	62.0	44.7	31.0[1]	29.8	29.5

Source: *Labour Canada*   (1) Does not include directly chartered unions and independent local organizations.

Canadian Labour Unions Directory

(as of Sept. 1, 1994)

☐ **Alberta Teachers' Association (ATA):** 11010-142 St, Edmonton, Alta T5N 2R1

☐ **British Columbia Teachers' Federation (BCTF):** 100-550 W 6th Ave, Vancouver, BC V52 4P2

☐ **Canadian Brotherhood of Railway, Transport and General Workers (CBRT&GW):** 2300 Carling Ave, Ottawa, Ont. K2B 7G1

☐ **Canadian Union of Postal Workers (CUPW):** 377 Bank St, Ottawa, Ont. K2P 1Y3

☐ **Canadian Union of Public Employees (CUPE):** 21 Florence St, Ottawa, Ont. K2P 0W6

☐ **Communications, Energy and Paperworkers (CEP):** 350 Albert St, 19th Flr, Ottawa, Ont. K1R 1A4

☐ **Fédération CSN–Construction (CSN):** 1594 ave de Lorimier, Montréal, Qué. H2K 3W5

☐ **Fédération des affaires sociales inc. (FAS):** 1601 ave de Lorimier, Montréal, Qué. H2K 4M5

☐ **Fédération des employées et employés de services publics inc. (FEESP):** 1601 ave de Lorimier, Montréal, Qué. H2K 4M5

☐ **Fédération des enseignantes et enseignants des commissions scolaires (FCECS):** 300–1170 boul. Lebourgneuf, Québec, Qué. G2K 2G1

☐ **Fédération des infirmières et infirmiers du Québec (FIIQ):** 4e étage, 2050, rue De Bleury, Montréal, Qué. H3A 2J5

☐ **Fédération du commerce inc. (FC):** 122-1601 ave de Lorimier, Montréal, Qué. H2K 4M5

☐ **Federation of Women Teachers' Associations of Ontario (FWTAO):** 3rd Flr, 1260 Bay St, Toronto, Ont. M5R 2B8

☐ **Hospital Employees' Union (HEU):** 2006 West 10th Ave, Vancouver, BC V6J 4P5

☐ **Hotel Employees and Restaurant Employees International Union (HERE):** 1150–1140, boul. de Maisonneuve o., Montréal, Qué. H3A 1M8

☐ **International Association of Machinists and Aerospace Workers (IAMAW):** 300-100 Metcalfe St, Ottawa, Ont. K1P 5M1

☐ **International Brotherhood of Electrical Workers (IBEW):** 401-45 Sheppard Ave E, Willowdale, Ont. M2N 5Y1

☐ **International Brotherhood of Teamsters (IB of T):** 804-2540 Daniel Johnson, Laval, Qué. H7T 2S3

☐ **International Union of Operating Engineers (IUOE):** 401–4211 Kingsway, Burnaby, BC V5H 1Z6

☐ **IWA-Canada (IWA):** 500-1285 West Pender St, Vancouver, BC V6E 4B2

☐ **Labourers' International Union of North America (LIUNA):** 44 Hughson St S, Hamilton, Ont. L8N 2A7

☐ **National Automobile, Aerospace and Agricultural Implement Workers Union of Canada (CAW):** 205 Placer Court, Willowdale, Ont. M2H 3H9

☐ **National Union of Public and General Employees (NUPGE):** 204-2841 Riverside Dr., Ottawa, Ont. K1V 8N4

☐ **Office and Professional Employees International Union (OPEIU):** 630–1265 rue Berri, Montréal, Qué. H2L 4C6

☐ **Ontario English Catholic Teachers' Association (OECTA):** 400–65 St Clair Ave E, Toronto, Ont. M4T 2Y8

▶

☐ **Ontario Nurses Association (ONA):** 600-85 Grenville St, Toronto, Ont. M5S 3A2

☐ **Ontario Public School Teachers' Federation (OPSTF):** 1260 Bay St, Toronto, Ont. M5R 2B7

☐ **Ontario Secondary School Teachers' Federation (OSSTF):** 60 Mobile Dr., Toronto, Ont. M4A 2P3

☐ **Professional Institute of the Public Service of Canada (PIPS):** 53 Auriga Dr., Nepean, Ont. K2E 8C3

☐ **Public Service Alliance of Canada (PSAC):** 233 Gilmour St, Ottawa, Ont. K2P 0P1

☐ **Service Employees International Union (SEIU):** 1 Credit Union Dr., Toronto, Ont. M4A 2S6

☐ **Syndicat de la fonction publique du Québec (SFPQ):** 5100, boul. des Gradins, Québec, Que. G2J 1N4

☐ **United Association of Journeymen and Apprentices of the Plumbing and Pipe Fitting Industry of the United States and Canada (UA):** 316, 1959-152nd St, Surrey, BC V4A 9E3

☐ **United Brotherhood of Carpenters and Joiners of America (UBC):** 807-5799 Yonge St, Willowdale, Ont. M2M 3V3

☐ **United Food and Commercial Workers International Union (UFCW):** 300-61 International Blvd, Rexdale, Ont. M9W 6K4

☐ **United Steelworkers of America (USWA):** 7th Flr, 234 Eglinton Ave E, Toronto, Ont. M4P 1K7

Source: *Labour Canada*

Labour Income

(millions of dollars)

	1950	1955	1960	1965	1970	1975	1980
Total labour income	8 998	13 930	19 582	28 953	48 035	95 277	169 736
Agriculture, fishing and trapping	163	185	245	327	403	745	1325
Forestry	285	365	349	402	525	918	1 608
Mines, quarries and oil wells	283	424	556	650	1 067	2 000	4 442
Manufacturing	3 022	4 548	5 759	8 095	11 765	20 038	34 341
Construction	645	1 018	1 491	2 142	3 125	7 713	11 102
Transportation, communications and utilities	1 226	1 814	2 412	3 218	5 012	9 180	16 611
Trade	1 134	1 821	2 640	3 874	6 359	12 619	21 322
Finance, insurance and real estate	374	611	910	1 451	2 472	5 497	11 084
Community, business and personal services	1 021	1 722	3 037	5 529	10 955	22 284	41 075
Public administration	511	867	1 316	1 863	3 400	7 204	12 425

	1987	1988	1989	1990	1991	1992	1993
Total labour income	295 691	324 412	349 848	368 090	376 660	388 058	398 235
Agriculture, fishing and trapping	2 422	2 517	2 586	2 647	2 676	2 638	2 687
Forestry	2 145	2 313	2 564	2 735	2 779	2 788	2 994
Mines, quarries and oil wells	6 553	7 329	7 213	7 429	7 490	7 099	7 019
Manufacturing	54 397	59 131	61 760	61 470	60 735	60 713	62 440
Construction	16 766	19 672	22 219	22 730	21 139	20 241	19 685
Transportation, communications and utilities	26 263	27 847	30 024	31 513	32 460	33 359	33 759
Trade	36 616	41 394	45 115	47 333	47 111	47 806	48 937
Finance, insurance and real estate	22 445	24 898	26 910	27 819	28 306	29 211	30 493
Community, business and personal services	77 676	85 166	93 629	100 804	105 969	110 529	114 515
Public administration	21 438	22 352	24 255	26 328	27 255	28 614	28 892

Source: *Statistics Canada*

PERSONAL FINANCE

What's a Dollar Worth?[1]

This table shows how many current (1994) dollars it would take to equal the purchasing power of a single dollar in earlier years. For example, if you lived on $50 a week in 1950 and want to know what that would be by today's standards, multiply $50 times the relative value of a 1950 dollar ($6.85) and you have your answer: $342.50. The relative value of a dollar for the years listed was calculated according to changes in the cost of living in Canada as measured by the Consumer Price Index.

Year	Value	Year	Value	Year	Value	Year	Value
1915	$13.85	1956	$5.97	1969	$4.34	1982	$1.56
1920	7.53	1957	5.79	1970	4.20	1983	1.47
1925	9.37	1958	5.64	1971	4.08	1984	1.41
1930	9.37	1959	5.56	1972	3.90	1985	1.36
1935	11.73	1960	5.49	1973	3.62	1986	1.30
1940	10.67	1961	5.45	1974	3.26	1987	1.25
1945	9.37	1962	5.38	1975	2.95	1988	1.20
1950	6.85	1963	5.29	1976	2.74	1989	1.14
1951	6.17	1964	5.19	1977	2.54	1990	1.09
1952	6.03	1965	5.07	1978	2.33	1991	1.03
1953	6.08	1966	4.89	1979	2.13	1992	1.02
1954	6.06	1967	4.72	1980	1.94	1993	1.00
1955	6.06	1968	4.54	1981	1.72	1994	1.00

(1) Based on June Consumer Price Index

Average Income in Selected Canadian Cities, 1991

City	Average Income[1]	Total Income ($000)	Number of Tax Returns	City	Average Income[1]	Total Income ($000)	Number of Tax Returns
West Vancouver, BC	57 866	1 290 410	22 300	Vancouver, BC	35 604	9 511 200	267 140
Oakville, Ont.	45 733	2 914 450	63 730	Newcastle, Ont.	35 405	921 863	26 040
Markham, Ont.	43 707	4 466 687	102 200	Brampton, Ont.	33 736	4 176 966	123 820
Richmond Hill, Ont.	41 093	1 872 535	45 570	London, Ont.	33 706	5 498 979	163 150
Burlington, Ont.	39 758	2 903 551	73 030	Halifax, NS	33 217	2 143 906	64 540
Nepean, Ont.	39 634	2 290 242	57 790	Victoria, BC	32 891	4 688 214	142 540
Whitby, Ont.	39 414	1 280 143	32 480	Edmonton, Alta.	32 723	10 482 178	320 330
Toronto, Ont.	39 283	21 396 112	544 670	Regina, Sask.	32 029	3 014 917	94 130
North York, Ont.	38 814	9 085 661	234 080	Scarborough, Ont.	31 920	8 423 234	263 880
Newmarket, Ont.	38 531	1 048 556	27 210	Fredericton, NB	31 617	1 096 084	34 670
Pickering, Ont.	38 318	1 350 680	35 250	St. John's, Nfld	31 505	1 506 632	47 820
Waterloo, Ont.	38 294	1 513 452	39 520	Saskatoon, Sask.	31 159	2 932 610	94 120
Vaughan, Ont.	38 228	1 407 397	36 820	Laval, Que.	30 563	5 094 330	166 680
St. Albert, Alta.	38 213	921 320	24 110	Hamilton, Ont.	30 381	4 975 751	163 780
Gloucester, Ont.	38 169	2 502 266	65 560	Winnipeg, Man.	30 258	10 079 671	333 130
Ottawa, Ont.	37 776	7 100 810	187 970	Quebec, Que.	29 371	2 539 101	86 450
North Vancouver, BC	37 236	2 415 664	64 870	Montreal, Que.	29 169	15 090 087	517 340
Halton Hills, Ont.	36 909	815 715	22 100	Saint John, NB	29 152	1 148 894	39 410
Etobicoke, Ont.	36 515	4 563 961	124 990	Sydney, NS	28 526	512 245	17 960
Calgary, Alta	36 458	14 269 553	391 400	Brandon, Man.	27 742	582 951	21 010
Ajax, Ont.	36 449	1 079 341	29 610	Drummondville, Que.	27 127	631 384	23 280
Mississauga, Ont.	36 370	9 037 876	248 500	Montreal-Nord, Que.	25 086	912 770	36 390
Dollard-des-Ormeaux, Que.	36 206	814 593	22 500				

Source: *Revenue Canada*   (1) Average total income after business deductions, but before personal deductions.

Average Income in Canada

This table shows actual average income from 1971 to 1992 in addition to average income in constant dollars over the same period. Constant dollars are adjusted to remove the effects of inflation, thereby providing a realistic way of comparing incomes for different years. An increase in constant dollar income means that incomes have increased faster than the cost of living; a decrease in constant dollar income means that incomes have not kept pace with inflation.

| | Families[1] | | | | Individuals | | | |
| | Female Head | | Male Head | | Females | | Males | |
	Actual	Constant[2]	Actual	Constant[2]	Actual	Constant[2]	Actual	Constant[2]
1971....	$5 486	$22 393	$10 486	$42 804	$3 597	$14 683	$5 136	$20 965
1973 ...	6 687	26 066	12 910	50 323	4 267	16 633	6 206	24 191
1975 ...	8 528	25 158	16 993	50 129	5 450	16 078	7 964	23 494
1977 ...	10 691	27 134	20 544	52 141	6 923	17 571	9 919	25 174
1979 ...	12 663	27 023	24 946	53 235	8 754	18 681	12 427	26 519
1980 ...	13 982	27 083	28 533	55 268	8 364	16 201	16 917	32 768
1981 ...	16 704	28 898	31 655	54 763	9 833	17 011	19 041	32 941
1982 ...	17 439	27 205	34 357	53 596	10 551	16 460	19 905	31 052
1983 ...	17 135	25 188	36 008	52 932	10 985	16 148	20 756	30 511
1984 ...	19 578	27.605	37 487	52 857	11 764	16 587	21 125	29 786
1985 ...	20 541	27 936	39 982	54 376	12 375	16 830	22 563	30 686
1986 ...	21 396	27 858	42 390	55 192	13 247	17 248	23 846	31 047
1987 ...	22 818	28 454	44 885	55 972	14 028	17 493	24 903	31 054
1988 ...	23 656	28 364	47 763	57 268	14 886	17 848	26 403	31 657
1989 ...	26 802	30 608	51 413	58 714	16 321	18 639	28 238	32 248
1990 ...	26 721	29 099	53 264	58 004	17 269	19 198	29 108	31 699
1991	31 701	32 715	55 946	57 736	18 040	18 581	29 820	30 715
1992 ...	30 914	32 208	56 948	57 859	18 779	19 079	30 078	30 559

Source: *Statistics Canada*

(1) Based on the Census family definition: a husband and wife (without children or with children who never married) or a parent with one or more children who never married, living together in the same home. (2) Converted to 1993 dollars using the CPI with 1986 = 100.

Taxes of the Average Canadian Family[1], 1994[2]

Province	Total Taxes	Average Cash Income	Income Tax	Sales Tax	Property Tax	Liquor, Tobacco, Amusement and other Excise Taxes	Auto, Fuel and Motor Vehicle Licence Taxes	Social Security, Pension, Medical and Hospital Taxes	Other Taxes[3]
Canada ..	27 203	57 696	11 037	4 284	2 041	1 274	926	5 011	2 630
Nfld.	118 732	44 181	6 984	4 282	525	1 232	931	3 111	1 666
P.E.I.	16 864	47 122	6 540	3 633	760	1 152	774	2 910	1 095
N.S.	20 976	48 121	8 819	4 044	1 135	1 028	895	3 426	1 630
N.B.	18 678	47 394	7 541	4 341	352	1 085	915	3 591	854
Que.	24 816	52 348	10 068	4 309	1 227	948	823	5 773	1 668
Ont.	29 102	63 628	12 119	4 603	2 680	1 241	957	4 934	2 568
Man.	24 785	55 153	8 904	3 808	2 354	1 473	846	3 985	3 417
Sask.	24 159	48 701	8 032	3 836	2 542	1 452	1 326	3 206	3 765
Alta.	25 952	60 230	11 228	2 013	1 530	1 671	827	5 235	3 449
BC	30 209	60 809	11 898	4 637	1 794	1 715	856	5 465	3 843

Source: *The Fraser Institute*

(1) The family unit is an economic family of two or more individuals. (2) Preliminary estimates. (3) Includes profits tax, natural resource taxes, import duties and other taxes.

Canadian Income Tax

Income tax was introduced in 1917 as a temporary measure to finance Canada's participation in World War I. The law introducing the tax (the Income War Tax Act) was shorter and much simpler than our current legislation. It imposed tax at graduated rates, ranging from 4% on the first $1 500 to 25% for income over $100 000.

This "temporary" tax was not repealed when the war ended. But on Jan. 1, 1949, the federal government removed "war" from the title and gave the statute the name it has today—the Income Tax Act. This act has been amended many times—most notably in 1972 when a major overhaul of the tax system broadened the tax base and introduced a tax on capital gains. This is still the basis of our federal income tax laws today.

In 1988, all personal exemptions and many deductions were changed to non-refundable tax credits. Unlike deductions, which reduce taxable income, credits are used to reduce the amount of tax payable. The term "non-refundable" refers to the fact that, although you can use these credits to reduce or eliminate your federal tax payable, any unused portion is not refundable to you. In some cases, however, you may be able to transfer the unused portion of the credits to someone else.

Because the credits are calculated by multiplying eligible amounts by 17%—the same as the lowest personal tax rate—the change makes no difference to those whose income falls within the lowest tax bracket. But it increases taxes for most of those with higher incomes.

For 1994, the federal income tax rates for individuals were: 17% on income up to $29 590; 26% on income between $29 590 and $59 180; and 29% on income in excess of $59 180.

Provincial Income Tax

Every province except Quebec collects income tax from its residents by "piggy-backing" on the federal tax. Each province imposes tax of a fixed percentage based on the amount of income tax an individual must pay to the federal government. The federal government collects the tax, then remits the appropriate amounts to the provincial governments.

Quebec, however, chooses to collect its own provincial income tax, so Quebec residents must file both the federal return filed by all Canadian taxpayers, and the Quebec provincial income tax return.

Filing Tax Returns

Though corporations must file tax returns each year, individuals need only file if they owe taxes or if they are eligible to claim tax credits such as the Child Tax Credit or the Goods and Services Tax Credit. Persons owing money must file a return by Apr. 30 of the year following the taxation year. Failure to do so makes the taxpayer liable to a late-filing penalty of 5% of unpaid tax plus an additional penalty of 1% per month on the amount outstanding, to a maximum of 12 months, plus interest on amounts owing.

Source: *Revenue Canada*

Taxes Paid by Province, 1991

	Returns Filed	Total Income Assessed ($million)	Net Federal Tax Payable ($million)	Net Provincial Tax Payable ($million)
Canada	13 710 450	442 529.9	60 270.1	24 077.9
Newfoundland	239 720	6 250.2	737.0	432.5
Prince Edward Island	61 670	1 543.9	174.9	98.1
Nova Scotia	419 290	12 162.3	1 549.9	881.2
New Brunswick	334 890	9 110.7	1 109.3	634.6
Quebec	3 376 070	101 423.1	13 071.1	23.6
Ontario	5 271 280	182 723.9	26 120.4	13 151.2
Manitoba	516 530	14 954.3	1 842.2	1 140.8
Saskatchewan	447 020	12 865.1	1 577.9	984.2
Alberta	1 268 600	42 099.2	5 875.6	2 764.9
British Columbia	1 704 170	56 644.9	7 769.8	3 824.7
Yukon	13 430	497.4	61.9	26.6
Northwest Territories	22 100	925.0	128.9	53.9
Outside Canada	35 680	1 329.7	251.2	61.6

Source: *Taxation Statistics, Revenue Canada*

Individual Income Tax Rates, 1994

Federal Tax

Taxable Income	Basic Federal Tax	Marginal Rate[1]
$ 1	$ 0	17%
29 590	5 030	26%
59 180	12 724	29%

(1) Excludes the federal surtax of 3 % of Basic Federal Tax which generally constitutes the tax payable after deducting personal and dividend tax credits, but before deducting other credits. A further surtax of 5% applies to basic federal tax in excess of $12 500 (taxable income in excess of $62,193 assuming no other credits.

Quebec Tax[1]

Taxable Income	Basic Federal Tax	Marginal Rate[1]
$ 0	$ —	16%
7 000	1 120	19%
14 000	2 450	21%
23 000	4 340	23%
50 000	10 550	24%

(1) Residents of Quebec (as at Dec. 31) are entitled to a federal tax abatement of 16.5% of Basic Federal Tax (after deducting personal and dividend tax credits), but must pay Quebec income tax at the indicated rates. Surtaxes at 5% of provincial tax over $5,000 plus 5% of provincial tax over $10,000 and a tax reduction of 2% of the excess of $10,000 over provincial tax also apply.

Provincial Tax
(rates applied to basic federal tax)

Newfoundland	69.0%	Saskatchewan	50.0%	[6]
Prince Edward Island	59.5%[1]	Alberta	45.5%	[7]
Nova Scotia	59.5%[2]	British Columbia	52.5%	[8]
New Brunswick	64.0%[3]	Northwest Territories	45.0%	
Ontario	58.0%[4]	Yukon Territories	50.0%	[9]
Manitoba	52.0%[5]	Non-residents	52.0%	[10]

(1) To be increased by 10% of basic provincial tax in excess of $12 500.(2) To be increased by 20% of basic provincial tax in excess of $6 999 but not over $10 499 plus 30% of provincial tax in excess of $10 499. (3) Basic rate increased from 62% to 64% effective Jan. 1, 1994. To be increased by 8% of provincial tax in excess of $13 500. (4) To be increased by 20% of provincial tax in excess of $5 500 plus 10% of provincial tax in excess of $8 000. (5) To be increased by a flat tax of 2% of net income plus, where net income exceeds $30 000, a surtax equal to the flat tax minus $600 and several other credits. (6) To be increased by a flat tax of 2% of net income plus a surtax of 15% of provincial tax (including the 2% flat tax) in excess of $4 000 and a surtax of 10% of provincial tax and flat tax. (7) To be increased by 8% of basic provincial tax in excess of $3 500, plus an additional tax equal to 0.5% of taxable income. (8) To be increased 30% of provincial tax in excess of $5 300 plus 20% of provincial tax in excess of $9 000. (9) To be increased by 5% of provincial tax in excess of $6 000.(10) Non-residents are subject to an additional federal tax of 52% in lieu of provincial tax.

Source: *Coopers & Lybrand*

Tax Freedom Day

Tax freedom day is the day of the year on which Canadians begin to work for themselves. Until that point, everything they earn is paid out in taxes levied by federal, provincial and municipal governments.

The concept of tax freedom day was developed by the Fraser Institute, a Vancouver-based, independent Canadian economic research organization. According to the Institute's calculations, the average Canadian family in 1994 had an income of $57,696, out of which it paid taxes totalling $27,203—a rate of 47 percent. This corresponds to the 173rd day of the year, June 22. In 1961, the earliest year covered by the Institute's calculations, the average Canadian family had earned enough to pay its taxes by May 3.

Tax freedom day falls on a different date in each province due to variations in provincial and municipal taxes. The earliest tax freedom day—May 11— is in Prince Edward Island; the latest—July 1—is in British Columbia. Dates for all provinces are listed below.

Newfoundland	June 4	Quebec	June 22
Prince Edward Island	May 11	Manitoba	June 13
Nova Scotia	June 8	Saskatchewan	June 30
New Brunswick	May 24	Alberta	June 7
Ontario	June 16	British Columbia	July 1

Source: *The Fraser Institute*

1994 Personal Tax Credits

	Basic Amount	Federal Credit	Quebec Credit
Basic	$6 456	$1 098	$1 180
Age 65[1]	3 482	592	440
Disability[2]	4 233	720	440
Married[2]	5 380	915	1 180
Dependants[3] — 1st	—	—	520
— Other	—	—	480
Disabled dependant[4]	1 583	269	1 180
Single parent	—	—	260
Living alone	—	—	210
Charitable donations:			
First $250	—	17%	20%
Remainder	—	29%	20%
Medical expenses[5]	—	17%	20%
Education credit[6]	640	109	660
CPP/QPP/UIC	—	17%	20%
Tuition	—	17%	(8)
Pension income	1 000	170	200
Dividends[7]	—	13.33%	8.87%

Source: *Coopers & Lybrand*

(1) Federal Credit reduced where net income exceeds $25 921. (2) The credit is reduced where the spouse or qualifying dependant has income in excess of $538. (3) Includes only those under 19 years of age at the end of the year. (4) Those over 18 years of age at the end of the year. Income in excess of $2 690 reduces the credit. (5) Based upon the amount by which qualifying expenses exceed the lesser of $1 614 or 3% of net income. (6) The credit is actually $13.60 per month for federal purposes and $330 per term (not more than 2) for Quebec purposes. (7) The credit for taxable Canadian dividends is applied at the specified percentages to the grossed-up amount (125%) of dividends. (8) For Quebec, this amount is deductible from income.

1994 Individual Tax Tables

This table shows the combined federal and provincial income taxes, including surtaxes and flat taxes, payable on the assumption that only the basic personal tax credit is available. The political contribution tax credit and provincial credits for homeowners, renters, sales tax, cost of living, children, and venture capital have not been taken into account.

Taxable Income

	$20 000	$30 000	$40 000	$50 000	$60 000	$70 000	$80 000	$90 000	$100 000
Nfld.	3 960	6 947	11 419	15 891	20 407	25 508	30 641	35 774	40 907
P.E.I.	3 742	6 564	10 789	15 014	19 279	24 105	28 963	33 820	38 824
N.S.	3 742	6 564	10 789	15 014	19 291	24 462	29 666	35 041	40 416
N.B.	3 845	6 745	11 087	15 429	19 813	24 770	29 758	34 746	39 855
Que.-Prov.[1]	2 381	4 665	7 112	9 575	12 197	14 837	17 477	20 117	22 757
Que.-Fed.[1]	1 992	3 494	5 743	7 992	10 263	12 884	15 538	18 191	20 845
Ont.	3 707	6 503	10 689	14 875	19 378	24 553	29 871	35 190	40 508
Man.[2]	3 939	6 861	11 291	15 721	20 190	25 198	30 238	35 278	40 318
Sask.[3]	4 078	7 042	11 388	15 941	20 535	25 698	30 893	36 087	41 282
Alta.[4]	3 519	6 148	10 059	14 026	18 070	22 646	27 253	31 860	36 467
BC	3 580	6 281	10 324	14 367	18 728	23 807	28 973	34 389	39 805
Yukon	3 523	6 180	10 158	14 136	18 152	22 772	27 426	32 081	36 735
N.W.T.	3 408	5 978	9 826	13 674	17 559	21 964	26 401	30 838	35 275

Source: *Coopers & Lybrand*

(1) Because taxable income may differ for Federal and Quebec purposes, Quebec taxpayers may have to determine the tax payable to each jurisdiction on separate lines of the table before totalling. (2) The tax payable for Manitoba includes the additional tax of 2% of net income on the assumption that net income is the same as taxable income. Where net income exceeds taxable income, the tax payable should be increased by 2% of the excess to more accurately approximate the liability. (3) The tax payable for Saskatchewan includes the flat tax of 2% on the assumption that net income is the same as taxable income. Where net income exceeds taxable income, the tax payable should be increased by 2% of the excess to more accurately approximate the liability. (4) The tax payable for Alberta includes the flat tax of 0.5% of taxable income.

Average Canadian Income and Taxes by Occupation, 1991

Occupation	Average Income[1]	Average Federal Tax	Number[2]	Occupation	Average Income[1]	Average Federal Tax	Number[2]
Self-employed doctors and surgeons	129 206	28 469	41 790	Other self-employed professionals	33 869	5 095	89 080
Self-employed dentists	109 343	22 583	8 770	Municipal government employees	32 733	4 433	751 000
Self-employed lawyers and notaries	94 537	19 531	25 340	Investors	30 965	3 699	1 318 630
Self-employed accountants	68 643	12 203	14 590	Institutional employees	28 734	3 635	1 062 060
Teachers and professors	47 265	7 154	239 440	Business employees	28 053	3 910	7 577 190
Self-employed engineers and architects	46 324	7 503	6 290	Property owners	23 470	3 015	192 320
Provincial crown corp. employees	43 506	6 703	154 710	Self-employed salespeople	23 392	3 018	54 610
Federal crown corp. employees	38 855	5 458	131 320	Fishermen	21 539	2 288	32 110
Armed forces employees	37 627	5 459	88 280	Unclassified business employees	20 155	2 348	666 230
Federal government employees	37 240	5 410	324 250	Farmers	17 510	1 511	244 750
Provincial government employees	35 946	4 960	386 610	Pensioners	16 161	1 233	2 522 780
				Self-employed entertainers and artists	16 028	1 807	20 810
				Business proprietors	15 729	1 656	647 870
				Unclassified	6 613	580	2 449 990

Source: *Revenue Canada*

(1) Average total income after business expense deductions, but before personal deductions. (2) Based on number of tax returns.

Income Tax Collected from Individuals and Corporations

(millions of dollars)[1]

Year[2]	Total Tax Collected[3]	Individual Income Tax	% of Total	Corporate Income Tax	% of Total
1950	6 846.3	3 373.7	47.8	3 174.7	46.4
1955	11 427.9	5 974.0	52.3	4 960.5	43.4
1960	13 283.5	7 393.2	55.7	5 207.6	39.2
1965	19 239.5	11 308.0	58.8	7 026.5	36.5
1970	35 480.8	24 739.7	69.7	9 945.1	28.0
1975	52 658.4	39 450.0	74.9	12 186.4	23.1
1980	55 548.7	41 570.1	74.8	12 666.1	22.8
1985	69 670.8	55 362.4	79.5	10 465.3	15.0
1986	72 857.7	59 658.8	81.9	9 983.0	13.7
1987	77 298.6	65 268.6	84.4	10 142.1	13.1
1988	86 477.7	74 207.5	85.8	11 082.1	12.8
1989	86 230.7	73 008.2	84.7	11 517.5	13.4
1990	91 216.2	77 595.0	85.1	12 247.3	13.4
1991	98 731.7	87 538.7	88.7	9 812.7	9.9
1992	97 091.1	87 600.9	90.2	7 416.4	7.6

Source: *Revenue Canada.*

(1) All money figures in millions of dollars are in constant dollars where 1986 Base Year = 100. (2) For fiscal year ending Mar. 31. (3) Includes non-resident tax, excess profits and special taxes, miscellaneous tax revenue, Canada Pension Plan contributions and Unemployment Insurance premiums for individuals and corporations.

Retail Car Sales by Province – 1993

Manufacturer	Total	Nfld	PEI	NS	NB	Que
BMW	4 528	14	—	27	—	1 201
Chrysler	108 288	2 524	486	3 143	5 102	33 796
Ford	129 987	2 071	639	4 838	4 347	29 407
General Motors	238 475	5 532	963	7 799	6 107	58 107
Honda	68 459	716	143	1 806	1 027	23 885
Hyundai	20 286	440	257	1 415	435	9 906
Jaguar	630	—	—	1	—	172
Lada	1 275	27	42	26	15	680
Mazda	41 404	608	87	1 372	555	15 873
Mercedes-Benz	3 246	7	—	14	15	686
Nissan	26 730	172	86	869	335	10 712
Peugeot	—	—	—	—	—	—
Subaru	5 515	65	—	194	64	2 268
Suzuki	6 762	55	—	87	113	3 944
Toyota	55 367	717	182	1 506	1 132	19 559
Volkswagen	22 982	180	54	732	406	10 007
Volvo	5 117	30	—	112	41	1 152

Manufacturer	Ont.	Man	Sask	Alta	BC
BMW	2 017	37	25	230	977
Chrysler	42 599	2 736	1 657	9 912	6 333
Ford	56 278	3 826	2 990	12 261	13 330
General Motors	104 087	6 767	5 439	20 530	23 144
Honda	25 008	1 224	806	3 890	9 954
Hyundai	5 428	145	194	628	1 438
Jaguar	276	13	2	39	127
Lada	283	3	7	82	110
Mazda	14 784	593	360	1 808	5 364
Mercedes-Benz	1 564	35	20	208	697
Nissan	9 089	526	332	1 713	2 896
Peugeot	—	—	—	—	—
Subaru	1 429	98	39	317	1 041
Suzuki	1 621	239	74	190	439
Toyota	19 084	1 200	736	3 048	8 203
Volkswagen	7 646	386	200	988	2 383
Volvo	2 175	71	23	257	1 256

Source: *Motor Vehicle Manufacturers' Association*

Mortgage Rates by Year

	1-Year[1]	3-Year	5-Year
1981	18.1	18.19	18.38
1982	17.15	17.85	18.04
1983	11.17	12.67	13.23
1984	12.08	13.24	13.58
1985	10.44	11.65	12.13
1986	10.12	10.88	11.21
1987	9.86	10.71	11.17
1988	10.74	11.36	11.65
1989	12.77	12.17	12.06
1990	13.44	13.35	13.35
1991	10.22	11.00	11.13
1992	7.93	8.97	9.50
1993	7.70	n.a.	9.5

Sources: *Bank of Canada Review; Canada Mortgage and Housing Corp.; Canadian Bankers' Association*

(1) Does not include 1-year open.

The Effect of Interest Rate Changes on Mortgage Payments

The table below shows the monthly mortgage payment (principal and interest) for each $1 000 of mortgage debt. To calculate your payments at a given interest rate, choose the corresponding amount in the amortization column you select and multiply the amount by the number of thousands of dollars of debt. Example: if you want to know the cost per month to carry an $85 000 mortgage amortized over 25 years at 12.25%, multiply $10.49 by 85 and the result, $891.65, is your monthly payment. If the same mortgage was coming up for renewal at 12.75%, the new payment would be $922.25 ($10.85 × 85) or $30.60 more each month.

Monthly Payments for Each $1 000 of Mortgage

Interest Rate (%)	Amortization Period							
	1 Year	2 Years	3 Years	5 Years	10 Years	15 Years	20 Years	25 Years
7.00	$86.48	$44.73	$30.83	$19.75	$11.56	$ 8.93	$7.69	$7.00
7.25	86.59	44.84	30.94	19.87	11.68	9.07	7.84	7.16
7.50	86.70	44.95	31.05	19.98	11.81	9.21	7.99	7.32
7.75	86.82	45.06	31.16	20.10	11.94	9.34	8.13	7.47
8.00	86.93	45.17	31.28	20.21	12.06	9.48	8.28	7.63
8.25	87.04	45.28	31.39	20.33	12.19	9.62	8.43	7.79
8.50	87.15	45.39	31.50	20.45	12.32	9.76	8.59	7.95
8.75	87.26	45.50	31.61	20.56	12.45	9.90	8.74	8.12
9.00	87.38	45.61	31.72	20.68	12.58	10.05	8.89	8.28
9.25	87.49	45.72	31.84	20.80	12.71	10.19	9.05	8.44
9.50	87.60	45.83	31.95	20.91	12.84	10.33	9.20	8.61
9.75	87.71	45.94	32.06	21.03	12.97	10.48	9.36	8.78
10.00	87.82	46.05	32.17	21.15	13.10	10.62	9.52	8.94
10.25	87.93	46.16	32.28	21.27	13.24	10.77	9.68	9.11
10.50	88.04	46.27	32.40	21.38	13.37	10.92	9.83	9.28
10.75	88.16	46.38	32.51	21.50	13.50	11.06	10.00	9.45
11.00	88.27	46.49	32.62	21.62	13.64	11.21	10.16	9.63
11.25	88.38	46.61	32.74	21.74	13.77	11.36	10.32	9.80
11.50	88.49	46.72	32.85	21.86	13.91	11.51	10.48	9.97
11.75	88.60	46.83	32.96	21.98	14.04	11.66	10.65	10.14
12.00	88.71	46.94	33.08	22.10	14.18	11.82	10.81	10.32
12.25	88.82	47.05	33.19	22.22	14.32	11.97	10.98	10.49
12.50	88.94	47.16	33.30	22.34	14.46	12.12	11.14	10.67
12.75	89.05	47.27	33.42	22.46	14.59	12.28	11.31	10.85
13.00	89.16	47.38	33.53	22.58	14.73	12.43	11.48	11.02
13.25	89.27	47.49	33.65	22.70	14.87	12.59	11.64	11.20
13.50	89.38	47.61	33.76	22.82	15.01	12.74	11.81	11.38
13.75	89.49	47.72	33.87	22.94	15.15	12.90	11.98	11.56
14.00	89.60	47.83	33.99	23.07	15.29	13.06	12.15	11.74
14.25	89.71	47.94	34.10	23.19	15.43	13.21	12.32	11.92
14.50	89.82	48.05	34.22	23.31	15.58	13.37	12.49	12.10
14.75	89.94	48.16	34.33	23.43	15.72	13.53	12.67	12.28
15.00	90.05	48.27	34.45	23.56	15.86	13.69	12.84	12.46
15.25	90.16	48.39	34.56	23.68	16.00	13.85	13.01	12.64
15.50	90.27	48.50	34.68	23.80	16.15	14.01	13.18	12.83
15.75	90.38	48.61	34.79	23.92	16.29	14.17	13.36	13.01
16.00	90.49	48.72	34.91	24.05	16.44	14.33	13.53	13.19

Source: *The Royal Bank of Canada*

Housing Affordability Table

The table below shows how expensive a home an individual or family could likely afford, using various income levels and mortgage interest rates — assuming a downpayment of 25% of the purchase price. As income rises, housing becomes more affordable; but it becomes less affordable as interest rates increase.

For example: most couples with a combined annual income of $60 000 would qualify for a mortgage on a home costing $186 916 at an 11% interest rate—provided they had a downpayment of $46 729 (25% of the purchase price). But at a 13% interest rate, the same couple earning the same income could only afford a $163 339 home.

The table assumes that mortgage payments, property taxes, heating costs and 50% of condominium fees should not exceed 32% of gross income (net income if self- employed). Most lending institutions use this percentage when calculating how large a mortgage you can afford. For this table, we have estimated annual costs of $1 800 for property taxes and $1 200 for heating. Most lenders will also require that your Total Debt Service Ratio (mortgage payments, property tax, heating costs, 50% of condo fees plus any other liabilities such as car loans or other debts) does not exceed 40% of gross income.

Mortgage Interest Rate (%)[1]	Annual Income							
	$30 000	$40 000	$50 000	$60 000	$70 000	$80 000	$90 000	$100 000
9.00	$88 567	$131 562	$174 396	$217 391	$260 386	$303 2 21	$346 216	$389 211
9.25	86 887	129 068	171 090	213 270	255 450	297 4 72	339 652	381 832
9.50	85 172	126 519	167 712	209 059	250 406	291 5 99	332 946	374 293
9.75	83 523	124 070	164 465	205 011	245 558	285 9 53	326 500	367 046
10.00	82 028	121 849	161 521	201 344	241 163	280 8 35	320 656	360 477
10.25	80 498	119 575	158 507	197 585	236 663	275 5 95	314 672	353 750
10.50	79 023	117 385	155 603	193 965	232 328	270 5 46	308 908	347 270
10.75	77 601	115 273	152 804	190 476	228 148	265 6 79	303 351	341 023
11.00	76 151	113 119	149 948	186 916	223 884	260 7 13	297 681	334 649
11.25	74 830	111 156	147 347	183 673	220 000	256 1 90	292 517	328 843
11.50	73 554	109 261	144 834	180 542	216 249	251 8 22	287 529	323 236
11.75	72 321	107 429	142 406	177 515	212 623	247 6 00	282 709	317 817
12.00	71 059	105 555	139 222	174 419	208 915	243 2 82	277 778	312 274
12.25	69 908	103 845	137 654	171 592	205 529	239 3 39	273 276	307 213
12.50	68 729	102 093	135 333	168 697	202 062	235 3 01	268 666	302 030
12.75	67 588	100 399	133 087	165 899	198 710	231 3 98	264 209	297 020
13.00	66 546	98 851	131 034	163 339	195 644	227 8 28	260 133	292 438
13.25	65 476	97 262	129 928	160 714	192 500	224 1 67	255 952	287 738
13.50	64 441	95 723	126 889	158 172	189 455	220 6 21	251 904	283 187
13.75	63 437	94 233	124 913	155 709	186 505	217 1 86	247 981	278 777

Source: *The Royal Bank of Canada*

(1) Compounded semi-annually. Mortgage payments based on a 25-year amortization.

Average Resale Value of Canadian Homes[1]

The average value of resale homes in Canada rose by $2 780 between 1992 and 1993, a small increase after two years of declining. The pattern varied widely from city to city: in Ontario, major cities continued to register a drop in average prices, while home values in such cities as Ottawa, Edmonton, Victoria and St. John's continued the decade's upward trend.

	1975	1980	1985	1990	1992	1993
Canada	$47 201	$67 044	$80 775	$143 379	$150 725	153 504
Toronto, Ont.	57 583	75 620	109 093	254 890	214 971	206 490
Vancouver, B.C.	57 763	100 065	112 852	226 385	245 260	279 758
Mississauga, Ont.	61 977	80 340	99 674	224 449	195 762	189 550
Victoria, B.C.	n.a.	85 066	88 451	160 743	194 666	210 650
Hamilton, Ont.	45 103	54 834	72 972	165 742	151 038	143 433
Ottawa, Ont.	49 633	63 177	107 640	141 562	143 869	145 626
Calgary, Alta.	48 341	93 977	80 462	128 484	129 506	133 998
Montreal, Que.	35 266	49 419	70 563	111 956	113 688	114 293
Edmonton, Alta.	43 846	84 622	74 309	101 040	109 602	111 823
Halifax, N.S.	n.a.	53 160	79 350	97 238	99 975	102 500
St. John's, Nfld.	n.a.	53 246	66 642	88 939	91 959	92 319
Winnipeg, Man.	33 463	50 490	62 478	81 740	81 990	83 058
Saint John, N.B.	35 884	45 170	57 088	78 041	81 560	85 398
Regina, Sask.	33 880	48 628	61 403	71 054	72 372	72 897

Source: *The Canadian Real Estate Association*

(1) Average price of all homes sold on the Multiple Listing Service. (n.a.) not available.

Personal Income and Savings

	Personal Income ($millions)	Annual % Change in Personal Income	Personal Disposable ($millions)	Personal Saving ($millions)	Personal Saving Rate
1926	4 057	n.a	3 988	433	10.9
1930	4 392	(5.9)	4 294	(87)	(2.0)
1935	3 398	7.0	3 294	(59)	(1.8)
1940	4 972	14.3	4 798	300	6.3
1945	9 292	3.1	8 354	1 351	16.2
1950	14 388	6.5	13 411	770	5.7
1955	21 438	7.9	19 504	815	4.2
1960	29 883	5.4	26 855	854	3.2
1965	42 118	10.4	37 317	2 281	6.1
1970	79 222	8.0	55 616	3 049	5.5
1975	138 578	16.7	113 321	14 146	12.5
1980	248 890	13.4	203 653	27 160	13.3
1981	393 215	17.8	237 682	35 744	15.0
1982	324 837	10.8	262 861	46 777	17.8
1983	343 052	5.6	276 013	40 303	14.6
1984	372 239	8.5	300 346	44 410	14.8
1985	400 199	7.5	321 337	42 047	13.1
1986	427 262	6.8	338 093	35 517	10.5
1987	461 191	7.9	361 435	32 769	9.1
1988	506 042	9.7	394 235	37 384	9.5
1989	550 180	8.7	432 135	44 200	10.3
1990	587 529	6.8	451 976	42 865	9.5
1991	604 859	3.0	464 866	44 025	9.5
1992	619 293	2.4	475 655	45 774	9.6
1993	633 223	2.3	487 651	44 560	9.2

Source: *Statistics Canada*

INVESTMENT

Investment: A Glossary of Terms

Annual report: A report issued by a company to its shareholders at the end of the fiscal year. It contains a report on company operations and formal financial statements.

Bankers' acceptance: A commercial draft backed by the guarantee of a bank. The bankers' acceptance promises repayment on a certain date, usually not more than 90 days away, and bears a rate of return competitive with other chartered bank securities.

Bear market: A market in which prices are falling.

Bid and ask: The bid price is the highest price anyone is willing to pay to buy a stock; the ask is the lowest price anyone will accept to sell a stock. Together, the bid and ask prices are a "quote."

Blue chip stocks: Stocks with good investment qualities, usually common shares of well-established companies with good earnings records and long-time dividend payments.

Board Lot: A unit of trading. Board lots on The Toronto Stock Exchange are: under 10 cents each—1000 shares; between 10 cents and 99 cents each—500 shares; at and above $1 each—100 shares.

Bond: A written promise or IOU by the issuer to repay a fixed amount of borrowed money on a specified date, and to pay a set annual rate of interest in the meantime, generally at semi-annual intervals. Bonds are usually considered a safe investment because the borrower (whether a company or the government) must make interest payments before its money is spent on anything else.

Bull market: A market in which prices are rising.

Call: An option to buy a fixed amount of a certain stock at a specified price within a specified time.

Canada Savings Bonds: These are issued each fall, and are popular with small investors, because they come in denominations starting at $100. They are not traded. They have a term of several years, and a minimum guaranteed rate of interest. However, the government sets an effective rate during the issuing period each year, and adjusts it when necessary to conform with interest rate trends. Interest can be awarded yearly or compounded, depending upon which type of bond the purchaser buys.

Capital gain or loss: Profit or loss resulting from the sale of an asset, such as a security. The gain or loss is the difference between the buying and selling price of the security, with commissions figured in.

Commercial paper: Short-term negotiable securities issued by corporations which call for the payment of a specific amount of money at a given time.

Common shares: Securities issued by the company which represent part-ownership in the company. Common shares sometimes carry a voting privilege and entitle the holder to a share in the company's profits, usually issued in the form of dividends.

Convertible bond: A corporate bond (see below) which may be converted into a stated number of shares of the corporation's common stock. Its price tends to fluctuate with the price of the stock, as well as with changes in interest rates.

Corporate bonds: Evidence of debt by a corporation. The bond bears interest much like a government bond, and matures at a certain date in the future. Considered safer than the common or preferred stock of the same company.

Day Order: An order to buy or sell a security valid only for the day the order is given.

Dividend: A portion of a company's profit paid to the common and preferred shareholders. The amount is decided upon by the company's board of directors, and may be paid in cash or stock.

Equities: Common and preferred stocks, which represent a share in the ownership of a company.

Ex-dividend: Without dividend. The buyer of shares quoted ex-dividend is not entitled to receive an already declared dividend. When shares are un-dividend, the purchaser will receive the declared dividend.

Floor trader: A brokerage firm employee who works on the stock exchange trading floor, and is responsible for executing buy and sell orders on behalf of the firm and its clients.

Futures: Contracts to buy or sell specific quantities of a commodity or financial instrument with delivery delayed until some agreed-upon time in the future.

Government of Canada Bonds: These bear a fixed rate of interest and a maturation date in the future, and are traded on the market, with the price rising and falling in response to interest rate trends. ▶

▶ Long-term government bonds are considered a safe investment. Provinces and municipalities may also issue long-term bonds.

Index: Statistical measure of the state of the stock market or economy, based on the performance of stocks or other components. Examples are the TSE 300 Composite Index and the Toronto 35 Index.

Limit order: An order to buy or sell securities in which the client has specified the price. The order can be executed only at the specified price or a better one.

Liquidity: The measure of how quickly an investor can turn securities into cash. A security is liquid if it can be bought and sold quickly with small price changes between transactions.

Long: A term signifying ownership of securities. "I am long 100 XYZ" means that the speaker owns 100 shares of XYZ.

Margin: The amount paid by clients when they use credit to buy a security, the balance being loaned by their brokers.

Market order: An order to buy a security immediately at the best possible price.

Money market: Part of the capital market established for short-term borrowing and lending of funds. Money market dealers conduct business over the telephone, and trade securities such as short-term (3 years and less) government bonds, government treasury bills and commercial paper.

Mutual fund: A portfolio, or selection, of professionally bought and managed stocks in which the investor pools money along with thousands of other people. A share price is based on net asset value, or the value of all the investments owned by the fund, less any debt, and divided by the total number of shares. The major advantage is less risk—an investment is spread out over many stocks, and if one or two do badly, the remainder may shield the investor from the losses. Bond funds are mutual funds that deal in the bond market exclusively. Money market mutual funds concentrate on debt instruments sold on the money market. Equity mutual funds place their investments in the common shares of companies.

Odd lot: A number of shares less than a board lot.

Open order: An order to buy or sell a security at a specified price, valid until executed or cancelled.

Over-The-Counter: The over-the-counter (OTC) or unlisted market is the market maintained by securities dealers for issues not listed on a stock exchange.

Penny stock: Low-priced, often speculative issues selling at less than $1 a share.

Preferred shares: Shares that carry dividends at fixed rates which must be paid before any dividends are paid to common shareholders.

Price/earnings ratio: A common stock's current market price divided by the company's annual per share earnings.

Prospectus: A legal document describing securities being offered for sale to the public. It must be prepared in accordance with provincial securities commission regulations.

Put: An option to sell a fixed amount of a certain stock at a specified price within a specified time.

Registered representative: A salesperson or broker employed by an investment firm. Salespersons must be registered with the provincial securities commission.

Right: A temporary privilege granted to existing common shareholders to purchase additional shares directly from the company at a stated price.

Settlement date: The date on which a securities buyer must pay for a purchase or a seller must deliver the securities sold. In general, settlement must be made on or before the fifth business day following the transaction date.

Short sale: The sale of shares which the seller does not own. The seller is speculating that the stock price will fall, in the hope of later purchasing the same number of securities at a lower price, thereby making a profit. Sellers must advise their brokers when they are selling short.

Stock yield: The percentage of the dividend paid in relation to the price of the stock. For example, a stock selling at $40 a share with an annual dividend of $2 a share yields five percent.

Transfer agent: A trust company appointed by a company to keep a record of the names, addresses and numbers of shares held by its shareholders. Transfer agents are often responsible for distributing dividend cheques.

Underwriting: The purchase for resale of a new issue of securities by an investment dealer or group of dealers.

Warrant: A certificate giving the holder the right to purchase securities at a stipulated price within a specified period of time. They are often detachable and may be traded separately.

Canadian Stock Exchange Trading

	Value traded	% of Canadian Total	% Value Change From Previous Year	Volume Traded	% of Canadian Total
Toronto					
1982	$17 670 332 337	80.0	-29.6	1 576 708 792	47.0
1987	100 224 304 252	77.3	+57.4	7 393 698 717	49.5
1992	76 161 051 067	74.8	+12.4	7 326 389 140	53.2
Montreal					
1982	2 773 415 534	12.5	-16.1	208 180 664	6.2
1987	21 875 596 915	16.9	+36.9	2 022 147 963	13.5
1992	21 063 915 203	20.7	+14.9	1 683 111 409	12.2
Vancouver					
1982	1 558 481 345	7.0	-59.6	1 442 747 544	43.0
1987	6 659 301 038	5.1	+48.3	4 795 142 825	32.1
1992	3 571 936 377	3.5	+3.1	3 899 206 755	28.3
Alberta					
1982	120 499 563	0.5	+71.8	126 130 894	3.7
1987	971 991 022	0.7	+104.2	740 753 453	4.9
1992	980 005 497	1.0	+72.9	867 960 979	6.3
Winnipeg					
1982	2 700 892	(1)	+195.4	2 017 108	0.1
1987	424 776	(1)	-23.2	150 032	(1)
1992	2 348 078	(1)	+100.5	15 112	(1)

Source: *Toronto Stock Exchange*

(1) Less than 1%.

Most Actively Traded Stocks, 1992

(based on Toronto Stock Exchange transactions)

Company	Shares Traded (millions)	Closing Price	High	Low
			(for 52 weeks)	
Nova Corp. Rv	118.8	8\frac{3}{4}$	9\frac{1}{8}$	6\frac{3}{4}$
Transcan Pipelines	96.9	17$\frac{5}{8}$	18$\frac{1}{2}$	16
Laidlaw Cl B Nv	94.1	11$\frac{5}{8}$	13$\frac{1}{8}$	$ 8$\frac{5}{8}$
Toronto Dominion Bank	94.0	16$\frac{5}{8}$	19$\frac{3}{4}$	15$\frac{3}{4}$
Placer Dome	93.5	14$\frac{3}{4}$	15$\frac{1}{2}$	10$\frac{3}{4}$
Bank of Nova Scotia	89.6	23$\frac{3}{4}$	24$\frac{3}{4}$	19$\frac{1}{8}$
Canadian Pacific Ltd.	87.0	16$\frac{1}{8}$	19$\frac{3}{8}$	13$\frac{1}{2}$
Royal Bank	82.5	24 $\frac{5}{8}$	29	21$\frac{1}{2}$
BCE Inc.	78.7	41$\frac{1}{2}$	50	40$\frac{7}{8}$
Alcan Aluminium	78.5	22$\frac{5}{8}$	26$\frac{3}{8}$	19$\frac{1}{8}$

Source: *Toronto Stock Exchange*

Nv = Non-voting; Rv = Restricted voting.

Top 10 Stock Gainers and Losers, TSE 1992

52-Week Price Climb				52-Week Price Slide			
Name of Stock	Open	Close	% Gain	Name of Stock	Open	Close	% Loss
United Reef Petroleums Ltd J	0.035	3.30	10 900	Society Minhourem J	3.00	0.15	95
Southernera Resouces Ltd. J	0.08	5.0	6 150	Claude Resources Inc. Pr J	3.40	0.25	93
Lytton Minerals Ltd J	0.07	2.08	3 367	Danio Industries	10.00	1.10	90
Canhorn Mining Corp J	0.11	3.05	2 673	Peoples Jewellers Ltd	10.00	1.05	90
Osborn and Chappel Goldfields Ltd US, J	0.01	0.22	2 100	Timmins Nickel Inc. J	0.67	0.08	88
Pure Gold Resources Inc. J	0.03	0.44	2 100	Claude Resources Inc. J	1.40	0.23	86
Queenstake Resources Ltd.	0.07	1.42	1 929	Petroleum Capital Energy Inc. J	0.10	0.03	85
CanCapital Corp.	0.03	0.26	1 633	Dynalta Energy Copr 10%RJ	3.00	0.50	82
Tyler Resources Inc. J	0.06	0.76	1 167	Coscan Development	8.125	1.50	82
Exall Resources Ltd J	0.15	1.38	1 050	Pan Pacific Pete Inc. J	0.60	0.12	80

Source: *Toronto Stock Exchange*

Government of Canada Average Bond Yields, 1981–93

Year	1 to 3 Years	3 to 5 Years	5 to 10 Years	10 Years and Over
1981	15.97	15.68	15.29	15.22
1982	13.95	14.00	14.03	14.26
1983	10.18	10.61	11.11	11.79
1984	11.67	11.91	12.42	12.75
1985	10.12	10.39	10.78	11.04
1986	9.09	9.21	9.37	9.52
1987	9.19	9.42	9.55	9.95
1988	9.67	9.77	9.76	10.22
1989	10.71	10.20	9.83	9.92
1990	11.65	11.19	10.82	10.85
1991	8.99	9.16	9.36	9.76
1992	7.03	7.43	8.16	8.77
1993	5.89	6.46	7.24	7.85

Source: *Bank of Canada*

Value of RRSP Holdings by Canadians

(millions of dollars)

Year	Value	Year	Value	Year	Value
1961	29	1972	403	1983	5 766
1962	33	1973	661	1984	6 647
1963	38	1974	931	1985	7 769
1964	45	1975	1 229	1986	8 787
1965	59	1976	1 598	1987	9 813
1966	79	1977	2 064	1988	11 212
1967	96	1978	2 400	1989	12 604
1968	116	1979	2 765	1990	13 645
1969	145	1980	3 355	1991	12 923
1970	187	1981	4 347	1992	14 688
1971	249	1982	5 068	1993	14 860

Source: *Statistics Canada*

Toronto Stock Exchange (TSE) Price Index,[1] 1971–92

Year	High[2]	Date	Low[2]	Date	Year End	Net Change	Percent Change
1971	1 036.09	Apr. 16	879.80	Nov. 12	990.54	43.00	4.54
1972	1 226.58	Dec. 29	1 044.60	Jan. 7	1 226.58	236.04	23.83
1973	1 329.28	Oct. 31	1 122.34	May 18	1 193.56	-33.02	-2.69
1974	1 276.81	Mar. 15	821.10	Dec. 6	844.48	-349.08	-29.25
1975	1 081.96	July 18	862.74	Jan. 3	953.54	109.06	12.91
1976	1 106.17	May 13	920.15	Nov. 30	1 011.52	57.98	6.08
1977	1 068.53	July 20	957.58	Oct. 26	1 059.59	48.07	4.75
1978	1 336.34	Oct. 12	996.88	Jan. 30	1 309.99	250.40	23.63
1979	1 813.48	Dec. 31	1 310.31	Jan. 2	1 813.17	503.18	38.41
1980	2 405.65	Dec. 1	1 670.89	Mar. 27	2 268.70	455.53	25.12
1981	2 393.33	July 17	1 752.70	Sept. 28	1 954.24	-314.46	-13.86
1982	1 958.08	Dec. 31	1 332.22	July 8	1 958.08	3.84	0.20
1983	2 611.79	Sept. 12	1 926.44	Jan. 4	2 552.35	594.27	30.35
1984	2 594.59	Jan. 9	2 077.36	July 25	2 400.33	-152.02	-5.96
1985	2 902.17	Dec. 31	2 347.49	Jan. 7	2 900.60	500.27	20.84
1986	3 134.50	Apr. 29	2 744.00	Jan. 23	3 066.18	165.58	5.71
1987	4 118.94	Aug. 13	2 783.25	Nov. 10	3 160.05	93.87	3.06
1988	3 478.94	July 6	2 976.32	Feb. 8	3 389.99	229.94	7.28
1989	4 037.83	Oct. 6	3 353.13	Jan. 3	3 969.79	579.80	17.10
1990	4 020.86	Jan. 3	3 007.80	Oct. 16	3 256.75	-713.04	-17.96
1991	3 604.09	Nov. 12	3 150.88	Jan. 16	3 512.36	255.61	7.85
1992	3 672.58	Jan. 16	3 149.97	Oct. 5	3 350.44	-161.92	-4.61

Source: *Toronto Stock Exchange*

(1) A composite index of 300 leading stocks. The rise or fall of the index shows stock market trends. (2) High and low values are selected from the following time frames: 1958–70, month-end; 1971–75, month-end or weekly; 1976, daily close; 1977 on, intra-day values.

Canada's International Investment Position

• Statistics Canada's preliminary 1993 estimates placed a book value of $313 billion on Canada's net liability position.

• In 1993 the United States continued to be the largest foreign net investor in Canada at $138 billion. Other major investors included Japan at $55 billion, and the United Kingdom at $51 billion.

• Foreign holdings of Canadian bonds amounted to $266 billion, and American investors were the major foreign holders of Canadian bonds, with 42% of them.

On the asset side, Canada's international assets grew by 13%, to $275 billion, at the end of 1993, the highest growth since 1988.

• The United States remained by far the most important country for Canadian direct investment, with $65 billion at the end of 1993.

• 83% of Canadian direct investment went to industrial countries in 1992.

Global Superlatives

Largest continent	Asia	44 485 900 sq. km
Smallest continent	Australia	7 682 300 sq. km
Largest ocean	Pacific	166 241 000 sq. km
Smallest ocean	Arctic	9 485 000 sq. km
Deepest point of any ocean	Mariana Trench, Pacific Ocean	10 924 m
Largest sea	South China Sea	2 974 600 sq. km
Largest lake	Caspian Sea, CIS-Iran	371 000 sq. km
Deepest lake	Lake Baykal, Russia	1 620 m
Largest freshwater lake	Lake Superior, North America	82 100 sq. km
Highest major lake	Lake Titicaca, Bolivia-Peru, South America	3 809 m
Lowest major lake	Caspian Sea, CIS-Iran	-28 m
Largest island	Greenland, Denmark	2 175 600 sq. km
Longest reef	Great Barrier Reef, Australia-Papua New Guinea	2 027 km
Longest river	Nile, Africa	6 671 km
Largest nation	Russia	17 075 272 sq. km
Smallest nation	Vatican City	.44 ha. km
Most populous nation	People's Republic of China (1993)	pop. 1 185 170 000
Oldest city	Damascus, Syria	continuously inhabited since c. 2500 B.C.
Highest point	Mount Everest, Nepal-Tibet	8 848 m
Lowest point	Dead Sea, Israel-Jordan	-400 m
Highest city	Bogotá, Colombia	2 639 m
Coldest city	Norilsk, Russia	average temp. -10.9°C
Hottest city	Djibouti, Djibouti	average temp. 30°C
Coldest place	Plateau Station, Antarctica	-56.7°C
Hottest place	Dalol, Danakil Depression, Ethiopia	35°C avg.
Coldest recorded temperature	Vostok, Antarctica (Australian territory), July 21, 1983	-89.2°C
Hottest recorded temperature (shade)	Al-Aziziyah, Libya, Sept. 13, 1922	58°C
Wettest spot	Mount Waialeale, Kauai, Hawaii	avg. ann. rainfall of 16 800 mm
Driest spot	Atacama Desert, Chile	avg. ann. precipitation barely measurable
Greatest snowfall in 24 hrs	Silver Lake, Colorado, U.S., Apr. 14–15, 1921	193 cm
Greatest rainfall in 24 hrs	Cilaos, Reunion Island, Indian Ocean, Mar. 15–16, 1952	1 870 cm
Largest desert	Sahara, Africa	9 million sq. km
Largest waterfall (by volume)	Khone, Kampuchea-Laos	11 610 cu. m/sec.
Tallest waterfall	Angel Falls, Venezuela	807 m
Largest gorge	Grand Canyon, Colorado River, Arizona	349 km long; 6–20 km wide; 1.6 km deep
Deepest gorge	Colca River Canyon, Peru	3 223 m
Oldest tree	a bristlecone pine, Wheeler's Peak, Nevada	approx. age of 5 100 yrs.
Greatest tides	Bay of Fundy, Nova Scotia	14.5 m
Most devastating volcanic eruption	Tambora, Sumbawa, Indonesia, Apr. 5–7, 1815	92 000 deaths
Longest covered bridge	Hartland, New Brunswick	390.8 m
Longest bridge	Humber, crossing the River Humber, near Hull, England	(main span length) 1 410 m
Largest man-made lake	Owen Falls, Uganda	2 700 000 cu. m
Longest street	Yonge Street, from Toronto, Ont. to Rainy River (at. Man. border)	1 896.2 km
Tallest building	Sears Tower, Chicago, Illinois	110 storeys, 443 m
Tallest free-standing structure	CN Tower, Toronto, Ont.	553.34 m
Most common language	Mandarin	approx. 750 million speakers
Most common religion	Christianity	(approx. 1/3 of world's pop.) 1 669 520 000

GEOGRAPHY

The Continents

Continent	Area (sq. km)	% of Earth's Land	Population	% of World Total
Asia	44 485 900	30.0	3 132 638 000	59.9
Africa	30 269 680	20.4	646 389 000	12.4
North America	24 235 280	16.3	416 664 500	8.0
South America	17 820 770	12.0	290 014 900	5.5
Antarctica	13 209 000	8.9	uninhabited	
Europe	10 530 750	7.1	715 233 800	13.7
Australia	7 682 300	5.2	16 820 000	.3
Islands of the Pacific	148 382	.1	9 636 000	.2

Source: *National Geographic Atlas of the World (1990)*

Highest and Lowest Points on Each Continent

Continent	Highest Point	(metres)	Lowest Point	(metres)
Asia	Everest	8 848	Dead Sea	-400
South America	Aconcagua	6 960	Valdés Peninsula	-40
North America	McKinley (Denali)	6 194	Death Valley	-86
Africa	Kilimanjaro	5 895	Lake Assal	-156
Europe	El'brus	5 642	Caspian Sea	-28
Antarctica	Vinson Massif	4 897	—	-2 538
Australia	Kosciusko	2 228	Lake Eyre	-16

Source: *National Geographic Atlas of the World (1990)*

World's Highest Cities

City	Altitude	City	Altitude
Bogotá, Colombia	2 639 m	Calgary, Alta.	1 045 m
Addis Ababa, Ethiopia	2 450 m	Sao Paulo, Brazil	776 m
Mexico City, Mexico	2 309 m	Ankara, Turkey	686 m
Nairobi, Kenya	1 820 m	Edmonton, Alta.	666 m
Johannesburg, South Africa	1 734 m	Madrid, Spain	655 m

Source: *Global Atlas, Gage Educational Publishing Co.*

Oceans' Area and Depth

Ocean	Area (sq. km)	% of Earth's Water Area	Deepest Point	Depth (metres)
Pacific	166 241 000	46.0	Mariana Trench	10 924
Atlantic	86 557 000	23.9	Puerto Rico Trench	8 605
Indian	73 427 000	20.3	Java Trench	7 258
Arctic	9 485 000	2.6	Eurasia Basin	5 122

Source: *National Geographic Atlas of the World (1990)*

Major Seas of the World

Sea	Area (sq. km)	Average Depth (metres)	Sea	Area (sq. km)	Average Depth (metres)
South China	2 974 600	1 464	Sea of Japan	1 012 900	1 667
Caribbean	2 515 900	2 575	Hudson Bay	730 100	93
Mediterranean	2 510 000	1 501	East China	664 600	189
Bering	2 261 100	1 491	Andaman	564 900	1 118
Gulf of Mexico	1 507 600	1 615	Black	507 900	1 191
Sea of Okhotsk	1 392 100	973	Red	453 000	538

Source: *National Geographic Atlas of the World (1990)*

Largest Lakes of the World

Lake	Location	Area sq. mi.	Area sq. km
Caspian (Sea)	Iran/CIS	146 100	378 400
Superior	Canada/U.S.	31 760	82 260
Aral (Sea)	Kazakhstan-Uzbekistan	24 750	64 100
Victoria	Kenya/Tanzania/Uganda	24 300	62 940
Huron	Canada/U.S.	23 000	59 580
Michigan	U.S.	22 400	58 020
20 Tanganyika	Burundi/Tanzania/Zaire/Zambia	12 350	32 000
Baykal	Russia	12 160	31 500
Great Bear	**NWT, Canada**	**12 030**	**31 150**
Great Slave	**NWT, Canada**	**11 030**	**28 570**

Source: *World Facts and Figures, 1989; Victor Showers; John Wiley & Sons, Inc.*

Major Islands of the World

Island	Area (sq. km)	Island	Area (sq. km)
Greenland (Denmark)	2 175 600	Sumatra (Indonesia)	427 300
New Guinea (independent)	792 500	Honshu (Japan)	227 400
Borneo (Indonesia)	725 500	Great Britain (independent)	218 100
Madagascar (independent)	587 000	**Victoria (Canada)**	**217 300**
Baffin (Canada)	**507 500**	Ellesmere (Canada)	196 200

Source: *National Geographic Atlas of the World (1990)*

Highest Waterfalls in the World

Fall/Country	Height[1] (m)	Fall/Country	Height[1] (m)
Angel, Venezuela	807	Pilao, Brazil	524
Monge, Norway	774	Montoya, Venezuela	505
Itatinga, Brazil	628	Ribbon, United States	491
Ormeli, Norway	563	Great, Guyana	488
Tusse, Norway	533	Vestre Mardals, Norway	468

Source: *World Facts and Figures, 1989; Victor Showers; John Wiley & Sons Inc.*

(1) Height of the greatest individual leap.

Highest Mountains by Continent

Peak	Mountain Range or System	Location	Elevation[1] ft	Elevation[1] m	First Ascent
■ Africa					
Kibo	n.a.	Tanganyika, Tanzania	19 340	5 890	1889
Mawensi	n.a.	Tanganyika, Tanzania	17 100	5 210	1912
Batian	n.a.	Kenya	17 050	5 200	1899
Nelion	n.a.	Kenya	17 020	5 190	1929
Margherita	Ruwenzori	Uganda/Zaire	16 760	5 110	1906
Alexandra	Ruwenzori	Uganda/Zaire	16 700	5 090	1906
Albert	Ruwenzori	Zaire	16 690	5 090	1932
Savoia	Ruwenzori	Uganda	16 330	4 980	1906
Elena	Ruwenzori	Uganda	16 300	4 970	1906
Elizabeth	Ruwenzori	Uganda	16 170	4 930	1953
■ Antarctica					
—	Sentinel	Antarctica	16 860	5140	1966
Tyree	Sentinel	Antarctica	16 290	4970	1967
Shinn	Sentinel	Antarctica	15 750	4800	1966
Gardner	Sentinel	Antarctica	15 370	4690	1966
Epperly	Sentinel	Antarctica	15 100	4600	n.a.
Kirkpatrick	Queen Alexandra	Antarctica	14 850	4530	n.a.
Elizabeth	Queen Alexandra	Antarctica	14 700	4480	n.a.
Markham	Queen Elizabeth	Antarctica	14 290	4360	n.a.
Bell	Queen Alexandra	Antarctica	14 120	4300	n.a.
Mackellar	Queen Alexandra	Antarctica	14 100	4300	n.a.
■ Asia					
Everest (alt Qomolangma, Chumulangma)	Nepal Himalaya	China/Nepal	29 030	8 850	1953
K2 (alt Chogori, Dapsang, Godwin Austen)	Karakoram	Pakistan-held Kashmir	28 250	8 610	1954
Kangchenjunga (alt Kanchenjunga): highest peak	Nepal Himalaya	India/Nepal	28 170	8 590	1955
Lhotse (alt E1, Luozi, Lotzu)	Nepal Himalaya	China/Nepal	27 890	8 500	1956
Kangchenjunga: S peak	Nepal Himalaya	India/Nepal	27 800	8 470	n.a.
Makalu I	Nepal Himalaya	China/Nepal	27 790	8 470	1955
Kangchenjunga: W peak	Nepal Himalaya	India/Nepal	27 620	8 420	1973
Lhotse Shar (alt Lhotse: E peak)	Nepal Himalaya	China/Nepal	27 500	8 380	1970
Dhaulagiri I (alt Daulagiri I)	Nepal Himalaya	Nepal	26 810	8 170	1960
Cho Oyu (alt Zhuoaoyu, Choaoyu): highest peak	Nepal Himalaya	China/Nepal	26 750	8 150	1954
■ Europe					
Elbrus (for Elborus): W peak	Caucasus (off Kavkaz)	Russia	18 480	5630	1874
Elbrus: E peak	Caucasus	Russia	18 360	5 590	1829
Shkhara: E peak	Caucasus	Georgia/Russia	17 060	5 200	1888
Dykh(-Tau): W peak	Caucasus	Russia	17 050	5 200	1888
Dykh(-Tau): E peak	Caucasus	Russia	16 900	5 150	1938
Koshtan(-Tau)	Caucasus	Russia	16 880	5 140	1888
Shkhara: W peak	Caucasus	Georgia/Russia	16 880	5 140	n.a.
Pushkina	Caucasus	Russia	16 730	5 100	1938
Dzhangi(-Tau): NW peak	Caucasus	Georgia	16 570	5 050	1903
Kazbek: E peak	Caucasus	Georgia	16 560	5 050	1868 ▶

▶ ■ **North America**

McKinley: S peak	Alaska	Alaska, U.S.	20 320	6 190	1913
Logan: central peak	Saint Elias	Yukon, Canada	19 520	5 959	1925
Logan: W peak	Saint Elias	Yukon, Canada	19 470	5 930	1925
McKinley: N peak	Alaska	Alaska, U.S.	19 470	5 930	1910
Logan: E peak	Saint Elias	Yukon, Canada	19 420	5 920	1957
Citlaltepetl (alt Orizaba)	Neovolcanica	Puebla-Veracruz, Mexico	18 410	5 610	1848
Logan: N peak	Saint Elias	Yukon, Canada	18 270	5 570	1959
Saint Elias	Saint Elias	Canada/U.S.	18 010	5 490	1897
Popocatepetl	Neovolcanica	Puebla, Mexico	17 930	5 460	1520
Foraker	Alaska	Alaska, U.S.	17 400	5 300	1934

■ **Oceania**

Jaya (for Carstensz, Djaja, Sukarno)	Sudirman (for Nassau)	Irian Jaya, Indonesia	16 500	5 030	1936
Daam	Jayawijaya (for Djajawidjaja, Orange)	Irian Jaya, Indonesia	16 150	4 920	n.a.
Pilimsit (for Idenburg)	Sudirman	Irian Jaya, Indonesia	15 750	4 800	1962
Trikora (for Wilhelmina)	Jayawijaya	Irian Jaya, Indonesia	15 580	4 750	1913
Mandala (for Juliana)	Jayawijaya	Irian Jaya, Indonesia	15 420	4 700	1959
Wilhelm	Bismarck	Papua New Guinea	15 400	4 690	n.a.
Wisnumurti (for Jan Pieterszoon Coen)	Jayawijaya	Irian Jaya, Indonesia	15 080	4 590	n.a.
Yamin (for Prins Hendrik)	Jayawijaya	Irian Jaya, Indonesia	14 860	4 530	n.a.
Kubor	Kubor	Papua New Guinea	14 300	4 360	n.a.
Herbert	Bismarck	Papua New Guinea	14 000	4 270	n.a.

■ **South America**

Aconcagua	Andes	Mendoza, Argentina	22 840	6 960	1897
Ojos del Salado: SE peak	Andes	Argentina/Chile	22 560	6 870	1937
Bonete	Andes	La Rioja, Argentina	22 550	6 870	1913
Pissis	Andes	Catamarca, La Rioja, Argentina	22 240	6 780	1937
Huascaran: S peak	Blanca (Andes)	Peru	22 210	6 770	1932
Mercedario	Andes	San Juan, Argentina	22 210	6 770	1934
Llullaillaco	Andes	Argentina/Chile	22 100[1]	6 730	bef 1550
Libertador (for Cachi: N peak)	Andes	Salta, Argentina	22 050	6 720	1950
Ojos del Salado: NW peak	Andes	Argentina/Chile	22 050	6 720	1937
Tupungato	Andes	Argentina/Chile	21 900	6 670	1897

Source: *World Facts and Figures, 1989; Victor Showers; John Wiley & Sons, Inc.*

(1) Rounded figures except from some Canadian peaks from Energy, Mines and Resources Canada. n.a. not available or not applicable.

Longest Rivers in The World

River	Outflow and Location	Length mi.	Length km
Nile-Kagera-Ruvuvu-Luvironza	Mediterranean Sea, Egypt	4 140	6 670
Amazon-Ucayali-Tambo-Ene-Apurimac	Atlantic Ocean, Amapa-Para, Brazil	4 080	6 650
Yangtze	East China Sea, Jiangsu, China	3 720	5 980
Mississippi-Missouri-Jefferson-Beaverhead-Red Rock	Gulf of Mexico, Louisiana, U.S.	3 710	5 970
Yenisey-Angara-Selenga-Ider	Yenisey Gulf of Kara Sea, Russia	3 650	5 870
Amur-Argun-Kerulen	Tatar Strait, Russia	3 590	5 780
Ob-Irtysh	Gulf of Ob of Kara Sea, Russia	3 360	5 410
Plata-Parana-Grande	Atlantic Ocean, Argentina-Uruguay	3 030	4 880
Huang	Gulf of Chihli of Yellow Sea, Shandong, China	3 010	4 840
Congo-Lualaba	Atlantic Ocean, Angola-Zaire	2 880	4 630

Source: *World Facts and Figures, 1989; Victor Showers; John Wiley & Sons, Inc.*

POPULATION

The World's Most Populous Nations, 1992

China	1 188 000 000	Brazil	154 100 000
India	879 500 000	Pakistan	124 800 000
USSR (former)	284 500 000	Japan	124 500 000
United States	255 200 000	Bangladesh	119 300 000
Indonesia	191 200 000	Nigeria	115 700 000

Source: *The State of the World Population, 1993, U.N. Population Fund*

World's 20 Largest Cities, Ranked by Population Size, 1950–90

(millions of people)

	1950 City	Pop		1970 City	Pop		1990 City	Pop
1	New York, USA	12.3	1	New York, USA	16.2	1	Mexico City, Mexico	20.2
2	London, UK	8.7	2	Tokyo, Japan	14.9	2	Tokyo, Japan	18.1
3	Tokyo, Japan	6.7	3	Shanghai, China	11.2	3	Sao Paulo, Brazil	17.4
4	Paris, France	5.4	4	Mexico City, Mexico	9.4	4	New York, USA	16.2
5	Shanghai, China	5.3	5	London, UK	8.6	5	Shanghai, China	13.4
6	Buenos Aires, Argen.	5.0	6	Buenos Aires, Argen.	8.4	6	Los Angeles, USA	11.9
7	Chicago, USA	4.9	7	Los Angeles, USA	8.4	7	Calcutta, India	11.8
8	Moscow, USSR	4.8	8	Paris, France	8.3	8	Buenos Aires, Argen.	11.5
9	Calcutta, India	4.4	9	Beijing, China	8.1	9	Bombay, India	11.2
10	Los Angeles, USA	4.0	10	Sao Paulo, Brazil	8.1	10	Seoul, Korea	11.0
11	Beijing, China	3.9	11	Osaka, Japan	7.6	11	Beijing, China	10.8
12	Osaka, Japan	3.8	12	Moscow, USSR	7.1	12	Rio de Janeiro, Brazil	10.7
13	Milan, Italy	3.6	13	Rio de Janeiro, Brazil	7.0	13	Tianjin, China	9.4
14	Mexico City, Mexico	3.1	14	Calcutta, India	6.9	14	Jakarta, Indonesia	9.3
15	Philadelphia, USA	2.9	15	Chicago, USA	6.7	15	Cairo, Egypt	9.0
16	Bombay, India	2.9	16	Bombay, India	5.8	16	Moscow, USSR	8.8
17	Rio de Janeiro, Brazil	2.9	17	Milan, Italy	5.5	17	Delhi, India	8.8
18	Detroit, USA	2.8	18	Cairo, Egypt	5.3	18	Osaka, Japan	8.5
19	Naples, Italy	2.8	19	Seoul, Korea	5.3	19	Paris, France	8.5
20	Leningrad, USSR	2.6	20	Tianjin, China	5.2	20	Metro Manila, Philip.	8.5

Source: *The State of World Population, 1993, UN Population Fund*

20 Most Populous Cities (millions of people) in the Year 2000

*T*he UN Population Fund estimates that by the year 2000, the 20 most populous cities will be:

	City	Pop.		City	Pop.
1	Mexico City, Mexico	25.6	11	Delhi, India	13.2
2	Sao Paulo, Brazil	22.1	12	Buenos Aires, Argentina	12.9
3	Tokyo, Japan	19.0	13	Lagos, Nigeria	12.9
4	Shanghai, China	17.0	14	Tianjin, China	12.7
5	New York, USA	16.8	15	Seoul, Korea	12.7
6	Calcutta, India	15.7	16	Rio de Janeiro, Brazil	12.5
7	Bombay, India	15.4	17	Dhaka, Bangladesh	12.2
8	Beijing, China	14.0	18	Cairo, Egypt	11.8
9	Los Angeles, USA	13.9	19	Metro Manila, Philippines	11.8
10	Jakarta, Indonesia	13.7	20	Karachi, Pakistan	11.7

Population Projections, by Region and for Selected Countries: 1990 to 2025

(in millions)

Region and Country	1990	2025
World total	**5 295.3**	**8 472.4**
More developed[1]	1 211.1	1 403.3
Less developed[1]	4 084.2	7 069.2
Africa	**642.6**	**1 582.5**
Eastern Africa[2]	194.8	516.0
Burundi	5.5	13.4
Comoros	0.5	1.6
Djibouti	0.4	1.2
Ethiopia	49.8	130.7
Kenya	23.6	63.8
Madagascar	12.0	33.7
Malawi	9.6	24.9
Mauritius	1.1	1.4
Mozambique	14.2	36.3
Reunion	0.6	0.9
Rwanda	7.0	20.1
Seychelles	0.1	0.1
Somalia	8.7	23.4
Uganda	17.6	45.9
Tanzania	26.0	74.2
Zambia	8.1	21.0
Zimbabwe	9.9	22.9
Middle Africa	70.5	190.0
Angola	9.2	26.6
Cameroon	11.5	29.2
Cen. African Rep.	3.0	7.0
Chad	5.6	12.9
Congo	2.2	5.8
Equatorial Guinea	0.4	0.8
Gabon	1.2	2.9
Sao Tome and Principe	0.1	0.2
Zaire	37.4	104.5
Northern Africa[2]	140.5	280.4
Algeria	25.0	51.8
Egypt	52.4	93.5
Libya	4.5	12.8
Morocco	25.1	47.5
Sudan	25.2	60.6
Tunisia	8.1	13.4
Southern Africa	43.1	85.3
Botswana	1.2	2.9
Lesotho	1.7	3.8
Namibia	1.4	3.8
South Africa	37.9	73.2
Swaziland	0.8	1.7
Western Africa[2]	193.7	510.8
Benin	4.6	12.4
Burkina Faso[3]	9.0	22.6
Cape Verde	0.4	0.8
Côte d'Ivoire	12.0	37.9
Gambia	0.9	1.9
Ghana	15.0	38.0
Guinea	5.8	15.1
Guinea-Bissau	1.0	2.0
Liberia	2.6	7.2
Mali	9.2	24.6

Region and Country	1990	2025
Mauritania	2.0	5.0
Niger	7.7	21.3
Nigeria	108.5	285.8
Senegal	7.3	17.1
Sierra Leone	4.2	9.8
Togo	3.5	9.4
Latin America	**441.1**	**701.6**
Caribbean[2]	33.6	50.4
Antigua and Barbuda	0.1	0.1
Aruba	0.1	0.1
Bahamas	0.3	0.4
Barbados	0.3	0.3
Cuba	10.6	13.0
Dominica	0.1	0.1
Dominican Rep.	7.2	11.4
Grenada	0.1	0.1
Haiti	6.5	13.1
Jamaica	2.4	3.5
Puerto Rico	3.5	4.7
Saint Kitts and Nevis	...	...
Saint Lucia	0.1	0.2
St. Vincent & the Grenadines	0.1	0.2
Trinidad and Tobago	1.2	1.8
Central America	113.3	199.2
Belize	0.2	0.3
Costa Rica	3.0	5.6
El Salvador	5.2	9.7
Guatemala	9.2	21.7
Honduras	5.1	11.5
Mexico	84.5	137.5
Nicaragua	3.7	9.1
Panama	2.4	3.9
South America[2]	294.1	451.9
Argentina	32.3	45.5
Bolivia	7.2	14.1
Brazil	149.0	219.7
Chile	13.2	19.8
Colombia	32.3	49.4
Ecuador	10.5	18.6
Guyana	0.8	1.1
Paraguay	4.3	9.2
Peru	21.6	37.4
Suriname	0.4	0.7
Uruguay	3.1	3.7
Venezuela	19.3	32.7
Northern America[2]	**276.7**	**360.5**
Canada	26.6	38.4
United States	250.0	322.0
Asia	**3 117.8**	**4 900.3**
Eastern Asia[2]	1 350.5	1 762.2
China	1 153.5	1 539.8
Hong Kong	5.7	6.4
Japan	123.5	127.0
North Korea	21.8	33.3
South Korea	43.4	50.3 ▶

Mongolia	2.2	4.6
South-Eastern Asia[2]	444.1	715.6
Brunei Darussalam	0.3	0.4
Cambodia	8.3	16.7
Indonesia	184.3	283.3
Laos	4.2	9.4
Malaysia	17.9	31.3
Myanmar	41.8	75.6
Philippines	62.4	105.1
Singapore	2.7	3.3
Thailand	54.7	72.3
Vietnam	66.7	117.0
Southern Asia	1 191.1	2 135.8
Afghanistan	16.6	45.8
Bangladesh	113.7	223.3
Bhutan	1.5	3.4
India	846.2	1 393.9
Iran	58.3	144.6
Maldives	0.2	0.5
Nepal	19.6	40.1
Pakistan	118.1	259.6
Sri Lanka	17.2	24.7
Western Asia[2]	131.9	286.6
Bahrain	0.5	1.0
Cyprus	0.7	0.9
Iraq	18.1	46.3
Israel	4.7	8.1
Jordan	4.0	10.8
Kuwait	2.1	2.8
Lebanon	2.7	4.5
Oman	1.5	4.7
Qatar	0.4	0.7
Saudi Arabia	14.9	40.4
Syria	12.3	35.3
Turkey	56.0	92.9
United Arab Emirates	1.6	2.8
Yemen	11.7	34.2
Europe (excl. Soviet Union)	**509.0**	**541.8**
Eastern Europe	96.6	107.2
Bulgaria	9.0	8.8
Czechoslovakia	15.7	17.9
Hungary	10.6	10.4
Poland	38.2	43.8
Romania	23.2	26.3
Northern Europe[2]	92.4	97.8
Denmark	5.1	5.1
Estonia	1.6	1.6
Finland	5.0	5.2
Iceland	0.3	0.3
Ireland	3.5	3.6
Latvia	2.7	2.8
Lithuania	3.7	4.1
Norway United Kingdom	57.4	60.3
Southern Europe[2]	144.1	148.2
Albania	3.3	4.5
Andorra	...	0.1
Greece	10.1	10.1
Italy	57.7	56.2
Malta	0.4	0.4
Portugal	9.9	10.1
San Marino	...	...
Spain	39.0	40.6
Yugoslavia	23.8	26.0
Western Europe	176.0	188.7
Austria	7.7	8.3
Belgium	10.0	9.9
France	56.7	60.8
Germany	79.5	83.9
Liechtenstein	...	...
Luxembourg	0.4	0.4
Monaco	...	...
Netherlands	14.9	17.7
Switzerland	6.7	7.7
Soviet Union (former)	**281.3**	**344.5**
Oceania[2]	**26.7**	**41.3**
Australia	17.1	25.2
Fiji	0.7	1.0
Kiribati	0.1	0.1
Nauru	...	...
New Zealand	3.4	4.3
Papua New Guinea	3.9	7.8
Solomon Islands	0.3	0.8
Tonga	0.1	0.1
Tuvalu	...	...
Vanautu	0.2	0.3

Source: *World Population Prospects: The 1992 Revision, Population Division of the United Nations*

(1) Regions. (2) Includes areas not shown separately. (3) Formerly Upper Volta. (. . .) = too small to be included.

UN Conference on Population

*D*elegates from 180 countries met in Cairo in Sept., 1994 to discuss limiting population growth. Demographers predict that the present average global birthrate of 3.3 children per woman will bring world population to 9 billion by 2030. Many experts suggest this level is close to the limit or beyond the ability of the earth to sustain and will have serious environmental and social consequences.

The conference hoped to encourage policies that would lower the average global birthrate to 2 children per woman, and keep the population under 8 billion by 2050.

The World's Largest Industrial Corporations, 1994

Company (Ranked by 1993 Sales)	Country	Sales (millions)	Profits (millions)	Employees
General Motors (1)	U.S.	$133 621.9	$2 465.8	710 800
Ford Motor (3)	U.S.	108 521.0	2 529.0	322 200
Exxon (2)	U.S.	97 825.0	5 280.0	91 000
Royal Dutch/Shell Group (4)	Brit./Netherlands	95 134.4	4 505.2	117 000
Toyota Motor (5)	Japan	85 283.2	1 473.9	109 279
Hitachi (10)	Japan	68 581.8	605.0	330 637
Intl. Business Machines (7)	U.S.	62 716.0	(8 101.0)	267 196
Matsushita Electric Industrial (12)	Japan	61 384.5	227.0	254 059
General Electric (9)	U.S.	60 823.0	4 315.0	222 000
Daimler-Benz (8)	Germany	59 102.0	364.0	366 736
Mobil (13)	U.S.	56 576.0	2 084.0	61 900
Nissan Motor (16)	Japan	53 759.8	(805.5)	143 310
British Petroleum (11)	Britain	52 485.4	923.6	72 600
Samsung (18)	South Korea	51 345.2	519.7	191 303
Philip Morris (17)	U.S.	50 621.0	3 091.0	173 000
IRI (6)	Italy	50 488.1	n.a.	366 471
Siemens (15)	Germany	50 381.3	1 112.6	391 000
Volkswagen (14)	Germany	46 311.9	(1 232.4)	251 643
Chrysler (28)	U.S.	43 600.0	(2 551.0)	128 000
Toshiba (25)	Japan	42 917.2	112.5	175 000
Unilever (20)	Brit./Netherlands	41 842.6	1 946.2	302 000
Nestlé (23)	Switzerland	38 894.5	1 953.3	209 755
Elf Aquitaine (22)	France	37 016.3	188.9	94 000
Honda Motor (30)	Japan	35 797.9	219.6	91 300
ENI (21)	Italy	34 791.3	266.6	106 391

Source: *Fortune, ©1994 Time Inc. All rights reserved*

The Biggest Companies in the World by Industry [1]

Industry	Company	Country	Sales (million)	Profits (million)
Aerospace	Boeing	U.S.	$ 25 285	$ 1 244
Apparel	Levi Strauss Associates	U.S.	5 892	492
Beverages	Pepsico	U.S.	25 021	1 588
Building materials	Saint-Gobain	France	12 630	232
Chemicals	E.I. Du Pont de Nemours	U.S.	32 621	555
Computers (incl. office equipment)	IBM	U.S.	62 716	-8 101
Electronics	Hitachi	Japan	68 582	605
Food	Philip Morris	U.S.	50 621	3 091
Forest products	International Paper	U.S.	13 685	289
Industrial and farm equipment	Mitsubishi Heavy Industries	Japan	25.804	740
Jewelry, watches	Citizen Watch	Japan	3 501	69
Metal Products	Pechiney	France	11 127	-173
Metals	IRI	Italy	50 488	n.a.
Mining, crude oil production	Ruhrkohle	Germany	14 155	7
Motor vehicles and parts	General Motors	U.S.	133 622	2 466
Petroleum refining	Exxon	U.S.	97 825	5 280
Pharmaceuticals	Johnson & Johnson	U.S.	14 138	1 787
Publishing, printing	Bertelsmann	Germany	10 957	289
Rubber and plastics products	Bridgestone	Japan	14 377	255
Scientific and photo. equipment	Eastman Kodak	U.S.	20 059	-1 515
Soaps, cosmetics	Procter & Gamble	U.S.	30 433	-656
Textiles	Toray Industries	Japan	8 193	132
Tobacco	RJR Nabisco Holdings	U.S.	15 104	-145
Toys, sporting goods	Nintendo	Japan	4 500	488
Transportation equipment	Hyundai Heavy Industries	S. Korea	6 735	158

Source: *Fortune, ©1994 Time Inc. All rights reserved*

(1) Ranked by sales.

World Agricultural Production

(thousands of metric tons)

	1987 Total	1992 Total		1987 Total	1992 Total
■ Total Cereals			**■ Coarse Grains**		
World production	1 771 845	1 952 224	World production	803 042	863 101
North America (dev.)	332 432	492 591	North America (dev.)	243 246	297 588
Europe	275 000	255 616	Europe	156 467	137 861
Oceania (dev.)	20 959	25 758	Oceania (dev.)	7 727	9 459
Other developed	26 226	19 348	Other developed	8 631	3 761
Africa developing	57 329	58 364	Africa developing	42 956	41 890
Latin America	111 875	114 058	Latin America	71 376	77 515
Near East developing	64 203	80 392	Near East developing	22 127	28 395
Far East developing	698 771	809 993	Far East developing	145 245	172 404
Other developing	28	39	Other developing	4	5
Former USSR	185 021	186 155	Former USSR	105 262	94 224
EEC	168 176	170 780	EEC	90 478	82 987
■ Wheat			**■ Corn**		
World production	504 865	563 649	World production	450 902	526 410
North America (dev.)	83 307	96 790	North America (dev.)	188 157	245 305
Europe	116 382	115 498	Europe	54 789	52 824
Oceania (dev.)	12 624	15 171	Oceania (dev.)	383	370
Other developed	4 308	2 329	Other developed	7 361	3 128
Africa developing	6 408	6 376	Africa developing	17 096	15 560
Latin America	22 319	18 214	Latin America	56 394	64 281
Near East developing	37 198	44 923	Near East developing	6 782	8 268
Far East developing	144 988	174 422	Far East developing	105 129	129 308
Other developing	·	1	Other developing	3	5
Former USSR	77 331	89 925	Former USSR	14 808	7 362
EEC	75 815	85 646	EEC	25 864	29 193
■ Rice (paddy)			**■ Barley**		
World production	463 939	525 475	World production	175 475	160 134
North America (dev.)	5 879	8 123	North America (dev.)	25 311	20 855
Europe	2 151	2 257	Europe	69 280	59 777
Oceania (dev.)	608	1 128	Oceania (dev.)	3 818	5 885
Other developed	13 287	13 258	Other developed	653	450
Africa developing	7 965	10 098	Africa developing	4 069	4 071
Latin America	18 181	18 329	Latin America	1 596	1 737
Near East developing	4 878	7 075	Near East developing	11 792	13 333
Far East developing	408 538	463 167	Far East developing	5 614	4 397
Other developing	24	34	Other developing	3	5
Former USSR	2 428	2 006	Former USSR	53 342	49 630
EEC	1 883	2 148	EEC	51 578	43 400

NOTES: The country categories are defined as follows: **North America (dev.):** Canada, US; **Europe:** Albania, Andorra, Austria, Belgium-Luxembourg, Bulgaria, former Czechoslovakia, Denmark, Faeroe Islands, Finland, France, Germany, Gibralter, Greece, Holy See, Hungary, Iceland, Ireland, Italy, Liechtenstein, Malta, Monaco, Netherlands, Norway, Poland, Portugal, Romania, San Marino, Spain, Sweden, Switzerland, United Kingdom, former Yugoslavia SFR; **Oceania (dev.):** Australia, New Zealand; **Other developed:** Israel, Japan, South Africa; **Africa developing:** all African countries except South Africa, Egypt, Libya and Sudan; **Latin America:** all countries in South or Central America or the Caribbean unless otherwise noted; **Near East developing:** Afghanistan, Bahrain, Cyprus, Egypt, Gaza Strip, Islamic Republic of Iran, Iraq, Jordan, Kuwait, Lebanon, Libyan Arab Jamahiriya, Oman, Qatar, Kingdom of Saudi Arabia, Sudan, Syrian Arab Republic, Turkey, United Arab Emirates, Yemen; **Far East developing:** Bangladesh, Bhutan, Brunei Darussalam, Cambodia, China, East Timor, Hong Kong, India, Indonesia, North and South Korea, Laos, Macau, Malaysia, Maldives, Mongolia, Myanmar, Nepal, Pakistan, Philippines, Singapore, Sri Lanka, Thailand, Viet Nam; **Other developing:** Bermuda, Greenland, Saint Pierre & Miquelon, American Samoa, Canton and Enderbury Is., Christmas Is., Cocos Is., Cook Is., Fiji, French Polynesia, Guam, Johnston Is., Kiribati, Midway Is., Nauru, New Caledonia, Niue Is., Norfolk Is., ▶

	1987 Total	1992 Total
■ Root Crops		
World production	574 986	586 124
North America (dev.)	21 222	22 736
Europe	105 564	83 204
Oceania (dev.)	1 311	1 453
Other developed	7 317	7 082
Africa developing	87 412	112 862
Latin America	46 102	46 286
Near East developing	10 281	11 215
Far East developing	218 249	226 535
Other developing	1 620	1 727
Former USSR	75 908	73 024
EEC	55 013	46 977

	1987 Total	1992 Total
■ Potatoes		
World production	279 403	268 492
North America (dev.)	20 692	22 200
Europe	105 463	83 119
Oceania (dev.)	1 297	1 433
Other developed	5 189	5 065
Africa developing	4 046	4 366
Latin America	11 542	12 329
Near East developing	9 908	10 846
Far East developing	45 350	56 101
Other developing	9	8
Former USSR	75 908	73 024
EEC	54 916	46 895

	1987 Total	1992 Total
■ Total Pulses		
World production	53 531	57 455
North America (dev.)	2 374	2 166
Europe	6 421	7 031
Oceania (dev.)	1 608	1 726
Other developed	245	200
Africa developing	5 114	6 289
Latin America	4 545	5 344
Near East developing	3 355	3 415
Far East developing	21 037	23 144
Other developing	5	5
Former USSR	8 827	8 135
EEC	4 545	5 218

	1987 Total	1992 Total
■ Vegetables and Melons		
World production	436 381	456 170
North America (dev.)	30 067	32 307
Europe	67 461	66 796
Oceania (dev.)	1 789	2 101
Other developed	18 191	16 799
Africa developing	17 765	19 094
Latin America	20 894	22 618
Near East developing	48 811	47 281
Far East developing	197 049	219 159
Other developing	406	445
Former USSR	33 949	29 572
EEC	48 125	50 967

	1987 Total	1992 Total
■ Fruit		
World production	335 356	369 518
North America (dev.)	26 529	27 722
Europe	71 060	75 069
Oceania (dev.)	3 017	3 456
Other developed	11 628	10 000
Africa developing	32 842	36 272
Latin America	69 366	83 814
Near East developing	25 071	29 698
Far East developing	79 894	89 870
Other developing	1 627	1 899
Former USSR	14 321	11 720
EEC	58 180	61 671

	1987 Total	1992 Total
■ Apples		
World production	38 418	43 087
North America (dev.)	5 378	5 397
Europe	12 573	15 527
Oceania (dev.)	663	719
Other developed	1 504	1 724
Africa developing	243	409
Latin America	2 644	3 285
Near East developing	3 376	4 140
Far East developing	6 540	7 385
Other developing	-	-
Former USSR	5 496	4 500
EEC	8 711	10 810

▶ Pacific Is., Papua New Guinea, Pitcairn, Samoa, Solomon Is., Tokelau, Tonga, Tuvalu, Vanuatu, Wake Is., Wallis and Futuna Is.; **Former USSR:** Armenia, Azerbaijan, Georgia, Kazakhstan, Kyrgyzstan, Tajikistan, Turkmenistan, Uzbekistan, Belarus, Estonia, Latvia, Lithuania, Moldova, Russian Federation, Ukraine. **Total cereals** include dry grain only, including mixed grains and buckwheat. Not including hay, feed, silage, grazing grain. **Wheat** does not include spelt, except for former USSR figures. **Root crops** does not incl. crops grown for feed such as turnips, mangels and swedes. **Pulses** incl. the edible seeds of peas, beans, lentils. **Vegetables and Melons** incl. crops grown for human consumption, and excl. crops grown in kitchen gardens or small family gardens.

Source: Food and Agriculture Organization of the UN, *FAO Production Yearbook , 1992*

Beverage Crops	1987 Total	1992 Total
■ Cocoa Beans		
World production	2 063	2 329
North America (dev.)	-	-
Europe	-	-
Oceania (dev.)	-	-
Other developed	-	-
Africa developing	1 219	1 259
Latin America	572	620
Near East developing	-	-
Far East developing	236	408
Other developing	37	42
Former USSR	-	-
EEC	-	-
■ Green Coffee		
World production	6 378	5 919
North America (dev.)	1	1
Europe	-	-
Oceania (dev.)	-	-
Other developed	-	-
Africa developing	1 242	1 216
Latin America	4 255	3 710
Near East developing	5	8
Far East developing	812	945
Other developing	63	48
Former USSR	-	-
EEC	-	-
■ Tea		
World production	2 391	2 473
North America (dev.)	-	-
Europe	-	-
Oceania (dev.)	-	-
Other developed	106	99
Africa developing	257	286
Latin America	64	65
Near East developing	184	187
Far East developing	1 616	1 719
Other developing	8	9
Former USSR	156	109
EEC	-	-

	1987 Total	1992 Total
■ Total Meat		
World production	162 877	182 064
North America (dev.)	29 790	33 779
Europe	42 977	42 110
Oceania (dev.)	4 066	4 495
Other developed	5 064	5 060
Africa developing	5 421	6 016
Latin America	16 791	20 125
Near East developing	4 381	5 007
Far East developing	35 419	48 928
Other developing	84	89
Former USSR	18 884	16 455
EEC	30 347	30 981
■ Total Milk		
World production	520 743	182 064
North America (dev.)	72 815	76 346
Europe	177 178	158 707
Oceania (dev.)	13 655	15 080
Other developed	10 731	11 723
Africa developing	12 102	11 137
Latin America	39 207	44 352
Near East developing	21 243	21 585
Far East developing	70 457	97 777
Other developing	64	76
Former USSR	103 792	89 247
EEC	123 659	114 200
■ Hen Eggs		
World production	32 580	36 111
North America (dev.)	4 494	4 493
Europe	7 256	6 875
Oceania (dev.)	231	259
Other developed	2 661	2 916
Africa developing	853	980
Latin America	3 563	4 108
Near East developing	1 162	1 383
Far East developing	7 764	11 087
Other developing	10	11
Former USSR	4 587	4 000
EEC	5 122	5 008

NOTES: The country categories are defined as follows: **North America (dev.):** Canada, US; **Europe:** Albania, Andorra, Austria, Belgium-Luxembourg, Bulgaria, former Czechoslovakia, Denmark, Faeroe Islands, Finland, France, Germany, Gibralter, Greece, Holy See, Hungary, Iceland, Ireland, Italy, Liechtenstein, Malta, Monaco, Netherlands, Norway, Poland, Portugal, Romania, San Marino, Spain, Sweden, Switzerland, United Kingdom, former Yugoslavia SFR; **Oceania (dev.):** Australia, New Zealand; **Other developed:** Israel, Japan, South Africa; **Africa developing:** all African countries except South Africa, Egypt, Libya and Sudan; **Latin America:** all countries in South or Central America or the Caribbean unless otherwise noted; **Near East developing:** Afghanistan, Bahrain, Cyprus, Egypt, Gaza Strip, Islamic Republic of Iran, Iraq, Jordan, Kuwait, Lebanon, Libyan Arab Jamahiriya, Oman, Qatar, Kingdom of Saudi Arabia, Sudan, Syrian Arab Republic, Turkey, United Arab Emirates, Yemen; **Far East developing:** Bangladesh, Bhutan, Brunei Darussalam, Cambodia, China, East Timor, Hong Kong, India, Indonesia, North and South ▶

	1987 Total	1992 Total		1987 Total	1992 Total
■ Nuts			**■ Tobacco**		
World production	4 083	4 535	World production	6 175	7 965
North America (dev.)	897	837	North America (dev.)	601	827
Europe	964	945	Europe	612	644
Oceania (dev.)	8	19	Oceania (dev.)	14	14
Other developed	52	40	Other developed	132	115
Africa developing	279	352	Africa developing	291	448
Latin America	193	232	Latin America	691	890
Near East developing	876	1 269	Near East developing	252	385
Far East developing	640	689	Far East developing	3 079	4 409
Other developing	5	5	Other developing	-	-
Former USSR	118	147	Former USSR	303	233
EEC	837	824	EEC	403	413
■ Oil Crops			**■ Natural Rubber**		
World production	67 838	78 162	World production	4 732	5 304
North America (dev.)	13 409	14708	North America (dev.)	-	-
Europe	8 369	7 754	Europe	-	-
Oceania (dev.)	191	245	Oceania (dev.)	-	-
Other developed	330	216	Other developed	-	-
Africa developing	4 572	4 973	Africa developing	260	270
Latin America	7 893	9 888	Latin America	48	52
Near East developing	1 563	1 749	Near East developing	-	-
Far East developing	27 413	34 732	Far East developing	4 419	4 978
Other developing	470	520	Other developing	5	4
Former USSR	3 628	3 377	Former USSR	-	-
EEC	6 377	5 915	EEC	-	-
■ Sugar (raw)			**■ Vegetable Fibres**		
World production	102 521	115 939	World production	23 127	23 893
North America (dev.)	6 780	7 099	North America (dev.)	3 284	3 574
Europe	20 586	21 577	Europe	542	572
Oceania (dev.)	3 439	4 260	Oceania (dev.)	218	432
Other developed	3 174	2 787	Other developed	127	65
Africa developing	4 124	3 752	Africa developing	906	978
Latin America	27 667	29 410	Latin America	1 804	1 850
Near East developing	4 076	4 382	Near East developing	1 348	1 399
Far East developing	22 655	35 486	Far East developing	11 946	12 660
Other developing	456	455	Other developing	1	1
Former USSR	9 565	6 731	Former USSR	2 951	2 362
EEC	14 810	17 113	EEC	394	468

▶ Korea, Laos, Macau, Malaysia, Maldives, Mongolia, Myanmar, Nepal, Pakistan, Philippines, Singapore, Sri Lanka, Thailand, Viet Nam; **Other developing:** Bermuda, Greenland, Saint Pierre & Miquelon, American Samoa, Canton and Enderbury Is., Christmas Is., Cocos Is., Cook Is., Fiji, French Polynesia, Guam, Johnston Is., Kiribati, Midway Is., Nauru, New Caledonia, Niue Is., Norfolk Is., Pacific Is., Papua New Guinea, Pitcairn, Samoa, Solomon Is., Tokelau, Tonga, Tuvalu, Vanuatu, Wake Is., Wallis and Futuna Is.; **Former USSR:** Armenia, Azerbaijan, Georgia, Kazakhstan, Kyrgyzstan, Tajikistan, Turkmenistan, Uzbekistan, Belarus, Estonia, Latvia, Lithuania, Moldova, Russian Federation, Ukraine. **Total meat** incl. beef and veal, lamb and mutton, pork, poultry, goat, buffalo. **Oil crops** incl. canola, linseed, cottonseed, olive oil, palm kernels and coconuts.

Source: Food and Agriculture Organization of the UN, *FAO Production Yearbook , 1992*

INTERNATIONAL ORGANIZATIONS

United Nations

The first United Nations declaration was signed by 22 Allied governments on January 1, 1942, and was an alliance against Germany, Italy and Japan. This anti-Axis coalition was converted into an international body in 1945 when 51 nations agreed to sign a United Nations Charter and form an organization that would "save succeeding generations from the scourge of war," as stated in the UN Charter. The Charter was drawn up at the Conference on International Organization held in San Francisco from Apr. 25 to June 26, 1945 and took effect Oct. 24, 1945. The UN succeeded the ineffectual League of Nations, taking over its physical assets. UN membership has grown to 184.

The UN has six principal parts, with the General Assembly—the central organ—acting as a world parliament. General Assembly meetings have been held in New York since 1946 when UN Headquarters were established there. The International Court of Justice in The Hague, Netherlands, is the only major UN organ not based in New York. Specialized agencies are located throughout the world.

General Information on the UN may be requested from the Public Inquiries Unit, Dept. of Public Information, Room GA-057A, United Nations, New York, NY 10017; or from the United Nations Association in Canada, 900-130 Slater St., Ottawa, Ont., K1P 6E2.

■ Structure of the United Nations

General Assembly The General Assembly is the UN's forum for discussing issues, reviewing UN activities and setting the agenda for initiatives. All member states are represented, and each is entitled to one vote. Resolutions require a majority vote before adoption. A president, 21 vice-presidents and six committee chairs head the Assembly, which sits from mid-September to mid-December. The six committees study issues relating to: disarmament and security; economy and finance; social, humanitarian and cultural issues; UN administrative and budgetary matters; legal issues; and political and security issues such as peacekeeping, and report back to a plenary session of the Assembly.

The General Assembly sets UN policies, admits new members on recommendation of the Security Council, approves the budget and receives reports from all other UN bodies.

Security Council The Security Council has the power to act for the maintenance of peace and security. It can enforce military action or economic sanctions, and it can send peacekeeping units (the Blue Berets) to troubled areas. The Security Council may also try to negotiate a ceasefire in the case of conflicts.

The Council has 15 members, five permanent and 10 elected by the General Assembly for two- year terms. Decisions require nine affirmative votes, but all permanent members have the right to veto. The permanent members are: China, France, the United Kingdom, the United States and the Russian Federation. Canada served a fifth term as a member in 1989–1990. The Security Council is permanently in session and representatives are on call 24 hours a day, ready to confer in the event of an international crisis. The Secretary-General is an active participant in the Security Council.

Economic and Social Council The Economic and Social Council co-ordinates the economic and social work of the UN and its related agencies. It encourages economic growth in developing countries. The Council's 54 members hold two month- long sessions each year: one in New York, the other in Geneva. Each member is elected by the General Assembly for a three-year term.

Trusteeship Council The Trusteeship Council ensures that trust territories are preparing for self-government or independence. The Pacific Islands (administered by the US) is the only remaining trusteeship of the original 11.

International Court of Justice (World Court) The International Court of Justice is the UN's judicial body. The Security Council elects 15 judges to the Court for nine-year terms. No two members may be from the same nation. The Court, located in The Hague, Netherlands, only sits in judgement on disputes between states. Both member and non- member states may submit grievances (border disputes, resource access, breach of treaty, etc.). Countries can opt out of any proceeding, unless required to participate by treaty provisions. But after agreeing to become a party in a case, a nation must comply with the Court's decision, enforced by the Security Council.

Secretariat The Secretariat administers the programs and policies laid out by other UN bodies. The Secretary-General, heading the Secretariat, is responsible for the UN's administration and for alerting the Security Council to any threats to international peace and security, and acts as spokesperson for the UN. The Secretary-General is elected by the General Assembly on the recommendation of the Security Council and cannot be from one of the five permanent members of the Security Council.

United Nations Secretaries-General

Secretary, Nation	Date Installed	Secretary, Nation	Date Installed
Trygve Lie, Norway	Feb. 1946	Kurt Waldheim, Austria	Dec. 1971
Dag Hammarskjold, Sweden	Apr. 1953	Javier Perez de Cuellar, Peru	Dec. 1981
U Thant, Burma	Nov. 1961	Boutros Boutros-Ghali, Egypt[1]	Jan. 1992

(1) Term ends Dec. 31, 1996

Canadian Ambassadors to the United Nations

Ambassador	Date Appointed	Ambassador	Date Appointed
Andrew McNaughton	Jan. 1948	Yvon Beaulne	Jan. 1969
John Holmes	Jan. 1950	Saul Forbes Rae	June 1972
Gerald Riddell	June 1950	William Barton	May 1976
David Johnson	Oct. 1951	Michel Dupuy	Mar. 1980
Robert MacKay	June 1955	Gérard Pelletier	Aug. 1981
Charles Ritchie	Nov. 1957	Stephen H. Lewis	Oct. 1984
Paul Tremblay	May 1962	Yves Fortier	July 1988
George Ignatieff	Mar. 1966	Louise Fréchette	Jan. 1992

Source: *Dept. of External Affairs*

Canadian Representatives to International Organizations

(As of Oct. 1994)

European Union, Brussels	Jacques Roy
FAO (Food and Agriculture Organization), Rome	Robert Andrigo, P.R.
Habitat (U.N. Centre for Human Settlements), Nairobi	Lucie Edwards, P.R.
International Civil Aviation Organization, Montreal	Gilles H.J. Duguay, R.
Conference on Security and Cooperation in Europe	Peter F. Walker, H.D., Amb
North Atlantic Council, Brussels	Admiral John R. Anderson
Office of the U.N.; Conference on Disarmament, Geneva	Gerald E. Shannon, P.R., Amb.
Office of the U.N.; U.N. Industrial Development Organization, International Atomic Energy Agency, Vienna	Peter F. Walker, P.R., Amb.
Organization of American States, Washington	Brian Dickson, Q.C., P.R., Amb.
Organization for Economic Co-Operation and Development, Paris	Anne-Marie Doyle, P.R., Amb.
UNEP (U.N. Environment Program), Nairobi	Lucie Edwards, P.R.
UNESCO (U.N. Educational, Scientific and Cultural Organization), Paris	Jacques Demers, P.R., Amb.
United Nations, New York	Louise Fréchette, P.R., Amb.

Source: *Dept. of External Affairs*

H.D. = Head of Delegation; H.M. = Head of Mission; Amb. = Ambassador; P.R. = Permanent Representative; P.O. = Permanent Observer; P.D. = Permanent Delegate; R.A. = Roving Ambassador; R. = Representative.

United Nations and Related Organizations

■ General Assembly

IAEA: International Atomic Energy Agency

INSTRAW: International Research and Training Institute for the Advancement of Women

UNCHS/HABITAT: UN Centre for Human Settlements

UNCTAD: UN Conference on Trade and Development

UNDP: UN Development Programme

UNEP: UN Environment Programme

UNFPA: United Nations Population Fund

UNHCR: Office of the UN High Commissioner for Refugees

UNICEF: UN Children's Fund

UNITAR: UN Institute for Training and Research

UNRWA: UN Relief and Works Agency for Palestine Refugees in the Near East

UNU: UN University

WFC: World Food Council

■ Security Council

MINURSO: UN Mission for the Referendum in Western Sahara

ONUMOZ: UN Operation in Mozambique

ONUSAL: UN Observer Mission in El Salvador

UNAMIR: UN Assistance Mission for Rwanda

UNAVEM II: UN Angola Verification Mission II

UNDOF: UN Disengagement Observer Force

UNFICYP: UN Peace-keeping Force in Cyprus

UNIFIL: UN Interim Force in Lebanon

UNIKOM: UN Iraq-Kuwait Observation Mission

UNMIH: UN Mission in Haiti

UNMOGIP: UN Military Observer Group in India and Pakistan

UNOMIG: UN Observer Mission in Georgia

UNOMIL: UN Observer Mission in Liberia

UNOMUR: UN Observer Mission in Uganda-Rwanda

UNOSOM II: United Nations Operation in Somalia

UNPROFOR: UN Protection Force

UNTSO: UN Truce Supervision Organization

■ Secretariat

UNDRO: UN Disaster Relief Coordinator

■ Economic and Social Council

FAO: Food and Agriculture Organization

GATT: General Agreement on Tariffs and Trade

ICAO: International Civil Aviation Organization

IFAD: International Fund for Agricultural Development

ILO: International Labour Organization

IMF: International Monetary Fund

IMO: International Maritime Organization

ITU: International Telecommunications Union

UNESCO: UN Educational, Scientific and Cultural Organization

UNIDO: UN Industrial Development Organization

UPU: Universal Postal Union

WFP: World Food Programme

WHO: World Health Organization

WIPO: World Intellectual Property Organization

WMO: World Meteorological Organization

□ World Bank

IBRD: International Bank for Reconstruction and Development

IDA: International Development Association

IFC: International Finance Corporation

■ International Court of Justice

■ Trusteeship Council

The United Nations System

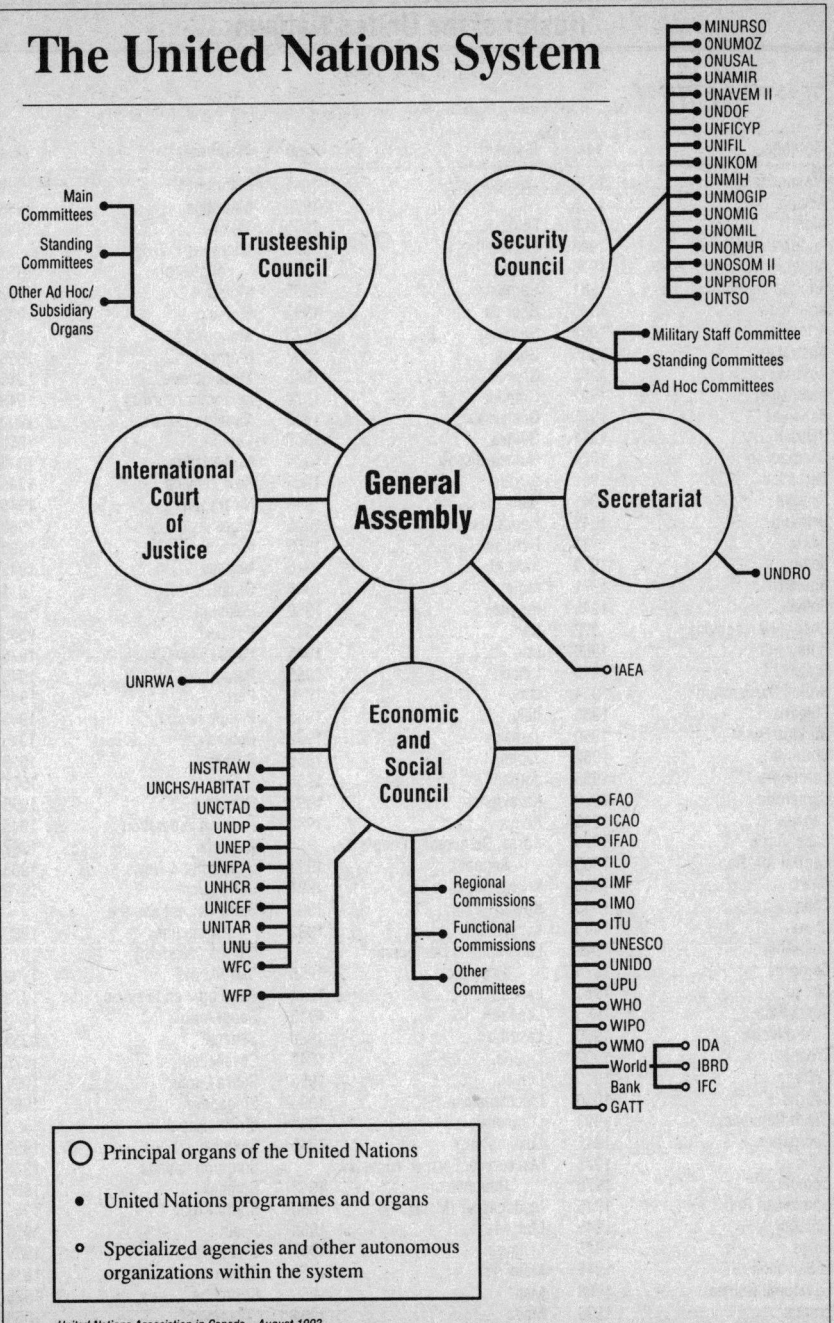

MINURSO
ONUMOZ
ONUSAL
UNAMIR
UNAVEM II
UNDOF
UNFICYP
UNIFIL
UNIKOM
UNMIH
UNMOGIP
UNOMIG
UNOMIL
UNOMUR
UNOSOM II
UNPROFOR
UNTSO

Main Committees
Standing Committees
Other Ad Hoc/ Subsidiary Organs

Trusteeship Council

Security Council

Military Staff Committee
Standing Committees
Ad Hoc Committees

International Court of Justice

General Assembly

Secretariat

UNDRO

UNRWA

IAEA

Economic and Social Council

INSTRAW
UNCHS/HABITAT
UNCTAD
UNDP
UNEP
UNFPA
UNHCR
UNICEF
UNITAR
UNU
WFC
WFP

Regional Commissions
Functional Commissions
Other Committees

FAO
ICAO
IFAD
ILO
IMF
IMO
ITU
UNESCO
UNIDO
UPU
WHO
WIPO
WMO
World Bank
GATT

IDA
IBRD
IFC

○ Principal organs of the United Nations

● United Nations programmes and organs

○ Specialized agencies and other autonomous organizations within the system

United Nations Association in Canada – August 1993

Roster of the United Nations

(As of Sept. 1994)

The 184 members of the United Nations, with the years in which they became members.

Member	Year	Member	Year	Member	Year
Afghanistan	1946	Ethiopia	1945	Mauritania	1961
Albania	1955	Fiji	1970	Mauritius	1968
Algeria	1962	Finland	1955	Mexico	1945
Andorra	1993	France	1945	Micronesia, Federated	
Angola	1976	Gabon	1960	States of	1991
Antigua and Barbuda	1981	Gambia	1965	Moldova	1992
Argentina	1945	Georgia	1992	Monaco	1993
Armenia	1992	Germany	1973	Mongolia	1961
Australia	1945	Ghana	1957	Morocco	1956
Austria	1955	Greece	1945	Mozambique	1975
Azerbaijan	1992	Grenada	1974	Myanmar (Burma)	1948
Bahamas	1973	Guatemala	1945	Namibia	1990
Bahrain	1971	Guinea	1958	Nepal	1955
Bangladesh	1974	Guinea-Bissau	1974	Netherlands	1945
Barbados	1966	Guyana	1966	New Zealand	1945
Belarus	1945	Haiti	1945	Nicaragua	1945
Belgium	1945	Honduras	1945	Niger	1960
Belize	1981	Hungary	1955	Nigeria	1960
Benin	1960	Iceland	1946	Norway	1945
Bhutan	1971	India	1945	Oman	1971
Bolivia	1945	Indonesia	1950	Pakistan	1947
Bosnia-Hercegovina	1992	Iran	1945	Panama	1945
Botswana	1966	Iraq	1945	Papua New Guinea	1975
Brazil	1945	Ireland	1955	Paraguay	1945
Brunei Darussalam	1984	Israel	1949	Peru	1945
Bulgaria	1955	Italy	1955	Philippines	1945
Burkina-Faso	1960	Jamaica	1962	Poland	1945
Burundi	1962	Japan	1956	Portugal	1955
Cambodia	1955	Jordan	1955	Qatar	1971
Cameroon	1960	Kazakhstan	1992	Romania	1955
Canada	1945	Kenya	1963	Russian Federation	1945
Cape Verde	1975	Korea, Democratic People's		Rwanda	1962
Central Afr. Rep.	1960	Republic of	1991	Saint Kitts & Nevis	1983
Chad	1960	Korea, Republic of	1991	Saint Lucia	1979
Chile	1945	Kuwait	1963	Saint Vincent and the	
China	1945	Kyrgyzstan	1992	Grenadines	1980
Colombia	1945	Lao People's Democratic		Samoa (Western)	1976
Comoros	1975	Republic	1955	San Marino	1992
Congo	1960	Latvia	1991	Sao Tome and Principe	1975
Costa Rica	1945	Lebanon	1945	Saudi Arabia	1945
Côte d'Ivoire	1960	Lesotho	1966	Senegal	1960
Croatia	1992	Liberia	1945	Seychelles	1976
Cuba	1945	Libya	1955	Sierra Leone	1961
Cyprus	1960	Liechtenstein	1990	Singapore	1965
Czech Republic	1993	Lithuania	1991	Slovak Republic	1993
Denmark	1945	Luxembourg	1945	Slovenia	1992
Djibouti	1977	Macedonia, Former Yugoslav		Solomon Islands	1978
Dominica	1978	Republic of	1993	Somalia	1960
Dominican Rep.	1945	Madagascar (Malagasy)	1960	South Africa	1945
Ecuador	1945	Malawi	1964	Spain	1955
Egypt	1945	Malaysia	1957	Sri Lanka	1955
El Salvador	1945	Maldives	1965	Sudan	1956
Equatorial Guinea	1968	Mali	1960	Suriname	1975
Eritrea	1993	Malta	1964	Swaziland	1968
Estonia	1991	Marshall Islands	1991	Sweden	1946

Member	Year	Member	Year	Member	Year
Syria	1945	Turkmenistan	1992	Vanuatu	1981
Tajikistan	1992	Uganda	1962	Venezuela	1945
Tanzania	1961	Ukraine	1945	Vietnam	1977
Thailand	1946	United Arab Emirates	1971	Yemen	1947
Togo	1960	United Kingdom	1945	Yugoslavia[1]	1945
Trinidad & Tobago	1962	United States	1945	Zaire	1960
Tunisia	1956	Uruguay	1945	Zambia	1964
Turkey	1945	Uzbekistan	1992	Zimbabwe	1980

Source: *United Nations Association*

(1) Not permitted to participate in General Assembly deliberations.

Other International Organizations in the News

Association of Southeast Asian Nations (ASEAN) was created in 1967 to further the social, economic and agricultural progress of the region's non-communist countries. Original members are Indonesia, Malaysia, Philippines, Singapore and Thailand; Brunei joined in 1984. Based in Jakarta, ASEAN works for greater peace and security in the area. Summit meetings of heads of government, ministerial conferences and various committees organize for cooperation in research, trade and tourism of the member countries.

Caribbean Community (CARICOM) was created in 1973 as a common market for Barbados, Guyana, Jamaica and Trinidad and Tobago. It coordinates foreign policies of member states and organizes common services. Members now include Belize, Dominica, Grenada, St. Lucia, St. Vincent, Montserrat, Antigua and St. Kitts-Nevis.

La Francophonie is a term that was first used at the end of the 19th century. Then linked to the notion of France's influence in the world, it now signifies a French-language environment that has arisen from the will of 47 countries having the use of French in common to cooperate with one another. The heads of state and of government in these countries meet every two years, the first Francophone Summit having taken place in Paris in 1986. The international political situation, the world economy and major cooperation projects in fields that are priorities for those speaking French lie at the heart of their discussions. The presence of numerous countries from the southern hemisphere is a determining factor in setting priorities. Canada, Québec and New Brunswick, play the role of pacesetters within the group, which accounts for 20% of the world trade and over 200 million consumers,

by insisting on democratization and economic development.

League of Arab States (Arab League) was established in 1945 in Cairo to give Arab nations a united voice on political and economic issues and to mediate internal disputes. The original treaty was signed by Egypt, Iraq, Lebanon, Saudi Arabia, Syria, Jordan and Yemen. Membership now stands at 21 including: Algeria, Bahrain, Djibouti, Kuwait, Libya, Mauritania, Morocco, Oman, the Palestine Liberation Organization, Qatar, Somalia, Sudan, Tunisia and the United Arab Emirates. In 1948, the League opposed the formation of a Jewish state (Israel) in Palestine. In 1979, Egypt was suspended from the league for signing a peace treaty with Israel. As a result, the headquarters for the League moved from Cairo to Tunis. Egypt was re-admitted in 1989.

The North Atlantic Treaty Organization (NATO) provides common security for its members through cooperation and consultation in political, military and economic as well as scientific and other non-military fields. It was established on the basis of the 1949 North Atlantic Treaty. The 16 member nations include: Belgium, Canada, Denmark, France, Germany, Greece, Iceland, Italy, Luxembourg, The Netherlands, Norway, Portugal, Spain, Turkey, the UK, and the US. With the demise of the Warsaw Pact and the end of the Cold War, NATO began transforming its structures and policies to meet the new security challenges in Europe at the Brussels Summit in January 1994. The innovations include a new Strategic Concept with provisions for: a reduced and more flexible force structure; increased coordination and cooperation with other international institutions; active involvement in international crisis management and peacekeeping operations, including the provision of concrete support for UN peacekeeping efforts in former Yugoslavia; cooperation and consultation

with the countries of central and Eastern Europe and the former Soviet Union through the establishment of the North Atlantic Cooperation Council (NACC) in December 1991; and the Partnership for Peace programme inaugurated in January 1994, which serves to strengthen and deepen the process of cooperation betwen NATO and other countries participating in the programme.

Organization for Economic Cooperation and Development (OECD) was established in 1961 to promote economic growth and to increase employment and standards of living in member nations. Its 25 members also work to expand world trade and provide aid for developing countries. Members are: Australia, Austria, Belgium, Canada, Denmark, Finland, France, Germany, Greece, Iceland, Ireland, Italy, Japan, Luxembourg, Mexico, Netherlands, New Zealand, Norway, Portugal, Spain, Sweden, Switzerland, Turkey, the United Kingdom and the United States.

Organization of American States (OAS) was established in 1948 to promote peace and development in the Western hemisphere. Based in Washington D.C., its 35 members include all the independent countries of the hemisphere. Cuba has been suspended from participation since 1962. Canada joined the OAS in 1990. The mandate of the OAS is based on a principle in the Monroe Doctrine, which defines an attack on one American state as an attack on all. The OAS tries to settle internal disputes independently, discouraging foreign intervention.

Organization of Petroleum Exporting Countries (OPEC) was founded in 1960 by major oil-producing nations to gain more control over the pricing and production of oil. Original members are Iran, Iraq, Kuwait, Saudi Arabia and Venezuela. Additional members include Algeria, Gabon, Indonesia, Libya, Nigeria, Qatar and the United Arab Emirates. Together they have up to 75 percent of the world's recoverable oil reserves. In the 1970s, OPEC raised oil prices, causing rapid inflation in the industrialized nations.

The European Union

The term European Union (EU) represents a unique relationship among twelve democratic nations, with the aim of constructing a united

Europe. The EU is more than an international organization, but not a full-blown federation. Since it has 349 million people and accounts for nearly 20% of world trade, it is the largest trading entity in the world.

The European Community was the brainchild of Jean Monnet of France. In May 1950 French Foreign Minister Robert Schuman proposed pooling the coal and steel industries of France and West Germany. The plan was open to all democratic countries in Europe. The result was the European Coal and Steel Community (ECSC), formed in 1951 by France, West Germany, Italy, the Netherlands, Belgium and Luxembourg.

The ECSC boosted internal trade in coal and steel by 129% in five years. Its success spurred the six to apply the same approach to the entire economy. In 1957, the same six countries formed the European Economic Community (EEC), extending the common market to all sectors of the economy. The EEC committed the six to dismantle trade barriers and to allow the free movement of goods, services, capital and people between member countries. At the same time the six formed the European Atomic Energy Community (Euratom) to further the use of nuclear energy for peaceful purposes in Europe.

In 1967, the institutions of the ECSC, Euratom and the EEC were merged. In 1973, Denmark, Ireland and the United Kingdom became members, as did Greece in 1981 and Spain and Portugal in 1986.

From its inception, the EC has been dedicated to "reducing the differences existing between the various regions and the backwardness of the less-favoured regions." To that end, the EC can use three main sources of finance, known as the Structural Funds: The European Regional Development Fund, the European Social Fund and the European Agricultural Guidance and Guarantee Fund. Greece, Portugal, Ireland and parts of Spain and Italy have been targeted for aid to bring their standards of living closer to that of the other member states.

The Europe 1992 project to complete the common market and create an internal market by dismantling the remaining physical, technical and fiscal barriers among the member states was part of the Single European Act which came into force in 1987.

The Maastricht Treaty on European Union was signed in 1992 and came into effect in November 1993. It is one further step on the road to a European constitution and integrates the previous EC structures. The treaty is intended to facilitate the development of the EC into a political union as well as an economic and monetary union. It is intended that by 1999, at the latest, a European currency will replace the national currencies. A common foreign and security policy is being developed, to be followed by a common defence policy.

The Treaty on European Union encourages the union members to:

- establish a European Central Bank and introduce a common currency by 1999 at the latest;
- introduce a common foreign and security policy; the European Political Cooperation Secretariat is merged with the General Secretariat of the Council; the Western European Union (WEU) becomes the defence component of the European Union;
- increase powers for the European Parliament; involvement in the enactment of legislation; right of approval prior to appointment of the commission; and power of assent for major international agreements;
- establish closer cooperation on justice and home affairs, including visa policy and immigration;
- introduce new responsibilities to the European Community in the area of social policy, public health, education, culture, environment and research and development;
- establish a new Cohesion Fund to increase aid to the union's less favoured regions;
- establish a Committee of Regions, to give the regions a part to play in the Community;
- introduce the principle of subsidiarity, according to which the EC should deal only with enactment of the matters it is better equipped to deal with than the member states and the regional and local authorities.

In early August 1993, progress toward a common currency was dealt a severe setback when the diverging economic goals of EC member countries (high interest rates in Germany to keep inflation in check vs. low interest rates needed to spur growth in France, Denmark, Spain and Belgium) made the restrictions on the variance in exchange rates (exchange-rate mechanism or ERM) unworkable. The pressure of buying and selling activity by currency speculators and investors forced the EC's monetary authorities to let the currencies float within very broad limits against each other in the market, thereby virtually abandoning the ERM that was the cornerstone of the proposed European Monetary System.

The EU consists of three pillars. The first pillar is the European Community with its common supranational institutions. The two others are intergovernmental cooperation in foreign and security policy and intergovernmental cooperation in home and justice affairs.

Institutions of the EC

As part of the Union, the European Community creates its own laws and policies through the following institutions:

The European Commission proposes legislation, implements policy and enforces the treaties. It has investigative powers and can take legal action. It also represents the EU in trade negotiations. The commission is headed by 17 commissioners: France, Germany, Italy, Spain and the U.K. each have two commissioners to represent them and the other member states are represented by one commissioner each. Commissioners are appointed for five years by mutual agreement of national governments.

The European Parliament is directly elected by the citizens of the union. Its 567 members debate issues, question the commission and council, and scrutinize proposed legislation. It can dismiss the commission and has final approval over the EC budget. Elections take place every five years. The number of MPs from each country are: Germany 99, U.K. 87, France 87, Italy 87, Spain 64, Netherlands 31, Belgium 25, Portugal 25, Greece 25, Denmark 16, Ireland 15 and Luxembourg 6. MPs sit according to political affiliation and not nationality.

The Council of the European Union is composed of ministers from the 12 member countries. The Council acts on Commission proposals and is the final decision-making body. Participation in the meetings change according to the agenda. Agricultural ministers, for instance, decide on agricultural matters and economic and finance ministers on economic and monetary matters. Ministers represent and defend the interest of their countries, while seeking agreements that promote the union's goals.

The presidency of the council rotates among the member states every six months. In one of the EC's most important reforms, the Single European Act provided for majority voting in the council in certain areas that previously required unanimity. Areas for majority voting were extended again in the Maastricht Treaty.

The European Council is comprised of the heads of state or government of the EU member states and the commission president. The group meets at least twice a year to define major internal and foreign policy orientations. The European Council does not legislate but its written conclusions provide guidance and impetus for the union.

The Court of Justice is the EC's supreme court. It interprets EC law and it rules on legal questions. The court comprises 13 judges, assisted by 6 advocates-general. Both groups are appointed for six years by mutual consent of the member states.

The Court of Auditors audits the accounts of the EC and EC bodies.

The Committee of the Regions and the **Economic and Social Committee** must be consulted by the commission and the council on policies and and proposals for legislation.

Roster of the European Community

(As of Sept. 1994)

Member	Year Joined	Member	Year Joined
Belgium	1957	Italy	1957
Denmark	1973	Luxembourg	1957
France	1957	Netherlands	1957
Germany	1957	Portugal	1986
Greece	1981	Spain	1986
Ireland	1973	United Kingdom	1973

Source: *Commission of the European Communities*

United Nations—50 Years Old in 1995

F ifty-one countries, including Canada, signed the United Nations Charter in 1945, vowing to "save succeeding generations from the scourge of war." The world body has grown to 186 members since its inception and will mark its 50th anniversary in 1995. Plans are underway to mark the event, including commemorative books, curriculum materials and many celebrations.

Conferences during the anniversary year will further the UN's goal of world development: the World Summit on Social Development will be held in Copenhagen March 6-12; delegates will gather for the Fourth World Conference on Women in Beijing September 4-15; and the Food and Agricultural Organization's 50th Anniversary Symposium will be held in Quebec City October 11-13.

The Canadian Committee for the 50th anniversary notes that the event offers both an opportunity to recognize the organization's achievements and an opportunity to consider reform of the world body. The Canada's UN Reform Satellite Committee has already prepared a draft paper detailing Canadian priorities on this matter and they include: the creation of UN peace-enforcement units; an increase in the membership of the Security Council and some curbs on the powers of permanent members; the creation of an Auditor-General with the power to reduce inefficiency; the strengthening of the UN Register of Conventional Arms; a plan of action of the UN High Commissioner for Human Rights and the creation of a Sustainable Development Security Council.

For more information on UN/50 plans contact the Canadian Committee for the 50th Anniversary at 900-130 Slater St., Ottawa, ON. H1P 6E2

The Commonwealth

The Commonwealth is an association of 50 independent states which once formed part of the British Empire. Its roots can be traced to the early 1900s and the concept of autonomous nations within the Empire cooperating in such matters as foreign policy, out of a common allegiance to the Crown. The Commonwealth was more formally established in 1931 when the *Statute of Westminster* legally granted self-government to the Dominions within the Empire. Founding members were Britain, Canada, Newfoundland (which ceased to be an independent member upon entering Confederation in 1949), Australia, New Zealand and South Africa.

The number of members grew through the late 1940s into the 1960s as many Asian and African countries gained independence. In more recent years, many small Caribbean, Indian Ocean and Pacific Island countries have become member states. Current membership represents about a quarter of the world's population and about a third of the countries in the United Nations.

The Commonwealth has no written charter. It is a forum for pooling experience and expressing viewpoints. The highest level of Commonwealth consultation is the Heads of Government Meetings, held every 2 years. In 1971, the Commonwealth adopted 5 principles: the pursuit of international peace and order through the United Nations; the promotion of representative institutions and guarantees for personal freedom under the law; the recognition of racial equality and the need to combat racial discrimination; opposition to all forms of colonial domination and racial oppression; and dedication to lessening the disparities in wealth between different sections of humanity.

The Commonwealth Secretariat was established in 1965 to coordinate all areas of Commonwealth joint endeavor. Funded by members under a system of assessed contributions, the Secretariat carries out economic, social and educational programs primarily in developing Commonwealth countries.

Source: *Department of Foreign Affairs and International Trade*

Commonwealth Members[1]

Country	Year Joined	Country	Year Joined
Antigua and Barbuda	1981	Mauritius	1968
Australia	1931	Namibia	1990
Bahamas	1973	Nauru [2]	1968
Bangladesh	1972	New Zealand	1931
Barbados	1966	Nigeria	1960
Belize	1981	Pakistan [3]	1989
Botswana	1966	Papua New Guinea	1975
Britain	1931	St. Kitts and Nevis	1983
Brunei Darussalam	1984	St. Lucia	1979
Canada	1931	St.Vincent and The Grenadines	1979
Cyprus	1961	Seychelles	1976
Dominica	1978	Sierra Leone	1961
The Gambia	1965	Singapore	1965
Ghana	1957	Solomon Islands	1978
Grenada	1974	South Africa [4]	1934
Guyana	1966	Sri Lanka	1948
India	1947	Swaziland	1968
Jamaica	1962	Tanzania	1961
Kenya	1963	Tonga	1970
Kiribati	1979	Trinidad and Tobago	1962
Lesotho	1966	Tuvalu [2]	1978
Malawi	1964	Uganda	1962
Malaysia	1957	Vanuatu	1980
Maldives	1982	Western Samoa	1970
Malta	1964	Zambia	1964
Mauritius	1968	Zimbabwe	1980

(1) As of Sept. 1994. (2) Special Member of the Commonwealth. Participates in all meetings and activities except meetings of Commonwealth Heads of Government. (3) Left in 1972 in a dispute over the recognition of Bangladesh; rejoined Oct. 1, 1989. (4) In 1961, the Union of South Africa requested membership as a republic but withdrew the application due to mounting opposition to apartheid. Ties resumed June 1, 1994.

Focus on GATT

■ General Agreement on Tarrifs and Trades

The General Agreement on Tarrifs and Trade (GATT) is a contract defining rules for international trade. Altogether, the 125 governments under contract account for 90 percent of merchandise trade. The agreement intends to produce a predictable and liberalized trading environment in order to stimulate global trade, investment and job creation.

GATT operates in three ways—as a set of rules for multilateral trade, as a forum for trade negotiations, and as an international court for trade disputes. Participants include contracting parties, observers, and applicants for membership.

GATT began in 1946 as a provisional organization designed to reduce the high protectionist tariffs of the 1930s. At the first meeting, 23 countries (11 developing) made 45 000 trade concessions. Since then, the GATT organization has sponsored a series of global trade negotiations called "rounds." Negotiations for the recent Uruguay Round ended December 15, 1993 and the agreement was signed at Marrakesh on April 15, 1994.

■ Uruguay Round

The Uruguay Round began its seven-year negotiation in September of 1986 in Punta del Este, Uruguay. The resulting Final Act deals with trade in goods (reducing tariffs by over one-third) and suggests expanding GATT into a permanent institution. New rules are proposed for trade in services, trade-related intellectual property rights (TRIPs) and trade-related investments (TRIMs).

■ Principles of GATT

The General Agreement contains 38 articles plus added agreements on anti-dumping, subsidies, and non-tariff issues. The articles are based on these fundamental principles:
- The "most-favoured-nation" clause insists that contracting parties treat each other equally when trading.
- Customs tariffs should replace commercial measures to protect domestic industries.
- Members are bound to follow tariff schedules fixed in the GATT.
- GATT is concerned not with free-trade, but with open, fair and undistorted competition.
- Quantitative restrictions on imports are prohibited except in balance-of-payment situations.
- A waiver may release a member from obligations in cases of trade or economic emergency.
- In exception to the most-favoured-nation clause, regional trading agreements are allowed provided that participants do not raise trade barriers to excluded nations.
- GATT includes special conditions for developing countries (two-thirds of members)
- The Multi-Fibre Arrangement (MFA) allows industrial countries to impose quotas on textiles imported from more competitive developing nations. The Uruguay Round will dismantle the MFA.

■ Structure of GATT

GATT activities are directed by a Secretariat in Geneva, funded by contracting parties. The staff of 400 services the standing bodies of GATT and analyzes trade policy and its application. Along with the International Trade Centre (run by GATT and the UN), the Secretariat advises developing countries on trade policy.

The Session of Contracting Parties, GATT's senior body, meets annually. The Council of Representatives, made up of delegates from contracting parties takes care of daily operations. Under the Trade Policy Review Mechanism, the Council examines members' trade policies to ensure they honour agreements. A panel judges trade disputes, but cannot enforce decisions.

■ From GATT to WTO

The World Trade Organization (WTO) will replace the provisional GATT as a permanent institution for trade negotiations. Assuming that the 22 000 page, 385-pound Uruguay Round agreement is ratified by participating governments, the WTO will take over on January 1, 1995, working with the International Monetary Fund (IMF) and the World Bank to oversee the global economy. The General Council of the WTO will implement the results of the Uruguay Round, and provide a Dispute Settlement Body and a Trade Policy Mechanism.

Unlike previous agreements, members must accept all the terms of the Uruguay Round in order to belong to the WTO. This institution will have more authority than GATT to settle trade disputes, using panels and an Appellate Body. The WTO will be able to enforce decisions with sanctions.

Common GATT Terms

accession: refers to a country's entrance into the General Agreement

anti-dumping: restrictions on selling goods abroad for less than the original price (and injuring the importing country's domestic industry)

balance-of-payment: countries may impose restrictions on imports in the least disruptive way to balance payment owing

contracting parties: governments agreeing to be bound by the terms of GATT

multilateral: describes an agreement or treaty with three or more participants

non-tariff measures: designed to reduce practices other than quantitative restrictions which form barriers to trade (e.g. dumping, technical barriers to trade, subsidies)

tariff: a duty or custom paid on an import or export

GATT Members

Antigua and	Denmark	Lesotho	Rwanda
Barbuda	Dominican Republic	Luxembourg	Senegal
Argentina	Egypt	Macau	Sierra Leone
Australia	El Salvador	Madagascar	Singapore
Austria	Finland	Malawi	South Africa
Bangladesh	France	Malaysia	Spain
Barbados	Gabon	Maldives	Sri Lanka
Belgium	Gambia	Malta	Suriname
Belize	Germany	Mauritania	Sweden
Benin	Ghana	Mauritius	Switzerland
Bolivia	Greece	Mexico	Tanzania
Botswana	Guatemala	Morocco	Thailand
Brazil	Guyana	Mozambique	Togo
Burkina Faso	Haiti	Myanmar	Trinidad and Tobago
Burundi	Hong Kong	Namibia	Tunisia
Cameroon	Hungary	Netherlands	Turkey
Canada	Iceland	New Zealand	Uganda
Central African Rep.	India	Nicaragua	United Kingdom
Chad	Indonesia	Niger	United States
Chile	Ireland	Nigeria	Uruguay
Colombia	Israel	Norway	Venezuela
Congo	Italy	Pakistan	Yugoslavia
Costa Rica	Jamaica	Peru	Zaire
Cote d'Ivoire	Japan	Philippines	Zambia
Cuba	Kenya	Poland	Zimbabwe
Cyprus	Korea, Rep. of	Portugal	
Czech Republic	Kuwait	Romania	

HISTORY IN HEADLINES

■ Ancient History 5000 BC to AD 476

5000–3501: The earliest known cities are in Mesopotamia—in southwest Asia between the Tigris and Euphrates Rivers—a plain rendered fertile by canals; the Egyptian calendar is regulated by the sun and moon; Sumerian writing exists, in southern Mesopotamia on clay tablets, consisting of 2,000 pictograph signs; the Neolithic period in western Europe is characterized by polished stone weapons and tools and agriculturally-based settlements; Cretan ships appear in the Mediterranean Sea; copper alloys are used, and there is smelting of gold and silver in Sumer and Egypt; harps and flutes are played in Egypt; painted pottery appears along the Mediterranean; coloured ceramic ware from Russia reaches China.

3500–2001: The Middle Eastern Bronze Age begins (c. 3500 BC); the height of Sumerian civilization (in the region of the Euphrates River valley) is noted for having a numerical system, irrigated agriculture, poetry, potters' wheels, linen, wheeled vehicles, wedge-shaped (cuneiform) script, barley, bread, beer, use of metal coins as legal tender, oil-burning lamps, brick temples and medicine; the dynasty of Pharoahs as god-kings in Egypt begins (2200–525 BC); the Great Sphinx of Gizeh is built; wrestling is the first highly developed sport; glass beads are worn in Egypt; the bow and arrow is first used in warfare; the Yao dynasty is the first recorded in China (2500–2300); the Indus civilization begins in India; the earliest Egyptian mummies are made; equinoxes and solstices are calculated in China; the first library is in Egypt.

2000–1501: The Egyptian height of power and achievement (18th dynasty) features an irrigation system, contraceptives, bathrooms with a water supply, an alphabet of 24 signs, and the oldest form of a novel (*Story of Sinuhe*); the Persian empire begins (1750–1550); the first legal system and laws of a kingdom are set up by Hammurabi, king of Babylonia; the first of seven periods of Chinese literature begins; Stonehenge is built; Abraham, the patriarch of the Jewish religion, lives (c. 1800); Babylonia uses geometry as the basis for astronomical measurements, and

describes the signs of the Zodiac; religious dances are performed in Crete.

1500–1001: The Israelites, led by Moses, leave bondage in Egypt (eventually settling in Canaan in 1250), and receive the Ten Commandments and the world's first monotheistic belief at Mt Sinai; the decline of Egyptian power begins (1200–1090); Troy is destroyed during the Trojan War (1193–83) over Helen of Sparta (Greek legend); the Iron Age begins in the Mediterranean area (1000); obelisk structures are used as sundials in Egypt; the first Chinese dictionary is written; silk fabrics appear in China; leprosy spreads in India and Egypt; Phoenicia is the dominant trading power in the Mediterranean; the Mexican Sun Pyramid is built in Teotihuacan.

1000–901: Asiatic and Greek civilizations are linked by Phoenician trading; David is the king of the united kingdom of Judah and Israel (1000–960) with Jerusalem as its capital; David is succeeded by his son Solomon who presides over the height of Israel's ancient civilization (960–25); classical paganism reigns in Greece; pantheistic belief reigns in India (teaching reincarnation and the caste system); the Chou dynasty's rational philosophy reigns in China; Pinto Indians build huts in southwest North America; brush and ink painting appears in China; gold vessels and jewellery are made in northern Europe; the Hebrew alphabet and literature are developed; the Germanic peoples begin to migrate en masse.

900–601: Carthage is founded as a trading centre (813); *Iliad* and *Odyssey* are written and credited to the poet Homer (c. 800); according to legend, Rome is founded by the twins Romulus and Remus (753); the first recorded Olympic Games are held in Greece (776), and every four years thereafter during ancient times; the earliest record of music is a hymn on a Sumerian tablet; arts and crafts flourish in Asia Minor and Greece; a canal between the Nile River and the Red Sea is started under Pharoah Nechos; Etruscan art forms emerge in Tuscany; the Assyrians destroy Babylon and divert the Euphrates River to cover the site of the city; the Babylonians and their allies later destroy the Assyrian empire, which is then divided among the conquerors; the Acropolis, a fortified hill and religious centre, is built in Athens; limestone and marble are used in the construction of Greek temples; flutes and lyres accompany song; Greek choral and lyric poetry use strophe and antistrophe; Zoroaster, a religious teacher and prophet of ancient Persia, lives (c. 628–c. 551).

600–451: The Mayan civilization flourishes in Mexico; Nebuchadnezzer builds what may be the terraced Hanging Gardens of Babylon (600); Babylonian troops destroy the Jewish Temple at Jerusalem and take many Jews as slaves; Jews write the early books of the Bible during the Babylonian Captivity; Siddhartha Gautama, who becomes Buddha, the "enlightened" Indian philosopher and religious teacher, is born (563): at age 29 he renounces world luxuries and searches for enlightenment, which he attains at age 35 while meditating under a pipal tree at Bodh Gaya, and he teaches monks to continue his work; Confucius, the Chinese philosopher and teacher, is born (551); his moral and religious system governs China and is contained in the sayings of *Analects*; Cyrus II the Great of Persia conquers Babylon and surrounding areas and transforms Persia into a vast empire (c. 540): he frees the Jews from Babylon (536) and aids their return to Israel; Darius I divides the Persian empire into 20 provinces and introduces reforms including a common currency, regular taxes and a standing army; Solon's laws are adopted in Athens; Milo of Crotona, a legendary athlete, is crowned six times at the Olympic Games (536); Chinese feudal structure begins to weaken during Chou dynasty (c. 500–451); Greek cities are freed from Persian domination when the Greeks in Cyprus win the Persian Wars (490–49); the marble temple of Apollo is built at Delphi (478); the statue of Zeus, the centrepiece of the temple of Olympia, is built (460); Aeschylus writes *Prometheus Bound* (460); the *Fables of Aesop* is written by a former Phrygian slave.

450–301: The Greek Periclean Age unfolds with the philosophers Socrates and (his pupil) Plato, the dramatists Sophocles and Euripides and historians Thucydides and Herodotus; the beginning of the Indian empire is centred at Magadha (the "cradle of Buddhism"); the Torah becomes the moral code of the Jewish people; Celtic settlements begin in the British Isles; the Spartans use chemicals in warfare (charcoal, sulphur and pitch); the Parthenon,

the masterpiece of Greek architecture, is built (447–32); the population of Greece reaches two million citizens and one million slaves; indigenous Indian civilization ends in Mexico; the Peloponnesian Wars between Athens and Sparta (431–04) end when the Spartan navy destroys the Athenian navy at Aegospotami: this leads to the decline of Athens as a great power; the first horoscopes are developed in Mesopotamia (c. 410); Socrates is put to death for state offences (399); Brennus leads the Gauls from northern Italy to sack Rome (390); Rome is rebuilt (387) and city walls are built around it (377); Plato, a Greek philosopher, founds the most influential school in the world, the Academy (c. 387); the use of catapults as weapons of war begins; Aristotle, the Greek philosopher, is born (384); Alexander the Great, son of Philip II of Macedon, is born (356); Shung-tse founds Chinese monist philosophy (the doctrine that the universe can be explained by one principle) (350); Corinth becomes a trading centre (338); Philip II is assassinated (336); Alexander succeeds his father and conquers Persia, Jerusalem and Tyre, extending his empire to the Indus River in India where his generals force him to turn back; Alexander dies in Babylon (323) and his empire is divided among his generals who fight civil wars for a time (beginning in 321); the Hellenistic period of Greek arts begins (330–20) and the leading Greek schools of thought are: Stoics, Epicureans and Cynics; Euclid writes *Elements*, a standard work on geometry (323); Alexandria is the centre of Greek learning.

300–151: The Mexican sun temple Atetello is built at Teotihuacan (300); accurate star maps are compiled by Chinese astronomers (c. 300); full equality between patricians and plebeians is mandated in Rome (287); Archimedes, the Greek mathematician, is born (287); the practical end of the history of Babylon coincides with Babylonian re-establishment in the new city of Seleucia (275); Manetho, the high priest of Egypt, writes a history of Egypt in Greek (275); the Colossus at Rhodes is completed (275); the Lighthouse of Pharos is completed at Alexandria (275); the First Punic War between the Carthaginians and the Romans (264–41) arises out of a dispute involving the Sicilian cities of Messana and Syracuse: the Romans win naval battles at Mylae (260) and Cape Ecnomus

(256) but lose in Africa (255); a Roman victory of the Aegadian Isles (241) brings a peace treaty that gives Sicily to Rome, but Rome reneges on the treaty and invades Sardinia and Corsica; the leap year is introduced into the Egyptian calendar (239); the Greeks and Romans play ball games, roll dice and play board games; the death of Sun-tsi marks the end of Chinese classical philosophy; the Great Wall of China (2,400 km long) is built to keep out invaders (215); the Second Punic War (218–01) opens when Hannibal and the Carthaginians conquer the Spanish city Saguntum, a Roman ally, and Rome declares war: Hannibal successfully invades Italy from the north (217) and makes an alliance with Philip V of Macedon (216), but is later defeated by the Romans at Zama (202) in Africa; Carthage surrenders its war fleet to Rome as well as its Spanish province; the Second Macedonian War (200–197) ends with the Romans under Flamius defeating Philip V of Macedon; the use of gears leads to the invention of the ox-driven water wheel for irrigation (200); an inscription is engraved on the Rosetta Stone (c. 200); Antiochus IV of Syria persecutes the Jews in Israel and desecrates their Temple of Jerusalem (168); the Jews revolt under Judas Maccabeus and repel the Syrians, then rededicate (Chanukah) the Temple (165); the inventor of trigonometry, Hipparchus of Nicaea, is born (160).

150–1 BC: During the Third Punic War (149–46) the Romans destroy Corinth and massacre the inhabitants of Carthage (due to alleged breach of treaty); the Roman Empire now consists of seven provinces; the Venus of Milo is sculpted (140); Cicero, the greatest Roman orator, is born (106); the first Chinese ships reach the east coast of India (100); the greatest of Roman poets, Virgil, is born (70): he pens the epic *Aeneid*; Horace, the lyric poet, is born (65); Julius Caesar, Roman military commander, organizes the First Triumvirate (60) with Pompey, commander-in-chief of the army, and Marcus Crassus; Caesar conquers the northern Gauls (55) and the Britons; Caesar and Pompey battle for control of Rome after Caesar crosses the Rubicon River and provokes a civil war; Caesar emerges victorious (48); the Julian calendar and leap year are adopted in Rome (46); Cleopatra, the last queen of Egypt, orders the death of Pompey; Caesar, now the dictator of Rome, is murdered by a group headed by Brutus and Cassius Longinus (44); Mark Antony, Octavian and Lepidus form the Second Triumvirate and defeat Brutus and Cassius at Phillipi (42); Mark Antony returns to Egypt (38) where he and Cleopatra commit suicide after being defeated by Octavian at Actium (31); Octavian, retitled Augustus, is a virtual emperor of Rome (30–AD 14); Herod the Great is appointed king of Judea by the Romans (c. 40); the probable date of the birth of Jesus, the Jewish son of Mary, in Bethlehem (AD 4).

AD 1–150: Jesus, who is revered as the Son of God by his followers, the Christians, preaches for three years in Galilee (c. 30); in the third year of his preaching, Jesus is crucified in Jerusalem by Roman authorities at the request of local political and religious leaders; Caligula becomes emperor of Rome (37) and is known for his ruthlessness and insanity: he is assassinated by the Praetorian Guard (42) and is succeeded by Claudius I, who consolidates and reinvigorates the empire despite a paralysis (dies in 54); the apostle Paul sets out on his missionary travels (45) and spreads Christianity; Nero, emperor of Rome, is the first to persecute the Christians, for allegedly burning half of Rome (64); the Gospels according to Matthew, Mark and John are written; Jews revolt against Rome and the Romans destroy the second Temple at Jerusalem and enslave many inhabitants (70); 1,000 Jewish Zealots hold off the 15,000-member Roman legion for three years on the mountaintop fortress of Masada, and the Zealots commit suicide to escape capture (73); under Emperor Trajan, the Roman Empire reaches its greatest geographical extent when he conquers Dacia and much of Parthia (98–116); paper is made by the Chinese, though not for writing (by 100); Hadrian's Wall is built as the northern boundary and defence line of the Roman Empire (122–26); the medical authority up to the 16th century, Greek physician and writer Galen, (c. 130–200) demonstrates that arteries carry blood (not air) and establishes the importance of the spinal cord by correlating earlier medical knowledge with his discoveries based on experiments and animal dissection; the earliest known Sanskrit inscriptions are made in India (150).

151–300: Ptolemy, a Greco-Egyptian thinker, compiles *Almagest*, the 13-volume work on ancient astronomy (earth-centred universe), mathematics, geography and science, which is influential to the 16th century; the oldest known Maya monuments are built (c. 164); the period of Neo-Platonism, the last of the Greek philosophies, begins (c. 200); silk-worms are exported from Korea to China and then to Japan (c. 200); citizenship is granted to every freeborn subject in the Roman Empire (212); Afghanistan is invaded by the Huns (200); the Goths invade Asia Minor and the Balkan Peninsula (220); the end of the Han dynasty in China is followed by four centuries of division (220); the southern part of India breaks into several kingdoms; Rome celebrates its 1,000th anniversary (248); persecution of Christians increases and martyrs are revered as saints (c. 250); the first book of algebra is written by Diophantus of Alexandria (c. 250); the Goths attack the Black Sea area (257) as well as Athens, Sparta and Corinth (268); Pappus of Alexandria documents use of cogwheel, lever, pulley, screw and wedge (c. 285); Rome is partitioned into a western and an eastern empire; five distinct German dukedoms emerge (Saxons, Franks, Alemanni, Thuringians and Goths) (c. 300).

301–400: Constantine the Great reunites the western and eastern Roman Empires and becomes sole emperor (310–37); Constantine establishes toleration of Christianity with the Edict of Milan (313); the seat of the Roman Empire is moved to Constantinople (c. 331); the Basilican Church of St Peter is erected (330); Emperor Constantine is baptized on his deathbed (337) and is succeeded by his three sons, who again split Rome into two empires; the Huns invade Europe (360) and Russia (376); books begin to replace scrolls (360); Lo-Tsun, a Chinese monk, founds the Caves of the Thousand Buddhas in Kansu (360); Theodosius the Great becomes the last emperor of a united Roman Empire (392); Alaric, king of the Visigoths, invades Greece (396) and plunders Athens and the Balkans (398); the first definite records of Japanese history appear (400), although legend claims Japan was founded in 660 BC.

401–76: The Visigoths invade Italy (401); Alaric sacks Rome (410); Roman legions withdraw from Britain to defend Italy from the Visigoths (410); barbarians settle in Roman provinces (425); Attila becomes ruler of the Huns (433); St Augustine, Christian theologian, writes *The City of God* (411);

alchemy begins with the search for the Philosopher's Stone and the Elixir of Life as chief objects; pre-Inca culture develops in Peru; Venice is founded by refugees from Attila's Huns (452); the Vandals sack Rome (455) and destroy the Roman fleet at Cartegena (460); the Huns leave Europe (470); the Mayan civilization flourishes in southern Mexico (c. 470); the first Shinto religious shrines are built in Japan (478): they deal primarily with nature and ancestor worship; the German barbarian Odoacer takes Ravenna and deposes Emperor Romulus Augustulus, thereby ending the Western Roman Empire (476); Aryabhata, Hindu astronomer and mathematician, studies powers and roots of numbers (b. 476).

■ Middle or Dark Ages: 477–1450

477–529: Chi dynasty in southern China (479–502); Clovis, leader of the Franks (since 481), converts to Christianity (496); the first schism between the Western and Eastern Churches occurs when Pope Felix III excommunicates Patriarch Acacius of Constantinople (484–519); Armenian Church separates from Byzantium and Rome (491); the Moshica culture of the Chimic Indians flowers in Peru with agriculture, pottery and textiles; the Vatican Palace in Rome is first planned (500); Tamo carries tea from India to China (c. 500); Clovis kills Alaric II and annexes the Visigoth kingdom of Toulouse (507), and Clovis's realm is divided among his four sons upon his death (511); Emperor Wu-Ti converts to Buddhism and encourages the new religion in central China (517); Justinian I becomes the Byzantine Emperor (527): he is known for heavy taxes, public works and codifying Roman law; the Saxon kingdoms of Essex and Middlesex appear; Chosroes I is king of Persia (531–79) and encourages culture and art.

530–99: Arthur, the semi-legendary king of the Britons, is first mentioned at the Battle of Mt Badon (c. 540); the earliest Chinese roll paintings appear in Tun-huang (landscapes); war breaks out between Persia and the Byzantine Empire (539–62); St Gildas writes the first important source of early British history, *De excido et conquestu Brittaniae* (542); disastrous earthquakes occur around the world (543); the plague of Constantinople, imported by rats from Egypt and Syria, spreads throughout Europe and reaches Britain (547); the Golden Era of Byzantine art begins (550); Poles settle in western Galacia, Ukrainians in eastern Galacia (550); chess begins in India (c. 550); Buddhism is introduced into Japan by Emperor Shotoko Taishi (c.552–621), and the first Buddhist monastery in Japan is founded (587); Japanese prehistory ends and the Asuka period begins; Justinian sends missionaries to China and Ceylon to smuggle out silkworms and the European silk industry becomes a Byzantine state monopoly (553); Mohammed, the founder of Islam, is born (570); war is renewed between Persia and the Byzantine Empire (572–91), and again when Chosroes II ascends the throne of Persia (590–628); the plague ends after killing half the population of Europe (542–94); first verified account of decimal number system in India (595); probably the first English school is established at Canterbury (598); the authoritative Talmud Babli, a compilation of Jewish Oral Law with rabbinical interpretations, is compiled (c. 6th century).

600–749: Books printed in China (600); Czechs and Slovaks take up land in Bohemia and Moravia, Yugoslavs in Serbia (c. 600); smallpox spreads from India, via China and Asia Minor, to southern Europe; the oldest surviving wooden building in the world, the Horyuji temple and hospital, is completed in Japan (607); Mohammed experiences a religious vision on Mt Hira (610); "burning water" (petroleum) is used in Japan (615); orchestras are formed in China (619); porcelain is produced in China (620); the Hegira is named after Mohammed's flight from hostile Mecca to Yathrib (later renamed Medina), and is year one in the Muslim calendar (622); an encyclopedia of arts and sciences is written by Isidore of Seville (622); Shaka Trinity, the famous altarpiece of the Kondo in Japan, is built by Tori (623); Mohammed begins to dictate the Koran (the sacred book of Islam) in Arabic (625); the Byzantines decisively defeat the Persians at Nineveh (627); Mohammed captures Mecca and writes letters to world leaders explaining the Muslim faith (628); cotton is introduced in Arab countries (630); Buddhism becomes the state religion in Tibet (632); Medina is the seat of the first caliph (religious and political leader of Muslims) who is Abu Bekr, Mohammed's father-in-law; the Arabs attack Persia (633); Damascus is the new capital of the caliphs (635–70);

Jerusalem is conquered by the Arabs (637); the book-copying industry of the west is destroyed by the Arabs and the Alexandrian school ceases to be the centre of Western culture (641); the Arabs under Omar destroy the Persian Empire: the caliphs rule the area (until 1258), and Islam replaces the religion of Zoroaster; the Eastern Roman Empire is weakened by the Arab conquest of Egypt, Mesopotamia and Syria (642); the Dome of the Rock, a Muslim mosque, is begun in Jerusalem (643); the Muslim fleet destroys the Byzantine fleet at Lycia (655); Croats and Serbs settle in Bosnia (650); Chinese artists invent lamp-black ink and wood block printing (c. 650); Caliphs organize first news service (650); Japanese Buddhism and Shintoism are reconciled by the Korean-born priest Gyogi (c. 668–749); the Byzantines use "Greek Fire," a missile weapon of sulphur, rock, salt, resin and petroleum, against the Arabs at the siege of Constantinople (671–78); glass windows appear in English churches (674); the first Arab coinage is introduced (695); the Arabs destroy Carthage (697); Greek, instead of Latin, becomes the official language of the Eastern Roman Empire (700); the Arabs conquer Algiers (700) and virtually eliminate Christianity in northern Africa; mass migration of European peoples is followed by their subjection at the hands of property owners; China's population grows rapidly (700) and the first large urban developments appear there; the Great Mosque of Damascus is built (705); Buddhist monasteries in Japan become centres of civilization (710); the first written history of Japan, *Kojiki*, is compiled (712); the Lombard kingdom in northern Italy reaches its height (c. 600–c. 799); the Muslim empire now extends from the Pyrenees to China, with Damascus as its capital (715); the earliest Islamic paintings appear (715); Caliph Omar II grants tax exemption to all Muslim believers (717); the Chinese capital Ch'ang-an is the largest city in the world and Constantinople is the second largest (725); Casa Grande, a North American Indian fort and large irrigation works, is built in Arizona (725); Charles Martel (mayor of the Frankish court) wins victory over the Arabs in the battle of Tours and halts their westward advance (732); first printed newspaper published in Beijing (748).

750–849: Pueblos are built in southwest North America (750–900); Spain, under Arab influence, excels in mathematics, optics and chemistry (c. 750); Kiev, Russia, becomes known as a trading centre (750); the Turkish Empire is founded by a Tartar tribe in Armenia (760); Charlemagne becomes ruler of the Franks after the death of his father (Pepin the Short, son of Charles Martel) (768) and brother Carloman (771); Arabic learning flourishes under Harun-al-Rashid (790), peaks during reign of Caliph Mamun (813–33); the Byzantine Empress Irene overthrows her son Constantine (797), an act heralded by the Greek Church; Charlemagne is crowned Holy Roman Emperor (Western Empire) at Rome (800); the earliest records of Persian poetry and literature appear (800); the Vikings dominate Ireland (802); Arabic numerals are created under Indian influence (814); the Arabs conquer Crete, proceed as far as the Greek isles (826) and begin their conquest of Italy and Sardinia (827); Prince Mimir founds the Great Moravian Empire (830) from a confederation of Slavs in Bohemia, Moravia, Slovakia, Hungary and Transylvania; the Treaty of Verdun divides the Frankish Empire into France, Germany and Italy (843); paper currency in China creates inflation and state bankruptcy (845); Abu Tamman writes *Hamasa*, a collection of Arabian legends, proverbs and heroic stories (845); the Arabs sack Rome (846), damage the Vatican and destroy the Venetian fleet.

850–99: Salerno University is founded (850); the discovery of coffee is credited to Arabia (850); Jews settling in Germany develop the Yiddish language (c. 850); the first important Japanese painter, Kudara Kuwanari, dies (853); Norse pirates enter the Mediterranean and sack the coast up to Asia Minor (859); Iceland is discovered by the Northmen (861); Russian Northmen sack parts of France (861) and attack Constantinople (865); Basil I, the Byzantine Emperor, compiles the Basilican code (reforming finance and law and restoring the prestige of the military), and begins the Macedonian dynasty (867); Alfred the Great, king of England, recaptures London from the Danes (878); Emperor Charles III becomes king of France and once more unites the empire of Charlemagne (884), he is deposed (887) and there is a final separation of Germany and France; England's King Alfred establishes a regular militia and navy, extends the power of the king's courts and institutes fairs and markets (890).

900–99: The Vikings discover Greenland (900); the Mayans relinquish their settlements in the lowlands of Mexico and emigrate to the Yucatan peninsula (900); England is divided into shires with county courts in order to safeguard the civil rights of the inhabitants (900); the Arabian tales *A Thousand and One Nights* is begun (900); castles become the seats of the European nobility (900); Cordoba, Spain, is the seat of Arab learning, science, commerce and industry (930); Yenching becomes new capital city of China, later known as Beijing (938); revolts against imperial rule in Japan set off a period of civil war (939–1185); the Arab empire creates advanced postal and news services (942); the earliest record of the existence of a London bridge (963); a Chinese encyclopedia of 1,000 volumes is begun (978–84); the rule of nobles in Rome ends (980); Venice and Genoa carry on a flourishing trade between Asia and Western Europe (983); systematic musical notation develops (990); canonization of Christian saints begins.

1000–99: The heroic poem *Beowulf* is written in Old English by an unknown author (1000); Leif Ericsson, son of Eric the Red, sails to North America (1000); the Chinese invent gunpowder (1000); Mayan culture on the Yucatan peninsula achieves its zenith (1000); Sridhara, Indian mathematician, describes the importance of zero (1000); the Holy Sepulchre in Jerusalem is sacked by Muslims (1009); Danes under Canute control England (1016); Canute conquers Norway (1028); Jaroslav the Wise, Prince of Kiev (1020–54), codifies Russian law and builds cities, schools and churches; Byzantine power begins to decline (1025); Canute dies (1035) and his kingdom of England, Norway and Denmark is divided among his three sons; after murdering Duncan of Scotland, Macbeth becomes king (1040) and is later murdered by Malcolm (1057); time values are given to musical notes (1050); the separation of the Roman and Eastern Churches becomes permanent (1054); Westminster Abbey is consecrated (1065); William of Normandy is crowned William the Conqueror, of England (1066); the comet, later known as Halley's comet, appears (1066); She-tsung, Emperor of China, nationalizes agricultural production and distribution (1068); Constantine the African brings Greek medicine to the Western world (1071); the original Tower of London is built (1078); the Domesday Book, a survey of assessment for tax purposes, is compiled (1086); the start of the First Crusade (1096) is proclaimed by Pope Urban II to recapture the Holy Land from the Turks; Crusaders take Jerusalem (1099).

1100–99: Middle English supercedes Old English (1100); Islamic science begins to decline; secular music first appears; Robert of Normandy is appeased after invading England in the Treaty of Alton (1101); colonization of eastern Germany begins (1105); the earliest record of a miracle play is from Dunstable, England (1110): based on Scriptures and the lives of saints, they are widely performed until the 16th century; Bologna University founded (1119); the earliest account of a mariner's compass is by Alexander Neckham (1125); the Second Crusade begins (1146) and fails one year later; Paris University is founded (1150); Bologna Medical School is founded (1150); the first recorded fire and plague insurance is in Iceland (1151); the Japanese clans Taira and Minamoto fight each other (1156); Eric of Sweden conquers Finland (1157); Thomas à Becket is elected Archbishop of Canterbury (1162) in an effort to curb church power, but he later quarrels with King Henry II over growing royal power; Becket is murdered by Norman knights (1170) and buried at Canterbury; jails are ordered erected in all English counties and boroughs (1166); Oxford University is founded (1167); rules for the canonization of saints are established by Pope Alexander III (1170); first authenticated influenza epidemics occur (1173); the Campanile ("Leaning Tower") of Pisa is built (1174); Walter Map organizes the Arthurian legends in their present form (1176); all Jews are banished from France (1182); the Third Crusade (1189–93) fails to recapture Jerusalem from the Muslims; Moses Maimonides, Jewish philosopher, introduces Aristotle to modern western philosophy when he attempts to reconcile Aristotle's theories with those of Jewish philosophy in *Guide to the Perplexed* (1190), and he is also credited with organizing all Jewish law for the layman as well as religious educators.

1200–49: Cambridge University founded (1200); Islam takes root in India; the Fourth Crusade begins with crusaders from Venice fighting Constantinople and establishing a Latin Kingdom of Jerusalem (1204); St Francis of Assisi issues the first rules of his brotherhood of educators and missionaries, the Franciscans (1209); in the Children's Crusade (1212), thousands of children from Europe leave for the Holy Land, but most are either sold as slaves or die of hunger or disease; Genghis Khan becomes chief prince of the Mongols (1206) and conquers most of the Chinese empire of north China (1213–15) as well as Turkistan, Afghanistan and Transoxania (1218–24), and he raids Persia and Eastern Europe; Genghis Khan's empire is divided among his descendants upon his death (1227); the Council of St Albans is the precursor to the British Parliament (1213); King John puts his seal on England's Magna Carta at Runnymede under compulsion by the barons (1215): it defines the limitations of royal power and sets out basic civil rights; the Fifth Crusade fails in Egypt (1217–21); the oldest national flag in the world, Danneborg, is adopted by Denmark (1218); the form of the sonnet develops in Italian poetry (1221); Thomas Aquinas (1225–74) theorizes philosophical proofs for the existence of God and reconciles Greek ideas with Christian theology; the Sixth Crusade is led by Emperor Frederick II (1228); crusaders bring back leprosy to Europe (1230), and they secure a temporary truce with the Muslims; three later crusades against Muslims in the 13th century fail; coal is mined for the first time in Newcastle, England (1233); the Inquisition begins as the pope makes Dominicans responsible for putting an end to heresy (1233); Alexander Nevski made Grand Duke of Novgorod (1236).

1250–99: Kublai Khan becomes governor of China (1251) and ruler of the Mongol peoples (1259–94); he fails to conquer Japan (1274), southeast Asia and Indonesia, but he defeats the Sung dynasty of China (1279); instruments of torture are first used in the Inquisition (1252); the Sorbonne is founded by Robert de Sorbon as the Paris School of Theology (1254); the House of Commons is established in England (1258); Mongols control Baghdad, end caliphate (1258); Roger Bacon writes *"De computo naturali"* (1264); the glass mirror is invented (1278); Marco Polo, the Venetian explorer, journeys to China (1271–95) and is in the diplomatic service of Kublai Khan (1275–92); Florence, Italy, is the leading European city in commerce and finance (c. 1282); the Teutonic Order, a German military and religious order, conquers Prussia (1283) after killing the native "heathens" and replacing them with Germans; spectacles (eyeglasses) are invented (1290); the crusades end and the Knights of St John of Jerusalem settle in Cyprus (1291).

1300–99: Trade fairs at Bruges, Antwerp, Lyons and Geneva (c. 1300); Edward I of England standardizes the yard and the acre (1305); Dante composes his *Divina Commedia* (1307–21); mechanical clocks are driven by weights in Europe; Salic Law, excluding women from succession to the throne, is adopted in France (1317); No plays originate in Japan (1325); the Aztecs establish Mexico City (1327); the sawmill is invented (1328); weaving at York first documented (1331); the Hundred Years War between France and England begins (1337) as a dispute over lands held by the English crown in France: it later becomes a dispute over the French crown itself; the first scientific weather forecasts are attempted by William Merlee of Oxford (1337); the Black Death (bubonic plague) devastates Europe, killing about 75 million people, more than one-third of the population (1347–51); Boccaccio writes *Decameron* (1348–53), which is intended to be a diversion from the horrors of the plague; Timur the Lame (Tamerlaine) begins his conquest of Asia (1363); the Aztecs of Mexico build their capital, Tenochtitlan (1364); the Mongol Yüan dynasty in China is overthrown by the national Ming dynasty (1368–1644); the building of the Bastille begins in Paris (1369); "Robin Hood," the legendary hero who robbed the rich to help the poor, appears in English ballads and literature; The Great Schism in the Catholic Church begins (1378–1417) when, after the death of Pope Gregory XI, two popes are elected, one each at Rome and Avignon; Venice wins its Hundred Years War against Genoa (1256–1381); Briton John Wyclif calls for the reform of church practices (1379); he is condemned as a heretic (1380, 1382) and inspires the first English translation of the Latin Bible, the Wyclif Bible; Chaucer writes *The Canterbury Tales*; the rival southern and northern courts of Japan's divided imperial family reunite after 50 years of strife; Denmark, Sweden and Norway unite under Queen Margaret of Denmark (1397) in the Union of Kalmar.

1400–39: Russia's greatest icon painter,

Andrei Rublex, creates *Trinity* (1411); England and France sign a perpetual peace treaty upon the marriage of Henry V and Catherine of Valois (1420); Joan of Arc and her French followers defeat the British at Orleans (1429) and march triumphantly to Paris: she is then taken prisoner by the Burgundians (1430) and condemned and executed (1431) in a political inquisition and trial; complete suits of metal armor plate replace chain mail in Europe (1430); China shuts out the western world and bans voyages there (1433) because Confucian doctrine sees little merit in trade; the Portugese find the way round Cape Bojador (on the west coast of Africa) under Henry the Navigator (1434); the Greek (Eastern or Byzantine) Church unites with the Roman church (1439) in order to save itself from the Turkish threat; Montezuma becomes ruler of the Aztecs in Mexico (1440) and begins to conquer surrounding tribes.

■ Renaissance: 1440–1650

1440–69: The rise of the Italian city-states heralds the Renaissance (1440–50), and the richest families (such as the Medici) vie with each other as patrons of art and learning (mainly in Florence); the first oil painter, Jan van Eyck, dies in Flanders (1441); France defeats England at Castillion, ending the Hundred Years War (1453), and the English give up everything except Calais, thus ending English rule in France; Zimbabwe, the great African kingdom, declines after 200 years of expansion (1450) because of food shortages; Constantinople, the old capital of the Byzantine empire, falls to the Ottomans (1453); a treaty unites rival Italian city-states (1454), requiring them to protect each other from outside aggression; Ming porcelain pottery appears in Europe (1460); the Bible is printed mechanically with metal type faces and oil-based ink by Johann Gutenberg (1455); the Wars of the Roses begin in England (1455) as a struggle for the throne between the houses of York and Lancaster, and end (1485) when Henry VII of the house of Lancaster prevails over Richard III; Plato's writings are translated into Latin at the Platonic Academy in Florence (1469).

1470–99: Music sheets, maps and posters are mechanically printed (1470s); Vlad the Impaler dies in Transylvania (1477) and the mass murderer becomes the source for

Dracula legends; Peruvian-centred Inca rule expands to include the entire Andean region (3,200 sq. km) under Pachacuti, and his son Topa Inca (1470), and it is characterized by terracing, irrigation, pantheistic religion with human sacrifice, advanced metalwork, tapestry making and construction; the Spanish Catholic Inquisition begins (1478); King Ferdinand V of Aragón and Queen Isabella I of Castile unite their crowns in Spain to ward off Alfonso V of Portugal (1479); Ivan the Great declares Russian independence (1480) from the Mongols when he refuses to continue paying them tribute; the first European manual of navigation and nautical almanac is prepared in Portugal by mathematical experts (1484) who calculate the latitude of the sun, based on the work of the Jewish astronomer Abraham Zacuto; the spread of witchcraft and heresy in Germany is attacked by Pope Innocent VIII (1484) and he authorizes Dominican inquisitors to torture and burn witches; the publication of an encyclopedia of witchcraft, *Malleus Maleficarum* (1486), adds to witch hunt hysteria; the Genoese seaman Christopher Columbus secures the sponsorship of Queen Isabella of Spain (1486) for his expedition to discover a western route to Asia (he sets sail with his three ships: Santa María, Pinta and Niña in 1492); the Aztecs of Mexico inaugurate the Great Temple of Tenochtitlan (1487) when they ritually sacrifice the hearts of 20,000 people; the Portugese explorer Bartholomew Dias rounds the Cape of Good Hope off South Africa (1488); Leonardo da Vinci is in his prime in Italy (1488) as an artist, scientist, inventor and philosopher, with inventions centuries ahead of their time (e.g., he conceives of flying machines and an apparatus to enable humans to breathe under water); the Great Wall of China is rebuilt by Ming emperors as a defence against attacks by northern Barbarians (1488); the first terrestrial globe is made by Martin Behaim, a German (1492); Jews are ordered by Spain's Catholic rulers to choose between expulsion or forced conversion (1492), and the rulers change the options to conversion or death (1498); Spain conquers Granada (1492), the last Muslim kingdom in Spain; Spain and Portugal sign a treaty dividing lands discovered in the new world, but Spain benefits the most from the treaty (1494); French armies in Italy bring a virus later identified as syphilis to Naples and the epidemic spreads through Europe (1495);

Columbus brings tobacco back from the new world (1496); the Chinese invent a toothbrush (1498); Vasco da Gama discovers a sea route round the Cape of Good Hope to India via the Indian Ocean (1498); the Italian navigator Amerigo Vespucci explores the northeast coast of South America (1499) and reports cannibals (1502); Portugal's Pedro Cabral discovers the east coast of Brazil and observes natives using stone to cut wood (1499).

1500–25: The discovery of plays and poems by Hroswitha of Gandersheim, a 10th-century saxoness, makes her the first European playwright since the Classical Age (1500); King Ferdinand of Spain sanctions a system of levying tribute payments from Indians in the new world and using Indians as forced labour (1501); Shi'ism becomes the state religion in Persia (1502) and Sunni Muslim dissenters are executed there; a hand-held timepiece, made possible by the invention of the coiled mainspring, is constructed by German locksmith Peter Henlein (1502); *David*, a 13-foot statue, is completed by Michelangelo Buonarrotti (1504) in Florence, Italy; Leonardo da Vinci paints the *Mona Lisa* (1505); Venice dominates Mediterranean trade (c. 1507); a map calls the new world "America" after Amerigo Vespucci (1507) and shows it as a distinct continent; the first great German artist, Albrecht Dürer (painter/engraver), creates his *Adam and Eve* oil painting (1507); Michelangelo paints the ceiling of the Sistine Chapel (1508–12); Sebastian Cabot sails around Cuba, proving it is an island (1508) and later reaches Hudson Bay in search of a northwest passage; the first African slaves are brought to the Americas (Cuba) (1510); Erasmus, the Dutch humanist, writes the satirical *In Praise of Folly* (1511); Juan Ponce de Léon claims Florida for Spain (1513) while searching for the Fountain of Youth; Niccolo Machiavelli writes *The Prince* (1513) which discusses the uses and abuses of power; Vasco Núñez de Balboa discovers the "South Sea," or Pacific Ocean, for Spain (1513); Spain orders new world natives to convert to Christianity under threat of enslavement or death (1514); Henry VIII of England puts forth measures to protect peasants from enclosure—the dividing and closing off of common land (1515); Sir Thomas More writes *Utopia*, which depicts an ideal state (1516); Martin Luther, a German Augustinian monk, writes his *95 Theses*, attacking the Catholic church's sale of indulgences granting the forgiveness of sins (1517) and nails it to the door of the Wittenberg church; English sailors complain to King Henry VIII about the growing number of French cod fishermen in Newfoundland (1517); the rule of Suleiman I the Magnificent sees the Ottoman Turks reach the zenith of their empire with the conquest of Egypt, Syria and Hungary (1520); Ferdinand Magellan begins a three-year voyage to circumnavigate the globe (1519); Hernando Cortes lands at Vera Cruz, Mexico, where Montezuma II and the Aztecs surrender (1519); chocolate is introduced to Europe from Mexico (1520); Nicholas Copernicus publishes his "Commentariolus" stating his theory that the earth revolves around the sun (1521); Martin Luther translates the Bible into German (1522).

1526–49: Lutheran German troops sack and burn Rome (1527); Hippocrates' ancient idea of the four humours governing bodily health is first disputed (1528); Henry VIII separates from the Church of Rome and becomes head of the English Church (1534) after he is refused an annulment of his first marriage; the Jesuit order of missionaries is founded by Ignatius Loyola (1534); Jacques Cartier searches for riches in North America along the St Lawrence River (1535); John Calvin, the French leader of the Protestant Reformation in Geneva, theorizes the concepts of predestination and God's omniscience (1536); the first mechanical artificial limbs appear for crippled war veterans (1539); the founder of the Sikh religion, Guru Nanak, dies in India (1539); Henry VIII becomes King of Ireland and Head of the Irish Church (1541); John Knox leads the Calvinist Reformation in Scotland (1541); oil is discovered in North America by the Spaniards (1543); Portugese traders are the first to sell guns to Japan (1543); Nostradamus, the French astrologer, begins making predictions (1547); Ivan IV (the Terrible) is crowned the first czar of Russia (1547); he calls the first national assembly (1549).

1550–99: Jesuit missionaries protect natives in the new world from slavery (1551); Ivan the Terrible defeats the Mongols (1552), and conquers as far as the Caspian Sea (1556); Lady Jane Grey is executed for treason in England by Queen Mary Tudor (1554), who becomes known as "Bloody Mary" after persecuting Protestants (1555); Mary restores papal authority in England and Wales (1554); Charles V relinquishes the Holy Roman Empire and Spain to his brother and son, and goes to a monastery (1556); an influenza epidemic hits Europe (1557); Elizabeth I becomes Queen of England (1558) and rejects papal power in England (1559); the Huguenot (Calvinist French Protestant) conspiracy occurs at Amboise: liberty of worship is promised in France (1560); the Edict of Orleans suspends persecution of Huguenots (1561); the Peace of Amboise ends the first War of Religion in France and the Huguenots are granted limited toleration (1563); Andreas Vesalius, the Flemish founder of modern anatomy, dies (1564); Nobunaga deposes the Japanese shogunate and centralizes the government (1567); the Iroquois Confederacy of five North American nations (Mohawk, Oneida, Onondaga, Cayuga, Seneca) is founded (c. 1570); Huguenots are massacred on St Bartholomew's Day in Paris (1572); the Dutch War of Independence begins (1572); the Union of Utrecht is the foundation of the Dutch Republic (1579); William of Orange accepts the sovereignty of northern Netherlands and is assassinated (1584); the first English colony in Newfoundland is founded (1582); Elizabeth of England orders Mary Queen of Scots beheaded for treason (1587); Christopher Marlowe completes *Dr. Faustus* (1588); the first Spanish Armada leaves for England and is defeated by the English under Charles Howard (1588); Sir Francis Drake, with 18,000 men, fails to take Lisbon for England (1589); William Shakespeare completes the play *Romeo and Juliet* (1594); the Second Spanish Armada leaves for England but is scattered by storms (1597); an English Act of Parliament calls for convicted criminals to serve their terms in the colonies (1597).

1600–49: France boasts the largest population in central Europe, with 16 million persons (1600); William Shakespeare completes *Hamlet* (1600); Dutch opticians invent the telescope (1600); the first modern public company is founded, the Dutch East India Company (1602); Guy Fawkes is arrested and accused of trying to blow up the House of Lords during James I's state opening of Parliament (The Gunpowder Plot, 1605); Fawkes is sentenced to death (1606); the first English settlement on the American mainland is founded at Jamestown, Virginia (1607);

Shakespeare writes his *Sonnets* (1609); the first cheques appear in Netherlands as "cash letters" (1608); the *King James Bible* is published (1611); Peter Paul Rubens paints *Descent from the Cross* (1611); the North American Indian princess Pocahantas marries English colonist John Rolfe (1614); Galileo Galilei, Italian astronomer, faces the Inquisition for the first time for renouncing the Ptolemaic system of the earth-centred universe and embracing the Copernican sun-centred system (1615); the Thirty Years War begins in Prague as Protestants rebel against Catholic oppression (1618); slavery in North America begins when the first Africans are brought to Virginia (1619) and the triangular slave trade starts (British goods are sent to west Africa and are traded for slaves, who are traded for agricultural staples in the new world, which are sent back to Britain); pilgrims arriving on the *Mayflower* found Plymouth Colony, Massachusetts (1620); patent law is created in England to protect inventors (1623); construction begins on the Taj Mahal mausoleum in Agra, North India (1628); Charles I dissolves the English Parliament for 11 years (1629); Cardinal Richelieu, chief minister of Louis XIII of France, rules France (1630–42); Galileo is forced by the Inquisition to cease promulgating the theories of Copernicus (1633); Japan forbids foreign books, Christianity and any European contacts (1637); René Descartes, called the father of modern philosophy, writes *Discourse on Method* (1637); the Ming dynasty in China ends and the Manchu dynasty takes power (1644–1912); Charles I of England, after a long struggle for power with Parliament (English Civil War 1642–48), is beheaded by Oliver Cromwell for treason (1649).

1650–99: Bishop James Ussher dates the creation of the world at Oct. 23, 4004 BC (1650); the wholesale massacre of North American Indians by European settlers begins (1650); Thomas Hobbes writes *Leviathan*, a defence of absolute monarchy in England (1651); Oliver Cromwell becomes Lord Protector in England, dissolves Parliament, divides England into 11 districts, prohibits Anglican services (1653) and readmits Jews to England after 365 years (1655); Blaise Pascal (French) develops the basic laws of probability (1654); the Portugese drive the Dutch out of Brazil (1654); the first London opera house opens (1656); Dutch peasants (Boers) first settle in South Africa (1660); the Royal Society is founded in London to promote scientific discussion among great thinkers (1660); the earliest condemnation of industrial pollution, *The Inconvenience of the Air and Smoke of London Dissipated*, is written by John Evelyn (1661); Louis XIV (the Sun King) begins to build the palace at Versailles (1662); Jean Baptiste Colbert forms the North American colony of New France with Quebec as its capital (1663); the British annex New Netherlands from the Dutch and rename the main city New York (1664); Isaac Newton begins to experiment with gravity and develops calculus (1664–66); the cell is named and described by Briton Robert Hooke (1665); the French army uses the first hand grenades (1667); Portugal gains independence from Spain through the Treaty of Lisbon (1668); microorganisms are discovered by Anton van Leeuwenhoek (Dutch, 1669) who later observes bacteria (1683) for the first time; the Hudson's Bay Company is incorporated by a British royal charter to trade in the region of North America defined by those rivers which drain into Hudson Bay (1670); Dutch philosopher Baruch Spinoza writes *Ethics* (1675); the poems of Bashu (a pseudonym) popularize Japanese haiku poetry (1675); the *Declaration of the People of Virgina* by Nathaniel Bacon lends support to rebellion against authorities in the colonies (1676); Roman Catholics are excluded from both houses of Parliament in England (1678); the Habeas Corpus Amendment Act in England protects citizens from unjust imprisonment (1679); the French colonial empire of North America, reaching from Quebec to the mouth of the Mississippi River, is organized (1680); the large dodo bird with small, flightless wings becomes extinct (1680); Sir Isaac Newton writes *Principles of Natural Philosophy* (1687), which discusses universal gravitation; the Glorious Revolution establishes the constitutional monarchy in England (1688–89) and William of Orange III and Mary II ascend the throne; Peter the Great becomes Czar of Russia (1689); John Locke writes *Essay Concerning Human Understanding* and *Two Treatises on Civil Government* (1690).

1700–49: The War of the Spanish Succession to the childless Charles II, Hapsburg king of Spain, is fought (1701–14) between the

French Bourbons and Austrian Hapsburgs; rebellion occurs in Astrakhan against Czar Peter's westernization of Russia (1705); England and Scotland form Great Britain (1707); the Peace of Utrecht is signed between Spain and England: Spain cedes Gibraltar and Minorca to England (1713) and Philip of France retains the Spanish crown; D.G. Fahrenheit constructs a mercury thermometer with a temperature scale (1714); George F. Handel writes *Water Music* for King George I (1717); Daniel Defoe writes *The Life and Strange Surprising Adventures of Robinson Crusoe* (1719); the German composer and virtuoso organist J.S. Bach composes *The Brandenburg Concertos* (1721); Johnathan Swift writes *Gulliver's Travels* (1726); Benjamin Franklin, American statesman, scientist, printer and writer, writes *Poor Richard's Almanack* (1732); John Kay patents the fly shuttle loom, which revolutionizes weaving (1733); Alexander Pope, poet and English verse satirist, writes *Essay on Man* (1733); the modern classification system of plants and animals is introduced by Carolus Linnaeus (Swedish, 1735); Alaska is discovered by Victor Behring (1740); Frederick the Great introduces freedom of the press and freedom of worship in Prussia (1740); sign language for the deaf is created by Rodriguez Pereire (1749).

■ Industrial Revolution: 1750–1850

1750–99: Benjamin Franklin experimented with static electricity and invented the lightning conductor (1752); in the Seven Years War (1756–63) Britain declares war on France and, in the North American colonies, the French drive the British from the Great Lakes area (1756); the French lose Quebec to the British (1759) during the battle on the Plains of Abraham; Voltaire writes the philosophical novel *Candide* (1759); Catherine II (the Great) becomes czarina of Russia (1762); Swiss-French philosopher Jean Jacques Rousseau writes *Social Contract* (1762) which discusses his theory of "natural man"; the Peace of Paris (1763) ends the war between England and France and gives Canada to England; eight-year-old Mozart writes his first symphony (1764); the spinning jenny, which spins up to 120 threads at once is invented by Briton James Hargreaves (1764); the British Parliament passes the

Stamp Act for taxing American colonies: Virginia and New York challenge the right of Britain to taxation without representation (1766); the Mason-Dixon Line is drawn by English surveyors between Pennsylvania and Maryland (1767) and is later the boundary between "slave" and "free" states; Daniel Rutherford and Joseph Priestley independently discover nitrogen (1772); the Bolshoi Ballet is founded in Russia (1773); during the Boston Tea Party American colonists protesting British taxes dress as Indians and dump the cargo of three tea ships in the Boston, Mass., harbor (1773); James Watt, Scottish inventor, perfects the steam engine (1775); the American Revolution begins (1775); the Second Continental Congress assembles at Philadelphia and appoints George Washington commander-in-chief of the American forces; the Americans proclaim the *Declaration of Independence* (July 4, 1776); Edward Gibbon writes *Decline and Fall of the Roman Empire* (1776); Adam Smith completes *Wealth of Nations* (1776); after the American victory in the Saratoga Campaign (1777) France entered into an alliance with the Americans (1778); Washington's army suffers at Valley Forge (1778); Hawaii is discovered by James Cook (1778); Franz Mesmer practices mesmerism (hypnotism) (1778); Spain joins the American War of Independence against Britain (1779); the Dutch support the American side (1780); Sir William Herschel discovers Uranus (1781); British General Cornwallis surrenders to the Americans (Oct. 1781) at the end of the Yorktown Campaign, and the Treaty of Paris recognizes American independence (1783); John Wesley writes the *Deed of Declaration*, the charter of Wesleyan Methodism (1784); the British colony of Australia is founded (1788); the French Revolution begins (1789); a Paris mob opposing the monarchy storms the Bastille jail; French royalists begin to emigrate; the French revolutionaries proclaim the Decrees of Aug. 4 and the *Declaration of the Rights of Man and of the Citizen;* the government limits the monarchy's power, abolishes the French feudal system, extends religious tolerance to Jews and protestants and reorganizes the Catholic Church; A.L. Lavoisier completes the *Table of Thirty-One Chemical Elements* (1790); the Constitutional Act divides Britain's Canadian colony into Upper Canada (English-speaking) and Lower Canada (French-speaking) (1791); Thomas Paine writes *The Rights of Man* in defence of the French Revolution (1791); the French King Louis XIV and Queen Marie Antoinette are beheaded for treason (Jan., 1793); the Reign of Terror (guillotine executions of prisoners) under the Jacobin government ends with the execution of Maximilien Robespierre; Robert Burns' *Auld Lang Syne* is published (1794); Edward Jenner discovers a smallpox vaccine (1796).

1800–09: Ottawa is founded (1800); Eli Whitney makes muskets with interchangeable parts (1800); the Library of Congress is established in Washington, DC by Thomas Jefferson (1800); the first battery is produced from zinc and copper plates by Alessandro Volto (1800); William Herschel discovers the existence of infrared solar rays (1800); the first submarine *Nautilus* is made by American civil engineer Robert Fulton (1801); the atomic theory of chemistry is put forth by John Dalton (1802); the US buys land from France in the Louisiana Purchase (1803); Henry Shrapnel invents the shell used in warfare (1803); Napoleon crowns himself emperor of the French empire (1804) and king of Italy (1805); modern Egypt is established when Mehemet Ali becomes Pasha (1805); morphine is isolated by F.W.A. Satürner (1805); Napoleon wins his greatest victory, at Austerlitz, over the Austrians and Russians allied against him (1805); the American frigate *Chesapeake* is stopped and boarded by British naval officers looking for deserters, almost causing a war (1807); Ludwig van Beethoven, the great German composer who brought together Classical and Romantic styles, performs his *Fifth Symphony* (written for Napoleon) and *Sixth Symphony* (1808); the first part of J.W. von Goethe's *Faust* is published (1808); Washington Irving writes *Rip van Winkle* (1809).

1810–19: Simón Bolívar becomes a leading figure in South American politics (1810) and liberates Greater Colombia (Panama, Venezuela, Ecuador and Colombia) (1819) and Peru (1824) from Spanish rule; a machine for spinning flax is invented by Philippe Girard (1812); German folklorist Jakob Grimm completes *Grimm's Fairy Tales* (1812–15); Napoleon Bonaparte's first military setback is in the Peninsular War (1808–14); and he later retreats from an unsuccessful invasion of Russia; the War of 1812 (1812–14) between Britain and the United States is foreshadowed

by the battle at Tippecanoe (1811); Jane Austen writes *Pride and Prejudice* (1813), depicting English country life and mores; Austria, Russia and Prussia form an alliance against Napoleon and defeat him at Leipzig (1813) and recapture Paris (1814); Napoleon abdicates and is exiled to Elba Island; the War of 1812 continues in North America as the British capture Washington, DC (1814) but the Americans win battles at Fort McHenry, Thames (killing Tecumseh, an Indian ally of the British) and at Plattsburgh (1814); the British initiate peace in the Treaty of Ghent (1814) but this news travels too slowly to stop the Battle of New Orleans (1815), won by the Americans; Napoleon escapes from exile and returns to march on Paris; he is defeated at Waterloo (1815), abdicates again and is banished to St Helena Island; the German Confederation, dominated by Austria and Prussia, is created to replace the Holy Roman Empire (1815); Argentina declares its independence from Spain (1816); the classical economist David Ricardo (British) writes *The Principles of Political Economy and Taxation* (1817), discussing the determination of wage and value; Georg Hegel writes his all-embracing *Encyclopedia of the Philosophical Sciences* (1817); Mary Wollstonecraft Shelley writes *Frankenstein* (1818); Lord Byron begins *Don Juan* (1818–23); Chile proclaims its independence from Spain (1818); electromagnetism is discovered by Danish physicist Hans C. Oersted (1819); Greater Colombia (including Panama, Venezuela, Ecuador and Colombia) declares independence from Spain (1819).

1820–29: Andre Ampere (French) writes *Laws of Electrodynamic Action* (1820); Liberia is founded by the Washington Colonization Society, for the repatriation of black slaves (1820); Sir Walter Scott writes *Ivanhoe* (1820); John Keats writes *Ode to a Nightingale* (1820); an electric recording device for sound reproduction is invented by Sir Charles Wheatstone (1821); Peru and Guatemala declare their independence from Spain (1821); the Reign of Terror begins between the Greeks and the Turks (1821); Franz Liszt, the Hungarian pianist who revolutionizes Romantic music and invents the symphonic poem, makes his debut at age 11 in Vienna (1822); Brazil declares itself independent from Portugal (1822); the Monroe Doctrine closes the American continent to colonial settlement by European powers (1823); Spanish are defeated and Paris independence recognized (1824); Simón Bolívar creates his namesake, Bolivia (1825); the first steam-powered railroads carrying freight and passengers, operated by the the Stockton and Darlington Railway, run in England (1825); the Erie Canal opens, linking the Hudson River and the Great Lakes (1825); the first major American author, James Fenimore Cooper, writes *The Last of the Mohicans* (1826); Felix Mendelssohn composes the Overture to *A Midsummer Night's Dream* (1826); the great cholera epidemic begins in India (1826) and spreads from Russia into Central Europe; J. J. Audubon writes *Birds of North America* (1827); Noah Webster writes the *American Dictionary of the English Language* (1828); Uruguay declares independence from Brazil (1828); the Peace of Adrianople ends the Russo-Turkish war and Turkey acknowledges the independence of Greece (1829); Frederic Chopin, the Polish pianist, debuts in Vienna (1829); Venezuela withdraws from Greater Colombia and becomes independent (1829).

1830–39: Charles Lyell of Scotland divides the geological system into three groups: Eocene, Miocene and Pliocene (1830); Ecuador declares independence (1830); mass demonstrations in Swiss cities lead to liberal reforms (1831); Charles Darwin sails on the HMS *Beagle* as a naturalist, surveying South America, New Zealand and Australia (1831–36); the leading anti-slavery leader in the United States, W. L. Garrison, begins publishing *The Liberator* in Boston (1831); the wealthy middle classes emerging from the Industrial Revolution are enfranchised in Britain, doubling the number of voters (1832); the New England anti-slavery society is founded in Boston (1832); slavery is abolished in the British Empire (1833); the Spanish Inquisition, begun during the 13th century, is finally abolished (1834); France's leading writer, Victor Hugo, writes *The Hunchback of Notre Dame* (1834); the Poor Law Amendment Act decrees that no able-bodied person (displaced by the Industrial Revolution) in Great Britain shall receive assistance unless he or she enters a workhouse (1834); Hans Christian Anderson writes his first stories for children (1835); the American writer Ralph Waldo Emerson writes *Nature* (1836); the People's Charter initiates Britain's

first national working-class movement, calling for universal suffrage for men and voting by ballot (1836); the Dutch (Afrikaner) farmers begin "The Great Trek" of emigration across the Orange and Vaal Rivers, South Africa (1836); the first botanical textbook, *The Elements of Botany*, is written by American Asa Gray (1836); Victoria becomes Queen of Great Britain (1837); citizens stage unsuccessful rebellions in Lower and Upper Canada (1837); Louis Braille invents his reading system for the blind (1837); Charles Dickens's *Oliver Twist*, a critique of British industrial society, is a bestseller (1838); the first bicycle is invented by a Scot, Kirkpatrick Macmillan (1839); the cell-growth theory is put forth by Theodor Schwann (1839); ozone is discovered by Christian Schönbein, a German-Swiss chemist (1839); American Charles Goodyear develops the process of vulcanization, making the commercial use of rubber possible (1839); a photograph produced on a silver-coated copperplate treated with iodine vapor, the daguerreotype, is invented by Louis Daguerre and J. Niepce (French) (1839); the First Opium War between Britain and China begins (1839).

1840–49: New Zealand becomes a British colony (1840); philosopher Thomas Carlyle writes *On Heroes, Hero-Worship and the Heroic in History* in support of strong government (1841); the father of the guided tour, Thomas Cook (British), arranges his first trip (1841); showman P.T. Barnum gains fame after opening his American Museum of freak exhibitions (1841); the Webster-Ashburton Treaty between Britain and the US settles American border disputes with Canada (1842); the Treaty of Nanking ends the Opium War between Britain and China and confirms the cession of Hong Kong to Great Britain (1842); riots and strikes erupt in northern England's industrial areas (1842); Richard Wagner (German) finishes the opera *The Flying Dutchman* (1843); the amount of work required to produce a unit of heat, the joule, is determined by English physicist James P. Joule (1843); American social reformer Dorothea Dix reports on the shocking conditions in prisons and asylums, influencing the establishment of state hospitals for the insane in Europe and North America (1843); Samuel Morse's telegraph is used for the first time between Baltimore and Washington (1844); US troops are victorious over the Mexicans at

Palo Alto (1846), Congress formally declares war, US forces take Santa Fe and annex New Mexico; the Smithsonian Institution, a research and educational centre, is founded in Washington, DC (1846); ether is first used as an anaesthetic by dentist W.T. Morton (1846); sisters Charlotte and Emily Brontë publish *Jane Eyre* and *Wuthering Heights* respectively (1847); US forces capture Mexico City (1847) and the Treaty of Guadalupe Hidalgo ends the Mexican-US war (1848), the US acquires Texas and much of the surrounding territory in return for $15 million; gold discoveries in California lead to the first gold rush (1848); a revolt in Paris causes Louis Philippe to abdicate (1848); a revolution in Vienna brings Metternich's resignation (1848); revolutions in Venice, Berlin, Milan, Rome and Parma (1848); the first Public Health Act is introduced in Britain (1848); the first women's rights convention, organized by Elizabeth Stanton and Lucretia Mott, is held in Seneca Falls, New York (1848); the *Communist Manifesto* is issued by Germans Karl Marx and Friedrich Engels (1848), championing the working class and establishing socialist theory.

1850–59: Harriet Beecher Stowe writes her anti-slavery novel *Uncle Tom's Cabin* (1852); the Transvaal is granted self-government (1852); the Crimean War (1853–56) begins when Russia occupies Moldavia and Walachia and Turkey declares war, the Russians destroy the Turkish fleet off Sinope, and England, France and Sardinia join Turkey's fight; after a long siege the Russian base Sevastopol falls to the allied forces (1855), and after the allied victory at Balaklava, Russia recognizes the integrity of Turkey (1856); English nurse Florence Nightingale founds modern nursing while tending soldiers during the Crimean War (1853–56); the first hypodermic syringe is used by Alexander Wood (1853); Samuel Colt revolutionizes the manufacture of small arms (1853); Commander Matthew Perry negotiates the first American-Japanese treaty, permitting US ships to use two Japanese ports (1854); the Elgin Reciprocity Treaty between Great Britain and the US implements free trade between Canada and the US (1854); steel making becomes inexpensive when Henry Bessemer introduces a converter into his process for making steel (1855); pure cocaine is extracted from coca leaves (1856);

Gustave Flaubert, the French master of realistic novels, writes *Madame Bovary* (1856); Louis Pasteur discovers that fermentation is caused by micro-organisms (1857), and later invents pasteurization and discovers a vaccine for rabies; the first Neanderthal skeleton is found in a cave in Neander Valley (near Düsseldorf, Germany); the Indian Mutiny against British rule (1857) causes the British siege and capture of Delhi; the British Royal Navy destroys the Chinese fleet, and Britain and France take Canton (1857); Guiseppe Garibaldi forms the Italian National Association for the unification of Italy (1857); the Treaty of Tientsin ends the Anglo-Chinese war (1858); Charles Darwin writes *On the Origin of Species by Natural Selection*, explaining his theory of evolution (1859); the German National Association is formed to unite Germany under Prussia (1859); John Stuart Mill (British) writes his essay *On Liberty* (1859).

■ Modern Era

1860–64: Garibaldi and his redshirts sail from Genoa to take Palermo and Naples; Victor Emmanuel II (King of Sardinia) invades the Papal States and defeats the Papal troops, Garibaldi proclaims Emmanuel II king of Italy (1860); Anglo-French troops defeat the Chinese at Pa-li-Chau (1860) and sign the Treaty of Peking; the first Food and Drugs Act is enacted in Britain (1860); Lenoir constructs the first internal-combustion engine (1860); a primitive form of typewriter is created by American Christopher L. Sholes (1860); hundreds of thousands of Irish and British citizens flee their homelands following the potato famine (by 1860); Russian troops fire at anti-Russian demonstrators in Poland during the Warsaw Massacre (1861); the first machine-chilled cold storage unit is built by T. S. Mort (1861); Krupp begins arms production in Essen, Germany (1861); the Archaeopteryx, the skeleton linking reptiles and birds, is discovered at Solnhofen, Germany (1861); the American Civil War (1861–65) begins after Abraham Lincoln, who views slavery as evil, is elected president; South Carolina secedes in protest, followed by 10 other southern states, to form the Confederacy fighting for states' rights and opposing the abolition of slavery; Lincoln issues the Emancipation Proclamation (1862) calling for the freeing of black slaves in Confederate territory; the Red Cross voluntary relief organization is proposed by Jean Henri Dunant, a Swiss humanist (1862); the first form of a machine gun is invented by the American Richard Gatling (1862); Otto von Bismarck becomes the prime minister of Prussia (1862) and begins his system of alliances and alignments that result in German preeminence in Europe; Victor Hugo writes *Les Miserables* (1862); Leo Tolstoy writes *War and Peace* (1864); the Geneva Convention establishes the neutrality of battlefield medical facilities (1864); liberalism, socialism and rationalism are condemned in *Syllabus Errorum*, issued by Pope Pius IX (1864); Cheyenne and Arapahoe Indians are massacred at Sand Creek, Colorado (1864); the First International Workingmen's Association is founded by Karl Marx in London and New York (1864); Confederate forces surrender finally at Appomattox, Virginia (1865) marking the end of the war and victory for the Union; slavery in the US is abolished by the Thirteenth Amendment; US Pres. Lincoln is assassinated by the actor John Wilkes Booth (1865).

1865–69: Lewis Carroll (British) writes *Alice's Adventures in Wonderland* (1865); Joseph Lister initiates antiseptic surgery by using carbolic acid on a compound wound (1865); line geometry is invented by German mathematician Julius Plücker (1865); Gregor Mendel, an Austrian monk, describes his Law of Heredity (1865); Bismarck, the Prussian foreign minister, provoked the brief Austro-Prussian War by invading the duchies of Schleswig-Holstein and overrunning the German states allied with Austria; after seven weeks a peace settlement gave Schleswig-Holstein, Hanover, Hesse, Nasau and Frankfurt to Prussia and excluded Austria from influence in German affairs (1866); *Crime and Punishment* by Feodor Dostoevsky is published (1866); Alfred Nobel invents dynamite (1866); Johann Strauss popularizes the Viennese waltz with Blue Danube (1866); the underwater torpedo is invented by Robert Whitehead, an English engineer (1866); the fundamental law of biogenetics, *General Morphology,* is published by Ernst Haeckel (1866); Claude Monet, a French founder of Impressionism, paints *Camille* (1866); Russia sells Alaska to the US for $7.2 million (1867); Karl Marx writes *Das Kapital,* volume I (1867); the British North America Act establishes the Dominion of Canada and John A. Macdonald becomes prime minister (1867); Louisa May Alcott describes Victorian American life in *Little Women* (1868); a skeleton of Cro Magnon man from the Upper Paleolithic age (the first Homo sapiens in Europe, successor to the Neanderthal man) is found in France by Louis Lartet (1868); the first regular Trades Union Congress is held at Manchester, England (1868); Dmitri Mendeleyev formulates his periodic law for the classification of the elements (1869); John Stuart Mill writes *On the Subjection of Women* (1869); the major early treatise on eugenics, *Hereditary Genius,* is published by Francis Galton (1869); J.W. Hyatt invents celluloid (plastic) (1869); the First Nihilist Congress is held at Basel, Switzerland (1869); the strategically important Suez Canal opens (1869); the doctrine of papal infallibility is established by Pope Pius IX during Vatican Council I (1869–79).

1870–79: US industrialist John D. Rockefeller founds the Standard Oil Company (1870); T.H. Huxley, English biologist and educator, writes the *Theory of Biogenesis* (1870); the Franco-Prussian War begins (1870) and France under Napoleon III capitulates; William I, king of Prussia, is proclaimed the German Emperor at Versailles, and in the Peace of Frankfurt France cedes Alsace-Lorraine to Germany (1871); the Italian Law of Guarantees allows the Pope possession of the Vatican (1871); labour unions become legal in Britain (1871); Charles Darwin writes *The Descent of Man* (1871); the Great Fire ravages Chicago (1871); explorer Sir Henry M. Stanley is sent to find David Livingstone in Africa (1871); the first modern luxury liner, SS *Oceanic*, is launched (1871); Civil War in Spain ends with the Carlists' defeat (1872); the Three Emperors League is established in Berlin as an alliance between Germany, Russia and Austria-Hungary (1872); colour photographs are first developed (1873); James C. Maxwell writes *Electricity and Magnetism* (1873); Willhelm Wundt, known for the experimental method, writes *Physiological Psychology* (1873); under the direction of Benjamin Disraeli as prime minister, Britain expands its imperial power by annexing the Fiji islands (1874); Johannes Brahms composes the *Hungarian Dances* (1874); Johann Strauss II performs the operetta *Die Fleder-*

maus in Vienna (1874); Bosnia and Herzegovina rebel against Turkish rule (1875); Turkish sultan promises reforms (1875); Mary Baker Eddy writes *Science and Health* (1875) and she founds the Christian Science movement (1879); Georges Bizet performs *Carmen* in Paris (1875); British Queen Victoria is crowned empress of India (1876); Britain annexes the Transvaal (1877); US General George Custer is killed along with his cavalry by Cheyenne Indians in the Battle of the Little Bighorn (1876); Alexander Graham Bell constructs a telephone (1876); first national lawn tennis championship played at Wimbledon (1877); German historian Heinrich Treitschke begins a racial antisemite movement (1878); Gilbert and Sullivan write *HMS Pinafore* (1878); British troops are massacred by Zulus in Isandhlwana, Africa (1879); the British occupy the Khyber Pass near Afghanistan and are massacred in Kabul (1879); Norwegian Henrik Ibsen completes the play *A Doll's House* (1879); Chile invades Bolivia and its ally Peru after Bolivia cancels a Chilean company's contract to exploit Bolivia's nitrate deposits (1879).

1880–84: Auguste Rodin sculpts *The Thinker* (1880); France annexes Tahiti (1880); Transvaal declares its independence from Britain and the Boers establish a republic after a brief war with Britain (1880–81); the first practical electrical lights are independently made by Thomas Edison and J.W. Swan (1880); the malaria parasite is discovered by Charles Laveran (1880); the first large steel furnace is developed by American steel baron Andrew Carnegie (1880); the Vatican opens its archives to scholars (1881); the first Japanese political parties are founded (1881); violent government-condoned attacks (pogroms) are carried out against Russian Jews (1881–1917) causing large-scale Jewish emigration to North America; the Federation of Organized Trades and Labor Unions of the US and Canada is formed (1881); Germany, Austria and Italy form an alliance (1882); the three-mile limit for territorial waters is agreed upon at the Hague Convention (1882); Peter I. Tchaikovsky composes the *1812 Overture* (1882); psychoanalysis begins when Joseph Breuer (Austrian) uses hypnosis to treat hysteria (1882); Thomas Edison designs the first hydroelectric plant in Wisconsin (1882); the Orient Express train between Paris and Istanbul makes its first run (1883); *On the Size of Atoms* is published by British scientist William Thomson, later Lord Kelvin (1883); peace is restored between Peru and Chile (1883); Friedrich Nietzsche (German philosopher) begins *Thus Spake Zarathustra* (1884–91); gold is discovered in the Transvaal (1884) and this leads to the rise of Johannesburg; a truce is signed between Bolivia and Chile, with Bolivia forced to cede its only coastal territory to Chile (1884); the *Oxford English Dictionary* begins publication (1884–1928); the Berlin Conference of 14 nations on African affairs is held (1884).

1885–89: Karl Benz builds the single-cylinder engine for motor cars (1885); the individuality of fingerprints is proved by Sir Francis Galton (1885); the first Indian National Congress meets (1886); the Statue of Liberty is presented to the US by France (1886); steam is first used to sterilize surgical instruments by Ernst von Bergmann (1886); Irish politician Charles Parnell, the Fenians, and British Prime Min. William Gladstone try unsuccessfully to pass the first Irish Home Rule Bill to give Ireland control over domestic affairs (1886); Sir Arthur Conan Doyle writes the first Sherlock Holmes story, *A Study in Scarlet* (1887); William II (the Kaiser) becomes emperor of Germany (1888); Vincent Van Gogh paints the series of sunflowers (1888) and later, *Starry Night*; the electric motor is first constructed by Nikola A. Tesla and manufactured by George Westinghouse (1888); radio waves are discovered to be of the same family as light waves by the independently working Heinrich Hertz and Oliver Lodge (1888); Kodak box camera produced by George Eastman (1888); "Jack the Ripper" murders six women in London (1888); Alexander G. Eiffel designs the Eiffel Tower for the Paris World Exhibition (1889).

1890–94: The first Japanese general election is held (1890); German Chancellor Bismarck dismissed by Emperor William II (1890); the first moving picture shows appear in New York (1890); Oscar Wilde writes *The Picture of Dorian Gray* (1890); antitoxins are discovered by Emil von Behring (1890); the first entirely steel-framed building is erected in Chicago (1890); the Triple Alliance between Austria, Germany and Italy is renewed for 12 years (1891); Briton Thomas Hardy writes *Tess of the D'Ubervilles* (1891); Henri

Toulouse-Lautrec produces his first music hall posters (1891); *Experiments in Aerodynamics* is published by Samuel P. Langley (1891); the All-Deutschland Verband (Pan-Germany League) is founded (1891); Russia experiences widespread famine (1891); an earthquake in Japan kills ten thousand people (1891); the Java Man (*Pithecanthropus homo erectus*) is discovered by Dutch anthropologist Eugène Dubois, in Java (1891); Paul Gauguin (French) paints *By the Sea* in Tahiti (1892); Rudolph Diesel (German) patents his internal-combustion engine (1892); Tchaikovsky performs his *The Nutcracker* ballet score in St Petersburg (1892); Karl Benz constructs his four-wheel car (1893); Jewish French army captain Alfred Dreyfus is arrested under controversy and convicted of spying for Germany (1894); Rudyard Kipling writes *The Jungle Book* (1894); after Japan sends troops to Seoul, Korea, Japan declares war on China and defeats the Chinese at Port Arthur (1894); Emil Berliner develops a horizontal gramophone disc, replacing the record cylinder for sound reproduction (1894).

1895–99: The Chinese-Japanese war ends with Japan victorious: Formosa and Port Arthur are first ceded to Japan and later returned to China for payment (1895); H.G. Wells writes *The Time Machine* (1895); William B. Yeats writes *Poems* (1895); x-rays are discovered by William Röntgen (1895); Marchese Marconi invents radio telegraphy (1895); the principle of rocket reaction propulsion is developed by Konstantin Isiolkovski (1895); the first modern Olympics is held in Athens, Greece (1896); Anton Chekhov (Russian) writes *The Sea Gull* (1896); five annual Nobel prizes are established by Alfred Nobel for persons who have contributed the most in the fields of physics, physiology and medicine, chemistry, literature and peace (1896); Wilfrid Laurier becomes the first French Canadian prime minister of Canada (1896–1911); the Klondike gold rush in Bonanza Creek, Canada, begins (1896); Edmond Rostand writes *Cyrano de Bergerac* (1897); Queen Victoria celebrates her Diamond Jubilee (1897); French writer Emile Zola writes an open letter, *J'accuse*, condemning the Dreyfus espionage trial and he is imprisoned (1898), Col. Henry admits forging documents in the case (1898), and Captain Dreyfus is pardoned after a retrial (1899)—the case polarized French politics for

a decade; the US declares war on Spain over Cuba and destroys the Spanish fleet at Manila (1898); Spain cedes Cuba, Puerto Rico, Guam and the Philippines to the US for $20 million at the Treaty of Paris; Chinese Boxers, an anti-Western organization, is formed (1898); the Boer War begins as the South African Republic (Transvaal) and the Orange Free State unite against the British (1898); Marie and Pierre Curie discover radium and polonium (1898); German Count Ferdinand von Zeppelin builds his airship (1898); photographs using artificial light are first taken (1898); Marchese Marconi invents the radio (1899).

1900: The Boer War continues and Canadian troops set sail for South Africa to fight for England in their first foreign war; Boxer rebellion against Western influence, supported by the Dowager Empress Tzu-hsi, continues in China against Christian missionaries and foreigners; Sigmund Freud, the founder of psychoanalysis (Austrian), completes *The Interpretation of Dreams*; Wilhelm Wundt writes *Comparative Psychology*; Shintoism is reinstated in Japan to counter Buddhist influence; Commonwealth of Australia is created; Max Planck formulates the quantum theory; human speech is first transmitted via radio waves by the American scientist R.A. Fessenden; Holland's senate creates an international arbitration court at The Hague; millions are reported starving in India; botanist Hugo de Vries rediscovers Gregor Mendel's laws of heredity after 30 years; 10,000 Ashanti natives attack a British force of 400 at Cape Coast, Ghana, and are defeated.

1901: Queen Victoria dies and is succeeded by her son Edward VII; the Dutch Boers begin organized guerrilla warfare against the British; the Cuba Convention makes Cuba a US protectorate; US Pres. William McKinley is assassinated and is succeeded by Theodore Roosevelt; a treaty is signed to build the Panama Canal under US supervision; the hormone adrenaline is first isolated; Walter Nernst postulates the "third law of thermodynamics"; John Pierpont Morgan organizes the US Steel Corp., the first billion-dollar corporation; the Peace of Peking ends the Boxer uprising and China is forced to pay an indemnity of $333 million to the Allies to amend commercial treaties in favor of foreign nationals and to allow foreign troops to be posted in Peking; French physicist Henri Becquerel determines that atoms have internal structure; there are racial riots in New Orleans when American black leader Booker T. Washington is invited to the White House; the Trans-Siberian railroad reaches Port Arthur on the east coast of Russia; oil drilling begins in Persia (Iran).

1902: An Anglo-Japanese treaty recognizes the independence of China and Korea; the Treaty of Vereeniging ends the Boer War and the Orange Free State becomes a British colony; the Triple Alliance between Germany, Austria and Italy is renewed for another six years; the US acquires perpetual control over the Panama Canal; the Colonial Conference meets in London; the Committee of Imperial Defence meets in London for the first time; Jean Sibelius, Finnish composer and conductor, completes *Symphony No. 2*; Egypt's Aswan Dam is opened.

1903: The "Entente Cordiale" between England and France is established to counter German imperialism; the Russian Social Democratic Party splits into Mensheviks (led by Plechanoff) and Bolsheviks (led by Vladimir Lenin and Leon Trotsky); *The Conduction of Electricity through Gases* is published by Joseph John Thomson; Briton George Bernard Shaw writes *Man and Superman*; Orville and Wilbur Wright successfully fly a powered airplane near Kitty Hawk, North Carolina; the electrocardiograph, which records heart action, is invented by William Einthoven; Briton Emmeline Pankhurst founds the National Women's Social and Political Union and campaigns for women's right to vote; Albert I, Prince of Monaco, founds the International Peace Institute; Henry Ford founds the Ford Motor Company.

1904: The Russo-Japanese War breaks out over Korea and Manchuria; the Japanese besiege Port Arthur and occupy Seoul; the Russian fleet is partially destroyed off Port Arthur; the Russians are defeated at Mukden and Toushima Straits; Max Weber writes *The Protestant Ethic and the Birth of Capitalism*; the first performance of Giacomo Puccini's opera *Madame Butterfly* in Milan; the first radio transmission of music is at Graz, Austria; the general theory of radioactivity is postulated by Ernest Rutherford and Frederick Soddy; W.C. Gorgas eradicates yellow fever in the Panama Canal Zone; sili-

cones are discovered by F.S. Kipping.

1905: Albert Einstein publishes four papers detailing his special theory of relativity, the relationship between mass and energy, the Brownian theory of motion and another formulating the photon theory of light; the Russian city of Port Arthur surrenders to the Japanese; in Russia troops fire at peaceful protest marchers heading for the czar's Winter Palace in St Petersburg, and the event becomes known as "Bloody Sunday"; William II of Germany and Nicholas II of Russia sign the Treaty of Bjorko for mutual help in Europe; the Treaty of Portsmouth ends the Russo-Japanese War; a general strike in Russia in response to Bloody Sunday includes a sailors' mutiny on the battleship *Potemkin* and the creation of the first workers soviet in St Petersburg; Czar Nicholas establishes a constitutional government (the Imperial Duma); the Norwegian Parliament decides to separate from Sweden; the Anglo-Japanese alliance is renewed for 10 years; the Sinn Fein nationalist party is formed in Ireland; George Santayana writes his philosophical work *The Life of Reason*.

1906: Reform laws are proposed in Russia and the Imperial Duma is dissolved by the czar to end the radical change; the All India Muslim League is founded by Aga Khan; the term "allergy" is introduced by Clemens von Pirquet; the position of the magnetic North Pole is determined by Norwegian explorer Roald Amundsen; night-shift work for women is forbidden in many countries; the San Francisco earthquake kills 700 people and causes $400 million in property loss; Transvaal and Orange River colonies are granted self-government.

1907: The second Russian Duma meets in March; its radical proposals lead to its dissolution five months later; the US prohibits Japanese immigration; Lenin leaves Russia and founds the newspaper *The Proletarian*; Grigori Rasputin, a Russian mystic, gains influence with the royal family when he treats the hemophiliac son of Nicholas II; New Zealand becomes a dominion within the British Empire; Baden-Powell forms the Boy Scout movement; Korea becomes a Japanese protectorate; Russian artist Marc Chagall paints *Peasant Women*; Gustav Mahler (Austrian) composes *Symphony No. 8*; Ivan Pavlov (Russian) studies conditioned reflexes in dogs; the SS *Lusitania* beats the SS *Mauritania* in a race from Ireland to New York.

1908: Austria occupies Bosnia and Herzegovina; Bulgaria declares independence from Turkey; Isadora Duncan emerges as a popular modern dancer; the Zeppelin airship crashes near Echterdingen; General Motors Corporation is formed in the US; Henry Ford designs the inexpensive, standardized Model T automobile while pioneering assembly line techniques for autos; an earthquake in Sicily and Calabria kills 150,000; American Gertrude Stein writes *Three Lives*; French writer Anatole France completes the political satire *Penguin Island*; Canadian Lucy Maud Montgomery writes *Anne of Green Gables*.

1909: Turkey and Serbia acknowledge Austrian control of Bosnia and Herzegovina; sultan of Turkey is deposed and replaced by his brother; Ezra Pound writes *Exultations*; the first newsreels appear and director D.W. Griffith features Canadian-born Mary Pickford, who becomes the first film star; Sergei Diaghilev presents his *Ballets Russes*, revolutionizing dance, in Paris; Blériot flies from Calais to Dover in 37 minutes, Farman makes the first 100-mile flight; W.E. Du Bois cofounds the National Negro Committee which becomes the National Association for the Advancement of Colored People in 1910; Girl Guides organized in Britain; Thomas Hunt Morgan begins research in genetics; US explorer Robert E. Peary reaches the North Pole.

1910: The Union of South Africa becomes a dominion within the British Empire with Louis Botha as premier; China abolishes slavery; Japan takes over Korea; Montenegro becomes an independent kingdom; Portugal becomes a republic after a revolution ends the monarchy; Albania rebels against Turkish rule; Roger Fry arranges the Post-Impressionist Exhibition in London with works by Cezanne, van Gogh and Matisse; Igor Stravinsky performs his ballet score *The Firebird* in Paris; the South American tango is the dance craze in Europe and North America; the first deep-sea research expedition is undertaken by Murray and Hjort; the five-day work week is instituted in the US, making the "week-end" possible.

1911: US-Japanese and Anglo-Japanese commercial treaties are signed; Diaz surrenders

power in Mexico but revolutions continue; the Kaiser's Hamburg speech promises Germany's "Place in the Sun"; war erupts between Turkey and Italy and aircraft are first used for offensive measures; a revolution in Central China is followed by the fall of the Manchu dynasty (in power since 1644) and the proclamation of a Chinese Republic; Sun Yat-sen is elected president and he appoints Chiang Kai-shek as his military adviser; Russian premier, Peter Stolypin, is assassinated; Roald Amundsen reaches the South Pole; Marie Curie is the first person to win a second Noble Prize, in chemistry; Rutherford formulates his theory of atomic structure.

1912: British dock workers, coal miners and transport workers strike; the German-Austro-Italian alliance is renewed again; Lenin becomes editor of *Pravda*; Sun Yat-sen founds Kuomintang (Chinese National Party); Montenegro declares war against Turkey and Bulgaria, Greece and Serbia mobilize; Carl Jung writes *The Theory of Psychoanalysis*; the term "vitamin" is coined by Polish chemist Kasimir Funk; Stefansson and Anderson explore Arctic Canada; Wilson's cloud chamber (particle detector) photographs lead to the detection of protons and electrons; the Royal Flying Corps (later RAF) is established in Britain; SS *Titanic* sinks on its first voyage after colliding with an iceberg: 1,513 people drown.

1913: The London Peace Treaty ending the First Balkan War is signed and Turkey loses all possessions in Europe except E. Thrace; the Second Balkan War breaks out as Bulgaria attacks Serbia and Greece; Russia declares war on Bulgaria, Bulgaria and Turkey settle a peace treaty and Turkey regains Thrace, Serbia invades Albania; Greece and Turkey make peace; police crack down on suffragette demonstrations led by Emmeline Pankhurst in London; Maxim Gorki, the father of Soviet literature, writes *My Childhood*; Charlie Chaplin first stars in movies; Niels Bohr formulates his theory of atomic structure; Albert Schweitzer, medical missionary, opens his famous hospital in Lambaréné, French Congo.

1914: Archduke Francis Ferdinand, heir to the Austrian throne, is assassinated in Sarajevo (capital of the Austro-Hungarian province of Bosnia) by a Serbian nationalist (June 28); Austria-Hungary challenges Serbia and declares war (July 28); Russia and France support Serbia and mobilize troops; Austria's ally Germany declares war on Russia and France in response; the members of the Triple Entente (Britain, France, Russia) declare war on Turkey after Turks attack Russia; Germany, Austria-Hungary and the Ottoman Empire (Turkey) form alliance of Central Powers, they are opposed by UK, members of British Empire, France, Russia, Belgium, Japan and Serbia (Allied Powers); Germany invades Belgium, attacks France, and establishes the Eastern Front against the Russians at Tannenberg and the Masurian Lakes; on the Western Front the Germans are held in check after battles at Marne River, France (Sept. 6); the First Battle of Ypres, Belgium, is waged to prevent the Germans from cutting British supply lines to France; Austria-Hungary fails in three attacks on Serbia and, after the Russians capture the province of Galicia, retreats to its own territory; by Nov. 14, 1914 there is a deadlock along the Western Front (stretching 720 km across Belgium and northeast France to the Swiss border) that remains throughout the war; Irish writer James Joyce writes *Dubliners* (1914); John B. Watson writes *Behavior: an Introduction to Comparative Psychology* (1914); the first successful heart surgery is performed on a dog by Dr. Alexis Carrel (1914); the Panama Canal opens (1914); millions of immigrants leave southern and eastern Europe between 1905 and 1914.

1915: The Allied Gallipoli Campaign to neutralize Turkey fails and Australian and New Zealand troops suffer heavy losses; the first German submarine (U-boat) attack is at Le Havre; the German blockade of England begins; at the Second Battle of Ypres, Canadian forces hold off the German advance while under heavy fire and attacks from chlorine gas and newly-introduced flame throwers; Italy joins the Allied Powers, declares war on Austria-Hungary (May 23) and an Italian Front soon opens; a German submarine sinks the *Lusitania* (May 7); the first Zeppelin air attack takes place on London; Ottoman-controlled Mesopotamia (now Iraq) surrenders to Britain; Italians fight Austria-Hungary in continuous battles at Isonzo (1915–17); Germans invade Warsaw and Brest-Litovsk; Allied troops land at Salonika; the first fighter airplane is constructed by Hugo Junkers; Henry Ford develops a farm tractor; the

dysentery bacillus is isolated by British chemist James Kendall; the first book advocating birth control, by American Margaret Sanger, is published, and the author is sent to jail.

1916: Germany stages a Zeppelin raid on Paris and declares war on Portugal; Portugal and Rumania later join the Allied Powers; in the Middle East, T.E. Lawrence leads an Arab revolt against Turkey; heavy casualties occur at Verdun (Feb. 21); British and German fleets clash at the Battle of Jutland (May 31–June 1); the 1st Newfoundland Regiment is annihilated along with 624,000 Allied troops during the offensive at the Somme (launched July 1); HMS *Hampshire* is sunk; Italy declares war on Germany; the Germans first use gas masks and steel helmets; peace notes are exchanged between Germany and the Allies; Lloyd George becomes British prime minister; blood for transfusion is first refrigerated; the theory of shell shock is put forth by F.W. Mott; an underwater ultrasonic source for submarine detection is built by Paul Langevin; Britain initiates daylight-saving time; US purchases the Virgin Islands for $25 million.

1917: The United States enters the war on the Allied side (Apr. 6); Germans withdraw on the Western Front; the Russian Black Sea fleet mutinies at Sebastopol; there is revolution in Russia in Feb. and the Czar abdicates (Mar. 16); Kerensky becomes Russian premier and continues the war effort; Canadian forces seize Vimy Ridge in northern France; Germany stages air attacks on England; Greece joins the Allies (July); China declares war on Germany and Austria; the British-led offensive at the Third Battle of Ypres (Passchendaele) fails (July 31); the Italian army is defeated at Caporetto by Austria-Hungary; Kerensky's government is overthrown in Petrograd in Oct. and Lenin is appointed Chief Commissar, Trotsky becomes Commissar for Foreign Affairs and Russia seeks peace with Germany; the first tank battle is at Cambrai; starvation sweeps Germany; Finland declares independence from Russia; the Allies execute dancer Mata Hari as a spy; Lord Arthur Balfour, the British Foreign Secretary, issues the Balfour Declaration stating British support for a Jewish national homeland in Palestine; women are arrested for suffrage activities in the US.

1918: Russia, the Ukraine and the Central Powers conclude the Treaties of Brest-Litovsk: the first one establishes the independence of the Ukraine, the second strips Russia of its Baltic and Polish possessions; Turks surrender to British at Jerusalem; US Pres. Wilson puts forth Fourteen Points for world peace (including a proposal for a League of Nations); Rumania signs a peace treaty with the Central Powers; Germany launches three final offensives on the Western Front (Mar. 21); Germans bomb Paris; the Second Battle of the Marne (July 15–Aug. 6) is won by the Allies; the Allies win victories on all fronts in the fall; the Japanese push into Siberia; Germany and Austria agree to retreat to their own territory before an armistice is signed; the Hungarian premier is assassinated; the Turkish and Austro-Hungarian empires and Bulgaria surrender to the Allies (Nov. 3); the German fleet mutinies at Kiel and the emperor flees; an armistice between the Allies and Germany is signed (Nov. 11); Germany agrees to the provisions of the Treaty of Versailles after the Allies threaten to invade; Emperor Charles of Austria loses the throne; the map of Europe is reshaped: Austria becomes a republic and the Serbo-Croatian-Slovene Kingdom of Yugoslavia is proclaimed, Poland and Czechoslovakia are created; Iceland becomes independent state; the Russian Revolution continues as Bolshevik workers take over government buildings, the Winter Palace and later Moscow and other cities; civil war between the Bolshevik (Red) and anti-Bolshevik (White) continues (until 1920); British, French and American troops intervene against the Reds; the British government abandons Home Rule for Ireland; ex-Czar Nicholas II and family are executed by Russian revolutionaries; Hsu-Shih-Chang becomes president of the Chinese Republic; women over 30 get the vote in Britain; controversy rages over the psychology of Freud and Jung; the true dimensions of the Milky Way are discovered by Harlow Shapley, an American astronomer.

1919: US Pres. Woodrow Wilson heads the first League of Nations meeting in Paris; the Peace Conference opens at Versailles; Benito Mussolini founds the Fasci del Combattimento in Italy; socialist governments are founded in Austria and Budapest, Hungary; the Treaty of Versailles is signed with Germany; the final treaty exacts heavy financial penalties on Germany, restricts the German army and navy, blames Germany for provoking the war and establishes the League of Nations; US refusal to ratify the treaty excludes it from League membership; the Allied peace treaty with Austria is signed at St Germain; the Treaty of Neuilly with Bulgaria is signed; the International Labor Congress in Washington endorses the eight-hour workday; the Red (Soviet) forces win successive battles in the Russian civil war; Soviets attack Finland; the first nonstop flight across the Atlantic is made from Newfoundland to Ireland by J.W. Alcock and A. Whitten Brown; Lady Astor is elected to Britain's Parliament, becoming the first female MP.

1920: The League of Nations is founded in Paris and establishes headquarters in Geneva; Russian civil war ends with Soviet victory; Great Britain gains control of Palestine from the Turks; The Hague becomes the International Court of Justice; the Little Entente between Czechoslovakia, Yugoslavia and Rumania is formed; the Treaty of Trianon is signed with Hungary; the Treaty of Sevres is signed with the Ottoman Empire; the 19th Amendment gives American women the vote; 200,000 Chinese die in an earthquake in Kansu province; the world population is 1.8 billion; Britain establishes separate parliaments for Northern and Southern Ireland; Adolph Hitler founds the Nazi party in Munich, Germany, and announces his 25-point program, blaming Germany's war defeat on Jews and Communists; Mohandas (Mahatma) Ghandi becomes India's leader in its struggle for independence from Britain; Prohibition goes into effect in the US, banning the sale and consumption of alcoholic beverages; a worldwide influenza epidemic, which began in 1918, leaves 22 million dead

1921: The first Indian Parliament meets; German reparations payments totalling $33.3 million are fixed by the Allies at a Paris conference; Hitler's storm troopers (SA) begin to terrorize ideological opponents; Mackenzie King is elected prime minister of Canada; British Broadcasting Company is founded (changed to the British Broadcasting Corporation in 1927); the Spanish prime minister and Japanese premier are assassinated; founder of Portuguese republic is murdered; ex-emperor Charles stages two failed coup attempts to regain Hungarian throne; Britain and Ireland sign a peace treaty; German mark falls and rapid inflation plagues the economy; coal is successfully hydrogenated into oil by Friedrich Bergius; the tuberculosis vaccine (B-C-G) is developed by Albert Calmette and Camille Guerin; the chromosome theory of heredity is put forth by American biologist Thomas Morgan; Albert Einstein wins Nobel Prize for Physics; Ku Klux Klan members terrorize blacks and black sympathizers in the southern US; one of the founders of modern aeronautics, Hermann J. Oberth, writes *The Rocket into Interplanetary Space*.

1922: Gandhi is sentenced to six years imprisonment for civil disobedience; German reconstruction minister Walter Rathenau is assassinated by German nationalists; the Arab Congress at Nablus rejects the British control of Palestine; Austria denounces "Anschluss" (union with Germany); Mussolini stages the March on Rome and forms a Fascist government; Irish Free State is proclaimed; the tomb of Tutankhamen is discovered by Lord Carnarvaron and Howard Carter; a self-winding wristwatch is invented by John Harwood (patented in 1924); a stock market "boom" begins in the US; Soviet states form the USSR; insulin, prepared by Canadian physicians Frederick Banting, Charles Best and John Macleod, is first given to diabetic patients.

1923: An earthquake kills 120,000 people in Tokyo and Yokohama; Adolph Hitler tries (and fails) to overthrow the German government ("Beer Hall Putsch"); Greek army overthrows monarch; Jewish philosopher Martin Buber writes the theological *I and Thou*; the theory of acids and bases is postulated by J.N. Brönsted; Lee de Forest demonstrates the process for motion pictures with sound; the first commercial airline, Aeroflot, is founded in the USSR.

1924: Ramsay MacDonald forms the first Labour government in Britain; Adolph Hitler writes *Mein Kampf* during an eight-month jail term; R.C. Andrews discovers skulls and skeletons of Mesozoic dinosaurs in the Gobi desert; Winston Churchill, having switched from the Liberals to the Conservatives, is named Chancellor of the Exchequer in Britain; in Russia, Lenin dies and Stalin, Zinoviev and Kamenev ally against Trotsky; the "Zinoviev letter," purported to be calling for a communist revolution in Britain, is pub-

lished by the British Foreign Office; Greece becomes a republic; elections are held in Italy and Mussolini wins support of 65% of the electorate; leader of Italian socialists is murdered; Albanian Republic is founded; Sigmund Freud begins *Collected Writings* (12 vols. 1924–39); Ghandi fasts for 21 days, protesting feuding between Hindus and Muslims in India; British astronomer Arthur Eddington discovers that the luminosity of a star is approximately related to its mass; insecticides are used for the first time; a patent application for iconoscope (television) is filed by Russian-American inventor V.K. Zworkin; Danish polar explorer Knud Rasmussen completes the longest dog-sled journey ever made across the North American Arctic; British Imperial Airways begins commercial air flights.

1925: Locarno Conference creates a series of treaties between Germany, France, Belgium, Poland, UK, Italy and Czechoslovakia that set up a demilitarized zone in the Rhineland and confirmed borders between Belgium, France and Germany; Mrs Nellie Tayloe Ross of Wyoming becomes the first woman governor in the US; the United Church of Canada is founded; recognizable human features are transmitted by television by Scottish inventor John Logie Baird; Walter P. Chrysler founds the Chrysler Corporation; the (Franz) Fischer and (Hans) Tropsch synthesis leads to the industrial development of synthetic oil; Heisenberg, Bohr and Jordan develop quantum mechanics for atoms; the presence of cosmic rays in the upper atmosphere is discovered by US physicist Robert Andrews Millikan; the "flapper" era takes hold; an international convention condemns the illegal narcotics trade.

1926: Fascist youth organizations appear: "Balilla" in Italy and "Hitlerjugend" in Germany; Josef Pilsudski successfully stages a coup d'état in Poland and begins a military dictatorship; commerce in Britain is stopped by a general strike; Trotsky is expelled from Moscow; Hirohito succeeds his father Taisho as Emperor of Japan; Robert H. Goddard fires the first liquid fuel rocket; vitamin B is isolated by B. Jansen and W. Donath; Kodak produces the first 16mm movie film; British Imperial Chemical Industries (ICI) begins operations; H.L. Mencken writes *Notes on Democracy*; Turkish reforms include the abolition of polygamy, modernization of female attire and adoption of Latin alphabet (1926–28).

1927: The Allied military control of Germany ends; an economic conference in Geneva is attended by 52 nations; the economic system in Germany collapses ("Black Friday"); Trotsky expelled from the Communist Party in the USSR; Nazis on trial in Austria for political murder are acquitted and socialists riot in Venice to protest; the first film with sound, a "talkie," *The Jazz Singer*, stars Al Jolson; Lev Theremin invents the earliest electronic musical instrument; Charles Lindbergh flies the monoplane *Spirit of St Louis* in the first solo transatlantic flight, nonstop from New York to Paris in 33.5 hours; Canadian forests are the first sprayed with insecticides by airplanes; the first vehicular tunnel, the Holland Tunnel, links New York and New Jersey.

1928: The Supreme Court of Canada rules that women may not hold public office because they are not "persons" as defined by the British North America Act, but the British Privy Council overturns the decision in a landmark Commonwealth case in 1929; the Kellogg-Briand Pact outlawing war is signed by 65 states; Josef Stalin emerges as leader of Soviet Union; the first economic five-year plan begins in the USSR; Chiang Kai-Shek is elected president of China; over-production of coffee leads to the collapse of Brazil's economy; penicillin is discovered by Alexander Fleming (Scottish); American anthropologist Margaret Mead writes *Coming of Age in Samoa;* the first colour motion pictures are exhibited by George Eastman in Rochester, New York; J.L. Baird presents colour television; Mickey Mouse makes his Disney debut.

1929: The US Stock Exchange collapses on Oct. 28, Black Friday; the Great Depression, a world economic crisis, begins and is primarily caused by easy credit and stock market over-speculation, overproduction of goods and tariff and war-debt policies; six Chicago-area gangsters are machine-gunned to death in the St Valentine's Day Massacre; a dictatorship is established in Serbo-Croat-Slovene kingdom by the monarch and the country's name is changed to Yugoslavia; Trotsky is exiled from USSR; talks on Indian sovereignty begin betweeen Indian leaders and the Viceroy; the Lateran Treaty establishes the independence of Vatican City; precise timekeeping is made possible with the quartz-crystal clocks by W.A. Morrison; the airship *Graf Zeppelin* flies around the world in 21 days.

1930: Austria and Italy sign a treaty of friendship; Britain, the US, Japan, France and Italy sign a treaty on naval disarmament; right-wing coalition comes to power in Germany, Nazis later capture 107 more seats in an election; right-wing government is formed in Poland; Catholic-Fascist units are established in Austria; revolution in Argentina brings new military dictatorship to power; the planet Pluto is discovered by C.W. Tombaugh at Lowell Observatory; a yellow fever vaccine is developed by South African microbiologist Max Theiler; photoflash bulb is introduced; the word "technocracy," meaning the domination of technology, comes into use.

1931: A financial crisis in central Europe is caused by the collapse of Austria's Credit-Anstalt; all German banks close following the bankruptcy of the German Danatbank; Britain abandons the gold standard; Fascist party is formed in Britain; the Statute of Westminster established the British Commonwealth of Nations as a free association of autonomous nations sharing a common allegiance to the British crown, and declared that British Parliament could no longer legislate for any member states unless requested to do so; US Pres. Hoover proposes a one-year moratorium for reparations and war debts; the first trans-African railroad line is completed, Benguella-Katanga; the northern face of the Matterhorn is climbed for the first time by Franz and Toni Schmid.

1932: The Indian National Congress, a nationalist party dedicated to home rule, is declared illegal and its leader, Mahatma Gandhi, is arrested; the US criticizes Japanese aggression in Manchuria; the Nazis sweep the German Reichstag (Parliament) elections while WWI hero Hindenburg wins the Presidential election; Hitler refuses Hindenburg's offer to become Vice Chancellor, and the Austrian-born Hitler receives German citizenship; Franklin D. Roosevelt wins the US presidential election and proposes domestic reform programs to provide recovery and relief from the Great Depression ("New Deal"); the USSR suffers famine; Zuider Zee, a huge dam and drainage project in Holland, is completed; Amelia Earheart is the first woman to fly solo across the Atlantic; Japan conquers world markets by undercutting prices; about 30 million people are unemployed worldwide; the neutron is discovered by James Chadwick; vitamin D is discovered.

1933: Reichstag building is burned in Berlin and Hitler uses the event to justify banning opposition parties and labour unions; Hitler is appointed German Chancellor and granted dictatorial powers with the Enabling Law; Nazi Hermann Goering is named Prussian prime minister; Parliamentary government is suspended in Austria; starvation spreads in USSR; Paul Joseph Goebbels is named Hitler's Minister of Propaganda; Japan withdraws from the League of Nations; the first concentration camps are built by the Nazis in Germany to hold Jews and ideological opponents; books by non-Nazi and Jewish authors are burned in Germany; Germans begin to boycott and restrict Jewish services; an anti-Nazi treatise, *Judaism-Christendom-Germanism*, is published by Cardinal von Faulhaber in Munich; Assyrian Christians are massacred in Iraq; US goes off the gold standard and tries to stimulate its economy by creating The Tennessee Valley Authority to construct dams and generate electricity.

1934: A revolution in Austria overturns the Social Democrats and Austrian Chancellor is assassinated by the Nazis; a general strike takes place in France; the USSR is admitted to the League of Nations; Winston Churchill warns the British Parliament of the German air menace; Hitler oversees purge of his associates and many are executed; a national vote grants him the title Führer (leader); Stalin's purge of the Soviet Communist party begins and he reportedly oversees the murder of millions of people; German scientist Albert Einstein is persecuted by the Nazis for being Jewish and he flees, settling in the US; Japan renounces the Washington treaties of 1922 and 1930; Mao Tse-tung, leader of the Chinese Communists, heads the Long March.

1935: Nazis repudiate the Treaty of Versailles and reintroduce compulsory military service; the autonomous territory of Saarland votes for reunion with Germany; an Anglo-German Naval Agreement is concluded; Nazis implement the Nuremburg Laws against Jews, stripping them of civic rights and forbidding intermarriage with non-Jews; Mussolini invades Ethiopia, and the League of Nations retaliates by imposing sanctions; the Chaco War, a bitter conflict between Paraguay and Bolivia begun in 1932 and fought over oil-rich but otherwise barren territory, ended after 100,000 lives were lost and both sides were exhausted (treaty not concluded until 1938); radar equipment to detect aircraft is built by Robert Watson Watt; oil pipelines between Iraq, Haifa and Tripoli open; Persia changes its name to Iran.

1936: King George V of England dies and is succeeded by Edward VIII; German troops occupy the Rhineland and Hitler wins the German elections with 99 percent of the vote; Italy, Austria and Hungary sign the Rome Pact; Britain, France and the US sign the London Naval Convention; an Austro-German convention acknowledges Austrian independence; the Spanish Civil War begins and Francisco Franco is appointed Chief of State by the Nationalist insurgents against the government's Loyalist republicans; Franco begins the siege of Madrid, rebels take Malaga and destroy Guernica and Gijon and Franco begins a naval blockade (1937); Heinrich Himmler is appointed head of the Gestapo, responsible for Nazi concentration camps (1936–45); King Edward VIII abdicates in order to marry American divorcee Wallis Simpson; Mussolini and Hitler proclaim the Rome-Berlin Axis; the Anti-Comintern Pact is signed by Germany and Japan; Chiang Kai-shek declares war on Japan; Dr Alexis Carrel develops an artificial heart; the airship *Hindenburg* burns at Lakehurst, New Jersey, after a transatlantic flight; black American athlete Jesse Owens upsets the Nazis when he wins four gold medals at the Olympic Games in Berlin.

1937: Poland refuses to return Danzig to Germany; the first worldwide radio broadcast is heard when George VI is crowned King of Great Britain; Roosevelt signs a US Neutrality Act, intended to keep the US out of a possible European war; Trotsky, exiled from Russia in 1929, is forced to leave Norway and settles in Mexico; aggressive Japanese war policy begins when Prince Konoye is named the Japanese premier, and the Japanese seize major Chinese cities (Beijing, Tianjin, Shanghai, Nanjing and Hangzhou), forcing Chiang Kai-shek and the Communists, under Mao Tse-tung and Chou En-lai, to unite; the Chinese government makes Chungking its capital; the Royal Commission on Palestine recommends the establishment of Arab and Jewish states; Stalin initiates a purge of Soviet generals and show trials of political leaders; Britain signs naval agreements with Germany and the USSR; Germany guarantees Belgian sovereignty; Italy joins the Anti-Comintern Pact and withdraws from the League of Nations; Japanese planes sink US gunboat in Chinese waters; Amelia Earheart disappears during a Pacific flight.

1938: Germany annexes Austria, "Anschluss" (Mar.); France calls up reservists; Great Britain, France and Italy agree to let Germany absorb the Sudetenland, Czechoslovakia, in a policy of appeasement (Munich Pact, Sept.) and Germany promises to cease its aggressive expansion; British foreign minister Anthony Eden resigns in protest against the appeasement policy and Winston Churchill also voices opposition; Franco begins an offensive against the Spanish Loyalists in Catalonia; anti-Jewish legislation is enacted in Italy; Kristallnacht, or "Night of Broken Glass," is a large-scale pogrom by the Nazis against German Jews; the US and Germany recall their respective ambassadors; Japan withdraws from the League of Nations and sets up a puppet Chinese government in Nanking; Howard Hughes flies around the world in less than four days.

1939: US Pres. Roosevelt demands assurances from Hitler and Mussolini that they have no plans to attack other states; Germany breaks the Munich Pact and occupies Bohemia and Moravia; Slovakia is placed under "protection"; Italy invades Albania; Germany renounces the nonaggression pact with Poland and naval agreement with England, and concludes a 10-year alliance with Italy and a nonaggression pact with the USSR, secretly dividing Poland; Germany stages a surprise (blitzkrieg) invasion of Poland, and annexes Danzig (Sept. 1); Britain and France declare war on Germany (Sept. 3); the Allied powers are Britain and France and the Axis powers are led by Germany; Canada declares war (Sept. 10); US Pres. Roosevelt announces US neutrality; Soviets invade Poland from the east (Sept. 17); Germans overrun western Poland and reach Brest-Litovsk and Warsaw and a puppet government is installed; France masses troops along the Maginot Line on the eastern frontier of France and Germany sends troops to its parallel Siegfried Line; the British Expeditionary Force is sent to France; the USSR invades Finland and is expelled from the League of Nations; Japan occupies Hainan and blockades the British at Tientsin; the US renounces the Japanese trade agreement of 1911; the Spanish Civil War ends with Franco's Nationalists (supported by Hitler and Mussolini) victorious over the Loyalists (supported by the USSR); Spain joins the Anti-Comintern Pact and leaves the League of Nations; England and Poland sign a treaty of mutual assistance; women and children are first evacuated from London; the first helicopter is built by Russian-American Igor Sikorsky; the US economy booms from arms sales to Europe.

1940: Food rationing begins in Britain; Finland surrenders (Mar.) and signs a peace treaty with the USSR; Germany invades Norway and Denmark (Apr. 9); Winston Churchill becomes British prime minister (May 10); Norway falls (June); Germany invades Belgium, Luxembourg and the Netherlands (May 10); Holland and Belgium surrender to Germany and 340,000 Allied forces are trapped in Belgium, but most are evacuated from Dunkirk, a French seaport on the English channel (May 29 to June 3); Italy declares war on France and Britain; Germans attack France from the north and enter Paris (June 14); France concludes an armistice with Germany; southern France remains unoccupied until 1942 and is ruled by the Vichy government; USSR seizes Estonia, Latvia and Lithuania (summer); the Royal Navy sinks the French fleet in Oran; the Royal Air Force begins night bombing of Germany; the Battle of Britain in Aug. is the first battle fought completely in the air; Hitler begins bombing England (all-night blitzes) throughout fall and winter; Japan, Germany and Italy sign a military and economic pact; US destroyers are sold to Britain; Germany intensifies U-boat warfare; Italian forces attempt to take Egypt and Libya in order to cut off British access to Middle East oil and the Suez Canal; the British Eighth Army opens an offensive in North Africa and defeats the Italian forces; Trotsky is murdered in Mexico; Batista becomes president of Cuba; wall paintings dating to about 20,000 BC are discovered in France, the Lascaux caves; a giant cyclotron is built at the University of California for producing mesotrons from atomic nuclei.

1941: The British invade Ethiopia and defeat the Italians (by May); Germany opens a counter-offensive in North Africa to aid Italy; German General Rommel regains Libya and Egypt; Germans launch an airborne invasion against Crete, thereby securing an important base in the Mediterranean (by the end of May); England sinks the German battleship *Bismarck* in an effort to protect vital US shipments to Great Britain; Allies develop radar and sonar to track U-boats; German air raids over London continue; US freezes German and Italian assets in that country; Germans invade Russia (Operation Barbarossa, June 22); Churchill and Roosevelt sign the Atlantic charter (Aug. 14); German troops surround Leningrad and Moscow (Nov.), but an early, harsh winter saves the USSR; Marshal Timoshenko launches the Russian counter-offensive; the US ambassador to Japan warns Pres. Roosevelt of possible Japanese attack; Japanese bomb Pearl Harbor (Dec. 7) and the US and Britain declare war on Japan (Dec. 8); China declares war on the Axis (Dec. 9); Japan invades the Philippines; Germany and Italy declare war on the US; the US declares war on Germany and Italy; British Hong Kong surrenders to the Japanese; Henry Moore draws refugees in London air raid shelters while an official war artist; Dmitri Shostakovich writes *Symphony No. 7* during the German siege of Leningrad; German dramatist Bertolt Brecht writes *Mother Courage and Her Children* while in exile from the Nazis.

1942: Hitler's Final Solution, the systematic murder of Jews in the Nazi gas chambers (Holocaust) is in full force at death camps such as Auschwitz and Dachau; the 26 Allied nations agree not to make separate treaties with the Axis powers; Rommel breaks through British lines and reaches El Alamein (320 km from the Suez Canal); Montgomery (British Eighth Army) scores the first decisive defeat of Rommel at El Alamein; Germans reach Stalingrad, Russia; 400,000 American troops land in French North Africa; Rommel, in full retreat, loses Tobruk and Benghazi; Japan invades Burma, the Dutch East Indies, and captures Singapore; the British bomb Cologne and Lübeck; the US and Canada intern residents of Japanese heritage in camps; many American and Philippine prisoners die in the Japanese-forced Bataan Death March; Americans bomb Tokyo; Americans begin successful island-hopping strategy against Japan and win the battles of the Coral Sea and Midway; French navy loses in Toulon; British and Indian troops advance in Burma; Fermi achieves the first controlled nuclear chain reaction when he splits the atom; the Manhattan Project of intensive US atomic research begins; the first electronic brain or automatic computer is developed in the US; a recorder using plastic magnetic recording tape is invented by German engineers; Gandhi demands independence from Britain and is arrested.

1943: German troops surrender at Stalingrad (Feb. 2) and begin to withdraw from the Caucasus; Churchill and Roosevelt meet in Casablanca; the Japanese are driven from Guadalcanal by US troops; the British Eighth Army reaches Tripoli; Axis powers surrender in North Africa (Tunisia, May 13); Russians destroy the German army southwest of Stalingrad; Russians recapture Rostov and Kharkov; the Royal Air Force raids Berlin; US planes sink the 22-ship Japanese convoy in the Battle of the Bismarck Sea; British and US armies in Africa link up and Rommel retreats; an armed Jewish uprising begins in the overcrowded Warsaw ghetto, but it is crushed by German troops (1943–44) who massacre Jewish inhabitants; the RAF bombs Ruhr dams; US forces land in New Guinea; US recaptures Aleutians; Allies land in Sicily (July 10); Churchill, Roosevelt and Mackenzie King meet in Quebec; US troops bomb Ploesti oil fields in Rumania and enter Messina; Allies land in Salerno Bay and invade Italy, which surrenders unconditionally (Sept. 8); Russians take Kiev; Chinese Gen. and Mme Chiang Kai-shek meet with Roosevelt and Churchill in Cairo and pledge to liberate Korea after Japan is defeated; Churchill, Stalin and Roosevelt hold the Teheran Conference; Allied round-the-clock bombing of Germany begins; the first fully electronic computer is used by the British government to crack German military codes; penicillin is used to treat chronic diseases; Bengal is swept by famine; rationing of selected foods begins in the US; major US cities are troubled by race riots.

1944: Germany continues air raids on London; Russian offensives continue in the Ukraine and Crimea; Allies bomb Berlin; Monte Cassino and Rome are liberated by the Allies June 4; D-day landings in Normandy

(France, June 6): over 700 ships and 4,000 landing craft are involved and Canadian troops lead the trek from the Normandy beaches; Germans drop first flying bomb (V-1) on London; southern Japan is bombed by the US; US troops take Saigon; Russians capture 100,000 Germans at Minsk; German officers unsuccessfully attempt to assassinate Hitler; Russians reach Brest-Litovsk; Americans capture Guam from the Japanese; the British Eighth Army takes Florence; creation of a United Nations is discussed at the Dunbarton Oaks conference in Washington; Charles De Gaulle leads the Free French into Paris (Aug. 25); Allies liberate Belgium; the first V-2 rockets land in Britain; Churchill and Roosevelt meet in Quebec; Americans cross the German frontier near Trier; British airborne forces land at Eindhoven and Arnheim but have to withdraw; US troops land in the Philippines; Russians and Yugoslavs enter Belgrade; Russian Army occupies Hungary; Japanese suffer heavy losses in Battle of Leyte Gulf; Battle of the Bulge (Ardennes Forest) results in Allied victory; France regains Lorraine; Rommel commits suicide; Vietnam, under Ho Chi Minh, declares independence from France; American playwright Tennessee Williams completes *The Glass Menagerie*; quinine is synthesized; Richard Strauss completes the opera *Die Liebe der Danae* in Austria but its performance is cancelled when the Nazis shut down the theatres; French playwright Jean-Paul Sartre writes the existentialist work *Being and Nothingness*.

1945: Britain begins major offensive in Burma; Russians take Warsaw, Cracow and reach Oder River; Churchill, Roosevelt and Stalin meet at the Yalta Conference; Americans enter Manila; Russians take Budapest; British troops reach the Rhine; US air raids on Tokyo, Cologne and Danzig; Okinawa is captured; the British Second Army crosses the Rhine; the last German V-2 rocket falls on Britain; Franklin D. Roosevelt dies and is succeeded by Harry S. Truman; Russians reach Berlin; Bologna is captured; US and Soviet troops meet at Torgau and both liberate Nazi death camps, finding gas chambers and crematoriums; anti-Axis coalition agrees to set up new international body to replace ineffective League of Nations; new United Nations charter drawn up at conference in San Francisco (Apr.–June); Bremen, Genoa, Verona and Venice are captured by

the Allies; the Allies cross the Elbe; Mussolini is killed by Italian partisans; Hitler commits suicide (Apr. 30); the German army on the Italian front surrenders; Berlin surrenders to the Russians (May 2) and Germany capitulates to the Allies (May 7); V-E Day (Victory in Europe) ends the war in Europe (May 8); Germany is divided into four zones by the Allies and the three-power occupation of Berlin begins; Churchill, Truman and Stalin meet at Potsdam; Clement Attlee replaces Churchill as prime minister of Great Britain in a Liberal landslide; the first atomic bomb is detonated near Alamogordo, New Mexico after being developed by J. Robert Oppenheimer, Enrico Fermi and others (July 16); the Soviet Union declares war on Japan and occupied Manchuria; the US drops atomic bombs on Hiroshima (Aug. 6) and Nagasaki (Aug. 9); Japan surrenders and World War II ends; war dead are estimated at 35 million plus victims of Nazi concentration camps; the Nuremburg trials of Nazi war criminals begin; the League of Nations holds its final meeting in Geneva and turns over its assets to the UN (Oct.); Charles De Gaulle is elected president of the French provisional government; Tito is chief of state of the newly created Federal People's Republic of Yugoslavia; Nationalists and Communists resume civil war in north China; the Arab League is founded to oppose the creation of a Jewish state; Shintoism is abolished in Japan; vitamin A is synthesized; black markets for food, clothing and cigarettes develop in Europe; the UN World Bank (International Bank for Reconstruction and Development) is founded with authorized share capital of $27 billion.

1946: Albania, Bulgaria, Hungary and Transjordan become sovereign states; the UN General Assembly holds its first session in London (Jan. 7), electing Trygve Lie of Norway as its first Secretary-General, and its permanent headquarters is made in New York; Juan Perón is elected president of Argentina; a Peace Conference of 21 nations is held in Paris; 12 leading Nazis are sentenced to death following the Nuremburg trials and others get life imprisonment; power in Japan is transferred from the Emperor to an elected assembly; the UN Atomic Energy Commission is formed to monitor member nations; after a referendum in Italy, the king abdicates, Italy becomes a republic and de

Gasperi becomes head of state; xerography (photocopying) is invented by Chester Carlson; Dr Benjamin Spock writes *Baby and Child Care*, the "baby boom" reference book.

1947: British coal industry is nationalized; *The Diary of Anne Frank* is published by Anne's father, the only member of the German-Jewish Frank family to survive the Holocaust; Burma proclaims its independence; Paris Peace treaties signed; the Dead Sea Scrolls, dating from about 22 BC to AD 100, are discovered in Wadi Qumran, Palestine; American Chuck Yeager flies the first airplane at supersonic speeds; the transistor is invented by Bell Telephone Laboratory scientists; the UN divides Palestine, which is under British mandate, into a Jewish and an Arab state (Nov. 1947) and the British withdraw six months later; India gains independence from Great Britain and is partitioned into India and East and West Pakistan.

1948: Gandhi is assassinated by a Hindu opposing his tolerance of Muslims; a Communist coup d'état takes place in Czechoslovakia (Feb. 25); the Marshall Plan providing $17 billion in aid for Europe is passed by the US Congress; Winston Churchill chairs the Hague Congress for European unity; the Jewish state of Israel is proclaimed with Chaim Weizmann as president and David Ben-Gurion as premier (May 14); neighbouring Arab states declare war (1948–49) on Israel but by the end of the conflict Israel succeeds in increasing its territory; the Berlin airlift by the west begins after the USSR imposes a land and water blockade (1948–Sept. 1949); bread rationing ends in Britain; the World Council of Churches is organized in Amsterdam; American biologist Alfred C. Kinsey writes *Sexual Behavior in the Human Male*; the first World Health Assembly meets in Geneva; the first port radar system is installed in Liverpool, England.

1949: Tianjin, China, falls to the Communists, Chiang Kai-shek resigns as president of China, and removes his Nationalist forces to Formosa; the Communist People's Republic is proclaimed under Mao Tse-tung, with Chou En-lai as premier; the North Atlantic Treaty establishing a defence alliance (NATO) is signed by all parties (Belgium, Canada, Denmark, France, Iceland, Italy, Luxembourg, the Netherlands, Norway, Portugal, UK and US) in Washington; the Berlin blockade by the Soviet Union is lifted; the German Federal Republic (West Germany) comes into being with Bonn as its capital and Konrad Adenauer as Chancellor; republic of Eire is proclaimed with its capital in Dublin; Transjordan is renamed the Hashemite Kingdom of Jordan; the state of Vietnam, under Ho Chi Minh, is established at Saigon; civil war looms in Korea; the apartheid program of official racial discrimination is established in South Africa; the Democratic Republic is established in East Germany with Pieck as president; India becomes a federal republic with Pandit Nehru as prime minister; Indonesia gains sovereignty from Holland; the USSR tests its first atomic bomb; the US launches a guided missile to a height of 400 km, the highest altitude yet; George Orwell publishes *Nineteen Eighty-Four*.

1950: Communist China and Russia sign a treaty of friendship and mutual assistance, Britain also recognizes Communist China; 18 protesters are killed in anti-apartheid riots in South Africa; Vietnam, Laos and Cambodia gain independence from France; North Korea invades South Korea, capturing Seoul and forcing Pres. Syngman Rhee to flee; US Atomic Energy Commission begins work on hydrogen bomb; UN forces under Gen. Douglas MacArthur land in South Korea and push north of the 38th parallel, prompting Communist China to enter the war; US recognizes Vietnam, sends military supplies and instructors and signs pact for military assistance with Vietnam, Laos, Cambodia and France.

1951: North Korean forces reach the 38th parallel and capture Seoul: attempts to negotiate peace fail; Gen. MacArthur is replaced as commander in Korea for threatening massive retaliation against China; Winston Churchill forms the government in Britain; Remington Rand produces UNIVAC, the first large-scale, general-purpose computer; electricity is produced from atomic energy in the US; heart-lung machine devised by J. Andre-Thomas; penicillin and streptomycin available in US.

1952: Dwight D. Eisenhower is elected US president; Britain produces an atomic bomb; Elizabeth II becomes Queen of England; Egypt rocked by anti-British riots: premier resigns and the army seizes power; Mau-maus rebel in Kenya and government declares a state of emergency; first hydrogen bomb at Eniwetok Atoll in the Pacific; British Overseas Airways introduces the world's first jet passenger service from London to Rome; the first pocket-sized transistor radio is marketed by Sony in Japan.

1953: An armistice ending the Korean War is signed at Panmunjom; Soviet leader Joseph Stalin dies and is replaced by Malenkov; Sweden's Dag Hammarskjöld is elected UN secretary-general; the Soviet Union explodes a hydrogen bomb; Yugoslavia proclaims a new constitution and Marshall Tito becomes president; Egyptian generals establish a dictatorship and proclaim a republic; rebels from Vietnam attack Laos; Fidel Castro begins a campaign to overthrow Cuban dictator Fulgencio Batista; Ethel and Julius Rosenberg are executed after being convicted of passing American atomic secrets to the Soviet Union; Edmund Hillary and Tenzing Norgay become the first to scale Mt Everest; the first successful open heart surgery is performed in the US; researchers associate lung cancer with cigarette smoking.

1954: Vietnamese Communists defeat the French at Dien Bien Phu; racial segregation in public schools is banned by the US Supreme Court; Gammal Abdel Nasser becomes leader in Egypt; the US Senate censures Sen. Joseph McCarthy for launching a Communist witch-hunt; Canada and the US plan a joint radar defence system in the north (Distant Early Warning, DEW Line); the US *Nautilus* becomes the first nuclear-powered submarine; Dr Jonas Salk begins inoculating children against polio; the oral contraceptive pill is introduced in the US; the first successful kidney transplant is performed in the US; Roger Bannister becomes the first to run a mile in less than four minutes.

1955: Churchill resigns in Britain and is succeeded by Anthony Eden; Bulganin succeeds Malenkov as Soviet premier; eight east-European Communist bloc countries adopt the Warsaw Pact mutual defence treaty; West Germany joins NATO; border clashes between Israel and Jordan increase; Juan Perón is ousted by a military coup in Argentina; the first optical fibres are produced in Britain.

1956: Nasser elected Egyptian president; Egypt seizes control of the Suez Canal; Israeli troops invade Egypt and push towards the canal; British and French forces invade Egypt; a United Nations force arrives in Egypt, prompting a cease-fire; UN truce proposals for dispute between Jordan and Israel accepted; Soviet Communist leader Nikita Khrushchev denounces Joseph Stalin's "cult of personality"; Soviet tanks and troops crush an anti-Communist rebellion in Hungary; Sudan becomes a democratic republic; Pakistan becomes an Islamic republic; Martin Luther King, Jr, leads the campaign against racial segregation in the US South; transatlantic telephone service begins; the first computer programming language (FORTRAN) is developed in the US.

1957: Israeli troops withdraw from Egypt and the Gaza Strip comes under UN jurisdiction; UN reopens the Suez Canal; the space race begins as the USSR launches the first earth-orbiting satellite *Sputnik 1*; Belgium, France, Italy, Luxembourg, the Netherlands and West Germany sign the Rome Treaty to extend the common market established for the steel industry to all sectors of the economy; Pres. Eisenhower warns that the US will oppose Communist takeovers in the Middle East; Harold Macmillan leads the new Conservative government in Britain; John Diefenbaker becomes Canada's prime minister.

1958: Nikita Khrushchev becomes Soviet premier; Charles De Gaulle is elected president of France; Pope Pius XII dies and is succeeded by John XXIII; the first US space satellite, *Explorer I*, is launched; scientists in the USSR send two dogs into space and return them safely; Egypt and Syria form the United Arab Republic; Iraq's King Faisal is assassinated in a military coup; Alaska becomes the 49th US state.

1959: Fidel Castro overthrows Fulgencio Batista and establishes a Communist government in Cuba, expropriating sugar mills owned by the US; Soviet Prem. Khrushchev visits the US; American Vice-Pres. Richard Nixon visits the Soviet Union and has the "kitchen debate" with Khrushchev; the USSR sends a space probe to the moon and photographs its hidden side; the St Lawrence Seaway opens; the first commercial photocopier is introduced; the Dalai Lama flees Tibet; Hawaii becomes the 50th state of the US.

1960: An American U-2 spy plane is shot

down over the USSR, prompting Soviet Prem. Nikita Khrushchev to cancel a Soviet-American summit meeting; 50 South African black protesters are massacred at Sharpeville; the Congo (Zaïre) gains independence from Belgium, sparking political instability and UN intervention; Cyprus becomes independent and Archbishop Makarios wins the first presidential election; Israeli agents capture former Gestapo chief Adolf Eichmann in Argentina and smuggle him to Israel for trial; Germany bans Neo-Nazi political groups; John F. Kennedy is elected US president; the first weather and communications satellites are launched in the US; the first heart pacemaker is developed.

1961: Soviet Major Yuri Gagarin becomes the first man in space; US breaks off diplomatic ties with Cuba; the US-backed Bay of Pigs invasion by Cuban exiles fails to topple Cuba's Fidel Castro; astronaut Alan Shepard becomes the first American in space with a sub-orbital flight; East Germany builds the Berlin Wall to stop its citizens from moving to the West; Kuwait becomes independent from Britain, which sends troops to counter Iraqi annexation threats; UN Sec.-Gen. Dag Hammarskjöld dies in a plane crash over Northern Rhodesia; UK applies for membership in the Common Market; the silicon chip is patented by Texas Instruments in the US.

1962: Fearing nuclear war, many North Americans build fallout shelters; John Glenn becomes the first American to orbit the earth; US establishes a military council in South Vietnam; the discovery of Soviet missile bases in Cuba leads to a US naval blockade; the Cuban Missile Crisis ends when Soviet leader Khrushchev agrees to dismantle the bases; UN troops quell rebellion in the Congo's Katanga province; Algeria, Uganda and Jamaica gain independence; the UN votes in favor of economic sanctions against South Africa; Pope John XXIII opens the Second Vatican Council which will modernize the Catholic church; the TV satellite *Telstar* is launched in the US.

1963: US Pres. John Kennedy is assassinated in Dallas and Lyndon Johnson succeeds him; the US, Soviet Union and Britain ban nuclear tests in the atmosphere; South Vietnamese leader Ngo Dinh Diem is assassinated following a military coup; US sends financial aid to South Vietnam; Zanzibar and Kenya gain

independence; Dr. Martin Luther King leads the March on Washington seeking equality for US blacks; the "hot line" emergency communications link is established between the White House and the Kremlin; UK application to Common Market rejected after French opposition; British government rocked by the Profumo affair and the scandal forces the resignation of a senior minister; Pope John XXIII dies and is succeeded by Paul VI; archaeologists find the remains of a thousand-year-old Viking settlement in Newfoundland; the first liver and lung transplants are performed; Valentina Tereshkova becomes the first female astronaut.

1964: Harold Wilson becomes prime minister in Britain; Communist China announces it has developed an atomic bomb; the US escalates its military involvement in Vietnam following a reported North Vietnamese attack on US destroyers in the Gulf of Tonkin; the Palestine Liberation Organization (PLO) is formed; Zambia, Malta and Malawi become independent; the sultan of Zanzibar is banished and the country is declared a republic; Zanzibar unites with Tanganyika to form Tanzania; Northern Rhodesia declares independence and adopts the name Zambia; Leonid Brezhnev and Alexei Kosygin become Soviet leaders after Khrushchev is deposed; the first word processor is developed by IBM; the Beatles appear on the Ed Sullivan Show as "Beatlemania" sweeps North America.

1965: Ferdinand Marcos is elected president of the Philippines; Gambia and Rhodesia declare independence from Britain; Rhodesia's declaration is met by an oil embargo; a massive power failure blacks out most of the northeast US and eastern Canada; Pope Paul VI reaffirms the Catholic Church's opposition to birth control; a Soviet cosmonaut is the first to leave a spacecraft and "float" in space; two US Gemini capsules rendezvous in space.

1966: China's Red Guards demonstrate against western influences as Mao launches the Cultural Revolution; Indira Gandhi becomes India's prime minister; floods destroy art treasures in Florence, Italy; De Gaulle asks that NATO forces leave France; South African Pres. Hendrik Verwoerd is stabbed to death during a Parliamentary session; Lesotho and Guyana become independent; civilian protests against the Vietnam

War escalate in the US; government in Ghana overthrown by military coup; an artificial heart is successfully implanted for the first time by Dr Michael De Bakey in Houston; the Soviet Union lands an unmanned spacecraft on the moon.

1967: Israel defeats Egypt, Syria and Jordan in the Six Day War and occupies the Sinai Peninsula, Golan Heights, Gaza Strip and the east bank of the Suez Canal; Expo 67 world fair opens in Montreal; a Soviet cosmonaut becomes the first reported casualty of the space race; US manned space flights are suspended after astronauts Grissom, White and Chaffee die in Apollo capsule fire; race riots erupt in US cities during the "long hot summer"; Canada celebrates its centennial; Dr Christiaan Barnard of South Africa performs the world's first successful human heart transplant: the patient survives for 18 days.

1968: The US intelligence ship *Pueblo* is captured by North Korea; US civil rights leader Martin Luther King is assassinated in Memphis; presidential candidate Robert Kennedy is assassinated in Los Angeles; Soviet troops crush liberal reform in Czechoslovakia; a treaty limiting military use of outer space is signed by 62 nations; university student protest movement spreads worldwide; Richard Nixon is elected US president; Pierre Trudeau becomes prime minister in Canada; peace talks between the US and North Vietnam begin in Paris; British colony of Mauritius becomes independent; Pope Paul VI issues an encyclical banning artificial birth control; three US astronauts circle the moon and return to Earth; *Surveyor 7*, uncrewed, lands on moon.

1969: US astronaut Neil Armstrong becomes the first man to walk on the moon as *Apollo 12* lands on the lunar surface; Yasir Arafat becomes PLO chairman; North Vietnamese leader Ho Chi Minh dies at age 79; the International Red Cross estimates that 1.5 million Biafrans have died, mostly by starvation, in the civil war with Nigeria; the US begins withdrawal of troops from Vietnam; Golda Meir becomes Israeli prime minister; the Concorde supersonic airliner makes its first flight; *Mariner* space probes transmit pictures of Mars back to earth.

1970: An earthquake kills about 30,000 people in Peru; US National Guardsmen kill four Kent State University students during anti-war protests at the campus and two students are killed at Jackson State following similar demonstrations; the first complete synthesis of a gene is announced by University of Wisconsin scientists; Arab commandos hijack three jets bound for New York from Europe; the civil wars in Nigeria end when Biafra capitulates to the federal government; the Front de Libération du Québec (FLQ) kidnaps British trade commissioner James Cross, and kidnaps and murders Quebec cabinet minister Pierre Laporte; the Canadian federal government responds to this "October Crisis" by invoking the War Measures Act, temporarily suspending civil liberties in Canada; Israel and United Arab Republic declare a 99-day truce in latest conflict; Gambia becomes a republic; a cyclone and tidal wave hit the offshore islands in the Ganges Delta of East Pakistan, leaving at least 168,000 people dead and about 1 million homeless.

1971: US planes bomb Cambodia, attacking Vietcong supply routes; fighting in Indochina spreads to Laos and Cambodia; the US conducts large-scale bombing raids against North Vietnam; mainland China is admitted to the United Nations; women are granted the right to vote in Switzerland; violence in Northern Ireland escalates after Britain introduces policies of internment without trial; India fights with the Bengali rebels against Pakistan; the US and USSR sign a treaty banning nuclear weapons on the ocean floor; Algeria seizes majority control of all French oil and gas interests within its borders but promises restitution; Idi Amin takes control over Uganda; Mao Zedong's heir-apparent, Lin Piao, dies in a mysterious air crash; the USSR soft-lands a space capsule on Mars; a Los Angeles earthquake kills 60 people and causes $1 billion in damage; the hormone that controls human growth is synthesized by Dr. Choh Hao Li at the University of California.

1972: The world's largest diamond (969.8 carats) is unearthed in Sierra Leone; US Pres. Richard Nixon meets Mao Zedong in China; Britain imposes direct rule on Northern Ireland and 467 people are killed in violence between Catholics and Protestants; Ceylon becomes a republic and changes its name to Sri Lanka; Philippine Pres. Ferdinand Marcos assumes near-dictatorial powers; a Soviet spacecraft soft-lands on Venus; more than 70 nations sign a treaty prohibiting the stockpiling of biological weapons; the US conducts its heaviest B-52 bombing raids of the war against North Vietnam but continues to withdraw troops, despite lack of progress at Paris peace talks; Arab terrorists massacre 11 Israeli Olympic athletes in a stand-off with West German police at the summer Olympic games in Munich; Richard Leakey and Glynn Isaac discover a 2.5-million-year-old human skull in northern Kenya; a US federal grand jury indicts seven persons, including two former White House aids, on charges of conspiracy to break into the Democratic national headquarters (in the Watergate building) in Washington, DC; Richard Nixon is reelected as US president.

1973: A cease-fire agreement, intended to end the Vietnam war, is signed in Paris; fighting in the Middle East between Israeli and Arab forces (Yom Kippur War) is resolved by a shaky ceasefire; Arab oil-producing states cut petroleum exports to the US, western Europe and Japan because of their support of Israel; the US Senate begins televised hearings on the Watergate scandal and it is revealed that Pres. Nixon had secretly taped all conversations in his White House office; US vice-president resigns in an unrelated scandal; US combat involvement in Indochina officially ends as American planes halt their bombing of Cambodia; typhoon "Nora" leaves 800,000 Filipinos homeless on the island of Luzon; Great Britain, Ireland and Denmark formally join the Common Market; the Bahamas are granted independence from Britain after three centuries of colonial rule; Chilean Marxist Pres. Salvadore Allende is overthrown by a CIA-backed military junta which claims Allende commits suicide; Shah of Iran nationalizes foreign-owned oil companies.

1974: Oil-producing nations boost their prices and worldwide inflation accelerates as economic growth slows to near zero in most industrialized nations; the government of China launches a new "Cultural Revolution" program aimed at condemning both the Chinese philosopher Confucius and former Defence Minister Lin Piao; West German Chancellor Willy Brandt resigns after a scandal involving an East German spy; the Tower of London and the British Houses of Parliament are bombed by the Irish Republican Army; Soviet Nobel prize-winning author Aleksandr Solzhenitsyn is stripped of his citizenship and exiled; Portuguese dictatorship ended by military

coup and democratic reforms are initiated; rebels supported by Greece overthrow government in Cyprus; Turkish forces invade and take over much of the island; India explodes a nuclear device; Syria and Israel agree to the boundaries of a demilitarized zone in the Golan Heights and they begin troop withdrawals from the region; US Pres. Richard Nixon resigns to avoid impeachment by Congress for his coverup of the Watergate scandal; Gerald Ford is sworn in to replace Nixon; the US and Soviet Union reach a tentative agreement to limit the numbers of strategic offensive nuclear weapons and delivery vehicles; severe drought threatens millions in Africa; scientists warn of the effects of chloroflourocarbons (CFCs) on the ozone layer.

1975: Portugal's new constitution grants most power to the military; Angola, Cape Verde, São Tomé and Principe and Mozambique gain independence from Portugal; Turkish Cypriots declare the establishment of a separate state in the northern half of the island; US evacuates as North Vietnam seizes Saigon; Egypt reopens the Suez Canal, which had been closed since the 1967 Arab-Israeli war; a UN Security Council resolution calling for the imposition of an arms embargo against South Africa is vetoed by the US, Great Britain and France; Generalissimo Franco, Spain's chief of state, dies and is replaced by King Juan Carlos I; Peru's president is ousted in a military coup and replaced by a general; a democratic republic is proclaimed in Laos; Papua New Guinea and Surinam become independent; civil war breaks out in Beirut between Christians and Muslims; rebels in Eritrea provoke battles with Ethiopian government.

1976: Chinese Prem. Chou En-lai and Communist Chinese leader Mao Zedong die within months of each other; riots against apartheid take place in the all-black township of Soweto outside of Johannesburg and spread to Cape Town in black townships and white areas; first reports surface that Libyan leader Col. Moammar Qaddafi is financing, training and arming a widespread terrorist network; the Parti Québécois wins power in Quebec's provincial election, raising the possibility of Quebec's secession from Canada; worldwide earthquakes kill an estimated 780,000 people; the Gang of Four (Mao Zedong's widow and three others) unsuccessfully attempt a coup in China; Venezuela nationalizes petroleum industry; president of Argentina overthrown by military junta; Spanish Sahara released from Spain's jurisdiction and divided between Morocco and Mauritania; North and South Vietnam reunited under Communist government; a military coup in Thailand topples the government; 9,000 refugees flee Angolan civil war.

1977: Cambodian refugees report economic and social disaster following the Communists' capture of Phnom Penh; Egypt severs diplomatic relations with Syria, Iraq, Libya, Algeria and South Yemen for attempting to disrupt its peace overtures to Israel; over 570 die in the world's worst aviation disaster when two Boeing 747s collide on the runway on the Canary Island of Tenerife; black South African leader Steven Biko dies in jail; French territories of Afars and Issa unite to form independent Republic of Djibouti; government of Pakistan is overthrown and martial law is imposed; Leonid Brezhnev becomes USSR president and Communist Party chief; Somalia-backed Eritrean guerrillas are stopped by Ethiopian army; Thailand government seized by military junta; Rhodesia's white government announces it will begin negotiations with black majority; cyclone in India leaves 20,000 dead and 2 million homeless; US unmanned spacecrafts *Voyager I* and *II* begin journeys to explore the outer solar system; the neutron bomb, which causes great loss of life but little property damage, is developed in the US.

1978: A Soviet-supported military junta takes power in Afghanistan and Soviet troops occupy the country; Lebanon is torn by Christian and Muslim militia activity as well as Palestinian guerrilla activity, and Arab League intervenes to restore peace; Israeli forces withdraw; Syria declares a unilateral cease-fire in and around Beirut, Lebanon; Egyptian Pres. Anwar Sadat and Israeli Prem. Menachem Begin sign peace accords, mediated by US Pres. Jimmy Carter; Shah Mohammed Riza Pahlevi of Iran imposes martial law to suppress anti-government demonstrations; leftist Sandinista guerrillas attempt to overthrow the government of Nicaraguan Pres. Anastasio Somoza; US establishes full diplomatic relations with Communist China; the first peaceful transfer of power takes place in Dominican Republic; Zaïre invaded by secessionist rebels: defence aid comes from other African nations, and

France and Belgium after the massacre of Europeans; military junta seizes power in Honduras; army seizes government power in Bolivia; former Italian Prem. Aldo Moro is kidnapped and murdered by the Red Brigades, a revolutionary terrorist group; John Paul II (Karol Wojtyla) of Poland becomes the first non-Italian Pope in four centuries; the first "test-tube baby" (human baby conceived outside the womb) is born in England.

1979: Armed Islamic revolutionary followers of Ayatollah Khomeini overthrow the government of Iran and the Shah flees; students demanding the Shah's return to stand trial seize hostages at US embassy; a malfunction in the cooling system of a nuclear reactor at Three Mile Island in Pennsylvania, US, closes down the reactor and radiation escapes into the air; Conservative Margaret Thatcher becomes Britain's first female prime minister; a black government is formally installed in Rhodesia and its name is changed to Zimbabwe; China and the US establish formal commercial relations for the first time since 1949; Vietnamese army invades Cambodia and installs new government; St Lucia, St Vincent and the Grenadines become independent; coup in Grenada replaces government leader; president of Uganda, Idi Amin, overthrown; Egypt is expelled from Arab League after signing Camp David peace treaty; first elections for European Parliament held; the US-USSR SALT (Strategic Arms Limitation Treaty) Agreement is signed in Vienna; Iran nationalizes remaining privately-owned industries without compensation; sharp oil price increases contribute to high inflation worldwide; South Korean Pres. Park Chung Hee and his chief body guard are assassinated by a government official; emperor of Central African Empire overthrown; president of El Salvador is ousted by military coup.

1980: Soviet dissident Andrei Sakharov, a Nobel prize-winning physicist, is arrested in Moscow; human interferon, a promising natural disease-fighting substance, is made by gene splicing; Mt St Helens erupts in Washington, in a blast that sends debris 20 km up into the atmosphere and is heard over 300 km away; in a political comeback, Indira Gandhi wins a landslide victory in India's parliamentary elections; Soviet war in Afghanistan escalates as the US imposes an embargo on the sale of grain and high technology to the Soviet Union in response to the continued occupation of Afghanistan, and 50 nations boycott the Moscow Olympics in protest; Roman Catholic Archbishop Oscar Arnulfo Romero, an El Salvadoran reformer, is assassinated while saying mass; some 10,800 Cubans seek asylum in Peru's Cuban embassy and more than 125,000 Cubans escape by boat to the US; Liberian Pres. William Tolbert, Jr, is killed in a coup; military coup in Turkey unseats government; Zimbabwe gains independence from Britain; 350 Bengalis are massacred by native tribal people in India; black guerrillas successfully bomb two South African petroleum plants and a refinery; mass labour strikes in Poland force the government to allow independent trade unions, including Solidarity, led by Lech Walesa; 20 terrorist bomb attacks take place in France; the Iran-Iraq war begins when Iraqi fighter-bombers attack Iranian airfields and lay siege to its southwestern cities; 3,000 are killed in earthquakes centred in southern Italy; 20,000 die in two strong earthquakes in Algeria; *Voyager I* sends back the first pictures of Saturn; wreck of the *Titanic* found in North Atlantic.

1981: Aquired Immune Deficiency Syndrome (AIDS) is first recognized, in the US; in El Salvador, heavy fighting occurs between the government and leftist insurgents; the world's first reusable spacecraft, the Space Shuttle *Columbia*, is sent into space; clashes between Syrian troops and Christian militiamen in Lebanon are followed by Israeli bombing in support of Christian forces; artificial bone and skin are developed in the US; Pope John Paul II is shot and seriously wounded outside the Vatican by a Turkish terrorist; Israel is condemned worldwide after Israeli warplanes destroy an Iraqi atomic reactor near Baghdad; Irish prisoners in Belfast stage hunger strikes to force the British government to grant political prisoner status to Irish nationalist inmates, and some die; South African troops invade Angola in pursuit of guerrillas; Belize, formerly British Honduras, becomes independent from Britain; Pres. Anwar el-Sadat of Egypt is assassinated by Muslim extremists during a military parade; Israel formally annexes the Golan Heights; a five-day war between Ecuador and Peru erupts over a border dispute; Greece joins the European Community; Italian government rocked by revelation that nearly 1,000 key government, army and business leaders support a secret outlawed Masonic lodge; president of Bangladesh assassinated; Iranian president, prime minister and 29 others killed in bomb attack; 5,000 die when Indonesian ferry sinks in Java Sea; martial law is instituted in Poland in the face of continued labour unrest; the personal computer is introduced by IBM in the US.

1982: Argentina moves to reclaim Malvinas (the Falkland Islands) from UK by invading the territory; Britain defeats Argentina in the subsequent war; Canada gains the power to amend its own constitution from Britain; Israel withdraws from the Sinai and turns it over to Egypt, fulfilling their 1979 peace treaty; Israel invades Lebanon and the PLO leadership leaves Lebanon under UN protection; Lebanese Christian militiamen massacre Palestinians in refugee camps and Israel is accused of indirectly aiding the attack; Iran invades Iraq, but Iraq claims to have killed 27,000 Iranians in 18 days of battle; a series of IRA bombs explode in London, killing nine and wounding 51; western nations debate a proposed Soviet oil pipeline to western Europe; Lech Walesa, former leader of Solidarity, the outlawed Polish labour union, is freed after 11 months of imprisonment; military coups in Bangladesh and Guatemala force changes in government; Soviet leader Leonid Brezhnev dies and Yuri Andropov succeeds him; in Cambodia, support for Khmer Rouge grows as coalition against Vietnamese-backed government joined by Prince Sihanouk; up to 1,200 Afghan civilians and Soviet soldiers die in a tunnel explosion caused by the collision of two trucks; the first permanent artificial heart is transplanted into Dr Barney B. Clark, 61, in Utah; Mexican volcano, El Chichón, erupts, blasting debris into the stratosphere.

1983: Klaus Barbie, former chief of the German Gestapo in Lyons, France, during WW II is deported to France from Bolivia to face charges of "crimes against humanity"; Soviet citizens and diplomats accused of espionage are expelled from France, Spain, the US and Britain; the US government is accused of having illegally aided Nicaraguan rebels; anti-government protests increase in Chile, governed by Gen. Pinochet; Ethiopia appeals for aid to 4 million victims of drought and famine; Sri Lankan Sinhalese and Tamil forces clash, killing hundreds and destroying the homes of thousands of others; 1,200 die in an earthquake in Turkey; martial law is formally lifted in Poland; the Organization of Petroleum Exporting Countries (OPEC) agrees to cut crude oil prices for the first time in its 23-year-history; all 269 people aboard are killed when the Soviet Union shoots down a South Korean airliner, claiming that the plane had been on a spying mission and strayed into Soviet airspace; Benigno Aquino, opponent of Philippine Pres. Marcos, returns to Manila and is assassinated; 241 US Marines and sailors and 40 French paratroopers, members of a multinational peacekeeping force in Lebanon, are killed by suicide terrorists; the US and France support Chad's government against Libyan-supported guerrillas; Israeli withdrawal from Lebanon is followed by full-scale fighting between Lebanese ethnic and religious groups; US-led forces invade the small island of Grenada; US Cruise missiles in Europe are deployed in Britain despite Soviet and civilian opposition; white South Africans approve a new constitution granting limited political participation for persons of mixed race and Asians, but not for blacks, in a new tricameral legislature; Yasir Arafat and PLO guerrillas are evacuated from Lebanon to Tunis, under UN sponsorship; riots in Assam, India claim 5,000 lives and 300,000 refugees flee; the compact disc is introduced; after an 11-year journey, the *Pioneer 10* spacecraft leaves the solar system.

1984: Cholesterol is linked to heart disease following a 10-year study by US researchers; the Apple Macintosh with mouse enters the personal computer market; Konstantin Chernenko becomes Soviet leader following the death of Yuri Andropov; US astronauts fly free of the space shuttle *Challenger*, the first humans to do so without a tether; US and UN forces are withdrawn from Lebanon; French and American researchers, working separately, report that they have identified viruses which appear to be the cause of AIDS; Saudi, Greek and Swiss tankers are attacked by both Iran and Iraq in the Persian Gulf and Saudi Arabia shoots down two Iranian jets; hundreds die during a battle for the Golden Temple in Amritsar between Sikh militants and police in India; Indian Prime Min. Indira Gandhi is slain by two of her Sikh bodyguards in New Delhi and widespread violence follows; Daniel Ortega, Sandinista leader, wins in Nicaraguan elections; the international community sends aid to starving

Ethiopians; in a secret operation, Israel airlifts 25,000 Ethiopian Jews (Falashas) out of the Sudan; Britain and China finalize an agreement on Hong Kong's future, guaranteeing its capitalist system for 50 years after it is turned over to China in 1997; a Union Carbide chemical plant leak kills 2,500 in Bhopal, India; the European Space Agency launches the largest telecommunications satellite in the world.

1985: South African police kill 18 blacks commemorating the Sharpville massacre in 1960, 19 more are killed while participating in a funeral procession and later the government declares a state of emergency; Daniel Ortega becomes president of Nicaragua; US president urges military aid to Nicaraguan opposition forces but only humanitarian aid is approved; Mikhail Gorbachev succeeds Konstantin Chernenko as Soviet leader and he opens disarmament talks with the US; Iraq turns back an Iranian offensive, allegedly killing 30,000 to 50,000 Iranians; Shiite Muslim hijackers release hostages after 17 days of captivity in Beirut, having demanded the release of hundreds of Shiites detained by Israeli forces; Argentine president imposes drastic economic measures to cut 1,010 percent inflation rate; top French officials are linked to the bombing of a ship owned by Greenpeace; two leading Soviet KGB officials defect to Britain and the US, where both name Soviet spies in the two countries; a cyclone and tidal waves hit Bangladesh, killing 10,000; a Mexican earthquake kills more than 7,000 and causes widespread destruction, leaving thousands homeless; border dispute between Mali and Burkina Faso leads to war but is eventually referred to International Court of Justice; Nicaragua suspends civil rights; four Palestinians seize the Italian cruise ship *Achille Lauro* off the coast of Egypt, murdering a wheelchair-bound American; Reagan and Gorbachev meet at the first superpower summit in six years; 95 Colombians die when 60 rebels seize the Palace of Justice in Bogotá and take more than 300 persons hostage; 60 die when Arab gunmen hijack an Egyptian jetliner, in an act allegedly backed by Libya's leader Col. Muammar Qaddafi; a Colombian volcanic eruption kills 20,000 people; Guatemala elects its first civilian president following three decades of military rule; Uruguay's military government replaced by civilian government; Sudanese and Ugandan presidents ousted by military coups; terrorists kill 20 people at two airports (in Rome and Vienna), both at the ticket counters of El Al, Israel's national airline; Live Aid rock concert in London, UK and Philadelphia, US raises over $60 million for African famine relief.

1986: Portugal and Spain join the European Community; Jean-Claude Duvalier, Haiti's "president for life," flees to France in the face of nationwide protest; Portugal elects its first civilian president in 60 years; Gorbachev calls for "radical reform" of Soviet economy and reshapes the leadership of the Communist party; Philippine Pres. Ferdinand Marcos flees to the US after allegations of electoral fraud; his opponent, Corazon Aquino, succeeds Marcos as president; Swedish Prime Min. Olof Palme is assassinated; former UN secretary general Kurt Waldheim is elected president of Austria; US planes bomb Libya citing retaliatory measures after missile attacks; radiation is spread following the meltdown of the Chernobyl nuclear power plant in the USSR; South African forces attack alleged African National Congress (ANC) bases in neighbouring Botswana, Zambia and Zimbabwe; the *New York Times* first links Panama's General Manuel Noriega with drug and arms trafficking; US president acknowledges a secret and illegal arms deal with Iran: the "Iran-Contra Affair" involving the US sale of arms in exchange for hostages is first reported in a Lebanese newspaper; The US space shuttle *Challenger* explodes one minute after liftoff and all seven crew members die instantly; *Voyager 2* spacecraft passes Uranus.

1987: Soviet leader Mikhail Gorbachev begins a campaign for openness (glasnost) and reconstruction (perestroika); Tamil separatists kill hundreds of Sri Lankans, mostly Sinhalese, and clash with government forces; German pilot Mathias Rust, 19, embarrasses Soviets when he lands his single-engine Cessna in Red Square, Moscow; Moscow's Communist Party chief, Boris Yeltsin, is dismissed after criticizing Soviet leader Gorbachev; South Africa withdraws its troops from Angola; an Iraqi warplane's missile kills 37 US sailors in the Persian Gulf, and the US escorts Kuwaiti oil tankers despite danger posed by the Iran-Iraq war; 402 Iranian pilgrims to Mecca die in battles with Saudi police; 24 nations sign a treaty to protect the ozone layer; Portugal and China agree that the Portuguese colony of Macao will be returned to China in 1999; stock market prices plunge worldwide; the Palestinian intifadah (uprising) begins against Israeli authorities in the Gaza Strip and West Bank, and thousands of protesters are imprisoned; Syrian troops enter Beirut in an attempt to bring a cease-fire; Lebanese prime minister dies in a bomb attack; a military coup ousts coalition government in Chad; 2,000 die in the Philippines when a ferry sinks.

1988: Nicaraguan contras and the Sandinista government reach a cease-fire agreement; the US and Soviet Union sign a treaty on intermediate-range nuclear forces (INF); Soviet troops begin to pull out of Afghanistan after a nine-year occupation; nationalist groups in Soviet-controlled Azerbaijan and Armenia clash; Colombian drug cartels defy government attempts to bring them to justice, and fight among themselves; prime minister of Poland promises co-operation with non-communist groups; a US navy warship accidentally shoots down a commercial Iranian airliner over the Persian Gulf, killing all 290 persons aboard; the Soviet communist party backs Gorbachev's plan for perestroika; Canadian and US governments ratify a free trade agreement, to take effect Jan. 1, 1989; Iran and Iraq agree on a cease-fire to end their eight-year war; Iraq uses poison gas on its Kurdish minority and razes Kurdish villages; Libya and Chad formally end their war; Thailand and Laos do battle in a brief border dispute; Ethiopia and Somalia end 11 years of disputes over borders with a peace treaty; Solidarity supporters stage widespread strikes in Poland; Vietnamese troops leave Kampuchea; a military coup in Burma causes a change in leadership; Yugoslavia's inflation rate tops 250%, ethnic Albanians in Kosovo province demand freedom from Serbian rule; Benazir Bhutto, daughter of a former Pakistani president, becomes prime minister of Pakistan; 270 people die when a bomb blows up a Pan Am jetliner over Lockerbie, Scotland; 25,000 Armenians die during an earthquake.

1989: Iran's Ayatollah Khomeini calls for the execution of author Salman Rushdie for blaspheming the prophet Mohammed; the Soviet Union holds historic multicandidate parliamentary elections and Boris Yeltsin emerges as Russian leader; Japanese Prime Min.

Noboru Takeshita is toppled by financial scandal, Emperor Hirohita dies and is succeeded by his son; Chinese students lead more than one million in demonstrations for democratic reforms, but spreading unrest is checked by a government crackdown in Tiananmen Square that is suspected to have killed thousands; Hungary opens its border with Austria and moves toward political and economic reform; anti-Communist forces continue to battle the government in Afghanistan; fighting between Christians and Muslims in Beirut intensifies; 90 people die in ethnic violence in Soviet Uzbekistan; Poles participate in their first open election in 40 years and Solidarity wins a solid victory; the three Baltic states (Estonia, Latvia and Lithuania) protest Soviet domination; a Colombian presidential candidate is slain, prompting a renewed crackdown on illegal drug traffickers; thousands of East Germans flee to West Germany and the East German government proposes political reforms; Vietnamese forces withdraw from Cambodia; East German communist leader Erich Honecker is removed from power, he is later charged with corruption; thousands demonstrate in Czech-oslovakia and force the communist government to resign, Vaclav Havel is elected president; the spaceship *Atlantis* is launched on a journey to Jupiter; East Germany opens the Berlin wall after 28 years and lifts visa and emigration restrictions; Panama's General Noriega annuls presidential elections after an opposition party victory, the US invades Panama and Noriega goes into hiding; Romanian Pres. Nicolae Ceausescu is overthrown and executed with his wife for genocide, abuse of power and theft; 80 nations sign an agreement to limit production of chorofluorocarbons (CFCs) to protect the ozone layer; Paraguay's president is toppled by a military coup; the Exxon *Valdez* runs aground in Alaska and spills thousands of litres of oil; *Voyager 2* spacecraft reaches Neptune.

1990: Panama's Manuel Noriega surrenders to US authorities; violence erupts in Soviet Azerbaijan as Azerbaijanis attack Armenians; Bulgaria and Yugoslavia switch to multiparty systems; Violeta Chamorro defeats Sandinista leader Daniel Ortega to become the Nicaraguan president; South African government lifts restrictions on opposition organizations and declares amnesty for political pris-

oners, black leader Nelson Mandela is freed after 27 years in prison; the US, France, Great Britain and the Soviet Union reach agreement on a reunited Germany; Lithuania proclaims its sovereignty and Soviet troops move in; many Soviet communists are defeated by reformers in city council elections; Namibia gains independence from South Africa; newly-released Soviet documents prove Soviet secret police killed 15,000 Polish military officers in the Katyn forest massacre of 1940; the $1.5-billion Hubble Space Telescope is sent into space, but flawed light-gathering mirrors distort transmissions; Iran's worst earthquake kills 40,000; more than 1,400 Muslim pilgrims to Mecca suffocate in a stampede in an overcrowded tunnel; the Ukraine declares its sovereignty within the Soviet Union; the two Germanys reunite, merging their economic, legal and political systems; Czechoslovakia and Romania hold their first free elections in the postwar era (Aug. 2); Iraq invades Kuwait over disagreements regarding oil production levels and appears ready to invade Saudi Arabia; the UN passes sweeping trade and financial sanctions against Iraq, and aid and troops pour into Saudi Arabia; Pakistani Prime Min. Benazir Bhutto is overthrown on charges of corruption and nepotism; civil war in black South African townships kills hundreds; the first human gene therapy for disease is done by blood transfusion; South Africa bans racial discrimination in public places; following a political challenge from within her own party, British Prime Min. Margaret Thatcher resigns and is succeeded by John Major; India's National Front coalition government is defeated and Chandra Shekhar becomes prime minister; Mozam-bique adopts a constitution allowing for a multiparty democracy; civil war in Chad ends with overthrow of president; a military coup in Bangladesh unseats the president; Soviet Pres. Mikhail Gorbachev proposes Union Treaty to restructure Soviet Union; Helmut Kohl elected Chancellor of Unified Germany; Lech Walesa elected president of Poland; African National Congress (ANC) holds first conference in South Africa in 31 years; Rev. Jean-Bertrand Aristide elected president of Haiti; Edward Shevardnadze resigns as Soviet foreign minister; Slovenia and Croatia initiate secession from Yugoslavian republic.

1991: Iraq ignores Jan. 15 deadline for withdrawal from Kuwait and Allied forces (including the US, Canada, Britain, France, Italy, Japan, Pakistan and members of the Arab League) launch a six-week air attack; Soviets suppress independence movements in Baltic republics; US and Italy begin rescue of foreigners trapped in Somalian civil war; limited integration of schools begins in South Africa and sweeping reforms of apartheid law are proposed; Allies launch ground assault on Iraqi forces and informal cease-fire follows; 1,200 killed in major earthquake in Pakistan and Afghanistan; Lithuanians vote to secede from Soviet Union; military seizes power in Thailand; Canada, the US and Mexico begin trade talks; Estonia and Latvia vote for independence from the Soviet Union; violent protests held in Belgrade to topple Yugoslavian government; Kuwaiti government forced to resign in wake of failure to establish post-war order; Mali government overthrown; UN cease-fire formally ends Gulf War (Apr.) and Kurds flee from Iraq; Soviet republic of Georgia votes for independence; thousands killed in cyclone in Bangladesh; cease-fire declared in Angola's 16-year civil war; Ethiopian Pres. Mengistu deposed; Rajiv Ghandi assassinated during Indian national election campaign; Albania's first non-Communist government confirmed; Boris Yeltsin elected president of Russia; Mt Pinatubo volcano erupts in Philippines; P.V. Narasimha Rao elected prime minister of India; Population Registration Act repealed in South Africa; fighting between Yugoslav military and Slovenian nationalists escalates; Israel agrees to take part in Middle East peace talks; Soviet hardliners attempt a coup against Mikhail Gorbachev: its failure results in the dissolution of the Communist party and a power struggle between Gorbachev and Russian leader Boris Yeltsin; rebels oust Haitian Pres. Jean-Bertrand Aristide; Serbia and Croatia reach political settlement but civil war continues; peace accord signed in El Salvador, paving the way to end of 11-year civil war; failed coup in Soviet Union speeds disintegration of the country as Lithuania, Estonia and Latvia act to enforce their independence; civil war in Croatia escalates; Philippine senate refuses to renew lease on US naval base; warring factions in Cambodia sign peace accord; members of EC and European Free Trade Area agree to create world's largest common market (European Economic Area) in 1993; Kiichi Miyazawa unseats Toshiki Kaifu as party leader and becomes prime minister of Japan; talks on new constitution begin in South Africa; rebels fighting in Somalia claim to have taken over Mogadishu and deposed the president; last oil well fire in Kuwait capped; Gorbachev resigns as USSR formally dissolved and CIS created; North and South Korea sign non-aggression pact; fighting escalates in Somalia; Slovenia and Croatia recognized as independent states by Germany; Islamic Salvation Front leads in Algerian elections; by year-end, cholera epidemic has killed 3,500 in Latin America and 12,500 in Africa.

1992: A Jan. military coup in Algeria gave power to a committee, which cancelled elections and outlawed its political rival, the Islamic Salvation Front (Mar.); in June the Algerian president was assassinated and power was assumed by the defense minister. In Afghanistan, the communist government backed by the former Soviet Union fell in Apr., after 14 years of fighting; interfactional fighting among the victorious mujaheddin continued throughout most of the year as rivals sought to secure power. Brazil was the site of the Earth Summit (June), which saw 100 world leaders and 30,000 participants gather in Rio de Janeiro to discuss worldwide environmental protection; the country was rocked by political unrest in Aug., which resulted in the end of the presidency of President Fernando Collor de Mello over an influence-peddling and bribery scandal. The European Community's Maastricht Treaty was first rejected by Denmark (June), then ratified by Irish (June) and French (Sept.) voters, and the Italian senate (Sept.). The leader of Colombia's drug cartel, Pablo Escobar, escaped from his custom-built prison during a bungled transfer (July) and stayed at large for the rest of the year. Czechoslovakia's president, Vaclav Havel, resigned on July 20 and the Parliament of Slovakia declared its sovereignty. An earthquake on Oct. 12 left 300 dead and thousands injured in Egypt. The Uruguay round of the GATT (General Agreement on Tariffs and Trade) negotiations remained stalled over the issue of farm subsidies. The president of Georgia was driven from office by fierce fighting around the capital (Jan.); by Mar., former Soviet foreign minister Eduard Shevardnadze had returned to assume legislative and executive power. Germany was plagued by riots and firebombings staged by right-wing extremists attacking foreign-born workers and refugees; German citizens rallied to protest. The OAS (Organization of American States) continued to try and reinstate Haiti's exiled president, Jean-Bertrand Aristide, without success. Israel's June national election resulted in a victory for the Labour Party and its leader, Yitzhak Rabin; in Aug., Rabin began to hint that compromise in the area of peace and territorial disputes might be possible. Italy continued an anti-Mafia crackdown despite the assassination of two prominent judges and a police investigator. In Iraq, the year was marked by a series of stand-offs with UN monitors attempting to enforce the terms of the Gulf War cease-fire. Jamaica's president Michael Manley resigned due to ill health and Percival Patterson was elected leader of the ruling party. Libya was the target of sanctions early in the year in an effort to force the surrender of suspects in the 1988 bombing of a Pan Am jet that crashed near Lockerbie, Scotland. A ruptured petrol pipeline in Mexico's working-class district of Guadalajara was blamed for an explosion that killed 200 and injured nearly 1,500 in Apr.. On Oct. 4, an El Al cargo plane crashed into two nine-storey apartment buildings close to the Netherland's Schipol airport. Nicaragua was hit by a powerful earthquake in Sept., which unleashed a series of tidal waves that killed 56 and left thousands homeless. Heavy rains and flash floods killed at least 650 people in northern and eastern Pakistan in Sept.. Peru's president, Alberto Fujimori, suspended sections of the country's constitution in Apr. and seized power, citing a need to root out corruption and combat the combined forces of the Shining Path guerrillas and various drug barons. Russia's first experiments with free markets triggered soaring inflation and shortages. Civil war in Somalia brought 4.5 million of its people to the brink of starvation; by Aug. the UN brought in forces to ensure that food was distributed to the hungry, but was unable to restore order; by Sept. the flights were targeted to remote villages in an effort to ensure that the hungry received the food and Canadians and US Marines arrived in Dec. in an attempt to restore order. The government in South Africa continued to work towards a power-sharing agreement with the black majority after receiving nearly 70% support in a Mar. whites-only referendum; negotiations were broken off after hundreds of armed blacks attacked residents of the Boipatong settlement in June, killing 42 and tarnishing President de Klerk's government with charges of collusion with the killers; in Sept. troops from the Ciskei homeland opened fire on ANC supporters massed at the border and talks on democratic reform were again delayed. Citizens in Thailand took to the streets in a series of demonstrations that forced Gen. Suchinda Kraprayoon to resign as the head of government by the end of May; at least 40 people were killed during the unrest but constitutional reforms were instituted and democratic elections were scheduled. In the United Kingdom, John Major's Conservative party won reelection to a fourth term with a reduced majority (Apr.); by Aug. the scandals of the royal family began to threaten the credibility of the monarchy; uncertainty over the fate of the Maastricht Treaty and pressure on UK currency forced a withdrawal from the European Monetary System in Sept. and a devaluation of the UK pound. In the United States, riots in Los Angeles in late Apr./early May left 42 dead, and damage was high; the US state of Florida was devastated by Hurricane Andrew (Aug.) which did an estimated $15 billion damage; on Oct. 12, the *Pioneer* spacecraft plunged into the scorching atmosphere surrounding the planet Venus and ended a 14-year space mission; in Nov., Republicans George Bush and Dan Quayle were defeated in their bid for reelection as the Democrats, under Bill Clinton and Al Gore, were elected to a four-year term. Yugoslavia continued to disintegrate: the UN Security Council deployed peacekeepers in Jan.; Croatia and Slovenia were given diplomatic recognition by the European community as well as 20 other countries (including Canada); by Feb., Serbia and Montenegro reached agreement on a common state retaining the Yugoslav flag, anthem and joint parliament; in Mar., citizens of the republic of Bosnia-Hercegovina voted for independence; however, ethnic fighting over Bosnian territory escalated throughout the year amid charges of "ethnic cleansing" and atrocities, and a series of cease-fires that rarely held for more than a few days; by the end of May, refugees began to arrive in neighbouring countries; in Sept., an attack on an Italian relief plane delivering supplies to Sarajevo forced the suspension of all flights for a month; on Sept. 22, Yugoslavia (Serbia and Montenegro) was expelled from the UN General Assembly.

1993: Both sides in the Bosnia-Hercegovina conflict rejected peace plans to settle the conflict; by Oct. repeated failure of the peace process led the US to propose lifting the arms embargo on the Muslims; in November Croatian gunners destroyed the16th century bridge at Mostar. Brazilian Pres. Fernando Collor de Mello resigned just as his Jan. impeachment trial began; Itamar Franco took over the presidency. In Burundi an abortive Oct. coup left the President and 6 ministers dead before the army decided to back the existing government and order was restored. Despite opposition and active interference by the Khmer Rouge, 90% of registered voters cast their ballots in Cambodia's national election in May. Colombian police killed fugitive drug baron Pablo Escobar after a 16-month manhunt and a rooftop shoot-out in Dec. One of the longest civil wars in Africa ended when the separation of Eritrea from Ethiopia was approved in a referendum. In the European Union, both Britain and Denmark voted in favour of the Maastricht Treaty, clearing another roadblock on the road to European union, however by August pressure on member currencies forced the scrapping of the exchange rate mechanism designed to ready member countries for a common currency; in Oct. Germany's federal court declared the Maastricht Treat to conform to the German constitution; this was the last obstacle in the unity process. After 7 years of negotiation, the latest version of the GATT agreement was approved by 117 countries in late Dec. German military forces took part in missions outside its borders for the first time since WWII; the German parliament bowed to right-wing pressures and placed limits on their liberal immigration laws. After a ceasefire was proposed in Jan. to end the civil conflict in Guatemala, the country was rocked by a series of coups in June which eventually saw the former human rights ombudsman, Ramiro de Leon Carpio, inaugurated as president. Neither the OAS nor the UN was able to restore Haiti's deposed president Jean-Bertrand Aristide to power despite intense negotiations and increased blockades. On Sept 13, PLO leader yasser Arafat and Israeli Prime Min. Yitzak Rabin met in Washington to sign a peace agreement secretly negotiated in Norway; the agreement granted Palestinian autonomy over certain lands and recognized Israel's right to exist. The balance of power in the Japanese parliament shifted as Prime Minister Miyazawa was forced to resign on a non-confidence vote after a series of political scandals; Morihiro Hosokawa assembled a coalition to form a government and took over as prime minister. The results of the June election in Nigeria were nullified by the long-time dictator, despite protests which included a 3-day general strike. A battle for power in the Russian parliament saw Pres. Boris Yeltsin strip Vice-Pres. Rutskoi of his powers and dissolve parliament to call Dec. elections; parliamentarians responded by barricading themselves in the building which was then surrounded by government troops; the seige was lifted when the insurgents surrendered on Oct. 4; a new parliament was elected in Dec. and a new constitution was approved. Slovakia and the Czech republic declared independence on Jan 1. UK Prime Min. John Major and his Irish counterpart announced a tentative peace plan for Northern Ireland that would allow the people to decide their own fate. US troops in Somalia handed the mission to re-establish order over to a UN force made up of personnel from 20 countries and announced they would pull out at the end of Mar. 1994. The first few months were marked by skirmishes between UN forces and those of General Mohammed Farrah Aidid. In Sept. an agreement was reached in South Africa that paved the way for a multi-party transitional council that included blacks; in Oct. the United Nations lifted economic sanctions; in Nov. a new constitution was approved and national all-race elections where scheduled for Apr. 27/94; white rule ended officially in Dec. The United Nations received payment of US$5333 million in outstanding dues from the United States. In the United States, a standoff outside the compound of a religious group in Waco Texas ended in tragedy when authorities stormed the area and the buildings erupted in flames. (Apr.); a rainy summer led to record-breaking floods in nine states along the Mississippi River and in Oct. brush fires devasted six counties in California; in Nov. Pres. Clinton secured approval for NAFTA in the House of Representatives.

1994: For 1994, see *News Events of the Year.*

NATIONS OF THE WORLD

THE STATISTICS SHOWN ARE INTENDED TO PRESENT an informative and comparative picture of the various nations of the world and their dependent territories. All data, including the geographic, population and government data, are taken from the latest available sources. The economic and finance/trade data indicate the size of the national economies and the amount of economic activity in the respective countries; health and education data, and communications and transportation data give some evidence of the quality of life and the state of the infrastructure in each nation. All dollar amounts are in US dollars.

The information contained in this section reflects data available up to and including October 1, 1994. Sources used for information include:

CIA World Fact Book 1993 • *"Facts on File"* • *Demographic Yearbook (UN)* • *Encyclopedia Britannica* • *Foreign Affairs Canada* • *Government Finance Statistics Yearbook (International Monetary Fund)* • *"Human Development Report" (UN Development Programme)* • *International Financial Stats Yearbook (International Monetary Fund)* • *"Keesing's Record of World Events"* • *Monthly Bulletin of Statistics (UN Statistical Division)* • *"Population and Vital Statistics Report" (UN Dept. of International Economic and Social Affairs)* • *"Social Indicators of Development" (World Bank)* • *Statesman's Yearbook (Macmillan)* • *The World Media Handbook 1992-1994 (UN Programme Evaluation and Communication Research Unit)* • *World Bank Atlas (World Bank)* • *World Book Encyclopedia* • *"World Debt Tables 1992-1993" (World Bank)* • *"World Development Report 1993-94" (World Bank)* • *"World Motor Vehicle Data" (Motor Vehicle Manufacturers Assoc. of the US Inc.)* • *"World Population" (UNESCO)* • *"World Population Data Sheet" (Population Reference Bureau Inc.)* • *World Resources 1992-1993 (World Resources Institute)* • *"World Tables 1992" (John Hopkins UP)* • *Worldwide Government Directory with International Organizations (Belmont Publications)* • *Year Book of Labour Statistics, (International Labour Office, Geneva).*

Afghanistan

Long-Form Name: Islamic State of Afghanistan
Capital: Kabul
Population: 17,400,000 (1993 est.)

■ GEOGRAPHY

Area: 652,090 sq. km
Coastline: none: landlocked
Climate: arid to semi-arid; cold winters and hot summers, considerable snowfall
Environment: damaging earthquakes occur in Hindu Kush mountains; poor soil, flooding, desertification, overgrazing, deforestation, pollution
Terrain: mostly rugged mountains; plains in north and southwest
Land Use: 12% arable land; negligible permanent crops; 46% meadows and pastures; 3% forest and woodland; 39% other; includes negligible irrigated
Location: SW Asia (Middle East)

■ PEOPLE

Nationality: Afghan
Ethnic Groups: 38% Pathan, 25% Tajik, 6% Uzbek, 19% Hazara; minor ethnic groups include Charar Aimaks, Turkoman, Baloch and others
Languages: 35% Pushtu (official), 50% Afghan Persian (Dari), 11% Turkic languages (primarily Uzbek and Turmen), 4% thirty minor languages (primarily Balochi and Pahai); much bilingualism
Religions: Islam (nearly 100%–majority Sunni Muslim)
Marriages: n.a.
Divorces: n.a.

■ GOVERNMENT

Leader(s): Pres. Burhanuddin Rabbani; Premier Gulbuddin HekMatyar
Government Type: transitional government
Administrative Divisions: 31 provinces
Independence: Aug. 19, 1919 (from UK)
National Holiday: Victory of the Muslim Nation, Apr. 28

■ ECONOMY

Overview: a poor country, largely dependent on farming (wheat) and livestock (sheep and goats). The economy is adversely affected by political and military disruptions
GNP: $3 billion, per capita $200; real growth rate n.a. (1989 est.)
Inflation: 56.7% (1991)
Industries: small-scale production of textiles, soap, furniture, shoes, fertilizer and cement; handwoven carpets; natural gas, oil, coal, copper

Labour Force: 6,230,000 (1992); 61% agriculture and animal husbandry, 14% industry, 25% services and other
Unemployment: n.a.
Agriculture: largely subsistence farming and nomadic animal husbandry; cash products–wheat, fruit, nuts, karakul pelts, wool, mutton, barley, corn; production is limited due to the shortage of modern machinery, high-grade seed, and fertilizer
Natural Resources: natural gas, crude oil, copper, coal, salt, talc, barites, sulphur, lead, zinc, iron ore, slate, precious and semi-precious stones, especially lapis lazuli, amethysts, rubies

■ **FINANCE/TRADE**

Currency: afghani (Af)
International Reserves Excluding Gold: $227 million (1992)
Gold Reserves: 0.96 million fine troy ounces (1992)
Budget: revenues $962 million (1990); expenditures $3.2 billion, including capital expenditures of $296 million
Defence Expenditures: $286.56 million (1985)
External Debt: $1.8 billion (1989)
Exports: $243 million (1991); commodities: natural gas 55%, fruit and nuts 24%, handwoven carpets, wool, cotton, hides; partners: mostly USSR and Eastern Europe
Imports: $737 million (1991); commodities: food and petroleum products; partners: mostly USSR and Eastern Europe

■ **HEALTH**

Births: 49/1,000 population (1993)
Deaths: 22/1,000 population (1993)
Infant Mortality: 168 deaths/1,000 live births (1993)
Life Expectancy at Birth: 42 years male, 43 years female (1993)
No. of Physicians: 1.6/10,000 population (1992)

■ **EDUCATION**

Govt. Expenditure: 4.0% of govt. expenditure (1987)
Literacy: 29.4% (1992)

■ **COMMUNICATIONS**

Daily newspapers: 14 (1992)
Televisions: 8.1/1,000 inhabitants (1992)
Radios: 104/1,000 inhabitants (1992)
Telephones: 0.21/100 persons (1992)

■ **TRANSPORTATION**

Motor Vehicles: 70,000; 36,000 passenger cars
Roads: 20,867 km; 2,608 km paved

Railway: 9.6 km from Kushka (Turkmenistan) t Towraghondi and 15.0 km from Terme (Uzbekistan) to Kheyrabad
Air Traffic: 212,000 passengers carried (1991)
Airports: 41, of which 36 are usable

Canadian Embassy: c/o Canadian Hig Commission, Diplomatic Sector G-5 Islamabad; mailing address: GPO Box 1042 Islamabad, Pakistan. Tel: (011-92-51) 21-11-01

Albania

Long-Form Name: Republic of Albania
Capital: Tirana
Population: 3,300,000 (1993 est.)

■ **GEOGRAPHY**

Area: 28,750 sq. km
Coastline: 362 km
Climate: mild temperate; cool, cloudy, wet winters; hot, clear, dry summers; interior is coole and wetter, with severe winters
Environment: subject to destructive earthquakes tsunami occur along southwestern coast; defor estation seems to be slowing
Terrain: mostly mountains and hills; small plain along coast
Land Use: 21% arable land; 4% permanen crops; 15% meadows and pastures; 38% fores and woodland, including 30% scrub forest; 22% other; includes 1% irrigated
Location: SC Europe, bordering on Adriatic Sea

■ **PEOPLE**

Nationality: Albanian
Ethnic Groups: 90% Albanian, 8% Greek, 2% others (Vlachs, Gypsies, Serbs and Bulgarians (1989 est.)
Languages: Albanian (Tosk is official dialect also Gheg dialect), Greek
Religions: 70% Muslim, 20% Greek Orthodox. 10% Roman Catholic. From April 1991, freedom of religion replaced official atheism.
Marriages: 8.6 (per 1,000) (1989)
Divorces: 0.82 (per 1,000) (1989)

■ **GOVERNMENT**

Leader(s): Pres. Sali Berisha, Prime Min. Aleksander Meksi
Government Type: in transition to democracy
Administrative Divisions: 26 districts
Independence: Nov. 28, 1912 (from Ottoman Empire); People's Socialist Republic of Albania declared Jan. 11, 1946
National Holiday: Liberation Day, Nov. 29

■ ECONOMY

Overview: the poorest country in Europe, it is a Stalinist-type economy (central planning and state ownership of the means of production). Though largely self-sufficient in food until 1990, the recent break-up of cooperative farms and the general economic decline has forced Albania to rely increasingly on foreign aid
GNP: n.a., GDP $2.5 billion (1992 est.)
Inflation: n.a.
Industries: food processing, textiles and clothing, lumber, oil, cement, chemicals, basic metals, hydroelectricity; most industries produce at only fraction of past levels.
Labour Force: 1,591,000 (1992); about 56% agriculture, 26% industry, 18% service (1989)
Unemployment: 40% (1993 est.)
Agriculture: arable land per capita among lowest in Europe; one-half of work force engaged in farming; produces wide range of temperate-zone crops and livestock; claims self-sufficiency in grain output; over 60% of all arable land is now in private ownership
Natural Resources: crude oil, natural gas, coal, chromium, copper, timber, nickel, petroleum

■ FINANCE/TRADE

Currency: lek (L)
International Reserves Excluding Gold: n.a.
Gold Reserves: n.a.
Budget: revenues $1.1 billion; expenditures $1.4 billion, including capital expenditures $70 million (1991 est.)
Defence Expenditures: $171.2 million (1990)
External Debt: $625 million (1992)
Exports: $45 million (1992 est.); commodities: asphalt, bitumen, petroleum products, metals and metallic ores, electricity, oil, vegetables, fruit, tobacco; partners: Italy, Yugoslavia, Germany, Greece, Czechoslovakia, Poland, Romania, Bulgaria, Hungary
Imports: $120 million (1992 est.); commodities: machinery, machine tools, iron and steel products, textiles, chemicals, pharmaceuticals; partners: Italy, Yugoslavia, Germany, Czechoslovakia, Romania, Poland, Hungary, Bulgaria

■ HEALTH

Births: 25/1,000 population (1993)
Deaths: 6/1,000 population (1993)
Infant Mortality: 28.3 deaths/1,000 live births (1993)
Life Expectancy at Birth: 69 years male, 75 years female (1993)
No. of Physicians: 10.5/10,000 population (1975)

■ EDUCATION

Govt. Expenditure: 9.1% of government expenditure (1990)
Literacy: 72%

■ COMMUNICATIONS

Daily newspapers: 2 (1992)
Televisions: 83.1/1,000 inhabitants (1992)
Radios: 172/1,000 inhabitants (1992)
Telephones: n.a.

■ TRANSPORTATION

Motor Vehicles: n.a.
Roads: 17,509 km; paved n.a.
Railway: 569 km (1992)
Air Traffic: n.a.
Airports: 12, of which 10 are usable; 3 have permanent-surface runways (1993)

Canadian Embassy: c/o Budakeszi ut. 32, 1121 Budapest. Tel: (011-36-1) 1767-312
Representative to Canada: Embassy of the People's Republic of Albania, 320 East 79th St, New York, NY 10021, USA. Tel. (212) 249-2059.

Algeria

Long-Form Name: Democratic and Popular Republic of Algeria
Capital: Algiers
Population: 27,300,000 (1993 est.)

■ GEOGRAPHY

Area: 2,381,740 sq. km
Coastline: 998 km
Climate: arid to semi-arid; mild, wet winters with hot, dry summers along coast; drier with cold winters and hot summers on high plateau; sirocco is a hot, dust/sand-laden wind especially common in summer
Environment: mountainous areas subject to severe earthquakes; desertification
Terrain: mostly high plateau and desert; some mountains; narrow, discontinuous coastal plain
Land Use: 3% arable land; negligible permanent crops; 13% meadows and pastures; 2% forest and woodland; 82% other; cattle, sheep and goat grazing on grassland and shrub regions; includes negligible irrigated
Location: N Africa, bordering on Mediterranean Sea

■ PEOPLE

Nationality: Algerian
Ethnic Groups: 99% Arab-Berber, less than 1% European

Languages: Arabic (official), French, Berber dialects
Religions: 99% Sunni Moslem (state religion); 1% Christian and Jewish
Marriages: n.a.
Divorces: n.a.

■ GOVERNMENT

Leader(s): Pres. Lamine Zeroual, Prem. Mokdad Sifi
Government Type: republic
Administrative Divisions: 48 "wilayat" (provinces) (1993)
Independence: July 5, 1962 (from France)
National Holiday: Anniversary of the Revolution, Nov. 1

■ ECONOMY

Overview: the economy is largely based on the exploitation of oil and natural gas products. Dropping oil and gas prices have contributed to bringing Algeria to its most serious social and economic crisis since independence. Recently, reforms have been implemented to combat social and economic problems
GNP: n.a., GDP $42 billion (1992 est.)
Inflation: 31.8% (1992)
Industries: petroleum, light industries, natural gas, mining, electrical, petrochemical, food processing
Labour Force: 5,819,000 (1992); 11% industry, 14% agriculture, 75% services (1989)
Unemployment: 35% (1992 est.)
Agriculture: accounts for 10.8% of GDP and employs 22% of labour force; products include wheat, barley, grapes, oats, olives, fruit, livestock; must import more than 1/3 of its food
Natural Resources: crude oil, natural gas, iron ore, phosphates, uranium, lead, zinc, mercury

■ FINANCE/TRADE

Currency: dinar (DA)
International Reserves Excluding Gold: $1,526 million (as of Jan. 1994)
Gold Reserves: 5.58 million fine troy ounces (as of Jan. 1994)
Budget: revenues $14.4 billion; expenditures $14.6 billion, including capital expenditures of $3.5 billion (1992 est.)
Defence Expenditures: 5% of total expenditures (1988)
External Debt: $26.349 billion (1992)
Exports: $11.137 billion (1992); commodities: petroleum and natural gas 98%; partners: Netherlands, Czechoslovakia, Romania, Italy, France, US
Imports: $8.648 billion (1992); commodities:

capital goods 35%, consumer goods 36%, food 20%; partners: France 25%, Italy 8%, Germany 8%, US 6–7%

■ HEALTH

Births: 34/1,000 population (1993)
Deaths: 7/1,000 population (1993)
Infant Mortality: 61 deaths/1,000 live births (1993)
Life Expectancy at Birth: 65 years male, 67 years female (1993)
No. of Physicians: 4.3/10,000 population (1992)

■ EDUCATION

Govt. Expenditure: 27.0% of govt. expenditure (1989)
Literacy: 57.4% (1992)

■ COMMUNICATIONS

Daily newspapers: 12 (1992)
Televisions: 72.8/1,000 inhabitants (1992)
Radios: 232/1,000 inhabitants (1992)
Telephones: 3.8/100 inhabitants (1992)

■ TRANSPORTATION

Motor Vehicles: 1,250,000; 750,000 passenger cars (1990)
Roads: 90,031 km; 38,108 km paved (1990)
Railway: 4,060 km (1993)
Air Traffic: 3,385,000 passengers carried (1991)
Airports: 141 airfields, of which 124 are usable; 53 have permanent-surface runways (1993)

Canadian Embassy: 27 bis, rue Ali Massoudi, Hydra, Algiers; mailing address: P.O. Box 225, Gare Alger, Algiers, Algeria. Tel: (011-213-2) 60-66-11
Representative to Canada: Embassy of the People's Democratic Republic of Algeria, 435 Daly Ave, Ottawa ON K1N 6H3. Tel: (613) 789-8505.

American Samoa

Dependent Territory of the United States

Long-Form Name: Territory of American Samoa
Capital: Pago Pago (on Tutuila Island)
Population: 53,139 (1993 est.); in 1990, some 85,000 Samoans lived in the US

■ GEOGRAPHY

Area: 199 sq. km
Climate: tropical maritime, plentiful rainfall, temperatures consistent throughout the year
Land Use: 10% arable land, 5% permanent crops, 0% meadows and pastures, 75% forest

and woodland, 10% other
Location: S Pacific Ocean, NW of Australia and New Zealand

■ PEOPLE

Nationality: American Samoan; nationals of the United States
Ethnic Groups: Samoan (Polynesian) 89%, Caucasian 2%, Tongan 4%, other 5%
Languages: Samoan (a Polynesian dialect), English

■ GOVERNMENT

Leader(s): Gov. A.P. Lutali elected Nov. 3, 1992; next elections scheduled for Nov. 1996
Government Type: US dependency with democratically elected governor: unorganized unincorporated territory
National Holiday: Territorial Flag Day, April 17, 1900

■ ECONOMY

Overview: agriculture: taro, bread-fruit, yams, bananas, coconuts; livestock includes pigs, goats, poultry; industries: fish (tuna) canning; economic activity is closely tied to US; tourism is slowly developing

■ FINANCE/TRADE

Currency: American dollar (US$)

Andorra

Long-Form Name: Principality of Andorra
Capital: Andorra-la-Vella
Population: 61,962 (1993 est.)

■ GEOGRAPHY

Area: 450 sq. km
Coastline: none: landlocked
Climate: temperate; snowy, cold winters and warm, dry summers
Environment: deforestation, overgrazing
Terrain: rugged mountains dissected by narrow valleys
Land Use: 2% arable land; 0% permanent crops; 56% meadows and pastures; 22% forest and woodland; 20% other
Location: SW Europe

■ PEOPLE

Nationality: Andorran
Ethnic Groups: Catalan stock; 61% Spanish, 30% Andorran, 6% French, 3% other
Languages: Catalan (official); many also speak some French and Spanish
Religions: virtually all Roman Catholic

Marriages: 3.0 (per 1,000) (1990)

■ GOVERNMENT

Leader(s): co-Chiefs of State: François Mitterand (France) and Felipe González Márquez (Spain); Premier Oscar Ribas Reig
Government Type: unique co-principality under formal sovereignty of president of France and Spanish bishop of Seo de Urgel, who are represented locally by officials called verguers
Administrative Divisions: 7 parishes
Independence: 1278 (from France and Spain)
National Holiday: Mare de Deu de Meritxell, Sept. 8

■ ECONOMY

Overview: tourism is the backbone of the economy, due to its duty-free status and year-round resorts. Most food is imported due to a scarcity of arable land
GNP: n.a., GDP $760 million (1992 est.), per capita $14,000
Industries: tourism (particularly skiing), sheep, timber, tobacco, banking
Unemployment: 0% (1993)
Agriculture: sheep raising, small quantities of tobacco, rye, wheat, barley, buckwheat, maize, oats and some vegetables, especially potatoes
Natural Resources: hydroelectricity, mineral water, timber, iron ore, lead

■ FINANCE/TRADE

Currency: French Franc, Spanish peseta (F Ptas)
Budget: revenues $119.4 million, expenditures $190 million, capital expenditures n.a. (1990)
Exports: $2.3 million (1989); commodities: electricity; partners: France and Spain
Imports: $888.7 million (1989); commodities: n.a.; partners: France and Spain

■ HEALTH

Births: 13.78/1,000 population (1993 est.)
Deaths: 6.99/1,000 population (1993 est.)
Infant Mortality: 8.1 deaths/1,000 live births (1993 est.)
Life Expectancy at Birth: 75 years male, 81 years female (1993 est.)
No. of Physicians: 112/10,000 population (1988)

■ EDUCATION

Govt. Expenditure: 15.8% of govt. expenditure (1986)
Literacy: 100%

■ COMMUNICATIONS

Daily newspapers: n.a.; 4 non-daily (1988)
Televisions: 148.9/1,000 inhabitants (1989)

Radios: 219/1,000 inhabitants (1989)

■ TRANSPORTATION

Motor Vehicles: 38,691; 34,168 passenger cars (1990)
Roads: 96 km (1993)

Canadian Embassy: c/o 35, av Montaigne, 75008 Paris, France. Tel: (011-33-1) 44-43-29-00.

Angola

Long-Form Name: Republic of Angola
Capital: Luanda
Population: 9,500,000 (1993 est.)

■ GEOGRAPHY

Area: 1,246,700 sq. km
Coastline: 1,600 km
Climate: semi-arid in south and along coast to Luanda; north has cool, dry season (May to October) and hot, rainy season (Nov. to Apr.)
Environment: locally heavy rainfall causes periodic flooding on plateau; desertification, especially on coastal plain
Terrain: narrow coastal plain rises abruptly to vast interior plain
Land Use: 2% arable land; negligible permanent crops; 23% meadows and pastures; 43% forest and woodland; 32% other
Location: SW Africa

■ PEOPLE

Nationality: Angolan
Ethnic Groups: 37% Ovimbundu, 25% Kimbundu, 13% Bakongo, 2% Mestiço, 1% European, 22% other
Languages: Portuguese (official); Bantu dialects spoken include Ovimbundu, Kimbundu, Bakongo and Chokwe
Religions: 38% Roman Catholic, 15% Protestant, 47% Animist
Marriages: n.a.
Divorces: n.a.

■ GOVERNMENT

Leader(s): Pres. José Eduardo dos Santos; Premier Marcolino José Carlos Moco
Government Type: transitional government, nominally a democracy with strong presidential system
Administrative Divisions: 18 provinces
Independence: Nov. 11, 1975 (from Portugal)
National Holiday: Independence Day, Nov. 11

■ ECONOMY

Overview: subsistence agriculture is the main livelihood of the population, but oil production is the most lucrative activity. Recent internal war has weakened the economy, and food must be imported
GNP: $5.1 billion, per capita $950; real growth rate 1.7% (1991 est.)
Inflation: n.a.
Industries: petroleum, mining (phosphate rock, uranium, gold, iron ore, bauxite, feldspar, diamonds), fish processing, brewing, tobacco, sugar, textiles, cement, food processing, building construction
Labour Force: 4,081,000 economically active (1992); 74% agriculture, 10% industry, 16% services (1989)
Unemployment: 18.9% (1986)
Agriculture: cash crops–coffee, sisal, corn, cotton, sugar, manioc, tobacco; food crops–cassava, corn, vegetables, plantains, bananas and other local foodstuffs
Natural Resources: petroleum, diamonds, iron ore, phosphates, copper, feldspar, gold, bauxite, uranium

■ FINANCE/TRADE

Currency: kwanza (Kz)
International Reserves Excluding Gold: n.a.
Gold Reserves: n.a.
Budget: revenues $2.1 billion; expenditures $3.6 billion, including capital expenditures of $963 million (1991 est.)
Defence Expenditures: $2.69 billion (1989)
External Debt: $9.641 billion (1992)
Exports: $3.410 billion (1991); commodities: oil, coffee, diamonds, sisal, fish and fish products, timber, cotton; partners: US, USSR, Cuba, Portugal, Brazil
Imports: $1.14 billion (1990); commodities: capital equipment (machinery and electrical equipment), food, vehicles and spare parts, textiles and clothing, medicines, substantial military deliveries; partners: US, USSR, Cuba, Portugal, Brazil

■ HEALTH

Births: 51/1,000 population (1993)
Deaths: 20/1,000 population (1993)
Infant Mortality: 131 deaths/1,000 live births (1993)
Life Expectancy at Birth: 44 years male, 47 years female (1993)
No. of Physicians: 0.6/10,000 population (1992)

■ EDUCATION

Govt. Expenditure: 10.7% of govt. expenditure (1990)
Literacy: 42% (1993)

■ COMMUNICATIONS

Daily newspapers: 1 (1992)
Televisions: 5.6/1,000 inhabitants (1992)
Radios: 53/1,000 inhabitants (1992)
Telephones: 0.76/100 inhabitants (1992)

■ TRANSPORTATION

Motor Vehicles: 175,000; 130,000 passenger cars (1990)
Roads: 73,828 km; 8,727 km paved
Railway: 3,189 km
Air Traffic: 456,000 passengers carried (1991)
Airports: 302 airfields, of which 173 are usable; 32 have permanent-surface runways

Canadian Embassy: c/o The Canadian High Commission, 45 Baines Ave, Harare; mailing address: P.O. Box 1430, Harare, Zimbabwe. Tel. (011-263-4) 73-38-81.

Anguilla

Dependent Territory of the United Kingdom

Long-Form Name: Territory of Anguilla
Capital: The Valley
Population: 7,006 (1993 est.)

■ GEOGRAPHY

Area: 91 sq. km
Climate: dry and sunny, tropical with moderating northeast trade winds
Land Use: mostly rock, with sparse scrub, few trees, some commercial salt ponds; low rainfall limits agricultural potential
Location: West Indies

■ PEOPLE

Nationality: Anguillan
Ethnic Groups: of English ancestry, black/mixed-black African
Languages: English (official)

■ GOVERNMENT

Leader(s): Gov. Alan W. Share, Chief Min. Emile Gumbs
Government Type: separate dependency of Great Britain
National Holiday: Anguilla Day, May 30

■ ECONOMY

Overview: agriculture: pigeon peas, corn, sweet potatoes; fishing; livestock includes sheep, goats, cattle, poultry; tourism; main trading partner: United Kingdom

■ FINANCE/TRADE

Currency: Eastern Caribbean dollar (EC$)

Antigua and Barbuda

Long-Form Name: Antigua and Barbuda
Capital: Saint John's
Population: 100,000 (1993 est.)

■ GEOGRAPHY

Area: 440 sq. km; includes Redonda (1.3 sq km)
Coastline: 153 km
Climate: tropical marine; little seasonal temperature variation
Environment: subject to hurricanes and tropical storms (July to Oct.); insufficient freshwater resources; occasional long periods of drought; deeply indented coastline provides many natural harbours
Terrain: mostly low-lying limestone and coral islands with some higher volcanic areas
Land Use: 18% arable land; 0% permanent crops; 7% meadows and pastures; 16% forest and woodland; 59% other
Location: Caribbean islands

■ PEOPLE

Nationality: Antiguan, Barbudan
Ethnic Groups: almost entirely of black African origin; some British, Portuguese, Lebanese and Syrian origin
Languages: English (official), local dialects
Religions: Anglican (predominant), other Protestant sects, some Roman Catholic
Marriages: 4.1 (per 1,000) (1987)
Divorces: n.a.

■ GOVERNMENT

Leader(s): Prime Min. Lester Bird, Gov. Gen. James B. Carlisle
Government Type: parliamentary democracy
Administrative Divisions: 6 parishes, 2 dependencies
Independence: Nov. 1, 1981 (from UK)
National Holiday: Independence Day, Nov. 1

■ ECONOMY

Overview: tourism is the backbone of this service-oriented economy, although the drop in tourism caused by the Persian Gulf war and the US recession has had adverse effects. A labour shortage is plaguing some sectors of the economy
GNP: $355 million, per capita $4,770; real growth rate 4.4% (1991)
Inflation: 7.1% (1988 est.)

Industries: tourism, construction, light manufacturing (clothing, alcohol, household appliances)
Labour Force: n.a.
Unemployment: 5.0% (1988 est.)
Agriculture: expanding output of cotton, fruit, vegetables and livestock; other crops—bananas, coconuts, cucumbers, mangoes; not self-sufficient in food
Natural Resources: negligible; pleasant climate and beautiful beaches foster tourism

■ FINANCE/TRADE

Currency: East Caribbean dollar ($EC)
International Reserves Excluding Gold: $37 million (as of Oct. 1993)
Gold Reserves: n.a.
Budget: revenues $105 million; expenditures $161 million, including capital expenditures of $56 million (1992)
Defence Expenditures: n.a.
External Debt: $250 million (1990 est.)
Exports: $32.0 million (1991); commodities: petroleum products 46%, manufactures 23%, food and live animals 4%, machinery and transport equipment 17%; partners: Trinidad and Tobago 2%, Barbados 15%, US 0.3%, others 26%
Imports: $317.5 million (1991); commodities: food and live animals, machinery and transport equipment, manufactures, chemicals, oil; partners: US 27%, UK 16%, OECS 3%, Canada 4%, other 50%

■ HEALTH

Births: 18/1,000 population (1993)
Deaths: 6/1,000 population (1993)
Infant Mortality: 24.4 deaths/1,000 live births (1993)
Life Expectancy at Birth: 70 years male, 74 years female (1993)
No. of Physicians: n.a.

■ EDUCATION

Govt. Expenditure: 4.0% of GNP (1988)
Literacy: 89% (1993)

■ COMMUNICATIONS

Daily newspapers: 1 (1992)
Televisions: 289.5/1,000 inhabitants (1992)
Radios: 276/1,000 inhabitants (1992)
Telephones: 14.4/100 inhabitants (1992)

■ TRANSPORTATION

Motor Vehicles: 17,000; 13,500 passenger cars (1990)
Roads: 240 km (1993)
Railway: 64 km

Air Traffic: 755,000 passengers carried (1991)
Airports: 3

Canadian Embassy: c/o The Canadian High Commission, Bishop's Court Hill, St. Michael; mailing address: P.O. Box 404, Bridgetown, Barbados
Representative to Canada: High Commission for Antigua and Barbuda, 112 Kent St, Ste 205, Place de Ville, Tower B, Ottawa ON K1P 5P2. Tel: (613) 234-9143, Fax: (613) 232-0539.

Argentina

Long-Form Name: Argentine Republic
Capital: Buenos Aires
Population: 33,500,000 (1993 est.)

■ GEOGRAPHY

Area: 2,766,890 sq. km
Coastline: 4,989 km
Climate: mostly temperate; arid in southeast; sub-antarctic in southwest
Environment: Tucamán and Mendoza areas in Andes subject to earthquakes; pamperos are violent windstorms that can strike the Pampas and northeast; irrigated soil degradation; desertification; air and water pollution in Buenos Aires
Terrain: rich plains of the Pampas in northern half, flat to rolling plateau of Patagonia in south, rugged Andes along western border
Land Use: 9% arable land; 4% permanent crops; 52% meadows and pastures; 22% forest and woodland; 13% other; includes 1% irrigated
Location: SE South America

■ PEOPLE

Nationality: Argentine or Argentinian
Ethnic Groups: 85% white, 15% mestizo, Indian, or other nonwhite groups
Languages: Spanish (official), English, Italian, German, French
Religions: 90% nominally Roman Catholic (less than 20% practising), 2% Protestant, 2% Jewish, 6% other
Marriages: 5.8 (per 1,000) (1990)
Divorces: n.a.

■ GOVERNMENT

Leader(s): Pres. Carlos Saùl Menem, V. Pres. vacant
Government Type: republic
Administrative Divisions: 22 provinces, 1 national territory and 1 district
Independence: Independence: July 9, 1816 (from Spain)
National Holiday: Revolution Day, May 25

■ ECONOMY

Overview: though the country possesses abundant natural resources and a diversified industrial base, high inflation and burgeoning debt are weakening the economy
GNP: n.a., GDP $112 billion, per capita $3,400; real growth rate 7% (1992 est.)
Inflation: 24.9% (1992)
Industries: food processing (especially meat packing), motor vehicles, consumer durables, textiles, chemicals and petrochemicals, printing, metallurgy, steel
Labour Force: 12,305,346 (1992); 13% agriculture, 34% industry, 53% services (1989)
Unemployment: 6.9% (1992)
Agriculture: accounts for 8% of GNP (including fishing); produces abundant food for both domestic consumption and exports; among world's top five exporters of grain and beef; principal crops—wheat, corn, sorghum, soybeans, sugar beets
Natural Resources: fertile plains of the Pampas, lead, zinc, tin, copper, iron ore, manganese, crude oil, uranium

■ FINANCE/TRADE

Currency: peso
International Reserves Excluding Gold: $11,960 million (as of Nov. 1993)
Gold Reserves: 4.37 million fine troy ounces (as of Nov. 1993)
Budget: revenues $33.1 billion; expenditures $35.8 billion, including capital expenditures of $3.5 billion (1992)
Defence Expenditures: $770.98 million (1990)
External Debt: $67.569 billion (1992)
Exports: $11.972 billion (1992); commodities: meat, wheat, corn, oil seed, hides, wool; partners: US 14%, USSR, Italy, Brazil, Japan, Netherlands
Imports: $8.090 billion (1992); commodities: machinery and equipment, metals, chemicals, fuels and lubricants, agricultural products; partners: US 25%, Brazil, Germany, Bolivia, Japan, Italy, Netherlands

■ HEALTH

Births: 21/1,000 population (1993)
Deaths: 8/1,000 population (1993)
Infant Mortality: 25.6 deaths/1,000 live births (1993)
Life Expectancy at Birth: 67 years male, 74 years female (1993)
No. of Physicians: 26.7/10,000 population (1992)

■ EDUCATION

Govt. Expenditure: 10.9% of govt. expenditure (1990)
Literacy: 95% (1993)

■ COMMUNICATIONS

Daily newspapers: 194 (1992)
Televisions: 219.3/1,000 inhabitants (1992)
Radios: 673/1,000 inhabitants (1992)
Telephones: 12.13/100 inhabitants (1992)

■ TRANSPORTATION

Motor Vehicles: 5,784,500; 4,283,700 passenger cars (1990)
Roads: 208,350 km total; 47,550 km paved (1993)
Railway: 34,172 km (1993)
Air Traffic: 4,532,000 passengers carried (1991)
Airports: 1,700 airfields, of which 1,451 are usable; 137 have permanent-surface runways (1993)

Canadian Embassy: 2828 Tagle, 1425, Buenos Aires; mailing address: Casilla de Correo 1598, Buenos Aires, Argentina. Tel: (011-54-1) 805-3032
Representative to Canada: Embassy of the Argentine Republic, Royal Bank Centre, 90 Sparks St, Ste 620, Ottawa ON K1P 5B4. Tel: (613) 236-2351, -4. Fax: (613) 235-2659.

Armenia

Long-Form Name: Republic of Armenia
Capital: Yerevan
Population: 3,600,000 (1993 est.)

■ GEOGRAPHY

Area: 29,800 sq. km
Coastline: none: landlocked
Climate: severe winters; hot summers; dry year-round
Environment: prone to earthquakes; little land suitable for cultivation; air and water pollution; deforestation
Terrain: rugged highlands; 70% is mountains; little forest land; fast-flowing rivers; Aras River valley has good soil
Land Use: 29% arable, negligible permanent crops, 15% meadows and pasture, 56% other; most farmland lies in the Aras Valley; animal herding predominant in the highlands
Location: SE Europe

■ PEOPLE

Nationality: Armenian
Ethnic Groups: 93.3% Armenians, 1.6% Russians, 2.6% Azerbaijanis, 1.7% Kurds
Languages: Armenian (official), Azerbaijan,

Russian
Religions: predominantly Eastern Orthodox
Marriages: n.a.
Divorces: n.a.

■ GOVERNMENT

Leader(s): Pres. Levon Ter-Petrosyan, V. Pres. Gagik Arutyunyan, Prime Min. Hrant Bagratian
Government Type: republic
Administrative Divisions: none; direct republic jurisdiction is universal
Independence: Sept. 23, 1991 (from Soviet Union)
National Holiday: n.a.

■ ECONOMY

Overview: predominantly manufacturing and agriculture; production has dropped sharply since 1991
GNP: $7.2 billion (1991), n.a. for 1992; real growth -34% (1992)
Inflation: 20% per month (1993)
Industries: electrical equipment and machinery, chemicals, machine tools, vehicles, textiles
Labour Force: 1.63 million; 42% industry and construction, 18% agriculture and forestry, 40% other (1990)
Unemployment: 2%, but large numbers of under-employed (1993)
Agriculture: accounts for approximately 20% of GDP; only 29% of land is arable; fruit, grapes, vegetables, tobacco, grains, beetroot, potatoes, geranium oil, cattle and sheep herding
Natural Resources: marble, precious metals, iron, tufa, small deposits of gold, copper, molybdenum, zinc, alumina

■ FINANCE/TRADE

Currency: rouble (rbl.)
International Reserves Excluding Gold: n.a.
Gold Reserves: n.a.
Budget: 1989 revenues, 2,460 million roubles
Defence Expenditures: $650 million (1991 est.)
External Debt: $10 million (1992)
Exports: $30 million to outside the successor states of the former USSR (1992); commodities include cotton, fruit, olives, pomegranates, machine tools, instruments, shoes
Imports: $300 million from outside the successor states of the former USSR (1992); commodities include machinery, energy, consumer goods (1991)

■ HEALTH

Births: 23/1,000 population (1993)
Deaths: 7/1,000 population (1993)
Infant Mortality: 22 deaths/1,000 live births

(1993)
Life Expectancy at Birth: 68 years male, 75 years female (1993)
No. of Physicians: n.a.

■ EDUCATION

Govt. Expenditure: n.a.
Literacy: 100% (1993)

■ COMMUNICATIONS

Daily newspapers: 85 papers of all circulation types (1989)
Televisions: n.a.
Radios: n.a.
Telephones: 260,000 total (1993), approximately 8 per 10 population

■ TRANSPORTATION

Motor Vehicles: n.a.
Roads: 11,300 km; 10,500 km hard-surfaced (1990)
Railway: 840 km (does not include industrial lines) (1990)
Air Traffic: n.a.
Airports: 12, of which 10 are usable and 6 have permanent-surface runways (1993)

Canadian Embassy: c/o Starokonyushenny Per 23, Moscow 121002, Russian Federation. Tel: (011-7-095) 241-1111. Fax: (011-7-95) 241-4400
Representative to Canada: c/o Embassy of the Russian Federation, 285 Charlotte St, Ottawa ON K1N 8L5. Tel: (613) 235-4341. Fax: (613) 236-6342.

Aruba

Dependent Territory of the Netherlands

Long-Form Name: Aruba
Capital: Oranjestad
Population: 65,117 (1993 est.)

■ GEOGRAPHY

Area: 193 sq. km
Climate: tropical marine; little seasonal temperature variation
Land Use: 0% arable land; 0% permanent crops; 0% meadows and pastures; 0% forest and woodland; 100% other
Location: off N coast of South America

■ PEOPLE

Nationality: Aruban
Ethnic Groups: 80% mixed European/Caribbean Indian

Languages: Dutch (official), Papiamento (a Spanish, Portuguese, Dutch, English dialect), English (widely spoken), Spanish

■ **GOVERNMENT**

Leader(s): Prime Min. Nelson Oduber
Government Type: part of the Dutch realm; autonomy in internal affairs obtained in 1986
National Holiday: Flag Day, Mar. 18

■ **ECONOMY**

Overview: tourism is the mainstay; banking and oil refinery are also important

■ **FINANCE/TRADE**

Currency: Aruban florin (Af)

Australia

Long-Form Name: Commonwealth of Australia
Capital: Canberra
Population: 17,800,000 (1993 est.)

■ **GEOGRAPHY**

Area: 7,686,850 sq. km; includes Macquarie Island
Coastline: 25,760 km
Climate: generally arid to semi-arid; temperate in south and east; tropical in north
Environment: subject to severe droughts and floods; cyclones along coast; limited freshwater availability; irrigated soil degradation; regular, tropical, invigorating, sea breeze known as "the Doctor" occurs along west coast in summer; desertification
Terrain: mostly low plateau with deserts; fertile plain in southeast
Land Use: 6% arable land; negligible permanent crops; 58% meadows and pastures; 14% forest and woodland; 22% other; includes negligible irrigated
Location: divides Indian and Pacific Oceans

■ **PEOPLE**

Nationality: Australian
Ethnic Groups: 95% Caucasian, 4% Asian, 1% Aboriginal and other
Languages: English, native languages
Religions: 26% Anglican, 26% Roman Catholic, 24% other Christian; most of the rest do not profess a religion
Marriages: 6.8 (per 1,000) (1990)
Divorces: 2.49 (per 1,000) (1990)

■ **GOVERNMENT**

Leader(s): Prime Min. Paul Keating, Gov. Gen. William Hayden

Government Type: federal parliamentary state
Administrative Divisions: 6 states, 2 territories; dependent areas inc.: Ashmore and Cartier Islands (uninhabited), Australian Antarctic Territory (uninhabited except for scientific staff), Cocos (Keeling) Islands, Coral Sea Islands Territory (uninhabited), Christmas Island (uninhabited), Heard and McDonald Islands (uninhabited), Norfolk Island
Independence: Jan. 1, 1901 (federation of UK colonies)
National Holiday: Australia Day, Jan. 26

■ **ECONOMY**

Overview: successful Western-style capitalist economy and a major exporter of natural resources and agricultural products. Is looking to increase exports of manufactured goods
GNP: n.a., GDP $293.5 billion, per capita $16,700; real growth rate 2.5% (1992)
Inflation: 1.0% (1992)
Industries: mining, industrial and transportation equipment, food processing, chemicals, steel, motor vehicles
Labour Force: 7,963,000 (1992); 78.3% services, 16.4% industry, 5.3% agriculture (1989)
Unemployment: 11.3% (1992)
Agriculture: accounts for 5% of GNP and 37% of export revenues; world's largest exporter of beef and wool, second-largest for mutton, and among top wheat exporters; major crops—wheat, barley, sugar cane, fruit; livestock—cattle, sheep, poultry
Natural Resources: bauxite, coal, iron ore, copper, tin, silver, uranium, nickel, tungsten, mineral sands, lead, zinc, diamonds, natural gas, crude oil

■ **FINANCE/TRADE**

Currency: dollar ($A)
International Reserves Excluding Gold: $11,154 million (Jan. 1994)
Gold Reserves: 7.90 million fine troy ounces (Jan. 1994)
Budget: revenues $68.5 billion; expenditures $78.0 billion, including capital expenditures (1993)
Defence Expenditures: 8.56% of total govt. expenditure (1991)
External Debt: $130.4 billion (1991)
Exports: $41.272 billion (1993 est.); commodities: wheat, barley, beef, lamb, dairy products, wool, coal, iron ore; partners: Japan 26%, US 11%, New Zealand 6%, S Korea 4%, Singapore 4%, USSR 3%
Imports: $42.338 billion (1993 est.); commodities: manufactured raw materials, capital equip-

ment, consumer goods; partners: US 22%, Japan 22%, UK 7%, Germany 6%, New Zealand 4%

■ HEALTH

Births: 15/1,000 population (1993)
Deaths: 7/1,000 population (1993)
Infant Mortality: 6.9 deaths/1,000 live births (1993)
Life Expectancy at Birth: 74 years male, 80 years female (1993)
No. of Physicians: 22.9/10,000 population (1992)

■ EDUCATION

Govt. Expenditure: 7.03% of govt. expenditure (1991)
Literacy: 100% (1993)

■ COMMUNICATIONS

Daily newspapers: 68 (1992)
Televisions: 483.9/1,000 inhabitants (1992)
Radios: 1,262/1,000 inhabitants (1992)
Telephones: 51.72/100 inhabitants (1992)

■ TRANSPORTATION

Motor Vehicles: 9,776,600; 7,672,300 passenger cars (1990)
Roads: 837,872 km; 430,464 km paved (1993)
Railway: 40,478 km
Air Traffic: 21,244,000 passengers carried (1991)
Airports: 481, of which 439 are usable and 243 have permanent-surface runways

Canadian Embassy: The Canadian High Commission, Commonwealth Ave, Canberra A.C.T. 2600, Australia. Tel: (011-61-6) 273-3844
Representative to Canada: Australian High Commission, 50 O'Connor St, Ste 710, Ottawa ON K1P 6L2. Tel: (613) 236-0841.

Austria

Long-Form Name: Republic of Austria
Capital: Vienna
Population: 7,900,000 (1993 est.)

■ GEOGRAPHY

Area: 83,850 sq. km
Coastline: none: landlocked
Climate: temperate; continental, cloudy; cold winter with frequent rain in lowlands and snow in mountains; cool summers with occasional showers
Environment: because of steep slopes, poor soils and cold temperatures, population is concentrated on eastern lowlands
Terrain: mostly mountains with Alps in west and south; flat, with gentle slopes along eastern and northern margins
Land Use: 17% arable land; 1% permanent crops; 24% meadows and pastures; 39% forest and woodland; 19% other; includes negligible irrigated
Location: SC Europe

■ PEOPLE

Nationality: Austrian
Ethnic Groups: 99% German, 0.3 % Croatian, 0.2% Slovene, 0.1% others
Languages: German (official); Slovene, Hungarian, and a Croatian dialect also spoken
Religions: 85% Roman Catholic, 6% Protestant, 9% other
Marriages: 5.6 (per 1,000) (1991)
Divorces: 2.11 (per 1,000) (1990)

■ GOVERNMENT

Leader(s): Chanc. Franz Vranitzky, Pres. Thomas Klestil
Government Type: federal republic
Administrative Divisions: 9 states
Independence: Nov. 12, 1918 (from Austro-Hungarian Empire)
National Holiday: National Day, Oct. 26

■ ECONOMY

Overview: prosperous, Western capitalist economy, as well as substantial welfare benefits and extensive nationalized industry
GNP: n.a., GDP $141.3 billion, per capita $18,000; real growth rate 1.8% (1992)
Inflation: 4.0% (1992)
Industries: foods, iron and steel, machines, textiles, chemicals, electrical, paper and pulp, tourism, mining
Labour Force: 3,570,000 (1992); 64.7% services, 27.5% industry, 7.8% agriculture; an estimated 200,000 Austrians are employed in other European countries; foreign labourers in Austria number 177,840, about 6% of labour force (1989)
Unemployment: 5.8% (1992)
Agriculture: accounts for 3.2% of GDP (including forestry); principal crops and animals—grains, fruit, potatoes, sugar beets, sawn wood, cattle, pigs, poultry; 80–90% self-sufficient in food
Natural Resources: iron ore, crude oil, timber, magnesite, aluminum, lead, coal, lignite, copper, hydroelectricity

■ FINANCE/TRADE

Currency: schilling (S)
International Reserves Excluding Gold: $15,920

million (Jan. 1994)
Gold Reserves: 18.62 million fine troy ounces (Jan. 1994)
Budget: revenues $47.8 billion; expenditures $53 billion, including capital expenditures (1992 est.)
Defence Expenditures: 2.4% of total govt. expenditure (1991)
External Debt: $11.8 billion (1990)
Exports: $44.430 billion (1992); commodities: machinery and equipment, iron and steel, lumber, textiles, paper products, chemicals; partners: Germany 35%, Italy 10%, Eastern Europe 9%, Switzerland 7%, US 4%, OPEC 3%
Imports: $54.116 billion (1992); commodities: petroleum, foodstuffs, machinery and equipment, vehicles, chemicals, textiles and clothing, pharmaceuticals; partners: Germany 44%, Italy 9%, Eastern Europe 6%, Switzerland 5%, US 4%, USSR 2%

■ **HEALTH**

Births: 12/1,000 population (1993)
Deaths: 10/1,000 population (1993)
Infant Mortality: 7.5 deaths/1,000 live births (1993)
Life Expectancy at Birth: 73 years male, 79 years female (1993)
No. of Physicians: 25.8/10,000 population (1992)

■ **EDUCATION**

Govt. Expenditure: 9.45% of govt. expenditure (1991)
Literacy: 99% (1993)

■ **COMMUNICATIONS**

Daily newspapers: 34 (1992)
Televisions: 475.3/1,000 inhabitants (1992)
Radios: 622/1,000 inhabitants (1992)
Telephones: 50.0/100 inhabitants (1992)

■ **TRANSPORTATION**

Motor Vehicles: 3,691,749; 2,991,284 passenger cars (1990)
Roads: 108,586 km paved
Railway: 5,749 km (1993)
Air Traffic: 2,606,000 passengers carried (1991)
Airports: 55 airfields, all of which are usable, and 20 have permanent-surface runways (1993)

Canadian Embassy: Schubertring 10, A-1010 Vienna, Austria. Tel: (011-43-222) 533-3691
Representative to Canada: Embassy of the Republic of Austria, 445 Wilbrod St, Ottawa

ON K1N 6M7. Tel: (613) 789-1444. Fax: (613) 789-3431.

Azerbaijan

Long-Form Name: Azerbaijani Republic
Capital: Baku
Population: 7,200,000 (1993 est.)

■ **GEOGRAPHY**

Area: 86,600 sq. km
Coastline: none; landlocked. Inland coastline (Caspian Sea) approximately 800 km.
Climate: Alpine to subtropical; dry, semi-arid steppe subject to drought
Environment: severe air and water pollution render Aspheron Peninsula, including Baku and Sumgait, the "most ecologically devastated area in the world," according to local scientists
Terrain: fertile central lowlands; large flat Kura-Aras Lowland; Caucasus Mountains in north; western uplands
Land Use: 18% arable, negligible permanent crops and forests, 25% meadows and pastures, 57% other; grazing land in the Caucasus mountains; farming in lowlands
Location: SE Europe, bordering on Caspian Sea

■ **PEOPLE**

Nationality: Azerbaijani
Ethnic Groups: 82.7% Azerbaijani, 5.6% Russians, 5.6% Armenians, 3.2% Daghestanis, 2.9% other
Languages: Azerbaijani (official), Armenian, Russian
Religions: Muslim 87%, Russian Orthodox 5.6%, Armenian Orthodox 5.6%, other 1.8%
Marriages: 10.1 (per 1,000) (1989)
Divorces: 1.61 (per 1,000) (1989)

■ **GOVERNMENT**

Leader(s): Pres. Haydar Aliyev, Premier Surat Huseynov
Government Type: republic
Administrative Divisions: 1 autonomous republic
Independence: Aug. 30, 1991 (from Soviet Union)
National Holiday: n.a.

■ **ECONOMY**

Overview: cotton and refining industries are most prominent; Azerbaijan is least industrially developed of the Transcaucasian States
GNP: $12.065 billion, per capita $1,670 (1991); real growth rate -25% (1992)
Inflation: n.a.
Industries: oil extraction and refining, steel,

cement, textiles, chemicals, petrochemicals
Labour Force: 2.789 million; 32% agriculture and forestry, 26% industry and construction, 42% other (1990)
Unemployment: 0.2%, but large numbers of underemployed
Agriculture: cotton, grain, grapes, tea, citrus fruit, vegetables, sheep and horse breeding
Natural Resources: oil reserves, minerals, iron, aluminum

■ FINANCE/TRADE

Currency: rouble (rbl.), manat
International Reserves Excluding Gold: n.a.
Gold Reserves: n.a.
Budget: 1989 revenue, 3,808 million roubles
Defence Expenditures: n.a.
External Debt: $1.3 billion (1991)
Exports: $821 million to outside the successor states of the former USSR; oil and gas and related equipment, textiles, cotton. Partners: European and CIS countries (1992)
Imports: $300 million from outside the successor states of the former USSR; machinery and parts, foodstuffs, textiles, consumer durables (1992)

■ HEALTH

Births: 27/1,000 population (1993)
Deaths: 6/1,000 population (1993)
Infant Mortality: 33 deaths/1,000 live births (1993)
Life Expectancy at Birth: 67 years male, 75 years female (1993)
No. of Physicians: n.a.

■ EDUCATION

Govt. Expenditure: n.a.
Literacy: 100% (1993)

■ COMMUNICATIONS

Daily newspapers: 158 daily newspapers of all circulation types (1989)
Televisions: n.a.
Radios: n.a.
Telephones: n.a.

■ TRANSPORTATION

Motor Vehicles: n.a.
Roads: 36,700 km; 31,800 km hard-surfaced (1990)
Railway: 2,090 km (does not include industrial lines) (1990)
Air Traffic: n.a.
Airports: 65 airfields, of which 33 are usable and 26 have permanent-surface runways (1993)

Canadian Embassy: c/o Nenehatun Caddesi No.

75, Gaziosmanpasa 06700, Ankara, Turkey. Tel: (011-90-312) 436-1275. Fax: (011-90-312) 446-4437.
Representative to Canada: c/o Embassy of the Republic of Azerbaijan, 927 15th St. NW, Suite 700, Washington, DC 20005, USA. Tel: (202) 842-0001. Fax: (202) 842-0004.

Bahamas

Long-Form Name: Commonwealth of The Bahamas
Capital: Nassau
Population: 300,000 (1993 est.)

■ GEOGRAPHY

Area: 13,940 sq. km
Coastline: 3,542 km
Climate: tropical marine; moderated by warm waters of Gulf Stream
Environment: subject to hurricanes and other tropical storms that cause extensive flood damage
Terrain: long, flat coral formations with some low rounded hills
Land Use: 1% arable land; negligible permanent crops; negligible meadows and pastures; 32% forest and woodland; 67% other
Location: Caribbean islands

■ PEOPLE

Nationality: Bahamian
Ethnic Groups: 85% black, 15% white
Languages: English; some Creole among Haitian immigrants
Religions: 32% Baptist, 20% Anglican, 19% Roman Catholic, smaller groups of other Protestants, Greek Orthodox and Jews
Marriages: 8.6 (per 1,000) (1990)
Divorces: 1.10 (per 1,000) (1989)

■ GOVERNMENT

Leader(s): Prime Min. Hubert Alexander Ingraham, Gov. Gen. Clifford Darling
Government Type: commonwealth
Administrative Divisions: 21 districts
Independence: July 10, 1973 (from UK)
National Holiday: National Day, July 10

■ ECONOMY

Overview: tourism and offshore banking are features of this stable, middle-income developing nation
GNP: $3.044 billion, per capita $11,720; real growth rate 3.3% (1991)
Inflation: 5.7% (1992)
Industries: banking, tourism, cement, oil refining

and transshipment, salt production, rum, aragonite, pharmaceuticals, spiral welded steel pipe
Labour Force: 134,700 (1992); 30% government,
25% hotels and restaurants, 10% business services, 5% agriculture (1986)
Unemployment: 16% (1991 est.)
Agriculture: accounts for less than 5% of GDP;
dominated by small-scale producers; principal
products—citrus fruit, vegetables, poultry; large
net importer of food
Natural Resources: salt, aragonite, timber

■ FINANCE/TRADE

Currency: Bahamian dollar ($B)
International Reserves Excluding Gold: $187 mil-
lion (Jan. 1994)
Gold Reserves: none
Budget: revenues $627.5 million; expenditures
$727.5 million, including capital expenditures
of $100 million (1992 est.)
Defence Expenditures: n.a.
External Debt: $1.2 billion (1990)
Exports: $306 million (1991 est.); commodities:
pharmaceuticals, cement, rum, crawfish; part-
ners: US 90%, UK 10%
Imports: $1.14 billion (1991 est.); commodities:
foodstuffs, manufactured goods, mineral fuels;
partners: Nigeria 21%, US 35%, Japan 13%,
Angola 11%

■ HEALTH

Births: 20/1,000 population (1993)
Deaths: 5/1,000 population (1993)
Infant Mortality: 28.4 deaths/1,000 live births
(1993)
Life Expectancy at Birth: 68 years male, 75 years
female (1993)
No. of Physicians: 9.4/10,000 population (1992)

■ EDUCATION

Govt. Expenditure: 17.4% of govt. expenditure
(1991)
Literacy: 90% (1993)

■ COMMUNICATIONS

Daily newspapers: 3 (1992)
Televisions: 224.9/1,000 inhabitants (1992)
Radios: 538/1,000 inhabitants (1992)
Telephones: 63.59/100 inhabitants (1992)

■ TRANSPORTATION

Motor Vehicles: 85,000; 70,000 passenger cars
(1990)
Roads: 2,400 km; 1,350 km paved (1993)
Railway: n.a.
Air Traffic: 1,090,000 passengers carried (1991)
Airports: 60, of which 55 are usable and 31 have

permanent-surface runways

Canadian Embassy: Consulate of Canada, No. 21
Out Island Traders Building, Ernest Street,
Nassau; mailing address: Consulate of Canada,
P.O. Box SS-6371, Nassau, Bahamas. Tel: (1-
809) 393-4271. Fax: (1-809) 393-1305
Representative to Canada: High Commission for
the Commonwealth of the Bahamas, 360 Albert
St, Ste 1020, Ottawa ON K1R 7X7. Tel: (613)
232-1724. Fax: (613) 232-0097.

Bahrain

Long-Form Name: State of Bahrain
Capital: Manama
Population: 500,000 (1993 est.)

■ GEOGRAPHY

Area: 620 sq. km
Coastline: 161 km
Climate: arid; mild, pleasant winters; very hot,
humid summers
Environment: subsurface water sources being
rapidly depleted (requires development of
desalination facilities); dust storms; desertification
Terrain: mostly low desert plain rising gently to
low central escarpment
Land Use: 2% arable land; 2% permanent crops;
6% meadows and pastures; 0% forest and woodland; 90% other; includes negligible irrigated
Location: Persian Gulf

■ PEOPLE

Nationality: Bahraini
Ethnic Groups: 63% Bahraini, 13% Asian, 10%
other Arab, 8% Iranian, 6% other
Languages: Arabic (official); English also wide-
ly spoken; Farsi, Urdu
Religions: Moslem (70% Shi'a, 30% Sunni)
Marriages: 5.8 (per 1,000) (1990)
Divorces: 1.17 (per 1,000) (1990)

■ GOVERNMENT

Leader(s): Prime Min. Khalifa bin Salman Al
Khalifa, Amir 'Isa bin Sulman Al Khalifa
Government Type: traditional monarchy
Administrative Divisions: 12 districts
Independence: Aug. 15, 1971 (from UK)
National Holiday: Independence Day, Dec. 16

■ ECONOMY

Overview: petroleum production and processing
are the backbone of the economy and any
change in the world oil market affects the economy

GNP: $4.3 billion, per capita $7,800; real growth rate 3% (1992 est.)
Inflation: -0.2% (1992)
Industries: petroleum processing and refining, aluminum smelting, offshore banking, ship repairing
Labour Force: 220,000 (1992); 42% of labour force is Bahraini; 35% industry, 3% agriculture, 62% services (1989)
Unemployment: 8%–10% (1989)
Agriculture: including fishing, accounts for less than 2% of GDP; not self-sufficient in food production; heavily subsidized sector produces fruit, vegetables, poultry, dairy products, shrimp and fish
Natural Resources: oil, associated and non-associated natural gas, fish

■ FINANCE/TRADE

Currency: Bahraini dinar (BD)
International Reserves Excluding Gold: $1,245 million (Jan. 1994)
Gold Reserves: 0.15 million fine troy ounces (Jan. 1994)
Budget: revenues $1.2 billion; expenditures $1.32 billion, including capital expenditures (1991)
Defence Expenditures: 17.24% of total govt. expenditure (1992)
External Debt: $1.8 billion (1991)
Exports: $1.002 billion (1992); commodities: petroleum 80%, aluminum 7%, other 13%; partners: US, United Arab Emirates, Japan, Singapore, Saudi Arabia
Imports: $3.289 billion (1992); commodities: non-oil 59%, crude oil 41%; partners: UK, Saudi Arabia, US, Japan

■ HEALTH

Births: 27/1,000 population (1993)
Deaths: 3/1,000 population (1993)
Infant Mortality: 20 deaths/1,000 live births (1993)
Life Expectancy at Birth: 70 years male, 74 years female (1993)
No. of Physicians: 12.2/10,000 population (1992)

■ EDUCATION

Govt. Expenditure: 15.51% of govt. expenditure (1991)
Literacy: 77.4% (1992)

■ COMMUNICATIONS

Daily newspapers: 3 (1992)
Televisions: 401.6/1,000 inhabitants (1992)
Radios: 527/1,000 inhabitants (1992)
Telephones: 28.91/100 inhabitants (1992)

■ TRANSPORTATION

Motor Vehicles: 128,086; 104,585 passenger cars (1990)
Roads: 203 km paved
Railway: n.a.
Air Traffic: 876,000 passengers carried (1991)
Airports: 3 airfields, all usable; 2 have permanent-surface runways (1993)

Canadian Embassy: c/o The Canadian Embassy, Block 4, House No. 24, Al-Mutawakel St, Da'Aiyah, Kuwait City; mailing address: P.O. Box 25281, 13113 (Safat), Kuwait City, Kuwait. Tel: (011-965) 256-3025
Representative to Canada: c/o The Embassy of the State of Bahrain, 3502 International Drive NW, Washington, DC 20008, USA. Tel: (202) 342-0741; Fax: (202) 362-2192.

Bangladesh

Long-Form Name: People's Republic of Bangladesh
Capital: Dhaka
Population: 113,900,000 (1993 est.)

■ GEOGRAPHY

Area: 144,000 sq. km
Coastline: 580 km
Climate: tropical; cool, dry winter (Oct. to Mar.); hot, humid summer (Mar. to June); warm, rainy monsoon (June to Oct.)
Environment: vulnerable to droughts; much of country routinely flooded during summer monsoon season; overpopulation; deforestation
Terrain: mostly flat alluvial plain; hilly in southeast
Land Use: 67% arable land; 2% permanent crops; 4% meadows and pastures; 16% forest and woodland; 11% other
Location: S Asia, bordering on Bay of Bengal

■ PEOPLE

Nationality: Bangladeshi
Ethnic Groups: 98% Bengali, 250,000 Biharis, less than 1 million tribals
Languages: Bangla (official), English widely used, 5% tribal dialects
Religions: 83% Moslem, 16% Hindu, less than 1% Buddhist, Christian and other
Marriages: 11.3 (per 1,000) (1988)
Divorces: n.a.

■ GOVERNMENT

Leader(s): Pres. Abdur Rahman Biswas, Prime Min. Khaleda Ziaur Rahman

Government Type: republic
Administrative Divisions: 64 districts
Independence: Dec. 16, 1971 (from Pakistan; Bangladesh formerly known as East Pakistan)
National Holiday: Independence Day, Mar. 26

■ ECONOMY

Overview: one of the poorest nations in the world; the economy is based on a small number of agricultural exports which are vulnerable to natural disasters. Few natural resources. Frequent cyclones and floods, a rapidly growing labour force that cannot be absorbed by agriculture, a low level of industrialization, government interference with the economy, failure to exploit energy reserves, and inadequate power supplies all contribute to stifling economic growth
GNP: $23.8 billion, per capita $200; real growth rate 3.8% (1992)
Inflation: 4.3% (1992)
Industries: jute manufacturing, food processing, cotton textiles, petroleum, urea fertilizer
Labour Force: 33,000,000 (1992); 56.5% agriculture, 33.7% services, 9.8% industry; extensive export of labour to Saudi Arabia, United Arab Emirates, Oman and Kuwait (1989)
Unemployment: 30% (1988 est.)
Agriculture: accounts for about 40% of GDP, 60% of employment and 20% of exports; imports 10% of food grain requirements; world's largest exporter of jute; commercial products—jute, rice, wheat, tea, sugar cane, potatoes, beef, milk, poultry
Natural Resources: natural gas, arable land, timber

■ FINANCE/TRADE

Currency: taka (Tk)
International Reserves Excluding Gold: $2,561 million (Jan. 1994)
Gold Reserves: 0.09 million fine troy ounces (Jan. 1994)
Budget: revenues $2.5 billion; expenditures $3.7 billion, including capital expenditures (1992)
Defence Expenditures: $321.69 million (1990)
External Debt: $13.189 billion (1992)
Exports: $2.176 billion (1992); commodities: jute, tea, leather, shrimp, manufacturing; partners: US 25%, Western Europe 22%, Middle East 9%, Japan 8%, Eastern Europe 7%
Imports: $3.474 billion (1992); commodities: food, petroleum and other energy, nonfood consumer goods, semiprocessed goods and capital equipment; partners: Western Europe 18%, Japan 14%, Middle East 9%, US 8%

■ HEALTH

Births: 37/1,000 population (1993)
Deaths: 13/1,000 population (1993)
Infant Mortality: 116 deaths/1,000 live births (1993)
Life Expectancy at Birth: 54 years male, 53 years female (1993)
No. of Physicians: 1.6/10,000 population (1992)

■ EDUCATION

Govt. Expenditure: 10.3% of govt. expenditure (1990)
Literacy: 35.3% (1992)

■ COMMUNICATIONS

Daily newspapers: 72 (1992)
Televisions: 4.4/1,000 inhabitants (1992)
Radios: 41/1,000 inhabitants (1992)
Telephones: 0.1/100 inhabitants (1992)

■ TRANSPORTATION

Motor Vehicles: 128,000; 66,000 passenger cars (1990)
Roads: 8,064 km; 4,176 paved
Railway: 3,038 km (1988)
Air Traffic: 1,080,000 passengers carried (1991)
Airports: 16, of which 12 are usable and have permanent-surface runways (1993)

Canadian Embassy: The Canadian High Commission, House CWN 16/A, Rd. 48, Gulshan; mailing address: G.P.O. Box 569, Dhaka, Bangladesh. Tel: (011-880-2) 88-36-39. Fax: (011-880-2) 88-30-43
Representative to Canada: High Commission for the People's Republic of Bangladesh, 85 Range Rd, Ste 402, Ottawa ON K1N 8J6. Tel: (613) 236-0138. Fax: (613) 567-3213.

Barbados

Long-Form Name: Barbados
Capital: Bridgetown
Population: 300,000 (1993 est.)

■ GEOGRAPHY

Area: 430 sq. km
Coastline: 97 km
Climate: tropical; rainy season (June to Oct.)
Environment: subject to hurricanes, especially June to Oct.
Terrain: relatively flat; rises gently to a central highland region
Land Use: 77% arable land; 0% permanent crops; 9% meadows and pastures; 0% forest and woodland; 14% other

Location: Caribbean islands

■ PEOPLE

Nationality: Barbadian
Ethnic Groups: 80% African, 16% mixed, 4% European
Languages: English
Religions: 67% Protestant, 9% Methodist, 4% Roman Catholic, 9% other, including Moravian
Marriages: 8.0 (per 1,000) (1989)
Divorces: 1.63 (per 1,000) (1989)

■ GOVERNMENT

Leader(s): Gov. Gen. Dame Nita Barrow, Prime Min. Lloyd Erskine Sandiford
Government Type: parliamentary democracy
Administrative Divisions: 11 parishes
Independence: Nov. 30, 1966 (from UK)
National Holiday: Independence Day, Nov. 30

■ ECONOMY

Overview: has one of the highest standards of living of islands in the region; the tourist industry and traditional sugar cane cultivation are main parts of the economy; manufacturing has become increasingly important in recent years
GNP: $1.711 billion, per capita $6,630; real growth rate 1.6% (1991)
Inflation: 6.1% (1992)
Industries: tourism, sugar, light manufacturing, component assembly for export
Labour Force: 137,000 (1992); 84.1% services, 10.2% industry, 5.7% agriculture (1989)
Unemployment: 23% (1992)
Agriculture: accounts for 8% of GDP; major cash crop is sugar cane; other crops—vegetables and cotton; not self-sufficient in food
Natural Resources: crude oil, fishing, natural gas

■ FINANCE/TRADE

Currency: Barbadian dollar ($BDS)
International Reserves Excluding Gold: $148 million (Jan. 1994)
Gold Reserves: none (Jan. 1994)
Budget: revenues $547 million; expenditures $620 million, including capital expenditures of $60 million (1992–93)
Defence Expenditures: 1.87% of total govt. expenditure (1989)
External Debt: $621 million (1992)
Exports: $190 million (1992); commodities: sugar and molasses, electrical components, clothing, rum, machinery and transport equipment; partners: US 30%, CARICOM, UK, Puerto Rico, Canada
Imports: $471 million (1992); commodities: foodstuffs, consumer durables, raw materials, crude oil; partners: US 34%, CARICOM, Japan, UK, Canada

■ HEALTH

Births: 16/1,000 population (1993)
Deaths: 9/1,000 population (1993)
Infant Mortality: 11.8 deaths/1,000 live births (1993)
Life Expectancy at Birth: 72 years male, 77 years female (1993)
No. of Physicians: 8.9/10,000 population (1992)

■ EDUCATION

Govt. Expenditure: 18.64% of govt. expenditure (1989)
Literacy: 99% (1993)

■ COMMUNICATIONS

Daily newspapers: 2 (1992)
Televisions: 262.7/1,000 inhabitants (1992)
Radios: 878/1,000 inhabitants (1992)
Telephones: 57.46/100 inhabitants (1992)

■ TRANSPORTATION

Motor Vehicles: 45,000; 39,500 passenger cars (1990)
Roads: 1,570 km; 1,475 paved
Railway: none
Air Traffic: 1,320,000 passengers carried (1990)
Airports: 1, usable and with a permanent-surface runway

Canadian Embassy: The Canadian High Commission, Bishop's Court Hill, St. Michael, Barbados; mailing address: P.O. Box 404, Bridgetown, Barbados. Tel: (809) 429-3550. Fax: (809) 429-3780
Representative to Canada: High Commission for Barbados, 124 O'Connor St, Suite 500, Ottawa ON K1P 5M9. Tel: (613) 236-9517. Fax: (613) 230-4362.

Belarus

Long-Form Name: Republic of Belarus
Capital: Minsk
Population: 10,300,000 (1993 est.)

■ GEOGRAPHY

Area: 207,600 sq. km
Coastline: none; landlocked
Climate: mild and moist, transitional between continental and maritime
Environment: southern region is badly contaminated with nuclear fallout from 1986 Chernobyl reactor accident
Terrain: a hilly land of forests, lakes, rivers, and

marshes; soil poor and sandy
Land Use: 29% arable, negligible permanent crops and forest, 15% meadows and pastures, 56% other
Location: NC Europe

■ PEOPLE

Nationality: Byelorussian
Ethnic Groups: 78% Byelorussian, 13% Russian, 4% Polish, 2% Ukrainian, 1% Jewish, 2% other
Languages: Byelorussian, Russian
Religions: predominantly Roman Catholic and Eastern Orthodox
Marriages: 9.6 (per 1,000) (1989)
Divorces: 3.38 (per 1,000) (1989)

■ GOVERNMENT

Leader(s): President Mechislav Grib, Premier Vyacheslav M. Kebich
Government Type: republic
Administrative Divisions: 6 regions ("oblasts")
Independence: Aug. 25, 1991 (from Soviet Union)
National Holiday: Aug. 24

■ ECONOMY

Overview: strong emphasis on mining and agriculture, with growing manufacturing (heavy machinery, chemicals, fertilizer) and services sector
GNP: n.a.
Inflation: n.a.
Industries: machinery, tools, refineries, fertilizer production
Labour Force: 5,327,000 (1989)
Unemployment: 0.5%, but large numbers of underemployed (1993)
Agriculture: accounts for almost 25% of GDP; potatoes, flax, rye, oats, barley, wheat, cattle breeding, milk, vegetables, pigs, potatoes, peat, forest resources
Natural Resources: oil, potassium, forest land, peat deposits

■ FINANCE/TRADE

Currency: rouble (rbl.)
International Reserves Excluding Gold: n.a.
Gold Reserves: n.a.
Budget: 1989 revenue, 11,022 million roubles
Defence Expenditures: n.a.
External Debt: $181 million (1992)
Exports: $751 million (1992) agricultural and transport machinery, computers, refrigerators
Imports: $1,061 million (1992)

■ HEALTH

Births: 13/1,000 population (1993)

Deaths: 11/1,000 population (1993)
Infant Mortality: 15 deaths/1,000 live births (1993)
Life Expectancy at Birth: 66 years male, 76 years female (1993)
No. of Physicians: 41,400 (1989)

■ EDUCATION

Govt. Expenditure: 17.61% of govt. expenditure (1992)
Literacy: 100% (1993)

■ COMMUNICATIONS

Daily newspapers: 220 papers of all circulation types (1989), 28 dailies (1992)
Televisions: 255/1,000 inhabitants (1992)
Radios: 303/1,000 inhabitants (1992)
Telephones: approximately 17 per 100 persons (1993)

■ TRANSPORTATION

Motor Vehicles: n.a.
Roads: 98,200 km; 66,100 km hard-surfaced (1990)
Railway: 5,590 km (does not include industrial lines) (1990)
Air Traffic: n.a.
Airports: 124 airfields, of which 55 are usable and 31 have permanent-surface runways (1993)

Canadian Embassy: c/o Starokonyushenny Per 23, Moscow 121002, Russian Federation. Tel: (011-7-095) 241-1111. Fax: (011-7-095) 241-4400.
Representative to Canada: c/o Embassy of the Russian Federation, 285 Charlotte St, Ottawa ON K1N 8L5. Tel: (613) 235-4341. Fax: (613) 236-6342.

Belau (Palau)

Dependent Territory of the United States

Long-Form Name: Republic of Belau (Palau), Trust Territory of the Pacific Islands
Capital: Koror (on Koror Island)
Population: 16,071 (1993 est.)

■ GEOGRAPHY

Area: 458 sq. km (26 islands and 300+ islets)
Climate: tropical, warm year-round; wet season, May to Dec., dry season, Jan. to April; typhoon-prone with violent winds and heavy rain, esp. in July
Land Use: northern islands of volcanic origin, fertile and extensively cultivated; southern islands too rugged for habitation

Location: W Pacific Ocean (Micronesia)

■ PEOPLE

Nationality: Palauan
Ethnic Groups: Polynesian, Malayan, Melanesian, mixtures
Languages: English (official in all states), Sonsorolese, Angaur, Japanese, Tobi, Palauan

■ GOVERNMENT

Leader(s): Pres. Kuniwo Nakamura, V. Pres. Tommy Remengesau, next election scheduled for Nov. 1996
Government Type: UN trusteeship administered by the US
National Holiday: Constitution Day, July 9

■ ECONOMY

Overview: subsistence agriculture and fishing; some tourism; government is main employer; phosphate deposits on northern islands; largely dependent on imports from US

■ FINANCE/TRADE

Currency: American dollar (US$)

Belgium

Long-Form Name: Kingdom of Belgium
Capital: Brussels
Population: 10,100,000 (1993 est.)

■ GEOGRAPHY

Area: 30,510 sq. km
Coastline: 64 km
Climate: temperate; mild winters, cool summers; rainy, humid, cloudy
Environment: air and water pollution
Terrain: flat coastal plains in northwest central rolling hills, rugged mountains of Ardennes Forest in southeast
Land Use: 24% arable land; 1% permanent crops; 20% meadows and pastures; 21% forest and woodland; 34% other; includes negligible irrigated
Location: NW Europe, bordering on North Sea

■ PEOPLE

Nationality: Belgian
Ethnic Groups: 55% Flemish, 33% Walloon, 12% mixed or other
Languages: Dutch or Flemish spoken in north (Flanders), French in south (Wallonia), both languages official; small English-speaking minority in the east, German 1%
Religions: 75% Roman Catholic, remainder Protestant or other

Marriages: 6.2 (per 1,000) (1991)
Divorces: 1.9 (per 1,000) (1986)

■ GOVERNMENT

Leader(s): King Albert II, Prime Min. Jean-Luc Dehaene
Government Type: constitutional monarchy
Administrative Divisions: 9 provinces
Independence: Oct. 4, 1830 (from the Netherlands)
National Holiday: National Day, July 21

■ ECONOMY

Overview: a small, private-enterprise-based economy possessing few natural resources, it is therefore highly vulnerable to the state of world markets
GNP: n.a., GDP $177.9 billion, per capita $17,800; real growth rate 0.8% (1992)
Inflation: 2.4% (1992)
Industries: engineering and metal products, processed food and beverages, chemicals, basic metals, textiles, glass, petroleum, coal
Labour Force: 4,151,000 (1992); 78% services, 19.5% industry, 2.5% agriculture (1989)
Unemployment: 9.8% (1992)
Agriculture: accounts for 2.3% of GDP; emphasis on livestock production—beef, veal, pork, milk; major crops are sugar beets, fresh vegetables, fruit, grain and tobacco; net importer of farm products
Natural Resources: coal, natural gas

■ FINANCE/TRADE

Currency: Belgian franc (BF)
International Reserves Excluding Gold: $12,338 million (Jan. 1994)
Gold Reserves: 25.04 million fine troy ounces (Jan. 1994)
Budget: revenues $97.8 billion; expenditures $109.3 billion, including capital expenditures (1989)
Defence Expenditures: $3.07 billion (1991)
External Debt: $31.3 billion (1992 est.)
Exports: $123.066 billion (1992) Belgium-Luxembourg Economic Union; commodities: iron and steel, transportation equipment, tractors, diamonds, petroleum products; partners: European Community 74%, US 5%, communist countries 2%
Imports: $125.058 billion (1992) Belgium-Luxembourg Economic Union; commodities: fuels, grains, chemicals, foodstuffs; partners: European Community 72%, US 5%, oil-exporting, less-developed countries 4%, communist countries 3%

■ HEALTH

Births: 13/1,000 population (1993)
Deaths: 11/1,000 population (1993)
Infant Mortality: 8.4 deaths/1,000 live births (1993)
Life Expectancy at Birth: 73 years male, 79 years female (1993)
No. of Physicians: 30.2/10,000 population (1992)

■ EDUCATION

Govt. Expenditure: 12% of govt. expenditure (1988)
Literacy: 99% (1993)

■ COMMUNICATIONS

Daily newspapers: 23 (1992)
Televisions: 447.1/1,000 inhabitants (1992)
Radios: 776/1,000 inhabitants (1992)
Telephones: 51.72/100 inhabitants (1992)

■ TRANSPORTATION

Motor Vehicles: 4,276,737; 3,833,294 passenger cars (1990)
Roads: 129,454 km; 124,267 km paved
Railway: 3,600 km
Air Traffic: 3,018,000 passengers carried (1991)
Airports: 42 airfields, all usable; 24 have permanent-surface runways

Canadian Embassy: 2, Avenue de Tervuren, 1040 Brussels, Belgium. Tel: (011-32-2) 735-6040. Fax: (011-32-2) 735-3383
Representative to Canada: Embassy of the Kingdom of Belgium, 80 Elgin St, 4th Floor, Ottawa ON K1P 1B7. Tel: (613) 236-7267. Fax: (613) 236-7882.

Belize

Long-Form Name: Belize
Capital: Belmopan
Population: 200,000 (1993 est.)

■ GEOGRAPHY

Area: 22,960 sq. km
Coastline: 386 km
Climate: tropical; very hot and humid; rainy season (May to Feb.)
Environment: frequent devastating hurricanes (Sept. to Dec.) and coastal flooding, especially in south; deforestation
Terrain: flat, swampy coastal plain; low mountains in south
Land Use: 2% arable land; negligible permanent crops; 2% meadows and pastures; 44% forest and woodland; 52% other; includes negligible irrigated
Location: Central (Latin) America, bordering on Caribbean Sea

■ PEOPLE

Nationality: Belizean
Ethnic Groups: 30% Creole, 44% Mestizo, 11% Maya, 7% Garifuna, 8% other
Languages: English (official), Spanish, Maya, Garifuna (Carib)
Religions: 62% Roman Catholic, 30% Protestant sects, 2% none, 6% other
Marriages: 6.3 (per 1,000) (1991)
Divorces: 0.62 (per 1,000) (1989)

■ GOVERNMENT

Leader(s): Gov. Gen. Colville Young, Prime Min. Manuel Esquivel
Government Type: parliamentary democracy
Administrative Divisions: 6 districts
Independence: Sept. 21, 1981 (from UK; Belize formerly known as British Honduras)
National Holiday: Independence Day, Sept. 21

■ ECONOMY

Overview: economy primarily based on agriculture and merchandising; sugar is the main crop; tourism and construction are becoming increasingly important
GNP: $389 million, per capita $2,050; real growth rate 5.3% (1991)
Inflation: 2.8% (1992)
Industries: sugar refining, clothing, timber and forest products, furniture, rum, soap, beverages, cigarettes, tourism, garment production, citrus concentrates
Labour Force: 51,500; 30% agriculture, 16% services, 15.4% government, 11.2% commerce, 10.3% manufacturing; shortage of skilled labour and all types of technical personnel (1985)
Unemployment: 12% (1991 est.)
Agriculture: accounts for 22% of GDP (including fish and forestry); commercial crops include sugar cane, bananas, cocoa, citrus fruit; expanding output of lumber and cultured shrimp; net importer of basic foods
Natural Resources: arable land potential, timber, fish

■ FINANCE/TRADE

Currency: Belizean dollar ($BZ)
International Reserves Excluding Gold: $37 million (Jan. 1994)
Gold Reserves: n.a.
Budget: revenues $126.8 million; expenditures $123.1 million, including capital expenditures of $44.8 million (1991)

Defence Expenditures: 3.12% of total govt. expenditure (1993)
External Debt: $170 million (1992)
Exports: $141 million (1992); commodities: sugar, clothing, seafood, molasses, citrus, wood and wood products; partners: US 47%, UK, Trinidad and Tobago, Canada
Imports: $273 million (1992); commodities: machinery and transportation equipment, food, manufactured goods, fuels, chemicals, pharmaceuticals; partners: US 55%, UK, Netherlands Antilles, Mexico

■ HEALTH

Births: 38/1,000 population (1993)
Deaths: 5/1,000 population (1993)
Infant Mortality: 23 deaths/1,000 live births (1993)
Life Expectancy at Birth: 65 years male, 69 years female (1993)
No. of Physicians: 4.5/10,000 population (1992)

■ EDUCATION

Govt. Expenditure: 17.00% of govt. expenditures (1993)
Literacy: 91.2% (1993)

■ COMMUNICATIONS

Daily newspapers: 5 (1992)
Televisions: 164.8/1,000 inhabitants (1992)
Radios: 580/1,000 inhabitants (1992)
Telephones: 15,917 (1990)

■ TRANSPORTATION

Motor Vehicles: 4,465; 1,692 passenger cars (1990)
Roads: 2,710 km; 500 km paved (1993)
Railway: none
Air Traffic: 765,430 passengers carried (1988)
Airports: 42 airfields, of which 32 are usable and 3 have permanent-surface runways (1993)

Canadian Embassy: Consulate of Canada, 85 North Front St, Belize City. Tel: (011-501-02) 33-722. Fax: (011-501-02) 30-060
Representative to Canada: Closed December 15, 1993; to be relocated.

Benin

Long-Form Name: Republic of Benin
Capital: Porto Novo (official); Cotonou (de facto)
Population: 5,100,000 (1993 est.)

■ GEOGRAPHY

Area: 112,620 sq. km

Coastline: 121 km
Climate: tropical; hot, humid in south; semi-arid in north
Environment: hot, dry, dusty harmattan wind may affect north in winter; deforestation; desertification; recent droughts have severely affected marginal agriculture in north
Terrain: mostly flat to undulating plain; some hills and low mountains
Land Use: 12% arable land; 4% permanent crops; 4% meadows and pastures; 35% forest and woodland; 45% other; includes negligible irrigated
Location: WC Africa, bordering on South Atlantic Ocean

■ PEOPLE

Nationality: Beninese
Ethnic Groups: 99% African (42 ethnic groups, most important being Fon, Adja, Yoruba, Bariba); 5,500 Europeans
Languages: French (official); also Fon, Yoruba, Fulami, Bariba
Religions: majority Animist, 13% Islam, 15% Christian
Marriages: n.a.
Divorces: n.a.

■ GOVERNMENT

Leader(s): Pres. Nicéphore Soglo
Government Type: republic under multi-party democratic rule
Administrative Divisions: 6 provinces
Independence: Aug. 1, 1960 (from France; Benin formerly Dahomey)
National Holiday: National Day, Aug. 1

■ ECONOMY

Overview: one of the least developed countries in the world; limited natural resources and an underdeveloped infrastructure characterize the economy; agricultural products are a major export
GNP: $1.848 billion, per capita $380; real growth rate 2.1% (1991)
Inflation: 4.3% (1988)
Industries: palm oil and palm kernel oil processing, textiles, beverages, petroleum, cigarettes, construction materials, foodstuffs
Labour Force: 2,200,000 (1992); 70.2% agriculture, 23.1% services, 6.6% industry (1989)
Unemployment: n.a.
Agriculture: accounts for 35% of GDP; small farms produce 90% of agricultural output; production is dominated by food crops—corn, sorghum, cassava, beans and rice; cash crops include cotton, palm oil and peanuts; poultry

and livestock output has not kept up with consumption

Natural Resources: small offshore oil deposits, limestone, marble, timber

■ FINANCE/TRADE

Currency: Communauté financière africaine franc (CFAF)

International Reserves Excluding Gold: $279 million (Sept. 1993)

Gold Reserves: 0.01 million fine troy ounces (1991)

Budget: revenues $194 million; expenditures $390 million, including capital expenditures of $104 million (1990 est.)

Defence Expenditures: $38.36 million (1988)

External Debt: $1.367 billion (1992)

Exports: $97 million (1989); commodities: crude oil, fuels, cotton, palm products, cocoa; partners: Germany 36%, France 16%, Spain 14%, Italy 8%, UK 7%

Imports: $207 million (1989); commodities: foodstuffs, beverages, tobacco, petroleum products, cereals, chemicals, miscellaneous manufactured goods, intermediate goods, capital goods, light consumer goods; partners: France 34%, Netherlands 10%, Japan 7%, Italy 6%, US 5%

■ HEALTH

Births: 49/1,000 population (1993)

Deaths: 19/1,000 population (1993)

Infant Mortality: 89 deaths/1,000 live births (1993)

Life Expectancy at Birth: 44 years male, 48 years female (1993)

No. of Physicians: 0.6/10,000 population (1990)

■ EDUCATION

Govt. Expenditure: n.a.

Literacy: 23.4% (1992)

■ COMMUNICATIONS

Daily newspapers: 1 (1992)

Televisions: 4.5/1,000 inhabitants (1992); 2 TV stations

Radios: 89/1,000 inhabitants (1992); 4 radio stations

Telephones: 0.37/100 inhabitants (1992)

■ TRANSPORTATION

Motor Vehicles: 38,000; 25,000 passenger cars (1990)

Roads: 5,050 km; 920 km paved

Railway: 578 km

Air Traffic: 64,000 passengers carried (1991)

Airports: 7 airfields, of which 5 are usable; 1 has permanent-surface runway (1993)

Canadian Embassy: The Canadian High Commission, P.O. Box 1639, Accra, Ghana. Tel: (011-233-21) 77-37-91. Fax: (011-233-21) 77-37-92

Representative to Canada: Embassy of the Republic of Benin, 58 Glebe Ave, Ottawa ON K1S 2C3. Tel: (613) 233-4429. Fax: (613) 233-8952.

Bermuda

Dependent Territory of the United Kingdom

Long-Form Name: Bermuda

Capital: Hamilton

Population: 60,686 (1993 est.)

■ GEOGRAPHY

Area: 50 sq. km

Climate: subtropical; mild, humid; gales, strong winds common in winter

Land Use: 0% arable land; 0% permanent crops; 0% meadows and pastures; 20% forest and woodland; 80% other

Location: North Atlantic Ocean

■ PEOPLE

Nationality: Bermudian

Ethnic Groups: 61% black, 39% white and other

Languages: English

■ GOVERNMENT

Leader(s): Gov. Lord Waddington, Prem. John W.D. Swan

Government Type: dependent territory of the UK

National Holiday: Bermuda Day, May 22

■ ECONOMY

Overview: a successful tourist industry accounts for its high per capita income; most food is imported; the industrial sector is small, and agriculture is limited by the lack of suitable land

■ FINANCE/TRADE

Currency: Bermudian dollar ($Ber)

Canadian Embassy: The Canadian Commission to Bermuda, c/o The Canadian Consulate General, 1251 Avenue of the Americas, 16th Floor, New York, NY, USA 10020-1175. Tel: (212) 596-1600. Fax: (212) 596-1790.

Bhutan

Long-Form Name: Kingdom of Bhutan
Capital: Punakha (winter), Thimphu (summer)
Population: 800,000 (1993 est.)

■ GEOGRAPHY

Area: 47,000 sq. km
Coastline: none: landlocked
Climate: varies; tropical in southern plains; cool winters and hot summers in central valleys; severe winters and cool summers in Himalayas
Environment: violent storms coming from the Himalayas were the source of the country name which translates as Land of the Thunder Dragon
Terrain: mostly mountainous with some fertile valleys and savanna
Land Use: 2% arable land; negligible permanent crops; 5% meadows and pastures; 70% forest and woodland; 23% other
Location: S Asia

■ PEOPLE

Nationality: Bhutanese
Ethnic Groups: 50% Bhote, 35% ethnic Nepalese, 15% indigenous or migrant tribes
Languages: Bhotes speak various Tibetan dialects—most widely spoken dialect is Dzongkha (official); Nepalese speak various Nepalese dialects
Religions: 75% Mahayana Buddhism (state religion), Hinduism (25%, mainly ethnic Nepalese)
Marriages: n.a.
Divorces: n.a.

■ GOVERNMENT

Leader(s): King Jigme Singye Wangchuk
Government Type: monarchy; special treaty relationship with India
Administrative Divisions: 18 districts
Independence: Aug. 8, 1949 (from India)
National Holiday: National Day, Dec. 17

■ ECONOMY

Overview: agriculture and forestry are the bedrock of the economy; it is poorly developed due to omnipresent rugged topography
GNP: n.a., GDP: $320 million, per capita $200; real growth rate 3.1% (1991)
Inflation: 11.8% (1991)
Industries: cement, chemical products, mining, distilling, food processing, handicrafts, wood products, calcium carbide
Labour Force: 700,000 (1992); 92.5% agriculture, 2.8% industry; 4.7% services (1989)
Unemployment: n.a.
Agriculture: accounts for 45% of GDP; based on subsistence farming and animal husbandry; self-sufficient in food except for foodgrains; other production—rice, corn, root crops, citrus fruit, dairy and eggs
Natural Resources: timber, hydroelectricity, gypsum, calcium carbide, tourism potential

■ FINANCE/TRADE

Currency: ngultrum (Nu)
International Reserves Excluding Gold: $69 million (1991)
Gold Reserves: n.a.
Budget: revenues $112 million; expenditures $121 million, including capital expenditures of $58 million (1991 est.)
Defence Expenditures: negligible
External Debt: $84 million (1992)
Exports: $70.9 million (1989); commodities: cardamon, gypsum, timber, handicrafts, cement, fruit; partners: India 93%
Imports: $138.3 million (1989); commodities: fuel and lubricants, grain, machinery and parts, vehicles, fabrics; partners: India 67%

■ HEALTH

Births: 40/1,000 population (1993)
Deaths: 17/1,000 population (1993)
Infant Mortality: 130 deaths/1,000 live births (1993)
Life Expectancy at Birth: 50 years male, 48 years female (1993)
No. of Physicians: 1.0/10,000 population (1992)

■ EDUCATION

Govt. Expenditure: 10.66% of GNP (1991)
Literacy: 38.4% (1992)

■ COMMUNICATIONS

Daily newspapers: 1 (1992)
Televisions: n.a.
Radios: 15/1,000 inhabitants (1992)
Telephones: service is poor, and very few telephones are in use

■ TRANSPORTATION

Motor Vehicles: 7,002 registered vehicles (1989)
Roads: 2,165 km; 1,703 km surfaced
Railway: n.a.
Air Traffic: 8,000 passengers carried (1991)
Airports: 2, both usable; 1 has permanent-surface runway (1993)

Canadian Embassy: The Canadian High Commission, 7/8 Shantipath, Chanakyapuri, New Delhi 110021; mailing address: P.O. Box 5207, New Delhi, India. Tel: (011-91-11) 687-6500.

Bolivia

Long-Form Name: Republic of Bolivia
Capital: La Paz (seat of government); Sucre (legal capital and seat of judiciary)
Population: 7,800,000 (1993 est.)

■ GEOGRAPHY

Area: 1,098,580 sq. km
Coastline: none: landlocked
Climate: varies with altitude; humid and tropical to cold and semi-arid
Environment: cold, thin air of high plateau is obstacle to efficient fuel combustion; overgrazing, soil erosion, desertification
Terrain: Andes Mountains, high plateau, hills, lowland plains in Amazon basin
Land Use: 3% arable land; negligible permanent crops; 25% meadows and pastures; 52% forest and woodland; 20% other; includes negligible irrigated
Location: W South America

■ PEOPLE

Nationality: Bolivian
Ethnic Groups: 30% Quenchua, 25% Aymara, 25–30% mixed, 5–15% European
Languages: Spanish, Quechua and Aymara (all official)
Religions: 95% Roman Catholic; 5% Protestant, especially Methodist
Marriages: n.a.
Divorces: n.a.

■ GOVERNMENT

Leader(s): Pres. Gonzalo Sanchez de Lozada Bustamente
Government Type: republic
Administrative Divisions: 9 departments
Independence: Aug. 6, 1825 (from Spain)
National Holiday: Independence Day, Aug. 6

■ ECONOMY

Overview: a poor economy vulnerable to price fluctuations for its small number of exports, it relies heavily on coca, used for cocaine processing
GNP: n.a., GDP: $4.9 billion, per capita $670; real growth rate 3.8% (1992)
Inflation: 21.4% (1991)
Industries: mining, smelting, petroleum, food and beverage, tobacco, handicrafts, clothing; illicit drug industry reportedly produces the largest revenues
Labour Force: 2,283,000 (1992); 46.5% agriculture, 33.9% services, 19.2% industry (1989)
Unemployment: 5% (1992)
Agriculture: accounts for 21% of GDP (including forestry and fisheries); principal commodities–coffee, coca, cotton, corn, sugar cane, rice, potatoes, timber; self-sufficient in food
Natural Resources: tin, natural gas, crude oil, zinc, tungsten, antimony, silver, iron ore, lead, gold, timber

■ FINANCE/TRADE

Currency: Boliviano ($b)
International Reserves Excluding Gold: $232 million (Jan. 1994)
Gold Reserves: 0.89 million fine troy ounces (Jan. 1994)
Budget: revenues $1.5 billion; expenditures $1.57 billion, including capital expenditures of $627 million (1993 est.)
Defence Expenditures: 9.77% of total govt. expenditure (1992)
External Debt: $4.243 billion (1992)
Exports: $737 million (1992); commodities: metals 45%, natural gas 32%, coffee, soyabeans, sugar, cotton, timber and illicit drugs; partners: US 23%, Argentina
Imports: $1.181 billion (1992); commodities: food, petroleum, consumer goods, capital goods; partners: US 15%

■ HEALTH

Births: 37/1,000 population (1993)
Deaths: 10/1,000 population (1993)
Infant Mortality: 89 deaths/1,000 live births (1993)
Life Expectancy at Birth: 59 years male, 64 years female (1993)
No. of Physicians: 6.5/10,000 population (1992)

■ EDUCATION

Govt. Expenditure: 16.65% of govt. expenditure (1992)
Literacy: 78% (1993)

■ COMMUNICATIONS

Daily newspapers: 16 (1992)
Televisions: 98.4/1,000 inhabitants (1992)
Radios: 574/1,000 inhabitants (1992)
Telephones: 2.87/100 inhabitants (1992)

■ TRANSPORTATION

Motor Vehicles: 316,969; 261,082 passenger cars

(1990)
Roads: 38,836 km; 1,300 km paved
Railway: 3,864 km
Air Traffic: 1,200,000 passengers carried (1991)
Airports: 1,225 airfields, of which 1,043 are usable and 9 have permanent-surface runways (1993)

Canadian Embassy: c/o The Canadian Embassy, Antes Calle Libertad 130, Miraflores, Lima; mailing address: Casilla 18-1126, Correo Miraflores, Lima, Peru. Tel: (011-51-14) 44-40-15. Fax (011-51-14) 44-43-47
Representative to Canada: Embassy of Bolivia, 130 Albert St, Ste 504, Ottawa ON K1P 5G4. Tel: (613) 236-8237. Fax: (613) 230-9937.

Bosnia and Herzegovina

Long-Form Name: Republic of Bosnia and Herzegovina
Capital: Sarajevo
Population: 4,618,804 (1993 est.)

■ GEOGRAPHY

Area: 51,233 sq. km
Coastline: 20 km
Climate: hot summers and cold winters; regions with high elevation have short, cool summers and long, severe winters; mild, rainy winters along the coast
Environment: air pollution; scarce water; waste disposal sites limited; subject to frequent destructive earthquakes
Terrain: mountains and valleys
Land Use: 20% arable, 2% permanent crops, 25% meadows and pastures, 36% forests, 17% other
Location: SE Europe

■ PEOPLE

Nationality: Bosnian, Herzegovinian
Ethnic Groups: 44% Muslim, 31% Serb, 17% Croat, 8% other
Languages: 99% Serbo-Croatian
Religions: 40% Muslim, 31% Orthodox, 15% Catholic, 4% Protestant, 10% other
Marriages: n.a.
Divorces: n.a.

■ GOVERNMENT

Leader(s): Pres. Alija Izetbegovic, Prime Min. Haris Silajdzic
Government Type: emerging democracy
Administrative Divisions: 109 districts
Independence: April 1992 (from Yugoslavia)
National Holiday: n.a.

■ ECONOMY

Overview: though farms are almost entirely privately owned, they are small and inefficient, and food must be imported; inter-ethnic warfare has caused sharp decreases in industrial output and soaring unemployment; reliable economic statistics are not yet available for 1992
GNP: $14 billion; $3,200 per capita; real growth rate -37% (1991 est.)
Inflation: 80% per month (1991)
Industries: steel production, mining (esp. coal, iron ore, lead, zinc), manufacturing (esp. vehicle assembly, textiles, tobacco products, wood furniture), oil refining
Labour Force: 1,026,254 (1991 est.); 2% agriculture, 45% industry and mining
Unemployment: 28% (1992)
Agriculture: regularly produces less than half the region's food needs; foothills of northern Bosnia support orchards, vineyards, livestock and some wheat and corn; long winters and heavy precipitation reduce agricultural output in mountains; farms are generally not very productive
Natural Resources: coal, iron, bauxite, manganese, timber, copper

■ FINANCE/TRADE

Currency: Croatian dinar is used in ethnic Croat areas, "Yugoslav" dinar used in all other regions
International Reserves Excluding Gold: n.a.
Gold Reserves: n.a.
Budget: n.a.
Defence Expenditures: n.a.
External Debt: n.a.
Exports: n.a.
Imports: n.a.

■ HEALTH

Births: 14/1,000 population (1993)
Deaths: 6/1,000 population (1993)
Infant Mortality: 15.2 deaths/1,000 live births (1993)
Life Expectancy at Birth: 69 years male, 75 years female (1993)
No. of Physicians: n.a.

■ EDUCATION

Govt. Expenditure: n.a.
Literacy: n.a.

■ COMMUNICATIONS

Daily newspapers: n.a.
Televisions: 1,012,094 total; 6 TV stations (1993)
Radios: 840,000 total; 11 radio stations (1993)
Telephones: 727,000 total (1993)

■ TRANSPORTATION

Motor Vehicles: n.a.
Roads: 21,168 km; 11,436 km paved (1991)
Railway: n.a.
Air Traffic: n.a.
Airports: 27 airfields, of which 22 are usable; 8 have permanent-surface runways (1993).

Botswana

Long-Form Name: Republic of Botswana
Capital: Gaborone
Population: 1,400,000 (1993 est.)

■ GEOGRAPHY

Area: 600,370 sq. km
Coastline: none: landlocked
Climate: sub-tropical to semi-arid; warm winters and hot summers
Environment: rains in early 1988 broke six years of drought that had severely affected the important cattle industry; overgrazing; desertification
Terrain: predominantly flat to gently rolling tableland; Kalahari Desert in southwest
Land Use: 2% arable land; 0% permanent crops; 75% meadows and pastures; 2% forest and woodland; 21% other; includes negligible irrigated
Location: SC Africa

■ PEOPLE

Nationality: Motswana (sing.), Batswana (pl.)
Ethnic Groups: 95% Batswana; about 4% Kalanga, Basarwa and Kgalagadi; about 1% white
Languages: English (official), Setswana
Religions: 50% indigenous beliefs, 50% Christian
Marriages: n.a.
Divorces: n.a.

■ GOVERNMENT

Leader(s): Pres. Sir Quett Ketumile J. Masire, V. Pres. Festus Mogae
Government Type: parliamentary republic
Administrative Divisions: 10 districts
Independence: Sept. 30, 1966 (from UK; Botswana formerly known as Bechuanaland)
National Holiday: Independence Day, Sept. 30

■ ECONOMY

Overview: economy based on mining (diamonds) and traditionally, cattle raising and crops, exhibits high unemployment
GNP: n.a., GDP $3.6 billion, per capita $2,450; real growth rate 5.8% (1992 est.)

Inflation: 16.2% (1992)
Industries: livestock processing; mining of diamonds, copper, nickel, coal, salt, soda ash, potash; tourism
Labour Force: 446,000 (1992); 52% services, 43.2% agriculture, 4.8 industry; 19,000 are employed in various mines in South Africa (1989)
Unemployment: 25% (1989)
Agriculture: plagued by erratic rainfall and poor soil; accounts for only 5% of GDP; subsistence farming predominates; cattle raising supports 50% of the population; must import large share of food needs
Natural Resources: diamonds, copper, nickel, salt, soda ash, potash, coal, iron ore, silver, natural gas

■ FINANCE/TRADE

Currency: pula (P)
International Reserves Excluding Gold: $4,107 million (Nov. 1993)
Gold Reserves: n.a.
Budget: revenues $1.7 billion; expenditures $1.99 billion, including capital expenditures of $652 million (1994)
Defence Expenditures: 13.34% of govt. expenditure (1991)
External Debt: $545 million (1992)
Exports: $1.358 billion (1991); commodities: diamonds 88%, copper and nickel 5%, meat 4%, cattle, animal products; partners: Switzerland, US, UK, other European Community—associated members of Southern African Customs Union
Imports: $2.433 billion (1992); commodities: foodstuffs, vehicles, textiles, petroleum products; partners: Switzerland

■ HEALTH

Births: 37/1,000 population (1993)
Deaths: 9/1,000 population (1993)
Infant Mortality: 45 deaths/1,000 live births (1993)
Life Expectancy at Birth: 58 years male, 64 years female (1993)
No. of Physicians: 1.5/10,000 population (1990)

■ EDUCATION

Govt. Expenditure: 21.00% of total govt. expenditures (1991)
Literacy: 72% (1993)

■ COMMUNICATIONS

Daily newspapers: 1 (1992)
Televisions: 11.9/1,000 inhabitants (1992)
Radios: 111/1,000 inhabitants (1992)

Telephones: 2.86/100 inhabitants (1992)

■ TRANSPORTATION

Motor Vehicles: 60,000; 25,000 passenger cars (1990)
Roads: 13,968 km; 2,328 km paved
Railway: 757 km
Air Traffic: 102,000 passengers carried (1991)
Airports: 100 airfields, of which 87 are usable and 8 have permanent-surface runways (1993)

Canadian Embassy: c/o The Canadian High Commission, 45 Baines Ave, Harare; mailing address: P.O. Box 1430, Harare, Zimbabwe. Tel: (011-263-4) 73-38-81. Fax: (011-263-4) 73-29-17
Representative to Canada: c/o Embassy of the Republic of Botswana, Intelsat Bldg, 3400 International Dr NW, Suite 7M, Washington, DC 20008 USA. Tel: (202) 244-4990. Fax: (202) 244-4164.

Brazil

Long-Form Name: Federative Republic of Brazil
Capital: Brasilia
Population: 152,000,000 (1993 est.)

■ GEOGRAPHY

Area: 8,511,965 sq. km; includes Arquipélago de Fernando de Noronha, Atol das Rocas, Ilha da Trindade, Ilhas Martin Vaz and Penedos de São Pedro e São Paulo
Coastline: 7,491 km
Climate: mostly tropical, but temperate in south
Environment: recurrent droughts in northeast; floods and frost in south; deforestation in Amazon basin; air and water pollution in Rio de Janeiro and São Paulo and several other large cities
Terrain: mostly flat to rolling lowlands in north; some plains, hills, mountains and narrow coastal belt
Land Use: 7% arable land; 1% permanent crops; 19% meadows and pastures; 67% forest and woodland; 6% other; includes negligible irrigated
Location: E South America

■ PEOPLE

Nationality: Brazilian
Ethnic Groups: Portuguese, Italian, German, Japanese, black, Amerindian; 55% white, 38% mixed, 6% black, 1% other
Languages: Portuguese (official), Spanish, English, French
Religions: 90% Roman Catholic (nominal)
Marriages: 5.6 (per 1,000) (1989)

Divorces: 0.45 (per 1,000) (1989)

■ GOVERNMENT

Leader(s): Pres. Itamar Franco; Fernando Henrique Cardoso (as of Jan. 1)
Government Type: federal republic
Administrative Divisions: 26 states and 1 federal district
Independence: Sept. 7, 1822 (from Portugal)
National Holiday: Independence Day, Sept. 7

■ ECONOMY

Overview: despite abundant natural resources, the economy has experienced runaway inflation and large foreign debt; Brazil's natural resources remain a major, long-term economic strength
GNP: n.a., GDP: $369 billion, per capita $2,350; real growth rate -0.2% (1992)
Inflation: 1,008.7% (1992)
Industries: textiles and other consumer goods, shoes, chemicals, cement, lumber, iron ore, steel, motor vehicles and auto parts, metalworking, capital goods, tin
Labour Force: 55,026,000 (1992); 54.7% services, 29.3% agriculture, 16% industry (1989)
Unemployment: 5.9% (1992)
Agriculture: accounts for 11% of GDP; world's largest producer and exporter of coffee and orange juice concentrate and second-largest exporter of soybeans; self-sufficient in food, except for wheat
Natural Resources: iron ore, manganese, bauxite, nickel, uranium, phosphates, tin, hydroelectricity, gold, platinum, crude oil, timber

■ FINANCE/TRADE

Currency: real (replaced the cruzeiro on July 1, 1994
International Reserves Excluding Gold: $30,604 million (Dec. 1993)
Gold Reserves: 2.93 million fine troy ounces (Dec. 1993)
Budget: revenues $164.3 billion; expenditures $170.6 billion, including capital expenditures of $32.9 billion (1990)
Defence Expenditures: 2.99% of govt. expenditure (1991)
External Debt: $121.11 billion (1992)
Exports: $35.862 billion (1992); commodities: coffee, metallurgical products, foodstuffs, iron ore, automobiles and parts; partners: US 28%, European Community 26%, Latin America 11%, Japan 6%
Imports: $20.559 billion (1992); commodities: crude oil, capital goods, chemical products, foodstuffs, coal; partners: Middle East and Africa 24%, European Community 22%, US

21%, Latin America 12%, Japan 6%

■ HEALTH

Births: 23/1,000 population (1993)
Deaths: 7/1,000 population (1993)
Infant Mortality: 63 deaths/1,000 live births (1993)
Life Expectancy at Birth: 64 years male, 71 years female (1993)
No. of Physicians: 9.3/10,000 population (1992)

■ EDUCATION

Govt. Expenditure: 3.75% of government expenditure (1991)
Literacy: 81% (1993)

■ COMMUNICATIONS

Daily newspapers: 366 (1992)
Televisions: 203.6/1,000 inhabitants (1992)
Radios: 373/1,000 inhabitants (1992)
Telephones: 9.54/100 inhabitants (1992)

■ TRANSPORTATION

Motor Vehicles: 13,063,345; 12,127,562 passenger cars (1990)
Roads: 1,448,000 km; 48,000 km paved
Railway: 30,643 km
Air Traffic: 19,015,000 passengers carried (1991)
Airports: 3,613 airfields, of which 3,031 are usable, and 431 have permanent-surface runways (1993)

Canadian Embassy: Avendia das Nacoes, Lote 16, Brasilia–DF 70410-900; mailing address: Caixa Postal 00961, Brasilia DF 70359-900, Brazil. Tel: (011-55-61) 321-2171. Fax: (011-55-61) 321-4529
Representative to Canada: Embassy of the Federative Republic of Brazil, 450 Wilbrod St, Ottawa ON K1N 6M8. Tel: (613) 237-1090. Fax: (613) 237-6144.

British Indian Ocean Territory

Dependent Territory of the United Kingdom

Long-Form Name: British Indian Ocean Territory
Capital: None; Victoria (Seychelles) is administrative headquarters
Population: 2,000 (1992); no indigenous inhabitants; US and UK military personnel

■ GEOGRAPHY

Area: 60 sq. km
Climate: tropical maritime, hot and humid, moderated by trade winds
Location: Indian Ocean, the Chagos Archipelago

island group NE of Madagascar

■ PEOPLE

Languages: English

■ GOVERNMENT

Leader(s): Comm. T.G. Harris, Administrator R.G. Wells; both reside in the UK
Government Type: dependency of Great Britain

■ ECONOMY

Overview: fishing, coconuts, guano fertilizer; all economic activity takes place on the largest island, Diego Garcia, where joint US-UK defence facilities are located; there are no industrial or agricultural activities on the islands

■ FINANCE/TRADE

Currency: pound sterling (£ or £ stg)

British Virgin Islands

Dependent Territory of the United Kingdom

Long-Form Name: British Virgin Islands
Capital: Road Town (on Tortola Island)
Population: 12,707 (1993 est.)

■ GEOGRAPHY

Area: 150 sq. km; 40 islands and numerous small rocks and reefs
Climate: humid, sub-tropical with modifying sea winds
Land Use: 20% arable, 7% permanent crops, 33% meadows and pastures, 7% forest and woodland, 33% other
Location: West Indies, NE of Puerto Rico

■ PEOPLE

Nationality: British Virgin Islander
Ethnic Groups: 90% black, Asian, white, various Hispanic strains, descendants of European settlers
Languages: English (official)

■ GOVERNMENT

Leader(s): Gov. Peter A. Penfold
Government Type: self-governing territory of United Kingdom
National Holiday: Territory Day, July 1

■ ECONOMY

Overview: very small export trade, mostly with American Virgin Islands and UK; very limited agriculture: fruit, vegetables, livestock, poultry; construction industry; economy is highly dependent on the tourist industry, which accounts for approximately 21% of the GDP

■ FINANCE/TRADE

Currency: American dollar ($US)

Brunei Darussalam

Long-Form Name: Negara Brunei Darussalam
Capital: Bandar Seri Begawan
Population: 300,000 (1993 est.)

■ GEOGRAPHY

Area: 5,770 sq. km
Coastline: 161 km
Climate: tropical; hot, humid, rainy
Environment: typhoons, earthquakes and severe floods occasionally occur
Terrain: flat coastal plain rises to mountainous east; hilly lowland in west
Land Use: 1% arable land; 1% permanent crops; 1% meadows and pastures; 79% forest and woodland; 18% other; includes negligible irrigated
Location: Indonesia (island of Borneo), bordering on South China Sea

■ PEOPLE

Nationality: Bruneian
Ethnic Groups: 64% Malay, 20% Chinese, 16% other
Languages: Malay (official), English and Chinese
Religions: Islam (official, mainly Sunni Muslims); majority of Chinese are Buddhist, Confucian or Taoist
Marriages: 7.2 (per 1,000) (1989)
Divorces: 0.76 (per 1,000) (1989)

■ GOVERNMENT

Leader(s): Sultan, Prime Minister and Minister of Defence Sir Hassanal Bolkiah
Government Type: constitutional sultanate
Administrative Divisions: 4 districts
Independence: Jan. 1, 1984 (from UK)
National Holiday: National Day, Feb. 23

■ ECONOMY

Overview: economy is based on crude oil and natural gas exports and the per capita GDP is one of the highest for under-developed nations; almost totally supported by exports of crude oil and natural gas
GNP: n.a., GDP $3.5 billion, per capita $8,800; real growth rate 1.3% (1990 est.)
Inflation: 2.5% (1989 est.)
Industries: petroleum, liquefied natural gas, construction
Labour Force: 89,000 (includes members of the army); 33% of labour force is foreign (1988); 50.4% production of oil, natural gas and construction; 47.6% trade, services and other; 2.0% agriculture, forestry and fishing
Unemployment: 3.7%, shortage of skilled labour (1989)
Agriculture: imports about 80% of its food needs; principal crops and livestock include rice, cassava, bananas, buffaloes and pigs
Natural Resources: crude oil, natural gas, timber

■ FINANCE/TRADE

Currency: Brunei dollar ($B)
International Reserves Excluding Gold: n.a.
Gold Reserves: n.a.
Budget: revenues $1.3 billion; expenditures $1.5 billion, including capital expenditures of $255 million (1989 est.)
Defence Expenditures: $229.025 million (1988)
External Debt: none
Exports: $2.370 billion (1992); commodities: crude oil, liquefied natural gas, petroleum products; partners: Japan 55%
Imports: $1.176 billion (1992); commodities: machinery and transport equipment, manufactured goods, food, beverages, tobacco, consumer goods; partners: Singapore 31%, US 20%, Japan 6%

■ HEALTH

Births: 29/1,000 population (1993)
Deaths: 3/1,000 population (1993)
Infant Mortality: 9.0 deaths/1,000 live births (1993)
Life Expectancy at Birth: 69 years male, 72 years female (1993)
No. of Physicians: 5.5/10,000 population (1992)

■ EDUCATION

Govt. Expenditure: n.a.
Literacy: 77.8% (1992)

■ COMMUNICATIONS

Daily newspapers: 1 (1992)
Televisions: 224.6/1,000 inhabitants (1992)
Radios: 234/1,000 inhabitants (1992)
Telephones: 19.38/100 inhabitants (1992)

■ TRANSPORTATION

Motor Vehicles: 112,087; 100,114 passenger cars (1990)
Roads: 1,090 km; 370 km paved
Railway: 13 km
Air Traffic: 307,000 passengers carried (1991)
Airports: 2, both usable; 1 has a permanent-surface runway

Canadian Embassy: c/o The Canadian High Commission, 80 Anson Rd, 14th and 15th Floors, IBM Towers, Singapore 0207; mailing address: Robinson Rd, P.O. Box 845, Singapore 9016. Tel: (011-65) 225-6363. Fax (011-65) 225-2450

Representative to Canada: c/o High Commission for Brunei, 866 United Nations Plaza, Room 248, New York, NY 10017 USA. Tel: (212) 838-1600. Fax: (212) 980-6478.

Bulgaria

Long-Form Name: Republic of Bulgaria
Capital: Sofia
Population: 9,000,000 (1992)

■ GEOGRAPHY

Area: 110,910 sq. km
Coastline: 354 km
Climate: temperate; cold, damp winters; hot, dry summers
Environment: subject to earthquakes, landslides, deforestation, air pollution
Terrain: mostly mountains with lowlands in north and south
Land Use: 34% arable land; 3% permanent crops; 18% meadows and pastures; 35% forest and woodland; 10% other; includes 10 sq. km irrigated
Location: SC Europe, bordering on Black Sea

■ PEOPLE

Nationality: Bulgarian
Ethnic Groups: 85% Bulgarian, 9% Turk, 3% Gypsy, 3% Macedonian, 0.3% Armenian, 0.2% Russian, 0.6% other
Languages: Bulgarian (official), Turkish; secondary languages closely correspond to ethnic breakdown
Religions: 85% Bulgarian Orthodox, 13% Moslem (practised by Turkish and Pomak minorities), 0.8% Jewish, 0.7% Roman Catholic, 0.5% Protestant, Gregorian-Armenian and other
Marriages: 5.4 (per 1,000) (1991)
Divorces: 1.26 (per 1,000) (1990)

■ GOVERNMENT

Leader(s): Pres. Zhelyu Zhelev, Prime Min. Lyuben Berov
Government Type: caretaker government, emerging democracy
Administrative Divisions: 9 provinces, 1 city
Independence: Sept. 22, 1908 (from Turkey)
National Holiday: March 3

■ ECONOMY

Overview: heavily in debt with low growth, the economy is also hindered by antiquated industrial plants
GNP: n.a., GDP: $34.1 billion, per capita $3,800; real growth rate -7.7% (1992)
Inflation: 80% (1992)
Industries: food processing, machine building and metal working, electronics, chemicals
Labour Force: 4,475,000 (1992); 37.9% industry, 16.5% agriculture, 45.6% services (1989)
Unemployment: 15% (1992)
Agriculture: accounts for 22% of GNP; climate and soil conditions support livestock raising and the growing of various grain crops, oilseeds, vegetables, fruit and tobacco; more than one-third of the arable land devoted to grain; world's fourth-largest tobacco exporter; surplus food producer
Natural Resources: bauxite, copper, lead, zinc, coal, timber, arable land

■ FINANCE/TRADE

Currency: lev (pl. leva) (Lv)
International Reserves Excluding Gold: n.a.
Gold Reserves: n.a.
Budget: revenues $8 billion; expenditures $5 billion, including capital expenditures (1991 est.)
Defence Expenditures: 5.6% of total govt. expenditure (1990)
External Debt: $12.146 billion (1992)
Exports: $4.071 billion (1992); commodities: machinery and equipment 60.5%, agricultural products 14.7%, manufactured consumer goods 10.6%, fuels, minerals, raw materials and metals 8.5%, other 5.7%; partners: socialist countries 82.5%, developed countries 6.8%, less developed countries 10.7%
Imports: $4.239 billion (1992); commodities: fuels, minerals, raw materials 45.2%, machinery and equipment 39.8%, manufactured consumer goods 4.6%, agricultural products 3.8%, other 6.6%; partners: socialist countries 80.5%, developed countries 15.1%, less developed countries 4.4%

■ HEALTH

Births: 11/1,000 population (1993)
Deaths: 12/1,000 population (1993)
Infant Mortality: 16.7 deaths/1,000 live births (1993)
Life Expectancy at Birth: 68 years male, 75 years female (1993)
No. of Physicians: 36.2/10,000 population (1992)

■ EDUCATION

Govt. Expenditure: 6.21% of govt. expenditure

(1990)
Literacy: 95%

■ COMMUNICATIONS

Daily newspapers: 20 (1992)
Televisions: 249.1/1,000 inhabitants (1992)
Radios: 436/1,000 inhabitants (1992)
Telephones: 20/100 inhabitants (1992)

■ TRANSPORTATION

Motor Vehicles: 1,500,000; 1,300,000 passenger cars (1990)
Roads: 36,908 km; 33,535 km hard-surface
Railway: 4,314 km
Air Traffic: 646,000 passengers carried (1991)
Airports: 380 airfields, all usable; 120 have permanent-surface runways

Canadian Embassy: c/o The Canadian Embassy, Budakeszi ut. 32, 1121 Budapest, Hungary. Tel: (011-36-1) 1767-312. Fax (011-36-1): 1767-689
Representative to Canada: Embassy of the Republic of Bulgaria, 325 Stewart St, Ottawa ON K1N 6K5. Tel: (613) 789-3215. Fax: (613) 789-3524.

Burkina Faso

Long-Form Name: Burkina Faso
Capital: Ouagadougou
Population: 10,000,000 (1993 est.)

■ GEOGRAPHY

Area: 274,200 sq. km
Coastline: none: landlocked
Climate: tropical; warm, dry winters; hot, wet summers
Environment: recent droughts and desertification severely affecting marginal agricultural activities, population distribution, economy; overgrazing; desertification
Terrain: mostly flat to dissected, undulating plains; hills in west and southeast
Land Use: 10% arable land; negligible permanent crops; 37% meadows and pastures; 26% forest and woodland; 27% other; includes negligible irrigated
Location: WC Africa

■ PEOPLE

Nationality: Burkina-be
Ethnic Groups: more than 50 tribes; principal tribe is Mossi (about 2.5 million); other important groups are Gurunsi, Senufo, Lobi, Bobo, Mande and Fulani
Languages: French (official); tribal languages belong to Sudanic family, spoken by 90% of population
Religions: 65% indigenous beliefs, about 25% Moslem, 10% Christian (mainly Roman Catholic)
Marriages: n.a.
Divorces: n.a.

■ GOVERNMENT

Leader(s): Head of State, Head of Government & Chairman, Capt. Blaise Compaoré, Prime Min. Roch Christian Kabore
Government Type: parliamentary democracy
Administrative Divisions: 30 provinces
Independence: Aug. 5, 1960 (from France; Burkina Faso formerly known as Upper Volta)
National Holiday: Anniversary of the Revolution, Aug. 4

■ ECONOMY

Overview: a poor economy with high population density and few natural resources, it relies heavily on subsistence agriculture; economic development is hindered by a poor communication network; agriculture provides approximately 40% of national income
GNP: $3.213 billion, per capita $350; real growth rate 4% (1991)
Inflation: -1.4% (1992)
Industries: agricultural processing plants; brewery, cement and brick plants; soap, cigarettes, textiles, gold mining and extraction; a few other small consumer goods enterprises
Labour Force: 4,170,000 (1992); 86.6% agriculture, 4.3% industry, 9.1% services; 20% of male labour force migrates annually to neighbouring countries for seasonal employment (1989)
Unemployment: n.a.
Agriculture: accounts for 30-40% of GDP; cash crops—peanuts, shea nuts, sesame, cotton; food crops—sorghum, millet, corn, rice; livestock; not self-sufficient in food grains
Natural Resources: manganese, limestone, marble; small deposits of gold, antimony, copper, nickel, bauxite, lead, phosphates, zinc, silver

■ FINANCE/TRADE

Currency: Communauté financière africaine franc (CFAF)
International Reserves Excluding Gold: $405 million (Sept. 1993)
Gold Reserves: 0.01 million fine troy ounces (1991)
Budget: revenues $495 million; expenditures $786 million, including capital expenditures (1991)
Defence Expenditures: $76.40 million (1990)
External Debt: $1.055 billion (1992)

Exports: $105 million (1991); commodities: oilseeds, cotton, live animals, gold; partners: European Community 42%, Taiwan 17%, Ivory Coast 15%
Imports: $566 million (1991); commodities: grain, dairy products, petroleum, machinery; partners: European Community 37%, Africa 31%, US 15%

■ HEALTH

Births: 50/1,000 population (1993)
Deaths: 16/1,000 population (1993)
Infant Mortality: 119 deaths/1,000 live births (1993)
Life Expectancy at Birth: 52 years male, 53 years female (1993)
No. of Physicians: 0.2/10,000 population (1992)

■ EDUCATION

Govt. Expenditure: 17.5% of government expenditure (1989)
Literacy: 18% (1993)

■ COMMUNICATIONS

Daily newspapers: 4 (1992)
Televisions: 5.1/1,000 inhabitants (1992)
Radios: 26/1,000 inhabitants (1992)
Telephones: 0.2/100 inhabitants (1992)

■ TRANSPORTATION

Motor Vehicles: 25,000; 12,000 passenger cars (1990)
Roads: 16,500 km; 1,300 km paved (1993)
Railway: 620 km (1993)
Air Traffic: 124,000 passengers carried (1991)
Airports: 48, of which 38 are usable; 2 have permanent-surface runways (1993)

Canadian Embassy: Canadian Development Centre, Ouagadougou; mailing address: Office of the Canadian Embassy, P.O. Box 548, Ouagadougou, Province du Kadiogo, Burkina Faso. Tel: (011-226) 31-18-94. Fax (011-226) 31-19-00
Representative to Canada: Embassy of Burkina Faso, 48 Range Rd, Ottawa ON K1N 8J4. Tel: (613) 238-4796. Fax: (613) 238-3812.

Burundi

Long-Form Name: Republic of Burundi
Capital: Bujumbura
Population: 5,800,000 (1993 est.)

■ GEOGRAPHY

Area: 27,830 sq. km
Coastline: none: landlocked

Climate: temperate; warm; occasional frost in uplands
Environment: soil exhaustion; soil erosion; deforestation
Terrain: mostly rolling to hilly highland; some plains
Land Use: 43% arable land; 8% permanent crops; 35% meadows and pastures; 2% forest and woodland; 12% other; includes negligible irrigated
Location: EC Africa

■ PEOPLE

Nationality: Burundian
Ethnic Groups: Africans: 85% Hutu (Bantu), 14% Tutsi (Hamitic), 1% Twa (Pygmy); non-Africans: 3,000 Europeans, 2,000 South Asians
Languages: Kirundi and French (official); Swahili used commercially
Religions: about 67% Christian (62% Roman Catholic, 5% Protestant), 32% indigenous beliefs, 1% Moslem
Marriages: n.a.
Divorces: n.a.

■ GOVERNMENT

Leader(s): Prime Min. Anatole Kanyenkino, Pres. Sylvestre Ntibantunganya (acting)
Government Type: republic
Administrative Divisions: 15 provinces
Independence: July 1, 1962 (from UN trusteeship under Belgian administration)
National Holiday: Independence Day, July 1

■ ECONOMY

Overview: economy is heavily dependent on the coffee crop and therefore vulnerable to market conditions; there are only a few basic industries
GNP: $1.210 billion, per capita $210; real growth rate 4.3% (1991)
Inflation: 4.7% (1992)
Industries: light consumer goods such as blankets, shoes, soap; assembly of imports; public works construction; food processing
Labour Force: 2,820,000 (1992); 93% agriculture, 1.5% industry and commerce, 5.5% services (1989)
Unemployment: 14,471 (1990)
Agriculture: accounts for 60% of GDP; 90% of population dependent on subsistence farming; marginally self-sufficient in food production; cash crops–coffee, cotton, tea; food crops–corn, sorghum, sweet potatoes, bananas, manioc; livestock–meat, milk, hides and skins
Natural Resources: nickel, uranium, rare earth oxide, peat, cobalt, copper, platinum (not yet exploited), vanadium

■ FINANCE/TRADE

Currency: Burundi franc (FBu)
International Reserves Excluding Gold: $163 million (Dec. 1993)
Gold Reserves: 0.02 million fine troy ounces (Dec. 1993)
Budget: revenues $318 million; expenditures $326 million, including capital expenditures of $150 million (1991 est.)
Defence Expenditures: $32.05 million (1988)
External Debt: $1.023 billion (1992)
Exports: $76 million (1992); commodities: coffee 88%, tea, hides and skins; partners: European Community 83%, US 5%, Asia 2%
Imports: $230 million (1992); commodities: capital goods 31%, petroleum products 15%, foodstuffs, consumer goods; partners: European Community 57%, Asia 23%, US 3%

■ HEALTH

Births: 47/1,000 population (1993)
Deaths: 15/1,000 population (1993)
Infant Mortality: 109 deaths/1,000 live births (1993)
Life Expectancy at Birth: 50 years male, 54 years female (1993)
No. of Physicians: 0.5/10,000 population (1992)

■ EDUCATION

Govt. Expenditure: 17.7% of govt. expenditure (1991)
Literacy: 50.0% (1993)

■ COMMUNICATIONS

Daily newspapers: 1 (1992)
Televisions: 0.6/1,000 inhabitants (1992)
Radios: 57/1,000 inhabitants (1992)
Telephones: 0.2/100 inhabitants (1992)

■ TRANSPORTATION

Motor Vehicles: 19,500; 8,500 passenger cars (1990)
Roads: 5,900 km; 400 km paved
Railway: n.a.
Air Traffic: 8,000 passengers carried (1991)
Airports: 5, of which 4 are usable; 1 has a permanent-surface runway (1993)

Canadian Embassy: c/o The Canadian High Commission, P.O. Box 30481, Nairobi, Kenya. Tel: (011-254-2) 21-48-04. Fax: (011-254-2) 22-69-87
Representative to Canada: Embassy of the Republic of Burundi, 151 Slater St, Ste 800, Ottawa ON K1P 5H3. Tel: (613) 236-8483.

Fax: (613) 563-1827.

Cambodia

Long-Form Name: Cambodia
Capital: Phnom Penh
Population: 9,000,000 (1993 est.)

■ GEOGRAPHY

Area: 181,040 sq. km
Coastline: 443 km
Climate: tropical; rainy, monsoon season (May to Oct.); dry season (Dec. to Mar.); little seasonal temperature variation
Environment: a land of paddies and forests dominated by Mekong River and Tonle Sap
Terrain: mostly low, flat plains; mountains in southwest and north
Land Use: 16% arable land; 1% permanent crops; 3% meadows and pastures; 76% forest and woodland; 4% other; includes 1% irrigated
Location: SE Asia, bordering on the Gulf of Siam

■ PEOPLE

Nationality: Cambodian
Ethnic Groups: 90% Khmer (Cambodian), 5% Vietnamese, 1% Chinese, 5% other minorities
Languages: Khmer (official), French
Religions: 95% Theravada Buddhism, 5% Christianity
Marriages: n.a.
Divorces: n.a.

■ GOVERNMENT

Leader(s): King Norodom Sihanouk, First Premier Norodom Ranariddh, Second Premier Hun Sen
Government Type: transitional government
Administrative Divisions: 20 provinces, 1 autonomous municipality
Independence: Nov. 9, 1949 (from France)
National Holiday: NGC-Independence Day, Apr. 17; SOC-Liberation Day, Jan. 7

■ ECONOMY

Overview: a desperately poor country; the economy has suffered badly due to internal war; the country has not been able to feed its people; economy remains essentially rural, with 90% of the population dependent mainly on subsistence agriculture
GNP: $1.725 billion, per capita $200; real growth rate 0% (1991)
Inflation: 250-300% (1992 est.)
Industries: rice milling, fishing, wood and wood products, rubber, cement, gem mining

Labour Force: 3.76 million (1992); 74.4% agriculture, 6.7% industry, 18.9% services (1989)
Unemployment: n.a.
Agriculture: mainly subsistence farming except for rubber plantations; main crops—rice, rubber, corn; food shortages—rice, meat, vegetables, dairy products, sugar, flour
Natural Resources: timber, gemstones, some iron ore, manganese, phosphates, hydroelectricity potential

■ **FINANCE/TRADE**

Currency: riel (KR)
International Reserves Excluding Gold: n.a.
Gold Reserves: n.a.
Budget: revenues $120 million, expenditures n.a. (1992)
Defence Expenditures: n.a.
External Debt: $717 million (1990)
Exports: $32 million (1988); commodities: natural rubber, rice, pepper, wood; partners: Vietnam, USSR, Eastern Europe, Japan, India
Imports: $147 million (1988); commodities: international food aid, fuels, consumer goods; partners: Vietnam, USSR, Eastern Europe, Japan, India

■ **HEALTH**

Births: 41/1,000 population (1993)
Deaths: 15/1,000 population (1993)
Infant Mortality: 123 deaths/1,000 live births (1993)
Life Expectancy at Birth: 48 years male, 51 years female (1993)
No. of Physicians: n.a.

■ **EDUCATION**

Govt. Expenditure: n.a.
Literacy: 35% (1993)

■ **COMMUNICATIONS**

Daily newspapers: 1 (1992)
Televisions: 8.1/1,000 inhabitants (1992)
Radios: 107/1,000 inhabitants (1992)
Telephones: n.a.

■ **TRANSPORTATION**

Motor Vehicles: n.a.
Roads: 13,759 km; 2,716 km paved
Railway: 670 km, much inoperational since 1973
Air Traffic: n.a.
Airports: 15 airfields, of which 9 are usable; 5 have permanent-surface runways (1993)

Canadian Embassy: The Canadian Office, c/o The Australian Embassy, Villa II, Street 254, Chartaumuk, Daun Penh District, Phnom Penh.

Tel: (011-855-23) 26-000. **Fax:** (011-855-23) 26-003.

Cameroon

Long-Form Name: Republic of Cameroon
Capital: Yaoundé
Population: 12,800,000 (1993 est.)

■ **GEOGRAPHY**

Area: 475,440 sq. km
Coastline: 402 km
Climate: varies with terrain from tropical along coast to semi-arid and hot in north
Environment: recent volcanic activity with release of poisonous gases; deforestation; overgrazing; desertification
Terrain: diverse with coastal plain in southwest, dissected plateau in centre, mountains in west, plains in north
Land Use: 13% arable land; 2% permanent crops; 18% meadows and pastures; 54% forest and woodland; 13% other; includes negligible irrigated
Location: WC Africa, bordering on South Atlantic Ocean

■ **PEOPLE**

Nationality: Cameroonian
Ethnic Groups: over 200 tribes of widely differing background; 31% Cameroon Highlanders, 19% Equatorial Bantu, 11% Kirdi, 10% Fulani, 8% Northwestern Bantu, 7% Eastern Nigritic, 13% other African, less than 1% non-African
Languages: English and French (official), 24 major African language groups, including Fang, Bamileke, Duala
Religions: 51% indigenous beliefs, 33% Christian, 16% Moslem
Marriages: n.a.
Divorces: n.a.

■ **GOVERNMENT**

Leader(s): Pres. Paul Biya, Prime Min. Simon Achidi Achu
Government Type: unitary republic; multi-party presidential regime (opposition parties legalized in 1990)
Administrative Divisions: 10 provinces
Independence: Jan. 1, 1960 (from UN trusteeship under French administration; Cameroon formerly known as French Cameroon)
National Holiday: National Day, May 20

■ **ECONOMY**

Overview: an offshore oil industry has boosted the economy but the government is now emphasizing diversification, particularly in agriculture

GNP: $11.320 billion, per capita $940; real growth rate 2.1% (1991)
Inflation: -2.3% (1989)
Industries: crude oil products, small aluminum plant, food processing, light consumer goods industries, textiles, sawmills
Labour Force: 4.365 million (1992); 74% agriculture, 4.5% industry, 21.5% services (1989)
Unemployment: 25% (1990 est.)
Agriculture: the agriculture and forestry sectors provide employment for the majority of the population, contributing nearly 25% to GDP and providing a high degree of self-sufficiency in staple foods
Natural Resources: crude oil, bauxite, iron ore, timber, hydroelectricity potential

■ **FINANCE/TRADE**

Currency: Communauté financière africaine franc (CFAF)
International Reserves Excluding Gold: $2 million (Dec. 1993)
Gold Reserves: 0.30 million fine troy ounces (Oct. 1993)
Budget: revenues $1.7 billion; expenditures $2.4 billion, capital expenditures $422 million (1990 est.)
Defence Expenditures: $142.7 million (6.67% of total govt. expenditure) (1989)
External Debt: $6.554 billion (1992)
Exports: $1.815 billion (1992); commodities: petroleum products 56%, coffee, cocoa, timber, manufacturing; partners: European Community 50%, US 3%
Imports: $1.175 billion (1992); commodities: machines and electrical equipment, transport equipment, chemical products, consumer goods; partners: France 42%, Japan 7%, US 4%

■ **HEALTH**

Births: 41/1,000 population (1993)
Deaths: 12/1,000 population (1993)
Infant Mortality: 82 deaths/1,000 live births (1993)
Life Expectancy at Birth: 54 years male, 58 years female (1993)
No. of Physicians: 0.7/10,000 inhabitants (1980)

■ **EDUCATION**

Govt. Expenditure: 16.9% of govt. expenditure (1991)
Literacy: 54.1% (1992)

■ **COMMUNICATIONS**

Daily newspapers: 2 (1992)
Televisions: 2.1/1,000 inhabitants (1992)
Radios: 131/1,000 inhabitants (1992)

Telephones: 0.6/100 inhabitants (1992)

■ **TRANSPORTATION**

Motor Vehicles: 175,000; 93,000 passenger cars (1990)
Roads: 65,000 km; 2,682 km paved (1993)
Railway: 1,115 km
Air Traffic: 357,000 passengers carried (1991)
Airports: 59 airfields, of which 51 are usable; 11 have permanent-surface runways (1993)

Canadian Embassy: Canadian Embassy, Édifice Stamatiades, Place de l'Hôtel de Ville, Yaoundé; mailing address: CP 572, Yaoundé, Cameroon. Tel: (011-237) 23-02-03. Fax: (011-237) 22-10-90
Representative to Canada: Embassy of the Republic of Cameroon, 170 Clemow Ave, Ottawa ON K1S 2B4. Tel: (613) 236-1522.

Canada

Long-Form Name: Canada
Capital: Ottawa
Population: 28,100,000 (1993 est.)

■ **GEOGRAPHY**

Area: 9,976,140 sq. km
Coastline: 243,791 km
Climate: varies from temperate in south to sub-arctic and arctic in north
Environment: 80% of population concentrated within 160 km of US border; continuous permafrost in north a serious obstacle to development
Terrain: mostly plains with mountains in west and lowlands in southeast
Land Use: 5% arable land; negligible permanent crops; 3% meadows and pastures; 35% forest and woodland; 57% other; includes negligible irrigated
Location: N North America, bordering on North Atlantic Ocean, Arctic Ocean, North Pacific Ocean

■ **PEOPLE**

Nationality: Canadian
Ethnic Groups: 40% British, 27% French, 20% other European, 11.5% other, 1.5% indigenous
Languages: English and French (both official)
Religions: 46% Roman Catholic, 16% United Church, 10% Anglican, 28% other
Marriages: 7.3 (per 1,000) (1989)
Divorces: 3.08 (per 1,000) (1989)

■ **GOVERNMENT**

Leader(s): Gov. Gen. Ramon John Hnatyshyn,

Prime Min. Jean Chrétien
Government Type: confederation with parliamentary democracy
Administrative Divisions: 10 provinces, two territories
Independence: July 1, 1867 (from UK)
National Holiday: Canada Day, July 1

■ ECONOMY

Overview: abundant natural resources, skilled labour force, and high-tech industrialization characterize a market-oriented economy
GNP: n.a., GDP $537.1 billion, per capita $19,600; real growth rate 0.9% (1992)
Inflation: 1.5% (1992)
Industries: processsed and unprocessed minerals, food products, wood and paper products, transportation equipment, chemicals, fish products, petroleum, natural gas
Labour Force: 13,360,000 (1992); 77.2% services, 19.4% industry, 3.4% agriculture (1989)
Unemployment: 11.5% (1992)
Agriculture: accounts for 3% of GDP; one of the world's major producers and exporters of grain (wheat and barley); key source of US agricultural imports; large forest resources cover 35% of total land area
Natural Resources: nickel, zinc, copper, gold, lead, molybdenum, potash, silver, fish, timber, wildlife, coal, crude oil, natural gas

■ FINANCE/TRADE

Currency: dollar ($ or $Can)
International Reserves Excluding Gold: $12,790 million (Jan. 1994)
Gold Reserves: 5.96 million fine troy ounces (Jan. 1994)
Budget: revenues $105.8 billion; expenditures $131.6 billion, capital expenditures n.a. (1990)
Defence Expenditures: $11.42 billion (1991)
External Debt: $247 billion (1987)
Exports: $144.072 billion (1993); commodities: newsprint, wood pulp, timber, grain, crude petroleum, natural gas, ferrous and nonferrous ores, motor vehicles; partners: US, Japan, UK, Germany, other European Community, USSR
Imports: $131.167 billion (1993); commodities: processed foods, beverages, crude petroleum, chemicals, industrial machinery, motor vehicles, durable consumer goods, electronic computers; partners: US, Japan, UK, Germany, other European Community, Taiwan, S Korea, Mexico

■ HEALTH

Births: 15/1,000 population (1993)
Deaths: 7/1,000 population (1993)

Infant Mortality: 6.8 deaths/1,000 live births (1993)
Life Expectancy at Birth: 74 years male, 81 years female (1993)
No. of Physicians: 19.6/10,000 population (1992)

■ EDUCATION

Govt. Expenditure: 15.6% of govt. expenditure (1990)
Literacy: 99% (1993)

■ COMMUNICATIONS

Daily newspapers: 107 (1992)
Televisions: 626.3/1,000 inhabitants (1992)
Radios: 1,023/1,000 inhabitants (1992)
Telephones: 78.02/100 inhabitants (1992)

■ TRANSPORTATION

Motor Vehicles: 16,553,385; 12,622,038 passenger cars (1990)
Roads: 884,272 km; 712,936 km surfaced, 250,023 km paved (1993)
Railway: 146,444 km
Air Traffic: 16,586,000 passengers carried (1991)
Airports: 1,420 airfields, of which 1,142 are usable; 457 have permanent-surface runways (1993)

Cape Verde

Long-Form Name: Republic of Cape Verde
Capital: Praia
Population: 400,000 (1993 est.)

■ GEOGRAPHY

Area: 4,030 sq. km
Coastline: 965 km
Climate: temperate; warm, dry, very erratic summer precipitation
Environment: subject to prolonged droughts; harmattan wind can obscure visibility; volcanically and seismically active; deforestation; overgrazing
Terrain: steep, rugged, rocky, volcanic
Land Use: 9% arable land; negligible permanent crops; 6% meadows and pastures; negligible forest and woodland; 85% other; includes 1% irrigated
Location: Atlantic Ocean W of Africa

■ PEOPLE

Nationality: Cape Verdean
Ethnic Groups: approx. 71% Creole (mulatto), 28% African, 1% European
Languages: Portuguese and Crioulo, a blend of Portuguese and West African tongues
Religions: Roman Catholicism fused with

indigenous beliefs
Marriages: n.a.
Divorces: n.a.

■ GOVERNMENT

Leader(s): Pres. Antonio Mascarenhas Monteiro, Prime Min. Carlos Alberto Wahnon de Carvalho Veiga
Government Type: republic
Administrative Divisions: 14 districts
Independence: July 5, 1975 (from Portugal)
National Holiday: Independence Day, July 5

■ ECONOMY

Overview: a service-oriented economy which suffers from a poor natural resource base, a high birth rate and a long-term drought
GNP: $285 million, per capita $750; real growth rate 4.8% (1991)
Inflation: 3.8% (1987)
Industries: fish processing, salt mining, clothing factories, ship repair, construction materials, food and beverage production
Labour Force: 141,000 (1992); 52% agriculture (mostly subsistence), 25% services, 23% industry (1989)
Unemployment: 25% (1988)
Agriculture: accounts for 20% of GDP; largely subsistence farming; bananas are the only export crop; annual food imports required; growth potential limited by poor soils and limited rainfall
Natural Resources: salt, basalt rock, pozzolana, limestone, kaolin, fish

■ FINANCE/TRADE

Currency: Cape Verdean escudo (C.V. Esc.)
International Reserves Excluding Gold: $71 million (July 1993)
Gold Reserves: n.a.
Budget: revenues $104 million; expenditures $133 million, including capital expenditures of $72 million (1991 est.)
Defence Expenditures: n.a.
External Debt: $160 million (1992)
Exports: $5 million (1992); commodities: fish, bananas, salt; partners: Portugal, Angola, Algeria, Belgium/Luxembourg, Italy
Imports: $180 million (1992); commodities: petroleum, foodstuffs, consumer goods, industrial products; partners: Portugal, Netherlands, Spain, France, US, Germany

■ HEALTH

Births: 36/1,000 population (1993)
Deaths: 8/1,000 population (1993)
Infant Mortality: 47 deaths/1,000 live births

(1993)
Life Expectancy at Birth: 66 years male, 68 years female (1993)
No. of Physicians: 1.9/10,000 population (1990)

■ EDUCATION

Govt. Expenditure: 19.9% of govt. expenditure (1991)
Literacy: 66.5% (1992)

■ COMMUNICATIONS

Daily newspapers: 0; 3 non-daily
Televisions: n.a.
Radios: 158/1,000 inhabitants (1992)
Telephones: 0.81/100 inhabitants (1992)

■ TRANSPORTATION

Motor Vehicles: 14,500; 10,000 passenger cars (1990)
Roads: 2,249 km; 601 km paved
Railway: n.a.
Air Traffic: 177,000 passengers carried (1991)
Airports: 6 airfields, all usable and with permanent-surface runways (1993)

Canadian Embassy: c/o The Canadian Embassy, 45 av. de la République, Dakar; mailing address: P.O. Box 3373, Dakar, Senegal. Tel: (011-221) 23-92-90. Fax: (011-221) 23-87-49.
Representative to Canada: c/o Embassy of the Republic of Cape Verde, 3415 Massachusetts Ave NW, Washington, DC 20007 USA. Tel: (202) 965-6820. Fax: (202) 965-1207.

Cayman Islands

United Kingdom Crown Colony

Long-Form Name: Cayman Islands
Capital: George Town (on Grand Cayman Island)
Population: 30,440 (1993 est.)

■ GEOGRAPHY

Area: 260 sq. km (three islands: Grand Cayman, Little Cayman, Cayman Brac)
Climate: tropical maritime; warm, rainy summers (May to Oct.); cool season: Nov. to March, hurricane-prone July to Nov.
Land Use: negligible arable, permanent crops; 8% meadows and pastures; 23% forest and woodland; 69% other
Location: Caribbean Sea, S of Cuba

■ PEOPLE

Nationality: Caymanian
Ethnic Groups: 40% mixed, 20% white, 20%

black, 20% expatriates of various ethnic groups, various Hispanic strains, descendants of European settlers
Languages: English (official)

■ **GOVERNMENT**

Leader(s): Gov. Michael Gore
Government Type: United Kingdom Crown Colony
National Holiday: Constitution Day (first Monday in July)

■ **ECONOMY**

Overview: chiefly tourism (70% of GDP and 75% of export earnings), financial services; main export turtle products; imports: foodstuffs, manufactured items, textiles, building materials, cars, petroleum products

■ **FINANCE/TRADE**

Currency: Caymanian dollar (CI$)

Central African Republic

Long-Form Name: Central African Republic
Capital: Bangui
Population: 3,100,000 (1993 est.)

■ **GEOGRAPHY**

Area: 622,980 sq. km
Coastline: none: landlocked
Climate: tropical; hot, dry winters; mild to hot, wet summers
Environment: hot, dry, dusty harmattan winds affect northern areas; poaching has diminished reputation as one of last great wildlife refuges; desertification
Terrain: vast, flat to rolling, monotonous plateau; scattered hills in northeast and southwest
Land Use: 3% arable land; negligible permanent crops; 5% meadows and pastures; 64% forest and woodland; 28% other
Location: C Africa

■ **PEOPLE**

Nationality: Central African
Ethnic Groups: about 80 ethnic groups, the majority of which have related ethnic and linguistic characteristics; 34% Baya, 27% Banda, 10% Sara, 21% Mandjia, 4% Mboum, 4% m'Baka; 6,500 Europeans, of whom 3,600 are French
Languages: French (official); Sangho (lingua franca and national language); Arabic, Hunsa, Swahili
Religions: 24% indigenous beliefs, 25% Protestant, 25% Roman Catholic, 15% Moslem,

11% other; animistic beliefs and practices strongly influence the Christian majority
Marriages: n.a.
Divorces: n.a.

■ **GOVERNMENT**

Leader(s): Pres. Ange Felix Patassé, Prime Min. Jean-Luc Mandaba
Government Type: republic, one-party presidential regime since 1986
Administrative Divisions: 16 prefectures, 1 capital commune
Independence: Aug. 13, 1960 (from France; formerly known as Central African Empire)
National Holiday: National Day (proclamation of the republic), Dec. 1

■ **ECONOMY**

Overview: subsistence agriculture is the backbone of the economy (mainly forestry). It suffers from a poor transportation infrastructure and a weak human resource base; diamond industry accounts for 30% of export earnings
GNP: $1.218 billion, per capita $390; real growth rate 1.2% (1991)
Inflation: -2.8% (1991)
Industries: sawmills, breweries, diamond mining, textiles, footwear, assembly of bicycles and motorcycles
Labour Force: 1.38 million (1992); 83.7% agriculture, 13.5% services, 2.8% industry (1989)
Unemployment: 30% (1988)
Agriculture: accounts for 40% of GDP; self-sufficient in food production except for grain; commercial crops—cotton, coffee, tobacco, timber; food crops—manioc, yams, millet, corn, bananas
Natural Resources: diamonds, uranium, timber, gold, oil

■ **FINANCE/TRADE**

Currency: Communauté financière africaine franc (CFAF)
International Reserves Excluding Gold: $112 million (Dec. 1993)
Gold Reserves: 0.01 million fine troy ounces (1991)
Budget: revenues $175 million; expenditures $312 million, including capital expenditures of 122 million (1991 est.)
Defence Expenditures: $18.67 million (1988)
External Debt: $901 million (1992)
Exports: $74 million (1991); commodities: diamonds, cotton, coffee, timber, tobacco; partners: France, Belgium, Italy, Japan, US
Imports: $145 million (1991); commodities: food, textiles, petroleum products, machinery,

electrical equipment, motor vehicles, chemicals, pharmaceuticals, consumer goods, industrial products; partners: France, other European Community, Japan, Algeria, Yugoslavia

■ **HEALTH**

Births: 44/1,000 population (1993)
Deaths: 18/1,000 population (1993)
Infant Mortality: 140 deaths/1,000 live births (1993)
Life Expectancy at Birth: 45 years male, 48 years female (1993)
No. of Physicians: 0.5/10,000 population (1990)

■ **EDUCATION**

Govt. Expenditure: 16.8% of govt. expenditure (1989)
Literacy: 27% (1993)

■ **COMMUNICATIONS**

Daily newspapers: 1 (1992)
Televisions: 3.4/1,000 inhabitants (1992)
Radios: 61/1,000 inhabitants (1992)
Telephones: 0.26/100 inhabitants (1992)

■ **TRANSPORTATION**

Motor Vehicles: 22,000; 12,000 passenger cars (1984)
Roads: 22,000 km; 458 km paved (1993)
Railway: none, but line of 800 km proposed for construction (1985)
Air Traffic: 118,000 passengers carried (1991)
Airports: 66 airfields, of which 51 are usable; 3 have permanent-surface runways (1993)

Canadian Embassy: c/o Canadian Embassy, Édifice Stamatiades, Place de l'Hôtel de Ville, Yaoundé; mailing address: CP 572, Yaoundé, Cameroon. Tel: (011-237) 23-02-03. Fax: (011-237) 22-10-90.
Representative to Canada: c/o Embassy of the Central African Republic, 1618-22nd St NW, Washington, DC 20008 USA. Tel: (202) 483-7800.

Chad

Long-Form Name: Republic of Chad
Capital: N'Djamena
Population: 5,400,000 (1993)

■ **GEOGRAPHY**

Area: 1,284,000 sq. km
Coastline: none: landlocked
Climate: tropical in south, desert in north
Environment: hot, dry, dusty harmattan winds occur in north; drought and desertification adversely affecting south; subject to plagues of locusts
Terrain: broad, arid plains in centre, desert in north, mountains in northwest, lowlands in south
Land Use: 2% arable land; negligible permanent crops; 36% meadows and pastures; 11% forest and woodland; 51% others; includes negligible irrigated
Location: NC Africa

■ **PEOPLE**

Nationality: Chadian
Ethnic Groups: some 200 distinct ethnic groups, most of whom are Moslems in the north and centre, and non-Moslems in the south; some 150,000 non-indigenous, of whom 1,000 are French
Languages: French and Arabic (official); Sara and Sango in south; more than 100 different languages and dialects are spoken
Religions: 44% Moslem, 33% Christian, remainder indigenous beliefs, animism
Marriages: n.a.
Divorces: n.a.

■ **GOVERNMENT**

Leader(s): Pres. Col. Idriss Deby, Prime Min. Delwa Kassire Koumakoye
Government Type: republic
Administrative Divisions: 14 prefectures
Independence: Aug. 11, 1960 (from France)
National Holiday: Aug. 11

■ **ECONOMY**

Overview: Chad is one of the world's most underdeveloped countries; civil war, drought and food shortages have adversely affected the economy which is based on subsistence farming and fishing
GNP: $1.212 billion, per capita $220; real growth rate 6.3% (1991)
Inflation: -4.1% (1992)
Industries: cotton textile mills, slaughterhouses, soap, cigarettes, brewery, natron (sodium carbonate)
Labour Force: 1.97 million (1992); 83% agriculture (engaged in unpaid subsistence farming, herding and fishing), 12% services, 5% industry (1989)
Unemployment: 10,715 (1989)
Agriculture: accounts for 45% of GDP; largely subsistence farming; cotton most important cash crop; food crops include sorghum, millet, peanuts, rice, potatoes, manioc; livestock—cattle, sheep, goats, camels; self-sufficient in food in years of adequate rainfall

Natural Resources: small quantities of crude oil (unexploited but exploration beginning), uranium, natron, kaolin, fish (Lake Chad)

■ FINANCE/TRADE

Currency: Communauté financière africaine franc (CFAF)
International Reserves Excluding Gold: $84 million (1991)
Gold Reserves: 0.01 million fine troy ounces (1990)
Budget: revenues $115 million; expenditures $412 million, not including capital expenditures of $218 million that are mostly financed by foreign aid donors (1991 est.)
Defence Expenditures: $57.99 million (1989)
External Debt: $729 million (1992)
Exports: $194 million (1991); commodities: cotton 43%, cattle 35%, textiles 5%, fish; partners: France, Nigeria, Cameroon
Imports: $297 million (1991); commodities: machinery and transportation equipment 39%, industrial goods 20%, petroleum products 13%, foodstuffs 9%; partners: US, France

■ HEALTH

Births: 44/1,000 population (1993)
Deaths: 19/1,000 population (1993)
Infant Mortality: 127 deaths/1,000 live births (1993)
Life Expectancy at Birth: 45 years male, 48 years female (1993)
No. of Physicians: 0.3/10,000 population (1992)

■ EDUCATION

Govt. Expenditure: 2.3% of GNP (1991)
Literacy: 30% (1993)

■ COMMUNICATIONS

Daily newspapers: 1 (1992)
Televisions: 1.0/1,000 inhabitants (1992)
Radios: 237/1,000 inhabitants (1992)
Telephones: 0.18/100 inhabitants (1992)

■ TRANSPORTATION

Motor Vehicles: 15,000; 8,500 passenger cars (1990)
Roads: 32,100 km; 32 km paved
Railway: n.a.
Air Traffic: 81,000 passengers carried (1991)
Airports: 69 airfields, of which 55 are usable; 5 have permanent-surface runways (1993)

Canadian Embassy: c/o The Canadian Embassy, Édifice Stamatiades, Place de l'Hôtel de Ville, Yaoundé; mailing address: CP 572, Yaoundé, Cameroon. Tel: (011-237) 23-02-03. Fax: (011-

237) 22-10-90.
Representative to Canada: c/o Embassy of the Republic of Chad, 2002 R St NW, Washington, DC 20009 USA. Tel: (202) 462-4009.

Channel Islands

Dependent Territory of the United Kingdom

Long-Form Name: Channel Islands; Guernsey: Bailiwick of Guernsey; Jersey: Bailiwick of Jersey
Capital: St. Helier (Jersey), St. Peter Port (Guernsey)
Population: Jersey: 85,450; Guernsey: 63,075 (1993 est.)

■ GEOGRAPHY

Area: Jersey: 117 sq. km; Guernsey: 194 sq. km
Climate: temperate, with mild winters and cool summers
Land Use: Jersey: 57% arable, remainder n.a.; Guernsey: n.a.
Location: English Channel, off the coast of France

■ PEOPLE

Nationality: Channel Islander
Ethnic Groups: English, French
Languages: English (official), French (official only on Jersey), Norman-French dialect

■ GOVERNMENT

Leader(s): Jersey: Lt. Gov. & Commander-in-Chief Air Marshal Sir John Sutton; Guernsey: Lt. Gov. & Commander-in-Chief Capt. D.P.L. Hodgetts
Government Type: largely self-governing British Crown dependency
National Holiday: Liberation Day, May 9

■ ECONOMY

Overview: Jersey: economy is based chiefly on financial services, agriculture and tourism, vegetable and flower exports, Jersey cattle; Guernsey: tourism, financial services, Guernsey cattle, and tomato and flower exports make up backbone of the economy

■ FINANCE/TRADE

Currency: Jersey pound, Guernsey pound; both are at par with the British pound

Chile

Long-Form Name: Republic of Chile

Capital: Santiago
Population: 13,500,000 (1993 est.)

■ GEOGRAPHY

Area: 756,950 sq. km
Coastline: 6,435 km
Climate: temperate; desert in north; cool and damp in south
Environment: subject to severe earthquakes, active volcanism, tsunami; Atacama Desert one of world's driest regions; desertification
Terrain: low coastal mountains; fertile central valley; rugged Andes in east
Land Use: 7% arable land; negligible permanent crops; 16% meadows and pastures; 21% forest and woodland; 56% other; includes 2% irrigated
Location: W South America

■ PEOPLE

Nationality: Chilean
Ethnic Groups: 95% European and European-Indian, 3% Indian, 2% other
Languages: Spanish
Religions: 89% Roman Catholic, 11% Protestant and small Jewish population
Marriages: 7.5 (per 1,000) (1990)
Divorces: 0.46 (per 1,000) (1990)

■ GOVERNMENT

Leader(s): Pres. Eduardo Frei Ruiz-Tagle
Government Type: republic
Administrative Divisions: 13 regions
Independence: Sept. 18, 1810 (from Spain)
National Holiday: Independence Day, Sept. 18

■ ECONOMY

Overview: copper is the single largest export in this economy which has benefited from growth in industry, agriculture and construction
GNP: n.a., GDP $34.7 billion, per capita $2,550; real growth rate 10.4% (1992 est.)
Inflation: 15.4% (1992)
Industries: copper, other minerals, foodstuffs, fish processing, iron and steel, wood and wood products, transport equipment, textiles, cement
Labour Force: 4,753,000 (1992); 38.3% services (including government), 33.8% industry, 19.2% agriculture, forestry and fishing, 2.3% mining, 6.4% construction (1990)
Unemployment: 4.9% (1992)
Agriculture: accounts for about 9% of GDP (including fishing and forestry); major exporter of fruit, fish and timber products; major crops—wheat, corn, grapes, beans, sugar beets, potatoes, fruit; net agricultural importer
Natural Resources: copper, timber, iron ore, nitrates, precious metals, molybdenum

■ FINANCE/TRADE

Currency: peso ($CH)
International Reserves Excluding Gold: $9,963 million (Jan. 1994)
Gold Reserves: 1.87 million fine troy ounces (Jan. 1994)
Budget: revenues $10.9 billion; expenditures $10.9 billion, including capital expenditures of $1.2 billion (1993)
Defence Expenditures: 9.65% of total govt. expenditure (1992)
External Debt: $19.36 billion (1992)
Exports: $10.126 billion (1992); commodities: copper 48%, industrial products 33%, molybdenum, iron ore, wood pulp, fishmeal, fruit; partners: European Community 34%, US 22%, Japan 10%, Brazil 7%
Imports: $9.670 billion (1992); commodities: petroleum, wheat, capital goods, spare parts, raw materials; partners: European Community 23%, US 20%, Japan 10%, Brazil 9%

■ HEALTH

Births: 21/1,000 population (1993)
Deaths: 6/1,000 population (1993)
Infant Mortality: 15.4 deaths/1,000 live births (1993)
Life Expectancy at Birth: 70 years male, 76 years female (1993)
No. of Physicians: 8.1/10,000 population (1992)

■ EDUCATION

Govt. Expenditure: 13.28% of govt. expenditure (1992)
Literacy: 93.4% (1992)

■ COMMUNICATIONS

Daily newspapers: 39 (1992)
Televisions: 200.6/1,000 inhabitants (1992)
Radios: 340/1,000 inhabitants (1992)
Telephones: 6.7/100 inhabitants (1992)

■ TRANSPORTATION

Motor Vehicles: 1,016,641; 706,641 passenger cars (1990)
Roads: 79,025 km; 9,913 km paved (1993)
Railway: 7,766 km (1993)
Air Traffic: 1,406,000 passengers carried (1991)
Airports: 396 airfields, of which 351 are usable; 48 have permanent-surface runways (1993)

Canadian Embassy: Ahumada 11, 10th Fl, Santiago, Chile; mailing address: Casilla 427, Santiago, Chile. Tel: (011-56-2) 696-2256. Fax: (011-56-2) 696-2424
Representative to Canada: Embassy of the Republic of Chile, 151 Slater St, Ste 605,

Ottawa ON K1P 5H3. Tel: (613) 235-9940, -4402. Fax: (613) 235-1176.

China

Long-Form Name: People's Republic of China
Capital: Beijing (formerly Peking)
Population: 1,178,500,000 (1993 est.)

■ GEOGRAPHY

Area: 9,596,960 sq. km
Coastline: 14,500 km
Climate: extremely diverse; tropical in south to subarctic in north
Environment: frequent typhoons (about five times per year along southern and eastern coasts), damaging floods, tsunamis, earthquakes; deforestation; soil erosion; industrial pollution; water pollution; desertification
Terrain: mostly mountains, high plateaus, deserts in west; plains, deltas and hills in east
Land Use: 10% arable land; negligible permanent crops; 31% meadows and pastures; 14% forest and woodland; 45% other; includes 5% irrigated
Location: SE Asia, bordering on South China Sea, Yellow Sea

■ PEOPLE

Nationality: Chinese
Ethnic Groups: 91.9% Han Chinese; 8.1% Zhuang, Uigur, Hui, Yi, Tibetan, Miao, Manchu, Mongol, Buyi, Korean and other nationalities
Languages: Standard Chinese (Putonghua) or Mandarin (based on the Beijing dialect), Yue (Cantonese), Wu (Shanghainese), Minbei (Fuzhou), Minnan. The Tibetans, Uigurs, Mongols, and others have their own languages
Religions: officially atheist, but traditionally pragmatic and eclectic; Confucianism, Taoism and Buddhism; approx. 2–3% Moslem, 1% Christian
Marriages: n.a.
Divorces: n.a.

■ GOVERNMENT

Leader(s): Pres. Jiang Zemin, V. Pres. Rong Yiren, Premier Li Peng
Government Type: Communist Party-led state
Administrative Divisions: 23 provinces, 5 autonomous regions, 3 government-controlled municipalities
Independence: People's Republic established Oct. 1, 1949
National Holiday: National Day, Oct. 1

■ ECONOMY

Overview: the Soviet-style centrally planned economy has been recently altered to include increased local authority which has increased production; population control is vital
GNP: $424.012 billion, per capita $370; real growth rate 9.4% (1991)
Inflation: 1.3% (1990)
Industries: iron, steel, coal, machine building, armaments, textiles, petroleum, chemical fertilizer, cement, consumer durables, food processing
Labour Force: 680,000,000 (1992); 73.7% agriculture and forestry, 13.6% industry, 12.7% services (1989)
Unemployment: 2.3% in urban areas (1992)
Agriculture: accounts for 26% of GNP; among the world's largest producers of rice, potatoes, sorghum, peanuts, tea, millet, barley and pork; commercial crops include cotton, other fibres and oilseeds; produces variety of livestock products; self-sufficient in food
Natural Resources: coal, iron ore, crude oil, mercury, tin, tungsten, antimony, manganese, molybdenum, vanadium, magnetite, aluminum, lead, zinc, uranium, world's greatest hydroelectric potential

■ FINANCE/TRADE

Currency: yuan (¥RMB)
International Reserves Excluding Gold: $22,076 million (Nov. 1993)
Gold Reserves: 12.7 million fine troy ounces (Nov. 1993)
Budget: deficit $16.3 billion (1992)
Defence Expenditures: $6.06 billion (1990)
External Debt: $69.321 billion (1992)
Exports: $91.721 billion (1993); commodities: manufactured goods, agricultural products, oilseeds, grain (rice and corn), oil, minerals; partners: Hong Kong, US, Japan, USSR, Singapore, Germany
Imports: $103.943 billion (1993); commodities: grain (mostly wheat), chemical fertilizer, steel, industrial raw materials, machinery, equipment; partners: Hong Kong, Japan, US, Germany, USSR

■ HEALTH

Births: 18/1,000 population (1993)
Deaths: 7/1,000 population (1993)
Infant Mortality: 53 deaths/1,000 live births (1993)
Life Expectancy at Birth: 68 years male, 71 years female (1993)
No. of Physicians: 9.9/10,000 population (1992)

■ EDUCATION

Govt. Expenditure: 12.4% of government expenditure (1989)
Literacy: 73.3% (1992)

■ COMMUNICATIONS

Daily newspapers: 78 (1992)
Televisions: 26.7/1,000 inhabitants (1992)
Radios: 184/1,000 inhabitants (1992)
Telephones: 0.97/100 inhabitants (1992)

■ TRANSPORTATION

Motor Vehicles: 5,835,865; 1,664,010 passenger cars (1990)
Roads: 1,029,000 km; 170,000 km paved (1993)
Railway: 64,000 km (1993)
Air Traffic: 19,520,000 passengers carried (1991)
Airports: 330 airfields, all usable; 260 have permanent-surface runways (1993)

Canadian Embassy: 19 Dong Zhi Men Wai St, Chao Yang District, Beijing 100600, China. Tel: (011-86-1) 532-3536. Fax (011-86-1) 532-4311
Representative to Canada: Embassy of the People's Republic of China, 515 St. Patrick St, Ottawa ON K1N 5H3. Tel: (613) 789-3434. Fax: (613) 789-1911.

Christmas Island

Dependent Territory of Australia

Long-Form Name: Territory of Christmas Island
Capital: The Settlement
Population: 1,685 (1993 est.)

■ GEOGRAPHY

Area: 135 sq. km (land area); includes one of the largest coral islands in the Pacific
Climate: tropical, with little seasonal variation, heat and humidity moderated by trade winds
Land Use: dry sandy soil does not permit much cultivation
Location: Indian Ocean (Line Islands), between Australia and Indonesia

■ PEOPLE

Nationality: Christmas Islander
Ethnic Groups: 61% Chinese, 25% Malay, 24% Austrian/European origin
Languages: English, Chinese, Oriental and European-speaking minorities

■ GOVERNMENT

Leader(s): administrator appointed by Australian Commonwealth Govt.

Government Type: dependency
Independence: none

■ ECONOMY

Overview: extraction and export of rock phosphate dust was the only significant economic activity until 1987, when the mine was closed. There are plans to reopen it, as well as to develop tourism

■ FINANCE/TRADE

Currency: Australian dollar

Cocos (Keeling) Islands

Dependent Territory of Australia

Long-Form Name: Territory of Cocos (Keeling) Islands
Capital: West Island
Population: 593 (1993 est.)

■ GEOGRAPHY

Area: 14.2 sq. km
Climate: tropical maritime modified by southeast trade wind for 9 months of the year; moderate rainfall
Land Use: primarily subsistence agriculture
Location: Indian Ocean, SW of Sumatra

■ PEOPLE

Nationality: Cocos Islander
Ethnic Groups: West Island: Europeans; Home Island: Cocos Malays
Languages: English, local and tribal

■ GOVERNMENT

Leader(s): Administrator appointed by Gov.-Gen. of Australia
Government Type: territory of Australia; dependency placed under Australian govt. authority by Cocos (Keeling) Islands Act of 1955

■ ECONOMY

Overview: little industrial activity; agriculture limited to copra and coconut cultivation

■ FINANCE/TRADE

Currency: Australian dollar

Colombia

Long-Form Name: Republic of Colombia
Capital: Bogotá
Population: 34,900,000 (1993 est.)

■ GEOGRAPHY

Area: 1,138,910 sq. km; includes Isla de Malpelo, Roncador Cay, Serrana Bank, and Serranilla Bank
Coastline: 3,208 km total (1,448 km North Pacific Ocean; 1,760 Caribbean Sea)
Climate: tropical along coast and eastern plains; cooler in highlands
Environment: highlands subject to volcanic eruptions; deforestation; soil damage from overuse of pesticides; periodic droughts
Terrain: mixture of flat coastal lowlands, plains in east, central highlands, some high mountains (Andes)
Land Use: 4% arable land; 2% permanent crops; 29% meadows and pastures; 49% forest and woodlands; 16% other; includes negligible irrigated
Location: NW South America, bordering on Caribbean Sea, Pacific Ocean

■ PEOPLE

Nationality: Colombian
Ethnic Groups: 58% mestizo, 20% white, 14% mulatto, 5% black, 7% Indian
Languages: Spanish
Religions: 95% Roman Catholic
Marriages: n.a.
Divorces: n.a.

■ GOVERNMENT

Leader(s): Pres. Ernesto Samper Pizano
Government Type: republic; executive branch dominates government structure
Administrative Divisions: 23 departments, 5 commissariats and 4 intendancies
Independence: July 20, 1810 (from Spain)
National Holiday: Independence Day, July 20

■ ECONOMY

Overview: traditionally coffee has been the main export though other industries such as oil and coal are developing; drug-related violence is an increasing threat to economic growth
GNP: n.a., GDP $51 billion, per capita $1,500; real growth rate 3.3% (1992 est.)
Inflation: 27.0% (1992)
Industries: textiles, food processing, oil, clothing and footwear, beverages, chemicals, metal products, cement; mining—gold, coal, emeralds, iron, nickel, silver, salt
Labour Force: 10,394,000 (1992); 76.9% services, 1.7% agriculture, 21.4% industry (1989)
Unemployment: 10% (1992)
Agriculture: accounts for 22% of GDP; crops make up two-thirds and livestock one-third of agricultural output; climate and soils permit a wide variety of crops, such as coffee, rice, tobacco, corn, sugar cane, cocoa beans, oilseeds, vegetables; forest products and shrimp farming are increasing in importance
Natural Resources: crude oil, natural gas, coal, iron ore, nickel, gold, copper, emeralds

■ FINANCE/TRADE

Currency: peso ($Col)
International Reserves Excluding Gold: $7,917 million (June 1993)
Gold Reserves: 0.38 million fine troy ounces (June 1993)
Budget: revenues $5.0 billion; expenditures $5.1 billion, including capital expenditures of $964 million (1991 est.)
Defence Expenditures: $630 million (1.3% of GDP) (1993 est.)
External Debt: $17.204 billion (1992)
Exports: $7.052 billion (1992); commodities: coffee 30%, petroleum 24%, coal, bananas, fresh cut flowers; partners: US 36%, European Community 21%, Japan 5%, Netherlands 4%, Sweden 3%
Imports: $6.686 billion (1992); commodities: industrial equipment, transportation equipment, foodstuffs, chemicals, paper products; partners: US 34%, European Community 16%, Brazil 4%, Venezuela 3%, Japan 3%

■ HEALTH

Births: 26/1,000 population (1993)
Deaths: 5/1,000 population (1993)
Infant Mortality: 34 deaths/1,000 live births (1993)
Life Expectancy at Birth: 68 years male, 73 years female (1993)
No. of Physicians: 8.1/10,000 population (1992)

■ EDUCATION

Govt. Expenditure: 10.9% of govt. expenditure (1991)
Literacy: 86.7% (1992)

■ COMMUNICATIONS

Daily newspapers: 45 (1992)
Televisions: 108.1/1,000 inhabitants (1992)
Radios: 167/1,000 inhabitants (1992)
Telephones: 8.11/100 inhabitants (1992)

■ TRANSPORTATION

Motor Vehicles: 1,380,618; 715,315 passenger cars (1990)
Roads: 75,450 km; 9,350 km paved (1993)
Railway: 3,386 km (1993)
Air Traffic: 5,540,000 passengers carried (1991)
Airports: 1,233 airfields, of which 1,059 are

usable and 69 have permanent-surface runways (1993)

Canadian Embassy: Calle 76, No. 11-52, Bogotá, Colombia; mailing address: Apartado Aereo 53531, Bogotá 2, Colombia. Tel: (011-57-1) 217-5555. Fax (011-57-1) 310-4509
Representative to Canada: Embassy of Colombia, 360 Albert St, Ste 1130, Ottawa ON K1R 7X7. Tel: (613) 230-3761. Fax: (613) 230-4416.

Comoros

Long-Form Name: Federal Islamic Republic of the Comoros
Capital: Moroni
Population: 500,000 (1993 est.)

■ GEOGRAPHY

Area: 2,170 sq. km
Coastline: 340 km
Climate: tropical marine; rainy season (Nov. to May)
Environment: soil degradation and erosion; deforestation; cyclones possible during rainy season
Terrain: volcanic islands, interiors vary from steep mountains to low hills
Land Use: 35% arable; 8% permanent; 7% meadows; 16% forest; 34% other
Location: Indian Ocean E of Africa

■ PEOPLE

Nationality: Comoran
Ethnic Groups: Antalote, Cafre, Makoa, Oimatsaha, Sakalava
Languages: French and Arabic (both official), Shaafi Islam (a Swahili dialect), Malagasy, majority speaks Comoran
Religions: 86% Sunni Moslem, 14% Roman Catholic
Marriages: n.a.
Divorces: n.a.

■ GOVERNMENT

Leader(s): Pres. Said Mohamed Djohar, Prem. Mohamed Abdou Madi
Government Type: independent republic
Administrative Divisions: 3 islands
Independence: July 6, 1975 (from France)
National Holiday: Independence Day, July 6

■ ECONOMY

Overview: agriculture is the main sector of the economy though it does not feed citizens adequately; lack of natural resources makes Comoros one of the world's poorest countries

GNP: $245 million, per capita $500; real growth rate 2.6% (1991)
Inflation: 8.3% (1986)
Industries: perfume distillation, textiles, furniture, jewelry, soft drinks, construction materials
Labour Force: 230,000 (1992); 83% agriculture, 6% industry, 11% services (1989)
Unemployment: over 16% (1988 est.)
Agriculture: accounts for 40% of GDP; most of population works in subsistence agriculture and fishing; plantations produce cash crops for export–vanilla, cloves, perfume essences and copra; principal food crops–coconuts, bananas, cassava; large net food importer
Natural Resources: negligible

■ FINANCE/TRADE

Currency: Comoran franc (CFAF)
International Reserves Excluding Gold: $33 million (June 1993)
Gold Reserves: n.a.
Budget: revenues $96 million; expenditures $88 million, including capital expenditures of $33 million (1991 est.)
Defence Expenditures: n.a.
External Debt: $173 million (1992)
Exports: $16 million (1990); commodities: vanilla, cloves, perfume oil, copra; partners: US 53%, France 41%, Africa 4%, Germany 2%
Imports: $41 million (1990); commodities: rice and other foodstuffs, cement, petroleum products, consumer goods; partners: Europe 62% (France 22%, other 40%), Africa 5%, Pakistan, China

■ HEALTH

Births: 48/1,000 population (1993)
Deaths: 12/1,000 population (1993)
Infant Mortality: 89 deaths/1,000 live births (1993)
Life Expectancy at Birth: 54 years male, 58 years female (1993)
No. of Physicians: 0.8/10,000 population (1992)

■ EDUCATION

Govt. Expenditure: 13.2% of govt. expenditure (1989)
Literacy: 47.9% (1992)

■ COMMUNICATIONS

Daily newspapers: 1 (1992)
Televisions: 0.3/1,000 inhabitants (1992)
Radios: 115/1,000 inhabitants (1992)
Telephones: 0.88/100 inhabitants (1992)

■ TRANSPORTATION

Motor Vehicles: 5,600 motor vehicles (1983)

Roads: 750 km; 210 km paved
Railway: n.a.
Air Traffic: 26,000 passengers carried (1991)
Airports: 4, all usable and with permanent-surface runways (1993)

Canadian Embassy: c/o The Canadian High Commission, Comcraft House, Hailé Sélassie Ave, Nairobi; mailing address: P.O. Box 30481, Nairobi, Kenya. Tel: (011-254-2) 21-48-04. Fax: (011-254-2) 22-69-87.
Representative to Canada: c/o 336 East 45th St, 2nd Floor, New York, NY 10021 USA. Tel: (212) 972-8010. Fax: (212) 983-4712.

Congo

Long-Form Name: People's Republic of the Congo
Capital: Brazzaville
Population: 2,400,000 (1993 est.)

■ GEOGRAPHY

Area: 342,000 sq. km
Coastline: 169 km
Climate: tropical; rainy season (Mar. to June); dry season (June to Oct.); constant high temperatures and humidity; particularly enervating climate astride the Equator
Environment: deforestation; about 70% of the population lives in Brazzaville, Pointe Noire or along the railroad between them
Terrain: coastal plain, southern basin, central plateau, northern basin
Land Use: 2% arable land; negligible permanent; 29% meadows; 62% forest; 7% other
Location: WC Africa, bordering on South Atlantic Ocean

■ PEOPLE

Nationality: Congolese
Ethnic Groups: about 15 ethnic groups divided into some 75 tribes, almost all Bantu; most important ethnic groups are Kongo (48%) in south, Sangha (20%) and M'Bochi (12%) in the north, Teke (17%) in the centre; about 8,500 Europeans, mostly French
Languages: French (official); many African languages with Lingala and Kikongo most widely used
Religions: 50% Christian, 48% animist, 2% Moslem
Marriages: n.a.
Divorces: n.a.

■ GOVERNMENT

Leader(s): Pres. Pascal Lissouba, Prem. Jacques Joachim Yhombi-Opango
Government Type: republic
Administrative Divisions: 9 regions, 1 commune
Independence: Aug. 15, 1960 (from France; formerly known as Congo/Brazzaville)
National Holiday: National Day, Aug. 15

■ ECONOMY

Overview: oil revenues are responsible for one of the highest growth rates in Africa, though the country faces increasing foreign debt and is vulnerable to the oil market
GNP: $2.623 billion, per capita $1,120; real growth rate 3.1% (1991)
Inflation: 2.9% (1992)
Industries: petroleum, lumbering, cement, sawmills, brewery, sugar mills, palm oil, soap, cigarettes
Labour Force: 781,000 (1992); 62.4% agriculture, 25.6% services, 11.9% industry (1989)
Unemployment: n.a.
Agriculture: accounts for 13% of GDP (including fishing and forestry); cassava accounts for 90% of food output; other crops—rice, corn, peanuts, vegetables; cash crops include coffee and cocoa; forest products important export earner; imports over 90% of food needs
Natural Resources: petroleum, timber, potash, lead, zinc, uranium, copper, phosphate, natural gas

■ FINANCE/TRADE

Currency: Communauté financière africaine franc (CFAF)
International Reserves Excluding Gold: $1 million (Jan. 1994)
Gold Reserves: 0.01 million fine troy ounces (1991)
Budget: revenues $765 million; expenditures $952 million, including capital expenditures of $65 million (1990)
Defence Expenditures: $100.51 million (1987)
External Debt: $4.751 billion (1992)
Exports: $1.110 billion (1991); commodities: crude petroleum 72%, lumber, plywood, coffee, cocoa, sugar, diamonds; partners: US, France, other European Community
Imports: $1.095 billion (1991); commodities: foodstuffs, consumer goods, intermediate manufactures, capital equipment; partners: France, Italy, other European Community, US, Germany, Spain, Japan, Brazil

■ HEALTH

Births: 42/1,000 population (1993)
Deaths: 14/1,000 population (1993)
Infant Mortality: 114 deaths/1,000 live births

(1993)
Life Expectancy at Birth: 52 years male, 55 years female (1993)
No. of Physicians: 1.3/10,000 population (1990)

■ EDUCATION

Govt. Expenditure: 14.4% of govt. expenditure (1990)
Literacy: 56.6% (1992)

■ COMMUNICATIONS

Daily newspapers: 1 (1992)
Televisions: 4.5/1,000 inhabitants (1992)
Radios: 109/1,000 inhabitants (1992)
Telephones: 1.29/100 inhabitants (1992)

■ TRANSPORTATION

Motor Vehicles: 48,000; 27,000 passenger cars (1990)
Roads: 11,970 km; 684 km paved
Railway: 797 km (1993)
Air Traffic: 227,000 passengers carried (1991)
Airports: 44, of which 41 are usable and 5 have permanent-surface runways (1993)

Canadian Embassy: c/o The Canadian Embassy, 17 Pumbe Zone de Gombe Ave, Kinshasa; mailing address: c/o Embassy of the United States of America (Canadian Office), 310, avenue des Aviateurs, Kinshasa, Zaïre. Tel: (011-243-12) 21-532. Fax: (011-243-88) 43-805.
Representative to Canada: c/o Embassy of the Republic of the Congo, 4891 Colorado Ave NW, Washington, DC 20011 USA. Tel: (202) 726-5500. Fax: (202) 726-1860.

Cook Islands

Dependent Territory of New Zealand

Long-Form Name: Cook Islands
Capital: Avarua (on Rarotonga Island)
Population: 18,903 (1993 est.)

■ GEOGRAPHY

Area: 240 sq. km
Climate: mild year-round, moderated by trade winds
Land Use: 4% arable, 22% permanent crops, negligible meadows and pastures, negligible forest and woodland, 74% other
Location: S Pacific Ocean, NE of New Zealand

■ PEOPLE

Nationality: Cook Islander
Ethnic Groups: Polynesian 81.3%, Polynesian-European mixture 7.7%, Polynesian-other mix-

ture 7.7%, European 2.4%, other 0.9%
Languages: English (official), Cook Islands Maori

■ GOVERNMENT

Leader(s): Prime Min. Hon. Geoffrey A. Henry
Government Type: self-governing territory in free association with New Zealand; Cook Island is fully responsible for internal affairs; New Zealand retains responsibility for external affairs, in consultation with the Cook Islands
National Holiday: Constitution Day, Aug. 4

■ ECONOMY

Overview: agriculture provides the backbone of the economy: copra, fruits, tomatoes; livestock: pigs, goats; fishing; manufacturing is limited

■ FINANCE/TRADE

Currency: New Zealand dollar (NZ$)

Costa Rica

Long-Form Name: Republic of Costa Rica
Capital: San José
Population: 3,300,000 (1993 est.)

■ GEOGRAPHY

Area: 51,100 sq. km; includes Isla del Coco
Coastline: 1,290 km
Climate: tropical; dry season (Dec. to Apr.); rainy season (May to Nov.)
Environment: subject to occasional earthquakes, hurricanes along Atlantic coast; frequent flooding of lowlands at onset of rainy season; active volcanoes; deforestation; soil erosion
Terrain: coastal plains separated by rugged mountains
Land Use: 6% arable; 7% permanent; 45% meadows; 34% forest; 8% other
Location: Central (Latin) America, bordering on Caribbean Sea, Pacific Ocean

■ PEOPLE

Nationality: Costa Rican
Ethnic Groups: 96% white (including mestizo), 2% black, 1% Indian, 1% Chinese
Languages: Spanish (official), English is spoken around Puerto Limon
Religions: 95% Roman Catholic
Marriages: 7.6 (per 1,000) (1990)
Divorces: 1.10 (per 1,000) (1990)

■ GOVERNMENT

Leader(s): Pres. José Maria Figueres
Government Type: democratic republic
Administrative Divisions: 7 provinces

Independence: Sept. 15, 1821 (from Spain)
National Holiday: Independence Day, Sept. 15

■ ECONOMY

Overview: inflation and external debt are high, many people are underemployed; coffee and banana crops are vital
GNP: n.a., GDP $6.4 billion, per capita $2,000; real growth rate 5.4% (1991 est.)
Inflation: 21.8% (1992)
Industries: food processing, textiles and clothing, plastics products, construction materials, fertilizer, tourism
Labour Force: 1.023 million (1992); 18.2% industry and commerce, 56.4% services, 25.4% agriculture (1989)
Unemployment: 4%, but there is much underemployment (1992)
Agriculture: accounts for 17% of GDP and 70% of exports; cash commodities—coffee, beef, bananas, sugar; normally self-sufficient in food except for grain; depletion of forest resources resulting in lower timber output
Natural Resources: hydroelectricity potential

■ FINANCE/TRADE

Currency: colón (pl. colones) (C/)
International Reserves Excluding Gold: $1,039 million (Jan. 1994)
Gold Reserves: 0.03 million fine troy ounces (Jan. 1994)
Budget: revenues $1.1 billion; expenditures $1.34 billion, including capital expenditures of $110 million (1991 est.)
Defence Expenditures: $62.67 million (1990)
External Debt: $3.963 billion (1992)
Exports: $1.834 billion (1992); commodities: coffee, bananas, textiles, sugar; partners: US 75%, Germany, Guatemala, Netherlands, UK, Japan
Imports: $2.458 billion (1992); commodities: petroleum, machinery, consumer durables, chemicals, fertilizer, foodstuffs; partners: US 35%, Japan, Guatemala, Germany

■ HEALTH

Births: 27/1,000 population (1993)
Deaths: 4/1,000 population (1993)
Infant Mortality: 15.3 deaths/1,000 live births (1993)
Life Expectancy at Birth: 74 years male, 78 years female (1993)
No. of Physicians: 10.5/10,000 population (1992)

■ EDUCATION

Govt. Expenditure: 19.14% of govt. expenditure (1991)

Literacy: 93% (1993)

■ COMMUNICATIONS

Daily newspapers: 4 (1992)
Televisions: 136.1/1,000 inhabitants (1992)
Radios: 259/1,000 inhabitants (1992)
Telephones: 16.7/100 inhabitants (1992)

■ TRANSPORTATION

Motor Vehicles: 250,000; 150,000 passenger cars (1990)
Roads: 15,400 km; 7,030 km paved (1993)
Railway: 950 km (1993)
Air Traffic: 504,000 passengers carried 1991
Airports: 162 airfields, of which 144 are usable; 28 have permanent-surface runways (1993)

Canadian Embassy: Cronos Building, Calle 3 y Avenida Central; mailing address: Apartado Postal 10303, San José, Costa Rica. Tel: (011-506) 55-35-22. Fax: (011-506) 23-23-95
Representative to Canada: Embassy of the Republic of Costa Rica, 135 York St, Ste 208, Ottawa ON K1N 5T4. Tel: (613) 562-2855. Fax: (613) 562-2582.

Côte d'Ivoire (Ivory Coast)

Long-Form Name: Republic of Côte d'Ivoire
Capital: Yamoussoukro
Population: 13,400,000 (1993 est.)

■ GEOGRAPHY

Area: 322,460 sq. km
Coastline: 515 km
Climate: tropical along coast, semi-arid in far north; three seasons: warm and dry (Nov. to Mar.), hot and dry (Mar. to May), hot and wet (June to Oct.)
Environment: coast has heavy surf and no natural harbours; severe deforestation
Terrain: mostly flat to undulating plains; mountains in northwest
Land Use: 9% arable; 4% permanent; 9% meadows; 26% forest; 52% other
Location: WC Africa, bordering on South Atlantic Ocean

■ PEOPLE

Nationality: Ivorian
Ethnic Groups: over 60 ethnic groups; most important are the Baoule 23%, Bete 18%, Senoufou 15%, Malinke 11% and Agni; about 2 million foreign Africans mostly Burkinabe; about 130,000 to 330,000 non-Africans (30,000 French and 100,000–300,000 Lebanese)
Languages: French (official), 60 native dialects,

of which Dioula is the most widely spoken
Religions: 63% indigenous, 25% Moslem, 12% Christian
Marriages: n.a.
Divorces: n.a.

■ **GOVERNMENT**

Leader(s): Pres. Henri Konan Bédié, Prime Min. Kablan Daniel Duncan
Government Type: republic; multi-party presidential regime established 1960
Administrative Divisions: 49 departments
Independence: Aug. 7, 1960 (from France)
National Holiday: National Day, Dec. 7

■ **ECONOMY**

Overview: despite attempts to diversify, the economy is largely dependent on agriculture and related industries; highly sensitive to fluctuations in world prices for coffee and cocoa and to weather conditions; a 1986 collapse of world cocoa and coffee prices threw the economy into a recession from which it is still only slowly recovering
GNP: $8.523 billion, per capita $690; real growth rate 0.3% (1991)
Inflation: 4.4% (1992)
Industries: foodstuffs, wood processing, oil refinery, automobile assembly, textiles, fertilizer, beverage
Labour Force: 4,599,000 (1992), 65.2% agriculture, 8.3% industry, 26.5% services (1989)
Unemployment: 140,250 (1990)
Agriculture: most important sector, contributing one-third to GDP and 80% to exports; cash crops include coffee, cocoa beans, timber, bananas, palm kernels, rubber; food crops; not self-sufficient in bread grain and dairy products
Natural Resources: crude oil, diamonds, manganese, iron ore, cobalt, bauxite, copper

■ **FINANCE/TRADE**

Currency: Communauté financière africaine franc (CFAF)
International Reserves Excluding Gold: $4 million (Sept. 1993)
Gold Reserves: 0.04 million fine troy ounces (Sept. 1993)
Budget: revenues $2.3 billion; expenditures $3.6 billion, including capital expenditures of $274 million (1990 est.)
Defence Expenditures: $119.68 million (1987)
External Debt: $17.997 billion (1992)
Exports: $2.8 billion (1990); commodities: cocoa 30%, coffee 20%, tropical woods 11%, cotton, bananas, pineapples, palm oil; partners: France, Germany, Netherlands, US, Belgium, Spain

Imports: $1.6 billion (1990); commodities: manufactured goods and semifinished products 50%, consumer goods 40%, raw materials and fuels 10%; partners: France, other European Community, Nigeria, US, Japan

■ **HEALTH**

Births: 50/1,000 population (1993)
Deaths: 15/1,000 population (1993)
Infant Mortality: 95 deaths/1,000 live births (1993)
Life Expectancy at Birth: 50 years male, 53 years female (1993)
No. of Physicians: n.a.

■ **EDUCATION**

Govt. Expenditure: n.a.
Literacy: 54% (1993)

■ **COMMUNICATIONS**

Daily newspapers: 2 (1992)
Televisions: 58.5/1,000 inhabitants (1992)
Radios: 139/1,000 inhabitants (1992)
Telephones: 1.06/100 inhabitants (1992)

■ **TRANSPORTATION**

Motor Vehicles: 262,000; 170,000 passenger cars (1990)
Roads: 54,496 km; 3,870 km paved
Railway: 677 km
Air Traffic: 175,000 passengers carried (1991)
Airports: 42 airfields, of which 37 are usable; 7 have permanent-surface runways (1993)

Canadian Embassy: Immeuble Trade-Center, 23 rue Nogues, Le Plateau, Abidjan; mailing address: BP 4104, Abidjan 01, Côte d'Ivoire. Tel: (011-225) 21-20-09. Fax: (011-225) 21-77-28
Representative to Canada: Embassy of the Republic of Côte d'Ivoire, 9 Marlborough Ave, Ottawa ON K1N 8E6. Tel: (613) 236-9919. Fax: (613) 563-8287.

Croatia

Long-Form Name: Republic of Croatia
Capital: Zagreb
Population: 4,400,000 (1993)

■ **GEOGRAPHY**

Area: 56,538 sq. km
Coastline: 5,790 km
Climate: hot summers and cold winters; along coast, mild winters and dry summers
Environment: air pollution, damaged forests, coastal pollution; subject to frequent and

destructive earthquakes

Terrain: flat plains along Hungarian border, low mountains and highlands along Adriatic coast, coastline, and islands

Land Use: 32% arable, 20% permanent crops, 18% meadows and pastures, 15% forests and woodland, 15% other

Location: S Europe, bordering on Adriatic Sea

■ PEOPLE

Nationality: Croatian

Ethnic Groups: 78% Croat, 12% Serb, 0.9% Muslim, 0.5% Hungarian, 0.5% Slovenian, 8.1% other

Languages: Serbo-Croatian 96%, other 4%

Religions: 76.5% Catholic, 11.1% Orthodox, 1.2% Slavic Muslim, 1.4% Protestant, 9.8% others and unknown

Marriages: 29,399 (1989)

■ GOVERNMENT

Leader(s): Pres. Franjo Tudjman, Prime Min. Nikica Valentic

Government Type: parliamentary democracy

Administrative Divisions: 100 districts

Independence: June 1991, secession from federal Yugoslovia

National Holiday: Statehood Day, May 30

■ ECONOMY

Overview: tourism, manufacturing including chemicals, food products, petroleum, ships and textiles. War and internal strife have severely disrupted economy

GNP: n.a., GDP $26.3 billion, $5,600 per capita; real growth rate 25% (1991 est.)

Inflation: 50% per month (1992)

Industries: mining, fertilizers, plastics, chemicals, fabricated metal, pig iron and rolled steel products, paper, wood products, shipbuilding, food processing, beverages, sugar, cotton fabrics, machinery

Labour Force: 3,049,000 (1989); 61% agriculture and animal husbandry, 14% industry, 25% services and other

Unemployment: 20% (1991 est.)

Agriculture: Croatia normally produces a food surplus, but much land has been put out of production by fighting; products include wheat, maize, potatoes, plums, fish, livestock, esp. cattle, sheep, pigs, poultry, cereal grains, citrus fruit, vegetables

Natural Resources: oil, salt, coal, bauxite, brown coal and lignite, iron ore, china clay

■ FINANCE/TRADE

Currency: Croatian dinar

International Reserves Excluding Gold: n.a.

Gold Reserves: n.a.

Budget: n.a.

Defence Expenditures: n.a.

External Debt: $2.6 billion (1993)

Exports: $2.9 billion (1990); machiney and transportation equipment and other manufactured goods; partners: mostly Italy, Germany, United States, Commonwealth of Independent States

Imports: $4.4 billion (1990); machinery and transportation equipment, chemicals, raw materials

■ HEALTH

Births: 12/1,000 population (1993)

Deaths: 11/1,000 population (1993)

Infant Mortality: 10.6 deaths/1,000 live births (1993)

Life Expectancy at Birth: 68 years male, 76 years female (1993)

No. of Physicians: n.a.

■ EDUCATION

Govt. Expenditure: n.a.

Literacy: n.a.

■ COMMUNICATIONS

Daily newspapers: n.a.

Televisions: n.a.; 12 TV stations (1993)

Radios: n.a.; 22 radio stations (1993)

Telephones: 350,000 total (1993)

■ TRANSPORTATION

Motor Vehicles: n.a.

Roads: 32,071 km; 23,305 km paved

Railway: 2,592 km

Air Traffic: n.a.

Airports: 75 airfields, of which 72 are usable; 15 have permanent-surface runways (1993)

Canadian Embassy: Hotel Esplanade, Mihanovicva 1, 4100 Zagreb. Tel: (011-385-41) 450-785. Fax: (011-385-41) 450-913

Representative to Canada: To be opened at a later date.

Cuba

Long-Form Name: Republic of Cuba

Capital: Havana

Population: 11,000,000 (1993 est.)

■ GEOGRAPHY

Area: 110,860 sq. km

Coastline: 3,735 km

Climate: tropical; moderated by trade winds; dry season (Nov. to Apr.); rainy season (May to

Oct.)

Environment: averages one hurricane every two years

Terrain: mostly flat to rolling plains with rugged hills and mountains in the southeast

Land Use: 23% arable; 6% permanent; 23% meadows; 17% forest; 31% other

Location: West Indies, bordering on Caribbean Sea, Atlantic Ocean

■ PEOPLE

Nationality: Cuban

Ethnic Groups: 51% mulatto, 37% white, 11% black, 1% Chinese

Languages: Spanish

Religions: Christianity (majority Roman Catholic)

Marriages: 15.0 (per 1,000) (1991)

Divorces: 4.05 (per 1,000) (1991)

■ GOVERNMENT

Leader(s): Pres. of the Council of State Fidel Castro Ruz

Government Type: communist state

Administrative Divisions: 14 provinces and 1 special municipality

Independence: May 20, 1902 (from Spain Dec. 10, 1898; administered by the US from 1898 to 1902)

National Holiday: Rebellion Day, July 26

■ ECONOMY

Overview: the Soviet-style, centrally planned and largely state-owned economy depends on agriculture and foreign trade (sugar); Soviet foreign aid used to be an important boost for the economy; between 1989 and 1992 the economy contracted by about one-third due to the loss of $4 billion of annual economic aid from the former Soviet Union and other Eastern European countries

GNP: $14.9 billion, per capita $1,370; real growth rate -15% (1992 est.)

Inflation: n.a.

Industries: sugar milling, petroleum refining, food and tobacco processing, textiles, chemicals, paper and wood products, metals (particularly nickel), cement, fertilizers, consumer goods, agricultural machinery

Labour Force: 4,461,000 (1992); 47.7% services, 28.5% industry, 23.8% agriculture (1989)

Unemployment: 6% overall, 10% for women (1989)

Agriculture: accounts for 11% of GNP (including fishing and forestry); key commercial crops–sugar cane, tobacco and citrus fruit; other products–coffee, rice, potatoes, meat, beans;

world's largest sugar exporter; not self-sufficient in food

Natural Resources: cobalt, nickel, iron ore, copper, manganese, salt, timber, silica, petroleum

■ FINANCE/TRADE

Currency: peso ($)

International Reserves Excluding Gold: n.a.

Gold Reserves: n.a.

Budget: revenues $12.46 billion; expenditures $14.45 billion, including capital expenditures (1990)

Defence Expenditures: $1.83 billion (1989)

External Debt: $6.8 billion (1989)

Exports: $2.1 billion (1992 est.); commodities: sugar, nickel, shellfish, citrus, tobacco, coffee; partners: Russia 30%, China 9%, Canada 10%, Japan 6%, Spain 4%

Imports: $2.2 billion (1992 est.); commodities: capital goods, industrial raw materials, food, petroleum; partners: Russia 10%, China 9%, Spain 9%, Mexico 5%, Italy 5%, Canada 4%, France 4%

■ HEALTH

Births: 16/1,000 population (1993)

Deaths: 7/1,000 population (1993)

Infant Mortality: 10.7 deaths/1,000 live births (1993)

Life Expectancy at Birth: 74 years male, 79 years female (1993)

No. of Physicians: 18.9/10,000 population (1992)

■ EDUCATION

Govt. Expenditure: 12.3% government expenditure (1990)

Literacy: 94.0% (1992)

■ COMMUNICATIONS

Daily newspapers: 1 (1992)

Televisions: 203.4/1,000 inhabitants (1992)

Radios: 343/1,000 inhabitants (1992)

Telephones: 5.6/100 inhabitants (1992)

■ TRANSPORTATION

Motor Vehicles: 229,500 passenger cars (1987)

Roads: 26,477 km; 14,477 km paved

Railway: 12,915 km

Air Traffic: 831,000 passengers carried (1991)

Airports: 186 airfields, of which 166 are usable and 73 have permanent-surface runways (1993)

Canadian Embassy: Calle 30, No. 518 Esquina a7a, Avenida Miramar, Havana, Cuba. Tel: (011-53-7) 33-20-44. Fax: (011-53-7) 33-25-16

Representative to Canada: Embassy of the Republic of Cuba, 388 Main St, Ottawa ON

K1S 1E3. Tel: (613) 563-0141. Fax: (613) 563-0068.

Cyprus

Long-Form Name: Republic of Cyprus
Capital: Nicosia
Population: 723,371 (1993 est.)

■ GEOGRAPHY

Area: 9,250 sq. km
Coastline: 648 km
Climate: temperate, Mediterranean with hot, dry summers and cool, wet winters
Environment: moderate earthquake activity; water resource problems (no natural reservoir catchments, seasonal disparity in rainfall and most potable resources concentrated in the Turkish-Cypriot area)
Terrain: central plain with mountains to north and south
Land Use: 40% arable; 7% permanent; 10% meadows; 18% forest; 25% other
Location: Mediterranean Sea

■ PEOPLE

Nationality: Cypriot
Ethnic Groups: 78% Greek; 18% Turkish; 4% other
Languages: 80% Greek, Turkish, English
Religions: 78% Greek Orthodox; 18% Moslem; 4% Maronite, Armenian, Apostolic and other
Marriages: 9.9 (per 1,000) (1991)
Divorces: 0.42 (per 1,000) (1991)

■ GOVERNMENT

Leader(s): Pres. Glafcos Clerides
Government Type: republic; Greek Cypriots control the only internationally recognized government
Administrative Divisions: 6 districts
Independence: Aug. 16, 1960 (from UK)
National Holiday: Independence Day, Oct. 1 (Nov. 15 is celebrated as Independence Day in the Turkish area)

■ ECONOMY

Overview: a high growth rate, low inflation rate and manageable deficit characterize the economy
GNP: $6.135 billion, per capita $8,640; real growth rate 6% (1991)
Inflation: 6.5% (1992)
Industries: mining (iron pyrites, gypsum, asbestos); manufactured products–beverages, footwear, clothing and cement–are principally for local consumption, tourism

Labour Force: 326,000 (1992); 67.4% services, 18.9% industry, 13.7% agriculture (1989)
Unemployment: 3.0% (1991)
Agriculture: accounts for 6% of GDP and employs 14% of labour force; major crops—potatoes, vegetables, barley, grapes, olives and citrus fruit; vegetables and fruit provide 25% of export revenues
Natural Resources: copper, pyrites, asbestos, gypsum, timber, salt, marble, clay earth pigment

■ FINANCE/TRADE

Currency: Cypriot pound (£ or £C)
International Reserves Excluding Gold: $1,155 million (Nov. 1993)
Gold Reserves: 0.46 million fine troy ounces (Nov. 1993)
Budget: revenues $1.7 billion; expenditures $2.2 billion, including capital expenditures of $350 million (1993)
Defence Expenditures: 3.21% of total govt. expenditure (1991)
External Debt: $2.8 billion (1988)
Exports: $1.012 billion (1992); commodities: citrus, potatoes, grapes, wine, cement, clothing and shoes; partners: Middle East and North Africa 37%, UK 27%, other European Community 11%, US 2%
Imports: $3.313 billion (1992); commodities: consumer goods 23%, petroleum and lubricants 12%, food and feed grains, machinery; partners: European Community 60%, Middle East and North Africa 7%, US 4%

■ HEALTH

Births: 17.4/1,000 population (1993 est.)
Deaths: 7.74/1,000 population (1993 est.)
Infant Mortality: 9.3 deaths/1,000 live births (1993 est.)
Life Expectancy at Birth: 73.75 years male, 78.31 years female (1993 est.)
No. of Physicians: n.a.

■ EDUCATION

Govt. Expenditure: 11% of govt. expenditure (1991)
Literacy: 94% (1993)

■ COMMUNICATIONS

Daily newspapers: 14 (1992)
Televisions: 141.4/1,000 inhabitants (1992)
Radios: 289/1,000 inhabitants (1992)
Telephones: 33.3/100 inhabitants (1992)

■ TRANSPORTATION

Motor Vehicles: 192,700 passenger cars (1989)
Roads: 10,780 km; 5,170 km paved (1993)

Railway: n.a.
Air Traffic: 820,000 passengers carried (1991)
Airports: 13 airfields, all usable; 10 have permanent-surface runways (1993)

Canadian Embassy: The Canadian High Commission to Cyprus, c/o The Canadian Embassy, 220 Rehov Hayarkon, Tel Aviv, 63405; mailing address: P.O. Box 6410, Tel Aviv 61063, Israel. Tel: (011-972-3) 527-2929. Fax: (011-972-3) 527-2333
Representative to Canada: c/o Embassy of Cyprus, 2211 R St, NW, Washington, DC 20008 USA.

Czech Republic

Long-Form Name: Czech Republic
Capital: Prague
Population: 10,300,000 (1993 est.)

■ GEOGRAPHY

Area: 78,703 sq. km
Coastline: none: landlocked
Climate: temperate; cool summers; cold, cloudy, humid winters
Environment: n.a.
Terrain: two main regions: Bohemia in the west consists of rolling plains, hills, and plateaus surrounded by low mountains; Moravia in east consists of very hilly country
Land Use: n.a.
Location: EC Europe

■ PEOPLE

Nationality: Czech
Ethnic Groups: 94.4% Czech, 3% Slovak, 0.2% Hungarian, 0.5% German, 0.6% Polish, 0.3% Ukrainian, 0.1% Russian, 0.3% Gypsy, 1% other
Languages: Czech and Slovak
Religions: 70% Roman Catholic, 15% Protestant, 2% Orthodox, 13% other
Marriages: 6.7 (per 1,000) (1991)
Divorces: 2.39 (per 1,000) (1991)

■ GOVERNMENT

Leader(s): Prime Min. Vaclav Klaus
Government Type: parliamentary democracy
Administrative Divisions: 7 regions
Independence: Jan. 1, 1993 (from Czechoslovakia)
National Holiday: n.a.

■ ECONOMY

Overview: economy is beginning the transition from a command to a market economy; deficient in energy and has an obsolete capital plant, though a skilled work force
GNP: n.a., GDP $75.3 billion, per capita $7,300; real growth rate -5% (1992 est.)
Inflation: 10.8% (1992)
Industries: fuels, ferrous metallurgy, machinery and equipment, coal, motor vehicles, glass, armaments
Labour Force: 5,389,000 (1990); 37.9% industry, 8.1% agriculture, 8.8% construction, 45.2% communications and other
Unemployment: 3.1% (1992 est.)
Agriculture: largely self-sufficient in food production; diversified crop and livestock production, including grains, sugar beets, potatoes, hops, fruit, hogs, cattle and poultry
Natural Resources: hard coal, kaolin, clay, graphite

■ FINANCE/TRADE

Currency: koruna (pl. koruny) (Kcs)
International Reserves Excluding Gold: n.a.
Gold Reserves: n.a.
Budget: n.a.
Defence Expenditures: 5.46% of total govt. expenditure (1991)
External Debt: $9.328 billion (1992)
Exports: $11.656 billion (1992); commodities: machinery and equipment 58.5%, industrial consumer goods 15.2%, fuels, minerals and metals 10.6%, agricultural and forestry products 6.1%, other products 15.2%; partners: USSR, Germany, Poland, Hungary, Yugoslavia, Austria, Bulgaria, Romania, US
Imports: $12.530 billion (1992); commodities: machinery and equipment 41.6%, fuels, minerals, metals 32.2%, agricultural and forestry products 11.5%, industrial consumer goods 6.7%, other products 8%; partners: USSR, Germany, Poland, Hungary, Yugoslavia, Austria, Bulgaria, Romania, US

■ HEALTH

Births: 13/1,000 population (1993)
Deaths: 12/1,000 population (1993)
Infant Mortality: 10.4 deaths/1,000 live births (1993)
Life Expectancy at Birth: 68 years male, 76 years female (1993)
No. of Physicians: 36.1/10,000 population (1992)

■ EDUCATION

Govt. Expenditure: 7.48% of govt. expenditure (1991)
Literacy: 99%

■ COMMUNICATIONS

Daily newspapers: n.a.
Televisions: n.a.
Radios: n.a.
Telephones: n.a.

■ TRANSPORTATION

Motor Vehicles: n.a.
Roads: 55,890 km
Railway: 9,434 km
Air Traffic: n.a.
Airports: 75 airfields, all usable; 8 have permanent-surface runways (1993)

Canadian Embassy: Mickiewiczova 6, 125 33 Prague 6, Czech Republic. Tel: (011-42-2) 2431-1108. Fax: (011-42-2) 2431-0294
Representative to Canada: Embassy of the Czech Republic, 541 Sussex Dr, Ottawa ON K1N 6Z6. Tel: (613) 562-3877. Fax: (613) 562-3878.

Denmark

Long-Form Name: Kingdom of Denmark
Capital: Copenhagen
Population: 5,200,000 (1993 est.)

■ GEOGRAPHY

Area: 43,070 sq. km; includes the island of Bornholm in the Baltic Sea and the rest of metropolitan Denmark, but excludes the Faeroe Islands and Greenland
Coastline: 3,379 km
Climate: temperate; humid and overcast; mild, windy winters and cool summers
Environment: air and water pollution
Terrain: low and flat to gently rolling plains
Land Use: 61% arable land; negligible permanent; 6% meadows; 12% forest; 21% other
Location: N Europe, bordering on North Sea, Baltic Sea

■ PEOPLE

Nationality: Danish, Dane
Ethnic Groups: Scandinavian, Eskimo, Faroese, German
Languages: Danish, Faroese, Greenlandic (an Eskimo dialect); small German-speaking minority
Religions: 91% Evangelical Lutheran, 2% other Protestant and Roman Catholic, 7% other
Marriages: 6.0 (per 1,000) (1991)
Divorces: 2.95 (per 1,000) (1989)

■ GOVERNMENT

Leader(s): Prime Min. Nyrup Rasmussen, Queen Margrethe II
Government Type: constitutional monarchy
Administrative Divisions: 14 counties and 1 city; dependent areas inc.: Faeroe Islands, Greenland (see Greenland entry for details)
Independence: became a constitutional monarchy in 1849
National Holiday: Birthday of the Queen, Apr. 16

■ ECONOMY

Overview: advanced agriculture and industry; extensive government welfare measures; highly dependent on foreign trade
GNP: n.a., GDP $94.2 billion, per capita $18,200; real growth rate 1% (1992)
Inflation: 2.1% (1992)
Industries: food processing, machinery and equipment, textiles and clothing, chemical products, electronics, construction, furniture and other wood products
Labour Force: 2,852,000 (1992); 74.7% services, 20% industry, 5.3% agriculture (1989)
Unemployment: 11.4% (1992)
Agriculture: accounts for 4% of GNP and employs 5.6% of labour force (includes fishing); farm products account for nearly 15% of export revenues; principal products—meat, dairy, grain, potatoes, rape, sugar beets, fish; self-sufficient in food production
Natural Resources: crude oil, natural gas, fish, salt, limestone

■ FINANCE/TRADE

Currency: krone (pl. kroner) (DKr)
International Reserves Excluding Gold: $9,530 million (Jan. 1994)
Gold Reserves: 1.64 million fine troy ounces (Jan. 1994)
Budget: revenues $48.8 billion; expenditures $55.3 billion, including capital expenditures (1992)
Defence Expenditures: $2.6 billion (5.0% of total govt. expenditure) (1990)
External Debt: $40 billion (1992)
Exports: $36.884 billion (1993 est.); commodities: meat and meat products, dairy products, transport equipment, fish, chemicals, industrial machinery; partners: US 6%, Germany, Norway, Sweden, UK, other European Community, Japan
Imports: $30.540 billion (1993 est.); commodities: petroleum, machinery and equipment, chemicals, grain and foodstuffs, textiles, paper; partners: US 7%, Germany, Netherlands, Sweden, UK, other European Community

■ HEALTH

Births: 13/1,000 population (1993)
Deaths: 12/1,000 population (1993)
Infant Mortality: 7.5 deaths/1,000 live births (1993)
Life Expectancy at Birth: 72 years male, 78 years female (1993)
No. of Physicians: 25.1/10,000 population (1992)

■ EDUCATION

Govt. Expenditure: 9.71% of govt. expenditure (1990)
Literacy: 99% (1993)

■ COMMUNICATIONS

Daily newspapers: 46 (1992)
Televisions: 528.3/1,000 inhabitants (1992)
Radios: 1,012/1,000 inhabitants (1992)
Telephones: 85.65/100 inhabitants (1992)

■ TRANSPORTATION

Motor Vehicles: 1,892,624; 1,590,570 passenger cars (1990)
Roads: 66,482 km; 64,551 km hard surface
Railway: 2,770 km (1993)
Air Traffic: 4,582,000 passengers carried (1991)
Airports: 118 airfields, of which 109 are usable; 28 have permanent-surface runways (1993)

Canadian Embassy: Kr. Bernikowsgade 1, 1105 Copenhagen K, Denmark. Tel: (011-45-33) 12-22-99. Fax: (011-45-33) 14-05-85
Representative to Canada: Embassy of the Kingdom of Denmark, 85 Range Rd, Ste 702, Ottawa ON K1N 8J6. Tel: (613) 234-0704. Fax: (613) 234-7368.

Djibouti

Long-Form Name: Republic of Djibouti
Capital: Djibouti
Population: 500,000 (1993 est.)

■ GEOGRAPHY

Area: 23,200 sq. km
Coastline: 314 km
Climate: desert; torrid, dry
Environment: vast wasteland
Terrain: coastal plain and plateau separated by central mountains
Land Use: 0% arable; 0% permanent; 9% meadows; negligible forest; 91% other
Location: E Africa, bordering on Gulf of Aden

■ PEOPLE

Nationality: Djiboutian

Ethnic Groups: 60% Somali (Issa); 35% Afar, 5% French, Arab, Ethiopian and Italian
Languages: French and Arabic (both official); Somali and Afar widely used
Religions: 94% Moslem, 6% Christian
Marriages: n.a.
Divorces: n.a.

■ GOVERNMENT

Leader(s): Pres. Hassan Gouled Aptidon, Prime Min. Barkat Gourad Hamadou
Government Type: republic
Administrative Divisions: 5 districts
Independence: June 27, 1977 (from France; formerly known as French Territory of the Afars and Issas)
National Holiday: Independence Day, June 27

■ ECONOMY

Overview: based on service activities related to country's strategic location and status as a free trade zone; unemployment rate of over 30%; Djibouti is heavily dependent on foreign aid
GNP: n.a., GDP $358 million, $1,030 per capita; real growth rate 1.2% (1990 est.)
Inflation: 7.7% (1991 est.)
Industries: limited to a few small-scale enterprises, such as dairy products and mineral-water bottling
Labour Force: n.a.
Unemployment: over 30% (1989)
Agriculture: accounts for only 3% of GDP; scanty rainfall limits crop production to mostly fruit and vegetables; half of population pastoral nomads herding goats, sheep and camels; imports bulk of food needs
Natural Resources: geothermal areas

■ FINANCE/TRADE

Currency: Djibouti franc (DF)
International Reserves Excluding Gold: $76 million (Jan. 1994)
Gold Reserves: n.a.
Budget: revenues $170 million; expenditures $203 million, including capital expenditures of $70 million (1991 est.)
Defence Expenditures: $26 million (1989)
External Debt: $190 million (1992)
Exports: $17 million (1991); commodities: hides and skins, coffee (in transit); partners: Middle East 50%, Africa 43%, Western Europe 7%
Imports: $214 million (1991); commodities: foods, beverages, transport equipment, chemicals, petroleum products; partners: European Community 36%, Africa 21%, Bahrain 14%, Asia 12%, US 2%

■ HEALTH

Births: 47/1,000 population (1993)
Deaths: 17/1,000 population (1993)
Infant Mortality: 117 deaths/1,000 live births (1993)
Life Expectancy at Birth: 46 years male, 50 years female (1993)
No. of Physicians: 2.4/10,000 population (1992)

■ EDUCATION

Govt. Expenditure: 11.1% of government expenditure (1991)
Literacy: 48% (1993)

■ COMMUNICATIONS

Daily newspapers: 1 (1992)
Televisions: 55.4/1,000 inhabitants (1992)
Radios: 88/1,000 inhabitants (1992)
Telephones: 2.4/100 inhabitants (1992)

■ TRANSPORTATION

Motor Vehicles: 15,000; 13,000 passenger cars (1990)
Roads: 2,900 km; 280 km paved
Railway: 100 km
Air Traffic: 131,000 passengers carried (1991)
Airports: 13 airfields, of which 11 are usable; 2 have permanent-surface runways (1993)

Canadian Embassy: c/o The Canadian Embassy, Old Airport Area, Higher 23, Kebele 12, House Number 122, Addis Ababa; mailing address: P.O. Box 1130, Addis Ababa, Ethiopia. Tel: (011-251-1) 71-30-22. Fax: (011-251-1) 71-30-33
Representative to Canada: c/o Embassy of the Republic of Djibouti, 1156 15th St, NW, Ste 515, Washington, DC 20005 USA. Tel: (202) 331-0270. Fax: (202) 331-0302.

Dominica

Long-Form Name: Commonwealth of Dominica
Capital: Roseau
Population: 100,000 (1993 est.)

■ GEOGRAPHY

Area: 750 sq. km
Coastline: 148 km
Climate: tropical; moderated by northeast trade winds; heavy rainfall
Environment: flash floods a constant hazard; occasional hurricanes
Terrain: rugged mountains of volcanic origin
Land Use: 9% arable; 13% permanent; 3% meadows; 41% forest; 34% other

Location: Caribbean Islands

■ PEOPLE

Nationality: Dominican
Ethnic Groups: mostly black; some Carib Indians
Languages: English (official); French patois widely spoken
Religions: 77% Roman Catholic; 15% Protestant, 2% none, 1% unknown, 5% other
Marriages: 2.7 (per 1,000) (1990)
Divorces: n.a.

■ GOVERNMENT

Leader(s): Prime Min. (Mary) Eugenia Charles, Pres. Crispin Anselm Sorhaindo
Government Type: parliamentary democracy
Administrative Divisions: 10 parishes
Independence: Nov. 3, 1978 (from UK)
National Holiday: Independence Day, Nov. 3

■ ECONOMY

Overview: dependent on agriculture and vulnerable to climatic conditions; tourist potential (undeveloped)
GNP: $175 million, per capita $2,440; real growth rate 4.4% (1991)
Inflation: 1.4% (1990)
Industries: agricultural processing, tourism, soap and other coconut-based products, cigars, pumice mining, cement blocks, shoes
Labour Force: 30,600 (1989); 40% agriculture, 32% industry and commerce, 28% services
Unemployment: 15% (1991)
Agriculture: accounts for 30% of GDP; principal crops—bananas, citrus fruit, coconuts, root crops; bananas provide the bulk of export earnings; forestry and fisheries potential not exploited
Natural Resources: timber

■ FINANCE/TRADE

Currency: East Caribbean dollar ($EC)
International Reserves Excluding Gold: $19 million (Oct. 1993)
Gold Reserves: n.a.
Budget: revenues $70 million; expenditures $84 million, including capital expenditures of $26 million (1991 est.)
Defence Expenditures: n.a.
External Debt: $93 million (1992)
Exports: $56 million (1992); commodities: bananas, coconuts, grapefruit, soap, galvanized sheets; partners: UK 72%, Jamaica 10%, OECS 6%, US 3%, other 9%
Imports: $111 million (1992); commodities: food, oils and fats, chemicals, fuels and lubricants, manufactured goods, machinery and

equipment; partners: US 23%, UK 18%, CARI-COM 15%, OECS 15%, Japan 5%, Canada 3%, other 21%

■ HEALTH

Births: 20/1,000 population (1993)
Deaths: 7/1,000 population (1993)
Infant Mortality: 18.4 deaths/1,000 live births (1993)
Life Expectancy at Birth: 73 years male, 79 years female (1993)
No. of Physicians: 3.4/10,000 population (1992)

■ EDUCATION

Govt. Expenditure: 10.6% of government expenditure (1989)
Literacy: 94.1% (1993)

■ COMMUNICATIONS

Daily newspapers: 2 (1992)
Televisions: 49.4/1,000 inhabitants (1992)
Radios: 507/1,000 inhabitants (1992)
Telephones: 9.1/100 inhabitants (1992)

■ TRANSPORTATION

Motor Vehicles: 4,250; 2,700 passenger cars (1990)
Roads: 750 km; 370 km paved
Railway: n.a.
Air Traffic: n.a.
Airports: 2 airfields, both usable and with permanent-surface runways

Canadian Embassy: c/o The Canadian High Commission, Bishop's Court Hill, St. Michael, Barbados; mailing address: P.O. Box 404, Bridgetown, Barbados. Tel: (809) 429-3550. Fax: (809) 429-3780.
Representative to Canada: c/o High Commission for the Countries of the Organization of Eastern Caribbean States, 112 Kent St, Ste 1610, Place de Ville, Tower B, Ottawa, ON K1P 5P2. Tel: (613) 236-8952. Fax: (613) 236-3042.

Dominican Republic

Long-Form Name: Dominican Republic
Capital: Santo Domingo
Population: 7,600,000 (1993 est.)

■ GEOGRAPHY

Area: 48,730 sq. km
Coastline: 1,288 km
Climate: tropical maritime; little seasonal temperature variation
Environment: subject to occasional hurricanes (July to Oct.); deforestation

Terrain: rugged highlands and mountains with fertile valleys interspersed
Land Use: 23% arable; 7% permanent; 43% meadows; 13% forest; 14% other
Location: West Indies, bordering on Caribbean Sea, Atlantic Ocean

■ PEOPLE

Nationality: Dominican
Ethnic Groups: 73% mixed, 16% white, 11% black
Languages: Spanish
Religions: 95% Roman Catholic
Marriages: 3.3 (per 1,000) (1985)
Divorces: 1.2 (per 1,000) (1985)

■ GOVERNMENT

Leader(s): Pres. Joaquín Balaguer Ricardo
Government Type: republic
Administrative Divisions: 29 provinces and 1 district
Independence: Feb. 27, 1844 (from Haiti)
National Holiday: Independence Day, Feb. 27

■ ECONOMY

Overview: agriculture is the backbone of the economy (sugar cane); tourism and a free trade zone help
GNP: $8.4 billion, per capita $1,120; real growth rate 5% (1992 est.)
Inflation: 53.9% (1991)
Industries: tourism, sugar processing, ferronickel and gold mining, textiles, cement, tobacco
Labour Force: 2,187,000 (1992); 45.7% agriculture, 38.8% services, 15.5% industry (1989)
Unemployment: 30% (1992 est.)
Agriculture: accounts for 15% of GDP and employs 49% of labour force; sugar cane most important commercial crop, followed by coffee, cotton and cocoa; food crops; animal output; not self-sufficient in food
Natural Resources: nickel, bauxite, gold, silver

■ FINANCE/TRADE

Currency: Dominican peso ($RD)
International Reserves Excluding Gold: $603 million (Jan. 1994)
Gold Reserves: 0.02 million fine troy ounces (Jan. 1994)
Budget: revenues $1.4 billion; expenditures $1.8 billion, including capital expenditures (1993 est.)
Defence Expenditures: 4.84% of govt. expenditure (1990)
External Debt: $4.649 billion (1992)
Exports: $112 million (1992); commodities: sugar, coffee, cocoa, gold, ferronickel; partners:

US (including Puerto Rico) 74%
Imports: $566 million (1992); commodities: foodstuffs, petroleum, cotton and fabrics, chemicals and pharmaceuticals; partners: US (including Puerto Rico) 36%

■ HEALTH

Births: 28/1,000 population (1993)
Deaths: 6/1,000 population (1993)
Infant Mortality: 43 deaths/1,000 live births (1993)
Life Expectancy at Birth: 65 years male, 70 years female (1993)
No. of Physicians: 5.7/10,000 population (1992)

■ EDUCATION

Govt. Expenditure: 10.17% of government expenditure (1990)
Literacy: 83.3% (1992)

■ COMMUNICATIONS

Daily newspapers: 10 (1992)
Televisions: 81.9/1,000 inhabitants (1992)
Radios: 168/1,000 inhabitants (1992)
Telephones: 2.1/100 inhabitants (1980).

■ TRANSPORTATION

Motor Vehicles: 270,000; 160,000 passenger cars (1990)
Roads: 17,390 km; 4,941 km paved
Railway: 1,655 km total in numerous segments and 4 different gauges
Air Traffic: 648,000 passengers carried (1991)
Airports: 36 airfields, of which 30 are usable; 12 have permanent-surface runways (1993)

Canadian Embassy: c/o The Canadian Embassy, Maximo Gomez 30, Santo Domingo; mailing address: Apartado 2054, Santo Domingo 1, Dominican Republic. Tel: (809) 689-0002. Fax: (809) 682-2691.
Representative to Canada: c/o Consulate General, 1055 St. Mathieu Central Tower Bur. 241, Montreal, Quebec, H3H 2S3. Tel: (514) 933-9008. Fax: (514) 933-2070.

Ecuador

Long-Form Name: Republic of Ecuador
Capital: Quito
Population: 10,300,000 (1993 est.)

■ GEOGRAPHY

Area: Area can only be estimated, as a portion of the frontier has not been delimited. One estimate is 270,670 sq. km, which excludes the litigation zone between Ecuador and Peru, but includes the Galapagos Islands
Coastline: 2,237 km
Climate: tropical along coast becoming cooler inland
Environment: subject to frequent earthquakes, landslides, volcanic activity; deforestation; desertification; soil erosion; periodic droughts
Terrain: coastal plain, inter-Andean central highlands and flat to rolling eastern jungle
Land Use: 6% arable; 3% permanent; 17% meadows; 51% forest; 23% other
Location: NW South America, bordering on Pacific Ocean

■ PEOPLE

Nationality: Ecuadorian
Ethnic Groups: 55% mestizo (mixed Indian and Spanish), 25% Indian, 10% Spanish, 10% black
Languages: Spanish (official), Indian languages, especially Quechua
Religions: 95% Roman Catholic
Marriages: 6.7 (per 1,000) (1990)
Divorces: 0.54 (per 1,000) (1989)

■ GOVERNMENT

Leader(s): Pres. Sixto Duran Ballen, V. Pres. Alberto Dahik Garzoni
Government Type: republic
Administrative Divisions: 21 provinces
Independence: May 24, 1822 (from Spain; Battle of Pichincha)
National Holiday: Independence Day, Aug. 10

■ ECONOMY

Overview: recovering from a major earthquake in 1987 which halted oil exports; vulnerable to international oil prices; the banana crop, second in importance only to oil, has been hurt by EC import quotas and banana blight
GNP: n.a., GDP $11.8 billion, per capita $1,100; real growth rate 3.0% (1991)
Inflation: 54.6% (1992)
Industries: food processing, textiles, metal works, paper products, chemicals, fishing, timber, petroleum
Labour Force: 3,287,000 (1992); 38.5% agriculture, 19.8% industry, 41.6% services and other activities (1989)
Unemployment: 8.0% (1992)
Agriculture: accounts for 18% of GDP and 35% of labour force (including fishing and forestry); leading producer and exporter of bananas and balsawood; crop and livestock sector; net importer of food-grain, dairy products and sugar
Natural Resources: petroleum, fish, timber

■ FINANCE/TRADE

Currency: sucre (S/)
International Reserves Excluding Gold: $1,306 million (Oct. 1993)
Gold Reserves: 0.41 million fine troy ounces (Oct. 1993)
Budget: revenues $1.9 billion; expenditures $1.9 billion, including capital expenditures (1992)
Defence Expenditures: $251.38 million (12.95% of total govt. expenditure) (1990)
External Debt: $12.28 billion (1992)
Exports: $3.008 billion (1992); commodities: petroleum 47%, coffee, bananas, cocoa products, shrimp, fish products; partners: US 58%, Latin America, Caribbean, European Community countries
Imports: $2.500 billion (1992); commodities: transport equipment, vehicles, machinery, chemicals, petroleum; partners: US 28%, Latin America, Caribbean, European Community, Japan

■ HEALTH

Births: 31/1,000 population (1993)
Deaths: 6/1,000 population (1993)
Infant Mortality: 53 deaths/1,000 live births (1993)
Life Expectancy at Birth: 65 years male, 69 years female (1993)
No. of Physicians: 12.3/10,000 population (1992)

■ EDUCATION

Govt. Expenditure: 17.5% of government expenditure (1991)
Literacy: 86% (1993)

■ COMMUNICATIONS

Daily newspapers: 26 (1992)
Televisions: 82.3/1,000 inhabitants (1992)
Radios: 314/1,000 inhabitants (1992)
Telephones: 3.7/100 inhabitants (1992)

■ TRANSPORTATION

Motor Vehicles: 240,000; 77,000 passenger cars (1990)
Roads: 28,000 km; 3,600 km paved
Railway: 950 km
Air Traffic: 752,000 passengers carried (1991)
Airports: 174 airfields, of which 173 are usable; 52 have permanent-surface runways (1993)

Canadian Embassy: c/o The Canadian Embassy, Calle 76, No. 11-52, Bogotá, Colombia; mailing address: Apartado Aereo 53531, Bogotá 2, Colombia. Tel: (011-57-1) 217-5555. Fax (011-57-1) 310-4509
Representative to Canada: Embassy of the Republic of Ecuador, 50 O'Connor St, Ste 1311, Ottawa ON K1P 6L2. Tel: (613) 563-8206. Fax: (613) 235-5776.

Egypt

Long-Form Name: Arab Republic of Egypt
Capital: Cairo
Population: 58,300,000 (1993 est.)

■ GEOGRAPHY

Area: 1,001,450 sq. km
Coastline: 2,450 km
Climate: desert; hot, dry summers with moderate winters
Environment: Nile is only perennial water source; increasing soil salinization below Aswan High Dam; hot, driving windstorm called khamsin occurs in spring; water pollution; desertification
Terrain: vast desert plateau interrupted by Nile valley and delta
Land Use: 3% arable; 2% permanent; 0% meadows; negligible forest; 95% other
Location: NE Africa, bordering on Mediterranean Sea, Red Sea

■ PEOPLE

Nationality: Egyptian
Ethnic Groups: 90% Eastern Hamitic stock; 10% Greek, Italian, Syro-Lebanese
Languages: Arabic (official); English and French
Religions: 94% Moslem (mostly Sunni), 6% Coptic Christian and other
Marriages: 9.1 (per 1,000) (1985)
Divorces: 1.6 (per 1,000) (1985)

■ GOVERNMENT

Leader(s): Prime Min. Atef Muhamed Sidki, Pres. Mohammad Hosni Mubarak
Government Type: republic
Administrative Divisions: 26 governorates
Independence: Feb. 28, 1922 (from UK; formerly known as United Arab Republic)
National Holiday: Anniversary of the Revolution, July 23

■ ECONOMY

Overview: urban population growth puts pressure on the agricultural sector; having difficulty with its debt servicing; vulnerable to oil prices; unemployment has become a growing problem
GNP: $41.2 billion, per capita $730; real growth rate 2.1% (1992 est.)
Inflation: 13.6% (1992)
Industries: textiles, food processing, tourism, chemicals, petroleum, construction, cement,

metals
Labour Force: 16,033,600 (1989); 54.1% services; 33.9% agriculture; 12% industry (1989); 2,500,000 Egyptians work abroad, mostly in Iraq and the Gulf Arab states
Unemployment: 20% (1992 est.)
Agriculture: accounts for 20% of GNP and employs more than one-third of labour force; dependent on irrigation water from the Nile; world's fifth-largest cotton exporter; other crops include rice, corn, wheat, beans, fruit, vegetables; not self-sufficient in food
Natural Resources: crude oil, natural gas, iron ore, phosphates, manganese, limestone, gypsum, talc, asbestos, lead, zinc

■ FINANCE/TRADE

Currency: Egyptian pound (LE)
International Reserves Excluding Gold: $12,904 million (Dec. 1993)
Gold Reserves: 2.43 million fine troy ounces (Dec. 1993)
Budget: revenues $12.6 billion; expenditures $15.2 billion, including capital expenditures of $4 billion (1992 est.)
Defence Expenditures: $2.05 billion, 5% of GDP (1992-93)
External Debt: $40.018 billion (1992)
Exports: $3.071 billion (1992); commodities: raw cotton, crude and refined petroleum, cotton yarn, textiles; partners: US, European Community, Japan, Eastern Europe
Imports: $8.357 billion (1992); commodities: foods, machinery and equipment, fertilizers, wood products, durable consumer goods, capital goods; partners: US, European Community, Japan, Eastern Europe

■ HEALTH

Births: 31/1,000 population (1993)
Deaths: 8/1,000 population (1993)
Infant Mortality: 56 deaths/1,000 live births (1993)
Life Expectancy at Birth: 59 years male, 62 years female (1993)
No. of Physicians: 13/10,000 population (1992)

■ EDUCATION

Govt. Expenditure: 13.39% of government expenditure (1989)
Literacy: 48% (1993)

■ COMMUNICATIONS

Daily newspapers: 8 (1992)
Televisions: 97.7/1,000 inhabitants (1992)
Radios: 322/1,000 inhabitants (1992)
Telephones: 2.9/100 inhabitants (1992)

■ TRANSPORTATION

Motor Vehicles: 725,000; 450,000 passenger cars (1990)
Roads: 51,925 km; 17,900 km paved (1993)
Railway: 5,110 km
Air Traffic: 2,602,000 passengers carried (1991)
Airports: 92 airfields, of which 82 are usable; 66 have permanent-surface runways (1993)

Canadian Embassy: 6 Mohamed Fahmi el Sayed St, Garden City, Cairo; mailing address: P.O. Box 2646, Cairo, Egypt. Tel: (011-20-2) 354-3110. Fax: (011-20-2) 356-3548
Representative to Canada: Embassy of the Arab Republic of Egypt, 454 Laurier Ave E, Ottawa ON K1N 6R3. Tel: (613) 234-4931. Fax: (613) 234-9347.

El Salvador

Long-Form Name: Republic of El Salvador
Capital: San Salvador
Population: 5,200,000 (1993 est.)

■ GEOGRAPHY

Area: 21,040 sq. km
Coastline: 307 km
Climate: tropical; rainy season (May to Oct.), dry season (Nov. to Apr.)
Environment: The Land of Volcanoes; subject to frequent and sometimes very destructive earthquakes; deforestation; soil erosion; water pollution
Terrain: mostly mountains with narrow coastal belt and central plateau
Land Use: 27% arable; 8% permanent; 29% meadows; 6% forest; 30% other
Location: Central (Latin) America, bordering on Pacific Ocean

■ PEOPLE

Nationality: Salvadoran
Ethnic Groups: 94% mestizo, 5% Indian, 1% white
Languages: Spanish, Nahua spoken among some Indians
Religions: approx. 75% Roman Catholic, with activity by Protestant groups throughout the country
Marriages: 4.4 (per 1,000) (1990)
Divorces: 0.43 (per 1,000) (1989)

■ GOVERNMENT

Leader(s): Pres. Armando Calderon Sol
Government Type: republic
Administrative Divisions: 14 departments

Independence: Sept. 15, 1821 (from Spain)
National Holiday: Independence Day, Sept. 15

ECONOMY

Overview: agricultural sector accounts for one-quarter of GDP and employs majority of labour force; major crop is coffee; economic losses due to guerrilla sabotage are extensive
GNP: n.a., GDP $5.9 billion, per capita $1,060; real growth rate 4.6% (1992 est.)
Inflation: 11.2% (1992)
Industries: food processing, textiles, non-metallic products, tobacco, beverages, clothing, petroleum products, cement
Labour Force: 2,155,000 (1992); 8.2% agriculture, 21.8% industry, 70% services (1989)
Unemployment: 7.5% (1992)
Agriculture: accounts for 24% of GDP and 40% of labour force (including fishing and forestry); coffee most important commercial crop; other products—sugar cane, corn, rice, beans, oilseeds, beef, dairy products, shrimp; not self-sufficient in food
Natural Resources: hydroelectricity and geothermal power, crude oil

FINANCE/TRADE

Currency: colón (pl. colones) (C/)
International Reserves Excluding Gold: $512 million (Jan. 1994)
Gold Reserves: 0.47 million fine troy ounces (Jan. 1994)
Budget: revenues $846 million; expenditures $890 million, including capital expenditures (1992 est.)
Defence Expenditures: 16.04% of total govt. expenditure (1992)
External Debt: $2.131 billion (1992)
Exports: $555 million (1992); commodities: coffee 60%, sugar, cotton, shrimp; partners: US 49%, Germany 24%, Guatemala 7%, Costa Rica 4%, Japan 4%
Imports: $1.544 billion (1992); commodities: petroleum products, consumer goods, foodstuffs, machinery, construction materials, fertilizer; partners: US 40%, Guatemala 12%, Venezuela 7%, Mexico 7%, Germany 5%, Japan 4%

HEALTH

Births: 34/1,000 population (1993)
Deaths: 8/1,000 population (1993)
Infant Mortality: 53 deaths/1,000 live births (1993)
Life Expectancy at Birth: 61 years male, 68 years female (1993)
No. of Physicians: 3.5/10,000 population (1992)

EDUCATION

Govt. Expenditure: 12.8% of govt. expenditure (1992)
Literacy: 73% (1992)

COMMUNICATIONS

Daily newspapers: 5 (1992)
Televisions: 87.1/1,000 inhabitants (1992)
Radios: 403/1,000 inhabitants (1992)
Telephones: 2.8/100 inhabitants (1992)

TRANSPORTATION

Motor Vehicles: 160,000; 80,000 passenger cars (1990)
Roads: 12,562 km; 1,798 km paved
Railway: 621 km
Air Traffic: 590,000 passengers carried (1991)
Airports: 105 airfields, of which 74 are usable; 5 have permanent-surface runways (1993)

Canadian Embassy: c/o The Canadian Embassy, 10 Avenida 21-25, Zona 14, Guatemala City; mailing address: P.O. Box 400, Guatemala, C.A. Tel: (011-502-2) 33-61-02. Fax: (011-502-2) 33-61-61
Representative to Canada: Embassy of the Republic of El Salvador, 209 Kent St, Ste 504, Ottawa ON K2P 1Z8. Tel: (613) 238-2939. Fax: (613) 238-6940.

Equatorial Guinea

Long-Form Name: Republic of Equatorial Guinea
Capital: Malabo
Population: 400,000 (1993 est.)

GEOGRAPHY

Area: 28,050 sq. km
Coastline: 296 km
Climate: tropical; always hot, humid
Environment: subject to violent windstorms
Terrain: coastal plains rise to interior hills; islands are volcanic
Land Use: 8% arable; 4% permanent; 4% meadows; 51% forest; 33% other
Location: WC Africa, bordering on South Atlantic Ocean

PEOPLE

Nationality: Equatorial Guinean or Equatoguinean
Ethnic Groups: indigenous population of Bioko, primarily Bubi, some Fernandinos; Rio Muni, primarily Fang; less than 1,000 Europeans, mostly Spanish
Languages: Spanish (official), pidgin English,

Fang, Bubi, Ndowe, Bujeba, Anobones and Corisqueño
Religions: natives all nominally Christian and predominantly Roman Catholic; some pagan practices retained (5%)
Marriages: n.a.
Divorces: n.a.

■ GOVERNMENT

Leader(s): Pres. Teodoro Obiang Nguema Mbasogo, Prime Min. Silvestre Siale Bileka
Government Type: republic in transition to multi-party democracy
Administrative Divisions: 7 provinces
Independence: Oct. 12, 1968 (from Spain; formerly Spanish Guinea)
National Holiday: Independence Day, Oct. 12

■ ECONOMY

Overview: the economy is recovering from destruction by a past regime; subsistence agriculture, forestry and fishing predominate; little industry; undeveloped natural resources
GNP: $142 million, per capita $330; real growth rate 5.8% (1991)
Inflation: -3.2% (1991)
Industries: fishing, sawmilling
Labour Force: 180,000 (1992); 66% agriculture, 23% services, 11% industry (1989)
Unemployment: n.a.
Agriculture: cash crops—timber and coffee from Rio Muni, cocoa from Bioko; food crops—rice, yams, cassava, bananas, oil, palm nuts, manioc, livestock
Natural Resources: timber, crude oil, small unexploited deposits of gold, manganese, uranium

■ FINANCE/TRADE

Currency: Communauté financière africaine franc (CFAF)
International Reserves Excluding Gold: $0 (Dec. 1993)
Gold Reserves: n.a.
Budget: revenues $26 million; expenditures $30 million, including capital expenditures of $3 million (1991 est.)
Defence Expenditures: n.a.
External Debt: $246 million (1992)
Exports: $36 million (1991); commodities: coffee, timber, cocoa beans; partners: Spain 44%, Germany 19%, Italy 12%, Netherlands 11%
Imports: $70 million (1991); commodities: petroleum, food, beverages, clothing, machinery; partners: Spain 34%, Italy 16%, France 14%, Netherlands 8%

■ HEALTH

Births: 43/1,000 population (1993)
Deaths: 16/1,000 population (1993)
Infant Mortality: 112 deaths/1,000 live births (1993)
Life Expectancy at Birth: 48 years male, 52 years female (1993)
No. of Physicians: n.a.

■ EDUCATION

Govt. Expenditure: 3.9% of government expenditure (1990)
Literacy: 50.2% (1992)

■ COMMUNICATIONS

Daily newspapers: 1 (1992)
Televisions: 8.7/1,000 inhabitants (1992)
Radios: 374/1,000 inhabitants (1992)
Telephones: n.a.

■ TRANSPORTATION

Motor Vehicles: 9,000; 5,500 passenger cars (1990)
Roads: 2,760 km
Railway: n.a.
Air Traffic: 14,000 passengers carried (1991)
Airports: 3 airfields, all usable; 2 have permanent-surface runways (1993)

Canadian Embassy: The Canadian Embassy to Equatorial Guinea, c/o P.O. Box 4037, Libreville, Gabon. Tel: (011-241) 74-34-64. Fax (011-241) 74-34-66.

Eritrea

Long-Form Name: State of Eritrea
Capital: Asmara (formerly Asmera)
Population: 3,467,087 (1993 est.)

■ GEOGRAPHY

Area: 121,320 sq. km
Coastline: 1,151 km; 2,234 km including island coastlines
Climate: hot, dry desert along Red Sea coast, cooler and wetter in central highlands, semi-arid in west
Environment: frequent droughts, famine, deforestation, soil erosion, overgrazing
Terrain: highlands descending to coastal desert in east, hilly in northwest, flat to rolling plains in southwest
Land Use: 3% arable, 2% permanent crops, 40% meadows and pastures, 5% forests, 50% other
Location: E Africa

■ PEOPLE

Nationality: Eritrean
Ethnic Groups: 50% ethnic Tigrays, 40% Tigre and Kunama, 4% Afar, 3% Saho
Languages: Tigre and Kunama, Cushitic dialects, Tigre, Nora Bana, Arabic
Religions: Muslim, Coptic Christian, Roman Catholic, Protestant
Marriages: n.a.
Divorces: n.a.

■ GOVERNMENT

Leader(s): Pres. Issaias Afewerki (March 4)
Government Type: transitional govt.
Administrative Divisions: n.a.
Independence: April 27, 1993 (from Ethiopia)
National Holiday: National Day (independence from Ethiopia), May 25

■ ECONOMY

Overview: with independence from Ethiopia, Eritrea faces the bitter economic problems of a small and desperately poor nation; subsistence farming will continue to be the people's economic mainstay; production is augmented by remittances from abroad, and there are long-term prospects for revenue from offshore oil development, offshore fishing, and tourism; Ethiopia is largely dependent on Eritrean ports for foreign trade
GNP: n.a., GDP $400 million, $115 per capita; real growth rate n.a. (1992 est.)
Inflation: n.a.
Industries: food processing, beverages, textiles, clothing manufacture
Labour Force: n.a.
Unemployment: n.a.
Agriculture: n.a.
Natural Resources: gold, potash, copper, zinc, salt, fish

■ FINANCE/TRADE

Currency: n.a.
International Reserves Excluding Gold: n.a.
Gold Reserves: n.a.
Budget: n.a.
Defence Expenditures: n.a.
External Debt: n.a.
Exports: n.a.
Imports: n.a.

■ HEALTH

Births: n.a.
Deaths: n.a.
Infant Mortality: n.a.
Life Expectancy at Birth: n.a.
No. of Physicians: n.a.

■ EDUCATION

Govt. Expenditure: n.a.
Literacy: n.a.

■ COMMUNICATIONS

Daily newspapers: n.a.
Televisions: n.a.
Radios: n.a.
Telephones: n.a.

■ TRANSPORTATION

Motor Vehicles: n.a.
Roads: 3,845 km; 807 km paved (1993)
Railway: 307 km (1993)
Air Traffic: n.a.
Airports: 5 airfields, all usable; 2 have permanent-surface runways (1993)

Canadian Embassy: c/o Old Airport Area, Higher 23, Kebele 12, House Number 122, Addis Ababa; mailing address: P.O. Box 1130, Addis Ababa, Ethiopia. Tel: (011-251-1) 71-30-22. Fax: (011-251-1) 71 30 33
Representative to Canada: c/o Embassy of the State of Eritrea, 910 17th St NW, Ste 400, Washington, DC 20006 USA. Tel: (202) 429-1991. Fax: (202) 429-9004.

Estonia

Long-Form Name: Republic of Estonia
Capital: Tallinn
Population: 1,600,000 (1993 est.)

■ GEOGRAPHY

Area: 45,100 sq. km
Coastline: 1,393 km
Climate: wet, moderate winter; long windy autumn; warm sunny summer; late and short spring
Environment: severe air pollution, soil and ground water contamination (chemicals and petroleum products), radioactive wastes
Terrain: marshy, lowlands, sloping coastal plain; islands account for 10% of the region
Land Use: 22% arable, negligible permanent crops, 11% meadows and pastures, 31% forest and woodland, 36% other
Location: NE Europe, bordering on Baltic Sea

■ PEOPLE

Nationality: Estonian
Ethnic Groups: 61.5% Estonian, 30.3% Russian, 3% Ukrainian, 2% Byelorussian, 2% other
Languages: Estonian (official), Russian, Latvian, Lithuanian, English and German also spoken

Religions: Lutheran
Marriages: 7.5 (per 1,000) (1990)
Divorces: 3.68 (per 1,000) (1990)

■ GOVERNMENT

Leader(s): Pres. Lennart Meri, Premier Mart Laar
Government Type: republic
Administrative Divisions: none; all districts are under direct republic jurisdiction
Independence: Sept. 6, 1991 (from Soviet Union)
National Holiday: Independence Day, Feb. 24

■ ECONOMY

Overview: mining and manufacturing accounts for 75% of the country's economic output; only about 20% of the labour force is engaged in agriculture
GNP: $6.088 billion, $3,830 per capita; real growth rate 2.8% (1991)
Inflation: n.a.
Industries: accounts for approximately 30% of labour force; electronics, electrical engineering, textiles, clothing, footwear
Labour Force: 795,500 (1990)
Unemployment: 3% (1993); large numbers of underemployed
Agriculture: dairy products, pork, poultry, eggs, fruit, vegetables; net exports of meat, fish, dairy products, potatoes
Natural Resources: fish, shale, phosphorites, amber, limestone, peat, dolomite

■ FINANCE/TRADE

Currency: kroon (pl. kroons)
International Reserves Excluding Gold: n.a.
Gold Reserves: n.a.
Budget: revenues $223 million, expenditures $142 million, including capital expenditures (1992)
Defence Expenditures: negligible (1991)
External Debt: $51 million (1992)
Exports: dairy products, fish, furniture, electrical power, meat; partners: Russia and other former Soviet republics 50%, West 50%
Imports: machinery 45%, oil 13%, chemicals 12%; partners: Finland, Russia

■ HEALTH

Births: 12/1,000 population (1993)
Deaths: 13/1,000 population (1993)
Infant Mortality: 14/1,000 live births (1993)
Life Expectancy at Birth: 65 years male, 75 years female (1993)
No. of Physicians: n.a.

■ EDUCATION

Govt. Expenditure: 7.05% of govt. expenditure (1991)
Literacy: 100% (1993)

■ COMMUNICATIONS

Daily newspapers: 52 papers of all circulation types (1988)
Televisions: n.a.; 3 TV stations (1993)
Radios: n.a.
Telephones: 300,000 total (1990); 21/100 persons (1991)

■ TRANSPORTATION

Motor Vehicles: n.a.
Roads: 30,300 km; 29,200 km hard-surfaced (1990)
Railway: 1,030 km
Air Traffic: n.a.
Airports: 29 airfields, of which 18 are usable; 11 have permanent-surface runways (1993)

Canadian Embassy: The Canadian Embassy to Estonia, c/o The Canadian Embassy, Elizabetes 45-47, Riga LV 1010, Latvia. Tel: (011-371-88) 301-41. Fax (011-371-88) 301-40.
Representative to Canada: c/o Embassy of the Republic of Estonia, 1030 15th St NW, Ste 100, Washington, DC 20005, USA. Tel: (202) 789-0320. Fax: (202) 789-0471.

Ethiopia

Long-Form Name: Ethiopia
Capital: Addis Ababa
Population: 56,700,000 (1993 est.)

■ GEOGRAPHY

Area: 1,127,127 sq. km
Coastline: none; landlocked
Climate: tropical with wide topographic-induced variation; prone to extended droughts
Environment: geologically active Great Rift Valley susceptible to earthquakes, volcanic eruptions; deforestation; overgrazing; soil erosion; desertification; frequent droughts; famine
Terrain: high plateau with central mountain range divided by Great Rift Valley
Land Use: 12% arable; 1% permanent; 41% meadows; 24% forest; 22% other
Location: E Africa, between Somalia and Sudan

■ PEOPLE

Nationality: Ethiopian
Ethnic Groups: 40% Oromo, 32% Amhara and Tigrean, 9% Sidamo, 6% Shankella, 6% Somali,

4% Afar, 2% Gurage, 1% other
Languages: Amharic (official), Tigrinya, Orominga, Arabic, English (major foreign language taught in schools)
Religions: 45-50% Moslem, 35-40% Ethiopian Orthodox, 12% animist, 5% other
Marriages: n.a.
Divorces: n.a.

■ GOVERNMENT

Leader(s): Pres. Meles Zenawi, Premier Tamirat Layne
Government Type: transitional government
Administrative Divisions: 24 administrative regions
Independence: oldest (at least 2,000 years) independent country in Africa and one of the oldest in the world
National Holiday: National Day, April 28

■ ECONOMY

Overview: with the independence of Eritrea on April 27, 1993, Ethiopia continues to face difficult economic problems as one of the poorest and least developed countries in Africa; a centrally-planned state-run economy is based on subsistence agriculture and is vulnerable to climatic conditions
GNP: $6.6 billion, per capita $130; real growth rate 6% (1992 est.)
Inflation: 10.5% (1992)
Industries: cement, textiles, food processing, beverages, chemicals, metals processing, oil refinery
Labour Force: 21,000,000 (1992); 80% agriculture, 12% services, 8% industry (1989)
Unemployment: 44,310 (1991); shortage of skilled labour
Agriculture: accounts for 47% of GDP even though frequent droughts, poor cultivation practices and state economic policies keep farm output low; famines not uncommon; estimated 50% of agricultural production at subsistence level
Natural Resources: small reserves of gold, platinum, copper, potash

■ FINANCE/TRADE

Currency: birr (Br)
International Reserves Excluding Gold: $444 million (Jan. 1994)
Gold Reserves: 0.11 million fine troy ounces (Jan. 1994)
Budget: revenues $1.4 billion; expenditures $2.3 billion, including capital expenditures of $565 million (1991)
Defence Expenditures: $536.30 million (34.98% of total govt. expenditure) (1989)

External Debt: $4.354 billion (1992)
Exports: $169 million (1992); commodities: coffee 60%, hides; partners: US, Germany, Djibouti, Japan, Yemen, France, Italy
Imports: $707 million (1992); commodities: food, fuels, capital goods; partners: USSR, Italy, Germany, Japan, UK, US, France

■ HEALTH

Births: 47/1,000 population (1993)
Deaths: 20/1,000 population (1993)
Infant Mortality: 127 deaths/1,000 live births (1993)
Life Expectancy at Birth: 44 years male, 48 years female (1993)
No. of Physicians: 0.1/10,000 population (1992)

■ EDUCATION

Govt. Expenditure: 9.4% of govt. expenditure (1990)
Literacy: 62% (1993)

■ COMMUNICATIONS

Daily newspapers: 2 (1992)
Televisions: 2.1/1,000 inhabitants (1992)
Radios: 188/1,000 inhabitants (1992)
Telephones: 0.3/100 inhabitants (1992)

■ TRANSPORTATION

Motor Vehicles: 64,000; 43,000 passenger cars (1990)
Roads: 39,150 km; 2,776 km paved (excluding urban roads)
Railway: 781 km
Air Traffic: 636,000 passengers carried (1991)
Airports: 121 airfields, of which 82 are usable; 9 have permanent-surface runways (1993)

Canadian Embassy: Old Airport Area, Higher 23, Kebele 12, House Number 122, Addis Ababa; mailing address: P.O. Box 1130, Addis Ababa, Ethiopia. Tel: (011-251-1) 71-30-22. Fax: (011-251-1) 71 30 33
Representative to Canada: Embassy of Ethiopia, 151 Slater St, Ste 210, Ottawa ON K1P 5H3. Tel: (613) 235-6637. Fax: (613) 235-4638.

Faeroe Islands

Dependent Territory of Denmark

Long-Form Name: Faeroe Islands
Capital: Tórshavn (island of Stremoy)
Population: 48,065 (1993 est.)

■ GEOGRAPHY

Area: 1,399 sq. km (total of 18 islands and some

reefs)
Climate: cold and windy, mild winters, cool
summers, foggy
Land Use: 2% arable; potatoes are important
crop; grazing, esp. for sheep and cattle
Location: Norwegian Sea (N Atlantic Ocean), N
of Scotland

■ PEOPLE

Nationality: Faeroese
Ethnic Groups: Scandinavian
Languages: Faeroese (derived from Old Norse),
Danish

■ GOVERNMENT

Leader(s): three-party ruling coalition: Maria
Petersen, Signer Hansen, Hilmar Kass
Government Type: dependency with some degree
of self-rule
National Holiday: Birthday of the Queen, Apr. 16

■ ECONOMY

Overview: fishing main industry, now in decline,
which poses great danger to the economy; steep
coastline and treacherous currents make trading
by sea difficult; exports: fish and fish products;
partners: Denmark, Norway, Sweden, Germany,
United States

■ FINANCE/TRADE

Currency: Danish krone (kr)

Falkland Islands

Dependent Territory of the United Kingdom

Long-Form Name: Colony of the Falkland Islands
Capital: Stanley (on East Falkland)
Population: 2,206 (1993 est.)

■ GEOGRAPHY

Area: numerous islands covering 12,225 sq. km
of ocean; total land area 12,170 sq km
Climate: damp, cool, temperate, strong winds
esp. in spring, occasional snow all year
Land Use: 99% pastureland
Location: South Atlantic Ocean

■ PEOPLE

Nationality: Falkland Islander
Ethnic Groups: almost 100% British descent
Languages: English

■ GOVERNMENT

Leader(s): Gov. David Everard Tatham
Government Type: dependent territory of the UK,
although in 1990 Argentina declared Falklands

and other British-held South Atlantic Islands
part of new Argentine province Tierra del Fuego
Independence: none
National Holiday: Liberation Day, June 14

■ ECONOMY

Overview: heavily agricultural, esp. sheep farming, with wool main product; fishing: illex
squid; exports tend to outweigh imports in
value; chief trading partner: United Kingdom
Natural Resources: fish, wildlife

■ FINANCE/TRADE

Currency: Falkland Islands pound (FKP), at parity with the British pound sterling

---

Fiji

Long-Form Name: Republic of Fiji
Capital: Suva
Population: 800,000 (1993 est.)

■ GEOGRAPHY

Area: 18,270 sq. km
Coastline: 1,129 km
Climate: tropical marine; only slight seasonal
temperature variation
Environment: subject to hurricanes from Nov. to
Jan.; includes 332 islands of which approx. 110
are inhabited
Terrain: mostly mountains of volcanic origin
Land Use: 8% arable; 5% permanent; 3% mead-
ows; 65% forest; 19% other
Location: Pacific Ocean, N of New Zealand

■ PEOPLE

Nationality: Fijian
Ethnic Groups: 46% Indian, 49% Fijian, 5%
European, other Pacific Islanders, overseas
Chinese and others
Languages: English (official); Fijian; Hindi
Religions: Christianity 52%, Hinduism 38%,
Islam 8%, other 2%
Marriages: 9.3 (per 1,000) (1988)
Divorces: n.a.

■ GOVERNMENT

Leader(s): Pres. Kamisese Mara, Prime Min.
Sitiveni Rabuka
Government Type: republic
Administrative Divisions: 14 provinces and 1
dependency
Independence: Oct. 10, 1970 (from UK)
National Holiday: Independence Day, Oct. 10

■ ECONOMY

Overview: the economy, based on agriculture,

has recovered from military coups, droughts and a drop in tourism; sugar exports are a major source of income

GNP: $1.4 billion, per capita $1,900; real growth rate 3% (1992 est.)

Inflation: 4.9% (1992)

Industries: sugar, copra, tourism, gold, silver, fishing, clothing, lumber, small cottage industries

Labour Force: 250,000 (1992); 44.1% agriculture, 47.8% services, 8.1% industry (1989)

Unemployment: 5.9% (1991)

Agriculture: accounts for 23% of GDP; principal cash crop is sugar cane; coconuts, cassava, rice, sweet potatoes and bananas; small livestock sector includes cattle, pigs, horses and goats

Natural Resources: timber, fish, gold, copper, offshore oil potential

■ FINANCE/TRADE

Currency: Fiji dollar ($F)

International Reserves Excluding Gold: $264 million (Jan. 1994)

Gold Reserves: none (1991)

Budget: revenues $455 million; expenditures $546 million, including capital expenditures (1993 est.)

Defence Expenditures: 5.56% of total govt. expenditure (1993)

External Debt: $337 million (1992)

Exports: $435 million (1992); commodities: sugar 49%, copra, processed fish, lumber; partners: UK 45%, Australia 21%, US 4.7%

Imports: $624 million (1992); commodities: food 15%, petroleum products, machinery, consumer goods; partners: US 48%, New Zealand, Australia, Japan

■ HEALTH

Births: 25/1,000 population (1993)

Deaths: 5/1,000 population (1993)

Infant Mortality: 10 deaths/1,000 live births (1993)

Life Expectancy at Birth: 62 years male, 66 years female (1993)

No. of Physicians: 4.9/10,000 population (1990)

■ EDUCATION

Govt. Expenditure: 19.64% of govt. expenditure (1993)

Literacy: 79% (1992)

■ COMMUNICATIONS

Daily newspapers: 2 (1992)

Televisions: 14.0/1,000 inhabitants (1992)

Radios: 573/1,000 inhabitants (1992)

Telephones: 8.3/100 inhabitants (1992)

■ TRANSPORTATION

Motor Vehicles: 56,000; 30,000 passenger cars (1990)

Roads: 3,300 km; 1,590 km paved

Railway: 643 km

Air Traffic: 414,000 passengers carried (1991)

Airports: 25 airfields, of which 22 are usable; 2 have permanent-surface runways (1993)

Canadian Embassy: c/o The Canadian High Commission, 61 Molesworth St, 3rd Floor, Thorndon, Wellington; mailing address: P.O. Box 12-049, Thorndon, Wellington, New Zealand. Tel: (011-64-4) 473-9577. Fax: (011-64-4) 352-3902

Representative to Canada: c/o Embassy of the Republic of Fiji, One United Nations Plaza, 26th Floor, New York, NY 10017 USA. Tel: (212) 355-7316. Fax: (212) 319-1896.

Finland

Long-Form Name: Republic of Finland

Capital: Helsinki

Population: 5,100,000 (1993 est.)

■ GEOGRAPHY

Area: 337,030 sq. km

Coastline: 1,126 km excluding islands and coastal indentations

Climate: cold temperate; potentially subarctic, but comparatively mild because of moderating influence of the North Atlantic Current, Baltic Sea and more than 60,000 lakes

Environment: permanently wet ground covers approx. 30% of land

Terrain: mostly low, flat to rolling plains interspersed with lakes and low hills

Land Use: 8% arable; 0% permanent; negligible meadows; 76% forest; 16% other

Location: N Europe, bordering on Baltic Sea

■ PEOPLE

Nationality: Finn

Ethnic Groups: Finn, Swede, Lapp, Gypsy, Tatar

Languages: 94% Finnish, 6% Swedish (both official); small Lapp-and Russian-speaking minorities; business language is English

Religions: 89% Evangelical Lutheran, 9% atheist, 1% Eastern Orthodox, 1% other

Marriages: 4.7 (per 1,000) (1991)

Divorces: 2.89 (per 1,000) (1989)

■ GOVERNMENT

Leader(s): Pres. Martti Ahtisaari, Prime Min. Esko Aho

Government Type: republic
Administrative Divisions: 12 provinces
Independence: Dec. 6, 1917 (from Soviet Union)
National Holiday: Independence Day, Dec. 6

■ ECONOMY

Overview: the manufacturing sector and trade are vital to this highly industrialized, largely free market economy; because of the climate, agricultural development is limited to maintaining self-sufficiency in basic products
GNP: $79.4 billion, per capita $15,900; real growth rate -3.5% (1992)
Inflation: 2.6% (1992)
Industries: metal manufacturing and shipbuilding, forestry and wood processing (pulp, paper), copper refining, foodstuffs, textiles, clothing
Labour Force: 2,552,000 (1992); 70.6% services, 21.1% industry, 8.3% agriculture (1989)
Unemployment: 7.5% (1992)
Agriculture: accounts for 5% of GNP (including forestry); livestock production, especially dairy cattle, predominates; forestry is an important export earner; main crops—cereals, sugar beets, potatoes; 85% self-sufficient, but short of food and fodder grains
Natural Resources: timber, copper, zinc, iron ore, silver

■ FINANCE/TRADE

Currency: markkaa, or Fin mark
International Reserves Excluding Gold: $6,991 million (Jan. 1994)
Gold Reserves: 2.0 million fine troy ounces (Jan. 1994)
Budget: revenues $26.8 billion; expenditures $40.6 billion, including capital expenditures (1992)
Defence Expenditures: 4.26% of total govt. expenditure (1991)
External Debt: $25 billion (1992)
Exports: $22.814 billion (1993 est.); commodities: timber, paper and pulp, ships, machinery, clothing and footwear; partners: European Community 44.2% (UK 13%, Germany 10.8%), USSR 14.9%, Sweden 14.1%, US 5.8%
Imports: $18.116 billion (1993 est.); commodities: foodstuffs, petroleum and petroleum products, chemicals, transport equipment, iron and steel, machinery, textile yarn and fabrics, fodder grains; partners: European Community 43.5% (Germany 16.9%, UK 6.8%), Sweden 13.3%, USSR 12.1%, US 6.3%

■ HEALTH

Births: 13/1,000 population (1993)
Deaths: 10/1,000 population (1993)

Infant Mortality: 5.8 deaths/1,000 live births (1993)
Life Expectancy at Birth: 71 years male, 79 years female (1993)
No. of Physicians: 22.6/10,000 population (1992)

■ EDUCATION

Govt. Expenditure: 13.90% of government expenditure (1991)
Literacy: 100% (1993)

■ COMMUNICATIONS

Daily newspapers: 66 (1992)
Televisions: 488.3/1,000 inhabitants (1992)
Radios: 998/1,000 inhabitants (1992)
Telephones: 61.66/100 inhabitants (1992)

■ TRANSPORTATION

Motor Vehicles: 2,217,729; 1,926,326 passenger cars (1990)
Roads: 103,000 km; 35,000 km paved
Railway: 5,924 km (1993)
Air Traffic: 3,999,000 passengers carried (1991)
Airports: 160 airfields, of which 157 are usable; 66 have permanent-surface runways (1993)

Canadian Embassy: Pohjois Esplanadi, 25B, 00100 Helsinki; mailing address: Box 779, 00101 Helsinki, Finland. Tel: (011-358-0) 17-11-41. Fax (011-358-0) 60-10-60
Representative to Canada: Embassy of Finland, 55 Metcalfe St, Ste 850, Ottawa ON K1P 6L5. Tel: (613) 236-2389. Fax: (613) 238-1474.

France

Long-Form Name: French Republic
Capital: Paris
Population: 57,700,000 (1993 est.)

■ GEOGRAPHY

Area: 547,030 sq. km; includes Corsica and the rest of metropolitan France, but excludes the overseas administrative divisions
Coastline: 3,427 km (includes Corsica, 644 km)
Climate: generally cool winters and mild summers, but mild winters and hot summers along the Mediterranean
Environment: most of large urban areas and industrial centres in Rhône, Garonne, Seine or Loire River basins; occasional warm tropical winds known as mistrals are in central south; air and water pollution
Terrain: mostly flat plains or gently rolling hills in north and west; remainder is mountainous, especially Pyrenees in south and Alps in east
Land Use: 32% arable; 2% permanent; 23%

meadows; 27% forest; 16% other
Location: W Europe, bordering on Atlantic Ocean, Mediterranean Sea

■ PEOPLE

Nationality: French
Ethnic Groups: Celtic and Latin with Teutonic, Slavic, North African, Indochinese and Basque minorities
Languages: French (100% of population); rapidly declining regional dialects (Provençal, Breton, Alsatian, Corsican, Catalan, Basque, Flemish)
Religions: 90% Roman Catholic, 2% Protestant, 1% Jewish, 1% Moslem (North African workers), 6% unaffiliated
Marriages: 5.0 (per 1,000) (1991)
Divorces: 1.87 (per 1,000) (1990)

■ GOVERNMENT

Leader(s): Pres. François Mitterand, Prime Min. Edouard Balladur
Government Type: republic
Administrative Divisions: 22 regions; dependent areas inc.: French Polynesia, Guadeloupe, Guiana (French Guiana), Martinique, Mayotte, New Caledonia, Réunion, St. Pierre and Miquelon, Southern and Antarctic Territories, Wallis and Futuna Islands
Independence: unified by Clovis in 486, First Republic proclaimed in 1792
National Holiday: Taking of the Bastille, July 14

■ ECONOMY

Overview: one of the world's most developed economies; largely self-sufficient in agricultural products; the leading agricultural producer in Western Europe; highly diversified industrial sector; economic integration into the European Community has unknown consequences
GNP: n.a., GDP $1.8 trillion, per capita $18,900; real growth rate 1.1% (1992)
Inflation: 2.4% (1992)
Industries: steel, machinery, chemicals, automobiles, metallurgy, aircraft, electronics, mining, textiles, food processing, tourism
Labour Force: 25,404,000 (1992); 73.5% services, 19.8% industry; 6.7% agriculture (1989)
Unemployment: 10.5% (1992)
Agriculture: accounts for 4% of GNP (including fishing and forestry); one of the world's top five wheat producers; self-sufficient for most temperate-zone foods; shortages include fats and oils and tropical produce, but overall net exporter of farm products
Natural Resources: coal, iron ore, bauxite, fish, timber, zinc, potash

■ FINANCE/TRADE

Currency: franc (F or FF)
International Reserves Excluding Gold: $22,649 million (Dec. 1993)
Gold Reserves: 81.85 million fine troy ounces (Dec. 1993)
Budget: revenues $220.5 billion; expenditures $249.1 billion, including capital expenditures of $47 billion (1993 budget)
Defence Expenditures: $37.34 billion (1991)
External Debt: $270 billion (1992)
Exports: $206.231 billion (1993); commodities: machinery and transportation equipment, chemicals, foodstuffs, agricultural products, iron and steel products, textiles and clothing; partners: Germany 15.8%, Italy 12.2%, UK 9.8%, Belgium/Luxembourg 8.9%, Netherlands 8.7%, US 6.7%, Spain 5.6%, Japan 1.8%, USSR 1.3%
Imports: $200.728 billion (1993); commodities: crude oil, machinery and equipment, agricultural products, chemicals, iron and steel products; partners: Germany 19.4%, Italy 11.5%, Belgium/ Luxembourg 9.2%, US 7.7%, UK 7.2%, Netherlands 5.2%, Spain 4.4%, Japan 4.1%, USSR 2.1%

■ HEALTH

Births: 13/1,000 population (1993)
Deaths: 9/1,000 population (1993)
Infant Mortality: 7.3 deaths/1,000 live births (1993)
Life Expectancy at Birth: 73 years male, 81 years female (1993)
No. of Physicians: 31.3/10,000 population (1992)

■ EDUCATION

Govt. Expenditure: 6.9% of govt. expenditure (1990)
Literacy: 99% (1993)

■ COMMUNICATIONS

Daily newspapers: 96 (1992)
Televisions: 35.6/1,000 inhabitants (1992)
Radios: 138/1,000 inhabitants (1992)
Telephones: 60.87/100 inhabitants(1992)

■ TRANSPORTATION

Motor Vehicles: 28,460,000; 23,550,000 passenger cars (1990)
Roads: 1,551,400 km; 803,000 km paved (1993)
Railway: 34,055 km
Air Traffic: 31,665,000 passengers carried (1991)
Airports: 471 airfields, of which 461 are usable; 256 have permanent-surface runways (1993)

Canadian Embassy: 35 av Montaigne, 75008 Paris France. Tel: (011-33-1) 44-43-29-00. Fax:

(011-33-1) 44-43-29-99
Representative to Canada: Embassy of France, 42 Sussex Dr, Ottawa ON K1M 2C9. Tel: (613) 789-1795. Fax: (613) 789-3484.

French Guiana

Overseas Department of France

Long-Form Name: Department of Guiana
Capital: Cayenne
Population: 133,376 (1993 est.)

■ GEOGRAPHY

Area: 91,000 sq. km
Coastline: 378 km
Climate: tropical, warm and humid, little seasonal temperature variation
Environment: mostly an unsettled wilderness
Terrain: low-lying coastal plains rising to hills and small mountains
Land Use: interior is uncultivated wilderness, with mineral and forest resources which have not been tapped; 31,000 acres under cultivation
Location: N South America, bordering on Atlantic Ocean

■ PEOPLE

Nationality: French Guianese
Ethnic Groups: 66% black or mulatto, 12% Caucasian, 12% East Indian, Chinese, Amerindian, 10% other
Languages: French (official), Creole patois
Religions: Roman Catholic

■ GOVERNMENT

Leader(s): Prefect of French Govt. Jean-Pierre Lacroix, Pres. of General Council Elie Castor, Pres. of Regional Council Georges Othily
Government Type: overseas department of France
Administrative Divisions: none
Independence: none
National Holiday: Taking of the Bastille, July 14`

■ ECONOMY

Overview: economy is closely tied to that of France through subsidies and imports; agriculture: rice, manioc, sugar cane, livestock; forestry, fisheries, food processing industry; chief trading partners: France, EC countries, Japan, US
GNP: n.a., GDP $421 million, per capita $4,390; real growth rate n.a. (1986)
Inflation: 4.1% (1987)
Industries: construction, shrimp processing, forestry products, rum, gold, mining
Unemployment: 13% (1990)

Agriculture: some vegetables for local consumption, rice, corn, cocoa, manioc, bananas, sugar, cattle, pigs, poultry
Natural Resources: bauxite, timber, gold, cinnabar, kaolin, fish

■ FINANCE/TRADE

Currency: French franc
Budget: revenues $735 million; expenditures $735 million, including capital expenditures (1987)
External Debt: $1.2 billion (1988)
Exports: $96 million (1992)
Imports: $669 million (1992)

■ HEALTH

Births: 26.46/1,000 population (1993 est.)
Deaths: 4.72/1,000 population (1993 est.)
Infant Mortality: 16.6 deaths/1,000 live births (1993 est.)
Life Expectancy at Birth: 71.59 years male, 78.32 years female (1993 est.)

■ EDUCATION

Literacy: 82% (1993)

■ COMMUNICATIONS

Televisions: n.a.; 9 TV stations (1993)
Radios: n.a.; 12 radio stations (1993)
Telephones: 18,100 total (1993)

■ TRANSPORTATION

Roads: 680 km; 510 km paved (1993)
Airports: 10 airfields, all usable; 4 have permanent-surface runways (1993).

French Polynesia

Overseas Department of France

Long-Form Name: Territory of French Polynesia
Capital: Papeete (Windward Islands)
Population: 200,000 (1993 est.)

■ GEOGRAPHY

Area: 3,941 sq. km, consisting of five island archipelagoes scattered widely over Eastern Pacific; uninhabited Clipperton Territory is a dependency of French Polynesia but does not form part of the territory
Climate: warm and humid, tropical but moderate
Land Use: 1% arable, 19% permanent crops, 5% meadows and pastures, 31% forest and woodland, 44% other
Location: eastern Pacific Ocean

■ PEOPLE

Nationality: French Polynesian
Ethnic Groups: 78% Polynesian, 12% Chinese, 6% local French, 4% metropolitan French
Languages: French and Tahitian (both official)

■ GOVERNMENT

Leader(s): Pres. of Territorial Council Gaston Flosse
Government Type: French overseas territory
National Holiday: Taking of the Bastille, July 14

■ ECONOMY

Overview: agriculture: copra, tropical fruits grown for local consumption; tourism accounts for approximately 20% of GDP and is primary source of revenue; trading partners: France, UK, US

■ FINANCE/TRADE

Currency: CFP franc

Gabon

Long-Form Name: Gabonese Republic
Capital: Libreville
Population: 1,100,000 (1993 est.)

■ GEOGRAPHY

Area: 267,670 sq. km
Coastline: 885 km
Climate: tropical; always hot, humid
Environment: deforestation
Terrain: narrow coastal plain; hilly interior; savanna in east and south
Land Use: 1% arable; 1% permanent; 18% meadows; 78% forest; 2% other
Location: WC Africa, bordering on South Atlantic Ocean

■ PEOPLE

Nationality: Gabonese
Ethnic Groups: about 40 Bantu tribes, including four major tribal groupings (Fang, Eshira, Bapounou, Bateke); approx. 100,000 expatriate Africans and Europeans, including 27,000 French
Languages: French (official), Fang, Myene, Bateke, Bapounou/Eschira, Bandjabi
Religions: 55-75% Roman Catholic, 1% Muslim, remainder animist
Marriages: n.a.
Divorces: n.a.

■ GOVERNMENT

Leader(s): Prime Min. Casimir Oye-Mba, Pres.

El Hadj Omar Bongo
Government Type: republic; multi-party presidential regime (opposition parties legalized in 1990)
Administrative Divisions: 9 provinces
Independence: Aug. 17, 1960 (from France)
National Holiday: Renovation Day (Gabonese Democratic Party established), Mar. 12

■ ECONOMY

Overview: economy is dependent on oil, which has contributed to an increase in per capita income; agricultural and industrial sectors are relatively underdeveloped
GNP: $4.6 billion, per capita $4,200; real growth rate 1.3% (1991)
Inflation: -9.5% (1992)
Industries: sawmills, cement, petroleum, food and beverages; mining of increasing importance (especially manganese and uranium)
Labour Force: 536,000 (1992); 75.5% agriculture, 10.8% industry, 13.7% services
Unemployment: n.a.
Agriculture: accounts for 10% of GDP (including fishing and forestry); cash crops—cocoa, coffee, palm oil; livestock not developed; importer of food; okoume (a tropical softwood) is the most important timber product
Natural Resources: crude oil, manganese, uranium, gold, timber, iron ore

■ FINANCE/TRADE

Currency: Communauté financière africaine franc (CFAF)
International Reserves Excluding Gold: $1 million (Dec. 1993)
Gold Reserves: n.a.
Budget: revenues $1.1 billion; expenditures $1.5 billion, including capital expenditures of $277 million (1990)
Defence Expenditures: $145.79 million (1989)
External Debt: $3.798 billion (1992)
Exports: $2.273 billion (1991); commodities: crude oil 70%, manganese 11%, wood 12%, uranium 6%; partners: France 53%, US 22%, Germany, Japan
Imports: $884 million (1991); commodities: foodstuffs, chemical products, petroleum products, construction materials, manufacturers, machinery; partners: France 48%, US 2.6%, Germany, Japan, UK

■ HEALTH

Births: 41/1,000 population (1993)
Deaths: 16/1,000 population (1993)
Infant Mortality: 99 deaths/1,000 live births (1993)
Life Expectancy at Birth: 51 years male, 54 years

female (1993)
No. of Physicians: 3.6/10,000 population (1990)

■ EDUCATION

Govt. Expenditure: n.a.
Literacy: 60.7% (1992)

■ COMMUNICATIONS

Daily newspapers: 1 (1992)
Televisions: 35.6/1,000 inhabitants (1992)
Radios: 138/1,000 inhabitants (1992)
Telephones: 1.12/100 inhabitants (1992)

■ TRANSPORTATION

Motor Vehicles: 38,000; 22,000 passenger cars (1990)
Roads: 7,762 km; 535 km paved
Railway: 649 km (1993)
Air Traffic: 398,000 passengers carried (1991)
Airports: 68 airfields, of which 56 are usable; 10 have permanent-surface runways (1993)

Canadian Embassy: P.O. Box 4037 Libreville, Gabon. Tel: (011-241) 74-34-64. Fax: (011-241) 74-34-66
Representative to Canada: Embassy of the Gabonese Republic, 4 Range Rd, Ottawa ON K1N 8J5. Tel: (613) 232-5301. Fax: (613) 232-6916.

Gambia

Long-Form Name: Republic of the Gambia
Capital: Banjul
Population: 900,000 (1993 est.)

■ GEOGRAPHY

Area: 11,300 sq. km
Coastline: 80 km
Climate: tropical; hot, rainy season (June to Nov.); cooler, dry season (Nov. to May)
Environment: deforestation
Terrain: flood plain of the Gambia River flanked by some low hills
Land Use: 16% arable; 0% permanent; 9% meadows; 20% forest; 55% other
Location: W Africa, bordering on Atlantic Ocean

■ PEOPLE

Nationality: Gambian
Ethnic Groups: 99% African (42% Mandinka, 18% Fula, 16% Wolof, 10% Jola, 9% Serahuli, 4% other); 1% non-Gambian
Languages: English (official); Mandinka, Wolof, Fula, other indigenous vernaculars
Religions: 90% Moslem, 9% Christian, 1% indigenous beliefs

Marriages: n.a.
Divorces: n.a.

■ GOVERNMENT

Leader(s): Pres. Sir Dawda Kairaba Jawara, Prime Min. Saihou S. Sabally
Government Type: republic
Administrative Divisions: 5 divisions and 1 city (Banjul)
Independence: Feb. 18, 1965 (from UK)
National Holiday: Independence Day, Feb. 18

■ ECONOMY

Overview: a poor country, lacking in natural resources and possessing a limited agricultural base of peanut products; tourism is growing; small-scale manufacturing activity accounts for less than 10% of GDP
GNP: n.a., GDP $292 million, per capita $325; real growth rate 3% (1991 est.)
Inflation: 9.5% (1992)
Industries: peanut processing, tourism, beverages, agricultural machinery assembly, woodworking, metalworking, clothing
Labour Force: 330,000 (1992) 84% agriculture, 7% industry, 9% services
Unemployment: n.a.
Agriculture: accounts for 30% of GDP and employs about 75% of the population; imports one-third of food requirements; major export crop is peanuts; forestry and fishing resources not fully exploited
Natural Resources: fish

■ FINANCE/TRADE

Currency: dalasi (D)
International Reserves Excluding Gold: $104 million (Nov. 1993)
Gold Reserves: n.a.
Budget: revenues $94 million; expenditures $80 million, including capital expenditures of $25 million (1991 est.)
Defence Expenditures: 4% of total govt. expenditure (1990)
External Debt: $379 million (1992)
Exports: $66.25 million (1992 est.); commodities: peanuts and peanut products, fish, cotton lint, palm kernels; partners: Ghana 49%, Europe 27%, Japan 12%, US 1%
Imports: $207.5 million (1992 est.); commodities: foodstuffs, manufacturers, raw materials, fuel, machinery and transport equipment; partners: Europe 55%, (European Community 39%, other 16%), Asia 20%, US 11%, Senegal 4%

■ HEALTH

Births: 46/1,000 population (1993)

Deaths: 20/1,000 population (1993)
Infant Mortality: 138 deaths/1,000 live births (1993)
Life Expectancy at Birth: 42 years male, 46 years female (1993)
No. of Physicians: 0.9/10,000 population (1990)

■ EDUCATION

Govt. Expenditure: 12.9% of government expenditure (1991)
Literacy: 27.2% (1992)

■ COMMUNICATIONS

Daily newspapers: 2 (1992)
Televisions: n.a.
Radios: 168/1,000 inhabitants (1992)
Telephones: 0.5/100 inhabitants (1992)

■ TRANSPORTATION

Motor Vehicles: 8,000; 6,500 passenger cars (1990)
Roads: 3,083 km; 431 paved km
Railway: none
Air Traffic: n.a.
Airports: 1, usable and with permanent-surface runway (1993)

Canadian Embassy: c/o 45 boul. de la République, Dakar; mailing address: P.O. Box 3373, Dakar, Senegal. Tel: (011-221) 23-92-90. Fax: (011-221) 23-87-49
Representative to Canada: c/o High Commission for the Republic of the Gambia, 1155 15th St NW, Ste 1000, Washington DC 20005 USA. Tel: (202) 785-1399. Fax: (202) 785-1430.

Georgia

Long-Form Name: Republic of Georgia
Capital: Tbilisi
Population: 5,500,000 (1993 est.)

■ GEOGRAPHY

Area: 69,700 sq. km
Coastline: 310 km
Climate: Alpine to subtropical with warm, humid coastlands
Environment: air and water pollution
Terrain: largely mountainous in north and south; lowlands open to Black Sea in west; Kura River Basin in east; good soils in river valley, flood plains and lowlands
Land Use: 35% forests and woodlands; 65% cultivated
Location: SE Europe, bordering on Black Sea

■ PEOPLE

Nationality: Georgian
Ethnic Groups: 70.1% Georgian, 8.1% Armenian, 6.3% Russian, 5.7% Azerbaijani, 3% Ossetian, 1.9% Greek, 1.8% Abkhazian, 1% Ukrainian
Languages: Armenian 7%, Azerbaijani 6%, Georgian 71% (official), Russian 9%, other 7%
Religions: Georgian Orthodox 65%, Russian Orthodox 10%, Muslim 11%, Armenian Orthodox 8%, unknown 6%
Marriages: 7.0 (per 1,000) (1989)
Divorces: 1.35 (per 1,000) (1989)

■ GOVERNMENT

Leader(s): Chairman of Parliament Eduard A. Shevardnadze, Prime Minister Otar Patsatsia
Government Type: republic
Administrative Divisions: 2 autonomous regions
Independence: April 9, 1991 (from Soviet Union)
National Holiday: Independence Day, April 9

■ ECONOMY

Overview: steel processing and light industry predominate; agriculture hindered by extensive wooded areas
GNP: $9 billion, $1,640 per capita; real growth rate 2.9% (1991)
Inflation: 50% per month (1993 est.)
Industries: coal and non-ferrous metals refining, machinery and instruments, electrical engineering, chemical production, food processing, cloth, hosiery, shoes, vehicles, mining, esp. manganese, coal, baryta
Labour Force: 2.763 million; 31% industry and construction, 25% agriculture and forestry, 44% other (1990)
Unemployment: 3% (1993), but large numbers of underemployed
Agriculture: grapes, tobacco, bay leaves, tea, citrus fruit, sugar, vegetables, grains, tobacco, tung, silk, orchard fruit
Natural Resources: manganese deposits; sulphur and other medicinal springs, forest resources, hydropower, coal and oil

■ FINANCE/TRADE

Currency: Russian rouble remains official currency until introduction of the "lari" at undetermined future date
International Reserves Excluding Gold: n.a.
Gold Reserves: n.a.
Budget: 4,067 million roubles (1989 revenues)
Defence Expenditures: n.a.
External Debt: $85 million (1992)
Exports: grain, fruit, vegetables, tea, electric mine cars, seamless pipes

Imports: n.a.

■ HEALTH

Births: 15/1,000 population (1993)
Deaths: 8/1,000 population (1993)
Infant Mortality: 16 deaths/1,000 live births (1993)
Life Expectancy at Birth: 69 years male, 76 years female (1993)
No. of Physicians: 31,700 (1989)

■ EDUCATION

Govt. Expenditure: n.a.
Literacy: 100% (1993)

■ COMMUNICATIONS

Daily newspapers: 149 papers of all circulation types (1989)
Televisions: n.a.
Radios: n.a.
Telephones: approximately 12/100 persons (1992)

■ TRANSPORTATION

Motor Vehicles: n.a.
Roads: 33,900 km; 29,500 km hard-surfaced (1993)
Railway: 1,570 km
Air Traffic: n.a.
Airports: 37 airfields, of which 26 are usable; 19 have permanent-surface runways (1993)

Canadian Embassy: c/o Nenehatun Caddesi No. 75, Gaziosmanpasa 06700, Ankara, Turkey. Tel: (011-90-312) 436-1275. Fax: (011-90-312) 446-4437.

Germany

Long-Form Name: Federal Republic of Germany
Capital: Berlin; seat of government, Bonn
Population: 81,100,000 (1993 est.)

■ GEOGRAPHY

Area: 356,910 sq. km
Coastline: 2,389 km
Climate: temperate; cool, wet summers; cool to cold, cloudy winters with frequent rain and snow; occasional warm, tropical föhn wind; high relative humidity
Environment: air and water pollution; significant deforestation in mountain regions due to environmental pollution
Terrain: flat plains; lowlands in north; central uplands; Bavarian Alps in southwest
Land Use: 34% arable land; 1% permanent crops; 16% meadows and pastures; 30% forest and woodland; 19% other
Location: NC Europe, bordering on North Sea, Baltic Sea

■ PEOPLE

Nationality: German
Ethnic Groups: German 95.1%, Turkish 2.3%, Italian 0.7%, Greek 0.4%, Polish 0.4%, other 1.1%
Languages: German
Religions: 45% Protestant, 37% Roman Catholic, 18% unaffiliated
Marriages: 6.5/1,000 population (1990)
Divorces: 2.5/1,000 population (1989)

■ GOVERNMENT

Leader(s): Chanc. Helmut Kohl, Pres. Roman Herzog
Government Type: federal republic
Administrative Divisions: 16 states
Independence: former Federal Republic of Germany (west) had come into existence on Sept. 21, 1949; former German Democratic Republic (east), Oct. 1949; eastern and western halves were reunified on Oct. 3, 1990
National Holiday: German Unity Day, Oct. 3

■ ECONOMY

Overview: Former W Germany: highly urbanized with advanced market economy and strong exports; manufacturing and service industries dominate with imported raw materials and semi-manufactured products. Former E Germany: outmoded economy, slow pace of economic reform deters outside investors; FRG's legal, social welfare, and economic systems have been extended to the east. Unified Germany: slight nation-wide post-reunification recession.
GNP: $1.398 trillion, per capita $17,400; real growth rate 1.5% (1992)
Inflation: 4.0% (1992)
Industries: iron, steel, coal, chemicals, vehicles, ships, machinery, food and beverages, electronics, brown coal, shipbuilding, textiles, petroleum refining
Labour Force: 48,651,000 (1992); 30.2% industry, 66.3% services, 3.5% agriculture (1989)
Unemployment: former W Germany 7.1% (1992); former E Germany 13.5% (1992)
Agriculture: agriculture, including fishing and forestry, accounts for about 3% of GDP; diversified crop and livestock farming, inc. wheat, potatoes, barley, sugar beets, fruit, livestock products; net importer of food
Natural Resources: iron ore, coal, potash, natural gas, salt, nickel, timber

■ FINANCE/TRADE

Currency: Deutsche Mark (DM)
International Reserves Excluding Gold: $81,083 million (Jan. 1994)
Gold Reserves: 95.18 million fine troy ounces (Jan. 1994)
Budget: former W Germany: revenues, $684 billion; expenditures, $704 billion, including capital expenditures; former E Germany: revenues n.a., expenditures n.a., capital expenditures n.a. (1990)
Defence Expenditures: $35.61 billion (1991)
External Debt: n.a.
Exports: $370.85 billion (1993 est.)
Imports: $342.576 billion (1993 est.)

■ HEALTH

Births: 10/1,000 population (1993)
Deaths: 11/1,000 population (1993)
Infant Mortality: 6.7 deaths/1,000 live births (1993)
Life Expectancy at Birth: 72 years male, 78 years female (1993)
No. of Physicians: former W Germany: 26.5/10,000 population (1990); former E Germany: 22.8/10,000 population (1990)

■ EDUCATION

Govt. Expenditure: 8.6% of govt. expenditure (1990)
Literacy: 99% (1993)

■ COMMUNICATIONS

Daily newspapers: 358 (1992)
Televisions: 642.7/1,000 (1992)
Radios: 868/1,000 (1992)
Telephones: 46.04/100 (1992)

■ TRANSPORTATION

Motor Vehicles: 38,276,274; 35,512,083 passenger cars (1990)
Roads: 690,909 km
Railway: 45,468 km (1993)
Air Traffic: 24,830,000 passengers carried (1991)
Airports: 499 airfields, of which 492 are usable; 271 have permanent-surface runways (1993)

Canadian Embassy: Friedrich-Wilhelm-Strasse 18, 53113 Bonn, Germany. Tel. (011-49-228) 968 0. Fax: (011-49-228) 968-3904
Representative to Canada: Embassy of the Federal Republic of Germany, 275 Slater St,
14th Floor, Ottawa ON K1P 5H9. Tel: (613) 232-1101. Fax: (613) 594-9330.

Ghana

Long-Form Name: Republic of Ghana
Capital: Accra
Population: 16,400,000 (1993 est.)

■ GEOGRAPHY

Area: 238,540 sq. km
Coastline: 539 km
Climate: tropical; warm and comparatively dry along southeast coast; hot and humid in southwest; hot and dry in north
Environment: recent drought in north severely affecting marginal agricultural activities; deforestation; overgrazing; soil erosion; dry, northeasterly harmattan wind (Jan. to Mar.)
Terrain: mostly low plains with dissected plateau in south-central area
Land Use: 5% arable; 7% permanent; 15% meadows; 37% forest; 36% other
Location: WC Africa, bordering on South Atlantic Ocean

■ PEOPLE

Nationality: Ghanaian
Ethnic Groups: 99% black African (major tribes–44% Akan, 16% Moshi-Dagomba, 13% Ewe, 8% Ga), 0.2% European and other
Languages: English (official); African languages include Akan, Moshi-Dagomba, Ewe and Ga
Religions: 38% indigenous beliefs, 30% Moslem, 24% Christian, 8% other
Marriages: n.a.
Divorces: n.a.

■ GOVERNMENT

Leader(s): Pres. Flt. Lt. (Ret.) Jerry John Rawlings
Government Type: constitutional democracy
Administrative Divisions: 10 regions
Independence: Mar. 6, 1957 (from UK, formerly known as Gold Coast)
National Holiday: Independence Day, Mar. 6

■ ECONOMY

Overview: heavily dependent on cocoa, gold and timber exports; international assistance boosts this economy, which depends on good harvests; population growth is a burden
GNP: n.a., GDP $6.6 billion, per capita $410; real growth rate 3.9% (1992 est.)
Inflation: 10.1% (1992)
Industries: mining, lumbering, light manufacturing, fishing, aluminum, food processing

Labour Force: 5,690,000 (1992); 59.3% agriculture, 11.1% industry, 29.6% services (1989)
Unemployment: 10% (1991)
Agriculture: accounts for more than 50% of GDP; major cash crop is cocoa; other crops: rice, coffee, cassava, peanuts, corn; normally self-sufficient in food
Natural Resources: gold, timber, industrial diamonds, bauxite, manganese, fish, rubber

■ **FINANCE/TRADE**

Currency: cedi (C/)
International Reserves Excluding Gold: $313 million (Sept. 1993)
Gold Reserves: 0.27 million fine troy ounces (Sept. 1993)
Budget: revenues $1.0 billion; expenditures $905 million, including capital expenditures of $200 million (1991 est.)
Defence Expenditures: $45.39 million (1990)
External Debt: $4.275 billion (1992)
Exports: $880 million (1989); commodities: cocoa 60%, timber, gold, tuna, bauxite, and aluminum; partners: US 23%, UK, other European Community
Imports: $1,200 million (1989); commodities: petroleum 16%, consumer goods, foods, intermediate goods, capital equipment; partners: US 10%, UK, W Germany, France, Japan, S Korea, E Germany

■ **HEALTH**

Births: 43/1,000 population (1993)
Deaths: 12/1,000 population (1993)
Infant Mortality: 86 deaths/1,000 live births (1993)
Life Expectancy at Birth: 53 years male, 57 years female (1993)
No. of Physicians: 0.5/10,000 population (1992)

■ **EDUCATION**

Govt. Expenditure: 24.3% of govt. expenditure (1990)
Literacy: 60.3% (1993)

■ **COMMUNICATIONS**

Daily newspapers: 3 (1992)
Televisions: 14.5/1,000 inhabitants (1992)
Radios: 295/1,000 inhabitants (1992)
Telephones: 0.63/100 inhabitants (1992)

■ **TRANSPORTATION**

Motor Vehicles: 124,264; 82,152 passenger cars (1990)

Roads: 32,250 km; 6,084 km hard-surfaced (1993)
Railway: 953 km
Air Traffic: 192,000 passengers carried (1991)
Airports: 10 airfields, of which 9 are usable; 5 have permanent-surface runways (1993)
Canadian Embassy: Canadian High Commission, 42 Independence Ave, Accra; P.O. Box 1639, Accra. Tel: (011-233-21) 77 37 91. Fax: (011-233-21) 77-37-92
Representative to Canada: High Commission for Ghana, 1 Clemow Ave, Ottawa ON K1S 2A9. Tel: (613) 236-0871. Fax: (613) 236-0874.

Gibraltar

Dependent Territory of United Kingdom

Long-Form Name: Gibraltar
Capital: Gibraltar
Population: 31,508 (1993 est.)

■ **GEOGRAPHY**

Area: 6.5 sq. km
Climate: warm, temperate, low precipitation, mild winters, warm summers
Land Use: almost 100% bare limestone (Rock of Gibraltar) and/or built up; no farmland
Location: Iberian Peninsula of S Spain, bordering on Mediterranean Sea

■ **PEOPLE**

Nationality: Gibraltarian
Ethnic Groups: Portuguese, Maltese, Spanish, Italian, English
Languages: English (used in schools and for official purposes), Spanish, Italian, Portuguese, Russian

■ **GOVERNMENT**

Leader(s): Gov. and Commander-in-Chief Adm. Sir Derek Reffell; Chief Min. José (Joe) Bossano
Government Type: dependent territory of the UK
National Holiday: Commonwealth Day (second Monday in March)

■ **ECONOMY**

Overview: tourism most important; industries: construction materials, beverage bottling; re-exports: tobacco, petroleum, wine; exports of local products negligible; must import all food; more than 70% of the economy is in the public sector

■ **FINANCE/TRADE**

Currency: Gibraltar pound

Greece

Long-Form Name: Hellenic Republic
Capital: Athens
Population: 10,500,000 (1993 est.)

■ **GEOGRAPHY**

Area: 131,940 sq. km
Coastline: 13,676 km
Climate: temperate; mild, wet winter; hot, dry summer
Environment: subject to severe earthquakes; air pollution; archipelago of 2,000 islands
Terrain: mostly mountainous with ranges extending into sea as peninsulas or chains of islands
Land Use: 23% arable; 8% permanent; 40% meadows; 20% forest; 9% other
Location: S Europe, bordering on Adriatic Sea

■ **PEOPLE**

Nationality: Greek
Ethnic Groups: 98% Greek, 2% others
Languages: Greek (official); English, German and French widely understood
Religions: 98% Greek Orthodox, 1% Moslem, 1% other
Marriages: 5.9 (per 1,000) (1990)
Divorces: 0.9 (per 1,000) (1986)

■ **GOVERNMENT**

Leader(s): Prime Min. Andreas Papandreou, Pres. Constantine Karamanlis
Government Type: presidential parliamentary government; monarchy rejected by referendum Dec. 8, 1974
Administrative Divisions: 52 prefectures (nomoi, singular–nomós)
Independence: 1829 (from the Ottoman Empire)
National Holiday: Independence Day (proclamation of the war of independence), Mar. 25

■ **ECONOMY**

Overview: a large commodity trade deficit is offset by the successful tourism industry; a mixed capitalistic economy was administered by a socialist government in the 1980s
GNP: $82.9 billion, per capita $8,200; real growth rate 1.2% (1992)
Inflation: 15.8% (1992)
Industries: food and tobacco processing, textiles, chemicals, metal products, tourism, mining, petroleum

Labour Force: 3.825 million (1992); 56% services, 24.7% agriculture, 19.3% industry (1989)
Unemployment: 9.1% (1992)
Agriculture: accounts for 15% of GNP (including fishing and forestry); self sufficient in food; principal products—wheat, corn, barley, sugar beets, olives, tomatoes, wine, tobacco, potatoes, beef, mutton, pork, dairy products
Natural Resources: bauxite, lignite, magnesite, crude oil, marble

■ **FINANCE/TRADE**

Currency: drachma (Dr)
International Reserves Excluding Gold: $8,653 million (Jan. 1994)
Gold Reserves: 3.44 million fine troy ounces (Jan. 1994)
Budget: revenues $37.6 billion; expenditures $45.1 billion, including capital expenditures of $5.4 billion (1993)
Defence Expenditures: $4.2 billion (5.1% of GDP) (1992)
External Debt: $23.7 billion (1991)
Exports: $9.488 billion (1992); commodities: manufactured goods, food and live animals, fuels and lubricants, raw materials; partners: Germany 24%, Italy 14%, non-oil developing countries 11.8%, France 9.5%, US 7.1%, UK 6.8%
Imports: $23.203 billion (1992); commodities: machinery and transport equipment, light manufactures, fuels and lubricants, foodstuffs, chemicals; partners: Germany 22%, non-oil-developing countries 14%, oil-exporting countries 13%, Italy 12%, France 8%, US 3.2%

■ **HEALTH**

Births: 10/1,000 population (1993)
Deaths: 9/1,000 population (1993)
Infant Mortality: 10 deaths/1,000 live births (1993)
Life Expectancy at Birth: 74 years male, 79 years female (1993)
No. of Physicians: 28.5/10,000 population (1992)

■ **EDUCATION**

Govt. Expenditure: 5.6% of govt. expenditure (1988)
Literacy: 93.2% (1993)

■ **COMMUNICATIONS**

Daily newspapers: 117 (1992)
Televisions: 194.5/1,000 inhabitants (1992)
Radios: 419/1,000 inhabitants (1992)
Telephones: 50/100 inhabitants (1992)

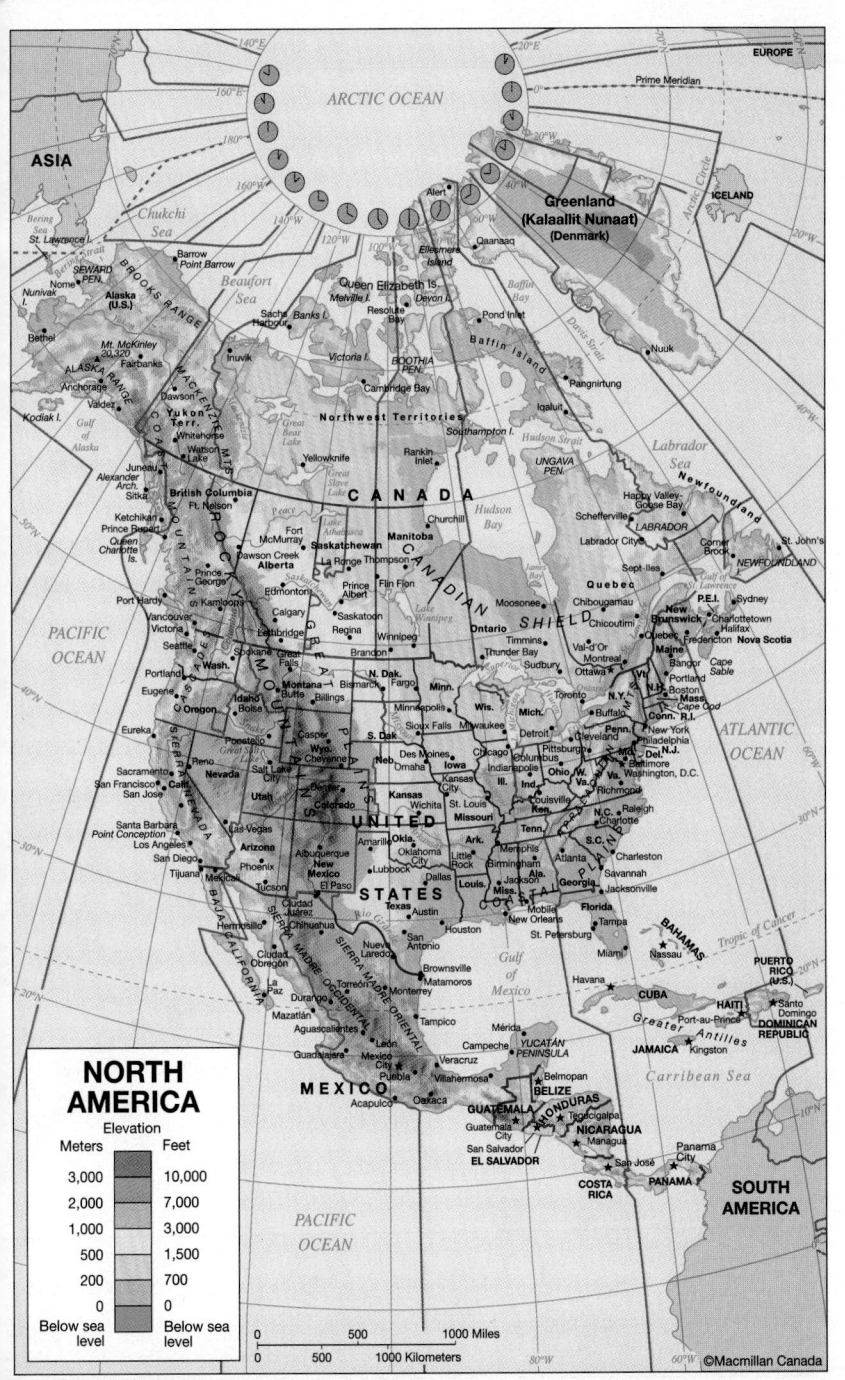

NORTH AMERICA

Elevation

Meters	Feet
3,000	10,000
2,000	7,000
1,000	3,000
500	1,500
200	700
0	0
Below sea level	Below sea level

©Macmillan Canada

ARCTIC OCEAN

Beaufort
Sea

Queen Elizabeth Islands

Prince
Patrick
I.

Heiber

Melville I.

Banks
Island

Alaska
(U.S.)

Inuvik

Gulf
of
Alaska

Dawson

Victoria
Island

Princ
of Wal
I.

Mount Logan
19,524

Yukon
Territory

MACKENZIE MOUNTAINS

Great Bear
Lake

ST. ELIAS MTS.

Whitehorse

Northwest
Territories

ROCKY

COAST MOUNTAINS

British
Columbia

Great Slave
Lake

Yellowknife

Queen
Charlotte Is.

Prince Rupert

Kitimat

Williston L.

Peace

Dawson Creek

Mount Waddington
13,260

Prince
George

Grande-
Prairie

GREAT

Lake
Athabasca

Fort
McMurray

Mount Robson
12,972

MOUNTAINS

Alberta

PLAINS

Athabasca

C

Vancouver
Island

Kamloops

Edmonton

Saskatchewan

Manitoba

Thompson

Nanaimo

Vancouver
Kelowna

Red Deer

Prince Albert

Saskatchewan

Lake
Winnipeg

PACIFIC
OCEAN

Victoria

Nelson

Calgary

North Battleford
Saskatoon

Trail

Lethbridge

Medicine
Hat

Swift Current

Lake
Manitoba

Moose
Jaw

Regina

Portage-
la-Prairie

K

Brandon

Winnipeg

UNITED STATES

60°N

50°N

40°N

160°W   150°W   140°W   130°W   120°W 110°W

110°W   100°W

©Macmillan Canada

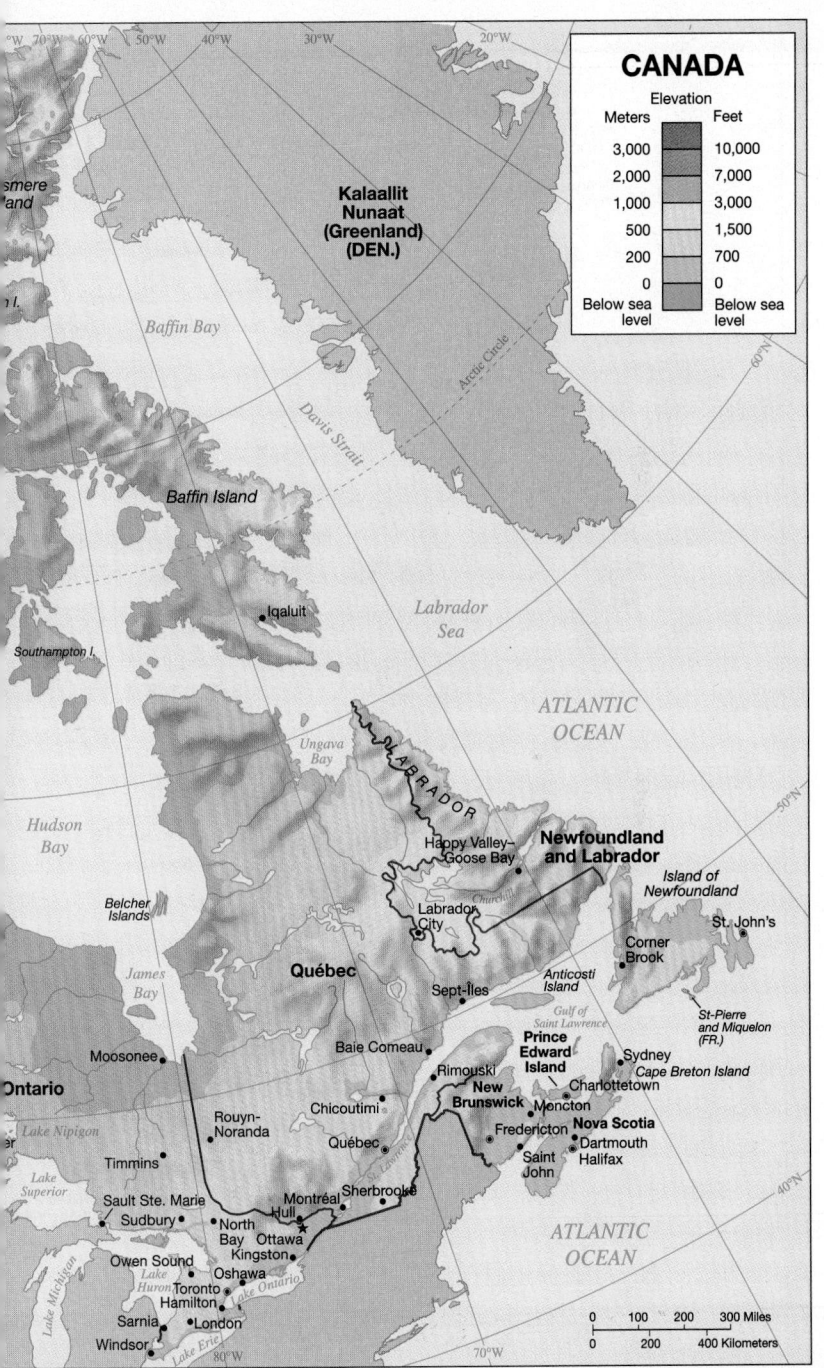

CANADA

Elevation

Meters		Feet
3,000		10,000
2,000		7,000
1,000		3,000
500		1,500
200		700
0		0
Below sea level		Below sea level

Kalaallit Nunaat (Greenland) (DEN.)

Baffin Bay

Ellesmere Island

Baffin Island

Davis Strait

Arctic Circle

Igaluit

Labrador Sea

Southampton I.

ATLANTIC OCEAN

Hudson Bay

LABRADOR

Ungava Bay

Happy Valley–Goose Bay

Newfoundland and Labrador

Churchill

Island of Newfoundland

Belcher Islands

Labrador City

St. John's

James Bay

Québec

Corner Brook

Sept-Îles

Anticosti Island

St-Pierre and Miquelon (FR.)

Moosonee

Baie Comeau

Gulf of Saint Lawrence

Prince Edward Island

Sydney

Cape Breton Island

Ontario

Rouyn-Noranda

Rimouski

New Brunswick

Charlottetown

Lake Nipigon

Chicoutimi

Moncton

Nova Scotia

Timmins

Québec

Fredericton

Dartmouth

Lake Superior

Sault Ste. Marie

Saint John

Halifax

Sudbury

Montréal

Sherbrooke

North Bay

Hull

Ottawa

Kingston

ATLANTIC OCEAN

Owen Sound

Lake Huron

Oshawa

Lake Ontario

Toronto

Hamilton

Sarnia

London

Lake Michigan

Windsor

Lake Erie

0	100	200	300 Miles
0	200		400 Kilometers

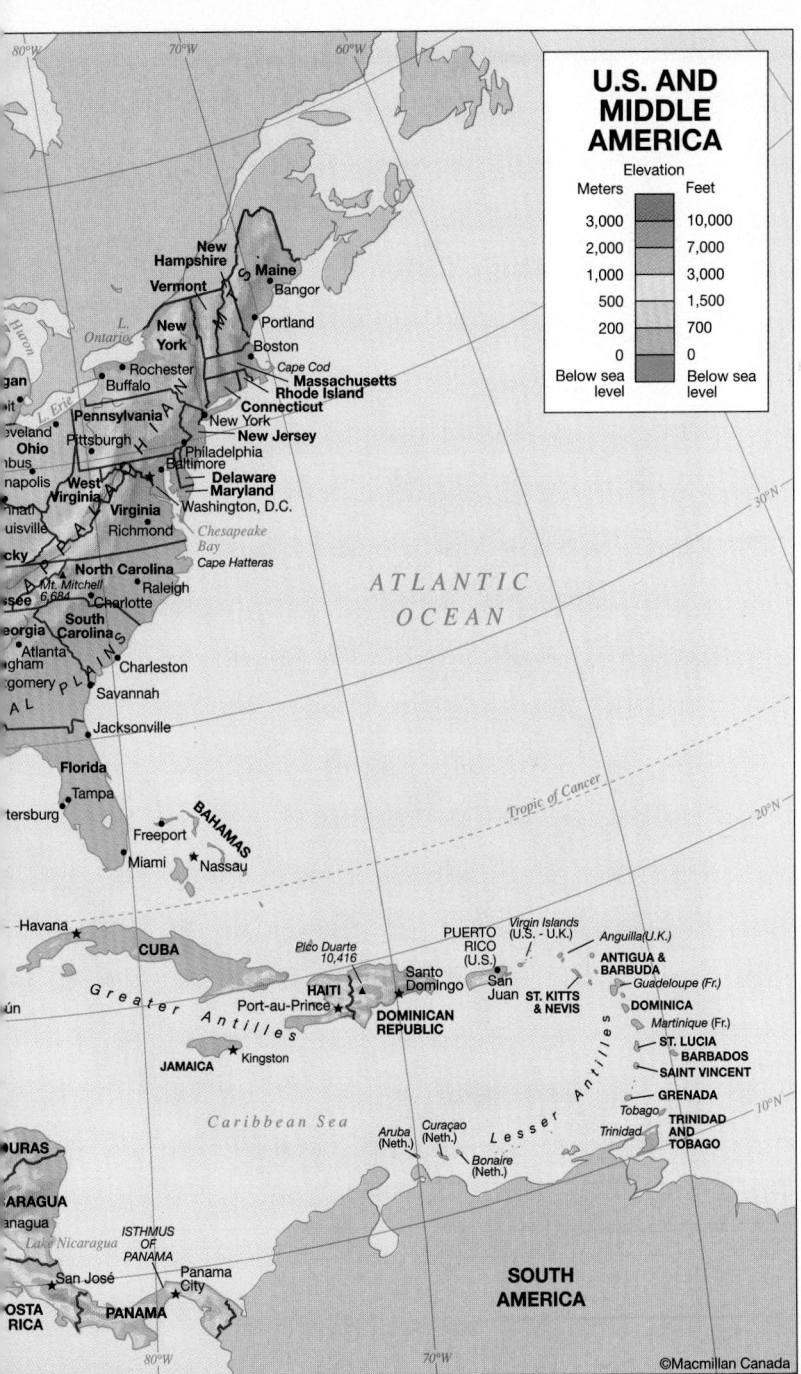

U.S. AND MIDDLE AMERICA

Elevation

Meters	Feet
3,000	10,000
2,000	7,000
1,000	3,000
500	1,500
200	700
0	0
Below sea level	Below sea level

80°W 70°W 60°W

L. Huron

L. Ontario

L. Erie

New Hampshire
Vermont
Maine
• Bangor
• Portland
New York
• Boston
• Rochester
Cape Cod
• Buffalo
Massachusetts
Rhode Island
Connecticut
New York
Pennsylvania
New Jersey
Philadelphia
eveland
Pittsburgh
Baltimore
Ohio
bus
West
napolis
Virginia
Delaware
Maryland
Washington, D.C.
hati
Virginia
uisville
Richmond
Chesapeake Bay
cky
North Carolina
Cape Hatteras
Mt. Mitchell
6,684
• Raleigh
see
• Charlotte
eorgia
South Carolina
• Atlanta
gham
• Charleston
gomery
• Savannah
AL
• Jacksonville

Florida
• Tampa
tersburg

ATLANTIC OCEAN

BAHAMAS
• Freeport
• Miami
★ Nassau

Tropic of Cancer

30°N

20°N

• Havana
CUBA

Greater Antilles

Pico Duarte
10,416

PUERTO RICO (U.S.)
Santo Domingo
San Juan

Virgin Islands (U.S. - U.K.)

Anguilla(U.K.)

ANTIGUA & BARBUDA
Guadeloupe (Fr.)

HAITI
Port-au-Prince ★
DOMINICAN REPUBLIC

ST. KITTS & NEVIS

DOMINICA
Martinique (Fr.)
ST. LUCIA
BARBADOS
SAINT VINCENT

Lesser Antilles

GRENADA
Tobago
TRINIDAD AND TOBAGO
Trinidad

JAMAICA
★ Kingston

Caribbean Sea

Aruba (Neth.)
Curaçao (Neth.)
Bonaire (Neth.)

10°N

ún

URAS

ARAGUA
anagua
Lake Nicaragua

ISTHMUS OF PANAMA
• San José
Panama City

OSTA RICA
PANAMA

SOUTH AMERICA

80°W 70°W

©Macmillan Canada

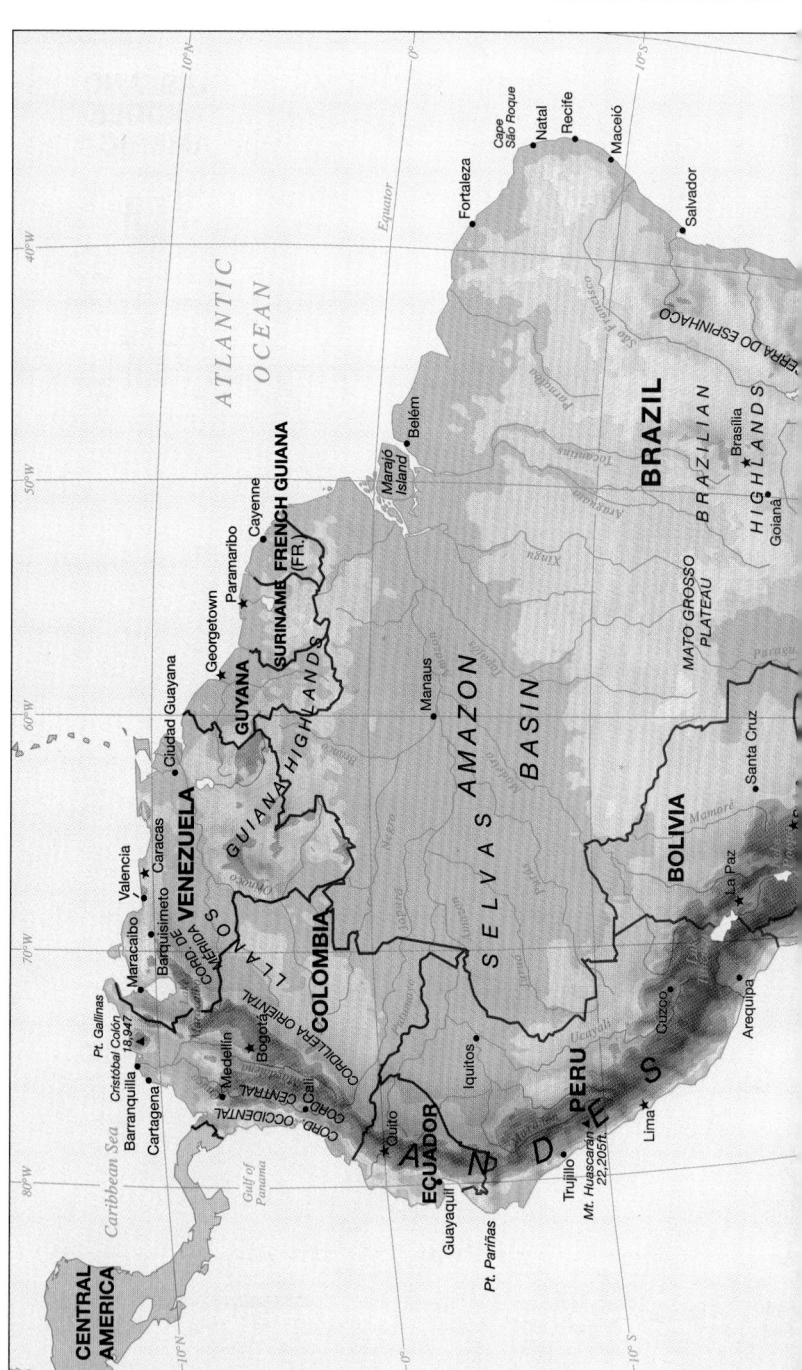

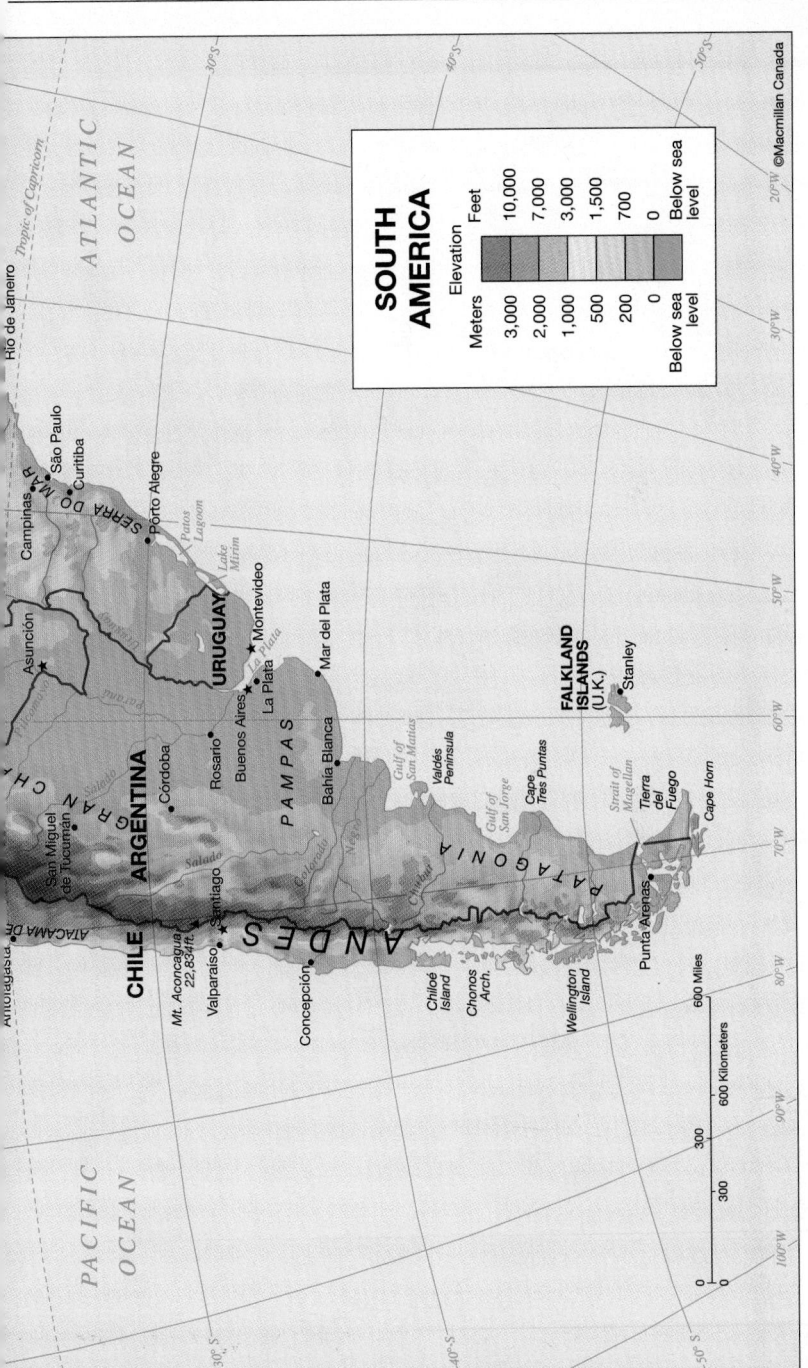

SOUTH
AMERICA

Elevation

Meters	Feet
3,000	10,000
2,000	7,000
1,000	3,000
500	1,500
200	700
0	0
Below sea level	Below sea level

ATLANTIC OCEAN

PACIFIC OCEAN

Tropic of Capricorn

Rio de Janeiro

São Paulo

Campinas

Curitiba

SERRA DO MAR

Asunción

Pôrto Alegre

Patos Lagoon

Lake Mirim

URUGUAY

Montevideo

La Plata

Buenos Aires

Mar del Plata

Córdoba

Rosario

ARGENTINA

GRAN CHACO

San Miguel de Tucumán

Salado

Salado

CHILE

ATACAMA DE

Antofagasta

Mt. Aconcagua 22,834 ft.

Valparaíso

Santiago

Concepción

ANDES

PAMPAS

Bahía Blanca

Colorado

Negro

Chubut

PATAGONIA

Gulf of San Matías

Valdés Peninsula

Gulf of San Jorge

Cape Tres Puntas

Strait of Magellan

Tierra del Fuego

Cape Horn

Punta Arenas

Chiloé Island

Chonos Arch.

Wellington Island

FALKLAND ISLANDS (U.K.)

Stanley

0	300	600 Miles
0	300	600 Kilometers

100°W 90°W 80°W 70°W 60°W 50°W 40°W 30°W 20°W

30°S 40°S 50°S

30°W 20°W 70°N 10°W 0° 10°E 20°E

Arctic Circle

60°N

Reykjavík ★ **ICELAND**

N o r w e g i a n
Sea

Faeroe Is.
(Den.)

Trondheim •

Shetland Is.
(U.K.)

Bergen •

ATLANTIC

Hebrides *Orkney Is.*

OCEAN

50°N

HIGHLANDS

Glasgow • • Edinburgh
Belfast •

IRELAND **UNITED**
Dublin ★ Manchester • **KINGDOM**
Liverpool • • Leeds
• Sheffield

North
Sea

JUTLAND
DENMARK
Copenhagen ★ • Malmö

Oslo ★ Uppsala •
Västeras •
Stockholm ★

Göteborg •
GÖTALAND

NORWAY **SWEDEN** *KJÖLEN MTS.*

Gulf of Bo

Baltic Se

Kaliningrac
Gdansk •

Birmingham • **NETHERLANDS** Bremen • • Hamburg
Cardiff • Bristol • Amsterdam • • Hannover Berlin
• Rotterdam • Utrecht ★
London ★ Antwerp • • Essen
Portsmouth • Dover • • Düsseldorf Leipzig
English Channel Lille **BELGIUM** Cologne •
Brussels • Bonn • **GERMANY**
Brest • Le Havre • *NORMANDY* **LUX.** • Frankfurt
★ Paris Mannheim •
Nantes • *Loire* Strasbourg • Nuremberg •
BRITTANY Stuttgart •
Bay *JURA MTS.* Basel • Munich •
of **FRANCE** Bern ★ • Zürich **LIECH.**
Biscay Geneva • **SWITZ.** A

Poznan •
POLA
NORTH Warsa
• Wrocław
Dresden • Katov
Prague • **SLO**
CZECH REP. Brno • Kc
Vienna ★ Bratislav
•Linz • Mi
• Salzburg **HUNGARY**
AUSTRIA Budapest★

La Coruña •
Oviedo • Bordeaux •
• León *MASSIF* Lyon •
Bilbao • *CENTRAL* Mt. Blanc
Porto • Toulouse • 15,770ft.
Duero *PYRENEES* Turin •
• Salamanca **ANDORRA** Nice •
PORTUGAL *IBERIAN* Marseille •
Lisbon ★ Madrid ★ **MONACO**
Tagus Barcelona •
SPAIN
PENINSULA • Valencia
Guadalquivir *Balearic Is.*
Seville •
Cádiz • • Granada
Strait of
Gibraltar

SLOVENIA
Ljubljana •
Milan • Venice • Zagreb • **CROATIA**
Genoa • **BOSNIA &**
Bologna • **HERCEG.** B
ITALY *SAN* Sarajevo • **Y**
Florence • *MARINO*
Pisa • • Ancona
APENNINES *Adriatic Sea*

Corsica
(Fr.) Rome ★
Naples • • Bari Tirar
Sardinia • Brindisi **ALB**
(It.)

Tyrrhenian *Ionian*
Sea *Sea*

Palermo • • Messina
Sicily • *Mt. Etna*
10,902ft.
Valletta
★ **MALTA**

Mediterranean Sea

AFRICA

0 200 400 Miles
0 200 400 Kilometers

0° 10°E

EUROPE

Elevation

Meters		Feet
4,000		14,000
2,000		7,000
1,000		3,000
500		1,500
200		700
0		0
Below sea level		Below sea level

©Macmillan Canada

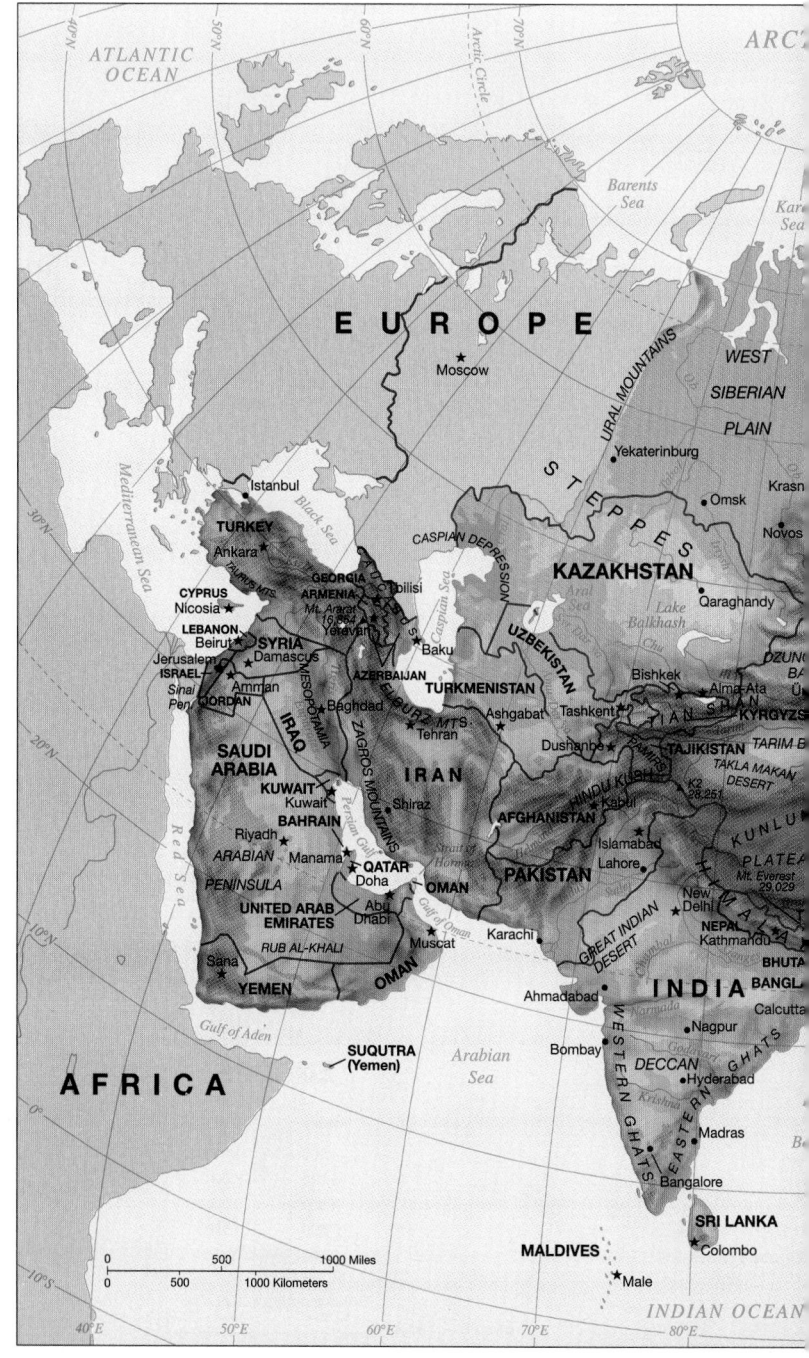

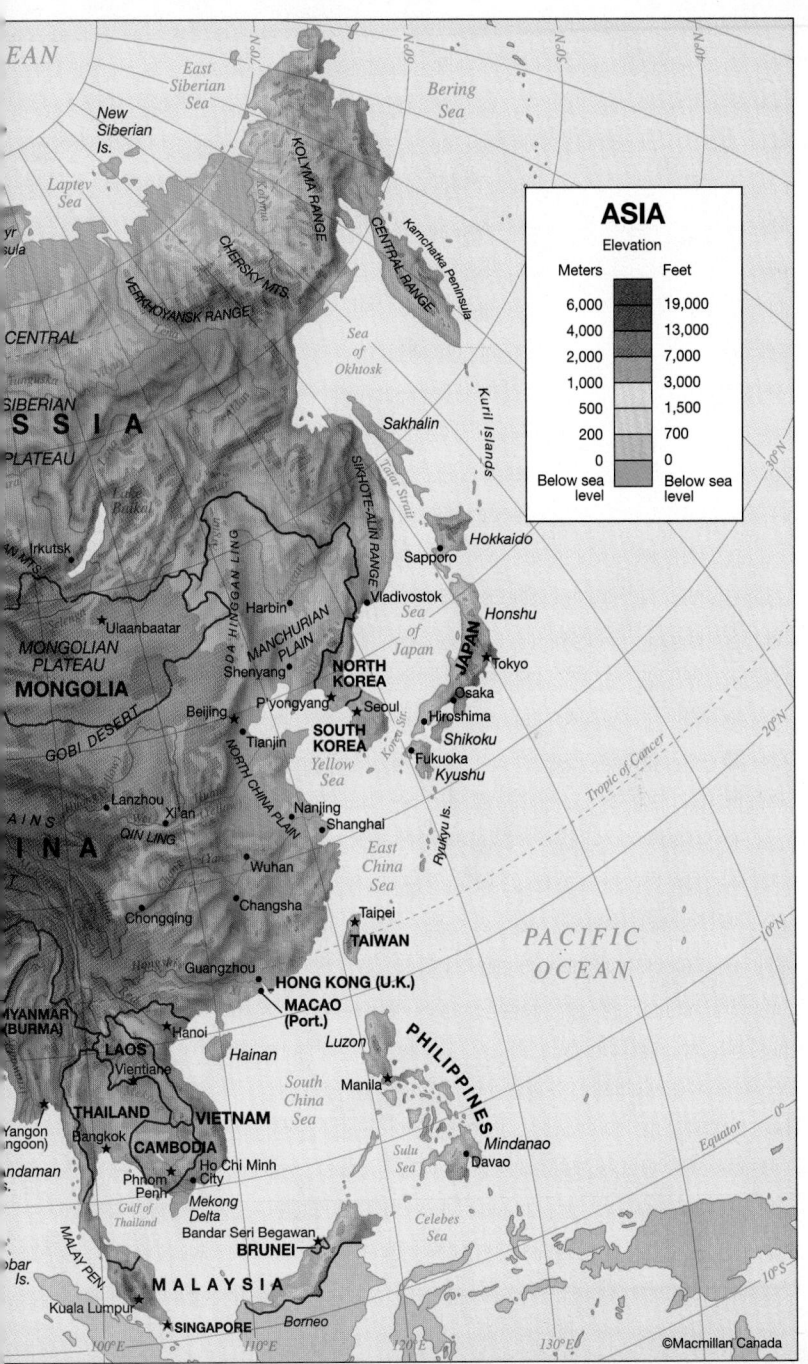

ASIA

Elevation

Meters		Feet
6,000		19,000
4,000		13,000
2,000		7,000
1,000		3,000
500		1,500
200		700
0		0
Below sea level		Below sea level

©Macmillan Canada

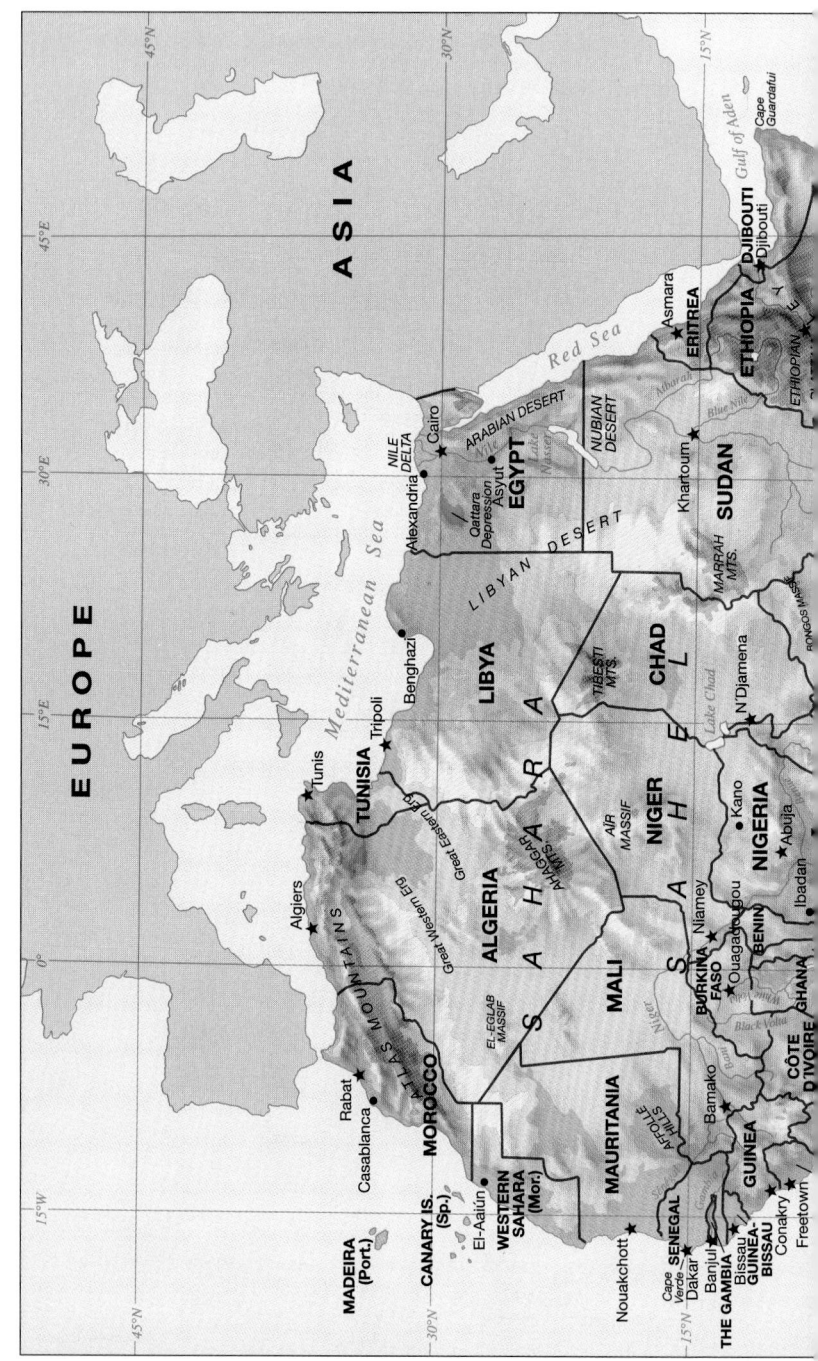

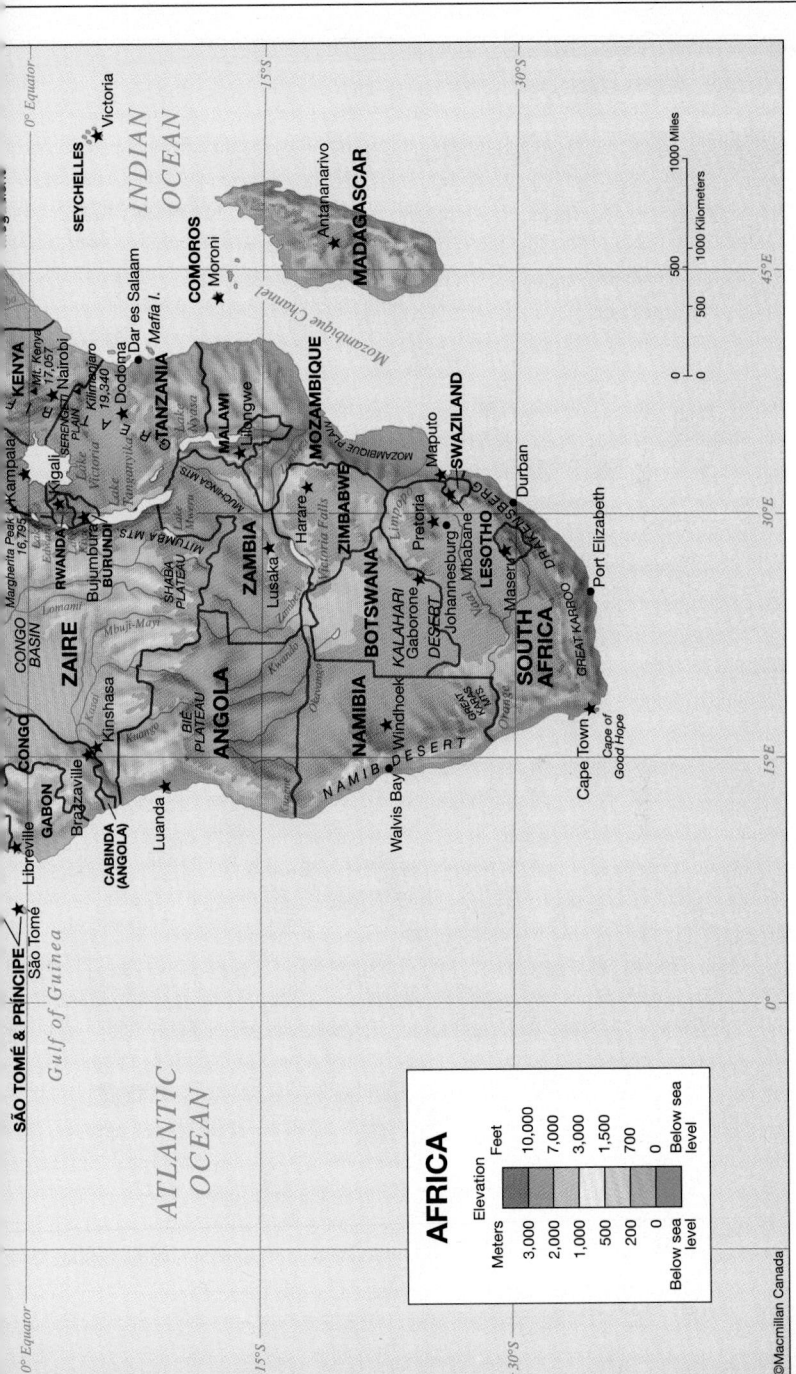

AFRICA

Elevation

Meters	Feet
3,000	10,000
2,000	7,000
1,000	3,000
500	1,500
200	700
0	0
Below sea level	Below sea level

1000 Miles
1000 Kilometers

ASIA

Tropic of Cancer

Taiwan

Hainan

South

China

Sea

Philippine
Islands

Philippine

Sea

NORTHERN
MARIANA
ISLANDS
(U.S.)

Mariana Is.

Tinian

Guam (U.S.)

FEDERATED STATES
OF MICRONESIA

Yap

Palau (U.S.)

Truk ★ Palikir

Caroline Islands

Leuser
11,371ft.
▲ •Medan

Sumatra

Celebes Sea

Manado

Molucca
Is.

Bismarck Arch.

0° Padang
Kerinci
12,467ft. Jambi
Palembang

Pontianak

Bangka

Borneo

Banjarmasin

Celebes

Ujung
Pandang

Buru

Ceram

Ambon

WEST
IRIAN
Jaya Peak
16,499ft.
Aru

Jayapura

MACKE MTS.

New Guinea

Bismarck

Sea

New Britain

PAPUA NEW GUINEA

Solomon
Sea

Jakarta

Bandung *Java*

Yogyakarta Malang

Surabaya

Java Sea

INDONESIA

Banda Sea

Bali

Sumbawa Flores

Arafura

Sea

Torres Strait

Pt. Moresby

Lombok

Sumba

Timor

Cape York

Timor

Sea

Darwin

ARNHEM
LAND

Gulf of
Carpentaria

CAPE
YORK
PENINSULA

15°S

KIMBERLEY
PLATEAU

Northern
Territory

Great Barrier Reef

Ca
Se

North
West
Cape

GREAT SANDY
DESERT

AUSTRALIA

Townsville

GREAT DIVIDING

Tropic of Capricorn

HAMERSLEY RA.

MACDONNELL RANGES

Alice Springs

Queensland

GIBSON
DESERT

Ayers Rock
▲4,954ft.

MUSGRAVE RANGES

SIMPSON
DESERT

GREAT
ARTESIAN
BASIN

Brisba

RANGE

30°S

GREAT
VICTORIA
DESERT

South
Australia

Western
Australia

Victoria

•Perth

NULLARBOR PLAIN

Newcastle

AUSTRALIAN ALPS

Sydney

Canberra, A.C.T.

Cape
Leeuwin

Great Australiulian

Bight

Adelaide

New
South
Wales

Mt. Kosciusko
7,310ft.

Cape Howe

Melbourne

Bass Strait

Ta

INDIAN OCEAN

Tasmania

Hobart

45°S

South
East
Cape

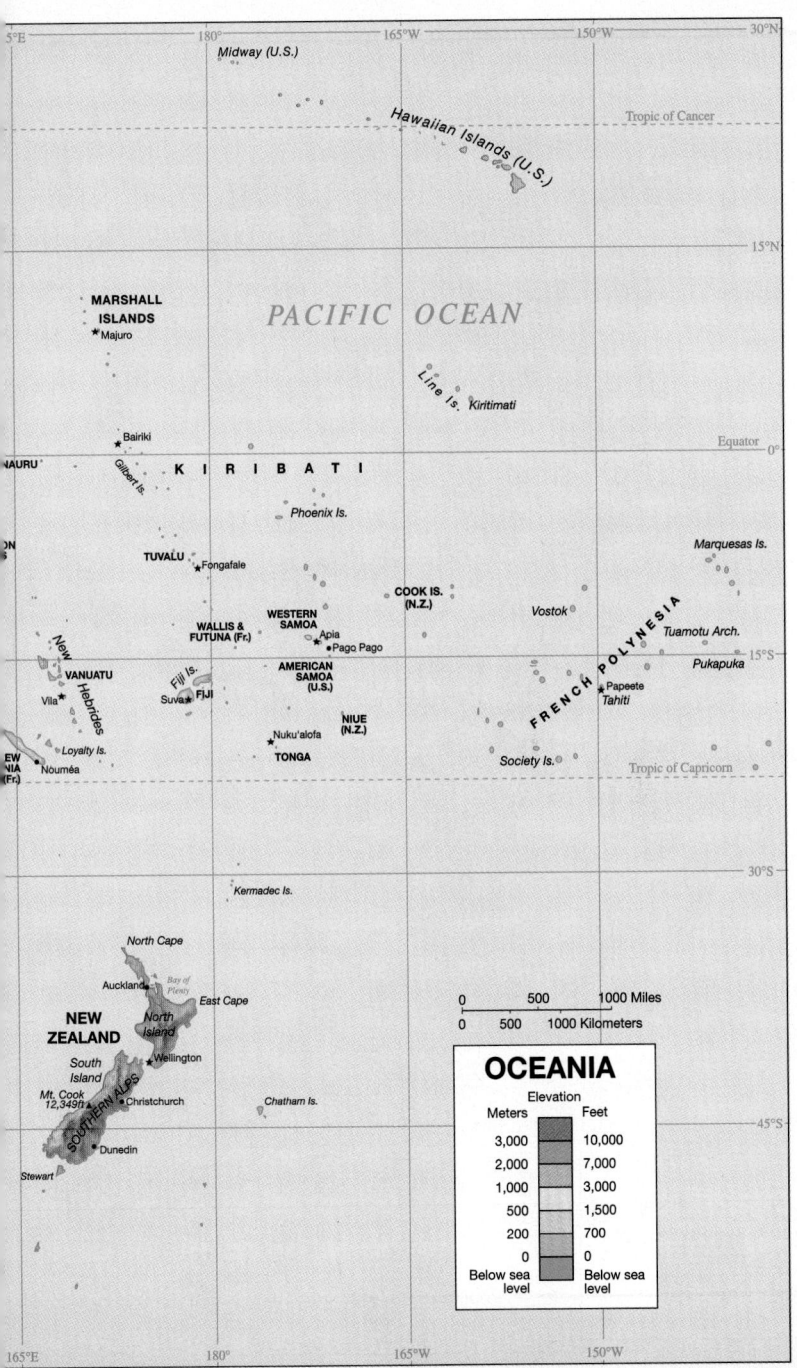

5°E 180° 165°W 150°W 30°N

Midway (U.S.)

Hawaiian Islands (U.S.)

Tropic of Cancer

15°N

MARSHALL
ISLANDS
★ Majuro

PACIFIC OCEAN

NAURU

★ Bairiki

Gilbert Is.

K I R I B A T I

Line Is.

Kiritimati

Equator 0°

Phoenix Is.

Marquesas Is.

TUVALU ★ Fongafale

COOK IS.
(N.Z.)

Vostok

FRENCH POLYNESIA

Tuamotu Arch.

WALLIS &
FUTUNA (Fr.)

WESTERN
SAMOA

★ Apia
● Pago Pago

Pukapuka

15°S

New Hebrides

VANUATU

Fiji Is.

AMERICAN
SAMOA
(U.S.)

Papeete
Tahiti

Vila ★

Suva ★ FIJI

NIUE
(N.Z.)

EW
NIA
(Fr.)

Loyalty Is.

● Nouméa

★ Nuku'alofa

TONGA

Society Is.

Tropic of Capricorn

30°S

Kermadec Is.

North Cape

Auckland ★

Bay of
Plenty

East Cape

NEW
ZEALAND

North
Island

South
Island

★ Wellington

Mt. Cook
12,349ft ▲ ● Christchurch

Chatham Is.

45°S

SOUTHERN ALPS

● Dunedin

Stewart

| 0 | | 500 | 1000 Miles |
| 0 | 500 | 1000 Kilometers | |

OCEANIA

Elevation

Meters		Feet
3,000		10,000
2,000		7,000
1,000		3,000
500		1,500
200		700
0		0
Below sea level		Below sea level

165°E 180° 165°W 150°W

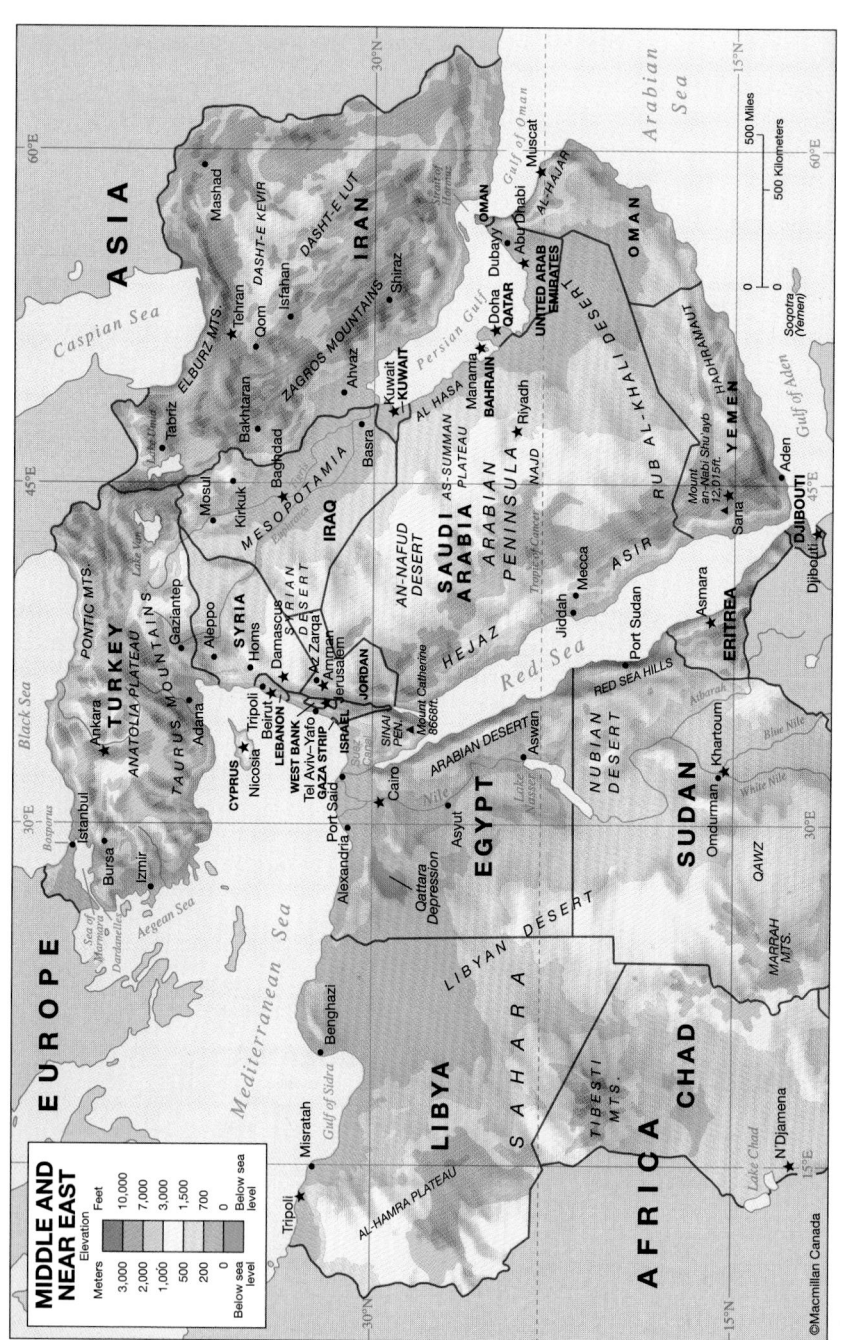

MIDDLE AND NEAR EAST

Elevation

Meters	Feet
3,000	10,000
2,000	7,000
1,000	3,000
500	1,500
200	700
0	0
Below sea level	Below sea level

©Macmillan Canada

■ TRANSPORTATION

Motor Vehicles: 2,522,628; 1,729,683 passenger cars (1990)
Roads: 34,832 km; 29,027 km paved
Railway: 2,494 km
Air Traffic: 4,937,000 passengers carried (1991)
Airports: 78 airfields, of which 77 are usable; 63 have permanent-surface runways (1993)

Canadian Embassy: 4 Ioannou Gennadiou St, Athens 115 21. Tel: (011-30-1) 725-4011. Fax: (011-30-1) 725-3994
Representative to Canada: Embassy of the Hellenic Republic, 76-80 MacLaren St, Ottawa ON K2P 0K6. Tel: (613) 238-6271. Fax: (613) 238-5676.

Greenland

Dependent Territory of Denmark

Long-Form Name: Grønland (Kalaallit Nunaat)
Capital: Nuuk (Godthab)
Population: 56,533 (1993 est.)

■ GEOGRAPHY

Area: 2,175,600 sq. km
Coastline: 44,087 km
Climate: arctic to subarctic; cool summers, cold winters
Environment: sparse population confined to small settlements along coast; continuous permafrost over northern two-thirds of the island
Terrain: flat to gradually sloping icecap covers all but a narrow, mountainous, barren, rocky coast
Land Use: 0% arable land; 0% permanent crops; 1% meadow and pastures; negligible forest and woodland; 99% other
Location: N North America, bordering on Atlantic Ocean, Greenland Sea, Arctic Ocean, Baffin Bay

■ PEOPLE

Nationality: Greenlander
Ethnic Groups: 86% Greenlander (Inuit and Greenland-born Caucasians), 14% Danish
Languages: Inuit dialects, Danish
Religions: Evangelical Lutheran
Marriages: 7.1/1,000 population (1989)
Divorces: 2.38/1,000 population (1989)

■ GOVERNMENT

Leader(s): Queen Margrethe II represented by High Commissioner Torben Hede Pedersen
Government Type: part of the Danish realm; self-governing overseas administrative division
Administrative Divisions: 3 municipalities
Independence: none
National Holiday: Birthday of the Queen, Apr. 16

■ ECONOMY

Overview: dependent on annual subsidy from the Danish government; unemployment is on the increase; fishing is the most important industry; mineral resource exploitation is limited to lead and zinc
GNP: $500 million, per capita $9,000; real growth rate 5% (1988)
Inflation: n.a.
Industries: fish processing, lead and zinc mining, handicrafts, small shipyards, potential for platinum and gold mining
Labour Force: 22,800, largely engaged in fishing, hunting, sheep breeding (1993)
Unemployment: 9% (1990 est.)
Agriculture: fishing, sheep raising, crops limited to forage and small-garden vegetables
Natural Resources: zinc, lead, iron ore, coal, molybdenum, cryolite, uranium, fish

■ FINANCE/TRADE

Currency: danish krone (DKr)
International Reserves Excluding Gold: n.a.
Gold Reserves: n.a.
Budget: revenues $381 million, expenditures $381 million, including capital expenditures of $36 million (1989)
Defence Expenditures: n.a.
External Debt: $480 million (1990)
Exports: $341 million (1991); fish and fish products
Imports: $408 million (1991); manufactured goods, machinery and transport equipment

■ HEALTH

Births: 19.62/1,000 population (1993 est.)
Deaths: 7.66/1,000 population (1993 est.)
Infant Mortality: 28.4 deaths/1,000 live births (1993 est.)
Life Expectancy at Birth: 61.79 years male, 70.6 years female (1993 est.)
No. of Physicians: n.a.

■ EDUCATION

Govt. Expenditure: n.a.
Literacy: 93% (1993)

■ COMMUNICATIONS

Daily newspapers: n.a.
Televisions: n.a.; 4 TV stations (1993)
Radios: n.a.; 12 radio stations (1993)
Telephones: 17,900 total

■ TRANSPORTATION

Motor Vehicles: n.a.
Roads: 80 km
Railway: n.a.
Air Traffic: n.a.
Airports: 11 airfields, of which 8 are usable; 5 have permanent-surface runways (1993)

Canadian Embassy: c/o Kr. Bernikowsgade 1, 1105 Copenhagen K, Denmark. Tel: (011-45-33) 12-22-99. Fax: (011-45-33) 14-05-85.

Grenada

Long-Form Name: Grenada
Capital: Saint George's
Population: 100,000 (1993 est.)

■ GEOGRAPHY

Area: 340 sq. km
Coastline: 121 km
Climate: tropical; tempered by northeast trade winds
Environment: lies on edge of hurricane belt; hurricane season lasts from June to Nov.
Terrain: volcanic in origin with central mountains
Land Use: 15% arable; 26% permanent; 3% meadows; 9% forest; 47% other
Location: Caribbean Islands

■ PEOPLE

Nationality: Grenadian
Ethnic Groups: mainly of black African descent
Languages: English (official); some French patois
Religions: largely Roman Catholic; Anglican; other Protestant sects
Marriages: n.a.
Divorces: n.a.

■ GOVERNMENT

Leader(s): Prime Min. Nicholas Braithwaite, Gov. Gen. Reginald Palmer
Government Type: parliamentary democracy
Administrative Divisions: 6 parishes and 1 dependency
Independence: Feb. 7, 1974 (from UK)
National Holiday: Independence Day, Feb. 7

■ ECONOMY

Overview: the economy is based on agriculture (spices, tropical plants) and tourism; unemployment is high
GNP: n.a., GDP $250 million, per capita $3,000; real growth rate -0.4% (1992 est.)

Inflation: 2.6% (1991)
Industries: food and beverage, textiles, light assembly operations, tourism, construction
Labour Force: 36,000; 31% services, 24% agriculture, 8% construction, 5% manufacturing, 32% other (1985)
Unemployment: 25% (1992 est.)
Agriculture: accounts for 16% of GDP, 80% of exports and employs 24% of the labour force; bananas, cocoa, nutmeg and mace are major crops; small-scale farms predominate
Natural Resources: timber, tropical fruit, deepwater harbours

■ FINANCE/TRADE

Currency: East Caribbean dollar ($EC)
International Reserves Excluding Gold: $27 million (Dec. 1993)
Gold Reserves: n.a.
Budget: revenues $78 million; expenditures $51 million, including capital expenditures of $22 million (1991)
Defence Expenditures: n.a.
External Debt: $109 million (1992)
Exports: $23 million (1991); commodities: nutmeg 35%, cocoa beans 15%, bananas 13%, mace 7%, textiles; partners: US 4%, UK, Germany, Netherlands, Trinidad and Tobago
Imports: $117 million (1991); commodities: machinery 24%, food 22%, manufactured goods 19%, petroleum 8%; partners: US 32%, UK, Trinidad and Tobago, Japan, Canada

■ HEALTH

Births: 33/1,000 population (1993)
Deaths: 8/1,000 population (1993)
Infant Mortality: 15.9 deaths/1,000 live births (1993)
Life Expectancy at Birth: 67 years male, 72 years female (1993)
No. of Physicians: 4.7/10,000 population (1992)

■ EDUCATION

Govt. Expenditure: n.a.
Literacy: 98% (1993)

■ COMMUNICATIONS

Daily newspapers: n.a.
Televisions: 148/1,000 inhabitants (1986)
Radios: 624/1,000 inhabitants (1989)
Telephones: 6.3/100 inhabitants (1992)

■ TRANSPORTATION

Motor Vehicles: 12,198 registered vehicles (1988)
Roads: 1,000 km; 600 km paved (1993)
Railway: n.a.

Air Traffic: n.a.
Airports: 3 airfields, all usable; 2 have permanent-surface runways (1993)

Canadian Embassy: c/o The Canadian High Commission, Bishop's Court Hill, St. Michael, Barbados; mailing address: P.O. Box 404, Bridgetown, Barbados. Tel: (809) 429-3550. Fax: (809) 429-3780.
Representative to Canada: c/o High Commission for the Countries of the Organization of Eastern Caribbean States, 112 Kent St, Ste 1610, Place de Ville, Tower B, Ottawa, ON K1P 5P2. Tel: (613) 236-8952. Fax: (613) 236-3042.

Guadeloupe

Dependency of France

Long-Form Name: Department of Guadeloupe
Capital: Basse-Terre (seat of govt.); each of the 7 inhabited islands has its own chief town
Population: 400,000 (1993 est.)

■ GEOGRAPHY

Area: 1,779 sq. km (2 main islands, 5 small islands, one small island group called Iles des Saintes)
Climate: subtropical tempered by trade winds; hot and humid May–Dec., cool and dry Dec.–April
Land Use: 18% arable, 5% permanent crops, 13% meadows and pastures, 40% forests and woodland, 24% other
Location: Lesser Antilles

■ PEOPLE

Nationality: Guadeloupian
Ethnic Groups: 90% black or mulatto, 5% white, less than 5% East Indian, Lebanese, Chinese
Languages: French, Creole dialect

■ GOVERNMENT

Leader(s): Prefect Franck Perriez
Government Type: overseas department of France
National Holiday: Taking of the Bastille, July 14

■ ECONOMY

Overview: economy depends on agriculture, tourism, light industry and services; agriculture: includes bananas, sugar cane, rum, flowers, livestock; vegetables and tobacco grown for local consumption; forestry, fisheries, tourism, food processing; partners: France, Martinique

■ FINANCE/TRADE

Currency: French franc

Guam

Unincorporated Outlying Territory of the United States

Long-Form Name: Territory of Guam
Capital: Agana
Population: 145,935 (1993 est.)

■ GEOGRAPHY

Area: 541.3 sq. km
Climate: tropical maritime, with little seasonal variation, but typhoon-prone and suffers from earthquakes; wet all year
Land Use: 11% arable, 11% permanent crops, 15% meadows and pastures, 18% forest and woodland, 45% other; interior is mountainous and volcanic hills dominate the south, but many forests in northern Guam have been cleared for farming and the construction of airfields; coconut trees grow throughout the island
Location: N Pacific Ocean, E of the Philippines

■ PEOPLE

Nationality: Guamanian
Ethnic Groups: 47% Chamorro, 25% Filipino, 10% Caucasian, 18% Chinese, Japanese, Korean and other
Languages: English (official), Chamorro, Japanese

■ GOVERNMENT

Leader(s): Gov. Joseph F. Ada
Government Type: unincorporated outlying territory of the US; executive powers of the legislature similar to those of an American state legislature
National Holiday: Guam Discovery Day (first Monday in March); also Liberation Day, July 21

■ ECONOMY

Overview: economy depends mainly on US military spending and on tourism; agriculture: corn, coconuts, sweet potatoes, cucumbers, watermelons, beans, livestock, esp. cattle and pigs, fruit, vegetables, fish; industry: textile manufacture, cement, petroleum, printing, plastics, ship repair; tourism of growing importance

■ **FINANCE/TRADE**

Currency: American dollar

Guatemala

Long-Form Name: Republic of Guatemala
Capital: Guatemala
Population: 10,000,000 (1993 est.)

■ **GEOGRAPHY**

Area: 108,890 sq. km
Coastline: 400 km
Climate: tropical; hot, humid in lowlands; cooler in highlands
Environment: numerous volcanoes in mountains, with frequent violent earthquakes; Caribbean coast subject to hurricanes and other tropical storms; deforestation; soil erosion; water pollution
Terrain: mostly mountainous with narrow coastal plains and rolling limestone plateau (Petén)
Land Use: 12% arable; 4% permanent; 12% meadows; 40% forest; 32% other
Location: Central (Latin) America, bordering on Caribbean Sea, Pacific Ocean

■ **PEOPLE**

Nationality: Guatemalan
Ethnic Groups: 56% Ladino (mestizo-mixed Indian and European ancestry), 44% Indian
Languages: Spanish, but over 40% of the population speaks an Indian language as a primary tongue (20 Indian dialects, including Quiche, Cakchiquel, Kekchi)
Religions: predominantly Roman Catholic; also Protestant, traditional Mayan
Marriages: 5.3 (per 1,000) (1988)
Divorces: 0.18 (per 1,000) (1988)

■ **GOVERNMENT**

Leader(s): Pres. Ramiro de Leon Carpio, V Pres. Arturo Herbruger
Government Type: republic
Administrative Divisions: 22 departments (departamento, pl. departamentos)
Independence: Sept. 15, 1821 (from Spain)
National Holiday: Independence Day, Sept. 15

■ **ECONOMY**

Overview: the inflation rate has dropped significantly as a result of government economic reforms, but political uncertainty casts a shadow over the agriculturally based economy
GNP: n.a., GDP $12.6 billion, per capita $1,300; real growth rate 4.2% (1991)

Inflation: 10.0% (1992)
Industries: sugar, textiles and clothing, furniture, chemicals, petroleum, metals, rubber, tourism
Labour Force: 2,628,000 (1992); 49.8% agriculture, 12.3% industry, 37.9% services (1989)
Unemployment: 6.5%, with 30–40% underemployment (1991 est.)
Agriculture: accounts for 26% of GDP; principal crops—sugar cane, corn, bananas, coffee, beans, cardamon; livestock—cattle, sheep, pigs, chickens; food importer
Natural Resources: crude oil, nickel, rare woods, fish, chicle

■ **FINANCE/TRADE**

Currency: quetzal (pl. quetzalas) (Q)
International Reserves Excluding Gold: $899 million (Jan. 1994)
Gold Reserves: 0.21 million fine troy ounces (Jan. 1994)
Budget: revenues $604 million; expenditures $808 million, including capital expenditures of $134 million (1990 est.)
Defence Expenditures: $121 million (1% of GDP) (1993)
External Debt: 2.749 billion (1992)
Exports: $1.295 billion (1992); commodities: coffee 38%, bananas 7%, sugar 7%, cardamon 4%; partners: US 29%, El Salvador, Germany, Costa Rica, Italy
Imports: $2.463 billion (1992); commodities: fuel and petroleum products, machinery, grain, fertilizers, motor vehicles; partners: US 38%, Mexico, Germany, Japan, El Salvador

■ **HEALTH**

Births: 39/1,000 population (1993)
Deaths: 7/1,000 population (1993)
Infant Mortality: 59 deaths/1,000 live births (1993)
Life Expectancy at Birth: 61 years male, 66 years female (1993)
No. of Physicians: 4.6/10,000 population (1992)

■ **EDUCATION**

Govt. Expenditure: 11.8% of govt. expenditure (1990)
Literacy: 55.1% (1993)

■ **COMMUNICATIONS**

Daily newspapers: 5 (1992)
Televisions: 44.7/1,000 inhabitants (1992)
Radios: 64/1,000 inhabitants (1992)
Telephones: 1.61/100 inhabitants (1992)

■ **TRANSPORTATION**

Motor Vehicles: 230,000; 130,000 passenger cars

(1990)
Roads: 26,429 km; 2,868 km paved (1993)
Railway: 1,019 km (1993)
Air Traffic: 165,000 passengers carried (1991)
Airports: 478 airfields, of which 418 are usable; 11 have permanent-surface runways (1993)

Canadian Embassy: 10 Avenida 21-25, Zona 14, Guatemala City; mailing address: P.O. Box 400, Guatemala City, Guatemala; C.A. Tel: (011-502-2) 33 61 02. Fax: (011-502-2) 33-61-61
Representative to Canada: Embassy of Guatemala, 130 Albert St, Ste 1010, Ottawa ON K1P 5G4. Tel: (613) 233-7237. Fax: (613) 233-0135.

Guinea

Long-Form Name: Republic of Guinea
Capital: Conakry
Population: 6,200,000 (1993 est.)

■ GEOGRAPHY

Area: 245,860 sq. km
Coastline: 320 km
Climate: generally hot and humid; monsoonal-type rainy season (June to Nov.) with south-westerly winds; dry season (Dec. to May) with northeasterly harmattan winds
Environment: hot, dry, dusty harmattan haze may reduce visibility during dry season; deforestation
Terrain: generally flat coastal plain, hilly to mountainous interior
Land Use: 6% arable; negligible permanent, 12% meadows; 42% forest; 40% other
Location: W Africa, bordering on Atlantic Ocean

■ PEOPLE

Nationality: Guinean
Ethnic Groups: 35% Fulani, 30% Malinke, 20% Sousou, 15% smaller tribes
Languages: French (official); each tribe has its own language; 8 official languages are taught in schools, including Fulani, Malinke, Soussou
Religions: 85% Moslem, 7% indigenous beliefs, 8% Christian
Marriages: n.a.
Divorces: n.a.

■ GOVERNMENT

Leader(s): Pres. Gen. Lansana Conté
Government Type: republic
Administrative Divisions: 33 administrative regions
Independence: Oct. 2, 1958 (from France; formerly known as French Guinea)

National Holiday: Anniversary of the Second Republic, Apr. 3

■ ECONOMY

Overview: although possessing numerous natural resources and potential for agricultural development, it is one of the poorest countries in the world
GNP: $2.669 billion, per capita $450; real growth rate n.a. (1991)
Inflation: 19.6% (1990 est.)
Industries: bauxite mining, alumina, diamond mining, light manufacturing and agricultural processing industries
Labour Force: 3,100,000 (1992); 78.1% agriculture, 1.3% industry, 20.6% services (1989)
Unemployment: n.a.
Agriculture: accounts for 40% of GDP (includes fishing and forestry); mostly subsistence farming; principal products—rice, coffee, pineapples, palm kernels, cassava, sweet potatoes, timber; livestock—cattle, sheep and goats
Natural Resources: bauxite, iron ore, diamonds, gold, uranium, hydroelectricity, fish

■ FINANCE/TRADE

Currency: Guinean franc
International Reserves Excluding Gold: n.a.
Gold Reserves: n.a.
Budget: revenues $449 million; expenditures $708 million, including capital expenditures of $361 million (1990 est.)
Defence Expenditures: n.a.
External Debt: 2.651 billion (1992)
Exports: $788 million (1990); commodities: alumina, bauxite, diamonds, coffee, pineapples, bananas, palm kernels; partners: US 33%, European Community 33%, Eastern Europe 20%, Canada
Imports: $692 million (1990); commodities: petroleum products, metals, machinery, transport equipment, foodstuffs, textiles and other grain; partners: US 16%, France, Brazil

■ HEALTH

Births: 47/1,000 population (1993)
Deaths: 22/1,000 population (1993)
Infant Mortality: 149 deaths/1,000 live births (1993)
Life Expectancy at Birth: 40 years male, 44 years female (1993)
No. of Physicians: 0.2/10,000 population (1990)

■ EDUCATION

Govt. Expenditure: 21.5% of govt. expenditure (1988)
Literacy: 24.0% (1993)

■ COMMUNICATIONS

Daily newspapers: 1 (1992)
Televisions: 5.4/1,000 inhabitants (1992)
Radios: 41/1,000 inhabitants (1992)
Telephones: 15,000 total (1993)

■ TRANSPORTATION

Motor Vehicles: 26,000; 13,500 passenger cars (1990)
Roads: 30,100 km; 1,145 km paved (1993)
Railway: 1,057 km
Air Traffic: 41,000 passengers carried (1991)
Airports: 15 airfields, all usable; 4 have permanent-surface runways (1993)

Canadian Embassy: mailing address: P.O. Box 99, Conakry, Guinea. Tel: (011-224) 41-23-95. Fax: (011-224) 41-42-36
Representative to Canada: Embassy of the Republic of Guinea, 483 Wilbrod St, Ottawa ON K1N 6N1. Tel: (613) 789-8444. Fax: (613) 789-7560.

Guinea-Bissau

Long-Form Name: Republic of Guinea-Bissau
Capital: Bissau
Population: 1,000,000 (1993 est.)

■ GEOGRAPHY

Area: 36,120 sq. km
Coastline: 350 km
Climate: tropical; generally hot and humid; monsoon-type rainy season (June to Nov.) with southwesterly winds; dry season (Dec. to May) with northeasterly harmattan winds
Environment: hot, dry, dusty harmattan haze may reduce visibility during dry season
Terrain: mostly low coastal plain rising to savanna in east
Land Use: 11% arable; 1% permanent; 43% meadows; 38% forest; 7% other
Location: W Africa, bordering on Atlantic Ocean

■ PEOPLE

Nationality: Guinea-Bissauan
Ethnic Groups: approx. 99% African (30% Balanta, 20% Fula, 14% Manjaca, 13% Mandinga, 7% Papel); less than 1% European and mulatto
Languages: Portuguese (official); Crioulo (a Portuguese-based Creole), Balante and numerous African languages
Religions: 65% indigenous beliefs, 30% Moslem, 5% Christian
Marriages: n.a.

Divorces: n.a.

■ GOVERNMENT

Leader(s): Pres. Brig. Gen. João Bernardo Vieira, Prime Min. Carlos Correira
Government Type: republic; highly centralized one-party regime since Sept. 1974
Administrative Divisions: 9 regions (regiões, singular–região)
Independence: Sept. 10, 1974 (from Portugal; formerly known as Portuguese Guinea)
National Holiday: Independence Day, Sept. 10

■ ECONOMY

Overview: this poor country is focusing on agricultural development; exploitation of mineral deposits is hampered by a weak infrastructure and high costs
GNP: $194 million, per capita $190; real growth rate 3.3% (1991)
Inflation: n.a.
Industries: agricultural processing, beer, soft drinks
Labour Force: 460,000 (1992); 82% agriculture, 4% industry, 14% services (1989)
Unemployment: n.a.
Agriculture: accounts for over 50% of GDP, nearly 100% of exports and 90% of employment; rice is the staple; not self-sufficient in food; fishing and forestry not fully exploited; crops include corn, beans, cassava, cashew nuts, peanuts, palm kernels and cotton
Natural Resources: unexploited deposits of petroleum, bauxite, phosphates; fish, timber

■ FINANCE/TRADE

Currency: Guinea-Bissauan peso (PG)
International Reserves Excluding Gold: $15 million (Dec. 1993)
Gold Reserves: n.a.
Budget: revenues $33.6 million; expenditures $44.8 million, including capital expenditures of 5.7 million (1991 est.)
Defence Expenditures: $4.43 billion (4.22% of total govt. expenditure) (1989)
External Debt: $634 million (1992)
Exports: $6 million (1992); commodities: cashews, fish, peanuts, palm kernels; partners: Portugal, Spain, Switzerland, Cape Verde, China
Imports: $84 million (1992); commodities: capital equipment, consumer goods, semiprocessed goods, foods, petroleum; partners: Portugal, USSR, European Community, other Europe, Senegal, US

■ HEALTH

Births: 43/1,000 population (1993)
Deaths: 22/1,000 population (1993)
Infant Mortality: 146 deaths/1,000 live births (1993)
Life Expectancy at Birth: 41 years male, 44 years female (1993)
No. of Physicians: 1.4/10,000 population (1992)

■ EDUCATION

Govt. Expenditure: 2.7% of govt. expenditure (1989)
Literacy: 36% (1993)

■ COMMUNICATIONS

Daily newspapers: 1 (1992)
Televisions: n.a.; 1 TV station (1993)
Radios: 39/1,000 inhabitants (1992)
Telephones: 3,000 total (1993)

■ TRANSPORTATION

Motor Vehicles: 5,700; 3,300 passenger cars (1990)
Roads: 3,218 km; 2,698 km paved
Railway: n.a.
Air Traffic: 21,000 passengers carried (1991)
Airports: 33 airfields, of which 15 are usable; 4 have permanent-surface runways (1993)

Canadian Embassy: c/o 45 boul. de la République; mailing address: P.O. Box 3373, Dakar, Senegal. Tel: (011-221) 23-92-90. Fax: (011-221) 23-87-49
Representative to Canada: c/o Embassy of the Republic of Guinea-Bissau, 211 East 43rd St, Ste 604, New York, NY 10017 USA. Tel: (212) 661-3977.

Guyana

Long-Form Name: Co-operative Republic of Guyana
Capital: Georgetown
Population: 800,000 (1993 est.)

■ GEOGRAPHY

Area: 214,970 sq. km
Coastline: 459 km
Climate: tropical; hot, humid, moderated by northeast trade winds; two rainy seasons (May to mid-Aug., mid-Nov. to mid-Jan.)
Environment: flash floods a constant threat during rainy seasons; water pollution
Terrain: mostly rolling highlands; low coastal plain; savanna in south
Land Use: 3% arable; negligible permanent; 6% meadows; 83% forest; 8% other
Location: N South America, bordering on Atlantic Ocean

■ PEOPLE

Nationality: Guyanese
Ethnic Groups: 51% East Indian, 43% black and mixed, 4% Amerindian, 2% European and Chinese
Languages: English, Hindi, Urdu, Amerindian dialects
Religions: 57% Christian, 33% Hindu, 9% Moslem, 1% other
Marriages: n.a.
Divorces: n.a.

■ GOVERNMENT

Leader(s): Prime Min. Sam Hinds, Pres. Cheddi Jagan
Government Type: republic
Administrative Divisions: 10 regions
Independence: May 26, 1966 (from UK; formerly known as British Guyana)
National Holiday: Republic Day, Feb. 23

■ ECONOMY

Overview: Guyana is one of the world's poorest countries, with a per capita income less than one-fifth the South American average; the government is focusing on an austere stabilization program after economic trouble in the 1980s
GNP: n.a., GDP $267.5 million, per capita $370; real growth rate 7% (1992 est.)
Inflation: 15% (1992)
Industries: bauxite mining, sugar, rice milling, timber, fishing (shrimp), textiles, gold mining
Labour Force: 380,000 (1992) 26% industry, 27% agriculture, 47% services (1989)
Unemployment: 12-15% (1991 est.)
Agriculture: most important sector, accounting for 25% of GDP; sugar and rice are main crops; not self-sufficient in food; development potential exists for fishing and forestry
Natural Resources: bauxite, gold, diamonds, hardwood timber, shrimp, fish

■ FINANCE/TRADE

Currency: Guyana dollar ($G)
International Reserves Excluding Gold: $238 million (Dec. 1993)
Gold Reserves: n.a.
Budget: revenues $121 million; expenditures $225 million, including capital expenditures of $50 million (1990 est.)
Defence Expenditures: $14.4 million (1988)
External Debt: $1.879 billion (1992)
Exports: $293 million (1992); commodities:

bauxite, sugar, rice, shrimp, gold, molasses, timber, rum; partners: UK 37%, US 12%, Canada 10.6%, CARICOM 4.8%

Imports: $382 million (1992); commodities: manufactures, machinery, food, petroleum; partners: CARICOM 41%, US 18%, UK 9%, Canada 3%

■ HEALTH

Births: 25/1,000 population (1993)
Deaths: 7/1,000 population (1993)
Infant Mortality: 48 deaths/1,000 live births (1993)
Life Expectancy at Birth: 62 years male, 68 years female (1993)
No. of Physicians: 1.6/10,000 population (1992)

■ EDUCATION

Govt. Expenditure: 8.9% of govt. expenditure (1989)
Literacy: 95% (1993)

■ COMMUNICATIONS

Daily newspapers: 2 (1992)
Televisions: 31.4/1,000 inhabitants (1992)
Radios: 486/1,000 inhabitants (1992)
Telephones: 4.2/100 inhabitants (1992)

■ TRANSPORTATION

Motor Vehicles: 33,000; 24,000 passenger cars (1990)
Roads: 7,665 km; 550 km paved (1993)
Railway: 187 km
Air Traffic: 112,000 passengers carried (1991)
Airports: 53 airfields, of which 48 are usable; 5 have permanent-surface runways (1993)

Canadian Embassy: Canadian High Commission, High and Young Streets, Georgetown; mailing address: P.O. Box 10880, Georgetown, Guyana. Tel: (011-592-2) 72081. Fax: (011-592-2): 58380
Representative to Canada: High Commission for the Co-operative Republic of Guyana, Burnside Bldg, 151 Slater St, Ste 309, Ottawa ON K1P 5H3. Tel: (613) 235-7249. Fax: (613) 235-1447.

Haiti

Long-Form Name: Republic of Haiti
Capital: Port-au-Prince
Population: 6,500,000 (1993 est.)

■ GEOGRAPHY

Area: 27,750 sq. km
Coastline: 1,771 km
Climate: tropical; semi-arid where mountains in east cut off trade winds
Environment: lies in the middle of the hurricane belt and subject to severe storms from June to Oct.; occasional flooding and earthquakes; deforestation
Terrain: mostly rough and mountainous
Land Use: 20% arable; 13% permanent; 18% meadows; 4% forest; 45% other
Location: West Indies, bordering on Caribbean Sea, Atlantic Ocean

■ PEOPLE

Nationality: Haitian
Ethnic Groups: 95% black, 5% mulatto and European
Languages: French (official) spoken by only 10% of population; all speak Creole
Religions: 80% Roman Catholic (of which an overwhelming majority also practice Voodoo), 16% Protestant, 4% other
Marriages: n.a.
Divorces: n.a.

■ GOVERNMENT

Leader(s): Pres. Jean-Bertrand Aristide
Government Type: republic
Administrative Divisions: 9 departments (départements)
Independence: Jan. 1, 1804 (from France)
National Holiday: Independence Day, Jan. 1

■ ECONOMY

Overview: about 75% of the population live in absolute poverty, and do not have access to safe drinking water, medical care, or sufficient food; agriculture based on small-scale subsistence farming; trade sanctions have further damaged the economy
GNP: $2.471 billion, per capita $370; real growth rate -0.6% (1991)
Inflation: 15.4% (1991)
Industries: sugar refining, textiles, flour milling, cement manufacturing, bauxite mining, tourism, light assembly industries based on imported parts
Labour Force: 3,130,000 (1992); 50.4% agriculture, 43.9% services, 5.7% industry (1989)
Unemployment: 25-50% (1991)
Agriculture: accounts for 28% of GDP and employs 70% of work force; mostly small-size subsistence farms; commercial crops include coffee and sugar cane; staple crops include rice, corn, sorghum and mangoes
Natural Resources: bauxite

■ FINANCE/TRADE

Currency: gourde (G)
International Reserves Excluding Gold: $18 million (1992)
Gold Reserves: 0.19 million fine troy ounces (1992)
Budget: revenues $300 million; expenditures $416 million, including capital expenditures of $145 million (1990)
Defence Expenditures: $16.9 million (1990)
External Debt: $773 million (1992)
Exports: $130 million (1992 est.); commodities: light manufactures 65%, coffee 17%, other agriculture 8%, other products 10%; partners: US 77%, France 5%, Italy 4%, Germany 3%, other industrial 9%, less developed countries 2%
Imports: $445 million (1992 est.); commodities: machines and manufactures 36%, food and beverages 21%, petroleum products 11%, fats and oils 12%, chemicals 12%; partners: US 65%, Netherlands Antilles 6%, Japan 5%, France 4%, Canada 2%, Asia 2%

■ HEALTH

Births: 43/1,000 population (1993)
Deaths: 15/1,000 population (1993)
Infant Mortality: 105 deaths/1,000 live births (1993)
Life Expectancy at Birth: 52 years male, 55 years female (1993)
No. of Physicians: 1.4/10,000 population (1992)

■ EDUCATION

Govt. Expenditure: 20.0% of govt. expenditure (1990)
Literacy: 53.0% (1993)

■ COMMUNICATIONS

Daily newspapers: 4 (1992)
Televisions: 4.5/1,000 inhabitants (1992)
Radios: 42/1,000 inhabitants (1992)
Telephones: 0.91/100 inhabitants (1992)

■ TRANSPORTATION

Motor Vehicles: 55,000; 33,000 passenger cars (1990)
Roads: 4,024 km; 944 km paved
Railway: 42 km
Air Traffic: n.a.
Airports: 13 airfields, of which 10 are usable; 3 have permanent-surface runways (1993)

Canadian Embassy: Édifice Banque de Nova Scotia, route de Delmas, Port-au-Prince, Haiti, WI; mailing address: C.P. 826, Port-au-Prince, Haiti. Tel: (011-509-1) 23-2358. Fax: (011-509-1) 23-8720

Representative to Canada: Embassy of the Republic of Haiti, 112 Kent St, Ste 212, Place de Ville, Tower B, Ottawa ON K1P 5P2. Tel: (613) 238-1628. Fax (613) 238-2986.

Honduras

Long-Form Name: Republic of Honduras
Capital: Tegucigalpa
Population: 5,600,000 (1993 est.)

■ GEOGRAPHY

Area: 112,090 sq. km
Coastline: 820 km
Climate: subtropical in lowlands, temperate in mountains
Environment: subject to frequent, but generally mild, earthquakes; damaging hurricanes along Caribbean coast; deforestation; soil erosion
Terrain: mostly mountainous in interior, narrow coastal plains
Land Use: 14% arable; 2% permanent; 30% meadows; 34% forest; 20% other
Location: Central (Latin) America, bordering on Caribbean Sea, Pacific Ocean

■ PEOPLE

Nationality: Honduran
Ethnic Groups: 90% mestizo (mixed Indian and European), 7% Indian, 2% black, 1% white
Languages: Spanish, Indian dialects
Religions: about 97% Roman Catholic; small Protestant minority
Marriages: n.a.
Divorces: n.a.

■ GOVERNMENT

Leader(s): Pres. Carlos Roberto Reina
Government Type: republic
Administrative Divisions: 18 departments (departamentos)
Independence: Sept. 15, 1821 (from Spain)
National Holiday: Independence Day, Sept. 15

■ ECONOMY

Overview: one of the poorest countries in the Western hemisphere, with a high population growth rate, a high unemployment rate, a lack of basic services, and an export sector vulnerable to world prices (coffee, bananas)
GNP: $5.5 billion, per capita $1,090; real growth rate 3.6% (1992 est.)
Inflation: 8.8% (1992)
Industries: agricultural processing (sugar and coffee), textiles, clothing, wood products
Labour Force: 1,580,000 (1992); 60.4% agriculture, 23.4% services, 16.1% industry (1989)

Unemployment: 72,135 unemployed, 30–40% underemployed (1991)
Agriculture: most important sector, accounting for more than 25% of GDP, over 60% of the labour force and two-thirds of exports; main products include bananas, coffee, timber, beef, citrus fruit, shrimp; importer of wheat
Natural Resources: timber, gold, silver, copper, lead, zinc, iron ore, antimony, coal, fish

■ FINANCE/TRADE

Currency: lempira (L)
International Reserves Excluding Gold: $90 million (Jan.1994)
Gold Reserves: 0.02 million fine troy ounces (Jan. 1994)
Budget: revenues $1.4 billion; expenditures $1.9 billion, including capital expenditures of $511 million (1990 est.)
Defence Expenditures: $45 million (1993 est.)
External Debt: 3.573 billion (1992)
Exports: $801 million (1992); commodities: bananas, coffee, shrimp, lobster, minerals, lumber; partners: US 52%, Germany 11%, Japan, Italy, Belgium
Imports: $1.043 billion (1992 est.); commodities: machinery and transport equipment, chemical products, manufactured goods, fuel and oil, foodstuffs; partners: US 39%, Japan 9%, CACM, Venezuela, Mexico

■ HEALTH

Births: 39/1,000 population (1993)
Deaths: 8/1,000 population (1993)
Infant Mortality: 61 deaths/1,000 live births (1993)
Life Expectancy at Birth: 63 years male, 67 years female (1993)
No. of Physicians: 6.6/10,000 population (1992)

■ EDUCATION

Govt. Expenditure: 15.9% of govt. expenditure (1989)
Literacy: 73.1% (1992)

■ COMMUNICATIONS

Daily newspapers: 4 (1992)
Televisions: 70.3/1,000 inhabitants (1992)
Radios: 384/1,000 inhabitants (1992)
Telephones: 1.42/100 inhabitants (1992)

■ TRANSPORTATION

Motor Vehicles: 133,000; 42,000 passenger cars (1990)
Roads: 12,106 km; 1,906 km paved
Railway: 785 km
Air Traffic: 447,000 passengers carried (1991)

Airports: 165 airfields, of which 137 are usable 11 have permanent-surface runways (1993)

Canadian Embassy: Office of the Canadian Embassy, Edificio Comercial Los Castanos, 6C Piso, Boulevard Morazan, Tegucigalpa; mailing address: Apartado Postal 3552, Tegucigalpa, Honduras. Tel: (011-504) 31-45-45. Fax: (011-504) 31-5793
Representative to Canada: Embassy of the Republic of Honduras, 151 Slater St, Ste 908, Ottawa ON K1P 5H3. Tel: (613) 233-8900. Fax: (613) 232-0193.

Hong Kong

Dependent Territory of United Kingdom

Long-Form Name: Hong Kong
Capital: Victoria
Population: 5,800,000 (1993 est.)

■ GEOGRAPHY

Area: 1,040 sq. km
Climate: tropical monsoon; cool and humid in winter, hot and rainy from spring through summer, warm and sunny in fall
Land Use: 7% arable land; 1% permanent; 1% meadows; 12% forest; 79% other
Location: SE Asia, bordering on South China Sea

■ PEOPLE

Nationality: Chinese
Ethnic Groups: 98% Chinese, 2% other
Languages: Chinese (Cantonese), English

■ GOVERNMENT

Leader(s): Gov. Chris Patten; Chief Secretary Sir D.R. Ford
Government Type: colony of the UK; scheduled to revert to China July 1, 1997
National Holiday: Liberation Day, Aug. 29

■ ECONOMY

Overview: has a free-market economy and is autonomous in financial affairs; manufacturing is the base of the economy; natural resources are limited and food and raw materials must be imported; economic future unclear due to Chinese takeover in 1997

■ FINANCE/TRADE

Currency: Hong Kong dollar (HK$)

Canadian Embassy: Office of the Commission for Canada, 11-14th Floors, Tower One,

Exchange Square, 8 Connaught Place, Hong Kong; mailing address: Office of the Commission for Canada, GPO Box 11142, Hong Kong. Tel: (011-852) 810-4321. Fax: (011-852) 810-6736.

Hungary

Long-Form Name: Republic of Hungary
Capital: Budapest
Population: 10,300,000 (1993 est.)

■ GEOGRAPHY

Area: 93,030 sq. km
Coastline: none: landlocked
Climate: temperate; cold, cloudy, humid winter; warm summer
Environment: levees are common along many streams, but flooding occurs almost every year
Terrain: mostly flat to rolling plains
Land Use: 50.7% arable; 6.1% permanent; 12.6% meadows; 18% forest; 12.3% other
Location: C Europe

■ PEOPLE

Nationality: Hungarian
Ethnic Groups: 89.9% Hungarian, 4% Gypsy, 2% Serb, 2.6% German, 0.8% Slovak, 0.7% Romanian
Languages: Hungarian (Magyar, official)
Religions: 67.5% Roman Catholic, 20% Calvinist, 5% Lutheran, 7.5% atheist and other
Marriages: 5.7 (per 1,000) (1991)
Divorces: 2.40 (per 1,000) (1990)

■ GOVERNMENT

Leader(s): Prime Min. Gyula Horn, Pres. Arpad Goncz
Government Type: republic
Administrative Divisions: 38 counties and 1 capital city (Budapest)
Independence: 1001 (unification by King Stephen I)
National Holiday: Oct. 23 (anniversary of the Hungarian uprising, 1956)

■ ECONOMY

Overview: Soviet-style economy which is attempting to decentralize and implement market-oriented enterprises; hampered by old capital plant and lack of funds
GNP: n.a., GDP $55.4 billion, per capita $5,380; real growth rate -5% (1992 est.)
Inflation: 18.5% (1992)
Industries: mining, metallurgy, engineering industries, processed foods, textiles, chemicals (especially pharmaceuticals)

Labour Force: 5,276,000 (1992); 47.8% services, 31.3% industry, 20.9% agriculture (1989)
Unemployment: 12.3% (1992)
Agriculture: accounts for about 15% of GNP (including forestry) and 16% of employment; highly diversified crop-livestock farming; main crops—wheat, corn, sunflowers, potatoes, sugar beets; livestock—hogs, cattle, poultry and dairy products; self-sufficient in food
Natural Resources: bauxite, coal, natural gas, fertile soils

■ FINANCE/TRADE

Currency: forint (Ft)
International Reserves Excluding Gold: $5,193 million (July 1993)
Gold Reserves: 0.25 million fine troy ounces (Aug. 1993)
Budget: revenues $13.2 billion; expenditures $15.4 billion, including capital expenditures (1993 est.)
Defence Expenditures: $1.45 billion (1990)
External Debt: $21.9 billion (1992)
Exports: $10.68 billion (1992); commodities: capital goods 36%, foods 24%, consumer goods 18%, fuels and minerals 11%, other 11%; partners: USSR 48%, Eastern Europe 25%, developed countries 16%, less developed countries 8%
Imports: $11.122 billion (1992); commodities: machinery and transport 28%, fuels 20%, chemical products 14%, manufactured consumer goods 16%, agriculture 6%, other 16%; partners: USSR 43%, Eastern Europe 28%, less developed countries 23%, US 3%

■ HEALTH

Births: 12/1,000 population (1993)
Deaths: 14/1,000 population (1993)
Infant Mortality: 15.1 deaths/1,000 live births (1993)
Life Expectancy at Birth: 65 years male, 74 years female (1993)
No. of Physicians: 32.6/10,000 population (1992)

■ EDUCATION

Govt. Expenditure: 7.8% of govt. expenditure (1991)
Literacy: 99% (1993)

■ COMMUNICATIONS

Daily newspapers: 28 (1992)
Televisions: 403.9/1,000 inhabitants (1992)
Radios: 592/1,000 inhabitants (1992)
Telephones: 16.94/100 inhabitants (1992)

■ TRANSPORTATION

Motor Vehicles: 2,195,338; 1,944,553 passenger

cars (1990)
Roads: 130,218 km; 52,934 km paved
Railway: 7,759 km
Air Traffic: 911,000 passengers carried (1991)
Airports: 92 airfields, all usable; 25 have permanent-surface runways (1993)

Canadian Embassy: Budakeszi ut 32, 1121 Budapest, Hungary. Tel.: (011-36-1) 1767-312. Fax: (011-36-1) 1767-689
Representative to Canada: Embassy of the Republic of Hungary, 7 Delaware Ave, Ottawa ON K2P 0Z2. Tel: (613) 232-1711. Fax: (613) 232-5620.

Iceland

Long-Form Name: Republic of Iceland
Capital: Reykjavik
Population: 300,000 (1993 est.)

■ GEOGRAPHY

Area: 103,000 sq. km
Coastline: 4,988 km
Climate: temperate; moderated by North Atlantic Current; mild, windy winters; damp, cool summers
Environment: subject to earthquakes and volcanic activity
Terrain: mostly plateau interspersed with mountain peaks, ice fields; coast deeply indented by bays and fjords
Land Use: 1% arable; 0% permanent; 23% meadows; 1% forest; 76% other
Location: NW Europe, bordering on Norwegian Sea, Atlantic Ocean

■ PEOPLE

Nationality: Icelander
Ethnic Groups: homogeneous mixture of descendants of Norwegians and Celts
Languages: Icelandic
Religions: Christianity (predominantly Protestant)
Marriages: 5.0 (per 1,000) (1991)
Divorces: 2.25 (per 1,000) (1991)

■ GOVERNMENT

Leader(s): Prime Min. David Oddsson, Pres. Vigdis Finnbogadóttir
Government Type: republic
Administrative Divisions: 23 counties and 14 independent towns
Independence: June 17, 1944 (from Denmark)
National Holiday: Anniversary of the Establishment of the Republic, June 17

■ ECONOMY

Overview: basically capitalistic but with extensive welfare measures and low but rising unemployment; heavily dependent on fishing industry
GNP: $5.814 billion, per capita $22,580; real growth rate 2.4% (1991)
Inflation: 3.7% (1992)
Industries: fish processing, aluminum smelting, ferro-silicon production, hydroelectricity
Labour Force: 136,000 (1992); 55% commerce, finance and services, 14% other manufacturing, 6% agriculture, 8% fish processing, 5% fishing
Unemployment: 5% (1993)
Agriculture: accounts for about 25% of GDP (including fishing); fishing is the most important economic activity, contributing nearly 75% to export earnings; principal crops include potatoes and turnips; livestock—cattle, sheep; self-sufficient in crops
Natural Resources: fish, hydroelectric and geothermal power, diatomite

■ FINANCE/TRADE

Currency: króna (pl. krónur) (ISK)
International Reserves Excluding Gold: $431 million (Jan. 1994)
Gold Reserves: 0.05 million fine troy ounces (Jan. 1994)
Budget: revenues $1.8 billion; expenditures $1.9 billion, including capital expenditures of $191 million (1992)
Defence Expenditures: negligible
External Debt: $3.9 billion (1992 est.)
Exports: $1.515 billion (1992); commodities: fish and fish products, animal products, aluminum, diatomite; partners: European Community 58.9% (UK 23.3%, Germany 10.3%), US 13.6%, USSR 3.6%
Imports: $1.692 billion (1992); commodities: machinery and transportation equipment, petroleum, foodstuffs, textiles; partners: European Community 58% (Germany 16%, Denmark 10.4%, UK 9.2%), US 8.5%, USSR 3.9%

■ HEALTH

Births: 18/1,000 population (1993)
Deaths: 7/1,000 population (1993)
Infant Mortality: 5.5 deaths/1,000 live births (1993)
Life Expectancy at Birth: 75 years male, 81 years female (1993)
No. of Physicians: 23/10,000 population (1990)

■ EDUCATION

Govt. Expenditure: 12.19% of govt. expenditure (1991)
Literacy: 100% (1993)

■ COMMUNICATIONS

Daily newspapers: 3 (1992)
Televisions: 318.7/1,000 inhabitants (1992)
Radios: 785/1,000 inhabitants (1992)
Telephones: 52.50/100 inhabitants (1992)

■ TRANSPORTATION

Motor Vehicles: 134,181; 119,731 passenger cars (1990)
Roads: 11,742 km; 2,163 km paved
Railway: n.a.
Air Traffic: 773,000 passengers carried (1991)
Airports: 90 airfields, of which 84 are usable; 8 have permanent-surface runways (1993)
Canadian Embassy: c/o The Canadian Embassy, Oscars Gate 20, 0244 Oslo, Norway; mailing address: 0244 Oslo, Norway. Tel: (011-47) 22-46-69-55. Fax: (011-47) 22-69-34-67
Representative to Canada: c/o Embassy of the Republic of Iceland, 2022 Connecticut Ave NW, Washington DC 20008 USA. Tel: (202) 265-6653. Fax: (202) 265-6656.

India

Long-Form Name: Republic of India
Capital: New Delhi
Population: 879,400,000 (1993 est.), excluding the occupied areas of Jammu and Kashmir

■ GEOGRAPHY

Area: 3,287,590 sq. km
Coastline: 7,000 km
Climate: varies from tropical monsoon in south to temperate in north
Environment: deforestation; soil erosion; overgrazing; air and water pollution; desertification; droughts, flash floods, severe thunderstorms common
Terrain: upland plain (Deccan Plateau) in south, flat to rolling plain along the Ganges, deserts in west, Himalayas in north
Land Use: 55% arable; 1% permanent; 4% meadows; 23% forest; 17% other
Location: S Asia, bordering on Arabian Sea, Indian Ocean, Bay of Bengal

■ PEOPLE

Nationality: Indian
Ethnic Groups: 72% Indo-Aryan, 25% Dravidian, 3% Mongoloid and other
Languages: Hindi (official, spoken by 30%), English, 19 regional languages, including Bengali, Tlegu, Marathi, Tamil, Urdu, Gujarati, Malayalam, Kannada, Oriya, Punjabi, Assamese, Kashmiri, Sindhi and Sanskrit; 24 languages spoken by a million or more persons each; numerous other languages
Religions: 82.6% Hindu, 11.4% Moslem, 2.4% Christian, 2% Sikh, 0.7% Buddhist, 0.5% Jains, 0.4% other
Marriages: are not registered in India
Divorces: are not registered in India

■ GOVERNMENT

Leader(s): Pres. Shankar Dayal Sharma, Prime Min. P.V. Narasimha Rao
Government Type: federal republic
Administrative Divisions: 25 states and 7 union territories
Independence: Aug. 15, 1947 (from UK)
National Holiday: Anniversary of the Proclamation of the Republic, Jan. 26

■ ECONOMY

Overview: a mixture of traditional village farming and handicrafts, modern agriculture, old and new branches of industry and a multitude of support services; millions still live in poverty, hoping to benefit from modern farming techniques
GNP: n.a., GDP $240 billion, per capita $270; real growth rate 4% (1993 est.)
Inflation: 11.8% (1992)
Industries: textiles, food processing, steel, machinery, transportation equipment, cement, jute manufactures, mining, petroleum, power, chemicals, pharmaceuticals, electronics
Labour Force: 323,000,000 (1992); 62.6% agriculture, 10.8% industry, 26.6% services (1989)
Unemployment: 36,300,000 (1991)
Agriculture: accounts for 30% of GNP and employs 67% of labour force; self-sufficient in food grains; main crops—rice, wheat, oilseeds, cotton, jute, tea, sugar cane, potatoes; livestock— cattle, buffaloes, sheep, goats and poultry; in top 10 of fishing nations
Natural Resources: coal, iron ore, manganese, mica, bauxite, titanium ore, chromite, natural gas, diamonds, crude oil, limestone

■ FINANCE/TRADE

Currency: rupee (Rs)
International Reserves Excluding Gold: $10,937 million (Jan. 1994)
Gold Reserves: 11.46 million fine troy ounces (Jan. 1994)
Budget: revenues $39.2 billion; expenditures $41.06 billion, including capital expenditures of $10.2 billion (1992)
Defence Expenditures: 15.02% of total govt. expenditure (1992)
External Debt: $76.983 billion (1992)

Exports: $17.935 billion (1992); commodities: tea, coffee, iron ore, fish products, manufactures; partners: European Community 25%, USSR and Eastern Europe 17%, US 19%, Japan 10%

Imports: $23.264 billion (1992); commodities: petroleum, edible oils, textiles, clothing, capital goods; partners: European Community 33%, Middle East 19%, Japan 10%, US 9%, USSR and Eastern Europe 8%

■ HEALTH

Births: 31/1,000 population (1993)
Deaths: 10/1,000 population (1993)
Infant Mortality: 91 deaths/1,000 live births (1993)
Life Expectancy at Birth: 58 years male, 59 years female (1993)
No. of Physicians: 4.0/10,000 population (1992)

■ EDUCATION

Govt. Expenditure: 2.05% of govt. expenditure (1992)
Literacy: 48.2% (1993)

■ COMMUNICATIONS

Daily newspapers: 1,978 (1992)
Televisions: 27.0/1,000 inhabitants (1992)
Radios: 78/1,000 inhabitants (1992)
Telephones: 0.6/100 inhabitants (1992)

■ TRANSPORTATION

Motor Vehicles: 4,350,000; 2,300,000 passenger cars (1990)
Roads: 1,970,000 km; 960,000 km hard-surfaced (1989)
Railway: 132,373 km
Air Traffic: 10,859,000 passengers carried (1991)
Airports: 336 airfields, of which 285 are usable; 205 have permanent-surface runways (1993)

Canadian Embassy: The Canadian High Commission, 7/8 Shantipath, Chanakyapuri, New Delhi 110 021; mailing address: The Canadian High Commission, P.O. Box 5208, New Delhi, India. Tel: (011-91-11) 687-6500. Fax: (011-91-11) 687-6579
Representative to Canada: High Commission for the Republic of India, 10 Springfield Rd, Ottawa ON K1M 1C9. Tel: (613) 744-3751. Fax: (613) 744-0913.

Indonesia

Long-Form Name: Republic of Indonesia
Capital: Jakarta
Population: 187,600,000 (1993 est.)

■ GEOGRAPHY

Area: (13,677 islands) 1,919,440 sq. km
Coastline: 54,716 km
Climate: tropical; hot, humid; more moderate in highlands
Environment: archipelago of 13,500 islands (6,000 inhabited); occasional floods, severe droughts and tsunamis; deforestation
Terrain: mostly coastal lowlands; larger islands have interior mountains
Land Use: 8% arable; 3% permanent crops; 7% meadows; 67% forest; 15% other
Location: SE Asia, bordering on Indian Ocean

■ PEOPLE

Nationality: Indonesian
Ethnic Groups: majority of Malay stock comprising 45% Javanese, 14% Sundanese, 7.5% Madurese, 7.5% coastal Malays, 26% other
Languages: Bahasa Indonesia (modified form of Malay; official); English and Dutch leading foreign languages; 25 local dialects, the most widely spoken of which is Javanese
Religions: 87% Muslim, 6% Protestant, 3% Roman Catholic, 2% Hindu, 1% Buddhist, 1% other
Marriages: n.a.
Divorces: n.a.

■ GOVERNMENT

Leader(s): Pres. Gen. (Ret.) Suharto, V. Pres. Gen. (Ret.) Sutrisno
Government Type: republic
Administrative Divisions: 24 provinces, 2 special regions and 1 special capital city district
Independence: Aug. 17, 1945 (from Netherlands; formerly known as Netherlands or Dutch East Indies)
National Holiday: Independence Day, Aug. 17

■ ECONOMY

Overview: a mixed economy with many socialist institutions and central planning but with a recent emphasis on deregulation and private enterprise; hampered by large population growth; possesses abundant natural wealth
GNP: $133 billion, per capita $680; real growth rate 6% (1992 est.)
Inflation: 7.5% (1992)
Industries: petroleum, textiles, mining, cement, chemical fertilizer production, timber, food, rubber
Labour Force: 71 million (1992); 54.4% agriculture, 8% industry, 37.6 % services (1989)
Unemployment: 3% (1991 est.); 45% underemployment
Agriculture: subsistence food production; small-

holder and plantation production for export; rice, cassava, peanuts, rubber, cocoa, coffee, copra, other tropical products; the staple crop is rice; once the world's largest rice importer, Indonesia is now nearly self-sufficient
Natural Resources: crude oil, tin, natural gas, nickel, timber, bauxite, copper, fertile soils, coal, gold, silver

■ FINANCE/TRADE

Currency: rupiah (Rp)
International Reserves Excluding Gold: $11,366 million (Jan. 1994)
Gold Reserves: 3.10 million fine troy ounces (Jan. 1994)
Budget: revenues $17.2 billion; expenditures $23.4 billion, including capital expenditures of $8.9 billion (1991)
Defence Expenditures: 6.83% of total govt. expenditure (1991)
External Debt: $84.385 billion (1992)
Exports: $33.861 billion (1992); commodities: petroleum and liquefied natural gas 40%, timber 15%, textiles 7%, rubber 5%, coffee 3%; partners: Japan 42%, US 16%, Singapore 9%, European Community 11%
Imports: $27.305 billion (1992); commodities: machinery 39%, chemical products 19%, manufactured goods 16%; partners: Japan 26%, European Community 19%, US 13%, Singapore 7%,

■ HEALTH

Births: 26/1,000 population (1993)
Deaths: 9/1,000 population (1993)
Infant Mortality: 68 deaths/1,000 live births (1993)
Life Expectancy at Birth: 58 years male, 61 years female (1993)
No. of Physicians: 1/10,000 population (1990)

■ EDUCATION

Govt. Expenditure: 9.07% of government expenditure (1990)
Literacy: 77.0% (1993)

■ COMMUNICATIONS

Daily newspapers: 60 (1992)
Televisions: 55.3/1,000 inhabitants (1992)
Radios: 144/1,000 inhabitants (1992)
Telephones: 0.58/100 inhabitants (1992)

■ TRANSPORTATION

Motor Vehicles: 2,591,087; 1,199,665 passenger cars (1990)
Roads: 232,252 km; 143,958 km paved
Railway: 6,910 km

Air Traffic: 10,386,000 passengers carried (1991)
Airports: 435 airfields, of which 411 are usable; 119 have permanent-surface runways (1993)

Canadian Embassy: Flr 5 Wisma Metropolitan-I, Jalan Jendral Sudirman, Jakarta; mailing address: P.O. Box 1052, Jakarta 10110, Indonesia. Tel: (011-62-21) 525-0709. Fax: (011-62-21) 571-2251
Representative to Canada: Embassy of the Republic of Indonesia, 287 MacLaren St, Ottawa ON K2P 0L9. Tel: (613) 236-7403. Fax: (613) 563-2858.

Iran

Long-Form Name: Islamic Republic of Iran
Capital: Tehran
Population: 62,800,000 (1993 est.)

■ GEOGRAPHY

Area: 1,648,000 sq. km
Coastline: 2,440 km
Climate: mostly arid or semi-arid, subtropical along Caspian coast
Environment: deforestation; overgrazing; desertification
Terrain: rugged mountainous rim; high, central basin with deserts, mountains; small, discontinuous plains along both coasts
Land Use: 8% arable; negligible permanent; 27% meadows; 11% forest; 54% other
Location: SW Asia (Middle East), bordering on Persian Gulf

■ PEOPLE

Nationality: Iranian
Ethnic Groups: 51% Persian, 24% Azerbaijani, 7% Kurd, 8% Gilaki and Mazandarani, 2% Lur, 2% Baloch, 3% Arab, 2% Turkmen, 1% other
Languages: Farsi (Persian, official, 58%), Turkish 26%, Kurdish 9%, Arabic 1%
Religions: Islam (95% Shia, 4% Sunni), Christianity, Judaism, Zoroastrianism 1%
Marriages: 8.3 (per 1,000) (1990)
Divorces: 0.69 (per 1,000) (1990)

■ GOVERNMENT

Leader(s): Pres. Hojatolislam Ali Akbar Hashemi Rafsanjani, Supreme Religious Leader Ayatollah Mohammed Ali Hoseini Khamenei
Government Type: theocratic republic
Administrative Divisions: 24 provinces
Independence: Apr. 1, 1979, Islamic Republic of Iran proclaimed
National Holiday: Islamic Republic Day, Apr. 1

■ ECONOMY

Overview: many aspects of economy were nationalized following the 1979 revolution but the new five-year plan (passed Jan. 1990) calls for many to be returned to the public sector; economy hurt by war with Iraq and lower world oil prices; country is looking to secure foreign loans

GNP: $127.366 billion, per capita $2,320; real growth rate 2.5% (1991)

Inflation: 22.9% (1992)

Industries: petroleum, petrochemicals, textiles, cement and other building materials, food processing (particularly sugar refining and vegetable oil production), metal fabricating (steel and copper)

Labour Force: 15,253,000 (1992); 36.4% agriculture, 32.8% industry, 30.8% services (1989)

Unemployment: 30% (1991)

Agriculture: accounts for approximately 20% of GDP; principal products—rice, other grains, sugar beets, fruits, nuts, cotton, dairy products, wool, caviar; not self-sufficient in food

Natural Resources: petroleum, natural gas, coal, chromium, copper, iron ore, lead, manganese, zinc, sulphur

■ FINANCE/TRADE

Currency: rial (RIs)

International Reserves Excluding Gold: n.a.

Gold Reserves: 4.34 million fine troy ounces (Sept. 1993)

Budget: revenues $63 billion, expenditures $80 billion, including capital expenditures of $23 billion (1990)

Defence Expenditures: 6.99% of total govt. expenditure (1993)

External Debt: $14.167 billion (1992)

Exports: $15.916 billion (1991); commodities: petroleum 90%, carpets, fruit, nuts, hides; partners: Japan, Turkey, Italy, Netherlands, Spain, France, Germany

Imports: $21.688 billion (1991); commodities: machinery, military supplies, metal works, foodstuffs, pharmaceuticals, technical services, refined oil products; partners: Germany, Japan, Turkey, UK, Italy

■ HEALTH

Births: 45/1,000 population (1993)

Deaths: 10/1,000 population (1993)

Infant Mortality: 76 deaths/1,000 live births (1993)

Life Expectancy at Birth: 62 years male, 62 years female (1993)

No. of Physicians: 3.4/10,000 population (1992)

■ EDUCATION

Govt. Expenditure: 20.9% of govt. expenditure (1993)

Literacy: 54.0% (1993)

■ COMMUNICATIONS

Daily newspapers: 11 (1992)

Televisions: 65.8/1,000 inhabitants (1992)

Radios: 245/1,000 inhabitants (1992)

Telephones: 3.8/100 inhabitants (1992)

■ TRANSPORTATION

Motor Vehicles: 2,200,000; 1,600,000 passenger cars (1990)

Roads: 140,200 km; 42,694 km paved (1993)

Railway: 4,779 km

Air Traffic: 5,353,000 passengers carried (1991)

Airports: 219 airfields, of which 194 are usable; 83 have permanent-surface runways (1993)

Canadian Embassy: 57 Shahid Javad-e-Sarafraz, Ostad-Motahari Ave, Tehran; mailing address: P.O. Box 11365-4647, Tehran, Iran. Tel: (011-98-21) 62-26-23. Fax: (011-98-21) 62-32-02

Representative to Canada: Embassy of the Islamic Republic of Iran, 245 Metcalfe St, Ottawa ON K2P 2K2. Tel: (613) 235-4726. Fax: (613) 232-5712.

Iraq

Long-Form Name: Republic of Iraq

Capital: Baghdad

Population: 19,200,000 (1993 est.)

■ GEOGRAPHY

Area: 437,072 sq. km

Coastline: 58 km

Climate: desert; mild to cool winters with dry, hot, cloudless summers

Environment: development of Tigris-Euphrates river systems contingent upon agreements with upstream riparians (Syria and Turkey); air and water pollution; soil degradation (salinization) and erosion; desertification

Terrain: mostly broad plains; reedy marshes in southeast; mountains along borders with Iran and Turkey

Land Use: 12% arable; 1% permanent; 9% meadows; 3% forest; 75% other

Location: SW Asia (Middle East), bordering on Persian Gulf

■ PEOPLE

Nationality: Iraqi

Ethnic Groups: 75–80% Arab, 15–20% Kurdish,

5% Turkoman (small minority)
Languages: Arabic (official), Kurdish (official in Kurdish region)
Religions: 97% Moslem (60–65% Shi'a, 32–37% Sunni), 3% Christian or other
Marriages: n.a.
Divorces: n.a.

■ GOVERNMENT

Leader(s): Pres. and Premier Saddam Hussein at-Takriti, Deputy Prem. Tariq Aziz
Government Type: republic
Administrative Divisions: 18 provinces
Independence: Oct. 3, 1932 (from League of Nations mandate under British administration)
National Holiday: Anniversary of the Revolution, July 17

■ ECONOMY

Overview: industrial production and foreign trade is centrally planned and managed while some small-scale industry and services and most agriculture is left to private enterprise; war with Iran in the 1980s and the Gulf War have caused economic problems; per capita output is far below previous levels
GNP: $35 billion, per capita $1,940; real growth rate 5% (1989 est.)
Inflation: 30–40% (1989 est.)
Industries: petroleum, chemicals, textiles, construction materials, food processing
Labour Force: 5,119,000 (1992) 79.7% services, 12.5% agriculture, 7.8% industry (1989)
Unemployment: less than 5% (1989 est.)
Agriculture: accounts for 11% of GNP but 30% of labour force; principal products— wheat, barley, rice, vegetables, dates, other fruit, cotton, wool; livestock—cattle, sheep; not self-sufficient in food output
Natural Resources: crude oil, natural gas, phosphates, sulphur

■ FINANCE/TRADE

Currency: dinar
International Reserves Excluding Gold: n.a.
Gold Reserves: n.a.
Budget: revenues n.a., expenditures $35 billion, including capital expenditures (1989)
Defence Expenditures: $8.61 billion (1990)
External Debt: $45 billion (1989), excluding debt to Persian Gulf Arab States
Exports: $392 million (1990); commodities: crude oil and refined products, machinery, chemicals, dates; partners: US, Brazil, USSR, Italy, Turkey, France, Japan, Yugoslavia
Imports: $4.834 billion (1990); commodities: manufactures, food; partners: Turkey, US,

Germany, UK, France, Japan, Romania, Yugoslavia, Brazil

■ HEALTH

Births: 45/1,000 population (1993)
Deaths: 8/1,000 population (1993)
Infant Mortality: 79 deaths/1,000 live births (1993)
Life Expectancy at Birth: 63 years male, 64 years female (1993)
No. of Physicians: 5.5/10,000 population (1992)

■ EDUCATION

Govt. Expenditure: 6.4% of government expenditure (1987)
Literacy: 60% (1993)

■ COMMUNICATIONS

Daily newspapers: 5 (1992)
Televisions: 68.4/1,000 inhabitants (1992)
Radios: 202/1,000 inhabitants (1992)
Telephones: 5.6/100 inhabitants (1992)

■ TRANSPORTATION

Motor Vehicles: 1,040,730; 672,205 passenger cars (1990)
Roads: 34,700 km; 17,500 km paved (1993)
Railway: 2,457 km
Air Traffic: 28,000 passengers carried (1991)
Airports: 114 airfields, of which 99 are usable; 74 have permanent-surface runways (1993)

Canadian Embassy: Hay Al-Mansour, Mahalla 609, Street 1, House 33, Baghdad; mailing address: P.O. Box 323, Central Post Office, Bagdad, Iraq. Tel: (011-964-1) 542-1459
Representative to Canada: Embassy of the Republic of Iraq, 215 McLeod St, Ottawa ON K2P 0Z8. Tel: (613) 236-9177. Fax: (613) 567-1101.

Ireland

Long-Form Name: Ireland
Capital: Dublin
Population: 3,600,000 (1993 est.)

■ GEOGRAPHY

Area: 70,280 sq. km
Coastline: 1,448 km
Climate: temperate maritime; modified by North Atlantic Current; mild winters, cool summers; consistently humid; overcast about half the time
Environment: deforestation
Terrain: mostly level to rolling interior plains surrounded by rugged hills and low mountains; sea cliffs on west coast

Land Use: 14% arable; negligible permanent; 71% meadows; 5% forest; 10% other
Location: NW Europe, bordering on Atlantic Ocean

■ PEOPLE

Nationality: Irish
Ethnic Groups: Celtic, with English minority
Languages: Irish (official first language, but use is limited) and English; English is the language generally used, with Gaelic spoken in a few areas, mostly along the western seaboard
Religions: 93% Roman Catholic, 5% Protestant, 2% other
Marriages: 5.2 (per 1,000) (1989)
Divorces: illegal under Irish law

■ GOVERNMENT

Leader(s): Prime Min. Albert Reynolds, Pres. Mary Robinson
Government Type: republic
Administrative Divisions: 26 counties
Independence: Dec. 6, 1921 (from UK)
National Holiday: St. Patrick's Day, Mar. 17

■ ECONOMY

Overview: a small, open economy that is trade dependent; unemployment is high but inflation has been considerably lowered and the deficit burden relieved
GNP: $42.4 billion, per capita $12,000; real growth rate 2% (1992)
Inflation: 3.1% (1992)
Industries: food products, brewing, textiles, clothing, chemicals, pharmaceuticals, machinery, transportation equipment, glass and crystal
Labour Force: 1,481,000 (1992) 68.6% services, 18.4% industry, 13% agriculture (1989)
Unemployment: 22.7% (1992)
Agriculture: accounts for 11% of GNP and 13% of the labour force; principal crops include turnips, barley, potatoes, sugar, beets, wheat; livestock— meat and dairy products; 85% self-sufficient in food; food shortages include bread grain, fruits, vegetables
Natural Resources: zinc, lead, natural gas, crude oil, barite, copper, gypsum, limestone, dolomite, peat, silver

■ FINANCE/TRADE

Currency: Irish pound (£ or £Ir)
International Reserves Excluding Gold: $5,626 million (Jan. 1994)
Gold Reserves: 0.36 million fine troy ounces (Jan. 1994)
Budget: revenues $16.0 billion; expenditures $16.6 billion, including capital expenditures of $1.6 billion (1992 est.)
Defence Expenditures: $507.50 million (3.32% of total govt. expenditure) (1990)
External Debt: $15.0 billion (1990)
Exports: $28.295 billion (1992); commodities: live animals, animal products, chemicals, data processing equipment, industrial machinery; partners: European Community 74% (U.K. 35%, Germany 11%, France 9%), US 8%
Imports: $22.478 billion (1992); commodities: food, animal feed, chemicals, petroleum and petroleum products, machinery, textiles, clothing; partners: European Community 66% (U.K. 42%, Germany 9%, France 4%), US 16%

■ HEALTH

Births: 15/1,000 population (1993)
Deaths: 9/1,000 population (1993)
Infant Mortality: 8.6 deaths/1,000 live births (1993)
Life Expectancy at Birth: 72 years male, 77 years female (1993)
No. of Physicians: 14.7/10,000 population (1992)

■ EDUCATION

Govt. Expenditure: 12.24% of govt. expenditure (1990)
Literacy: 98% (1993)

■ COMMUNICATIONS

Daily newspapers: 4 (1992)
Televisions: 271.0/1,000 inhabitants (1992)
Radios: 583/1,000 inhabitants (1992)
Telephones: 26.52/100 inhabitants (1992)

■ TRANSPORTATION

Motor Vehicles: 1,028,667; 796,408 passenger cars (1990)
Roads: 92,313 km; 87,422 km paved
Railway: 1,950 km
Air Traffic: 4,765,000 passengers carried (1990)
Airports: 40 airfields, of which 39 are usable; 13 have permanent-surface runways (1993)

Canadian Embassy: 65 St Stephen's Green, Dublin 2, Ireland. Tel: (011-353-1) 478-1285
Representative to Canada: Embassy of Ireland, 170 Metcalfe St, Ottawa ON K2P 1P3. Tel: (613) 233-6281. Fax: (613) 233-5835.

Isle of Man

Dependency of United Kingdom

Long-Form Name: Isle of Man
Capital: Douglas
Population: 71,263 (1993 est.)

■ GEOGRAPHY

Area: 588 sq. km
Climate: temperate maritime, cool summers and mild winters, humid, overcast about half the time
Land Use: most of island covered by farmland and moors; low mountain chain extends through island; 85% of cultivated land area used for farming, 68,000 acres farmland, 37,000 acres grazing
Location: Irish Sea, between Great Britain and Northern Ireland

■ PEOPLE

Nationality: Manxman, Manxwoman
Ethnic Groups: Manx (Norse-Celtic descent), Briton
Languages: English, Manx, Gaelic

■ GOVERNMENT

Leader(s): Pres. Sir Charles Kerruish
Government Type: Crown dependency administered in accordance with its own laws
National Holiday: Tynwald Day, July 5

■ ECONOMY

Overview: tourism, fishing; agriculture provides for local consumption only; banking now contributes over 20% to GNP and manufacturing about 15%

■ FINANCE/TRADE

Currency: Manx pound, on a par with British pound sterling

Israel

Long-Form Name: State of Israel
Capital: Jerusalem
Population: 5,300,000 (1993 est.)

■ GEOGRAPHY

Area: 20,770 sq. km
Coastline: 273 km
Climate: temperate; hot and dry in desert areas
Environment: sandstorms may occur during spring and summer; limited arable land and natural water resources pose serious constraints; deforestation
Terrain: Negev desert in the south; low coastal plain; central mountains; Jordan Rift Valley
Land Use: 17% arable; 5% permanent; 40% meadows; 6% forest; 32% other
Location: SW Asia (Middle East), bordering on Mediterranean Sea

■ PEOPLE

Nationality: Israeli
Ethnic Groups: 83% Jewish, 17% non-Jewish (mostly Arab)
Languages: Hebrew (official); Arabic used officially for Arab minority; European languages (mostly English)
Religions: 82% Judaism, 14% Islam (mostly Sunni Moslem), 2% Christian and Druze, 2% other
Marriages: 7.0 (per 1,000) (1990)
Divorces: 1.29 (per 1,000) (1990)

■ GOVERNMENT

Leader(s): Pres. Ezer Weizman, Prime Min. Yitzhak Rabin
Government Type: republic
Administrative Divisions: 6 districts
Independence: May 14, 1948 (from League of Nations mandate under British administration)
National Holiday: Independence Day, May 14; the Jewish calendar is lunar and the holiday may occur in Apr. or May

■ ECONOMY

Overview: a market economy with government participation; despite limited natural resources, country has strong agriculture and industry sectors; transfer payments and foreign loans offset the deficit; the Palestinian uprising and Russian immigration stifle growth
GNP: n.a., GDP $57.4 billion, per capita $12,100; real growth rate 6.4% (1992 est.)
Inflation: 11.9% (1992)
Industries: food processing, diamond cutting and polishing, textiles, clothing, chemicals, metal products, military equipment, transport equipment, electrical equipment, miscellaneous machinery, potash mining, high-technology electronics, tourism
Labour Force: 1,806,000 (1992); 75.3% services, 20.8% industry, 3.9% agriculture
Unemployment: 11% (1992 est.)
Agriculture: accounts for 3% of GDP; largely self-sufficient in food production, except for bread grains; principal products—citrus and other fruit, vegetables, cotton; livestock products—beef, dairy and poultry
Natural Resources: copper, phosphates, bromide, potash, clay, sand, sulphur, asphalt, manganese, small amounts of natural gas and crude oil

■ FINANCE/TRADE

Currency: shekel (IS)
International Reserves Excluding Gold: $6,207 million (Jan. 1994)
Gold Reserves: 0.01 million fine troy ounces

(Jan. 1994)

Budget: revenues $33.9 billion; expenditures $36.8 billion, including capital expenditures of $9.3 billion (1993)

Defence Expenditures: 22.12% of total govt. expenditure (1992)

External Debt: $25 billion (1992 est.)

Exports: $13.082 billion (1992); commodities: polished diamonds, citrus and other fruit, textiles and clothing, processed foods, fertilizer and chemical products, military hardware, electronics; partners: US, UK, Germany, France, Belgium, Luxembourg, Italy

Imports: $20.261 billion (1992); commodities: military equipment, rough diamonds, oil, chemicals, machinery, iron and steel, cereals, textiles, vehicles, ships, aircraft; partners: US, Germany, UK, Switzerland, Italy, Belgium, Luxembourg

■ HEALTH

Births: 21/1,000 population (1993)
Deaths: 7/1,000 population (1993)
Infant Mortality: 9.4 deaths/1,000 live births (1993)
Life Expectancy at Birth: 75 years male, 78 years female (1993)
No. of Physicians: 29/10,000 population (1990)

■ EDUCATION

Govt. Expenditure: 11.08% of govt. expenditure (1992)
Literacy: 92% (1993)

■ COMMUNICATIONS

Daily newspapers: 30 (1992)
Televisions: 265.5/1,000 inhabitants (1992)
Radios: 468/1,000 inhabitants (1992)
Telephones: 50.11/100 inhabitants (1992)

■ TRANSPORTATION

Motor Vehicles: 944,152; 786,266 passenger cars (1988)
Roads: 4,736 km paved
Railway: 600 km
Air Traffic: 2,047,000 passengers carried (1991)
Airports: 53 airfields, of which 46 are usable; 28 have permanent-surface runways (1993)

Canadian Embassy: 220 Hayarkon St, Tel Aviv, 63405; mailing address: P.O. Box 6410, Tel Aviv 61063, Israel. Tel: (011-972-3) 527-2929. Fax: (011-972-3) 527-2333

Representative to Canada: Embassy of Israel, 50 O'Connor St, Ste 1005, Ottawa ON K1P 6L2

Tel: (613) 237-6450. Fax: (613) 237-8865.

Italy

Long-Form Name: Italian Republic
Capital: Rome
Population: 57,800,000 (1993 est.)

■ GEOGRAPHY

Area: 301,230 sq. km; includes Sardinia and Sicily
Coastline: 4,996 km
Climate: predominantly Mediterranean; Alpine in far north; hot, dry in south
Environment: regional risks include landslides, mudflows, snowslides, earthquakes, volcanic eruptions, flooding, pollution; land sinkage in Venice; serious air and water pollution
Terrain: mostly rugged and mountainous; some plains, coastal lowlands
Land Use: 32% arable; 10% permanent; 17% meadows; 22% forest; 19% other
Location: S Europe, bordering on Adriatic Sea, Mediterranean Sea

■ PEOPLE

Nationality: Italian
Ethnic Groups: primarily Italian but population includes small clusters of German-, French- and Slovene-Italians in the north and Albanian-Italians in the south; Sicilians; Sardinians
Languages: Italian; parts of Trentino-Alto Adige region are predominantly German-speaking; significant French-speaking minority in Valle d'Aosta region; Slovene-speaking minority in the Trieste-Gorizia area
Religions: almost 100% nominally Roman Catholic
Marriages: 5.4 (per 1,000) (1990)
Divorces: 0.48 (per 1,000) (1990)

■ GOVERNMENT

Leader(s): Pres. Oscar Luigi Scalfaro, Prime Min. Silvio Berlusconi
Government Type: republic
Administrative Divisions: 20 regions
Independence: Mar. 17, 1861, Kingdom of Italy proclaimed
National Holiday: Anniversary of the Republic, June 2

■ ECONOMY

Overview: country is divided into a developed industrial north, and an undeveloped agricultural south; services account for 48% of GDP, industry 35%
GNP: $1.012 trillion, per capita $17,500; real

growth rate 0.9% (1992)
Inflation: 5.2% (1992)
Industries: machinery and transportation equipment, iron and steel, chemicals, food processing, textiles, motor vehicles
Labour Force: 23,339,000 (1992); 70.5% services, 20.4% industry, 9.1% agriculture (1989)
Unemployment: 11.0% (1992)
Agriculture: accounts for about 4% of GNP and 10% of the work force; self-sufficient in foods other than meat and dairy products; principal crops—fruit, vegetables, grapes, potatoes, sugar beets, soybeans, grain, olives
Natural Resources: mercury, potash, marble, sulphur, dwindling natural gas and crude oil reserves, fish, coal

■ FINANCE/TRADE

Currency: lira (Lit)
International Reserves Excluding Gold: $31,132 million (Jan. 1994)
Gold Reserves: 66.67 million fine troy ounces (Jan. 1994)
Budget: revenues $447 billion; expenditures $581 billion, including capital expenditures of 46 billion (1992 est.)
Defence Expenditures: $24.5 billion (1992)
External Debt: $42 billion (1992)
Exports: $178.471 billion (1992); commodities: textiles, wearing apparel, metals, transportation equipment, chemicals; partners: European Community 57%, US 9%, OPEC 4%
Imports: $188.712 billion (1992); commodities: petroleum, industrial machinery, chemicals, metals, foods, agricultural products; partners: European Community 57%, OPEC 6%, US 6%

■ HEALTH

Births: 10/1,000 population (1993)
Deaths: 10/1,000 population (1993)
Infant Mortality: 8.3 deaths/1,000 live births (1993)
Life Expectancy at Birth: 73 years male, 80 years female (1993)
No. of Physicians: 42.7/10,000 population (1992)

■ EDUCATION

Govt. Expenditure: 8% of government expenditure (1988)
Literacy: 97.1% (1993)

■ COMMUNICATIONS

Daily newspapers: 73 (1992)
Televisions: 422.9/1,000 inhabitants (1992)
Radios: 794/1,000 inhabitants (1992)
Telephones: 53.33/100 inhabitants (1992)

■ TRANSPORTATION

Motor Vehicles: 29,727,000; 27,300,000 passenger cars (1990)
Roads: 298,000 km, 270,000 km paved (1993)
Railway: 20,011 km (1993)
Air Traffic: 18,910,000 passengers carried (1991)
Airports: 137 airfields, of which 133 are usable; 92 have permanent-surface runways (1993)

Canadian Embassy: Via G.B. de Rossi 27, 00161 Rome, Italy. Tel: (011-39-6) 44598.1. Fax: (011-39-6) 44598.912
Representative to Canada: Embassy of the Italian Republic, 275 Slater St, 21st Flr, Ottawa ON K1P 5H9. Tel: (613) 232-2401.

Jamaica

Long-Form Name: Jamaica
Capital: Kingston
Population: 2,400,000 (1993 est.)

■ GEOGRAPHY

Area: 10,990 sq. km
Coastline: 1,022 km
Climate: tropical; hot, humid; temperate interior
Environment: subject to hurricanes (especially July to Nov.); deforestation; water pollution
Terrain: mostly mountainous with narrow, discontinuous coastal plain
Land Use: 19% arable; 6% permanent; 18% meadows; 28% forest; 29% other
Location: West Indies, bordering on Caribbean Sea

■ PEOPLE

Nationality: Jamaican
Ethnic Groups: 76% African, 15% Afro-European, 3% East Indian and Afro-East Indian, 3% white, 1% Chinese and Afro-Chinese, 0.8% other
Languages: English (official), Creole
Religions: 55.9% Protestant, 5% Roman Catholic, 39.1% other
Marriages: 5.4 (per 1,000) (1990)
Divorces: 0.28 (per 1,000) (1989)

■ GOVERNMENT

Leader(s): Prime Min. Percival J. Patterson, Gov. Gen. Howard Cooke
Government Type: parliamentary democracy
Administrative Divisions: 14 parishes
Independence: Aug. 6, 1962 (from UK)
National Holiday: Independence Day, first Monday in Aug.

■ ECONOMY

Overview: economy based on sugar, bauxite and tourism, and to a decreasing extent on illicit drugs
GNP: $3.7 billion, per capita $1,500; real growth rate 1.5% (1992 est.)
Inflation: 51.1% (1991)
Industries: tourism, bauxite mining, textiles, food processing, light manufactures
Labour Force: 1,246,000 (1992); 25.3% agriculture, 11.5% industry, 63.2% services (1989)
Unemployment: 15.4% (1992)
Agriculture: accounts for about 9% of GDP, 22% of work force and 17% of exports; principal crops–sugar cane, bananas, coffee, citrus, potatoes and vegetables; not self-sufficient in grain, meat and dairy products
Natural Resources: bauxite, gypsum, limestone

■ FINANCE/TRADE

Currency: Jamaican dollar ($J)
International Reserves Excluding Gold: $151 million (1992)
Gold Reserves: none (1991)
Budget: revenues $600 million; expenditures $736 million, including capital expenditures (1991 est.)
Defence Expenditures: $19.3 million (1992)
External Debt: $4.303 billion (1992)
Exports: $1.047 billion (1992); commodities: bauxite, alumina, sugar, bananas; partners: US 40%, UK, Canada, Trinidad and Tobago, Norway
Imports: $1.672 billion (1992); commodities: petroleum, machinery, food, consumer goods, construction goods; partners: US 46%, UK, Venezuela, Canada, Japan, Trinidad and Tobago

■ HEALTH

Births: 25/1,000 population (1993)
Deaths: 6/1,000 population (1993)
Infant Mortality: 17 deaths/1,000 live births (1993)
Life Expectancy at Birth: 71 years male, 76 years female (1993)
No. of Physicians: 4.9/10,000 population (1992)

■ EDUCATION

Govt. Expenditure: 7.9% of govt. expenditure (1991)
Literacy: 98.2% (1993)

■ COMMUNICATIONS

Daily newspapers: 4 (1992)
Televisions: 123.5/1,000 inhabitants (1992)
Radios: 409/1,000 inhabitants (1992)
Telephones: 7.13/100 inhabitants (1992)

■ TRANSPORTATION

Motor Vehicles: 112,000; 95,000 passenger cars (1990)
Roads: 18,200 km; 12,600 km paved (1993)
Railway: 310 km
Air Traffic: 894,000 passengers carried (1991)
Airports: 36 airfields, of which 23 are usable; 10 have permanent-surface runways (1993)

Canadian Embassy: The Canadian High Commission, Mutual Security Bank Bldg, 30-36 Knutsford Blvd, Kingston 5; mailing address: The Canadian High Commission, P.O. Box 1500, Kingston 10, Jamaica, WI. Tel: (809) 926-1500. Fax: (809) 926-1702
Representative to Canada: Jamaican High Commission, Standard Life Bldg, 275 Slater St, Ste 800, Ottawa ON K1P 5H9. Tel: (613) 233-9311. Fax: (613) 233-0611.

Japan

Long-Form Name: Japan
Capital: Tokyo
Population: 124,800,000 (1993 est.)

■ GEOGRAPHY

Area: 377,835 sq. km; includes Bonin Islands (Ogasawara-gunto), Daito-shoto, Minamijima, Okinotori-shima, Ryukyu Islands (Nansei-shoto) and Volcano Islands (Kazan-retto)
Coastline: 29,751 km
Climate: varies from tropical in south to cool temperate in north
Environment: many dormant and some active volcanoes; about 1,500 seismic occurrences (mostly tremors) every year; subject to tsunamis
Terrain: mostly rugged and mountainous
Land Use: 13% arable; 1% permanent; 1% meadows; 67% forest and woodland; 18% other
Location: NE Asia, bordering on Sea of Japan, North Pacific Ocean

■ PEOPLE

Nationality: Japanese
Ethnic Groups: 99.4% Japanese, 0.6% other (mostly Korean)
Languages: Japanese
Religions: most Japanese observe both Shinto and Buddhist rites; about 16% belong to other faiths, including 0.8% Christian
Marriages: 6.0 (per 1,000) (1991)
Divorces: 1.27 (per 1,000) (1990)

■ GOVERNMENT

Leader(s): Emperor Tsegu no Miya Akihito;

Prime Min. Tsutomu Hata took office on April 25, 1994, but resigned on June 25. Prem. Tomiichi Murayama succeeded Hata on June 29
Government Type: constitutional monarchy
Administrative Divisions: 47 prefectures
Independence: 660 BC, traditional founding by Emperor Jimmu; May 3, 1947 constitutional monarchy established
National Holiday: Birthday of the Emperor, Dec. 23

■ ECONOMY

Overview: impressive economic growth and status as the third largest industrial economy in the world is due to government-industry cooperation and a strong work ethic; known for high-tech industry
GNP: n.a., GDP $2.468 trillion, per capita $19,800; real growth rate 1.5% (1992)
Inflation: 1.7% (1992)
Industries: metallurgy, engineering, electrical and electronic, textiles, chemicals, automobiles, fishing
Labour Force: 62,202,000 (1992); 69.2% services, 23.7% industry; 7.1% agriculture (1989)
Unemployment: 2.2% (1992)
Agriculture: accounts for 2% of GNP; highly subsidized and protected sector, with crop yields among highest in the world; main crops—rice, sugar beets, vegetables, fruit; animal products include pork, poultry, dairy and eggs; about 50% self-sufficient in food
Natural Resources: negligible mineral resources, fish

■ FINANCE/TRADE

Currency: yen (pl. yen) (¥)
International Reserves Excluding Gold: $98,926 million (Jan. 1994)
Gold Reserves: 24.23 million fine troy ounces (Jan. 1994)
Budget: revenues $490 billion; expenditures $579 billion, including capital expenditures $68 billion (1993)
Defence Expenditures: $37 billion (1993-94)
External Debt: n.a.
Exports: $350.700 billion (1993 est.); commodities: manufactures 97% (including machinery 38%, motor vehicles 17%, consumer electronics 10%); partners: US 34%, Southeast Asia 22%, Western Europe 21%, communist countries 5%, Middle East 5%
Imports: $235.972 billion (1993 est.); commodities: manufactures 42%, fossil fuels 30%, foodstuffs 15%, nonfuel raw materials 13%; partners: Southeast Asia 23%, US 23%, Middle East 15%, Western Europe 16%, communist coun-

tries 7%

■ HEALTH

Births: 10/1,000 population (1993)
Deaths: 7/1,000 population (1993)
Infant Mortality: 4.4 deaths/1,000 live births (1993)
Life Expectancy at Birth: 76 years male, 82 years female (1993)
No. of Physicians: 15.1/10,000 population (1992)

■ EDUCATION

Govt. Expenditure: 16.5% of government expenditure (1989)
Literacy: 99% (1993)

■ COMMUNICATIONS

Daily newspapers: 158 (1992)
Televisions: 610.4/1,000 inhabitants (1992)
Radios: 895/1,000 inhabitants (1992)
Telephones: 55.53/100 inhabitants (1992)

■ TRANSPORTATION

Motor Vehicles: 57,697,669; 34,924,172 passenger cars (1990)
Roads: 1,113,860 km; 757,560 km paved
Railway: 27,327 km
Air Traffic: 68,347,000 passengers carried (1991)
Airports: 162 airfields, of which 159 are usable; 132 have permanent-surface runways (1993)

Canadian Embassy: 3-38 Akasaka 7-chome, Minato-ku, Tokyo 107, Japan. Tel: (011-81-3) 3408-2101. Fax: (011-81-3) 3479-5320
Representative to Canada: Embassy of Japan, 255 Sussex Dr, Ottawa ON K1N 9E6. Tel: (613) 236-8541. Fax: (613) 563-9047.

Jordan

Long-Form Name: Hashemite Kingdom of Jordan
Capital: Amman
Population: 3,800,000 (1993 est.)

■ GEOGRAPHY

Area: 89,213 sq. km
Coastline: 26 km
Climate: mostly arid desert; rainy season in west (Nov. to Apr.)
Environment: lack of natural water resources; deforestation; overgrazing; soil erosion; desertification
Terrain: mostly desert plateau in east, highland area in west; Great Rift Valley separates East and West Banks of the Jordan River
Land Use: 4% arable land; 0.5% permanent; 1% meadows; 0.5% forest; 94% other

Location: SW Asia (Middle East)

■ PEOPLE

Nationality: Jordanian
Ethnic Groups: 98% Arab, 1% Circassian, 1% Armenian
Languages: Arabic (official); English widely understood among upper and middle classes
Religions: Islam (over 90% Sunni Moslem, Shia minority)
Marriages: 8.1 (per 1,000) (1989)
Divorces: 1.21 (per 1,000) (1989)

■ GOVERNMENT

Leader(s): Prime Min. Abd al-Salam al-Majali, King Hussein ibn Talal I
Government Type: constitutional monarchy
Administrative Divisions: 8 governorates
Independence: May 25, 1946 (from League of Nations mandate under British administration; formerly known as Trans-Jordan)
National Holiday: Independence Day, May 25

■ ECONOMY

Overview: imports are outweighing exports and foreign aid makes up the difference; droughts are a potential threat; economic recovery is unlikely without substantial foreign aid, debt relief, and economic reform
GNP: $3.881 billion, per capita $1,120; real growth rate 0.6% (1991)
Inflation: 4.0% (1992)
Industries: phosphate mining, petroleum refining, cement, potash, light manufacturing
Labour Force: 992,000 (1992); 10.2% agriculture, 64.2% services, 25.6% industry (1989)
Unemployment: 40% (1991 est.)
Agriculture: accounts for 7% of GDP; principal products are wheat, barley, citrus fruit, tomatoes, melons, olives; livestock—sheep, goats, poultry; large net importer of food
Natural Resources: phosphates, potash, shale oil

■ FINANCE/TRADE

Currency: Jordanian dinar (JD)
International Reserves Excluding Gold: $540 million (Jan. 1994)
Gold Reserves: 0.79 million fine troy ounces (Jan. 1994)
Budget: revenues $1.3 billion; expenditures $1.9 billion, including capital expenditures of $440 million (1992 est.)
Defence Expenditures: 26.73% of total govt. expenditure (1991)
External Debt: $7.929 billion (1992)
Exports: $1.22 billion (1992); commodities: fruit and vegetables, phosphates, fertilizers; partners: Iraq, Saudi Arabia, India, Kuwait, Japan, China, Yugoslavia, Indonesia
Imports: $3.257 billion (1992); commodities: crude oil, textiles, capital goods, motor vehicles, foodstuffs; partners: European Community, US, Saudi Arabia, Japan, Turkey, Romania, China, Taiwan

■ HEALTH

Births: 40/1,000 population (1993)
Deaths: 4/1,000 population (1993)
Infant Mortality: 34 deaths/1,000 live births (1993)
Life Expectancy at Birth: 70 years male, 73 years female (1993)
No. of Physicians: 11.6/10,000 population (1992)

■ EDUCATION

Govt. Expenditure: 12.86% of govt. expenditure (1991)
Literacy: 80.1% (1993)

■ COMMUNICATIONS

Daily newspapers: 4 (1992)
Televisions: 77.2/1,000 inhabitants (1992)
Radios: 252/1,000 inhabitants (1992)
Telephones: 9.1/100 inhabitants (1992)

■ TRANSPORTATION

Motor Vehicles: 248,311; 161,884 passenger cars (1990)
Roads: 7,493 km; 5,530 km paved
Railway: 794 km
Air Traffic: 797,000 passengers carried (1991)
Airports: 19 airfields, of which 15 are usable; 14 have permanent-surface runways (1993)

Canadian Embassy: Pearl of Shmeisani Bldg, Shmeisani, Amman, Jordan; mailing address: P.O. Box 815403, Amman, Jordan. Tel: (011-962-6) 66-61-24. Fax: (011-962-6) 68-92-27
Representative to Canada: Embassy of the Hashemite Kingdom of Jordan, 100 Bronson Ave, Ste 701, Ottawa ON K1R 6G8. Tel: (613) 238-8090. Fax: (613) 232-3341.

Kazakhstan

Long-Form Name: Republic of Kazakhstan
Capital: Alma-Ata
Population: 17,200,000 (1993 est.)

■ GEOGRAPHY

Area: 2,717,300 sq. km
Coastline: none; landlocked; Kazakhstan borders the Aral Sea (1,015 km) and the Caspian Sea (1,894 km)

Climate: dry desert climate; arid and semi-arid; hot summers and cold winters

Environment: drought and desertification; lack of fresh water; drying up of Aral Sea is causing increased concentrations of chemical pesticides and natural salts; industrial pollution

Terrain: desert and steppe; plains in western Siberia to oasis and desert in Central Asia

Land Use: 15% arable, negligible permanent crops, 57% meadows and pastures, 4% forests, 24% other

Location: S Asia, bordering on Caspian Sea

■ PEOPLE

Nationality: Kazakhstani

Ethnic Groups: 41.9% Kazakh, 37% Russian, 5.2% Ukrainian, 4.7% German, 2.1% Uzbek, 2% Tatar, 7.1% other

Languages: Kazakh (official), Russian, German, Ukrainian

Religions: primarily Sunni Muslim (47%) and Eastern Orthodox (15%)

Marriages: 10.00 (per 1,000) (1989)

Divorces: 2.75 (per 1,000) (1989)

■ GOVERNMENT

Leader(s): President Nursultan A. Nazarbayev, Premier Sergei Tereshchenko

Government Type: republic

Administrative Divisions: 19 oblasts

Independence: Dec. 16, 1991 (from Soviet Union)

National Holiday: Independence Day, Dec. 16

■ ECONOMY

Overview: predominantly mining and manufacturing; agriculture possible only with irrigation; serious pollution problems, lack of modern technology, and little experience in foreign markets hamper economic progress

GNP: $41.691 billion, $2,470 per capita; real growth rate 2.1% (1991)

Inflation: n.a.

Industries: coal refining, oil and natural gas extraction, mining, agricultural machinery, electric motors, construction materials

Labour Force: 7.563 million; 32% industry and construction, 23% agriculture and forestry, 45% other (1990)

Unemployment: 0.4%; large numbers of under-employed (1993)

Agriculture: accounts for almost 40% of net material product and employs one quarter of labour force; wheat, cotton, rice, vineyard and orchard crops, sheep, cattle

Natural Resources: fish, oil, natural gas, zinc, coal, lead, iron ore, rare metals, tungsten, copper, zinc, manganese

■ FINANCE/TRADE

Currency: rouble (rbl.)

International Reserves Excluding Gold: n.a.

Gold Reserves: n.a.

Budget: 1989 revenues: $14,254 million roubles

Defence Expenditures: n.a.

External Debt: $25 million (1992)

Exports: $1.271 billion (1993): heat, karakul fleece, wool

Imports: $358 million (1993)

■ HEALTH

Births: 21/1,000 population (1993)

Deaths: 8/1,000 population (1993)

Infant Mortality: 32 deaths/1,000 live births (1993)

Life Expectancy at Birth: 64 years male, 73 years female (1993)

No. of Physicians: 68,000 (1989)

■ EDUCATION

Govt. Expenditure: n.a.

Literacy: 100% (1993)

■ COMMUNICATIONS

Daily newspapers: 443 papers of all circulation types (1989)

Televisions: n.a.

Radios: n.a.

Telephones: approximately 6/100 persons (1993)

■ TRANSPORTATION

Motor Vehicles: n.a.

Roads: 189,000 km; 108,100 km hard-surfaced (1993)

Railway: 14,460 km

Air Traffic: n.a.

Airports: 365 airfields, of which 152 are usable; 49 have permanent-surface runways (1993)

Canadian Embassy: Hotel Kazakhstan, Rooms 912 and 914, 52 Leina St, 480110, Almaty, Kazakhstan. Tel: (011-7-3272) 61-91-07.

Kenya

Long-Form Name: Republic of Kenya

Capital: Nairobi

Population: 27,700,000 (1993 est.)

■ GEOGRAPHY

Area: 582,650 sq. km

Coastline: 536 km

Climate: varies from tropical along coast to arid in interior

Environment: unique physiography supports abundant and varied wildlife of scientific and economic value; deforestation; soil erosion; desertification; glaciers on Mt. Kenya
Terrain: low plains rise to central highlands bisected by Great Rift Valley; fertile plateau in west
Land Use: 3% arable; 1% permanent; 7% meadows; 45% forest; 85% other
Location: E Africa, bordering on Indian Ocean

■ PEOPLE

Nationality: Kenyan
Ethnic Groups: 21% Kikuyu, 14% Luhya, 13% Luo, 11% Kalenjin, 11% Kamba, 6% Kisii, 6% Meru, 1% Asian, European and Arab
Languages: English and Swahili (official); Kikuyu and Luo are widely spoken, numerous indigenous languages
Religions: 28% Roman Catholic, 6% Islam, 18% indigenous beliefs, 26% Protestant
Marriages: n.a.
Divorces: n.a.

■ GOVERNMENT

Leader(s): Pres. Daniel Tarap Moi, V. Pres. George Saitoti
Government Type: republic
Administrative Divisions: 8 provinces
Independence: Dec. 12, 1963 (from UK; formerly known as British East Africa)
National Holiday: Independence Day, Dec. 12

■ ECONOMY

Overview: a large annual population growth and a shortage of arable land threaten economic growth; vulnerable to weather conditions
GNP: n.a., GDP $8.3 billion, per capita $320; real growth rate -1% (1992 est.)
Inflation: 30% (1992 est.)
Industries: small-scale consumer goods (plastic, furniture, batteries, textiles, soap, cigarettes, flour), agricultural processing, oil refining, cement, tourism
Labour Force: 10,010,000 (1992); 81% agriculture, 6.8% industry, 12.1% services (1989)
Unemployment: n.a., but there is a high level of unemployment and underemployment
Agriculture: accounts for 25% of GDP, about 80% of the work force and over 65% of exports; cash crops include coffee, tea, sisal, pineapple; food products—corn, wheat, sugar cane, fruit, vegetables, dairy products; food output not keeping pace with population growth
Natural Resources: gold, limestone, diatomite, salt barytes, magnesite, feldspar, sapphires, fluorspar, garnets, wildlife

■ FINANCE/TRADE

Currency: Kenya shilling (KSh)
International Reserves Excluding Gold: $146 million (Oct. 1993)
Gold Reserves: 0.08 million fine troy ounces (Jan. 1994)
Budget: revenues $2.4 billion; expenditures $2.8 billion, including capital expenditures of $0.74 billion (1990)
Defence Expenditures: 9.25% of total govt. expenditure (1991)
External Debt: $6.366 billion (1992)
Exports: $1.247 billion (1992); commodities: coffee 20%, tea 18%, manufactures 15%, petroleum products 10%; partners: Western Europe 45%, Africa 22%, Far East 10%, US 4%, Middle East 3%
Imports: $1.713 billion (1992); commodities: machinery and transportation equipment 36%, raw materials 33%, fuels and lubricants 20%, food and consumer goods 11%; partners: Western Europe 49%, Far East 20%, Middle East 19%, US 7%

■ HEALTH

Births: 45/1,000 population (1993)
Deaths: 9/1,000 population (1993)
Infant Mortality: 72 deaths/1,000 live births (1993)
Life Expectancy at Birth: 60 years male, 64 years female (1993)
No. of Physicians: 1.0/10,000 population (1992)

■ EDUCATION

Govt. Expenditure: 20.14% of government expenditure (1991)
Literacy: 69.0% (1993)

■ COMMUNICATIONS

Daily newspapers: 5 (1992)
Televisions: 8.6/1,000 inhabitants (1992)
Radios: 95/1,000 inhabitants (1992)
Telephones: 1.54/100 inhabitants (1992)

■ TRANSPORTATION

Motor Vehicles: 300,000; 150,000 passenger cars (1990)
Roads: 65,840 km; 8,157 km paved
Railway: 2,040 km (1993)
Air Traffic: 760,000 passengers carried (1991)
Airports: 247 airfields, of which 208 are usable; 18 have permanent-surface runways (1993)

Canadian Embassy: The Canadian High Commission, Comcraft House, Hailé Sélassie Ave, Nairobi; mailing address: The Canadian High Commission, P.O. Box 30481, Nairobi,

Kenya. Tel: (011-254-2) 21-48-04. Fax: (011-254-2) 22-69-87
Representative to Canada: High Commission for the Republic of Kenya, 415 Laurier Ave E, Ottawa ON K1N 6R4. Tel: (613) 563-1773. Fax: (613) 233-6599.

Kiribati

Long-Form Name: Republic of Kiribati
Capital: Tarawa
Population: 76,320 (1993 est.)

■ GEOGRAPHY

Area: 717 sq. km
Coastline: 1,143 km
Climate: tropical; marine, hot and humid, moderated by trade winds
Environment: typhoons can occur anytime, but usually Nov. to Mar.; 10 of the 33 islands are inhabited
Terrain: mostly low-lying coral atolls surrounded by extensive reefs
Land Use: negligible arable; 51% permanent; 0% meadows; 3% forest; 46% other
Location: SW Pacific Ocean

■ PEOPLE

Nationality: I-Kiribati
Ethnic Groups: Micronesian
Languages: English (official), Gilbertese
Religions: 52% Roman Catholic, 41% Protestant (Congregational), some Seventh-Day Adventist and Baha'i
Marriages: n.a.
Divorces: n.a.

■ GOVERNMENT

Leader(s): Pres. Teatao Teannaki, V. Pres. Taomaki T. Iuta
Government Type: republic
Administrative Divisions: 3 units
Independence: July 12, 1979 (from UK; formerly known as Gilbert Islands)
National Holiday: Independence Day, July 12

■ ECONOMY

Overview: the economy has fluctuated widely in recent years and copra production and a good fish catch have provided a boost
GNP: $53 million, per capita $750; real growth rate 2.4% (1991)
Inflation: 3.1% (1988)
Industries: fishing, handicrafts
Labour Force: 40,000 (1992)
Unemployment: n.a.
Agriculture: accounts for 15% of GDP (including fishing); copra and fish contribute 95% to exports; subsistence farming predominates; food crops—taro, breadfruit, sweet potatoes, vegetables; not self-sufficient in food
Natural Resources: tuna fishing

■ FINANCE/TRADE

Currency: Australian dollar ($A)
International Reserves Excluding Gold: n.a.
Gold Reserves: n.a.
Budget: revenues $29.9 million; expenditures $16.3 million, including capital expenditures of $14.0 million (1990)
Defence Expenditures: n.a.
External Debt: $2 billion (1987)
Exports: $5.1 million (1988); commodities: fish 55%, copra 42%; partners: European Community 20%, Marshall Islands 12%, US 8%, American Samoa 4%
Imports: $21.5 million (1988); commodities: foodstuffs, fuel, transportation equipment; partners: Australia 39%, Japan 21%, New Zealand 6%, UK 6%, US 3%

■ HEALTH

Births: 32.03/1,000 population (1993)
Deaths: 12.31/1,000 population (1993)
Infant Mortality: 98.4 deaths/1,000 live births (1993)
Life Expectancy at Birth: 52.56 years male, 55.78 years female (1993)
No. of Physicians: 5.1/10,000 population (1992)

■ EDUCATION

Govt. Expenditure: 14.8% of government expenditure (1991)
Literacy: 90% (1993)

■ COMMUNICATIONS

Daily newspapers: 0 (1989)
Televisions: n.a.
Radios: 225/1,000 inhabitants (1989)
Telephones: 1,400 total (1993)

■ TRANSPORTATION

Motor Vehicles: n.a.
Roads: 640 km
Railway: none
Air Traffic: 25,000 passengers carried (1991)
Airports: 21 airfields, of which 20 are usable; 4 have permanent-surface runways (1993)

Canadian Embassy: The Canadian High Commission to Kiribati, c/o The Canadian High Commission, 61 Molesworth St, 3rd Fl, Thorndon, Wellington; mailing address: P.O. Box 12-049, Thorndon, Wellington, New

Zealand. Tel: (011-64-4) 473-9577. Fax: (011-64-4) 471-2082.

Korea (North)

Long-Form Name: Democratic People's Republic of Korea
Capital: Pyongyang
Population: 22,618,000 (1993 est.)

■ GEOGRAPHY

Area: 120,540 sq. km
Coastline: 2,495 km
Climate: temperate with rainfall concentrated in summer
Environment: isolated mountainous interior, nearly inaccessible and sparsely populated; late spring droughts often followed by severe flooding
Terrain: mostly hills and mountains separated by deep, narrow valleys; coastal plains wide in west, discontinuous in east
Land Use: 18% arable; 1% permanent; negligible meadows; 74% forest; 7% other
Location: NE Asia, bordering on Yellow Sea, Sea of Japan

■ PEOPLE

Nationality: Korean
Ethnic Groups: Korean (racially homogeneous)
Languages: Korean
Religions: Buddhism and Confucianism; Taoism, Shamanism, Chonodogyu; autonomous religious activities are now almost non-existent; government-sponsored religious groups exist to provide an illusion of religious freedom
Marriages: n.a.
Divorces: n.a.

■ GOVERNMENT

Leader(s): Premier Kang Song San, Pres. Kim Jong Il
Government Type: communist state; Stalinist dictatorship
Administrative Divisions: 9 provinces and 3 special cities
Independence: Sept. 9, 1948
National Holiday: Independence Day (DPRK Foundation Day), Sept. 9

■ ECONOMY

Overview: a command economy which is almost completely socialized, with state-owned industry, and collectivization of agriculture; state control over economic affairs is unusually tight even for a communist country
GNP: $22 billion, per capita $1,000; real growth rate -10 to -15% (1992 est.)
Inflation: n.a.
Industries: machine building, military products, electric power, chemicals, mining, metallurgy, textiles, food processing
Labour Force: 10,470,000 (1992); 42.8% agricultural, 26.9% services, 30.3% industry
Unemployment: officially none
Agriculture: accounts for about 25% of GNP and 36% of work force; principal crops—rice, corn, potatoes, soybeans, pulses; fish; livestock and livestock products—cattle, hogs, pork, eggs; not self-sufficient in grain
Natural Resources: coal, lead, tungsten, zinc, graphite, magnesite, iron ore, copper, gold, pyrites, salt, fluorspar, hydroelectricity

■ FINANCE/TRADE

Currency: won (pl. won) (Wn)
International Reserves Excluding Gold: n.a.
Gold Reserves: n.a.
Budget: revenues $18.5 billion; expenditures $18.4 billion, including capital expenditures (1992)
Defence Expenditures: $5 billion (1991); the officially announced but suspect figure is $1.9 billion
External Debt: $8 billion (1992 est.)
Exports: $1.3 billion (1992); commodities: minerals, metallurgical products, agricultural products, manufactures; partners: USSR, China, Japan, Germany, Hong Kong, Singapore
Imports: $1.9 billion (1992); commodities: petroleum, machinery and equipment, coking coal, grain; partners: USSR, Japan, China, Germany, Hong Kong, Singapore

■ HEALTH

Births: 24/1,000 population (1993)
Deaths: 6/1,000 population (1993)
Infant Mortality: 30 deaths/1,000 live births (1993)
Life Expectancy at Birth: 66 years male, 72 years female (1993)
No. of Physicians: 23.9/10,000 population (1990)

■ EDUCATION

Govt. Expenditure: n.a.
Literacy: 99% (1993)

■ COMMUNICATIONS

Daily newspapers: 11 (1986)
Televisions: 14.0/1,000 inhabitants (1989)
Radios: 117/1,000 inhabitants (1989)
Telephones: n.a.

■ TRANSPORTATION

Motor Vehicles: 180,000 motor vehicles (1982)
Roads: approx. 30,000 km; 7.5% paved
Railway: 8,510 km (1992)
Air Traffic: 223,000 passengers carried (1991)
Airports: 55 airfields (est.), all usable; 30 (est.)
have permanent-surface runways (1993)

Canadian Embassy: none.

Korea (South)

Long-Form Name: Republic of Korea
Capital: Seoul
Population: 44,600,000 (1993 est.)

■ GEOGRAPHY

Area: 98,480 sq. km
Coastline: 2,413 km
Climate: temperate, with rainfall heavier in summer than winter
Environment: occasional typhoons bring high winds and floods; earthquakes in southwest; air pollution in large cities
Terrain: mostly hilly and mountains; wide coastal plains in west and south
Land Use: 21% arable; 1% permanent; 1% meadows; 67% forest; 10% other
Location: E Asia, bordering on Yellow Sea, Sea of Japan (also known as the East Sea)

■ PEOPLE

Nationality: Korean
Ethnic Groups: homogeneous; small Chinese minority (about 20,000)
Languages: Korean; English widely taught in high school
Religions: 48.6% Christianity, 47.4% Buddhism, 3% Confucianism, 0.2% other
Marriages: 7.3 (per 1,000) (1989)
Divorces: 0.77 (per 1,000) (1989)

■ GOVERNMENT

Leader(s): Pres. Kim Young Sam, Prime Min. Lee Young Duk
Government Type: republic
Administrative Divisions: 9 provinces and 6 special cities
Independence: Aug. 15, 1945
National Holiday: Independence Day, Aug. 15

■ ECONOMY

Overview: dynamic growth is attributed to the planned development of an export-oriented economy in a strongly entrepreneurial society; labour unrest threatens to hurt its record of non-inflationary growth; economic growth has slowed somewhat in recent years
GNP: $287 billion, per capita $6,500; real growth rate 5% (1992 est.)
Inflation: 6.2% (1992)
Industries: textiles, clothing, footwear, food processing, chemicals, steel, electronics, automobile production, ship building
Labour Force: 18,660,000 (1992); 58.5% services, 25.5% industry, 16.0% agriculture (1992)
Unemployment: 2.3% (1992)
Agriculture: accounts for 8% of GNP and 21% of work force (including fishing and forestry); main crops—rice, root crops, barley, vegetables, fruit; livestock and livestock products—cattle, hogs, chickens, milk, eggs; self-sufficient in food, except for wheat; fish catch is seventh-largest in the world
Natural Resources: coal, tungsten, graphite, molybdenum, lead, hydroelectricity

■ FINANCE/TRADE

Currency: won (pl. won) (W)
International Reserves Excluding Gold: $20,511 million (Jan. 1994)
Gold Reserves: 0.32 million fine troy ounces (Jan. 1994)
Budget: revenues $48.4 billion; expenditures $48.4 billion, including capital expenditures (1993)
Defence Expenditures: 22.11% of total govt. expenditure (1992)
External Debt: $42.999 billion (1992)
Exports: $82.451 billion (1993); commodities: textiles, clothing, electronic and electrical equipment, footwear, machinery, steel, automobiles, ships, fish; partners: US 33%, Japan 21%
Imports: $83.748 billion (1993); commodities: machinery, electronics and electronic equipment, oil, steel, transport equipment, textiles, organic chemicals, grains; partners: Japan 28%, US 25%

■ HEALTH

Births: 16/1,000 population (1993)
Deaths: 6/1,000 population (1993)
Infant Mortality: 15 deaths/1,000 live births (1993)
Life Expectancy at Birth: 67 years male, 75 years female (1993)
No. of Physicians: 8.7/10,000 population (1992)

■ EDUCATION

Govt. Expenditure: 16.2% of govt. expenditure (1992)
Literacy: 96% (1993)

■ COMMUNICATIONS

Daily newspapers: 39 (1992)
Televisions: 207.3/1,000 inhabitants (1992)
Radios: 1,003/1,000 inhabitants (1992)
Telephones: 33.49/100 inhabitants (1992)

■ TRANSPORTATION

Motor Vehicles: 3,394,803; 2,074,922 passenger cars (1990)
Roads: 63,201 km; 34,173 km paved
Railway: 3,142 km
Air Traffic: 16,908,000 passengers carried (1991)
Airports: 103 airfields, of which 93 are usable; 59 have permanent-surface runways (1993)

Canadian Embassy: Flr 10 & 11, Kolon Building, 45 Mugyo-Dong, Jung-Ku, Seoul 100-170; mailing address: P.O. Box 6299, Seoul 100-662 Korea. Tel: (011-82-2) 753-2605. Fax: (011-82-2) 755-0686
Representative to Canada: Embassy of the Republic of Korea, 151 Slater St, Flr 5, Ottawa ON K1P 5H3. Tel: (613) 232-1715. Fax: (613) 232-0928.

Kuwait

Long-Form Name: State of Kuwait
Capital: Kuwait
Population: 1,700,000 (1993 est.)

■ GEOGRAPHY

Area: 17,820 sq. km
Coastline: 499 km
Climate: dry desert; intensely hot summers; short, cool winters
Environment: some of world's largest and most sophisticated desalination facilities provide most of the water; air and water pollution; desertification
Terrain: flat to slightly undulating desert plain
Land Use: negligible arable; 0% permanent; 8% meadows; negligible forest; 92% other
Location: SW Asia (Middle East), bordering on Persian Gulf

■ PEOPLE

Nationality: Kuwaiti
Ethnic Groups: 45% Kuwaiti, 35% other Arab, 9% South Asian, 4% Iranian, 7% other
Languages: Arabic (official); Kurdish, Farsi, English (commercial) widely spoken
Religions: 85% Moslem (30% Shi'a, 45% Sunni, 10% other), 15% Christian, Hindu, Parsi and other
Marriages: 5.4 (per 1,000) (1989)

Divorces: 1.46 (per 1,000) (1989)

■ GOVERNMENT

Leader(s): Prime Min. Shaikh Saad al-Abdullah as-Salim as-Sabah; Emir: Shaikh Jabir al-Ahmad al-Jabir al-Sabah
Government Type: nominal constitutional monarchy
Administrative Divisions: 5 governorates
Independence: June 19, 1961 (from UK)
National Holiday: National Day, Feb. 25

■ ECONOMY

Overview: the oil-dominated economy has been heavily dependent on foreign labour (about 80% of the work force); Iraq's invasion and the Gulf War have probably drastically affected the economy, as will calls for democratic reforms to this monarchic government
GNP: $15.3 billion, per capita $11,100; real growth rate 80% (1992 est.)
Inflation: 5% (1992 est.)
Industries: petroleum, petrochemicals, desalination, food processing, salt, construction
Labour Force: 835,000 (1992); 45% services, 20% construction, 12% trade, 9% manufacturing, 3% finance and real estate, 2% agriculture, 2% power and water, 1% mining and quarrying
Unemployment: negligible (1992)
Agriculture: virtually none; dependent on imports for food; about 75% of potable water must be distilled (adversely affected by the Gulf War) or imported
Natural Resources: petroleum, fish, shrimp, natural gas

■ FINANCE/TRADE

Currency: dinar (KD)
International Reserves Excluding Gold: $4,272 million (Jan. 1994)
Gold Reserves: 2.54 million fine troy ounces (Jan. 1994)
Budget: revenues $7.1 billion; expenditures $10.5 billion, including capital expenditures of $3.1 billion (1988)
Defence Expenditures: 22.10% of total govt. expenditure (1992)
External Debt: $7.2 billion (1989)
Exports: $6.690 billion (1992); commodities: oil 90%; partners: Japan, Italy, Germany, US
Imports: $7.505 billion (1992); commodities: food, construction material, vehicles and parts, clothing; partners: Japan, US, Germany, UK

■ HEALTH

Births: 32/1,000 population (1993)
Deaths: 2/1,000 population (1993)

Infant Mortality: 14 deaths/1,000 live births (1993)
Life Expectancy at Birth: 72 years male, 77 years female (1993)
No. of Physicians: 15.6/10,000 population (1992)

■ **EDUCATION**

Govt. Expenditure: 13.68% of government expenditure (1992)
Literacy: 73.0% (1993)

■ **COMMUNICATIONS**

Daily newspapers: 8 (1992)
Televisions: 280.6/1,000 inhabitants (1992)
Radios: 337/1,000 inhabitants (1992)
Telephones: 18.92/100 inhabitants (1992)

■ **TRANSPORTATION**

Motor Vehicles: 630,000; 490,000 passenger cars (1990)
Roads: 4,277 km; 3,000 km paved
Railway: none
Air Traffic: 840,000 passengers carried (1991)
Airports: 7 airfields, of which 4 are usable and have permanent-surface runways (1993)

Canadian Embassy: Da'Aiyah - Block 4, House No. 24, Al-Mutawakel St, Kuwait City; mailing address: P.O. Box 25281, Safat, Kuwait City, 13113, Kuwait. Tel: (011-965) 256-3025. Fax: (011-965) 256-4167.
Representative to Canada: Embassy of the State of Kuwait, Suite 410, 360 Albert St, Ottawa, ON K1R 7X7. Tel: (613) 780-9999. Fax: (613) 780-9905.

Kyrgyzstan

Long-Form Name: Kyrgyz Republic
Capital: Bishkek (Frunze)
Population: 4,600,000 (1993 est.)

■ **GEOGRAPHY**

Area: 198,500 sq. km
Coastline: none: landlocked
Climate: dry continental to polar in high Tien Shan; subtropical in south; glacial Alpine; moderate in valley regions
Environment: frequent severe earthquakes
Terrain: mountainous; 75% of land covered by snow and glaciers; peaks of Tien Shan rise to 7,000 meters, and associated valleys and basins encompass the entire nation
Land Use: land is cultivated mainly in valleys, less than 25%
Location: S Asia

■ **PEOPLE**

Nationality: Kirghiz
Ethnic Groups: 52.4% Kirghiz, 21.5% Russian, 12.9% Uzbeks, 2.5% Ukrainian, 2.4% German, 1.6% Tatars
Languages: Kirghiz (official), Russian, Dungan
Religions: predominantly Sunni Muslim and Eastern Orthodox
Marriages: 9.7 (per 1,000) (1989)
Divorces: 1.9 (per 1,000) (1989)

■ **GOVERNMENT**

Leader(s): Pres. Askar Akayev; Chairman, Supreme Soviet: Medetkan Sherimkulov
Government Type: republic
Administrative Divisions: 6 oblasts
Independence: August 31, 1991 (from Soviet Union)
National Holiday: National Day, Dec. 2

■ **ECONOMY**

Overview: Kyrgyzstan's small economy (less than 1% of the total for the former Soviet Union) is oriented toward agriculture, producing mainly livestock as well as cotton, grain, and tobacco; over 500 large, modern, industrial enterprises including sugar refineries, tanneries, cotton and wool-cleansing works, flour mills, tobacco factories; agricultural sector of the economy predominates
GNP: $6.9 billion, $1,550 per capita; real growth rate 4.1% (1991)
Inflation: n.a.
Industries: small machinery, cement, shoes, furniture and appliances, electronics, electrical engineering, silk making
Labour Force: 1,748,000; 33% agriculture and forestry, 28% industry and construction, 39% other (1990)
Unemployment: 0.1%; large numbers of underemployed (1993)
Agriculture: wheat, barley, beets, cotton, fruit, vegetables, yaks, potatoes, cotton, grain, tobacco, livestock (mainly sheep); irrigation required;
Natural Resources: mercury, antimony, zinc, tungsten deposits, coal, natural gas, oil, nepheline, bismuth

■ **FINANCE/TRADE**

Currency: som was introduced as national currency on May 10, 1993
International Reserves Excluding Gold: n.a.
Gold Reserves: n.a.
Budget: 1989 revenues: 2,692 million roubles
Defence Expenditures: n.a.
External Debt: $0 (1992)
Exports: agricultural products, antimony, silk,

carpets, non-ferrous metals, electrical equipment
Imports: n.a.

■ HEALTH

Births: 29/1,000 population (1993)
Deaths: 7/1,000 population (1993)
Infant Mortality: 40 deaths/1,000 live births (1993)
Life Expectancy at Birth: 65 years male, 73 years female (1993)
No. of Physicians: 15,800 (1989)

■ EDUCATION

Govt. Expenditure: n.a.
Literacy: 100% (1993)

■ COMMUNICATIONS

Daily newspapers: 122 papers of all circulation types (1989)
Televisions: n.a.
Radios: n.a.
Telephones: approximately 5.6/100 inhabitants (1993)

■ TRANSPORTATION

Motor Vehicles: n.a.
Roads: 30,300 km; 22,600 km paved or graveled (1993)
Railway: 370 km
Air Traffic: n.a.
Airports: 52 airfields, of which 27 are usable; 12 have permanent-surface runways (1993)

Canadian Embassy: c/o Hotel Kazakhstan, Rooms 912 and 914, 52 Leina St, 480110, Almaty, Kazakhstan. Tel: (011-7-3272) 61-91-07.

Representative to Canada: c/o Embassy of the Republic of Kyrgyzstan, 1511 K St NW, Ste 705, Washington DC 20005 USA. Tel: (202) 347-3732. Fax: (202) 347-3718.

Laos

Long-Form Name: Lao People's Democratic Republic
Capital: Vientiane
Population: 4,600,000 (1993 est.)

■ GEOGRAPHY

Area: 236,800 sq. km
Coastline: none: landlocked
Climate: tropical monsoon; rainy season (May to Nov.); dry season (Dec. to Apr.)
Environment: deforestation; soil erosion; subject to floods
Terrain: mostly rugged mountains; some plains and plateaus
Land Use: 4% arable land; negligible permanent crops; 3% meadows; 58% forest; 35% other
Location: SE Asia

■ PEOPLE

Nationality: Laotian or Lao
Ethnic Groups: 50% Laotian; Vietnamese, Kha, Thai, Meo, Hmong, Yao, Chinese, European, Indian and Pakistani minorities
Languages: Lao (official), French, English, tribal languages
Religions: 85% Buddhist, 15% animist and other
Marriages: n.a.
Divorces: n.a.

■ GOVERNMENT

Leader(s): Pres. Nouhak Phoumsavan, Prime Min. Khamtai Siphandon
Government Type: communist state
Administrative Divisions: 16 provinces and 1 municipality (Vientiane)
Independence: July 19, 1949 (from France)
National Holiday: National Day (proclamation of the Lao People's Democratic Republic), Dec. 2

■ ECONOMY

Overview: one of the world's poorest nations, landlocked with a primitive infrastructure; while traditionally a communist centrally planned economy with government ownership and control of productive enterprises, the government is now decentralizing control and encouraging some private enterprise; heavily dependent on foreign aid
GNP: $965 million, per capita $230; real growth rate 4.2% (1991)
Inflation: 35% (1989 est.)
Industries: tin mining, timber, electric power, agricultural processing
Labour Force: 2,240,000 (1992) 75.7% agriculture, 7.1% industry, 17.2% services (1989)
Unemployment: 21% (1989)
Agriculture: accounts for 60% of GDP and employs most of the labour force; subsistence farming predominates; normally self-sufficient; principal crops—rice (80% of cultivated land), potatoes, vegetables, coffee, sugar cane, cotton
Natural Resources: timber, hydroelectricity, gypsum, tin, gold, gemstones

■ FINANCE/TRADE

Currency: new kip (NK)
International Reserves Excluding Gold: $43 million (1990)
Gold Reserves: n.a.
Budget: revenues $83 million; expenditures

$188.5 million, including capital expenditures of $94 million (1990)
Defence Expenditures: $18.94 million (1989)
External Debt: $1.952 billion (1992)
Exports: $57.5 million (1989); commodities: electricity, wood products, coffee, tin; partners: Thailand, Malaysia, Vietnam, USSR, US
Imports: $219 million (1989); commodities: food, fuel oil, consumer goods, manufactures; partners: Thailand, USSR, Japan, France, Vietnam

■ HEALTH

Births: 45/1,000 population (1993)
Deaths: 16/1,000 population (1993)
Infant Mortality: 110 deaths/1,000 live births (1993)
Life Expectancy at Birth: 49 years male, 52 years female (1993)
No. of Physicians: 7.3/10,000 population (1992)

■ EDUCATION

Govt. Expenditure: 6.6% of government expenditure (1986)
Literacy: 84% (1993)

■ COMMUNICATIONS

Daily newspapers: 3 (1992)
Televisions: 5.0/1,000 inhabitants (1992)
Radios: 124/1,000 inhabitants (1992)
Telephones: 0.23/100 inhabitants (1992)

■ TRANSPORTATION

Motor Vehicles: 22,000; 18,000 passenger cars (1990)
Roads: 28,180 km; 1,895 km paved
Railway: none
Air Traffic: 115,000 passengers carried (1991)
Airports: 54 airfields, of which 41 are usable; 8 have permanent-surface runways (1993)

Canadian Embassy: The Canadian Embassy to Laos, c/o 11th Floor, Boonmitr Bldg, 138 Silom Rd, Bangkok 10500; mailing address: P.O. Box 2090, Bangkok 10500, Thailand. Tel: (011-66-2) 237-4125. Fax: (011-66-2) 236-6463
Representative to Canada: c/o Embassy of the Lao People's Democratic Republic, 222 S St NW, Washington DC 20008 USA. Tel: (202) 332-6416. Fax: (202) 332-4923.

Latvia

Long-Form Name: Republic of Latvia
Capital: Riga
Population: 2,600,000 (1993 est.)

■ GEOGRAPHY

Area: 64,100 sq. km
Coastline: 531 km
Climate: maritime, wet, moderate winters
Environment: air and water pollution, soil and groundwater contaminated with chemicals and petroleum products at military bases
Terrain: hilly, forested land with many lakes and shallow valleys
Land Use: 27% arable, negligible permanent crops, 13% meadows and pastures, 39% forest, 21% other
Location: NE Europe, bordering on Baltic Sea

■ PEOPLE

Nationality: Latvian
Ethnic Groups: 51.8% Latvian, 33.8% Russian, 4.5% Belorussian, 3.4% Ukrainian, 2.3% Polish, 4.2% other
Languages: Latvian (official), Lithuanian, Russian
Religions: Lutheran, Catholic, Russian Orthodox
Marriages: 9.1 (per 1,000) (1989)
Divorces: 4.19 (per 1,000) (1989)

■ GOVERNMENT

Leader(s): Pres. Guntis Ulmanis, Prem. Valdis Birkavs
Government Type: republic
Administrative Divisions: none (all districts under direct republic jurisdiction)
Independence: Sept. 6, 1991 (from Soviet Union)
National Holiday: Independence Day, Nov. 18

■ ECONOMY

Overview: Latvia lacks natural resources, aside from its arable land and small forests; its most valuable economic asset is its work force, which is better educated and disciplined than in most of the former Soviet republics
GNP: $9.913 billion, per capita $3,410; real growth rate 3.4%
Inflation: 2% per month (1993)
Industries: accounts for 33% of labour force; manufacturing of railroad cars, paper, woolen goods, electronics and engineering, food processing
Labour Force: 1,407,000; 41% industry and construction, 16% agriculture and forestry, 43% other (1990)
Unemployment: 3.6% (1993), but large numbers of underemployed
Agriculture: employs 16% of labour force; poor soil hinders agriculture products inc. grain, beets, potatoes, cattle and dairy farming, poultry, fishing

Natural Resources: forests, peat deposits, amber, dolomite

■ FINANCE/TRADE

Currency: lat
International Reserves Excluding Gold: n.a.
Gold Reserves: n.a.
Budget: n.a.
Defence Expenditures: n.a.
External Debt: $61 million (1992)
Exports: vehicles, household appliances, electric power
Imports: n.a.

■ HEALTH

Births: 12/1,000 population (1993)
Deaths: 14/1,000 population (1993)
Infant Mortality: 17/1,000 live births (1993)
Life Expectancy at Birth: 64 years male, 75 years female (1993)
No. of Physicians: n.a.

■ EDUCATION

Govt. Expenditure: n.a.
Literacy: 100% (1993)

■ COMMUNICATIONS

Daily newspapers: 121 papers of all circulation types (1988)
Televisions: n.a.
Radios: n.a.
Telephones: n.a.

■ TRANSPORTATION

Motor Vehicles: n.a.
Roads: 59,500 total; 33,000 km hard-surfaced (1993)
Railway: 2,400 km, which does not include industrial lines (1990)
Air Traffic: n.a.
Airports: 50 airfields, of which 15 are usable; 11 have permanent-surface runways (1993)

Canadian Embassy: c/o The Canadian Embassy, Elizabetes 45-47, Riga LV 1010. Tel: (011-371-88) 301-41. Fax: (011-371-88) 301-40.
Representative to Canada: Consulate General, 230 Clemow Ave, Ottawa, ON K1S 2B6. Tel: (613) 238-6868. Fax: (613) 238-7044.

Lebanon

Long-Form Name: Republic of Lebanon
Capital: Beirut
Population: 3,600,000 (1993 est.)

■ GEOGRAPHY

Area: 10,400 sq. km
Coastline: 225 km
Climate: Mediterranean; mild to cool, wet winters with hot, dry summers
Environment: rugged terrain historically helped isolate, protect and develop numerous factional groups based on religion, clan, and ethnicity; deforestation; soil erosion; air and water pollution; desertification
Terrain: narrow coastal plain; al Biqa' separates Lebanon and Anti-Lebanon Mountains
Land Use: 21% arable; 9% permanent; 1% meadow; 8% forest; 61% other
Location: SW Asia (Middle East), bordering on Mediterranean Sea

■ PEOPLE

Nationality: Lebanese
Ethnic Groups: 95% Arab, 4% Armenian, 1% other
Languages: Arabic and French (both official); Armenian, English, Kurdish
Religions: Islam 70% (Sunni, Shia and Druse), Christian 30% (mainly Maronite; also, Armenian, Greek and Syrian sects and Protestants)
Marriages: n.a.
Divorces: n.a.

■ GOVERNMENT

Leader(s): Pres. Elias Hrawi, Prime. Min. Rafiq al-Hariri
Government Type: republic
Administrative Divisions: 5 governorates
Independence: Nov. 22, 1943 (from League of Nations mandate under French administration)
National Holiday: Independence Day, Nov. 22

■ ECONOMY

Overview: factional infighting has led to deterioration of the infrastructure and disrupted normal economic activity in what used to be the centre for Middle Eastern banking; high unemployment; growing shortages; international aid is vital
GNP: n.a., GDP $4.8 billion, per capita $1,400 (1991 est.)
Inflation: 100% (1992 est.)
Industries: banking, food processing, textiles, cement, oil refining, chemicals, jewelry, some metal fabricating
Labour Force: 914,000 (1992); 27.4% industry, 58.4% services, 14.3% agriculture (1989)
Unemployment: 35% (1991 est.)
Agriculture: accounts for about one-third of GDP; principal products—citrus fruit, vegeta-

bles, potatoes, olives, tobacco, hemp (hashish), sheep and goats; not self-sufficient in grain
Natural Resources: limestone, iron ore, salt; water-surplus state in a water-deficit region

■ FINANCE/TRADE

Currency: Lebanese pound (LL)
International Reserves Excluding Gold: $2,260 million (Dec. 1993)
Gold Reserves: 9.22 million fine troy ounces (Dec. 1993)
Budget: revenues $533 million; expenditures $1.3 billion, including capital expenditures (1991 est.)
Defence Expenditures: $271 million (1992 budget)
External Debt: $1.81 billion (1992)
Exports: $490 million (1991); commodities: agricultural products, chemicals, textiles, metals and jewelry; partners: 21% Saudi Arabia, 9.5% Switzerland, 6% Jordan, 12% Kuwait, 5% US
Imports: $3.7 billion (1991); commodities: consumer goods, machinery and transport equipment, petroleum products; partners: 14% Italy, 12% France, 6% US, 5% Turkey, 3% Saudi Arabia

■ HEALTH

Births: 28/1,000 population (1993)
Deaths: 7/1,000 population (1993)
Infant Mortality: 46 deaths/1,000 live births (1993)
Life Expectancy at Birth: 66 years male, 70 years female (1993)
No. of Physicians: 14.9/10,000 population (1990)

■ EDUCATION

Govt. Expenditure: 8.5% of government expenditure (1988)
Literacy: 80.1% (1993)

■ COMMUNICATIONS

Daily newspapers: 10 (1992)
Televisions: 326.5/1,000 inhabitants (1992)
Radios: 834/1,000 inhabitants (1992)
Telephones: 9.5/100 inhabitants (1993)

■ TRANSPORTATION

Motor Vehicles: 300,000 passenger cars (1985)
Roads: 7,300 km; 6,200 km paved
Railway: 226 km; railroad system in disrepair, considered inoperable
Air Traffic: 536,000 passengers carried (1991)
Airports: 9 airfields, of which 8 are usable; 6 have permanent-surface runways (1993)

Canadian Embassy: c/o The Canadian Embassy, P.O. Box 3394, Damascus, Syria. Tel: (011-963-11) 2236-851. Fax: (011-963-11) 2228-034.
Representative to Canada: Embassy of the Lebanese Republic, 640 Lyon St S, Ottawa ON K1S 3Z5. Tel: (613) 236-5825. Fax: (613) 232-1609.

Lesotho

Long-Form Name: Kingdom of Lesotho
Capital: Maseru
Population: 1,900,000 (1993 est.)

■ GEOGRAPHY

Area: 30,350 sq. km
Coastline: none: landlocked
Climate: temperate; cool to cold, dry winters; hot, wet summers
Environment: population pressure forcing settlement in marginal agricultural areas results in overgrazing, severe soil erosion, soil exhaustion; desertification
Terrain: mostly highland with some plateaus, hills and mountains
Land Use: 10% arable; 0% permanent; 66% meadows; 0% forest; 24% other
Location: S Africa

■ PEOPLE

Nationality: Mosotho/Basotho (pl.)
Ethnic Groups: 99.7% Sotho; 1,600 Europeans, 800 Asians
Languages: Sesotho (southern Sotho) and English (official); also Zulu and Xhosa
Religions: 80% Christian, indigenous beliefs
Marriages: n.a.
Divorces: n.a.

■ GOVERNMENT

Leader(s): King Letsie III, Prime Min. Ntsu Mokhele
Government Type: constitutional monarchy
Administrative Divisions: 10 districts
Independence: Oct. 4, 1966 (from UK: formerly known as Basutoland)
National Holiday: Independence Day, Oct. 4

■ ECONOMY

Overview: the economy is hampered by the geography of the country (small, landlocked and mountainous) and the lack of natural resources other than water; subsistence farming is the main occupation; labourers in South Africa make remittances
GNP: $1.053 billion, per capita $580; real growth rate 2.7% (1991)

Inflation: 15% (1989)
Industries: light manufacturing, milling, canning, leather, jute production, textiles, clothing, light engineering, food, beverages, handicrafts, tourism
Labour Force: 810,000 (1992); 23.3% agriculture, 33.1% industry, 43.6% services (1989)
Unemployment: 55+% (1991 est.)
Agriculture: accounts for 19% of GDP; very primitive, mostly subsistence farming and livestock; principal crops are corn, wheat, pulses, sorghum and barley
Natural Resources: some diamonds and other minerals, water, agricultural and grazing land

■ FINANCE/TRADE

Currency: loti, maloti (pl.)
International Reserves Excluding Gold: $260 million (Nov. 1993)
Gold Reserves: n.a.
Budget: revenues $388 million; expenditures $399 million, including capital expenditures of $132 million (1993)
Defence Expenditures: 6.47% of total govt. expenditures (1991)
External Debt: $472 million (1992)
Exports: $57 million (1991); commodities: wool, mohair, wheat, cattle, peas, beans, corn, hides, skins, baskets; partners: South Africa 53%, European Community 30%, North and South America 13%
Imports: $805 million (1991); commodities: corn, building materials, clothing, vehicles, machinery, medicines, petroleum, oil and lubricants; partners: South Africa 95%, European Community 2%

■ HEALTH

Births: 35/1,000 population (1993)
Deaths: 10/1,000 population (1993)
Infant Mortality: 84 deaths/1,000 live births (1993)
Life Expectancy at Birth: 57 years male, 62 years female (1993)
No. of Physicians: 0.5/10,000 population (1992)

■ EDUCATION

Govt. Expenditure: 21.93% of government expenditure (1991)
Literacy: 59% (1993)

■ COMMUNICATIONS

Daily newspapers: 4 (1992)
Televisions: 2.9/1,000 inhabitants (1992)
Radios: 68/1,000 inhabitants (1992)
Telephones: 0.9/100 inhabitants (1992)

■ TRANSPORTATION

Motor Vehicles: 6,700 passenger cars (1986)
Roads: 7,215 km; 572 km paved
Railway: 3 km, owned, operated by, and included in the statistics for South Africa
Air Traffic: 56,000 passengers carried (1991)
Airports: 28 airfields, all usable; 3 have permanent-surface runways (1993)

Canadian Embassy: c/o Canadian Embassy, mailing address: P.O. Box 26006, Arcadia, Pretoria 0007, South Africa. Tel: (011-27-12) 324-3970. Fax (011-27-12) 323-1564
Representative to Canada: High Commission for the Kingdom of Lesotho, 202 Clemow Ave, Ottawa ON K1S 2B4. Tel: (613) 236-9449. Fax: (613) 238-3341.

Liberia

Long-Form Name: Republic of Liberia
Capital: Monrovia
Population: 2,800,000 (1993 est.)

■ GEOGRAPHY

Area: 111,370 sq. km
Coastline: 579 km
Climate: tropical; hot, humid; dry winters with hot days and cool to cold nights; wet, cloudy summers with frequent heavy showers
Environment: West Africa's largest tropical rain forest, subject to deforestation
Terrain: mostly flat to rolling coastal plains rising to rolling plateau and low mountains in northeast
Land Use: 1% arable; 3% permanent; 2% meadows; 39% forest; 55% other
Location: WC Africa, bordering on South Atlantic Ocean

■ PEOPLE

Nationality: Liberian
Ethnic Groups: 95% indigenous African tribes, including Kpelle, Bassa, Gio, Kru, Grego, Mano, Krahn, Gola, Gbandi, Lom, Kissi, Vai and Bella; 5% descendants of repatriated slaves known as Americo-Liberians
Languages: English (official); 20 local languages of the Niger-Congo language group; English used by approx. 20%
Religions: 70% traditional, 20% Moslem, 10% Christian
Marriages: n.a.
Divorces: n.a.

■ GOVERNMENT

Leader(s): David Kpormakpor is leader of the new transitional government, the Council of State, established March 7, 1994
Government Type: republic
Administrative Divisions: 13 counties
Independence: July 26, 1847
National Holiday: Independence Day, July 26

■ ECONOMY

Overview: Since 1990, civil war has destroyed much of Liberia's economy, especially the infrastructure in and around Monrovia; the flight of businessmen has caused a capital and brain drain, and stability is not likely to return until the civil conflict has been settled
GNP: $988 million, per capita $395; real growth rate 1.5% (1988)
Inflation: 9.1% (1989)
Industries: rubber processing, food processing, construction materials, furniture, palm oil processing, mining (iron ore, diamonds)
Labour Force: 910,000 (1992); 74.2% agriculture, 16.4% services, 9.4% industry (1989)
Unemployment: 43% urban (1988)
Agriculture: accounts for 40% of GDP (including fishing and forestry); principal products—rubber, timber, coffee, cocoa, rice, cassava, palm oil, sugar cane, bananas, sheep and goats; not self-sufficient in food, imports 25% of rice consumption
Natural Resources: iron ore, timber, diamonds, goldi

■ FINANCE/TRADE

Currency: Liberian dollar ($L)
International Reserves Excluding Gold: $6 million (1989)
Gold Reserves: n.a.
Budget: revenues $242.1 million; expenditures $435.4 million, including capital expenditures of $29.5 million (1989)
Defence Expenditures: $28.07 million (9.35% of total govt. expenditure) (1988)
External Debt: $1.952 billion (1992)
Exports: $550 million (1989); commodities: iron ore 61%, rubber 20%, timber 11%, coffee; partners: US, European Community, Netherlands
Imports: $335 million (1989); commodities: rice, mineral fuels, chemicals, machinery, transportation equipment, other foodstuffs; partners: US, European Community, Japan, China, Netherlands and ECOWAS

■ HEALTH

Births: 47/1,000 population (1993)
Deaths: 15/1,000 population (1993)

Infant Mortality: 134 deaths/1,000 live births (1993)
Life Expectancy at Birth: 53 years male, 56 years female (1993)
No. of Physicians: 1.1/10,000 population (1990)

■ EDUCATION

Govt. Expenditure: 11.04% of govt. expenditure (1988)
Literacy: 39.5% (1993)

■ COMMUNICATIONS

Daily newspapers: 7 (1992)
Televisions: 18/1,000 inhabitants (1992)
Radios: 225/1,000 inhabitants (1992)
Telephones: n.a.

■ TRANSPORTATION

Motor Vehicles: 12,000; 8,000 passenger cars (1990)
Roads: 10,087 km; 603 km paved
Railway: 480 km (1993)
Air Traffic: 32,000 passengers carried (1991)
Airports: 59 airfields, of which 41 are usable; 2 have permanent-surface runways (1993)

Canadian Embassy: c/o Canadian High Commission, 42 Independence Ave, Accra; mailing address: P.O. Box 1639, Accra, Ghana. Tel: (011-233-21) 77-37-91. Fax: (011-233-21) 77-37-92
Representative to Canada: Embassy of the Republic of Liberia, Royal Trust Building, 160 Elgin St, Ste 2600, Ottawa ON K1N 8S3. Tel: (613) 232-1781. Fax: (613) 563-9869.

Libya

Long-Form Name: Socialist People's Libyan Arab Jamahiriya
Capital: Tripoli
Population: 4,900,000 (1993 est.)

■ GEOGRAPHY

Area: 1,759,540 sq. km
Coastline: 1,770 km
Climate: Mediterranean along coast; dry, extreme desert interior
Environment: hot, dry, dust-laden ghibli is a southern wind lasting one to four days in spring and fall; desertification; sparse natural surface-water resources
Terrain: mostly barren, flat to undulating plains, plateaus, depressions
Land Use: 2% arable; 0% permanent; 8% meadows; 0% forest; 90% other

Location: N Africa, bordering on Mediterranean Sea

■ PEOPLE

Nationality: Libyan
Ethnic Groups: 97% Berber and Arab; some Greeks, Maltese, Italians, Egyptians, Pakistanis, Turks, Indians and Tunisians
Languages: Arabic (official); Italian and English widely understood in major cities, Berber
Religions: 97% Sunni Moslem, 2.5% Christian
Marriages: 4.5 (per 1,000) (1988)
Divorces: 0.6 (per 1,000) (1988)

■ GOVERNMENT

Leader(s): Col. Mu'ammar Abu Minyar al-Qadhafi (de facto chief of state)
Government Type: Jamahiriya (a state of the masses); in theory, governed by the populace through local councils; in fact, a military dictatorship
Administrative Divisions: 25 municipalities
Independence: Dec. 24, 1951 (from Italy)
National Holiday: Revolution Day, Sept. 1

■ ECONOMY

Overview: a socialist-oriented economy depends largely on revenues from the oil sector; cutbacks on imports due to declining oil revenues have led to shortages of foodstuffs and basic goods; must import 75% of its food needs
GNP: n.a., GDP $26.1 billion, per capita $5,800; real growth rate 0.2% (1992 est.)
Inflation: 7% (1991 est.)
Industries: petroleum, food processing, textiles, handicrafts, cement
Labour Force: 1,076,000 (1992); 28.9% industry, 53% services, 18.1% agriculture (1989)
Unemployment: 2% (1988 est.)
Agriculture: accounts for 5% of GNP; cash crops— wheat, barley, olives, dates, citrus fruit, peanuts; 75% of food is imported
Natural Resources: crude oil, natural gas, gypsum

■ FINANCE/TRADE

Currency: Libyan dinar (LD)
International Reserves Excluding Gold: 5,886 million (June 1993)
Gold Reserves: 3.6 million fine troy ounces (1992)
Budget: revenues $8.1 billion; expenditures $9.8 billion, including capital expenditures of $3.1 billion (1989)
Defence Expenditures: $1.51 billion (1989)
External Debt: $3.5 billion (1991)
Exports: $11.212 billion (1991); commodities:

petroleum, peanuts, hides; partners: Italy, USSR, Germany, Spain, France, Belgium/Luxembourg, Turkey
Imports: $5.358 billion (1991); commodities: machinery, transport equipment, food, manufactured goods; partners: Italy, USSR, Germany, UK, Japan

■ HEALTH

Births: 42/1,000 population (1993)
Deaths: 8/1,000 population (1993)
Infant Mortality: 68 deaths/1,000 live births (1993)
Life Expectancy at Birth: 62 years male, 66 years female (1993)
No. of Physicians: 14.4/10,000 population (1990)

■ EDUCATION

Govt. Expenditure: 20.8% of govt. expenditure (1986)
Literacy: 63.8% (1993)

■ COMMUNICATIONS

Daily newspapers: 1 (1992)
Televisions: 91.3/1,000 inhabitants (1992)
Radios: 224/1,000 inhabitants (1992)
Telephones: 13.19/100 inhabitants (1992)

■ TRANSPORTATION

Motor Vehicles: 775,000; 450,000 passenger cars (1990)
Roads: 19,300 km; 10,800 km paved (1993)
Railway: no railroads in operation since 1965
Air Traffic: 1,884,000 passengers carried (1991)
Airports: 138 airfields, of which 124 are usable; 56 have permanent-surface runways (1993)

Canadian Embassy: c/o Canadian Embassy, 3 rue du Sénégal, Place d'Afrique, Tunis; mailing address: CP 31, Le Belvédère, 1002, Tunis, Tunisia. Tel: (011-216-1) 798-004. Fax: (011-216-1) 792-371
Representative to Canada: c/o Permanent Mission of Socialist People's Libyan Arab Jamahiriya to the UN, 309–315 St. East 48th St, New York, New York 10017 USA. Tel: (212) 752-5775. Fax: (212) 593-4787.

Liechtenstein

Long-Form Name: Principality of Liechtenstein
Capital: Vaduz
Population: 30,000 (1993 est.)

■ GEOGRAPHY

Area: 160 sq. km
Coastline: none: landlocked

Climate: continental; cold, cloudy winters with frequent snow or rain; cool to moderately warm, cloudy, humid summers
Environment: variety of microclimatic variations based on elevation
Terrain: mostly mountainous (Alps) with Rhine Valley in western third
Land Use: 25% arable; 0% permanent; 38% meadows; 19% forest; 18% other
Location: W Europe

■ **PEOPLE**

Nationality: Liechtensteiner
Ethnic Groups: 95% Alemannic, 5% Italian and other
Languages: German (official), also Alemannic dialect
Religions: 87% Roman Catholic, 8.3% Protestant, 2.8% other, 1.6% unknown
Marriages: 11.3 (per 1,000) (1989)

■ **GOVERNMENT**

Leader(s): Prime Min. Mario Frick, Head of State Prince Hans Adam von und zu Liechtenstein II
Government Type: hereditary constitutional monarchy
Administrative Divisions: 11 communes
Independence: Jan. 23, 1719, Imperial Principality of Liechtenstein established
National Holiday: Assumption Day, Aug. 15

■ **ECONOMY**

Overview: a prosperous economy based mainly on small-scale light industry and some farming; economy closely tied to that of Switzerland in a customs union; known for low business taxes and easy incorporation rules
GNP: n.a., GDP $630 million, $22,300 per capita; real growth rate n.a. (1990 est.)
Inflation: 5.4% (1990)
Industries: electronics, metal manufacturing, textiles, ceramics, pharmaceuticals, food products, precision instruments, tourism
Labour Force: 19,905, of which 11,933 are foreigners; 54% industry, trade and building, 42% services, 4% agriculture, fishing, forestry and horticulture
Unemployment: 1.5% (1990)
Agriculture: livestock, vegetables, corn, wheat, potatoes, grapes
Natural Resources: hydroelectric potential

■ **FINANCE/TRADE**

Currency: Swiss franc (SwF)
Budget: revenues $259 million; expenditures $292 million, including capital expenditures (1990)
Exports: $1.6 billion (1990); commodities: small specialty machinery, dental products, stamps, hardware, pottery; partners: European Community 40%, EFTA 26% (Switzerland 19%)
Imports: n.a.; commodities: machinery, metal goods, textiles, foodstuffs, motor vehicles; partners: n.a.

■ **HEALTH**

Births: 14/1,000 population (1993)
Deaths: 6/1,000 population (1993)
Infant Mortality: 5 deaths/1,000 live births (1991)
Life Expectancy at Birth: 66 years male, 73 years female (1993)

■ **EDUCATION**

Literacy: 99.7% (1992)

■ **COMMUNICATIONS**

Daily newspapers: 2 (1992)
Televisions: 342.9/1,000 inhabitants (1992)
Radios: 718/1,000 inhabitants (1992)
Telephones: 25,400 total (1993)

■ **TRANSPORTATION**

Roads: 130.66 km
Railway: 18.5 km

Lithuania

Long-Form Name: Republic of Lithuania
Capital: Vilnius
Population: 3,800,000 (1993 est.)

■ **GEOGRAPHY**

Area: 65,200 sq. km
Coastline: 108 km
Climate: mild, with moderate precipitation
Environment: risk of accidents from the two Chernobyl-type reactors; at military bases, contamination of soil and ground water with chemicals and petroleum products
Terrain: undulating glacial terrain; rivers, lakes, and swamps predominate
Land Use: 49.1% arable, negligible permanent crops, 22.2% meadows and pastures, 16.3% forest, 12.4% other
Location: NE Europe, bordering on Baltic Sea

■ **PEOPLE**

Nationality: Lithuanian
Ethnic Groups: 80.1% Lithuanian, 8.6% Russian, 7.7% Polish, 1.5% Byelorussian, 2.1% other
Languages: Lithuanian (official), Russian, Polish
Religions: predominantly Protestant, Roman

Catholic, Russian Orthodox
Marriages: 9.2 (per 1,000) (1991)
Divorces: 3.33 (per 1,000) (1989)

■ GOVERNMENT

Leader(s): Pres. Algirdas Brazauskas, Prime Min. Adolfas Slezevicius
Government Type: republic
Administrative Divisions: districts, number n.a.
Independence: Sept. 6, 1991 (from Soviet Union)
National Holiday: Independence Day, Feb. 16

■ ECONOMY

Overview: arable land and strategic location are Lithuania's only important natural resources; Lithuania remains highly dependent on Russia for energy, raw materials, grains, and markets for its products; industrial activity accounts for 65% of economic output; agriculture makes up only 20%
GNP: $10.220 billion, $2,710 per capita; real growth rate for 1992 -30%
Inflation: 10-20% per month (1993)
Industries: employs 25% of labour force; heavy engineering, shipbuilding, production of building materials, nuclear and electric power production; electric motors, television sets, appliances, refining, fertilizer
Labour Force: 1,836,000; 42% industry and construction, 18% agriculture and forestry, 40% other (1990)
Unemployment: 1% (1993); large numbers of underemployed
Agriculture: employs approximately 20% of labour force; beef and dairy cattle and related products, pigs, poultry, grains, flax, potatoes, and other vegetables, eggs, fish, dairy products; net exporter of meat, milk, and eggs
Natural Resources: amber, oil reserves, peat

■ FINANCE/TRADE

Currency: using talonas as temporary currency, but planning introduction of convertible litas
International Reserves Excluding Gold: n.a.
Gold Reserves: n.a.
Budget: revenues $258.5 million, expenditures $270.2 million, including capital expenditures (1992 est.)
Defence Expenditures: 5.5% of GDP (1993 est.)
External Debt: $38 million (1992)
Exports: $n.a.; 18% electronics, 5% petroleum products, 10% food, 6% chemicals; partners: 40% Russia, 16% Ukraine, 32% other former Soviet republics, 12% West (1989)
Imports: $n.a.; 24% oil, 14% machinery, 8% chemicals, grain; partners: 62% Russia, 18%

Belarus, 10% other former Soviet republics, 10% West (1989)

■ HEALTH

Births: 15/1,000 population (1993)
Deaths: 11/1,000 population (1993)
Infant Mortality: 14/1,000 live births (1993)
Life Expectancy at Birth: 65 years male, 76 years female (1993)
No. of Physicians: n.a.

■ EDUCATION

Govt. Expenditure: n.a.
Literacy: 100% (1993)

■ COMMUNICATIONS

Daily newspapers: 147 papers of all circulation types (1988)
Televisions: n.a.; 3 TV stations (1993)
Radios: n.a.; 41 radio stations (1993)
Telephones: 22.4/100 inhabitants (1993)

■ TRANSPORTATION

Motor Vehicles: n.a.
Roads: 44,200 km; 35,500 km hard-surfaced (1993)
Railway: 2,100 km, not including industrial lines (1990)
Air Traffic: n.a.
Airports: 96 airfields, of which 19 are usable; 12 have permanent-surface runways (1993)

Canadian Embassy: c/o The Canadian Embassy, Elizabetes 45-47, Riga LV 1010. Tel: (011-371-88) 301-41. Fax: (011-371-88) 301-40.
Representative to Canada: Consulate General, 235 Yorkland Blvd., Willowdale, ON M2J 4Y8. Tel: (416) 494-8313. Fax: (416) 494-4382.

Lithuania

Long-Form Name: Republic of Lithuania
Capital: Vilnius
Population: 3,800,000 (1993 est.)

■ GEOGRAPHY

Area: 65,200 sq. km
Coastline: 108 km
Climate: mild, with moderate precipitation
Environment: risk of accidents from the two Chernobyl-like reactors; at military bases, contamination of soil and ground water with chemicals and petroleum products
Terrain: undulating glacial terrain; rivers, lakes, and swamps predominate
Land Use: 49.1% arable, negligible permanent crops, 22.2% meadows and pastures, 16.3% for-

est, 12.4% other
Location: NE Europe, bordering on Baltic Sea

■ PEOPLE

Nationality: Lithuanian
Ethnic Groups: 80.1% Lithuanian, 8.6% Russian, 7.7% Poles, 1.5% Byelorussian, 2.1% other
Languages: Lithuanian (official), Russian, Polish
Religions: predominantly Protestant, Roman Catholic, Russian Orthodox
Marriages: 9.2 (per 1,000) (1991)
Divorces: 3.33 (per 1,000) (1989)

■ GOVERNMENT

Leader(s): Pres. Algirdas Brazauskas, Prime Min. Adolfas Slezevicius
Government Type: republic
Administrative Divisions: districts, number n.a.
Independence: Sept. 6, 1991 (from Soviet Union)
National Holiday: Independence Day, Feb. 16

■ ECONOMY

Overview: arable land and strategic location are Lithuania's only important natural resources; Lithuania remains highly dependent on Russia for energy, raw materials, grains, and markets for its products; industrial activity accounts for 65% of economic output; agriculture makes up only 20%
GNP: $10.220 billion, $2,710 per capita; real growth rate for 1992 15-30%
Inflation: 10-20% per month (1993)
Industries: employs 25% of labour force; heavy engineering, shipbuilding, production of building materials, nuclear and electric power production; electric motors, television sets, appliances, refining, fertilizer
Labour Force: 1,836,000; 42% industry and construction, 18% agriculture and forestry, 40% other (1990)
Unemployment: 1% (1993); large numbers of underemployed
Agriculture: employs approximately 20% of labour force; beef and dairy cattle and related products, pigs, poultry, grains, flax, potatoes, and other vegetables, eggs, fish, dairy products; net exporter of meat, milk, and eggs
Natural Resources: amber, oil reserves, peat

■ FINANCE/TRADE

Currency: using talonas as temporary currency, but planning introduction of convertible litas
International Reserves Excluding Gold: n.a.
Gold Reserves: n.a.
Budget: revenues $258.5 million, expenditures $270.2 million, including capital expenditures

(1992 est.)
Defence Expenditures: 5.5% of GDP (1993 est.)
External Debt: $38 million (1992)
Exports: $n.a.; 18% electronics, 5% petroleum products, 10% food, 6% chemicals; partners: 40% Russia, 16% Ukraine, 32% other former Soviet republics, 12% West (1989)
Imports: $n.a.; 24% oil, 14% machinery, 8% chemicals, grain; partners: 62% Russia, 18% Belarus, 10% other former Soviet republics, 10% West (1989)

■ HEALTH

Births: 15/1,000 population (1993)
Deaths: 11/1,000 population (1993)
Infant Mortality: 14/1,000 live births (1993)
Life Expectancy at Birth: 65 years male, 76 years female (1993)
No. of Physicians: n.a.

■ EDUCATION

Govt. Expenditure: n.a.
Literacy: 100% (1993)

■ COMMUNICATIONS

Daily newspapers: 147 papers of all circulation types (1988)
Televisions: n.a.; 3 TV stations (1993)
Radios: n.a.; 41 radio stations (1993)
Telephones: 22.4/100 inhabitants (1993)

■ TRANSPORTATION

Motor Vehicles: n.a.
Roads: 44,200 km; 35,500 km hard-surfaced (1993)
Railway: 2,100 km, not including industrial lines (1990)
Air Traffic: n.a.
Airports: 96 airfields, of which 19 are usable; 12 have permanent-surface runways (1993)

Canadian Embassy: c/o The Canadian Embassy, Tegelbacken 4 (Flr 7); mailing address: P.O. Box 16129; S-103 23 Stockholm 5, Sweden. Tel: (011-46-8) 613-9900. Fax: (011-46-8) 24 24 91.
Representative to Canada: Consulate General, 235 Yorkland Blvd., Ste 502, Willowdale, ON M2J 4Y8. Tel: (416) 494-8313.

Luxembourg

Long-Form Name: Grand Duchy of Luxembourg
Capital: Luxembourg
Population: 400,000 (1993 est.)

■ GEOGRAPHY

Area: 2,586 sq. km
Coastline: none: landlocked
Climate: modified continental with mild winters, cool summers
Environment: deforestation
Terrain: mostly gently rolling uplands with broad, shallow valleys; uplands to slightly mountainous in the north; steep slope down to Moselle floodplain in the southeast
Land Use: 24% arable; 1% permanent; 20% meadows; 21% forest; 34% other
Location: NW Europe

■ PEOPLE

Nationality: Luxembourger
Ethnic Groups: Celtic base, with French and German blend; also guest and worker residents
Languages: Luxembourgisch (official), German (written language of commerce and press), French (administrative), English
Religions: 97% Roman Catholic, 3% Protestant and Jewish
Marriages: 6.2 (per 1,000) (1990)
Divorces: 2.27 (per 1,000) (1989)

■ GOVERNMENT

Leader(s): Prime Min. Jacques Santer, Head of State, Jean, Grand Duke of Luxembourg
Government Type: constitutional monarchy
Administrative Divisions: 3 districts
Independence: 1839 (Grand Duchy)
National Holiday: National Day (public celebration of the Grand Duke's birthday), June 23

■ ECONOMY

Overview: a stable economy featuring moderate growth, low inflation and negligible unemployment; is in an economic union with Belgium for trade and most financial matters and is also closely connected economically with the Netherlands; financial sector is strong; industrial sector is becoming increasingly diversified
GNP: $8.5 billion, per capita $21,700; real growth rate 2.5% (1992)
Inflation: 3.2% (1992)
Industries: banking, iron and steel, food processing, chemicals, metal products, engineering, tires, glass, aluminum
Labour Force: 155,000 (1992); 77.2% services, 19.1% industry, 3.7% agriculture (1989)
Unemployment: 1.4% (1991)
Agriculture: accounts for less than 3% of GDP (including forestry); principal products—barley, oats, potatoes, wheat, fruits, wine grapes; cattle-raising widespread
Natural Resources: iron ore (no longer exploited)

■ FINANCE/TRADE

Currency: Luxembourg franc (LuxF)
International Reserves Excluding Gold: n.a.
Gold Reserves: 0.31 million fine troy ounces (Oct. 1993)
Budget: revenues $2.5 billion; expenditures $2.3 billion, including capital expenditures (1988)
Defence Expenditures: $100.23 million (1990)
External Debt: $131.6 million (1989)
Exports: $6.4 billion (1991 est.); commodities: finished steel products, chemicals, rubber products, glass, aluminum, other industrial products; partners: European Community 75%, US 6%
Imports: $8.3 billion (1991); commodities: minerals, metals, foodstuffs, quality consumer goods; partners: Germany 40%, Belgium 35%, France 15%, US 3%

■ HEALTH

Births: 13/1,000 population (1993)
Deaths: 10/1,000 population (1993)
Infant Mortality: 9.2 deaths/1,000 live births (1993)
Life Expectancy at Birth: 72 years male, 79 years female (1993)
No. of Physicians: 18.1/10,000 population (1992)

■ EDUCATION

Govt. Expenditure: 9.96% of govt. expenditure (1990)
Literacy: 100% (1993)

■ COMMUNICATIONS

Daily newspapers: 5 (1992)
Televisions: 252.0/1,000 inhabitants (1992)
Radios: 623/1,000 inhabitants (1992)
Telephones: 50/100 inhabitants (1980)

■ TRANSPORTATION

Motor Vehicles: 211,123; 191,588 passenger cars (1990)
Roads: 5,100 km; 4,995 km paved
Railway: 273 km
Air Traffic: 406,000 passengers carried (1991)
Airports: 2 airfields, both usable; 1 has a permanent-surface runway (1993)

Canadian Embassy: c/o 2, Avenue de Tervuren, 1040 Brussels, Belgium. Tel: (011-32-2) 735-6040. Fax: (011-32-2) 735-3383
Representative to Canada: c/o Embassy of the Grand Duchy of Luxembourg, 2200 Massachusetts Ave NW, Washington DC 20008

USA. Tel: (202) 265-4171. Fax: (202) 328-8270.

Macau

Dependent Territory of Portugal

Long-Form Name: Macau
Capital: Macau
Population: 492,000 (1992)

■ GEOGRAPHY

Area: 16 km (a peninsula and three small islands)
Climate: subtropical maritime; marine with cool winters, warm summers
Land Use: almost 100% built-up; almost no agricultural lands or fresh water resources
Location: SE coast of China, bordering on South China Sea

■ PEOPLE

Nationality: Macanese
Ethnic Groups: Chinese 95%, Portuguese 3%, other 2%
Languages: Portuguese (official), Cantonese, English widely spoken

■ GOVERNMENT

Leader(s): Head of State Mario Soares (Pres. of Portugal), Gov. Gen. Vasco Rocha Vieira
Government Type: overseas territory of Portugal scheduled to revert to China in 1999
National Holiday: Day of Portugal, June 10

■ ECONOMY

Overview: gambling and tourism; industry confined to textiles, fireworks, toy-making, plastics; imports almost all energy, food and water from China

■ FINANCE/TRADE

Currency: pataca (pl. patacas)

Macedonia

Long-Form Name: Republic of Macedonia
Capital: Skopje
Population: 2,193,951 (1993 est.)

■ GEOGRAPHY

Area: 25,333 sq. km
Coastline: none: landlocked
Climate: hot, dry summers and autumns; winters relatively cold with heavy snowfall

Environment: high earthquake hazard; air pollution
Terrain: mountainous, with deep valleys and basins; three large lakes
Land Use: 5% arable land, 5% permanent crops, 20% meadows and pastures, 30% forests, 40% other
Location: S Europe

■ PEOPLE

Nationality: Macedonian
Ethnic Groups: 67% Macedonian, 21% Albanian, 4% Turkish, 2% Serb, 6% other
Languages: 70% Macedonian, 21% Albanian, 3% Turkish, 2% Serbo-Croatian, 3% other
Religions: 59% Eastern Orthodox, 26% Muslim, 4% Catholic, 1% Protestant, 10% other
Marriages: n.a.
Divorces: n.a.

■ GOVERNMENT

Leader(s): Pres. Kiro Gligorov, Prime Min. Branko Crvenkovski
Government Type: emerging democracy
Administrative Divisions: 34 districts
Independence: Nov. 20, 1991 (from Yugoslavia)
National Holiday: n.a.

■ ECONOMY

Overview: although it is the poorest of the six republics of the dissolved Yugoslav federation, Macedonia can meet its basic food requirements; new economic ties are necessary, however, to keep living standards from falling to a bare subsistence level; all oil, gas, modern machinery and parts must be imported; continued political upheaval prevents return to settled economic conditions
GNP: n.a., GDP $7.1 billion, $3,110 per capita; real growth rate -18% (1991 est.)
Inflation: 114.9% (1991 est.)
Industries: level of technology is generally low; basic liquid fuels, coal, metallic chromium, lead, zinc; Macedonia is one of the seven legal cultivators of the opium poppy for the world pharmaceutical industry
Labour Force: 507,324 (1990); 8% agriculture, 40% manufacturing and mining
Unemployment: 20% (1991 est.)
Agriculture: highly labour-intensive
Natural Resources: chromium, lead, zinc, manganese, tungsten, nickel, timber

■ FINANCE/TRADE

Currency: denar
International Reserves Excluding Gold: n.a.
Gold Reserves: n.a.

Budget: n.a.
Defence Expenditures: n.a.
External Debt: $845.8 million (1993)
Exports: $578 million (1990); manufactured goods, machinery and transportation equipment, raw materials, food and livestock, tobacco and beverages, chemicals; partners: mostly the former Yugoslav republics, Germany, Albania, Greece
Imports: $1,112 million (1990); fuel and lubricants, machinery and transport equipment, food and livestock, chemicals, raw materials, manufactures; partners: other former Yugoslav republics, Germany, Albania, Greece, Bulgaria

■ HEALTH

Births: 17/1,000 population (1993)
Deaths: 7/1,000 population (1993)
Infant Mortality: 35.3 deaths/1,000 live births (1993)
Life Expectancy at Birth: 70 years male, 73 years female (1993)
No. of Physicians: n.a.

■ EDUCATION

Govt. Expenditure: n.a.
Literacy: n.a.

■ COMMUNICATIONS

Daily newspapers: n.a.
Televisions: 325,000 total; 5 TV stations (1993)
Radios: 370,000 total; 8 radio stations (1993)
Telephones: 125,000 total (1993)

■ TRANSPORTATION

Motor Vehicles: n.a.
Roads: 10,591; 5,091 km paved (1991)
Railway: n.a.
Air Traffic: n.a.
Airports: 17 airfields, all usable; 9 have permanent-surface runways (1993).

Madagascar

Long-Form Name: Democratic Republic of Madagascar
Capital: Antananarivo
Population: 13,300,000 (1993 est.)

■ GEOGRAPHY

Area: 587,040 sq. km
Coastline: 4,828 km
Climate: tropical along coast, temperate inland, arid in south
Environment: subject to periodic cyclones; deforestation; overgrazing; soil erosion; desertification

Terrain: narrow coastal plain, high plateau and mountains in centre
Land Use: 4% arable; 1% permanent; 58% meadow; 26% forest; 11% other
Location: Indian Ocean, E of Africa

■ PEOPLE

Nationality: Malagasy
Ethnic Groups: basic split between highlanders of predominantly Malayo-Indonesian origin (Merina and Betsileo) and coastal tribes, collectively termed the Côtiers, with mixed African, Malayo-Indonesian and Arab ancestry (Betsimisaraka, Tsimihety, Antaiska, Sakalava)
Languages: French and Malagasy (official)
Religions: 52% indigenous beliefs; approx. 41% Christian, 7% Moslem
Marriages: n.a.
Divorces: n.a.

■ GOVERNMENT

Leader(s): Pres. Albert Zafy, Prime Min. Francisque Ravony
Government Type: republic
Administrative Divisions: 6 provinces
Independence: June 26, 1960 (from France; formerly known as Malagasy Republic)
National Holiday: Independence Day, June 26

■ ECONOMY

Overview: a poor country, hampered by high population growth and a GDP growth rate which is not keeping pace; agriculture is the basis of the economy; industrial development is hurt by government policies restricting imports of equipment and spare parts
GNP: $2.5 billion, per capita $200; real growth rate 1% (1992 est.)
Inflation: 14.5% (1992)
Industries: agricultural processing (meat canneries, soap factories, breweries, tanneries, sugar refining), light consumer goods industries (textiles, glassware), cement, automobile assembly plant, paper, petroleum
Labour Force: 5,000,000 (1992); 80.9% agriculture, 6% industry, 13.2% services (1989)
Unemployment: n.a.
Agriculture: accounts for 31% of GDP; cash crops–coffee, vanilla, sugar cane, cloves, cocoa; food crops—rice, cassava, beans, bananas, peanuts; almost self-sufficient in rice
Natural Resources: graphite, chromite, coal, bauxite, salt, quartz, tar sands, semi-precious stones, mica, fish

■ FINANCE/TRADE

Currency: Malagasy franc (FMG)
International Reserves Excluding Gold: $123 million (1992)
Gold Reserves: n.a.
Budget: revenues $250 million; expenditures $265 million, including capital expenditures of $180 million (1991)
Defence Expenditures: 7.54% of total govt. expenditure (1991)
External Debt: $4.385 billion (1992)
Exports: $267 million (1992); commodities: coffee 45%, vanilla 15%, cloves 11%, sugar, petroleum products; partners: France, Japan, Italy, Germany, US
Imports: $452 million (1992); commodities: intermediate manufactures 30%, capital goods 28%, petroleum 15%, consumer goods 14%, food 13%; partners: France, Germany, UK, other European Community, US

■ HEALTH

Births: 46/1,000 population (1993)
Deaths: 13/1,000 population (1993)
Infant Mortality: 93 deaths/1,000 live births (1993)
Life Expectancy at Birth: 53 years male, 56 years female (1993)
No. of Physicians: 1.0/10,000 population (1992)

■ EDUCATION

Govt. Expenditure: 17.23% of govt. expenditure (1991)
Literacy: 80.2% (1993)

■ COMMUNICATIONS

Daily newspapers: 8 (1992)
Televisions: 19.8/1,000 inhabitants (1992)
Radios: 198/1,000 inhabitants (1992)
Telephones: 0.44/100 inhabitants (1992)

■ TRANSPORTATION

Motor Vehicles: 79,792; 46,636 passenger cars (1990)
Roads: 40,000 km; 4,694 km paved
Railway: 1,057 km
Air Traffic: 315,000 passengers carried (1991)
Airports: 146 airfields, of which 103 are usable; 30 have permanent-surface runways (1993)

Canadian Embassy: The Canadian High Commission, 38 Mirambo St, Dar-es-Salaam; mailing address: P.O. Box 1022, Dar-es-Salaam, Tanzania. Tel: (011-255-51) 46000. Fax: (011-255-51) 46000
Representative to Canada: Embassy of the Democratic Republic of Madagascar, 282 Somerset St W, Ottawa ON K2P 0J6. Tel: (613) 563-2506.Fax: (613) 231-3261.

Malawi

Long-Form Name: Republic of Malawi
Capital: Lilongwe
Population: 9,831,935 (1993 est.)

■ GEOGRAPHY

Area: 118,480 sq. km
Coastline: none: landlocked
Climate: tropical; rainy season (Nov. to May); dry season (May to Nov.)
Environment: deforestation
Terrain: narrow elongated plateau with rolling plains, rounded hills, some mountains
Land Use: 25% arable; negligible permanent; 20% meadows; 50% forest; 5% other
Location: SE Africa

■ PEOPLE

Nationality: Malawian
Ethnic Groups: Chewa, Nyanja, Tumbuko, Yao, Lomwe, Sena, Tonga, Ngoni, Ngonde, Asian, European
Languages: English and Chichewa (official); other languages important regionally
Religions: 55% Protestant, 20% Roman Catholic, 20% Muslim, traditional indigenous beliefs
Marriages: n.a.
Divorces: n.a.

■ GOVERNMENT

Leader(s): Pres. Bakili Muluzi
Government Type: one-party republic
Administrative Divisions: 24 districts
Independence: July 6, 1964 (from UK; formerly known as Nyasaland)
National Holiday: Independence Day, July 6

■ ECONOMY

Overview: the economy is predominantly agricultural, with about 90% of the population living in rural areas; economy depends heavily on foreign aid; drought has adversely affected agriculture
GNP: n.a., GDP $1.9 billion, per capita $200 real growth rate -7.7% (1992 est.)
Inflation: 23.1% (1992)
Industries: agricultural processing (tea, tobacco, sugar), sawmilling, cement, consumer goods
Labour Force: 3,500,000 (1992); 81.8% agriculture, 3% industry, 15.2% services (1989)
Unemployment: n.a.
Agriculture: 40% of GDP; crops: tobacco, sugar

cane, cotton, tea, corn; subsistence crops: cattle and goats
Natural Resources: limestone; unexploited deposits of uranium, coal and bauxite

■ FINANCE/TRADE

Currency: kwacha (K)
International Reserves Excluding Gold: $39 million (Oct. 1993)
Gold Reserves: 0.01 million fine troy ounces (1991)
Budget: revenues $398 million; expenditures $510 million, including capital expenditures of $154 million (1991)
Defence Expenditures: $20.73 million (5.28% of total govt. expenditure) (1988)
External Debt: $1.699 billion (1992)
Exports: $376 million (1992); commodities: tobacco, tea, sugar, coffee, peanuts; partners: US, UK, Zambia, South Africa, Germany
Imports: $699 million (1992); commodities: food, petroleum, semimanufactures, consumer goods, transportation equipment; partners: South Africa, Japan, US, UK, Zimbabwe

■ HEALTH

Births: 53/1,000 population (1993)
Deaths: 19/1,000 population (1993)
Infant Mortality: 138 deaths/1,000 live births (1993)
Life Expectancy at Birth: 46 years male, 49 years female (1993)
No. of Physicians: 0.9/10,000 population (1992)

■ EDUCATION

Govt. Expenditure: 10.3% of government expenditure (1990)
Literacy: 22% (1993)

■ COMMUNICATIONS

Daily newspapers: 1 (1992)
Televisions: n.a.; no TV stations
Radios: 237/1,000 inhabitants (1992)
Telephones: 0.3/100 inhabitants (1992)

■ TRANSPORTATION

Motor Vehicles: 32,000; 16,000 passenger cars (1990)
Roads: 13,135 km; 2,364 km paved
Railway: 789 km (1993)
Air Traffic: 118,000 passengers carried (1991)
Airports: 47 airfields, of which 41 are usable; 5 have permanent-surface runways (1993)

Canadian Embassy: c/o The Canadian High Commission, 5199 United Nations Ave, Lusaka; mailing address: P.O. Box 31313 Lusaka,

Zambia. Tel: (011-260-1) 26-10-07. Fax: (011-260-1) 26-11-72
Representative to Canada: High Commission for Malawi, 7 Clemow Ave, Ottawa ON K1S 2A9. Tel: (613) 236-8931. Fax: (613) 236-1054.

Malaysia

Long-Form Name: Malaysia
Capital: Kuala Lumpur
Population: 18,792,000 (1992)

■ GEOGRAPHY

Area: 329,750 sq. km; inc. Sabah and Sarawak
Coastline: 4,675 km total (2,068 km Peninsular Malaysia, 2,607 km East Malaysia)
Climate: tropical; annual southwest (Apr. to Oct.) and northeast (Oct. to Feb.) monsoons
Environment: subject to flooding; air and water pollution
Terrain: coastal plains rising to hills and mountains
Land Use: 3% arable; 10% permanent; negligible meadows; 63% forest; 24% other
Location: SE Asia, bordering on South China Sea

■ PEOPLE

Nationality: Malaysian
Ethnic Groups: 59% Malay and other indigenous, 32% Chinese, 9% Indian
Languages: Peninsular Malaysia: Malay (official), English, Chinese dialects, Tamil; State of Sabah: English, Malay, numerous tribal dialects; Chinese State of Sarawak: English, Malay, Mandarin, numerous tribal languages
Religions: Peninsular Malaysia: Muslim (Malays), Buddhist (Chinese), Hindu (Indians); State of Sabah: 38% Muslim, 17% Christian, 45% other; Chinese State of Sarawak: 35% tribal religions, 24% Buddhist and Confucianist, 20% Muslim, 16% Christian, 5% other
Marriages: 3.2 (per 1,000) (1988)
Divorces: n.a.

■ GOVERNMENT

Leader(s): Prime Min. Mahathir Sultan bin Mohamad, Paramount Ruler (King) Jaafarbin Abdul Rahman
Government Type: constitutional monarch nominally headed by the paramount ruler (king) and a bicameral Parliament
Administrative Divisions: 13 states and 2 federal territories
Independence: Aug. 31, 1957 (from UK)
National Holiday: National Day, Aug. 31

■ ECONOMY

Overview: the economy is vulnerable to recession or a fall in world commodity prices because of its high export dependence; the world's largest producer of semiconductor devices; the majority of the rural population subsists at the poverty level
GNP: n.a., GDP $54.5 billion, per capita $2,960; real growth rate 8% (1992 est.)
Inflation: 4.8% (1992)
Industries: rubber and oil palm processing and manufacturing, light manufacturing industries, electronics, tin mining and smelting, logging and processing timber, logging, petroleum production, agriculture processing, petroleum production and refining, logging
Labour Force: 7,070,000 (1992); 41.6% agriculture, 19.1% industry, 39.3% services (1989)
Unemployment: 4.1% (1992 est.)
Agriculture: accounts for 20% of GDP; Peninsular Malaysia—natural rubber, palm oil, rice; Sabah—mainly subsistence; main crops—rubber, timber, coconut, rice; Sarawak—main crops—rubber, timber, pepper; there is a deficit of rice in all areas
Natural Resources: tin, crude oil, timber, copper, iron ore, natural gas, bauxite

■ FINANCE/TRADE

Currency: ringgit ($M)
International Reserves Excluding Gold: $27,249 million (Dec. 1993)
Gold Reserves: 2.39 million fine troy ounces (Dec. 1993)
Budget: revenues $15.6 billion; expenditures $18.0 billion, including capital expenditures of $4.5 billion (1992 est.)
Defence Expenditures: 11.74% of total govt. expenditure (1993)
External Debt: $19.837 billion (1992)
Exports: $40.711 billion (1992); commodities: natural rubber, palm oil, tin, timber, petroleum, electronics, light manufactures; partners: Singapore, Japan, USSR, European Community, Australia, US
Imports: $39.964 billion (1992); commodities: food, crude oil, consumer goods, intermediate goods, capital equipment, chemicals; partners: Japan, Singapore, Germany, UK, Thailand, China, Australia, US

■ HEALTH

Births: 28/1,000 population (1993)
Deaths: 5/1,000 population (1993)
Infant Mortality: 14 deaths/1,000 live births (1993)
Life Expectancy at Birth: 69 years male, 73 years female (1993)
No. of Physicians: 5.2/10,000 population (1992)

■ EDUCATION

Govt. Expenditure: 20.59% of government expenditure (1993)
Literacy: 78.4% (1993)

■ COMMUNICATIONS

Daily newspapers: 47 (1992)
Televisions: 143.6/1,000 inhabitants (1992)
Radios: 428/1,000 inhabitants in (1992)
Telephones: 9.68/100 inhabitants (1992)

■ TRANSPORTATION

Motor Vehicles: 2,426,799; 1,811,141 passenger cars (1987)
Roads: Peninsular Malaysia: 23,600 km; 19,352 km paved; Sabah: 3,782 km; Sarawak: 1,644 km (1993)
Railway: Peninsular Malaysia: 1,665 km; Sabah: 136 km; Sarawak: none (1993)
Air Traffic: 11,838,000 passengers carried (1991)
Airports: 111 airfields, of which 102 are usable; 32 have permanent-surface runways (1993)

Canadian Embassy: Flr 7, Plaza MBF, 172 Jalan Ampang, 50450 Kuala Lumpur, Malaysia; mailing address: P.O. Box 10990, 50732 Kuala Lumpur, Malaysia. Tel: (011-60-3) 261-2000. Fax: (011-60-3) 261-3428
Representative to Canada: High Commission for Malaysia, 60 Boteler St, Ottawa ON K1N 8Y7. Tel: (613) 237-5182. Fax: (613) 237-4852.

Maldives

Long-Form Name: Republic of Maldives
Capital: Malé
Population: 227,000 (1992)

■ GEOGRAPHY

Area: 300 sq. km
Coastline: 644 km
Climate: tropical; hot, humid; dry, northeast monsoon (Nov. to Mar.); rainy, southwest monsoon (June to Aug.)
Environment: 1,200 coral islands grouped in 19 atolls, future rise in ocean level could obliterate large parts of the country
Terrain: flat with elevations only as high as 2.5 metres
Land Use: 10% arable; 0% permanent; 3% meadows; 3% forest; 84% other
Location: Indian Ocean, S of India

■ PEOPLE

Nationality: Maldivian
Ethnic Groups: mixtures of Sinhalese, Dravidian, Arab and black
Languages: Dhivehi (Maldivian dialect of Sinhara; script derived from Arabic); English spoken by most government officials
Religions: Sunni Moslem
Marriages: 10.6 (per 1,000) (1990)
Divorces: 7.93 (per 1,000) (1990)

■ GOVERNMENT

Leader(s): Pres. Maumoun Abdul Gayoom
Government Type: republic
Administrative Divisions: 19 districts
Independence: July 26, 1965 (from UK)
National Holiday: Independence Day, July 26

■ ECONOMY

Overview: based on fishing, tourism and shipping; fishing is the largest industry; tourism has become one of the largest and most important sources of revenue
GNP: $101 million, per capita $460; real growth rate 10.2% (1991)
Inflation: 11.5% (1991 est.)
Industries: fishing and fish processing, tourism, shipping, boat building, some coconut processing, garments, woven mats, coir (rope), handicrafts
Labour Force: 25% agriculture, 15.8% industry, 59.2% services
Unemployment: negligible
Agriculture: accounts for almost 25% of GDP (including fishing); fishing more important than farming; limited production of coconuts, corn, sweet potatoes; most staple foods must be imported
Natural Resources: fish

■ FINANCE/TRADE

Currency: rufiyaa (Rf)
International Reserves Excluding Gold: $16 million (1991)
Gold Reserves: none (1991)
Budget: revenues $52 million; expenditures $83 million, including capital expenditures of $39 million (1991 est.)
Defence Expenditures: negligible
External Debt: $97 million (1992)
Exports: $40 million (1992); commodities: fish 57%, clothing 39%; partners: Thailand, Western Europe, Sri Lanka
Imports: $189 million (1992); commodities: intermediate and capital goods 47%, consumer goods 42%, petroleum products 11%; partners: Japan, Western Europe, Thailand

■ HEALTH

Births: 41/1,000 population (1993)
Deaths: 6/1,000 population (1993)
Infant Mortality: 34 deaths/1,000 live births (1993)
Life Expectancy at Birth: 62 years male, 59 years female (1993)
No. of Physicians: 0.7/10,000 population (1990)

■ EDUCATION

Govt. Expenditure: 11.27% of government expenditure (1990)
Literacy: 91.3% (1993)

■ COMMUNICATIONS

Daily newspapers: 2 (1992)
Televisions: 24.0/1,000 inhabitants (1992)
Radios: 115/1,000 inhabitants (1992)
Telephones: 1.4/100 inhabitants (1992)

■ TRANSPORTATION

Motor Vehicles: 509
Roads: Male has 9.5 km of coral highways within the city
Railway: none
Air Traffic: 9,000 passengers carried (1991)
Airports: 2 airfields, both usable and with permanent-surface runways (1993)

Canadian Embassy: c/o 6 Gregory's Rd, Cinnamon Gardens, Colombo 7; mailing address: P.O. Box 1006, Colombo, Sri Lanka. Tel: (011-94-1) 69-58-41. Fax: (011-94-1) 68-70-49.

Mali

Long-Form Name: Republic of Mali
Capital: Bamako
Population: 9,000,000 (1993 est.)

■ GEOGRAPHY

Area: 1,240,000 sq. km
Coastline: none: landlocked
Climate: subtropical to arid; hot and dry Feb. to June; rainy, humid and mild June to Nov.; cool and dry Nov. to Feb.
Environment: hot, dust-laden harmattan haze common during dry seasons; desertification
Terrain: mostly flat to rolling northern plains covered by sand; savanna in south, rugged hills in northeast
Land Use: 2% arable; negligible permanent; 25% meadows; 7% forest; 66% other
Location: NW Africa

■ PEOPLE

Nationality: Malian
Ethnic Groups: 50% Mande (Bambara, Malinke, Sarakole), 17% Peul, 12% Voltaic, 6% Songhai, 5% Tuareg and Moor, 10% other
Languages: French (official); Bambara spoken by about 80% of the population; numerous African languages
Religions: 90% Moslem, 9% indigenous beliefs, 1% Christian
Marriages: n.a.
Divorces: n.a.

■ GOVERNMENT

Leader(s): Pres. Alpha Oumar Konare, Prime Min. Ibrahim Boubakar Keita
Government Type: republic
Administrative Divisions: 8 regions
Independence: Sept. 22, 1960 (from France; formerly French Sudan)
National Holiday: Anniversary of the Proclamation of the Republic, Sept. 22

■ ECONOMY

Overview: a poor country, 70% of its land area is desert or semidesert; 80% of the labour force is involved in agriculture and fishing; 10% of the population live as nomads; industrial activity is confined to processing farm commodities
GNP: $2.412 billion, per capita $280; real growth rate 2.5% (1991)
Inflation: n.a.
Industries: small local consumer goods and processing, construction, phosphate, gold, fishing
Labour Force: 2,960,000 (1992); 85.5% agriculture, 12.5% services, 2% industry (1989)
Unemployment: n.a.
Agriculture: accounts for 50% of GDP; most production based on small subsistence farms; cotton and livestock products account for over 70% of exports; other crops—millet, rice, corn, vegetables, peanuts; livestock—cattle, sheep and goats
Natural Resources: gold, phosphates, kaolin, salt, limestone, uranium; bauxite, iron ore, manganese, tin and copper deposits are known but not exploited

■ FINANCE/TRADE

Currency: Communauté financière africaine franc (CFAF)
International Reserves Excluding Gold: $324 million (Sept. 1993)
Gold Reserves: 0.02 million fine troy ounces (Sept. 1993)
Budget: revenues $329 million; expenditures $519 million, including capital expenditures of $178 million (1989)
Defence Expenditures: $63.82 million (8.01% of total govt. expenditure) (1988)
External Debt: $2.595 billion (1992)
Exports: $320 million (1991); commodities: livestock, peanuts, dried fish, cotton, skins; partners: mostly franc zone and Western Europe
Imports: $390 million (1991); commodities: textiles, vehicles, petroleum products, machinery, sugar, cereals; partners: mostly franc zone and Western Europe

■ HEALTH

Births: 52/1,000 population (1993)
Deaths: 22/1,000 population (1993)
Infant Mortality: 111 deaths/1,000 live births (1993)
Life Expectancy at Birth: 43 years male, 46 years female (1993)
No. of Physicians: 0.4/10,000 population (1992)

■ EDUCATION

Govt. Expenditure: 9.04% of govt. expenditure (1988)
Literacy: 32.0% (1993)

■ COMMUNICATIONS

Daily newspapers: 2 (1992)
Televisions: 0.4/1,000 inhabitants (1992)
Radios: 39/1,000 inhabitants (1992)
Telephones: 0.17/100 inhabitants (1992)

■ TRANSPORTATION

Motor Vehicles: 31,000; 22,000 passenger cars (1990)
Roads: 16,120 km; 1,240 km paved
Railway: 642 km
Air Traffic: n.a.
Airports: 34 airfields, of which 27 are usable; 8 have permanent-surface runways (1993)

Canadian Embassy: P.O. Box 198, Bamako, Mali. Tel: (011-223) 22-22-36. Fax: (011-223) 22-43-62.
Representative to Canada: Embassy of the Republic of Mali, 50 Goulburn Ave, Ottawa ON K1N 8C8. Tel: (613) 232-1501. Fax: (613) 232-7429.

Malta

Long-Form Name: Republic of Malta
Capital: Valletta
Population: 400,000 (1993 est.)

■ GEOGRAPHY

Area: 320 sq. km

Coastline: 140 km
Climate: Mediterranean with mild, rainy winters and hot, dry summers
Environment: numerous bays provide good harbours; fresh water very scarce, increasing reliance on desalination
Terrain: mostly low, rocky, flat to dissected plains; many coastal cliffs
Land Use: 38% arable; 3% permanent; 0% meadows; 0% forest; 59% other
Location: Mediterranean Sea, S of Sicily

■ PEOPLE

Nationality: Maltese
Ethnic Groups: mixture of Arab, Sicilian, Norman, Spanish, Italian, English
Languages: Maltese and English (official), Italian widely spoken
Religions: 98% Roman Catholic
Marriages: 7.4 (per 1,000) (1987)
Divorces: n.a.

■ GOVERNMENT

Leader(s): Prime Min. Eddie Fenech Adami, Pres. Vincent (Censu) Tabone
Government Type: parliamentary democracy
Administrative Divisions: none
Independence: Sept. 21, 1964 (from UK)
National Holiday: Freedom Day, Mar. 31; Independence Day, Sept. 21

■ ECONOMY

Overview: manufacturing and tourism are important; economy is dependent on foreign trade and services (food, water and energy); Malta produces only 20% of its food needs, has a limited supply of fresh water, and lacks domestic energy sources
GNP: $2.598 billion, per capita $6,850; real growth rate 3.5% (1991)
Inflation: 1.6% (1992)
Industries: tourism, ship repair yard, clothing, construction, food manufacturing, textiles, footwear, clothing, beverages, tobacco
Labour Force: 146,000 (1992); 28.1% industry, 2.5% agriculture, 69.4% services (1989)
Unemployment: 3.6% (1992)
Agriculture: 20% self-sufficient overall; main products—potatoes, cauliflower, grapes, wheat, barley, tomatoes, citrus, cut flowers, green peppers, hogs, poultry, eggs; adequate supplies of vegetables, poultry, milk, pork products; seasonal or periodic shortages
Natural Resources: limestone, salt

■ FINANCE/TRADE

Currency: Maltese lira (LM)

International Reserves Excluding Gold: $1,365 million (Jan. 1994)
Gold Reserves: 0.10 million fine troy ounces (Jan. 1994)
Budget: revenues $1.1 billion; expenditures $1.1 billion, including capital expenditures of $161 million (1992 est.)
Defence Expenditures: 1.8% of total govt. expenditure (1991)
External Debt: $603 million (1992)
Exports: $1.536 billion (1992); commodities: clothing, textiles, footwear, ships; partners: Germany 31%, UK 14%, Italy 14%
Imports: $2.339 billion (1992); commodities: food, petroleum, nonfood raw materials; partners: Germany 19%, UK 17%, Italy 17%, US 11%

■ HEALTH

Births: 15/1,000 population (1993)
Deaths: 8/1,000 population (1993)
Infant Mortality: 9.1 deaths/1,000 live births (1993)
Life Expectancy at Birth: 74 years male, 78 years female (1993)
No. of Physicians: 11.4/10,000 population (1990)

■ EDUCATION

Govt. Expenditure: 9.03% of govt. expenditure (1991)
Literacy: 84% (1993)

■ COMMUNICATIONS

Daily newspapers: 3 (1992)
Televisions: 740.7/1,000 inhabitants (1992)
Radios: 396/1,000 inhabitants (1992)
Telephones: 49.08/100 inhabitants (1992)

■ TRANSPORTATION

Motor Vehicles: 135,919; 114,682 passenger cars (1990)
Roads: 1,291 km; 1,179 km paved
Railway: none
Air Traffic: 649,000 passengers carried (1991)
Airports: 1 airfield, usable and with a permanent-surface runway (1993)

Canadian Embassy: c/o Via G.B. de Rossi 27, 00161 Rome, Italy. Tel: (011-39-6) 44598.1, Fax: (011-39-6) 44598.912
Representative to Canada: c/o High Commission for the Republic of Malta, 2017 Connecticut

Ave NW, Washington DC 20008 USA. Tel:
(202) 462-3611. Fax: (202) 387-5470.

Marshall Islands

Long-Form Name: Republic of the Marshall
Islands
Capital: Majuro
Population: 51,982 (1993 est.)

■ GEOGRAPHY

Area: 181.3 sq. km
Coastline: 370.4 km
Climate: islands border typhoon belt; wet season,
May to Nov.; hot and humid
Environment: occasional typhoons; 2 island
chains of 30 atolls and 1,152 islands
Terrain: low coral limestone and sand islands
Land Use: 0% arable, 60% permanent crops, 0%
meadows or forests, 40% other
Location: Oceania, in North Pacific Ocean

■ PEOPLE

Nationality: Marshallese
Ethnic Groups: Micronesian
Languages: English (official), two major
Marshallese dialects, Japanese
Religions: Christian
Marriages: n.a.
Divorces: n.a.

■ GOVERNMENT

Leader(s): Pres. Amata Kabua
Government Type: constitutional government in
free association with US
Administrative Divisions: none
Independence: Oct. 21, 1986 (from US-adminis-
tered UN trusteeship)
National Holiday: Proclamation of the Republic
of the Marshall Islands, May 1

■ ECONOMY

Overview: agriculture and tourism are the back-
bone of the economy; industry is on a small
scale, limited to handicrafts, copra, and fish pro-
cessing; imports far exceed exports
GNP: n.a., GDP $63 million, $1,500 per capita;
real growth rate n.a. (1989)
Inflation: n.a.
Industries: copra, fish, tourism, crafts
Labour Force: n.a.
Unemployment: n.a.
Agriculture: coconuts, taro, cacao, breadfruit,
fruits, poultry
Natural Resources: phosphate, marine products,
minerals

■ FINANCE/TRADE

Currency: US currency is used
International Reserves Excluding Gold: n.a.
Gold Reserves: n.a.
Budget: n.a.
Defence Expenditures: none
External Debt: n.a.
Exports: n.a.
Imports: n.a.

■ HEALTH

Births: 43/1,000 population (1993)
Deaths: 9/1,000 population (1993)
Infant Mortality: 57 deaths/1,000 live births
(1993)
Life Expectancy at Birth: 60 years male, 63 years
female (1993)
No. of Physicians: n.a.

■ EDUCATION

Govt. Expenditure: n.a.
Literacy: 93% (1993)

■ COMMUNICATIONS

Daily newspapers: n.a.
Televisions: n.a.; 1 TV station (1993)
Radios: n.a.; 3 radio stations (1993)
Telephones: 756 telephone lines (1993)

■ TRANSPORTATION

Motor Vehicles: n.a.
Roads: paved roads on major islands only
Railway: none
Air Traffic: n.a.
Airports: 16 airfields, all usable; 4 have perma-
nent-surface runways (1993).

Martinique

Overseas Department of France

Long-Form Name: Department of Martinique
Capital: Fort-de-France
Population: 400,000 (1993 est.)

■ GEOGRAPHY

Area: 1,100 sq. km
Climate: tropical, moderated by trade winds;
rainy season (June to Oct.)
Land Use: 10% arable; 8% permanent; 30%
meadows; 26% forest; 26% other
Location: Windward Islands, Caribbean

■ PEOPLE

Nationality: Martiniquais
Ethnic Groups: majority black, remainder a mix

of black African and Latin ancestry, Caucasian 5%

Languages: French (official), majority speak Creole

Religions: 95% Roman Catholic, 5% Hindu and pagan African

Marriages: 4.3 (per 1,000) (1990)

Divorces: 0.73 (per 1,000) (1990)

■ GOVERNMENT

Leader(s): Chief of State President Francois Mitterand, Govt. Commissioner Jean Claude Roure

Government Type: overseas department of France

National Holiday: Taking of the Bastille, National Day, July 14

■ ECONOMY

Overview: most of the meat, vegetable and grain requirements must be imported; industry: food processing, oil refining, chemical engineering; agriculture: pineapples, tobacco, cotton, bananas, sugar, rum, livestock; forest products; fishing; chief trading partners: France, UK, Guadeloupe

■ FINANCE/TRADE

Currency: French franc (F)

Mauritania

Long-Form Name: Islamic Republic of Mauritania

Capital: Nouakchott

Population: 2,200,000 (1993 est.)

■ GEOGRAPHY

Area: 1,030,700 sq. km

Coastline: 754 km

Climate: desert; constantly hot, dry, dusty

Environment: hot, dry, dust/sand-laden sirocco wind blows primarily in Mar. and Apr.; desertification; only perennial river is the Senegal

Terrain: mostly barren, flat plains of the Sahara; some central hills

Land Use: 38% meadows; 5% forest; 56% other, 1% arable

Location: NW Africa, bordering on Atlantic Ocean

■ PEOPLE

Nationality: Mauritanian

Ethnic Groups: 30% Maur, 40% mixed Maur-black, 30% black

Languages: Hasaniya Arabic (national), Wolof (official), Pular, Soninke

Religions: nearly 100% Moslem

Marriages: n.a.

Divorces: n.a.

■ GOVERNMENT

Leader(s): Pres., Military Committee for National Salvation (CMSN), Chief of State Col. Maaouya Ould Sid'Ahmend Taya

Government Type: republic; military seized power in bloodless coup July 10, 1978; a palace coup that took place on Dec. 24, 1984 brought President Taya to power

Administrative Divisions: 12 regions

Independence: Nov. 28, 1960 (from France)

National Holiday: Independence Day, Nov. 28

■ ECONOMY

Overview: most of the population is engaged in agricultural and livestock production; substantial iron ores; threatened by foreign overexploitation of fishing areas; in recent years, droughts, conflicts with Senegal, rising energy costs, and economic mismanagement have resulted in a substantial build-up of foreign debt

GNP: $1.026 billion, per capita $510; real growth rate 0.6% (1991)

Inflation: 10.1% (1992)

Industries: fishing, fish processing, mining of iron ore and gypsum

Labour Force: 680,000 (1992) 69.4% agriculture, 21.7% services, 8.9% industry

Unemployment: 20% (1991 est.)

Agriculture: accounts for 50% of GDP (including fishing); largely subsistence farming, nomadic cattle and sheep herding except in Senegal river valley; crops—dates, millet, sorghum, root crops; fish products number-one export; large food deficit in years of drought

Natural Resources: iron ore, gypsum, fish, copper, phosphate

■ FINANCE/TRADE

Currency: ouguiya (UM)

International Reserves Excluding Gold: $50 million (Jan. 1994)

Gold Reserves: 0.01 million fine troy ounces (1991)

Budget: revenues $280 million; expenditures $364 million, including capital expenditures of $61 million (1989)

Defence Expenditures: 4.2% GDP (1987)

External Debt: $2.301 billion (1992)

Exports: $469 million (1990); commodities: iron ore, processed fish, small amounts of gum arabic and gypsum, unrecorded but numerically significant cattle exports to Senegal; partners: European Community 57%, Japan 39%, Ivory Coast 2%

Imports: $639 million (1990); commodities: foodstuffs, consumer goods, petroleum products, capital goods; partners: European Community 79%, Africa 5%, US 4%, Japan 2%

■ HEALTH

Births: 46/1,000 population (1993)
Deaths: 18/1,000 population (1993)
Infant Mortality: 122 deaths/1,000 live births (1993)
Life Expectancy at Birth: 45 years male, 49 years female (1993)
No. of Physicians: 0.8/10,000 population (1992)

■ EDUCATION

Govt. Expenditure: 33.2% of govt. expenditure (1985)
Literacy: 34% (1993)

■ COMMUNICATIONS

Daily newspapers: 1 (1992)
Televisions: 22.9/1,000 inhabitants (1992)
Radios: 143/1,000 inhabitants (1992)
Telephones: 0.3/100 inhabitants (1992)

■ TRANSPORTATION

Motor Vehicles: 15,000; 10,000 passenger cars (1990)
Roads: 7,525 km; 1,685 km paved (1993)
Railway: 690 km
Air Traffic: 210,000 passengers carried (1991)
Airports: 29 airfields, all usable; 9 have permanent-surface runways (1993)

Canadian Embassy: c/o 45 av de la République; mailing address: P.O. Box 3373, Dakar, Senegal. Tel: (011-221) 23-92-90. Fax: (011-221) 23-87-49
Representative to Canada: Embassy of the Islamic Republic of Mauritania, 249 McLeod St, Ottawa, ON K2P 1A1. Tel: (613) 237-3283. Fax: (613) 237-3287.

Mauritius

Long-Form Name: Mauritius
Capital: Port Louis
Population: 1,100,000 (1993 est.)

■ GEOGRAPHY

Area: 1,860 sq. km; includes Agalega Islands, Cargados Carajos Shoals (St. Brandon) and Rodriques
Coastline: 177 km
Climate: tropical modified by southeast trade winds; warm, dry winter (May to Nov.); hot, wet, humid summer (Nov. to May)

Environment: subject to cyclones (Nov. to Apr.); almost completely surrounded by reefs
Terrain: small coastal plain rising to discontinuous mountains encircling central plateau
Land Use: 54% arable; 4% permanent; 4% meadows; 31% forest; 7% other
Location: Indian Ocean, E of Africa

■ PEOPLE

Nationality: Mauritian
Ethnic Groups: 68% Indo-Mauritian, 27% Creole, 3% Sino-Mauritian, 2% Franco-Mauritian
Languages: English (official), Creole, French, Hindi, Urdu, Hakka, Bojpoori
Religions: 55% Hindu, 28% Christian (mostly Roman Catholic with a few Anglicans), 17% Moslem
Marriages: 10.6 (per 1,000) (1991)
Divorces: 0.67 (per 1,000) (1990)

■ GOVERNMENT

Leader(s): Pres. Cassam Uteem, Prime Min. Sir Anerood Jugnauth
Government Type: parliamentary democracy
Administrative Divisions: 9 administrative districts
Independence: Mar. 12, 1968 (from UK)
National Holiday: Independence Day, Mar. 12

■ ECONOMY

Overview: based on sugar, manufacturing (textiles) and tourism; features low unemployment and a high real growth rate
GNP: $2.623 billion, per capita $2,420; real growth rate 7.2% (1991)
Inflation: 4.6% (1992)
Industries: food processing (largely sugar milling), textiles, wearing apparel, chemical and chemical products, metal products, transport equipment, nonelectrical machinery, tourism
Labour Force: 440,000 (1992); 19% agriculture, 31.1% industry, 49.9% services (1989)
Unemployment: 2.4% (1991)
Agriculture: accounts for 10% of GDP; about 90% of cultivated land in sugar cane; other products—tea, corn, potatoes, bananas, pulses, cattle, goats, fish; net food importer, especially rice and fish
Natural Resources: arable land, fish

■ FINANCE/TRADE

Currency: rupee (Mau Rs)
International Reserves Excluding Gold: $764 million (Jan. 1994)
Gold Reserves: 0.06 million fine troy ounces (Jan. 1994)

Budget: revenues $557 million; expenditures $607 million, including capital expenditures of $111 million (1990)
Defence Expenditures: 1.59% of total govt. expenditure (1993)
External Debt: $1.049 billion (1992)
Exports: $1.290 billion (1992); commodities: textiles 44%, sugar 40%, light manufactures 10%; partners: European Community 77%, US 15%
Imports: $1.623 billion (1992); commodities: manufactured goods 50%, capital equipment 17%, foodstuffs 13%, petroleum products 8%, chemicals 7%; partners: European Community, US, South Africa, Japan

■ HEALTH

Births: 21/1,000 population (1993)
Deaths: 7/1,000 population (1993)
Infant Mortality: 18.6 deaths/1,000 live births (1993)
Life Expectancy at Birth: 65 years male, 73 years female (1993)
No. of Physicians: 5.3/10,000 population (1992)

■ EDUCATION

Govt. Expenditure: 14.73% of govt. expenditure (1993)
Literacy: 61% (1993)

■ COMMUNICATIONS

Daily newspapers: 7 (1992)
Televisions: 214.6/1,000 inhabitants (1992)
Radios: 354/1,000 inhabitants (1992)
Telephones: 7.20/100 inhabitants (1992)

■ TRANSPORTATION

Motor Vehicles: 55,981; 46,793 passenger cars (1990)
Roads: 7,215 km; 2,060 km paved
Railway: none
Air Traffic: 535,000 passengers carried (1991)
Airports: 5 airfields, of which 4 are usable; 2 have permanent-surface runways (1993)

Canadian Embassy: c/o The Canadian High Commission, 38 Mirambo St, Dar-es-Salaam; mailing address: P.O. Box 1022, Dar-es-Salaam, Tanzania. Tel: (011-255-51) 46000. Fax: (011-255-51) 46005
Representative to Canada: c/o Embassy of Mauritius, Suite 441, Van Ness Center, 4301 Connecticut Avenue NW, Washington DC 20008 USA.

Mayotte

Territorial Collectivity of France

Long-Form Name: Territorial Collectivity of Mayotte
Capital: Mamoundzou
Population: 89,983 (1993 est.)

■ GEOGRAPHY

Area: 375 sq. km
Climate: tropical maritime; hot, humid rainy season during northeastern monsoon (Nov. to May), dry season is cooler (May to Nov.)
Land Use: 20,000 acres under agricultural cultivation
Location: Mozambique Channel, off W coast of Africa

■ PEOPLE

Nationality: Mahorais
Ethnic Groups: Antalote, Cafre, Makoa, Oimatsaha, Sakalava
Languages: French (official), Mahorian (a Swahili dialect)

■ GOVERNMENT

Leader(s): Pres. General Council Younoussa Bamana, French Govt. Commissioner Jean-Paul Coste
Government Type: territorial collectivity
National Holiday: Taking of the Bastille, July 14

■ ECONOMY

Overview: industry: lobster, shrimp; agriculture: pineapples, bananas, mangoes, breadfruit, cassava, ylang-ylang, vanilla, coffee, spices; Mayotte must import a large portion of its food requirements, mainly from France; chief trading partners: France, UK, South Africa, Bahrain, Thailand, Réunion

■ FINANCE/TRADE

Currency: French franc (F)

Mexico

Long-Form Name: United States of Mexico
Capital: Mexico
Population: 90,000,000 (1993)

■ GEOGRAPHY

Area: 1,972,550 sq. km

Coastline: 9,330 km
Climate: varies from tropical to desert
Environment: subject to tsunamis along the Pacific coast and destructive earthquakes in the centre and south; natural water resources scarce and polluted in centre and extreme southeast; deforestation; erosion widespread; desertification; serious air pollution
Terrain: high, rugged mountains, low coastal plains, high plateaus and desert
Land Use: 12% arable, 1% permanent; 39% meadows; 24% forest; 24% other
Location: Central (Latin) America, bordering on Gulf of Mexico, Pacific Ocean

■ PEOPLE

Nationality: Mexican
Ethnic Groups: 60% mestizo (Indian-Spanish), 30% Amerindian or predominantly Amerindian, 9% white or predominantly white, 1% other
Languages: Spanish, also indigenous (Mayan) languages
Religions: 89% Roman Catholic, 6% Protestant, 5% other
Marriages: 7.4 (per 1,000) (1990)
Divorces: 0.63 (per 1,000) (1990)

■ GOVERNMENT

Leader(s): Pres. Ernesto Zedillo Ponce de Léon
Government Type: federal republic operating under a centralized government
Administrative Divisions: 31 states and 1 federal district
Independence: Sept. 16, 1810 (from Spain)
National Holiday: Independence Day, Sept. 16

■ ECONOMY

Overview: a mixture of state-owned industrial plants (mainly oil), private manufacturing and services, and both large-scale and traditional agriculture; suffers from rapid population growth and large external debts due to falling petroleum prices
GNP: $328 billion, per capita $3,600; real growth rate 11.9% (1992)
Inflation: 15.5% (1992)
Industries: food and beverages, tobacco, chemicals, iron and steel, petroleum, mining, textiles, clothing, transportation equipment, tourism
Labour Force: 30,487,000 (1992); 57% services, 22.9% agriculture, 20.1% industry (1989)
Unemployment: 14-17% (1991)
Agriculture: accounts for 9% of GDP and over 25% of labour force; large number of small farms at subsistence level; major food crops—corn, wheat, rice, beans; cash crops—cotton, coffee, fruit, tomatoes

Natural Resources: crude oil, silver, copper, gold, lead, zinc, natural gas, timber

■ FINANCE/TRADE

Currency: peso ($Mex)
International Reserves Excluding Gold: $23,224 million (Oct. 1993)
Gold Reserves: 0.50 million fine troy ounces (Oct. 1993)
Budget: revenues $58.9 billion; expenditures $48.3 billion, including capital expenditures of $6.5 billion (1991)
Defence Expenditures: $678.41 million (2.36% of total govt. expenditure) (1990)
External Debt: $113.378 billion (1992)
Exports: $27.531 billion (1992); commodities: crude oil, oil products, coffee, shrimp, engines; cotton; partners: US 66%, European Community 16%, Japan 11%
Imports: $48.138 billion (1992); commodities: grain, metal manufactures, agricultural machinery, electrical equipment; partners: US 62%, European Community 18%, Japan 10%

■ HEALTH

Births: 29/1,000 population (1993)
Deaths: 6/1,000 population (1993)
Infant Mortality: 38 deaths/1,000 live births (1993)
Life Expectancy at Birth: 66 years male, 73 years female (1993)
No. of Physicians: 6.7/10,000 population (1992)

■ EDUCATION

Govt. Expenditure: 13.86% of govt. expenditure (1990)
Literacy: 87.3% (1993)

■ COMMUNICATIONS

Daily newspapers: 286 (1992)
Televisions: 126.8/1,000 inhabitants (1992)
Radios: 242/1,000 inhabitants (1992)
Telephones: 11.08/100 inhabitants (1992)

■ TRANSPORTATION

Motor Vehicles: 9,882,490; 6,819,305 passenger cars (1990)
Roads: 212,000 km; 65,000 km paved, 30,000 km semi-paved or cobblestone
Railway: 24,500 km
Air Traffic: 14,901,000 passengers carried (1991)
Airports: 1,841 airfields, of which 1,478 are usable; 200 have permanent-surface runways (1993)

Canadian Embassy: Calle Schiller no. 529, Rincon del Bosque, 11560 Polanco Mexico,

D.F.; mailing address: Apartado Postal 105-05, 11580 Mexico, Mexico. Tel: (011-52-5) 724-7900. Fax: (011-52-5) 724-7980
Representative to Canada: Embassy of Mexico, 130 Albert St, Ste 1800, Ottawa ON K1P 5G4. Tel: (613) 233-8988. Fax: (613) 235-9123.

Moldova

Long-Form Name: Republic of Moldova
Capital: Kishinev
Population: 4,400,000 (1993 est.)

■ GEOGRAPHY

Area: 33,700 sq. km
Coastline: none: landlocked
Climate: mild sunny winters; warm rainy summers; long dry autumns
Environment: heavy use of agricultural chemicals, including banned pesticides such as DDT, has contaminated ground water and soil; erosion severe due to poor farming methods
Terrain: hilly plains in north; southern steppe
Land Use: 50% arable, negligible permanent crops, 9% meadows and pastures, negligible forest, 41% other
Location: SE Europe

■ PEOPLE

Nationality: Moldovan
Ethnic Groups: 64.5% Moldavian, 13.9% Ukrainian, 13% Russian, 3.5% Gagauz, 1.5% Jews, 2% other
Languages: Moldavian (official), Russian, Ukrainian
Religions: 98.5% Eastern Orthodox, 1.5% Jewish, 1,000 Baptists (note that almost all churchgoers are ethnic Moldovan; the Slavic population are not churchgoers)
Marriages: n.a.
Divorces: n.a.

■ GOVERNMENT

Leader(s): Pres. Mircea Snegur, Prime Min. Andrei Sangheli
Government Type: republic
Administrative Divisions: previously divided into 40 rayons; to be divided into fewer, larger districts at unspecified future date
Independence: Aug. 27, 1991 (from Soviet Union)
National Holiday: Independence Day, Aug. 27

■ ECONOMY

Overview: predominantly mining and manufacturing, with important agricultural sector; Moldova has a climate favourable to agriculture, and this is where the bulk of economic development has taken place
GNP: $9.529 billion, $2,170 per capita; real growth rate 2.7%
Inflation: n.a.
Industries: machinery and appliances, hosiery, refined sugar, vegetable oil, canned food, shoes, textiles
Labour Force: 2,117,592 (1989)
Unemployment: 0.7%; also large numbers of underemployed (1993)
Agriculture: grapes and other fruits, vegetables, sugar, wheat and cereal grains, tobacco, oil, essential oil crops
Natural Resources: lignite, phosphorites, gypsum

■ FINANCE/TRADE

Currency: rouble (rbl.), soon to be replaced by the lei (presently in preparation)
International Reserves Excluding Gold: n.a.
Gold Reserves: n.a.
Budget: 1989 revenues: 3,396 million roubles
Defence Expenditures: n.a.
External Debt: $38 million (1992)
Exports: $109 million (1992); wine, grapes, other agricultural products, machinery, pumps
Imports: $141 million (1992)

■ HEALTH

Births: 17/1,000 population (1993)
Deaths: 11/1,000 population (1993)
Infant Mortality: 23 deaths/1,000 live births (1993)=
Life Expectancy at Birth: 65 years male, 72 years female (1993)
No. of Physicians: 17,500 doctors (1989)

■ EDUCATION

Govt. Expenditure: n.a.
Literacy: 100% (1993)

■ COMMUNICATIONS

Daily newspapers: 200 papers of all circulation types (1989)
Televisions: n.a.
Radios: n.a.
Telephones: 11.1/100 inhabitants (1993)

■ TRANSPORTATION

Motor Vehicles: n.a.
Roads: 20,000 km; 13,900 km hard-surfaced (1993)
Railway: 1,150 km, which does not include industrial lines
Air Traffic: n.a.
Airports: 26 airfields, of which 16 are usable; 6 have permanent-surface runways (1993)

Canadian Embassy: c/o 36 Nicolae Iorga, Bucharest; mailing address: P.O. Box 2966 Post Office No. 22, 71118 Bucharest, Romania. Tel: (011-40-1) 312.03.65. Fax: (011-40-1) 312.03.66.

Monaco

Long-Form Name: Principality of Monaco
Capital: Monaco
Population: 31,008 (1993 est.)

■ GEOGRAPHY

Area: 1.9 sq. km
Coastline: 4.1 km
Climate: Mediterranean with mild, wet winters and hot, dry summers
Environment: almost entirely urban
Terrain: hilly, rugged, rocky
Land Use: 0% arable; 0% permanent; 0% meadows; 0% forest; 100% other
Location: S Europe, bordering on Mediterranean Sea

■ PEOPLE

Nationality: Monegasque or Monacan
Ethnic Groups: 47% French, 16% Monegasque, 16% Italian, 21% other
Languages: French (official), English, Italian, Monegasque
Religions: 95% Roman Catholic

■ GOVERNMENT

Leader(s): Chief of State Prince Rainier III, Min. of State Jacques Dupont
Government Type: constitutional monarchy
Administrative Divisions: 4 districts (quarters)
Independence: 1419, rule by the House of Grimaldi
National Holiday: National Day, Nov. 19

■ ECONOMY

Overview: a popular resort, attracting tourists to its casinos and pleasant climate; no income tax and low business taxes make it a tax haven; no data is published on the economy
GNP: $475 million, per capita $16,000, real growth rate n.a. (1991 est.)
Industries: pharmaceuticals, food processing, precision instruments, glassmaking, printing, tourism
Unemployment: negligible (1993)
Natural Resources: none

■ FINANCE/TRADE

Currency: French franc (F)
Budget: revenues $424 million; expenditures $376 million; including capital expenditures (1991)

■ HEALTH

Births: 10.8/1,000 population (1993)
Deaths: 12.32/1,000 population (1993)
Infant Mortality: 7.3 deaths/1,000 live births (1993)
Life Expectancy at Birth: 73.7 years male, 81.49 years female (1993)
No. of Physicians: 21.9/10,000 population (1982)

■ EDUCATION

Govt. Expenditure: 5.3% of govt. expenditure (1989)
Literacy: 99% (1993)

■ COMMUNICATIONS

Daily newspapers: 2 (1988)
Televisions: 785.7/1,000 inhabitants (1989)
Radios: 1,084/1,000 inhabitants (1989)
Telephones: 131.4/100 inhabitants (1985)

■ TRANSPORTATION

Motor Vehicles: 20,800; 17,000 passenger cars (1990)
Roads: none; city streets only
Railway: 1.6 km
Air Traffic: 43,000 passengers carried (1991)
Airports: 1 airfields, usable and with a permanent-surface runway (1993)

Canadian Embassy: c/o 35 av Montaigne, 75008 Paris, France. Tel: (011-33-1) 44-43-29-00. Fax: (011-33-1) 44-43-29-99
Representative to Canada: c/o Consulate of Monaco, 1155 Sherbrooke St W, Ste 1500, Montreal, PQ H3A 2W1. Tel: (514) 849-0589. Fax: (514) 631-2771.

Mongolia

Long-Form Name: Mongolia
Capital: Ulan Bator
Population: 2,310,000 (1993)

■ GEOGRAPHY

Area: 1,565,000 sq. km
Coastline: none: landlocked
Climate: desert; continental (large daily and seasonal temperature ranges)
Environment: harsh and rugged
Terrain: vast semidesert and desert plains; mountains in west and southwest; Gobi desert in southeast
Land Use: 1% arable; 0% permanent; 79% meadows; 10% forest; 10% other

Location: EC Asia

■ PEOPLE

Nationality: Mongolian
Ethnic Groups: 90% Mongol, 4% Kazakh, 2% Chinese, 2% Russian, 2% other
Languages: Kazakh and Khalkha Mongol is spoken by over 90% of population; minor languages include Turkic, Russian, Chinese and English
Religions: no state religion; predominantly Buddhist Lamaism and Shamanism, Islam 4%
Marriages: 7.5 (per 1,000) (1989)
Divorces: 0.48 (per 1,000) (1989)

■ GOVERNMENT

Leader(s): Prime Min. Puntsagiyn Jasray, Pres. Punsalmaagiyn Ochirbat
Government Type: republic
Administrative Divisions: 18 provinces and 3 municipalities
Independence: Mar. 13, 1921 (from China; formerly known as Outer Mongolia)
National Holiday: National Day, July 11

■ ECONOMY

Overview: severe climate, widely dispersed population and largely unproductive land have hindered economic development; traditionally based on agriculture and the breeding of livestock (has highest number of livestock per person in the world); recently extensive mineral resources have been developed
GNP: n.a., GDP $1.8 billion, per capita $800; average real growth rate -15% (1992 est.)
Inflation: 325% (1992 est.)
Industries: processing of animal products, building materials, food and beverage, mining (particularly coal), copper
Labour Force: 1,030,000 (1992); 39.9% agriculture, 21% industry, 39.2% services (1989)
Unemployment: 15% (1991)
Agriculture: accounts for 20% of GDP, 90% of exports, and provides livelihood for about 50% of the population; livestock raising predominates (sheep, goats, horses); crops—wheat, barley, potatoes, forage
Natural Resources: coal, copper, molybdenum, tungsten, phosphates, tin, nickel, zinc, wolfram, fluorspar, gold

■ FINANCE/TRADE

Currency: tughrik (Tug)
International Reserves Excluding Gold: n.a.
Gold Reserves: n.a.
Budget: deficit of $67 million (1991)
Defence Expenditures: $249.44 million (1987)

External Debt: $375 million (1992)
Exports: $347 million (1991); commodities: livestock, animal products, wool, hides, fluorspar, nonferrous metals, minerals; partners: USSR 80%
Imports: $501 million (1991); commodities: machinery and equipment, fuels, food products, industrial consumer goods, chemicals, building materials, sugar, tea; partners: USSR 80%

■ HEALTH

Births: 36/1,000 population (1993)
Deaths: 9/1,000 population (1993)
Infant Mortality: 50 deaths/1,000 live births (1993)
Life Expectancy at Birth: 62 years male, 67 years female (1993)
No. of Physicians: n.a.

■ EDUCATION

Govt. Expenditure: n.a.
Literacy: 80% (1993)

■ COMMUNICATIONS

Daily newspapers: 3 (1992)
Televisions: 37.5/1,000 inhabitants (1992)
Radios: 131/1,000 inhabitants (1992)
Telephones: n.a.

■ TRANSPORTATION

Motor Vehicles: n.a.
Roads: 46,950 km; 1,565 km paved
Railway: 1,878 km
Air Traffic: 554,000 passengers carried (1991)
Airports: 81 airfields, of which 31 are usable; 11 have permanent-surface runways (1993)

Canadian Embassy: c/o 19 Dong Zhi Men Wai St, Chao Yang District, Beijing 100600, China. Tel: (011-86-1) 532-3536. Fax: (011-86-1) 532-4311
Representative to Canada: c/o Embassy of Mongolia, 2833 M St NW, Washington, DC 20007 USA. Tel: (202) 333-7117. Fax: (202) 298-9227.

Montserrat

Crown Colony of the United Kingdom

Long-Form Name: Montserrat
Capital: Plymouth
Population: 12,661 (1993 est.)

■ GEOGRAPHY

Area: 100 sq. km
Climate: tropical, no well-defined rainy season;

June-Nov. hottest, prone to hurricanes
Land Use: 20% arable, 0% permanent crops, 10% meadows and pastures, 40% forests, 30% other
Location: West Indies

■ **PEOPLE**

Nationality: Montserratian
Ethnic Groups: descendants of British, French, Irish settlers, also black
Languages: English (official)

■ **GOVERNMENT**

Leader(s): Gov. David G.P. Taylor; Chief Min. Reuben Meade
Government Type: dependent territory of the UK
National Holiday: Celebration of the Birthday of the Queen, second Saturday in June

■ **ECONOMY**

Overview: manufacturing accounts for 85% of exports: leather goods, cotton clothing, electronics, plastic bags, herbal teas, ornamental plants, tropical fruit; the economy is heavily dependent on imports, making it vulnerable to fluctuations in world prices

■ **FINANCE/TRADE**

Currency: Eastern Caribbean dollar

Morocco

Long-Form Name: Kingdom of Morocco
Capital: Rabat
Population: 28,000,000 (1993 est.)

■ **GEOGRAPHY**

Area: 446,550 sq. km
Coastline: 1,835 km
Climate: Mediterranean, becoming more extreme in the interior
Environment: northern mountains geologically unstable and subject to earthquakes; desertification
Terrain: mostly mountains with rich coastal plains
Land Use: 18% arable; 1% permanent; 28% meadows; 12% forest; 41% other
Location: N Africa, bordering on Atlantic Ocean

■ **PEOPLE**

Nationality: Moroccan
Ethnic Groups: 99.1% Arab-Berber, 0.7% non-Morrocan, 0.2% Jewish
Languages: Arabic (official); several Berber dialects; French is language of business, government, diplomacy and post-primary education

Religions: 98.7% Sunni Moslem, 1.1% Christian, 0.2% Jewish
Marriages: n.a.
Divorces: n.a.

■ **GOVERNMENT**

Leader(s): Prime Min. Mohammed Karim Larmani, King Hassan II
Government Type: constitutional monarchy
Administrative Divisions: 36 provinces and 8 urban prefectures; 4 new governorates (wilayats) were created in early February 1994
Independence: Mar. 2, 1956 (from France)
National Holiday: National Day (anniversary of King Hassan II's accession to the throne), Mar. 3

■ **ECONOMY**

Overview: the economy is suffering due to high foreign debt, high unemployment and the country's vulnerability to external forces
GNP: $28.1 billion, per capita $1,060; real growth rate 0% (1992 est.)
Inflation: 4.9% (1992)
Industries: phosphate rock mining and processing, food processing, leather goods, textiles, construction, tourism
Labour Force: 7,824,000 (1992); 45.6% agriculture, 29.4% services, 25% industry (1989)
Unemployment: 19% (1992 est.)
Agriculture: 50% of employment and 30% of export value; not self-sufficient in food; cereal farming and livestock raising predominate; barley, wheat, citrus fruit, wine, vegetables, olives
Natural Resources: phosphates, iron ore, manganese, lead, zinc, fish, salt

■ **FINANCE/TRADE**

Currency: dirham (DH)
International Reserves Excluding Gold: $3,671 million (Jan. 1994)
Gold Reserves: 0.7 million fine troy ounces (Jan. 1994)
Budget: revenues $7.5 billion; expenditures $7.7 billion, including capital expenditures of $1.9 billion (1992)
Defence Expenditures: $1.34 billion (12.83% of total govt. expenditure) (1990), $1.1 billion (1993 budget)
External Debt: $21.305 billion (1992)
Exports: $3.977 billion (1992); commodities: food and beverages 30%, semi-processed goods 23%, consumer goods 21%, phosphates 17%; partners: European Community 58%, India 7%, Japan 5%, USSR 3%, US 2%
Imports: $7.358 billion (1992); commodities: capital goods 24%, semi-processed goods 22%,

raw materials 16%, fuel and lubricants 16%, food and beverages 13%, consumer goods 10%; partners: European Community 53%, US 11%, Canada 4%, Iraq 3%, USSR 3%, Japan 2%

■ HEALTH

Births: 31/1,000 population (1993)
Deaths: 8/1,000 population (1993)
Infant Mortality: 57 deaths/1,000 live births (1993)
Life Expectancy at Birth: 64 years male, 67 years female (1993)
No. of Physicians: 2.1/10,000 population (1992)

■ EDUCATION

Govt. Expenditure: 26.3% of govt. expenditure (1991)
Literacy: 49.5% (1993)

■ COMMUNICATIONS

Daily newspapers: 16 (1992)
Televisions: 69.6/1,000 inhabitants (1992)
Radios: 209/1,000 inhabitants (1992)
Telephones: 1.55/100 inhabitants (1992)

■ TRANSPORTATION

Motor Vehicles: 945,752; 663,802 passenger cars (1990)
Roads: 61,047 km; 29,835 km paved
Railway: 1,928 km
Air Traffic: 1,430,000 passengers carried (1991)
Airports: 73 airfields, of which 65 are usable; 26 have permanent-surface runways (1993)

Canadian Embassy: 13 bis, rue Jaafar As-Sadik; Rabat-Agdal; mailing address: CP 709, Rabat-Agdal, Morocco. Tel: (011-212-7) 67-28-80. Fax: (011-212-7) 67-21-87
Representative to Canada: Embassy of the Kingdom of Morocco, 38 Range Rd, Ottawa ON K1N 8J4. Tel: (613) 236-7391. Fax: (613) 236-6164.

Mozambique

Long-Form Name: Republic of Mozambique
Capital: Maputo
Population: 15,300,000 (1993 est.)

■ GEOGRAPHY

Area: 801,590 sq. km
Coastline: 2,470 km
Climate: tropical to subtropical
Environment: severe drought and floods occur in south; desertification
Terrain: mostly coastal lowlands, uplands in centre, high plateaus in northwest, mountains in west

Land Use: 4% arable; negligible permanent; 56% meadows; 20% forest; 20% other
Location: SE Africa, bordering on Mozambique Channel

■ PEOPLE

Nationality: Mozambican
Ethnic Groups: majority from indigenous tribal groups; about 10,000 Europeans, 35,000 Euro-Africans, 15,000 Indians
Languages: Portuguese (official); English; many indigenous dialects
Religions: 60% indigenous beliefs, 30% Christian, 10% Moslem
Marriages: n.a.
Divorces: n.a.

■ GOVERNMENT

Leader(s): Prime Min. Mário da Graça Machungo, Pres. Joaquím Alberto Chissano
Government Type: republic
Administrative Divisions: 10 provinces
Independence: June 25, 1975 (from Portugal)
National Holiday: Independence Day, June 25

■ ECONOMY

Overview: internal disorder, lack of government administrative control and a growing foreign debt have contributed to the country's failure to exploit the economic potential of its agricultural, hydropower and transportation resources; depends on much foreign aid; industry operates at only 20-40% of capacity
GNP: n.a., GDP $1.75 billion, per capita $115; real growth rate 0.3% (1992 est.)
Inflation: 50% (1992)
Industries: food, beverages, chemicals (fertilizer, soap, paints), petroleum products, textiles, non-metallic mineral products (cement, glass, asbestos), tobacco
Labour Force: 8,440,000 (1992); 84.5% agriculture, 7.4% industry, 8.1% services (1989)
Unemployment: 50% (1988)
Agriculture: accounts for 50% of GDP, over 80% of labour force and about 90% of exports; cash crops—cotton, cashew nuts, sugar cane, tea, shrimp; other crops—cassava, corn, rice, tropical fruit; not self-sufficient in food
Natural Resources: coal, titanium

■ FINANCE/TRADE

Currency: metical (pl. meticais) (Mt)
International Reserves Excluding Gold: $253 million (1991)
Gold Reserves: n.a.
Budget: revenues $252 million; expenditures

$607 million, including capital expenditures (1992 est.)
Defence Expenditures: $118 million (1993 est.)
External Debt: $4.928 billion (1992)
Exports: $162 million (1991); commodities: shrimp 48%, cashews 21%, sugar 10%, copra 3%, citrus 3%; partners: US, Western Europe, Germany, Japan
Imports: $899 million (1991); commodities: food, clothing, farm equipment, petroleum; partners: US, Western Europe, USSR

■ HEALTH

Births: 45/1,000 population (1993)
Deaths: 19/1,000 population (1993)
Infant Mortality: 151 deaths/1,000 live births (1993)
Life Expectancy at Birth: 45 years male, 48 years female (1993)
No. of Physicians: 0.3/10,000 population (1990)

■ EDUCATION

Govt. Expenditure: 12% of govt. expenditure (1990)
Literacy: 32.9% (1993)

■ COMMUNICATIONS

Daily newspapers: 2 (1992)
Televisions: 2.3/1,000 inhabitants (1992)
Radios: 41/1,000 inhabitants (1992)
Telephones: 0.41/100 inhabitants (1992)

■ TRANSPORTATION

Motor Vehicles: 111,500; 87,500 passenger cars (1990)
Roads: 26,453 km; 5,610 km paved
Railway: 3,367 km
Air Traffic: 283,000 passengers carried (1991)
Airports: 194 airfields, of which 131 are usable; 25 have permanent-surface runways (1993)

Canadian Embassy: rue Tomas Nduda, 1345, Maputo; mailingb address: P.O. Box 1578, Maputo, Mozambique. Tel: (011-258-1) 492-623. Fax: (011-258-1) 492-667
Representative to Canada: c/o Embassy of the People's Republic of Mozambique, 1900 M St NW, Ste 570, Washington DC 20036 USA. Tel: (202) 293-7146.

Myanmar

Long-Form Name: Union of Myanmar (formerly Burma)
Capital: Rangoon
Population: 43,668,000 (1993 est.)

■ GEOGRAPHY

Area: 678,500 sq. km
Coastline: 1,930 km
Climate: tropical monsoon; cloudy, rainy, hot, humid summers (southwest monsoon, June to Sept.); less cloudy, scant rainfall, mild temperatures, lower humidity during winter (northeast monsoon, Dec. to Apr.)
Environment: subject to destructive earthquakes and cyclones; flooding and landslides common during rainy season (June to Sept.); deforestation
Terrain: central lowlands ringed by steep, rugged highlands
Land Use: 15% arable land; 1% permanent crops; 1% meadows and pastures; 49% forest and woodland; 34% other; includes 2% irrigated
Location: SC Asia, bordering on Bay of Bengal

■ PEOPLE

Nationality: Burmese
Ethnic Groups: 68% Burmese, 9% Shan, 7% Karen, 4% Rakhine, 3% Chinese, 2% Mon, 2% Indian, 5% other
Languages: Myanmar (Burmese); minority ethnic groups have their own languages
Religions: 89% Buddhist, 11% animist beliefs, Moslem, Christian or other
Marriages: n.a.
Divorces: n.a.

■ GOVERNMENT

Leader(s): Prime Min. General Than Shwe
Government Type: military regime
Administrative Divisions: 7 divisions, 7 states
Independence: Jan. 4, 1948 (from UK)
National Holiday: Independence Day, Jan. 4

■ ECONOMY

Overview: economy is dependent on agriculture and is vulnerable to world market conditions (especially for rice); Myanmar has been unable to achieve much improvement in export earnings due to falling prices for many of its export commodities
GNP: $28 billion, per capita $660; real growth rate 1.3% (1992)
Inflation: 21.9% (1992)
Industries: agricultural processing; textiles and footwear; wood and wood products; petroleum refining; mining of copper, tin, tungsten, iron; construction materials; pharmaceuticals; fertilizer
Labour Force: 18,000,000 (1992); 63.9% agriculture, 9.1% industry, 27% services (1989)
Unemployment: 555,250 (1990)
Agriculture: accounts for about 40% of GDP;

self-sufficient in food; principal crops: rice, corn, oilseed, sugar cane, pulses; world's largest stand of hardwood trees; rice and teak account for 55% of exports; world's largest producer of opium poppies
Natural Resources: crude oil, timber, tin, antimony, zinc, copper, tungsten, lead, coal, some marble, limestone, precious stones, natural gas

■ **FINANCE/TRADE**

Currency: kyat (K)
International Reserves Excluding Gold: $300 million (Jan. 1994)
Gold Reserves: 0.25 million fine troy ounces (Jan. 1994)
Budget: revenues $8.1 billion; expenditures $11.6 billion, including capital expenditures (1992)
Defence Expenditures: 22.03% of total govt. expenditure (1991)
External Debt: $5.326 billion (1992)
Exports: $533 million (1992); commodities: teak, rice, oilseed, metals, rubber, gems; partners: Southeast Asia, India, China, European Community, Africa
Imports: $653 million (1992); commodities: machinery, transport equipment, chemicals, food products; partners: Japan, European Community, CEMA, China, Southeast Asia

■ **HEALTH**

Births: 30/1,000 population (1993)
Deaths: 11/1,000 population (1993)
Infant Mortality: 72 deaths/1,000 live births (1993)
Life Expectancy at Birth: 56 years male, 60 years female (1993)
No. of Physicians: 2.7/10,000 population (1992)

■ **EDUCATION**

Govt. Expenditure: 17.41% of govt. expenditure (1991)
Literacy: 81% (1993)

■ **COMMUNICATIONS**

Daily newspapers: 2 (1992)
Televisions: 1.7/1,000 inhabitants (1992)
Radios: 81/1,000 inhabitants (1992)
Telephones: 0.21/100 inhabitants (1992)

■ **TRANSPORTATION**

Motor Vehicles: 73,000; 30,000 passenger cars (1990)
Roads: 27,820 km; 3,393 km paved
Railway: 3,991 km
Air Traffic: 319,000 passengers carried (1991)
Airports: 83 airfields, of which 78 are usable; 26

have permanent-surface runways (1993)

Canadian Embassy: c/o The Canadian Embassy, 11th Floor, Boonmitr Bldg, 138 Silom Rd, Bangkok 10500; mailing address: P.O. Box 2090, Bangkok 10500, Thailand. Tel: (011-66-2) 237-4125. Fax: (011-66-2) 236-6463
Representative to Canada: Embassy of the Union of Myanmar, 85 Range Rd, Ste 902, Ottawa ON K1N 8J6. Tel: (613) 232-6434. Fax: (613) 232-6435.

Namibia

Long-Form Name: Republic of Namibia
Capital: Windhoek
Population: 1,600,000 (1993)

■ **GEOGRAPHY**

Area: 824,290 sq. km
Coastline: 1,489 km
Climate: desert; hot, dry; rainfall sparse and erratic
Environment: inhospitable with very limited natural water resources; desertification
Terrain: mostly high plateau; Namib Desert along coast; Kalahari Desert in east
Land Use: 1% arable; negligible permanent crops; 64% meadows; 22% forest; 13% other
Location: SW Africa, bordering on South Atlantic Ocean

■ **PEOPLE**

Nationality: Namibian
Ethnic Groups: 86% black, 7% white, 8% mixed; about 50% of the population belong to the Ovambo tribe and 9% to the Kavangos tribe
Languages: white population: 60% Afrikaans, 33% German, 7% English (all official); several indigenous languages
Religions: 90% Christian, 10% traditional religions
Marriages: n.a.
Divorces: n.a.

■ **GOVERNMENT**

Leader(s): Prime Min. Hage Geingob, Pres. Sam Nujoma
Government Type: republic
Administrative Divisions: 13 newly organized districts
Independence: Mar. 21, 1990 (from South Africa)
National Holiday: Independence Day, Mar. 21

■ **ECONOMY**

Overview: economy is very dependent on the

mining industry to extract and process minerals for export; world's fifth largest producer of uranium; rich diamond deposits; more than 50% of the population depends on subsistence agriculture

GNP: $2 billion, per capita $1,300; real growth rate 2% (1992)

Inflation: 10% in urban areas (1992)

Industries: meat packing, fish processing, dairy products, mining (copper, lead, zinc, diamonds, uranium)

Labour Force: 537,000 (1992); 43.5% agriculture, 21.9% industry, 34.8% services (1989)

Unemployment: 25-35% (1992)

Agriculture: accounts for 15% of GDP (including fishing); mostly subsistence farming; livestock raising major source of cash income; crops: millet, sorghum, peanuts; large unfulfilled fish catch potential

Natural Resources: diamonds, copper, uranium, gold, lead, tin, zinc, salt, vanadium, natural gas, fish; suspected deposits of coal and iron ore

■ FINANCE/TRADE

Currency: rand (R)

International Reserves Excluding Gold: $182 million (Jan. 1994)

Gold Reserves: n.a.

Budget: revenues $864 million; expenditures $1,112 million, including capital expenditures of $144 million (1992)

Defence Expenditures: 6.5% of total govt. expenditure (1991)

External Debt: $227 million (1990)

Exports: $1.184 billion (1991); commodities: diamonds, uranium, zinc, copper, meat, processed fish, karakul skins; partner: South Africa

Imports: $1.238 billion (1991); commodities: foodstuffs, manufactured consumer goods, machinery and equipment; partners: South Africa, Germany, UK, US

■ HEALTH

Births: 43/1,000 population (1993)

Deaths: 11/1,000 population (1993)

Infant Mortality: 75 deaths/1,000 live births (1993)

Life Expectancy at Birth: 56 years male, 59 years female (1993)

No. of Physicians: n.a.

■ EDUCATION

Govt. Expenditure: 22.20% of govt. expenditure (1991)

Literacy: 38.4% (1993)

■ COMMUNICATIONS

Daily newspapers: 5 (1989)

Televisions: 15.7/1,000 population (1989)

Radios: 133/1,000 population (1989)

Telephones: 4/100 inhabitants (1980)

■ TRANSPORTATION

Motor Vehicles: 103,715 registered motor vehicles (1986)

Roads: 54,400 km; 4,120 km paved

Railway: 2,390 km

Air Traffic: 455,000 passengers carried (1991)

Airports: 137 airfields, of which 112 are usable; 21 have permanent-surface runways (1993)

Representative to Canada: c/o High Commission for the Republic of Namibia, 1605 New Hampshire Ave NW, Washington DC 20009 USA. Tel: (202) 986-0540. Fax: (202) 986-0443.

Nauru

Long-Form Name: Republic of Nauru

Capital: no capital city as such; government offices in Yaren

Population: 9,882 (1993 est.)

■ GEOGRAPHY

Area: 21 sq. km

Coastline: 30 km

Climate: tropical; monsoonal; rainy season (Nov. to Feb.)

Environment: only 53 km south of equator

Terrain: sandy beach rises to fertile ring around raised coral reefs with phosphate plateau in centre

Land Use: 0% arable; 0% permanent; 0% meadows; 0% forest; 100% other

Location: Melanesia, Pacific Ocean

■ PEOPLE

Nationality: Nauruan

Ethnic Groups: 58% Nauruan, 26% other Pacific Islander, 8% Chinese, 8% European

Languages: Nauruan, a distinct Pacific Island language (official); English widely understood, spoken and used for most government and commercial purposes

Religions: Christian (two-thirds Nauruan Protestant, one-third Roman Catholic)

Marriages: n.a.

Divorces: n.a.

■ GOVERNMENT

Leader(s): Pres. Bernard Dowiyogo

Government Type: republic
Administrative Divisions: 14 districts
Independence: Jan. 31, 1968 (from UN trustee-ship under Australia, New Zealand and UK; for-merly known as Pleasant Island)
National Holiday: Independence Day, Jan. 31

■ ECONOMY

Overview: economy depends on revenues from the export of phosphates, the reserves of which are expected to be exhausted by the year 2000; most other resources are imported; has one of the highest per capita incomes in the Third World; the rehabilitation of mined land and the replacement of income from phosphates are serious long-term considerations
GNP: over $90 million, per capita $10,000; real growth rate n.a. (1989)
Inflation: n.a.
Industries: phosphate mining, financial services, coconuts
Labour Force: n.a.
Unemployment: 0% (1993)
Agriculture: coconuts; other agricultural activi-ties are negligible; almost completely dependent on imports for food and water
Natural Resources: phosphates

■ FINANCE/TRADE

Currency: Australian dollar ($A)
International Reserves Excluding Gold: n.a.
Gold Reserves: n.a.
Budget: revenues $69.7 million; expenditures $51.5 million, including capital expenditures (1986)
Defence Expenditures: n.a.
External Debt: $33.3 million
Exports: n.a.
Imports: n.a.

■ HEALTH

Births: 18.92/1,000 population (1993)
Deaths: 5.1/1,000 population (1993)
Infant Mortality: 40.6 deaths/1,000 live births (1993)
Life Expectancy at Birth: 64.3 years male, 69.18 years female (1993)
No. of Physicians: n.a.

■ EDUCATION

Govt. Expenditure: n.a.
Literacy: 99% (1993)

■ COMMUNICATIONS

Daily newspapers: n.a.
Televisions: n.a.
Radios: 633/1,000 inhabitants (1989)

Telephones: 1,600 total (1993)

■ TRANSPORTATION

Motor Vehicles: n.a.
Roads: 27 km; 21 km paved
Railway: 3.9 km
Air Traffic: 59,000 passengers carried (1991)
Airports: 1 airfield, usable and with a permanent-surface runway (1993)

Nepal

Long-Form Name: Kingdom of Nepal
Capital: Kathmandu
Population: 20,577,000 (1992)

■ GEOGRAPHY

Area: 140,800 sq. km
Coastline: none: landlocked
Climate: varies from cool summers and severe winters in north to subtropical summers and mild winters in south
Environment: contains eight of the world's 10 highest peaks; deforestation; soil erosion; water pollution
Terrain: flat river plain of the Ganges in south, central hilly region, rugged Himalayas in north
Land Use: 17% arable; negligible permanent; 13% meadows; 33% forest; 37% other
Location: SC Asia

■ PEOPLE

Nationality: Nepalese
Ethnic Groups: Newars, Indians, Tibetans, Gurungs, Magars, Tamangs, Bhotias, Rais, Limbus, Sherpas, as well as many smaller groups
Languages: Nepali (official); 20 languages divided into numerous dialects
Religions: 90% Hindu, 5% Buddhist, 3% Muslim, 2% other; only official Hindu state in the world, although no sharp distinction between many Hindu and Buddhist groups; small groups of Moslems and Christians
Marriages: n.a.
Divorces: n.a.

■ GOVERNMENT

Leader(s): King Birendra Bir Bikram Shah Dev, Prime Min. Girija Prasad Koirala (interim until Nov. 94 election); Pres. Krishna Prasad Bhattarai
Government Type: parliamentary democracy as of May 12, 1991
Administrative Divisions: 14 zones
Independence: 1768, unified by Prithvi Narayan Shah

National Holiday: Birthday of His Majesty the King, Dec. 28

■ ECONOMY

Overview: agriculture is the basis of this poor economy; suffers from an ongoing trade/transit dispute with India; agricultural production hasn't kept pace with high population growth; more than 40% of the population is undernourished, partly because of poor distribution network

GNP: $3.4 billion, per capita $170; real growth rate 3.1% (1992)

Inflation: 17.1% (1992)

Industries: small rice, jute, sugar and oilseed mills, cigarette, textiles, cement, brick; tourism

Labour Force: 7,730,000 (1992); 93% agriculture, 6.5% services, 0.6% industry (1989)

Unemployment: 5%; underemployment estimated at 25–40% (1987)

Agriculture: accounts for 60% of GDP and 90% of work force; farm products—rice, corn, wheat, sugar cane, root crops, milk, buffalo meat; not self-sufficient in food, particularly in drought years

Natural Resources: quartz, water, timber, hydroelectric potential, scenic beauty; small deposits of lignite, copper, cobalt, iron ore

■ FINANCE/TRADE

Currency: rupee (NRs)

International Reserves Excluding Gold: $602 million (Oct. 1993)

Gold Reserves: 0.15 million fine troy ounces (Oct. 1993)

Budget: revenues $308.0 million; expenditures $672 million, including capital expenditures of $396 million (1992 est.)

Defence Expenditures: 5.87% of total govt. expenditure (1991)

External Debt: $1.797 billion (1992)

Exports: $374 million (1992); commodities: clothing, carpets, leather goods, grain; partners: India 38%, US 23%, UK 6%, other Europe 9%

Imports: $792 million (1992); commodities: petroleum products 20%, fertilizer 11%, machinery 10%; partners: India 36%, Japan 13%, Europe 4%, US 1%

■ HEALTH

Births: 41/1,000 population (1993)

Deaths: 16/1,000 population (1993)

Infant Mortality: 107 deaths/1,000 live births (1993)

Life Expectancy at Birth: 55 years male, 53 years female (1993)

No. of Physicians: 0.3/10,000 population (1992)

■ EDUCATION

Govt. Expenditure: 10.95% of govt. expenditure (1991)

Literacy: 26% (1993)

■ COMMUNICATIONS

Daily newspapers: 28 (1992)

Televisions: 1.6/1,000 inhabitants (1992)

Radios: 33/1,000 inhabitants (1992)

Telephones: 0.36/100 inhabitants (1992)

■ TRANSPORTATION

Motor Vehicles: n.a.

Roads: 7,080 km; 2,898 km paved (1993)

Railway: 103 km

Air Traffic: 672,000 passengers carried (1991)

Airports: 37 airfields, all of which are usable; 5 have permanent-surface runways (1993)

Canadian Embassy: c/o The Canadian High Commission, 7/8 Shantipath, Chanakyapuri, New Delhi 110 021; mailing address: The Canadian High Commission, P.O. Box 5207, New Delhi, India. Tel: (011-91-11) 687-6500. Fax: (011-91-11) 687-6579

Representative to Canada: c/o Embassy of the Kingdom of Nepal, 2131 Leroy Place NW, Washington DC 20008 USA. Tel: (202) 667-4550. Fax: (202) 667-5534.

Netherlands

Long-Form Name: Kingdom of the Netherlands

Capital: Amsterdam; seat of government: The Hague

Population: 15,200,000 (1993 est.)

■ GEOGRAPHY

Area: 37,330 sq. km

Coastline: 451 km

Climate: temperate; marine; cool summers and mild winters

Environment: 27% of the land area is below sea level and protected from the North Sea by dikes

Terrain: mostly coastal lowland and reclaimed land (polders); some hills in southeast

Land Use: 26% arable; 1% permanent; 32% meadows; 9% forest; 32% other

Location: NC Europe, bordering on North Sea

■ PEOPLE

Nationality: Dutch

Ethnic Groups: 96% Dutch, 4% Moroccans, Turks and others (1988)

Languages: Dutch, Frisian

Religions: 62% Christianity, of which Roman

Catholic 36%, Protestant 26%; most of the rest do not profess a religion
Marriages: 6.3 (per 1,000) (1991)
Divorces: 1.88 (per 1,000) (1991)

■ GOVERNMENT

Leader(s): Prime Min. Wim Kok, Queen Beatrix
Government Type: constitutional monarchy
Administrative Divisions: 12 provinces. Dependent areas: Aruba, Netherland Antilles
Independence: 1579 (from Spain)
National Holiday: Queen's Day, Apr. 30

■ ECONOMY

Overview: a highly developed and affluent economy based on private enterprise; numerous government-backed welfare programs; trade and financial sectors are the strongest part of the economy; has a sizable budget deficit
GNP: n.a., GDP $259.8 billion, per capita $17,200; real growth rate 1.6% (1992)
Inflation: 3.7% (1992)
Industries: agro-industries, metal and engineering products, electrical machinery and equipment, chemicals, petroleum, fishing, construction, microelectronics
Labour Force: 6,153,000 (1992); 78.4% services, 17.4% industry, 4.2% agriculture
Unemployment: 5.3% (1992 est.)
Agriculture: accounts for 4.6% of GDP; animal production predominates; crops—grains, potatoes, sugar beets, fruits, vegetables; shortages of grain, fats and oils
Natural Resources: natural gas, crude oil, fertile soil

■ FINANCE/TRADE

Currency: guilder, gulden or florin (f.)
International Reserves Excluding Gold: $31,863 million (Jan. 1994)
Gold Reserves: 33.39 million fine troy ounces (Jan. 1994)
Budget: revenues $109.9 billion; expenditures $122.1 billion, including capital expenditures (1992 est.)
Defence Expenditures: 4.62% of govt. expenditure (1992)
External Debt: none
Exports: $139.944 billion (1992); commodities: agricultural products, processed foods and tobacco, natural gas, chemicals, metal products, textiles, clothing; partners: European Community 74.9% (Germany 28.3%, Belgium-Luxembourg 14.2%, France 10.7%, UK 10.2%), US 4.7%
Imports: $134.475 billion (1992); commodities: raw materials and semifinished products, consumer goods, transportation equipment, crude oil, food products; partners: European Community 63.8% (Germany 26.5%, Belgium-Luxembourg 23.1%, UK 8.1%), US 7.9%

■ HEALTH

Births: 13/1,000 population (1993)
Deaths: 9/1,000 population (1993)
Infant Mortality: 6.5 deaths/1,000 live births (1993)
Life Expectancy at Birth: 74 years male, 80 years female (1993)
No. of Physicians: 22.2/10,000 population (1992)

■ EDUCATION

Govt. Expenditure: 10.83% total govt. expenditures (1992)
Literacy: 99% (1993)

■ COMMUNICATIONS

Daily newspapers: 86 (1992)
Televisions: 484.8/1,000 inhabitants (1992)
Radios: 902/1,000 inhabitants (1992)
Telephones: 65.86/100 inhabitants (1992)

■ TRANSPORTATION

Motor Vehicles: 6,091,294; 5,509,174 passenger cars (1990)
Roads: 108,360 km; 92,525 km paved (1993)
Railway: 2,828 km (1993)
Air Traffic: 8,893,000 passengers carried (1991)
Airports: 28 airfields, all of which are usable; 20 have permanent-surface runways (1993)

Canadian Embassy: Sophialaan 7, The Hague, Netherlands. Tel: (011-31-70) 361-4111. Fax: (011-31-70) 356-1111
Representative to Canada: Royal Netherlands Embassy, 350 Albert St, Ste 2020, Ottawa ON K1R 1A4. Tel: (613) 237-5030. Fax: (613) 237-6471.

Netherlands Antilles

Dependent Territory of the Netherlands

Long-Form Name: Netherlands Antilles
Capital: Willemstad
Population: 200,000 (1993 est.)

■ GEOGRAPHY

Area: 960 sq. km, 2 island groups
Climate: tropical maritime, moderated by northeasterly trade winds, short rainy season
Land Use: islands mostly too rocky for agriculture; only 8% is arable land; 0% permanent crops, 0% meadows and pastures, 0% forest,

92% other
Location: West Indies

■ PEOPLE

Nationality: Netherlands Antillean
Ethnic Groups: mixed African 85%, Carib Indian, European, Latin, Oriental
Languages: Dutch (official), Papiamento (derived from Dutch, Spanish, Portuguese), English

■ GOVERNMENT

Leader(s): Chief of State Queen Beatrix, Gov. Dr. Jaime M. Saleh; Prime Min. Maria Liberia-Peters
Government Type: dependency with internal self-government
National Holiday: Queen's Day, April 30

■ ECONOMY

Overview: unlike many Latin American countries, the Netherlands Antilles has avoided crushing external debt; Curaçao has one of the largest ship-repair dry docks in western hemisphere; chief trading partner: UK

■ FINANCE/TRADE

Currency: Netherlands Antilles guilder

New Caledonia

Overseas Territory of France

Long-Form Name: Territory of New Caledonia and Dependencies
Capital: Nouméa
Population: 200,000 (1993 est.)

■ GEOGRAPHY

Area: 19,060 sq. km (a peninsula and three small islands)
Climate: humid, subtropical maritime, modified by southeast trade winds
Land Use: 0% arable, 0% permanent crops, 14% meadow and pasture, 51% forest and woodland, 35% other
Location: SW Pacific Ocean (Melanesia)

■ PEOPLE

Nationality: New Caledonian
Ethnic Groups: 42.5% Melanesian, 37.1% European, 8.4% Wallisian, 3.8% Polynesian, 3.6% Indonesian, 1.6% Vietnamese, 3% other
Languages: French (official), 28 Melanesian and Polynesian languages

■ GOVERNMENT

Leader(s): Head of Govt. Alain Christnacht, Pres. of Territorial Congress Simon Loueckhote
Government Type: overseas territory
National Holiday: Taking of the Bastille, July 14

■ ECONOMY

Overview: only a negligible portion of the land is arable, and most food must be imported; the backbone of the economy is nickel export

■ FINANCE/TRADE

Currency: CFP franc

New Zealand

Long-Form Name: New Zealand
Capital: Wellington
Population: 3,455,000 (1993 est.)

■ GEOGRAPHY

Area: 268,680 sq. km
Coastline: 15,134 km
Climate: temperate with sharp regional contrasts
Environment: earthquakes are common though usually not severe
Terrain: predominantly mountainous with some large coastal plains
Land Use: 2% arable, 0% permanent, 53% meadows and pastures, 38% forest and woodland, 7% other
Location: SE of Australia, bordering on Tasman Sea, Pacific Ocean

■ PEOPLE

Nationality: New Zealander
Ethnic Groups: 88% European, 8.9% Maori, 2.9% Pacific Islander, 0.2% other
Languages: English (official), Maori
Religions: 75% Christian, 18% unspecified, 7% Hindu, Confucian, other
Marriages: 6.8 (per 1,000) (1991)
Divorces: 2.7 (per 1,000) (1991)

■ GOVERNMENT

Leader(s): Gov. Gen. Catherine Tizard, Prime Min. Jim Bolger
Government Type: parliamentary democracy
Administrative Divisions: 93 counties, 9 districts, 3 town districts; dependent areas inc.: the Cook Islands, the Kermadec Islands, Niue, the Ross Dependency (uninhabited except for scientific personnel), Tokelau
Independence: Sept. 26, 1907 (from UK)
National Holiday: Waitangi Day, Feb. 6

■ ECONOMY

Overview: government has been reorienting from an agrarian to an open free market economy that can compete in the global community; inflation has been reduced; growth has been sluggish, unemployment has been at an all-time high
GNP: $49.8 billion, per capita $14,900; real growth rate 3% (1992)
Inflation: 1.0% (1992)
Industries: food processing, wool production, wood and paper products, textiles, machinery, transportation equipment, banking and insurance, tourism, mining
Labour Force: 1,570,900 (1992); 69.9% services, 20.1% industry, 10% agriculture (1989)
Unemployment: 10.1% (1992)
Agriculture: accounts for 9% of GNP and 10% of work force; livestock predominates: wool, meat, dairy products; crops: wheat, barley, potatoes, pulses, fruit and vegetables; fish; surplus producer of farm products
Natural Resources: natural gas, iron ore, sand, coal, timber, hydroelectricity, gold, limestone

■ FINANCE/TRADE

Currency: New Zealand dollar (NZ$)
International Reserves Excluding Gold: $3,846 million (Jan. 1994)
Gold Reserves: 0.00 million fine troy ounces (Jan. 1994)
Budget: revenues $14.0 billion; expenditures $15.2 billion, including capital expenditures (1992)
Defence Expenditures: 3.76% of total govt. expenditure (1993)
External Debt: $17 billion (1989)
Exports: $10.936 billion (1993 est.); commodities: wool, lamb, mutton, beef, fruit, fish, cheese, manufactures, chemicals, forestry products; partners: European Community 18.3%, Japan 17.9%, Australia 17.5%, US 13.5%
Imports: $8.628 billion (1993 est.); commodities: petroleum, consumer goods, motor vehicles, industrial equipment; partners: Australia 19.7%, Japan 16.9%, European Community 16.9%, US 15.3%, Taiwan 3%

■ HEALTH

Births: 18/1,000 population (1993)
Deaths: 8/1,000 population (1993)
Infant Mortality: 8.3 deaths/1,000 live births (1993)
Life Expectancy at Birth: 72 years male, 78 years female (1993)
No. of Physicians: 17.4/10,000 population (1992)

■ EDUCATION

Govt. Expenditure: 13% of govt. expenditure (1988)
Literacy: 99% (1993)

■ COMMUNICATIONS

Daily newspapers: 35 (1992)
Televisions: 371.6/1,000 inhabitants (1992)
Radios: 922/1,000 inhabitants (1992)
Telephones: 71.74/100 inhabitants (1992)

■ TRANSPORTATION

Motor Vehicles: 1,867,745; 1,557,074 passenger cars (1990)
Roads: 93,232 km; 51,319 km paved
Railway: 4,716 km
Air Traffic: 5,371,000 passengers carried (1991)
Airports: 120 airfields, all of which are usable; 33 have permanent-surface runways (1993)

Canadian Embassy: The Canadian High Commission, 61 Molesworth St, 3rd Floor, Thorndon, Wellington; mailing address: P.O. Box 12049, Thorndon, Wellington, New Zealand. Tel: (011-64-4) 473-9577. Fax: (011-64-4) 471-2082
Representative to Canada: New Zealand High Commission, Metropolitan House, 99 Bank St, Ste 727, Ottawa ON K1P 6G3. Tel: (613) 238-5991. Fax: (613) 238-5707.

Nicaragua

Long-Form Name: Republic of Nicaragua
Capital: Managua
Population: 4,100,000 (1993 est.)

■ GEOGRAPHY

Area: 129,494 sq. km
Coastline: 910 km
Climate: tropical in lowlands, cooler in highlands
Environment: subject to destructive earthquakes, volcanoes, landslides and occasional severe hurricanes; deforestation; soil erosion; water pollution
Terrain: extensive Atlantic coastal plains rising to central interior mountains; narrow Pacific coastal plain interrupted by volcanoes
Land Use: 9% arable; 1% permanent; 43% meadows; 35% forest; 12% other
Location: Central (Latin) America, bordering on Caribbean Sea, Pacific Ocean

■ PEOPLE

Nationality: Nicaraguan

Ethnic Groups: 69% mestizo, 17% white, 9% black, 5% Indian
Languages: Spanish (official); English- and Indian-speaking minorities on Atlantic coast
Religions: 95% Roman Catholic, 5% Protestant
Marriages: 3.3 (per 1,000) (1987)
Divorces: 0.22 (per 1,000) (1990)

■ GOVERNMENT

Leader(s): Pres. Violeta Chamorro, V. Pres. Virgilio Godoy Reyes
Government Type: republic
Administrative Divisions: 17 departments
Independence: Sept. 15, 1821 (from Spain)
National Holiday: Independence Day, Sept. 15

■ ECONOMY

Overview: the economy is based on the export of coffee and cotton; government control is extensive, including the financial system, wholesale purchasing, production, sales, foreign trade and distribution of goods; many shortages; high inflation; large debt
GNP: $1.7 billion, per capita $425; real growth rate 0.5% (1992 est.)
Inflation: 8% (1992)
Industries: food processing, chemicals, metal products, textiles, clothing, petroleum refining and distribution, beverages, footwear
Labour Force: 1,204,000 (1992); 37.7% services, 46.5% agriculture, 15.8% industry (1989)
Unemployment: 14.0% (1992); underemployment approximately 50%
Agriculture: accounts for 15% of GDP and 44% of work force; cash crops—coffee, bananas, sugar cane, cotton; food crops—rice, corn, cassava, citrus fruit, beans; variety of animal products—beef, veal, pork, poultry, dairy; war has lowered self-sufficiency in food
Natural Resources: gold, silver, copper, tungsten, lead, zinc, timber, fish

■ FINANCE/TRADE

Currency: córdoba ($C)
International Reserves Excluding Gold: n.a.
Gold Reserves: n.a.
Budget: revenues $347 million; expenditures $499 million, including capital expenditures (1991)
Defence Expenditures: $318 million (1990)
External Debt: $11.126 billion (1992)
Exports: $218 million (1992); commodities: coffee, cotton, sugar, bananas, seafood, meat, chemicals; partners: CEMA 15%, OECD 75%, others 10%
Imports: $892 million (1992); commodities: petroleum, food, chemicals, machinery, clothing; partners: CEMA 55%, European Community 20%, Latin America 10%, others 10%

■ HEALTH

Births: 38/1,000 population (1993)
Deaths: 7/1,000 population (1993)
Infant Mortality: 59 deaths/1,000 live births (1993)
Life Expectancy at Birth: 60 years male, 65 years female (1993)
No. of Physicians: 6.4/10,000 population (1992)

■ EDUCATION

Govt. Expenditure: 12.0% of govt. expenditure (1987)
Literacy: 57.5% (1993)

■ COMMUNICATIONS

Daily newspapers: 3 (1992)
Televisions: 61.4/1,000 inhabitants (1992)
Radios: 247/1,000 inhabitants (1992)
Telephones: 1.65/100 inhabitants (1992)

■ TRANSPORTATION

Motor Vehicles: 74,085; 31,111 passenger cars (1990)
Roads: 25,930 km; 4,000 km paved (1993)
Railway: 373 km
Air Traffic: 130,000 passengers carried (1991)
Airports: 226 airfields, of which 151 are usable; 11 have permanent-surface runways (1993)

Canadian Embassy: c/o Cronos Building, Calle 3 y Avenida Central, San José; mailing address: Apartado Postal 10303, San José, Costa Rica. Tel: (011-506) 55-35-22. Fax: (011-506) 23-23-95
Representative to Canada: Embassy of the Republic of Nicaragua, 130 Albert St, Ste 407, Ottawa ON K1P 5G4. Tel: (613) 234-9361. Fax: (613) 238-7666.

Niger

Long-Form Name: Republic of Niger
Capital: Niamey
Population: 8,500,000 (1993 est.)

■ GEOGRAPHY

Area: 1,267,000 sq. km
Coastline: none: landlocked
Climate: mostly hot, dry, dusty; tropical in extreme south
Environment: recurrent drought and desertification severely affecting marginal agricultural activities; overgrazing; soil erosion

Terrain: desert and sand dunes; hills in north
Land Use: 3% arable land; 0% permanent; 7% meadows; 2% forest; 88% other
Location: NC Africa

■ PEOPLE

Nationality: Nigerien
Ethnic Groups: 56% Hausa; 22% Djerma; 9% Fula; 8% Tuareg; 4% Beri Beri (Kanouri); 1% Arab, Toubou and Gourmantche; about 4,000 French expatriates
Languages: French (official); Hausa (50%), Djerma, also Tuareg, Fulani
Religions: 80% Moslem, remainder indigenous beliefs and Christians
Marriages: n.a.
Divorces: n.a.

■ GOVERNMENT

Leader(s): Pres. Mahamane Ousmane, Prime Min. Mahamadou Issoufou
Government Type: transitional govt. as of Nov. 1991; scheduled to turn over power to democratically elected govt. in March 1993
Administrative Divisions: 7 departments
Independence: Aug. 3, 1960 (from France)
National Holiday: Republic Day, Dec. 18

■ ECONOMY

Overview: about 90% of the population is engaged in livestock rearing and farming; depends heavily on exploitation of uranium deposits, thus vulnerable to demand for uranium; increasing external debt is a problem
GNP: $2.361 billion, per capita $300; real growth rate -0.9% (1991)
Inflation: -4.5% (1992)
Industries: cement, brick, rice mills, small cotton gins, textiles, chemicals, oilseed presses, slaughterhouses and a few other small light industries; uranium production began in 1971
Labour Force: 3,620,000 (1992); 85% agriculture, 2.7% industry, 12.3% services (1989)
Unemployment: 46.8% (1989)
Agriculture: accounts for roughly 40% of GDP and 90% of labour force; cash crops—cowpeas, cotton, peanuts; food crops—millet, sorghum, cassava, rice; livestock—cattle, sheep, goats; self-sufficient in food except in drought years
Natural Resources: uranium, coal, iron ore, tin, phosphates

■ FINANCE/TRADE

Currency: Communauté financière africaine franc (CFAF)
International Reserves Excluding Gold: $194 million (Sept. 1993)

Gold Reserves: 0.01 million fine troy ounces (1991)
Budget: revenues $193 million; expenditures $355 million, including capital expenditures of $106 million (1991 est.)
Defence Expenditures: $17.21 million (1989)
External Debt: $1.711 billion (1992)
Exports: $312 million (1991); commodities: uranium 76%, livestock, cowpeas, onions, hides, skins; partners: n.a.
Imports: $355 million (1991); commodities: petroleum products, primary materials, machinery, vehicles and parts, electronic equipment, pharmaceuticals, chemical products, cereals, foodstuffs; partners: n.a.

■ HEALTH

Births: 52/1,000 population (1993)
Deaths: 20/1,000 population (1993)
Infant Mortality: 123 deaths/1,000 live births (1993)
Life Expectancy at Birth: 43 years male, 46 years female (1993)
No. of Physicians: 0.2/10,000 population (1992)

■ EDUCATION

Govt. Expenditure: 9.0% of government expenditure (1989)
Literacy: 28.4% (1993)

■ COMMUNICATIONS

Daily newspapers: 1 (1992)
Televisions: 4/1,000 inhabitants (1992)
Radios: 59/1,000 inhabitants (1992)
Telephones: 0.2/100 inhabitants (1992)

■ TRANSPORTATION

Motor Vehicles: 35,000; 17,000 passenger cars (1990)
Roads: 39,970 km; 3,170 km paved (1993)
Railway: n.a.
Air Traffic: 64,000 passengers carried (1991)
Airports: 28 airfields, of which 26 are usable; 9 have permanent-surface runways (1993)

Canadian Embassy: Sonara II Bldg, avenue du Premier Pont, Niamey; mailing address: Box 362, Niamey, Niger. Tel: (011-227) 73-36-86. Fax: (011-227) 73-50-64.
Representative to Canada: Embassy of the Republic of Niger, 38 Blackburn Ave, Ottawa

ON K1N 8A2. Tel: (613) 232-4291. Fax: (613) 230-9808.

Nigeria

Long-Form Name: Federal Republic of Nigeria
Capital: Abuja
Population: 95,100,000 (1993 est.)

■ GEOGRAPHY

Area: 923,770 sq. km
Coastline: 853 km
Climate: varies; equatorial in south, tropical in centre, arid in north
Environment: recent droughts in north severely affecting marginal agricultural activities; desertification; soil degradation, rapid deforestation
Terrain: southern lowlands merge into central hills and plateaus; mountains in southeast, plains in north
Land Use: 31% arable; 3% permanent; 23% meadows; 15% forest; 28% other
Location: WC Africa, bordering on North Atlantic Ocean

■ PEOPLE

Nationality: Nigerian
Ethnic Groups: more than 250 tribal groups; Hausa and Fulani of the north, Yoruba of the southwest and Ibos of the southeast make up 65% of the population; about 27,000 non-Africans
Languages: English (official); Hausa, Yoruba, Ibo, Fulani and several other languages also widely used
Religions: 50% Moslem, 40% Christian, 10% indigenous beliefs
Marriages: n.a.
Divorces: n.a.

■ GOVERNMENT

Leader(s): Head of State Sani Abacha
Government Type: military government from Dec. 1983 to Aug. 27, 1993 when interim government announced
Administrative Divisions: 30 states and 1 territory
Independence: Oct. 1, 1960 (from UK)
National Holiday: Independence Day, Oct. 1

■ ECONOMY

Overview: the economy is dependent on oil and vulnerable to oil prices; agricultural production has been poor recently; high inflationary pressures are a concern; government efforts to reduce Nigeria's dependence on oil exports and to sustain noninflationary economic growth have been hampered by inadequate new invest-ment and endemic corruption

GNP: $35 billion, per capita $300; real growth rate 3.6% (1992 est.)
Inflation: 44.6% (1992)
Industries: crude oil, natural gas, coal, tin, columbite; palm oil, peanut, cotton, rubber, petroleum, wood, hides and skins; textiles, cement, building materials, food products, footwear, chemicals, printing, ceramics, steel
Labour Force: 42,000,000 (1992); 44.6% agriculture, 51.2% services, 4.2% industry (1989)
Unemployment: 28% (1992 est.)
Agriculture: accounts for 32% of GNP and half of labour force; inefficient small-scale farming dominates; once a large net exporter of food and now an importer; cash crops—cocoa, peanuts, palm oil, rubber; food crops—corn, rice, sorghum, millet, cassava, yams, fishing and forestry
Natural Resources: crude oil, tin, columbite, iron ore, coal, limestone, lead, zinc, natural gas

■ FINANCE/TRADE

Currency: naira (N)
International Reserves Excluding Gold: $1,316 million (Nov. 1993)
Gold Reserves: 0.69 million fine troy ounces (Nov. 1993)
Budget: revenues $9 billion; expenditures $10.8 billion, including capital expenditures (1992)
Defence Expenditures: $172 million (1992)
External Debt: $30.959 billion (1992)
Exports: $11.886 billion (1992); commodities: oil 95%, cocoa, palm kernels, rubber; partners: European Community 51%, US 32%
Imports: $8.276 billion (1992); commodities: consumer goods, capital equipment, chemicals, raw materials; partners: European Community, US

■ HEALTH

Births: 45/1,000 population (1993)
Deaths: 14/1,000 population (1993)
Infant Mortality: 84 deaths/1,000 live births (1993)
Life Expectancy at Birth: 52 years male, 54 years female (1993)
No. of Physicians: 1.6/10,000 population (1992)

■ EDUCATION

Govt. Expenditure: 2.81% of govt. expenditure (1987)
Literacy: 51% (1993)

■ COMMUNICATIONS

Daily newspapers: 31 (1992)
Televisions: 28.6/1,000 inhabitants (1992)

Radios: 171/1,000 inhabitants (1992)
Telephones: 0.3/100 inhabitants (1992)

■ TRANSPORTATION

Motor Vehicles: 1,410,000; 785,000 passenger cars (1986)
Roads: 109,930 km; 30,484 km paved
Railway: 3,510 km
Air Traffic: 930,000 passengers carried (1991)
Airports: 76 airfields, of which 63 are usable; 34 have permanent-surface runways (1993)

Canadian Embassy: The Canadian High Commission, Committee of Vice-Chancellors Bldg, Plot 8A, 4 Idowu Taylor St, Victoria Island, Lagos; mailing address: The Canadian High Commission, P.O. Box 54506, Ikoyi Station, Lagos, Nigeria. Tel: (011-234-1) 269-2915. Fax: (011-234-1) 269-2919
Representative to Canada: High Commission for the Federal Republic of Nigeria, 295 Metcalfe St, Ottawa ON K2P 1R9. Tel: (613) 236-0521. Fax: (613) 236-0529.

Niue

Territory of New Zealand

Long-Form Name: Niue
Capital: Alofi
Population: 1,977 (1993 est.)

■ GEOGRAPHY

Area: 260 sq. km, world's largest uplifted coral island
Climate: tropical maritime, modified by south-easterly trade winds
Land Use: 61% arable, 4% permanent crops, 4% meadows and pastures, 19% forest, 12% other
Location: Pacific Ocean, NE of New Zealand

■ PEOPLE

Nationality: Niuean
Ethnic Groups: Polynesian
Languages: English, Polynesian closely related to Tongan and Samoan

■ GOVERNMENT

Leader(s): Prem. Young Vivian
National Holiday: Waitangi Day, Feb. 6

■ ECONOMY

Overview: heavily dependent on aid from New Zealand; govt. expenditures regularly exceed revenues; agriculture includes coconuts, honey, limes, root crops; chief trading partner: New Zealand

■ FINANCE/TRADE

Currency: New Zealand dollar

Norfolk Island

Dependent Territory of Australia

Long-Form Name: Territory of Norfolk Island
Capital: Kingston (administrative center), Burnt Pine (commercial center)
Population: 2,665 (1993 est.)

■ GEOGRAPHY

Area: 34.6 sq. km
Climate: subtropical, mild, little seasonal variation
Land Use: 0% arable, 0% permanent crops, 25% meadows and pastures, 0% forests, 75% other
Location: S Pacific Ocean, NE of Australia

■ PEOPLE

Nationality: Norfolk Islander
Ethnic Groups: majority descendants of Polynesians and British (the latter crew members of the British naval ship Bounty)
Languages: English (official), Norfolk (a mixture of 18th-century English and ancient Tahitian)

■ GOVERNMENT

Leader(s): Admin. A.G. Kerr; head of legislative assembly John Brown
Government Type: a largely self-governing dependency, territory of Australia
National Holiday: Pitcairners Arrival Day Anniversary, June 8

■ ECONOMY

Overview: tourism is backbone of economy; revenues from tourism have helped the agricultural sector become self-sufficient in beef, poultry and eggs; export of indigenous fruit and vegetables

■ FINANCE/TRADE

Currency: Australian dollar

Northern Marianas

Outlying Territory of the United States

Long-Form Name: The Commonwealth of the Northern Mariana Islands
Capital: Saipan
Population: 48,581 (1993 est.)

■ GEOGRAPHY

Area: 477 sq. km (combined land area of 16 islands)
Climate: tropical maritime, moderated by north-easterly trade winds; little seasonal temperature variation
Land Use: 5% arable on Saipan island; volcanic islands too mountainous for cultivation; chief agricultural use is grazing; 19% meadows and pastures
Location: Pacific Ocean, E of the Philippines

■ PEOPLE

Nationality: n.a. (no descriptive term); American citizenship
Ethnic Groups: Chamorro, Carolinians and other Micronesians, Caucasian, Japanese, Chinese, Korean
Languages: English (official), Chamorro, Carolinian, Japanese; 86% of the population speaks a language other than English at home

■ GOVERNMENT

Leader(s): Gov. Lorenzo (Larry) De Leon Guerrero; Lieut.-Gov. Benjamin Manglona
Government Type: commonwealth in political union with the US; self-governing with locally elected governing body
National Holiday: Commonwealth Day, Jan. 8

■ ECONOMY

Overview: economy benefits from US financial assistance, but the rate of funding has declined as local revenues have increased; tourism is growing in importance and now employs approximately 50% of the work force; agriculture: cattle, coconuts, breadfruit, vegetables

■ FINANCE/TRADE

Currency: American dollar

Norway

Long-Form Name: Kingdom of Norway
Capital: Oslo
Population: 4,300,000 (1993 est.)

■ GEOGRAPHY

Area: 324,220 sq. km
Coastline: 21,925 km (3,491 km mainland; 2,413 km large islands; 16,093 km long fjords; numerous small islands and minor indentations); one of the longest and most rugged coastlines in the world
Climate: temperate along coast, modified by North Atlantic Current; colder interior; rainy year-round on west coast
Environment: air and water pollution; acid rain
Terrain: glaciated; mostly high plateaus and rugged mountains broken by fertile valleys; small, scattered plains; coastline deeply indented by fjords; arctic tundra in north
Land Use: 3% arable; 0% permanent crops; negligible meadows, 27% forest; 70% other
Location: N Europe, bordering on Norwegian Sea, North Sea

■ PEOPLE

Nationality: Norwegian
Ethnic Groups: Germanic (Nordic, Alpine, Baltic) and racial-cultural minority of 20,000 Lapps
Languages: Norwegian (official); small Lapp- and Finnish-speaking minorities
Religions: Christianity (predominantly Protestant)
Marriages: 5.2 (per 1,000) (1990)
Divorces: 2.4 (per 1,000) (1990)

■ GOVERNMENT

Leader(s): Prime Min. Gro Harlem Brundtland, King Harald V
Government Type: constitutional monarchy
Administrative Divisions: 19 provinces; dependent areas inc.: Bouvet Island (uninhabited), Jan Mayen (uninhabited), Peter I Island (uninhabited), Queen Maud Land (uninhabited), Svalbard
Independence: Oct. 26, 1905 (from Sweden)
National Holiday: Constitution Day, May 17

■ ECONOMY

Overview: a small country with high dependence on international trade; a prosperous capitalist nation which has extensive welfare measures; concerns are the aging population, increased economic integration with Europe and the balance between private and public influence in economic decisions
GNP: $76.1 billion, per capita $17,700; real growth rate 2.9% (1992)
Inflation: 2.3% (1992)
Industries: petroleum and gas, food processing, shipbuilding, pulp and paper products, metal, chemicals, timber, mining, textiles, fishing
Labour Force: 2,128,000 (1992); 77.8% services, 16.1% industry, 6.1% agriculture (1989)
Unemployment: 5.9% (1992)
Agriculture: accounts for 2.6% of GDP and 5.5% of labour force; among world's top 10 fishing nations; livestock output exceeds value of crops; over half of food needs imported
Natural Resources: crude oil, copper, natural gas, pyrites, nickel, iron ore, zinc, lead, fish, timber,

hydropower

■ FINANCE/TRADE

Currency: krone (pl. kroner) (NKr)
International Reserves Excluding Gold: $19,873 million (Jan. 1994)
Gold Reserves: 1.18 million fine troy ounces (Jan. 1994)
Budget: revenues $50.6 billion; expenditures $57.0 billion, including capital expenditures (1992)
Defence Expenditures: $3.76 billion (1991)
External Debt: $3.8 billion (1992)
Exports: $32.311 billion (1993); commodities: petroleum and petroleum products 25%, natural gas 11%, fish 7%, aluminum 6%, ships 3.5%, pulp and paper; partners: UK 26%, EFTA 16.3%, less developed countries 14%, Sweden 12%, Germany 12%, US 6%, Denmark 5%
Imports: $24.303 billion (1993); commodities: machinery, fuels and lubricants, transportation equipment, chemicals, foodstuffs, clothing, ships; partners: Sweden 18%, less developed countries 18%, Germany 14%, Denmark 8%, UK 7%, Japan 5%

■ HEALTH

Births: 14/1,000 population (1993)
Deaths: 11/1,000 population (1993)
Infant Mortality: 7.8 deaths/1,000 live births (1993)
Life Expectancy at Birth: 73 years male, 80 years female (1993)
No. of Physicians: 22.2/10,000 population (1992)

■ EDUCATION

Govt. Expenditure: 14.8% of govt. expenditure (1991)
Literacy: 100% (1993)

■ COMMUNICATIONS

Daily newspapers: 83 (1992)
Televisions: 422.7/1,000 inhabitants (1992)
Radios: 796.7/1,000 inhabitants (1992)
Telephones: 62.20/100 inhabitants (1992)

■ TRANSPORTATION

Motor Vehicles: 1,942,558; 1,613,037 passenger cars (1990)
Roads: 79,540 km; 38,580 km paved
Railway: 4,280 km
Air Traffic: 8,857,000 passengers carried (1991)
Airports: 103 airfields, of which 102 are usable; 63 have permanent-surface runways (1993)

Canadian Embassy: The Canadian Embassy, Oscars Gate 20, 0244 Oslo, Norway; mailing address: Oscars Gate 20, 0244 Oslo, Norway. Tel: (011-47) 22-46-69-55. Fax: (011-47) 22-69-34-67
Representative to Canada: Embassy of the Kingdom of Norway, Royal Bank Centre, 90 Sparks St, Ste 532, Ottawa ON K1P 5B4. Tel: (613) 238-6571. Fax: (613) 238-2765.

Oman

Long-Form Name: Sultanate of Oman
Capital: Masqat or Muscat
Population: 1,637,000 (1993 est.)

■ GEOGRAPHY

Area: 212,460 sq. km
Coastline: 2,092 km along the Arabian Sea and Gulf of Oman
Climate: dry desert; hot, humid along coast; hot, dry interior; strong southwest summer monsoon (May to Sept.) in far south
Environment: summer winds often raise large sandstorms and dust storms in interior; sparse natural freshwater resources
Terrain: vast central desert plain, rugged mountains in north and south
Land Use: less than 2% arable; negligible permanent; 5% meadows; 0% forest; 93% other
Location: SW Asia (Middle East), bordering on Arabian Sea

■ PEOPLE

Nationality: Omani
Ethnic Groups: almost entirely Arab, with small Balochi, Zanzibari and Indian groups
Languages: Arabic (official); English, Balochi, Urdu, Indian dialects
Religions: 75% Ibadhi Moslem; remainder Sunni Moslem, Shi'a Moslem, Hindu minority
Marriages: n.a.
Divorces: n.a.

■ GOVERNMENT

Leader(s): Sultan and Prime Min. Qaboos bin Sa'id Al Said
Government Type: absolute monarchy; independent, with residual UK influence
Administrative Divisions: none per se, but there are 3 "muhafazah" (i.e., governorates)
Independence: 1650, expulsion of the Portuguese
National Holiday: National Day, Nov. 18

■ ECONOMY

Overview: economy depends on the success of its oil industry which has 20 years' supply at the current rate of extraction; subsistence agriculture is the major employment, and the general

populace relies on imported food
GNP: $8.787 billion, per capita $6,006; real growth rate 9.3% (1991)
Inflation: 1.6% (1991)
Industries: crude oil production and refining, natural gas production, construction, cement, copper
Labour Force: 405,100 (1992); 50% agriculture, 21.8% industry, 28.6% services (1989); 58% of labour force are non-Omani
Unemployment: n.a.
Agriculture: accounts for 6% of GDP and 40% of labour force (including fishing); less than 2% of land cultivated; largely subsistence farming (dates, limes, bananas, alfalfa, vegetables, camels, cattle); not self-sufficient in food
Natural Resources: crude oil, copper, asbestos, some marble, limestone, chromium, gypsum, natural gas

■ FINANCE/TRADE

Currency: Omani rial (RO)
International Reserves Excluding Gold: $1,609 million (1992)
Gold Reserves: 0.29 million fine troy ounces (1992)
Budget: revenues $4.1 billion; expenditures $4.8 billion, including capital expenditures of $1 billion (1991)
Defence Expenditures: 35.76% of total govt. expenditure (1992)
External Debt: $2.854 billion (1992)
Exports: $5.428 billion (1992); commodities: petroleum, re-exports, processed copper, dates, nuts, fish; partners: Japan, S Korea, Thailand
Imports: $3.769 billion (1992); commodities: machinery, transportation equipment, manufactured goods, food, livestock, lubricants; partners: Japan, United Arab Emirates, UK, Germany, US

■ HEALTH

Births: 42/1,000 population (1993)
Deaths: 7/1,000 population (1993)
Infant Mortality: 44 deaths/1,000 live births (1993)
Life Expectancy at Birth: 64 years male, 68 years female (1993)
No. of Physicians: 9.1/10,000 population (1990)

■ EDUCATION

Govt. Expenditure: 11.43% of government expenditure (1991)
Literacy: 20% (1992)

■ COMMUNICATIONS

Daily newspapers: 3 (1992)

Televisions: 761.8/1,000 inhabitants (1992)
Radios: 645/1,000 inhabitants (1992)
Telephones: 5.33/100 inhabitants (1992)

■ TRANSPORTATION

Motor Vehicles: 215,266; 140,000 passenger cars (1990)
Roads: 26,000 km; 6,000 km paved
Railway: n.a.
Air Traffic: 958,000 passengers carried (1991)
Airports: 138 airfields, of which 130 are usable; 6 have permanent-surface runways (1993)

Canadian Embassy: Da'Aiyah - Block 4, House No. 24, Al-Mutawakel St, Kuwait City; mailing address: P.O. Box 25281, Safat, Kuwait City, 13113, Kuwait. Tel: (011-965) 256-3025. Fax: (011-965) 256-4167.
Representative to Canada: c/o Embassy of the Sultanate of Oman, 2342 Massachusetts Ave NW, Washington, DC 20008 USA. Tel: (202) 387-1980. Fax: (202) 745-4933.

Pakistan

Long-Form Name: Islamic Republic of Pakistan
Capital: Islamabad
Population: 122,400,000 (1993 est.)

■ GEOGRAPHY

Area: 803,940 sq. km
Coastline: 1,046 km along Gulf of Oman and Arabian Sea
Climate: mostly hot, dry desert; temperate in northwest; arctic in north
Environment: frequent earthquakes, occasionally severe especially in north and west; flooding along the Indus after heavy rains (July and Aug.); deforestation; soil erosion; water logging; desertification
Terrain: flat Indus plain in east; mountains in north and northwest; Balochistan plateau in west
Land Use: 26% arable; negligible permanent; 6% meadows; 4% forest; 64% other
Location: SW Asia (Middle East), bordering on Arabian Sea

■ PEOPLE

Nationality: Pakistani
Ethnic Groups: Punjabi, Sindhi, Pashtun (Pathan), Baloch, Muhajir (immigrants from India and their descendents)
Languages: Urdu (national), Punjab, Sindhi, Pushto, English
Religions: 97% Moslem (77% Sunni, 20% Shi'a), 3% Christian, Hindu and other
Marriages: n.a.

Divorces: n.a.

■ GOVERNMENT

Leader(s): Pres. Farooq Leghari, Prime Min. Benazir Bhutto
Government Type: republic
Administrative Divisions: 4 provinces, 1 tribal area and 1 territory
Independence: Aug. 14, 1947 (from UK; formerly West Pakistan)
National Holiday: Pakistan Day (proclamation of the republic), Mar. 23

■ ECONOMY

Overview: a poor economy faced with rapidly increasing population, sizable government deficits and heavy dependence on foreign aid; small-scale industry and agriculture is in private hands and most large-scale industry is now publicly owned; living standards remain low because of the rapid population increase; at the current rate of growth the population will double in 25 years
GNP: $48.3 billion, per capita $410; real growth rate 6.4% (1992 est.)
Inflation: 9.5% (1992)
Industries: textiles, food processing, beverages, petroleum products, construction materials, clothing, paper products, international finance, shrimp
Labour Force: 34,000,000 (1992); 49.6% agriculture, 12.4% industry, 38% services (1989)
Unemployment: 6.3% (1991)
Agriculture: 24% of GNP, over 50% of labour force; world's largest continuous irrigation system; cotton, wheat, rice, sugar cane, fruits, vegetables, livestock (milk, beef, mutton, eggs); self-sufficient in food grain
Natural Resources: land, extensive natural gas reserves, limited crude oil, poor quality coal, iron ore, copper, salt, limestone

■ FINANCE/TRADE

Currency: Pakistani rupee (PRs)
International Reserves Excluding Gold: $1,227 million (Jan. 1994)
Gold Reserves: 2.04 million fine troy ounces (Jan. 1994)
Budget: revenues $9.4 billion; expenditures $10.9 billion, including capital expenditures of $3.1 billion (1993 est.)
Defence Expenditures: $3.2 billion (1991-1992)
External Debt: $24.072 billion (1992)
Exports: $7.273 billion (1992); commodities: rice, cotton, textiles, clothing; partners: European Community 31%, US 11%, Japan 11%

Imports: $9.365 billion (1992); commodities: petroleum, petroleum products, machinery, transportation, equipment, vegetable oils, animal fats, chemicals; partners: European Community 26%, Japan 15%, US 11%

■ HEALTH

Births: 44/1,000 population (1993)
Deaths: 13/1,000 population (1993)
Infant Mortality: 109 deaths/1,000 live births (1993)
Life Expectancy at Birth: 56 years male, 57 years female (1993)
No. of Physicians: 3.4/10,000 population (1992)

■ EDUCATION

Govt. Expenditure: 5.0% of government expenditure, or 2.0% of GNP in 1980; 2.6% of GNP in 1989
Literacy: 34.8% (1993)

■ COMMUNICATIONS

Daily newspapers: 183 (1992)
Televisions: 15.8/1,000 inhabitants (1992)
Radios: 86/1,000 inhabitants (1992)
Telephones: 0.7/100 inhabitants (1992)

■ TRANSPORTATION

Motor Vehicles: 909,576; 738,059 passenger cars (1990)
Roads: 114,640 km; 60,500 km paved
Railway: 8,773 km (1993)
Air Traffic: 5,198,000 million passengers carried (1991)
Airports: 111 airfields, of which 104 are usable; 75 have permanent-surface runways (1993)

Canadian Embassy: The Canadian High Commission, Diplomatic Enclave, Sector G-5, Islamabad; mailing address: The Canadian High Commission, G.P.O. Box 1042, Islamabad, Pakistan. Tel: (011-92-51) 21-11-01. Fax: (011-92-51) 21-15-40
Representative to Canada: High Commission for the Islamic Republic of Pakistan, Burnside Bldg, 151 Slater St, Ste 608, Ottawa ON K1P 5H3. Tel: (613) 238-7881. Fax: (613) 238-7296.

Panama

Long-Form Name: Republic of Panama
Capital: Panama City
Population: 2,500,000 (1993 est.)

■ GEOGRAPHY

Area: 78,200 sq. km
Coastline: 2,490 along Caribbean Sea and North

Pacific Ocean (Gulf of Panama)
Climate: tropical; hot, humid, cloudy; prolonged rainy season (May to Jan.), short dry season (Jan. to May)
Environment: dense tropical forest in east and northwest
Terrain: interior mostly steep, rugged mountains and dissected, upland plains; coastal areas largely plains and rolling hills
Land Use: 6% arable; 2% permanent; 15% meadows; 54% forest; 23% other
Location: Central (Latin) America, bordering on Caribbean Sea, Pacific Ocean

■ PEOPLE

Nationality: Panamanian
Ethnic Groups: 70% mestizo (mixed Indian and European ancestry), 14% West Indian, 10% white, 6% Indian
Languages: Spanish (official), 14% English; many Panamanians are bilingual
Religions: 85% Roman Catholic, 15% Protestant
Marriages: 5.2 (per 1,000) (1990)
Divorces: 0.79 (per 1,000) (1989)

■ GOVERNMENT

Leader(s): Pres. Guillermo Endara Galimany, V. Pres. Guillermo Ford Boyd
Government Type: centralized republic
Administrative Divisions: 9 provinces and 1 territory
Independence: Nov. 3, 1903 (from Colombia; became independent from Spain Nov. 28, 1821)
National Holiday: Independence Day, Nov. 3

■ ECONOMY

Overview: political instability, lack of credit and the erosion of business confidence have drastically hurt the economy; exports are stagnant; unemployment and economic reform are two of the greatest challenges the government must face
GNP: $6 billion, per capita $2,400; real growth rate 8% (1992 est.)
Inflation: 1.8% (1992)
Industries: manufacturing and construction activities, petroleum refining, brewing, cement and other construction materials, sugar mills, paper products
Labour Force: 873,000 (1992); 64.7% services, 25.4% agriculture, 9.9% industry (1989)
Unemployment: 15% (1992)
Agriculture: accounts for 10% of GDP and 27% of labour force; bananas, rice, corn, coffee, sugar cane, livestock, fishing, importer of food grain, vegetables, milk products
Natural Resources: copper, mahogany forests, shrimp

■ FINANCE/TRADE

Currency: balboa (B)
International Reserves Excluding Gold: $637 million (Jan. 1994)
Gold Reserves: n.a.
Budget: revenues $1.8 billion; expenditures $1.9 billion, including capital expenditures of $200 million (1992 est.)
Defence Expenditures: $75 million (4.91% of total govt. expenditure) (1991)
External Debt: $6.505 billion (1992)
Exports: $510 million (1992); commodities: bananas 40%, shrimp 27%, coffee 4%, sugar, petroleum products; partners: US 90%, Central America and Caribbean, European Community
Imports: $2.019 billion (1992); commodities: foodstuffs 16%, capital goods 9%, crude oil 16%, consumer goods, chemicals; partners: US 35%, Central America and Caribbean, European Community, Mexico, Venezuela

■ HEALTH

Births: 25/1,000 population (1993)
Deaths: 5/1,000 population (1993)
Infant Mortality: 21 deaths/1,000 live births (1993)
Life Expectancy at Birth: 71 years male, 75 years female (1993)
No. of Physicians: 10.0/10,000 population (1992)

■ EDUCATION

Govt. Expenditure: 16.10% of govt. expenditure (1991)
Literacy: 88.1% (1993)

■ COMMUNICATIONS

Daily newspapers: 6 (1992)
Televisions: 164.6/1,000 inhabitants (1992)
Radios: 222/1,000 inhabitants (1992)
Telephones: 10.63/100 inhabitants (1992)

■ TRANSPORTATION

Motor Vehicles: 223,647; 150,903 passenger cars (1990)
Roads: 8,633 km; 2,775 km paved
Railway: 239 km
Air Traffic: 398,000 passengers carried (1991)
Airports: 112 airfields, of which 104 are usable; 39 have permanent-surface runways (1993)

Canadian Embassy: c/o Cronos Building, Calle 3 y Avenida Central; mailing address: Apartado Postal 10303, San José, Costa Rica. Tel: (011-506) 55-35-22. Fax: (011-506) 23-23-95
Representative to Canada: c/o Embassy of the

Republic of Panama, 2862 McGill Terrace NW, Washington DC 20008 USA. Tel: (202) 483-1407. Fax: (202) 483-8413.

Papua New Guinea

Long-Form Name: Independent State of Papua New Guinea
Capital: Port Moresby
Population: 3,900,000 (1993 est.)

■ GEOGRAPHY

Area: 461,690 sq. km
Coastline: 5,152 km
Climate: tropical; northwest monsoon (Dec. to Mar.), southeast monsoon (May to Oct.); slight seasonal temperature variation
Environment: one of world's largest swamps along southwest coast; some active volcanos; frequent earthquakes
Terrain: mostly mountains with coastal lowlands and rolling foothills
Land Use: negligible arable; 1% permanent; negligible meadows; 71% forest; 28% other
Location: Pacific Ocean, Coral Sea N of Australia

■ PEOPLE

Nationality: Papua New Guinean
Ethnic Groups: predominantly Melanesian and Papuan; some Negrito, Micronesian and Polynesian
Languages: pidgin, English, Motu (all official); also 715 local languages
Religions: 22% Roman Catholic, 16% Lutheran, 8% Presbyterian/Methodist/London Missionary Society, 5% Anglican, 4% Evangelical Alliance, 1% Seventh-Day Adventists, 10% other Protestant sects, 34% indigenous beliefs
Marriages: n.a.
Divorces: n.a.

■ GOVERNMENT

Leader(s): Prime Min. Paias Wingti, Gov. Gen. Wiwa Korowi
Government Type: parliamentary democracy
Administrative Divisions: 20 provinces
Independence: Sept. 16, 1975 (from UN trusteeship under Australian administration)
National Holiday: Independence Day, Sept. 16

■ ECONOMY

Overview: country has abundant natural resources but exploitation has been hampered by the rugged terrain and the high cost of developing an infrastructure; subsistence agriculture is the livelihood for 85% of the population; mining accounts for about 60% of export earnings
GNP: $3.4 billion, per capita $850; real growth rate 8.5% (1992)
Inflation: 4.6% (1992)
Industries: copra crushing, oil palm processing, plywood processing, wood chip production, gold, silver, copper, construction, tourism
Labour Force: 1,570,000 (1992); 76.3% agriculture, 10.2% industry, 13.5% services
Unemployment: 5% (1988)
Agriculture: one-third of GDP; fertile soils and favourable climate permits cultivating a wide variety of crops; cash crops: coffee, cocoa, coconuts, palm kernels; other products: tea, rubber, sweet potatoes, fruit, vegetables, poultry, pork; net importer of food for urban centers
Natural Resources: gold, copper, silver, natural gas, timber, oil potential

■ FINANCE/TRADE

Currency: kina (K)
International Reserves Excluding Gold: $141 million (Jan. 1994)
Gold Reserves: 0.06 million fine troy ounces (Jan. 1994)
Budget: revenues $1.33 billion; expenditures $1.49 billion, including capital expenditures (1993 est.)
Defence Expenditures: 3.67% of total govt. expenditure (1993)
External Debt: $3.736 billion (1992)
Exports: $1.790 billion (1992); commodities: gold, copper ore, coffee, copra, palm oil, timber, lobster; partners: Germany, Japan, Australia, UK, Spain, US
Imports: $1.523 billion (1992); commodities: machinery and transport equipment, fuels, food, chemicals, consumer goods; partners: Australia, Singapore, Japan, US, New Zealand, UK

■ HEALTH

Births: 35/1,000 population (1993)
Deaths: 12/1,000 population (1993)
Infant Mortality: 99 deaths/1,000 live births (1993)
Life Expectancy at Birth: 54 years male, 56 years female (1993)
No. of Physicians: 1.6/10,000 population (1992)

■ EDUCATION

Govt. Expenditure: 16.95% of govt. expenditure (1993)
Literacy: 52.0% (1993)

■ COMMUNICATIONS

Daily newspapers: 1 (1992)
Televisions: 2.1/1,000 inhabitants (1992)

Radios: 69/1,000 inhabitants (1992)
Telephones: 2.03/100 inhabitants (1992)

■ TRANSPORTATION

Motor Vehicles: 17,100 passenger cars (1987)
Roads: 19,440 km; 640 km paved (1993)
Railway: none
Air Traffic: 907,000 passengers carried (1991)
Airports: 504 airfields, of which 457 are usable; permanent-surface runways n.a. (1993)

Canadian Embassy: c/o The Canadian High Commission, Commonwealth Ave, Canberra A.C.T. 2600, Australia. Tel: (011-61-6) 273-3844. Fax: (011-61-6) 273-3285
Representative to Canada: c/o High Commission for Papua New Guinea, 1615 New Hampshire Ave, Ste 300, Washington DC 20009 USA. Tel: (202) 745-3680. Fax: (202) 745-3679.

Paraguay

Long-Form Name: Republic of Paraguay
Capital: Asunción
Population: 4,200,000 (1993 est.)

■ GEOGRAPHY

Area: 406,750 sq. km
Coastline: none: landlocked
Climate: varies from temperate in east to semi-arid in far west
Environment: local flooding in southeast (early Sept. to June); poorly drained plains may become boggy (early Oct. to June)
Terrain: grassy plains and wooded hills east of Río Paraguay; Gran Chaco region west of Río Paraguay mostly low, marshy plain near the river and dry forest and thorny scrub elsewhere
Land Use: 20% arable; 1% permanent; 39% meadows; 35% forest; 5% other
Location: C South America

■ PEOPLE

Nationality: Paraguayan
Ethnic Groups: 95% mestizo (Spanish and Indian), 5% white and Indian
Languages: Spanish (official), Guarani
Religions: 90% Roman Catholic; 10% Mennonite and other Protestant denominations
Marriages: 4.5 (per 1,000) (1987)
Divorces: n.a.

■ GOVERNMENT

Leader(s): Pres. Juan Carlos Wasmosy
Government Type: republic
Administrative Divisions: 19 departments
Independence: May 14, 1811 (from Spain)

National Holiday: Independence Days, May 14–15

■ ECONOMY

Overview: in the absence of significant mineral or petroleum resources, the economy is based on agriculture; has a large hydropower potential; is vulnerable to climatic conditions and international commodity prices for agricultural exports
GNP: $7.3 billion, per capita $1,500; real growth rate 1.7% (1992 est.)
Inflation: 15.1% (1992)
Industries: meat packing, oilseed crushing, milling, brewing, textiles, other light consumer goods, cement, construction
Labour Force: 1,410,000 (1992); 48.6% agriculture, 20.5% industry, 30.9% services
Unemployment: 10% (1992 est.)
Agriculture: accounts for 25% GDP and 44% of labour force; cash crops: cotton, sugar cane; other crops: corn, wheat, tobacco, soybeans, cassava, fruit and vegetables; animal products: beef, pork, eggs, milk; surplus producer of timber; self-sufficient in most foods
Natural Resources: iron ore, manganese, limestone, hydropower, timber

■ FINANCE/TRADE

Currency: guaraní (pl. guaraníes) (G/)
International Reserves Excluding Gold: $590 million (Sept. 1993)
Gold Reserves: 0.03 million fine troy ounces (1992)
Budget: revenues $1.2 billion; expenditures $1.2 billion, including capital expenditures of $487 million (1991)
Defence Expenditures: 13.29% of total govt. expenditure (1990)
External Debt: $1.747 billion (1992)
Exports: $657 million (1992); commodities: cotton, soybeans, timber, vegetable oils, coffee, tung oil, meat products; partners: European Community 37%, Brazil 25%, Argentina 10%, Chile 6%, US 6%
Imports: $1.422 billion (1992); commodities: capital goods 35%, consumer goods 20%, fuels and lubricants 19%, raw materials 16%, foodstuffs, beverages and tobacco 10%; partners: Brazil 30%, European Community 20%, US 18%, Argentina 8%, Japan 7%

■ HEALTH

Births: 34/1,000 population (1993)
Deaths: 6/1,000 population (1993)
Infant Mortality: 48 deaths/1,000 live births (1993)
Life Expectancy at Birth: 65 years male, 69 years

female (1993)
No. of Physicians: 6.9/10,000 population (1992)

■ EDUCATION

Govt. Expenditure: 12.67% of govt. expenditure (1990)
Literacy: 90.1% (1993)

■ COMMUNICATIONS

Daily newspapers: 5 (1992)
Televisions: 48.2/1,000 inhabitants (1992)
Radios: 169/1,000 inhabitants (1992)
Telephones: 2.6/100 inhabitants (1992)

■ TRANSPORTATION

Motor Vehicles: 110,000; 75,000 passenger cars (1990)
Roads: 21,960 km; 1,788 km paved
Railway: 970 km
Air Traffic: 309,000 passengers carried (1991)
Airports: 862 airfields, of which 719 are usable; 7 have permanent-surface runways (1993)

Canadian Embassy: c/o Ahumada 11, 10th Flr, Santiago, Chile; mailing address: Casilla 771, Santiago, Chile. Tel: (011-56-2) 696-2256. Fax: (011-56-2) 696-2424
Representative to Canada: Embassy of the Republic of Paraguay, 151 Slater St, Ste 401, Ottawa, ON K1P 5H3. Tel: (613) 567-1283. Fax: (613) 567-1679.

Peru

Long-Form Name: Republic of Peru
Capital: Lima
Population: 22,900,000 (1993 est.)

■ GEOGRAPHY

Area: 1,285,220 sq. km
Coastline: 2,414 km along South Pacific Ocean
Climate: varies from tropical in east to dry desert in west
Environment: subject to earthquakes, tsunamis, landslides, mild volcanic activity; deforestation; overgrazing; soil erosion; desertification; air pollution in Lima; shares control of Lago Titicaca, world's highest navigable lake, with Bolivia
Terrain: western coastal plain (costa), high and rugged Andes in centre (sierra), eastern lowland jungle of Amazon Basin (selva)
Land Use: 3% arable; negligible permanent; 21% meadows; 55% forest; 21% other
Location: W South America, bordering on Pacific Ocean

■ PEOPLE

Nationality: Peruvian
Ethnic Groups: 45% Indian; 37% mestizo (mixed Indian and European ancestry); 15% white; 3% black, Japanese, Chinese and other
Languages: Spanish and Quechua (official), Ayamara
Religions: predominantly Roman Catholic
Marriages: n.a.
Divorces: n.a.

■ GOVERNMENT

Leader(s): Pres. Alberto Kenyo Fujimori, Prime Min. Efrain Goldenberg Schreiber
Government Type: republic
Administrative Divisions: 24 departments and 1 constitutional province
Independence: July 28, 1821 (from Spain)
National Holiday: Independence Day, July 28

■ ECONOMY

Overview: revival of growth in GDP continues to be restricted by the large amount of public and private resources being devoted to strengthening internal security; deficit spending and poor relations with international lenders are problems; labour unrest has cut production; food shortages; world's largest producer of coca (for cocaine)
GNP: $25 billion, per capita $1,100; real growth rate -2.8% (1992 est.)
Inflation: 73.5% (1992)
Industries: mining of metals, petroleum, fishing, textiles, clothing, food processing, cement, auto assembly, steel, shipbuilding, metal fabrication
Labour Force: 7.138 million (1992); 52.6% services, 35.1% agriculture, 12.3% industry (1989)
Unemployment: 15%; underemployment 70% (1992 est.)
Agriculture: accounts for 10% of GDP and 35% of labour force; commercial crops: coffee, cotton, sugar cane; other crops: rice, wheat, potatoes, plantains, coca; animal products: poultry, meats, dairy, wool; not self-sufficient in grain or vegetable oil; fish catch of 6.9 million metric tons
Natural Resources: copper, silver, gold, petroleum, timber, fish, iron ore, coal, phosphate, potash

■ FINANCE/TRADE

Currency: sol (pl. soles) (S/.)
International Reserves Excluding Gold: $3,408 million (Dec. 1993)
Gold Reserves: 1.30 million fine troy ounces (Dec. 1993)
Budget: revenues $2.0 billion; expenditures $2.7

billion, including capital expenditures of $300 million (1992 est.)
Defence Expenditures: $500 million (1991)
External Debt: $20.293 billion (1992)
Exports: $3.484 billion (1992); commodities: fishmeal, cotton, sugar, coffee, copper, iron ore, refined silver, lead, zinc, crude petroleum and byproducts; partners: European Community 22%, US 20%, Japan 11%, Latin America 8%, USSR 4%
Imports: $3.305 billion (1992); commodities: foodstuffs, machinery, transport equipment, iron and steel semimanufactures, chemicals, pharmaceuticals; partners: US 23%, Latin America 16%, European Community 12%, Japan 7%, Switzerland 3%

■ HEALTH

Births: 28/1,000 population (1993)
Deaths: 8/1,000 population (1993)
Infant Mortality: 81 deaths/1,000 live births (1993)
Life Expectancy at Birth: 63 years male, 66 years female (1993)
No. of Physicians: 9.6/10,000 population (1992)

■ EDUCATION

Govt. Expenditure: 22.9% of govt. expenditure (1987)
Literacy: 85.1% (1993)

■ COMMUNICATIONS

Daily newspapers: 12 (1992)
Televisions: 94.6/1,000 inhabitants (1992)
Radios: 251/1,000 inhabitants (1992)
Telephones: 3.38/100 inhabitants (1992)

■ TRANSPORTATION

Motor Vehicles: 625,000; 395,000 passenger cars (1990)
Roads: 69,942 km; 7,459 km paved
Railway: 1,801 km
Air Traffic: 1,491,000 passengers carried (1991)
Airports: 228 airfields, of which 199 are usable; 37 have permanent-surface runways (1993)

Canadian Embassy: Calle Libertad 130, Miraflores, Lima; mailing address: Casilla 18-1126, Correo Miraflores, Lima, Peru. Tel: (011-51-14) 44-40-15. Fax: (011-51-14) 44-43-47
Representative to Canada: Embassy of the Republic of Peru, 170 Laurier Ave W, Ste 1007,

Ottawa ON K1P 5V5. Tel: (613) 238-1777, -9. Fax: (613) 232-3062.

Philippines

Long-Form Name: Republic of the Philippines
Capital: Manila
Population: 64,600,000 (1992)

■ GEOGRAPHY

Area: 300,000 sq. km
Coastline: 36,289 km
Climate: tropical marine; northeast monsoon (Nov. to Apr.); southwest monsoon (May to Oct.)
Environment: astride typhoon belt, usually affected by 15 and struck by five to six cyclonic storms per year; subject to landslides, active volcanoes, destructive earthquakes, tsunami; deforestation; soil erosion; water pollution
Terrain: mostly mountains with narrow to extensive coastal lowlands
Land Use: 26% arable; 11% permanent; 4% meadows; 40% forest; 19% other
Location: SE of China, bordering on South China Sea, Pacific Ocean

■ PEOPLE

Nationality: Filipino
Ethnic Groups: 91.5% Christian Malay, 4% Moslem Malay, 1.5% Chinese, 3% other
Languages: Pilipino (native national language based on Tagalog) and English (both official); Spanish also spoken, also 76 indigenous languages inc. Cebuano, Tagalog, Iloco, Ifugao
Religions: 83% Roman Catholic, 9% Protestant, 5% Moslem, 3% Buddhist and other
Marriages: 5.0 (per 1,000) (1989)
Divorces: n.a.

■ GOVERNMENT

Leader(s): Pres. Fidel Ramos, Vice Pres. Joseph Estrada
Government Type: republic
Administrative Divisions: 14 regions, divided into 73 provinces and 61 chartered cities
Independence: July 4, 1946 (from US)
National Holiday: Independence Day (from Spain), June 12

■ ECONOMY

Overview: the agriculturally based economy is still recovering from the ouster of former President Marcos and several coup attempts; drought and power supply problems have hampered production; world's largest exporter of coconuts and coconut products

GNP: n.a., GDP $54.1 billion, per capita $860; real growth rate 0.6% (1992 est.)
Inflation: 8.9% (1992)
Industries: textiles, pharmaceuticals, chemicals, wood products, food processing, electronics assembly, petroleum refining, fishing
Labour Force: 22,000,000 (1992); 41.5% agriculture, 9.5% industry, 49% services (1989)
Unemployment: 9.8% (1992)
Agriculture: accounts for about one-third of GDP and 45% of labour force; major crops: rice, coconuts, corn, sugarcane, bananas, pineapples, mangoes; animal products: pork, eggs, beef: net exporter of farm products: fish catch of 2 million metric tons annually
Natural Resources: timber, crude oil, nickel, cobalt, silver, gold, salt, copper

■ FINANCE/TRADE

Currency: peso (P)
International Reserves Excluding Gold: $4,690 million (Jan. 1994)
Gold Reserves: 2.98 million fine troy ounces (Jan. 1994)
Budget: revenues $11.0 billion; expenditures $12.0 billion, including capital expenditures (1992 est.)
Defence Expenditures: 9.91% of total govt. expenditure (1992)
External Debt: $32.498 billion (1992)
Exports: $9.752 billion (1992); commodities: electrical equipment 19%, textiles 16%, minerals and ores 11%, farm products 10%, coconut 10%, chemicals 5%, fish 5%, forest products 4%; partners: US 36%, European Community 19%, Japan 18%, ESCAP 9%, ASEAN 7%
Imports: $15.459 billion (1992); commodities: raw materials 53%, capital goods 17%, petroleum products 17%; partners: US 25%, Japan 17%, ESCAP 13%, European Community 11%, ASEAN 10%, Middle East 10%

■ HEALTH

Births: 32/1,000 population (1993)
Deaths: 7/1,000 population (1993)
Infant Mortality: 43 deaths/1,000 live births (1993)
Life Expectancy at Birth: 63 years male, 66 years female (1993)
No. of Physicians: 1.5/10,000 population (1992)

■ EDUCATION

Govt. Expenditure: 15.03% of govt. expenditure (1992)
Literacy: 89.7% (1993)

■ COMMUNICATIONS

Daily newspapers: 38 (1992)
Televisions: 41.1/1,000 inhabitants (1992)
Radios: 136/1,000 inhabitants (1992)
Telephones: 1.64/100 inhabitants (1992)

■ TRANSPORTATION

Motor Vehicles: 1,219,471; 454,554 passenger cars (1990)
Roads: 158,400; 22,500 km paved
Railway: 1,080 km
Air Traffic: 5,438,000 passengers carried (1991)
Airports: 270 airfields, of which 238 are usable; 73 have permanent-surface runways (1993)

Canadian Embassy: 9th and 11th Flrs, Allied Bank Centre, 6754 Ayala Ave, Makati, Metro Manila, Philippines; mailing address: P.O. Box 2168, 1261 Makati CPO, Makati, Metro Manila, Philippines. Tel: (011-63-2) 810-8861. Fax: (011-63-2) 810-8839
Representative to Canada: Embassy of the Philippines, 130 Albert St, Ste 606 & 609, Ottawa ON K1P 5G4. Tel: (613) 233-1121. Fax: (613) 233-4165.

Pitcairn Islands

Dependent Territory of the United Kingdom

Long-Form Name: Pitcairn, Henderson, Ducie and Oeno Islands
Capital: Adamstown
Population: 52 (1993)

■ GEOGRAPHY

Area: 47 sq. km (Pitcairn and 3 small uninhabited islands)
Climate: tropical, hot, humid, modified by southeasterly trade winds, rainy season from Nov. to March
Land Use: rugged but fertile interior
Location: S Pacific Ocean, E of French Polynesia

■ PEOPLE

Nationality: Pitcairn Islander
Ethnic Groups: descendants of Polynesians and British (the latter crew members of the British naval ship Bounty)
Languages: English (official), Tahitian-English dialects
Religions: 100% Seventh-Day Adventists

■ GOVERNMENT

Leader(s): Gov. David J. Moss

Government Type: dependency of the UK
National Holiday: Celebration of the Birthday of the Queen, June 10/second Saturday in June

■ ECONOMY

Overview: inhabitants subsist on fishing and farming; fertile soil of the valleys produces wide variety of fruit and vegetables; bartering is an important part of the economy; imports: fuel oil, machinery, building materials; no exports other than small tourist trade with passing ships

■ FINANCE/TRADE

Currency: New Zealand dollar

Poland

Long-Form Name: Republic of Poland
Capital: Warsaw
Population: 38,500,000 (1993 est.)

■ GEOGRAPHY

Area: 312,680 sq. km
Coastline: 491 km along Baltic Sea
Climate: temperate with cold, cloudy, moderately severe winters with frequent precipitation; mild summers with frequent showers and thundershowers
Environment: plain crossed by a few north flowing, meandering streams; severe air and water pollution in south; historically, an area of conflict because of flat terrain and the lack of natural barrier on the North European Plain
Terrain: mostly flat plain, mountains along southern border
Land Use: 46% arable; 1% permanent; 13% meadows; 28% forest; 12% other
Location: NC Europe, bordering on Baltic Sea

■ PEOPLE

Nationality: Polish
Ethnic Groups: 97.6% Polish, 1.3% German, 0.6% Ukrainian, 0.5% Byelorussian
Languages: Polish
Religions: 95% Roman Catholic (about 75% practising), 5% Russian Orthodox, Protestant and other
Marriages: 6.1 (per 1,000) (1991)
Divorces: 0.91 (per 1,000) (1991)

■ GOVERNMENT

Leader(s): Pres. Lech Walesa, Prime Min. Waldemar Pawlak
Government Type: democratic state
Administrative Divisions: 49 provinces
Independence: Nov. 11, 1918, independent republic proclaimed

National Holiday: Constitution Day, May 3

■ ECONOMY

Overview: following sweeping political changes of 1989 which disrupted normal economic activity and increased shortages, the government adopted a "cold turkey" program for transforming the country to a market economy from a largely Soviet-style economy; as a result, consumer goods shortages have eased and inflation fell dramatically
GNP: n.a., GDP $167.6 billion, per capita $4,400; real growth rate 2% (1992 est.)
Inflation: 43% (1992)
Industries: machine building, iron and steel, extractive industries, chemicals, shipbuilding, food processing, glass, beverages, textiles
Labour Force: 19,704,000 (1992); 28.2% industry, 27.8% agriculture, 44% services (1989)
Unemployment: 13.6% (1992)
Agriculture: accounts for 15% GNP and 27% of labour force; 75% of output from private farms, 25% from state farms; low productivity; leading European producer of rye, rapeseed and potatoes; wide variety of other crops and livestock; major exporter of pork products
Natural Resources: coal, sulphur, copper, natural gas, silver, lead, salt

■ FINANCE/TRADE

Currency: zloty (pl. zlotys) (Zl)
International Reserves Excluding Gold: $4,104 million (Jan. 1994)
Gold Reserves: 0.47 million fine troy ounces (Jan. 1994)
Budget: revenues $17.5 billion; expenditures $22.0 billion, including capital expenditures of $1.5 billion (1992 est.)
Defence Expenditures: $2.54 billion (1990)
External Debt: $48.521 billion (1992)
Exports: $13.187 billion (1992); commodities: machinery and equipment 63%, fuels, minerals and metals 14%, manufactured consumer goods 14%, agricultural and forestry products 5%; partners: USSR 25%, Germany 12%, Czechoslovakia 6%
Imports: $15.913 billion (1992); commodities: machinery and equipment 36%, fuels, minerals and metals 35%, manufactured consumer goods 9%, agricultural and forestry products 12%; partners: USSR 23%, Germany 13%, Czechoslovakia 6%

■ HEALTH

Births: 13/1,000 population (1993)
Deaths: 10/1,000 population (1993)
Infant Mortality: 14.4 deaths/1,000 live births

(1993)
Life Expectancy at Birth: 67 years male, 76 years female (1993)
No. of Physicians: 20.5/10,000 population (1992)

■ EDUCATION

Govt. Expenditure: 14.6% of govt. expenditure (1991)
Literacy: 98% (1993)

■ COMMUNICATIONS

Daily newspapers: 45 (1992)
Televisions: 291.5/1,000 inhabitants (1992)
Radios: 428/1,000 inhabitants (1992)
Telephones: 12.78/100 inhabitants (1992)

■ TRANSPORTATION

Motor Vehicles: 6,304,000; 5,260,000 passenger cars (1990)
Roads: 370,525 km; 227,630 km paved
Railway: 26,250 km (1993)
Air Traffic: 1,051,000 passengers carried (1991)
Airports: 163 airfields, all usable; 100 have permanent-surface runways (1993)

Canadian Embassy: Ulica Jana Matejki 1/5, 00-481, Warsaw, Poland. Tel: (011-48-22) 29-80-51. Fax: (011-48-22) 29-64-57
Representative to Canada: Embassy of the Republic of Poland, 443 Daly Ave, Ottawa ON K1N 6H3. Tel: (613) 789-0468. Fax: (613) 789-1218.

Portugal

Long-Form Name: Portuguese Republic
Capital: Lisbon
Population: 9,866,000 (1993 est.)

■ GEOGRAPHY

Area: 92,080 sq. km; includes Azores and Madeira Islands
Coastline: 1,793 along North Atlantic Ocean
Climate: maritime temperature; cool and rainy in north, warmer and drier in south
Environment: Azores subject to severe earthquakes
Terrain: mountainous north, rolling plains in south
Land Use: 32% arable; 6% permanent; 6% meadows; 40% forest; 16% other
Location: SW Europe, bordering on North Atlantic Ocean

■ PEOPLE

Nationality: Portuguese
Ethnic Groups: homogeneous Mediterranean stock in mainland, Azores and Madeira Islands; citizens of black African descent who immigrated to mainland during decolonization number less than 100,000
Languages: Portuguese (official), English, French
Religions: 97% Roman Catholic, 1% Protestant, 2% other
Marriages: 6.8 (per 1,000) (1991)
Divorces: 1.01 (per 1,000) (1991)

■ GOVERNMENT

Leader(s): Prime Min. Aníbal Cavaco Silva, Pres. Mário Alberto Nobre Lopes Soares
Government Type: republic
Administrative Divisions: 18 districts and 2 autonomous regions; dependent areas: Macau (scheduled to become a Special Administrative Region of China in 1999)
Independence: 1140; independent republic proclaimed Oct. 5, 1910
National Holiday: Day of Portugal, June 10

■ ECONOMY

Overview: the economy has grown recently due to strong domestic consumption and investment spending; unemployment has declined but inflation remains high; government is promoting privatization measures; the global slowdown and tight financial policies to combat inflation have caused economic growth to slow
GNP: $93.7 billion, per capita $9,000; real growth rate 1.1% (1992)
Inflation: 8.9% (1992)
Industries: textiles and footwear; wood pulp, paper and cork; metalworking; oil refining; chemicals; fish canning; wine; tourism
Labour Force: 4,740,000 (1992); 57.3% services, 25.2% industry, 17.5% agriculture (1989)
Unemployment: 5% (1992)
Agriculture: accounts for 6.1% of GDP and 20% of labour force; small inefficient farms; imports more than half of food needs; major crops: grain, potatoes, olives, grapes; livestock sector: sheep, cattle, goats, poultry, meat, dairy products
Natural Resources: fish, forests (cork), tungsten, iron ore, uranium ore, marble

■ FINANCE/TRADE

Currency: escudo (Esc)
International Reserves Excluding Gold: $15,840 million (Dec. 1993)
Gold Reserves: 16.06 million fine troy ounces (Jan. 1994)
Budget: revenues $27.3 billion; expenditures $33.2 billion, including capital expenditures of

$4.5 billion (1991)
Defence Expenditures: $2.4 billion (1992)
External Debt: $32.046 billion (1992)
Exports: $16.376 billion (1993 est.); commodities: cotton textiles, cork and cork products, canned fish, wine, timber and timber products, resin, machinery, appliances; partners: European Community 72%, other developed countries 13%, US 6%
Imports: $26.320 billion (1993 est.); commodities: petroleum, cotton, foodgrains, industrial machinery, iron and steel, chemicals; partners: European Community 67%, other developed countries 13%, less developed countries 15%, US 4%

■ HEALTH

Births: 12/1,000 population (1993)
Deaths: 11/1,000 population (1993)
Infant Mortality: 10.8 deaths/1,000 live births (1993)
Life Expectancy at Birth: 70 years male, 77 years female (1993)
No. of Physicians: 24.3/10,000 population (1992)

■ EDUCATION

Govt. Expenditure: 11.96% of government expenditure (1990)
Literacy: 85.0% (1993)

■ COMMUNICATIONS

Daily newspapers: 28 (1992)
Televisions: 176.2/1,000 inhabitants (1992)
Radios: 216/1,000 inhabitants (1992)
Telephones: 21.91/100 inhabitants (1992)

■ TRANSPORTATION

Motor Vehicles: 2,198,000; 1,605,000 passenger cars (1988)
Roads: 73,661 km; 61,599 km surfaced (1993)
Railway: 3,625 km
Air Traffic: 3,572,000 passengers carried (1991)
Airports: 64 airfields, of which 62 are usable; 36 have permanent-surface runways (1993)

Canadian Embassy: Avendia da Liberdade 144/56, Flr 4, 1200 Lisbon, Portugal. Tel: (011-351-1) 347-4892. Fax: (011-351-1) 347-6466
Representative to Canada: Embassy of the Portuguese Republic, 645 Island Park Dr,
Ottawa ON K1Y 0B8. Tel: (613) 729-0883. Fax: (613) 729-4236.

Puerto Rico

Commonwealth associated with the United States

Long-Form Name: Commonwealth of Puerto Rico
Capital: San Juan
Population: 3,600,000 (1993 est.)

■ GEOGRAPHY

Area: 9,104 sq. km
Coastline: 501 km
Climate: tropical marine, mild, little seasonal temperature variation
Land Use: 8% arable; 9% permanent; 41% meadows; 20% forest; 22% other
Location: West Indies, bordering on Caribbean Sea, Atlantic Ocean

■ PEOPLE

Nationality: Puerto Rican
Ethnic Groups: almost entirely Hispanic
Languages: Spanish (official); English is widely understood

■ GOVERNMENT

Leader(s): Gov. Pedro J. Rossello
Government Type: commonwealth associated with US
National Holiday: Constitution Day, July 25; US Independence Day, July 4

■ ECONOMY

Overview: one of the most dynamic economies in the Caribbean region; economy has benefited from heavy US investment; new industries include pharmaceuticals and electronics; tourism is important; sugar production has lost out to dairy production and other livestock products as the main facet of the agricultural sector

---

Qatar

Long-Form Name: State of Qatar
Capital: Doha
Population: 500,000 (1993 est.)

■ GEOGRAPHY

Area: 11,000 sq. km
Coastline: 563 km
Climate: desert; hot, dry; humid and sultry in summer
Environment: haze, dust storms, sandstorms com-

mon; limited freshwater resources mean increasing dependence on large-scale desalination facilities

Terrain: mostly flat and barren desert covered with loose sand and gravel

Land Use: negligible arable; 0% permanent; 5% meadows; 0% forest; 95% other

Location: SW Asia (Middle East), bordering on Persian Gulf

▪ PEOPLE

Nationality: Qatari

Ethnic Groups: 40% Arab, 18% Pakistani, 18% Indian, 10% Iranian, 14% other

Languages: Arabic (official); English is commonly used as second language

Religions: Islam (native Qataris–less than one-third of the population–principally adhere to orthodox Wahhabi sect of Sunni Moslems)

Marriages: 2.8 (per 1,000) (1990)

Divorces: 0.74 (per 1,000) (1990)

▪ GOVERNMENT

Leader(s): Amir and Prime Min. Khalifa ibn Hamad Al Thani

Government Type: traditional monarchy

Administrative Divisions: 9 municipalities

Independence: Sept. 3, 1971 (from UK)

National Holiday: Independence Day, Sept. 3

▪ ECONOMY

Overview: has one of the highest per capita GDP's in the world, due to oil revenues; reserves should not be completely depleted for about 25 years; production and export of natural gas is becoming increasingly important

GNP: $6.968 billion, per capita $15,860; real growth rate -6.6% (1991)

Inflation: 3.0% (1990)

Industries: crude oil production and refining, fertilizers, petrochemicals, steel, cement

Labour Force: 186,000 (1992); 3% agriculture, 28% industry, 69% services; 85% of labour force in private sector is non-Qatari (1989)

Unemployment: n.a.

Agriculture: farming and grazing on small scale, less than 2% of GDP; commercial fishing increasing in importance; most food imported

Natural Resources: crude oil, natural gas, fish

▪ FINANCE/TRADE

Currency: Qatar riyal (QR)

International Reserves Excluding Gold: $662 million (Sept. 1993)

Gold Reserves: 0.84 million fine troy ounces (Sept. 1993)

Budget: revenues $2.5 billion; expenditures $3.0 billion, including capital expenditures of $440 million (1992 est.)

Defence Expenditures: $934.07 million (1990)

External Debt: $1.1 billion (1989)

Exports: $3.107 billion (1991); commodities: petroleum products 90%, steel, fertilizers; partners: France, Germany, Italy, Japan, Spain

Imports: $1.720 billion (1991); commodities: foodstuffs, beverages, animal and vegetable oils, chemicals, machinery and equipment; partners: European Community, Japan, Arab countries, US, Australia

▪ HEALTH

Births: 23/1,000 population (1993)

Deaths: 2/1,000 population (1993)

Infant Mortality: 26 deaths/1,000 live births (1993)

Life Expectancy at Birth: 69 years male, 74 years female (1993)

No. of Physicians: 17.4/10,000 population (1992)

▪ EDUCATION

Govt. Expenditure: n.a.

Literacy: 75.7% (1993)

▪ COMMUNICATIONS

Daily newspapers: 4 (1992)

Televisions: 514.3/1,000 inhabitants (1992)

Radios: 510/1,000 inhabitants (1992)

Telephones: 36.26/100 inhabitants (1992)

▪ TRANSPORTATION

Motor Vehicles: 162,377; 115,149 passenger cars (1990)

Roads: 1,555 km; 1,040 km paved

Railway: none

Air Traffic: 876,000 passengers carried (1991)

Airports: 4 airfields, all of which are usable; 1 has a permanent-surface runway (1993)

Canadian Embassy: Da'Aiyah - Block 4, House No. 24, Al-Mutawakel St, Kuwait City; mailing address: P.O. Box 25281, Safat, Kuwait City, 13113, Kuwait. Tel: (011-965) 256-3025. Fax: (011-965) 256-4167.

Representative to Canada: c/o The Permanent Mission of Qatar to the UN, 747 Third Ave, 22nd Flr, New York, New York 10017 USA. Tel: (212) 486-9335. Fax: (212) 458-4952.

Réunion

Overseas Department of France

Long-Form Name: Department of Réunion

Capital: Saint-Denis

Population: 639,000 (1993 est.)

■ GEOGRAPHY

Area: 2,512 sq. km; uninhabited islands of Juan de Nova, Europa, Bassas da India, Iles Glorieuses, Tromelin administered by Réunion but do not form part of the territory; Mauritius and the Seychelles claim Tromelin, Madagascar claims all 5 islands

Climate: tropical, but more moderate at higher elevations; May-Nov.: cool and dry; Nov.-April: hot and rainy

Land Use: volcanic island; some cultivation of indigenous plants and cash crops such as corn; 20% arable, 2% permanent crops, 4% meadows and pastures, 35% forest, 39% other

Location: Indian Ocean, E of Africa

■ PEOPLE

Nationality: Réunionese

Ethnic Groups: French Creoles, African, Malagasy, Pakistani, Indian and Chinese minorities

Languages: French (official), Creole vernacular

■ GOVERNMENT

Leader(s): Chief of State Francois Mitterand; Commissioner of the Republic Jacques Dewatre

Government Type: overseas department of France

National Holiday: Taking of the Bastille, July 14

■ ECONOMY

Overview: agriculture-based economy, of which sugarcane is the backbone; government is promoting the development of the tourist industry; socioeconomic tensions between classes with widely disparate living standards

■ FINANCE/TRADE

Currency: French franc

Romania

Long-Form Name: Romania
Capital: Bucharest
Population: 23,200,000 (1993 est.)

■ GEOGRAPHY

Area: 237,500 sq. km

Coastline: 225 km along Black Sea

Climate: temperate; cold, cloudy winters with frequent snow and fog; sunny summers with frequent showers and thunderstorms

Environment: frequent earthquakes most severe in south and southwest; geologic structure and climate promotes landslides, air pollution in south

Terrain: central Transylvanian Basin is separated from the plain of Moldavia on the east by the Carpathian Mountains and separated from the Walachian Plain on the south by the Transylvanian Alps

Land Use: 43% arable; 3% permanent; 19% meadows; 28% forest; 7% other

Location: SE Europe, bordering on Black Sea

■ PEOPLE

Nationality: Romanian

Ethnic Groups: 89% Romanian; 9% Hungarian; 0.4% German; 1.6% Ukrainian, Serb, Croat, Russian, Turk and Gypsy

Languages: Romanian (official), Hungarian, German; French and English also spoken

Religions: 70% Romanian Orthodox; 6% Roman Catholic; 24% Calvinist, Lutheran, Jewish, Baptist, unaffiliated

Marriages: 8.3 (per 1,000) (1990)

Divorces: 1.42 (per 1,000) (1990)

■ GOVERNMENT

Leader(s): Prime Min. Nicolae Vacaroiu, Pres. Ion Iliescu

Government Type: republic

Administrative Divisions: 40 counties and 1 municipality

Independence: 1881 (from Turkey); republic proclaimed Dec. 30, 1947

National Holiday: National Day of Romania, Dec. 1

■ ECONOMY

Overview: the new government is slowly loosening the tight central controls of Ceausescu's command economy; industry suffers from an aging capital plant and shortages of energy; agriculture sector has suffered from drought and mismanagement; private enterprise is increasing in importance

GNP: n.a., GDP $63.4 billion, per capita $2,700; real growth rate -15% (1992 est.)

Inflation: 200% (1992)

Industries: mining, timber, construction materials, metallurgy, chemicals, machine building, food processing, petroleum

Labour Force: 11,825,000 (1992); 43.5% industry, 30.5% agriculture, 26% services (1989)

Unemployment: 9% (1993)

Agriculture: 18% of GNP and 28% of labour force; major wheat and corn producer, sugar beets, sunflower seeds, potatoes, milk, eggs, meat

Natural Resources: crude oil (reserves being exhausted), timber, natural gas, coal, iron ore, salt

■ FINANCE/TRADE

Currency: leu (pl. lei)
International Reserves Excluding Gold: $926 million (Jan. 1994)
Gold Reserves: 2.38 million fine troy ounces (Jan. 1994)
Budget: revenues $19 billion; expenditures $20 billion, including capital expenditures of $2.1 billion (1991 est.)
Defence Expenditures: 10.31% of total govt. expenditure (1991)
External Debt: $3.520 billion (1992)
Exports: $4.536 billion (1993); commodities: machinery and equipment 34.7%, fuels, minerals and metals 24.7%, manufactured consumer goods 16.9%, agricultural materials and forestry products 11.9%, other 11.6%; partners: USSR 27%, Eastern Europe 23%, European Community 15%, US 5%, China 4%
Imports: $5.683 billion (1993); commodities: fuels, minerals and metals 51%, machinery and equipment 26.7%, agricultural and forestry products 11%, manufactured consumer goods 4.2%; partners: communist countries 60%, noncommunist countries 40%

■ HEALTH

Births: 12/1,000 population (1993)
Deaths: 11/1,000 population (1993)
Infant Mortality: 22.7 deaths/1,000 live births (1993)
Life Expectancy at Birth: 67 years male, 73 years female (1993)
No. of Physicians: 17.6/10,000 population (1992)

■ EDUCATION

Govt. Expenditure: 10.02% of govt. expenditure (1991)
Literacy: 98% (1993)

■ COMMUNICATIONS

Daily newspapers: 34 (1992)
Televisions: 193.8/1,000 inhabitants (1992)
Radios: 195/1,000 inhabitants (1992)
Telephones: 9.85/100 inhabitants (1993)

■ TRANSPORTATION

Motor Vehicles: 1,100,000; 850,000 passenger cars (1990)
Roads: 72,799 km; 35,970 km paved (1993)
Railway: 11,425 km
Air Traffic: 149,000 passengers carried (1987)
Airports: 158 airfields, all usable; 27 have permanent-surface runways (1993)

Canadian Embassy: 36, Nicolae Iorga, Bucharest 71118; mailing address: P.O. Box 117 Post Office No. 22, Bucharest, Romania. tel: (011-40-1) 312-83-45. Fax: (011-40-1) 312.03.66
Representative to Canada: Embassy of Romania, 655 Rideau St, Ottawa ON K1N 6A3. Tel: (613) 789-3709. Fax: (613) 789-4365.

Russia

Long-Form Name: Russian Federation
Capital: Moscow
Population: 149,000,000 (1993 est.)

■ GEOGRAPHY

Area: 17,075,200 sq. km
Coastline: 37,653 km
Climate: ranges from steppes in south through humid continental, subarctic in Siberia to tundra in polar north; winters vary—cool along Black Sea, frigid in Siberia; summers—warm in the steppes to cool along Arctic coast
Environment: cold desert in north; volcanic activity; only small percentage of land is arable—much is too far north; permafrost over much of Siberia; severe land, air and water pollution
Terrain: rolling western plains, north-south ridge of Ural Mountains, central plateau, rugged eastern uplands
Land Use: 30% forests and woodland; 25% cultivated; remainder steppe and cold desert; agricultural land accounts for only 13% of land area
Location: E Europe and N Asia, bordering on Barents Sea, Baltic Sea, Black Sea, Caspian Sea

■ PEOPLE

Nationality: Russian
Ethnic Groups: 81.5% Russians; 3.8% Tatars, 1.2% Chuvash, 0.9% Bashkir, 0.8% Belorussian, 3% Ukrainian, remainder inc. Chechens, Germans, Udmurts, Mari, Kazakhs, Avars, Jews, Moldavians and Armenians
Languages: Russian (official), Tartar, Ukrainian
Religions: Christianity (Russian Orthodox) with substantial Muslim populations and other religious minorities
Marriages: 9.4 (per 1,000) (1989)
Divorces: 3.94 (per 1,000) 1989)

■ GOVERNMENT

Leader(s): Pres. Boris N. Yeltsin, Prime Min. Viktor S. Chernomyrdin
Government Type: federation
Administrative Divisions: 21 autonomous republics
Independence: Aug. 24, 1991 (from Soviet Union)
National Holiday: Independence Day, June 12

■ ECONOMY

Overview: a vast country with a great many natural resources and a diverse industrial base; industry accounts for more than half of Russia's economic output; agriculture and service sector make up approximately 25% each; foreign trade and exports have dropped sharply since 1992; foreign aid is important

GNP: $479.546 billion, $3,220 per capita; real growth rate 2.0% (1991)

Inflation: 25% per month (1992)

Industries: natural gas refining, steel and coal production and processing, all forms of machine building, ship building, transportation equipment, consumer durables, communications and agricultural equipment, medical and scientific instruments

Labour Force: 75,000,000 (1993 est.); 83.9% production and economic services, 16.1% government

Unemployment: 3-4% (1993)

Agriculture: grain, sugar beets, sunflower seeds, meat, milk, vegetables, fruit

Natural Resources: iron ore, coal, oil, gold, platinum, copper, zinc, lead, tin, rare metals; climate, terrain and distance hinder exploitation

■ FINANCE/TRADE

Currency: rouble (rbl.)

International Reserves Excluding Gold: n.a.

Gold Reserves: n.a.

Budget: 1989 budget balanced at 126,471 million roubles; in 1991–92 budgets were set every 3 months

Defence Expenditures: n.a.

External Debt: $80 billion (1992 est.)

Exports: $39.967 billion (1992)

Imports: $34.981 billion (1992)

■ HEALTH

Births: 12/1,000 population (1993)

Deaths: 11/1,000 population (1993)

Infant Mortality: 20 deaths/1,000 live births (1993)

Life Expectancy at Birth: 64 years male, 74 years female (1993)

No. of Physicians: 697,000 (1989)

■ EDUCATION

Govt. Expenditure: n.a.

Literacy: 100% (1993)

■ COMMUNICATIONS

Daily newspapers: 4,772 papers of all circulation types (1989)

Televisions: 54.2 million total (1993)

Radios: 48.8 million total (1993)

Telephones: 24.4 million total, approximately 16.4/100 inhabitants (1993)

■ TRANSPORTATION

Motor Vehicles: n.a.

Roads: 893,000 km; 677,000 km paved (1993)

Railway: 158,100 km (1993)

Air Traffic: 128,275,000 passengers carried (1991)

Airports: 2,550 airfields, of which 964 are usable; 565 have permanent-surface runways (1993)

Canadian Embassy: 23 Starokonyushenny Per, Moscow, 121002 Russia. Tel: (011-7-095) 241-1111. Fax: (011-7-095) 241-4400.

Representative to Canada: Embassy of the Russian Federation, 285 Charlotte St, Ottawa ON K1N 8L5. Tel: (613) 235-4341, 236-1413. Fax: (613) 236-6342.

Rwanda

Data below does not reflect the effects of civil war which began in 1994.

Long-Form Name: Republic of Rwanda

Capital: Kigali

Population: 7,400,000 (1993 est.)

■ GEOGRAPHY

Area: 26,340 sq. km

Coastline: none: landlocked

Climate: temperate; two rainy seasons (Feb. to Apr., Nov. to Jan.); mild in mountains with frost and snow possible

Environment: deforestation; overgrazing; soil exhaustion; soil erosion; periodic droughts

Terrain: mostly grassy uplands and hills; mountains in west

Land Use: 29% arable; 11% permanent; 18% meadows; 10% forest; 32% other

Location: EC Africa

■ PEOPLE

Nationality: Rwandan

Ethnic Groups: 90% Hutu, 9% Tutsi, 1% Twa (Pygmoid)

Languages: Kinyarwanda, French (both official); Kiswahili used in commercial centres

Religions: 65% Christian (mostly Roman Catholic), 9% Protestant, 1% Muslim, 25% indigenous beliefs and other

Marriages: 2.6 (per 1,000) (1982)

Divorces: n.a.

■ GOVERNMENT

Leader(s): Pres. Pasteur Bizimungu
Government Type: republic; presidential system in which military leaders hold key offices
Administrative Divisions: 10 prefectures
Independence: July 1, 1962 (from UN trusteeship under Belgian administration)
National Holiday: Independence Day, July 1

■ ECONOMY

Overview: economy is dependent on coffee exports and foreign aid; deforestation and soil erosion are problems; industrial sector is small, and manufacturing focuses chiefly on the processing of agricultural products
GNP: n.a., GDP $2.35 billion, per capita $290; real growth rate 1.3% (1992 est.)
Inflation: 9.5% (1992)
Industries: mining of cassiterite (tin ore) and wolframite (tungsten ore), tin, cement, agricultural processing, small-scale beverage production, soap, furniture, shoes, plastic goods, textiles, cigarettes
Labour Force: 3,520,000 (1992); 92.8% agriculture, 4.3% services, 3% industry and commerce (1989)
Unemployment: n.a.
Agriculture: accounts for almost 50% of GDP and about 90% of labour force; cash crops: coffee, tea, pyrethrum (insecticide made from chrysanthemums); main food crops: bananas, beans, sorghum, potatoes; stock raising; self-sufficiency declining; country imports foodstuffs as farm production fails to keep up with population growth
Natural Resources: gold, cassiterite (tin ore), wolframite (tungsten ore), natural gas, hydropower

■ FINANCE/TRADE

Currency: Rwandan franc (RF)
International Reserves Excluding Gold: $47 million (Jan. 1994)
Gold Reserves: none (1991)
Budget: revenues $350 million; expenditures $453.7 million, including capital expenditures (1992 est.)
Defence Expenditures: $36.63 million (1990)
External Debt: $873 million (1992)
Exports: $68 million (1992); commodities: coffee 85%, tea, tin, cassiterite, wolframite, pyrethrum; partners: Germany, Belgium, Italy, Uganda, UK, France, US
Imports: $288 million (1992); commodities: textiles, foodstuffs, machines and equipment, capital goods, steel, petroleum products, cement and construction material; partners: US, Belgium, Germany, Kenya, Japan

■ HEALTH

Births: 40/1,000 population (1993)
Deaths: 17/1,000 population (1993)
Infant Mortality: 110 deaths/1,000 live births (1993)
Life Expectancy at Birth: 44 years male, 48 years female (1993)
No. of Physicians: 0.1/10,000 population (1992)

■ EDUCATION

Govt. Expenditure: 25.4% of govt. expenditure (1989)
Literacy: 50.2% (1993)

■ COMMUNICATIONS

Daily newspapers: 1 (1992)
Televisions: n.a.; no TV stations (1993)
Radios: 59/1,000 inhabitants (1992)
Telephones: 0.18/100 inhabitants (1992)

■ TRANSPORTATION

Motor Vehicles: 25,000; 15,000 passenger cars (1990)
Roads: 4,885 km; 460 km paved (1993)
Railway: n.a.
Air Traffic: 8,000 passengers carried (1991)
Airports: 8 airfields, of which 7 are usable; 3 have permanent-surface runways (1993)

Canadian Embassy: rue Akagera, P.O. Box 1177, Kigali, Rwanda. Tel: (011-250) 73210. Fax: (011-250) 72719
Representative to Canada: Embassy of the Rwandese Republic, 121 Sherwood Dr, Ottawa ON K1Y 3V1. Tel: (613) 722-5835. Fax: (613) 729-3291.

Saint Kitts and Nevis

Long-Form Name: Federation of St. Kitts and Nevis
Capital: Basseterre
Population: 40,000 (1993 est.)

■ GEOGRAPHY

Area: 269 sq. km
Coastline: 135 km
Climate: subtropical tempered by constant sea breezes; little seasonal temperature variation; rainy season (May to Nov.)
Environment: subject to hurricanes (July to Oct.)
Terrain: volcanic with mountainous interiors
Land Use: 22% arable; 17% permanent; 3% meadows; 17% forest; 41% other

Location: Caribbean Islands

■ PEOPLE

Nationality: Kittsian, Nevisian
Ethnic Groups: mainly of black African descent
Languages: English
Religions: Anglican, other Protestant sects, Roman Catholic
Marriages: n.a.
Divorces: n.a.

■ GOVERNMENT

Leader(s): Prime Min. Kennedy Alphonse Simmonds, Gov. Gen. Clement Athelston Arrindell
Government Type: constitutional monarchy
Administrative Divisions: 14 parishes
Independence: Sept. 19, 1983 (from UK)
National Holiday: Independence Day, Sept. 19

■ ECONOMY

Overview: traditionally dependent on the growing and processing of sugar cane and on remittances from overseas workers; tourism and export-oriented manufacturing are increasing
GNP: $156 million, per capita $3,960; real growth rate 4.5% (1991)
Inflation: 2.9% (1992)
Industries: sugar processing, tourism, cotton, salt, copra, clothing, footwear, beverages
Labour Force: n.a.
Unemployment: 12.2% (1990)
Agriculture: accounts for 7% of GDP; cash crop: sugar cane; subsistence crops: rice, yams, vegetables, bananas; fishing potential but not fully exploited; most food imported
Natural Resources: negligible

■ FINANCE/TRADE

Currency: East Caribbean dollar ($EC)
International Reserves Excluding Gold: $26 million (Oct. 1993)
Gold Reserves: n.a.
Budget: revenues $85.7 million; expenditures $85.8 million, including capital expenditures of $42.4 million (1993)
Defence Expenditures: n.a.
External Debt: $43 million (1992)
Exports: $24.6 million (1990); commodities: sugar, manufactures, postage stamps; partners: US 53%, UK 22%, Trinidad and Tobago 5%, OECS 5%
Imports: $103.2 million (1990); commodities: foodstuffs, intermediate manufactures, machinery, fuels; partners: US 36%, UK 12%, Trinidad and Tobago 6%, Canada 3%, Japan 3%, OECS 4%

■ HEALTH

Births: 23/1,000 population (1993)
Deaths: 11/1,000 population (1993)
Infant Mortality: 22.2 deaths/1,000 live births (1993)
Life Expectancy at Birth: 66 years male, 71 years female (1993)
No. of Physicians: 4.6/10,000 population (1992)

■ EDUCATION

Govt. Expenditure: 12.0% of govt. expenditure (1989)
Literacy: 98% (1993)

■ COMMUNICATIONS

Daily newspapers: n.a.
Televisions: 181.8/1,000 inhabitants (1992)
Radios: 580/1,000 inhabitants (1992)
Telephones: 7.61/100 inhabitants (1992)

■ TRANSPORTATION

Motor Vehicles: 4,903 passenger cars (1988)
Roads: 300 km; 125 km paved
Railway: 58 km
Air Traffic: 98,263 passengers carried (1987)
Airports: 2, both usable and with permanent-surface runways (1993)

Canadian Embassy: c/o The Canadian High Commission, Bishop's Court Hill, St. Michael, Barbados; mailing address: P.O. Box 404, Bridgetown, Barbados. Tel: (809) 429-3550. Fax: (809) 429-3780
Representative to Canada: c/o High Commission for the Countries of the Organization of Eastern Caribbean States, 112 Kent St, Ste 1610, Place de Ville, Tower B, Ottawa, ON K1P 5P2. Tel: (613) 236-8952. Fax: (613) 236-3042.

Saint Lucia

Long-Form Name: Saint Lucia
Capital: Castries
Population: 100,000 (1993 est.)

■ GEOGRAPHY

Area: 620 sq. km
Coastline: 158 km
Climate: tropical, moderated by northeast trade winds; dry season from Jan. to Apr., rainy season from May to Aug.
Environment: subject to hurricanes and volcanic activity; deforestation; soil erosion
Terrain: volcanic and mountainous with some broad, fertile valleys
Land Use: 8% arable; 20% permanent; 5%

meadow; 13% forest; 54% other
Location: Caribbean Islands

■ PEOPLE

Nationality: Saint Lucian
Ethnic Groups: 90% African descent, 6% mixed, 3% East Indian, 1% Caucasian
Languages: English (official), French patois
Religions: 90% Roman Catholic, 7% Protestant, 3% Anglican
Marriages: 2.7 (per 1,000) (1989)
Divorces: 0.4 (per 1,000) (1986)

■ GOVERNMENT

Leader(s): Prime Min. John Compton, Gov. Gen. Sir Stanislaus A. James
Government Type: parliamentary democracy
Administrative Divisions: 11 quarters
Independence: Feb. 22, 1979 (from UK)
National Holiday: Independence Day, Feb. 22

■ ECONOMY

Overview: depends on strong agricultural (bananas) and tourist industry sectors; expanding industrial base supported by foreign investment in manufacturing and activities such as data processing; vulnerable to droughts and tropical storms
GNP: $380 million, per capita $2,500; real growth rate 4.8% (1991)
Inflation: 5.1% (1992)
Industries: clothing, electronic component assembly, beverages, tourism, lime and coconut processing
Labour Force: n.a.
Unemployment: 16% (1988)
Agriculture: accounts for 12% GDP and 43% of labour force; crops: bananas, coconuts, vegetables, citrus fruit, root crops, cocoa; imports food for the tourist industry
Natural Resources: forests, sandy beaches, minerals (pumice), mineral springs, geothermal potential

■ FINANCE/TRADE

Currency: EC dollar (EC$)
International Reserves Excluding Gold: $51 million (1992)
Gold Reserves: n.a.
Budget: revenues $131 million; expenditures $149 million, including capital expenditures of $71 million (1990)
Defence Expenditures: n.a.
External Debt: $96 million (1992)
Exports: $123 million (1992); commodities: bananas 67%, cocoa, vegetables, fruit, coconut oil, clothing; partners: UK 55%, CARICOM

21%, US 18%, other 6%
Imports: $313 million (1992); commodities: manufactured goods 22%, machinery and transportation equipment 21%, food and live animals 20%, mineral fuels, foodstuffs, machinery and equipment, fertilizers, petroleum products; partners: US 33%, UK 16%, CARICOM 14.8%, Japan 6.5%, other 29.7%

■ HEALTH

Births: 23/1,000 population (1993)
Deaths: 6/1,000 population (1993)
Infant Mortality: 20.8 deaths/1,000 live births (1993)
Life Expectancy at Birth: 68 years male, 75 years female (1993)
No. of Physicians: 2.6/10,000 population (1992)

■ EDUCATION

Govt. Expenditure: 7.2% of GNP (1986)
Literacy: 67% (1993)

■ COMMUNICATIONS

Daily newspapers: 1 (1992)
Televisions: 18.4/1,000 inhabitants (1992)
Radios: 667/1,000 inhabitants (1992)
Telephones: 12.14/100 inhabitants (1992)

■ TRANSPORTATION

Motor Vehicles: 11,000; 7,000 passenger cars (1990)
Roads: 760 km; 500 km paved (1993)
Railway: none
Air Traffic: n.a.
Airports: 2, both usable and with permanent-surface runways (1993)

Canadian Embassy: c/o The Canadian High Commission, Bishop's Court Hill, St. Michael, Barbados; mailing address: P.O. Box 404, Bridgetown, Barbados. Tel: (809) 429-3550. Fax: (809) 429-3780.
Representative to Canada: c/o High Commission for the Countries of the Organization of Eastern Caribbean States, 112 Kent St, Ste 1610, Place de Ville, Tower B, Ottawa, ON K1P 5P2. Tel: (613) 236-8952. Fax: (613) 236-3042.

Saint Pierre and Miquelon

Territorial Collectivity of France

Long-Form Name: Territorial Collectivity of Saint Pierre et Miquelon
Capital: Saint Pierre
Population: 6,652 (1993 est.)

■ GEOGRAPHY

Area: 242 sq. km, 8 small islands
Climate: cold and wet, misty and foggy, windy spring and autumn, moist, temperate summers, cold and snowy winters
Land Use: 13% arable, 0% permanent crops, 0% meadows and pastures, 4% forest, 83% other
Location: N Atlantic Ocean, S of Newfoundland

■ PEOPLE

Nationality: French
Ethnic Groups: descendants of French settlers, Basques and Bretons (French fishermen)
Languages: French, English

■ GOVERNMENT

Leader(s): Prefect Karnel Khrissate; Pres. General Council Marc Plantegenest
Government Type: territorial collectivity with internal self-government
National Holiday: Taking of the Bastille, July 14

■ ECONOMY

Overview: fishing, and the servicing of fishing fleets operating off the coast of Newfoundland, have long been an important part of the economy; agriculture: some vegetables and livestock for local consumption; partners: UK, Canada, EEC

■ FINANCE/TRADE

Currency: French franc

Saint Vincent and the Grenadines

Long-Form Name: Saint Vincent and the Grenadines
Capital: Kingstown
Population: 100,000 (1993 est.)

■ GEOGRAPHY

Area: 344 sq. km
Coastline: 84 km
Climate: tropical; little seasonal temperature variation; rainy season (May to Nov.)
Environment: subject to hurricanes; Soufrière volcano is a constant threat
Terrain: volcanic, mountainous; Soufrière volcano on the island of Saint Vincent
Land Use: 38% arable; 12% permanent; 6% meadows; 41% forest; 3% other
Location: Caribbean Islands

■ PEOPLE

Nationality: Saint Vincentian or Vincentian
Ethnic Groups: mainly of black African descent; remainder mixed, with some white, East Indian, Carib Indian
Languages: English (official), some French patois
Religions: Anglican, Methodist, Roman Catholic, Seventh-Day Adventist
Marriages: 4.1 (per 1,000) (1988)
Divorces: n.a.

■ GOVERNMENT

Leader(s): Prime Min. James F. Mitchell, Gov. Gen. (Acting) David Jack
Government Type: constitutional monarchy
Administrative Divisions: 6 parishes
Independence: Oct. 27, 1979 (from UK)
National Holiday: Independence Day, Oct. 27

■ ECONOMY

Overview: overdependence on the weather-plagued banana crop as a major export earner has caused high unemployment; has been unsuccessful in diversifying into new industries
GNP: n.a., GDP $171 million, per capita $1,500; real growth rate 3% (1992 est.)
Inflation: 5.6% (1991)
Industries: food processing (sugar, flour), cement, furniture, rum, starch, sheet metal, beverage
Labour Force: n.a.
Unemployment: 35-40% (1992)
Agriculture: accounts for 15% of GDP and 60% of labour force; provides bulk of exports; products: bananas, arrowroot (world's largest producer), coconuts, sweet potatoes, spices; small numbers of cattle, sheep, hogs, goats; small fish catch used locally
Natural Resources: negligible

■ FINANCE/TRADE

Currency: EC dollar ($EC)
International Reserves Excluding Gold: $28 million (Oct. 1993)
Gold Reserves: n.a.
Budget: revenues $62 million; expenditures $67 million, including capital expenditures of $21 million (1990)
Defence Expenditures: 5.6% of total govt. expenditures (1990)
External Debt: $63 million (1992)
Exports: $65.7 million (1991); commodities: bananas, eddoes and dasheen (taro), arrowroot starch, copra; partners: CARICOM 37%, UK 43%, US 15%
Imports: $110.7 million (1991); commodities: foodstuffs, machinery and equipment, chemicals and fertilizers, minerals and fuels; partners: US 42%, CARICOM 19%, UK 15%

■ HEALTH

Births: 24/1,000 population (1993)
Deaths: 6/1,000 population (1993)
Infant Mortality: 21.7 deaths/1,000 live births (1993)
Life Expectancy at Birth: 70 years male, 73 years female (1993)
No. of Physicians: 2.7/10,000 population (1992)

■ EDUCATION

Govt. Expenditure: 18.08% of govt. expenditure (1990)
Literacy: 95.6% (1993)

■ COMMUNICATIONS

Daily newspapers: 1 (1992)
Televisions: 78.9/1,000 inhabitants (1992)
Radios: 636/1,000 inhabitants (1992)
Telephones: 9.1/100 inhabitants (1992)

■ TRANSPORTATION

Motor Vehicles: 8,000; 5,000 passenger cars (1990)
Roads: 1,000 km; 300 km paved (1993)
Railway: none
Air Traffic: n.a.
Airports: 6 airfields, all usable; 5 have permanent-surface runways (1993)

Canadian Embassy: c/o The Canadian High Commission, Bishop's Court Hill, St. Michael, Barbados; mailing address: P.O. Box 404, Bridgetown, Barbados. Tel: (809) 429-3550. Fax: (809) 429-3780.
Representative to Canada: c/o High Commission for the Countries of the Organization of Eastern Caribbean States, 112 Kent St, Ste 1610, Place de Ville, Tower B, Ottawa, ON K1P 5P2. Tel: (613) 236-8952. Fax: (613) 236-3042.

San Marino

Long-Form Name: Republic of San Marino
Capital: San Marino
Population: 23,855 (1993 est.)

■ GEOGRAPHY

Area: 60 sq. km
Coastline: none: landlocked
Climate: Mediterranean; mild to cool winters; warm, sunny summers
Environment: dominated by the Appenines
Terrain: rugged mountains
Land Use: 17% arable; 0% permanent; 0% meadows; 0% forest; 83% other
Location: S Europe (E Italy)

■ PEOPLE

Nationality: Sammarinese
Ethnic Groups: Sammarinese, Italian
Languages: Italian
Religions: Roman Catholic
Marriages: 7.4 (per 1,000) (1989)
Divorces: 1.0 (per 1,000) (1987)

■ GOVERNMENT

Leader(s): Secretary of State for Foreign & Political Affairs Gabriele Gatti
Government Type: republic
Administrative Divisions: 9 municipalities
Independence: 301 (by tradition)
National Holiday: Anniversary of the Foundation of the Republic, Sept. 3

■ ECONOMY

Overview: tourism and the sale of postage stamps are vital to the economy; key industries are clothing, electronics, ceramics, agricultural products, wine and cheese
GNP: n.a., GDP $465 million, per capita $20,000; real growth rate n.a. (1992 est.)
Inflation: 5% (1992)
Industries: wine, olive oil, cement, leather, textiles, tourism
Labour Force: 13,332 (1991)
Unemployment: 4.3% (1991)
Agriculture: employs 3% of labour force; products: wheat, grapes, corn, olives, meat, cheese, hides; small numbers of cattle, pigs, horses; depends on Italy for food imports
Natural Resources: building stone

■ FINANCE/TRADE

Currency: Italian lira (Lit); San Marino also mints its own coins
International Reserves Excluding Gold: n.a.
Gold Reserves: n.a.
Budget: n.a.
Defence Expenditures: n.a.
External Debt: n.a.
Exports: n.a.; trade data are included in the statistics for Italy
Imports: n.a.; see exports

■ HEALTH

Births: 12/1,000 population (1993)
Deaths: 7/1,000 population (1993)
Infant Mortality: 3.8 deaths/1,000 live births (1993)
Life Expectancy at Birth: 73 years male, 79 years female (1993)
No. of Physicians: n.a.

■ EDUCATION

Govt. Expenditure: n.a.
Literacy: 96% (1993)

■ COMMUNICATIONS

Daily newspapers: 16 (1988)
Televisions: 326.1/1,000 inhabitants (1989)
Radios: 583/1,000 inhabitants (1989)
Telephones: 62.5/100 inhabitants (1987)

■ TRANSPORTATION

Motor Vehicles: 22,519; 19,360 passenger cars (1990)
Roads: 104 km
Railway: none
Air Traffic: n.a.
Airports: none

Canadian Embassy: c/o The Canadian Embassy, Via G.B. de Rossi 27, 00161 Rome, Italy. Tel: (011-39-6) 44598.1. Fax: (011-39-6) 44598.912. **Representative to Canada:** c/o Consulate of San Marino, 27 McNider Ave, Montreal, PQ H2V 3X4. Tel: (514) 871-3838. Fax: (514) 876-4217.

Sao Tome and Principe

Long-Form Name: Democratic Republic of Sao Tome and Principe
Capital: Sao Tome
Population: 100,000 (1993 est.)

■ GEOGRAPHY

Area: 960 sq. km
Coastline: 209 km
Climate: tropical; hot, humid; one rainy season (Oct. to May)
Environment: deforestation; soil erosion
Terrain: volcanic, mountainous
Land Use: 1% arable; 20% permanent; 1% meadows; 75% forest; 3% other
Location: South Atlantic Ocean, off WC African Coast

■ PEOPLE

Nationality: Sao Tomean
Ethnic Groups: mestiço, angolares (descendents of Angolan slaves), forros (descendents of freed slaves), servicais (contract labourers from Angola, Mozambique and Cape Verde), tongas (children of servicais born on the islands) and European (primarily Portuguese)
Languages: Portuguese (official), Crioulo
Religions: Roman Catholic, Evangelical Protestant, Seventh-Day Adventist
Marriages: n.a.

Divorces: n.a.

■ GOVERNMENT

Leader(s): Prime Min. Norberto José d'Alva Costa Alegre, Pres. Miguel Trovoada
Government Type: republic
Administrative Divisions: 2 districts
Independence: July 12, 1975 (from Portugal)
National Holiday: Independence Day, July 12

■ ECONOMY

Overview: the economy is hampered by overdependence on cocoa production; the value of imports generally exceeds the value of exports by a ratio of 4 to 1; imports 90% of food needs as well as all fuels and most manufactured goods; government is attempting to restructure economy and reduce debt burden
GNP: $41.4 million, per capita $315; real growth rate 1.5% (1992 est.)
Inflation: 27% (1992)
Industries: light construction, shirts, soap, beer, fisheries, shrimp processing
Labour Force: n.a.; most of population engaged in subsistence agriculture and fishing
Unemployment: n.a.
Agriculture: dominant sector of economy, primary source of exports; cash crops: cocoa (85%), coconuts, palm kernels, coffee; food products: bananas, papayas, beans, poultry, fish; not self-sufficient in food grain and meat
Natural Resources: fish

■ FINANCE/TRADE

Currency: dobra (Db)
International Reserves Excluding Gold: n.a.
Gold Reserves: n.a.
Budget: revenues $10.2 million; expenditures $36.8 million, including capital expenditures of $22.5 million (1989)
Defence Expenditures: n.a.
External Debt: $190 million (1992)
Exports: $5.5 million (1991); commodities: cocoa 85%, copra, coffee, palm oil; partners: Germany, Netherlands, China
Imports: $24.5 million (1991); commodities: machinery and electrical equipment 54%, food products 23%, other 23%; partners: Portugal, Germany, Angola, China

■ HEALTH

Births: 35/1,000 population (1993)
Deaths: 10/1,000 population (1993)
Infant Mortality: 71.9 deaths/1,000 live births (1993)
Life Expectancy at Birth: 60 years male, 64 years female (1993)

No. of Physicians: 5.0/10,000 population (1990)

■ EDUCATION

Govt. Expenditure: 18.8% of govt. expenditure (1986)
Literacy: 57.4% (1993)

■ COMMUNICATIONS

Daily newspapers: 1 (1992)
Televisions: n.a.; no TV stations (1993)
Radios: 256/1,000 inhabitants (1992)
Telephones: 2.44/100 inhabitants (1992)

■ TRANSPORTATION

Motor Vehicles: 2,600 passenger cars (1987)
Roads: 300 km; 200 km paved (1993)
Railway: none
Air Traffic: 22,000 passengers carried (1991)
Airports: 2, both usable and with permanent-surface runways (1993)

Canadian Embassy: c/o P.O. Box 4037 Libreville, Gabon. Tel: (011-241) 74.34.64, 65. Fax: (011-241) 74.34.66
Representative to Canada: Consulate General, 4068 Beaconsfield Ave, Montreal, PQ H4A 2H3. (514) 484-2706.

Saudi Arabia

Long-Form Name: Kingdom of Saudi Arabia
Capital: Riyadh (royal); Jeddah (administrative)
Population: 17,500,000 (1993 est.)

■ GEOGRAPHY

Area: 1,960,582 sq. km
Coastline: 2,640 km along Red Sea and Persian Gulf
Climate: harsh, dry desert with great extremes of temperature
Environment: no perennial rivers or permanent water bodies; developing extensive coastal sea-water desalination facilities; desertification
Terrain: mostly uninhabited, sandy desert
Land Use: 1% arable; negligible permanent; 39% meadows; 1% forest; 59% other
Location: SW Asia (Middle East), bordering on Persian Gulf, Arabian Sea, Red Sea

■ PEOPLE

Nationality: Saudi
Ethnic Groups: 90% Arab, 10% Afro-Asian
Languages: Arabic (official); English (business language)
Religions: Islam (85% Sunni, 15% Shia)
Marriages: n.a.
Divorces: n.a.

■ GOVERNMENT

Leader(s): King and Prime Min. Fahd bin 'Abd al- 'Aziz Al Sa'ud
Government Type: monarchy
Administrative Divisions: 14 emirates
Independence: Sept. 23, 1932 (unification)
National Holiday: Unification of the Kingdom, Sept. 23

■ ECONOMY

Overview: has the largest reserves of petroleum in the world and is the largest exporter of petroleum; consumer prices have been dropping or showing little change in recent years; the government is working towards the privatization of the economy; 4 million foreign workers
GNP: $111 billion, per capita $6,500; real growth rate 3.6% (1992 est.)
Inflation: -0.1% (1992)
Industries: crude oil production, petroleum refining, basic petrochemicals, cement, small steel-rolling mill, construction, fertilizer, plastic
Labour Force: 5,000,000 (1993); 34% government, 28% industry, 22% services, 16% agriculture (1993)
Unemployment: 6.5% (1992)
Agriculture: accounts for about 10% of GDP; fastest growing economic sector; subsidized by government; products: wheat, barley, tomatoes, melons, dates, citrus fruit, mutton, chickens, eggs, milk; approaching self-sufficiency in food
Natural Resources: crude oil, natural gas, iron ore, gold, copper

■ FINANCE/TRADE

Currency: riyal (SRIs)
International Reserves Excluding Gold: $7,018 million (Jan. 1994)
Gold Reserves: 4.6 million fine troy ounces (Jan. 1994)
Budget: revenues $45.1 billion; expenditures $52.5 billion, including capital expenditures (1993 est.)
Defence Expenditures: $16.5 billion (1993 budget)
External Debt: $18.9 billion (1989)
Exports: $47.797 billion (1991); commodities: petroleum and petroleum products 89%; partners: Japan 26%, US 26%, France 6%, Bahrain 6%
Imports: $29.079 billion (1991); commodities: manufactured goods, transportation equipment, construction materials, processed food products; partners: US 20%, Japan 18%, UK 16%, Italy 11%

■ HEALTH

Births: 39/1,000 population (1993)
Deaths: 7/1,000 population (1993)
Infant Mortality: 65 deaths/1,000 live births (1993)
Life Expectancy at Birth: 64 years male, 67 years female (1993)
No. of Physicians: 13.5/10,000 population (1992)

■ EDUCATION

Govt. Expenditure: 17.8% of government expenditure (1990)
Literacy: 62.4% (1993)

■ COMMUNICATIONS

Daily newspapers: 12 (1992)
Televisions: 276.5/1,000 inhabitants (1992)
Radios: 280/1,000 inhabitants (1992)
Telephones: 15.74/100 inhabitants (1992)

■ TRANSPORTATION

Motor Vehicles: 4,500,000; 2,350,000 passenger cars (1990)
Roads: 74,000 km; 34,400 km paved
Railway: 1,390 km
Air Traffic: 9,409,000 passengers carried (1991)
Airports: 213 airfields, of which 193 are usable; 71 have permanent-surface runways (1993)

Canadian Embassy: Diplomatic Quarter, Riyadh; mailing address: P.O. Box 94321, Riyadh 11693, Saudi Arabia. Tel: (011-966-1) 488-2288. Fax: (011-966-1) 488-1997
Representative to Canada: Embassy of the Kingdom of Saudi Arabia, 99 Bank St, Suite 901, Ottawa ON K1P 6B9. Tel: (613) 234-4100. Fax: (613) 237-0567.

Senegal

Long-Form Name: Republic of Senegal
Capital: Dakar
Population: 7,900,000 (1993 est.)

■ GEOGRAPHY

Area: 196,190 sq. km
Coastline: 531 km along the North Atlantic Ocean
Climate: tropical; hot, humid; rainy season (Dec. to Apr.) has strong southeast winds; dry season (May to Nov.) dominated by hot, dry harmattan wind
Environment: lowlands seasonally flooded; deforestation; overgrazing; soil erosion; desertification
Terrain: generally low, rolling, plains rising to foothills in southeast
Land Use: 27% arable; 0% permanent; 30% meadows; 31% forest; 12% other
Location: W Africa, bordering on Atlantic Ocean

■ PEOPLE

Nationality: Senegalese
Ethnic Groups: 36% Wolof, 13% Fulani, 19% Serer, 9% Toucouleur, 8% Diola, 9% Mandingo, 1% European and Lebanese, 2% other
Languages: French (official); Wolof, Pulaar, Diola, Mandingo
Religions: 92% Moslem, 6% indigenous beliefs, 2% Christian (mostly Roman Catholic)
Marriages: n.a.
Divorces: n.a.

■ GOVERNMENT

Leader(s): Prime Min. Habib Thiam, Pres. Abdou Diouf
Government Type: republic under multi-party democratic rule
Administrative Divisions: 10 regions
Independence: Aug. 20, 1960 (from France)
National Holiday: Independence Day, Apr. 4

■ ECONOMY

Overview: tourism has emerged as a great boon to the economy; fishing is the main economic resource; mining (phosphate) has been hurt by reduced worldwide demand for fertilizers in recent years; agriculture represents only 12% of GDP
GNP: $5.550 billion, per capita $720; real growth rate 2.9% (1991)
Inflation: -0.1% (1992)
Industries: fishing, agricultural processing, phosphate mining, petroleum refining, building materials
Labour Force: 3,192,000 (1992); 80.6% agriculture, 6.2% industry, 13.1% services (1989)
Unemployment: 7.5% (1988)
Agriculture: including fishing, accounts for 12% of GDP; major products: peanuts (cash crop), millet, corn, sorghum, rice, cotton, tomatoes, green vegetables; estimated two-thirds self-sufficient in food; fish catch of 354,000 metric tons (1990)
Natural Resources: fish, phosphates, iron ore

■ FINANCE/TRADE

Currency: Communauté financière africaine franc (CFAF)
International Reserves Excluding Gold: $11 million (Sept. 1993)
Gold Reserves: 0.03 million fine troy ounces

(Sept. 1993)

Budget: revenues $921 million; expenditures $1 billion, including capital expenditures of $14 million (1989)

Defence Expenditures: $111.85 million (1990)

External Debt: $3.607 billion (1992)

Exports: $904 million (1991); commodities: manufactures 30%, fish products 27%, peanuts 11%, petroleum products 11%, phosphates 10%; partners: US, France, other European Community, Ivory Coast, India

Imports: $1.2 billion (1991); commodities: semi-manufactures 30%, food 27%, durable consumer goods 17%, petroleum 12%, capital goods 14%; partners: US, France, other European Community, Nigeria, Algeria, China, Japan

■ HEALTH

Births: 44/1,000 population (1993)

Deaths: 17/1,000 population (1993)

Infant Mortality: 84 deaths/1,000 live births (1993)

Life Expectancy at Birth: 47 years male, 49 years female (1993)

No. of Physicians: 0.7/10,000 population (1990)

■ EDUCATION

Govt. Expenditure: 24.1% of govt. expenditure (1988)

Literacy: 38.3% (1993)

■ COMMUNICATIONS

Daily newspapers: 1 (1992)

Televisions: 35.1/1,000 inhabitants (1992)

Radios: 113/1,000 inhabitants (1992)

Telephones: n.a.

■ TRANSPORTATION

Motor Vehicles: 135,000; 92,000 passenger cars (1990)

Roads: 14,007 km; 3,777 km paved (1993)

Railway: 1,034 km

Air Traffic: 136,000 passengers carried (1991)

Airports: 25 airfields, of which 19 are usable; 10 have permanent-surface runways (1993)

Canadian Embassy: 45 av. de la République; mailing address: P.O. Box 3373, Dakar, Senegal. Tel: (011-221) 23 92 90. Fax: (011-221) 23-87-49

Representative to Canada: Embassy of the Republic of Senegal, 57 Marlborough Ave, Ottawa ON K1N 8E8. Tel: (613) 238-6392. Fax: (613) 238-2695.

Serbia and Montenegro

Long-Form Name: Serbia and Montenegro

Capital: Belgrade

Population: 10,699,539 (1993 est.)

■ GEOGRAPHY

Area: 102,350 sq. km

Coastline: 199 km (Montenegro 199 km, Serbia 0 km)

Climate: continental in north, continental and Mediterranean in central region; south–Adriatic climate along coast, hot and dry summers, relatively cold winters, with heavy snowfall inland

Environment: coastal water pollution from sewage outlets, esp. in tourist-related areas; air and water pollution; subject to earthquakes

Terrain: varied: rich fertile plain in north, limestone ranges and basins in east, mountains and hills in southeast, high shoreline with no islands in southwest

Land Use: 30% arable, 5% permanent crops, 20% meadows and pastures, 25% forests, 20% other

Location: S Europe, bordering Adriatic Sea

■ PEOPLE

Nationality: Serb, Montenegrin

Ethnic Groups: 63% Serb, 14% Albanian, 6% Montenegrin, 4% Hungarian, 13% other

Languages: 95% Serbo-Croatian, 5% Albanian

Religions: 65% Orthodox, 19% Muslim, 4% Roman Catholic, 1% Protestant, 11% other

Marriages: n.a.

Divorces: n.a.

■ GOVERNMENT

Leader(s): Chief of State Zoran Lilic, Pres. Slobodan Milosevic

Government Type: republic

Administrative Divisions: 2 republics and 2 autonomous provinces

Independence: April 11, 1992 (from Yugoslavia)

National Holiday: n.a.

■ ECONOMY

Overview: bloody ethnic warfare has caused destabilization of republic boundaries and the break-up of important inter-republic trade connections; economic situation is complicated by the continuation in office of a communist government whose primary interest lies in political and military mastery rather than economic reform, as well as by the imposition of econom-

ic sanctions by the UN
GNP: n.a., GDP $27-$37 billion; $2,500-$3,500 per capita; real growth rate n.a. (1992 est.)
Inflation: 81% (1991)
Industries: machine building, metallurgy, mining, consumer goods, electronics, petroleum products, chemicals, pharmaceuticals
Labour Force: 2,640,909 (1990); 40% industry and mining, 5% agriculture
Unemployment: 25-40% (1991)
Agriculture: cereals, cotton, oilseed plants, chicory, fodder crops, fruit, vegetables, tobacco, olives, citrus, rice, livestock (sheep, goats)
Natural Resources: oil, gas, coal, antimony, copper, lead, gold, chrome

■ FINANCE/TRADE

Currency: Yugoslav New Dinar (YD)
International Reserves Excluding Gold: n.a.
Gold Reserves: n.a.
Budget: n.a.
Defence Expenditures: 4-6% of GDP (1992 est.)
External Debt: $4.2 billion (1993)
Exports: $4.4 billion (1990)
Imports: $6.4 billion (1990)

■ HEALTH

Births: n.a.
Deaths: n.a.
Infant Mortality: n.a.
Life Expectancy at Birth: n.a.
No. of Physicians: n.a.

■ EDUCATION

Govt. Expenditure: n.a.
Literacy: n.a.

■ COMMUNICATIONS

Daily newspapers: n.a.
Televisions: 1,000,000 total; 18 TV stations (1993)
Radios: 2,015,000 total; 35 radio stations (1993)
Telephones: 700,000 total (1993)

■ TRANSPORTATION

Motor Vehicles: n.a.
Roads: 46,019 km; 26,949 km paved (1990)
Railway: n.a.
Air Traffic: n.a.
Airports: 48 airfields, all usable; 16 have permanent-surface runways (1993).

Seychelles

Long-Form Name: Republic of Seychelles
Capital: Victoria
Population: 100,000 (1993 est.)

■ GEOGRAPHY

Area: 455 sq. km
Coastline: 491 km
Climate: tropical marine; humid; cooler season during southeast monsoon (late May to Sept.); warmer season during northwest monsoon (Mar. to May)
Environment: lies outside the cyclone belt, so severe storms are rare; short droughts possible; no fresh water, catchments collect rain; 40 granitic and about 50 coralline islands
Terrain: Mahé Group is granitic, narrow coastal strip, rocky, hilly; others are coral, flat, elevated reefs
Land Use: 4% arable; 18% permanent; 0% meadows; 18% forest; 60% other
Location: Indian Ocean, NE of Madagascar

■ PEOPLE

Nationality: Seychellois
Ethnic Groups: Seychellois (mixture of Asians, Africans, Europeans)
Languages: English, French (both official), Creole
Religions: 90% Roman Catholic, 8% Anglican, 2% other
Marriages: 13.5 (per 1,000) (1991)
Divorces: 0.6 (per 1,000) (1986)

■ GOVERNMENT

Leader(s): Pres. France Albert René
Government Type: republic
Administrative Divisions: 23 administrative districts
Independence: June 29, 1976 (from UK)
National Holiday: Liberation Day (anniversary of coup), June 5

■ ECONOMY

Overview: the government is moving to reduce the high dependence on tourism by promoting the development of farming, fishing and small-scale manufacturing, yet it is also encouraging foreign investment in order to upgrade hotels and other services
GNP: $350 million, per capita $5,110; real growth rate 3.2% (1991)
Inflation: 3.3% (1992)
Industries: tourism employs 30% of labour force and makes up 70+% of national income; mostly subsistence farming; cash crops: coconuts, cinnamon, vanilla; other products: sweet potatoes, cassava, bananas; broiler chickens; large share of food needs imported; expansion of tuna fishing under way
Labour Force: 31% industry and commerce, 21% services, 20% government, 12% agriculture,

forestry and fishing, 16% other (1985)
Unemployment: 9% (1987)
Agriculture: accounts for 7% of GDP, mostly subsistence farming; cash crops: coconuts, cinnamon, vanilla; large share of food needs imported; tuna fishing is increasing in importance
Natural Resources: fish, copra, cinnamon trees

■ FINANCE/TRADE

Currency: Seychelles rupee (Sr)
International Reserves Excluding Gold: $34 million (Jan. 1994)
Gold Reserves: n.a.
Budget: revenues $170 million; expenditures $173 million, including capital expenditures (1989)
Defence Expenditures: $12.4 million (1989)
External Debt: $181 million (1992)
Exports: $44 million (1992); commodities: fish, copra, cinnamon bark, petroleum products (re-exports); partners: France 63%, Pakistan 12%, Réunion 10%, UK 7%
Imports: $192 million (1992); commodities: manufactured goods, food, tobacco, beverages, machinery and transportation equipment, petroleum products; partners: UK 20%, France 14%, South Africa 13%, PDRY 13%, Singapore 8%, Japan 6%

■ HEALTH

Births: 25/1,000 population (1993)
Deaths: 8/1,000 population (1993)
Infant Mortality: 13 deaths/1,000 live births (1993)
Life Expectancy at Birth: 64 years male, 72 years female (1993)
No. of Physicians: 4.6/10,000 population (1992)

■ EDUCATION

Govt. Expenditure: 11.9% of govt. expenditure (1990)
Literacy: 57.7% (1992)

■ COMMUNICATIONS

Daily newspapers: 1 (1992)
Televisions: 73.5/1,000 inhabitants (1992)
Radios: 449/1,000 inhabitants (1992)
Telephones: 20.92/100 inhabitants (1992)

■ TRANSPORTATION

Motor Vehicles: 5,785; 4,301 passenger cars (1990)
Roads: 260 km; 160 km paved (1993)
Railway: none
Air Traffic: 243,000 passengers carried (1991)
Airports: 14 airfields, all of which are usable; 8 have permanent-surface runways (1993)

Canadian Embassy: c/o The Canadian High Commission, 38 Mirambo St, Dar-es-Salaam; mailing address: P.O. Box 1022, Dar-es-Salaam, Tanzania. Tel: (011-255-51) 46000. Fax: (011-255-51) 46005
Representative to Canada: c/o High Commissioner for the Seychelles, 820 Second Ave, Suite 900F, New York, NY 10017 USA. Tel: (212) 687-9766. Fax: (212) 922-9177.

Sierra Leone

Long-Form Name: Republic of Sierra Leone
Capital: Freetown
Population: 4,500,000 (1993 est.)

■ GEOGRAPHY

Area: 71,740 sq. km
Coastline: 402 km
Climate: tropical; hot, humid; summer rainy season (May to Dec.); winter dry season (Dec. to Apr.)
Environment: extensive mangrove swamps hinder access to sea; deforestation; soil degradation
Terrain: coastal belt of mangrove swamps, wooded hill country, upland plateau, mountains in east
Land Use: 25% arable; 2% permanent; 31% meadows; 29% forest; 13% other
Location: WC Africa, bordering on North Atlantic Ocean

■ PEOPLE

Nationality: Sierra Leonean
Ethnic Groups: 99% native African (31% Temne, 34% Mende); 1% Creole, European, Lebanese and Asian
Languages: English (official); regular use limited to literate minority; principal vernaculars are Mende in south and Temne in north; Krio is the language of the resettled ex-slave population of the Freetown area and is lingua franca
Religions: 30% Moslem, 10% Christian, 30% traditional beliefs, 30% other or none
Marriages: n.a.
Divorces: n.a.

■ GOVERNMENT

Leader(s): Pres. Valentine E.M. Strasser
Government Type: military government
Administrative Divisions: 3 provinces and 1 area
Independence: Apr. 27, 1961 (from UK)
National Holiday: Republic Day, Apr. 27

■ ECONOMY

Overview: the economic and social infrastructure is underdeveloped; subsistence agriculture is the backbone of the economy; problems include unemployment, rising inflation, large trade deficits; diamond mining is an important source of national income

GNP: n.a., GDP $1.4 billion, per capita $330; real growth rate -1% (1992 est.)

Inflation: 65.5% (1992)

Industries: mining (diamonds, bauxite, rutile), small-scale manufacturing (beverages, textiles, cigarettes, footwear), petroleum refinery

Labour Force: 1,440,000 (1992); 69.6% agriculture, 14.1% industry, 16.4% services (1989)

Unemployment: n.a.

Agriculture: accounts for over 30% of GDP and two-thirds of the labour force, largely subsistence farming; cash crops: coffee, cocoa, palm kernels; harvest of food staple rice meets 80% of domestic needs; annual fish catch averages 53,000 metric tons

Natural Resources: diamonds, titanium ore, bauxite, iron ore, gold, chromite

■ FINANCE/TRADE

Currency: leone (Le)

International Reserves Excluding Gold: $30 million (Jan. 1994)

Gold Reserves: n.a.

Budget: revenues $68 million; expenditures $118 million, including capital expenditures of $28 million (1992 est.)

Defence Expenditures: $6 million (1988)

External Debt: $1.265 billion (1992)

Exports: $149 million (1992); commodities: rutile 50%, bauxite 17%, cocoa 11%, diamonds 3%, coffee 3%; partners: US, UK, Belgium, Germany, other Western Europe

Imports: $128 million (1992); commodities: capital goods 40%, food 32%, petroleum 12%, consumer goods 7%, light industrial goods; partners: US, European Community, Japan, China, Nigeria

■ HEALTH

Births: 48/1,000 population (1993)

Deaths: 23/1,000 population (1993)

Infant Mortality: 148 deaths/1,000 live births (1993)

Life Expectancy at Birth: 40 years male, 44 years female (1993)

No. of Physicians: 0.7/10,000 population (1992)

■ EDUCATION

Govt. Expenditure: 13.28% of govt. expenditure (1990)

Literacy: 20.7% (1993)

■ COMMUNICATIONS

Daily newspapers: 1 (1992)

Televisions: 9.9/1,000 inhabitants (1992)

Radios: 220/1,000 inhabitants (1992)

Telephones: n.a.

■ TRANSPORTATION

Motor Vehicles: 47,659; 35,870 passenger cars (1990)

Roads: 7,550 km; 1,175 km paved

Railway: 88 km

Air Traffic: n.a.

Airports: 11 airfields, of which are 7 usable; 4 have permanent-surface runways (1993)

Canadian Embassy: c/o Canadian High Commission, 46 Independence Ave, Accra; mailing address: P.O. Box 1639, Accra, Ghana. Tel: (011-233-21) 77-37-91. Fax: (011-233-21) 77-37-92

Representative to Canada: c/o High Commission for the Republic of Sierra Leone, 1701-19th St NW, Washington DC 20009 USA. Tel: (202) 939-9261.

Singapore

Long-Form Name: Republic of Singapore

Capital: Singapore

Population: 2,800,000 (1993 est.)

■ GEOGRAPHY

Area: 632.6 sq. km

Coastline: 193 km

Climate: tropical; hot, humid, rainy; no pronounced rainy or dry seasons; thunderstorms occur on 40% of all days (67% of days in Apr.)

Environment: mostly urban and industrialized

Terrain: lowland; gently undulating central plateau contains water catchment area and nature preserve

Land Use: 4% arable; 7% permanent; 0% meadows; 5% forest; 84% other

Location: SE Asia, bordering on South China Sea

■ PEOPLE

Nationality: Singaporean

Ethnic Groups: 76% Chinese, 15% Malay, 6% Indian, 3% other

Languages: Chinese (Mandarin), Malay, Tamil and English (official); Malay (national)

Religions: majority of Chinese are Buddhists or atheists; Malays nearly all Moslem (minorities are Christians, Hindus, Sikhs, Taoists,

Confucianists)
Marriages: 9.0 (per 1,000) (1991)
Divorces: 1.60 (per 1,000) (1991)

■ GOVERNMENT

Leader(s): Prime Min. Goh Chok Tong, Pres. Ong Teng Cheong
Government Type: republic within Commonwealth
Administrative Divisions: none
Independence: Aug. 9, 1965 (from Malaysia)
National Holiday: National Day, Aug. 9

■ ECONOMY

Overview: has an open entrepreneurial economy with strong service and manufacturing sectors and good international trading links; growth has traditionally run at high rates; per capita GDP is among the highest in Asia; rising labour costs continue to adversely affect Singapore's competitiveness
GNP: n.a., GDP $45.9 billion, per capita $16,500; real growth rate 5.8% (1992)
Inflation: 2.3% (1992)
Industries: petroleum refining, electronics, oil drilling equipment, rubber processing and rubber products, processed food and beverages, ship repair, entrepôt trade, financial services, biotechnology
Labour Force: 1,298,000 (1992); 29% industry, 0.5% agriculture, 70.5% services (1989)
Unemployment: 2.7% (1992)
Agriculture: minor importance in the economy; self-sufficient in poultry and eggs; must import most other food; major crops: rubber, copra, fruit, vegetables
Natural Resources: fish, deepwater ports

■ FINANCE/TRADE

Currency: Singapore dollar ($S)
International Reserves Excluding Gold: $48,361 million (Dec. 1993)
Gold Reserves: n.a.
Budget: revenues $10.4 billion; expenditures $9.4 billion, including capital expenditures (1993)
Defence Expenditures: 22.07% of total govt. expenditure (1991)
External Debt: none; Singapore is a net creditor (1993)
Exports: $69.748 billion (1993 est.); commodities (includes transshipments to Malaysia): petroleum products, rubber electronics, manufactured goods; partners: US 24%, Malaysia 14%, Japan 9%, Thailand 6%, Hong Kong 5%, Australia 3%, Germany 3%
Imports: $81.332 billion (1993 est.); commodities (includes transshipments from Malaysia): capital equipment, petroleum, chemicals, manufactured goods, foodstuffs; partners: Japan 22%, US 16%, Malaysia 15%, European Community 12%, Kuwait 1%

■ HEALTH

Births: 17/1,000 population (1993)
Deaths: 5/1,000 population (1993)
Infant Mortality: 5.5 deaths/1,000 live births (1993)
Life Expectancy at Birth: 72 years male, 77 years female (1993)
No. of Physicians: 7.1/10,000 population (1992)

■ EDUCATION

Govt. Expenditure: 22.89% of govt. expenditure (1991)
Literacy: 88% (1993)

■ COMMUNICATIONS

Daily newspapers: 8 (1992)
Televisions: 372.4/1,000 inhabitants (1992)
Radios: 306/1,000 inhabitants (1992)
Telephones: 45.59/100 inhabitants (1992)

■ TRANSPORTATION

Motor Vehicles: 411,740; 286,756 passenger cars (1989)
Roads: 2,644 km; 2,600 km paved
Railway: 37 km
Air Traffic: 7,745,000 passengers carried (1991)
Airports: 10 airfields, all usable with permanent-surface runways (1993)

Canadian Embassy: Canadian High Commission, IBM Towers, 14th & 15th Flrs, 80 Anson Rd, Singapore 0207; mailing address: Robinson Rd, P.O. Box 845, Singapore 9016. Tel: (011-65) 225-6363. Fax: (011-65) 225-2450
Representative to Canada: c/o High Commission for the Republic of Singapore, 231 East 51st St, New York, New York 10022 USA. Tel: (212) 826-0840. Fax: (212) 826-2964.

Slovakia

Long-Form Name: Slovak Republic
Capital: Bratislava
Population: 5,375,501 (1993 est.)

■ GEOGRAPHY

Area: 48,845 sq. km
Coastline: none: landlocked
Climate: temperate: cool summers, cold, cloudy, humid winters

Environment: severe damage to forests from acid rain
Terrain: rugged mountains in central region and north, lowlands in south
Land Use: n.a.
Location: E Europe

■ PEOPLE

Nationality: Slovak
Ethnic Groups: 85.6% Slovak, 10.8% Hungarian, 1.5% Gypsy, 2.1% other
Languages: Slovak (official), Hungarian
Religions: 60.3% Roman Catholic, 9.7% atheist, 8.4% Protestant, 4.1% Orthodox, 17.5% other
Marriages: n.a.
Divorces: n.a.

■ GOVERNMENT

Leader(s): Pres. Michal Kovac, Prime Min. Jozef Moravcik (interim)
Government Type: parliamentary democracy
Administrative Divisions: 4 departments
Independence: Jan. 1, 1993 (from Czechoslovakia)
National Holiday: Slovak National Uprising, Aug. 29

■ ECONOMY

Overview: separation from Czechoslovakia has severely disrupted the economy, resulting in rising inflation and unemployment
GNP: n.a., GDP 32.1 billion, $6,100 per capita; real growth rate -7% (1992 est.)
Inflation: 8.7% (1992 est.)
Industries: mining, chemicals, metalworking, consumer appliances, plastics, armaments
Labour Force: 2,484,000; 33.2% industry, 12.2% agriculture, 10.3% construction, 44.3% other (1990)
Unemployment: 11.3% (1992 est.)
Agriculture: very diversified crop and livestock production; mostly self-sufficient in food
Natural Resources: brown coal and lignite, iron ore, copper, manganese, salt, gas

■ FINANCE/TRADE

Currency: koruna (pl. koruny) (Kc)
International Reserves Excluding Gold: n.a.
Gold Reserves: n.a.
Budget: n.a.
Defence Expenditures: n.a.
External Debt: $1.9 billion (1992)
Exports: $3.6 billion (1992); machinery and transport equipment, chemicals, fuels, minerals, agricultural products; partners: Czech Republic, CIS republics, Germany, Poland, Austria, France, US, UK

Imports: $3.6 billion (1992); machinery and transport equipment, fuels, lubricants, manufactured goods, chemicals, agricultural products

■ HEALTH

Births: 15/1,000 population (1993)
Deaths: 10/1,000 population (1993)
Infant Mortality: 13.2 deaths/1,000 live births (1993)
Life Expectancy at Birth: 67 years male, 75 years female (1993)
No. of Physicians: n.a.

■ EDUCATION

Govt. Expenditure: n.a.
Literacy: n.a.

■ COMMUNICATIONS

Daily newspapers: n.a.
Televisions: n.a.
Radios: n.a.
Telephones: n.a.

■ TRANSPORTATION

Motor Vehicles: n.a.
Roads: 17,650 km (1990)
Railway: 3,669 km (1990)
Air Traffic: n.a.
Airports: 34 airfields, all usable; 9 have permanent-surface runways (1993)

Canadian Embassy: c/o Mickiewiczova 6, 125 33 Prague 6, Czech Republic. Tel: (011-42-2) 2431-1108. Fax: (011-42-2) 2431-0294
Representative to Canada: Embassy of the Slovak Republic, 50 Rideau Terrace, Ottawa ON K1M 2A1. Tel: (613) 749-4442. Fax: (613) 749-4989.

Slovenia

Long-Form Name: Republic of Slovenia
Capital: Ljubljana
Population: 2,000,000 (1993 est.)

■ GEOGRAPHY

Area: 20,296 sq. km
Coastline: 32 km
Climate: Mediterranean climate on the coast, continental climate with mild to hot summers and cold winters in the plateaus and eastern valleys
Environment: pollution of Sava River; heavy metals and toxic chemicals along coast; forest damage from air pollution; subject to flooding and earthquakes
Terrain: short coastal strip, alpine mountain

region, mixed mountains and valleys and numerous rivers in east
Land Use: 10% arable, 2% permanent crops, 20% meadows and pastures, 45% forests and woodland, 23% other
Location: southern Europe, bordering on Adriatic Sea

■ PEOPLE

Nationality: Slovene
Ethnic Groups: 91% Slovene, 3% Croat, 2% Serb, 1% Muslim, 3% other
Languages: 91% Slovenian, 7% Serbo-Croatian, 2% other
Religions: 96% Roman Catholic, 1% Muslim, 3% other
Marriages: n.a.
Divorces: n.a.

■ GOVERNMENT

Leader(s): Pres. Milan Kucan, Prime Min. Janez Drnovsek
Government Type: emerging democracy
Administrative Divisions: 60 provinces
Independence: June 25, 1991 (from Yugoslavia)
National Holiday: Statehood Day, June 25

■ ECONOMY

Overview: tourism has suffered due to internal strife; destruction of trade channels and the influx of tens of thousands of refugees has interfered with economic recovery after secession from Yugoslavia; there are efforts towards the privatization of major industrial firms; chief trading partners: Germany, Italy, former Soviet countries, France, Austria, US
GNP: n.a., GDP $21 billion, $10,700 per capita; real growth rate -10% (1991 est.)
Inflation: 2.7% (1992)
Industries: metallurgy, furniture, sports equipment, steel, cars, sugar, cement, textiles, machine tools
Labour Force: 945,766 (1991)
Unemployment: 10% (1992)
Agriculture: products include wheat, maize, sugar beets, potatoes, cabbages, livestock (esp. cattle, sheep, pigs, poultry); fishing, forestry; many other agricultural products must be imported
Natural Resources: brown coal and lignite deposits, lead, zinc, mercury, uranium

■ FINANCE/TRADE

Currency: Slovenian tolar (at parity with Yugoslav dinar)
International Reserves Excluding Gold: n.a.
Gold Reserves: n.a.

Budget: n.a.
Defence Expenditures: 4.5% of GDP (1993)
External Debt: $2.5 billion (1993)
Exports: $4.12 billion dinars (1990), inc. machinery, semi-finished goods, raw materials, electric motors, transportation equipment, clothing, foodstuffs
Imports: $4.679 billion dinars (1990), inc. raw materials, semi-finished goods, machinery, foodstuffs

■ HEALTH

Births: 13/1,000 population (1993)
Deaths: 10/1,000 population (1993)
Infant Mortality: 8.9 deaths/1,000 live births (1993)
Life Expectancy at Birth: 69 years male, 77 years female (1993)
No. of Physicians: n.a.

■ EDUCATION

Govt. Expenditure: n.a.
Literacy: n.a.

■ COMMUNICATIONS

Daily newspapers: 3
Televisions: 330,000 total; 7 TV stations (1993)
Radios: n.a.; 11 radio stations (1993)
Telephones: 130,000 total (1993)

■ TRANSPORTATION

Motor Vehicles: 554,200 passenger cars (1989)
Roads: 14,553 km; 10,525 km paved
Railway: 1,200 km
Air Traffic: n.a.
Airports: 13 airfields, all of which are usable; 5 have permanent-surface runways (1993)

Canadian Embassy: c/o Budakeszi ut 32, 1121 Budapest, Hungary. Tel.: (011-36-1) 1767-312. Fax: (011-36-1) 1767-689
Representative to Canada: Embassy of the Republic of Slovenia, 150 Metcalfe St, Ste 2101, Ottawa, ON K2P 1P1. Tel: (613) 565-5781. Fax: (613) 565-5783.

Solomon Islands

Long-Form Name: Solomon Islands
Capital: Honiara (on island of Guadalcanal)
Population: 300,000 (1993 est.)

■ GEOGRAPHY

Area: 28,450 sq km; 27,540 sq. km (land area)
Coastline: 5,313 km
Climate: tropical monsoon; few extremes of temperature and weather

Environment: subject to typhoons, which are rarely destructive; geologically active region with frequent earth tremors
Terrain: mostly rugged mountains with some low coral atolls
Land Use: 1% arable; 1% permanent; 1% meadows; 93% pastures; 4% other
Location: Melanesia, Pacific Ocean

■ PEOPLE

Nationality: Solomon Islander
Ethnic Groups: 93% Melanesian, 4% Polynesian, 1.5% Micronesian, 0.8% European, 0.3% Chinese, 0.4% other
Languages: English (official), Pidgin, 120 local languages
Religions: 34% Anglican, 19% Roman Catholic, 17% South Seas Evangelical, 25% other Protestant
Marriages: n.a.
Divorces: n.a.

■ GOVERNMENT

Leader(s): Prime Min. Francis Billy Hilly, Gov. Gen. Sir George Lepping
Government Type: parliamentary democracy
Administrative Divisions: 7 provinces and 1 town
Independence: July 7, 1978 (from UK; formerly known as British Solomon Islands)
National Holiday: Independence Day, July 7

■ ECONOMY

Overview: about 90% of the population depend on subsistence agriculture, fishing and forestry for at least part of their livelihood; possesses an abundance of undeveloped mineral resources; little manufacturing activity–most manufactured goods must be imported
GNP: $184 million, per capita $560; real growth rate 6.7% (1991)
Inflation: 10.8% (1992)
Industries: copra, fish (tuna)
Labour Force: n.a.
Unemployment: n.a.
Agriculture: including fishing and forestry, accounts for approx. 70% of GDP; mostly subsistence farming; cash crops: cocoa, beans, coconuts, palm kernels, timber; other products: rice, potatoes, vegetables, fruit, cattle, pigs; not self-sufficient in food grains; 90% of fish catch is exported
Natural Resources: fish, forests, gold, bauxite, phosphates

■ FINANCE/TRADE

Currency: Solomon Islands dollar ($SI)
International Reserves Excluding Gold: $19 million (Jan. 1994)
Gold Reserves: n.a.
Budget: revenues $48 million; expenditures $107 million, including capital expenditures of $45 million (1991)
Defence Expenditures: negligible
External Debt: $91 million (1992)
Exports: $84 million (1991); commodities: fish 46%, timber 31%, copra 5%, palm oil 5%; partners: Japan 51%, UK 12%, Thailand 9%, Netherlands 8%, Australia 2%, US 2%
Imports: $87.1 million (1991); commodities: plant and machinery 30%, fuel 19%, food 16%; partners: Japan 36%, US 23%, Singapore 9%, UK 9%, New Zealand 9%, Australia 4%, Hong Kong 4%, China 3%

■ HEALTH

Births: 39/1,000 population (1993)
Deaths: 7/1,000 population (1993)
Infant Mortality: 44 deaths/1,000 live births (1993)
Life Expectancy at Birth: 60 years male, 61 years female (1992)
No. of Physicians: 1.3/10,000 population (1992)

■ EDUCATION

Govt. Expenditure: 22.38% of govt. expenditure (1988)
Literacy: 60% (1993)

■ COMMUNICATIONS

Daily newspapers: 1 (1992)
Televisions: n.a.
Radios: 117/1,000 inhabitants (1992)
Telephones: 2.19/100 inhabitants (1992)

■ TRANSPORTATION

Motor Vehicles: 3,629 registered motor vehicles (1986)
Roads: 2,066 km; 28 km paved (1992)
Railway: none
Air Traffic: 69,000 passengers carried (1991)
Airports: 30 airfields, of which 29 are usable; 2 have permanent-surface runways (1993)

Canadian Embassy: c/o The Canadian High Commission, Commonwealth Ave, Canberra ACT 2600, Australia. Tel: (011-61-6) 273-3844
Representative to Canada: c/o High Commission for the Solomon Islands, 820-2nd Ave,

Ste 800B, New York, NY 10017 USA. Tel: (212) 599-6194.

Somalia

Long-Form Name: Somalia
Capital: Mogadishu
Population: 9,500,000 (1993 est.)

■ GEOGRAPHY

Area: 637,660 sq. km
Coastline: 3,025 km
Climate: desert; northeast monsoon (Dec. to Feb.), cooler southwest monsoon (May to Oct.); irregular rainfall; hot, humid periods (tangambili) between monsoons
Environment: recurring droughts; frequent dust storms over eastern plains in summer; deforestation; overgrazing; soil erosion; desertification
Terrain: mostly flat to undulating plateau rising to hills in north
Land Use: 2% arable; negligible permanent crops; 46% meadows; 14% forest; 38% other
Location: E Africa, bordering on Gulf of Aden, Indian Ocean

■ PEOPLE

Nationality: Somali
Ethnic Groups: 85% Somali, rest mainly Bantu; 30,000 Arabs, 3,000 Europeans, 800 Asians
Languages: Somali (official); Arabic, Italian, English
Religions: almost entirely Sunni Moslem, small Christian community
Marriages: n.a.
Divorces: n.a.

■ GOVERNMENT

Leader(s): Interim government has not been recognized internationally; due to political violence throughout the country, no functioning government is in place
Government Type: republic
Administrative Divisions: 18 regions
Independence: July 1, 1960 (from a merger of British Somaliland, which became independent from the UK on June 26, 1960, and Italian Somaliland, which became independent from the Italian-administered UN trusteeship on July 1, 1960, to form the Somali Republic)
National Holiday: Anniversary of the Revolution, Oct. 21

■ ECONOMY

Overview: nomads or semi-nomads who are dependent upon livestock for their livelihoods make up about 50% of the population; one of the world's least developed countries, possessing few resources; problems include high external debt, double-digit inflation and bitter civil war which has devastated much of the economy
GNP: $946 million, per capita $150; real growth rate -5.5% (1990)
Inflation: 81.9% (1988)
Industries: based on processing of agricultural products; sugar refining, textiles, petroleum refining
Labour Force: 2,140,000 (1992); 75.6% agriculture, 8.4% industry, 16% services (1989)
Unemployment: n.a.
Agriculture: livestock raising dominant: cattle, sheep, goats; fishing potential largely unexploited; crops: bananas, sorghum, corn, mangoes, sugar cane; not self-sufficient in food
Natural Resources: uranium and largely unexploited reserves of iron ore, tin, gypsum, bauxite, copper, salt

■ FINANCE/TRADE

Currency: Somali shilling (So.Sh.)
International Reserves Excluding Gold: $12 million (1989)
Gold Reserves: 0.02 million fine troy ounces (1989)
Budget: revenues $190 million; expenditures $195 million, including capital expenditures of $111 million (1989)
Defence Expenditures: $18.05 million (1989)
External Debt: $2.447 billion (1992)
Exports: $58 million (1988); commodities: livestock, hides, skins, bananas, fish; partners: US 0.5%, Saudi Arabia, Italy, Germany
Imports: $354 million (1988); commodities: textiles, petroleum products, foodstuffs, construction materials; partners: US 13%, Italy, Germany, Kenya, UK, Saudi Arabia

■ HEALTH

Births: 50/1,000 population (1993)
Deaths: 19/1,000 population (1993)
Infant Mortality: 127 deaths/1,000 live births (1993)
Life Expectancy at Birth: 44 years male, 48 years female (1993)
No. of Physicians: 0.5/10,000 population (1992)

■ EDUCATION

Govt. Expenditure: 2.8% of government expenditure (1986)
Literacy: 24.1% (1993)

■ COMMUNICATIONS

Daily newspapers: 1 (1988)
Televisions: The public telecommunications sys-

tem was completely destroyed or dismantled by the civil war factions (1993)

■ TRANSPORTATION

Motor Vehicles: 32,000; 20,000 passenger cars (1990)
Roads: 22,500 km; 2,700 km paved (1993)
Railway: n.a.
Air Traffic: 46,000 passengers carried (1991)
Airports: 69 airfields, of which 48 are usable; 8 have permanent-surface runways (1993)

Canadian Embassy: c/o The Canadian High Commission, Comcraft House, Hailé Sélassie Ave, Nairobi; mailing address: The Canadian High Commission, P.O. Box 30481, Nairobi, Kenya. Tel: (011-254-2) 21-48-04. Fax: (011-254-2) 22-69-87.

South Africa

Long-Form Name: Republic of South Africa
Capital: Pretoria (administrative), Cape Town (legislative), Bloemfontein (judicial)
Population: 39,000,000 (1993 est.)

■ GEOGRAPHY

Area: 1,221,040 sq. km; includes Walvis Bay, Marion Island, and Prince Edward Island
Coastline: 2,881 km along Indian Ocean and South Atlantic Ocean
Climate: mostly semi-arid; subtropical along coast; sunny days, cool nights
Environment: lack of important arterial rivers or lakes requires extensive water conservation and control measures
Terrain: vast interior plateau rimmed by rugged hills and narrow coastal plain
Land Use: 10% arable; 1% permanent; 65% meadows; 3% forest; 21% other
Location: S Africa, bordering on Indian Ocean, South Atlantic Ocean

■ PEOPLE

Nationality: South African
Ethnic Groups: 75.2% black, 13.6% white, 8.6% coloured, 2.6% Indian
Languages: Afrikaans, English (official); many vernacular languages, including Zulu, Xhosa, North and South Sotho, Tswana
Religions: most of whites, coloureds and approx. 60% of blacks are Christian; approx. 60% of Indians are Hindu, 20% Moslem
Marriages: n.a.
Divorces: n.a.

■ GOVERNMENT

Leader(s): President Nelson Rolihlahla Mandela
Government Type: republic
Administrative Divisions: 9 provinces; after the election bringing Mandela to power, all 10 black homelands and 4 provinces existing earlier were dissolved
Independence: May 31, 1910 (from UK)
National Holiday: Republic Day, May 31

■ ECONOMY

Overview: there is great disparity in living standards between the white minority (favoured) and the black majority; international embargoes against the country (because of its policy of apartheid) hurt the economy; has rich mineral resources (diamonds)
GNP: n.a., GDP $115 billion, per capita $2,800; real growth rate -2% (1992)
Inflation: 13.9% (1992)
Industries: mining (world's largest producer of platinum, gold, chrome), automobile assembly, metalworking, machinery, textile, iron and steel, chemical, fertilizer, foodstuffs
Labour Force: 12,434,000 (1992); 62% services, 13.6% agriculture, 24.4% industry (1989)
Unemployment: 45%; well over 50% in some homelands (1992)
Agriculture: accounts for 5% of GDP and 30% of labour force; diversified agriculture, with emphasis on livestock; products: cattle, poultry, sheep, wool, milk, beef, corn, wheat; sugar cane, fruit, vegetables; self-sufficient in food
Natural Resources: gold, chromium, antimony, coal, iron ore, manganese, nickel, phosphates, tin, uranium, gem diamonds, platinum, copper, vanadium, salt, natural gas

■ FINANCE/TRADE

Currency: rand (R)
International Reserves Excluding Gold: $1,020 million (Dec. 1993)
Gold Reserves: 4.75 million fine troy ounces (Jan. 1994)
Budget: revenues $28 billion; expenditures $36 billion, including capital expenditures of 3 billion (1993 est.); $25 billion budget proposed for 1994-1995
Defence Expenditures: $2.9 billion (1993 budget)
External Debt: $18 billion (1992)
Exports: $22.073 billion (1992); commodities: gold 40%, minerals and metals 23%, food 6%, chemicals 3%; partners: Germany, Japan, UK, US, other European Community, Hong Kong
Imports: $18.236 billion (1992); commodities: machinery 27%, chemicals 11%, vehicles and aircraft 11%, textiles, scientific instruments,

base metals; partners: US, Germany, Japan, UK, France, Italy, Switzerland

■ HEALTH

Births: 34/1,000 population (1993)
Deaths: 8/1,000 population (1993)
Infant Mortality: 51 deaths/1,000 live births (1993)
Life Expectancy at Birth: 62 years male, 67 years female (1993)
No. of Physicians: 5.3/10,000 population (1980)

■ EDUCATION

Govt. Expenditure: n.a.
Literacy: 76% (1993)

■ COMMUNICATIONS

Daily newspapers: 22 (1988)
Televisions: 101.4/1,000 inhabitants (1989)
Radios: 324/1,000 inhabitants (1989) =
Telephones: 12.5/100 inhabitants (1992)

■ TRANSPORTATION

Motor Vehicles: 5,200,153; 3,375,277 passenger cars (1990)
Roads: 188,309 km; 54,013 km paved (1993)
Railway: 20,638 km (1993)
Air Traffic: 4,819,000 passengers carried (1991)
Airports: 899 airfields, of which 713 are usable; 136 have permanent-surface runways (1993)

Canadian Embassy: Canadian Embassy, 5th Flr, Nedbank Plaza, Church & Beatrix Streets, Arcadia, Pretoria 0007; mailing address: P.O. Box 26006, Arcadia, Pretoria 0007, South Africa. Tel: (011-27-12) 324-3970. Fax (011-27-12) 323-1564
Representative to Canada: Embassy of the Republic of South Africa, 15 Sussex Dr, Ottawa ON K1M 1M8. Tel: (613) 744-0330. Fax: (613) 741-1639.

Spain

Long-Form Name: Kingdom of Spain
Capital: Madrid
Population: 39,100,000 (1993 est.)

■ GEOGRAPHY

Area: 504,750 sq. km; includes Balaeric Islands, Canary Islands, Ceuta, Melilla, Islas Chafarinas, Peñón de Vélez de la Gomera
Coastline: 4,964 km along Mediterranean Sea, Balearic Sea, Bay of Biscay, Strait of Gibraltar and North Atlantic Ocean
Climate: temperate; clear, hot summers in interior, more moderate and cloudy along coast; cloudy, cold winters in interior, partly cloudy and cool along coast
Environment: deforestation; air pollution
Terrain: large, flat to dissected, rugged hills; Pyrenees in north
Land Use: 31% arable; 10% permanent; 21% meadows; 31% forest; 7% other
Location: SW Europe, bordering on Mediterranean Sea

■ PEOPLE

Nationality: Spanish
Ethnic Groups: composite of Mediterranean and Nordic types
Languages: Castilian Spanish; second languages include 17% Catalan (northeast),7% Galician (northwest), 2% Basque (north)
Religions: 99% Roman Catholic, 1% other sects
Marriages: 5.5 (per 1,000) (1990)
Divorces: 0.59 (per 1,000) (1991)

■ GOVERNMENT

Leader(s): Pres. Felipe Gonzalez Marquez, King Juan Carlos I
Government Type: parliamentary monarchy
Administrative Divisions: 17 autonomous communities
Independence: 1492 (expulsion of the Moors and unification)
National Holiday: National Day, Oct. 12

■ ECONOMY

Overview: has been the fastest growing member of the European Economic Community (since joining in 1986) due largely to increased foreign and domestic investment; problems include the highest unemployment rate in Europe and inflation
GNP: n.a., GDP $514.9 billion, per capita $13,200; real growth rate 1% (1992)
Inflation: 5.9% (1992)
Industries: textiles and apparel (including footwear), food and beverages, metals and metal manufacturing, chemicals, shipbuilding, automobiles, machine tools
Labour Force: 14,456,000 (1992); 67.7% services, 21.1% industry, 11.2% agriculture (1989)
Unemployment: 19% (1992)
Agriculture: accounts for 5% of GNP and 14% of labour force; major products: grain, vegetables, olives, wine grapes, sugar beets, citrus fruit, beef, pork, poultry, dairy; largely self-sufficient in food; fish catch of 1.4 million metric tons
Natural Resources: coal, lignite, iron ore, uranium, mercury, pyrites, fluorspar, gypsum, zinc, lead, tungsten, copper, kaolin, potash, hydropower

■ FINANCE/TRADE

Currency: peseta (Ptas)
International Reserves Excluding Gold: $41,336 million (Jan. 1994)
Gold Reserves: 15.62 million fine troy ounces (Jan. 1994)
Budget: revenues $122.9 billion; expenditures $140.2 billion, including capital expenditures (1992 est.)
Defence Expenditures: $9.6 billion (1992)
External Debt: $67.5 billion (1992 est.)
Exports: $64.329 billion (1992); commodities: foodstuffs, live animals, wood, footwear, machinery, chemicals; partners: European Community 66%, US 8%, other developed countries 9%
Imports: $99.766 billion (1992); commodities: petroleum, footwear, machinery, chemicals, grain, soybeans, coffee, tobacco, iron and steel, timber, cotton, transport equipment; partners: European Community 57%, US 9%, other developed countries 13%, Middle East 3%

■ HEALTH

Births: 10/1,000 population (1993)
Deaths: 9/1,000 population (1993)
Infant Mortality: 7.8 deaths/1,000 live births (1993)
Life Expectancy at Birth: 73 years male, 80 years female (1993)
No. of Physicians: 31.6/10,000 population (1992)

■ EDUCATION

Govt. Expenditure: 5.25% of govt. expenditure (1990)
Literacy: 95% (1993)

■ COMMUNICATIONS

Daily newspapers: 102 (1992)
Televisions: 388.7/1,000 inhabitants (1992)
Radios: 304/1,000 inhabitants (1992)
Telephones: 39.59/100 inhabitants (1992)

■ TRANSPORTATION

Motor Vehicles: 14,442,492; 11,995,640 passenger cars (1988)
Roads: 154,960 km; 151,930 km paved
Railway: 15,430 km
Air Traffic: 20,945,000 passengers carried (1991)
Airports: 105 airfields, of which 99 are usable; 60 have permanent-surface runways (1993)

Canadian Embassy: Calle Nunez de Balboa 35, Madrid; mailing address: Apartado 587, 28080 Madrid, Spain. Tel: (011-34-1) 431-4300. Fax: (011-34-1) 431-2367
Representative to Canada: Embassy of Spain, 350 Sparks St, Ste 802, Ottawa ON K1R 7S8. Tel: (613) 237-2193. Fax: (613) 236-9246.

Sri Lanka

Long-Form Name: Democratic Socialist Republic of Sri Lanka
Capital: Colombo
Population: 17,800,000 (1993 est.)

■ GEOGRAPHY

Area: 65,610 sq. km
Coastline: 1,340 km along Indian Ocean, Bay of Bengal, Gulf of Mannar, Palk Bay
Climate: tropical; monsoonal; northeast monsoon (Dec. to Mar.); southwest monsoon (June to Oct.)
Environment: occasional cyclones, tornados; deforestation; soil erosion
Terrain: mostly low, flat to rolling plain; mountains in south-central interior
Land Use: 16% arable; 17% permanent; 7% meadows; 37% forest; 23% other
Location: Indian Ocean, S of India

■ PEOPLE

Nationality: Sri Lankan
Ethnic Groups: 74% Sinhalese; 18% Tamil; 7% Moor; 1% Burgher, Malay and Veddha
Languages: Sinhala (official); Sinhala and Tamil are the national languages; Sinhala spoken by about 74% of population, Tamil spoken by about 18%; English commonly used in government and spoken by about 10% of the population
Religions: 69% Buddhist, 15% Hindu (Tamil speakers), 8% Christian, 8% Moslem
Marriages: 8.4 (per 1,000) (1989)
Divorces: 0.16 (per 1,000) (1988)

■ GOVERNMENT

Leader(s): Pres. Dingiri Banda Wijetunge, Prime Min. Ranil Wickremasinghe
Government Type: republic
Administrative Divisions: 8 provinces
Independence: Feb. 4, 1948 (from UK; formerly known as Ceylon)
National Holiday: Independence and National Day, Feb. 4

■ ECONOMY

Overview: economy based on agriculture, forestry and fishing; tea, rubber and coconuts provide about one-third of export earnings; has had high rates of unemployment since the late 1970s
GNP: n.a., GDP $7.75 billion, per capita $440;

real growth rate 4.5% (1992 est.)
Inflation: 11.4% (1992)
Industries: processing of rubber, tea, coconuts and other agricultural commodities; cement, petroleum refining, textiles, tobacco, clothing
Labour Force: 6,370,000 (1992); 42.6% agriculture, 11.7% industry, 45.7% services (1989)
Unemployment: 14.4% (1992)
Agriculture: accounts for 26% of GDP and almost 50% of labour force; most important staple crop is paddy rice; other field crops: sugar cane, grains, pulses, oilseeds, roots; spices; cash crops: tea, rubber, coconuts; animal products: milk, eggs, hides, meat; not self-sufficient in rice production
Natural Resources: limestone, graphite, mineral sands, gems, phosphates, clay

■ FINANCE/TRADE

Currency: rupee (SL Rs)
International Reserves Excluding Gold: $1,671 million (Jan. 1994)
Gold Reserves: 0.14 million fine troy ounces (Jan. 1994)
Budget: revenues $2.0 billion; expenditures $3.7 billion, including capital expenditures of $0.5 billion (1992)
Defence Expenditures: 8.54% of total govt. expenditure (1992)
External Debt: $6.401 billion (1992)
Exports: $2.487 billion (1992); commodities: tea, textiles and garments, petroleum products, coconut, rubber, agricultural products, gems and jewelry, marine products; partners: US 26%, Egypt, Iraq, UK, Germany, Singapore, Japan
Imports: $3.646 billion (1992); commodities: petroleum, machinery and equipment, textiles and textile materials, wheat, transportation equipment, electrical machinery, sugar, rice; partners: Japan, Saudi Arabia, US 5.6%, India, Singapore, Germany, UK, Iran

■ HEALTH

Births: 20/1,000 population (1993)
Deaths: 6/1,000 population (1993)
Infant Mortality: 19 deaths/1,000 live births (1993)
Life Expectancy at Birth: 68 years male, 74 years female (1993)
No. of Physicians: 1.8/10,000 population (1992)

■ EDUCATION

Govt. Expenditure: 10.14% of govt. expenditure (1992)
Literacy: 88.4% (1993)

■ COMMUNICATIONS

Daily newspapers: 21 (1992)
Televisions: 32.3/1,000 inhabitants (1992)
Radios: 194/1,000 inhabitants (1992)
Telephones: 1.01/100 inhabitants (1992)

■ TRANSPORTATION

Motor Vehicles: 320,235; 176,711 passenger cars (1990)
Roads: 75,749 km; 27,637 km paved
Railway: 1,948 km
Air Traffic: 893,000 passengers carried (1991)
Airports: 14 airfields, of which 13 are usable; 12 have permanent-surface runways (1993)

Canadian Embassy: 6 Gregory's Rd, Cinnamon Gardens, Colombo 7; mailing address: P.O. Box 1006, Colombo 7, Sri Lanka. Tel: (011-94-1) 69-58-41. Fax: (011-94-1) 68-70-49
Representative to Canada: High Commission for the Democratic Socialist Republic of Sri Lanka, 85 Range Rd, Ste 102-4 & 201, Ottawa ON K1N 8J6. Tel: (613) 233-8440. Fax: (613) 238-8448.

St. Helena

Dependent Territory of the United Kingdom

Long-Form Name: Saint Helena
Capital: Jamestown
Population: 6,720 (1993 est.)

■ GEOGRAPHY

Area: 410 sq. km
Climate: tropical marine; little seasonal variation
Land Use: 7% arable, 0% permanent crops, 7% meadows and pastures, 3% forests, 83% other
Location: Atlantic Ocean, SW of Africa

■ PEOPLE

Nationality: Saint Helenian
Ethnic Groups: Europeans, East Indians, Africans
Languages: English (official)

■ GOVERNMENT

Leader(s): Gov. and Commander-in-Chief Alan Hoole
Government Type: dependency
National Holiday: Celebration of the Birthday of the Queen, June 10

■ ECONOMY

Overview: depends primarily on financial assistance from UK; fishing, livestock raising and sale of handicrafts provide income for local population; due to the lack of jobs, many inhabitants have emigrated

■ FINANCE/TRADE

Currency: Saint Helenian pound (at par with British pound)

Sudan

Long-Form Name: Republic of the Sudan
Capital: Khartoum
Population: 27,400,000 (1993 est.)

■ GEOGRAPHY

Area: 2,505,810 sq. km
Coastline: 853 km along Red Sea
Climate: tropical in south; arid desert in north; rainy season (Apr. to Oct.)
Environment: dominated by the Nile and its tributaries; dust storms; desertification
Terrain: generally flat, featureless plain; mountains in east and west
Land Use: 5% arable; negligible permanent; 24% meadows; 20% forest; 51% other
Location: NE Africa, bordering on Red Sea

■ PEOPLE

Nationality: Sudanese
Ethnic Groups: 52% black, 39% Arab, 6% Beja, 2% foreigners, 1% other
Languages: Arabic (official), Nubian, Ta Bedawie, diverse dialects of Nilotic, Nilo-Hamatic and Sudanic languages, English; program of Arabization in process
Religions: 70% Sunni Moslem (in north), 25% indigenous beliefs, 5% Christian (mostly in south and Khartoum)
Marriages: n.a.
Divorces: n.a.

■ GOVERNMENT

Leader(s): Pres. Omar Hassan Ahmed al-Bashir
Government Type: military; civilian government suspended and martial law imposed after June 30, 1989, coup
Administrative Divisions: 26 states (as of Feb. 2, 1994)
Independence: Jan. 1, 1956 (from Egypt and UK; formerly known as Anglo-Egyptian Sudan)
National Holiday: Independence Day, Jan. 1

■ ECONOMY

Overview: a very poor country, hurt by civil war, chronic political instability, adverse weather and counterproductive governmental economic policies; agriculture is the economic base, employing 80% of the labour force; international aid is helping the country manage a high foreign debt but creditors want economic reform
GNP: n.a., GDP $5.2 billion, per capita $184; real growth rate 9% (1992 est.)
Inflation: 117.6% (1992)
Industries: cotton ginning, textiles, cement, edible oils, sugar, soap distilling, shoes, petroleum refining
Labour Force: 8,080,000 (1992); 63.4% agriculture, 4.3% industry, 32.3% services (1989)
Unemployment: 30% (1992)
Agriculture: accounts for 35% of GNP and 80% of labour force; untapped potential for higher farm production; water shortages; two-thirds of land area suitable for crops and livestock; major products: cotton, oilseeds, sorghum, millet, wheat, gum arabic, sheep; marginally self-sufficient in most foods
Natural Resources: modest reserves of crude oil, iron ore, copper, chromium ore, zinc, tungsten, mica, silver, crude oil

■ FINANCE/TRADE

Currency: Sudanese pound (LSd)
International Reserves Excluding Gold: $43 million (Nov. 1993)
Gold Reserves: n.a.
Budget: revenues $1.3 billion; expenditures $2.1 billion, including capital expenditures of $505 million (1991 est.)
Defence Expenditures: $460 million (1990)
External Debt: $16.193 billion (1992)
Exports: $315 million (1992); commodities: cotton 43%, sesame, gum arabic, peanuts; partners: Western Europe 46%, Saudi Arabia 14%, Eastern Europe 9%, Japan 9%, US 3%
Imports: $1.3 billion (1992); commodities: petroleum products, manufactured goods, machinery and equipment, medicines and chemicals; partners: Western Europe 32%, Africa and Asia 15%, US 13%, Eastern Europe 3%

■ HEALTH

Births: 45/1,000 population (1993)
Deaths: 14/1,000 population (1993)
Infant Mortality: 87 deaths/1,000 live births (1993)
Life Expectancy at Birth: 52 years male, 53 years female (1993)
No. of Physicians: 1/10,000 population (1992)

■ EDUCATION

Govt. Expenditure: 15% of govt. expenditure (1985)
Literacy: 27.1% (1993)

■ COMMUNICATIONS

Daily newspapers: 3 (1992)
Televisions: 61.3/1,000 inhabitants (1992)
Radios: 235/1,000 inhabitants (1992)
Telephones: 0.4/100 inhabitants (1992)

■ TRANSPORTATION

Motor Vehicles: 173,422; 116,473 passenger cars (1990)
Roads: 20,703 km; 2,000 km paved (1993)
Railway: 5,516 km (1993)
Air Traffic: 363,000 passengers carried (1991)
Airports: 68 airfields, of which 56 are usable; 10 have permanent-surface runways (1993)

Canadian Embassy: c/o Old Airport Area, Higher 23, Kebele 12, House Number 122, Addis Ababa; mailing address: P.O. Box 1130, Addis Ababa, Ethiopia. Tel: (011-251-1) 71-30-22. Fax: (011-251-1) 71 30 33
Representative to Canada: Embassy of the Republic of the Sudan, 85 Range Rd, Ste 407, Ottawa ON K1N 8J6. Tel: (613) 235-4000. Fax: (613) 235-6880.

Suriname

Long-Form Name: Republic of Suriname
Capital: Paramaribo
Population: 400,000 (1993 est.)

■ GEOGRAPHY

Area: 163,270 sq. km
Coastline: 386 km along Atlantic Ocean
Climate: tropical; moderated by trade winds
Environment: mostly tropical rain forest
Terrain: mostly rolling hills; narrow coastal plain with swamps
Land Use: negligible arable: negligible permanent; negligible meadows; 97% forest; 3% other
Location: N South America, bordering on Atlantic Ocean

■ PEOPLE

Nationality: Surinamer
Ethnic Groups: 37% Hindustani (East Indian), 31% Creole (black and mixed), 15% Javanese, 10% Bush black, 3% Amerindian, 2% Chinese, 1% European, 1% other
Languages: Dutch (official), Hindustani 32%, Javanese 15%; the majority can speak the native language Sranang Tongo (Taki-Taki)
Religions: 27.4% Hindu, 19.6% Moslem, 22.8% Roman Catholic, 25.2% Protestant (predominantly Moravian), about 5% indigenous beliefs
Marriages: n.a.

Divorces: n.a.

■ GOVERNMENT

Leader(s): Pres. Runaldo R. Venetiaan, V. Pres. Jules Ajodhia
Government Type: republic
Administrative Divisions: 10 districts
Independence: Nov. 25, 1975 (from Netherlands; formerly known as Netherlands Guiana or Dutch Guiana)
National Holiday: Independence Day, Nov. 25

■ ECONOMY

Overview: the economy is vulnerable to world prices for its product bauxite as well as guerrilla activity which has targeted the economic infrastructure; it has been hurt by the cut off of Dutch development aid in 1982; high inflation, high unemployment, widespread black-market activity, and hard currency shortfalls continue to characterize the economy
GNP: $1.649 billion, per capita $3,610; real growth rate -2.2% (1991)
Inflation: 50% (1988 est.)
Industries: bauxite mining, alumina and aluminum production, lumbering, food processing, fishing
Labour Force: 135,000 (1992); 20% agriculture, 20% industry, 60% services (1989)
Unemployment: 16.5% (1990)
Agriculture: accounts for 10.4% of GDP and 25% of export earnings; paddy rice planted on 85% of arable land and represents 60% of total farm output; other products: bananas, palm kernels, coconuts, plantains, peanuts, beef, chicken; shrimp and forestry products of increasing importance
Natural Resources: timber, hydropower potential, fish, shrimp, bauxite, iron ore and modest amounts of nickel, copper, platinum, gold

■ FINANCE/TRADE

Currency: Suriname guilder (Sf)
International Reserves Excluding Gold: $0 million (Aug. 1993)
Gold Reserves: 0.05 million fine troy ounces (Aug. 1993)
Budget: revenues $466 million; expenditures $716 million, including capital expenditures of $123 million (1989)
Defence Expenditures: $39 million (1989)
External Debt: $138 million (1990 est.)
Exports: $472 million (1990); commodities: alumina, bauxite, aluminum, rice, wood and wood products, shrimp and fish, bananas; partners: Netherlands 28%, US 22%, Norway 18%, Japan 11%, Brazil 10%, UK 4%

Imports: $472 million (1990); commodities: capital equipment, petroleum, foodstuffs, cotton, consumer goods; partners: US 34%, Netherlands 20%, Trinidad and Tobago 8%, Brazil 5%, UK 3%

■ HEALTH

Births: 24/1,000 population (1993)
Deaths: 7/1,000 population (1993)
Infant Mortality: 27 deaths/1,000 live births (1993)
Life Expectancy at Birth: 66 years male, 71 years female (1993)
No. of Physicians: 7.9/10,000 population (1992)

■ EDUCATION

Govt. Expenditure: 18% of govt. expenditure (1986)
Literacy: 94.9% (1993)

■ COMMUNICATIONS

Daily newspapers: 2 (1992)
Televisions: 132.9/1,000 inhabitants (1992)
Radios: 633/1,000 inhabitants (1992)
Telephones: 10.45/100 inhabitants (1992)

■ TRANSPORTATION

Motor Vehicles: 48,000; 35,000 passenger cars (1990)
Roads: 8,300 km; 500 km paved
Railway: 166 km
Air Traffic: 133,000 passengers carried (1991)
Airports: 46 airfields, of which 39 are usable; 6 have permanent-surface runways (1993)

Canadian Embassy: c/o Canadian High Commission, High and Young Streets, Georgetown; mailing address: P.O. Box 10880, Georgetown, Guyana. Tel: (011-592-2) 72081. Fax: (011-592-2): 58380
Representative to Canada: c/o Embassy of the Republic of Suriname, 4301 Connecticut Ave NW, Ste 108, Washington DC 20008 USA. Tel: (202) 244-7488. Fax: (202) 244-5878.

Svalbard

Dependent Territory of Norway

Long-Form Name: Svalbard
Capital: Longyearbyen
Population: 3,209 (1993 est.)

■ GEOGRAPHY

Area: 62,050 sq. km, 5 large islands, many smaller ones
Climate: arctic, tempered by mild Atlantic winds, cool suumers, cold winters
Land Use: undeveloped except for mining establishments; no trees–the only bushes are crowberry and cloudberry
Location: Arctic Ocean, midway between Norway and the North Pole

■ PEOPLE

Nationality: Norwegian
Ethnic Groups: 64% Russian, 35% Norwegian, 1% other
Languages: Norwegian, Russian

■ GOVERNMENT

Leader(s): under Norwegian govt. administration
Government Type: Territory of Norway

■ ECONOMY

Overview: tourism most important; coal mining only industry; some trapping of seal, polar bear, fox, and walrus

■ FINANCE/TRADE

Currency: Norwegian krone

Swaziland

Long-Form Name: Kingdom of Swaziland
Capital: Mbabane
Population: 800,000 (1993 est.)

■ GEOGRAPHY

Area: 17,360 sq. km
Coastline: none: landlocked
Climate: varies from tropical to near temperate
Environment: overgrazing; soil degradation; soil erosion
Terrain: mostly mountains and hills; some moderately sloping plains
Land Use: 8% arable; negligible permanent; 67% meadows; 6% forest; 19% other
Location: S Africa

■ PEOPLE

Nationality: Swazi
Ethnic Groups: 97% African, 3% European
Languages: English and siSwati (official); government business conducted in English
Religions: 60% Christian, 40% indigenous beliefs
Marriages: 4.1 (per 1,000) (1989)
Divorces: n.a.

■ GOVERNMENT

Leader(s): Prime Min. Prince Jameson Mbilini Dlamini, King Mswati III
Government Type: monarchy; independent mem-

ber of Commonwealth
Administrative Divisions: 4 districts
Independence: Sept. 6, 1968 (from UK)
National Holiday: Somhlolo (Independence) Day, Sept. 6

■ ECONOMY

Overview: the economy is based on subsistence agriculture and is closely tied to that of its neighbour, South Africa, from which it receives 90% of its imports and to which it sends about one-third of its exports; manufacturing focuses on the processing of agricultural products; mining is becoming less important
GNP: $874 million, per capita $1,060; real growth rate 6.8% (1991)
Inflation: 12.1% (1991)
Industries: mining (coal and asbestos), wood pulp, sugar
Labour Force: 306,000 (1992); 74% agriculture, 17% services, 9% industry (1989); 24,000–29,000 employed in South Africa
Unemployment: n.a.
Agriculture: accounts for 25% of GDP; mostly subsistence agriculture; cash crops: sugar cane, citrus fruit, cotton, pineapple; other crops and livestock: corn, sorghum, peanuts, cattle, goats, sheep; not self-sufficient in grain
Natural Resources: asbestos, coal, clay, tin, hydroelectric power, forests and small gold and diamond deposits

■ FINANCE/TRADE

Currency: lilangeni (pl. emalangeni) (E)
International Reserves Excluding Gold: $287 million (Jan. 1994)
Gold Reserves: n.a.
Budget: revenues $342 million; expenditures $410 million, including capital expenditures of $130 million (1994 est.)
Defence Expenditures: $22 million (1993-1994)
External Debt: $240 million (1992)
Exports: $524 million (1990); commodities: sugar, asbestos, wood pulp, citrus, canned fruit, soft drink concentrates; partners: South Africa, UK, US
Imports: $746 million (1991); commodities: motor vehicles, machinery, transport equipment, chemicals, petroleum products, foodstuffs; partners: South Africa, US, UK

■ HEALTH

Births: 44/1,000 population (1993)
Deaths: 12/1,000 population (1993)
Infant Mortality: 101 deaths/1,000 live births (1993)
Life Expectancy at Birth: 51 years male, 59 years

female (1993)
No. of Physicians: 0.5/10,000 population (1990)

■ EDUCATION

Govt. Expenditure: 27.37% of govt. expenditure (1990)
Literacy: 55.2% (1993)

■ COMMUNICATIONS

Daily newspapers: 2 (1992)
Televisions: 16.4/1,000 inhabitants (1992)
Radios: 154/1,000 inhabitants (1992)
Telephones: 2.95/100 inhabitants (1992)

■ TRANSPORTATION

Motor Vehicles: 33,019; 24,899 passenger cars (1987)
Roads: 2,743 km; 521 km paved
Railway: 297 km, plus 71 km disused (1993)
Air Traffic: 59,000 passengers carried (1991)
Airports: 23 airfields, of which 21 are usable; 1 has a permanent-surface runway (1993)

Canadian Embassy: c/o Canadian Embassy, 5th Flr, Nedbank Plaza, Church & Beatrix Streets, Arcadia, Pretoria 0007; mailing address: P.O. Box 26006, Arcadia, Pretoria 0007, South Africa. Tel: (011-27-12) 324-3970. Fax (011-27-12) 323-1564
Representative to Canada: High Commission for the Kingdom of Swaziland, 130 Albert St, Ste 1204, Ottawa ON K1P 5G4. Tel: (613) 567-1480. Fax: (613) 567-1058.

Sweden

Long-Form Name: Kingdom of Sweden
Capital: Stockholm
Population: 8,700,000 (1993 est.)

■ GEOGRAPHY

Area: 449,960 sq. km
Coastline: 3,218 km
Climate: temperate in south with cold, cloudy winters and cool, partly cloudy summers, sub-arctic in north
Environment: water pollution; acid rain
Terrain: mostly flat or gently rolling lowlands; mountains in west
Land Use: 7% arable; 0% permanent; 2% meadows; 64% forest; 27% other
Location: N Europe, bordering on Baltic Sea

■ PEOPLE

Nationality: Swedish
Ethnic Groups: homogeneous white population; small Lappish minority; about 12% foreign born

of first-generation immigrants (Finns, Yugoslavs, Danes, Norwegians, Greeks, Turks)
Languages: Swedish (official), small Lapp- and Finnish-speaking minorities; immigrants speak native languages
Religions: 94% Evangelical Lutheran, 1.5% Roman Catholic, 4.5% other
Marriages: 4.7 (per 1,000) (1991)
Divorces: 2.20 (per 1,000) (1991)

■ GOVERNMENT

Leader(s): Prime Min. Ingvar Carlsson, King Carl XVI Gustaf
Government Type: constitutional monarchy
Administrative Divisions: 24 provinces
Independence: June 6, 1809, constitutional monarchy established
National Holiday: Day of the Swedish Flag, June 6

■ ECONOMY

Overview: a mixed system of high-tech capitalism and extensive welfare benefits; has benefited from neutrality in world wars; has essentially full employment and excellent communications systems; but faces loss of competitive edge
GNP: n.a., GDP $145.6 billion, per capita $16,900; real growth rate -1.7% (1992)
Inflation: 2.3% (1992)
Industries: iron and steel, precision equipment (bearings, radio and telephone parts, armaments), wood pulp and paper products, processed foods, motor vehicles
Labour Force: 4,319,000 (1992); 3.3% agriculture, 21.8% industry, 74.9% services (1989)
Unemployment: 5.3% (1992)
Agriculture: animal husbandry predominates, with milk and dairy products accounting for 37% of farm income; main crops: grains, sugar beets, potatoes; 100% self-sufficient in grains and potatoes, 85% self-sufficient in sugar beets
Natural Resources: zinc, iron ore, lead, copper, silver, timber, uranium, hydropower potential

■ FINANCE/TRADE

Currency: krona (pl. kronor) (Skr)
International Reserves Excluding Gold: $19,050 million (Dec. 1993)
Gold Reserves: 6.07 million fine troy ounces (Jan. 1994)
Budget: revenues $70.4 billion; expenditures $82.5 billion, including capital expenditures (1992)
Defence Expenditures: 5.5% of total govt. expenditure (1992)
External Debt: $19.5 billion (1992 est.)
Exports: $49.9 billion (1993 est.); commodities: machinery, motor vehicles, paper products, pulp and wood, iron and steel products, chemicals, petroleum and petroleum products; partners: European Community 52.1%, (Germany 12.1%, UK 11.2%, Denmark 6.8%), US 9.8%, Norway 9.3%
Imports: $42.8 billion (1993 est.); commodities: machinery, petroleum and petroleum products, chemicals, motor vehicles, foodstuffs, iron and steel, clothing; partners: European Community 55.8%, (Germany 21.2%, UK 8.6%, Denmark 6.6%), US 7.5%, Norway 6%

■ HEALTH

Births: 14/1,000 population (1993)
Deaths: 11/1,000 population (1993)
Infant Mortality: 6.2 deaths/1,000 live births (1993)
Life Expectancy at Birth: 75 years male, 80 years female (1993)
No. of Physicians: 25.8/10,000 population (1992)

■ EDUCATION

Govt. Expenditure: 9.31% of govt. expenditure (1992)
Literacy: 99% (1993)

■ COMMUNICATIONS

Daily newspapers: 107 (1992)
Televisions: 470.5/1,000 inhabitants (1992)
Radios: 885/1,000 inhabitants (1992)
Telephones: 88.95/100 inhabitants (1992)

■ TRANSPORTATION

Motor Vehicles: 3,924,633; 3,600,518 passenger cars (1990)
Roads: 97,400 km; 51,899 km paved (1993)
Railway: 12,735 km
Air Traffic: 9,827,000 passengers carried (1991)
Airports: 253 airfields, of which 250 are usable; 139 have permanent-surface runways (1993)

Canadian Embassy: The Canadian Embassy, Tegelbacken 4 (Flr 7), Stockholm; mailing address: P.O. Box 16129; S-10323 Stockholm, Sweden. Tel: (011-46-8) 613-9900. Fax: (011-46-8) 24 24 91
Representative to Canada: Embassy of Sweden, Mercury Court, 377 Dalhousie St, Ottawa ON K1N 9N8. Tel: (613) 236-8553. Fax: (613) 236-5720.

Switzerland

Long-Form Name: Swiss Confederation
Capital: Bern
Population: 7,000,000 (1993 est.)

■ GEOGRAPHY

Area: 41,290 sq. km
Coastline: none: landlocked
Climate: temperate, but varies with altitude; cold, cloudy, rainy/snowy winters; cool to warm, cloudy, humid summers with occasional showers
Environment: dominated by Alps
Terrain: mostly mountains (Alps in south, Jura in northwest) with a central plateau of rolling hills, plains and large lakes
Land Use: 10% arable; 1% permanent; 40% meadows; 26% forest; 23% other
Location: SC Europe

■ PEOPLE

Nationality: Swiss
Ethnic Groups: total population: 65% German, 18% French, 10% Italian, 1% Romansch, 6% other; Swiss nationals: 74% German, 20% French, 4% Italian, 1% Romansch, 1% other
Languages: 65% German, 18% French, 12% Italian, 1% Raeto-Romansch (all official)
Religions: 47.6% Roman Catholic, 44.3% Protestant, 8.1% other
Marriages: 6.9 (per 1,000) (1991)
Divorces: 1.96 (per 1,000) (1990)

■ GOVERNMENT

Leader(s): Pres. Otto Stich, V. Pres. Kaspar Villiger
Government Type: federal republic
Administrative Divisions: 26 cantons
Independence: Aug. 1, 1291
National Holiday: Anniversary of the Founding of the Swiss Confederation, Aug. 1

■ ECONOMY

Overview: country has the highest per capita output, general living standards, education and science, healthcare and diet standards in Europe; important banking and tourist sectors; low inflation and negligible unemployment is due partly to government policies; has rejected membership in the European Economic Community
GNP: n.a., GDP $152.3 billion, per capita $22,300; real growth rate -0.6% (1992)
Inflation: 4.0% (1992)
Industries: machinery, chemicals, watches, textiles, precision instruments
Labour Force: 3,212,000 (1992); 63.8% services, 29.8% industry, 6.4% agriculture (1989)
Unemployment: 3% (1992)
Agriculture: dairy farming predominates; less than 50% self-sufficient; food shortages: fish, refined sugar, fats and oils (other than butter), grains, eggs, fruit, vegetables, meat

Natural Resources: hydropower potential, timber, salt

■ FINANCE/TRADE

Currency: Swiss franc (SwF)
International Reserves Excluding Gold: $29,052 million (Jan. 1994)
Gold Reserves: 83.28 million fine troy ounces (Jan. 1994)
Budget: revenues $24.0 billion; expenditures $23.8 billion, including capital expenditures (1990)
Defence Expenditures: $3.5 billion (1993 est.)
External Debt: n.a.
Exports: $63.204 billion (1993); commodities: machinery and equipment, precision instruments, metal products, foodstuffs, textiles and clothing; partners: Europe 64% (European Community 56%, other 8%) US 9%, Japan 4%
Imports: $60.851 billion (1993); commodities: agricultural products, machinery and transportation equipment, chemicals, textiles, construction materials; partners: Europe 79% (European Community 72%, other 7%), US 5%

■ HEALTH

Births: 13/1,000 population (1993)
Deaths: 9/1,000 population (1993)
Infant Mortality: 6.9 deaths/1,000 live births (1993)
Life Expectancy at Birth: 74 years male, 81 years female (1993)
No. of Physicians: 14.4/10,000 population (1992)

■ EDUCATION

Govt. Expenditure: 18.7% of govt. expenditure (1989)
Literacy: 99% (1993)

■ COMMUNICATIONS

Daily newspapers: 98 (1992)
Televisions: 405.8/1,000 inhabitants (1992)
Radios: 851/1,000 inhabitants (1992)
Telephones: 90.0/100 inhabitants (1992)

■ TRANSPORTATION

Motor Vehicles: 3,297,237; 2,993,529 passenger cars (1990)
Roads: 62,145 km, all paved (1993)
Railway: 4,418 km (1993)
Air Traffic: 7,974,000 passengers carried (1991)
Airports: 66 airfields, of which 65 are usable; 42 have permanent-surface runways (1993)

Canadian Embassy: Canadian Embassy, 88 Kirchenfeldstrasse, 3005 Berne, Switzerland; mailing address: Box 3000, Berne 6,

Switzerland. Tel: (011-41-31) 352-63-81. Fax: (011-41-31) 352-73-15
Representative to Canada: Embassy of Switzerland, 5 Marlborough Ave, Ottawa ON K1N 8E6. Tel: (613) 235-1837. Fax: (613) 563-1394.

Syria

Long-Form Name: Syrian Arab Republic
Capital: Damascus
Population: 13,500,000 (1993 est.)

■ GEOGRAPHY

Area: 185,180 sq. km; including 1,295 sq. km of Israeli-occupied territory
Coastline: 193 km along Mediterranean Sea
Climate: mostly desert; hot, dry, sunny summers (June to Aug.) and mild, rainy winters (Dec. to Feb.) along coast
Environment: deforestation; overgrazing; soil erosion; desertification
Terrain: primarily semi-arid and desert plateau; narrow coastal plain; mountains in west
Land Use: 28% arable; 3% permanent; 46% meadows; 3% forest; 20% other
Location: SW Asia (Middle East), bordering on Mediterranean Sea

■ PEOPLE

Nationality: Syrian
Ethnic Groups: 90% Arab; 10% Kurds, Armenians and other
Languages: Arabic (official), Kurdish, Armenian, Aramaic, Circassian; French widely understood
Religions: 74% Sunni, 16% Alawite, Druze and other Muslim sects, 10% Christian
Marriages: 7.50 (per 1,000) (1990)
Divorces: 0.69 (per 1,000) (1990)

■ GOVERNMENT

Leader(s): Pres. Lt.-Gen. Hafez al-Assad, V. Pres. Abdel Halim Khaddam, Mohammad Zuheir Masharqa and Col. Rifaat Assad, Prime Min. Mahmoud Zubi
Government Type: republic under leftwing military regime
Administrative Divisions: 14 provinces
Independence: Apr. 17, 1946 (from League of Nations mandate under French administration; formerly known as United Arab Republic)
National Holiday: National Day, Apr. 17

■ ECONOMY

Overview: economic difficulties are due, in part, to severe drought in several recent years, costly but unsuccessful attempts to match Israel's military strength, a fall-off in Arab aid and insufficient foreign exchange earnings to buy needed imports; agricultural output is poor; a major long-term concern is the additional drain of upstream Euphrates water by Turkey once its vast dam and irrigation projects are completed
GNP: $14.234 billion, per capita $1,110; real growth rate 1.4% (1991)
Inflation: 7.7% (1991)
Industries: textiles, food processing, beverages, tobacco, phosphate rock mining, petroleum
Labour Force: 3,101,000 (1992); 62.9% services, 22% agriculture, 15.1% industry (1989)
Unemployment: 5.7% (1989)
Agriculture: accounts for 27% of GDP; all major crops (wheat, barley, cotton, lentils, chickpeas) grown on rain-fed land causing wide swings in yields; animal products: beef, lamb, eggs, poultry, milk; not self-sufficient in grain or livestock products
Natural Resources: crude oil, phosphates, chrome and manganese ores, asphalt, iron ore, rock salt, marble, gypsum

■ FINANCE/TRADE

Currency: Syrian pound (LS)
International Reserves Excluding Gold: $143 million (1988)
Gold Reserves: 0.83 million fine troy ounces (May 1993)
Budget: revenues 5.4 billion; expenditures $7.5 billion, including capital expenditures of $2.9 billion (1991)
Defence Expenditures: $1.62 billion (31.51% of total govt. expenditure) (1990)
External Debt: $16.481 billion (1992)
Exports: $3.093 billion (1992); commodities: petroleum, textiles, fruit and vegetables, phosphates; partners: Italy, Romania, USSR, US, Iran, France
Imports: $3.490 billion (1992); commodities: petroleum, machinery, base metals, foodstuffs and beverages; partners: Iran, Germany, USSR, France, Libya, US

■ HEALTH

Births: 45/1,000 population (1993)
Deaths: 7/1,000 population (1993)
Infant Mortality: 48 deaths/1,000 live births (1993)
Life Expectancy at Birth: 64 years male, 66 years female (1993)
No. of Physicians: 7.7/10,000 population (1992)

■ EDUCATION

Govt. Expenditure: 14.2% of govt. expenditure

(1991)
Literacy: 64.5% (1993)

■ COMMUNICATIONS

Daily newspapers: 8 (1992)
Televisions: 58.7/1,000 inhabitants (1992)
Radios: 248/1,000 inhabitants (1992)
Telephones: 5.9/100 inhabitants (1992)

■ TRANSPORTATION

Motor Vehicles: 242,792; 112,259 passenger cars
(1990)
Roads: 30,000 km; 22,680 km paved
Railway: 1,998 km (1993)
Air Traffic: 661,000 passengers carried (1991)
Airports: 104 airfields, of which 100 are usable;
24 have permanent-surface runways (1993)

Canadian Embassy: The Canadian Embassy, Lot
12, Mezzah Autostrade, Damascus; mailing
address: P.O. Box 3394, Damascus, Syria. Tel:
(011-963-11) 2236-851. Fax: (011-963-11)
2228-034
Representative to Canada: c/o Embassy of the
Syrian Arab Republic, 2215 Wyoming Ave
NW, Washington DC 20008 USA. Tel: (202)
232-6313. Fax: (202) 232-5184.

Taiwan

Long-Form Name: Taiwan
Capital: Taipei
Population: 20,900,000 (1993 est.)

■ GEOGRAPHY

Area: 35,980 sq. km; includes the Pescadores,
Matsu and Quemoy
Coastline: 1,448 km
Climate: tropical; marine; rainy season during
southwest monsoon (June to Aug.); cloudiness
is persistent and extensive all year
Environment: subject to earthquakes and
typhoons
Terrain: eastern two-thirds mostly rugged moun-
tains; flat to gently rolling plains in west
Land Use: 24% arable; 1% permanent; 5%
meadows; 55% forest; 15% other
Location: SE of China, bordering on South and
East China Seas, Pacific Ocean

■ PEOPLE

Nationality: Chinese
Ethnic Groups: 84% Taiwanese, 14% mainland
Chinese, 2% aborigine
Languages: Mandarin Chinese (official);
Taiwanese and Hakka dialects also used
Religions: 93% mixture of Buddhist, Islam,
Confucian and Taoist, 5% Christian, 3% other
Marriages: n.a.
Divorces: n.a.

■ GOVERNMENT

Leader(s): Pres. Lee Teng-hui, Prem. Lien Chan
Government Type: multi-party democratic regime
Administrative Divisions: 16 counties, 5 munici-
palities, 2 special municipalities
Independence: n.a.
National Holiday: National Day (Anniversary of
the Revolution), Oct. 10

■ ECONOMY

Overview: capitalist economy with government
guidance of investment and foreign trade; ranks
as number 13 among major trading countries;
steady industrialization; agriculture now contributes only 4% to GNP, as opposed to 35% in
1952
GNP: $209 billion, per capita $10,000; real
growth rate 6.7% (1992 est.)
Inflation: 4.4% (1992)
Industries: textiles, clothing, chemicals, electronics, food processing, plywood, sugar
milling, cement, shipbuilding, petroleum
Labour Force: 41% industry and commerce, 32%
services, 20% agriculture, 7% civil administration (1986)
Unemployment: 1.6% (1992)
Agriculture: accounts for 4% of GNP; heavily
subsidized sector; major crops: rice sugar cane,
sweet potatoes, fruit, vegetables; livestock:
hogs, poultry, beef, milk, cattle; not self-sufficient in wheat, soybeans, corn; fish catch
expanding, 1.4 million metric ton
Natural Resources: small deposits of coal, natural gas, limestone, marble and asbestos

■ FINANCE/TRADE

Currency: New Taiwan dollar (NT$)
International Reserves Excluding Gold: $50,919
million (1990)
Gold Reserves: n.a.
Budget: revenues $30.3 billion; expenditures
$30.1 billion, including capital expenditures
(1991)
Defence Expenditures: $8.69 billion (1990)
External Debt: $620 million (1992)
Exports: $81.419 billion (1992); commodities:
textiles 16%, electrical machinery 19%, general
machinery and equipment 14%, telecommunications equipment 9%, basic metals and metal
products 5%, foodstuffs 0.9%, plywood and
wood products 1.3%; partners: US 36.2%, Japan
13.7%
Imports: $72.181 billion (1992); commodities:

machinery and equipment 15.9%, crude oil 5%, chemical and chemical products 11.1%, basic metals 7.4%, foodstuffs 2%; partners: Japan 31%, US 23%, Saudi Arabia 8.6%

■ HEALTH

Births: 16/1,000 population (1993)
Deaths: 5/1,000 population (1993)
Infant Mortality: 5.1 deaths/1,000 live births (1993)
Life Expectancy at Birth: 71 years male, 76 years female (1993)
No. of Physicians: 19,921 doctors (1990)

■ EDUCATION

Govt. Expenditure: n.a.
Literacy: 86% (1993)

■ COMMUNICATIONS

Daily newspapers: 139 (1990)
Televisions: 6.66 million (1991)
Radios: 13.6 million (1991)
Telephones: 14.7 million (1990)

■ TRANSPORTATION

Motor Vehicles: 2,800,000; 2,200,000 passenger cars (1990)
Roads: 20,041 km; 17,095 km paved (1993)
Railway: 4,875 km
Air Traffic: 17.21 million passengers carried (1989)
Airports: 40 airfields, of which 38 are usable; 36 have permanent-surface runways (1993)

Tajikistan

Long-Form Name: Republic of Tajikistan
Capital: Dushanbe
Population: 5,700,000 (1993 est.)

■ GEOGRAPHY

Area: 143,100 sq. km
Coastline: none; landlocked
Climate: continental; severe winters in east; extremely hot summers; wet spring; semi-arid to polar in Pamir mountains
Environment: lack of fresh water; little land suitable for cultivation
Terrain: mountains and glaciers constitute 93% of land area
Land Use: predominantly herding and nonagricultural; 6% arable, negligible permanent crops, 23% meadows and pastures, 0% forest and woodland, 71% other
Location: S Asia

■ PEOPLE

Nationality: Tajik
Ethnic Groups: 64.9% Tajik, 25% Uzbek, 3.5% Russian, 6.6% other
Languages: Tajik (official), Uzbek, Russian
Religions: predominantly Sunni Muslim
Marriages: 9.2 (per 1,000) (1989)
Divorces: 1.46 (per 1,000) (1989)

■ GOVERNMENT

Leader(s): Pres. (acting) Imamoli Rakhmanov, Prime Min. Abdujalil Samador
Government Type: republic
Administrative Divisions: 2 oblasts
Independence: Sept. 9, 1991 (from Soviet Union)
National Holiday: n.a.

■ ECONOMY

Overview: mostly mining and manufacturing with strong agricultural sector; throughout 1992, civil disturbances disrupted food imports, and several regions became very short of the barest necessities; industry and agriculture have been producing at reduced capacity due to civil unrest
GNP: $5.669 billion, per capita $1,050; real growth rate 2.9% (1991); real growth rate in 1992: -34%
Inflation: 35% per month (1993)
Industries: aluminum and electrochemical plants, textile machinery, silk and carpet mills; zinc, lead, chemicals and fertilizers, cement, vegetable oil, refrigerators and freezers
Labour Force: 1.938 million (1993); 43% agriculture and forestry, 22% industry and construction, 35% other
Unemployment: 0.4% (1993); also large numbers of underemployed
Agriculture: cotton, grapes, fruit, grains, silkworm farming, cattle breeding, sheep, goats, pigs
Natural Resources: coal, oil, rare metals, rock crystal, mica, gold, hydropower potential, uranium, mercury, zinc

■ FINANCE/TRADE

Currency: rouble (rbl.)
International Reserves Excluding Gold: n.a.
Gold Reserves: n.a.
Budget: 1989 revenues: 2.375 million roubles
Defence Expenditures: n.a.
External Debt: $10 million (1992)
Exports: $100 million to outside successor states of the former USSR (1992)
Imports: $100 million from outside successor states of the former USSR (1992)

■ HEALTH

Births: 40/1,000 population (1993)
Deaths: 6/1,000 population (1993)
Infant Mortality: 50 deaths/1,000 live births (1993)
Life Expectancy at Birth: 67 years male, 72 years female (1993)
No. of Physicians: 14,900 doctors (1989)

■ EDUCATION

Govt. Expenditure: n.a.
Literacy: 100% (1993)

■ COMMUNICATIONS

Daily newspapers: 74 daily newspapers of all circulation types (1989)
Televisions: n.a.
Radios: n.a.
Telephones: approximately 10/100 inhabitants in urban areas (1993)

■ TRANSPORTATION

Motor Vehicles: n.a.
Roads: 29,900 km; 21,400 km paved (1993)
Railway: 480 km, not including industrial lines (1993)
Air Traffic: n.a.
Airports: 58 airfields, of which 30 are usable; 12 have permanent-surface runways (1993)

Canadian Embassy: c/o Hotel Kazakhstan, Rooms 912 and 914, 52 Leina St, 480110, Almaty, Kazakhstan. Tel: (011-7-3272) 61-91-07.

Tanzania

Long-Form Name: United Republic of Tanzania
Capital: Dar es Salaam
Population: 27,800,000 (1993 est.)

■ GEOGRAPHY

Area: 945,090 sq. km
Coastline: 1,424 km along Indian Ocean, lakes
Climate: varies from tropical along coast to temperate in highlands
Environment: lack of water and tsetse fly limit agriculture; recent droughts affected marginal agriculture; Kilimanjaro is highest point in Africa
Terrain: plains along coast; central plateau; highlands in north, south
Land Use: 5% arable; 1% permanent; 40% meadows; 47% forest; 7% other
Location: E Africa, bordering on Indian Ocean

■ PEOPLE

Nationality: Tanzanian
Ethnic Groups: 99% native African consisting of well over 100 tribes; 1% Asian, European and Arab
Languages: Swahili and English (official); English primarily language of commerce, administration and higher education; Swahili widely understood and generally used for communication between ethnic groups
Religions: mainland: 40% Christian, 33% Moslem, 25% indigenous beliefs; Zanzibar: almost all Moslem
Marriages: n.a.
Divorces: n.a.

■ GOVERNMENT

Leader(s): Prime Min. John Malecela, Pres. Ali Hassan Mwinyi, V. Pres. John Malecela and Salmin Amour
Government Type: republic
Administrative Divisions: 25 regions
Independence: Tanganyika became independent on Dec. 9, 1961 (from UN trusteeship under British administration); Zanzibar became independent Dec. 19, 1963 (from UK); Tanganyika united with Zanzibar Apr. 26, 1964
National Holiday: Union Day, Apr. 26

■ ECONOMY

Overview: world aid is increasing the availability of imports and providing funds to rehabilitate this country's deteriorated economic infrastructure; this poor economy is heavily dependent on agriculture; industry accounts for less than 10% of GDP and is largely confined to processing agricultural products
GNP: $7.2 billion, per capita $260; real growth rate 4.5% (1992 est.)
Inflation: 22.1% (1992)
Industries: primarily agricultural processing (sugar, beer, cigarettes, sisal twine), diamond mines, oil refineries, shoes, cement, textiles, wood products, fertilizer
Labour Force: 12,600,000 (1992); 85.6% agriculture, 4.5% industry, 9.9% services (1989)
Unemployment: n.a.
Agriculture: accounts for over 58% of GDP; topography and climatic conditions limit cultivated crops to only 5% of land area; cash crops: coffee, sisal, tea, cotton, pyrethrum (insecticide made from chrysanthemums), cashews, tobacco, cloves (Zanzibar); corn, wheat, beans, fruit and vegetables grown for local consumption
Natural Resources: hydropower potential, tin, phosphates, iron ore, coal, diamonds, gemstones, gold, natural gas, nickel

■ FINANCE/TRADE

Currency: Tanzania shilling (TSh)
International Reserves Excluding Gold: $191 million (Jan. 1994)
Gold Reserves: n.a.
Budget: revenues $495 million, expenditures $631 million, including capital expenditures of $118 million (1990)
Defence Expenditures: $119.20 million (1989)
External Debt: $6.715 billion (1992)
Exports: $437 million (1992); commodities: coffee, cotton, sisal, cashew nuts, meat, tobacco, tea, diamonds, coconut products, pyrethrum, cloves; partners: Germany, UK, US, Netherlands, Japan
Imports: $1.502 billion (1992); commodities: manufactured goods, machinery and transportation equipment, cotton piece goods, crude oil, foodstuffs; partners: Germany, UK, US, Iran, Japan, Italy

■ HEALTH

Births: 46/1,000 population (1993)
Deaths: 15/1,000 population (1993)
Infant Mortality: 104 deaths/1,000 live births (1993)
Life Expectancy at Birth: 50 years male, 55 years female (1993)
No. of Physicians: 0.4/10,000 population (1992)

■ EDUCATION

Govt. Expenditure: 14.0% of government expenditure (1989)
Literacy: 46% (1993)

■ COMMUNICATIONS

Daily newspapers: 2 (1992)
Televisions: 1/1,000 inhabitants (1992)
Radios: 21/1,000 inhabitants (1992)
Telephones: 0.56/100 inhabitants (1992)

■ TRANSPORTATION

Motor Vehicles: 100,000; 45,000 passenger cars (1983)
Roads: 86,950 km; 3,780 km paved
Railway: 3,780 km
Air Traffic: 290,000 passengers carried (1991)
Airports: 103 airfields, of which 92 are usable; 12 have permanent-surface runways (1993)

Canadian Embassy: The Canadian High Commission, 38 Mirambo St, Dar-es-Salaam; mailing address: P.O. Box 1022, Dar-es-Salaam, Tanzania. Tel: (011-255-51) 46000. Fax: (011-255-51) 46000
Representative to Canada: High Commission for the United Republic of Tanzania, 50 Range Rd, Ottawa ON K1N 8J4. Tel: (613) 232-1500. Fax: (613) 232-5184.

Thailand

Long-Form Name: Kingdom of Thailand
Capital: Bangkok
Population: 57,200,000 (1993 est.)

■ GEOGRAPHY

Area: 514,000 sq. km
Coastline: 3,219 km
Climate: tropical; rainy, warm, cloudy southwest monsoon (mid-May to Sept.); dry, cool, northeast monsoon (Nov. to mid-Mar.); southern isthmus always hot and humid
Environment: air and water pollution; land subsidence in Bangkok area
Terrain: central plain; eastern plateau (Khorat); mountains elsewhere
Land Use: 34% arable; 4% permanent; 1% meadows; 30% forest; 31% other
Location: SE Asia, bordering on Bay of Bengal, South China Sea

■ PEOPLE

Nationality: Thai
Ethnic Groups: 75% Thai, 14% Chinese, 11% other
Languages: Thai; English is the secondary language of the elite; small minorities speak Chinese, Malay, indigenous languages
Religions: 95% Buddhist (Theravada), 3.8% Moslem, 0.5% Christianity, 0.1% Hinduism, 0.6% other
Marriages: 8.2 (per 1,000) (1990)
Divorces: 0.7 (per 1,000) (1986)

■ GOVERNMENT

Leader(s): Prime Min. Chuan Leekpai, King Phumiphon Adunlayadet (Rama IX)
Government Type: constitutional monarchy
Administrative Divisions: 73 provinces
Independence: 1238 (traditional founding date); never colonized
National Holiday: Birthday of His Majesty the King, Dec. 5

■ ECONOMY

Overview: improved weather, increased tourism, export-oriented investment and sound governmental fiscal and monetary policy have all contributed to impressive growth in this country; the government is refurbishing the infrastructure
GNP: $103 billion, per capita $1,800; real growth rate 7% (1992 est.)
Inflation: 4.1% (1990)

Industries: tourism is the largest source of foreign exchange; textiles and garments, agricultural processing, beverages, tobacco, cement, other light manufacturing, such as jewelry; electric appliances and components, integrated circuits, furniture, plastics
Labour Force: 30 million (1992); 69.8% agriculture, 5.9%, 24.3% services (1989)
Unemployment: 4.7% (1992)
Agriculture: accounts for 12% of GNP and 60% of labour force; leading producer and exporter of rice and cassava; other crops: rubber, corn, sugar cane, coconuts, soybeans; self-sufficient in food except for wheat
Natural Resources: tin, rubber, natural gas, tungsten, tantalum, timber, lead, fish, gypsum, lignite, fluorite

■ FINANCE/TRADE

Currency: baht (B)
International Reserves Excluding Gold: $24,393 million (Jan. 1994)
Gold Reserves: 2.47 million fine troy ounces (Jan. 1994)
Budget: revenues $21.36 billion; expenditures $22.40 billion, including capital expenditures of $6.24 billion (1993 est.)
Defence Expenditures: 17.20% of total govt. expenditure (1992)
External Debt: $39.424 billion (1992)
Exports: $32.207 billion (1992); commodities: textiles 12%, fishery products 12%, rice 8%, tapioca 8%, jewelry 6%, manufactured gas, corn, tin; partners: US 18%, Japan 14%, Singapore 9%, Netherlands, Malaysia, Hong Kong, China
Imports: $41.209 billion (1992); commodities: machinery and parts 23%, petroleum products 13%, chemicals 11%, iron and steel, electrical appliances; partners: Japan 26%, US 14%, Singapore 7%, Germany, Malaysia, UK

■ HEALTH

Births: 21/1,000 population (1993)
Deaths: 7/1,000 population (1993)
Infant Mortality: 40 deaths/1,000 live births (1993)
Life Expectancy at Birth: 66 years male, 71 years female (1993)
No. of Physicians: 1.6/10,000 population (1992)

■ EDUCATION

Govt. Expenditure: 21.06% of government expenditure (1992)
Literacy: 93.0% (1993)

■ COMMUNICATIONS

Daily newspapers: 40 (1992)
Televisions: 109.3/1,000 inhabitants (1992)
Radios: 182/1,000 inhabitants (1992)
Telephones: 1.9/100 inhabitants (1992)

■ TRANSPORTATION

Motor Vehicles: 2,813,865; 826,606 passenger cars (1990)
Roads: 77,697 km; 35,855 km paved (1993)
Railway: 3,960 km
Air Traffic: 7,709,000 passengers carried (1991)
Airports: 106 airfields, of which 95 are usable; 51 have permanent-surface runways (1993)

Canadian Embassy: The Canadian Embassy, 12th Floor, Boonmitr Bldg, 138 Silom Rd, Bangkok 10500; mailing address: P.O. Box 2090, Bangkok 10500, Thailand. Tel: (011-66-2) 237-4125. Fax: (011-66-2) 236-6463
Representative to Canada: Embassy of the Kingdom of Thailand, 180 Island Park Dr, Ottawa ON K1Y 0A2. Tel: (613) 722-4444. Fax: (613) 722-6624.

Togo

Long-Form Name: Republic of Togo
Capital: Lomé
Population: 4,100,000 (1993 est.)

■ GEOGRAPHY

Area: 56,790 sq. km
Coastline: 56 km along Bight of Benin
Climate: tropical; hot, humid in south; semi-arid in north
Environment: hot, dry harmattan wind can reduce visibility in north during winter; recent droughts affecting agriculture; deforestation
Terrain: gently rolling savanna in north, low coastal plain with extensive lagoons and marshes
Land Use: 25% arable; 1% permanent; 4% meadows; 28% forest; 42% other
Location: WC Africa, bordering on South Atlantic Ocean

■ PEOPLE

Nationality: Togolese
Ethnic Groups: 37 tribes; largest and most important are Ewe, Mina and Kabyè; under 1% European and Syrian-Lebanese
Languages: French, both official and language of commerce; major African languages are Ewe and Mina in the south and Dagomba and Kabyè in the north

Religions: about 70% indigenous beliefs, 20% Christian, 10% Moslem
Marriages: n.a.
Divorces: n.a.

■ GOVERNMENT

Leader(s): Pres. Gen. Gnassingbé Eyadéma, Prime Min. Edem Kodjo
Government Type: republic; one-party presidential regime under transition to multiparty democratic rule
Administrative Divisions: 21 circumscriptions
Independence: Apr. 27, 1960 (from UN trusteeship under French administration; formerly known as French Togo)
National Holiday: Independence Day, Apr. 27

■ ECONOMY

Overview: an underdeveloped country which is heavily dependent on subsistence agriculture and phosphate mining; self-sufficient in basic foodstuffs when harvests are normal
GNP: $1.530 billion, per capita $410; real growth rate 1.8% (1991)
Inflation: 0.4% (1991)
Industries: phosphate mining, agricultural processing, cement, handicrafts, textiles, beverages
Labour Force: 1,400,000 (1992); 64.3% agriculture, 6.3% industry, 29.4% services (1989)
Unemployment: 2% (1987)
Agriculture: accounts for 33% of GDP; cash crops: coffee, cocoa, cotton; food crops: yams, cassava, corn, beans, rice, millet, sorghum, fish
Natural Resources: phosphates, limestone, marble

■ FINANCE/TRADE

Currency: Communauté financière africaine franc (CFAF)
International Reserves Excluding Gold: $185 million (Sept. 1994)
Gold Reserves: 0.01 million fine troy ounces (1991)
Budget: revenues $284.8 million; expenditures $407 million, including capital expenditures (1991 est.)
Defence Expenditures: $43 million (1989)
External Debt: $1.356 billion (1992)
Exports: $253 million (1991); commodities: phosphates, cocoa, coffee, cotton, manufactures, palm kernels; partners: European Community 70%, Africa 9%, US 2%, other 19%
Imports: $444 million (1991); commodities: food, fuels, durable consumer goods, other intermediate goods, capital goods; partners: European Community 69%, Africa 10%, Japan 7%, US 4%, other 10%

■ HEALTH

Births: 49/1,000 population (1993)
Deaths: 13/1,000 population (1993)
Infant Mortality: 96 deaths/1,000 live births (1993)
Life Expectancy at Birth: 54 years male, 58 years female (1993)
No. of Physicians: 1.1/10,000 population (1992)

■ EDUCATION

Govt. Expenditure: 24.7% of govt. expenditure (1989)
Literacy: 43.3% (1993)

■ COMMUNICATIONS

Daily newspapers: 1 (1992)
Televisions: 5.8/1,000 inhabitants (1992)
Radios: 210/1,000 inhabitants (1992)
Telephones: 0.44/100 inhabitants (1992)

■ TRANSPORTATION

Motor Vehicles: 42,000; 26,000 passenger cars (1990)
Roads: 6,462 km; 1,762 km paved (1993)
Railway: 570 km
Air Traffic: 64,000 passengers carried (1991)
Airports: 9 airfields, all usable; 2 have permanent-surface runways (1993)

Canadian Embassy: c/o Canadian High Commission, 42 Independence Ave, Accra; P.O. Box 1639, Accra. Tel: (011-233-21) 77 37 91. Fax: (011-233-21) 77-37-92
Representative to Canada: Embassy of the Republic of Togo, 12 Range Rd, Ottawa ON K1N 8J3. Tel: (613) 238-5916. Fax: (613) 235-6425.

Tokelau

Overseas Territory of New Zealand

Long-Form Name: Tokelau
Capital: none; each atoll has its own administrative center
Population: 1,544 (1993 est.)

■ GEOGRAPHY

Area: 10 sq. km, 3 atolls
Climate: tropical maritime, moderated by trade winds (April-Nov.)
Land Use: 0% arable, permanent crops, meadows/pastures, or forests, 100% other
Location: S Pacific Ocean

■ PEOPLE

Nationality: Tokelauan
Ethnic Groups: Polynesian
Languages: Polynesian dialect, English

■ GOVERNMENT

Leader(s): Administrator N.D. Walter
Government Type: territory of New Zealand
National Holiday: Waitang Day, Feb. 6

■ ECONOMY

Overview: copra is only agricultural product of significance; the people rely on aid from New Zealand, supplemented by revenue from postage stamps, souvenir coins, and handicrafts

■ FINANCE/TRADE

Currency: New Zealand dollar

Tonga

Long-Form Name: Kingdom of Tonga
Capital: Nuku'alofa
Population: 103,949 (1993 est.)

■ GEOGRAPHY

Area: 748 sq. km
Coastline: 419 km
Climate: tropical; modified by trade winds; warm season (Dec. to May), cool season (May to Dec.)
Environment: subject to cyclones (Oct. to Apr.); deforestation
Terrain: most islands have limestone base formed from uplifted coral formation; others have limestone overlying volcanic base
Land Use: 25% arable; 55% permanent; 6% meadows; 12% forest; 2% other
Location: Pacific Ocean, NW of New Zealand

■ PEOPLE

Nationality: Tongan
Ethnic Groups: Polynesian; about 300 Europeans
Languages: Tongan, English
Religions: Christian; Free Wesleyan Church claims over 30,000 adherents
Marriages: 6.6 (per 1,000) (1985)
Divorces: 0.6 (per 1,000) (1985)

■ GOVERNMENT

Leader(s): Prime Min. Baron Vaea, King Taufa'ahau Tupou IV
Government Type: hereditary constitutional monarchy
Administrative Divisions: three island groups
Independence: June 4, 1970 (from UK; formerly known as Friendly Islands)
National Holiday: Emancipation Day, June 4

■ ECONOMY

Overview: the island remains dependent on external aid and remittances to sustain its trade deficit; the economy's base is agriculture though the country must import a high proportion of its food; tourism is the main source of hard currency; manufacturing accounts for only 11% of GDP
GNP: $110 million, per capita $1,100; real growth rate 2.2% (1991)
Inflation: 7.9% (1992)
Industries: tourism, fishing
Labour Force: 40,000 (1992); 70% agriculture, 30% mining
Unemployment: n.a.
Agriculture: 40% of GDP; dominated by coconut, copra and banana production; vanilla beans, cocoa, coffee, ginger, black pepper
Natural Resources: fish, fertile soil

■ FINANCE/TRADE

Currency: pa'anga (P)
International Reserves Excluding Gold: $37 million (Jan. 1994)
Gold Reserves: n.a.
Budget: revenues $36.4 million; expenditures $68.1 million, including capital expenditures of $33.2 million (1991)
Defence Expenditures: n.a.
External Debt: $43 million (1992)
Exports: $12 million (1992); commodities: coconut oil, desiccated coconut, copra, bananas, taro, vanilla beans, fruit, vegetables, fish; partners: New Zealand 54%, Australia 30%, US 8%, Fiji 5%
Imports: $63 million (1992); commodities: food products, beverages, tobacco, fuels, machinery, transport equipment, chemicals, building materials; partners: New Zealand 39%, Australia 25%, Japan 9%, US 6%, European Community 5%

■ HEALTH

Births: 25.16/1,000 population (1993)
Deaths: 6.75/1,000 population (1993)
Infant Mortality: 21.38 deaths/1,000 live births (1993)
Life Expectancy at Birth: 65.5 years male, 70.24 years female (1993)
No. of Physicians: 6.0/10,000 population (1990)

■ EDUCATION

Govt. Expenditure: 12.95% of government expenditure (1991)
Literacy: 57% (1993)

■ COMMUNICATIONS

Daily newspapers: 1 (1988)
Televisions: n.a.; no TV stations (1993)
Radios: 547/1,000 inhabitants (1989)
Telephones: 4.2/100 inhabitants (1992)none

■ TRANSPORTATION

Motor Vehicles: 1,400 passenger cars (1987)
Roads: 292 km; 198 km sealed (1993)
Railway: none
Air Traffic: 5,000 passengers carried (1991)
Airports: 6, all usable; 1 has a permanent-surface runway (1993)

Canadian Embassy: c/o The Canadian High Commission, 61 Molesworth St, 3rd Floor, Thorndon, Wellington; mailing address: P.O. Box 12-049, Thorndon, Wellington, New Zealand. Tel: (011-64-4) 473-9577. Fax: (011-64-4) 471-2082.

Trinidad and Tobago

Long-Form Name: Republic of Trinidad and Tobago
Capital: Port of Spain
Population: 1,300,000 (1993 est.)

■ GEOGRAPHY

Area: 5,130 sq. km
Coastline: 362 km
Climate: tropical; rainy season (June to Dec.)
Environment: outside usual path of hurricanes and other tropical storms
Terrain: mostly plains with some hills and low mountains
Land Use: 14% arable; 17% permanent; 2% meadows; 44% forest; 23% other
Location: Atlantic Ocean, off N coast of South America

■ PEOPLE

Nationality: Trinidadian, Tobagonian
Ethnic Groups: 43% black, 40% East Indian, 14% mixed, 2% white, Chinese, and other
Languages: English (official), Hindi, French, Spanish, Chinese
Religions: Christianity 60%, Hinduism 25%, Islam 6%
Marriages: 5.6 (per 1,000) (1989)
Divorces: 0.89 (per 1,000) (1989)

■ GOVERNMENT

Leader(s): Prime Min. Patrick Augustus Mervyn Manning, Pres. Noor Mohammed Hassanali
Government Type: parliamentary democracy

Administrative Divisions: 8 counties, 3 municipalities and 1 ward
Independence: Aug. 31, 1962 (from UK)
National Holiday: Independence Day, Aug. 31

■ ECONOMY

Overview: the economy has suffered in recent years because of the sharp decline in the price of oil; the unemployment rate has risen due to the government's austerity programs; the government is seeking to diversify the country's export base
GNP: $4.525 billion, per capita $3,620; real growth rate 3.9% (1991)
Inflation: 6.5% (1992)
Industries: petroleum, chemicals, tourism, food processing, cement, beverage, cotton textiles
Labour Force: 501,000 (1992); 14.9% industry, 73.3% services, 11.8% agriculture (1989)
Unemployment: 18.5% (1991)
Agriculture: accounts for approx. 3% of GDP; highly subsidized sector; major crops: cocoa and sugar cane; sugar cane acreage is being shifted into rice, citrus, coffee, vegetables; must import large share of food needs
Natural Resources: crude oil, natural gas, asphalt

■ FINANCE/TRADE

Currency: Trinidad and Tobago dollar ($TT)
International Reserves Excluding Gold: $171 million (Aug. 1993)
Gold Reserves: 0.05 million fine troy ounces (Aug. 1993)
Budget: revenues $1.6 billion; expenditures $1.6 billion, including capital expenditures of $158 million (1993 est.)
Defence Expenditures: $59 million (1989)
External Debt: $2.4 billion (1992)
Exports: $1.869 billion (1992); commodities (including re-exports): petroleum and petroleum products 70%, fertilizer, chemicals 15%, steel products, sugar, cocoa, coffee, citrus; partners: US 61%, European Community 15%, CARICOM 9%, Latin America 7%, Canada 3%
Imports: $1.431 billion (1992); commodities: raw materials 41%, capital goods 30%, consumer goods 29%; partners: US 42%, European Community 21%, Japan 10%, Canada 6%, Latin America 6%, CARICOM 4%

■ HEALTH

Births: 21/1,000 population (1993)
Deaths: 7/1,000 population (1993)
Infant Mortality: 10.2 deaths/1,000 live births (1993)
Life Expectancy at Birth: 68 years male, 73 years female (1993)

No. of Physicians: 10.6/10,000 population (1992)

■ EDUCATION

Govt. Expenditure: 11.6% of government expenditure (1990)
Literacy: 94.9% (1993)

■ COMMUNICATIONS

Daily newspapers: 2 (1992)
Televisions: 301.3/1,000 inhabitants (1992)
Radios: 460/1,000 inhabitants (1992)
Telephones: 17.40/100 inhabitants (1992)

■ TRANSPORTATION

Motor Vehicles: 342,000; 272,000 passenger cars (1986)
Roads: 8,000 km; 4,000 km paved (1993)
Railway: minimal agricultural railway system near San Fernando (1993)
Air Traffic: 1,345,000 passengers carried (1991)
Airports: 6 airfields, of which 5 are usable; 2 have permanent-surface runways (1993)

Canadian Embassy: The Canadian High Commission, Huggins Bldg, 72 South Quay; Port-of-Spain; mailing address: P.O. Box 1246, Port-of-Spain, Trinidad and Tobago. Tel: (809) 623-7254. Fax: (809) 624-4016
Representative to Canada: High Commission for the Republic of Trinidad and Tobago, 75 Albert St, Ste 508, Ottawa ON K1P 5E7. Tel: (613) 232-2418. Fax: (613) 232-4349.

Tunisia

Long-Form Name: Republic of Tunisia
Capital: Tunis
Population: 8,600,000 (1993 est.)

■ GEOGRAPHY

Area: 163,610 sq. km
Coastline: 1,148 km along the Mediterranean Sea
Climate: temperate in north with mild, rainy winters and hot, dry summers; desert in south
Environment: deforestation; overgrazing; soil erosion; desertification
Terrain: mountains in north; hot, dry central plain; semi-arid south merges into the Sahara
Land Use: 20% arable; 10% permanent; 19% meadows; 4% forest; 4% other
Location: N Africa, bordering on Mediterranean Sea

■ PEOPLE

Nationality: Tunisian
Ethnic Groups: 98% Arab-Berber, 1% European,
less than 1% Jewish
Languages: Arabic (official); Arabic and French (commerce)
Religions: 98% Moslem, 1% Christian, less than 1% Jewish
Marriages: 6.9 (per 1,000) (1990)
Divorces: 1.6 (per 1,000) (1989)

■ GOVERNMENT

Leader(s): Prime Min. Hamed Karoui, Pres. Gen. Zine El Abidine Ben Ali
Government Type: republic
Administrative Divisions: 23 governorates
Independence: Mar. 20, 1956 (from France)
National Holiday: National Day, Mar. 20

■ ECONOMY

Overview: two recent drought-induced crop failures have increased unemployment and strained the budget; increasing foreign debt is a problem but the country seems ready to implement structural reforms demanded by world creditors; economy depends on petroleum, phosphates, tourism, and exports of light manufactures
GNP: n.a., GDP $13.6 billion, per capita $1,650; real growth rate 8% (1992 est.)
Inflation: 5.4% (1992)
Industries: petroleum, mining (particularly phosphate and iron ore), textiles, footwear, food, beverages, tourism
Labour Force: 2,594,000 (1992); 21.6% agriculture, 16.3% industry, 62.1% services (1989)
Unemployment: 15.7% (1992)
Agriculture: accounts for 15% of GDP; output subject to severe fluctuations because of frequent droughts; export crops: olives, dates, oranges, almonds; other products: grain, sugar beets, wine grapes, poultry, beef, dairy; not self-sufficient in food
Natural Resources: crude oil, phosphates, iron ore, lead, zinc, salt

■ FINANCE/TRADE

Currency: Tunisian dinar (D)
International Reserves Excluding Gold: $786 million (Jan. 1994)
Gold Reserves: 0.22 million fine troy ounces (Jan. 1994)
Budget: revenues $4.3 billion; expenditures $5.5 billion, including capital expenditures (1993 est.)
Defence Expenditures: 5.39% of total govt. expenditure (1992)
External Debt: $7.7 billion (1992 est.)
Exports: $4.040 billion (1992); commodities: hydrocarbons, agricultural products, phosphates and chemicals; partners: European Community

73%, Middle East 9%, US 1%, Turkey, USSR
Imports: $6.415 billion (1992); commodities: industrial goods and equipment 57%, hyrocarbons 13%, food 12%, consumer goods; partners: European Community 68%, US 7%, Canada, Japan, USSR, China, Saudi Arabia, Algeria

■ HEALTH

Births: 25/1,000 population (1993)
Deaths: 6/1,000 population (1993)
Infant Mortality: 43 deaths/1,000 live births (1993)
Life Expectancy at Birth: 67 years male, 69 years female (1993)
No. of Physicians: 4.6/10,000 population (1992)

■ EDUCATION

Govt. Expenditure: 17.55% of government expenditure (1992)
Literacy: 65.3% (1993)

■ COMMUNICATIONS

Daily newspapers: 6 (1992)
Televisions: 75.1/1,000 inhabitants (1992)
Radios: 188/1,000 inhabitants (1992)
Telephones: 4.29/100 inhabitants (1992)

■ TRANSPORTATION

Motor Vehicles: 494,087; 320,101 passenger cars (1990)
Roads: 17,700 km; 9,100 km paved (1993)
Railway: 2,115 km (1993)
Air Traffic: 1,201,000 passengers carried (1991)
Airports: 29 airfields, of which 26 are usable; 13 have permanent-surface runways (1993)

Canadian Embassy: Canadian Embassy, 3, rue du Sénégal, Place d'Afrique, Tunis; mailing address: CP 31, Le Belvédère, 1002, Tunis, Tunisia. Tel: (011-216-1) 789-004. Fax: (011-216-1) 796-577
Representative to Canada: Embassy of the Republic of Tunisia, 515 O'Connor St, Ottawa ON K1S 3P8. Tel: (613) 237-0330. Fax: (613) 237-7939.

Turkey

Long-Form Name: Republic of Turkey
Capital: Ankara
Population: 60,700,000 (1993 est.)

■ GEOGRAPHY

Area: 780,580 sq. km
Coastline: 7,200 km along Black Sea and Mediterranean Sea
Climate: temperate; hot, dry summers with mild, wet winters; harsher in interior
Environment: subject to severe earthquakes, especially along major river valleys in west; air pollution; desertification
Terrain: mostly mountains; narrow coastal plain; high central plateau (Anatolia)
Land Use: 30% arable; 4% permanent; 12% meadows; 26% forest; 28% other
Location: SW Asia (Near East), bordering on Mediterranean Sea, Black Sea, Aegean Sea

■ PEOPLE

Nationality: Turk
Ethnic Groups: 80% Turkish, 20% Kurd
Languages: Turkish (official), Kurdish 7%, Arabic; English (business language)
Religions: 99.8% Moslem (mostly Sunni), 0.2% other (mostly Christian and Jewish)
Marriages: 7.9 (per 1,000) (1989)
Divorces: 0.45 (per 1,000) (1989)

■ GOVERNMENT

Leader(s): Pres. Suleyman Demirel, Prime Min.Tansu Ciller
Government Type: republican parliamentary democracy
Administrative Divisions: 73 provinces
Independence: Oct. 29, 1923 (successor state to the Ottoman Empire)
National Holiday: Anniversary of the Declaration of the Republic, Oct. 29

■ ECONOMY

Overview: the economy has grown steadily since the early 1980s but inflation and interest rates remain high; a large budget deficit may hamper efforts to move from a centrally controlled to a free market economy; agriculture remains an important economic sector, accounting for 50% of the labour force and 20% of exports
GNP: n.a., GDP $219 billion, per capita $3,670; real growth rate 5.9% (1992)
Inflation: 70.1% (1992)
Industries: textiles, food processing, mining (coal, chromite, copper, boron minerals), steel, petroleum, construction, lumber, paper
Labour Force: 23,696,000 (1992); 46.8% agriculture, 38.6% services, 14.6% industry; about 1,000,000 Turks work abroad (1989)
Unemployment: 11.1% (1992 est.)
Agriculture: accounts for 18% of GDP and half the labour force; products: tobacco, cotton, grain, olives, sugar beets, pulses, citrus fruit, variety of animal products; self-sufficient in food most years
Natural Resources: antimony, coal, chromium, mercury, copper, borate, sulphur, iron ore

■ FINANCE/TRADE

Currency: Turkish lira (LT)
International Reserves Excluding Gold: $7,258 million (Nov. 1993)
Gold Reserves: 4.03 million fine troy ounces (Jan. 1994)
Budget: revenues $40.5 billion; expenditures $46.8 billion, including capital expenditures of $5.5 billion (1993)
Defence Expenditures: 11.35% of total govt. expenditure (1992)
External Debt: $48.7 billion (1991)
Exports: $14.878 billion (1992); commodities: industrial products 70%, crops and livestock products 25%; partners: Germany 18.4%, Iraq 8.5%, Italy 8.2%, US 6.5%, UK 4.9%, Iran 4.7%
Imports: $22.579 billion (1992); commodities: crude oil, machinery, transport equipment, metals, pharmaceuticals, dyes, plastics, rubber, mineral fuels, fertilizers, chemicals; partners: Germany 14.3%, US 10.6%, Iraq 10.0%, Italy 7.0%, France 5.8%, UK 5.2%

■ HEALTH

Births: 29/1,000 population (1993)
Deaths: 7/1,000 population (1993)
Infant Mortality: 59 deaths/1,000 live births (1993)
Life Expectancy at Birth: 64 years male, 69 years female (1993)
No. of Physicians: 7.3/10,000 population (1992)

■ EDUCATION

Govt. Expenditure: 17.60% of govt. spending (1991)
Literacy: 80.7% (1993)

■ COMMUNICATIONS

Daily newspapers: 426 (1992)
Televisions: 173.6/1,000 inhabitants (1992)
Radios: 161/1,000 inhabitants (1992)
Telephones: 13.34/100 inhabitants (1992)

■ TRANSPORTATION

Motor Vehicles: 2,359,738; 1,649,879 passenger cars (1990)
Roads: 325,500 km; 46,050 km paved
Railway: 8,590 km
Air Traffic: 3,872,000 passengers carried (1991)
Airports: 110 airfields, of which 102 are usable; 65 have permanent-surface runways (1993)

Canadian Embassy: Nenehatun Caddesi 75, Gaziosmanpasa, 06700 Ankara, Turkey. Tel: (011-90-312) 436-1275. Fax: (011-90-312) 446-4437

Representative to Canada: Embassy of the Republic of Turkey, 197 Wurtemburg St, Ottawa ON K1N 8L9. Tel: (613) 789-4044. Fax: (613) 789-3442.

Turkmenistan

Long-Form Name: Turkmenistan
Capital: Ashkhabad
Population: 4,000,000 (1993 est.)

■ GEOGRAPHY

Area: 488,100 sq. km
Coastline: landlocked; 1,768 km coastline along Caspian Sea
Climate: subtropical desert; long, extremely hot summers; short and cold winters; rainfall occurs only in the mountains
Environment: soil and groundwater contaminated with chemicals and pesticides; salinization and waterlogging of soil due to poor irrigation methods; desertification in some areas; prone to earthquakes
Terrain: flat to rolling sandy desert; Caspian Sea in west
Land Use: 3% arable, 0% permanent crops, 69% pastures and meadows, 0% forests, 28% other
Location: SC Asia, bordering on Caspian Sea

■ PEOPLE

Nationality: Turkmen
Ethnic Groups: 73.3% Turkmen, 9.8% Russian, 9% Uzbek, 2% Kazakh, 5.9% other
Languages: 72% Turkmen (official), 12% Russian, 9% Uzbek, 7% other
Religions: predominantly Sunni Muslim
Marriages: 9.8 (per 1,000) (1989)
Divorces: 1.38 (per 1,000) (1989)

■ GOVERNMENT

Leader(s): Pres. Saparmurad Niyazov
Government Type: republic
Administrative Divisions: 5 regions ("velayets")
Independence: Oct. 27, 1991 (from Soviet Union)
National Holiday: Independence Day, Oct. 27

■ ECONOMY

Overview: mining produces the greatest part of Turkmenistan's economic production value, but agriculture is the chief occupation; industry leans heavily towards the energy sector (gas, oil)
GNP: $6.387 billion, per capita $1,700; real growth rate 3.2%
Inflation: n.a.
Industries: oil production and refining, natural

gas extraction, chemicals, electrical engineering, fertilizer, carpets, textiles and clothing, food processing
Labour Force: 1,542,000 (1990); 42% agriculture and forestry, 21% industry and construction, 37% other
Unemployment: 15-20% (1992 est.)
Agriculture: irrigation is mandatory for agriculture; products inc. cotton, grains, fruit, livestock, fishing, vegetables
Natural Resources: extensive mineral deposits, inc. the world's largest sulfur deposits; oil, natural gas, potassium, salts, sulphur

■ FINANCE/TRADE

Currency: rouble (rbl.); proposed introduction of new currency, the manat, at unspecified future date
International Reserves Excluding Gold: n.a.
Gold Reserves: n.a.
Budget: 1989 revenues: 1,934 million roubles
Defence Expenditures: n.a.
External Debt: $650 million (1991 est.)
Exports: $100 million to outside the successor states of the former USSR (1992): oil, electric power, clothing and textiles
Imports: $100 million from outside the successor states of the former USSR (1992)

■ HEALTH

Births: 34/1,000 population (1993)
Deaths: 7/1,000 population (1993)
Infant Mortality: 56 deaths/1,000 live births (1993)
Life Expectancy at Birth: 63 years male, 70 years female (1993)
No. of Physicians: 12,800 doctors (1989)

■ EDUCATION

Govt. Expenditure: n.a.
Literacy: 100% (1993)

■ COMMUNICATIONS

Daily newspapers: 66 papers of all circulation types (1989)
Televisions: n.a.
Radios: n.a.
Telephones: 6.5/100 inhabitants (1993)

■ TRANSPORTATION

Motor Vehicles: n.a.
Roads: 23,000 km; 18,300 km paved (1993)
Railway: 2,120 km
Air Traffic: n.a.
Airports: 7 airfields, all usable; 4 have permanent surface runways (1993)

Canadian Embassy: c/o Hotel Kazakhstan, Rooms 912 and 914, 52 Leina St, 480110, Almaty, Kazakhstan. Tel: (011-7-3272) 61-91-07.

Turks and Caicos

Colony of the United Kingdom

Long-Form Name: The Turks and Caicos Islands
Capital: Grand Turk
Population: 13,137 (1993 est.)

■ GEOGRAPHY

Area: 430 sq. km; 30+ small cays, of which only 8 are inhabited
Climate: sunny, relatively dry, equable climate with moderating winds; occasional hurricanes
Land Use: 2% arable, 0% permanent crops, meadows, forests, 98% other
Location: West Indies (S Atlantic Ocean), SE of Bahamas

■ PEOPLE

Nationality: British
Ethnic Groups: black majority
Languages: English (official)

■ GOVERNMENT

Leader(s): Gov. M.J. Bradley, Chief Min. Washington Missick
Government Type: dependent territory of the United Kingdom
National Holiday: Constitution Day, Aug. 30

■ ECONOMY

Overview: fishing is the most important activity; exports inc. lobster, conch, other fish products; imports inc. food and drink, tobacco, maufactured goods; tourism; chief trading partner: US

■ FINANCE/TRADE

Currency: US currency is used

Tuvalu

Long-Form Name: Tuvalu
Capital: Funafuti
Population: 9,666 (1993 est.)

■ GEOGRAPHY

Area: 26 sq. km
Coastline: 24 km
Climate: tropical; moderated by easterly trade winds (Mar. to Nov.); westerly gales and heavy rain (Nov. to Mar.)

Environment: severe tropical storms are rare
Terrain: very low-lying and narrow coral atolls
Land Use: 0% arable; 0% permanent; 0% meadows; 0% forest; 100% other
Location: S Pacific Ocean, NE of Australia

■ PEOPLE

Nationality: Tuvaluan
Ethnic Groups: 96% Polynesian
Languages: Tuvaluan, English
Religions: 96% Christian, predominantly Protestant, 4% other
Marriages: n.a.
Divorces: n.a.

■ GOVERNMENT

Leader(s): Prime Min. Kamuta Latasi, Gov. Gen. Tomu Malaefono Sione
Government Type: democracy
Administrative Divisions: none
Independence: Oct. 1, 1978 from UK (formerly known as Ellice Islands)
National Holiday: Independence Day, Oct. 1

■ ECONOMY

Overview: scattered group of 9 coral atolls with poor soil; a small economy, no known mineral resources and few exports; receives money from the sale of stamps and coins and worker remittances as well as an international trust fund; subsistence farming and fishing are the primary economic activities
GNP: $4.6 million, per capita $530; real growth rate n.a. (1989 est.)
Inflation: 3.9% (1990)
Industries: fishing, tourism, copra
Labour Force: n.a.
Unemployment: n.a.
Agriculture: coconuts, copra
Natural Resources: fish

■ FINANCE/TRADE

Currency: Australian dollar ($A) or Tuvaluan dollar ($T)
International Reserves Excluding Gold: n.a.
Gold Reserves: n.a.
Budget: revenues $4.3 million; expenditures $4.3 million, including capital expenditures (1989)
Defence Expenditures: n.a.
External Debt: n.a.
Exports: n.a.
Imports: n.a.

■ HEALTH

Births: 26.79/1,000 population (1993)
Deaths: 9.41/1,000 population (1993)

Infant Mortality: 26.8 deaths/1,000 live births (1993)
Life Expectancy at Birth: 61.27 years male, 63.82 years female (1993)
No. of Physicians: 3.8/10,000 population (1986)

■ EDUCATION

Govt. Expenditure: 16.2% of govt. expenditure (1990)
Literacy: less than 50%

■ COMMUNICATIONS

Daily newspapers: n.a.
Televisions: n.a.; no TV stations (1993)
Radios: 4,000 total (1993)
Telephones: 108 total (1993)

■ TRANSPORTATION

Motor Vehicles: n.a.
Roads: 8 km gravel roads (1993)
Railway: n.a.
Air Traffic: n.a.
Airports: 1, usable; no permanent-surface runway (1993)

Canadian Embassy: c/o The Canadian High Commission, 61 Molesworth St, 3rd Floor, Thorndon, Wellington; mailing address: P.O. Box 12-049, Thorndon, Wellington, New Zealand. Tel: (011-64-4) 473-9577. Fax: (011-64-4) 471-2082.

Uganda

Long-Form Name: Republic of Uganda
Capital: Kampala
Population: 18,100,000 (1993 est.)

■ GEOGRAPHY

Area: 236,040 sq. km
Coastline: none: landlocked
Climate: tropical; generally rainy with two dry seasons (Dec. to Feb., June to Aug.); semi-arid in northeast
Environment: straddles equator; deforestation; overgrazing; soil erosion
Terrain: mostly plateau with rim of mountains
Land Use: 23% arable; 9% permanent; 25% meadows; 30% forest; 13% other
Location: EC Africa

■ PEOPLE

Nationality: Ugandan
Ethnic Groups: 99% African, 1% European, Asian, Arab
Languages: English (official); Luganda and Swahili widely used; other Bantu and Nilotic

languages
Religions: 33% Roman Catholic, 33% Protestant, 16% Moslem, rest indigenous beliefs
Marriages: n.a.
Divorces: n.a.

■ GOVERNMENT

Leader(s): Prime Min. George Cosmas Adyebo, Pres. Yoweri Kaguta Museveni
Government Type: republic
Administrative Divisions: 10 provinces
Independence: Oct. 9, 1962 (from UK)
National Holiday: Independence Day, Oct. 9

■ ECONOMY

Overview: despite substantial natural resources, the economy has been ruined by years of political instability, mismanagement and civil war; the government has started a reform program which is partly aimed at lowering high inflation and increasing export earnings; agriculture is the most important economic sector
GNP: n.a., GDP $6 billion, per capita $300, real growth rate 4% (1992 est.)
Inflation: 52.4% (1992)
Industries: sugar, brewing, tobacco, cotton textile, cement
Labour Force: 8,130,000 (1992); 85.9% agriculture, 4.4% industry, 9.7% services (1989)
Unemployment: n.a.
Agriculture: accounts for 57% of GDP and more than 80% of the labour force; cash crops: coffee, tea, cotton, tobacco; food crops: cassava, potatoes, corn, millet, pulses; livestock products: beef, goat meat, milk, poultry; self-sufficient in food
Natural Resources: copper, cobalt, limestone, salt

■ FINANCE/TRADE

Currency: Uganda shilling (USh)
International Reserves Excluding Gold: $145 million (Dec. 1993)
Gold Reserves: n.a.
Budget: revenues $365 million; expenditures $545 million, including capital expenditures of $165 million (1989)
Defence Expenditures: $74.13 million (1990)
External Debt: $1.9 billion (1991 est.)
Exports: $143 million (1992); commodities: coffee 97%, cotton, tea; partners: US 25%, UK 18%, France 11%, Spain 10%
Imports: $516 million (1992); commodities: petroleum products, machinery, cotton piece goods, metals, transportation equipment, food; partners: Kenya 25%, UK 14%, Italy 13%

■ HEALTH

Births: 51/1,000 population (1993)
Deaths: 20/1,000 population (1993)
Infant Mortality: 106 deaths/1,000 live births (1993)
Life Expectancy at Birth: 42 years male, 45 years female (1993)
No. of Physicians: 0.01/10,000 population (1990)

■ EDUCATION

Govt. Expenditure: 22.5% government spending (1987)
Literacy: 48.3% (1993)

■ COMMUNICATIONS

Daily newspapers: 5 (1992)
Televisions: 8.3/1,000 inhabitants (1992)
Radios: 99/1,000 inhabitants (1992)
Telephones: 0.4/100 inhabitants (1992)

■ TRANSPORTATION

Motor Vehicles: 27,186; 12,284 passenger cars (1990)
Roads: 26,200 km; 1,970 km paved (1993)
Railway: 1,470 km
Air Traffic: 26,000 passengers carried (1991)
Airports: 31 airfields, of which 23 are usable; 5 have permanent-surface runways (1993)

Canadian Embassy: c/o The Canadian High Commission, Comcraft House, Hailé Sélassie Ave, Nairobi; mailing address: The Canadian High Commission, P.O. Box 30481, Nairobi, Kenya. Tel: (011-254-2) 21-48-04. Fax: (011-254-2) 22-69-87
Representative to Canada: High Commission for the Republic of Uganda, 231 Cobourg St, Ottawa ON K1N 8J2. Tel: (613) 789-7797. Fax: (613) 789-8909.

Ukraine

Long-Form Name: Ukraine
Capital: Kiev
Population: 51,900,000 (1993 est.)

■ GEOGRAPHY

Area: 603,700 sq. km
Coastline: 2,782 km
Climate: temperate continental; subtropical on southern Crimean coast; moderate rainfall in north; drier in southern regions
Environment: air and water pollution, deforestation, radiation contamination around Chernobyl nuclear power plant
Terrain: Carpathian mountains in west, marshy

in north, remainder flat fertile plains (steppes) and plateaux
Land Use: 56% arable, 2% permanent crops, 12% meadows and pastures, negligible forests, 30% other
Location: SE Europe, bordering on Black Sea

■ PEOPLE

Nationality: Ukrainian
Ethnic Groups: 73% Ukrainian, 22% Russian, 1% Jewish, 4% other
Languages: Ukrainian, Russian, Romanian, Polish
Religions: predominantly Eastern Orthodox and Roman Catholic; Uniate Church re-legalized in 1991; also, Autocephalous Orthodox Church, Greek rite Catholic
Marriages: 9.3 (per 1,000) (1990)
Divorces: 3.71 (per 1,000) (1990)

■ GOVERNMENT

Leader(s): Pres. Leonid Kuchma
Government Type: republic
Administrative Divisions: 24 oblasts, 1 autonomous republic, 2 municipalities with oblast status
Independence: December 1, 1991 (from Soviet Union)
National Holiday: August 24 (Independence Day)

■ ECONOMY

Overview: mining and heavy industry, with very strong agricultural sector; food surplus area of former USSR
GNP: $121.458 billion, per capita $2,340; real growth rate 2.7%
Inflation: n.a.
Industries: mining, manufacturing of machinery, food processing, chemicals, electric and electronic equipment, coal, electric power, food processing (esp. sugar)
Labour Force: 26,160,175 (1989)
Unemployment: n.a.
Agriculture: corn, wheat, sugar beets, sunflower seeds, barley, tobacco; livestock inc. cattle, pigs, goats, sheep, vegetables, milk, sugar beets
Natural Resources: coal, manganese, oil, gypsum, iron, lead, zinc, titanium, natural gas, oil, salt, sulphur, graphite

■ FINANCE/TRADE

Currency: Russian rouble was withdrawn from circulation Nov. 1992; karbovanets (pl. karbovantsi) sole legal tender; interim move pending introduction of a new currency (grivna)
International Reserves Excluding Gold: n.a.
Gold Reserves: n.a.

Budget: 1989 revenues: 36,885 million roubles
Defence Expenditures: n.a.
External Debt: $12 billion (1992 est.)
Exports: $3.173 billion (1992): minerals, agricultural products, heavy machinery, vehicles, airplanes
Imports: $1.953 billion (1992)

■ HEALTH

Births: 12.1/1,000 population (1993)
Deaths: 13/1,000 population (1993)
Infant Mortality: 18 deaths/1,000 live births (1993)
Life Expectancy at Birth: 66 years male, 75 years female (1993)
No. of Physicians: n.a.

■ EDUCATION

Govt. Expenditure: 21.1% of govt. expenditure (1985)
Literacy: 100% (1993)

■ COMMUNICATIONS

Daily newspapers: 1,763 papers of all circulation types (1989)
Televisions: 292/1,000 inhabitants (1992)
Radios: 781/1,000 inhabitants (1992)
Telephones: 13.5/100 inhabitants (1993)

■ TRANSPORTATION

Motor Vehicles: n.a.
Roads: 273,700 km; 236,400 km paved
Railway: 22,730 km
Air Traffic: n.a.
Airports: 694 airfields, of which 100 are usable; 111 have permanent-surface runways (1993)

Canadian Embassy: 31 Yaroslaviv Val St, Kiev, 252034 Ukraine. Tel: (011-7-044) 212-2112. Fax: (011-7-044) 212-2339.
Representative to Canada: Embassy of Ukraine, 331 Metcalfe St, Ottawa ON K2P 1S3. Tel: (613) 230-2961. Fax: (613) 230-2400.

United Arab Emirates

Long-Form Name: United Arab Emirates
Capital: Abu Dhabi
Population: 2,100,000 (1993 est.)

■ GEOGRAPHY

Area: 75,581 sq. km
Coastline: 1,318 km along Persian Gulf and Gulf of Oman
Climate: desert; cooler in eastern mountains
Environment: frequent dust and sand storms; lack of natural freshwater resources being overcome

by desalination plants; desertification
Terrain: flat, barren coastal plain; desert wasteland; mountains in east
Land Use: negligible arable; negligible permanent crops; 2% meadows; negligible forest; 98% other
Location: SW Asia (Middle East), bordering on Persian Gulf

■ PEOPLE

Nationality: Emirian
Ethnic Groups: 19% Emirian, 23% other Arab, 50% South Asian (fluctuating), 8% other expatriates (includes Westerners and East Asians); less than 20% of the population are United Arab Emirates citizens
Languages: Arabic (official); Farsi and English widely spoken in major cities; Hindi, Urdu
Religions: 96% Moslem (16% Shi'a); 4% Christian, Hindu and other
Marriages: n.a.
Divorces: n.a.

■ GOVERNMENT

Leader(s): Pres. Zayid bin Sultan Al Nuhayyan, Prime Min. Maktum bin Rashid al- Maktum,
Government Type: federation with specified powers delegated to the United Arab Emirates central government and other powers reserved to member emirates
Administrative Divisions: 7 emirates
Independence: Dec. 2, 1971 (from UK; formerly known as Trucial States)
National Holiday: National Day, Dec. 2

■ ECONOMY

Overview: has an open economy tied to the world prices for oil and gas; currently has a high standard of living; crude oil reserves should last for over 100 years at present levels of production
GNP: n.a., GDP $34.9 billion, per capita $13,800; real growth rate n.a. (1992)
Inflation: 1% (1990)
Industries: petroleum, fishing, petrochemicals, construction materials, some boat building, handicrafts, pearling
Labour Force: 784,000 (1992): 38% industry, 4.5% agriculture, 57.3% services (1989)
Unemployment: negligible (1988)
Agriculture: accounts for 2% of GNP; cash crop: dates; food products: vegetables, watermelons, poultry, eggs, dairy, fish; only 25% self-sufficient in food

Natural Resources: crude oil and natural gas

■ FINANCE/TRADE

Currency: UAE dirham (Dh)
International Reserves Excluding Gold: $5,748 million (Nov. 1993)
Gold Reserves: 0.80 million fine troy ounces (Nov. 1993)
Budget: revenues $4.3 billion; expenditures $4.8 billion, including capital expenditures (1993)
Defence Expenditures: $1.59 billion (1990)
External Debt: $11 billion (1989)
Exports: $21.2 billion (1991); commodities: crude oil 75%, natural gas, re-exports, dried fish, dates; partners: US, European Community, Japan, Singapore, Korea
Imports: $13.9 billion (1991); commodities: food, consumer and capital goods; partners: European Community, Japan, US

■ HEALTH

Births: 31/1,000 population (1993)
Deaths: 3/1,000 population (1993)
Infant Mortality: 25 deaths/1,000 live births (1993)
Life Expectancy at Birth: 69 years male, 74 years female (1993)
No. of Physicians: 9.8/10,000 population (1992)

■ EDUCATION

Govt. Expenditure: 15% of govt. expenditure (1991)
Literacy: 68% (1993)

■ COMMUNICATIONS

Daily newspapers: 8 (1992)
Televisions: 108.5/1,000 inhabitants (1992)
Radios: 322/1,000 inhabitants (1992)
Telephones: 24.52/100 inhabitants (1992)

■ TRANSPORTATION

Motor Vehicles: 459,000; 302,000 passenger cars (1990)
Roads: 2,000 km; 1,840 km paved
Railway: n.a.
Air Traffic: 2,042,000 passengers carried (1991)
Airports: 37 airfields, of which 34 are usable; 20 have permanent-surface runways (1993)

Canadian Embassy: c/o Da'Aiyah - Block 4, House No. 24, Al-Mutawakel St, Kuwait City; mailing address: P.O. Box 25281, Safat, Kuwait City, 13113, Kuwait. Tel: (011-965) 256-3025. Fax: (011-965) 256-4167.
Representative to Canada: c/o Embassy of the United Arab Emirates, 747 Third Ave, 36th Flr,

New York, NY 10017 USA. Tel: (212) 371-0480. Fax: (212) 371-4923.

United Kingdom

Long-Form Name: United Kingdom of Great Britain and Northern Ireland
Capital: London
Population: 58,000,000 (1993)

■ GEOGRAPHY

Area: 244,820 sq. km
Coastline: 12,429 km along English Channel, North Sea, North Atlantic Ocean, Irish Sea
Climate: temperate; moderated by prevailing southwest winds over the North Atlantic Current; more than half of the days are overcast
Environment: pollution control measures improving air, water quality; because of heavily indented coastline, no location is more than 125 km from tidal waters
Terrain: mostly rugged hills and low mountains; level to rolling plains in east and southeast
Land Use: 29% arable; negligible permanent; 48% meadows; 9% forest; 14% other
Location: NW Europe, bordering on North Sea, Atlantic Ocean

■ PEOPLE

Nationality: British
Ethnic Groups: 81.5% English, 9.6% Scottish, 2.4% Irish, 1.9% Welsh, 1.8% Ulster, 2.8% West Indian, Indian, Pakistani and other
Languages: English, Welsh (about 20% of population of Wales), Scottish form of Gaelic (about 60,000 in Scotland)
Religions: 27.0 million Anglican, 9 million Roman Catholic, 1 million Muslim, 400,000 Sikh, 800,000 Presbyterian, 760,000 Methodist, 300,000 Jewish
Marriages: 6.8 (per 1,000) (1989)
Divorces: 2.88 (per 1,000) (1990)

■ GOVERNMENT

Leader(s): Prime Min. and First Lord of the Treasury John Major, Queen Elizabeth II
Government Type: constitutional monarchy
Administrative Divisions: 47 counties, 7 metropolitan counties, 26 districts, 9 regions and 3 island areas; dependent areas inc.: Anguilla, Bermuda, British Antarctic Territory (uninhabited except for variable population of research stations – about 300 persons), British Indian Ocean Territory, British Virgin Islands, Cayman Islands, Channel Islands, Falkland Islands, Gibraltar, Guernsey, Hong Kong, Isle of Man, Jersey, Montserrat, Pitcairn, Saint Helena, South Georgia (uninhabited except for scientific station and 500 persons in a whaling/sealing settlement), South Sandwich Islands (uninhabited), Turks and Caicos Islands
Independence: Jan. 1, 1801, United Kingdom established
National Holiday: Celebration of the Birthday of the Queen, second Saturday in June

■ ECONOMY

Overview: capitalistic with social welfare programs and some government ownership; the 1980s saw increased privatization and continuous growth; is a great trading power and financial centre which is energy-rich; may be affected by European economic integration; agriculture is intensive, highly mechanized and efficient; services by far account for greatest proportion of GDP, while industry continues to decline in importance
GNP: n.a., GDP: $920.6 billion, per capita $15,900; real growth rate -0.6% (1992)
Inflation: 3.7% (1992)
Industries: machinery and transportation equipment, metals, food processing, paper and paper products, textiles, chemicals, clothing, other consumer goods, motor vehicles, aircraft, shipbuilding, petroleum, coal
Labour Force: 28,048,000; 62.8% services, 1.2% agriculture, 1.9% energy, 25% manufacturing and construction, 9.1% government (1992)
Unemployment: 9.8% (1992)
Agriculture: accounts for only 1.5% of GNP; highly mechanized and efficient farms; wide variety of crops and livestock products produced; about 60% self-sufficient in food and feed needs; fish catch of 665,000 metric tons (1987)
Natural Resources: coal, crude oil, natural gas, tin, limestone, iron ore, salt, clay, chalk, gypsum, lead, silica

■ FINANCE/TRADE

Currency: pound sterling (£ or £ stg)
International Reserves Excluding Gold: $38,329 million (Sept. 1993)
Gold Reserves: 18.45 million fine troy ounces (Sept. 1993)
Budget: revenues $367.6 billion; expenditures $439.3 billion, including capital expenditures of $32.5 billion (1992)
Defence Expenditures: 11.29% of total govt. expenditure (1991)
External Debt: $16.2 billion (1992)
Exports: $179.5 billion (1993 est.); commodities: manufactured goods, machinery, fuels, chemicals, semifinished goods, transport equipment;

partners: European Community 50.4% (Germany 11.7%, France 10.2%, Netherlands 6.8%), US 13%, communist countries 2.3%
Imports: $204.3 billion (1993 est.); commodities: manufactured goods, machinery, semifinished goods, foodstuffs, consumer goods; partners: European Community 52.5% (Germany 16.6%, France 8.8%, Netherlands 7.8%), US 10.2%, communist countries 2.1%

■ HEALTH

Births: 14/1,000 population (1993)
Deaths: 11/1,000 population (1993)
Infant Mortality: 7.1 deaths/1,000 live births (1993)
Life Expectancy at Birth: 73 years male, 78 years female (1993)
No. of Physicians: 16.4/10,000 population (1990)

■ EDUCATION

Govt. Expenditure: 3.18% of govt. expenditure (1990)
Literacy: 99% (1992)

■ COMMUNICATIONS

Daily newspapers: 104 (1992)
Televisions: 434.3/1,000 inhabitants (1992)
Radios: 1,145/1,000 inhabitants (1992)
Telephones: 52.36/100 inhabitants (1992)

■ TRANSPORTATION

Motor Vehicles: 26,301,748; 22,527,963 passenger cars (1990)
Roads: 362,982 km paved (1992)
Railway: 16,914 km (1993)
Air Traffic: 42,861,000 passengers carried (1991)
Airports: 496 airfields, of which 385 are usable; 249 have permanent-surface runways (1993)

Canadian Embassy: Macdonald House, 1 Grosvenor Square, London, W1X OAB, England, UK. Tel: (011-44-71) 258-6600
Representative to Canada: British High Commission, 80 Elgin St, Ottawa ON K1P 5K7. Tel: (613) 237-1530. Fax: (613) 237-7980.

United States

Long-Form Name: United States of America
Capital: Washington, D.C.
Population: 258,300,000 (1993 est.)

■ GEOGRAPHY

Area: 9,372,610 sq. km; includes only the 50 states and District of Columbia
Coastline: 19,924 km North Atlantic Ocean, Gulf of Mexico, North Pacific Ocean

Climate: mostly temperate, but varies from tropical (Hawaii) to arctic (Alaska); arid to semi-arid in west with occasional warm, dry chinook wind
Environment: pollution control measures improving air and water quality; acid rain; agricultural fertilizer and pesticide pollution; management of sparse natural water resources in west; desertification; tsunamis, volcanoes and earthquake activity around Pacific; permafrost in Alaska
Terrain: vast central plain, mountains in west, hills and low mountains in east; rugged mountains and broad river valleys in Alaska; rugged, volcanic topography in Hawaii
Land Use: 20% arable; negligible permanent; 26% meadows; 29% forest; 25% other
Location: North America, bordering on Pacific Ocean, Atlantic Ocean

■ PEOPLE

Nationality: American
Ethnic Groups: 83.4% white, 12.4% black, 4.1% other (1992)
Languages: predominantly English; sizable Spanish-speaking minority
Religions: 56% Protestant (including 21% Baptist, 12% Methodist, 8% Lutheran, 4% Presbyterian, 3% Episcopalian), 28% Roman Catholic, 2% Jewish, 4% other, 10% none
Marriages: 9.4 (per 1,000) (1991)
Divorces: 4.73 (per 1,000) (1991)

■ GOVERNMENT

Leader(s): Pres. William Jefferson Clinton
Government Type: federal republic
Administrative Divisions: 50 states and 1 district; dependent areas inc.: American Samoa, Baker Island, Federated States of Micronesia, Guam, Howland Island, Jarvis Island, Johnston Atoll, Kingman Reef, Marshall Islands, Midway Islands (inhabited by U.S. military personnel), Northern Marianas, Palau, Palymyra Atoll, Puerto Rico (for details see Puerto Rico entry), Virgin Islands (for details see Virgin Islands entry), Wake Island (military base)
Independence: July 4, 1776 (from England)
National Holiday: Independence Day, July 4

■ ECONOMY

Overview: a powerful and diversified economy, with high per capita GNP; the 1980s brought successive years of growth; problems may be the huge budget and trade deficits, large medical costs and inadequate investment in industry and infrastructure
GNP: $5.951 trillion, per capita $23,400; real growth rate 2.1% (1992)
Inflation: 3.0% (1992)

Industries: highly diversified industry; petroleum, steel, motor vehicles, aerospace, telecommunications, chemicals, electronics, food processing, consumer goods, fishing, lumber, mining
Labour Force: 122,005,000 (1992); 2.8% agriculture, 18.4% industry, 78.8% services (1989)
Unemployment: 7% (1991)
Agriculture: accounts for 2% of GNP; favourable climate and soils support a wide variety of crops and livestock production; world's second-largest producer and top exporter of grain; surplus food producer; fish catch of 4.4 million metric tons (1990)
Natural Resources: coal, copper, lead, molybdenum, phosphates, uranium, bauxite, gold, iron, mercury, nickel, potash, silver, tungsten, zinc, crude oil, natural gas, timber

■ FINANCE/TRADE

Currency: US dollar ($ or $US)
International Reserves Excluding Gold: $63,190 million (Jan. 1994)
Gold Reserves: 261.81 million fine troy ounces (Jan. 1994)
Budget: revenues $1,092 billion; expenditures $1,382 billion, including capital expenditures (1992)
Defence Expenditures: 20.58% of total govt. expenditure (1992)
External Debt: $532 billion (1988)
Exports: $464.610 billion (1993); commodities: capital goods, automobiles, industrial supplies and raw materials, consumer goods, agricultural products; partners: Canada 22.9%, Japan 11.8%
Imports: $603.365 billion (1993); commodities: crude and partly refined petroleum, machinery, automobiles, consumer goods, industrial raw materials, food and beverages; partners: Japan 19.6%, Canada 19.1%

■ HEALTH

Births: 16/1,000 population (1993)
Deaths: 9/1,000 population (1993)
Infant Mortality: 8.6 deaths/1,000 live births (1993)
Life Expectancy at Birth: 72 years male, 79 years female (1993)
No. of Physicians: 21.1/10,000 population (1992)

■ EDUCATION

Govt. Expenditure: 1.75% of govt. expenditure (1992)
Literacy: 97.9% (1993)

■ COMMUNICATIONS

Daily newspapers: 1,657 (1992)

Televisions: 813.6/1,000 inhabitants (1992)
Radios: 2,122/1,000 inhabitants (1992)
Telephones: 76.03/100 inhabitants (1992)

■ TRANSPORTATION

Motor Vehicles: 188,655,462; 143,549,627 passenger cars (1990)
Roads: 7,599,250 km; 3,627,000 km paved
Railway: 247,440 km
Air Traffic: 452,016,000 passengers carried (1991)
Airports: 14,177 airfields, of which 12,417 are usable; 4,820 have permanent-surface runways (1993)

Canadian Embassy: 501 Pennsylvania Ave, NW, Washington, DC 20001. Tel: (202) 682-1740. Fax: (202) 682-7726
Representative to Canada: Embassy of the United States of America, 100 Wellington St, P.O. Box 866, Station "B," Ottawa ON K1P 5T1. Tel: (613) 238-5335.

Uruguay

Long-Form Name: Oriental Republic of Uruguay
Capital: Montevideo
Population: 3,200,000 (1993 est.)

■ GEOGRAPHY

Area: 176,220 sq. km
Coastline: 660 km along South Atlantic Ocean
Climate: warm temperate; freezing temperatures almost unknown
Environment: subject to seasonally high winds, droughts, floods
Terrain: mostly rolling plains and low hills; fertile coastal lowland
Land Use: 8% arable; negligible permanent; 78% meadows; 4% forest; 10% other
Location: SE South America, bordering on Atlantic Ocean

■ PEOPLE

Nationality: Uruguayan
Ethnic Groups: 88% white, 8% mestizo, 4% black
Languages: Spanish
Religions: 66% nominally Roman Catholic, 2% Protestant, 2% Jewish, 30% other
Marriages: 7.0 (per 1,000) (1988)
Divorces: 2.08 (per 1,000) (1988)

■ GOVERNMENT

Leader(s): Pres. Luis Alberto Lacalle Herrera, V Pres. Gonzala Aguirre
Government Type: republic

Administrative Divisions: 19 departments
Independence: Aug. 25, 1828 (from Brazil)
National Holiday: Independence Day, Aug. 25

■ ECONOMY

Overview: a small economy with favorable climate, good soils, and considerable hydropower potential; economy is still recovering from a recession in the early 1980s; problems include high inflation rates, a large domestic debt and frequent strikes; growth in the agriculture and fishing sectors have spurred recovery
GNP: n.a., GDP $9.8 billion, per capita $3,100; real growth rate 8% (1992 est.)
Inflation: 68.5% (1992)
Industries: meat packing, oil refining, manufacturing, foodstuffs, engineering, transport equipment, sugar, textiles, leather apparel, tires
Labour Force: 1,216,000 (1992); 15.3% agriculture, 18.2% industry, 66.5% services (1989)
Unemployment: 9% (1992 est.)
Agriculture: meat processing, wool and hides, sugar, textiles, footwear, leather apparel, tires, cement, fishing, petroleum refining, wine, wheat, rice, corn, sorghum; self-sufficient in most basic foods
Natural Resources: soil, hydropower potential, minor minerals

■ FINANCE/TRADE

Currency: new peso (N$Ur)
International Reserves Excluding Gold: $758 million (Dec. 1993)
Gold Reserves: 1.70 million fine troy ounces (Dec. 1993)
Budget: revenues $2.9 billion; expenditures $3.0 billion, including capital expenditures of $388 million (1991)
Defence Expenditures: 6.54% of total govt. expenditure (1991)
External Debt: $4.1 billion (1991)
Exports: $1.701 billion (1992); commodities: hides and leather goods 17%, beef 10%, wool 9%, fish 7%, rice 4%; partners: Brazil 17%, US 15%, Germany 10%, Argentina 10%
Imports: $2.024 billion (1992); commodities: fuels and lubricants 15%, metals, machinery, transportation equipment, industrial chemicals; partners: Brazil 24%, Argentina 14%, US 8%, Germany 8%

■ HEALTH

Births: 19/1,000 population (1993)
Deaths: 10/1,000 population (1993)
Infant Mortality: 20.0 deaths/1,000 live births (1993)
Life Expectancy at Birth: 70 years male, 76 years female (1993)
No. of Physicians: 19.5/10,000 population (1992)

■ EDUCATION

Govt. Expenditure: 6.77% of govt. expenditure (1991)
Literacy: 96.2% (1993)

■ COMMUNICATIONS

Daily newspapers: 33 (1992)
Televisions: 227.2/1,000 inhabitants (1992)
Radios: 600/1,000 inhabitants (1992)
Telephones: 14.3/100 inhabitants (1992)

■ TRANSPORTATION

Motor Vehicles: 258,000; 175,000 passenger cars (1990)
Roads: 50,220 km; 6,700 km paved
Railway: 3,039 km
Air Traffic: 318,000 passengers carried (1991)
Airports: 88 airfields, of which 81 are usable; 16 have permanent-surface runways (1993)

Canadian Embassy: c/o 2828 Tagle, 1425, Buenos Aires; mailing address: Casilla de Correo 1598, Buenos Aires, Argentina. Tel: (011-54-1) 805-3032
Representative to Canada: Embassy of Uruguay, 130 Albert St, Ste 1905, Ottawa ON K1P 5G4. Tel: (613) 234-2727. Fax: (613) 233-4670.

Uzbekistan

Long-Form Name: Republic of Uzbekistan
Capital: Tashkent
Population: 21,700,000 (1993 est.)

■ GEOGRAPHY

Area: 447,400 sq. km
Coastline: landlocked; 420 km coastline along Aral Sea
Climate: dry continental; warm to hot summers; cool to cold winters; semi-arid grassland in east
Environment: drying up of the Aral Sea is resulting in increasing concentrations of chemical pesticides and natural salts
Terrain: flat to rolling deserts and semideserts, mountains, shrinking Aral Sea in west
Land Use: 10% arable, 0% permanent crops, 47% meadows and pastures, 0% forests, 43% other
Location: C Asia

■ PEOPLE

Nationality: Uzbek
Ethnic Groups: 70% Uzbek, 8.4% Russian, 2.4% Tartars, 4.7% Tajiks, 4.1% Kazakhs, 2.1%

Kara-Kalpaks, 1% Crimean Tatars
Languages: Uzbek (official), Russian, Kazakh, Tajik, Tartar, Jagatai Turkish
Religions: predominantly Sunni Muslim and Eastern Orthodox
Marriages: 10.0 (per 1,000) (1989)
Divorces: 1.49 (per 1,000) (1989)

■ GOVERNMENT

Leader(s): Pres. Islam A. Karimov, Prem. Abdulkhashum Mutalov
Government Type: republic
Administrative Divisions: 12 regions ("oblasts"), 1 autonomous republic
Independence: Aug. 31, 1991 (from Soviet Union)
National Holiday: Independence Day, Sept. 1

■ ECONOMY

Overview: despite the need for irrigation, agriculture is the predominant economic sector; small industrial sector, mining
GNP: $28.255 billion, per capita $1,350; real growth rate 3.4% (1991)
Inflation: 17+% per month (1993)
Industries: chemicals and gas, machine building, metalmaking, textile manufacture, clothing, butter, preserves, vegetable oil, textiles
Labour Force: 7,941,000 (1990); 39% agriculture and forestry, 24% industry and construction, 37% other
Unemployment: 0.1% (1993); also large numbers of underemployed
Agriculture: cotton, grains, almonds, fruit, livestock; 97% of all crops are grown on irrigated land
Natural Resources: gold, non-ferrous metals, coal, natural gas, petroleum, uranium, silver, copper

■ FINANCE/TRADE

Currency: rouble (rbl.)
International Reserves Excluding Gold: n.a.
Gold Reserves: n.a.
Budget: 1989 revenues: 10,029 million roubles
Defence Expenditures: n.a.
External Debt: $2 billion (1991 est.)
Exports: $869 million (1992): cotton, agricultural products, machinery
Imports: $926 million (1992)

■ HEALTH

Births: 35/1,000 population (1993)
Deaths: 6/1,000 population (1993)
Infant Mortality: 44 deaths/1,000 live births (1993)
Life Expectancy at Birth: 66 years male, 73 years female (1993)
No. of Physicians: 72,400 (1989)

■ EDUCATION

Govt. Expenditure: n.a.
Literacy: 100% (1993)

■ COMMUNICATIONS

Daily newspapers: 276 papers of all circulation types (1988)
Televisions: n.a.
Radios: n.a.
Telephones: 7.2/100 inhabitants (1993)

■ TRANSPORTATION

Motor Vehicles: n.a.
Roads: 78,400 km; 67,000 km hard-surfaced (1993)
Railway: 3,460 km
Air Traffic: n.a.
Airports: 265 airfields, of which 74 are usable; 30 have permanent-surface runways (1993)

Canadian Embassy: c/o Hotel Kazakhstan, Rooms 912 and 914, 52 Leina St, 480110, Almaty, Kazakhstan. Tel: (011-7-3272) 61-91-07.

Vanuatu

Long-Form Name: Republic of Vanuatu
Capital: Port Vila
Population: 200,000 (1993 est.)

■ GEOGRAPHY

Area: 14,760 sq. km
Coastline: 2,528 km
Climate: tropical; moderated by southeast trade winds
Environment: subject to tropical cyclones or typhoons (Jan. to Apr.); volcanism causes minor earthquakes
Terrain: mostly mountains of volcanic origin; narrow coastal plains
Land Use: 1% arable; 5% permanent; 2% meadows; 1% forest; 91% other
Location: South Pacific Ocean, E of Australia

■ PEOPLE

Nationality: Ni-Vanuatu
Ethnic Groups: 94% indigenous Melanesian, 4% French, remainder Vietnamese, Chinese and various Pacific Islanders
Languages: English and French (official); pidgin (known as Bislama or Bichelama)
Religions: 36.7% Presbyterian, 15% Anglican, 15% Catholic, 7.6% indigenous beliefs, 6.2%

Seventh-Day Adventist, 3.8% Church of Christ,
15.7% other
Marriages: n.a.
Divorces: n.a.

■ GOVERNMENT

Leader(s): Prime Min. Maxime Carlot Korman,
Pres. Jean-Marie Leye
Government Type: republic
Administrative Divisions: 11 island councils
Independence: July 30, 1980 (from France and
UK; formerly known as New Hebrides)
National Holiday: Independence Day, July 30

■ ECONOMY

Overview: economy is based on subsistence
farming, fishing and tourism; few mineral
deposits; tax revenues come largely from import
duties
GNP: $175 million, per capita $1,120; real
growth rate 2.6% (1991)
Inflation: 2.2% (1992)
Industries: food and fish freezing, meat canning,
wood processing
Labour Force: 61.1% agriculture, 1.3% industry,
37.6% services (1989)
Unemployment: n.a.
Agriculture: accounts for 40% of GDP; export
crops: cocoa, coffee and fish; subsistence crops:
copra, taro, yams, coconuts, fruit and vegetables
Natural Resources: manganese, hardwood
forests, fish

■ FINANCE/TRADE

Currency: vatu (VT)
International Reserves Excluding Gold: $42 mil-
lion (1992)
Gold Reserves: n.a.
Budget: revenues $90.0 million; expenditures
$103.0 million, including capital expenditures
of $45.0 million (1989)
Defence Expenditures: negligible
External Debt: $30 million (1990)
Exports: $20 million (1991); commodities: copra
37%, cocoa 11%, meat 9%, fish 8%, timber 4%;
partners: Netherlands 34%, France 27%, Japan
17%, Belgium 4%, New Caledonia 3%,
Singapore 2%
Imports: $83 million (1991); commodities:
machines and vehicles 25%, food and beverages
23%, basic manufactures 18%, raw materials
and fuels 11%, chemicals 6%; partners:
Australia 36%, Japan 13%, New Zealand 10%,
France 8%, Fiji 5%

■ HEALTH

Births: 40/1,000 population (1993)

Deaths: 7/1,000 population (1993)
Infant Mortality: 65 deaths/1,000 live births
(1993)
Life Expectancy at Birth: 67 years male, 72 years
female (1992)
No. of Physicians: 2.0/10,000 population (1992)

■ EDUCATION

Govt. Expenditure: 12.62% of govt. expenditure
(1989)
Literacy: 52.9% (1993)

■ COMMUNICATIONS

Daily newspapers: 1 (1992)
Televisions: 8.5/1,000 inhabitants (1992)
Radios: 267/1,000 inhabitants (1992)
Telephones: 2.31/100 inhabitants (1992)

■ TRANSPORTATION

Motor Vehicles: 7,000; 4,200 passenger cars
(1990)
Roads: 1,027 km; 240+ km sealed (1993)
Railway: none
Air Traffic: 19,000 passengers carried (1991)
Airports: 31 airfields, all usable; 2 have perma-
nent-surface runways (1993)

Canadian Embassy: c/o The Canadian High
Commission, Commonwealth Ave, Canberra
ACT 2600, Australia. Tel: (011-61-62) 273-
3844. Fax: (011-61-62) 273-3285
Representative to Canada: Australian High
Commission, 50 O'Connor St, Ste 710, Ottawa,
ON K1P 6L2. Tel: (613) 746-4914.

Vatican City

Long-Form Name: State of the Vatican City
Capital: Vatican City
Population: 1,000 (1992)

■ GEOGRAPHY

Area: 0.438 sq. km
Coastline: none: landlocked
Climate: temperate; mild, rainy winters (Sept. to
mid-May) with hot, dry summers (May to Sept.)
Environment: urban
Terrain: low hill
Land Use: 0% arable; 0% permanent; 0% mead-
ows; 0% forest; 100% other
Location: S Europe (W Italy)

■ PEOPLE

Nationality: n.a. (no descriptive word)
Ethnic Groups: primarily Italians but also many
other nationalities
Languages: Italian, Latin and various other lan-

guages
Religions: Roman Catholic
Marriages: n.a.
Divorces: n.a.

■ GOVERNMENT

Leader(s): Head, Roman Catholic Church, Pope John Paul II (Karol Wojtyla)
Government Type: monarchical-sacerdotal state
Administrative Divisions: none
Independence: Feb. 11, 1929 (from Italy)
National Holiday: Installation Day of the Pope (John Paul II), Oct. 22; also Christmas, Easter, Feast of Saints Peter and Paul (June 29), and other holy days of obligation

■ ECONOMY

Overview: economy is supported financially by contributions (known as Peter's pence) from Roman Catholics throughout the world, the sale of postage stamps, tourist mementos, fees for admission to museums and the sale of publications
GNP: n.a.
Inflation: n.a.
Industries: printing and production of a small amount of mosaics and staff uniforms; worldwide banking and financial activities
Labour Force: approx. 1,500 Vatican City employees divided into three categories: executives, office workers, salaried employees
Unemployment: n.a.
Agriculture: none
Natural Resources: none

■ FINANCE/TRADE

Currency: Vatican Lira (Lit) (at par with Italian lira)
International Reserves Excluding Gold: n.a.
Gold Reserves: n.a.
Budget: revenues $86 million; expenditures $178 million, including capital expenditures (1993 est.)
Defence Expenditures: n.a.
External Debt: n.a.
Exports: n.a.
Imports: n.a.

■ HEALTH

Births: n.a.
Deaths: n.a.
Infant Mortality: n.a.
Life Expectancy at Birth: n.a.
No. of Physicians: n.a.

■ EDUCATION

Govt. Expenditure: n.a.

Literacy: 100%

■ COMMUNICATIONS

Daily newspapers: 1 (1988)
Televisions: n.a.; no TV stations (1993)
Radios: n.a.; 7 radio stations (1993)
Telephones: 2,000 total (1993)

■ TRANSPORTATION

Motor Vehicles: n.a.
Roads: no highways, all city streets (1993)
Railway: 850 m
Air Traffic: none
Airports: none

Canadian Embassy: Via della Conciliazione 4/D, 00193 Rome, Italy. Tel. (011-39-6) 6830-7316. Fax: (011-39-6) 6880-6283
Representative to Canada: Apostolic Nunciature, 724 Manor Ave, Rockcliffe Park, Ottawa ON K1M 0E3. Tel: (613) 746-4914. Fax: (613) 746-4786.

Venezuela

Long-Form Name: Republic of Venezuela
Capital: Caracas
Population: 20,700,000 (1993 est.)

■ GEOGRAPHY

Area: 912,050 sq. km
Coastline: 2,800 km along Caribbean Sea
Climate: tropical; hot, humid; more moderate in highlands
Environment: subject to floods, rockslides, mud slides; periodic droughts; increasing industrial pollution in Caracas and Maracaibo
Terrain: Andes Mountains and Maracaibo lowlands in northwest; central plains (llanos); Guyana highlands in southwest
Land Use: 3% arable; 1% permanent; 20% meadows; 39% forest; 37% other
Location: N South America, bordering on Caribbean Sea

■ PEOPLE

Nationality: Venezuelan
Ethnic Groups: 67% mestizo, 21% white, 10% black, 2% Indian
Languages: Spanish (official); Indian dialects spoken by approx. 200,000 Amerindians in the remote interior
Religions: 96% nominally Roman Catholic, 2% Protestant, 2% other
Marriages: 5.9 (per 1,000) (1989)
Divorces: 1.16 (per 1,000) (1989)

■ GOVERNMENT

Leader(s): Pres. Rafael Caldera Rodríguez
Government Type: republic
Administrative Divisions: 21 states, 1 territory, 1 federal district and 1 federal dependency
Independence: July 5, 1811 (from Spain)
National Holiday: Independence Day, July 5

■ ECONOMY

Overview: petroleum is the backbone of the economy, accounting for 23% of GDP; after a brief decline in 1989, economy has partly recovered and is growing considerably
GNP: $57.8 billion, per capita $2,800; real growth rate 7.3% (1992 est.)
Inflation: 31.4% (1992)
Industries: petroleum, iron-ore mining, construction materials, food processing, textiles, steel, aluminum, motor vehicle assembly
Labour Force: 6,860,000 (1992); 70.2% services, 17.3% industry, 12.5% agriculture (1989)
Unemployment: 8.4% (1992 est.)
Agriculture: accounts for 6% GDP; products: corn, sorghum, sugar cane, rice, bananas, vegetables, coffee, beef, pork, milk, eggs, fish; not self-sufficient in food other than meat
Natural Resources: crude oil, natural gas, iron ore, gold, bauxite, other minerals, hydropower, diamonds

■ FINANCE/TRADE

Currency: bolívar (Bs)
International Reserves Excluding Gold: $8,481 million (Jan. 1994)
Gold Reserves: 11.46 million fine troy ounces (Jan. 1994)
Budget: revenues $13.2 billion; expenditures $13.1 billion, including capital expenditures (1992)
Defence Expenditures: $1.95 billion (1991)
External Debt: $27.1 billion (1992)
Exports: $13.239 billion (1992); commodities: petroleum 81%, bauxite and aluminum, iron ore, agricultural products, basic manufactures; partners: US 50.3%, Germany 5.3%, Japan 4.1%
Imports: $12.225 billion (1992); commodities: foodstuffs, chemicals, manufactures, machinery and transport equipment; partners: US 44%, Germany 8.5%, Japan 6%, Italy 5%, Brazil 4.4%

■ HEALTH

Births: 30/1,000 population (1993)
Deaths: 5/1,000 population (1993)
Infant Mortality: 20.4 deaths/1,000 live births (1993)
Life Expectancy at Birth: 67 years male, 73 years female (1993)
No. of Physicians: 14.3/10,000 population (1992)

■ EDUCATION

Govt. Expenditure: 19.0% of govt. expenditure (1990)
Literacy: 88.1% (1993)

■ COMMUNICATIONS

Daily newspapers: 56 (1992)
Televisions: 156.0/1,000 inhabitants (1992)
Radios: 432/1,000 inhabitants (1992)
Telephones: 9.33/100 inhabitants (1992)

■ TRANSPORTATION

Motor Vehicles: 2,184,000; 1,601,000 passenger cars (1990)
Roads: 77,785 km; 22,780 km paved (1993)
Railway: 542 km
Air Traffic: 6,626,000 passengers carried (1991)
Airports: 360 airfields, of which 331 are usable; 133 have permanent-surface runways (1993)

Canadian Embassy: Edificio Torre Europa, Septimo Piso, Avenida Francisco de Miranda, Campo Alegre, Caracas; mailing address: Apartado Postal 62302, Caracas 1060A, Venezuela. Tel: (011-58-2) 951-6166. Fax (011-58-2) 951-4950
Representative to Canada: Embassy of Venezuela, 32 Range Rd, Ottawa ON K1N 8J4. Tel: (613) 235-5151. Fax: (613) 235-3205.

Vietnam

Long-Form Name: Socialist Republic of Vietnam
Capital: Hanoi
Population: 71,800,000 (1993 est.)

■ GEOGRAPHY

Area: 329,560 sq. km
Coastline: 3,444 km (excluding islands) along the South China Sea (Gulf of Tonkin and Gulf of Thailand)
Climate: tropical in south; monsoonal in north with hot, rainy season (mid-May to mid-Sept.) and warm, dry season (mid-Oct. to mid-Mar.)
Environment: occasional typhoons (May to Jan.) with extensive flooding
Terrain: low, flat delta in south and north; central highlands; hilly, mountainous far north and northwest
Land Use: 22% arable; 2% permanent; 1% meadows; 40% forest; 35% other
Location: SE Asia, bordering on South China Sea

■ PEOPLE

Nationality: Vietnamese
Ethnic Groups: 85–90% predominantly Vietnamese; 3% Chinese; more than 60 ethnic minorities including Muong, Thai, Meo, Khmer, Man, Cham; other mountain tribes
Languages: Vietnamese (official), French, Chinese, English, Khmer, tribal languages (Mon- Khmer and Malayo-Polynesian)
Religions: Buddhist, Confucian, Taoist, Roman Catholic, indigenous beliefs, Islamic, Protestant
Marriages: n.a.
Divorces: n.a.

■ GOVERNMENT

Leader(s): Pres. Gen. Le Duc Anh, Prime Min. Gen. Vo Van Kiet
Government Type: communist state
Administrative Divisions: 50 provinces, 3 municipalities
Independence: Sept. 2, 1945 (from France)
National Holiday: Independence Day, Sept. 2

■ ECONOMY

Overview: is a centrally planned, developing economy with extensive government ownership and control of production facilities; is dependent on foreign aid; nearly three-quarters of total export earnings come from rice and crude oil; high rate of population growth and high unemployment combine to form the economy's most serious problem
GNP: $16 billion, per capita $230; real growth rate 7.4% (1992 est.)
Inflation: 15-20% (1992 est.)
Industries: food processing, textiles, machine building, mining, cement, chemical fertilizer, glass, tires, oil, fishing
Labour Force: 32.7 million; 65% agriculture, 11.8% industry, 20.7% services (1990)
Unemployment: 25% (1992 est.)
Agriculture: accounts for half of GNP; rice, corn, potatoes make up 50% of farm output; commercial crops (rubber, soybeans, coffee, tea, bananas) and animal products other 50%; not self-sufficient in rice; fish catch of 943,100 metric tons (1989 est.)
Natural Resources: phosphates, coal, manganese, bauxite, chromate, offshore oil deposits, forests

■ FINANCE/TRADE

Currency: dong (pl. dong) (D)
International Reserves Excluding Gold: n.a.
Gold Reserves: n.a.
Budget: revenues $892 million; expenditures $1.3 billion, including capital expenditures of $344 million (1990)

Defence Expenditures: $2.32 billion (1989)
External Debt: $16.8 billion (1990 est.)
Exports: $1.502 billion (1989); commodities: agricultural and handicraft products, coal, minerals, ores; partners: USSR, Eastern Europe, Japan, Singapore
Imports: $3.056 billion (1989); commodities: petroleum, steel products, railroad equipment, chemicals, medicines, raw cotton, fertilizer, grain; partners: USSR, Eastern Europe, Japan, Singapore

■ HEALTH

Births: 30/1,000 population (1993)
Deaths: 8/1,000 population (1993)
Infant Mortality: 45 deaths/1,000 live births (1993)
Life Expectancy at Birth: 62 years male, 66 years female (1993)
No. of Physicians: 10.6/10,000 population (1992)

■ EDUCATION

Govt. Expenditure: n.a.
Literacy: 87.6% (1993)

■ COMMUNICATIONS

Daily newspapers: 4 (1992)
Televisions: 38.3/1,000 inhabitants (1992)
Radios: 107/1,000 inhabitants (1992)
Telephones: 0.2/100 inhabitants (1992)

■ TRANSPORTATION

Motor Vehicles: n.a.
Roads: 86,000 km; 9,560 km paved
Railway: 3,059 km
Air Traffic: 89,000 passengers carried (1991)
Airports: 100 airfields, all usable; 50 have permanent-surface runways (1993)

Canadian Embassy: 39 Nguyen Dinh Chieu St, Hanoi. Tel: (011-84-4) 26-58-40. Fax: (011-84-4) 26-58-37

Representative to Canada: Embassy of the Socialist Republic of Vietnam, 25 B Davidson Dr, Gloucester, ON K1J 6L7. Tel: (613) 744-4963. Fax: (613) 744-1709.

Virgin Islands

Dependent Territory of the United States

Long-Form Name: Virgin Islands of the United States
Capital: Charlotte Amalie
Population: 98,130 (1993 est.)

■ GEOGRAPHY

Area: 352 sq. km
Climate: subtropical, tempered by easterly trade winds, relatively low humidity, little seasonal temperature variation; rainy season May to Nov.
Land Use: 15% arable; 6% permanent; 26% meadows; 6% forests; 47% other
Location: Caribbean Islands

■ PEOPLE

Nationality: Virgin Islander
Ethnic Groups: 74% West Indian (45% born in the Virgin Islands and 29% born elsewhere in the West Indies), 13% US mainland, 5% Puerto Rican, 8% other (80% black, 15% white, 5% other); 14% of Hispanic origin
Languages: English (official), but Spanish and Creole are widely spoken

■ GOVERNMENT

Leader(s): Gov. Alexander Farrelly, Lt. Gov. Derek Hodge
Government Type: organized, unincorporated territory of the US
National Holiday: Transfer Day March 31 (1917, from Denmark to US),

■ ECONOMY

Overview: tourism is the primary economic activity accounting for more than 70% of GDP and 70% of employment; some manufacturing; small agricultural sector; international business and financial services are a small but growing sector

■ FINANCE/TRADE

Currency: US dollar ($)

Wallis and Futuna

Overseas Territory of France

Long-Form Name: Territory of the Wallis and Futuna Islands
Capital: Matu-Utu
Population: 14,175 (1993 est.)

■ GEOGRAPHY

Area: 274 sq. km
Climate: tropical maritime, rainy season (Nov. to April); cool, dry season (May to Oct.)
Land Use: 5% arable, 20% permanent crops, 0% meadows and pastures, 0% forests, 75% other
Location: SW Pacific Ocean

■ PEOPLE

Nationality: Wallisian, Futunan, or Wallis and Futuna Islanders
Ethnic Groups: Polynesians, and descendants of French settlers
Languages: Wallisian, Futunian (Polynesian languages), French

■ GOVERNMENT

Leader(s): Chief Administrator Robert Pommies
Government Type: overseas territory of France

■ ECONOMY

Overview: agriculture includes copra, cassava, yams, taro roots, bananas; livestock inc. pigs and goats; considerable imports, few exports

■ FINANCE/TRADE

Currency: CFP franc

Western Sahara

Long-Form Name: Western Sahara
Capital: El Aaiún (since Western Sahara has been under Moroccan occupation, El Aaiún has lost its significance as a capital city)
Population: 200,000 (1993 est.); a further est. 165,000 Saharawis live in refugee camps in SW Algeria; large part of the population is nomadic

■ GEOGRAPHY

Area: 266,000 sq. km
Coastline: 1,110 km
Climate: Mediterranean to arid; hot, dry dessert; rain is rare; cold offshore air currents produce fog and heavy dew
Environment: desertification, sparse water and arable land; hot and dry and dust/sand-laden sirocco wind; harmattan haze
Terrain: mostly barren rocky desert
Land Use: 0% arable or permanent crops, 19% meadows and pastures, 0% forests, 81% other
Location: NW Africa, bordering on Atlantic Ocean

■ PEOPLE

Nationality: Sahrawi, Sahraoui
Ethnic Groups: Arabs, Berbers
Languages: Arabic, French, several Berber dialects
Religions: Islam (almost 100% Sunni Moslem)
Marriages: n.a.
Divorces: n.a.

■ GOVERNMENT

Leader(s): Pres. Mohammed Abdelaziz; Prime

Min. Mahfoud Ali Beiba
Government Type: under Moroccan occupation
Administrative Divisions: none (under de facto control of Morocco)
Independence: n.a.
National Holiday: n.a.

■ ECONOMY

Overview: economy severely disrupted by Moroccan occupation and ongoing guerrilla warfare; poor in natural resources and with inadequate rainfall, most food must be imported
GNP: n.a., GDP $60 million, $300 per capita; real growth rate n.a. (1991 est.)
Inflation: n.a.
Industries: phosphate mining, fishing, handicrafts
Labour Force: 12,000; 50% of the people are engaged in subsistence farming and animal husbandry
Unemployment: n.a.
Agriculture: limited to subsistence agriculture; some grain production, livestock (esp. sheep, goats, camels); cash economy exists largely for the garrison forces
Natural Resources: rich phosphate deposits, iron ore

■ FINANCE/TRADE

Currency: dirham (DH)
International Reserves Excluding Gold: n.a.
Gold Reserves: n.a.
Budget: n.a.
Defence Expenditures: n.a.
External Debt: n.a.
Exports: phosphates main export product
Imports: fuel for fishing fleet; most of the country's food supply must be imported

■ HEALTH

Births: 49/1,000 population (1993 est.)
Deaths: 21/1,000 population (1993 est.)
Infant Mortality: 155.5 deaths/1,000 live births (1993 est.)
Life Expectancy at Birth: 43.98 years male, 46.06 years female (1993 est.)
No. of Physicians: n.a.

■ EDUCATION

Govt. Expenditure: n.a.
Literacy: n.a.

■ COMMUNICATIONS

Daily newspapers: n.a.
Televisions: n.a.; 2 TV stations (1993)
Radios: n.a.; 2 radio stations (1993)
Telephones: 2,000 total (1993)

■ TRANSPORTATION

Motor Vehicles: n.a.
Roads: 6,200 km; 1,450 km surfaced (1993)
Railway: n.a.
Airports: 14 airfields, all usable; 3 have permanent-surface runways (1993).

Yemen

Long-Form Name: Republic of Yemen
Capital: Sana'a (political capital); Aden (commercial capital)
Population: 11,300,000 (1993 est.)

■ GEOGRAPHY

Area: 527,970 sq. km
Coastline: 1,906 km
Climate: hot, dry desert in the south to temperate in central region and north; harsh desert in the east
Environment: desertification, overgrazing, lack of natural fresh water, soil erosion
Terrain: narrow coastal plain; western mountains, northern desert interior
Land Use: 6% arable land; permanent crops negligible; 30% meadows & pastures; 7% forest & woodland; 57% other
Location: SW Asia (Middle East), bordering on Red Sea

■ PEOPLE

Nationality: Yemeni
Ethnic Groups: predominantly Arab; Afro-Arab, Indian, Somali and European minorities
Languages: Arabic
Religions: predominantly Moslem; Christian and Hindu minorities in the south
Marriages: n.a.
Divorces: n.a.

■ GOVERNMENT

Leader(s): Pres. Ali Abdallah Salih, V. Pres. Ali Salim al-Bid, Prime Min. Haydar Abu Bakr al-Attas
Government Type: republic
Administrative Divisions: 11 provinces in north, 6 governorates in south
Independence: May 22, 1990
National Holiday: Proclamation of the Republic, May 22

■ ECONOMY

Overview: future economic level depends heavily on Western assistance. North: low level of domestic industry, dependent on imports; South: economic growth among the poorest of all Arab countries
GNP: n.a., GDP $8 billion, per capita $775; real

growth rate n.a. (1992 est.)
Inflation: 100% (1992)
Industries: petroleum, cotton, textiles, leather goods, food processing, handicrafts, cement
Labour Force: 2,602,000; 62.5% agriculture, 11% industry, 26.4% services (1989)
Unemployment: 30% (1992)
Agriculture: in the north, agriculture accounts for 26% GDP and 7% of the labour force; main crops include fruit (grapes) and cotton; in the south, agriculture accounts for 17% GDP and 45% of the labour force; the main agricultural product is livestock (cattle, camels, sheep, goats, poultry)
Natural Resources: salt deposits, petroleum, fish, marble, coal, gold, lead

■ FINANCE/TRADE

Currency: during the transitional period following unification, the northern riyal and the southern dinar coexist
International Reserves Excluding Gold: North: $212 million, South: $58 million (1989)
Gold Reserves: North: n.a.; South: 0.04 million fine troy ounces (1988) n.a.
Budget: n.a.
Defence Expenditures: 20.57% of total govt. expenditure (1992)
External Debt: $5.040 billion (1990)
Exports: $908 million, inc. crude oil, cotton, coffee, animal hides, vegetables, cotton, animal hides, fish; partners: US, Japan, Singapore (1990)
Imports: $2.1 billion (1990), inc. textiles and other manufactured consumer goods, petroleum products, sugar, grain, flour, other foodstuffs, cement, grain, consumer goods, crude oil, machinery, chemicals; partners: nations of the former Soviet Union, UK, Ethiopia

■ HEALTH

Births: 53/1,000 population (1993)
Deaths: 21/1,000 population (1993)
Infant Mortality: 131/1,000 live births (1993)
Life Expectancy at Birth: 46 years male, 47 years female (1993)
No. of Physicians: North: 1.5/10,000 population (1990); South, n.a.

■ EDUCATION

Govt. Expenditure: 21.29% of govt. expenditure (1992)
Literacy: 38% (1993 est.)

■ COMMUNICATIONS

Daily newspapers: 4 (1992)
Televisions: 79/1,000 population (1992)
Radios: 188/1,000 population (1992)
Telephones: 65,000 total (1993 est.)

■ TRANSPORTATION

Motor Vehicles: 364,495; 145,390 psngr cars (1990)
Roads: 15,500 km; 4,000 km paved (1993)
Railway: n.a.
Air Traffic: 413,000 passengers carried (1991)
Airports: 45 airfields, of which 39 are usable; 10 have permanent-surface runways (1993)

Canadian Embassy: c/o Canadian Embassy, Diplomatic Quarter, Riyadh; mailing address: P.O. Box 94321, Riyadh 11693, Saudi Arabia. Tel: (011-966-1) 488-2288. Fax: (011-966-1) 488-1997
Representative to Canada: Embassy of the Republic of Yemen, 350 Sparks St, Ste 1100, Ottawa ON K1R 7S8. Tel: (613) 232-8525. Fax: (613) 232-8276.

Yugoslavia: see Serbia and Montenegro

Zaïre

Long-Form Name: Republic of Zaïre
Capital: Kinshasa
Population: 41,200,000 (1993 est.)

■ GEOGRAPHY

Area: 2,345,410 sq. km
Coastline: 37 km along South Atlantic Ocean
Climate: tropical; hot and humid in equatorial river basin; cooler and drier in southern highlands; cooler and wetter in eastern highlands
Environment: dense tropical rainforest in central river basin and eastern highlands; periodic droughts in south
Terrain: vast central basin is a low-lying plateau; mountains in east
Land Use: 3% arable; negligible permanent; 4% meadows; 78% forest; 15% other
Location: C Africa, just barely bordering on South Atlantic Ocean

■ PEOPLE

Nationality: Zairian
Ethnic Groups: over 200 African ethnic groups, the majority are Bantu; four largest tribes–Mongo, Luba, Kongo (all Bantu) and the Mangbetu-Azande (Hamitic)–make up 45% of the population
Languages: French (official), Lingala, Swahili, Kinggwana, Kikongo, Tshiluba
Religions: 50% Roman Catholic, 20% Protestant, 10% Kimbanguist, 10% Moslem, 10% other syncretic sects and traditional beliefs
Marriages: n.a.
Divorces: n.a.

■ GOVERNMENT

Leader(s): Prime Min. Etienne Tshisekedi, Pres.

Marshal Mobutu Sese Seko
Government Type: republic with a strong presidential system
Administrative Divisions: 10 regions and 1 town
Independence: June 30, 1960 (from Belgium; formerly known as Belgian Congo, then Congo/Leopoldville, then Congo/Kinshasa)
National Holiday: Anniversary of the Regime (Second Republic), Nov. 24

■ ECONOMY

Overview: despite large mineral resources and one of the most developed and diversified economies in Sub-Saharan Africa, the country has a very low per capita GDP; hyperinflation, the largest government deficit ever, and dropping mineral production have made Zaïre one of the world's poorest countries; increases in prices for copper and other minerals should help the economy
GNP: n.a., GDP $9.2 billion, per capita $235; real growth rate -6% (1992)
Inflation: 4,129.2% (1992)
Industries: mining, mineral processing, consumer products (including textiles, footwear and cigarettes), processed foods and beverages, cement, diamonds
Labour Force: 13,080,000 (1992); 71.5% agriculture, 12.9% industry, 15.6% services (1989)
Unemployment: n.a.
Agriculture: cash crops: coffee, palm oil, rubber, quinine; food crops: cassava, bananas, root crops, corn
Natural Resources: cobalt, copper, cadmium, crude oil, industrial and gem diamonds, gold, silver, zinc, manganese, tin, germanium, uranium, radium, bauxite, iron ore, coal, hydroelectric potential

■ FINANCE/TRADE

Currency: new zaire (NZ)
International Reserves Excluding Gold: $152 million (Nov. 1993)
Gold Reserves: 0.03 million fine troy ounces (Dec. 1993)
Budget: revenues $685 million; expenditures $1.1 billion, excludes capital expenditures largely funded by foreign aid donors (1990)
Defence Expenditures: $66.82 million (1988)
External Debt: $9.2 billion (1992 est.)
Exports: $426 million (1992); commodities: copper 37%, coffee 24%, diamonds 12%, cobalt, crude oil; partners: US, Belgium, France, Germany, Italy, UK, Japan
Imports: $420 million (1992); commodities: consumer goods, foodstuffs, mining and other machinery, transport equipment, fuels; partners: US, Belgium, France, Germany, Italy, Japan, UK

■ HEALTH

Births: 48/1,000 population (1993)
Deaths: 15/1,000 population (1993)
Infant Mortality: 98 deaths/1,000 live births (1993)
Life Expectancy at Birth: 50 years male, 53 years female (1993)
No. of Physicians: 0.7/10,000 population (1992)

■ EDUCATION

Govt. Expenditure: 6.4% of govt. expenditure (1988)
Literacy: 71.8% (1993)

■ COMMUNICATIONS

Daily newspapers: 7 (1992)
Televisions: 0.9/1,000 inhabitants (1992)
Radios: 101/1,000 inhabitants (1992)
Telephones: 0.09/100 inhabitants (1992)

■ TRANSPORTATION

Motor Vehicles: 190,000; 100,000 passenger cars (1990)
Roads: 146,500 km; 2,800 km paved (1993)
Railway: 5,254 km
Air Traffic: 150,000 passengers carried (1991)
Airports: 281 airfields, of which 235 are usable; 25 have permanent-surface runways (1993)

Canadian Embassy: The Canadian Office, c/o The Embassy of the United States of America, 310 avenue des Aviateurs, Kinshasa, Zaïre. Tel: (011-243-12) 21-532. Fax: (011-871-12) 43-805
Representative to Canada: 18 Range Rd, Ottawa, ON K1N 8J3. Tel: (613) 236-7103. Fax: (613) 236-9166.

Zambia

Long-Form Name: Republic of Zambia
Capital: Lusaka
Population: 8,600,000 (1993 est.)

■ GEOGRAPHY

Area: 752,610 sq. km
Coastline: none: landlocked
Climate: tropical; modified by altitude; rainy season (Oct. to Apr.)
Environment: deforestation; soil erosion; desertification
Terrain: mostly high plateau with some hills and mountains
Land Use: 7% arable; negligible permanent crops; 47% meadows; 27% forest; 19% other
Location: SC Africa

■ PEOPLE

Nationality: Zambian

Ethnic Groups: 98.7% African, 1.1% European, 0.2% other
Languages: English (official); about 70 indigenous languages
Religions: 50–75% Christian, 24-49% Moslem and Hindu, remainder indigenous beliefs
Marriages: n.a.
Divorces: n.a.

■ GOVERNMENT

Leader(s): Pres. Frederick Chiluba, Vice-Pres. Levy Mwanawasa
Government Type: republic
Administrative Divisions: 9 provinces
Independence: Oct. 24, 1964 (from UK; formerly known as Northern Rhodesia)
National Holiday: Independence Day, Oct. 24

■ ECONOMY

Overview: economy continues to decline due to a sustained drop in copper production and ineffective economic policies; problems include a high inflation rate, high population growth and severe drought
GNP: n.a., GDP $4.7 billion, per capita $550; real growth rate -3% (1992 est.)
Inflation: 170% (1992 est.)
Industries: copper mining and processing, transport, construction, foodstuffs, beverages, chemicals, textiles and fertilizer
Labour Force: 2,640,000 (1992); 37.9% agriculture, 7.8% industry, 54.9% services (1989)
Unemployment: 15,896 (1989)
Agriculture: accounts for 17% of GDP and 85% of labour force; crops: corn (food staple), sorghum, rice, peanuts, sunflower, tobacco, cotton, sugar cane, cassava; cattle, goats, beef, eggs produced; marginally self-sufficient in corn
Natural Resources: copper, cobalt, zinc, lead, coal, emeralds, gold, silver, uranium, hydropower potential

■ FINANCE/TRADE

Currency: kwacha (K)
International Reserves Excluding Gold: $54 million (Sept. 1993)
Gold Reserves: 0.00 million fine troy ounces (1991)
Budget: revenues $1.5 billion; expenditures $1.5 billion, including capital expenditures of $300 million (1991)
Defence Expenditures: $186.01 million (1989)
External Debt: $7.6 billion (1991)
Exports: $1.168 billion (1992); commodities: copper, zinc, cobalt, lead, tobacco; partners: European Community, Japan, South Africa, US
Imports: $870 million (1992); commodities: machinery, transportation equipment, foodstuffs, fuels, manufactures; partners: European

Community, Japan, South Africa, US

■ HEALTH

Births: 48/1,000 population (1993)
Deaths: 17/1,000 population (1993)
Infant Mortality: 107 deaths/1,000 live births (1993)
Life Expectancy at Birth: 46 years male, 47 years female (1993)
No. of Physicians: 1.4/10,000 population (1992)

■ EDUCATION

Govt. Expenditure: 8.7% of govt. expenditure (1990)
Literacy: 73% (1993)

■ COMMUNICATIONS

Daily newspapers: 3 (1992)
Televisions: 24.6/1,000 inhabitants (1992)
Radios: 74/1,000 inhabitants (1992)
Telephones: 1.2/100 inhabitants (1992)

■ TRANSPORTATION

Motor Vehicles: 165,000; 98,000 passenger cars (1990)
Roads: 36,370 km; 6,500 km paved (1993)
Railway: 1,266 km (1993)
Air Traffic: 293,000 passengers carried (1991)
Airports: 116 airfields, of which 104 are usable; 13 have permanent-surface runways (1993)

Canadian Embassy: The Canadian High Commission, 5199 United Nations Ave, Lusaka; mailing address: P.O. Box 31313, 10101 Lusaka, Zambia. Tel: (011-260-1) 26-10-07. Fax: (011-260-1) 26-11-72
Representative to Canada: High Commission for the Republic of Zambia, 130 Albert St, Ste 1610, Ottawa ON K1P 5G4. Tel: (613) 563-0712. Fax: (613) 235-0430.

Zimbabwe

Long-Form Name: Republic of Zimbabwe
Capital: Harare
Population: 10,700,000 (1993 est.)

■ GEOGRAPHY

Area: 390,580 sq. km
Coastline: none: landlocked
Climate: tropical; moderated by altitude; rainy season (Nov. to Mar.)
Environment: recurring droughts; floods and severe storms are rare; deforestation; soil erosion; air and water pollution; desertification
Terrain: mostly high plateau with higher central plateau (high veld); mountains in east
Land Use: 7% arable; negligible permanent; 12%

meadows; 62% forest; 19% other
Location: SC Africa

■ PEOPLE

Nationality: Zimbabwean
Ethnic Groups: 98% African (71% Shona, 16% Ndebele, 11% other), 1% white, 1% mixed and Asian
Languages: English (official); Shona and Ndebele
Religions: 50% syncretic (part Christian, part indigenous beliefs), 25% Christian, 24% indigenous beliefs, a few Moslem
Marriages: n.a.
Divorces: n.a.

■ GOVERNMENT

Leader(s): Exec. Pres. Robert Mugabe, V. Pres. Joshua Nkomo, Simon Vengesai Muzenda
Government Type: parliamentary democracy
Administrative Divisions: 8 provinces
Independence: Apr. 18, 1980 (from UK; formerly known as Southern Rhodesia)
National Holiday: Independence Day, Apr. 18

■ ECONOMY

Overview: the growth rate has been uneven in recent years due to year-to-year fluctuations in agricultural production; mining accounts for only 5% of GDP and employment, but supplies of minerals and metals make up 40% of exports; the annual population growth rate is running higher than economic growth
GNP: n.a., GDP $6.2 billion, per capita $545; real growth rate -10% (1992 est.)
Inflation: 46.3% (1992)
Industries: mining, steel, clothing and footwear, chemicals, foodstuffs, fertilizer, beverages, transportation equipment, wood products
Labour Force: 3,921,000 (1992); 64.7% agriculture, 5.6% industry, 29.7% services (1989)
Unemployment: at least 35% (1993 est.)
Agriculture: accounts for approximately 13% of GDP; 40% of land area divided into 4,500 large commercial farms and 42% in communal lands; crops: corn (food staple), cotton, tobacco, wheat, coffee, sugar cane, peanuts; livestock: cattle, sheep, goats, pigs; self-sufficient in food
Natural Resources: coal, chromium ore, asbestos, gold, nickel, copper, iron ore, vanadium, lithium, tin

■ FINANCE/TRADE

Currency: Zimbabwe dollar ($Z)
International Reserves Excluding Gold: $476 million (Jan. 1994)
Gold Reserves: 0.46 million fine troy ounces (Jan. 1994)
Budget: revenues $2.7 billion; expenditures $3.3 billion, including capital expenditures of $330 million (1991)
Defence Expenditures: $361.45 million (1990)
External Debt: $3.9 billion (1993)
Exports: $1.315 billion (1991); commodities: agriculture 34% (tobacco 21%, other 13%), manufactures 19%, gold 11%, ferrochrome 11%, cotton 6%; partners: Europe 55% (European Community 41%, Netherlands 6%, other 8%), Africa 22% (South Africa 12%, other 10%), US 8%, Japan 4%
Imports: $2.043 billion (1991); commodities: machinery and transportation equipment 37%, other manufactures 22%, chemicals 16%, fuels 15%; partners: European Community 31%, Africa 29% (South Africa 21%, other 8%), US 8%, Japan 4%

■ HEALTH

Births: 41/1,000 population (1993)
Deaths: 11/1,000 population (1993)
Infant Mortality: 59 deaths/1,000 live births (1993)
Life Expectancy at Birth: 54 years male, 57 years female (1993)
No. of Physicians: 1.4/10,000 population (1992)

■ EDUCATION

Govt. Expenditure: 23.45% of govt. expenditure (1989)
Literacy: 67% (1993)

■ COMMUNICATIONS

Daily newspapers: 2 (1992)
Televisions: 26.6/1,000 inhabitants (1992)
Radios: 85/1,000 inhabitants (1992)
Telephones: 3.23/100 inhabitants (1992)

■ TRANSPORTATION

Motor Vehicles: 260,000; 178,000 passenger cars (1990)
Roads: 85,237 km; 15,800 km paved (1993)
Railway: 2,775 km
Air Traffic: 606,000 passengers carried (1991)
Airports: 485 airfields, of which 403 are usable; 22 have permanent-surface runways (1993)

Canadian Embassy: The Canadian High Commission, 45 Baines Ave, Harare; mailing address: P.O. Box 1430, Harare, Zimbabwe. Tel: (011-263-4) 73-38-81. Fax: (011-263-4) 73-29-17
Representative to Canada: High Commission of the Republic of Zimbabwe, 332 Somerset St W, Ottawa ON K2P 0J9. Tel: (613) 237-4388. Fax: (613) 563-8269.

ASTRONOMY AND SPACE

Astronomy has taught us that the universe is more complex than the ancients thought. Though less dependent on the "patterns" in the sky, we continue the exploration. The skies act not simply as a guide, but have become our latest frontier.

The Solar System

The solar system consists of the sun, at least nine planets and smaller bodies such as asteroids, comets and moons. The dominant member of this family is the sun, our nearest star. The sun is an enormous ball of hot, glowing gas, mostly hydrogen and helium. Its powerful pull of gravity holds the planets, asteroids and comets in orbit around it.

The planets have been known since people first turned their gaze skyward. The ancient Greeks called them "wanderers" because they moved through the sky relative to the fixed stars. Five planets can be seen without a telescope: Mercury, Venus, Mars, Jupiter and Saturn. They are visible because they reflect the light of the sun.

Until 1999, in order of distance from the sun, the planets are Mercury, Venus, Earth, Mars, Jupiter, Saturn, Uranus, Pluto and Neptune. Pluto is *usually* the most remote planet, over seven billion kilometres from the sun at its maximum distance, but from 1979 to 1999, its strange orbit brings it closer to the sun than Neptune.

All the planets revolve (orbit) around the sun in the same counter-clockwise direction. The closer to the sun, the greater their speed. Except for Pluto, all the orbits lie in nearly the same plane in space, like marbles rolling on a table top.

Our Place in the Universe Although the solar system seems enormous, it is quite small compared to the whole universe. Our sun is only one star among the hundreds of billions that make up our spiral-shaped galaxy, the **Milky Way**. It takes our sun, with planets in tow, about 250 million years to orbit around the Milky Way just once. All the stars that we see at night are in a small, nearby portion of our galaxy. There may be billions of galaxies in the universe, each containing billions of stars of its own.

The Birth of the Solar System Approximately 4.6 billion years ago, (billions of years after the galaxies were formed), astronomers believe that a vast cloud of gas and dust collapsed and formed a spinning disk. Gravitation compacted so much material in the centre that extremely high pressures and temperatures lit a nuclear fire—our sun began to shine. Meanwhile, any remaining lumps of hot solids and gases slowly collected to become the planets, moons, asteroids and comets.

Our Solar System The planets of the solar system can be divided into two groups. The inner planets, Mercury, Venus, Earth and Mars, are the **terrestrial**, or Earth-like, planets. These are small rocky worlds with metal cores and thin atmospheres, except for airless Mercury. Jupiter, Saturn, Uranus and Neptune make up the realm of the **gas giants**. These planets do not have a solid surface, but are made up of layers of gases and clouds, possibly with rocky cores the size of Earth. The gas giants are huge: a thousand Earths could easily fit inside Jupiter. Saturn's rings may be the most famous feature of the solar system but rings are also found around Jupiter, Uranus and Neptune.

Pluto is unique and does not fit into either of these two groups. It is a tiny world of rock and ice, smaller than the Earth's moon, and with an extremely thin atmosphere.

Separating the terrestrial planets from the gas giants is the **asteroid belt**, a region of space between Mars and Jupiter where as many as 50 000 rocky objects may orbit the sun. Asteroids, often called minor planets, range from gravel-size, or smaller, to the 1000-km-wide Ceres. They may be the remains of a small, shattered planet.

Over 50 moons, or satellites, are found in the solar system. All the planets, except for Mercury and Venus, have at least one moon orbiting them. Some of these moons are fascinating worlds in their own right: **Phobos** and **Deimos**, the moons of Mars, may be captured asteroids; **Io**, one of Jupiter's moons, has many active volcanoes; **Europa**, another one of Jupiter's moons, may have a subterranean ocean; **Titan**, a moon of Saturn, has an atmosphere thicker than Earth's. Jupiter with its 16 known moons, Saturn with its 18 and Uranus with its 15 are like miniature solar systems.

Exploring the Solar System Most of the planets have been visited by space probes from Earth: Mercury was visited in 1974 by *Mariner 10*, Soviet *Venera* spacecraft landed on Venus several times in the 1970s while *Viking 1* and 2 landed on Mars in 1976. The best spacecraft views of Jupiter and Saturn were obtained by *Voyager 1* and 2 in 1979 and 1980/81 respectively. *Voyager 2* went on to Uranus in 1986 and Neptune in August 1989. These spacecraft made discoveries unobtainable from the Earth: craters on Mercury, volca-

noes and great valleys on Mars, Jupiter's ring and 10 new moons of Uranus were only a few.

Recent missions include the *Galileo* orbiter/atmospheric penetrator (Jupiter) and *Magellan* radar mapper (Venus), both of which were launched in 1989. *Magellan*'s mission is now complete. The probe has returned exquisitely-detailed images of the Venusian surface through the use of its imaging radar. *Galileo* is expected to reach Jupiter in December 1995. The *Ulysses* mission, launched in 1990, will send a space probe over the poles of the Sun in 1995 and 1996. The combined NASA/ESA (European Space Agency) *Cassini* mission to Saturn is expected to fly by Jupiter in the year 2000. Stereo imaging of Jupiter will be possible at that time as *Galileo* will still be in operation.

Solar System at a Glance

	Distance from Sun (million km)	Equatorial diameter (km)	Gravity (Earth=1)	Mass (Earth=1)	Period of Orbit about the Sun	Period of Rotation on Axis (days)	Number of known Moons
Sun	—	1 392 000	27.9	332 830	—	25.38	—
Mercury	57.9	4 878	0.38	0.06	88.0 days	58.60	0
Venus	108.2	12 104	0.91	0.8	224.7 days	243.00	0
Earth	149.6	12 756	1.00	1.0	365.3 days	0.99	1
Mars	227.9	6 787	0.38	0.1	1.88 years	1.02	2
Jupiter	778.4	142 800	2.54	317.8	11.86 years	0.41	16
Saturn	1 423.8	120 000	1.08	95.2	29.63 years	0.42	18
Uranus	2 868.7	51 200	0.91	14.5	83.97 years	0.45	15
Neptune	4 492.1	48 680	1.19	17.2	164.80 years	0.67	8
Pluto	5 926.5	2 300	0.06	0.002	248.63 years	6.38	1

Source: *Global Atlas, Gage Educational Publishing Co.; Observer's Handbook, 1991, The Royal Astronomical Society of Canada*

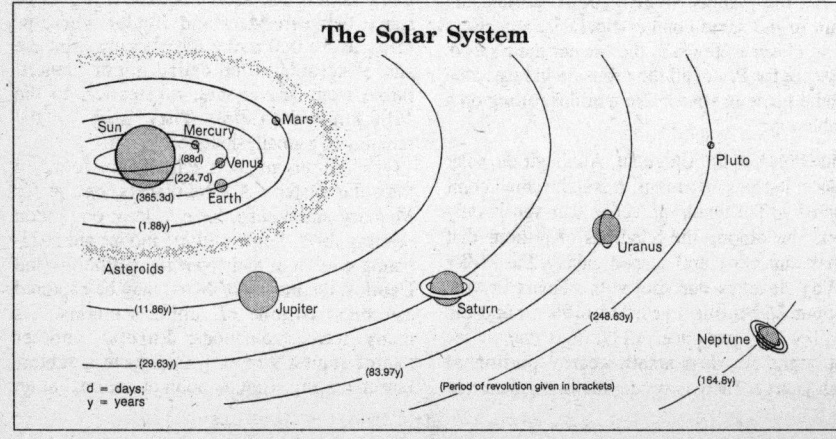

The Solar System

d = days; y = years

(Period of revolution given in brackets)

Jupiter: Profile of a Planet

The Planet Jupiter, the largest planet in the solar system, is a massive, colourful world composed mostly of hydrogen and helium in liquid form. It has more than twice the mass of all the other planets combined and its diameter is 11 times that of the earth. Appropriately, Jupiter is named for the most powerful of the Roman gods.

Jupiter is covered by dense layers of clouds, made largely of ammonia ice crystals and ammonium hydrosulfide. The atmosphere is 1 000 km thick and permanently hides deeper layers of the planet from our view. Jupiter rotates very quickly, once every ten hours, and this rapid motion pulls the orange, red, white and brown clouds into colourful swirls and long belts that run parallel to the equator. These belts are constantly moving with winds reaching 540 km/hour, twice as fast as the most severe hurricanes on Earth. Flashing through the clouds are giant lightning bolts and brilliant auroras.

The "surface" of Jupiter has never been seen, but it is thought to be entirely covered by a sluggish ocean of liquid hydrogen, something not found on the Earth. The pressure generated by the weight of the massive atmosphere and liquid hydrogen is unimaginable. Some 25 000 km beneath the clouds, the pressure is equivalent to three million Earth atmospheres and the temperature reaches 11 000°C. At the cloud tops, the temperature is a frosty -70°C.

Jupiter probably has a central core of rocky material which is about the size of the Earth, but this is not known for certain. Temperatures there are 30 000°. This tremendous heat is left over from the time of Jupiter's formation. If Jupiter had grown to be 10 times larger than its present size, it would have been a small star.

In 1979, the *Voyager* space probe discovered a tiny, thin ring around Jupiter. This ring is made largely of pieces of rock ranging in size from hundreds of metres across to tiny specks.

Surface Features Jupiter has no permanent, visible features; any solid surface is hidden by the dense atmosphere and clouds which are in constant motion. One feature that has existed for over 300 years, however, is the Great Red Spot. The GRS is a giant, red whirlpool the size of three Earths side-by-side. It is not a fixed feature, though, as it has altered its shape, colour and position over the years and has even occasionally faded from view.

Moons Jupiter has at least 16 moons. The four largest are planet-size, while the remaining 12 are mostly less than 100 km in diameter.

Io (3 630 km in diameter) has no visible craters. Instead, it has at least seven volcanoes that are continually erupting sulfur, giving this moon its unique orange, red and black colour. Sulfur lakes may also be present.

Because of a thick sheath of ice, **Europa** (3 140 km) is the smoothest object in the solar system and completely craterless. Under the ice, there may be an ocean of water hundreds of kilometres deep.

Ganymede (5 260 km) is the largest moon in the solar system (larger than the planet Mercury). Its surface is a mixture of ice and rock, and is heavily cratered in some areas.

Callisto (4 800 km) has a composition similar to Ganymede, but most of its surface consists of ice.

Exploring Jupiter The first visits to Jupiter by a spacecraft were made by *Pioneer 10* in 1973 and *Pioneer 11* in 1974. Both probes provided a great deal of information about Jupiter's magnetic field, its moons and the complex nature of the colourful cloud system. Five years later, *Voyager 1* and *2* flew by the planet. They discovered Jupiter's ring and studied the motions of the clouds and the Great Red Spot. Both the *Pioneer* and the *Voyager* probes sent back images of Jupiter and its moons. *Pioneer 11* and *Voyager 1* and *2* continued on and past Saturn. *Ulysses* flew by the planet en route to the Sun in 1992. *Galileo*, which will fly by Jupiter in 1995-6, will be able to make the closest observations possible of the July 1994 Comet Shoemaker-Levy 9 collision site. Although *Galileo*'s large antenna (its main link to Earth) failed to open fully, the back-up antenna will be able to record crash site data. Stereo imaging of Jupiter will be possible in the year 2000, as *Galileo* will still be in operation when the combined NASA/European Space agency *Cassini* mission passes the planet.

Some Astronomical Terms

Asteroid Any of the thousands of small, rocky objects that orbit the Sun. Some pass closer to the Sun than Earth does and others have orbits that take them well beyond Jupiter. The largest asteroid is one called Ceres.

Big Bang The primeval explosion that most astronomers think gave rise to the universe as we see it today, in which clusters of galaxies are moving apart from one another. Astronomers calculate the Big Bang happened about 15 to 20 billion years ago.

Black Hole An object whose gravitational pull is so strong that—within a certain distance of it— nothing can escape, not even light. Black holes are thought to result from the collapse of certain very massive stars, but other kinds have been postulated as well: **mini black holes,** for example, which might have been formed in the turbulence shortly after the Big Bang. **Supermassive black holes**—with masses millions of times the Sun's—may exist in the cores of large galaxies.

Comet A small chunk of ice, dust and rocky material (a few kilometres across) which, when it comes close enough to the Sun, can develop a tenuous "tail." The tail of a comet is made of gas and dust that have been driven off the comet's surface by the Sun's energy. The tail always points away from the Sun (no matter in what direction the comet is moving).

Eclipse The blocking of all or part of the light from one object by another.

Galaxy A large assemblage of stars (and sometimes interstellar gas and dust), typically containing millions to hundreds of billions of member stars. A galaxy is held together by the gravitational attraction of its member stars (and other material) to one another.

Light-Year The distance light travels in one year in a vacuum. Since light travels at a speed of about 300 000 km per second, a light-year is roughly 9.5 trillion km long.

Magnitude A way of expressing the brightness of astronomical objects, inherited from the Greeks. In the magnitude system, a lower number indicates a brighter object (for example, a 1st-magnitude star is brighter than a 3rd-magnitude star). Each step in magnitude corresponds to a brightness difference of about 2.5. Stars of the 6th magnitude are the faintest the unaided human eye can see.

Meteor A bit of solid debris from space, burning up in the Earth's atmosphere because of friction with the air. Before entering Earth's atmosphere, the body is called a meteoroid. If any of the object survives its fiery passage through the air, the parts that hit the ground are called **meteorites.**

Milky Way Galaxy A spiral galaxy, with a disk approximately 100 000 light-years across, containing roughly 400 billion stars. Our Sun is in the disk about two-thirds of the way from the centre. It takes about 200 million years to orbit the centre of the Milky Way once.

Neutron Star A crushed remnant left over when a very massive star explodes. Some neutron stars are known to spin very rapidly, at least at the beginning, and can be detected as **pulsars**: rapidly flashing sources of radio radiation or visible light. The pulses are produced by the spinning of a neutron star, much as a lighthouse beacon appears to flash off, on and off.

Nova A star that abruptly and temporarily increases its brightness by a factor of hundreds of thousands.

Orbit The path of one body around another (such as the Moon around the Earth) or around the centre of gravity of a number of objects (such as the Sun's 200-million-year path around the centre of our galaxy).

Planet A major object that orbits around a star.

Quasar One of a class of very distant (typically billions of light years away), extremely bright, and very small objects. Quasar means "quasi-star"— that is, something that looks like a star but can't actually be a star.

Red Giant A very large distended, and relatively cool star in the final stages of its life.

Solar System The Sun and all things orbiting it, including the nine major planets, their satellites, and all the asteroids and comets.

Supernova An explosion that marks the end of a very massive star's life. When it occurs, the star can outshine all the other stars in a galaxy in total for several days, and may leave behind a crushed core (perhaps a neutron star or a black hole).

White Dwarf The collapsed remnant of a relatively low-mass star (roughly one and a half times the Sun's mass and less), which has exhausted the fuel for its nuclear reactions and shines only by radiating its stored up heat.

Source: *The Astronomical Society of the Pacific, San Francisco, CA*

The Sky in 1995

Prepared by Ian G. McGregor, Educator
McLaughlin Planetarium, Toronto

■ The Planets

Mercury This elusive planet is never seen more than 28 degrees from the Sun and as a result most of the year the planet is too close to the Sun to be observed. Of the six apparitions of the planet in 1995, the evening appearance in the west after sunset during early January is good and in April, a second even better evening appearance will take place. As a morning object, only Mercury's appearance in the east before sunrise in the mid-autumn is favourable for observers.

Venus Like Mercury, the planet's position in the solar system means Venus never gets far from the Sun for Earth-based observers. Venus begins the year as a brilliant "morning star" in the east before sunrise and is visible low in the east until the early spring. As the months pass the planet disappears into the Sun's glare and is in superior conjunction on August 20. Venus emerges from the Sun's glare in the west after sunset in the autumn and becomes noticeable as a brilliant evening star by late in the season.

Mars The famous "Red Planet" comes to opposition in 1995, an event which occurs every two years, when the faster moving Earth overtakes Mars. At this time, Mars appears opposite the Sun in the sky and the planet is at its minimum distance from the Earth for the two year period. However, the 1995 opposition of Mars is the worst one in the period from 1980 to early into the 21st century as the planet is near its maximum distance from the Sun in March. Mars begins the year moving westwards relative to the background stars and after looping through the stars of Leo the Lion the planet resumes its motion to the west in April. After this, Mars fades in brightness and by year end the planet is in Sagittarius and disappearing into the sun's glare at sunset.

Jupiter Jupiter and Venus appear as two brilliant "stars" in the east before sunrise with Venus much the brighter object. Slow-moving Jupiter spends much of the year in the constellation of Scorpius as it moves roughly one zodiacal constellation per year through the sky. By June, the giant planet has reached opposition and will rise in the east as the Sun sets and will be visible all night long as a bright evening star for most of the summer. By the late summer, Jupiter will be disappearing into the Sun's glare. The planet is in conjunction with the Sun in December.

Saturn The famous ringed planet begins the year among the dim stars of Aquarius and it remains in Aquarius for the entire year. Saturn takes 29.5 years to complete one orbit of the Sun. During this time the appearance of the rings as seen from Earth gradually changes. The year 1987 marked the maximum inclination (27 degrees) of the north side of the rings to the Sun but this year the rings are presented to us edge-on and for part of the year are invisible. As a result at the time when Saturn reaches opposition in September and is visible all night long, Saturn will be much fainter than it usually is at opposition.

Uranus, Neptune and Pluto Uranus and Neptune had their first observed conjunction in 1993 in Sagittarius but these planets are so slow moving that they are still fairly close together in the sky in Sagittarius two years later. Uranus is slowly moving ahead of Neptune and the two planets will next be in conjunction in 170 years! Uranus is near the limit of naked-eye visibility and binoculars or telescopes are needed to see Neptune. Neptune is at opposition on July 17 and Uranus on July 21.

Pluto is currently closer to the Sun than Neptune but the tiny planet is very faint as it spends much of the year looping through the background stars along the Libra-Ophiuchus border. In 1999, Pluto will cross Neptune's orbit and resume being the outermost planet. The planet is at opposition on May 20.

Outer Solar System Objects Since 1992, astronomers have discovered a number of objects orbiting the Sun beyond the orbit of Neptune. Whether they should be called planets, asteroids or comets is still under debate. Currently, the six which have been found are no larger than about 200 km in size. They are moving in roughly circular orbits at distances between 35 and 50 astronomical units from the Sun. An astronomical unit is the average distance of the Earth from the Sun. For comparison, Neptune is about 30 astronomical units and Pluto about 40 astronomical units from the Sun. These newly-discovered objects lend observational support to the theory proposed almost 40 years ago that a reservoir of comets known as the "Kuiper Belt" exists just beyond the region occupied by the planets. More discoveries are expected.

▶ ■ **Events**

January

3-4	Quadrantid meteor shower (rate: 40-100/hour)
4	Earth at perihelion (147 099 900 km from the Sun)
13	Venus at greatest western elongation
14	Jupiter and Venus in conjunction in the east before sunrise
18-22	Mercury visible in west after sunset

February

12	Mars at opposition

March

6	Saturn in conjunction with the Sun
13	Mars at aphelion
20	Spring equinox (9:16 pm EST)

April

2	All provinces except Saskatchewan set clocks ahead one hour as of 2 am for daylight savings time. (Saskatchewan uses standard time all year long.)
13	Venus and Saturn in conjunction in Aquarius
15	Partial lunar eclipse (see Eclipse section)
22-23	Lyrid meteor shower (rate: 10-15/hour)
29	Annular solar eclipse (see Eclipse section)
30-May 21	Mercury visible in west after sunset

May

5-6	Eta Aquarid meteor shower (rate: 20/hour)

June

1	Jupiter at opposition in Scorpius
21	Summer solstice at 4:35 pm EDT

July

3	Earth at aphelion (152 102 400 km from the Sun)
29-30	South Delta Aquarid meteor shower (rate: 15-20/hour)

August

12-13	Perseid meteor shower (rate: 50/hour). The almost Full Moon will seriously interfere with the observation of this year's shower.

September

14	Saturn at opposition in Aquarius
23	Autumnal equinox (8:15 am EDT)

October

8	Penumbral lunar eclipse (see Eclipse section)
16-Nov 26	Mercury in east before sunrise
22-3	Orionid meteor shower (rate: 25/hour)
24	Total solar eclipse (see Eclipse section)
29	All provinces except Saskatchewan set clocks back one hour at 2 am for a return to standard time

November

3-5	Southern Taurid meteor shower (rate: 15/hour)
17-18	Leonid meteor shower (rate: 10-15/hour)

December

14	Geminid meteor shower (rate: 95 meteors/hour)
18	Jupiter in conjunction with the Sun
22	Winter solstice (3:19 am)

Phases of the Moon

(Eastern Standard Time)

New Moon		First Quarter		Full Moon		Last Quarter	
		Jan. 8	3:47 pm	Jan. 16	3:27 pm	Jan. 23	11:59 pm
Jan. 30	5:48 pm	Feb. 7	7:55 am	Feb. 15	7:16 am	Feb. 22	8:05 am
Mar. 1	6:49 am	Mar. 9	5:15 am	Mar. 16	9:26 am	Mar. 23	3:11 pm
Mar. 30	9:09 pm	Apr. 8	00:36 am	Apr. 15	8:09 am	Apr. 21	11:19 pm
Apr. 29	1:37 pm	May 7	5:45 pm	May 14	4:49 pm	May 21	7:36 am
May 29	5:28 pm	June 6	6:27 am	June 13	00:04 am	June 19	6:02 pm
June 27	8:51 pm	July 5	4:04 pm	July 12	6:50 am	July 19	7:11 am
July 27	11:15 am	Aug. 3	11:17 pm	Aug. 10	2:17 pm	Aug. 17	11:04 pm
Aug. 26	00:33 am	Sept. 2	5:04 am	Sept. 8	11:38 pm	Sept. 16	5:10 pm
Sept. 24	12:56 pm	Oct. 1	10:36 am	Oct. 8	11:53 am	Oct. 16	12:27 pm
Oct. 24	00:37 am	Oct. 30	4:18 pm	Nov. 7	2:21 pm	Nov. 15	6:41 pm
Nov. 22	10:44 am	Nov. 29	1:29 am	Dec. 6	8:28 pm	Dec. 15	00:33 am
Dec. 21	9:24 pm	Dec. 28	2:07 pm				

Source: *McLaughlin Planetarium, Toronto*

Organizations

Canadian Astronomical Society (CAS): An organization of professional astronomers. Contact: Norman Broten, CAS Secretary, 48 Pineglen Crescent, Nepean, Ontario K2E 6X9.

Planetarium Association of Canada (PAC): Organization of planetariums across Canada. Contact: Phil Mozel, PAC Secretary, c/o McLaughlin Planetarium, 100 Queen's Park, Toronto, Ontario M5S 2C6.

Royal Astronomical Society of Canada (RASC): The Society is devoted to the advancement of astronomy and the allied sciences and has twenty-two centres across Canada. Address: 136 Dupont Street, Toronto, Ontario M5R 1V2 Tel: (416) 924-7973.

Did You Know?

I n the weightless conditions of space flight, the absence of gravity causes astronauts to increase in height by as much as 7cm.

Eclipses in 1995

There are four eclipses of the Sun and Moon which take place in 1995. None are visible from North America. The April 29 eclipse across South America is similar to the May 10, 1994 eclipse across North America.

April 15	**Partial lunar eclipse**
	Visible from Pacific Ocean, Australia and eastern Asia
April 29	**Annular solar eclipse**
	Path of annularity goes through Ecuador, Peru and Brazil. All of South America experiences a partial eclipse. Maximum duration of annularity is 6 minutes 37 seconds.
October 8	**Penumbral lunar eclipse**
	Visible across central and eastern Asia and Australia
October 24	**Total solar eclipse**
	Path of totality goes through Iran, India and Thailand. All of central and eastern Asia and most of Australia experience a partial eclipse. Maximum duration of totality is 2 minutes 10 seconds.

Source: *McLaughlin Planetarium, Toronto*

Space Junk

T he consequence of thirty-five years of space exploration, more than 22,300 trackable pieces of space junk remain in orbit around the Earth. Of that number about 7,000 satellites have been catalogued but only 400-500 are active. The rest are used rocket bodies, dead payloads, leftover junk (such as optics covers and discarded payload hardware), and debris resulting from years of rocket and payload fragmentation. Space junk poses an ever increasing hazard to spacecraft. Objects only 1mm in diameter travelling at 10 km/sec can penetrate most satellites and spacecraft.

The behaviour of debris in orbit is closely monitored and "close approach" warnings are issued by the Space Defense Operations Centre in the US. An alert for collision avoidance is issued when two objects are within 5-8 km of each other. Shuttles are required to undertake avoidance procedures when debris is predicted within 2 km radially, 5 km downtrack, or 2 km out of orbital plane. Estimates are that space station "Freedom" would be required to make 20 such manoeuvres annually. The worst feature of the debris hazard is that there are now many thousands of pieces too small to be tracked, mostly resulting from the more than 100 explosions in space.

Common Space Terms

Deploy To place something into position.

End Effector A robotic grasping device, for example, the "hand" of Canadarm.

Extravehicular Activity (EVA) Work done outside the pressurized part of the spacecraft.

Flyby The passage of a spacecraft past a moon or planet, without going into orbit.

Footprint The area on the Earth's surface within which a satellite's signal can be received.

Geosynchronous Orbit (geostationary) An orbit, about 35 900 km above the Earth's equator, in which a satellite revolves around the Earth at the same rate as the Earth rotates on its axis. Consequentially, the satellite appears to be stationary over a point on the Earth's surface.

Ionosphere Region of the Earth's atmosphere made up of several layers of ionized gases.

Magnetosphere The region above the ionosphere in which the Earth's magnetic field forms a magnetic shell around our planet. The outermost region of our atmosphere, it contains the Van Allen Belts.

Orbiter The reusable, main section of the shuttle that carries the crew and payload.

Payload The cargo carried by a rocket or spacecraft.

Propellants The fuels and oxidizers burned in rocket engines to produce thrust.

Spacecraft Any vehicle designed to operate in space (placed in orbit or on a trajectory to another celestial body).

Space Shuttle The shuttle is a multipurpose vehicle which carries cargo to and from space.

Thrust The propulsive force produced by a rocket engine during firing.

Transponder A radio repeater (receives a signal and transmits a response) carried on board communications satellites.

Van Allen Radiation Belt Two belts of high-energy charged particles trapped in the Earth's magnetic field. These doughnut-shaped zones are the source of the Aurora Borealis and the Aurora Australis.

Weightlessness The condition in which no weight, caused by gravity or any other force, can be detected. A spacecraft in orbit falls endlessly around Earth or some other body, so that it and everything inside it is in freefall or weightless.

Major Satellite and Space Probe Launches

Space probes and satellites are instrument-carrying devices. Often overshadowed by crewed space-flight, theinformation they transmit has been the "engine" of space research.

Name	Launch	Accomplishment
Sputnik 1	Oct. 4, 1957	First artificial satellite to orbit Earth (USSR)
Explorer 1	Feb. 1, 1958	First US satellite; discovered Van Allen radiation belt
Score	Dec. 18, 1958	First satellite to send a recorded human voice into space (US)
Luna 3	Oct. 4, 1959	First photographic images of the dark side of the moon (USSR)
Tiros 1	Apr. 1, 1960	First weather satellite; crude cloud cover images (US)
Echo 1	Aug. 12, 1960	First communications satellite; voice and TV signals relayed by bouncing off satellite—a large balloon (US)
SO 1	Mar. 7, 1962	Orbiting Solar Observatory collected data on about 75 solar flares (US)
Telstar 1	July 10, 1962	Allowed first direct transmission of television images between the United Kingdom and the United States (US)
Mariner 2	Aug. 27, 1962	First successful interplanetary probe; passed Venus on Dec. 14 (109 days after launch) (US)
Alouette 1	Sept. 29, 1962	Launch of Canada's first satellite; first designed and built by a nation other than the US or the USSR; satellite gathered information on the ionosphere
Tiros 8	Dec. 21, 1963	Weather satellite carrying Automatic Picture Transmission (APT) equipment; allows local pictures to be received, using inexpensive portable ground stations (US)
Ariel 2	Mar. 27, 1964	First satellite to sample global distribution of ozone (UK/US)
Syncom 3	Aug. 19, 1964	First communications satellite in truly geostationary orbit (US)
Nimbus 1	Aug. 28, 1964	Earth orientation of weather satellite allows complete global cloud cover pictures every 24 hours; operated for 26 days (US)

▶

Name	Launch	Accomplishment
► **Early Bird 1**	Apr. 6, 1965	First commercial communications satellite; marked the beginning of global communications systems (US)
Molniya 1	Apr. 23, 1965	First Soviet communications satellite
Venera 3	Nov. 16, 1965	First space probe to make physical contact with another planet; probe crash landed on Venus (USSR)
Luna 9	Jan. 31, 1966	First photographic images transmitted from the surface of the Moon to Earth (USSR)
Surveyor 1	May 30, 1966	First successful soft lunar landing of a test vehicle (US)
Venera 7	Aug. 17, 1970	First probe to return signals from surface of Venus (USSR)
Mars 3	May 28, 1971	First soft landing of a probe on Mars (USSR)
Mariner 9	May 30, 1971	Enters Mars orbit on Nov. 13, and returns photographic images to Earth (US)
Pioneer 10	Mar. 3, 1972	First probe to explore Jupiter and its environment, and first to leave our solar system (US)
Landsat 1	July 23, 1972	First major Earth resources satellite; such satellites obtain (ERTS) information on Earth's land use, forestry, mineral, water and marine resources (US)
Anik A	Nov. 9, 1972	First domestic communications satellite in geostationary orbit (Canada)
Hermes (CTS)	Jan. 17, 1976	High-power communications satellite; first to demonstrate feasibility of direct-to-home television (Canada/US)
Voyager 2	Aug. 20, 1977	First scientific probe to study Jupiter and Saturn, including their satellites and the Rings of Saturn; first to flyby Uranus and Neptune; passed Neptune in late summer 1989 (US)
Seasat	June 26, 1978	Remote sensing satellite designed to study ocean currents and ice flow (US)
Solar Max	Feb. 14, 1980	Mission to study Sun activity during a period of maximum (SMM-A) activity for solar flares; failed satellite captured, repaired and successfully relaunched in April 1984 by astronauts on STS 41C shuttle mission (US)
SPOT	Feb. 21, 1986	*Système Probataire d'observation de la Terre*—remote sensing satellite designed to record surface detail images of Earth; the area can be as small as 10 metres square (France)
Hubble Space Telescope	Apr. 24, 1990	First optical telescope to be placed in orbit around Earth; on deployment encountered difficulty in opening aperture door of telescope; in partial operation only (US)
GRO	Apr. 4, 1991	Gamma Ray Observatory is heaviest satellite deployed from an orbiter, released from Atlantis by the Canadarm; satellite investigating the sources of gamma rays in outer space (US)
UARS	Sept. 12, 1991	Upper Atmosphere Research Satellite deployed to collect substantial information on Earth's upper atmosphere, including the ozone layer (US)

Crewed Spaceflights—Selected Firsts

Mission	Launch	First
Vostok 1	Apr. 12, 1961	First person in space; Soviet cosmonaut, Yuri Gagarin
Freedom 7	May 5, 1961	First American in space; Alan Shepherd with a sub-orbital flight of 15 min.
Friendship 7	Feb. 20, 1962	First orbital flight by an American; John Glenn, 3 orbits
Vostok 6	June 16, 1963	First woman in space; Valentina Tereshkova, 48 orbits
Voskhod 2	Mar. 18, 1965	First space walk; Soviet cosmonaut Aleksei Leonov
Gemini 4	June 3, 1965	First US space walk; first use of personal propulsion unit
Gemini 6-A	Dec. 15, 1965	First space capsule rendezvous; comes within 2 m of Gemini 7
Gemini 10	July 18, 1966	First dual rendezvous; first docked vehicle maneuvers
Apollo 8	Dec. 21, 1968	First spacecraft in orbit about the Moon
Apollo 11	July 16, 1969	First lunar landing; Neil Armstrong places first footprints on the Moon on July 20
Soyuz 10	Apr. 23, 1971	First space station; cosmonauts dock with Salyut 1
Skylab 2	May 25, 1973	First Skylab launch with crew; established the Skylab orbital assembly in Earth orbit, and conducted a series of medical experiments

Mission	Launch	First
Soyuz 34	June 6, 1979	First spacecraft to be launched without a crew, and to return with a crew (from Salyut 6)
STS-1	Apr. 12, 1981	First space shuttle flight; Columbia proves reusable orbiter viable; first US landing on land
STS-5	Nov. 11, 1982	First deployment of satellites from a shuttle orbiter
STS-7	June 18, 1983	First use of Canadarm (Remote Manipulator System), deployed two communications satellites on second flight of Challenger; Sally Ride becomes first American woman in space
STS-41B	Feb. 3, 1984	First untethered space walks
Soyuz T-12	July 18, 1984	First woman to walk in space; Svetlana Savitskaya
STS-41G	Oct. 5, 1984	First Canadian in space; Marc Garneau, as a payload specialist, carried out a series of experiments onboard the sixth flight of Challenger
STS-31	Apr. 24, 1990	First optical telescope placed in Earth orbit; Hubble Space Telescope launched from Discovery.
STS-61	Dec. 2, 1994	First Hubble Telescope servicing mission complete success.

Canadian Achievements in Space Technology

Alouette Canada launched its first satellite on September 9, 1962. **Alouette 1** was the first satellite to return useful information on the ionosphere, the layer of the upper atmosphere that affects long-distance radio transmissions. Although designed to last one year, the satellite successfully transmitted data for over a decade.

STEM Antenna The STEM (storage tubular extendible member) antenna was designed at the National Research Council for **Alouette**. It consisted of a thin ribbon of steel rolled onto a spool for launch and then extended to form a long tube in orbit. Later produced by Spar Aerospace for NASA, STEMs were used on early spacecraft, including a sub-orbital flight in 1961.

Anik Canada was the first country to launch a satellite for domestic communications. In 1972, **Anik A-1** made nation-wide, real-time television possible. Reliable telephone service came to the North for the first time. Despite a setback in 1994, Anik satellites continue to provide services to television networks, telephone systems to the Arctic, and allow a national newspaper to transmit copy to five printing plants across the country.

Hermes Canada worked with the United States on an experimental communications satellite system launched in 1976. Designed and built in Canada, **Hermes** operated at 10 times the power of previous communications satellites. Hermes proved that powerful satellites could bring low-cost television directly to remote areas anywhere on the globe. Teleconferencing was now feasible, and the world's first teleconferencing trials were carried out.

Canadarm Canadarm is the remote manipulator system designed and made in Canada for the US space shuttle program. It enables NASA astronauts to take satellites from their orbiter's cargo bay and position them accurately in space; is also designed to grapple satellites already in orbit and place them in the cargo bay for return to Earth. Operated by two hand controls from the comfort of the orbiter's cabin, Canadarm is one of the most advanced robots in existence.

Canadarm was developed by the National Research Council in coordination with Spar Aerospace in Toronto, and made its first flight in 1981.

Canada's Astronauts

*A*ll Canadians were invited to enter a nation-wide competition to become astronauts and 4 300 applied. In December 1983, six were chosen. Two have since resigned and four more were appointed in June 1992, for a total of eight. The Canadian astronauts are research scientists who fly as payload specialists on shuttle missions. Trained by NASA in flight procedures, they operate NASA payloads, as well as their own. Canada's astronauts are: Marc Garneau, Major Chris Hadfield, Steve MacLean, Captain Michael McKay, Julie Payette, Bob Thrisk, Bjarni Tryggvason and Dave Williams.

Constellations

Constellations are groups of stars that we on Earth see as patterns in the sky. Each pattern is named for a person, an animal or an object, usually from Greek mythology.

Astronomers use constellations to map directions in space. When citing a constellation to locate a star, astronomers use the possessive form instead of the common name; for example, Cancer (The Crab) is referred to as Cancri.

The largest constellation is Hydrus, followed by Virgo and Ursa Major. The smallest is Crux.

Constellation	Meaning
Andromeda	Daughter of Cassiopeia
Antlia	The Air Pump
Apus	Bird of Paradise
Aquarius	The Water-bearer
Aquila	The Eagle
Ara	The Altar
Aries	The Ram
Auriga	The Charioteer
Bootes	The Herdsman
Caelum	The Chisel
Camelopardalis	The Giraffe
Cancer	The Crab
Canes Venatici	The Hunting Dogs
Canis Major	The Big Dog
Canis Minor	The Little Dog
Capricornus	The Horned Goat
Carina	The Keel
Cassiopeia	The Queen
Centaurus	The Centaur
Cepheus	The King
Cetus	The Whale
Chamaeleon	The Chameleon
Circinus	The Compasses
Columba	The Dove
Coma Berenices	Berenice's Hair
Corona Australis	The Southern Crown
Corona Borealis	The Northern Crown
Corvus	The Crow
Crater	The Cup
Crux	The Cross
Cygnus	The Swan
Delphinus	The Dolphin
Dorado	The Goldfish
Draco	The Dragon
Equuleus	The Little Horse
Eridanus	A River
Fornax	The Furnace
Gemini	The Twins
Grus	The Crane (bird)
Hercules	The Son of Zeus
Horologium	The Clock
Hydra	The Water Snake (f)
Hydrus	The Water Snake (m)
Indus	The Indian

Constellation	Meaning
Lacerta	The Lizard
Leo	The Lion
Leo Minor	The Little Lion
Lepus	The Hare
Libra	The Balance
Lupus	The Wolf
Lynx	The Lynx
Lyra	The Lyre
Mensa	Table Mountain
Microscopium	The Microscope
Monoceros	The Unicorn
Musca	The Fly
Norma	The Square
Octans	The Octant
Ophiuchus	The Serpent-bearer
Orion	The Hunter
Pavo	The Peacock
Pegasus	The Winged Horse
Perseus	Rescuer of Andromeda
Phoenix	The Phoenix
Pictor	The Painter
Pisces	The Fishes
Piscis Austrinus	The Southern Fish
Puppis	The Stern
Pyxis	The Compass
Reticulum	The Reticle
Sagitta	The Arrow
Sagittarius	The Archer
Scorpius	The Scorpion
Sculptor	The Sculptor
Scutum	The Shield
Serpens	The Serpent
Sextans	The Sextant
Taurus	The Bull
Telescopium	The Telescope
Triangulum	The Triangle
Triangulum Australe	The Southern Triangle
Tucana	The Toucan
Ursa Major	The Great Bear[1]
Ursa Minor	The Little Bear[2]
Vela	The Sails
Virgo	The Maiden
Volans	The Flying Fish
Vulpecula	The Fox

(1) Commonly known as the Big Dipper. (2) Commonly known as The Little Dipper

Observatories in Canada

◼ Maritime Region:

Burke-Gaffney Observatory: Saint Mary's University, Halifax, NS B3H 3C3. Open: Oct.-Mar., Sat. 7 pm; Apr.-Sept., Sat. 9 pm. Mon. eve. or day tours by arrangement. Tel: (902) 420-5633.

◼ Central Canada:

David Dunlap Observatory: Richmond Hill, Ont. L4C 4Y6. open Tues. mornings 10 am throughout the year, Sat. evenings Apr.-Oct. by reservation. Tel: (416) 884-2112.

Helen B. Hogg Observatory: National Museum of Science and Technology. 1867 St. Laurent Blvd. Ottawa, Ont. K1A 0M8. Open: Oct.-June. Group tours Mon.-Thurs., Public visits Fri. (in French 2nd Fri.); Jul.-Aug.: Public visits: Tues. (French), Wed., Thurs. (English). Eve. tours by appt only. Tel: (613) 991-3073.

Hume Cronyn Observatory: University of Western Ontario, London, Ont. N6A 3K7. Tel: (519) 661-3183.

Observatoire astronomique du mont Mégantic: Notre-Dame-des-Bois, Que. J0B 2E0. Tel: (514) 343-6718 (information on summer programs).

Science North Solar Observatory: 100 Ramsey Lake Rd., Sudbury, Ont. P3A 2K3. Viewing of the solar spectrum and the Sun in hydrogen-alpha and white light in a darkened theatre. Open most days. Tel: (705) 522-3701.

◼ Western Canada:

Climenhaga Observatory: Dept. of Physics and Astronomy, University of Victoria, Victoria, BC V8W 2H2. Tel: (604) 388-0001. Open daily.

Rothney Astrophysical Observatory: Physics and Astronomy Dept., University of Calgary, Calgary, Alta. T2N 1N4. Tel: (403) 220-5385.

Dominion Astrophysical Observatory: 5071 West Saanich Rd., Victoria, BC V8X 4M6. Open: May-Aug., daily 9:15 am-4:30 pm; Sept.-Apr., Mon.-Fri. 9:15 am-4:30 pm. Public observing: Sat. eve., Apr.-Oct. Tel: (604) 497-5321.

Dominion Radio Astrophysical Observatory: Penticton, BC V2A 6K3. Conducted tours: Sun., July-Aug. only, 2-5 pm. Visitors' centre open year-round during daytime. Tel: (604) 497-5321.

Gordon MacMillan Southam Observatory: 1100 Chestnut St., Vancouver, B.C. V6J 3J9. Open Fri.-Sun., and statutory holidays 12 pm- 5 pm and 7 pm-11 pm, weather and volunteer staff permitting. Tel: (604) 738-2855.

Devon Observatory: Dept. of Physics, University of Alberta, Edmonton, Alta. T6G 2J1.

University of Saskatchewan Observatory: Saskatoon, Sask. S7N 0W0. Tel.: (306) 966-6434.

University of British Columbia Observatory: 2219 Main Mall, Van., BC V6T 1W5. Free public observing on clear Sat. eve. Tel: (604) 224-6186 (observing) or (604) 228-2802 (tours).

Planetariums

◼ Maritime Region:

Burke-Gaffney Planetarium: Saint Mary's University, Department of Astronomy, Halifax, NS B3H 3C3.

The Halifax Planetarium: The Education Section of the Nova Scotia Museum. Summer St., Halifax, NS B3H 3A6. Tel: (902) 429-1610. Located in the Sir James Dunn Building, Dalhousie Univeristy. Free public shows given on some evenings at 8 p.m. Group shows can be arranged.

◼ Central Canada:

Doran Planetarium: Laurentian University, Ramsey Lake Rd., Sudbury, Ont. P3E 2C8. tel: (705) 675-1151, ext. 2222.

Dow Planetarium: 1000 St. Jacques St. W., Montreal, Que. H3C 1G7. Tel: (514) 872-4530. Live shows in French and English. Open daily.

London Regional Children's Museum: 21 Wharncliffe Rd. S., London, Ont. N6J 4G5. Tel. (519) 434-5726. Features a planetarium.

McLaughlin Planetarium: 100 Queen's Park, Toronto, Ont. M5S 2C6. Tel: (416) 586-5736 (for show times) or (416) 586-5751 (for sky information). Public shows Tues.-Fri. at 3:00 and 7:30. Additional shows on weekends and during summer. School shows. Astrocentre with solar telescope, and evening courses are available.

Seneca Planetarium: Seneca College, 1750 Finch Ave. E. Willowdale, Ont. M2J 2X5. Tel: (416) 491-5050. Entrance fee. Open winter, spring and fall.

◼ Western Canada:

Calgary Centennial Planetarium: Alberta Science Centre, 701-11 St. S.W., P.O. Box 2100, Stn. M. Calgary, Alta. T2P 2M5. Tel: (403) 284-4060 or 221 3700.

Edmonton Space Sciences Centre: Coronation Park, 1121-142 St., Edmonton. Alta T5M 4A1. Tel: (403) 451-7722 or 452-9100. Features planetarium Star Theatre, IMAX film theatre, exhibit galleries, telescope shop and bookstore. Open daily.

H.R. MacMillan Planetarium: 1100 Chestnut St., Vancouver, B.C. V6J 3J9. Tel: (604) 736-3656. Open daily.

Manitoba Planetarium: Museum of Man and Nature. 190 Rupert Ave., Winnipeg, Man. R3B 0N2. Tel: (204) 956-2830 (switchboard). Shows daily except some Mondays. Museum gift shop has scientific books and equipment.

The Lockhart Planetarium: 394 University College, 500 Dysart Rd., Univesity of Manitoba, Winnipeg, Man. R3T 2M8. Tel: (204) 474-9785. By reservation only.

EARTH SCIENCES

The earth sciences include **geology** (the study of earth's origin and composition), **ocean-ography** (the study of ocean water, currents, life-forms and the ocean floor), **paleontology** (the study of fossils and ancient life-forms), and **meteorology** (the study of earth's atmosphere, including weather and climate). This section includes material on geology and paleontology. Meteorology can be found in the section on Climate (pp.11-29).

The Geological Survey of Canada

The Geological Survey of Canada (GSC) is Canada's first scientific agency, and one of the first of its kind in the world. The agency was created to survey and map mineral deposits in Canada's nearly 1 million square kilometres of land and freshwater lakes, and more than 6 million square kilometres of coastal boundaries.

The Survey began life in Montreal in 1842. Under the first director William Edmond Logan, a Canadian businessman turned geologist, its initial task was a search for coal, the main industrial fuel at the time. The search, throughout Upper and Lower Canada, was unsuccessful, but Logan did find mineable deposits of copper and other metallic minerals.

Soon Survey geologists were undertaking expeditions westward. In the 1880s another director, George Mercer Dawson, became a noted ethnologist in Western Canada, as well as pioneer geologist. His reports included observations of the Haida people of British Columbia. During his expeditions he took many photographs of settlements and totem poles, capturing a glimpse of a vanishing landscape.

In 1992 the Geological Survey marked its 150th anniversary. While the task of mapping Canada's geology remains its central focus, the computerized Survey of the 1990s is very different from the one started by Sir William Logan. The Survey now undertakes an ever-expanding range of research—from exploring questions related to global change to those concerning natural hazards such as earthquakes, landslides, volcanoes, floods and ground instability.

In the words of the GSC's former chief scientist, R.P. Riddihough, "They [GSC scientists] are pushing their science into new frontiers that are just as formidable as those that Logan faced, attempting to find out things that no one has ever found out before: When the Atlantic Ocean was closed many millions of years ago was Nova Scotia joined on to Spain? How far does the Canadian Shield stretch westwards under the Rocky Mountains? Is the Arctic really getting warmer? What happens when hot magma comes out under 2.5 km of sea water? Even though they are working with helicopters, submersibles, computers and electron microscopes, I am sure Logan would recognize their drive to explore and understand how the earth works so that all of us can better live on it."

For more information on the Geological Survey and its programs, contact: Communications Office, Geological Survey of Canada, 601 Booth Street, Ottawa, Ontatio K1A OE8.

Common Geological Terms

Continental shelf: Submerged edge of continent, extending to depths of less than 200 metres, and largely made up of sedimentary rock.

Earthquake: A sudden motion or trembling in the earth caused by the release of slowly accumulated strain along a fault line or through volcanic activity.

Echo Sounding: A determination of water depth by measuring the time required for a sonic or ultrasonic signal to travel to the bottom of a body of water and back to the ship emitting the signal.

Epicentre: Point on the earth's surface directly above the focus of an earthquake, usually the location of the most severe damage.

Erosion: Breakdown and wearing away of rocks on the earth's surface by the action of water, waves, glaciers, wind and underground water.

Fault: a fracture in the earth's crust along which there has been displacement of the rock on either side, relative to one another.

Geothermal energy: energy that can be extracted from the earth's internal heat, usually in the form of emissions of hot water, steam, and gas.

▶

▶ **Glacier:** a large ice mass formed on land by recrystallisation of compacted snow.

Ice Field: An extensive area of interconnected glaciers. An ice field is known as pack ice when floating on the sea.

Igneous Rock: Rock formed when a mass of molten magma cools and solidifies on or below earth's surface. One of three main classes of rock.

Magma: Molten rocky material (mostly silica) beneath the earth's surface. Reaching the surface red hot through volcanic activity, it cools and becomes lava.

Metamorphic Rock: Rock formed when preexisting rocks are altered by marked changes in temperature, pressure, or shearing stress. One of three major rock groups.

Sedimentary rock: Rock formed from the accumulation of loose material deposited by water, wind and ice, and solidified by compaction.

Seismograph: a device that records the seismic vibrations of an earthquake. The wave disturbances caused by earthquakes have different speeds and require different lengths of time to reach the surface.

Tectonic plates: Rigid outer layer of the earth's crust consists of about ten large plates, which "float" horizontally across the denser inner crust. The boundaries of these plates are zones of intense activity, and give rise to mountain building, volcanoes, changes in the ocean floor, and earthquakes.

Tsunami: Particular form of ocean wave produced by an earthquake in the ocean floor, noted for its destructive force.

Volcano: A vent in the earth's crust through which magma, rock fragments, dust, gases, and ash are ejected from below earth's surface.

Composition of the Earth

Core: The earth's core lies about 2,900 km below the surface, and consists of two layers: a solid inner core and an outer liquid layer. The inner core is a solid mass, 3,200 km in diameter, probably composed of compressed iron with small amounts of other metals such as nickel. The outer core (the only liquid layer) is about 3,470 km in radius and gives rise to earth's magnetic fields.

Mantle: Accounting for about 82% of earth's volume, the mantle is denser than the crust, and probably increases in density close to the core. The mantle extends from the core to about 90 km below the higher mountains, and to about 5 km beneath parts of the ocean crust.

Crust: The outside crust of planet earth ranges in thickness from 5 to 50 km. The relatively light, granite-like rock forming the continents overlies a thinner magnesium-iron layer that makes up the ocean floor. The continental blocks "float" on the denser layer forming the ocean bed.

Hydrosphere: A layer of water covering over 70% of the earth's crust, including all water on or near the surface of the planet.

Atmosphere: The lightest part of earth is the atmosphere, a gaseous envelope surrounding the planet. The atmosphere consists of nitrogen, oxygen, water vapour and argon. Less than 0.1% is composed of other gases. Gases have weight, so the atmosphere is densest near earth's surface, and thins towards the vacuum of space.

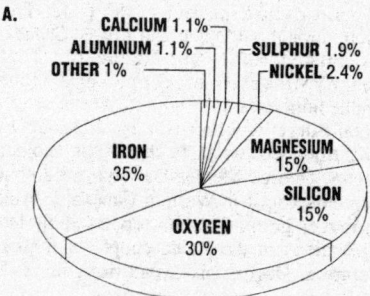

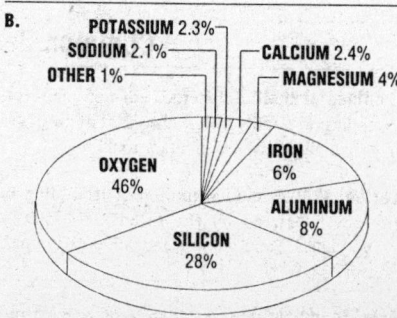

▲

Relative abundance of elements by weight of elements in the whole earth (A) and in the earth's crust (B).

LITHOPROBE: Probing Inner Space

Explorations of outer space have yielded an incredible amount of information on other planets. But what about our own? Lithoprobe, a pioneering earth sciences project launched in 1984, is probing Earth's outer shell to investigate our planet's "inner space." This geoscientific project is the largest in the world. More than 400 Canadian scientists from 28 universities and 13 provincial and federal agencies, as well the oil and mining industries are members of the multidisciplinary teams that include experts in seismology, geochemistry, geophysics, geology, geochronology, and remote sensing.

■ What is Lithoprobe?

The Lithoprobe project is examining the lithosphere (Earth's crust and outer mantle) that lies beneath Canada's landmass and surrounding oceans, down to depths of 100 km. The study hopes to reveal not only the present state of the lithosphere, but its evolution over more than 4 billion years. Its primary goal is to find out how the North American continent was formed. The results so far are changing geological models so much that geology textbooks will have to be rewritten.

Earth's lithosphere mostly consists of a mosaic of semi-rigid tectonic plates that move relative to each other, in different directions, and at rates ranging from one to ten cm a year. Their movement exerts stress on the lithosphere, resulting in faults and folding. For example, as rock foundations move against each other, some layers of rock are forced deep below, while others rise to the surface, giving birth to mountain ranges. Over billions of years, the constant collision, separation and side-slip of these plates, along with the accompanying recycling of earth material, have formed the planet's surface as we know it.

The lithosphere holds abundant stores of minerals, petroleum and natural gas, as well as geothermal energy. Knowing how the continent was formed not only shows scientists how mineral, oil and gas deposits form and where they lie, but helps them understand how earthquakes and volcanoes occur.

■ How Does the Project Work?

Spanning the country from Vancouver Island to Newfoundland and from the US border to the Yukon and Northwest Territories, Lithoprobe investigations are focused on ten carefully chosen study areas called transects. How were the sections chosen? Questions surrounding the convergence of two plates off the coast of British Columbia prompted the choice of that particular transect. Some geoscientists think the process ended millions of years ago; others believe it continues today.

The key method (but not the only one) being used by the research teams is called seismic reflection, and was adapted from the oil industry's more shallow investigations of sediments. Seismic reflection is an echo technique based on sonar, that is, bouncing sound waves off the boundaries between different types of material (either rock layers for crustal study, or water and bottom sediment for oceanic study). A pulse is produced on the surface. The resulting sound wave travels into the earth and back, bouncing against rock layers and other underground structures.

In the Lithoprobe project, researchers use 20-tonne trucks to generate sound waves. These so-called "thumper" trucks have been fitted with heavy vibrating platforms that emit pulses at specific frequencies, from 30 to 140 Hz.

Typically, a 50-person crew establishes survey points along a transect and plants groups of sensors (geophones) on the ground, at 50 m intervals over a 12 km length. Once the geophones are in place, four thumper trucks lower their vibrators in unison onto the surface at one survey point. The pulses travel into the Earth where they bounce off rock layers and rebound. The speed at which the waves travel depends on the density and elasticity of the rocks they pulse through.

Each period of vibration lasts 14 sec. and is followed immediately by a 18-sec. listening time that allows the geophones pick up the echo of the sound waves and transmit them to the recording truck. The crew repeats the vibrate-and-listen process eight times at each survey point, then moves to the next site along the survey line.

The responses (echoes) received by the geophones are recorded by a truck-mounted computer system. Echo results are analysed by the computer which then generates an image of the subsurface. Using the cross-sectional depth information to construct a three-dimensional picture, the resulting image represents a vertical slice through rocks below. Just as physicians interpret X-rays, seismologists working with geologists, interpret the computer images. Thus, geoscientists are able to "see" down to 100 km below Earth's surface.

Some transects include investigations of the ocean floor, such as off the coasts of British Columbia and Newfoundland. Pulses, generated by compressed air, are used at sea, and the echos are captured by floating "hydrophone" sensors towed behind a ship.

■ What Are the Results?

Among the many findings to date are the following:

- In the case of mineral deposits, Lithoprobe has confirmed the theory that Ontario's nickel belt was formed by a meteorite impact.

- About 1.8 billion years ago, most of present day Saskatchewan and northern Manitoba was a distinct micro-continent, now named Saskasedes (foundation of Saskatchewan), surrounded by ocean. Evidence shows that two plates, the Archean Superior (southeast of the Saskatchewan-Manitoba border) and the Rae-Hearne Craton (extending northwest of the provinces), collided with each other. Saskasedes was sandwiched between the two and pushed deep down into the lithosphere. Undetected for millions of years, the continent lies beneath the new plate formation.

- About 1 100 million years ago, a section of Earth's crust thinned so much that North America almost split in two. Molten rock from the earth's mantle bubbled up through an enormous fissure. The Keeweenawan Rift System, 35 km deep at some points, is now buried well below the surface under Lake Superior and the midwestern United States. Over millions of years, this rift, the deepest on the planet, has been filled in by magma seeping up from below and sediments from the surrounding land surface. The cause of the fissure is not known. Even more puzzling, scientists do not know why the rifting stopped.

- Scientists now know that about 180 million years ago, several huge islands floated out of the Pacific Ocean and crashed into the existing western shore of North America. The resulting upheaval caused the land and the sea bed to heave, buckle and fold. Much of British Columbia's landmass was created in this way, as well as successive ranges of the Rocky Mountains. This explains the Burgess Shale deposit, where fossilized sea creatures have been found in the mountain tops.

- The process that added two-thirds of western British Columbia during the last 180 million years continues in 1995, as the heavy Juan de Fuca Plate continues to slide under the lighter North American one. Our continent acts like a bulldozer, pushing sediment resting on the ocean plate into hills and ridges hundreds of metres high. Some of the scraped-off sediment is "plastered" to the west side of the continent, while the rest of the plate returns to Earth's mantle. More than 1 100 metres beneath the surface, the plate melts—only to have the molten material rise again and add new material to the land mass. As a result, North America continues to expand westward. Indeed, the British Columbia landmass is slowly increasing.

For more information about The Lithoprobe Project, contact: Lithoprobe Secretariat, 357 Geological Sciences Centre, 6339 Stores Road, University of British Columbia, Vancouver, BC V6T 1Z4

Who Discovered The Earth's Solid Inner Core?

*I*n 1936, Danish Seismologist Inge Lehmann put forward the theory that Earth has a solid inner core. Her discovery grew out of the realization that some seismic data could not be explained if the Earth's core was entirely molten.

Earthquakes

Although the earth's surface seems completely stable, it is constantly moving and changing. Layers of rock in the earth's crust, called plates, push and pull each other until they bend or stretch.

Vibrations or "seismic waves" emanate from the source of the breakage out through the earth, causing the planet to quiver or ring like a tuning fork. The waves can be so minor that the quake will not be felt by humans, or so severe it will change the physical landscape of the area.

Earthquakes can happen all over the world, but they tend to reoccur along weaknesses in the crust, called faults. By studying the patterns of earthquakes, scientists determine the areas at greatest risk and compile the information in seismic zoning maps. In this way, building regulations can be applied to earthquake zones to minimize possible damage.

The most common method of measuring an earthquake's magnitude is the Richter Scale. It estimates the force from recordings of seismic waves taken by an instrument called a seismometer. the scale is logarithmic, so that each numeric reading is ten times greater in recorded amplitude.

The intensity of an earthquake can also be measured through the Modified Mercalli Scale. In addition to mechanical recordings, it uses witness accounts to describe the effects of an earthquake.

Measuring Earthquakes

Richter		Modified Mercali	
2.5	Generally felt, but not recorded.	I	Not felt except by a very few
		II	Felt only by a few persons at rest, especially on upper floors of buildings
3.5	Felt by many people.	III	Felt noticeably indoors. Standing cars may rock slightly. Most people do not recognize.
		IV	During daytime felt by many indoors, outdoors by a few. Dishes, windows and doors disturbed; walls creak. At night, some awaken. Sensation like a heavy truck passing.
		V	Felt by nearly everyone; many awakened. Some dishes and windows broken; some objects over-turned. Trees, poles and other tall objects disturbed.
4.5	Some local damage may occur.	VI	Felt by all, many run outdoors. Heavy furniture moves; occasionally plaster falls and chimneys damaged. Overall damage slight.
		VII	Everyone runs outdoors. Well-built structures suffer negligible damage; slight to moderate damage in well-built homes; poorly constructed buildings suffer considerable damage. Noticed by people in moving cars.
6.0	A destructive earthquake	VIII	Damage slight in specially designed structures; considerable in ordinary substantial buildings, with partial collapse; great in poorly-built structures. Chimneys fall. Heavy furniture overturned. Disturbs people driving cars. Sand and mud ejected in small amounts.
		IX	Damage to specially designed structures considerable. Buildings shifted off foundations. Conspicuous ground cracks. Underground pipes broken.

▶

Richter		Modified Mercali
7.0	A major earthquake, about 10 occur each year	**X** Some well-built wooden structures destroyed; most masonry and frame structures destroyed. Ground badly cracked. Rails bent. Landslides considerable.
8.0	Great earthquake, occurs once every five to 10 years	**XI** Few masonry structures remain standing. Bridges destroyed. Broad fissures in ground. Underground pipelines out of service. Earth slumps, and land slips in soft ground.
		XII Damage total. Waves seen on ground surface. Lines of sight and levels distorted. Objects thrown upward into air.

World's Major Earthquakes

Date	Location	Deaths	Magnitude
1902 Dec. 16	Turkestan	4500	—
1905 Apr. 4	India, Kangra	19000	8.6
1905 Sep. 8	Italy, Calabria	2500	7.9
1906 Jan. 31	Colombia	1000	8.9
1906 Mar. 17	Formosa, Kaji	1300	7.1
1906 Apr. 18	U.S., San Francisco	700	8.5
1906 Aug. 17	Chile, Santiago	20000	8.6
1907 Jan. 14	Jamaica, Kingston	1600	6.5
1907 Oct. 21	Central Asia	12000	8.1
1908 Dec. 28	Italy, Messina	83000	7.5
1912 Aug. 9	Marmara Sea	1950	7.8
1915 Jan. 13	Italy, Avezzano	29980	7.5
1920 Dec. 16	China, Gansu	100000	8.6
1923 Sep. 1	Japan, Kwanto-Tokyo-Yokohama	143000	8.3
1925 Mar. 16	China, Yunnan	5000	7.1
1927 Mar. 7	Japan, Tango	3020	7.9
1927 May 22	China, near Xining	200000	8.3
1929 May 1	Iran	3300	7.4
1930 July 23	Italy	1430	6.5
1932 Dec. 25	China, Gansu	70000	7.6
1933 Mar. 2	Japan, Sanriku	2990	8.9
1934 Jan. 15	India, Behar-Nepal	10700	8.4
1935 Apr. 20	Formosa	3280	7.1
1935 May 30	Pakistan, Quetta	30000	7.6
1939 Jan. 25	Chile, Chillan	28000	8.3
1939 Dec. 26	Turkey, Erzincan	30000	7.6
1943 Sep. 10	Japan, Tottori	1190	7.4
1944 Dec. 7	Japan, Tonankai	1000	8.3
1945 Jan. 12	Japan, Mikawa	1900	7.1
1946 May 31	Turkey	1300	6.0
1946 Nov. 10	Peru, Ancash	1400	7.3
1946 Dec. 20	Japan, Tonankai	1330	8.4
1948 June 28	Japan, Fukui	5390	7.3
1949 Aug. 5	Ecuador, Ambato	6000	6.8
1950 Aug. 15	India, Assam, Tibet	1530	8.7
1954 Sep. 9	Algeria, Orleansville	1250	6.8
1956 June 9	Afghanistan	350–400	7.6
1957 July 2	Iran	1200	7.4
1957 Dec. 13	Iran	1130	7.3
1960 Feb. 29	Morocco, Agadir	15000	5.9
1960 May 22	Chile	5000	7.3
1963 July 26	Yugoslavia, Skopje	1100	6.0
1964 Mar. 27	Southern Alaska	131	9.2
1966 Aug. 19	Turkey, Varto	2520	7.1
1968 Aug. 31	Iran	20000	7.3

▶

Date		Location	Deaths	Magnitude
1969	July 25	Eastern China	3000	5.9
1970	Mar. 28	Turkey, Gediz	1100	7.3
1970	May 31	Peru	66000	7.8
1972	Apr. 10	Southern Iran	5054	7.1
1972	Dec. 23	Nicaragua, Managua	5000	6.2
1975	Sep. 6	Turkey	2300	6.7
1976	Feb. 4	Guatemala	23000	7.5
1976	May 6	Northeastern Italy	1000	6.5
1976	June 25	Western Iran	422	7.1
1976	July 27	China, Tangshan	255000	8.0
1976	Aug. 16	Philippines, Mindanao	8000	7.9
1976	Nov. 24	Northwest Iran-USSR	5000	7.3
1977	Mar. 4	Romania	1500	7.2
1977	Nov. 23	Argentina, San Juan Prov.	70	7.4
1978	Sep. 16	Iran	15000	7.8
1979	Dec. 12	near coast of Ecuador	600	7.9
1980	Oct. 10	Algeria	3500	7.7
1980	Nov. 23	Southern Italy	3000	7.2
1981	June 11	Southern Iran	3000	6.9
1981	July 28	Southern Iran	1500	7.3
1982	Dec. 13	Western Arabian Peninsula	2800	6.0
1983	Oct. 30	Turkey	1342	6.9
1985	Mar. 3	near coast of central Chile	177	7.8
1985	Sep. 19	Mexico, Michoacan	9500	8.1
1986	Oct. 10	El Salvador	1000	5.5
1987	Mar. 6	Colombia-Ecuador	1000	7.0
1988	Aug. 20	Nepal-India	1450	6.6
1988	Dec. 7	Turkey-USSR	25000	7.0
1989	Oct. 18	U.S., Southern California	62	7.1
1990	Apr. 26	China, Qinghai Province	126	6.9
1990	May 30	Northern Peru	135	6.5
1990	June 20	Western Iran	50000	7.7
1990	July 16	Luzon, Philippine Islands	1621	7.8
1990	Nov. 6	Southern Iran	22	6.8

Source: *Energy, Mines and Resources Canada*

Major Earthquakes in Canada, 1970–92*

Date	Location	Magnitude	Damage
1970 June 24	West of Vancouver Island	7.0	
1971 March 13	West of Vancouver Island	6.4	
1971 March 26	Yukon—Alaska Border	5.8	
1972 July 5	West of Vancouver Island	5.7	
1972 July 23	West of Vancouver Island	5.8	
1972 July 30	Southeast Alaska. Felt in BC and the Yukon	7.6	
1972 Nov. 21	Melville Island NWT	5.7	
1973 July 1	Southeast Alaska. Felt in BC and the Yukon	6.1	
1974 Oct. 16	East of Newfoundland	5.8	
1975 Oct. 6	South of Newfoundland	5.7	
1976 Feb. 23	West of Vancouver Island	6.0	
1976 Dec. 20	West of Vancouver Island	6.7	
1978 June 2	West of Vancouver Island	5.7	

▶

Date	Location	Magnitude	Damage
▶ 1979 Feb. 28	Yukon—Alaska Border	7.2	Minor
1980 Dec. 17	West of Vancouver Island	6.8	
1982 May 15	West of Vancouver Island	5.7	
1983 June 28	Yukon—Alaska Border	6.0	
1983 Oct. 28	Southern Utah. Felt in southern BC and Alberta	7.3	
1984 June 24	West of Vancouver Island	5.8	
1985 Oct. 5	Mackenzie Mountains, NWT	6.6	Major landslides
1985 Dec. 23	Mackenzie Mountains, NWT	6.9	
1987 Nov. 17	Gulf of Alaska. Felt in BC and the Yukon	6.9	
1987 Nov. 23	Yukon—Alaska Border	5.7	
1987 Nov. 30	Gulf of Alaska. Felt in BC and the Yukon	7.6	
1987 Nov. 30	Gulf of Alaska	5.9	
1987 Dec. 1	Gulf of Alaska	5.7	
1988 March 6	Gulf of Alaska. Felt in BC and the Yukon	7.6	
1988 March 6	Gulf of Alaska	6.2	
1988 March 25	Mackenzie Mountains, NWT	6.0	
1988 Nov. 25	southern Quebec	6.5	Widespread minor damage
1989 March 13	northern Quebec	5.7	
1989 Dec. 25	northern Quebec	6.1	
1990 July 11	BC—Alaska Border	5.8	
1991 Dec. 19	west of Vancouver Island	5.7	
1992 Jan. 2	west of Vancouver Island	6.0	
1992 Jan. 4	Keewatin District, NWT	6.0	
1992 April 6	west of Vancouver Island	6.8	
1992 April 6	west of Vancouver Island	6.0	
1992 April 23	west of Vancouver Island	5.7	
1992 Aug. 7	Gulf of Alaska. Felt in the Yukon	6.5	

Source: *Geophysics Division, Geological Survey of Canada*   *Earthquakes in or near Canada with a magnitude of 5.7 or higher.

Worldwide Earthquakes, per year

Magnitude	Average number	Magnitude	Average number
8	2	5	3 000
7	20	4	15 000
6	100	3	more than 100 00

Source: *Energy, Mines and Resources Canada*

Geological Time Periods

The story of planet earth is one of continuous change. Fossils, rock records and radioactive dating show three marked changes in the patterns of plant and animal life. These times of change in the most recent 570 million years of the earth's history are divided by geologists into three eras: Paleozoic (ancient life); Mesozoic (age of reptiles); and Cenozoic (age of mammals). The more than 4 billion years before the start of the Paleozoic era are referred to as Precambrian time. Each geological unit is divided further: the eras into periods, the periods into epochs.

The names of the time periods are taken either from the geographic locality where the fossil information was best displayed or first studied, or from some characteristic of the geological formations. For example, the Jurassic period is named from the Jura Mountains of France and Switzerland, and the Carboniferous is named from the coal-bearing sedimentary rocks.

Era	Period	Epoch	Years Ago	Changes and Characteristics
Precambrian Time			4.5 bil.?	Cooling and melting of the earth's crust. Evidence of bacteria, the first known living things, about 3.5 billion years ago.
Paleozoic	Cambrian		575 mil.	Seas spread across North America. First fishes appear. Greatest development of invertebrates.
	Ordovician		480 mil.	Floods sometimes cover two-thirds of North America. Jawless fish appear. Algae become plentiful.
	Silurian		435 mil.	Coral reefs are formed. First amphibians and forests of fernlike trees appear.
	Devonian		405 mil.	Gas and oil are formed. Many kinds of fish in seas and fresh water. First insects appear.
	Carboniferous —Mississippian		350 mil.	Warm, moist climate produces great forests that later become coal beds. Fish and amphibians plentiful.
	—Pennsylvanian		310 mil.	Appalachian Mountains are formed. Large amounts of coal are formed. First reptiles appear.
	Permian		270 mil.	Ural Mountains are formed. Glaciers in southern hemisphere melt. Gas, oil and salt are formed. Reptiles developing.
Mezozoic	Triassic		225 mil.	Reptiles dominate the earth. First mammals appear.
	Jurassic		180 mil.	Shallow seas invade continents. Dinosaurs reach their largest size. First birds appear.
	Cretaceous		130 mil.	Seas spread over the land. Flowering plants appear. Dinosaurs die out. Most chalk deposits are made.
Cenozoic	Tertiary	Paleocene	65 mil.	Mountains become higher. Climates less uniform. Mammals, flowering plants become common.
		Eocene	50 mil.	Climate mild. Seas flood shores of continents. Primitive apes, early horses and elephants appear.
		Oligocene	38 mil.	Climate mild. Alps and Himalayas begin to rise. Many volcanoes. Oil and natural gas are formed.
		Miocene	27 mil.	Climate mild. Rocky Mountains and Sierra Nevadas forming. Flowering plants and trees resemble modern kinds.
		Pliocene	10 mil.	Climate cooling. Mountains rising in western Canada. Many volcanoes. Birds and mammals spread around the world. Humans appear near end of epoch.
	Quaternary	Pleistocene	1.5 mil.	Great ice sheets cover northern hemisphere. Climate cool. Mountains continue to rise in North America. Early humans reach Europe and North America.
		Recent, or Holocene	10 000	Glaciers melt and Great Lakes are formed. Climate warm. Humans live in most parts of the earth, develop agriculture, use metals, domesticate animals.

The Quest for the Magnetic Pole

The first reference to the existence of a magnetic pole on the surface of the Earth was made in a letter written by Flemish geographer, Gerardus Mercator, in 1546. In that letter he dismissed the popular notion of the time that mariners' compasses were directed by the star Polaris. Mercator proposed the compass pointed directly at a magnetic pole, but finding the exact position of this pole proved more difficult than he first thought. His world map of 1569 shows two north magnetic poles, depicted as high mountains rising from the Arctic Sea.

In 1600 Sir William Gilbert, physician to Queen Elizabeth I, came up with a new theory. He believed the Earth itself to be a giant magnet. Using a sphere made from lodestone, a naturally magnetic mineral, Gilbert showed that a magnetized needle would stand vertically at two points—the North and South poles of the sphere. (At the magnetic poles, the earth's magnetic field lies perpendicular to the earth's surface.) Gilbert, however, took it for granted the magnetic and geographic poles were one and the same. Magnetic observations taken by explorers in subsequent years showed this was not true.

By the early nineteenth century, observations had proved the north magnetic pole to be somewhere in Canada's Arctic and the search for the exact position began in earnest. But the searchers never dreamed they might be looking for a moving target. The North magnetic pole was finally located in 1831 by James Ross while his ship was trapped in ice on the Boothia Peninsula in the Northwest Territories. The pole was found in almost the same position by Roald Amundsen in 1904 on his voyage through the Northwest Passage.

Subsequent expeditions have shown that the pole has moved about 750 km since 1904, an average of 9.4 km a year. From 1973 to 1994, the movement has been about 120 km, an average of 11.6 km annually.

■ Why does it move?

The flow of electric currents that originate in the Earth's liquid outer core is continually changing, so the magnetic field those currents produce also fluctuates. This means that at the surface of the Earth both the strength and direction of the magnetic field, as it lies perpendicular to Earth's surface, varies from year to year.

And there is another factor. If we record the Earth's magnetic field continually, we see changes over the course of a day—sometimes rapid, sometimes slow. These daily fluctuations are caused by the Sun. The Sun emits charged particles which, on encountering the Earth's magnetic field, cause electric currents to be produced in the upper atmosphere. These currents disturb the magnetic field, resulting in a shift in the pole's position. When scientists try to determine the average position of the pole, they must average out all these transient wanderings.

So where is the north magnetic pole now? As of October 1994, it was just south of Elles Rignes Island at 78.0° N latitude, 103.3°W longitude.

Source: *Energy Mines and Resources Canada, Geological Survey of Canada*

Head South Young Bee

Bees, which can travel for miles looking for food, orient themselves by means of the magnetic South pole. During experiments with an artificial magnetic field, scientists at the University of Sussex have found bees use magnetic orientation to establish a "landmark." They say the bees consistently face south while searching for the immediate location of food and also when returning to the same location.

Minerals

Minerals are all around us—everything from ice on the sidewalk in winter to the salt you sprinkle on French fries. Each mineral species has a definite chemical composition and a crystal structure.Therefore, ice is mineral because it is solid, but water is not because it is liquid. Sea shells are not minerals because, although they are solid, they are organic—formed by living creatures.

The physical properties of minerals—their form and hardness—are easy to recognize. Specimens may be composed of large showy crystals or millions of tiny crystals fused together. The external shape (or habit) is determined by the internal arrangement of atoms. The atoms are joined together in a framework to form minute building blocks. Called the crystal structure, the arrangement of atoms is unique for each mineral. The habit is also partly the result of the environment in which a mineral grows. If there is enough space during growth, the mineral develops smooth external crystals. However, conditions are seldom ideal and more often than not, minerals grow together as masses of fibres, grains, plates or spheres. The hardness of a mineral—its resistance to scratching—is measured by the Mohs scale.

The optical properties of minerals—lustre, colour and transparency—are easily observed by the unaided eye; other optical properties are determined with microscopes. Lustre is the quality of light reflected from the surface of a mineral. For instance, the highly reflective surfaces of pyrite produce the metallic lustre characteristics of most sulphide minerals. Many silicates, carbonates and otherminerals have a softer, but still bright, glassy or vitreous lustre. Minerals with surfaces that reflect light more diffusely, such as serpentine asbestos or cyanotrichite, are said to have silky or earthly lustres. Lustre is reliable means of distinguishing minerals.

Colour can also be very distinctive, but is not always reliable in identifying most minerals because even minerals of the same species can occur in many colours. Quartz, which is quite common, can be as clear as water or the deepest purple because of flaws in the mineral's crystal structure. Colour can also be affected by the presence of major elements in the mineral: copper in azurite produces an intense azure blue; arsenic makes realgar appear red; and curite is coloured orange by uranium. Colour can also be produced by physical structure. When light strikes very thin layers within the structure of labradorite, the mineral glows with iridescent colours, an effect much like that of sunlight striking a film of gasoline on a puddle, causing a rainbow of colour.

Determining the chemical composition and crystal structure of minerals requires laboratory techniques and tools such as the electron microbe, a reliable tool for analysing chemical composition. Crystal structure is determined using an X-ray diffractometer. Other mineral properties such as magnetism, fluorescence and radioactivity are more easily detected: magnetite and pyrrhotite are noticeably magnetic; some minerals, such as scheelite, fluoresce strongly in ultra-violet light; and all uranium and thorium-bearing minerals are radioactive. The radiation can easily be detected with a Geiger counter or scintillometer.

Mohs Scale of Hardness

Mohs scale indicates the relative hardness of minerals. Each mineral listed is hard enough to scratch a smooth surface of those below it. On this scale, a polymer-like polyethylene would have a hardness of about 1, a finger nail 2.5, a penny 5, window glass 5.5, and the blade of a pocket knife 6.5 Tool steel has a hardness of about 7, and easily cuts glass.

10	Diamond
9	Corundum
8	Topaz
7	Quartz
6	Orthoclase
5	Apatite
4	Fluorite
3	Calcite
2	Gypsum
1	Talc

Source: *Geological Survey of Canada*

Earth Sciences Museums*

Maritime Region:

☐ **St. Lawrence Miner's Museum**
St. Lawrence, Nfld A0E 2V0. (709) 873-2222. No charge. Open in summer.

☐ **Fundy Geological Museum**
4028 Eastern Avenue, Parrsboro, NS B0M 1S0. (902) 254-3814. No charge. Open May to June and Sept. to Oct. - 5 days; summer - 7 days; winter by appointment.

☐ **Inverness Miner's Museum**
Lower Railway Street, Inverness, NS B0E 1N0. (902) 258-2097. Entrance fee. Open all year.

☐ **Mineral and Gem Geological Museum**
1 Eastern Avenue, Parrsboro, NS B0M 1S0. (902) 254-2627. No charge. Open in summer and fall.

☐ **Springhill Miner's Museum**
Black River Road, Springhill, NS B0M 1X0. B0M 1X0 (902) 597-3449. Entrance fee. Open spring, summer and fall.

Central Canada:

☐ **Alcan Museum**
1188 Sherbrooke Street West, Montreal, Quebec H3A 3G2. (514) 848-8187. No charge. Open all year.

☐ **Logan Hall**
Geological Survey of Canada, 601 Booth Street, Ottawa, ON K1A 0E8. (613)995-4261. No charge. Open all year. Closed on weekends and holidays.

☐ **Musée de Géologie**
Laval University, Pavillon Pouliot, 4th floor, Sainte Foy, Quebec G1K 7P4. (418) 656-2193. No charge. Open all year.

☐ **Musée minéralogique d'Asbestos**
104 Letendre Street, Asbestos, Quebec J1T 1E3. (819) 879-6444. No charge. Open in summer.

☐ **Musée mineralogique et minier de la Région de l'amiante**
671 Smith Blvd. South, Thetford Mines, Quebec G6G 5T3. Entrance fee. Open all year.

☐ **Musée régional mines de Malartic**
650 rue da la Paix, Abitibi East, Malartic, Quebec J0Y 1Z0. (819) 757-4677. Entrance fee. Open all year.

☐ **Biology and Earth Sciences Museum**
University of Waterloo, Waterloo, Ontario N2L 3G1. (519) 885-1211, ext. 2469. No charge. Open all year.

☐ **Miller Museum of Geology and Minerology**
Queen's University, Dept. of Geological Sciences, Miller Hall, Kingston, Ontario K7L 3N6. (613) 545-2597. No charge. Open all year.

☐ **Oil Museum of Canada**
Oil Springs, 35 km southeast of Sarnia, Ontario N0N 1P0. (519) 834-2840. Entrance fee. Open in summer and fall. Tours all year.

☐ **The Petrolia Discovery Foundation**
Blind Line, Petrolia, Ontario N0N 1R0. (519) 882-0897. Entrance fee. Open in summer and fall.

☐ **Timmins Museum**
70 Legion Drive, South Porcupine, Ontario P4N 1B3. (705) 235-5066. No charge. Open all year.

Western Canada:

☐ **Stonewall Quarry Park**
299 North Main Street, Stonewall, Manitoba R0C 2Z0. (204) 467-5354. Entrance fee. Open all year.

☐ **Geological Museum**
University of Saskatchewan, Geological Sciences Building, Saskatoon, Saskatchewan S7N 0W0. (306) 966-5683. No charge. Open all year.

☐ **Frank Slide Interpretive Centre**
1 km north of Frank, Alberta T0K 0E0. (403) 562-7388. No charge. Open all year.

☐ **Museum of Geology**
University of Alberta, basement of Earth Sciences Building, Edmonton Alberta T6G 2E3. (403) 492-3265. No charge. Open all year.

☐ **Royal Tyrrell Museum of Palaeontology**
Midland Provincial Park, Drumheller, Alberta T0Y 0Y0. (403) 823-7707. Entrance fee. Open all year.

☐ **Field Station of the Tyrrell Museum**
Dinosaur Provincial Park, Patricia, Alberta T0J 2K0. (403) 378-4342. No charge. Open all year.

☐ **British Columbia Museum of Mining**
PO Box 188, Britannia Beach, BC V0N 1J0. Tel (604) 688-8735. Entrance fee. Open in summer and fall. All year for groups.

☐ **Manson Creek-Omenica Museum**
General Delivery, Manson Creek, BC V0J 2H0. Radio telephone only. No charge. Open all year.

☐ **M.Y. Williams Geological Museum**
University of British Columbia, 6339 Stores Road, Vancouver BC V6T 2B4. Tel (604) 228-5586 No charge. Open all year.

☐ **Princeton and District Museums**
167 Vermilion Street, Princeton BC V0X 1W0. Tel (604) 285-7588. No charge. Summer (30 June - 31 August)

☐ **Keno City Mining Museum**
Keno City, Yukon Y0B 1J0. (403) 995-2792. No charge. Open in summer.

*Small museums, devoted entirely to one or more areas of the Earth Sciences

PHYSICAL SCIENCES

Physics and chemistry constitute the physical sciences. **Chemistry** concerns itself with the composition, properties, and reactions of substances. Organic chemistry, one of the two main branches of chemistry, specializes in the composition, properties, and reactions of hydrocarbon compounds. The other branch, inorganic chemistry, deals primarily with the elements and compounds that do not include hydrocarbons. **Physics** concerns itself with universal aspects of nature—forces, energy, structure of matter, and their interactions. Some of its particular fields are: plasma physics, optics and quantum optics, particle physics, geophysics, biophysics, and acoustics. As basic sciences, physics and chemistry permeate all sciences and technologies.

Common Chemistry Terms

Acid: a substance that in liquid form will turn blue litmus paper red, react with alkalis (bases) to form salts, and dissolve metals to form salts.

Alkali: Any compound that has chemical qualities of a base, such as reacting with acid to form salts.

Atomic Weight (Mass): The relative mass of an atom, based on a scale in which a specific carbon atom is assigned a mass value of 12.

Base: an alkaline substance, either molecular or ionic in form, that will accept or receive a proton from another chemical unit.

Catalyst: a substance that accelerates a chemical reaction without becoming a part of the end product of the reaction.

Compound: A substance formed by the combination of two or more chemical elements that cannot be separated from the combination by physical means. The constituent atoms, however, can usually be separated by means of chemical reactions.

Electron: A negatively-charged particle that moves in orbit about the nucleus of an atom.

Element: A substance composed of atoms with the same atomic number or the same number of protons in their nuclei.

Isotope: One of two or more atoms having the same atomic number, but a different mass number.

Mass Number: the atomic weight of an isotope, calculated from the number of protons and neutrons in the nucleus.

Matter: Anything that has weight or fills space, such as a solid, liquid, or gas.

Polymer: a huge molecule composed of repeating units of the same molecule.

Valence: a number that represents the combining power of an element, ion, or radical.

Gairdner Awards

The Gairdner Foundation was established by James Arthur Gairdner, a Torontonian born in 1893. Gairdner was a scholar, an athlete and had a successful career in the investment business; he also had a lifelong interest in clinical medicine and medical research that led him to believe that the achievements of medical scientists should be recognized. The Gairdner Foundation has given awards to medical scientists from many countries since 1959. The Foundation has honoured 225 scientists during its history and 43 of those have subsequently received a Nobel Prize for their work as well. The winners of the 1994 Gairdner International Awards were announced in March.

Dr. Donald Metcalf (University of Melbourne) for his work on the treatment of diseases in which the control of blood cell formation is impaired.

Dr Anthony J. Pawson (Samuel Lunenfeld Research Institute, Mount Sinai Hospital) and Dr. Tony Hunter (The Salk Institute) for their characterization of a class of proteins—tyrosine kinases—that allow cells to signal one another. Tyrosine kinases are important in growth and development, and are often mutated in some forms of cancer.

Dr Don Wiley (Harvard University) and Dr Pamela Bjorkman (California Institute of Technology) who described the structure of molecules of the major histocompatibility complex on the cell surface and thus were able to show precisely how the body recognizes foreign invaders.

Common Physics Terms

Acceleration: the rate of change of velocity with respect to time.

Anode: The positive terminal of an electric current flow. In a vacuum tube, electrons flow from the cathode to the anode.

Cathode: The negative terminal of an electric current system. In vacuum tube, the filament serves as the source electrons.

Conduction: the transfer of heat by molecular motion from a source of high temperature to a region of lower temperature, tending towards a result of equalized temperatures.

Convection: The mechanical transfer of heated molecules of a gas or liquid from a source to another area, as when a room is warmed by the movement of air molecules heated by a radiator.

Electromotive Force: The force that causes the movement of electrons through an electrical circuit.

Energy: the ability to perform work. Energy may be changed from one form to another, as from heat to light, but normally it cannot be created or destroyed.

Force: the influence on a body that causes it to accelerate.

Heat: A form of energy that results from the disordered motion of molecules. As the motion becomes more rapid and disordered, the amount of heat is increased.

Mass: a measure of the amount of matter. Near the surface of earth, it is roughly equivalent to weight.

Momentum: the mathematical product of the mass of a moving object and its velocity.

Velocity: The speed with which an object travels over a specified distance during a measured amount of time.

Weight: The force on a body produced by the downward pull of gravity on it.

Blame It on Silicon

*T*he Philippines have had more than their fair share of natural disasters. Often battered by cyclones, the islands now have volcano trouble with Mount Pinatubo awakening from a 600-year snooze in the summer of 1991.

Without volcanoes like Pinatubo, the Philippines would not exist. Indeed, many oceanic islands share a common volcanic origin, but there are differences. Hawaii's volcanoes, for example, get on with the task of island building in an unspectacular way. Lava flows continuously and predictably. Such volcanoes seldom go in for the pyrotechnics of Pinatubo that scattered 120,000 Filipinos, killing 700 people.

Why? The difference between Hawaii's volcanoes and those in the Philippines and Japan is the amount of silicon at particular spots in the Earth's crust. In the middle of an ocean, volcanic lava arrives uncontaminated from deep below the earth's surface and flows freely. Lavas released where the oceans and continental rock come into contact melt and absorb the silicon in the rock. When the amount of silicon in the rock is high, the resulting lava becomes sticky. It gums up the works instead of flowing easily, until enough pressure has built up to blow the troublesome rocks, and anything surrounding them, away.

At Pinatubo, the eruption came from a weak spot on the volcano's north-west flank. A jumble of shattered rock, ash, hot mud, and lava, propelled by gases, was thrown out and down the Marella and Marauno river valleys. Geologists fear that the bubble of liquid rock under Pinatubo is still rising and as pressure builds will cause a much bigger explosion when the plug of lava in the main crater pops.

Basic Laws of Physics

■ Newton's Laws of Motion

Newton's laws apply to objects in a vacuum, and are difficult to observe in the "real" world where forces such as friction affect all objects.

First Law: Any object at rest tends to stay at rest, and a body in motion will continue that motion with a constant velocity unless acted upon by some external unbalanced force.

Second Law: The acceleration of an object is directly proportional to the force acting upon it, and is inversely proportional to the mass of the object.

Third Law: Every action generates an equal and opposite reaction.

■ Gravity

When an object is dropped near the surface of the earth, it increases in speed as it falls. By rolling balls down inclined planes Galileo discovered that acceleration due to gravity is the same for all objects, independent of their weight (mass). For example, if you drop this book and a heavy dictionary simultaneously, they will reach to floor at the same time. You can try the same experiment with a heavy book and a single sheet of paper. The paper is affected by the resistance of the air. Then crumple the paper, and try again.

Gravity is the force that tends to attract objects to the centre of a cellestial body, such as the earth, the moon or Mars. The weight of an object at the earth's surface is mainly due to the force of gravity between the earth and the object. The force exerted by the earth varies with the object's distance from the centre of the earth. Therefore the weight of an object is not the same at the earth's surface as it is on the moon or in space.

■ Laws of Thermodynamics

Sadi Carnot (1796-1832) stated in his work *Reflections on the Motive Power of Fire* that mechanical energy could be produced by the simple transfer of heat.

First Law: In a closed system, energy appears to be conserved in all but nuclear reactions and other extreme conditions.

Second Law: In a closed system, heat never travels from a low to a higher temperature in a self sustaining process. In a closed system, entropy (disorder) always increases.

■ Two Basic Laws of Quantum Physics

Heisenberg's Uncertainty Principle: It is impossible to specify completely the position and momentum of a particle, such as an electron.

Pauli's Exclusion Principle: No two electrons of the same atom can have identical values for all four quantum numbers: at least one quantum number must be different.

■ Electricity

Ohm's Law: Electric current is directly proportional to the potential difference and inversely proportional to resistance. If current (I) is measured in amperes; potential difference (V) in volts, and resistance (R) in volts, the formula is as follows: $I = V/R$

How Many Minerals Make Up Your Computer ?

I *t takes more than 31 elements and minerals to make a computer! Those vital ingredients are: aluminum, antimony, barite, beryllium, cobalt, columbium, copper, gallium, germanium, gold, indium, iron, lanthanides, lithium, manganese, mercury, mica, quartz crystals, rhenium, selenium, silver, strontium, tantalum, tellurium, tin, tungsten, vanadium, yttrium, zinc, and zirconium. And many of the components are housed in plastics.*

The Elements

(listed by name, symbol and atomic number)

An element is a substance composed of atoms that are chemically alike—each atom has an identical number of protons in its nucleus. Furthermore, there is no known process to break these elements down into more fundamental substances.

actinium	Ac	89	hafnium	Hf	72	promethium	Pm	61
aluminum	Al	13	helium	He	2	protactinium	Pa	91
americium	Am	95	holmium	Ho	67	radium	Ra	88
antimony	Sb	51	hydrogen	H	1	radon	Rn	86
argon	Ar	18	indium	In	49	rhenium	Re	75
arsenic	As	33	iodine	I	53	rhodium	Rh	45
astatine	At	85	iridium	Ir	77	rubidium	Rb	37
barium	Ba	56	iron	Fe	26	ruthenium	Ru	44
berkelium	Bk	97	krypton	Kr	36	samarium	Sm	62
beryllium	Be	4	lanthanum	La	57	scandium	Sc	21
bismuth	Bi	83	lawrencium	Lr	103	selenium	Se	34
boron	B	5	lead	Pb	82	silicon	Si	14
bromine	Br	35	lithium	Li	3	silver	Ag	47
cadmium	Cd	48	lutetium	Lu	71	sodium	Na	11
calcium	Ca	20	magnesium	Mg	12	strontium	Sr	38
californium	Cf	98	manganese	Mn	25	sulfur	S	16
carbon	C	6	mendelevium	Md	101	tantalum	Ta	73
cerium	Ce	58	mercury	Hg	80	technetium	Tc	43
cesium	Cs	55	molybdenum	Mo	42	tellurium	Te	52
chlorine	Cl	17	neodymium	Nd	60	terbium	Tb	65
chromium	Cr	24	neon	Ne	10	thallium	Tl	81
cobalt	Co	27	neptunium	Np	93	thorium	Th	90
copper	Cu	29	nickel	Ni	28	thulium	Tm	69
curium	Cm	96	niobium	Nb	41	tin	Sn	50
dysprosium	Dy	66	nitrogen	N	7	titanium	Ti	22
einsteinium	Es	99	nobelium	No	102	tungsten	W	74
erbium	Er	68	osmium	Os	76	unnilquadium	Unq	104[1]
europium	Eu	63	oxygen	O	8	unnilpentium	Unp	105[2]
fermium	Fm	100	palladium	Pd	46	uranium	U	92
fluorine	F	9	phosphorus	P	15	vanadium	V	23
francium	Fr	87	platinum	Pt	78	xenon	Xe	54
gadolinium	Gd	64	plutonium	Pu	94	ytterbium	Yb	70
gallium	Ga	31	polonium	Po	84	yttrium	Y	39
germanium	Ge	32	potassium	K	19	zinc	Zn	30
gold	Au	79	praseodymium	Pr	59	zirconium	Zr	40

Source: *Gage Canadian Dictionary*

(1) Proposed name is rutherfordium (2) Proposed name is hahnium.

Canines and Chemistry

Plagued by the high costs of the time-consuming task of locating leaks in underground pipelines, Imperial Oil developed a pungent chemical that could travel through a buried pipe, seep from the leak and rise directly to the surface from depths of up to six metres. The idea was to have a computerized chemical analyzer, like the one used on the Mars spaceprobe, sniff out the leak. But test trials were a failure. The computer just wasn't up to the job.

Following a hunch, a senior environmental scientist at Imperial Oil came up with a novel (and less expensive) approach. Knowing that rescue dogs use their keen sense of smell to uncover avalanche victims, he approached a Calgary firm that trains dogs to sniff out drugs and bombs. They brought the dogs and the chemical together. The result? Labrador retrievers can detect the equivalent of one drop of the chemical in 250 million barrels of oil—a sensitivity one billion times greater than the most sophisticated manufactured detector.

Periodic Table of Elements

																	gases
1 **H** 1.00																	2 **He** 4.00

non-metals

5 **B** 10.81	6 **C** 12.01	7 **N** 14.01	8 **O** 15.99	9 **F** 18.99	10 **Ne** 20.17
13 **Al** 26.98	14 **Si** 28.08	15 **P** 30.97	16 **S** 32.06	17 **Cl** 35.45	18 **Ar** 39.94

— transition metals —

3 **Li** 6.94	4 **Be** 9.01
11 **Na** 22.98	12 **Mg** 24.30

19 **K** 39.09	20 **Ca** 40.08	21 **Sc** 44.95	22 **Ti** 47.88	23 **V** 50.94	24 **Cr** 51.99	25 **Mn** 54.93	26 **Fe** 55.84	27 **Co** 58.93	28 **Ni** 58.69	29 **Cu** 63.54	30 **Zn** 65.39	31 **Ga** 69.72	32 **Ge** 72.59	33 **As** 74.92	34 **Se** 78.96	35 **Br** 79.90	36 **Kr** 83.80
37 **Rb** 85.46	38 **Sr** 87.62	39 **Y** 88.90	40 **Zr** 91.22	41 **Nb** 92.90	42 **Mo** 95.94	43 **Tc** (98)	44 **Ru** 101.07	45 **Rh** 102.90	46 **Pd** 106.42	47 **Ag** 107.87	48 **Cd** 112.41	49 **In** 114.82	50 **Sn** 118.71	51 **Sb** 121.75	52 **Te** 127.60	53 **I** 126.90	54 **Xe** 131.29
55 **Cs** 132.90	56 **Ba** 137.33	57 **La** 138.90	72 **Hf** 178.49	73 **Ta** 180.94	74 **W** 183.85	75 **Re** 186.20	76 **Os** 190.2	77 **Ir** 192.22	78 **Pt** 195.08	79 **Au** 196.96	80 **Hg** 200.59	81 **Tl** 204.38	82 **Pb** 207.2	83 **Bi** 208.98	84 **Po** (209)	85 **At** (210)	86 **Rn** (222)
87 **Fr** (223)	88 **Ra** 226.02	89 **Ac** 227.02	104 **Unq** (261)	105 **Unp** (262)	106 **Unh** (263)	107 **Uns** (262)	108 **Uno** (···)	109 **Une** (···)	110 **Uun** (···)								

other metals

— rare earth elements —

58 **Ce** 140.12	59 **Pr** 140.90	60 **Nd** 144.24	61 **Pm** (145)	62 **Sm** 150.36	63 **Eu** 151.96	64 **Gd** 157.25	65 **Tb** 158.93	66 **Dy** 162.50	67 **Ho** 164.93	68 **Er** 167.26	69 **Tm** 168.93	70 **Yb** 173.04	71 **Lu** 174.96
90 **Th** 232.03	91 **Pa** 231.03	92 **U** 238.02	93 **Np** 237.04	94 **Pu** (244)	95 **Am** (243)	96 **Cm** (247)	97 **Bk** (247)	98 **Cf** (251)	99 **Es** (252)	100 **Fm** (257)	101 **Md** (258)	102 **No** (259)	103 **Lr** (260)

This is a table which shows the properties of the elements, in the order of their atomic mass or number, and arranged in horizontal rows (periods) and vertical columns (groups) to illustrate the occurence of similarities in the structure of their atoms. When the elements are arranged in this order, their chemical and physical properties show repeatable trends. This pattern in properties occurs periodically; that is, the pattern is repeated in an orderly manner over time.

The order of the elements is that of their atomic numbers, the integers which are equal to the positive electrical charges of the atomic nuclei expressed in electronic units.

Loudness of Sounds

Sound is measured in decibels. A decibel is a unit for measuring the relative intensity of a sound, equal to one-tenth of a bel. A bel indicates the amount of energy in the form of sound transmitted to one sq cm of the ear. The bel was named after Alexander Graham Bell.

Source: *Dictionary of Science, Barnhardt, American Heritage Series*

The decibel scale advances geometrically instead of arithmetically. Twenty decibels represents not twice as much noise as ten, but 10 times as much. The 80-decibel level of a pneumatic drill is 100 times as noisy as the 60-decibel level of conversation.

Intensity (decibels)	Loudness	Intensity (decibels)	Loudness
0	Threshold of hearing	70	Loud conversation
10 (1 bel)	Virtual silence	80	Door slamming
20	Quiet room	90	Busy typing room
30	Watch ticking at 1 m	100	Near loud motor horn
40	Quiet street	100	Pneumatic drill
50	Quiet conversation	120	Near airplane engine
60	Quiet motor at 1 m	130	Threshold of pain

Science Centres and Museums

Maritime Region:

□ **Electrical Engineering Museum**
University of New Brunswick, Dept. of Electrical Engineering, Head Hall, Fredericton, NB No charge. Open winter, spring and fall.

Central Canada:

□ **Museum of Visual Science and Optometry**
University of Waterloo, Optometry Building, Columbia Street, Waterloo, Ontario N2L 3G1. Tel (519) 885-1211, ext. 3405. No charge. Open all year.

□ **Hamilton Museum of Steam and Technology**
900 Woodward Avenue, Hamilton, Ontario L8H 7N2. Tel (416) 549-5225. Entrance fee. Open all year.

□ **National Museum of Science and Technology**
1867 St. Laurent Blvd., Ottawa, Ontario K1G 5A3. Tel (613) 998-4566 Entrance fee. Open all year.

□ **Ontario Science Centre**
770 Don Mills Road, Toronto, Ontario M3C 1T3. Tel (416) 429-4100. Open daily (except Christmas Day).

□ **Science North**
100 Ramsay Lake Road, Sudbury, Ontario P3E 5S9. Tel (705) 522-3700 Entrance fee. Open all year.

Western Canada:

□ **Alberta Science Centre**
701-11 Street SW, Calgary, Alberta T2P 2M5. Tel(403) 221-3700 No charge. Open all year.

□ **Edmonton Space and Science Centre**
11211-142 Street, Edmonton, Alberta T5M 4A1. Tel(403) 452-9100 Entrance fee. Open all year.

□ **Energeum**
640-5th Avenue S.W., Main Floor, Energy Resources Building, Calgary, Alberta T2P 3G4. Tel (403) 297-4293 No charge. Open all year.

□ **Pacific Geoscience Centre**
9860 West Saanich Road, Sidney, BC V8L4B2. Tel(604) 363-6500 No charge. Open all year.

□ **Science World**
1455 Quebec Street, Vancouver, BC V6A 3Z7. Tel (604) 687-8414 Entrance fee. Open daily, except Christmas Day.

INVENTION AND SCIENTIFIC ACHIEVEMENT

Discoveries in technology, as well as achievements in science, are products of the human mind. Fascinated by ideas, inventors follow their curiosity. But they also possess the tenacity to overcome the many obstacles along the trail to discovery. Some remarkable Canadians and their contributions are noted in this section.

Canadian Nobel Laureates in Science and Medicine

1923	Dr. Frederick G. Banting Dr. J.J.R. Macleod	Medicine and Physiology	for the discovery of insulin
1971	Dr. Gerhard Herzberg	Chemistry	for his contributions to the knowledge of electronic structure and geometry of molecules, particularly free radicals
1986	Dr. John Polyani	Chemistry	for contributions concerning the dynamics of elementary chemical reactions
1993	Dr. Michael Smith	Chemistry	co-winner for work on genetic codes

Canadian Invention

The McIntosh Apple In 1811, Scottish-born John McIntosh discovered wild apple trees on his farm near Dundela, Ontario. Of the several trees he transplanted, one produced a superior fruit. His son Alan went on to develop the variety, and McIntosh apples are now grown in many parts of North America. The original tree continued to bear fruit for 90 years.

Undersea Cable Frederick Gisbourne developed a method of insulating wire to make it saltwater resistant. Then in 1852, he successfully laid the first undersea telegraph cable in North America, linking New Brunswick and Prince Edward Island. Gisbourne also proposed a cable linking North America and Europe. With the financial backing of American industrialist Cyrus Field, the Atlantic Cable, connecting Ireland and Newfoundland, was completed in 1866.

The Railway Sleeping Car In 1857, Samuel Sharp designed and built the world's first railway sleeping car. The car had berths with spring mattresses and curtains for privacy. Sharp's invention was improved on by the American, George Pullman.

Standard Time In 1878, Sir Sandford Fleming, Canada's foremost railway surveyor and construction engineer, realized the new national railroad made local timekeeping obsolete. He devised a method whereby the world is divided into 24 time zones. His system of Standard Time was adopted by the International Prime Meridian Conference in Washington, DC, in 1884, and is still used today.

First Radio Voice Message Reginald Fessenden, from East Bolton, Quebec, discovered a way to send actual sounds via radio waves. In 1906, he transmitted the world's first radio broadcast from his transmitter at Brant Rock, Massachusetts. Sailors aboard ships of the United Fruit Company in the Caribbean found themselves listening to a Christmas Eve broadcast of music and voice. Fessenden produced the program himself, and even sang and played carols on his violin.

Gas Mask In 1915, Dr. Cluny Macpherson designed the first gas mask to protect troops from gas attacks during World War I.

The Snowmobile Fifteen-year-old Armand Bombardier built a prototype snowmobile in 1922 at his home in Valcourt, Quebec. Over the years, he refined the design and was granted a patent in 1937. At first he produced commercial vehicles, but in 1959 Bombardier perfected a sports model, the Ski-doo.

The First AC Radio Tube In 1925, Ted Rogers, a Torontonian, introduced the world's first batteryless radio. Gone were the days when programs faded away as batteries "died." The modern "plug in" radio was born. Rogers also built the world's first all-electric, batteryless broadcast station, CFRB.

The Variable Pitch Propeller Wallace Turnbull, an aeronautical engineer, worked on the variable pitch propeller in his home workshop in Rothesay, New Brunswick. This propeller was the first that could be adjusted in the air and adapted to the differing aerodynamic conditions of takeoff, climbing ▶

▶ and diving. Pilots could adjust the propeller's blades for takeoff and again during flight. It was successfully tested by the RCAF at Camp Borden in 1927.

Pablum Toronto doctors Alan Brown, F. Tisdall and T. Drake, working at the Hospital for Sick Children, became concerned about infant nutrition during the Depression. After much research and testing, they produced a precooked cereal—the now famous Pablum.

Table Hockey Dan Munroe created and built the first table hockey game to amuse his three children. In 1932 he patented the game, and first sold it through the T. Eaton Company. The Munroe family manufactured the first games by hand.

The Bush Plane The world's first bush aircraft was designed and built in Montreal by Robert Noorduyn in 1935. Norseman aircraft are noted for their performance in rugged terrain, and were known as "workhorses" of the North. Some are still in use.

The Paint Roller In 1940, Norman Breakey invented the paint roller in Toronto. Breakey revolutionized home decorating, but was unable to reap the financial benefits of his invention.

Electronic Synthesizer In 1945, the world's first electronic synthesizer, the Sackbut, was designed and built by Hugh Le Caine in his home studio. A research physicist with the National Research Council, Le Caine was also a composer. His piece "Dripsody," using only the sound of single drop of water, is recognized as an electronic music classic.

Cobalt Bomb In 1951, Dr. Harold Johns, working with others, created the "Cobalt-60 bomb" for the treatment of cancer. Cobalt radiation therapy units have revolutionized cancer treatment worldwide.

Laser Sailboat The Laser sailboat was designed and built in 1970 by three Canadian Olympic sailors: Bruce Kirby, Hans Fogh and Ian Bruce. A stable, small pleasure craft, the Laser has given thousands of people their first introduction to sailing. The craft is now used throughout the world.

Steak Monitor The challenge of cooking T-bone steaks for hungry workers at the Great Lakes Power Company provided the impetus for Cathy Denomme of Wawa, Ontario to come up with a better way. Denomme is the inventor of No-Misteak, a handy device that, when pressed against cooking meat, registers its doneness.

Flat Electric Wall Plug In 1989, Bob Dickie of King City, Ontario invented a revolutionary wall plug—it's flat. The first major change to wall plugs in 75 years, the FlatPlug extends only one-quarter inch from the wall. The power cord exits and travels parallel to the wall. Dickie was motivated to create a safer plug while watching his two-year-old daughter at play.

Panoramic Camera John Connor of Elora, Ontario invented the world's first panoramic camera in 1887. The camera had the capability of photographing an entire circle at one exposure.

Infant Evacuation Stretcher Motivated by television images of rescuers scrambling to evacuate babies from the 1985 Mexico City earthquake, Toronto researcher Wendy Murphy developed the world's first stretcher for taking infants from disaster areas. Murphy's "Weevac 6" can transport six babies at a time.

Patents

If you have an idea for a new gizmo, what is required to have it patented? The Patent Office judges the idea based the following criteria:

1) the gizmo must be the first of its kind in the world;
2) the gizmo must be useful, and most importantly, it must work;
3) the gizmo must be obviously ingenious to others familiar with the field.

A patent gives you the right to exclude others from making, using or selling an invention from the day the patent is granted until 20 years after filing. Patents also provide useful technical information to the public.

Although individual inventors still apply for patents, the majority of applications now come from large corporations. Patents are granted by individual countries; so the protection of a Canadian patent extends throughout Canada alone. Patent rights in the United States or elsewhere must be applied for separately in the individual countries.

A list of the patents applied for and granted in Canada is issued once a week in The Patent Office Record. Among the 341 patents applied for during the week of 19 to 26 July 1994 are:

- Tear Resistant Fabric
- Post Hole Liner
- Ball Bearing Puck
- Device for Aligning Factured Bone
- Conversion of Methane and Carbon Dioxide Using Microwave Radiation
- Apparatus for Improving a Golfer's Putting Stroke

The distribution of applications to the Canadian Patent Office from 19 to 26 July 1994 are as follows.

Inventions by Country of Origin

Country	Percent of applications*
United States	48
Japan	15
Canada	12
Germany	8
France	5
Italy	3
Switzerland	2
United Kingdom	2

* The Netherlands, China, Taiwan, Australia, Denmark, South Africa, Sweden, Argentina, Finland, Israel, and Portugal share the remaining 5 percent.

Manning Awards

The Manning Awards were established to recognize and encourage innovation in Canada by honouring individuals who have created and promoted a new concept, process or product, which is beneficial to Canada and society. Administered by the Calgary-based, Ernest C. Manning Foundation, the awards are presented annually on the birthday of the former Alberta premier. Winners were announced October 27, 1994.

☐ **Dr. Michael Smith** (Vancouver, BC) won the 1994 Manning Principal Award for his work on re-programming genetic codes. His process permits the creation of specific and planned manipulation of genes and is considered to be instrumental in the fight against cancer, the treatment and cure of hereditary diseases, the creation of new agricultural crops and the engineering of synthetic blood products. Dr. Smith is Director of the Biotechnology Laboratory at the University of British Columbia and a co-winner of the 1993 Nobel Prize in Chemistry.

☐ **Drs. Michel Chrétien** and **Nabil Seidah** of the Institut de récherchés cliniques de Montréal were named co-winners of the Award of Distinction for their work on convertases. Convertases are enzymes within the human body that convert inactive substances to their active state. They play an important role in brain function, cell growth and many viral infections, but are also suspected to have harmful side affects. The co-winners' discovery is the result of 20 years of research and will aid in the understanding of brain chemistry and diseases such as epilepsy, Alzheimer's and many other neurological diseases.

Innovation Awards:

☐ **Al Rorison** (North Vancouver, BC) for developing highway repair equipment that removes old, damaged asphalt surfaces, processes the material, and lays it down again as a new surface at the rate of 20 feet per minute. The new process has greatly reduced highway repair costs and eliminated the need to dump old asphalt in landfill sites.

☐ **Normand Morin** (Parry Sound, Ont.) for developing an efficient conveyor belt cleaner that ensures that all the material to be dumped at the end of the belt in fact gets there and doesn't travel back on the underside of the belt. The innovation, a plastic blade that is continuously renewing itself, has received immediate acceptance in construction, mining and other industries.

Young Canadian Innovation Awards for 1994 chosen from 400 participants in the Canada-wide Youth Science Fair competitions held in Guelph.

☐ **Srimoyee Chaudhuri** (Calgary, Alta): sonolysis: ultrasonic irradiation of organic pollutants

☐ **Anie Galipeau** and **Paul Brown** (Ottawa, Ont.): green Walkman

☐ **Niladri Sarkar** and **Yuri Agrawal** (Brossard, Que.): fibre-optic micro-imaging scanner

☐ **Ram Puvanesasingham** and **Chris Heyn** (London, Ont.): plastic gas

A Special Award was given to the **Canadian Industrial Innovation Centre** of Waterloo, Ontario and to **Centennial High School** of Brossard, Quebec for work in developing and encouraging Canadian innovators.

Science and Engineering Hall of Fame

Sixteen Canadians have been inducted into the Canadian Science and Engineering Hall of Fame. The inductees are outstanding researchers, inventors, and innovators who have won worldwide recognition for their accomplishments. The Hall of Fame portrait gallery is located at the National Research Council laboratories on Sussex Drive in Ottawa. Inductees are announced each October.

The Inductees

Maude Abbott (1869-1940)	- pathologist and specialist in congenital heart disease
Sir Frederick Banting (1891-1941)	- co-discoverer of insulin and Nobel laureate
Alexander Graham Bell (1847-1922)	- inventor of the telephone
J. Armand Bombardier (1907-1964)	- inventor of the snowmobile
Reginald Fessenden (1866-1932)	- pioneer in the development of the radio
Sir Sandford Fleming (1827-1915)	- architect of the transcontinental railway and inventor of standard time
Gerhard Herzberg (1904-)	- astrophysicist and Nobel laureate
Sir William Logan (1798-1875)	- first director of the Geological Survey of Canada
Elsie MacGill	- aeronautical engineer, oversaw WWII production of Hawker Hurricane fighter aircraft
Frere Marie-Victorin (1885-1944)	- botanist, author and teache
Andrew GL MacNaughton (1887-1966)	- inventor of cathode-ray detection finder and military leader
Margaret Newton (1887-1971)	- plant pathologist, who developed techniques to combat wheat rust
Joseph-Alphonse Ouimet	- inventor, engineer and CBC president
Wilder Penfield (1891-1976)	- neurosurgeon who developed surgical treatments for epilepsy
John Polanyi (1929-)	- Nobel laureate whose work contributed to the development of laser chemistry
Edgar William Richard Steacie (1900-62)	- researcher (free radical chemistry), educator and former president of the National Research Council
Wallace Turnbull (1870-1954)	- inventor of the variable pitch propellor

Organizations

CISTI: Canada Institute for Scientific and Technical Information provides worldwide information in science, technology and medicine, using online databases, customized information services and publications. Address: Building M-55, Montreal Road, National Research Council Canada, Ottawa, K1A 0S2

Canadian Patent Office: A government agency that provides information to people wishing to file patents. Address: Commissioner of Patents, Consumer and Corporate Affairs Canada, 50 Victoria Street, Place du Portage, Phase 1, Hull, Québec. K1A 0C9

Canadian Industrial Innovation Centre: An organization helping Canadian innovators to develop their ideas. Address: 156 Columbia Street West, Waterloo, Ontario. N2I 3L3

Networks of Centres of Excellence in Canada: A federal program supporting the successful transfer of innovative research and development to private industry. Address: 200 Kent Street, Ottawa, Ontario. K1A 1H5

Women Inventors Project: A non-profit organization providing information to women inventors and to teachers. Address: 1 Greensboro Drive, Suite 302, Etobicoke, Ontario. M9W 1C8

The Computer

Some Common Computer Terms

ASCII (American Standard Code for Information Interchange): The common language in the form of a 7-bit, numerical code used by personal computers to translate the language of one software program to that of another.

Baud Rate: The transmission speed used to send data from one computer to another; a baud is roughly equal to one bit per second.

Bit: Contraction of "binary digit." The smallest unit of information: either "on" representing 1; or "off," representing 0.

Buffer: A storage device used to compensate for differences in the rate of data flow, or in the timing of events, when transmitting data from one device to another.

Bug: An error in a computer program that interferes with the processing the data.

Byte: A group of eight bits of data.

CD-ROM (Compact Disk: Read Only Memory): A type of compact disc system for the optical storage and retrieval of information. One CD can hold hundreds of thousands of pages of information, and combine text with sound, images and animation.

Character Set: The characters that may be coded and/or printed by a particular machine.

Character: A letter, figure, number, punctuation, or other symbol contained in a message or used in a control function.

CPU (Central Processing Unit): The CPU consists of the computer circuitry that interprets and executes program instructions and coordinates the interaction of input, output and storage devices.

Crash: An uncontrolled shutdown of a computer system.

Directory: A system of organizing or listing files; an inventory.

DPI (Dots per inch): A measure of resolution; that is the number of dots per square inch. The higher the number, the more detailed is the printed image.

Downloading: Retrieving a file from one computer and storing it on another, such as in downloading an E-mail file.

E-Mail: Electronic mail: messages exchanged between one computer and another on a local-area network (LAN: see below) or online service.

Expert System: A problem-solving, computer program modeled on human expertise.

Font: A complete set of numbers, letters or symbols in a particular style or size.

Gateway: Hardware and software that permits devices located on a local-area network (LAN) to access the facilities of another network.

Handshaking: Exchange of predetermined codes and signals between two data terminals to establish a connection.

Input: Information a computer receives from an external device, such as a keyboard or disk.

Kilobyte: A measurement of information storage capacity, equivalent to 1024 bytes.

LAN (Local-Area Network): A communications network connecting several computers and one or more printers, usually in the same building.

Math Coprocessor: A processor that handles some of the mathematical functions of the computer, enabling the main processor to handle other tasks; thereby increasing overall performance.

Megabyte: A measurement of information storage capacity: 1024 kilobytes or approximately one million bytes.

Memory: The location in the computer where information is stored. Memory is of two types: permanently stored information or ROM (Read Only Memory) ; and temporarily stored information or RAM (Random Access Memory)

Menu: The choice of commands given in on-screen lists.

Modem (Modulate/Demodulate):

A device that converts digital data to analog or voice-like frequencies that the telephone system can reproduce and use to transfer data.

Network: An interconnected group of computers that can exchange information or work together on different parts of the same problem.

Online: Computer operations carried out under direct control of a CPU (central processing unit) while the operator remains in communication with the computer.

Peripheral: A device such as a printer, scanner, or modem.

Pixel: The individual units that make up an on-screen image.

Platform: The primary hardware and operating system you work with, e.g., Macintosh, Windows, etc.

Program: A group of instructions that tells a computer to carry out a particular function. Also called software.

Protocol: A standard set of rules, providing a means to control the orderly communication of information between stations on a data link.

RAM: The random access memory chip stores information temporarily and is erased whenever the computer is turned off. It is the working memory of the computer—the more available RAM, the more tasks the computer will be able to perform.

ROM: The memory chips responsible for instructing the CPU to perform some basic tasks.

Server: A computer dedicated to "serving" all other computers on a network exclusively; for example, storing files that can be accessed by other users.

Utilities: Programs that perform housekeeping tasks like copying, renaming, deleting, and formatting.

Virus: A bug deliberately inserted into a computer system; it can be passed from computer to computer through infected disks.

Window: A portion of the screen display used to view simultaneously a different part of the file in use or part of a different file than the one in use.

Some Milestones in Information Processing

BC

1000 Abacus developed separately in China and in Egypt.

AD

1592 Leonardo da Vinci draws sketches for a mechanical adding machine, based on series of thirteen 10-digit wheels. The underlying concept is the basis of digital counting, adding one digit at a time to make any number.

1614 Scotsman John Napier develops logarithms. He also invents Rhabdology or Napier's bones—a quick multiplying device which laid out the multiplication tables 1-9 on strips of paper wood or bone so that they could be added diagonally. This made automatic carrying possible.

Logarithms: a system of calculation in mathematics using the concept of base numbers. For example if the base number is 10, then the log of 1 000 is 3 (10 x 10 x 10); the log of 10 000 is 4 (10 x 10 x 10 x 10), the log of 100 000 is 5 (10 x 10 x 10 x 10 x 10), etc. The system was developed to shorten calculations, particularly in multiplication and division.

1621 English clergyman, William Outred develops an early slide rule, a circular mechanical device graduated in a logarithmic scale of numbers.

1642 Blaise Pascal invents the first practical calculating machine capable of adding and subtracting, to help his father who was a tax collector.

1673 Gottfried Leibniz explores clockwork mechanisms and develops a general purpose, mechanical calculator that could not only add and subtract, but multiply, divide and extract square roots.

1777 English statesman and scientist, Charles Earl Stanhope develops the world's first logic machine. A simple mechanical device, it could solve simple problems of probability.

Logic—the science of getting new, valid information by reasoning from facts already known, without reference to meaning or context.

1801 Joseph-Marie Jacquard uses punch cards to control the lifting of thread on his mechanical loom. Sets of cards were each punched with a pattern of holes, and then linked together. In this way, an unlimited number of differing instructions could be stored and fed to the machine.

1820 French inventor Charles de Colmar perfects the first commercially successful calculating machine. He sells it to Parisian insurance houses.

1822 English gentleman, Charles Babbage designs a prototype "Difference Machine" for calculating logarithms.

1833 Charles Babbage designs the "Analytical Engine," a computing machine featuring printed card input, memory, and printed output. Never developed beyond the design stage, the machine would have been capable of being programmed to perform different tasks.

1833 English gentlewoman and mathematician, Ada, the Countess of Lovelace, daughter of Lord Byron, contributes to the development of the Analytical Engine. She works out a nearly complete program for the machine and solves problems related to programming "subroutines." She is referred to by some as the world's first computer programmer.

1892 American William Burroughs develops a keyboard for calculators.

1886 American statistician, Herman Hollerith's counting and sorting, punch card machine, is able to process the 1890 US census of 65-million people in two and a half years. Rough tabulation took six weeks. The machine was also capable of cross tabulation. For the first time a large, practical statistical problem is handled by machines.

1925 Efforts by Vanneval Bush, at MIT, to solve very difficult differential equations describing the behaviour of a power line network, results in a special mechanical, analog machine, called a differential analyser. Prior to World War II, several differential analysers are specifically designed to assist in calculating ballistic trajectories for artillery positions.

Analog computers are important when continuous monitoring and control are required. They are highly specialized computers, each one can only do the job for which it's designed.

1936 Englishman Alan Turing develops a theoretical model of a logic machine. In creating this imaginary machine, Turing laid out a working model for the general structure, feasibility, and limitations of digital computers.

1945 Designed by John Mauchey and Presper Eckert, the Electronic Numerical Integrator and Calculator (ENIAC) is the first large-scale, electronic computing device: except for input and output, it has no moving parts, all storage, number manipulation and operations control was by electronic circuit.

1946 John von Neumann puts forward the idea that the instructions given computers can themselves be stored as numbers. The numbers then could easily be converted to binary form— "0" and "1."

1948 Americans, John Bardeen, Walter Brattain, and William Shockley of Bell Labs invent the transistor. Small, reliable and cool, it eventually replaces the bulky, unreliable, heat-generating vacuum tube.

1950 Sergei A. Lebedev working at the Ukrainian Academy of Sciences in Kiev, builds the first Soviet electronic, digital stored-memory computer, the MESM (Malaia Elektronnaia Schnetnaia Mashina—Small Calculating Machine).

1951 Mauchey and Eckert's UNIVAC (Universal Automatic Computer) uses magnetic tape for input. It becomes the first commercially successful computer.

1955 CUC (Computer Usage Company), the world's first computer software company, is started by John Sheldon and Elmer Kubie in Sheldon's Manhattan apartment. All four of the company's first programmers were women.

1965 American's Kemeny and Kurtz develop the first "user friendly: programming language— BASIC (Beginner's All Purpose Instructions Code). Designed so the user could write programs in a conversational mode, it later becomes the standard language for personal computers.

1971 Intel Corporation develops the first microprocessor chip, the 4004; whereby several integrated circuits (ICs) are housed on one silicon chip. The microprocessor is programmable and performs core processing functions. This innovation paves the way for personal computers.

1975 The first personal computer, the MITS Altair 8800, is introduced. Memory capacity is 256 bytes.

1976 First Apple "mother boards" or main circuit board (from which do-it-yourself personal computers can be assembled) are sold to consumers.

1977 The first in the popular Apple II series of personal computers is introduced.

1981 IBM introduces the IBM PC. It soon becomes the personal computer industry standard. The first completely portable personal computer is introduced, the Osborne 1.

1984 Apple introduces Macintosh, the first personal computer that can be controlled by a hand-held device, the "mouse." Using the "mouse," items can be selected from pull-down menus on the screen rather than by typing lines of coded instructions.

1985 Personal computers, small laser printers and the Aldus PageMaker program make desktop publishing possible, whereby office workers can create documents, brochures, and books, eliminating the need for typesetting.

1987 IBM introduces OS/2 that allows multitasking; that is several programs can be run apparently simultaneously in different "windows" on the screen.

1989 Intel announces the 80860, a single chip containing one million transistors.

1991 Palmtop computers are introduced. The hand-held devices can run standard spreadsheets and word processing programs, and can communicate with other compatible machines.

1992 Microsoft introduces Video for Windows. The program enables any personal computer using Windows to integrate moving picture sequences into any application running on that PC. Macintosh had introduced a similar program, QuickTime in 1991.

Electronic Highways

Imagine being able to plug all of your home electronic equipment—television, telephone, fax, computer, central fire and burglar alarms, and more—into a single wall outlet.

This "everything connection," known as the "electronic highway system," may be coming closer to a reality in Canada. Like our road system, the electronic version would include major highways, secondary roads and urban streets. The "cars" and "trucks" would be bundles of information that can travel along all the roads with all kinds of cargo.

Once completed, it would be a "network of networks," joining telecommunications, broadcasting cable, wireless and satellite systems, all seamlessly and transparently interconnected so that hooking up to any one of them would give you, in effect, access to all.

This is possible because as more kinds of information are digitized, old technological boundaries between these services are blurring, although some regulatory boundaries remain.

Precedents for this type of seamless transparent connection already exist. Canadians who telephone Europe don't know or care if their voices are routed through land and undersea cable or satellite links, as long as they connect.

Similarly, television could come to you by cable, telephone, satellite, or a blend of all three.

■ Canadian Routes

Internet is the network of networks that links 20 million computer users in 60 countries. Internet came into being in 1969 as part of a US defence department strategy and has grown steadily, with businesses and individuals signing on in droves during the last three years.

What's been happening in Canada? During the mid-1980s, universities in Quebec, Ontario and BC began to link their computer networks with Internet. Then in 1990, under the direction of the National Research Council, the University of Toronto and IBM Canada set up CA*net to link provincially run computer networks and function as the Canadian part of Internet. Internet's rapid growth means a structural overhaul is due. An upgrade of CA*net is also proposed and CANARIE (the Canadian Network for the Advancement of Research, Industry and Education) has planned a $10 million upgrade of CA*net, part of a larger $115 million plan to expand our electronic infrastructure.

The World's Largest Fax Machine

*S*ending drawings and blueprints to clients by courier is an inconvenience and a costly item for many design, construction and engineering firms. Instead of simply complaining about it, Raja and Suneet Tuli, owners of a Mississauga consulting engineering firm, decided to do something. The result—a new technology, a new business, and a world record.

With the help of a National Research Council grant, the Tuli brothers hired a student who devoted her full time to developing their idea. The resulting WideFax machine can handle documents up to 24 inches wide and 200 feet long, and has been certified by the Guinness Book of World Records as the world's largest fax.

LIFE SCIENCES

The life sciences consist of diverse disciplines that share a knowledge base centered around the same fundamental question, "What is life?" Beginning with biology (the study of living organisms), the life sciences soon included: zoology (the study of animals), botany (the study of plants), and taxonomy (the study of the classification of living things).

Over this century, an ever increasing variety of subdisciplines and approaches to studying life have arisen: microbiology (the study of microorganisms), genetics (the study of heredity), biochemistry (the study of chemical compounds and reactions in living organisms), ecology (the study of the relationships between living things and their environment), and ethology (the study of animal behaviour); and most recently have been joined by biotechnology (the study and use of organisms or their components for the manufacture or production of commercial substances, aided by techniques of genetic manipulation).

Common Life Sciences Terms

Aerobic: Life processes that depend on the presence of oxygen.

Algae: Simple rootless plants that grow in bodies of water in relative proportion to the amount of nutrients available.

Allergen: Any of various sorts of material that as a result of coming into contact with appropriate tissues induce a state of sensitivity and/or resistance to infection or toxic substances.

Anaerobic: Life processes that occur in the absence of oxygen.

Animal: A vertebrate (having a bony skeleton or one made of cartilage) or invertebrate (lacking a spine or skeleton) species including, but not limited to, humans and other mammals, birds, fish, and shellfish.

Bacteria: Single cell microorganisms that possess cell walls. Some cause disease and some are beneficial.

Baleen: Horny plates with fringed inner edges attached to the upper jaw of Mysticeti type whales, such as right and blue whales. The baleen are used to filter plankton and other food from water.

Biodiversity: The total diversity within an ecosystem, including genetic variation among species, diversity of life forms, and ecosystem diversity.

Biomass: The amount of living matter in a given unit of the environment.

Biosphere: The portion of Earth (upwards at least to a height of 10,000 m and downward to the ocean floor and a 100 km below the planet's surface) and the atmosphere surrounding it that supports life.

Bloom: A seasonal, dense growth of small marine plants, i.e., phytoplankton.

Coniferous: Refers to a softwood, cone bearing tree.

Deciduous: Refers to a hardwood, leaf dropping tree.

Effluent Waste: Material discharged into the environment, treated or untreated.

Flood Tide: Interim period of tide between low and high water; a rising tide.

Lagoon: Shallow pond where sunlight, bacterial action and oxygen work to purify waste water.

Marsh: Wet, soft, low-lying land that provides a natural habitat for many plants and animals.

Molt: The periodic casting off or shedding of the outerbody covering (feathers, hair, skin, or cuticle) by birds, mammals, and reptiles.

Nutrients: Elements or compounds essential to growth and development of living things: carbon, oxygen, nitrogen, potassium, and phosphorus.

Osmosis: Tendency of a fluid to pass through a permeable membrane, such as the wall of a living cell, into a less concentrated solution, so as to equalize concentrations on both sides of the membrane.

Photosynthesis: A process of biochemical change in which plant cells, using light as an energy source, manufacture simple sugars from oxygen and carbon dioxide.

Regeneration (forests): The renewal of a forest by natural processes (self-sown seed or root suckers), as well as by sowing or planting new tree stock.

Synthesis: Production of a substance by the union of elements or simpler chemical compounds.

Tailings: Residue of raw materials or waste separated out during the processing of wood or minerals products.

Tidal Marsh: Low, flat marshlands crossed by interlaced channels and tidal sloughs, and subject to tidal inundation from the ocean, normally, the only vegetation present is salt-tolerant rushes and grasses.

Tide: Alternate rising and falling of water levels twice each lunar day, due to gravitational attraction of the moon and the sun in conjunction with the Earth's rotational force.

Major Groups of Living Organisms

All life forms are classified in a hierarchical series of groups. Taxonomy, the science of such classification, was introduced by Swedish scientist, Carolus Linneaus (1707-78). All plants, animals and organisms are identified, described, and named, according to their anatomy, physiology and biochemical information. The system of classification is flexible, allowing updating as more is learned about the organisms and their fossil history.

All living things are organized into five major groups, called kingdoms; that is:
• Monerans (bacteria and simple, one-celled organisms),
• Protists (complex, one-celled organisms),
• Fungi,
• Plants,
• Animals.

Organisms in a given kingdom are more closely related to one another than they are to organisms in a different kingdom.

Each kingdom is divided into sub-groups of two or more phyla. Organisms within one phylum are more closely related to one another than they are to members of other phyla. For example, the phylum Arthropoda, described as segmented animals with an external skeletons, includes insects, arachnids, millipedes, crustaceans, and crabs among others.

The phyla are also divided into parts, which are then further divided, each time on the basis of closer and closer relationships.

In descending order of size, the main divisions of the system are:

Kingdom
    Phylum
        Class
            Order
                Family
                    Genus
                        Species

The standard naming of species involves two Latin names. The first (generic) name designates the genus to which it belongs, while the second part of the name is particular to the species. Thus the wolf, *Canis lupus*, and the dog, *Canis familiaris*, are different species belonging to the same genus.

Order Cetacea

Cetaceans—whales, dolphins and porpoises—are the most intelligent creatures on the planet, apart from the higher primates, including humans. Among the largest animals ever known, present day cetaceans are divided into two main groups, called suborders—Odontoceti and Mysticeti. About a hundred species live in the oceans, seas and many rivers.

All cetaceans have flippers, a streamlined body, and a horizontally-flattened tail. They breathe through a blowhole on the top of the head. Unlike seals and walruses, cetaceans are powered completely by their tails. The flippers are used only for steering and balance, and in some species are actually folded away into "flipper pockets" or depressions in the body wall while swimming.

Cetaceans differ in shape, length, weight, colour and marking. These differences are important not only to distinguish between species, but for determining age, sex, and local variation within species. These mammals spend their entire life, including birth, in water. A young cetacean must be able to swim, surface for air, follow its mother and keep itself warm from the moment of its birth.Cetaceans have well developed and distinct voices. All speak by means of a series of clicks and squeals. The *Odontoceti* are considered the most vocal. The *Odontoceti* live primarily on a diet of fish; the *Mysticeti*, primarily on plankton and small crustaceans.

■ Cetacean Classification

The classification of species that live in the waters surrounding Canada is as follows:

ORDER: Cetacea
SUBORDER: Odontoceti or Toothed Whales
General characteristics include: single external blowhole and simple conical teeth which they use to catch fish and squid.

FAMILY: Ocean Dolphin
GENUS: Delphinidae
SPECIES: • Killer whale
• Long Finned Pilot Whale
• Atlantic White-sided Dolphin
• Pacific White-sided Dolphin
• White-Beaked Dolphin

FAMILY: Porpoise
GENUS: Phocoenidae
SPECIES: • Harbour Porpoise
• Dall's Porpoise

FAMILY: Sperm Whale
GENUS: Physeteidae
SPECIES: • Sperm Whale

FAMILY: Beluga / Narwhal
GENUS: Monodontidae
SPECIES: • Narval
• Beluga

ORDER: Cetacea
SUBORDER: Mysticeti or Baleen Whales
General characteristics include: paired blowholes and baleen instead of teeth. The baleen act as a sieve, allowing water to filter through and trap the tiny animals upon which the whales feed.

FAMILY: Rorqual
GENUS: Balaenopteridae
SPECIES: • Blue Whale
• Fin Whale
• Humpback Whale
• Minke Whale

FAMILY: Gray Whale
GENUS: Eschrichtidae
SPECIES • Gray Whale

FAMILY: Right Whale
GENUS: Balaenidae
SPECIES: • Right Whale
• Bowhead Whale

Whale Watching in Canada

Many people like to observe whales in their natural habitat. Fisheries and Oceans Canada has drawn up guidelines to ensure people do not modify whale behaviour, cause them injury, or keep them away from their habitat during mating, nursing and feeding periods. The lives and safety of observers can also be threatened if precautions are ignored.

■ Where to Go

Atlantic Region:

St Mary's Bay, Newfoundland
Trinity Bay, Newfoundland
Quoddy area of New Brunswick
Northeast coast of Cape Breton Island

Central Canada:

Saguenay area of Québec
Northshore of the St. Lawrence estuary, Québec

Western Canada:

Churchill, Manitoba
Pacific Rim National Park, BC
Johnstone Strait area of BC

The *North:*

Mackenzie Bay, NWT
Resolute, NWT
Pond Inlet, NWT
Frobisher Bay, NWT

■ When You Go

General Rule

• Do not hunt, chase, follow, disperse, drive or herd pods or individual whales.

Guidelines for Specific Areas and Species

Special precautions must be taken with some species and in some areas.

British Columbia: Robson Bight Ecological Reserve: This reserve was created to protect a portion of the killer whales' natural habitat. Rules for whale watching include:

• keep more than 300 m from the whales. Anyone wishing to observe whales at closer range must obtain a special permit. Outside the reserve, killer whales may be approached to within 100 m without a permit.

• avoid heading directly toward the whales. They will disperse. Instead, travel in a parallel course.

The permit may be obtained from: Ecological Reserves Unit, 1019 Wharf Street, Victoria BC, V8W 2Y9. Tel no.: (604) 387-1859

Québec: St. Lawrence Estuary: The beluga population of the St. Lawrence Estuary has been designated "endangered". Strict measures are in place.

Do not try to approach a pod, i.e., group of whales. If you find yourself near a pod take these added precautions:

• do not allow your boat to drift toward the

animals. Keeping your speed down, use your motor to maintain a distance of 300 m.

• be constantly on the lookout to ensure you are not breaking up pods or separating females from their young.

New Brunswick and Nova Scotia: In addition to rorquals, dolphins and porpoises frequent this area, right whales also visit during the summer months. Be very cautious while observing right whales. They are relatively slow-moving and can be easily disturbed or injured.

• Never approach right whales at a speed exceeding 4 knots. They may become frightened.

Source: *Based on* Whale Watching in Canada, *Fisheries and Oceans Canada*

The Right Whale

The right whale is an endangered species worldwide. So named by whalers because it was the "right" whale to kill, these whales have the dubious distinction of having launched the commercial whaling industry. Prized by whalers as early as the 12th century for its high oil yield from thick blubber and extra long baleen, the right whale was hunted to commercial extinction by the 19th century.

Although protected by international agreement since 1935, the world population has failed to show significant signs of recovery. Only an estimated 350 right whales remain in the North Atlantic. Evidence suggests their failure to recover can be attributed to:

• death from collision with ships and from fishing gear entanglements,
• loss of habitat,

• inbreeding,
• and a low reproductive rate.

Individual right whales can be recognized by natural skin growths on their heads. Since 1980, the New England Aquarium in Boston has been compiling a photo album/catalog of right whales that live off the east coast of North America. Being able to identify individual whales allows researchers in Canada and the United States to become familiar with their habits, behaviour, migration schedule, and social activities over many years. The scientists compile this data to assist in the recovery and survival of the North American right whale.

For information on observing the right whale aboard the vessel *Ocean Search* (from June to October), contact the Grand Mannan Whale and Seabird Research Station, PO Box 9, North Head, NB E0G 2M0

Source: *East Coast Ecosystems*

Whale Watching in Trinity Bay

Over two decades, Dr. Peter Beamish, his researchers and the whales in Trinity Bay, Newfoundland have developed a rhythm-based "language" of sound and movement. The whales and the researchers are now able to communicate simple messages. Ocean Contact, based in Trinity, gives visitors an opportunity to participate in this active cetacean-human research. During the summer months, research vessels will bring visitors and whales into eye-to-eye contact, as well as providing people with an opportunity to "talk" with the whales.

For further information, contact: Dr. Peter Beamish, Ocean Contact, PO Box 10, Trinity, Newfoundland A0C 2S0

Pollution of the World's Oceans

■ The Greenhouse Effect and Global Warming

Earth's atmosphere acts as a natural greenhouse by trapping the sun's heat near the planet's surface, which maintains an optimum temperature for plants and animals, including humans, to survive quite comfortably. Earth's atmosphere is made up primarily of nitrogen (78%) and oxygen (21%). The remainder consists of argon (0.99%), carbon dioxide (0.03%), traces of other gases, and small, variable amounts of water vapour. Together these natural "greenhouse" gases form a perfect gaseous envelope around the planet.

The composition of Earth's atmosphere has changed very little over thousands of years until the 20th century. Now an abrupt change appears to be taking place. Much of the energy we use to power our cars, to heat our homes, produce electricity, and manufacture products comes from fossil fuels such as coal, petroleum, peat or natural gas. These fuels were formed by the decomposition of prehistoric organisms. When burned, they produce large amounts of carbon dioxide, methane and nitrous oxide as byproducts, which are then added to the atmosphere.

Many scientists believe the marked increase in these gases, carbon dioxide in particular, is disrupting the natural balance of the envelope. Research into the composition of the atmosphere over the past 160 000 years, based on observations of ice core data from a deep drillhole at Vostok Station in Antarctica, shows links between past atmospheric concentrations of CO_2 and temperature. The departure from normal highs began in the 1830s—at the beginning of the Industrial Revolution.

Scientists now predict global temperatures will rise as the concentration of gases produced by fossil fuels continues to increase. If this theory is correct, not only will there be a global change in climate, but water supply, sea levels, and plant and animal life will all be affected.

Scientists seem to agree on a number of points:

- Global Warming—The degree of warming will not be uniform all over the planet, but will be highest at high latitudes.
- Water Supply—While some areas of Canada may receive more rain, others would be drier. This could mean increased drought on the prairies, melting permafrost in the North, shrinking glaciers, and a 25-50 per cent reduction in run-off in the Great Lakes-St. Lawrence Basin. The possible benefits of increased rainfall would be offset by increased evaporation.
- Sea Levels—Globally, with almost 50 per cent of the world's population located along ocean coastlines, the possibility of a 30 to 100 cm rise in sea levels by 2100 has ominous implications, particularly for low-lying areas such as Prince Edward Island, Bangladesh, and the Netherlands. Salt marsh habitats would also be affected.
- Plant and Animal Life—In Canada's North, where global warming could mean as much as a 10°C rise in average temperature, many animals could have difficulty adjusting. Recent research shows the treeline in the Northwest Territories and Northern Quebec and Labrador to be advancing northward, a process that began in the late sixties.

Source: *Environment Canada and* Wat on Earth.

Important Greenhouse Gases

*C*arbon Dioxide *(CO_2): the most important greenhouse gas (natural or manufactured). Plants and all animals, including humans, release CO_2 when breathing. The burning of fossil fuels (coal, oil, natural gas) and global deforestation is a major source of CO_2.*

Methane: produced when vegetation is burned, digested or rotted without the presence of oxygen. Large amounts of methane are released by rice paddies, grazing cattle, rotting material in garbage dumps or landfills, and by fossil fuels.

Nitrous Oxide: occurs naturally in the environment. Large amounts are released from the use of chemicals fertilizers and the burning of fossil fuels.

Endangered Species in Canada[1]

An endangered species is any native species of plant or animal whose existence in Canada is threatened with imminent exitinction.

Species	Critical habitat

■ Birds

Acadian Flycatcher	Ontario
Anatum Peregrine Falcon	throughout Canada, except PEI
Eskimo Curlew	for breeding: tundra and lichen woodland
Harlequin Duck, Eastern population	coastal waters of Maritimes and New England
Henslow's Sparrow	Ontario
King Rail	Ontario
Kirtland's Warbler	dense jack pine stands
Loggerhead Shrike	old fields in eastern Man., Ont. and Que.
Mountain Plover	flat, heavily grazed grasslands of southern Alta and Sask.
Northern Bobwhite	Ontario
Piping Plover	along beaches, close to the water
Sage Thrasher	breeds in southern interior BC, southeast Alta., southwest Sask.
Spotted Owl	old growth timber in southwest BC
Whooping Crane	breeding: generally Wood Buffalo National Park

■ Fish

Acadian Whitefish	Tusket and Petit rivers in southern NS
Aurora Trout	small lakes; however, no species left in wild
Salish Sucker	Campbell and Salmon rivers headwaters, BC

■ Mammals

Beluga (White Whale) St. Lawrence River stock	St. Lawrence estuary
Southeast Baffin stock	shallow coastal waters and river mouths; complete range unknown
Ungava Bay stock	Ungava Bay, northern Quebec
Bowhead Whale	winter: southern edge of pack ice
Eastern Cougar (mountain lion)	mixed and coniferous forest
Peary Caribou	Arctic tundra; with grasses and lichens
Right Whale	coasts of N. America, both Atlantic and Pacific, from tropics to sub-arctic
Sea Otter	Pacific Coast
Vancouver Island Marmot	alpine and subalpine areas, steep slopes, talus debris and open meadows
Wolverine, Eastern population	East of Hudson Bay and James Bay

■ Reptile

Blanchard's Cricket Frog	wet areas on Pelee Island and Point Pelee, Lake Erie
Blue Racer (snake)	Pelee Island, Ont.
Lake Erie Water Snake	western Lake Erie islands, Ont.
Leatherback Turtle	nesting: beaches

■ Plants

Cucumber Tree	9 sites in southwestern Ont.
Eastern Mountain Avens	generally in the Maritime provinces
Eastern Prickly Pear Cactus	southwestern Ont.
Engelmann's Quillwort	southern edge of Canadian Shield in Ont.
Furbish's Lousewort (herb)	banks of the upper Saint John R., NB
Gattinger's Agalinis	delta islands of St. Clair river in southwestern Ont.
Heart-Leaved Plantain	one site remains on the eastern shore of L. Huron; moist depressions in undisturbed deciduous woodland

▶

Species	Critical habitat
► Hoary Mountain Mint	one site in Ont.
Large Whorled Pogonia	only 2 known locations in Ont.
Pink Coreopsis (herb)	only in the Tusket R. valley, NS
Pink Milkwort (herb)	2 sites only in Lambton County, Ont.
Slender Bush Clover	one site in Windsor, Ont.
Slender Mouse-ear-cress	mixed grassland, southeast Alta to southwest Sask.
Small White Lady Slipper (orchid)	tall grass prairie, bogs, swampy meadows, remnant prairies, edge of thickets
Small Whorled Pogonia (orchid)	one site Elgin County, Ont.
Skinner's Agalinis	delta islands of St. Clair river in southwestern Ont.
Southern Maidenhair Fern	Fairmont Hot Springs, BC
Spotted Wintergreen	St. Williams and Wasaga areas in S. Ont.
Thread-leaved Sundew	only 3 small colonies in peat bogs in NS
Water-pennywort	only found at Wilson's Lake and Kejimkujik Lake in southeastern NS
White Prairie Gentian	only 20 plants in one southern Ont. site
Western Fringed Prairie Orchid	Manitoba
Wood Poppy	Ontario

Source: *Committee on the Status of Endangered Wildlife in Canada*

(1) Status as of April 1994.

Pollution of the World's Oceans

POLLUTANTS	North Sea	Mediterranean Sea	Indian Ocean	Southeast Pacific Ocean	North Atlantic Ocean	North Pacific Ocean	Caribbean Sea	South Atlantic Ocean	South Pacific Ocean
Agricultural pesticides and fertilizers, runoff		■	■	■	■	■			
Food and beverage processing	■	■			■	■	■	■	■
Industries, chemical	■	■			■	■			
Industries, metal	■	■			■	■		■	
Industries, petrochemical	■	■			■	■		■	
Mining			■		■				■
Petroleum, drilling	■	■			■	■	■	■	■
Petroleum, transportation	■	■		■	■	■	■	■	■
Pulp and paper manufacturing					■	■			
Radioactive wastes	■	■	■		■	■	■		
Sea-salt extraction								■	
Sewage	■	■	■		■	■	■	■	■
Sewage sludge, dumping	■								
Silt from coastal development			■	■			■		
Thermal sources			■		■		■	■	

Source: *Global Atlas*, Gage Educational Publishing Company

Names of Animal Babies

Adult name	A baby is known as:	Adult name	A baby is known as:
Ape or monkey	an infant	Harp or hooded seal	a whitecoat
Bat	a batling	Horse	a foal
Bear	a cub	Kangaroo	a joey
Beaver	a kit or pup	Koala	a cub or gum baby
Chicken	a chick	Moose	a calf
Crane	a craneling	Owl	an owlet
Dolphin	a cub	Parrot	a chick
Cat (domestic)	a cub, kit, kitling, kitten or pussy	Pheasant	a chick
Deer	a fawn	Pigeon	a squab
Dog (domestic)	a pup, puppy or whelp	Porcupine	a porcupette
Donkey	a colt or foal	Porpoise	a cub
Duck	a duckling	Rabbit	a fawn or kit
Eagle	an eaglet	Sheep	a lamb, hog, shearling, tag or teg
Elephant	a calf	Swan	a cygnet
Goat	a fawn or kid	Swine (domestic)	a garrow, grice, pigletor shoat
Goose	a gosling	Turkey	a poult
Hawk	an eyas	Zebra	a colt or fawn

Source: *Metro Toronto Zoo*

Animal Facts

Mammal group (species)	Length (avg. m)	Height (avg. m)	Weight (avg. kg)	Gestation (avg.)	Lifespan (avg.)	Status (in wild)
Ape (Barbary)	0.6	n.a.	7	7mo	20	OK
Baboon (Hamadryas)	0.7	n.a.	18	6mo	17	OK
Bear (Grizzly)	2.6	2.8	336	8mo	25	OK
Bear (Polar)	2.6	1.4	410	8mo	25	Vulnerable
Beaver (Canadian)	0.6	n.a.	23	128 d	20	OK
Bobcat	0.8	n.a.	8	80 d	11	OK
Caribou (Woodland)	1.7	1.3	214	140 d	15	OK
Cheetah (African)	1.7	.8	52	90 d	n.a.	Vulnerable
Cougar	2.1	n.a.	70	94 d	20	Endangered
Deer (White Tailed)	1.8	1.0	98	200 d	15	OK
Devil (Tasmanian)	0.7	n.a.	7	31 d	8	OK
Elephant (African)	n.a.	2.9	4615	20mo	60	Vulnerable
Gibbon (White-Handed)	0.5	n.a.	7	206 d	30	OK
Giraffe (Masai)	4.0	3.1	1175	450 d	18	OK
Gorilla (Lowland)	n.a.	1.5	208	9mo	43	Vulnerable
Hippo (River)	4.2	1.5	3750	234 d	n.a.	OK
Jaguar	1.7	n.a.	102	99 d	20	Endangered
Lion (African)	2.1	1.0	205	108 d	23	OK
Lynx (Canadian)	0.9	0.6	16	60 d	15	OK
Monkey (Spider)	0.5	n.a.	7	139 d	n.a.	Vulnerable
Moose	2.8	1.7	700	246 d	20	OK
Orangutan (Sumatran)	1.4	1.5	58	8–9mo	35	Endangered
Otter (River)	0.7	n.a.	10	11mo	19	OK
Panda (Red)	0.6	n.a.	5	120 d	n.a.	Unknown
Rhino (Indian)	3.2	1.6	3000	19mo	50+	Endangered
Sheep (Dall's)	1.5	1.0	83	165 d	18	Vulnerable
Tiger (Siberian)	2.3	n.a.	250	105 d	16	Endangered
Wolf (Arctic)	1.5	1.0	40	4mo	14	OK

Source: *Metro Toronto Zoo*

n.a. = not available or not applicable

Groups of Animals

Animal name	When you'd rather not say a "bunch of", try the group name:	Animal name	When you'd rather not say a "bunch of", try the group name:
Ants	colony	Martens	richness
Apes or monkeys	troop	Mice	nest
Bears	sloth or sleuth	Owls	parliament
Beavers	colony		
Boars	sounder	Pheasants	covey (on ground),
Butterflies	flight		bouquet (rising), nide
			(nye) (large covey), nest
Cats	clouder or clowder,		or brood (family)
	clutter, cluster (tame),	Pigs	drove or litter
	kindle (young)	Ponies	string
Chickens	brood	Porpoises	school
Colts	rag	Poultry	run
Crows	murder or murmuration	Prairie dogs	coterie
Deer	bevy	Ravens	unkindness
Dogs	kennel	Rhinoceroses	crash
Donkeys	pace	Roaches	shoal
Ducks	brace, flock, paddling		
	(swimming), raft or team	Salmon	run
	(in flight)	Sandpipers	murmuration
		Snakes	bed
Eagles	convocation	Sparrows	host
Eels	swarm	Squirrels	drag (dray)
Elephants	herd	Storks	mustering
Elk	gang	Swallows	flight
		Swine	den, drift, sounder
Ferrets	business		or doylt (tame)
Finches	charm		
Flies	business		
Frogs	army	Toads	knot
		Trout	hover
Goats	tribe	Turkeys	rafter
Gorillas	band	Turtles	bale
Grasshoppers	cluster		
Hens	brood	Wasps	nest
Hogs	drift	Whales	gam, pod, or herd
			(sperm)
Jackrabbits	husk	Woodpeckers	descent
Jays	band	Wrens	herd
Jellyfish	smack		
Kittens	kindle or litter		
Larks	exaltation, ascension		
	or bevy		
Leopards	leap		
Lions	pride		

Source: *Metro Toronto Zoo*

Zoos and Aquariums*

Maritime Region:

☐ **Aquarium and Marine Centre**
2nd Avenue, Shippigan, NB E0B 2P0. Tel: (506) 336-4771. Entrance fee. Open May to September.

☐ **Cherry Brook Zoo**
Saint John, NB E2L 3W2. Tel: (506) 634-1440. Entrance fee. Open all year.

Central Canada:

☐ **Aquarium du Québec**
1675, avenue du Parc, Sainte-Foy, Quebec G1W 4S3 Tel: (418) 659-5266. Entrance fee. Open all year.

☐ **The Biodôme de Montréal**
An environmental museum. 4777, avenue Pierre-de-Coubertin, Montréal, Quebec H1V 1B3. Entrance fee. Open all year.

☐ **Jardin Zoologique de Québec**
8191, avenue du Zoo, Charlesbourg, Quebec G1G 4G4. Tel: (418) 622-0313. Entrance fee. Open all year.

☐ **Parc safari Africain**
823 Rt. 202, Hemmingford, Quebec J0L 1H0 Tel: (514) 247-2727. Entrance fee. Open mid-May to Labour Day.

☐ **Société Zoologique de Granby**
347, rue Bourget, Granby, Quebec J2G 1E8. Tel: (514) 372-5531. Entrance fee. Open May to September.

☐ **African Lion Safari**
R.R#1, Cambridge, Ontario N1R 5S2. Tel: (519) 623-2620. Entrance fee. Open summer.

☐ **Jungle Cat World**
R.R.#1, Orono, Ontario L0B 1M0. Tel: (416) 983-5016. Entrance fee. Open March to November.

☐ **Metro Toronto Zoo**
Meadowvale Road, Scarborough, Ontario M1E 4R5. Tel; (416) 392-5900. Entrance fee. Open all year.

☐ **Riverview Park and Zoo**
Peterborough, Ontario K9J 6Z5. Tel: (705) 748-9300 No charge. Open all year.

Western Canada:

☐ **Assiniboine Park Zoo**
-2355 Corydon Avenue, Winnipeg, Manitoba R3P 0R5. Tel: (204) 888-3634. No charge. Open all year.

☐ **Forestry Farm Zoo**
Saskatoon, Saskatchewan S7N 2H0. Tel: (306) 975-3382. Entrance fee. Open all year.

☐ **Calgary Zoo, Botanical Garden and Prehistoric Park**
1300 Z00 Road, Calgary, Alberta T2E 7V6. Tel: (403) 232-9300. Entrance fee. Open all year.

☐ **Valley Zoo**
Edmonton, Alberta T5J 2R7. Tel: (403) 496-6911. Entrance fee. Open all year.

☐ **Crystal Garden**
713 Douglas Street, Victoria, BC V8W 1N8. Tel: (604) 386-1356. Entrance fee. Open all year.

☐ **Kamloops Wildlife Park**
East Trans Canada Highway, Kamloops, BC V2C 5L7. Tel: (604) 573-3242. Entrance fee. Open all year.

☐ **Okanagan Game Farm**
Kaleden, BC V2A 6J9. Tel: (604) 497-5405. Entrance fee. Open all year.

☐ **Vancouver Game Farm**
5048, 264 Street, Aldergrove, BC V0X 1A0. Tel: (604) 856-6825. Entrance fee. Open all year.

☐ **Vancouver Public Aquarium**
Stanley Park, Vancouver, BC V6B 3X8. Tel: (604) 658-3364. Entrance fee. Open all year.

*Accredited by the Canadian Association of Zoological Parks and Aquariums

ARTS AND ENTERTAINMENT

Arts and Entertainment Highlights, 1993–94

Oct 5: Lucien Bouchard, leader of the Bloc Québécois and leader of the Opposition, announces he wants the federal government to give Quebec responsibility for its own arts and culture. More than a hundred protestors march and chant outside the new Performing Arts Centre in North York, Ontario at the first preview performance of the musical "Showboat." The peaceful demonstration protests what the demonstrators claim are racist depictions of black people in the popular Jerome Kern/Oscar Hammerstein musical. The Governor General's Performing Arts Awards are announced in Toronto. The winners are Leonard Cohen, Gilles Vigneault, Lois Marshall, Don Haig, Ludmilla Chiriaeff and Monique Mercure.

Oct 13: Author Sandra Birdsell wins the Marian Engel Award.

Oct 18: The Supreme Court of Canada rules that viewers in Ontario and Eastern Quebec will finally be able to see "The Boys of St. Vincent," an NFB drama focussing on child abuse in a Catholic orphanage in Newfoundland. The film was originally scheduled for broadcast in these provinces on CBC television a year ago.

Oct 28: The Canadian Association of Broadcasters announce what it calls "the toughest television violence code in North America."

Nov 4: Michel Dupuy is sworn in as the new Minister of Canadian Heritage (which includes culture) in Ottawa.

Nov 16: The Governor General's Literary Awards are announced. Winners include Carol Shields for her novel *The Stone Diaries*, poet Don Coles for "Forests of the Medieval World," and novelist Nancy Huston for *Cantique des Plaines*.

Nov 25: Although in danger of closing, the Dalhousie University Art Gallery celebrates its 40th anniversary.

Dec 2: Editors from five Quebec publishing houses protest this year's choice for the Governor General's Award for French-language fiction, arguing that since the book is a translation of an English language novel, it should not have been considered.

Dec 8: The CBC, Bell Canada and a number of Canadian arts organizations jointly put in an application to the CRTC for a performing arts television channel to be called Festival. The Newfoundland Writers Guild celebrates its 25th Anniversary.

Dec. 12: The film *32 Short Films About Glenn Gould* wins several Genie Awards at the first Genie Award ceremony held in Montreal. John Pozer wins the first Claude Jutra Award for the direction of his first feature film, *The Grocer's Wife*.

Dec 22: A group of English speaking poets in Montreal plaster the city with poetry posters to celebrate the new law that allows outdoor signs to be in languages other than French.

Jan 6: Appointments to the Order of Canada include jazz artists Oliver Jones and Phil Nimmons, playwright Thomson Highway, singers Kate and Anna McGarrigle and writer Dennis Lee.

Jan 10: Anne Hébert wins the Giles Corbeil Prize, one of the richest literary awards in the world, which is given every three years to a Quebec writer.

Jan 31: The CBC's much-criticized "Prime Time News" gets a face-lift, but stays in the 9 pm time slot.

Feb 1: The Humour Museum in Montreal closes indefinitely. A private donor saves the Dalhousie Art Gallery from closing down.

Feb 2: Nomination rules for the Juno Awards deny rocker Brian Adams a nod for Single of the Year consideration for "Please Forgive Me." After loud protests, Juno organizers promise to correct the rule, which bases eligibility on airplay rather than sales, for the 1995 Awards.

Feb 16: Karen Kain marks 25 years with the National Ballet. A group of Quebec comedians team up with the Power Corporation to try to save the Humour Museum in Montreal.

Feb 22: The Federal budget is announced, and arts and culture groups are generally spared major cuts, but there are still reductions to grants to arts programs funded by the Heritage Ministry.

March 2: Saskatoon is named the reading capital of North America.

March 6: The controversial television film "The Boys of St. Vincent" sweeps Award honours at the Gemini Awards.

March 10: The federal government comes under attack in the House of Commons for its decision to sell Ginn Publishing to US-based Paramount Communications. Composer R. Murray Shafer wins the Molson Prize worth $50 000.

March 15: The federal opposition called for a public investigation of the government's sale of Ginn & Co., but the motion was defeated.

March 23: The all-Canadian, all-original musical *Napoleon* opens in Toronto at the Winter Garden theatre.

March 24: Deborah Joy Corey wins the Smithbooks/Books in Canada First Novel Award this year for her book *Losing Eddie.*

March 28: The first annual Stephen Leacock Poetry Awards are held on the anniversary of Leacock's death. The top prize of $5 000 is won by poet Linda Rogers.

May 11: CBC announces that "Prime Time News" will move back to the 10:00 pm slot next fall after a failed attempt to capture an audience at 9 pm.

May 24: Atom Egoyan wins the international critic's prize at Cannes for his new film *Exotica.*

June 1: Author Roch Carrier is named Director of the Canada Council with Donna Scott as its new Chairperson.

June 6: Three culture channels, Showcase, Bravo, and Arts et Divertissement, are among ten chosen for licenses by the CRTC.

June 14: Carol Shields named Author of the Year by the Canadian Booksellers Association.

June 28: Martin Short, Robert LePage, and Evelyn Hart are named to the Order Of Canada.

August 1: The Canada Council's Prix de Rome is given to Vancouver architect, Anthony Robins.

MOVIES

Genie Awards, 1983–93

The Genie Awards have been presented since 1980 by the Academy of Canadian Cinema and Television to honor achievement in the Canadian film industry. Awards apply to films released in the previous year. Voting is conducted in a two-step process whereby the winners are chosen by all academy members from among the five nominees selected in each category by their respective craft branches. These awards were presented Dec. 12, 1993.

1983

Picture . . . . *The Grey Fox*
Actor . . . . Donald Sutherland, *Threshold*
Actress . . . . Rae Dawn Chong, *Quest for Fire*
Sup. Actor . . . R. H. Thomson, *If You Could See What I Hear*
Sup. Actress . . . . Jackie Burroughs, *The Grey Fox*
Director. . . . . Phillip Borsos, *The Grey Fox*

1984

Picture . . . . *The Terry Fox Story*
Actor . . . . Eric Fryer, *The Terry Fox Story*
Actress. . . . . Martha Henry, *The Wars*
Sup. Actor . . . . Michael Zelniker, *The Terry Fox Story*
Sup. Actress. . . . . Jackie Burroughs, *The Wars*
Director . . . . Bob Clark, *A Christmas Story;*
David Cronenberg, *Videodrome*

1985

Picture . . . . *The Bay Boy*
Actor . . . . Gabriel Arcand, *Le Crime d'Ovide Plouffe*
Actress . . . . Louise Marleau, *La Femme de l'hôtel*
Sup. Actor . . . . Alan Scarfe, *The Bay Boy*
Sup. Actress . . . . Linda Sorensen, *Draw!*
Director . . . . Micheline Lanctôt, *Sonatine*

1986

Picture . . . . *My American Cousin*
Actor. . . . . John Wildman, *My American Cousin*
Actress . . . . Margaret Langrick, *My American Cousin*
Sup. Actor . . . . Alan Arkin, *Joshua Then and Now*
Sup. Actress . . . . . . Linda Sorensen, *Joshua Then and Now*
Director . . . . Sandy Wilson, *My American Cousin*

1987

Picture . . . . *The Decline of the American Empire*
Actor. . . . . Gordon Pinsent, *John and the Missus*
Actress. . . . . Martha Henry, *Dancing in the Dark*
Sup. Actor . . . . Gabriel Arcand, *The Decline of the American Empire*
Sup. Actress . . . . Louise Portal, *The Decline of the American Empire*
Director . . . . Denys Arcand, *The Decline of the American Empire*

1988

Picture . . . . *Un Zoo la nuit*
Actor . . . . Roger Le Bel, *Un Zoo la nuit*
Actress . . . . Sheila McCarthy, *I've Heard the Mermaids Singing*

▶ Sup. Actor . . . . Germaine Houde, *Un Zoo la nuit*
Sup. Actress . . . . Paule Baillargeon, *I've Heard the*
. . . . *Mermaids Singing*
Director . . . . Jean-Claude Lauzon, *Un Zoo la nuit*

1989
Picture . . . . *Dead Ringers*
Actor . . . . Jeremy Irons, *Dead Ringers*
Actress . . . . Jackie Burroughs, *A Winter Tan*
Sup. Actor . . . . Remy Girard, *Les Portes tournantes*
Sup. Actress . . . . Colleen Dewhurst, *Obsessed*
Director . . . . David Cronenberg, *Dead Ringers*

1990
Picture . . . . *Jesus de Montréal*
Actor . . . . Lothaire Bluteau, *Jesus de Montréal*
Actress . . . . Rebecca Jenkins, *Bye Bye Blues*
Sup. Actor . . . . Remy Girard, *Jesus de Montréal*
Sup. Actress . . . . Robyn Stevan, *Bye Bye Blues*
Director . . . . Denys Arcand, *Jesus de Montréal*

1991
Picture . . . . *Black Robe*
Actor . . . . Remy Girard, *Amoureux fou*
Actress . . . . Pascale Montpetit, *H*
Sup. Actor . . . . August Schellenberg, *Black Robe*
Sup. Actress . . . . Danielle Proulx, *Amoureux fou*
Director . . . . Bruce Beresford, *Black Robe*

1992
Picture . . . . *Naked Lunch*
Actor . . . . Tony Nardi, *La Sarrasine*
Actress . . . . Janet Wright, *Bordertown Café*

Sup. Actor . . . . Michael Hogan, *Solitaire*
Sup. Actress . . . . Monique Mercure, *Naked Lunch*
Director . . . . David Cronenberg, *Naked Lunch*

1993
Picture . . . . *Thirty-Two Short Films about Glenn Gould*
Actor . . . . Tom McCamus, *I Love A Man in Uniform*
Actress . . . . Sheila McCarthy, *The Lotus Eaters*
Sup. Actor . . . . Kevin Tighe, *I Love A Man in Uniform*
Sup. Actress . . . . Nicola Cavendish, *The Grocer's Wife*
Director . . . . François Girard, *Thirty-Two Short Films*
about Glenn Gould
Original Screenplay . . . . Peggy Thompson, *The Lotus Eaters*
Cinematography . . . . . Alain Dostie, *Thirty-Two Short Films*
about Glenn Gould
Film Editing . . . . Gaétan Huot, *Thirty-Two Short Films*
about Glenn Gould
Art Direction . . . . Wolf Kroeger, *Agaguk*
Costume Design . . . . Olga Dimitrov, *Agaguk*
Overall Sound . . . . Hans Peter Strobl, Richard Besse,
Jocelyn Caron, *Le sexe des étoiles*
Sound Editing . . . Gael Maclean, Anke Bakker, Alison Grace,
Ellen Gram, Maureen Wetteland,
The Lotus Eaters
Music Score . . . . Simon Kendall, *Cadillac Girls*
Feature Documentary . . . . *Forbidden Love*
Short Documentary . . . . *Le Singe bleu*
Live Action Short Drama . . . . *The Fairy Who Didn't*
Want To Be A Fairy Anymore
Animated Short . . . . *Pearl's Diner*

Toronto International Film Festival, 1994

(Festival of Festivals)

The 19th annual festival was held from Sept. 8 to 17 in 1994, showing 296 films from around the world. This is widely regarded as North America's major film festival.

People's Choice Award . . . . *Priest* (UK)
International Critics' Award . . . . *Les silences du palais* (Tunisia)
Best Canadian Feature Film . . . . *Exotica*
Metro Media Award . . . . *Heavenly Creatures* (New Zealand)
Best Canadian Short Film . . . . *Frank's Cock*

Source: *Toronto International Film Festival*

Montreal World Film Festival, 1994

The eighteenth annual Festival des Films du Monde was held from Aug. 25th to Sept. 5th in 1994.

Grand Prix of the Americas . . . . *Once Were Warriors* (New Zealand)
Special Grand Prix of the Jury . . . . *Cancion de Cuna (Cradle Song)* (Spain)
Best Director . . . . Jose Luis Garci, *Cancion de Cuna (Cradle Song)* (Spain)
Best Actress . . . . Rena Owen, *Once Were Warriors* (New Zealand)
Best Actor . . . . Alan Rickman, *Mesmer* (UK)
Best Screenplay . . . . Kevin Dowling, *The Sum of Us* (Australia)
Best Short Film . . . . *Scratch Ticket* (Canada)
International Critics Prize . . . . *Le Vent du Wyoming* (Canada)

Source: *Montreal World Film Festival*

The Cannes Film Festival Awards, 1984–94

1984

Best Film .... *Paris, Texas* (international collaboration)
Special Grand Jury Prize .... *Diary For My Children* (Hungary)
Best Director . Bertrand Tavernier, *A Sunday in the Country*
Best Actor .... Francisco Rabal, Alfredo Landa, *Los Santos Innocentes*
Best Actress .... Helen Mirren, *Cal*

1985

Best Film .... *Father's Gone on a Business Trip* (Yugoslavia)
Special Grand Jury Prize .... *Birdy* (USA)
Best Director .... André Techine, *Rendez-vous*
Best Actor ...... William Hurt, *Kiss of the Spider Woman*
Best Actress . Cher, *Mask;* Norma Aleandro, *Official Version*

1986

Best Film .... *The Mission* (Great Britain)
Special Grand Jury Prize .... *The Sacrifice* (Sweden)
Best Director................... Martin Scorsese, *After Hours*
Best Actor ... Michel Blanc, *Tenue de Soirée;* Bob Hoskins, *Mona Lisa*
Best Actress .... Barbara Sukowa, *Rosa Luxemburg;* Fernanda Torres, *Speak to Me of Love*

1987

Best Film .... *Under Satan's Sun* (France)
Special Grand Jury Prize.................. *Repent* (USSR)
Best Director........ Wim Wenders, *The Wings of Desire*
Best Actor ...... Marcello Mastroianni, *Black Eyes*
Best Actress.............. Barbara Hershey, *The Bayou*

1988

Best Film................ *Pelle The Conqueror* (Denmark)
Special Grand Jury Prize..... *A World Apart* (Great Britain)
Best Director........... Fernando E. Solanas, *The South*
Best Actor .... Forest Whitaker, *Bird*
Best Actress .Barbara Hershey, Jodhi May and Linda Mvusi, *A World Apart*

1989

Best Film................. *sex, lies and videotape* (USA)
Special Grand Jury Prize ..... *Trop Belle Pour Toi* (France); *Cinema Paradiso* (Italy)

Best Director......... Emir Kusturica, *Time of the Gypsies*
Best Actor........ James Spader, *sex, lies and videotape*
Best Actress .... Meryl Streep, *A Cry In The Dark*

1990

Best Film .... *Wild at Heart* (USA)
Special Grand Jury Prize ... *Tilaï* (Burkina Faso); *The Sting of Death* (Japan)
Best Director.................. Pavel Loungine, *Taxi Blues*
Best Actor........ Gerard Depardieu, *Cyrano de Bergerac*
Best Actress .... Krystyna Janda, *Interrogation*

1991

Best Film .... *Barton Fink* (USA)
Special Grand Jury Prize .... *La belle noiseuse* (France)
Best Director........ Joel Coen & Ethan Coen, *Barton Fink*
Best Actor .... John Turturro, *Barton Fink*
Best Actress..... Irène Jacob, *The Double Life of Veronica*

1992

Best Film .... *The Best Intentions* (Switzerland)
Special Grand Jury Prize........ *Il Ladro di Bambini* (Italy)
Best Director................. Robert Altman, *The Player*
Best Actor..................... Tim Robbins, *The Player*
Best Actress .... Pernilla August, *The Best Intentions*

1993

Best Film .. (tie) *The Piano,* (New Zealand), *Farewell To My Concubine* (China)
Special Grand Jury Prize ... *Faraway, So Close!* (Germany)
Best Director....................... Mike Leigh, *Naked*
Best Actor .... David Thewlis, *Naked*
Best Actress .... Holly Hunter, *The Piano*

1994

Best Film............................. *Pulp Fiction,* (USA)
Special Grand Jury Prize ... *Burnt by the Sun* (Russia) and *To Live!* (China)
Best Director .... Nanni Moretti, *Journal intime*
Best Actor........................... Ge You, *To Live!*
Best Actress .... Virna Lisi, *la Reine Margot*

Source: *Embassy of France*

(1) The Cannes Festival Jury is not obliged to select a winner in any category except that of Best Film.

Motion Picture Academy Awards (Oscars), 1927–93

1927–28

Picture......................... *Wings,* Paramount
Actor.............. Emil Jannings, *The Way of All Flesh*
Actress .... Janet Gaynor, *7th Heaven*
Director..... Frank Borzage, *7th Heaven;* Lewis Milestone, *Two Arabian Knights*

1928–29

Picture.................. *The Broadway Melody,* MGM
Actor .... Warner Baxter, *In Old Arizona*
Actress .... Mary Pickford, *Coquette*
Director................ Frank Lloyd, *The Divine Lady*

1929–30

Picture......... *All Quiet on the Western Front,* Universal
Actor .... George Arliss, *Disraeli*
Actress .... Norma Shearer, *The Divorcee*
Director ... Lewis Milestone, *All Quiet on the Western Front*

1930–31

Picture............................... *Cimarron,* RKO
Actor .... Lionel Barrymore, *A Free Soul*
Actress .... Marie Dressler, *Min and Bill*
Director .... Norman Taurog, *Skippy* ▶

1931–32

Picture . . . . *Grand Hotel*, MGM
Actor . . . . . Fredric March, *Dr. Jekyll and Mr. Hyde*; Wallace
Beery, *The Champ* (tie)
Actress . . . . Helen Hayes, *Sin of Madelon Claudet*
Director . . . . Frank Borzage, *Bad Girl*
Special . . . . Walt Disney, *Mickey Mouse*

1932–33

Picture . . . . *Cavalcade*, Fox
Actor . . . . Charles Laughton, *The Private Life of Henry VIII*
Actress . . . . Katharine Hepburn, *Morning Glory*
Director . . . . Frank Lloyd, *Cavalcade*

1934

Picture . . . . *It Happened One Night*, Columbia
Actor . . . . Clark Gable, *It Happened One Night*
Actress . . . . Claudette Colbert, *It Happened One Night*
Director . . . . Frank Capra, *It Happened One Night*

1935

Picture . . . . *Mutiny on the Bounty*, MGM
Actor . . . . Victor McLaglen, *The Informer*
Actress . . . . Bette Davis, *Dangerous*
Director . . . . John Ford, *The Informer*

1936

Picture . . . . *The Great Ziegfeld*, MGM
Actor . . . . Paul Muni, *The Story of Louis Pasteur*
Actress . . . . Luise Rainer, *The Great Ziegfeld*
Sup. Actor . . . . Walter Brennan, *Come and Get It*
Sup. Actress . . . . Gale Sondergaard, *Anthony Adverse*
Director . . . . Frank Capra, *Mr. Deeds Goes to Town*

1937

Picture . . . . *Life of Emile Zola*, Warner Bros.
Actor . . . . Spencer Tracy, *Captains Courageous*
Actress . . . . Luise Rainer, *The Good Earth*
Sup. Actor . . . . Joseph Schildkraut, *Life of Emile Zola*
Sup. Actress . . . . Alice Brady, *In Old Chicago*
Director . . . . Leo McCarey, *The Awful Truth*

1938

Picture . . . . *You Can't Take It With You*, Columbia
Actor . . . . Spencer Tracy, *Boys Town*
Actress . . . . Bette Davis, *Jezebel*
Sup. Actor . . . . Walter Brennan, *Kentucky*
Sup. Actress . . . . Fay Bainter, *Jezebel*
Director . . . . Frank Capra, *You Can't Take It With You*

1939

Picture . . . . *Gone With the Wind*, Selznick International
Actor . . . . Robert Donat, *Goodbye, Mr. Chips*
Actress . . . . Vivien Leigh, *Gone With the Wind*
Sup. Actor . . . . Thomas Mitchell, *StageCoach*
Sup. Actress . . . . . . Hattie McDaniel, *Gone With the Wind*
Director . . . . Victor Fleming, *Gone With the Wind*

1940

Picture . . . . Rebecca, Selznick International
Actor . . . . James Stewart, *The Philadelphia Story*
Actress . . . . Ginger Rogers, *Kitty Foyle*
Sup. Actor . . . . Walter Brennan, *The Westerner*
Sup. Actress . . . . Jane Darwell, *The Grapes of Wrath*
Director . . . . John Ford, *The Grapes of Wrath*

1941

Picture . . . . *How Green Was My Valley*, 20th Cent.-Fox
Actor . . . . Gary Cooper, *Sergeant York*
Actress . . . . Joan Fontaine, *Suspicion*
Sup. Actor . . . . . . Donald Crisp, *How Green Was My Valley*
Sup. Actress . . . . Mary Astor, *The Great Lie*
Director . . . . John Ford, *How Green Was My Valley*

1942

Picture . . . . *Mrs. Miniver*, MGM
Actor . . . . James Cagney, *Yankee Doodle Dandy*
Actress . . . . Greer Garson, *Mrs. Miniver*
Sup. Actor . . . . Van Heflin, *Johnny Eager*
Sup. Actress . . . . Teresa Wright, *Mrs. Miniver*
Director . . . . William Wyler, *Mrs. Miniver*

1943

Picture . . . . *Casablanca*, Warner Bros.
Actor . . . . Paul Lukas, *Watch on the Rhine*
Actress . . . . Jennifer Jones, *The Song of Bernadette*
Sup. Actor . . . . Charles Coburn, *The More the Merrier*
Sup. Actress . . . . . Katina Paxinou, *For Whom the Bell Tolls*
Director . . . . Michael Curtiz, *Casablanca*

1944

Picture . . . . *Going My Way*, Paramount
Actor . . . . Bing Crosby, *Going My Way*
Actress . . . . Ingrid Bergman, *Gaslight*
Sup. Actor . . . . Barry Fitzgerald, *Going My Way*
Sup. Actress . . . Ethel Barrymore, *None But the Lonely Heart*
Director . . . . Leo McCarey, *Going My Way*

1945

Picture . . . . *The Lost Weekend*, Paramount
Actor . . . . Ray Milland, *The Lost Weekend*
Actress . . . . Joan Crawford, *Mildred Pierce*
Sup. Actor . . . . James Dunn, *A Tree Grows in Brooklyn*
Sup. Actress . . . . Anne Revere, *National Velvet*
Director . . . . Billy Wilder, *The Lost Weekend*

1946

Picture . . . . . . *The Best Years of Our Lives*, Goldwyn, RKO
Actor . . . . Fredric March, *The Best Years of Our Lives*
Actress . . . . Olivia de Havilland, *To Each His Own*
Sup. Actor . . . Harold Russell, *The Best Years of Our Lives*
Sup. Actress . . . . Anne Baxter, *The Razor's Edge*
Director . . . . . . William Wyler, *The Best Years of Our Lives*

1947

Picture . . . . *Gentleman's Agreement*, 20th Century-Fox
Actor . . . . Ronald Colman, *A Double Life*
Actress . . . . Loretta Young, *The Farmer's Daughter*
Sup. Actor . . . . Edmund Gwenn, *Miracle on 34th Street*
Sup. Actress . . . . . Celeste Holm, *Gentleman's Agreement*
Director . . . . Elia Kazan, *Gentleman's Agreement*

1948

Picture . . . *Hamlet*, Two Cities Film, Universal International
Actor . . . . Laurence Olivier, *Hamlet*
Actress . . . . Jane Wyman, *Johnny Belinda*
Sup. Actor . . . . . . Walter Huston, *Treasure of Sierra Madre*
Sup. Actress . . . . Claire Trevor, *Key Largo*
Director . . . . John Huston, *Treasure of Sierra Madre*

1949

Picture . . . . *All the King's Men*, Columbia.
Actor . . . . Broderick Crawford, *All the King's Men*
Actress . . . . Olivia de Havilland, *The Heiress*▶

▶ Sup. Actor . . . . Dean Jagger, *Twelve O'Clock High*
Sup. Actress . . . Mercedes McCambridge, *All the King's Men*
Director . . . Joseph L. Mankiewicz, *A Letter to Three Wives*

1950

Picture . . . . *All About Eve*, 20th Century-Fox
Actor. . . . . Jose Ferrer, *Cyrano de Bergerac*
Actress. . . . . Judy Holliday, *Born Yesterday*
Sup. Actor. . . . . George Sanders, *All About Eve*
Sup. Actress . . . . Josephine Hull, *Harvey*
Director . . . . Joseph L. Mankiewicz, *All About Eve*

1951

Picture. . . . . *An American in Paris*, MGM
Actor . . . . Humphrey Bogart, *The African Queen*
Actress . . . . Vivien Leigh, *A Streetcar Named Desire*
Sup. Actor . . . . Karl Malden, *A Streetcar Named Desire*
Sup. Actress . . . . . Kim Hunter, *A Streetcar Named Desire*
Director . . . . George Stevens, *A Place in the Sun*

1952

Picture . . . . *The Greatest Show on Earth*, C.B. DeMille,
Paramount
Actor. . . . . Gary Cooper, *High Noon*
Actress . . . . Shirley Booth, *Come Back, Little Sheba*
Sup. Actor . . . . Anthony Quinn, *Viva Zapata!*
Sup. Actress . . Gloria Grahame, *The Bad and the Beautiful*
Director . . . . John Ford, *The Quiet Man*

1953

Picture . . . . *From Here to Eternity*, Columbia
Actor . . . . William Holden, *Stalag 17*
Actress . . . . Audrey Hepburn, *Roman Holiday*
Sup. Actor . . . . Frank Sinatra, *From Here to Eternity*
Sup. Actress . . . . Donna Reed, *From Here to Eternity*
Director . . . . Fred Zinnemann, *From Here to Eternity*

1954

Picture . . . *On the Waterfront*, Horizon-American, Columbia
Actor . . . . Marlon Brando, *On the Waterfront*
Actress . . . . Grace Kelly, *The Country Girl*
Sup. Actor . . . . . . Edmond O'Brien, *The Barefoot Contessa*
Sup. Actress. . . . . Eva Marie Saint, *On the Waterfront*
Director . . . . Elia Kazan, *On the Waterfront*

1955

Picture . . . *Marty*, Hecht and Lancaster's Steven Prods., U.A.
Actor . . . . Ernest Borgnine, *Marty*
Actress . . . . Anna Magnani, *The Rose Tattoo*
Sup. Actor . . . . Jack Lemmon, *Mister Roberts*
Sup. Actress. . . . . Jo Van Fleet, *East of Eden*
Director . . . . Delbert Mann, *Marty*

1956

Picture . . . *Around the World in 80 Days*, Michael Todd, U.A.
Actor . . . . Yul Brynner, *The King and I*
Actress . . . . Ingrid Bergman, *Anastasia*
Sup. Actor . . . . Anthony Quinn, *Lust for Life*
Sup. Actress . . . . . . Dorothy Malone, *Written on the Wind*
Director . . . . George Stevens, *Giant*

1957

Picture . . . . *The Bridge on the River Kwai*, Columbia
Actor. . . . . . . Alec Guinness, *The Bridge on the River Kwai*
Actress . . . . . Joanne Woodward, *The Three Faces of Eve*
Sup. Actor. . . . . Red Buttons, *Sayonara*
Sup. Actress. . . . . Miyoshi Umeki, *Sayonara*
Director . . . . David Lean, *The Bridge on the River Kwai*

1958

Picture . . . . *Gigi*, Arthur Freed Production, MGM
Actor . . . . David Niven, *Separate Tables*
Actress . . . . Susan Hayward, *I Want to Live*
Sup. Actor . . . . Burl Ives, *The Big Country*
Sup. Actress . . . . Wendy Hiller, *Separate Tables*
Director . . . . Vincente Minnelli, *Gigi*

1959

Picture . . . . *Ben-Hur*, MGM
Actor . . . . Charlton Heston, *Ben-Hur*
Actress . . . . Simone Signoret, *Room at the Top*
Sup. Actor . . . . Hugh Griffith, *Ben-Hur*
Sup. Actress . . . . Shelley Winters, *The Diary of Anne Frank*
Director . . . . William Wyler, *Ben-Hur*

1960

Picture. . . . . *The Apartment*, Mirisch Co., U.A.
Actor . . . . Burt Lancaster, *Elmer Gantry*
Actress . . . . Elizabeth Taylor, *Butterfield 8*
Sup. Actor . . . . Peter Ustinov, *Spartacus*
Sup. Actress . . . . Shirley Jones, *Elmer Gantry*
Director . . . . Billy Wilder, *The Apartment*

1961

Picture . . . . *West Side Story*, Mirisch Pictures, U.A.
Actor. . . . . Maximilian Schell, *Judgment at Nuremberg*
Actress. . . . . Sophia Loren, *Two Women*
Sup. Actor . . . . George Chakiris, *West Side Story*
Sup. Actress . . . . Rita Moreno, *West Side Story*
Director . . . Jerome Robbins, Robert Wise, *West Side Story*

1962

Picture . . . . *Lawrence of Arabia*, Columbia
Actor . . . . Gregory Peck, *To Kill a Mockingbird*
Actress . . . . Anne Bancroft, *The Miracle Worker*
Sup. Actor . . . . Ed Begley, *Sweet Bird of Youth*
Sup. Actress . . . . Patty Duke, *The Miracle Worker*
Director . . . . David Lean, *Lawrence of Arabia*

1963

Picture . . . *Tom Jones*, Woodfall Prod., U.A.-Lopert Pictures
Actor . . . . Sidney Poitier, *Lilies of the Field*
Actress . . . . Patricia Neal, *Hud*
Sup. Actor. . . . . Melvyn Douglas, *Hud*
Sup. Actress . . . . Margaret Rutherford, *The V.I.P.s*
Director . . . . Tony Richardson, *Tom Jones*

1964

Picture . . . . *My Fair Lady*, Warner Bros.
Actor . . . . Rex Harrison, *My Fair Lady*
Actress . . . . Julie Andrews, *Mary Poppins*
Sup. Actor . . . . Peter Ustinov, *Topkapi*
Sup. Actress . . . . Lila Kedrova, *Zorba the Greek*
Director. . . . . George Cukor, *My Fair Lady*

1965

Picture . . . . *The Sound of Music*, 20th Century-Fox
Actor . . . . Lee Marvin, *Cat Ballou*
Actress . . . . Julie Christie, *Darling*
Sup. Actor . . . . Martin Balsam, *A Thousand Clowns*
Sup. Actress. . . . . Shelley Winters, *A Patch of Blue*
Director . . . . Robert Wise, *The Sound of Music* ▶

1966

Picture . . . . *A Man for All Seasons*, Columbia
Actor . . . . Paul Scofield, *A Man for All Seasons*
Actress . . . Elizabeth Taylor, *Who's Afraid of Virginia Woolf?*
Sup. Actor . . . . Walter Matthau, *The Fortune Cookie*
Sup. Actress . . . . . Sandy Dennis, *Who's Afraid of Virginia Woolf?*
Director. . . . . Fred Zinnemann, *A Man for All Seasons*

1967

Picture . . . . . *In the Heat of the Night*, Mirisch Corp., U.A.
Actor . . . . Rod Steiger, *In the Heat of the Night*
Actress . . . . . Katharine Hepburn, *Guess Who's Coming to Dinner*
Sup. Actor . . . . George Kennedy, *Cool Hand Luke*
Sup. Actress . . . . Estelle Parsons, *Bonnie and Clyde*
Director . . . . Mike Nichols, *The Graduate*

1968

Picture . . . . *Oliver!*, Columbia
Actor . . . . Cliff Robertson, *Charly*
Actress . . . . Katharine Hepburn, *The Lion in Winter*, Barbra Streisand, *Funny Girl* (tie)
Sup. Actor . . . . Jack Albertson, *The Subject Was Roses*
Sup. Actress . . . . Ruth Gordon, *Rosemary's Baby*
Director . . . . Sir Carol Reed, *Oliver!*

1969

Picture . . . . *Midnight Cowboy*, United Artists
Actor . . . . John Wayne, *True Grit*
Actress . . . Maggie Smith, *The Prime of Miss Jean Brodie*
Sup. Actor . . . Gig Young, *They Shoot Horses, Don't They?*
Sup. Actress . . . . Goldie Hawn, *Cactus Flower*
Director . . . . John Schlesinger, *Midnight Cowboy*

1970

Picture . . . . *Patton*, 20th Century-Fox
Actor . . . . George C. Scott, *Patton* (refused)
Actress . . . . Glenda Jackson, *Women in Love*
Sup. Actor . . . . John Mills, *Ryan's Daughter*
Sup. Actress . . . . Helen Hayes, *Airport*
Director . . . . Franklin J. Schaffner, *Patton*

1971

Picture . . . . *The French Connection*, 20th Century-Fox
Actor . . . . Gene Hackman, *The French Connection*
Actress . . . . Jane Fonda, *Klute*
Sup. Actor . . . . Ben Johnson, *The Last Picture Show*
Sup. Actress . . . . Cloris Leachman, *The Last Picture Show*
Director . . . . William Friedkin, *The French Connection*

1972

Picture . . . . *The Godfather*, Paramount
Actor . . . . Marlon Brando, *The Godfather* (refused)
Actress . . . . Liza Minnelli, *Cabaret*
Sup. Actor . . . . Joel Grey, *Cabaret*
Sup. Actress . . . . Eileen Heckart, *Butterflies Are Free*
Director . . . . Bob Fosse, *Cabaret*

1973

Picture . . . . *The Sting*, Universal
Actor . . . . Jack Lemmon, *Save the Tiger*
Actress . . . . Glenda Jackson, *A Touch of Class*
Sup. Actor . . . . John Houseman, *The Paper Chase*
Sup. Actress . . . . Tatum O'Neal, *Paper Moon*
Director . . . . George Roy Hill, *The Sting*

1974

Picture . . . . *The Godfather Part II*, Paramount
Actor . . . . Art Carney, *Harry and Tonto*
Actress . . . Ellen Burstyn, *Alice Doesn't Live Here Anymore*
Sup. Actor . . . . Robert De Niro, *The Godfather Part II*
Sup. Actress . . . . . . Ingrid Bergman, *Murder on the Orient Express*
Director . . . . . Francis Ford Coppola, *The Godfather Part II*

1975

Picture . . . *One Flew Over the Cuckoo's Nest*, United Artists
Actor . . . Jack Nicholson, *One Flew Over the Cuckoo's Nest*
Actress . . . . . Louise Fletcher, *One Flew Over the Cuckoo's Nest*
Sup. Actor . . . . George Burns, *The Sunshine Boys*
Sup. Actress . . . . Lee Grant, *Shampoo*
Director . . . Milos Forman, *One Flew Over the Cuckoo's Nest*

1976

Picture . . . . *Rocky*, United Artists
Actor . . . . Peter Finch, *Network*
Actress . . . . Faye Dunaway, *Network*
Sup. Actor . . . . Jason Robards, *All the President's Men*
Sup. Actress . . . . Beatrice Straight, *Network*
Director . . . . John G. Avildsen, *Rocky*

1977

Picture . . . . *Annie Hall*, United Artists
Actor . . . . Richard Dreyfuss, *The Goodbye Girl*
Actress. . . . . Diane Keaton, *Annie Hall*
Sup. Actor . . . . Jason Robards, *Julia*
Sup. Actress. . . . . Vanessa Redgrave, *Julia*
Director. . . . . Woody Allen, *Annie Hall*

1978

Picture . . . . *The Deer Hunter*, Universal
Actor . . . . Jon Voight, *Coming Home*
Actress . . . . Jane Fonda, *Coming Home*
Sup. Actor . . . . Christopher Walken, *The Deer Hunter*
Sup. Actress . . . . Maggie Smith, *California Suite*
Director . . . . Michael Cimino, *The Deer Hunter*

1979

Picture . . . . *Kramer vs. Kramer*, Columbia
Actor . . . . Dustin Hoffman, *Kramer vs. Kramer*
Actress . . . . Sally Field, *Norma Rae*
Sup. Actor . . . . Melvyn Douglas, *Being There*
Sup. Actress . . . . Meryl Streep, *Kramer vs. Kramer*
Director . . . . Robert Benton, *Kramer vs. Kramer*

1980

Picture . . . . *Ordinary People*, Paramount
Actor . . . . Robert De Niro, *Raging Bull*
Actress . . . . Sissy Spacek, *Coal Miner's Daughter*
Sup. Actor . . . . Timothy Hutton, *Ordinary People*
Sup. Actress . . . . . Mary Steenburgen, *Melvin and Howard*
Director. . . . . Robert Redford, *Ordinary People*

1981

Picture . . . . *Chariots of Fire*, Warner Bros.
Actor . . . . Henry Fonda, *On Golden Pond*
Actress . . . . Katharine Hepburn, *On Golden Pond*
Sup. Actor . . . . John Gielgud, *Arthur*
Sup. Actress . . . . Maureen Stapleton, *Reds*
Director. . . . . Warren Beatty, *Reds* ▶

1982

Picture . . . . *Gandhi*, Columbia
Actor . . . . Ben Kingsley, *Gandhi*
Actress . . . . Meryl Streep, *Sophie's Choice*
Sup. Actor . . . . Louis Gossett, Jr., *An Officer and a Gentleman*
Sup. Actress . . . . Jessica Lange, *Tootsie*
Director . . . . Richard Attenborough, *Gandhi*

1983

Picture . . . . *Terms of Endearment*, Paramount
Actor . . . . Robert Duvall, *Tender Mercies*
Actress . . . . Shirley Maclaine, *Terms of Endearment*
Sup. Actor . . . . Jack Nicholson, *Terms of Endearment*
Sup. Actress . . . . Linda Hunt, *The Year of Living Dangerously*
Director . . . . James L. Brooks, *Terms of Endearment*

1984

Picture . . . . *Amadeus*, Orion
Actor . . . . F. Murray Abraham, *Amadeus*
Actress . . . . Sally Field, *Places in the Heart*
Sup. Actor . . . . Haing S. Ngor, *The Killing Fields*
Sup. Actress . . . . Peggy Ashcroft, *A Passage to India*
Director . . . . Milos Forman, *Amadeus*

1985

Picture . . . . *Out of Africa*, Universal
Actor . . . . William Hurt, *Kiss of the Spider Woman*
Actress . . . . Geraldine Page, *The Trip to Bountiful*
Sup. Actor . . . . Don Ameche, *Cocoon*
Sup. Actress . . . . Anjelica Huston, *Prizzi's Honor*
Director . . . . Sydney Pollack, *Out of Africa*

1986

Picture . . . . *Platoon*, Orion
Actor . . . . Paul Newman, *The Color of Money*
Actress . . . . Marlee Matlin, *Children of a Lesser God*
Sup. Actor . . . . Michael Caine, *Hannah and Her Sisters*
Sup. Actress . . . . . . Dianne Wiest, *Hannah and Her Sisters*
Director . . . . Oliver Stone, *Platoon*

1987

Picture . . . . *The Last Emperor*, Columbia
Actor . . . . Michael Douglas, *Wall Street*
Actress . . . . Cher, *Moonstruck*
Sup. Actor . . . . Sean Connery, *The Untouchables*
Sup. Actress . . . . Olympia Dukakis, *Moonstruck*
Director . . . . Bernardo Bertolucci, *The Last Emperor*

1988

Picture . . . . *Rain Man*, United Artists
Actor . . . . Dustin Hoffman, *Rain Man*
Actress . . . . Jodie Foster, *The Accused*
Sup. Actor . . . . Kevin Kline, *A Fish Called Wanda*
Sup. Actress . . . . Geena Davis, *The Accidental Tourist*
Director . . . . Barry Levinson, *Rain Man*

1989

Picture . . . . *Driving Miss Daisy*, Warner Bros.
Actor . . . . Daniel Day Lewis, *My Left Foot*
Actress . . . . Jessica Tandy, *Driving Miss Daisy*
Sup. Actor . . . . Denzel Washington, *Glory*
Sup. Actress . . . . Brenda Fricker, *My Left Foot*
Director . . . . Oliver Stone, *Born on the Fourth of July*

1990

Picture . . . . *Dances With Wolves*, Orion
Actor . . . . Jeremy Irons, *Reversal of Fortune*
Actress . . . . Kathy Bates, *Misery*
Sup. Actor . . . . Joe Pesci, *Good Fellas*
Sup. Actress . . . . Whoopi Goldberg, *Ghost*
Director . . . . Kevin Costner, *Dances With Wolves*

1991

Picture . . . . *The Silence of the Lambs*, Orion
Actor . . . . Anthony Hopkins, *The Silence of the Lambs*
Actress . . . . Jodie Foster, *The Silence of the Lambs*
Sup. Actor . . . . Jack Palance, *City Slickers*
Sup. Actress . . . . Mercedes Ruehl, *The Fisher King*
Director . . . . . Jonathan Demme, *The Silence of the Lambs*

1992

Picture . . . . *Unforgiven*, Clint Eastwood, producer
Actor . . . . Al Pacino, *Scent of A Woman*
Actress . . . . Emma Thompson, *Howards End*
Sup. Actor . . . . Gene Hackman, *Unforgiven*
Sup. Actress . . . . Marisa Tomei, *My Cousin Vinny*
Director . . . . Clint Eastwood, *Unforgiven*

1993

Picture . . . . *Schindler's List*, Steven Spielberg, Gerald R. Molen, Branko Lustig, producers
Actor . . . . Tom Hanks, *Philadelphia*
Actress . . . . Holly Hunter, *The Piano*
Sup. Actor . . . . Tommy Lee Jones, *The Fugitive*
Sup. Actress . . . . Anna Paquin, *The Piano*
Director . . . . Steven Spielberg, *Schindler's List*
Foreign-Language Film . . . . *Belle Epoque*, Spain
Original Screenplay . . . . Jane Campion, *The Piano*
Screenplay Adaptation . . . . Steven Zaillian, *Schindler's List*
Cinematography . . . . . . Janusz Kaminski, *Schindler's List*
Editing . . . . Michael Kahn, *Schindler's List*
Original Score . . . . John Williams, *Schindler's List*
Original Song . . . . Bruce Springsteen, "Streets of Philadelphia," *Philadelphia*
Art Direction . . . . Allan Starski, *Schindler's List*
Set Decoration . . . . Ewa Braun, *Schindler's List*
Costume Design . . . . Gabriella Pescucci, *The Age of Innocence*
Sound . . . . Gary Summers, Gary Rydstrom, Shawn Murphy, Ron Judkins, *Jurassic Park*
Sound Effects Editing . . . . Gary Rydstrom, Richard Hymns, *Jurassic Park*
Makeup . . . . . . Greg Cannom, Ve Neill, Yolanda Toussieng, *Mrs. Doubtfire*
Visual Effects . . Dennis Muren, Stan Winston, Phil Tippett, Michael Lantieri, *Jurassic Park*
Documentary Feature . . . Alan Raymond, Susan Raymond, producers, *I Am a Promise: The Children of Stanton Elementary School*
Documentary Short Subject . . . . *Defending Our Lives*, Margaret Lazarus and Renner Wunderlich, producers
Short Film, Animated . . . . . Nick Park, *The Wrong Trousers*
Short Film, Live . . . . Pepe Danquart, *Black Rider*

Source: *Academy of Motion Picture Arts and Sciences*

1993 Oscar Nominations

Picture: *The Fugitive; In the Name of the Father; The Piano; The Remains of the Day; Schindler's List.*

Actor: Daniel Day-Lewis, *In the Name of the Father*; Laurence Fishburne, *What's Love Got to Do With It*; Tom Hanks, *Philadelphia*; Anthony Hopkins, *The Remains of the Day*; Liam Neeson, *Schindler's List.*

Actress: Angela Bassett, *What's Love Got to Do With It*; Stockard Channing, *Six Degrees of Separation*; Holly Hunter, *The Piano*; Emma Thompson, *The Remains of the Day*; Debra Winger, *Shadowlands.*

Supporting Actor: Leonardo DiCaprio, *What's Eating Gilbert Grape*; Ralph Fiennes, *Schindler's List*; Tommy Lee Jones, *The Fugitive*; John Malkovich, *In the Line of Fire*; Pete Postelthwaite, *In the Name of the Father.*

Supporting Actress: Holly Hunter, *The Firm*; Anna Pequin, *The Piano*; Rosie Perez, *Fearless*; Winona Ryder, *The Age of Innocence*; Emma Thompson, *In the Name of the Father.*

Director: Jim Sheridan, *In the Name of the Father*; Jane Campion, *The Piano*; James Ivory, *The Remains of the Day*; Steven Spielberg, *Schindler's List*; Robert Altman, *Short Cuts.*

Foreign-Language Film: *Belle Epoque*, Spain; *Farewell My Concubine*, Hong Kong; *Hedd Wyn*, UK; *The Scent of Green Papaya*, Vietnam; *The Wedding Bouquet*, Taiwan.

Original Screenplay: Gary Ross, *Dave*; Jeff Maguire, *In the Line of Fire*; Ron Myswaner, *Philadelphia*; Jane Campion, *The Piano*; Nora Ephron, David S. Ward, Jeff Arch, *Sleepless in Seattle.*

Screenplay Adaptation: Jay Cocks, Martin Scorsese, *The Age of Innocence*; Terry George, Jim Sheridan, *In the Name of the Father*; Ruth Prawer Jhabvala, *The Remains of the Day*; Steven Zaillian, *Schindler's List*; William Nicholson, *Shawdowlands.*

Cinematography: Gu Changwei, *Farewell My Concubine*; Michael Chapman, *The Fugitive*; Stuart Dryburgh, *The Piano*; Janusz Kaminski, *Schindler's List*; Conrad L. Hall, *Searching for Bobby Fischer.*

Original Song: Janet Jackson, James Harris III, Terry Lewis, "Again," *Poetic Justice*; Carole Bayer Sager, James Ingram, Clif Magness, "The Day I Fall in Love," *Beethoven's 2nd*; Neil Young, "Philadelphia," *Philadelphia*; Bruce Springsteen, "The Streets of Philadelphia," *Philadelphia*; Marc Shaiman, Ramsey McLean, "A Wink and a Smile," *Sleepless in Seattle.*

Source: *Academy of Motion Picture Arts and Sciences*

TELEVISION AND RADIO

The Early Days of Canadian Television

Canadian television got off to a belated and somewhat shaky start in 1952 as stations signed on in Montreal Sept. 6 and two days later in Toronto, where the first image was the CBC logo upside down and backwards. As viewers huddled in front of flickering TV sets, the picture quickly faded to black while the logo was reversed and the countdown to sign-on was restarted.

Both the Toronto and Montreal stations—which were joined by a third in Vancouver by the end of 1952—began with 18 hours of weekly programming, almost all of it Canadian. Performers in early productions included Don Harron, Barbara Hamilton and Lorne Greene. A young Norman Jewison was stage director of "The Big Revue," a variety show. Hockey Night in Canada, with Foster Hewitt handling the play-by-play, was one of the first shows to compete in popularity with American-based programs such as the Jackie Gleason Show.

Before the start of CBC television broadcasts, there were fewer than 150 000 television sets in the country—all with antennas pointed towards the United States, where the first stations had been launched five years earlier. Sales doubled each year during the mid 1950s so that, by 1956, more than half of Canadian households owned a TV.

An early boost to sales was the coronation of Queen Elizabeth in 1953. The CBC rewarded its early viewers by winning the transatlantic race to be the first North American station to broadcast the royal event. The network recorded the seven-hour BBC broadcast on kinescope film and developed it in minutes using a special process called "hot kine." The film was flown across the Atlantic in three shipments by a combination of RAF bomber, RCAF jet and helicopter. It aired in Canada at 4:14 p.m. EDT, less than four hours after the ceremony had ended.

Other notable CBC broadcasts during the early years included exclusive coverage of Roger Bannister's "miracle mile" at the 1954 British Empire and Commonwealth Games in Vancouver and the first live coverage of a federal election in 1957.

The nation's first private station—Sudbury's CKSO—went on the air in Oct. 1953 and was quickly followed by others as the number of Canadian stations grew to 26 by 1955. By 1958, an electronic highway costing $50 million had linked stations on the east and west coasts.

The Gemini Awards, 1993

The Gemini Awards were established in 1986 to honor outstanding contributions to the Canadian television industry. Given out annually by the Academy of Canadian Cinema and Television, the Geminis grew out of the former ACTRA Awards, last presented in 1985. These awards were presented Mar. 7, 1993.

Drama series	**ENG**
Dramatic mini-series	**The Boys of St. Vincent**
Comedy series	**The Kids in the Hall**
Variety series	**The Trial of Red Riding Hood**
TV movie	**The Diviners**
Actor (dramatic series)	**James Purcell**, Counterstrike, "Going Home"
Actor (dramatic program or mini-series)	**Henry Czerny**, The Boys of St. Vincent
Supporting actor	**Wayne Robson**, The Diviners
Actress (drama series)	**Jackie Burroughs**, Road to Avonlea, "Hearts and Flowers"
Actress (dramatic program or mini-series)	**Kelly Rowan**, Adrift
Supporting actress	**Lise Roy**, The Boys of St. Vincent
Guest performance in a series	**Philip Granger**, Neon Rider, "Saint Walt"
Performance (performing arts program or series)	**Holly Cole**, The Holly Cole Trio, "My Foolish Heart"
Performance (comedy program or series)	**Mary Walsh, Cathy Jones, Tommy Sexton, Greg Malone**, CODCO, "Lil and Buster"
Performance (variety program or series)	**Jinny Jacinto, Laurence Racine Choiniere, Nadine Louis-Binette, Isabelle Chasse**, "1993 YTV Achievement Awards"
Animated program or series	**Jim Henson's Dog City**
Children's program or series	**Lamb Chop's Play-Along**
Documentary series	**Acts of War**
Information series	**Market Place**
Light information series	**MediaTelevision**
Sports program	**The Spirit of the Game**
Youth program or series	**Street Cents**
Documentary program	**Donald Brittain Filmmaker**
Performing arts program	**My War Years: Arnold Schoenberg**
Short dramatic program	**Letter From Francis**
Variety program	**The Trial of Red Riding Hood**

Source: *Academy of Canadian Cinema and Television*

The Most-Watched Television Programs in Canada[1]

(by adults 18+; Sept. 1993–April 1994)

Canadian Networks	American Networks
1. Roseanne (CTV)	1. Home Improvement (ABC)
2. America's Funniest Home Videos (CTV)	2. 60 Minutes (CBS)
3. CTV Sunday Movie (CTV)	3. Seinfeld (NBC)
4. NYPD Blue (CTV)	4. Roseanne (ABC)
5. CTV Monday Movie (CTV)	5. These Friends of Mine (ABC)
6. John Larroquette (CTV)	6. Grace Under Fire (ABC)
7. CTV Movie Special (CTV)	7. Frasier (NBC)
8. CTV News (CTV)	8. Coach (NBC)
9. America's Funniest People (CTV)	8. Murder, She Wrote (CBS)
10. Hockey Night in Canada (CBC)	9. NFL Monday Night Football (ABC)

Source: *Nielsen Marketing Research*

(1) Based on five or more telecasts.

The Emmy Awards, 1992–93

Drama Series	**Picket Fences**, CBS
Actor (drama series)	**Tom Skerritt,** Picket Fences, CBS
Actress (drama series)	**Sela Ward,** Sisters, NBC
Supporting actor (drama series)	**Fyvush Finkel,** Picket Fences, CBS
Supporting actress (drama series)	**Leigh Taylor-Young,** Picket Fences, CBS
Directing (drama series)	**Daniel Sackheim,** NYPD Blue, ABC
Writing (drama series)	**Ann Biderman,** NYPD Blue, ABC
Comedy Series	**Frasier,** NBC
Actor (comedy series)	**Kelsey Grammer,** Frasier, NBC
Actress (comedy series)	**Candice Bergen,** Murphy Brown, CBS
Supporting actor (comedy series)	**Michael Richards,** Seinfeld, NBC
Supporting actress (comedy series)	**Laurie Metcalf,** Roseanne, ABC
Directing (comedy series)	**James Burrows,** Frasier, "The Good Son", NBC
Writing (comedy series)	**David Angell, Peter Casey, David Lee,** Frasier, "The Good Son", NBC
Miniseries	**Prime Suspect 3,** PBS
Actor (miniseries or special)	**Hume Cronyn,** To Dance With The White Dog, CBS
Actress (miniseries or special)	**Kirstie Alley,** David's Mother, CBS
Supporting actor (miniseries or special)	**Michael Goorjian,** David's Mother, CBS
Supporting actress (miniseries or special)	**Cicely Tyson,** Oldest Living Confederate Widow Tells All, CBS
Directing (miniseries or special)	**John Frankenheimer,** Against the Wall, HBO
Variety (music or comedy) special	**The Kennedy Centre Honors,** CBS
Individual performance (variety or music)	**Tracey Ullman,** Tracey Ullman-Takes on New York, HBO
Directing (variety or music)	**Walter C. Miller,** The Tony Awards, CBS
Informational series	**Later With Bob Costas,** NBC
Animated program	**The Roman City,** PBS,
Children's program (special)	**Kids Killing Kids/Kids Saving Kids,** CBS/FOX
Outstanding TV Movie	**And The Band Played On,** HBO

Source: *Academy of Television Arts and Science*

Longest–Running Canadian TV Network Shows

(up to the end of the 1993–94 season)

Program (Network)	Seasons	Program (Network)	Seasons
Hockey Night in Canada (CBC)	41 (1952–)	Canada AM (CTV)	21 (1972–)
CFL Football	41 (1952–)	The Beachcombers	19 (1972–91)
Country Canada/Country Calendar	39 (1954–)	Market Place	21 (1972–)
Front Page Challenge	36 (1957–)	Meeting Place	21 (1972–)
The Nature of Things	33 (1960–)	What's New	18 (1972–90)
The Friendly Giant	27 (1958–85)	the 5th estate	18 (1975–)
Hymn Sing	28 (1965–)	Definition	16 (1974–90)
The Tommy Hunter Show	27 (1965–92)	Live It Up	13 (1977–90)
Romper Room	26 (1966–92)	Sportsweekend	14 (1979–)
W-5	27 (1966–)	What's Cooking	12 (1977–89)
Mr. Dressup	26 (1967–)	Headline Hunters	11 (1972–83)
Man Alive	26 (1967–)	Don Messer's Jubilee	10 (1959–69)
Expos Baseball (CBC)	19 (1971–90)	Juliette	10 (1956–66)
This Land	19 (1967–86)		

Source: *CBC, CTV, Global*

Television Networks and Cable Services

Alberta Educational Communications Authority (Access Network): 3720-76 Ave, Edmonton, Alta. T6B 2N9. (403) 440-7777

Allarcom Pay TV Ltd.: #200-5324 Calgary Trail, Edmonton, Alta. T6H 4J8. (403) 437-7744

American Broadcasting Company (ABC): 77 W 66th St, New York, NY 10023-6298. (212) 456-7777

Arts & Entertainment Network (A&E): 235 E 45th St, New York, NY 10017. (212) 210-1328

Atlantic Television System & Atlantic Satellite Network: Box 1653, 2885 Robie St, Halifax, N.S. B3J 2Z4. (902) 453-4000.

Baton Broadcasting Inc.: #9, Channel Nine Court, Scarborough, Ont. M1S 4B5. (416) 299-2000

C-SPAN (Cable Satellite Public Affairs Network): 400 N. Capitol St. NW, Suite 650, Washington, DC 20001. (202) 737-3220

Cable News Network (CNN): 1 CNN Centre, Box 105366, Atlanta, GA 30348-5366. (404) 827-1700

Canadian Broadcasting Corporation (CBC): Box 8478, Ottawa, Ont. K1G 3J5. (613) 724-1200

Canal Famille: 2100 Sainte-Catherine ouest, Bureau 800, Montreal, Que. H3H 2T3. (514) 939-3150

CanWest/Global Communications Corp.: 201 Portage Ave, 31st Flr, TD Centre, Winnipeg, Man. R3B 3L7. (204) 956-2025

Cathay International Television Inc.: 494 W 49th Ave, Vancouver, B.C. V5Y 2P7. (604) 321-5266

Chinavision Canada Corporation: 160 Duncan Mill Rd., Don Mills, Ont. M3B 1Z5. (416) 510-2850

CHUM Limited: 1331 Yonge St, Toronto, Ont. M4T 1Y1. (416) 925-6666.

Columbia Broadcasting System (CBS): 51 W 52nd St, New York, NY 10019. (212) 975-4321

Corporation for Public Broadcasting (PBS): 901 E St NW, Washington, DC 20004-2037. (202) 879-9600

CTV Television Network Ltd.: 42 Charles St E, Toronto, Ont. M4Y 1T5. (416) 928-6000

The Family Channel Inc.: BCE Place, 181 Bay St., Box 787, Toronto, Ont. M5J 2T3. (416) 956-2030

Fox Broadcasting Co.: 10201 W Pico Blvd, Los Angeles, CA 90035. (212) 203-3266

Global Television Network: 81 Barber Greene Rd, Don Mills, Ont. M3C 2A2 (416) 446-5311

Inuit Broadcasting Corporation: 251 Laurier Ave W, Ste 703, Ottawa, Ont. K1P 5J6. (613) 235-1892

Knowledge Network: 4355 Mathissi Place, Burnaby, B.C. V5G 4S8. (604) 431-3000

The Learning Channel: 7700 Wisconsin Ave, Bethesda, MD 20814-3539. (301) 986-1999

Maclean Hunter Limited: 777 Bay St, Toronto, Ont. M5W 1A7. (416) 596-5000

The Movie Network/First Choice: BCE Place, 181 Bay St., Box 787, Toronto, Ont. M5J 2T3. (416) 956-2010

MuchMusic Network: 299 Queen St W, Toronto, Ont. M5V 2Z5. (416) 591-5757

MusiquePlus Network: 209 Sainte-Catherine est, Montreal, Que. H2X 1L2. (514) 284-7587

The Nashville Network: 250 Harbor Plaza Dr, Box 10210, Stamford, CT 06904-2210. (203) 965-6000

National Broadcasting Company (NBC): 30 Rockefeller Plaza, New York, NY 10112. (212) 664-4444

Premier Choix TVEC Inc.: 2100 Sainte-Catherine ouest, #800 Montreal, Que. H3H 2T3. (514) 939-3150

Radio-Canada International: Box 6000, Montreal, Que. H3C 3A8. (514) 597-5000

Le Reseau des Sports: 1755 Boul. René-Lévesque est, Bur. 300, Montreal, Que. H2K 4P6. (514) 599-2244

Rogers Broadcasting Ltd.: 25 Adelaide St E, 10th Flr, Toronto, Ont. M5C 1H3. (416) 864-2000

Société de radio-télévision du Quebec (Radio-Quebec): 800, rue Fullum, Montreal, Que. H2K 3L7. (514) 521-2424

The Sports Network (TSN): 1155 Leslie St, Don Mills, Ont. M3C 2J6. (416) 449-2244

Superchannel: 200-5324 Calgary Trail, Edmonton, Alta. T6H 4J8. (403) 437-7744

Telelatino Network Inc.: 5125 Steeles Ave W, Weston, Ont. M5B 1M2. (416) 744-8200

TVOntario (TVO): Box 200, Stn Q, Toronto, Ont. M4T 2T1. (416) 484-2600

Vision TV: 315 Queen St E, Toronto, Ont. M5A 1S7. (416) 368-3194

The Weather Network: 1755 René-Lévesque Blvd E, #251, Montreal, Que. H2K 4P6. (514) 597-1700

YTV Canada Inc.: 64 Jefferson Ave, Unit 18, Toronto, Ont. M6K 3H3. (416) 534-1191

Ten Early Highlights of Canadian Radio

1919 . . . . First broadcast by XWA Montreal, the first licensed radio station in North America.
1920 . . . . XWA broadcast its first regularly scheduled programs.
1923 . . . . First hockey play-by-play on CKCK Regina.
1924 . . . . First Dominion Observatory time signals.
1924 . . . . First livestock market reports.
1924 . . . . First Stanley Cup broadcast.
1932 . . . . First Christmas Day broadcast from Buckingham Palace.
1933 . . . . Canadian Press began providing daily news bulletins.
1936 . . . . . Live telephone reports on trapped miners in Nova Scotia heard on 58 Canadian stations and 650 in the US.
1941 . . . . CBC National News Service began regular scheduled broadcasts.

POPULAR MUSIC

The Juno Awards, 1983–94

The Juno Awards were established in 1975 to honor achievement in the Canadian recording industry. The name was chosen to honor Pierre Juneau, former head of the Canadian Radio-television and Telecommunications Commission (CRTC) which instituted "Canadian content" requirements in the nation's broadcast industry.

Nominations for most major Juno categories are determined by record sales, although the actual winners are selected by a vote of members of the Canadian Academy of Recording Arts & Sciences.

There were no awards presented in 1988. Following the Nov. 1987 awards, the presentation of the Junos was moved from the fall to the spring so that the next awards were presented in the spring of 1989. The 1989 awards cover 1988 releases.

The 1993 awards were announced Mar. 20, 1994.

Canadian Entertainer of the Year

1987 . . . . Bryan Adams
1989 . . . . Glass Tiger
1990 . . . . The Jeff Healey Band
1991 . . . . The Tragically Hip
1992 . . . . Bryan Adams
1993 . . . . The Tragically Hip
1994 . . . . The Rankin Family

Album of the Year

1983/84 . . . . *Cuts Like a Knife*, Bryan Adams
1985 . . . . *Reckless*, Bryan Adams
1986 . . . . *The Thin Red Line*, Glass Tiger
1987 . . . . . *Shakin' Like A Human Being*, Kim Mitchell
1989 . . . . *Robbie Robertson*, Robbie Robertson
1990 . . . . *Alannah Myles*, Alannah Myles
1991 . . . . *Unison*, Celine Dion
1992 . . . . *Mad Mad World*, Tom Cochrane
1993 . . . . *Ingenue*, k.d. lang
1994 . . . . *Harvest Moon*, Neil Young

Single of the Year

1983/84 . . . . "Rise Up," The Parachute Club
1985 . . . . "Never Surrender," Corey Hart
1986 . . . . "Don't Forget Me (When I'm Gone)," Glass Tiger
1987 . . . . "Someday," Glass Tiger
1989 . . . . "Try," Blue Rodeo
1990 . . . . "Black Velvet," Alannah Myles
1991 . . . . "Just Came Back," Colin James
1992 . . . . "Life Is a Highway," Tom Cochrane
1993 . . . "Beauty and the Beast," Celine Dion/Peabo Bryson
1994 . . . . "Fare Thee Well Love," The Rankin Family

Female Vocalist of the Year

1983/84 . . . . Carole Pope
1985 . . . . Luba
1986 . . . . Luba
1987 . . . . Luba
1989 . . . . k.d. lang
1990 . . . . Rita MacNeil
1991 . . . . Celine Dion
1992 . . . . Celine Dion
1993 . . . . Celine Dion
1994 . . . . Celine Dion

Male Vocalist of the Year

1983/84 . . . . Bryan Adams
1985 . . . . Bryan Adams
1986 . . . . Bryan Adams
1987 . . . . Bryan Adams
1989 . . . . Robbie Robertson
1990 . . . . Kim Mitchell
1991 . . . . Colin James
1992 . . . . Tom Cochrane
1993 . . . . Leonard Cohen
1994 . . . . Roch Voisine

Group of the Year

1983/84 . . . . Loverboy
1985 . . . . The Parachute Club
1986 . . . . Honeymoon Suite
1987 . . . . Tom Cochrane & Red Rider
1989 . . . . Blue Rodeo
1990 . . . . Blue Rodeo
1991 . . . . Blue Rodeo ▶

▶ 1992 . . . . Crash Test Dummies
1993 . . . . Barenaked Ladies
1994 . . . . The Rankin Family

Songwriter of the Year
1985 . . . . Bryan Adams and Jim Vallance
1986 . . . . Jim Vallance
1987 . . . . Jim Vallance
1989 . . . . Rita MacNeil, Tom Cochrane (tie)
1990 . . . . Greg Keelor and Jim Cuddy
1991 . . . . David Tyson
1992 . . . . Tom Cochrane
1993 . . . . k.d. lang
1994 . . . . Leonard Cohen

Most Promising Female Vocalist of the Year
1983/84 . . . . Sherry Kean
1985 . . . . k.d. lang
1986 . . . . Kim Richardson
1987 . . . . Rita MacNeil
1989 . . . . Sass Jordan
1990 . . . . Alannah Myles
1991 . . . . Sue Medley
1992 . . . . Alanis
1993 . . . . Julie Masse

Most Promising Male Vocalist of the Year
1983/84 . . . . Zappacosta
1985 . . . . Paul Janz
1986 . . . . Billy Newton-Davis
1987 . . . . Tim Feehan
1989 . . . . Colin James
1990 . . . . Daniel Lanois
1991 . . . . Andy Curran
1992 . . . . Keven Jordan
1993 . . . . John Bottomley

Most Promising Group of the Year
1983/84 . . . . The Parachute Club
1985 . . . . Idle Eyes
1986 . . . . Glass Tiger
1987 . . . . Frozen Ghost
1989 . . . . Barney Bentall & The Legendary Hearts
1990 . . . . The Tragically Hip
1991 . . . . The Leslie Spit Treeo
1992 . . . . Infidels
1993 . . . . Skydiggers

Best New Solo Artist
1994 . . . . Jann Arden

Best New Group
1994 . . . . The Waltons

Best Selling Francophone Album
1994 . . . . *Album de Peuple: Tome 2*

Country Female Vocalist of the Year
1983/84 . . . . Anne Murray
1985 . . . . Anne Murray
1986 . . . . Anne Murray
1987 . . . . k.d. lang
1989 . . . . k.d. lang
1990 . . . . k.d. lang
1991 . . . . Rita MacNeil
1992 . . . . Cassandra Vasik
1993 . . . . Michelle Wright
1994 . . . . Cassandra Vasik

Country Male Vocalist of the Year
1983/84 . . . . Murray McLauchlan
1985 . . . . Murray McLauchlan
1986 . . . . Murray McLauchlan
1987 . . . . Ian Tyson
1989 . . . . Murray McLauchlan
1990 . . . . George Fox
1991 . . . . George Fox
1992 . . . . George Fox
1993 . . . . Gary Fjellgaard
1994 . . . . Charlie Major

Country Group or Duo of the Year
1983/84 . . . . The Good Brothers
1985 . . . . The Family Brown
1986 . . . . Prairie Oyster
1987 . . . . Prairie Oyster
1989 . . . . The Family Brown
1990 . . . . The Family Brown
1991 . . . . Prairie Oyster
1992 . . . . Prairie Oyster
1993 . . . . Tracey Prescott & Lonesome Daddy
1994 . . . . The Rankin Family

Best Hard Rock Album
1991 . . . . *Presto*, Rush
1992 . . . . *Roll the Bones*, Rush
1993 . . . . *Doin' the Nasty*, Slik Toxik
1994 . . . . *Dig*, I. Mother Earth

Rap Recording of the Year
1991 . . . . "Symphony in Effect," Maestro Fresh-Wes
1992 . . . "My Definition of a Boombastic Jazz Style,"
Dream Warriors
1993 . . . . *Keep It Slammin'*, Devon
1994 . . . . *One Track Mind*, TBTBT

Best Dance Recording
1990 . . . . "I Beg Your Pardon (I Never Promised You a
Rose Garden)," Kon Kan
1991 . . . . "Don't Wanna Fall in Love," Jane Child
1992 . . . . "Everyone's a Winner (Chocolate Movement
Mix)," Bootsauce
1993 . "Love Can Move Mountains (Club Mix)," Celine Dion
1994 . . . . "Thankful (Raw Club Mix)," Red Light

Best Jazz Album
1983/84 . . *All In Good Time*, Rob McConnell and The Boss
The Boss Brass
1985 . . . . *A Beautiful Friendship*, Don Thompson
1986 . . . . *Lights of Burgundy*, Oliver Jones
1987 . . *If You Could See Me Now*, The Oscar Peterson Four
1989 . . . . *Looking Up*, The Hugh Fraser Quintet
1990 . . . . *Skydance*, Jon Ballantyne Trio featuring Joe
Henderson
1991 . . . . *Two Sides*, Mike Murley
1992 . . . . . . *For the Moment*, Renee Rosnes; *In Transition* ,
Brian Dickinson; *The Brass Is Back*, Rob
McConnell and The Boss Brass
1993 . . . . *My Ideal*, P.J. Perry
1994 . . . . *Don't Smoke in Bed*, Holly Cole Trio

Best Mainstream Jazz Album
1994 . *Fables and Dreams*, Dave Young/Phil Dwyer Quartet ▶

Best R&B/Soul Recording

1985 .. "Lost Somewhere Inside Your Love," Liberty Silver
1986 ...... "Love Is a Contact Sport," Billy Newton-Davis
1987 .... "Peek-A-Boo," Kim Richardson
1989 .... "Angel," Erroll Star
1990 .... "Spellbound," Billy Newton-Davis
1991 .... "Dance to the Music (Work Your Body),"
Simply Majestic Featuring B. Kool
1992 .... "Call My Name," Love & Sas
1993 .... "Once in a Lifetime," Love & Sas
1994 .... "The Time is Right,"Rupert Gayle

Best Blues/Gospel Album

1994 .... *South at Eight/North at Nine*, Colin Linden

Best Reggae/Calypso Recording

1985 .... *Heaven Must Have Sent You*, Liberty Silver &
Otis Gayle
1986 .... *Revolutionary Tea Party*, Lillian Allen
1987 .... *Mean While*, Leroy Sibbles
1989 .... *Conditions Critical*, Lillian Allen
1990 ...... *Too Late To Turn Back Now*, Sattalites
1991 ...... *Soldiers We Are All*, Jayson & Friends
1994 .... *Informer*, Snow

Best World Beat Recording

1992 .... *The Gathering*, Various Artists
1993 .... *Spirits of Havana*, Jane Bunnett
1994 .... *El Camino Real*, Ancient Cultures

Best Roots and Traditional Album

1989 ...... *The Return of the Formily Brothers*, The Amos
Garrett, Doug Sahm, Gene Taylor Band
1990 .... *Je Voudrais Changer D'Chapeau*, La Bottine
Souriante
1991 .... *Dance & Celebrate*, Bourne & MacLeod
1992 ..... *Saturday Night Blues*, Various Artists; *The Visit*,
Loreena McKennitt
1993 ..... *Jusqu'aux P'tites Heures*, La Bouttine Souriante
1994 .... *My Skies*, James Keelaghan

Instrumental Artist(s) of the Year

1983/84 .... Liona Boyd
1985 .... The Canadian Brass
1986 .... David Foster
1987 .... David Foster
1989 .... David Foster
1990 .... Manteca
1991 .... Ofra Harnoy
1992 .... Shadowy Men on a Shadowy Planet
1993 .... Ofra Harnoy
1994 .... Ofra Harnoy

Best Classical Recording

1983/84 ..... *Ballades op. 10, Rhapsodies op. 79*, Glenn
Gould, A. Brahms

Best Classical Album (solo or chamber ensemble)

1985 .... *W.A. Mozart—String Quartets*, The Orford
String Quartet
1986 ... *Stolen Gems*, James Campbell and Eric Robertson
1987 .... *Schubert, Quintet in C*, The Orford String
Quartet, Ofra Harnoy
1989 .... *Schubert: Arpeggione Sonata*, Ofra Harnoy

1990 .... *20th Century Original Piano Transcriptions*,
Louis Lortie
1991 .. *Schafer: Five String Quartets*, Orford String Quartet
1992 ..... *Franz Liszt: Années de Pelerinage*, Louis Lortie
1993 .... *Beethoven: Piano Sonatas*, Louis Lortie
1994 .... *Beethoven: Piano Sonatas, Op. 10, No. 1-3*,
Louis Lortie

Best Classical Album (large ensemble)

1985 ..... *Ravel: Ma Mère L'oye/Pavane Pour Une Infante
Defunte/Valses Nobles et Sentimentales*,
l'Orchestre Symphonique de Montréal, Charle Dutoit
1986 .... *Holst: The Planets*, Toronto Symphony,
Andrew Davis
1987 ..... *Holst: The Planets*, l'Orchestre Symphonique de
Montréal, Charles Dutoit
1989 .... *Bartok: Concerto for Orchestra; Music for
Strings, Percussion and Celesta*, Montreal
Symphony and Orchestra, Charles Dutoit
1990 ...... *Boccherini: Cello Concertos and Symphonies*,
Tafelmusik Baroque Orchestra
1991 .... *Debussy: Images, Nocturnes*, Orchestre
.... Symphonique de Montréal, Charles Dutoit
1992 .... *Debussy: Pelleas et Melisande*, Orchestre
Symphonique de Montréal, Charles Dutoit
1993 .... *Handel: Excerpts from Floridante*, Tafelmusik
1994 .. *Handel: Concerti Grossi, Op. 3, No. 1-6*, Tafelmusik

Best Classical Album (vocal or choral performance)

1994 . *Debussy Songs*, Claudette Leblanc, soprano, Valerie
Tryon, piano

Best Classical Composition

1987 ...... *Pages of Solitary Delights*, Maureen Forrester
with the McGill Symphony Orchestra, Donal
Steven, Composer
1989 .... *Songs of Paradise*, Alexina Louie
1990 .... *Concerto For Harp and Chamber Orchestra/
Morawetz Harp Concertos*, Oskar Morawetz
1991 .... *String Quartet No. 5 'Rosalind'*
R. Murray Schafer
1992 .... *Concerto For Piano & Chamber Orchestra*,
Michael Conway Baker
1993 .... *Concerto for Flute and Orchestra*,
R. Murray Schafer
1994 .... *Among Friends*, Chan Ka Nin

Best Children's Album

1983/84 .... *Rugrat Rock*, Rugrats
1985 .... *Murmel Murmel Munsch*, Robert Munsch
1986 .... *10 Carrot Diamond*, Charlotte Diamond
1987 .... *Drums*, Bill Usher
1989 .... *Fred Penner's Place*, Fred Penner; *Lullaby
Berceuse*, Connie Kaldor & Carmen Campagne
1990 ...... *Beethoven Lives Upstairs*, Susan Hammond &
Barbara Nichol
1991 .... *Mozart's Magic Fantasy*, Susan Hammond/
Classical Kids
1992 .... *Vivaldi's Ring of Mystery*, Susan Hammond/
Classical Kids
1993 .... *Waves of Wonder*, Jack Grunsky
1994 .... *Tchaikovsky Discovers America*,
SusanHammond/Classical Kids

Composer of the Year

1985	Bryan Adams/Jim Vallance
1986	Jim Vallance
1987	Jim Vallance
1989	Tom Cochrane
1990	David Tyson, Christopher Ward
1991	David Tyson
1992	Tom Cochrane
1993	k.d. lang/Ben Mink

Producer of the Year

1983/84	Bryan Adams
1985	David Foster
1986	David Foster
1987	Daniel Lanois
1989	Daniel Lanois and Robbie Robertson
1990	Bruce Fairbairn
1991	David Tyson
1992	Bryan Adams
1993	k.d. lang/Ben Mink (Greg Penny, co-producer)
1994	Steve MacKinnon/Marc Jordan (Greg Penny, co-producer)

Best Video of the Year

1983/84	*Sunglasses At Night* (Corey Hart), Rob Quartly
1985	*A Criminal Mind* (Gowan), Rob Quartly
1986	*How Many (Rivers to Cross)* (Luba), Greg Masvak
1987	*Love Is Fire* (The Parachute Club), Ron Berti

1989	*Try* (Blue Rodeo), Michael Buckley
1990	*Boomtown* (Andrew Cash), Cosimo Cavallaro
1991	*Drop the Needle* (Maestro Fresh-Wes), Joel Goldberg
1992	*Into the Fire* (Sarah McLachlan), Phil Kates
1993	*Closing Time* (Leonard Cohen), Curtis Wehrfritz
1994	*I Would Die For You* (Jann Arden), Jeth Weinrich

Best Music of Aboriginal Canada Recording

1994	Wapistan

Hall of Fame Award

1978	Guy Lombardo, Oscar Peterson
1979	Hank Snow
1980	Paul Anka
1981	Joni Mitchell
1982	Neil Young
1983	Glenn Gould
1984	Crewcuts, Diamonds, Four Lads
1985	Wilf Carter
1986	Gordon Lightfoot
1987	The Guess Who
1989	The Band
1990	Maureen Forrester
1991	Leonard Cohen
1992	Ian & Sylvia
1993	Anne Murray
1994	Rush

Source: *Canadian Academy of Recording Arts & Sciences*

CASBY Awards, 1993

The CASBY (Canadian Artists Selected By You) Awards were established in 1981 by Toronto radio station CFNY to pay tribute to Canadian musicians with awards chosen by the audience, rather than by the industry. These awards were presented Oct. 17, 1993.

Favourite New Group	**Universal Honey**
Favourite New Release	*Crush*, **Doughboys**
Favourite New Song	*More*, **13 Engines**

Source: *CFNY*

Canadian Country Music Association Awards, 1994

Awards and citations from the CCMA are presented during Country Music Week, which was held in Calgary from Sept. 16th to 19th, 1994. These were the thirteenth annual awards, the second to be broadcast in the US and Europe.

Entertainer of the Year	**Prairie Oyster**
Single of the Year	**"I'm Gonna Drive You Out of My Mind,"** Charlie Major
Album of the Year	*The Other Side*, **Charlie Major**
Song of the Year	**"I'm Gonna Drive You Out of My Mind,"** Charlie Major
Female Vocalist of the Year	**Patricia Conroy**
Male Vocalist of the Year	**Charlie Major**
Vocal Duo or Group	**Prairie Oyster**
Vocal Collaboration	**Quartette**
Vista (Rising Star) Award	**Susan Aglukark**
Video of the Year	**"Stolen Moments,"** Jim Witter
Top Selling Album (Foreign or Domestic)	*In Pieces*, **Garth Brooks**

Source: *Canadian Country Music Association*

The Grammy Awards, 1983–93

Grammy winners are selected annually by the 6,000 voting members of The Recording Academy, based on artistic and/or technical excellence. The titles for song of the year are followed by the names of the songwriters. The 1994 Grammy winners will be announced Mar. 1, 1995.

Best Record

1983 "Beat It," Michael Jackson
1984 "What's Love Got to Do with It," Tina Turner
1985 "We Are the World," USA For Africa
1986 "Higher Love," Steve Winwood
1987 "Graceland," Paul Simon
1988 "Don't Worry, Be Happy," Bobby McFerrin
1989 "Wind Beneath My Wings," Bette Midler
1990 "Another Day In Paradise," Phil Collins
1991 "Unforgettable," Natalie Cole (with Nat King Cole)
1992 "Tears in Heaven," Eric Clapton
1993 "I Will Always Love You," Whitney Houston

Best Album

1983 *Thriller*, Michael Jackson
1984 *Can't Slow Down*, Lionel Richie
1985 *No Jacket Required*, Phil Collins
1986 *Graceland*, Paul Simon
1987 *The Joshua Tree*, U2
1988 *Faith*, George Michael
1989 *Nick of Time*, Bonnie Raitt
1990 *Back On The Block*, Quincy Jones
1991 *Unforgettable*, Natalie Cole
1992 *Unplugged*, Eric Clapton
1993 *The Bodyguard–Original Soundtrack Album*, Whitney Houston

Best Song

1983 "Every Breath You Take," Sting
1984 "What's Love Got to Do with It," Graham Lyle, Terry Britten
1985 "We Are the World," Michael Jackson, Lionel Richie
1986 "That's What Friends Are For," Burt Bacharach, Carole Bayer Sager
1987 "Somewhere Out There," Barry Mann, Cynthia Weil, James Horner
1988 "Don't Worry, Be Happy," Bobby McFerrin
1989 "Wind Beneath My Wings," Larry Henley, Jeff Silbar
1990 "From A Distance," Julie Gold
1991 "Unforgettable," Irving Gordon
1992 "Tears in Heaven," Eric Clapton, Will Jennings
1993 "A Whole New World (Aladdin's Theme)," Alan Menken, Tim Rice

Best Male Vocal

1983 *Thriller*, Michael Jackson
1984 "Against All Odds," Phil Collins
1985 *No Jacket Required*, Phil Collins
1986 "Higher Love," Steve Winwood
1987 *Bring On the Night*, Sting
1988 "Don't Worry, Be Happy," Bobby McFerrin
1989 "How Am I Supposed to Live Without You," Michael Bolton
1990 "Oh, Pretty Woman," Roy Orbison
1991 "When a Man Loves a Woman," Michael Bolton
1992 "Tears in Heaven," Eric Clapton
1993 "If I Ever Lose My Faith in You," Sting

Best Female Vocal

1983 "Flashdance…What a Feeling," Irene Cara
1984 "What's Love Got to Do with It," Tina Turner
1985 "Saving All My Love for You," Whitney Houston
1986 *The Broadway Album*, Barbra Streisand
1987 "I Wanna Dance with Somebody (Who Loves Me)," Whitney Houston
1988 "Fast Car," Tracy Chapman
1989 "Nick of Time," Bonnie Raitt
1990 "Vision Of Love," Mariah Carey
1991 "Something to Talk About," Bonnie Raitt
1992 "Constant Craving," k.d. lang
1993 "I Will Always Love You," Whitney Houston

Best New Artist

1983 Culture Club
1984 Cyndi Lauper
1985 Sade
1986 Bruce Hornsby and the Range
1987 Jody Watley
1988 Tracy Chapman
1989[1] Withdrawn
1990 Mariah Carey
1991 Mark Cohn
1992 Arrested Development
1993 Toni Braxton

Source: *National Academy of Recording Arts & Sciences*

(1) Initially awarded to Milli Vanilli who later admitted they had not performed on any of their recordings.

Top Records in Canada, 1993

Hit Singles

1. "I Will Always Love You," Whitney Houston
2. "Dream Lover," Mariah Carey
3. "That's the Way Love Goes," Janet Jackson
4. "If I Ever Lose My Faith in You," Sting
5. "I Don't Wanna Fight," Tina Turner
6. "Can't Help Falling in Love," UB40
7. "Ordinary World," Duran Duran
8. "Runaway Train," Soul Asylum
9. "Have I Told You Lately," Rod Stewart
10. "I'd Do Anything for Love (But I...)," Meat Loaf

Adult Contemporary Tracks

1. "I Don't Wanna Fight," Tina Turner
2. "The River of Dreams," Billy Joel
3. "Reason to Believe," Rod Stewart
4. "I Have Nothing," Whitney Houston
5. "Forever in Love," Kenny G
6. "A Whole New World," Peabo Bryson and Regina Belle
7. "I Will Always Love You," Whitney Houston
8. "Make Love to Me," Anne Murray
9. "To Love Somebody," Michael Bolton
10. "Run to You," Whitney Houston

Country Tracks

1. "In the Heart of A Woman," Billy Ray Cyrus
2. "I'm Gonna Drive You Out of My Mind," Charlie Major
3. "Ain't That Lonely Yet," Dwight Yoakam
4. "Almost Goodbye," Marc Chessnut
5. "Tell Me Why," Wynonna Judd
6. "Hard Workin' Man," Brooks & Dunn
7. "I Love the Way You Love Me," John Michael Montgomery
8. "Chatahoochee," Alan Jackson

9. "What's It to You," Clay Walker
10. "Take it Back," Reba McEntire

Albums

1. *Unplugged*, Eric Clapton
2. *Are You Gonna Go My Way*, Lenny Kravitz
3. *The Bodyguard Soundtrack*, Various Artists
4. *Pocket Full of Kryptonite*, Spin Doctors
5. *Get A Grip*, Aerosmith
6. *Unplugged*, Rod Stewart
7. *Bat Out of Hell II: Back Into Hell*, Meat Loaf
8. *Zooropa*, U2
9. *Janet*, Janet Jackson
10. *Dance Mix '93*, Various Artists

Dance Tracks

1. "Mr. Vain," Culture Beat
2. "What is Love," Haddaway
3. "Took My Love," Bizarre Inc.
4. "Rump Shaker," Wreckx n' Effect
5. "It's Gonna Be a Lovely Day," S.O.U.L. S.Y.S.T.E.M.
6. "More and More," Captain Hollywood Project
7. "I'm Gonna Get You," Bizarre Inc.
8. "Little Bird," Annie Lennox
9. "All That She Wants," Ace of Base
10. "Happy," Legacy of Sound

Canadian Content Albums

1. *Gordon*, Barenaked Ladies
2. *Fare Thee Well Love*, The Rankin Family
3. *Fully Completely*, The Tragically Hip
4. *Harvest Moon*, Neil Young
5. *The Future*, Leonard Cohen
6. *Bargainville*, Moxy Fruvous
7. *North Country*, The Rankin Family
8. *Unplugged*, Neil Young
9. *So Far So Good*, Bryan Adams
10. *Counterparts*, Rush

Source: *RPM Weekly*

Number of New Recordings

With Canadian Content

Type of music	1987–88	1989–90	1991–92
Adult-oriented Pop Music	74	198	244
Top 40/Rock, Disco	155	149	228
Classical and related	36	76	80
Jazz	19	24	18
Country and Folk	57	107	192
Children's	12	6	180
Other (includes unspecified)	68	55	159
Total	421	615	1,101

Without Canadian Content

Type of music	1987–88	1989–90	1991–92
Adult-oriented Pop Music	417	725	623
Top 40/Rock, Disco	801	1 741	2 818
Classical and related	267	607	1 362
Jazz	543	220	488
Country and Folk	177	150	233
Children's	35	24	135
Other (includes unspecified)	222	357	746
Total	2 462	3 824	6 405

Source: *Statistics Canada*

Top–Selling[1] Canadian Record Albums, 1975–94

1 Million + Sales
Bryan Adams, *Reckless*
Corey Hart, *Boy In The Box*

900 000 + Sales
Tom Cochrane, *Mad Mad World*

800 000 + Sales
Barenaked Ladies, *Gordon*

600 000 + Sales
Anne Murray, *Greatest Hits*
Alannah Myles, *Alannah Myles*
Bryan Adams, *So Far So Good*

500 000 + Sales
Loverboy, *Loverboy*
Platinum Blonde, *Alien Shores*
The Phantom of the Opera, Original Canadian Cast
The Tragically Hip, *Fully Completely*
Trooper, *Hot Shots*
Zamfir, *The Lonely Shepherd*
Celine Dion, *Celine Dion*
Celine Dion, *Unison*

400 000 + Sales
Glass Tiger, *The Thin Red Line*
Rush, *Moving Pictures*
The Rankin Family, *Fare Thee Well Love*
The Tragically Hip, *Apples*
Roch Voisine, *I'll Always Be There*

300 000 + Sales
Bryan Adams, *Cuts Like a Knife*
Bryan Adams, *Into The Fire*
Blue Rodeo, *Diamond Mine*
Corey Hart, *First Offense*
Harmonium, *L'Heptade*
Honeymoon Suite, *The Big Prize*
Honeymoon Suite, *Honeymoon Suite*
Loverboy, *Get Lucky*
Bob & Doug McKenzie, *The Great White North*
Rita MacNeil, *Now the Bells Ring*
Kim Mitchell, *Shakin' Like a Human Being*
Anne Murray, *Christmas Wishes*
Raffi, *Singable Songs For The Very Young*

The Rankin Family, *North Country*
Ginette Reno, *Je Ne Suis Qu'une Chanson*

200 000 + Sales
Aldo Nova, *Aldo Nova*
April Wine, *Greatest Hits*
April Wine, *The Nature of The Beast*
Angele Arsenault, *Libre*
Blue Rodeo, *Outskirts*
Gerry Boulet, *Rendez-vous doux*
Marie Carmen, *Miel Et Venin*
Chilliwack, *Hit Express*
Tom Cochrane and Red Rider, *Victory Day*
Burton Cummings, *Best of Burton Cummings*
Burton Cummings, *Dream of a Child*
Celine Dion, *Dion Chante Plamondon*
The Emeralds, *Bird Dance*
Glass Tiger, *Diamond Sun*
Gowan, *Strange Animal*
Harmonium, *Harmonium*
Corey Hart, *Fields of Fire*
Headpins, *Turn it Loud*
The Jeff Healey Band, *See The Light*
Heart, *Dreamboat Annie*
Dan Hill, *Longer Fuse*
Honeymoon Suite, *Racing After Midnight*
Colin James, *Colin James*
Gordon Lightfoot, *Gord's Gold*
Loverboy, *Keep it Up*
Rita MacNeil, *Flying On Your Own*
Rita MacNeil, *Home I'll Be*
Rita MacNeil, *Reason to Believe*
Rita MacNeil, *Rita*
Julie Masse, *Julie Masse*
Loreena McKennitt, *The Visit*
Marjo, *Celle Qui Va*
Alannah Myles, *Rockinghorse*
Platinum Blonde, *Standing in the Dark*
Powder Blues, *Uncut*
Prism, *Armageddon*
Raffi, *More Singable Songs*
Raffi, *Baby Beluga*
The Rankin Family, *North Country*

▶

▶ Robbie Robertson, *Robbie Robertson*
Roch Voisine, *Helene*
The Rovers, *The Rovers' 20th Anniversary*
Rush, *2112*

Sharon, Lois and Bram, *One Elephant, Deux Elephants*
Jennifer Warnes, *Famous Blue Raincoat*
Neil Young, *Harvest Moon*

Source: *Canadian Recording Industry Association*

(1) Includes only Canadian sales of over 200,000, based on certification by the Canadian Recording Industry Association, as of August 1994, of recordings that meet Canadian content standards by satisfying three of the following four criteria: music by a Canadian; performed by a Canadian artist; Canadian production; lyrics by a Canadian. Includes records, tapes and compact discs.

Top–Selling[1] Canadian Record Singles, 1975–94

Artist	Record Title	Canadian Sales
Northern Lights	"Tears Are Not Enough"	300 000+
The Rovers	"Wasn't That a Party"	200 000+
Bryan Adams	"Diana"[2]	100 000+
Alain Barrière	"Tue T'en Vas"	100 000+
Claudja Barry	"Boogie Woogie Dancin' Shoes"	100 000+
Corey Hart	"Never Surrender"	100 000+
Irish Rovers	"The Unicorn"	100 000+
Anne Murray	"You Needed Me"	100 000+
Platinum Blonde	"Crying Over You"	100 000+
J & R Williams	"La Danse des Canards"	100 000+

Source: *Canadian Recording Industry Association*

(1) Includes only Canadian sales of over 50,000, based on certification by the Canadian Recording Industry Association, as of August 1993, of recordings that meet Canadian content standards by satisfying three of the following four criteria: music by a Canadian; performed by a Canadian artist; Canadian production; lyrics by a Canadian. (2) An extended play single.

Canadian Music Video Awards, 1994

Best Director	Curtis Wehrfritz, "Hasn't Hit Me Yet," Blue Rodeo
Best Director of Photography	Doug Koch, "and if Venice is sinking," Spirit of the West
Best Editor	Jeth Weinrich, "Blame Your Parents," 54-40
Best Video	"Hasn't Hit Me Yet," Blue Rodeo
Best Rap Video	"X Marks the Spot," Devon
Best R&B/Soul Video	"Funkmobile," Bass is Base
Best Dance Video	"Music is My Life," Temperance
Best Alternative Video	"Push," Moist
Best Metal Video	"Not Quite Sonic," I Mother Earth
Best Adult Contemporary Video	"Possession," Sarah McLachlan
Best Country Music Video	"Distant Drum," Jim Witter
People's Choice–Favourite Video	"The River," The Tea Party

Source: *MuchMusic Network*

MTV Video Music Awards, 1994

Best Video of the Year	**"Cryin,"** Aerosmith
Best Male Video	**"Mary Jane's Last Dance,"** Tom Petty & The Heartbreakers
Best Female Video	**"If,"** Janet Jackson
Best Group Video	**"Cryin,"** Aerosmith
Best Metal/Hard Rock Video	**"Black Hole Sun,"** Soundgarden
Best New Artist in a Video	**"Mr. Jones,"** Counting Crows
Best Video from a Film	**"Streets of Philadelphia,"** Bruce Springsteen
Best Rap Video	**"Doggy Dogg World,"** Snoop Doggy Dogg
Best Dance Video	**"Whatta Man,"** Salt-N-Pepa w/En Vogue
Best R&B Video	**"Whatta Man,"** Salt-N-Pepa w/En Vogue
Best Direction in a Video	**"Everybody Hurts,"** R.E.M.
Best Choreography in a Video	**"Whatta Man,"** Salt-N-Pepa w/En Vogue
Best Special Effects in a Video	**"Kiss That Frog,"** Peter Gabriel
Breakthrough Video	**"Everybody Hurts,"** R.E.M.
Best Art Direction in a Video	**"Heart-Shaped Box,"** Nirvana
Best Editing in a Video	**"Everybody Hurts,"** R.E.M.
Best Cinematography in a Video	**"Everybody Hurts,"** R.E.M.
Viewer's Choice Award	**"Cryin,"** Aerosmith
International Winners, Japan	**"Eyes Love You,"** Hide
International Winners, Brasil	**"Territory,"** Sepultura
International Winners, Europe	**"Babe,"** Take That
International Winners, Latino	**"Matador,"** Los Fabulosos Cadillacsl

Source: *MTV: Music Television*

The Rock and Roll Hall of Fame

The Rock and Roll Hall of Fame was established in 1984 to preserve and enhance the status of rock and roll as an art form. The Rock and Roll Hall of Fame and Museum, featuring exhibits on each of the member performers, is scheduled to open in September 1995 in Cleveland, Ohio.

The members, chosen by a group of pop music experts, are listed below, followed by the years in which they were elected. Members in the early influences category are not listed.

■ **ARTISTS**

The Animals (1994)
LaVern Baker (1991)
Hank Ballard (1990)
The Band (1994)
The Beach Boys (1988)
The Beatles (1988)
Chuck Berry (1986)
Bobby "Blue" Bland (1992)
Booker T. & The MG's (1992)
James Brown (1986)
Ruth Brown (1993)
The Byrds (1991)
Johnny Cash (1992)
Ray Charles (1986)
The Coasters (1987)
Eddie Cochran (1987)
Sam Cooke (1986)
Cream (1993)
Creedence Clearwater Revival (1993)
Bobby Darin (1990)
Bo Diddley (1987)
Dion (1989)
Fats Domino (1986)
The Doors (1993)

The Drifters (1988)
Bob Dylan (1988)
Duane Eddy (1994)
The Everly Brothers (1986)
The Four Seasons (1990)
The Four Tops (1990)
Aretha Franklin (1987)
Marvin Gaye (1987)
Grateful Dead (1994)
Bill Haley (1987)
Buddy Holly (1986)
The Jimi Hendrix Experience (1992)
John Lee Hooker (1991)
The Impressions (1991)
The Isley Brothers (1992)
Etta James (1993)
Elton John (1994)
B.B. King (1987)
The Kinks (1990)
John Lennon (1994)
Jerry Lee Lewis (1986)
Little Richard (1986)
Frankie Lyman and the Teenagers (1993)
Bob Marley (1994)
Clyde McPhatter (1987)

▶

▶ Van Morrison (1993)
Ricky Nelson (1987)
Roy Orbison (1987)
Carl Perkins (1987)
Wilson Pickett (1991)
The Platters (1990)
Elvis Presley (1986)
Otis Redding (1989)
Jimmy Reed (1991)
Smokey Robinson (1987)
The Rolling Stones (1989)
Sam & Dave (1992)
Simon and Garfunkel (1990)
Sly and the Family Stone (1993)
Rod Stewart (1994)
The Supremes (1988)
The Temptations (1989)
Ike and Tina Turner (1991)
Big Joe Turner (1987)
Muddy Waters (1987)
The Who (1990)
Jackie Wilson (1987)
Stevie Wonder (1989)
The Yardbirds (1992)

Source: *Rock and Roll Hall of Fame Foundation*

■ **NON-PERFORMERS**
Dave Bartholomew (1991)
Ralph Bass (1991)
Leonard Chess (1987)
Dick Clark (1993)
Lamont Dozier, Brian Holland & Eddie Holland (1990)
Ahmet Ertegun (1987)
Leo Fender (1992)
Alan Freed (1986)
Milt Gabler (1993)
Gerry Goffin & Carole King (1990)
Berry Gordy, Jr. (1988)
Bill Graham (1992)
Jerry Leiber & Mike Stoller (1987)
Johnny Otis (1994)
Doc Pomus (1992)
Phil Spector (1989)
Sam Phillips (1986)
Jerry Wexler (1987)

■ **LIFETIME ACHIEVEMENT AWARDS**
Willie Dixon (1994)
Nesuhi Ertegun (1991)
John Hammond (1986)

PERFORMING ARTS

Governor General's Performing Arts Awards

The Governor General's Performing Arts Awards were inaugurated in 1992 to pay tribute to the lifetime achievements of outstanding artists in a variety of creative fields. The motto of the awards, "The Arts Engage and Inspire Us," reflects the cultural contribution made by recipients chosen from theatre, dance, classical music/opera, popular music, film and broadcasting. The awards are presented annually in November by the Governor General and are administered by the Governor General's Performing Arts Awards Foundation.

1992 WINNERS

■ **William Hutt,** *actor/director*
Rightly considered a giant of the theatre scene in Canada, William Hutt has been working at his craft for forty-five years, including twenty-nine at the Stratford Festival. Specializing in Shakespearean roles, he made classical theatre a strong component in Canadian culture. Hutt also championed new theatrical works and has taught throughout the country. He won a Genie Award as Best Actor in 1975 for his portrayal of Sir John A. Macdonald in the final episode of CBC's acclaimed series "The Last Spike."

■ **Gweneth Lloyd,** *choreographer*
Gweneth Lloyd and her student and friend Betty Farrally came to Canada in 1938 and began what would become our country's first professional ballet company, The Royal Winnipeg Ballet. Lloyd was a prolific creator despite the low profile of arts and culture during the pre-war period. In the thirteen years preceding the founding of The Royal Winnipeg Ballet, she produced 35 works. In 1991, one of her most famous pieces, "The Wise Virgins," originally created in 1942, was reconstructed and danced by the Royal Winnipeg. Gweneth Lloyd was a

choreographer with rich and complex ideas that have been well-documented, and has now been permanently recognized.

■ **Dominique Michel**, *singer, comedienne, actor*

For over thirty years, Dominique Michel has been one of the greatest popular performers in Quebec. And what has maintained her popularity has been her versatility. From her first hit song "En Veillant Sur le Perron," which entertained many spectators in the Montreal nightclubs, to her biting characterization as the academic whose revelations destroy the lives around her in Denys Arcand's "The Decline of the American Empire," Dominique Michel has always played a quintessential modern woman, one who can be funny, and humane, but who can also break hearts. Her solidarity with her public has been best captured in her annual role imitating leading Quebec figures on Radio Canada's year-end programme "Bye Bye." One of her colleagues, actress Denise Filiatrault, best described Dominique Michel as "a phenomenon....a living caricaturist." And by becoming well-known as the *animatrice* of Montreal's "Just For Laughs" Festival," she also adds the essence of Quebec "showbiz" to her eclectic repertoire.

■ **Mercedes Palomino**, *co-founder of Théatre du Rideau Vert*

When Mercedes Palomino emigrated to Montreal from Spain in 1947, she began a career that sparked the development of theatre in Quebec. Palomino received her education in the dramatic arts in Argentina, and she brought a passionate temperament to theatre production. After only a year in Montreal, she founded Le Théatre du Rideau Vert with actress Yvette Brind'amour, and Le Rideau Vert became synonymous with the creation of new and original work in Quebec drama. Being the architect of the repertoire, Palomino was daring and brave in her selections, including Michel Tremblay's "Les Belles-Soeurs" and Antonine Maillet's "La Sagouine."

Operating in the early years without the help of government grants, Mercedes Palomino's contributions to theatre in Quebec laid the foundations for its continued success to this day.

■ **Oscar Peterson**, *jazz pianist*

Oscar Peterson, world-renowned for his contributions to the art of jazz, began his career in Montreal. Rather than apprenticing as a sideman before taking on the role of leader, Oscar Peterson led his own combo from the beginning. In 1949 he recruited musicians like Ray Brown, Ed Thigpen, and Louis Hayes, and introduced his group to an international audience. Peterson has played in a style often referred to as "swinging," crediting Art Tatum and Bill Evans as his influences. As well as leading his own group, he has accompanied some of the best in jazz like Louis Armstrong and Lester Young. Oscar Peterson is equally accomplished as a composer. One of his first pieces to achieve fame was the "Canadiana Suite," and his "Hymn to Freedom" was an early musical statement that poignantly addressed the injustice of racism. Known as a private man who has lived a very public life, Oscar Peterson has earned the title of Canada's Musical Ambassador.

■ **Leopold Simoneau**, *tenor*

Calling his voice "the faithful servant of the music," singer Leopold Simoneau has sung in all the great opera houses from La Scala to the Met. Known primarily as a great interpreter of the music of Mozart, which earned him the title of Mr. Mozart, his voice produced a unique *lyrico leggiero* sound which allowed him to be a great interpreter of many other composers. After his stage career ended, Simoneau went on to teach his craft.

1993 WINNERS

■ **Ludmilla Chiriaeff**, *dancer*

Ludmilla Chiriaeff survived the loss of her Russian family and the ravages of a wartime concentration camp, and came to Montreal in the early fifties. By 1956 she was presenting dance to Quebecers through CBC French television, and her ballet productions electrified the cultural community. Montreal's mayor Jean Drapeau invited her to form a ballet company to rival Toronto's National Ballet and she founded Les Grands Ballets Canadiens. A dance school to train young Quebec dancers soon followed, later to become Quebec's Ecole superieure de danse. Her work eventually became the foundation of classical dance education at all levels in the province. Ludmilla Chiriaeff has been named a Companion of the Order of Canada and awarded Quebec's Prix Denise-Pelletier for the performing arts.

■ **Leonard Cohen,** *poet, singer, songwriter*
For over thirty years, Leonard Cohen has been presenting his mysterious vision of our inner lives in songs such as "Suzanne," "Bird on a Wire," "Dance Me to the End of Love," and "The Future." In eight volumes of poetry, two novels, and eleven record albums, his tales and images have earned him a following unlike any other Canadian popular performer. His lyrics and songs have been covered by artists as diverse as Neil Diamond, Diana Ross, Joan Baez and Joe Cocker. For this richly textured career, he has been honoured with the Order of Canada, literary awards, and in 1991, induction in the Juno Hall of Fame. At last year's Junos he won "Male Vocalist of the Year."

■ **Don Haig,** *film producer*
After establishing himself as a brilliant CBC film editor on such programs as "This Hour Has Seven Days" and "The Fifth Estate," Don Haig turned to film production. He began by opening his own post-production house called Film Arts and served in a variety of roles, helping some film-makers with advice on rough cuts and raising funds for others. Haig has bankrolled such films as Patricia Rozema's *I've Heard the Mermaids Singing,* and Brigette Berman's Academy Award-winning *Artie Shaw: Time is all You've Got.* Recently he was appointed Executive Producer for drama and documentary at the National Film Board. As a mentor for new film-makers, Don Haig describes himself as being lucky to work with so many talented people; the thousands of film-makers who've crossed his path know they've been lucky to meet Don Haig.

■ **Lois Maxwell,** *singer*
The power and quality of Lois Maxwell's three octave voice has left listeners like Glenn Gould speechless in awe of her gifts. Famed for her singing of the great oratorios, Lois Maxwell can move from the depths of the lower mezzo-soprano to the heights of the coloratura soprano. Many conductors she has worked with such as Thomas Beecham, Otto Klemperer, and Toscanini have sung her praises and she has received rave reviews from concertgoers from London to Moscow. In 1967 she was made a Companion of the Order of Canada. Like most great artists with a gift to express, she now spends her time teaching the next generation of singers.

■ **Monique Mercure,** *actor*
This talented and intuitive actress has starred in some of Canada's most memorable films including Claude Jutra's *Mon Oncle Antoine* , and Jean Beaudin's *J.A. Martin, photographe,* for which she won the *Palme d'or* for best actress at the Cannes Film Festival. Mecure has been a crucial ingredient in the development of the sensibilities of some of the most talented Québecois artists. In 1992 she won a Genie Award for her role in David Cronenberg's *Naked Lunch.* She was made an Officer of the Order of Canada in 1979 and now serves as head of our National Theatre School. Monique Mercure sums up her accomplishments modestly when she says, "I am a worker because artists must become good citizens and be tools in creating this country's culture."

■ **Gilles Vigneault,** *poet*
Whether his poems have been read aloud or put to music, Gilles Vigneault has helped Quebecers feel a love and commitment to their land. He has also created marvellous tales for children, and recently a collection of one hundred and one of his most beautiful songs was released. Quebecers have danced and rejoiced over such songs as "Mon Pays" and "Gens du Pays," while recognizing the important part they've played in shaping Quebec's cultural heritage. Gilles Vigneault's importance to Québécois culture was recognized when he was honoured with its *Legion d'honneur.*

Canadian Orchestras

MARITIMES

Chebucto Symphony Orchestra: 95 Victoria Road, Dartmouth, N.S. B3A 1V2. John Rapson, musical director

Newfoundland Symphony Orchestra: Arts & Culture Centre, Prince Philip Dr., St. John's, Nfld. A1C 5P9. Marc David, musical director

Prince Edward Island Symphony Orchestra: P.O. Box 185, Charlottetown, PEI C1A 7K4. Brian Ellard, musical director

Scotia Chamber Players: 1541 Barrington St., #317, Halifax, N.S. B3J 1Z5

Symphony New Brunswick: 32 King St., Saint John, N.B. E2L 1G3. Nurhan Arman, musical director

Symphony Nova Scotia: 1646 Barrington St., #401, Halifax, N.S. B3J 2A3. Georg Tintner, musical director

CENTRAL CANADA

Brampton Symphony Orchestra: 24A Alexander St., Brampton, Ont. L6V 1H6. Andrew Dittgin, musical director

Brantford Symphony Orchestra: P.O. Box 24012, 185 King George Road, Brantford, Ont. N3R 7X3. Stanley Saunders, musical director

Cathedral Bluffs Symphony: 16 Kingswood Road, Scarborough, Ont. M4E 3N5. Clifford Poole, musical director

Chamber Players of Toronto: 24 Ryerson Ave., #209, Toronto, Ont. M5T 2P3. Paavo Jarvi, musical director

Chatham Symphony Orchestra: P.O. Box 396, Chatham, Ont. N7M 5K5. Allen Kosmala, musical director

CJRT Radio Orchestra: 297 Victoria St., Toronto, Ont. M5B 1W1. Paul Robinson, musical director

Deep River Symphony Orchestra: P.O. Box 1496, Deep River, Ont. K0J 1P0. Peter Morris, musical director

East York Symphony Orchestra: 110 Rumsey Rd., Toronto, Ont. M4G 1P2. Douglas M. Sanford, musical director

Eastern Ontario Concert Orchestra: P.O. Box 102, Belleville, Ont. K8N 4Z9. Gordon Craig, musical director

Esprit Orchestra: Chalmers Bldg., 35 McCaul St., #401, Toronto, Ont. M5T 1V7. Alex Pauk, musical director

Etobicoke Philharmonic Orchestra: 19 Hilldowntree Rd., Etobicoke, Ont. M9A 2Z4. Tak-Ng Lai, musical director

Fanshawe Community Orchestra: 1551 Ryersie Rd., London, Ont. N6G 2S2. Douglas M. Sanford, musical director

Georgian Bay Symphony: P.O. Box 133, Owen Sound, Ont. N4K 5P1. John Barnum, musical director

Hamilton Philharmonic Orchestra: 25 Main St. W, 8th Floor, Hamilton, Ont. L8P 1H1. Akira Endo, musical director

Hart House Orchestra: Hart House, University of Toronto, 7 Hart House Circle, Toronto, Ont. M5S 1A1. Errol Gay, musical director

Huronia Symphony: P.O. Box 904, Barrie, Ont. L4M 4Y6. Claudio Vena, musical director

International Symphony Orchestra of Sarnia and Port Huron: 774 London Rd., Sarnia, Ont. N7T 4Y1. Stan Kopac, musical director

Kingston Symphony Orchestra: P.O. Box 1616, Kingston, Ont. K7L 5C8. Glen Fast, musical director

Kitchener-Waterloo Chamber Orchestra: P.O. Box 937, Waterloo, Ont. N2J 4C3. Graham Coles, musical director

Kitchener-Waterloo Community Orchestra: P.O. Box 938, Waterloo, Ont. N2J 4C3. Erna Van Daele, musical director

Kitchener-Waterloo Symphony: 101 Queen St. N., Kitchener, Ont. N2H 6P7. Chosei Komatsu, musical director

Korean Canadian Symphony Orchestra, 703 Bloor St. W, #203, Toronto, Ont. M6G 1L5. Sung-Soon Kim, musical director

London Community Orchestra: 1551 Ryersie Rd., London, Ont. N6G 2S2. Mariusz Debich, musical director

McGill Chamber Orchestra: 1745 Cedar Ave., Montreal, Que. H3G 1A7. Alexander Brott, musical director

Mississauga Symphony/Sinfonia Mississauga: 161 Lakeshore Rd. W., Mississauga, Ont. L5H 1G3. John Barnum, musical director

Montreal Chamber Orchestra: 5825 Esplanade Ave., Montreal, Que. H2T 3A2. Wanda Kaluzny, musical director

National Arts Centre Orchestra: P.O. Box 1534, Station B, 53 Elgin St., Ottawa, Ont. K1P 5W1. Trevor Pinnock, artistic director

National Youth Orchestra of Canada: 1032 Bathurst St., Toronto, Ont. M5R 3G7.

Niagara Symphony: P.O. Box 401, St. Catharines, Ont. L2R 6V9. Ermanno Florio, musical director

North Bay Symphony Orchestra: 269 Main St. W., #106, North Bay, Ont. P1B 2T8. Victor Sawa, musical director

North York Concert Orchestra: 10 Prestwick Cres., Willowdale, Ont. M2H 1M9. Steven Riches, musical director

North York Symphony: 1210 Sheppard Ave. E., Ste. 109, North York, Ont. M2K 1E3. Kerry Stratton, musical director

Northumberland Orchestra Society: P.O. Box 1012, Cobourg, Ont., K9A 4W4. Matthew Jaskiewicz, musical director

Orchestra London Canada: 520 Wellington St., London, Ont. N6A 3P9. Uri Mayer, musical director

Orchestre symphonique de Laval: 4, Place Laval, bureau 410, Laval, Que. H7N 5W1. Jacques Lacombe, musical director

Orchestre symphonique de Montréal: 85, rue St-Catherine ouest, #900, Montréal, Que. H2X 3P4. Charles S. Dutoit, musical director

Orchestre symphonique de Québec: 130, Grande-Allée ouest, Québec, Que. G1R 2G7. Pascal Verrot, musical director

Orchestra symphonique du Saguenay-Lac-St-Jean: 202, rue Jacques-Cartier est, Chicoutimi, Que. G7H 1R8. Jacques Clément, musical director

Orchestre des Jeunes du Québec: 1501 Jeanne-Mance, Montreal, Que. H2X 1G9

Orchestre de chambre de l'estrie Sherbrooke: 14, rue Alexandre, Sherbrooke, Que. J1H 4S6. Marc David, musical director

Orchestre symphonique de Trois-Rivières: C.P. 1281, Trois-Rivières, Que. G9A 5K8. Gilles Bellemare, musical director

Orchestre symphonique Régional d'Abitibi-Témiscamingue: C.P. 2305, Rouyn-Noranda, Que. J9X 5A9. Jacques Marchand, musical director

Oshawa Symphony Orchestra: P.O. Box 444, Oshawa, Ont. L1H 7L5. Winston Webber, musical director

Ottawa Symphony Orchestra: 309-1390 Prince of Wales Dr., Ottawa, Ont. K2C 3N6. David Currie, musical director

Pembroke Symphony Orchestra: P.O. Box 374, Pembroke, Ont. K8A 6X6. Caryl A. Clark, musical director

Peterborough Symphony Orchestra: P.O. Box 1135, Peterborough, Ont. K9J 7H4. Stan Kopac, musical director

Pro Arte Orchestra: 1692 Danforth Ave., Toronto, Ont. M4C 1H8. Victor Di Bello, musical director

Royal Conservatory Orchestra: 273 Bloor St. W., Toronto, Ont. M5S 1W2. Jose Luis Garcia, musical director

Sault Symphony Orchestra: 1520 Queen St. E, Sault Ste. Marie, Ont. P6A 2G4. John Wilkinson, musical director

Scarborough Philharmonic Orchestra: 2100 Ellesmere Rd., #302, Scarborough, Ont. M1N 2G2. Christopher Kitts, musical director

Sir Ernest MacMillan String Ensemble: 9 Suter Cres., Dundas, Ont., Marta Hidy, musical director

Sudbury Symphony Orchestra: 111 Larch Street, 3rd Fl., Sudbury, Ont. P3E 4T5. Metro Kozak, musical director

Symphony Hamilton: 2341 Sharron St., Burlington, Ont. L7R 1W8. Clyde H. Mitchell, musical director

Tafelmusik Baroque Orchestra: 427 Bloor St. W., Toronto, Ont. M5S 1X7. Jeanne Lamon, musical director

Te Deum Orchestra and Singers: 105 Victoria St., Dundas, Ont. L9H 2C1. Richard Birney-Smith, musical director

Thunder Bay Symphony Orchestra: P.O. Box 2004, 953 Oliver Road, Thunder Bay, Ont. P7B 5E7. Glenn Mossop, musical director

Timmins Symphony Orchestra: Box 1365, Timmins, Ont. P4N 7N2. Geoff Lee, musical director

Toronto Chinese Philharmonic Orchestra: 3330 Midland Ave., #39, Scarborough, Ont. M1V 5E7. Tak Ng-Lai, musical director

Toronto Philharmonic Orchestra: 35McCaul St., #411, Toronto, Ont. M5T 1V7. Jacob Harnoy, artistic director

Toronto Sinfonietta: 588 Spadina Ave., #210, Toronto, Ont. M8X 1A3. Mathew Jaskiewicz, musical director

The Toronto Symphony: 60 Simcoe St., Ste. C116, Toronto, Ont. M5J 2H5. Jukka-Pekka Saraste, musical director

University of Toronto Symphony Orchestra: Faculty of Music, U of T, 80 Queen's Park Cres., Toronto, Ont. M5S 1A1. Pierre Hétu, musical director

University of Western Ontario Orchestra: Faculty of Music, UWO, London, Ont. N6A 3K7. James McKay, musical director

Wilfrid Laurier University Symphony: Faculty of Music, 75 University Ave. W., Waterloo, Ont. N2L 3C5. Paul Pulford, musical director

Windsor Symphony Orchestra: 174-198 Pitt St. W., Windsor, Ont. N95 5L4. Susan Haig, musical director

Woodstock Strings: 236 Riddell St., Woodstock, Ont. N4S 6N4. Patrick Burroughs, musical director

York Symphony Orchestra: Box 355, Richmond Hill, Ont. L4C 4Y6. Roberto De Clara, musical director

WESTERN CANADA

Calgary Philharmonic Orchestra: 205-8th Ave. S.E., Calgary, Alta. T2G 0K9

Civic Orchestra of Victoria: P.O. Box 6478, Depot 1, Victoria, B.C. V8P 5M4. Robert Cooper, musical director

Crowsnest Pass Symphony: P.O. Box 268, Blairmore, Alta. T0K 0E0. Dick Burgman, musical director

Edmonton Philharmonic Society: 186 Oeming Rd. NW, Edmonton, Alta. T6R 2G2. George Naylor, musical director

Edmonton Symphony Orchestra: 10160-103 St., Edmonton, Alta. T5J 0X6. Uri Mayer, musical director

Fraser Valley Symphony: Box 122, Abbotsford, B.C. V2S 4N8. David R. Rushton, musical director

Kamloops Symphony Orchestra: Box 57, Kamloops, B.C. V2C 5K3. Bruce Rodney Dunn, musical director

Kootenay Chamber Orchestra: P.O. Box 512, Cranbrook, B.C. V1C 4J1. Ronald Edinger, musical director

Lethbridge Symphony: Yates Memorial Centre, 4th Ave & 10th St. S, Lethbridge, Alta. T1J 4A2. Stewart Grant, musical director

Manitoba Chamber Orchestra: 202-1317A Portage Ave., Winnipeg, Man. R3G 0V3. Simon Streatfield, musical director

Medicine Hat Youth & Community Orchestra: P.O. Box 1295, Medicine Hat, Alta. T1A 7N1. Carl Duguid, musical director

Nanaimo Symphony Orchestra: P.O. Box 661, Nanaimo, B.C. V9R 5L9. Lloyd Blackburn, musical director

Okanagan Symphony Orchestra: P.O. Box 1120, Kelowna, B.C. V1Y 7P8. Leonard Camplin, musical director

Prince George Symphony Orchestra: 2880-15th Ave., Prince George, B.C. V2M 1T1. Michael Reason, musical director

Red Deer Orchestra: P.O. Box 1116, Red Deer, Alta. T4N 6J5. Claude Lapalme, musical director

Regina Symphony Orchestra: 200 Lakeshore Dr., Regina, Sask. S4P 3V7. Vladimir Conta, musical director

Richmond Community Orchestra and Chorus: P.O. Box 94284, Richmond, B.C. V6Y 2A2. Wallace Leung, musical director

Saskatoon Symphony: P.O. Box 1361, 703 Delta Bessborough, Saskatoon, Sask. S7K 3N9. Dennis Simons, artistic director

Vancouver Philharmonic Orchestra: P.O. Box 27503, Oakridge Station, Vancouver, B.C. V5Z 4M4.

Vancouver Symphony Orchestra: 601 Smithe St., Vancouver, B.C. V6B 5G1. Sergiu Comissiona, musical director

Victoria Symphony Orchestra: 846 Broughton St., Victoria, B.C. V8W 1E4. Peter McCoppin, musical director

Winnipeg Symphony Orchestra: 555 Main St., Rm. 101, Winnipeg, Man. R3B 1C3. Bramwell Tovey, artistic director

Source: *Association of Canadian Orchestras*

Canadian Opera Companies

Calgary Opera Association: #800, 125-9 Ave. S.E., Calgary, Alta. T2G 0P8. David A. Speers, gen. dir.

Canadian Opera Co.: 227 Front St. E., Toronto, Ont., M5A 1E8. Richard Bradshaw, A.D.

Edmonton Opera Association: #320, 10232-112 St., Edmonton, Alta. T5K 1M4. Irving Guttman, gen. dir.

Manitoba Opera Association: Box 31027, 393 Portage Ave., Winnipeg, Man. R3B 3K9. Irving Guttman, A.D.

Opera Atelier: 2 Bloor St. W., Cumberland Terrace, Upper Level, Toronto, Ont. M4W 3E2.

Opera Hamilton: Stelco Tower, 100 King St. W., #200 Plaza Level, Hamilton, Ont. L8P 1A2. Daniel Lipton, art. dir.

Opera Lyra Ottawa: Arts Court, 2 Daly Avenue, Ottawa, Ont. K1N 6E2. Jeanette Aster, art. dir.

L'Opéra de Montréal: 260, Boulevard de Maisonneuve ouest, Montreal, Que. H2X 1Y9. Joanne Massicotte, gen. dir.

Opera Saskatchewan: 1870 Albert St. #270, Regina, Sask. S4P 4B7

Pacific Opera Victoria: 1316B Government St., Victoria, B.C. V8W 1Y8. Timothy Vernon, art. dir.

Prairie Opera Inc.: P.O. Box 7924, Saskatoon, Sask. S7K 4R6

Vancouver Opera Association: 500-845 Cambie St., Vancouver, B.C. V6B 4Z9. Robert Hallam, gen. dir.

Major Ballet Companies

(artistic director in brackets)

Ballet British Columbia: 502-68 Water St., Vancouver, B.C. V6B 1A4 (John Alleyne)

Les Grands Ballets Canadiens: 4816 rue Rivard, Montreal, Que. H2J 2N6 (Lawrence Rhodes)

The National Ballet of Canada: 157 King St. E., Toronto, Ont. M5C 1G9 (Reid Anderson)

Ottawa Ballet: P.O. Box 366, Stn. "A," Ottawa, Ont. K1N 8V3

Royal Winnipeg Ballet: 380 Graham Ave., Winnipeg, Man. R3C 4K2 (William Whitener)

Major Contemporary and Jazz Dance Companies

(artistic director in brackets)

Les Ballets Jazz de Montréal: 3450 rue St-Urbain, Montreal, Que. H2X 2N5

Contemporary Dancers Incorporated: 109 Pulford St., Winnipeg, Man. R3L 1X8 (Tom Stroud)

Dancemakers: 927 Dupont St., Toronto, Ont. M6H 1Z1 (Serge Bennathan)

Danse Partout: 880 Père-Marquette, Quebec, Que. G1S 2A4 (Luc Tremblay)

Decidedly Jazz Danceworks: P.O. Box 4626, Stn. "C," Calgary, Alta. T2T 5P1 (Vicki Willis)

Desrosiers Dance Theatre: 103-219 Broadview Ave., Toronto, Ont. M4M 2G3 (Robert Desrosiers)

Fortier Danse Création: Box 605, Stn. C., Montreal, Que. H2L 4L5

La Fondation de danse Margie Gillis: 3575 boul. St. Laurent, #502, Montreal, Que. H2X 2T7 (Margie Gillis)

Danny Grossman Dance Company: 511 Bloor St. W., Toronto, Ont. M5S 1Y4 (Danny Grossman)

Le Groupe de la Place Royale: 2 Daly Ave., Ste. 2, Ottawa, Ont. K1N 6E2 (Peter Boneham)

Karen Jamieson Dance Company: 242 E. 10th Ave., Vancouver, B.C. V5T 1Z5 (Karen Jamieson)

Kompany!: #810, 10136-100th St., Edmonton, Alta. T5J 0P1 (Ron Schuster)

Judith Marcuse Dance Company: 106-206 E. 6th Ave., Vancouver, B.C. V5T 1J8 (Judith Marcuse)

Mascall Dance: 1130 Jarvis St., Vancouver, B.C. V6E 2C7 (Jennifer Mascall)

Montanaro Danse: 24, ave. du Mont-Royal ouest, #601, Montreal, Que. H2T 2S2 (Michael Montanaro)

O Vertigo: 4455 rue de Rouen, Montreal, Que. H1V 1H1 (Ginette Laurin)

La Fondation Jean-Pierre Perreault: Rue Sherbrooke Est, Montreal, Que. H2K 1B9

Gina Lori Riley Dance Enterprises: 3277 Sandwich St., Windsor, Ont. N9C 1A9 (Gina Lori Riley)

Toronto Dance Theatre: 80 Winchester St., Toronto, Ont. M4X 1B2 (Christopher House)

Source: *Dance Umbrella of Ontario*

Major Theatre Companies in Canada

(artistic directors in brackets)

MARITIMES

Mermaid Theatre of Nova Scotia: Box 2697, 132 Garrish St, Windsor, N.S. B0N 2T0 (Sara Lee Lewis)

Mulgrave Road Co-op Theatre: Box 219, Main St, Guysborough, N.S. B0H 1N0 (Allana MacDonald)

Neptune Theatre Foundation: 1593 Argyle St, Halifax, N.S. B3J 2B2 (Linda Moore)

Ship's Company Theatre: P.O. Box 275, Parrsboro, N.S. B0M 1S0 (Michael Fuller)

Theatre New Brunswick: Box 566, Fredericton, N.B. E3B 5A6 (Michael Shamata)

CENTRAL CANADA

Buddies in Bad Times: 41 Britain St, Toronto, Ont. M5A 1R7 (Sky Gilbert)

Canadian Stage Company: 26 Berkeley St, Toronto, Ont. M5A 2W3 (Bob Baker)

Centaur Theatre Company: 453, rue Saint-François-Xavier, Montreal, Que. H2Y 2T1 (Maurice Podbrey)

La Compagnie Jean Duceppe: 1400 rue Saint-Urbain, Montreal, Que. H2X 2M5 (Louise Duceppe)

Company of Sirens: 438 Bloor St W, 2nd Flr., Toronto, Ont. M5S 1X5 (Cynthia Grant)

Factory Theatre: 125 Bathurst St, Toronto, Ont. M5V 2R2 (Jackie Maxwell)

Grand Theatre Company (Theatre London): 471 Richmond St, London, Ont. N6A 3E4 (Martha Henry)

Great Canadian Theatre Company: 910 Gladstone Ave, Ottawa, Ont. K1R 6Y4 (Arthur Milner)

Gryphon Theatre: Box 454, 1 Georgian Dr., Barrie, Ont. L4M 4T7 (Uwe Meyer)

Magnus Theatre Company: 101 N. Syndicate Ave., Ste. 303, Thunder Bay, Ont. P7C 3V4 (Mario Crudo)

National Arts Centre: Box 1534, Stn. B, Ottawa, Ont. K1P 5W1

Native Earth Performing Arts: 302-720 Bathurst St, Toronto, Ont. M5S 2R4 (Drew Hayden Taylor)

Nightwood Theatre: 6000-317 Adelaide St W, Toronto, Ont. M5V 1P9 (Diane Roberts, artistic coordinator)

The Piggery: Box 390, North Hatley, Que. J0B 2C0

Princess of Wales Theatre: 300 King St W, Toronto, Ont. M5V 1J2

Royal Alexandra Theatre: 260 King St W, Toronto, Ont. M5V 1H9

Sudbury Theatre Centre: P.O. Box 641, Stn. B, Sudbury, Ont. P3E 4P8 (Gord McCall)

Tarragon Theatre: 30 Bridgman Ave, Toronto, Ont. M5R 1X3 (Urjo Kareda)

Theatre Aquarius: 190 King William St., Hamilton, Ont. L8R 1A8 (Peter Mandia)

▶

Théâtre de la Bordée: 1105, rue Saint-Jean, #201, Quebec, Que. G1R 1S3 (Jean-Jacqui Boutet)

Théâtre du Nouveau Monde: 137, Saint-Ferdinand, #201, Montreal, Que. H4C 2S7 (Lorraine Pintal)

Théâtre du Rideau Vert: 269 Rene Levesque G, Que., Que. G1R 2B3 (Mercedes Palomino)

Le Théâtre du Trident: 580, ave Grande-Allée est, #20, Quebec, Que. G1R 2K2 (Serge Denoncourt)

Theatre Passe Muraille: 16 Ryerson Ave, Toronto, Ont. M5T 2P3 (Susan Serran)

Young People's Theatre: 165 Front St E, Toronto, Ont. M5A 3Z4 (Maja Ardal)

WESTERN CANADA

Alberta Theatre Projects: 220-9th Ave SE, Calgary, Alta. T2G 5C4 (Michael Dobbin)

Arts Club Theatre: 1585 Johnson St, Vancouver, B.C. V6H 3R9 (Bill Millerd)

Banff Centre: Box 1020, Banff, Alta. T0L 0C0

Belfry Theatre: 1292 Gladstone Ave, Victoria, B.C. V8T 1G5 (Glynis Leyshon)

Citadel Theatre: 9828-101A Ave, Edmonton, Alta. T5J 3C6 (Robin Phillips)

Globe Theatre: 1801 Scarth St, Regina, Sask. S4P 2G9 (Susan Ferley)

Manitoba Theatre Centre: 174 Market Ave, Winnipeg, Man. R3B 0P8 (Steven Schipper)

Manitoba Theatre for Young People: 89 Princess St, Winnipeg, Man. R3B 1K6 (Leslee Silverman)

New Bastion Theatre Company: 625 Superior St, Victoria, BC V8V 1V1 (Douglas Riske)

Nightcap Productions: 239-5th Ave. N, Saskatoon, Sask. S7K 2P3 (Henry Woolf)

Persephone Theatre: 2802 Rusholme Rd, Saskatoon, Sask. S7L 0H2 (Tibor Fehergyhazi)

Popular Theatre Alliance of Manitoba: 2-413 Selkirk Ave, Winnipeg, Man. R2W 2M4 (Margo Charlton)

Prairie Theatre Exchange: 389 Portage Ave, Portage Place, Unit Y300, Winnipeg, Man. R3B 3H6 (Michael Springate)

Rainbow Stage (1993) Inc.: 320 Sherbrook St, Ste 201, Winnipeg, Man. R3B 2W6

Sunshine Theatre Company: Box 443, Kelowna, B.C. V1Y 7P1 (Ken Kramer)

Tamahnous Theatre: 222-275 Woodland Ave., Vancouver, B.C. V5L 3S7 (Jackie Crossland)

Theatre Calgary: 220-9th Ave. SE, Calgary, Alta. T2G 5C4 (Brian Rintoul)

Theatre Network: 10708-124th St, Edmonton, Alta. T5M 0H1 (Ben Henderson)

Theatre Projects Manitoba: 393 Portage Ave, Unit Y-300, Winnipeg, Man. R3B 3H6 (Harry Rintoul)

25th Street Theatre: 7-420 Duchess St, Saskatoon, Sask. S7K 0R1 (Tom Bentley-Fisher)

Vancouver Playhouse: 810 West Broadway, Box 281, Vancouver, B.C. V5Z 4C9 (Susan Cox)

Western Canada Theatre Company: Box 329, Kamloops, BC V2C 5K9 (David Ross)

Source: *Canadian Actors Equity Association, Union des Artistes*

Summer Theatre in Canada

Blyth Festival: P.O. Box 10, Blyth, Ont. N0M 1H0 (Janet Amos)

Charlottetown Festival: Confederation Centre of Arts, 145 Richmond St., Charlottetown, P.E.I. C1A 1J1 (Jacques Lemay)

Huron Country Playhouse: R.R. #1, Grand Bend, Ont. N0M 1T0 (Max Reimer)

Kawartha Summer Theatre: P.O. Box 161, 2 Lindsay St. S, Lindsay, Ont. K9V 4S1 (Diane Nyland Proctor)

Lighthouse Festival Theatre: P.O. Box 1208, Port Dover, Ont. N0A 1N0 (Simon Johnston)

Muskoka Festival: P.O. Box 1055, Gravenhurst, Ont. P1P 1X2 (Lesley Ballantyne)

Nanaimo Festival: P.O. Box 626, 7-10 Commercial St., Nanaimo, B.C. V9R 5L9 (Michael McLaughlin)

Red Barn Theatre: P.O. Box 291, Jackson's Point, Ont. L0E 1L0

Shaw Festival Theatre: P.O. Box 774, Niagara-on-the-Lake, Ont. L0S 1J0 (Christopher Newton)

Showboat Festival Theatre: P.O. Box 454, Port Colborne, Ont. L3K 5X7 (Blake Heathcote)

Stephenville Festival: 129 Montana Dr., Stephenville, Nfld. A2N 2T4

Stratford Shakespearean Festival: P.O. Box 520, Stratford, Ont. L3V 6K8 (Richard Monette)

Thousand Islands Playhouse: P.O. Box 241, Gananoque, Ont. K7G 2T8 (Greg Wanless)

Upper Canada Playhouse: P.O. Box 852, Morrisburg, Ont. K0C 1X0 (Marshall Button)

Source: *Canadian Actors Equity Association, Union des Artistes*

GALLERIES AND MUSEUMS

The Group of Seven

The Group of Seven held its first exhibition at the Art Gallery of Toronto in May 1920. The original members included J.E.H. MacDonald, Lawren Harris, A.Y. Jackson, Arthur Lismer, F.H. Varley, Frank Johnston and Franklin Carmichael.

In 1924, Johnston resigned from the Group and, in 1926, A.J. Casson was invited to join. In the later years of the Group, two new members, Edwin Holgate and Lionel Lemoine FitzGerald, were added. The Group held its final exhibition in Dec. 1931 and disbanded in 1932.

Tom Thomson, who drowned in 1917, was never a member of the Group of Seven, though his boldly-colored works depicting the rugged landscape of northern Ontario became associated with its style of painting.

By breaking with the traditional, European, painting style popular in Canada in the 1920s, The Group of Seven made a huge impact on Canadian art. Although originally reviled by critics, the Group had gained wide acceptance and popularity by the 1930s. Today, the Group's paintings are exhibited in every major gallery in Canada.

J.E.H. **MacDonald** (1873–1932)

Lawren **Harris** (1885–1970)

Alexander Young (A.Y.) **Jackson** (1882–1974)

Arthur **Lismer** (1885–1969)

Frederick Horsman **Varley** (1881–1969)

Frank Hans **Johnston** (1888–1949)

Frank **Carmichael** (1890–1945)

Alfred Joseph (A.J.) **Casson** (1898–1992)

Edwin **Holgate** (1892–1977)

Lionel Lemoine **FitzGerald** (1890–1956)

Tom **Thomson** (1877–1917)

Source: *Looking at Landscape*, Dwight Siegner, The McMichael Canadian Art Collection

Major Public Art Galleries in Canada

Art Gallery of Greater Victoria: 1040 Moss St., Victoria, B.C. V8V 4P1

Art Gallery of Nova Scotia: P.O. Box 2262, Halifax, N.S. B3J 3C8

Art Gallery of Ontario: 317 Dundas St. W., Toronto, Ont. M5T 1G4

Art Gallery of Windsor: 445 Riverside Dr. W., Windsor, Ont. N9A 6T8

Beaverbrook Art Gallery: P.O. Box 605, Fredericton, N.B. E3B 5A6

Confederation Centre Art Gallery and Museum: P.O. Box 848, Charlottetown, P.E.I. C1A 7L9

Dunlop Art Gallery: P.O. Box 2311, Regina, Sask. S4P 3Z5

Edmonton Art Gallery: 2 Sir Winston Churchill Sq., Edmonton, Alta. T5J 2C1

London Regional Art and Historical Museums: 421 Ridout St. N., London, Ont. N6A 5H4

McMichael Canadian Collection: 10365 Islington Ave., Kleinburg, Ont. L0J 1C0

Montreal Museum of Fine Arts: CP 3000, Succursale H, Montreal, Que. H3G 2T9

Musée du Québec: Parc des Champs de Bataille, 1, rue Wolfe/Montcalm, Quebec, Que. G1R 5H3

National Gallery of Canada: 380 Sussex Dr., Ottawa, Ont. K1N 9N4

Thunder Bay Art Gallery: P.O. Box 1193, Station F, Thunder Bay, Ont. P7C 4X9

Vancouver Art Gallery: 750 Hornby St., Vancouver, B.C. V6Z 2H7

Winnipeg Art Gallery: 300 Memorial Blvd., Winnipeg, Man. R3C 1V1

Major Public Museums in Canada

Canadian Museum of Civilization: 100 Laurier St., Box 3100, Hull, Que. J8X 4H2

Canadian Museum of Contemporary Photography: P.O. Box 465, Station A, Ottawa, Ont. K1N 9N6

Canadian Museum of Nature: P.O. Box 3443, Station D, Ottawa, Ont. K1P 6P4

Canadian War Museum: 330 Sussex Dr., Ottawa, Ont. K1A 0M8

Glenbow-Alberta Institute: 130-9th Ave. SE, Calgary, Alta. T2G 0P3

Manitoba Museum of Man and Nature: 190 Rupert Ave., Winnipeg, Man. R3B 0N2

McCord Museum of Canadian History: 690, rue Sherbrooke ouest, Montreal, Que. H3A 1E9

Musée de la Civilisation: 16, rue Saint-Jacques, C.P. 155, Succursale B, Quebec, Que. G1K 7A6

New Brunswick Museum: 277 Douglas Ave., Saint John, N.B. E2K 1E5

Newfoundland Museum: 285 Duckworth St., St. John's, Nfld. A1C 1G9

Nova Scotia Museum: 1747 Summer St., Halifax, N.S. B3H 3A6

Prince of Wales Northern Heritage Centre: Dept. of Culture and Communications, Govt. of the Northwest Territories, Yellowknife, N.W.T. X1A 2L9

Provincial Museum of Alberta: 12845-102nd Ave., Edmonton, Alta. T5N 0M6

Royal British Columbia Museum: 675 Belleville St., Victoria, B.C. V8V 1X4

Royal Ontario Museum: 100 Queen's Park, Toronto, Ont. M5S 2C6

Saskatchewan Museum of Natural History: Wascana Park, Regina, Sask. S4P 3V7

Vancouver Museum: 1100 Chestnut St., Vancouver, B.C. V6J 3J9

Museum of the Regiments

A museum in Calgary highlights the history of its local regiments and the heroism of members. The Museum of the Regiments includes displays about Lord Strathcona's Horse (Royal Canadians), founded in 1900; Princess Patricia's Canadian Light Infantry, founded in 1914; The King's Own Calgary Regiment, founded in 1910 as the 103rd Calgary Regiment; and the Calgary Highlanders, which also dates from 1910. The museum is open 6 days a week (closed Wednesdays). There is no admission charge. 520 Crowchild Trail SW, Calgary, Alberta T3E 1T8 Tel: 403 240 7674

BOOKS, MAGAZINES, NEWSPAPERS

The Governor General's Literary Awards, 1983–93

The Governor General's Literary Awards, Canada's foremost literary prizes, are presented annually to recognize and reward Canadian writers. The awards were initiated in 1937 by the Canadian Authors' Association with the agreement of Governor General Baron Tweedsmuir (novelist John Buchan), and were administered by the Association until 1958.

The Awards are now administered by the Canada Council which appoints juries composed of literary specialists who select the best English and French-language works in each of 6 best categories: drama, fiction, poetry, non-fiction, and beginning in 1987, children's literature (text and illustration) and translation. The juries review all books by Canadian authors, illustrators and translators published in Canada or abroad during the previous year (Oct. 1—Sept. 30). In the case of translation, the original work must also be a Canadian-authored title. Winners receive a medal from the Governor General, $10,000 and a specially-bound copy of their award-winning book. The 1993 winners were announced Nov. 16, 1993.

English

—1983—

Fiction . . . . *Shakespeare's Dog*, Leon Rooke
Non-fiction . . . . *Byng of Vimy: General and Governor General*, Jeffrey Williams
Poetry . . . . *Settlements*, David Donnell
Drama . . . . *Quiet in the Land*, Anne Chislett

—1984—

Fiction . . . . *The Engineer of Human Souls*, Josef Skvorecky
Non-fiction . . . . *The Private Capital: Ambition and Love in the Age of Macdonald and Laurier*, Sandra Gwyn
Poetry . . . . *Celestial Navigation*, Paulette Jiles
Drama . . . . *White Biting Dog*, Judith Thompson

—1985—

Fiction . . . . *The Handmaid's Tale*, Margaret Atwood
Non-fiction . . . . *The Regenerators: Social Criticism in Late Victorian English Canada*, Ramsay Cook
Poetry . . . . *Waiting for Saskatchewan*, Fred Wah
Drama . . . . *Criminals in Love*, George F. Walker

—1986—

Fiction . . . . *The Progress of Love*, Alice Munro
Non-fiction . . . . *Northrop Frye on Shakespeare*, Northrop Frye
Poetry . . . . *The Collected Poems of Al Purdy*, Al Purdy
Drama . . . . *Doc*, Sharon Pollack

—1987—

Fiction . . . . *A Dream Like Mine*, M.T. Kelly
Non-fiction . . . . *The Russian Album*, Michael Ignatieff
Poetry . . . . *Afterworlds*, Gwendolyn MacEwen
Drama . . . . *Prague*, John Krizanc
Translation . . . . *Enchantment and Sorrow: The Autobiography of Gabrielle Roy*, Patricia Claxton
Children's Literature (Illustration) . . . . *Rainy Day Magic*, Marie-Louise Gay
Children's Literature (Text) . . . . *Galahad Schwartz and the Cockroach Army*, Morgan Nyberg

—1988—

Fiction . . . . *Nights Below Station Street*, David Adams Richards
Non-fiction . . . . *In the Sleep Room*, Anne Collins
Poetry . . . . *Furious*, Erin Mouré
Drama . . . . *Nothing Sacred*, George F. Walker
Translation . . . . *Second Chance*, Philip Stratford

Children's Literature (Illustration)............................*Amos's Sweater*, Kim LaFave
Children's Literature (Text) ....*The Third Magic*, Welwyn Wilton Katz

—1989—

Fiction...*Whale Music*, Paul Quarrington
Non-fiction ....*Willie: The Life of W. Somerset Maugham*, Robert Calder
Poetry ....*The Word for Sand*, Heather Spears
Drama.....................................*The Other Side of the Dark*, Judith Thompson
Translation ....*On the Eighth Day*, Wayne Grady
Children's Literature (Illustration)....................*The Magic Paintbrush*, Robin Muller
Children's Literature (Text).......................................*Bad Boy*, Diana Wieler

—1990—

Fiction ....*Lives of the Saints*, Nino Ricci
Non-fiction ....*Trudeau and Our Times*, Stephen Clarkson
Poetry ....*No Time*, Margaret Avison
Drama ....*Goodnight Desdemona (Good Morning Juliet)*, Ann-Marie MacDonald
Translation ....*Yellow-Wolf and Other Tales
of the Saint Lawrence*, Jane Brierley
Children's Literature (Illustration)...........................*The Orphan Boy*, Paul Morin
Children's Literature (Text).....................................*Redwork*, Michael Bedard

—1991—

Fiction ....*Such a Long Journey*, Rohinton Mistry
Non-fiction ....*Occupied Canada*, Robert Hunter and Robert Calihoo
Poetry ....*Night Field*, Don McKay
Drama ....*Amigo's Blue Guitar*, Joan MacLeod
Translation ....*A Dictionary of Literary Devices*, Albert W. Halsall
Children's Literature (Illustration) ....*Doctor Kiss Says Yes*, Joanne Fitzgerald
Children's Literature (Text) ....*Pick-Up Sticks*, Sarah Ellis

—1992—

Fiction ....*The English Patient*, Michael Ondaatje
Non-fiction ....*Revenge of the Land: A century of greed, tragedy
and murder on a Saskatchewan Farm*, Maggie Siggins
Poetry ....*Inventing the Hawk*, Lorna Crozier
Drama.........................*Possible Worlds, A Short History of Night*, John Mighton
Translation ....*Imagining the Middle East*, Fred A. Reed
Children's Literature (Illustration) ....*Waiting for the Whales*, Ron Lightburn
Children's Literature (Text) ....*Hero of Lesser Causes*, Julie Johnston

—1993—

Fiction..*The Stone Diaries*, Carol Shields
Non-fiction ....*Touch the Dragon*, Karen Connelly
Poetry.......................................*Forest of the Medieval World*, Don Coles
Drama.........................*Fronteras Americanas*, Guillermo Verdecchia
Children's Literature (Illustration) ....*Sleep Tight*, Mireille Levert
Children's Literature (Text) ....*Some of the Kinder Planets*, Tim Wynne-Jones

French

—1983—

Fiction .... *Laura Laur*, Suzanne Jacob
Non-fiction .... *Le contrôle social du crime*, Maurice Cusson
Poetry .... *Un goût de sel*, Suzanne Paradis
Drama .... *Syncope*, René Gingras

—1984—

Fiction .... *Agonie*, Jacques Brault
Non-fiction .... *Le XXe siècle: Histoire du catholicisme québécois*,
Jean Hamelin et Nicole Gagnon
Poetry .... *Double Impression*, Nicole Brossard
Drama .... *Ne blâmez jamais les Bédouins*, René-Daniel Dubois

—1985—

Fiction .... *Lucie ou un midi en novembre*, Fernand Ouellette
Non-fiction .... *La littérature contre elle-même*, François Ricard
Poetry .... *Action Writing*, André Roy
Drama .... *Duo pour voix obstinées*, Maryse Pelletier

—1986—

Fiction .... *Les silences du corbeau*, Yvon Rivard
Non-fiction .... *Le réalism socialiste: une esthétique impossible*,
Régine Robin
Poetry .... *L'écouté*, Cecile Cloutier
Drama .... *La visite des sauvages*, Anne Legault

—1987—

Fiction .... *L'Obsédante Obèse et autres agressions*,
Gilles Archambault
Non-fiction .... *La Petite Noirceur*, Jean Larose
Poetry .... *Les Heures*, Fernand Ouellette
Drama .... *Un oiseau vivant dans la gueule*, Jeanne-Mance Delisle
Translation .... *L'homme qui se croyait aimé, ou La vie secrete d'un
premier ministre*, Ivan Steenhout and Christiane Teasdale
Children's Literature (Illustration) .... *Venir au monde*, Darcia Labrosse
Children's Literature (Text) .... *Le Don*, David Schinkel and
Yves Beauchesne

—1988—

Fiction .... *Le Silence ou le Parfait Bonheur*, Jacques Folch-Ribas
Non-fiction .... *Écrire dans la maison du père*, Patricia Smart
Poetry .... *Papiers d'épidémie*, Marcel Labine
Drama .... *Le Chien*, Jean Marc Dalpé
Translation .... *Nucléus*, Didier Holtzwarth
Children's Literature (Illustration) .... *Les Jeux de Pic-mots*, Philippe Béha

Children's Literature (Text).................................. *Cassiopée ou L'été polonais*,
Michèle Marineau

—1989—

Fiction .... *La Rage*, Louis Hamelin
Non-fiction....................... *L'Intolérance : une problématique générale*, Lise Noël
Poetry... *Monème*, Pierre Desruisseaux
Drama .... *Mademoiselle Rouge*, Michel Garneau
Translation.............................. *Les Âges de l'amour*, Jean Antonin Billard
Children's Literature (illustration)........ *Benjamin et la saga des oreillers*, Stéphane Poulin
Children's Literature (Text) .... *Temps mort*, Charles Montpetit

—1990—

Fiction.. *La Mauvaise Foi*, Gérald Tougas
Non-fiction .... *Dans l'oeil de l'aigle*, Jean François Lisée
Poetry.. *Les Cendres bleues*, Jean-Paul Daoust
Drama......................... *Le Voyage magnifique d'Emily Carr*, Jovette Marchessault
Translation.................... *Le Second Rouleau*, Charlotte and Robert Melançon
Children's Literature (Illustration) .... *Les fantaisies de l'oncle Henri*,
Pierre Pratt
Children's Literature (Text) .... *La Vraie Histoire du chien de Clara Vic*,
Christiane Duchesne

—1991—

Fiction .... *La Croix du Nord*, André Brochu
Non-fiction .... *Le Jaguar et le Tamanoir*, Bernard Arcand
Poetry .... *Chant pour un Québec Iointain*, Madeleine Gagnon
Drama............. *Mon oncle Marcel qui vague vague près du métro Berri*, Gilbert Dupuis
Translation .... *Les Enfants d'Aataentsic: l'histoire du peuple huron*,
Jean-Paul Sainte-Marie and Brigitte Chabert Hacikyan
Children's Literature (Illustration) .... *Un champion*, Sheldon Cohen
Children's Literature (Text) .... *Deux heures et demie avant Jasmine*,
François Gravel

—1992—

Fiction .... *L'enfant chargé de songes*, Anne Hébert
Non-fiction....................... *La Radissonie. Le pays de la baie James*, Pierre Turgeon
Poetry.. *Andromède attendra*, Gilles Cyr
Translation................................... *La mémoire postmoderne. Essai sur l'art
canadien contemporain*, Jean Papineau
Children's Literature (Illustration) .... *Simon et la ville de carton*, Gille Tibo
Children's Literature (Text) .... *Victor*, Christiane Duchesne

—1993—

Fiction .... *Cartique des Plaines*, Nancy Huston
Non-fiction...................... *Le littérature de l'exiguité*, François Paré
Poetry.. *Le Saut de L'ange*, Denise Desautels
Translation................................ *L'oeuvre du Gallois*, Marie Josée Thariault
Children's Literature (Illustration) .... *Le monde salon jean de...*, Stéphane Jorisch
Children's Literature (Text)...................... *La Route de Chlifa*, Michele Marineau
Drama.. *Celle-la*, Daniel Danis

Source: *The Canada Council*

Bestselling Books in Canada, 1993

(Canadian books in bold type)

Fiction

1. *The Bridges of Madison County*, Robert James Waller
2. **The Robber Bride, Margaret Atwood**
3. **The English Patient, Michael Ondaatje**
4. **Griffin and Sabine, Nick Bantock**
5. **Headhunter, Timothy Findley**
6. *The Client*, John Grisham
7. **Sabine's Notebook, Nick Bantock**
8. *Like Water for Chocolate*, Laura Esquivel
9. **The Gates of Paradise, Alberto Manguel**
10. **The Stone Diaries, Carol Shields**

Non-fiction

1. **Memoirs, Pierre Elliott Trudeau**
2. *Women Who Run With the Wolves*, Clarissa Pinkola Estes
3. *SeinLanguage*, Jerry Seinfeld
4. **Shifting Gears, Nuala Beck**
5. **Peacekeeper, Lewis MacKenzie**
6. **The Wealthy Banker's Wife, Linda McQuaig**
7. *The Great Reckoning Revised*, James Dale Davidson and William Rees-Mogg
8. *The Downing Street Years*, Margaret Thatcher
9. **Canada First, Ralph Nader**
10. *Systems of Survival*, Jane Jacobs

Source: *The Globe and Mail*

The Booker Prize, 1981–93

The Booker Prize recognizes the best work of English fiction published in the Commonwealth, South Africa and Ireland. It is sponsored by Booker McConnell Ltd., an international food and agriculture business, and administered by the Booker Prize Book Trust, a British educational charity. Since 1984, the value of the Booker Prize has been £15,000.

Year	Author	Title
1981	Salman Rushdie	*Midnight's Children*
1982	Thomas Keneally	*Schindler's Ark*
1983	J.M. Coetzee	*Life & Times of Michael K*
1984	Anita Brookner	*Hotel du Lac*
1985	Keri Hulme	*The Bone People*
1986	Kingsley Amis	*The Old Devils*
1987	Penelope Lively	*Moon Tiger*
1988	Peter Carey	*Oscar and Lucinda*
1989	Kazuo Ishiguro	*The Remains of the Day*
1990	A.S. Byatt	*Possession*
1991	Ben Okri	*The Famished Road*
1992 (joint winners)	Michael Ondaatje	*The English Patient*
	Barry Unsworth	*Sacred Hunger*
1993	Roddy Doyle	*Paddy Clarke Ha Ha Ha*

Pulitzer Prizes, 1993

The winners of these annual American literary awards were announced on April 12, 1994.

Fiction	E. Annie Proulx, *The Shipping News*
Nonfiction	David Remnick, *Lenin's Tomb*
Poetry	Yusef Komunyakaa, *Neon Vernacular*
Drama	Edward Albee, *Three Tall Women*
Biography	David Levering Lewis, *W.E.B. Dubois*
Music	Gunther Schuller, *Of Reminiscences and Remembrances*

Top Canadian Daily Newspapers

Newspaper	Circulation[1]		
	Daily[2]	Weekend	
Toronto Star (all day)	502 846	743 026 (Sat.)	497 136 (Sun.)
The Globe and Mail (m)	317 972[5]		
Le Journal de Montréal (m)	277 344	331 651 (Sat.)	298 104 (Sun.)
Toronto Sun (m)	254 563	193 709 (Sat.)	455 125 (Sun.)
Montreal: La Presse (m)	196 529	329 761 (Sat.)	195 176 (Sun.)
Vancouver Sun (m)	193 646[3]	255 977 (Sat.)	258 548 (Fri)
Vancouver Province (m)	159 687		197 457 (Sun.)
Ottawa Citizen (all day)	166 639	220 089 (Sat.)	153 389 (Sun.)
Edmonton Journal (m)	161 376[4]	195 988 (Fri.)	153 716 (Sun.)
Winnipeg Free Press (e)	145 209	214 935 (Sat.)	148 926 (Sun.)
Montreal Gazette (m)	157 007	199 079 (Sat.)	145 658 (Sun.)
Hamilton Spectator (e)	128 841		
Calgary Herald (m)	119 947[3]	159 433 (Fri.)	142 216 (Sun.)
London Free Press (m)	110 308	137 363 (Sat.)	
Quebec: Le Journal (m)	103 655	116 220 (Sat.)	99 389 (Sun.)
Quebec: Le Soleil (m)	97 639	141 086 (Sat.)	89 366 (Sun.)
Halifax Chronicle-Herald (m)	96 907		
Windsor Star (e)	86 236		
Edmonton Sun (m)	80 203		121 854 (Sun.)
Victoria Times-Colonist (m)	80 424		78 190 (Sun.)

Sources: *Audit Bureau of Circulations; The Globe and Mail*

(1) Average paid daily circulation for 6 months ending Mar. 31, 1994, unless otherwise indicated. (2) Monday to Saturday unless otherwise indicated. (3) Monday to Thursday. (4) Monday to Thursday plus Saturday. (5) Based on audited circulation six days a week for 1993. (m) morning; (e) evening.

National Newspaper Awards, 1993

These annual awards were announced in Toronto on April 16, 1994.

Editorial Writing	Andrew Coyne, *The Globe and Mail*
Spot News Photography	Paul Watson, *The Toronto Star*
Feature Photography	Diana Nethercott, *The Hamilton Spectator*
Spot News Reporting	Beth Gorham and Michael Johansen, *Canadian Press*
International Reporting	Paul Watson, *The Toronto Star*
Sports Writing	Randy Starkman, *The Toronto Star*
Feature Writing	Michael Valpy, *The Globe and Mail*
Columns	Rick Salutin, *The Globe and Mail*
Sports Photography	Rick Eglinton, *The Toronto Star*
Enterprise Reporting	William Marsden, Andrew McIntosh and Carolyn Adolph, *Montreal Gazette*
Critical Writing	Lloyd Dykk, *Vancouver Sun*
Layout and Design	Lucie Lacava, *Le Devoir*
Editorial Cartooning	Bruce MacKinnon, *Halifax Chronicle-Herald and Mail-Star*
Business Reporting	Lawrence Surtees, *The Globe and Mail*
Special Projects	*Edmonton Journal*

Source: *Canadian Daily Newspaper Association*

Top Canadian Paid–Circulation Magazines[1]

Magazine	Circulation[2]
Reader's Digest (Canadian English edition)	1 280 410
Chatelaine (English language edition)	892 003
TV Guide	829 838
Maclean's	556 372
Time (Canadian edition)	329 269
Sélection du Reader's Digest (Canadian French edition)	320 360
TV Hebdo	229 152
Canadian Geographic	246 160
Chatelaine (French language edition)	197 164
Flare	184 294
L'Actualité	214 480
Select Homes Magazine	169 816
Equinox	149 109
Harrowsmith	141 013

Source: *Audit Bureau of Circulations*

(1) Paid circulation magazines are sold by subscription and delivered through the mail and/or sold at newsstands. (2) Average paid circulation per issue for 6 months ending June 30, 1994, unless otherwise indicated.

National Magazine Awards, 1994

These annual awards were presented on May 6 by the National Magazine Awards Foundation. In 1994 there were gold and silver awards in 28 categories, including writing, design and photography.

Profiles: Louise Gendron, "La mal élevé de La Presse," *L'Actualité*
Humour: Paul Quarrington, "Grinding It Out," *Harrowsmith*
Personal Journalism: Andrew Scott, "Between the Living and the Dead," *Western Living*
Business Writing: Ann Shortell, "Hard Times at Castle Hill," *Toronto Life*
Sports and Recreation: Ed Struzik, "Nanook Passage," *Equinox*
Science, Health and Medicine: John Bentley Mays, "In the Jaws of the Black Dogs," *Saturday Night*
Service Journalism: Brian Banks, "The non-conformist, his ex-wife, the gambler and the alien," *CA Magazine*
Illustration: Sandra Dionisi, "Women and Spirituality," *Images*
Arts and Entertainment: Robert Fulford, "The Trouble With Emily," *Canadian Art*
Words and Pictures: Ann Vanderhoof, Steve Manley, Andreas Zaretski, Robert Bowles, "What's on your screen at night?" *Cottage Life*
Fashion: Jean-Marc Martin, André Panneton, Véronique Droulez, "Femmes de Botero," *Elle Québec*
Art Direction for a Single Article: Mark Koudys and Arthur Niemi, "Ay, Caramba!" *Destinations*
Art Direction for an Entire Issue: Mark Koudys and Arthur Niemi, "November 1993" *Destinations*
Public Issues: Sally Armstrong, "Eva Witness for Women," *Homemaker's Magazine*
Poetry: Janice Kulyk Keefer, "Oranges/A rare photograph.../Massacre of the Innocents," *Event*
Still-Life Photography: Steven Evans, "Buildings that talk back," *Toronto Life*
Fiction: Irena Friedman Karafilly, "Family Portrait," *Saturday Night*
Column Writing: Benoît Aubin, "Casinus interruptus/Que faire d'une vieille poubelle?/L'homme qui jouait les uns contre les autres," *L'Actualité*
One-of-a-Kind Articles: Zoe Landale and Marjorie Simmins, "Remembering Karen," *Saturday Night*
Portrait Photography: Suzanne Langevin "Attila up against the Wall," *Saturday Night*
Magazine Covers: Susan McCallum, Claude Martel and Isaac Applebaum, "Biology Obsession Invention" *C Magazine*
Spot Illustration: Kathy Boake, "Rail On," *Destinations*
Editorial Package: Diana Swift and Derek Cassels, "Survey '93," *The Medical Post*
Travel Features: John Allemang, "Oxford after Class," *Destinations*
Essays: Terry Glavin, "The Fight for Fish," *The Georgia Straight*
Photojournalism: Larry Towell, "Donde Esta?" *Border Crossings*
University of Western Ontario President's Medal for Excellence in Magazine Articles: John Bentley Mays, "In the Jaws of the Black Dogs," *Saturday Night*
Foundation Award for Outstanding Achievement: Don Obe
Magazine of the Year: OWL and Chickadee Magazines

CANADIAN HALL OF FAME

The following list is not meant to be exhaustive, but rather a listing of prominent Canadians, and those whose reputations are inextricably linked with Canada, from all fields.

A

ABBOTT, Sir John, politics. St Andrews, Lower Canada, 1821–1893. Canada's third prime minister

ABERDEEN, Ishbel Gordon, Lady, reformer. Eng., 1857–1939. Helped create Natl Council of Women, Victorian Order of Nurses

ABERHART, William, politics. Hibbard Twp, Ont., 1878–1843. Founded Social Credit party; Alberta premier, 1935–43

ACORN, Milton, literary arts. Charlottetown, PEI, 1923–86. Radical poet. "The Island Means Minago"

ADAMS, Thomas, city planner. Scot., 1871–1940. Father of the Canadian Planning Movement

ADAMS, Bryan, performing arts. Kingston, Ont., 1959. Singer/songwriter; rock star. *Reckless*

AFFLECK, Raymond, visual arts. Penticton, BC, 1922. Architect; designed Place Ville Marie, Place Bonaventure

AGLUKARK, Susan, performing arts. Arviat, NWT, 1966. Singer/songwriter; first Inuit recording artist

AISLIN (Terry Mosher), visual arts. Ottawa, Ont., 1942. *Montreal Gazette* cartoonist; sports caricaturist

AITKEN, Max (Lord Beaverbrook), literary arts. Maple, Ont., 1879–1964. Publisher; newspaper magnate; British Conservative cabinet minister

AKEEAKTASHUK, visual arts. Hudson Bay, Ont., 1898–1954. Sculptor; first important Inuit carver

ALEXANDER, Lincoln, politics. Toronto, Ont., 1922. First Black in Parliament; Ont. lieutenant-governor

ALLAN, Sir Hugh, business. Scot., 1810–82. Railway promoter; suspected of electoral bribery for soliciting favours in Pacific Scandal (1873)

ALLEN, Ralph, literary arts. Winnipeg, Man., 1913–66. Influential *Maclean's* editor (1946–60)

ALMOND, Paul, visual arts. Montreal, Que., 1931. Mystical film director. *Act of the Heart*

AMIEL, Barbara, media. Eng., 1940s. Journalist; conservative political and social columnist

ANDERSON, Doris, literary arts. Toronto, Ont., 1921. Writer; feminist; editor, *Chatelaine*, 1958–77

ANDRE, Brother, religion. St Gregoire d'Iberville, Lower Canada, 1845–1937. Mystic; built Montreal's St Joseph's Oratory

ANKA, Paul, performing arts. Ottawa, Ont., 1941. Singer/songwriter; written over 400 songs. "My Way"

APPLEBAUM, Louis, performing arts. Toronto, Ont., 1918. Composer; writer of opera, concerts, film scores

APPLEYARD, Peter, performing arts. Eng., 1928. Jazz musician; vibraphonist; TV personality. "Swing Fever"

AQUIN, Hubert, literary arts. Montreal, Que., 1929–77. Novelist; modernist writer. *Neige Noire*

ARCAND, Denys, visual arts. Deschambault, Que., 1941. Film director. *Decline of the American Empire*

ARCHAMBAULT, Louis, visual arts. Montreal, Que., 1915. Sculptor; his work is in many museum collections

ASPER, Israel, business. Minnedosa, Man., 1932. Financier; founder, Global-TV; columnist; author

ATHANS, George Jr., sports. Kelowna, BC, 1952. Three-time world water ski champion

ATKINSON, Joseph, media. Newcastle, Ont., 1865–1948. Journalist; built *Toronto Star* into nation's largest newspaper

ATWOOD, Margaret, literary arts. Ottawa, Ont., 1939. Prolific novelist with international following. *The Handmaid's Tale*

AUBERT de GASPE, Philippe-Joseph, literary arts. Quebec, Que., 1814–41. Novelist; wrote first French-Cdn novel. *L'influence d'un livre* (1837)

AUGUSTYN, Frank, performing arts. Hamilton, Ont., 1953. Former principal dancer, National Ballet of Canada; director, Ottawa Ballet

AYKROYD, Dan, performing arts. Ottawa, Ont., 1952. Actor/comedian. "Saturday Night Live," *Ghostbusters*

B

BACHMAN, Randy, performing arts. Winnipeg, Man., 1946. Rock musician; guitarist for Guess Who, Bachman-Turner Overdrive. *American Woman*

BAKER, Carroll, performing arts. Bridgewater, NS, 1949. Singer; country music star

BALDWIN, Robert, politics. York, Ont., 1804–58. Proponent of responsible government; co-premier (with LaFontaine) of Upper Canada

BALLARD, Harold, sports. Toronto, Ont., 1903–1990. Sports capitalist; irascible owner of Toronto Maple Leafs, Hamilton Tiger Cats

BANTING, Sir Frederick, medicine. Alliston, Ont., 1891–1941. Medical researcher; co-discoverer of insulin; Nobel Prize for medicine, 1923

BARBEAU, Marius, ethnologist. St-Marie-de-Beauce, Que., 1883-1969. Eminent folklorist

BARR, Murray, medicine. Belmont, Ont., 1908. Anatomist; developed chromosome analysis to diagnose genetic disorders

BASINSKI, Zbigniew, science. Poland, 1928. Outstanding metal physics researcher

BASSETT, Carling, sports. Toronto, Ont., 1967. Top ranked Canadian tennis player

BASSETT, John, media. Ottawa, Ont., 1915. Media executive; chairman, Baton Broadcasting Inc; owner of TV and radio stations

BATA, Thomas, business. Czech, 1914. Industrialist; chairman, Bata Shoes; in over 70 countries

BATEMAN, Robert, visual arts. Toronto, Ont., 1930. Painter; major international wildlife artist

BAUER, Father David, sports. Kitchener, Ont., 1925–1988. Hockey coach; father of Cdn Olympic hockey

BAUMANN, Alex, sports. Czech, 1964. Swimmer; gold medals in 200 m, 400 m individual medley, 1984 Olympics; 1984 top male athlete

BEARDY, Jackson, visual arts. Island Lake, Man., 1944–84. Graphic stylist using Cree legends

BECK, Sir Adam, business. Baden, Canada W, 1857–1925. Hydro commissioner; built Ontario Hydro

BECKWITH, John, literary arts/performing arts. Victoria, BC, 1927. Composer; writer; critic. *The Shivaree*

BEDARD, Myriam, sports. Loretteville, Que., 1969. Biathlete; two gold medals, biathlon, '94 Olympics

BECKER, Abigail, military. Frontenac Cty, UC, 1831–1905. Heroine; saved men shipwrecked on Lake Erie

BEECROFT, Norma, performing arts. Oshawa, Ont., 1934. Composer; avant-garde musician. "From Dreams of Brass"

BEERS, William, medicine/sports. Montreal, Que., 1843–1900. Popularized lacrosse; dean, Canada's first dental college

BEGIN, Monique, politics. Italy, 1936. First Quebec woman in Commons; health minister

BELIVEAU, Jean, sports. Trois-Rivieres, Que., 1931. Hockey player; stylish Montreal Canadiens centre, 1953–71; 507 goals

BELL, Alexander Graham, exploration & discovery. Scot., 1847–1922. Invented telephone; worked on iron lung, phonograph, seawater desalination

BELL, Marilyn, sports. Toronto, Ont., 1937. First person to swim Lake Ontario (1954)

BELL, Max, business. Regina, Sask., 1912–72. Industrialist; principal, FP Publications, and sportsman

BELL, Robert, science. Ladner, BC, 1918. Nuclear physicist; discovered proton radioactivity

BELLOW, Saul, literary arts. Lachine, Que., 1915. Nobel Prize for Literature. *Herzog*

BELZBERG, Samuel, business. Calgary, Alta, 1928. Financier; developed real estate financing in W Canada; founder, First City Trust

BENNETT, Richard, politics. Hopewell, NB, 1870–1947. Became prime minister of Canada July 28, 1930

BENNETT, W.A.C., politics. Hastings, NB, 1900–79. Social Credit premier of BC, 1952–72

BENNETT, William, politics. Kelowna, BC, 1932. Social Credit premier of BC, 1975–86

BENOIT, Jehane, media. Montreal, Que., 1904–87. Food expert; cookbook writer; featured on TV; authority on Cdn/Quebecois cooking

BENY, Rolof, visual arts. Medicine Hat, Alta, 1924–84. Photographer; lavish travel books. *India*

BERESFORD-HOWE, Constance, literary arts. Montreal, Que., 1922. Novelist. *Night Studies*

BERGER, Thomas, politics. Victoria, BC, 1933. Jurist; proponent of aboriginal rights; commissioner, Mackenzie Valley Pipeline Inquiry

BERNARDI, Mario, performing arts. Kirkland Lake, Ont., 1930. Conductor, Calgary Philharmonic

BERNIER, Sylvie, sports. Quebec, Que., 1964. Diver; gold medal, 3 m springboard, 1984 Olympics

BERTON, Pierre, literary arts. Whitehorse, YT, 1920. Popular historian; author and media personality. *The Last Spike*

BESSETTE, Gerard, literary arts. Ste-Anne-de-Sabrevois, Que., 1920. Novelist. *L'incubation*

BEST, Charles, medicine. USA, 1899–1978. Physiologist; co-discoverer of insulin

BETHUNE, Norman, medicine. Gravenhurst, Ont., 1890–1939. Surgeon; hero in China, where he died helping revolutionary army

BIG BEAR, politics. Ft Carlton, Sask., 1825–88. Cree leader; opposed treaties on grounds they would destroy Cree way of life

BIGELOW, Dr Wilfred, medicine. Brandon, Man., 1913. Surgeon; developed first cardiac pacemaker

BIRNEY, Earle, literary arts. Calgary, Alta, 1904. Narrative poet and professor. *David and Other Poems*

BISHOP, Billy, literary arts. Owen Sound, Ont., 1894–1956. WWI flying ace; downed 72 enemy planes

BISSOONDATH, Neil, literary arts. Trinidad, 1955. Novelist, story writer. *A Casual Brutality*

BLAIS, Marie-Claire, literary arts. Quebec, Que., 1939. Influential novelist. *Une Saison dans la vie d'Emmanuel*

BLAISE, Clark, literary arts. USA, 1940. Writer; explorer of the displaced person. *Resident Alien*

BLACK, Conrad, business. Montreal, Que., 1944. financier; multi-faceted and controversial; particular interest in publishing, writing

BLAKE, Hector "Toe," sports. Victoria Mines, Ont., 1912. Hockey player; coached Montreal Canadiens to eight Stanley Cups, 1955–68

BLAKENEY, Allen, politics. Bridgewater, NS, 1925. NDP premier of Saskatchewan, 1971–82

BLOHM, Hans, visual arts. Germany, 1927. Photographer; author of many photography books. *The Beauty of the Maritimes*

BLUMENFELD, Hans, city planner. Germany, 1892-1988. Urban planner; author. *The Modern Metropolis*

BOGGS, Jean Sutherland, visual arts. Peru, 1922. Art curator; National Gallery curator, 1966–76

BOLDT, Arnie, sports. Osler, Sask., 1957. One-legged high jumper holds disabled world record (2.08 m)

BOLT, Carol, literary arts. Winnipeg, Man., 1941. Playwright; socially conscious writer. *One Night Stand*

BOMBARDIER, Armand, exploration & discovery. Valcourt, Que., 1908–64. Inventor; developer of snowmobiles

BONDAR, Roberta, exploration & discovery. Sault Ste Marie, Ont., 1945. Astronaut; first Canadian woman in space

BORDEN, Sir Robert, politics. Grand Pre, NS, 1854–1937. Canada's prime minister throughout WWI

BORDUAS, Paul-Emile, visual arts. St-Hilaire, Que., 1905-60. Painter; founded Automatistes. "L'etoile noire"

BOSSY, Michael, sports. Montreal, Que., 1957. Hockey player; NY Islanders winger; 9, 50-goal seasons

BOUCHARD, Lucien, politics. St-Couer-de-Marie, Que., 1938. Founder and leader of Bloc Quebecois since 1990

BOUCHER, Gaetan, sports. Charlesbourg, Que., 1958. Speedskater; two gold medals (1000 m, 1500 m) and a bronze medal (500 m), 1984 Winter Olympics

BOUEY, Gerald, business. Axford, Sask., 1920. Banker; governor, Bank of Canada, 1973–87

BOURASSA, Henri, politician. Montreal, Que., 1868–1952. Federalist; founded *Le Devoir* newspaper

BOURASSA, Robert, politics. Montreal, Que., 1933. Quebec premier, 1970–76, 1985–93

BOURGEOYS, Marguerite, religion. France, 1620–1700. Religious educator; canonized, 1982

BOURGET, Ignace, religion. Lauzon, Que., 1799–1885. Catholic bishop of Montreal; avid ultramontanist opposed secular Quebec

BOURQUE, Raymond, sports. Montreal, Que., 1960. Hockey player; Boston Bruins defenceman; 4-time Norris Trophy winner

BOWELL, Sir Mackenzie, politics. Eng., 1823–1917. Canada's fifth prime minister

BOWERING, George, literary arts. Penticton, BC, 1935. Prolific poet and prose writer. "Burning Water"

BOWMAN, Scotty, sports. Montreal, Que., 1933. Hockey coach; won six Stanley Cups; five with Montreal

BOYD, Liona, performing arts. Eng., 1950. Lionized classical guitarist. *The Guitar—Liona Boyd*

BOYLE, Joseph, exploration & discovery. Toronto, Ont., 1867–1923. Adventurer, "Klondike Joe"; mining entrepreneur; national hero in Rumania

BRACKEN, John, politics. Ellisville, Ont., 1883–1969. Cons. Manitoba premier, 1922–42

BRAND, Oscar, performing arts. Winnipeg, Man., 1920. Folksinger; recorded 80 albums; author, folk song collections. *Squid Jiggin' Ground*

BRANT, Joseph, politics/religion. USA, 1742-1807. Mohawk leader; British loyalist during American Revolution; translated Bible into Mohawk

BRASSARD, Jean-Luc, sports. Valleyfield, Que., 1972. Skier; gold medal, moguls, 1994 Olympics

BRASSEUR, Isabel, sports. Kingsbury, Que., 1970. Skater; with Lloyd Eisler, won 1993 pairs world title, two Olympic bronze medals (1992, 1994)

BRAULT, Jacques, literary arts. Montreal, Que., 1933. Poet; playwright; novelist. *Agonie*

BREBEUF, Jean de, religion. France, 1593–1649. Jesuit martyr; missionary at Sainte Marie among the Huron

BRILL, Debbie, sports. Mission, BC, 1953. High jumper; originated "Brill bend" jumping style

BRITTAIN, Donald, visual arts. Ottawa, Ont., 1928. Documentary film-maker. *On Guard for Thee*

BROADBENT, Ed, politics. Oshawa, Ont., 1936. National leader, NDP, 1975–89

BROADFOOT, Dave, performing arts. Toronto, Ont., 1925. Comedian; Sergeant Renfrew character in Royal Canadian Airfarce

BROCK, Sir Isaac, military. Eng., 1769–1812. Soldier; War of 1812 hero; died at Queenston Heights

BRONFMAN, Charles, business. Montreal, Que., 1931. Industrialist; chairman, Cemp Investments Ltd; former owner, Montreal Expos

BRONFMAN, Edgar, business. Montreal, Que., 1929. Industrialist; CEO, Seagram's Ltd; president, World Jewish Congress

BRONFMAN, Samuel, business. Brandon, Man., 1891–1971. Capitalist; distiller (Seagram Co. Ltd) and philanthropist

BROSSARD, Nicole, literary arts. Montreal, Que., 1943. Formalist poet. "Mecanique jongleuse suivi de masculin grammaticale"

BROWN, George, media/politics. Scot., 1818–80. Journalist; founded Toronto *Globe* (1844); as Reformer, played major role in Confederation

BROWN, John "Kootenai," exploration & discovery. Ire., 1839–1916. Adventurer; army official; prospector; whisky trader; established Waterton Lakes Natl Park

BROWN, Rosemary, politics. Jamaica, 1930. Activist; head, Ontario Human Rights Cssn; former NDP leadership candidate

BROWNING, Kurt, sports. Rocky Mountain House, Alta, 1966. World figure skating champion, 1989–91, 1993

BRUHN, Erik, performing arts. Denmark, 1928–86. Dancer; choreographer; guiding figure for National Ballet

BRULE, Etienne, exploration & discovery. France, 1592–1633. Explorer; first known European to reach Lake Superior

BUCHAN, John, first Baron Tweedsmuir, literary arts. Scot., 1875–1940. Thriller novelist, wrote *The 39 Steps*; governor general, 1935–40

BUCHANAN, John, politics. Sydney, NS, 1931. Conservative premier of NS, 1978–1990

BUCK, Tim, politics. Eng., 1891–1973. Radical politician; led Canadian Commmunist Party, 1929–61

BUCKE, Richard, medicine. Eng., 1837–1902. Physician; writer; advocate for the mentally ill; spiritual writer. *Cosmic Consciousness*

BUJOLD, Genevieve, performing arts. Montreal, Que., 1942. Actress; international star. "Dead Ringers"

BULL, Gerald, exploration & discovery. North Bay, Ont., 1928–1990. Inventor; weapons designer; murdered mysteriously

BURKA, Petra, sports. Holland, 1946. Figure skater; women's world champion, 1965

BURNS, Tommy, sports. Hanover, Ont., 1881–1955. Boxer; world heavyweight champion, 1906–08.

BURR, Raymond, performing arts. New Westminster, BC, 1917–93. Actor; TV's Perry Mason, 1957–66

BURROUGHS, Jackie, performing arts. Eng., 1942. Actress; versatile performer; Hetty in "Road to Avonlea"

BUSH, Jack, visual arts. Toronto, Ont., 1909–77. Abstract artist. "Bridge Passage"

BY, John, military. Eng., 1779–1836. Engineer; built Rideau Canal, Quebec fortifications

BYNG, Julian George, Viscount, military. Eng., 1862–1935. Soldier; governor general, 1921–26

CABOT, John, exploration & discovery. Italy, c. 1450–1499. First N American landing since the Vikings

CAIN, Larry, sports. Toronto, Ont., 1963. Canoeist; gold (500 m) & silver (1000 m) medals, 1984 Olympics

CALDER, Frank, politics. Nass Harbour, BC, 1915. Native politician; Nishga leader; BC MLA

CALLAGHAN, Morley, literary arts. Toronto, Ont., 1903–90. Novelist; memoirist. *The Loved and the Lost*

CALLBECK, Catherine, politics. Central Bedeque, PEI, 1939. Liberal premier of PEI since 1993

CALLWOOD, June, media. Chatham, Ont., 1924. Journalist; civil libertarian, AIDS activist

CAMERON, James, literary arts. Eng., 1910. Philosopher; essayist; poet. "Images of Authority"

CAMERON, Thomas, medicine. Scot., 1894–1947. Parasitologist; pioneered study of parasitic worms

CAMP, Dalton, media/politics. Woodstock, NB, 1920. PC consultant; newspaper columnist

CAMPBELL, Sir Alexander, politics. Eng., 1822–92. Tory leader; Father of Confederation

CAMPBELL, Clarence, sports. Fleming, Sask., 1905–84. Sports administrator; headed NHL, 1946–77

CAMPBELL, Kim, politics. Port Alberni, BC, 1947. Prime minister of Canada June 1993–December 1993

CAMPBELL, Norman, performing arts. USA, 1924. Music producer; innovative developer of ballet and musicals

CAMPEAU, Robert, business. Sudbury, Ont., 1923. Financier; exemplar of 1980s expansionist business mania; developer; retail store magnate

CANDY, John, performing arts. Toronto, Ont., 1950–94. Actor; comedian; bearish SCTV regular (Johnny LaRue, William B.); film star. *Uncle Buck*

CARDINAL, Douglas, visual arts. Red Deer, Alta, 1934. Metis architect; Canadian Museum of Civilization

CARLE, Gilles, visual arts. Maniwaki, Que., 1929. Film director. *La Vrai Nature de Bernadette*

CARLETON, Guy, Baron Dorchester, politics. Ire., 1724–1808. Quebec governor, 1768–78, 1785–95; supporter of French traditions

CARMAN, Bliss, literary arts/media. Fredericton, NB, 1861–1929. Poet; journnalist. "The Pipes of Pan"

CARMICHAEL, Frank, visual arts. Orillia, Ont., 1890–1945. Group of Seven founding member

CARR, Emily, visual arts. Victoria, BC, 1871–1945. Painter of NW coastal Indians and nature

CARRIER, Roch, literary arts. Beauce, Que., 1937. Novelist; playwright. *La Guerre, Yes Sir!*

CARSON, Jack, performing arts. Carmen, Man., 1910–63. Square-jawed film actor. *Mildred Pierce*

CARTER, Emmett Cardinal, religion. Montreal, Que., 1912. As Toronto Cardinal, helped get full funding for Catholic schools

CARTER, Wilf, performing arts. Port Hilford, NS, 1904. Singer; father of Canadian country music

CARTIER, Georges-Etienne, politics. St Antoine, UC, 1814–73. Father of Confederation; joint premier of United Canada, 1857–62

CARTIER, Jacques, exploration & discovery. France, 1491–1557. Credited with European discovery of Canada; first explorer of St Lawrence River

CASSON, A.J., visual arts. Toronto, Ont., 1898–1992. Member, Group of Seven. "Country Store"

CATHERWOOD, Ethel, sports. Haldimand Cty, Ont., 1909. High jumper; gold in high jump, 1928 Olympics

CHAMPLAIN, Samuel de, exploration & discovery. France, 1567–1635. Explorer; important cartographer/geographer; "Father of New France"

CHANG, Thomas Ming Sui, medicine/science. China, 1933. Physiologist; expert on artificial cells and organs

CHAPMAN, John, science. London, Ont., 1921–79. Physicist; lead role in Canada's satellite program

CHAPUT-ROLLAND, Solange, media. Montreal, Que., 1919. Writer; broadcaster; Quebecoise federalist

CHAREST, Jean, politics. Sherbrooke, Que., 1958. Led PC rump after '93 electoral debacle

CHARLEBOIS, Robert, performing arts. Montreal, Que., 1945. Singer/songwriter. "Solidaritude"

CHARLEVOIX, Pierre, literary arts. France, 1682–1761. Historian; first complete history of New France

CHERRY, Don, sports. Kingston, Ont., 1934. Hockey coach; commentator; feisty nationalist

CHEVALIER, Leo, business/visual arts. Montreal, Que., 1934. Fashion designer of international lines

CHIPMAN, Ward, justice. St John, NB, 1787–1851. Jurist; chief justice of NB; noted abolitionist

CHIRAEFF, Ludmilla, performing arts. Latvia, 1924. Choreographer; founder, Les Grands Ballets Canadiennes

CHISHOLM, G. Brock, medicine/science. Oakville, Ont., 1896–1971. Psychiatrist; early opponent of pollution, nuclear arms; first head of World Health Org.

CHONG, Rae Dawn, performing arts. Vancouver, BC, 1962. Film actress. *Quest for Fire*

CHONG, Tommy, performing arts. Edmonton, Alta, 1938. Actor; half of Cheech & Chong comedy team.

CHOUART DES GROSEILLIERS, Medard, exploration & discovery. France, 1618–90. Explorer; fur trader; with Radisson, opened western fur trade

CHRÉTIEN, Jean, politics. Shawinigan, Que., 1934. Became prime minister of Canada, general election 1993

CHRISTIE, William, business. Scot., 1829–1900. Biscuit manufacturer; Christie biscuits founder

CHUVALO, George, sports. Toronto, Ont., 1937. Boxer; fought three world champions; never knocked down

CLAIR, Frank, sports. USA, 1917. Football coach; 174 wins (Ottawa Rough Riders) tops CFL coaches

CLANCY, Francis "King," sports. Ottawa, Ont., 1903–1986. Hockey player; defenceman, Ottawa Senators, Toronto Maple Leafs; lively raconteur

CLARK, Joe, politics. High River, Alta, 1939. Prime minister of Canada 1979–80

CLARKSON, Adrienne, media. Hong Kong, 1939. Broadcaster; long-time CBC host. "Take Thirty"

CLAYTON-THOMAS, David, performing arts. Eng., 1941. Singer; member, Blood, Sweat & Tears. "Spinning Wheel"

COCKBURN, Bruce, performing arts. Ottawa, Ont., 1945. Singer/songwriter; politically conscious performer. *Dancing in the Dragon's Jaws*

COE-JONES, Dawn, sports. Lake Cowichan, BC, 1961. golfer; leading pro; 1993 LPGA title

COHEN, Leonard, literary arts/performing arts. Montreal, Que., 1934. Poet; singer. *Flowers for Hitler, I'm Your Man*

COHEN, Morris "Two-Gun," military. Eng., 1889–1970. China hand; confidant of Sun Yat-sen; general in Chinese army

COHEN, Nathan, literary arts. Sydney, NS, 1923–71. Critic; Canada's first serious drama critic

COHON, George, business. USA, 1937. CEO, Cdn McDonald's Restaurants; philanthropist

COLDWELL, M.J. (Major James), politics. Eng., 1888–1974. CCF founder; leader, 1942–60

COLEMAN, Kit, media/military. Toronto, Ont., 1864–1915. First woman war correspondent

COLICOS, John, performing arts. Toronto, Ont., 1928. Stage actor; Stratford Festival regular

COLLIP, James, medicine. Belleville, Ont., 1892–1965. Biochemist; co-discoverer of insulin

COLOMBO, John Robert, literary arts. Kitchener, Ont., 1936. Anthologist; prolific compiler of reference books. *Colombo's Canadian Quotations*

COLVILLE, Alex, visual arts. Toronto, Ont., 1920. Realistic painter; designed centennial coins

CONACHER, Lionel, sports. Toronto, Ont., 1901–54. Canada's Athlete of the Half-Century (1900-1950); gifted at many sports

CONNOR, Ralph, literary arts. Canada W, 1867–1937. Popular novelist of muscular Christianity. *The Sky Pilot*

CONNORS, "Stompin' Tom", performing arts. St John, NB, 1936. Country singer; nationalist performer. *Across This Land with Stompin' Tom*

COOK, James, exploration & discovery. Eng., 1728–79. Navigator; explored Newfoundland and Northwest coasts

COOKE, Jack Kent, business. Hamilton, Ont., 1912. Capitalist; flamboyant owner of newspapers, radio stations, sports teams (Washington Redskins)

COPPS, Sheila, politics. Hamilton, Ont., 1952. Liberal deputy prime minister

CORMIER, Ernest, visual arts. Montreal, Que., 1885–1980. Architect; designed University of Montreal

COSENTINO, Frank, sports. Hamilton, Ont., 1937. Football player; CFL quarterback, 1960–69; sports history writer; prof., physical education

COSTAIN, Thomas, literary arts. Brantford, Ont., 1885–1965. Historical novelist. *High Towers*

COULTHARD, Jean, performing arts. Vancouver, BC, 1908. Composer. "The Pines of Emily Carr"

COUPLAND, Douglas, literary arts. Vancouver, BC, 1961. Novelist; humorist. *Generation X*

COWAN, Garry, sports. Kitchener, Ont., 1938. Golfer; twice US amateur champion (1966, 1971)

CRANSTON, Toller, sports. Hamilton, Ont., 1949. Skater; brought innovation and artistry to men's figure skating.

CRAWLEY, Frank "Budge," visual arts. Ottawa, Ont., 1911–87. Film producer. *The Rowdyman*

CREAM, Dr Neal, murderer. Scot., 1850–92. Hanged as poisoner of London prostitutes

CREIGHTON, Donald, literary arts. Toronto, Ont., 1902–79. Historian; developed literary side of history

CREMAZIE, Octave, literary arts/visual arts. Quebec, Que., 1827–1879. Father of French Canadian poetry. "Le Drapeau de Carillon"

CROLL, David, politics. Russia, 1900–91. As mayor and senator, championed the poor and aged

CROMBIE, David, politics. Toronto, Ont., 1936. Civic reformer; Toronto mayor 1973-78

CRONENBURG, David, visual arts. Toronto, Ont., 1943. Film director; inventive horror; science fiction film-maker. *Videodrome*

CRONYN, Hume, performing arts. London, Ont., 1911. Stage actor; film character player. *Cocoon*

CROTHERS, Bill, sports. Markham, Ont., 1940. Runner; silver medal (800 m), 1964 Olympics.

CROW, John, business. Eng., 1937. Economist; governor of Bank of Canada, 1987–94

CROWFOOT, Blackfoot chief, military. Belly R, Alta, 1830–90. Diplomat, warrior, negotiator

CUMMINGS, Burton, performing arts. Montreal, Que., 1947. Rock singer; lead singer, The Guess Who; later solo artist. *My Own Way to Rock*

CUNARD, Sir Samuel, business. Halifax, NS, 1787–1865. Shipowner; founded Cunard Line forerunner

CURRIE, Sir Arthur, military. Strathroy, Ont., 1875–1933. Commander, Canadian corps, WWI

CURTOLA, Bobby, performing arts. Thunder Bay, Ont., 1944. Singer; early teen idol. "Fortune Teller"

CYR, Louis, sports. Napierville, Que., 1863–1912. World's strongest man, 1880–1990

DAFOE, John, media. Combermere, Ont., 1866–1944. Journalist; influential editor, *Winnipeg Free Press*

DANBY, Ken, visual arts. Sault Ste Marie, Ont., 1940. Painter of realistic sports figures

DAVEY, Keith, politics. Toronto, Ont., 1926. Long-time Liberal Party strategist

DAVIES, Robertson, literary arts. Thamesville, Ont., 1913. Novelist; playwright. *Fifth Business*

DAVIS, Victor, sports. Guelph, Ont., 1964–89. Swimmer; three medals, 1984 Olympics; gold in 200 m breaststroke.

DAVIS, William, politics. Brampton, Ont., 1929. Cons. premier of Ontario, 1971–85

DAWSON, George, science. Pictou, NS, 1849–1901. Geologist; surveyed much of north & west Canada

DAWSON, Sir John, science. Pictou, NS, 1820–99. Geologist; made McGill a leading university; founded Royal Society of Canada

DAY, James, sports. Thornhill, Ont., 1946. Equestrian; team gold medal, 1968 Olympics.

DE CARLO, Yvonne, performing arts. Vancouver, BC, 1924. Actress; film/TV star. "The Munsters"

DE LA ROCHE, Mazo, literary arts. Newmarket, Ont., 1879–1961. Prolific popular novelist. *Jalna*

DESCHENES, Jules, justice. Montreal, Que., 1923. Jurist; Que. chief justice; chairman, Inquiry of War Criminals in Canada

DESJARDINS, Alphonse, business. Levis, Que., 1854–1920. Banker; established first Caisse populaire (credit union) in 1900

DESMARAIS, Paul, business. Sudbury, Ont., 1927. Industrialist; chairman of Power Corp, controlling trust, insurance and paper companies

DEWAR, Marion, politics. Montreal, Que., 1928. Mayor, Ottawa, 1978–85; NDP MP

DICKENS, Francis, justice. Eng., 1844–86. Policeman; novelist's son; inspector in NWMP

DICKSON, Brian, justice. Yorkton, Sask., 1916. Chief justice of Canada, 1984–90

DIEFENBAKER, John, politics. Neustadt, Ont., 1895–1979. Prime minister of Canada 1957–63

DION, Celine, performing arts. Montreal, Que., 1968. Popular Quebec chanteuse. "Unison"

DIONNE, Marcel, sports. Drummondville, Que., 1951. Hockey player; centre; 731 goals, third all-time

DMYTRYK, Edward, visual arts. Grand Forks, BC, 1908. Film director; film noir specialist. *Detour*

DOHERTY, Denny, performing arts. Halifax, NS, 1941. Pop singer; founding member, The Mamas and the Papas

DOUGHTY, Sir Arthur, archivist. Eng., 1860-1936. Established Public Archives of Canada

DOUGLAS, Sir James, politics. British Guiana, 1803–1877. Administrator; governor of BC, 1858–64

DOUGLAS, Tommy, politics. Scot., 1904–86. Eloquent Socialist; Sask. premier, 1944–61; NDP federal leader, 1961–71

DRABINSKY, Garth, performing arts. Toronto, Ont., 1948. Impresario; Cineplex founder, theatrical producer. "Show Boat"

DRAPEAU, Jean, politics. Montreal, Que., 1916. Montreal mayor for 29 years; brought city Expo 67, 1976 Olympics, Montreal Expos

DRESSLER, Marie, performing arts. Coburg, Ont., 1869–1934. Actress; oversize film star. *Min and Bill*

DRYDEN, Ken, sports. Hamilton, Ont., 1947. Hockey goaltender; six-time all-star for Montreal; also lawyer and writer. *The Game*

DUDEK, Louis, literary arts. Montreal, Que., 1918. Socially aware poet; critic. "East of the City"

DUGUID, Don, sports. Winnipeg, Man., 1935. Curler; Canadian and world champion, 1970, 1971

DUMONT, Gabriel, military. Red River, 1837–1906. Metis leader; guerilla leader in NW Rebellion

DUPLESSIS, Maurice, politics. Trois-Rivieres, Que., 1890–1959. Powerful premier of Quebec, 1936–39, 1944–59

DURBIN, Deanna, performing arts. Winnipeg, Man., 1921. Actress; singer; teenage movie star. *3 Smart Girls*

DURHAM, John Lambton, Earl of, politics. Eng., 1792–1840. Statesman; "Radical Jack" urged union of English and French Canada

DURNAN, Bill, sports. Toronto, Ont., 1915–1972. Hockey goaltender; six-time Vezina Trophy winner for Montreal Canadiens

DWAN, Allan, visual arts. Toronto, Ont., 1885–1981. film director; from silent era, made over 200 Hollywood films. *Sands of Iwo Jima*

EATON, Cyrus, business. Pugwash, NS, 1883–1979. Financier; promoter of international peace

EATON, Fredrik, business. Toronto, Ont., 1938. Retailer; former chairman, T. Eaton Co.

EATON, Timothy, business. Ire., 1834–1907. Retailer; innovative founder of T. Eaton Co. in 1867

EDWARDS, Bob, media. Scot., 1864–1922. Journalist; published satirical Calgary *Eye Opener.*

EGOYAN, Atom, visual arts. Egypt, 1960. Film director; guitarist; playwright. *The Adjuster*

EISLER, Lloyd, sports. Seaforth, Ont., 1963. Figure skater; with Isabelle Brasseur, world pairs title, 1993; Olympic bronze medals, 1992, 1994

ELDER, Jim, sports. Toronto, Ont., 1934. Equestrian; team gold medal, 1968 Olympics

ELGAARD, Ray, sports. Edmonton, Alta, 1959. Football player; Sask. Roughriders star wide receiver

ELGIN, James Bruce, Earl of, politics. Eng., 1811–63. Governor general, 1847–54

EMERY, Vic, sports. Montreal, Que., 1933. Bobsledder; piloted 1964 Olympic gold medal team

ENGEL, Howard, literary arts. Toronto, Ont., 1931. Mystery writer. *Murder Sees the Light*

ENGEL, Marian, literary arts. Toronto, Ont., 1933–1985. Novelist. *Bear*

ERASMUS, Georges, politics. Ft Rae, NWT, 1948. Dene leader; former head, Assembly of First Nations

ERICKSON, Arthur, visual arts. Vancouver, BC, 1924. Architect; Simon Fraser University (Burnaby, BC)

ESPOSITO, Phil, sports. Sault Ste Marie, Ont., 1942. Hockey player; Boston centre; 717 goals, fourth all-time

ESTEY, Willard "Bud", justice. Saskatoon, Sask., 1919. Supreme Court justice, 1977–88; headed several royal commissions

ETROG, Sorel, visual arts. Romania, 1933. Monumental sculptor; designer. "Ritual Head"

EVANSHEN, Terry, sports. Montreal, Que., 1944. Football player; outstanding CFL receiver.

EYTON, Trevor, business. Quebec, Que., 1934. Executive; president, Brascan Ltd; many corporate boards

FACKENHEIM, Emil, literary arts. Germany, 1916. Philosopher; works on religon and the Holocaust. *Quest for Past and Future*

FAIRCLOUGH, Ellen, politics. Hamilton, Ont., 1905. First woman Cabinet minister (1957)

FAIRLEY, Barker, visual arts. Eng., 1887–1986. Critic; essential Goethe scholar; portrait painter

FAITH, Percy, performing arts. Toronto, Ont., 1908–76. Bandleader; top music arranger. "Canadian Sunset"

FALONEY, Bernie, sports. USA, 1932. Football player; long-time star QB for Edmonton, Hamilton

FEINBERG, Rabbi Abraham, politics. USA, 1899–1986. Peace activist; champion of radical causes

FERGUSON, Ivan, exploration & discovery. Toronto, Ont., 1929. Inventor; developed IMAX and OMINMAX film systems

FERGUSON, Max (Rawhide), media. Eng., 1924. Broadcaster; popular host of CBC-radio's "Rawhide"

FERGUSON, Maynard, performing arts. Verdun, Que., 1928. Jazz trumpeter; versatile stylist made 50 albums

FERRON, Jacques, literary arts/politics. Louiseville, Que., 1921–85. Playwright; *Contes du pays incertain*; Rhinoceros Party founder

FESSENDEN, Reginald, exploration & discovery. Milton-Est, Canada E, 1866–1932. Inventor; transmitted world's first radio broadcast (1906)

FILION, Herve, sports. Angers, Que., 1940. Harness driver; all-time leader in victories; 12,000+

FILMON, Gary, politics. Winnipeg, Man., 1942. Cons. Manitoba premier since 1988

FINDLEY, Timothy, literary arts. Toronto, Ont., 1930. Novelist; versatile writer. *The Wars*

FITZGERALD, Lionel Lemoine, visual arts. Winnipeg, Man., 1890–1956. Impressionist turned to abstracts. "Doc Snider's House"

FLAVELLE, Sir Joseph, business. Peterborough, Ont., 1858–1939. Financier; executive for Canada Packers, Bank of Commerce, National Trust

FLEMING, Sir Sandford, exploration & discovery. Scot., 1827–1915. Engineer; developed standard time; designed Canada's first postage stamp; built railways

FONYO, Steve, sports. Montreal, Que., 1965. Handicapped runner; "Journey for Lives" raised funds for cancer research, 1985

FORRESTER, Maureen, performing arts. Monteal, Que., 1930. Operatic contralto; Canada's prima Diva

FORSEY, Eugene, politics. Grand Bank, Nfld, 1904–91. Intellectual; commentator on public affairs; social radical; strong federalist

FOSTER, David, performing arts. Victoria, BC, 1949. Musician; produced many major acts (Chicago, Barbra Streisand); 12 Grammy awards

FOSTER, Sir George, politics. Carletton, NB, 1847–1931. Statesman; central in Cdn political life; acting PM during Borden's illness (1920)

FOTHERINGHAM, Alan, media. Hearne, Sask., 1932. Journalist; popular political columnist

FOX, Michael J., performing arts. Edmonton, Alta, 1961. Actor; diminutive leading man. *Back to the Future*

FOX, Terry, sports. Winnipeg, Man., 1958–81. Began "Marathon of Hope" cross-Canada run to raise funds for cancer research; Lou Marsh Trophy as Canada's top athlete, 1980

FRANCA, Celia, performing arts. Eng., 1921. Choreographer; founder of National Ballet of Canada

FRANKLIN, Sir John, exploration & discovery. Eng., 1786–1847. Bold, doomed arctic explorer

FRANKS, Wilbur, exploration & discovery. Weston, Ont., 1901–86. Inventor; devised pressure suit for airplane pilots

FRAPPIER, Armand, science. Valleyfield, Que., 1904–91. Influential microbiologist

FRASER, Simon, exploration & discovery. USA, 1776–1862. First white man to explore Fraser River

FRECHETTE, Sylvie, synchronized swimmer. Laval,Que., 1967. Received post-event gold medal in sychronized swimming, 1992 Olympics

FROBISHER, Martin, exploration & discovery. Eng., 1539–94. Mariner; discovered Frobisher Bay

FRONTENAC, Comte de, politics. France, 1622–98. Gov. gen., New France, 1672–82, 1689–98

FROST, Leslie, politics. Orillia, Ont., 1895–1973. Cons. premier of Ontario, 1949–61

FRUM, Barbara, media. USA, 1937–92. Broadcaster; interviewer. "As It Happens," "The Journal"

FRYE, Northrop, literary arts. Sherbrooke, Que., 1912–91. Canada's most influential literary critic. *Anatomy of Criticism*

FULFORD, Robert, media. Ottawa, Ont., 1932. Journalist; former editor, *Saturday Night*; columnist

FUNG, Lori, sports. Vancouver, BC, 1963. Rhythmic gymnast; gold medal, 1984 Olympics

FURST, Judith, performing arts. New Westminster, BC, 1943. Opera singer; internationally renowned Diva

G

GABRIEL, Tony, sports. Hamilton, Ont., 1948. Football player; CFL tight end; record 138 straight games with receptions.

GAGNON, Andre, performing arts. St Pacome de Kamouraska, Que., 1942. Pianist; composer."Le Saint-Laurent"

GALBRAITH, John Kenneth, business/literary arts. Iona Station, Ont., 1908. Economist; author; influential intellectual. *The Affluent Society*

GALLANT, Mavis, literary arts. Montreal, Que., 1922. Over 100 short stories. "A Fairly Good Time"

GALLIVAN, Danny, sports. Montreal, Que., 1917–93. Hockey announcer; voice of the Montreal Canadiens

GALT, Alexander, politics. Eng., 1817–93. Railway promoter; proposed union of all British colonies

GARNEAU, Francis, literary arts. Quebec, Que., 1809–1866. Writer; early historian. *Histoire du Canada*

GARNEAU, Hector de St Denys, literary arts. Montreal, Que., 1912–43. Poet. "Regards et jeux dans l'espace"

GARNEAU, Marc, exploration & discovery. Quebec, Que.,1949. First Canadian astronaut (1984)

GARNER, Hugh, literary arts. Eng., 1913–79. Working class novelist. *Cabbagetown*

GASCON, Jean, performing arts. Montreal, Que., 1921–88. Actor; director; influential man of the theatre; headed Stratford Festival, Natl Arts Centre

GELINAS, Gratien, performing arts. St Tite, Que., 1909. Actor; director; playwright; crucial to modern Quebec theatre

GEORGE, Dan, performing arts. Burrard Reserve, BC, 1899–1981. Actor; helped redefine image of Aboriginal Peoples in media. *Little Big Man*

GERUSSI, Bruno, performing arts. Medicine Hat, Alta, 1928. Actor; regular on "The Beachcombers"

GESNER, Abraham, exploration & discovery. Cornwallis, NS, 1797–1864. Inventor of kerosene oil

GETTY, Don, politics/sports. Montreal, Que., 1933. Edmonton Eskimos quarterback; Conservative premier of Alberta, 1985–92

GIBSON, George "Mooney," sports. London, Ont., 1880–1967. Baseball player; pro catcher, 1905–18

GILMOUR, Clyde, media. Calgary, Alta, 1912. Journalist; arts broadcaster. "Gilmour's Albums"

GISBOURNE, Frederick, exploration & discovery. Eng., 1824–92. Inventor; developed undersea telegraph cable (1852)

GOMEZ, Avelino, sports. Cuba, 1928–80. Jockey; over 4000 career wins, including 4 Queen's Plates

GORDON, Donald, business. Scot., 1901–1969. Executive; controversial head of CNR, 1950–66

GORDON, Walter, politics. Toronto, Ont., 1906–87. Economic nationalist; inspired creation of Committee for an Independent Canada

GORMAN, Charles, sports. St John, NB, 1897–1940. Speed skater; held seven world records

GOUIN, Jean-Lomer, politics. Canada E, 1861–1929. Liberal premier of Quebec, 1905–20

GOULD, Glenn, performing arts. Toronto, Ont., 1932–82. Classical pianist; "Goldberg Variations" stand out in brilliant, eccentric career

GOUZENKO, Igor, military. USSR, 1919–82. Spy; defector exposed Soviet espionage network

GRANT, Charles, justice. Toronto, Ont., 1902–80. Activist; fought anti-semitism, racism, bigotry

GRANT, George, literary arts. Toronto, Ont., 1918–88. Philosopher; influential pessimistic thinker and nationalist. *Lament for a Nation*

GRAY, George, sports. Canada W, 1865–1933. Shot putter; world record holder during 1880s

GREENE, Grahame, performing arts. Six Nations Reserve, Ont., 1952. Film/TV actor. *Dances with Wolves*

GREENE, Lorne, performing arts. Ottawa, Ont., 1915–87. Actor; Ben Cartwright on TV's "Bonanza" for 14 years

GREENE, Nancy, sports. Ottawa, Ont., 1943. Skier; World Cup winner, 1967, 1968; gold and silver slalom medals, 1968 Olympics

GREENOUGH, Gail, sports. Edmonton, Alta, 1960. Equestrian; 1986 world champion, individual show jumping

GREENSPAN, Edward, justice. Niagara Falls, Ont., 1944. Distinguished criminal lawyer

GRENFELL, Sir Wilfred, medicine. Eng., 1865–1940. Medical missionary; builder of hospitals in Nfld

GRETZKY, Wayne, sports. Brantford, Ont., 1961. Hockey player; all-time leading NHL scorer

GREY OWL (Archibald Belaney), literary arts. Eng., 1888–1938. Writer; conservationist who identified with Aboriginal Peoples. *Pilgrims of the Wild*

GRIERSON, John, visual arts. Scot., 1898–1972. Documentarist; creater of National Film Board

GROULX, Lionel, religion. Vaudreuil, Que., 1878–1967. Historian; Quebec religious nationalist

GROVE, Frederick Philip, literary arts. Prussia, 1879–1948. Writer. *In Search of Myself*

GWYNNE, Horace, "Lefty," sports. Toronto, Ont., 1912. Boxer; bantamweight gold medal, 1932 Olympics

GZOWSKI, Sir Casimir, exploration & discovery. Russia, 1813–98. Engineer; built roads, bridges, and railroads

GZOWSKI, Peter, media. Toronto, Ont., 1934. Broadcaster; author; long-time radio host. "Morningside"

H

HACKNER, Allan, sports. Nipigon, Ont., 1954. Curler; Canadian and world champion, 1982, 1985

HAILEY, Arthur, literary arts. Eng., 1920. Writer; produced string of best-sellers. *Airport*

HAIM, Corey, performing arts. Toronto, Ont., 1972. Actor

HALIBURTON, Thomas, literary arts. Windsor, NS, 1796–1865. Writer; social satirist. *The Clockmaker*

HALL, Glenn, sports. Humboldt, Sask., 1931. Hockey goaltender; 11-time all-star; record 502 consecutive games

HALL, Monty, media. Winnipeg, Man., 1925. Long-time TV host of "Let's Make a Deal" show

HAMEL, Theophile, visual arts. Ste-Foy, LC, 1817–70. Painted life-like official portraits

HANLAN, Ned, sports. Toronto, Ont., 1855–1908. World champion oarsman, 1880–84

HANSEN, Rick, sports. Port Alberni, BC, 1957. Wheelchair athlete; "Man in Motion" tour raised $20M for medical research

HANSON, Fritzie, sports. USA, 1912. Football player; led Winnipeg to first western Grey Cup (1935)

HARCOURT, Michael, politics. Edmonton, Alta, 1943. NDP Premier of BC since 1991

HARE, Frederick, science. Eng., 1919. Environmentalist; expert on climate change, greenhouse effect

HARNOY, Ofra, cellist. Israel, 1965. International virtuoso soloist

HARPER, Elijah, native legislator. Red Sucker L, Man. His vote killed Meech Lake Accord

HARPER, J. Russell, visual arts. Caledonia, Ont., 1914–83. Art historian; pioneered study of art history

HARRIS, Lawren, visual arts. Brantford, Ont., 1885–1970. Founder of Group of Seven; noted for stark landscapes, e.g. "Above Lake Superior"

HARRIS, Wayne, sports. USA, 1938. Football player; outstanding Calgary Stampeders linebacker

HARRON, Don, performing arts. Toronto, Ont., 1924. Actor; comedian; host of "Morningside," 1977–82; also noted for portraying farmer Charlie Farquharson

HART, Corey, performing arts. Montreal, Que., 1962. Pop singer; teen heartthrob. *Boy in the Box*

HART, Evelyn, performing arts. Toronto, Ont., 1956. Prima ballerina, Royal Winnipeg Ballet.

HARTMAN, Grace, business. Toronto, Ont., 1918. Labour leader; first woman to head Canadian Union of Public Employees (1975–83)

HARVEY, Doug, sports. Montreal, Que., 1924–1990. Hockey player; Montreal Canadiens defenceman; won seven Norris Trophies

HARWOOD, Vanessa, performing arts. Eng., 1947. National ballet soloist

HATFIELD, Richard, politics. Woodstock, NB, 1931. Conservative premier of NB, 1970–87

HAWKINS, Ronnie, performing arts. USA, 1935. Pop/country singer; pioneer of Canadian rock. "Mary Lou"

HAWLEY, Sandy, sports. Oshawa, Ont., 1949. Jockey; winner of more than 6000 races.

HAYDEN, Melissa, performing arts. Toronto, Ont., 1923. Virtuoso with New York City Ballet

HEALEY, Jeff, performing arts. Toronto, Ont., 1966. Pop singer; blind blues guitarist. "See the Light"

HEARNE, Samuel, exploration & discovery. Eng., 1745–1792. Explorer; *A Journey from Prince of Wales's Fort in Hudson's Bay to the Northern Ocean* is one of the great travel narratives

HEATH, Jeff, sports. Ft William, Ont., 1915–75. Baseball player; hit .293 in 14-year career

HEBB, Donald, science. Chester, NS, 1904–1985. Psychologist; developmental work showed importance of environmental stimulation

HEBERT, Anne, literary arts. Ste-Catherine-de-Fossambault, Que., 1916. Writer. *Kamouraska*

HEBERT, Louis-Phillipe, visual arts. Megantic, Que., 1850–1917. Commemorative sculptor of many public monuments. "Queen Victoria"

HEGGTVEIT, Anne, sports. Ottawa, Ont., 1939. Skier; Canada's first Olympic gold medal in skiing; women's slalom, 1960

HELLSTROM, Brig-Gen Sheila, military. Bridgewater, NS, 1935. Soldier; first Cdn woman general

HELWIG, David, literary arts. Toronto, Ont., 1938. Poet; novelist. "Figures in a Landscape"

HENNING, Douglas, performing arts/politics. Ft Garry, Man., 1947. Magician; co-founder, Natural Law Party

HENLEY, Garney, sports. USA, 1935. Football player; Hamilton star CFL's most versatile player

HENRY, Martha, performing arts. USA, 1938. TV/film actress; Stratford regular. "The Wars"

HENSON, Josiah, politics. USA, 1789–1883. Black leader; escaped slave; model for *Uncle Tom's Cabin*

HEPBURN, Doug, sports. Vancouver, BC, 1926. Weight lifter; world heavyweight title, 1953

HEPBURN, Mitch, politics. St Thomas, Ont., 1896–1953. Liberal Ontario premier, 1934–42

HERIOT, George, visual arts. Scot., 1759–1839. Watercolourist. "Lake St Charles Near Quebec"

HEROUX, Denis, visual arts. Montreal, Que., 1940. Film producer. "Atlantic City"

HERZBERG, Gerhard, medicine. Germany, 1904. Physicist; molecular analyst; Nobel Prize, chemistry, 1971

HEWITT, Foster, sports. Toronto, Ont., 1903–1985. Hockey announcer; voice of Toronto Maple Leafs

HIGHWAY, Thompson, literary arts. Brovchet, Man., 1951. Playwright. *Dry Lips Oughta Move to Kapuskasing*

HILL, Arthur, performing arts. Melfort, Sask., 1922. Stage and film performer. *The Ugly American*

HILL, Dan Jr, performing arts. Toronto, Ont., 1954. Romantic singer. "Sometimes When We Touch"

HILL, Dan Sr, politics. USA, 1923. Reformer; human rights, black history activist and writer

HILLER, Arthur, visual arts. Edmonton, Alta, 1923. Slick film-maker/director. *Love Story*

HILLIER, James, exploration & discovery. Brantford, Ont., 1915. Inventor; pioneered electron microscopes

HIRSCH, John, performing arts. Hungary, 1930–89. Stage director; founded Manitoba Theatre Centre; headed Stratford Fetsival, CBC television drama

HITSCHMANOVA, Lotte, politics. Czech, 1909–80. Activist; founding director, Unitarian Service Committee of Canada development agency

HNATYSHTN, Ramon, politics. Saskatoon, Sask., 1934. Governor general of Canada since 1990

HODGINS, Jack, literary arts. Comox, BC, 1938. Novelist. *The Resurrection of Joseph Bourne*

HODGSON, George, sports. Montreal, Que., 1893–1983. Swimmer; first Canadian Olympic gold medals in swimming; 400 m, 1500 m freestyle in 1912

HOFFMAN, Abbie, sports. Toronto, Ont., 1947. Sports feminist; director of Sport Canada

HOGG, Helen, science. USA, 1905–1993. Astronomer; star clusters expert; asteroid named for her

HOHL, Elmer, sports. Wellesley, Ont., 1919–87. Horseshoe pitcher; world champion, 1965–87

HOOD, Hugh, literary arts. Toronto, Ont., 1928. Novelist; essayist. *The Swing in the Garden*

HOWARD, Russ, sports. Penetang, Ont., 1955. Curler; Canadian and world champion, 1987, 1993

HOWE, Gordie, sports. Floral, Sask., 1928. Hockey player; Detroit Red Wings great; 801 NHL goals

HOWE, Joseph, politics. Halifax, NS, 1804–1873. Led fight against Nova Scotia entry into Confederation; later joined cabinet.

HULL, Bobby, sports. Pte Anne, Ont., 1939. Hockey player; "Golden Jet", left winger for Chicago and Winnipeg; 610 NHL goals

HUNGERFORD, George, sports. Vancouver, BC, 1944. Rower; gold medal, coxless pairs, 1964 Olympics

HUNTER, Tommy, performing arts. London, Ont., 1937. Country singer; "Tommy Hunter Show" on CBC, 1965–92

HUNTSMAN, Archibald, science. Tintern, Ont., 1883–1973. Biologist; pioneered fisheries science

HURTIG, Mel, literary arts. Edmonton, Alta, 1932. Publisher; Canadian nationalist; publisher of *The Canadian Encyclopedia*

HUSTON, Walter, performing arts. Toronto, Ont., 1884–1960. Actor. *Treasure of the Sierra Madre*

HUTT, William, performing arts. Toronto, Ont., 1920. Stage actor; distinguished Stratford leading player

IBERVILLE, Pierre d', military. Montreal, Que., 1661–1706. soldier; daring, often cruel, adventurer

IGNATIEFF, George, politics. Russia, 1913–89. Diplomat; expert in East-West relations; UN ambassador

IGNATIEFF, Michael, literary arts/media. Toronto, Ont., 1947. Writer; broadcaster. *The Russian Album*

INNIS, Harold, politics. Otterville, Ont., 1894–1952. Political economist; communications theorist. *Empire and Communications*

IRELAND, John, performing arts. Vancouver, BC, 1914. Actor; often played a heavy. *Red River*

IRVIN, Dick Sr, sports. Limestone Ridge, Ont., 1892–1957. Hockey executive; innovative coach/mgr of Montreal Canadiens, Toronto Maple Leafs

IRVING, Kenneth (K.C.), business. Buctouche, NB, 1899–1992. Industrialist; founder of NB business empire, from oil to broadcasting

ISRAEL, Werner, science. Germany, 1931. Physicist; pioneered study of black holes, gravitation

ISSAJENKO, Angella (Taylor), sports. Jamaica, 1958. Sprinter; many medals in 100 m races

JACKS, Terry, performing arts. Winnipeg, Man., 1944. Singer; founding member, the Poppy Family

JACKSON, A.Y., visual arts. Montreal, Que., 1882–1974. Painter; landscape artist; member, Group of Seven. "Barns"

JACKSON, Donald, sports. Oshawa, Ont., 1940. Figure skater; men's world champion, 1962

JACKSON, Roger, sports. Toronto, Ont., 1942. Rower; gold medal, coxless pairs, 1964 Olympics

JACKSON, Russ, sports. Hamilton, Ont., 1936. Football player; Ottawa quarterback; three-time Schenley Award winner as CFL top player

JACOBS, "Indian" Jack, sports . USA, 1920–74. Football player; fiery quarterback for Winnipeg Blue Bombers; helped popularize CFL

JACOBS, Jane, literary arts. USA, 1916. Urban critic; major urban thinker. *Systems of Survival*

JAMES, Gerry, sports. Regina, Sask., 1934. Football/hockey player; rare pro double; Winnipeg Blue Bombers, Toronto Maple Leafs

JELINEK, Otto, politics. Czech, 1940. PC minister won, with sister Maria, world pairs figure skating title (1972)

JENKINS, Ferguson, sports. Chatham, Ont., 1943. Baseball pitcher; only Canadian in Hall of Fame; 284 career wins

JENNESS, Diamond, literary arts. NZ, 1886–1969. Anthropolgist; author; expert on native Canadians. *The People of the Twilight*

JENNINGS, Peter, media. Toronto, Ont., 1938. Broadcaster; anchorman. "ABC Evening News"

JEROME, Harry, sports. Prince Albert, Sask., 1940–82. Sprinter; one-time world record holder in 100 m

JEWISON, Norman, visual arts. Toronto, Ont., 1926. Film director; founded Canadian Film Centre in Toronto. "In the Heat of the Night"

JOHANSSON, Herman "Jackrabbit," sports. Nwy, 1875–1986. Skier; developer of cross-country skiing

JOHN, Dr Harold, medicine. China, 1915. Physician; developed cobalt bomb for treating cancer

JOHNSON, Ben, sports. Jamaica, 1961. Sprinter; stripped of 100 m world record time gold medal in 1988 Olympics for using banned drug

JOHNSON, Pauline, literary arts. Six Nations Reserve, UC, 1861–1913. Her poetry celebrated Canada and her native heritage. "Flint and Feather"

JOHNSTON, Franz, visual arts. Toronto, Ont., 1888–1949. Early Group of Seven member. "Batchawana Falls"

JOHNSTON, Lynn, visual arts. Collingwood, Ont., 1947. Cartoonist; creator, "For Better or For Worse"

JOLLIET, Louis, exploration & discovery. Quebec, Que., 1645–1700. Co-discoverer of the Mississippi R.

JONAS, George, literary arts. Hungary, 1935. Versatile writer; producer. *Vengeance*

JONES KONIHOWSKI, Diane, sports. Vancouver, BC, 1951. Canadian pentathlon record holder

JORY, Victor, performing arts. Yukon, 1902–82. Actor; Hollywood villain. *Huckleberry Finn*

JULIETTE (Juliette Sysak), media/performing arts. Winnipeg, Man., 1927. Singer; early TV star; own show, 1954–66

JUNEAU, Pierre, media. Verdun, Que., 1922. Broadcast executive; headed CRTC, 1968–75

JUTRA, Claude, visual arts. Montreal, Que.,1930–1987. Film director. *Mon Oncle Antoine*

K

KAIN, Karen, performing arts. Hamilton, Ont., 1951. Prima ballerina, National Ballet of Canada

KANE, Paul, visual arts. Ire., 1810–1871. Painter of the Canadian West and native peoples

KARPIS, Alvin, justice. Montreal, Que., 1908–79. Barker Gang member; US Public Enemy No. 1

KARSH, Yousuf, visual arts. Armenia, 1908. Photographer; portraitist of the famous, e.g., Churchill

KEELER, Ruby, performing arts. Halifax, NS, 1909–1993. Actress; dancer. 42nd Street

KEITH, Vicki, sports. Winnipeg, Man., 1961. Swam all five great lakes in 1988

KELLY, Leonard "Red," sports. Simcoe, Ont., 1927. Hockey player; star defenseman with Detroit and Toronto; two-time Liberal MP

KELSO, John, politics. Ire., 1864–1935. Reformer; founded Toronto Humane Society, Children's Aid

KENOJUAK, Ashevak, visual arts. Baffin Island, NWT 1927. Noted for bird graphics

KHORANA, Gobind, medicine/science. India, 1922. Chemist; Nobel Prize in medicine (1968) for DNA research

KIDD, Bruce, sports. Ottawa, Ont., 1943. Runner; many wins at various distances; outstanding athlete in Canada, 1961 and 1962

KIDDER, Margot, performing arts. Yellowknife, NWT, 1948. Actress; Hollywood star. *Superman*

KIERENS, Eric, politics. Montreal, Que., 1914. Economist; outspoken nationalist

KILBOURN, William, literary arts. Toronto, Ont., 1926. Writer; historian; biographer of C.D. Howe

KILLAM, Isaac Walton, business. Yarmouth, NS, 1885–1955. Industrialist; built business empire; known for philanthropy

KING, Allan, visual arts. Vancouver, BC, 1930. Film-maker; documentarist. "Warrendale"

KING, Mackenzie, politics.. Kitchener, Ont., 1874–1950. Prime minister of Canada during WWII

KINSELLA, W.P., literary arts. Edmonton, Alta, 1935. Writer; known for poetic baseball fiction. *Shoeless Joe*

KLEIN, Abraham Moses, literary arts. Ukraine, 1909–72. Poet of Jewish themes. "The Rocking Chair"

KLEIN, George, exploration & discovery. Hamilton, Ont., 1904–92. Productive inventor: wind tunnels, gearing systems, Canadarm gear design, etc.

KNUDSON, George, sports. Winnipeg, Man., 1937–89. Golfer; Canada's top pro; 12 PGA tour victories

KOFFLER, Murray, business. Toronto, Ont., 1924. Entrepreneur; made Shopper's Drug Mart Canada's largest pharmacy chain

KOFFMAN, Moe, performing arts. Toronto, Ont., 1928. Jazz flautist. "Swinging Shepherd Blues"

KOTCHEFF, Ted, visual arts. Toronto, Ont., 1931. Film director. *The Apprenticeship of Duddy Kravitz*

KREINER, Kathy, sports. Timmins, Ont., 1957. Skier; gold medal, giant slalom, 1976 Olympics

KRIEGHOFF, Cornelius, visual arts. Holland, 1815–72. Known for paintings of Quebec life. "The Habitant Farm"

KROL, Joe, sports. Hamilton, Ont., 1919. Football player; Toronto Argos star; top athlete, 1946

KUERTI, Anton, performing arts. Austria, 1938. Leading pianist; composer; Beethoven specialist

KURELEK, William, visual arts. Whitfield, Alta, 1927–1977. Symbolist religious painter

L

LAFLEUR, Guy, sports. Thurso, Que., 1951. Hockey player; Canadiens' star right winger; 560 goals

LAFONTAINE, Sir Louis, politics. Boucherville, LC, 1807–64. In effect, Canada's first PM, 1848–51

LAMBERT, Natalie, sports. Montreal, Que., 1963. Speed skater; short track title, 500 m, 1993

LAMER, Antonio, justice. Montreal, Que., 1933. Chief justice of the Supreme Court since 1990

LAMPMAN, Archibald, literary arts. Morpeth, Canada W, 1861–99. Nature poet. "Lyrics of Earth"

LANCASTER, Ron, sports. USA, 1938. Football player; coach; quarterback set 30 CFL records

LANG, k.d., performing arts. Consort, Alta, 1961. Country-torch singer; vegetarian activist. *Shadowlands*

LANGFORD, Sam, sports. Weymouth Falls, NS, 1886–1956. Boxer; great fighter; denied title shot

LANOIS, Daniel, performing arts. Hamilton, Ont., 1953. Singer; producer of Peter Gabriel's "Sledgehammer" and, with Brian Eno, U2's *Joshua Tree*

LANTOS, Robert, visual arts. Hungary, 1949. Film producer; CEO, Alliance Communications. *Black Robe*

LAPIERRE Laurier, media. Megantic, Que., 1929. TV personality; co-host, "This Hour Has 7 Days"

LASKIN, Borah, justice. Ft William, 1912–84. Chief justice of Canada, 1973–84

LAUMANN, Silken, sports. Toronto, Ont., 1964. Rower; braved broken leg for bronze medal in 1992 Olympics; Athlete of the Year 1991, 1992

LAURE, Carole, performing arts. Montreal, Que., 1949. Actress; screen star. "Maria Chapdelaine"

LAURENCE, Margaret, literary arts. Neepawa, Man., 1926–1987. Writer; created fictional setting of Manawaka. *The Diviners*

LAURENT, Louis St, politics. Compton, Que., 1882–1973. Became prime minister of Canada on Nov. 15, 1948; one of the architects of NATO

LAURIER, Sir Wilfred, politics. St-Lin, Canada E, 1841–1919. Canada's first French-speaking prime minister

LAVAL, Francois, religion. France, 1623–1708. First bishop of Quebec (1674–88)

LAVALLEE, Callixa, performing arts. Vercheres, Canada E, 1842–1891. Composer of "O Canada"

LA VERENDRYE, Pierre, exploration & discovery. Trois-Rivieres, Que., 1685–1749. Explorer of W Canada

LAYTON, Irving, literary arts. Neamtz, Romania, 1912. Prolific, flamboyant poet. "A Red Carpet for the Sun"

LEACOCK, Steven, literary arts. Eng., 1869–1944. Humorist. *Sunshine Sketches of a Little Town*

LEBLOND, Charles, science. France, 1910. Anatomist; pioneer in cell biology

LE CAINE, Hugh, performing arts/science. Port Arthur, Ont., 1914–1977. Physicist; composer; designed the sackbut, the first musical synthesizer

LECLERC, Felix, performing arts. La Tuque, Que., 1914–88. Singer/songwriter; influential chansonnier and Quebec nationalist

LEE, Dennis, literary arts. Toronto, Ont., 1939. Children's writer. *Alligator Pie, Garbage Delight*

LEE, Geddy, performing arts. Toronto, Ont., 1953. Singer/songwriter; lead singer for Rush. *Moving Pictures*

LEE-GARTNER, Kerrin, sports. Trail, BC, 1966. Skier; gold medal, women's downhill, 1992 Olympics

LEGER, Jules, politics. St-Anicet, Que., 1913–80. Canada's governor general, 1974–79

LEGER, Paul-Emile, religion. Valleyfield, Que., 1904–91. Cardinal; eloquent, compassionate religious leader; became missionary in Africa

LEMELIN, Roger, literary arts. Quebec, Que., 1919–92. Writer; creator of the popular Plouffe family

LEMIEUX, Mario, sports. Montreal, Que.,1965. Hockey player; Pittsburgh Penguins' centre one of two players to average two points per game

LEONARD, Stan, sports. Vancouver, BC, 1915. Golfer; won many Canadian titles; 3 US tour wins

LESAGE, Jean, politics. Montreal, Que, 1912–80. Liberal premier of Quebec, 1960–66

LEVESQUE, Jean-Louis, business. Nouvelle, Que., 1911. Financier; co-founder of Levesque Beaubien Inc., Quebec's largest brokerage house

LEVESQUE, Rene, politics. New Carlisle, Que., 1922–87. Led Parti Quebecois; Quebec premier 1976–85

LEVY, Eugene, performing arts. Hamilton, Ont., 1946. Actor; comedian; SCTV regular (Earl Camembert, Bobby Bitman)

LEWIS, David, politics. Russia, 1909–81. Federal NDP leader, 1971–75; eloquent speaker

LEWIS, Lennox, sports. Eng., 1965. Boxer; super heavyweight gold medal, 1988 Olympics

LEWIS, Stephen, politics. Ottawa, Ont., 1937. Ont NDP leader; Cdn UN ambassador

LEWIS, W. Bennet, science. Eng., 1908–87. Physicist; prime role in developing CANDU reactor

LEYRAC, Monique, performing arts. Montreal, Que., 1928. Actress; popular Quebec chanteuse

LIGHTFOOT, Gordon, performing arts. Orillia, Ont., 1938. Singer/songwriter; popular vocalist with many hits. "Canadian Railroad Trilogy"

LILLIE, Beatrice, performing arts. Toronto, Ont., 1894–1989. Stage comedienne. "Auntie Mame"

LINKLETTER, Art, media. Moose Jaw, Sask., 1912. Radio/TV host. "People Are Funny"

LISMER, Arthur, visual arts. Eng., 1885–1969. Painter; Group of Seven founding member. "September Gale"

LITTLE, Rich, performing arts. Ottawa, Ont., 1938. Impersonator; night club and television performer

LIVESAY, Dorothy, literary arts. Winnipeg, Man., 1909. Poet; sensitive feminist writer. *Poems for People*

LOATES, Glen, visual arts. Toronto, Ont., 1945. Wildlife artist; painter and naturalist

LOGAN, William, science. Montreal, Que., 1798–1875. Geologist; first head of Geological Survey of Canada; first to map Laurentian Shield

LOMBARDO, Guy, performing arts. London, Ont., 1902–1977. Bandleader; his Royal Canadians most popular band in N America; 300 million records sold

LONGBOAT, Tom, sports. Brantford, Ont., 1887–1949. Runner; set record in 1907 Boston Marathon

LONGDEN, John, sports. Eng., 1910. Jockey; first N American with 4000 winners (career: 6032)

LOUGHEED,Peter, politics. Calgary, Alta, 1928. PC premier of Alberta, 1971–85; played strong role in federal politics

M

MacDONALD, Flora, politics. Sydney, NS, 1926. First woman to hold Sr cabinet post; external affairs in Clark govt (1979)

MacDONALD, J.E.H., visual arts. Eng., 1873–1932. Landscape painter; Group of Seven founder. "Mist Fantasy"

MacDONALD, Jock, visual arts. Scot., 1897–1960. Early abstract painter; member, Painters Eleven

MacDONALD, Sir John A., politics. Scot., 1815–1891. Canada's first official prime minister

MacEWEN, Gwendolyn, literary arts. Toronto, Ont., 1941–1987. Poet. "The Shadow-Maker"

MacKENZIE, Alexander, exploration & discovery. Scot., 1764–1820. Charted MacKenzie R. (1789); crossed from L. Athabasca to Pacific Ocean (1793)

MacKENZIE, Alexander, politics. Scot., 1822–1892. Canada's second prime minister

MacKENZIE, William Lyon, politics. Scot., 1795–1861. Led 1837 rebellion for reform in Upper Canada; Toronto's first mayor

MacLENNAN, Hugh, literary arts. Glace Bay, NS, 1907–1990. Respected Canadian novelist. *The Watch That Ends the Night*

MacMILLAN, Harvey (H.R.), business. Newmarket, Ont., 1885–1976. Industrialist; established forerunner of logging giant MacMillan Bloedel

MacMILLAN, Sir Ernest, performing arts. Mimico, Ont, 1893–1973. Renowned conductor, composer, arranger; championed Canadian works

MacNAUGHTON, Andrew, military. Moosomin, NWT, 1887–1966. Soldier; led Cdn army in WWII; endorsed Dieppe raid; diplomat; UN, Atomic Energy Cssn

MacPHAIL Agnes, politics. Proton Twp, Ont., 1890–1954. Only woman MP in 1921 (first women's vote); founded Elizabeth Fry Society

MacPHERSON, Cluny, exploration & discovery. St John's, Nfld, 1879–1966. Invented the gas helmet

MacPHERSON, Duncan, visual arts. Toronto, Ont., 1925–1993. Long-time *Toronto Star* cartoonist

MAGNUSSEN, Karen, sports. North Vancouver, BC, 1952. Figure skater; world champion, 1973

MAILLET, Antonine, literary arts. Buctouche, NB, 1929. Novelist of Acadian life. *La Sagouine*

MAISSONEUVE, Paul de Chomedey de, exploration & discovery/politcs. France, 1612–76. Montreal founder; founded city, 1642

MANDEL, Howie, performing arts. Toronto, Ont., 1955. Manic comic and TV actor. "St Elsewhere"

MANLEY, Elizabeth, sports. Belleville, Ont., 1965. Figure skater; silver medal, 1988 Olympics

MANNING, Preston, politics. Edmonton, Alta, 1942. Led Reform Party to breakthrough in 1993 federal election

MANSBRIDGE, Peter, media. Eng., 1948. Broadcaster; anchorman, CBC national news

MARCHAND, Len, politics. Vernon, BC, 1933. Native politician; first native federal cabinet minister

MARSHALL, Donald, justice. Sydney, NS, 1953. Victim; acquitted of murder after 11 years in prison

MARTIN, Clara, justice. Toronto, Ont., 1874–1923. First woman lawyer in British Empire

MARTIN, Paul, politics. Ottawa, Ont., 1903–92. Long-time Liberal cabinet minister

MARTIN, Paul, Jr, politics. Windsor, Ont., 1938. Liberal minister of finance

MARTINI, Paul, sports. Weston, Ont., 1960. Figure skater; world pairs champion (with Barbara Underhill), 1984

MASSEY, Hart, business. Haldemand Twp, Ont., 1823–1896. Capitalist; developed Massey-Ferguson Ltd

MASSEY, Raymond, performing arts. Toronto, Ont., 1896–1983. Craggy-faced actor often played Lincoln

MASSEY, Vincent, politics. Toronto, Ont., 1887–1967. First native-born governor general, 1952–59

McCAIN, H. Harrison, business. Florenceville, NB, 1927. Industrialist; turned potato-processing plant into international firm

McCLELLAND, Jack, literary arts. Toronto, Ont., 1922. Publisher; his McClelland & Stewart nurtured Canadian writing; over 5000 Canadian titles

McCLUNG, Nellie, justice. Chatsworth, Ont., 1873–1951. Reformer; fought for women's suffrage

McCONNELL, Rob, performing arts. London, Ont., 1935. Jazz musician; founded Boss Brass, major big band

McCRAE, John, literary arts. Guelph, Ont., 1872–1918. Poet; physician who wrote "In Flanders Field"

McCURDY, Howard, politics. London, Ont., 1932. Black activist; also biologist

McCURDY, John, exploration & discovery. Baddeck, NS, 1886–1961. Pilot; first airplane flight in British Empire in Silver Dart (1909)

McDERMOTT, Dennis, business. Eng., 1922. Labour leader; former president, Canadian Labour Congress

McGARRIGLE, Anna and Kate, performing arts. Montreal, Que., 1944, 1946. Songwriter/ singers; unique duo. "Love Over and Over"

McGEE, Thomas D'Arcy, politics. Ire., 1825–1868. Eloquent proponent of Confederation; assassinated 1868.

McGIBBON, Pauline, politics. Sarnia, Ont., 1910. Cda's first woman lieutenant-governor (Ont.,1974)

McINTOSH, John, exploration & discovery. USA, 1777–1845. Inventor; breeder of McIntosh apple

McKENNA, Frank, politics. Apolaqui, NB, 1948. Liberal premier of NB since 1987

McKENNITT, Loreena, performing arts. Morden, Man., 1957. Singer; harpist; repertoire includes mostly Celtic material

McKENZIE, Maj.-Gen. Lewis, military. Truro, NS, 1940. Soldier; led Cdn peace-keepers in Yugoslavia

McKOY, Mark, sports. Guyana, 1961. Hurdler; gold medal, 110 m hurdles, 1992 Olympics

McLAREN, Norman, visual arts. Scot., 1914–87. Filmmaker; innovative NFB animator. *Pas de deux*

McLARNIN, Jimmy, sports. Ire., 1907. Boxer; world welterweight champion, 1933–35

McLAUGHLIN, Audrey, politics. Dutton, Ont., 1936. NDP national leader since 1989

McLAUGHLIN, Col. Robert S., business. Enniskillen, Ont., 1871–1972. Industrialist; developed firm which became General Motors of Canada

McLUHAN, Marshall, media. Edmonton, Alta, 1911–1980. Media theorist; developed theory about "hot" and "cool" media. *The Gutenburg Galaxy*

McNAUGHTON, Duncan, sports. Cornwall, Ont., 1910. High jumper; 1932 Olympic high jump gold medal

McPHERSON, Aimee Semple, religion. Ingersoll, Ont., 1890–1944. Controversial evangelist

MEIGHAN, Arthur, politics. Anderson, Ont., 1874–1960. Succeeded Sir Robert Borden as prime minister of Canada

MESSER, Don, performing arts. Tweedside, NB, 1909–73. Bandleader; popular maker of traditional fiddle and dance music. "Don Messer's Jubilee"

MICHAELS, Lorne, media. Toronto, Ont., 1945. TV producer; founding producer, "Saturday Night Live"

MICHENER, Roland, politics. Lacombe, Alta, 1900–91. Governor general of Canada, 1967–74

MILLAR, Ian, sports. Halifax, NS, 1947. Equestrian

MILLAR, Margaret, literary arts. Kitchener, Ont., 1915. Thriller writer. *Beast in View*

MILNE, David, visual arts. Paisley, Ont., 1882–1953. Versatile painter. "Raspberry Jam"

MILNER, Brenda, medicine. Eng., 1915. Neuropsychologist; ground-breaking brain researcher

MINER, Jack, science. USA, 1865–1944. Conservationist; pioneered bird sanctuaries, migratory banding

MIRVISH, Ed, business. USA, 1914. Entrepreneur; retailer (Honest Ed's) and theatre owner

MITCHELL, Joni, performing arts. Ft Macleod, Alta, 1943. Singer/songwriter; influential lyricist. "Court and Spark"

MITCHELL, W.O., literary arts. Weyburn, Sask., 1914. Prairie novelist. *Who Has Seen the Wind?*

MOLSON, John, business. Eng., 1763–1836. Founded Molson brewery; built railroads, steamships

MONTCALM, Louis Joseph, Marquis de, military. France, 1712–59. Soldier; French commander in 7 Years' War; died on Plains of Abraham

MONTGOMERY, Lucy Maud, literary arts. Clifton, PEI, 1874–1942. Writer; creator of Anne of Green Gables

MOODIE, Susanna, literary arts. Eng., 1803–85. Writer; pioneer author of "Roughing it in the Bush"

MOORE, Brian, literary arts. N Ire., 1921. Novelist. *The Luck of Ginger Coffey*

MOORE, Mavor, media. Toronto, Ont., 1919. TV producer; librettist; columnist; critic

MOORES, Frank, politics. Carbonear, Nfld, 1933. PC premier of Newfoundland, 1972–79

MORANIS, Rick, performing arts. Toronto, Ont., 1953. Comedian; actor; SCTV regular. *Ghostbusters*

MORAWETZ, Oscar, performing arts. Czech, 1917. Composer. "From the Diary of Anne Frank"

MORENZ, Howie, sports. Mitchell, Ont., 1902–1937. Hockey player; centre; Canada's player of half century (CP), 1950; died of on-ice injuries

MORGENTALER, Henry, medicine. Poland, 1923. Physician; challenge of abortion laws led to supreme court ruling them unconstitutional

MORIYAMA, Raymond, visual arts. Vancouver, BC, 1929. Architect; Ontario Science Centre

MORRICE, J.W. (James), visual arts. Montreal, Que., 1865–1924. Artist; early modernist. "The Ice Bridge"

MORRISSEAU, Norval, visual arts. Sand Point Reserve, Ont., 1932. Ojibway artist originated pictographic style

MORSE, Barry, performing arts. Eng., 1918. Stage/film/TV actor; regular on "The Fugitive"

MORTON, W.L. (William), literary arts. Gladstone, Man., 1908–80. Historian. "Manitoba: A History"

MOWAT, Farley, literary arts. Belleville, Ont., 1921. Controversial, popular naturalist writer. "A Whale for the Killing"

MOWAT, Sir Oliver, politics. Kingston, UC, 1820–1903. Ontario premier, 1872–96; lieutenant-governor, 1897–1903

MULRONEY, Brian, politics. Baie Comeau, Que., 1939. Prime minister of Canada 1984–1993

MUNK, Peter, business. Hungary, 1927. Capitalist; CEO, American Barrick Resources gold mining co.

MUNRO, Alice, literary arts. Wingham, Ont., 1931. Short story writer. "Lives of Girls and Women"

MURPHY, Emily, justice. Cookstown, Ont., 1868–1933. Legal reformer; first woman magistrate in British Empire; fought for women's rights

MURRAY, Anne, performing arts. Springhill, NS, 1945. Singer; Canada's most successful performer; many Junos and Grammys. "Snowbird"

MURRAY, George, politics. Grand Narrows, NS, 1861–1929. Lib. premier of NS, 1896–1923

MURRAY, John, justice. Scot., 1840–1906. Detective; pioneered scientific crime detection.

MURRAY, Margaret "Ma", media. USA, 1888–1982. Journalist; pungent editorialist in own magazines

MUSTARD, Fraser, medicine. Toronto, Ont., 1927. Physician; medical humanitarian; found connection between Aspirin and blood clotting

MUSTARD, William, medicine. Clinton, Ont., 1914–87. Physician; beloved children's surgeon developed operations for blue babies, polio cripples

NAISMITH, James, sports. Almonte, Ont., 1861–1939. Physician; invented basketball in 1891

NASH, Knowlton, media. Toronto, Ont., 1927. Broadcaster; former anchorman, CBC national news

NATTRASS, Susan, sports. Medicine Hat, Alta, 1950. Shooter; six women's world trapshooting titles

NAULT, Fernand, performing arts. Montreal, Que., 1921. Dancer; choreographer, Les Grands Ballets Canadiens

NELLIGAN, Emile, literary arts. Montreal, Que., 1879–1941. Romantic poet. "Romance du Vin"

NELLIGAN, Kate, performing arts. London, Ont., 1951. Actor; appears on both stage and film. "Eleni"

NEWMAN, Peter, media. Austria, 1929. Journalist; popular historian. *The Canadian Establishment; Maclean's* editor, 1971–82

NICHOLAS, Cindy, sports. Toronto, Ont., 1957. Marathon swimmer; first woman to swim English Channel both ways

NICOL, Eric, media. Kingston, Ont., 1919. Humour columnist. "Girdle Me a Globe"

NIELSEN, Leslie, performing arts. Regina, Sask., 1926. Deadpan film/TV comedian. *The Naked Gun*

NORQUAY, John, politics. St Andrews, Man., 1841–89. Manitoba premier of mixed European and native ancestry, 1878–87

NORTHCOTT, Ron, sports. Innisfail, Alta, 1935. Curler; skipped three Brier and world champion rinks

NOWLAN, Alden, literary arts. Windsor, NS, 1933–83. Poet. "Bread, Wine and Salt"

ODJIG, Daphne, visual arts. Manitoulin Island, Ont., 1919. Blends western and native styles. "The Indian in Transition"

O'HARA, Catherine, performing arts. Toronto, Ont., 1954. Actor; comedian; SCTV regular (Lola Heatherton)

OLIPHANT, Betty, performing arts. Eng., 1918. Founded National Ballet School

ONDAATJE, Christopher, business/literary arts. Sri Lanka, 1933. Financier; author. *Leopard in the Afternoon*

ONDAATJE, Michael, literary arts. Sri Lanka, 1943. Poet; editor; novelist. *The English Patient* (Booker Prize)

O'NEILL, James "Tip", sports. Canada W, 1859–1918. Baseball player; batted .326 in 10-year career

ORR, Bobby, sports. Parry Sound, Ont., 1948. Hockey player; spectacular offensive defenceman; won eight consecutive Norris trophies

ORSER, Brian, sports. Belleville, Ont., 1961. Figure skater; 1987 world champion, twice Olympic silver medallist (1984, 1988)

ORTON, George, sports. Strathroy, Ont., 1873–1958. Runner; Canada's first Olympic gold medallist, winning for USA in 1900 (2500 m steeplechase)

OSLER, Sir William, medicine. Bond Head, UC, 1849–1919. Physician; renowned medical educator; writer of authoritative textbooks

OTTENBRITE, Anne, sports. Whitby, Ont., 1966. Swimmer; gold medal, 200 m, 1984 Olympics

OUIMET, Alphonse, media. Montreal, Que., 1908–88. TV executive; designed first Canadian TV receiver; CBC president, 1958–67

PACE, Kate, sports. North Bay, Ont., 1969. Skier; World Cup downhill champion, 1993.

PAGE, P.K. (Patricia), literary arts. Eng., 1916. Poet; novelist; artist. "The Metal and the Flower"

PANNETTON, Phillipe (Ringuet), literary arts. Trois-Rivieres, Que., 1895–1960. Man of letters; acclaimed Quebec writer. "Trente Arpents"

PAPINEAU, Louis, politics. Montreal, Que., 1786–1871. Led political reform movement in Lower Canada

PARIZEAU, Jacques, politics. Montreal, Que., 1930. Leader, Parti Quebecois since 1987

PARKER, Jackie, sports. USA, 1932. Football player; coach; Edmonton Eskimos star quarterback; named CFL outstanding player three times

PARROT, Jean-Claude, business. Montreal, Que., 1936. Labour leader; leader of militant postal union

PARTRIDGE, Edward, business. Canada W, 1862–1931. Farm reformer; visionary in grain industry fought monopolies, started growers' cooperative

PATRICK, Lester, sports. Drummondville, Que., 1883–1960. Hockey executive; NHL builder

PATTISON, James, business. Saskatoon, Sask., 1928. Industrialist; developed car dealership into business empire; chairman, Expo 86

PAUL, Robert, sports. Toronto, Ont., 1937. Figure skater; with Barbara Wagner, won 4 pairs titles, 1960 Olympic gold

PERSON, Lester, politics. Newtonbrook, Ont., 1897–1972. Prime minister of Canada 1963–1968; awarded Nobel Peace Prize in 1957

PECKFORD, Brian, politics. Whitbourne, Nfld, 1942. Cons. premier of Nfld, 1979–89

PELADEAU, Pierre, media. Outremont, Que., 1925. Publisher; heads newspaper giant Quebecor

PELLAN, Alfred, visual arts. Quebec, Que., 1906–88. Painter; cubist and surrealist artist.

PELLATT, Sir Henry, military. Kingston, Canada W, 1969–1939. Soldier; Builder of eccentric Toronto mansion, Casa Loma

PENFIELD, Dr Wilder, medicine. USA, 1891–1976. Neurologist; writer; pioneered mapping of brain functions; founded Montreal Neurological Inst.

PERCY, Karen, sports. Edmonton, Alta, 1966. Skier; won two bronze medals, 1988 Olympics

PERRAULT, Pierre, visual arts. Montreal, Que., 1927. Filmmaker; realist director. *L'Acadie, L'Acadie*

PETERSON, Oscar, performing arts. Montreal, Que., 1925. Jazz pianist; "Canadiana Suite"; over 90 albums

PEZER, Vera, sports. Melfort, Sask., 1939. Curler; Canadian women's champion, 1971–73

PHILLIPS, Robin, performing arts. Eng., 1942. Director, Stratford Festival, 1975–80, 86–87

PICKFORD, Mary, performing arts. Toronto, Ont., 1893–1979. Actress; "America's Sweetheart" was early movie star. *Sparrows*

PIDGEON, Walter, performing arts. E St John, NB, 1897–1984. Leading man. *Mrs Miniver*

PINSENT, Gordon, performing arts. Grand Falls, Nfld, 1930. Versatile actor. "The Rowdyman"

PITSEOLAK, Peter, visual arts. NWT, 1902–73. Photographer; recorded passing of traditional Inuit life

PITSEOLAK, Ashoona, visual arts. NWT, 1904–83. Artist of Inuit myth and legend

PLAMONDON, Antoine, visual arts. Lorette, Que., 1804–95. Portraitist and religious painter

PLANTE, Jacques, sports. Mt Carmel, Que., 1929–86. Hockey goaltender; seven-time Vezina winner; originated face mask

PLUMMER, Christopher, performing arts. Toronto, Ont., 1929. Stage and film star. "Murder By Decree"

PODBORSKI, Steve, sports. Toronto, Ont., 1957. Skier; world downhill champion, 1982

POLANYI, John, science. Germany, 1929. Chemist; Nobel Prize (1986) for work on infrared chemiluminescence

POLLOCK, Sam, sports. Montreal, Que., 1925. Hockey executive; built Montreal Canadiens dynasty

POLLOCK, Sharon, literary arts. Fredericton, NB, 1936. Playwright; writer of conscience. *Blood Relations*

POST, Sandra, sports. Oakville, Ont., 1943. Golfer; Canada's first woman touring professional

POTTS, Jerry, justice. USA, 1840–96. Native scout; Blackfoot became NWMP special constable

PRATT, Christopher, visual arts. St John's, Nfld, 1935. Artist; developed style of "conceptual realism"

PRATT, E.J. (Edwin), literary arts. Western Bay, Nfld, 1883–1964. Leading pre-WWII poet. "Newfoundland Verse"

PURDY, Alfred, literary arts. Wooler, Ont., 1918. Working-class poet. "The Cariboo Horses"

QUILICO, Louis, performing arts. Montreal, Que., 1925. Operatic baritone; appeared with most major companies

RADISSON, Pierre, exploration & discovery. France, 1636–1710. Explorer; fur trader; important in early history of Hudson's Bay Co as guide and advisor

RAE, Bob, politics. Ottawa, Ont., 1948. NDP premier of Ontario since 1990

RAFFI (Raffi Cavoukian), performing arts. Egypt, 1948. Singer. *Baby Beluga*

RASKY, Harry, visual arts. Toronto, Ont., 1928. Film-maker; noted documentarist. *The Dispossessed: The War Against the Indians*

RASMINSKY, Louis, business. Montreal, Que., 1908. Governor, Bank of Canada, 1961–72.

REANEY, James, literary arts. Easthope, Ont., 1926. Playwright; poet; critic. "A Suit of Nettles"

REBICK, Judy, politics. USA, 1945. Former head, Natl Action Cttee on Status of Women

REED, George, sports. USA, 1939. Football player; back with Sask. Roughriders; 44 CFL records

REAVES, Keanu, performing arts. Lebanon, 1965. Actor. *Bill and Ted's Excellent Adventure*

REGAN, Gerald, politics. Windsor, NS, 1928. Liberal premier of NS, 1970–78

REID, Kate, performing arts. Eng., 1930–1993. Primarily stage actress; Stratford mainstay

REICHMANN, Paul, business. Austria, 1930. Developer; philanthropist; with brothers Albert and Ralph, built Olympia & York into world's largest real estate developers in 1980s

REITMAN, Ivan, visual arts. Czech, 1946. Film director; producer; went from exploitation movies to blockbusters. *Ghostbusters*

RICHARD, Maurice "Rocket," sports. Montreal, Que., 1921. Hockey player; legendary right winger; hockey's first 50-goal, 500-goal scorer

RICHARDSON, Ernie, sports. Stoughton, Sask., 1931. Curler; skipped 4 Brier and world title rinks

RICHARDSON, James, business. Kingston, Ont., 1885–1939. Financier; founded family grain business and investment house

RICHLER, Mordecai, literary arts. Montreal, Que., 1931. Novelist; essayist; acerbic comic writer. *St Urbain's Horseman*

RIEL, Louis, politics. St Boniface, Man., 1844–85. Metis leader; led North West Rebellion, 1870 and 1885; hanged for treason

RIOPELLE, Jean-Paul, visual arts. Montreal, Que., 1923. Acclaimed painter, sculptor. "Autrich"

ROBARTS, John, politics. Banff, Alta, 1917–1982. Cons. premier of Ontario, 1961–71

ROBERTS, Charles G.D., literary arts. Douglas, NB, 1860–1943. Poet; animal story writer. "Eyes of the Wilderness"

ROBERTSON, John Ross, business. Toronto, Ont., 1841–1918. Financier; publisher and philanthropist

ROBERTSON, Lloyd, media. Stratford, Ont., 1934. Broadcaster; chief anchor, CTV news

ROBERTSON, Robbie, performing arts. Toronto, Ont., 1944. Singer/songwriter; founding member of The Band; later soloist. "Music from Big Pink"

ROBICHAUD, Louis, politics. St-Antoine, NB, 1925. Liberal premier of NB, 1960–70

ROBINETTE, J.J., justice. Toronto, Ont., 1906. Lawyer; prominent in criminal and constitutional law

ROBLIN, Duff, politics. Winnipeg, Man., 1917. Cons. premier of Manitoba, 1958–67

ROBLIN, Sir Rodmond, politics. Sophiasburg, Canada W, 1853–1937. Cons. premier of Manitoba, 1900–15

ROGERS, Edward, exploration & discovery. Toronto, Ont., 1900–1939. Radio inventor; perfected alternating current radio tube, revolutionizing the industry

ROGERS, Stan, performing arts. Hamilton, Ont., 1949–83. Folk singer/songwriter. "Between the Breaks"

ROGERS, Ted, media. Toronto, Ont., 1933. Cable TV executive; runs Canada's largest cable system; 1994 take-over of Maclean Hunter

ROLPH, John, medicine. Eng., 1793–1870. physician; ran medical school; constitutional reformer

ROMAN, Stephen, business. Slovakia, 1921–1988. Industrialist; founded Denison Mines Ltd

ROMANOW, Roy, politics. Sask., 1939. NDP premier of Sask. since 1991.

RONALD, William, visual arts. Stratford, Ont., 1926. Abstract artist; host, "As It Happens"

ROSE, Fred, politics. Poland, 1907–83. Only Canadian Communist MP (1945); jailed as spy

ROSENFIELD, Bobbie, sports. Russia, 1905–1969. Track star; Canada's female athlete of half century 1950 CP poll

ROSS, Sinclair, literary arts. Shellbrook, Sask., 1908. Novelist. *As For Me and My House*

ROTHSTEIN, Aser, science. Vancouver, BC, 1918. Physiologist; introduced radioisotopes in biology

ROULEAU, Joseph, performing arts. Matane, Que., 1929. Operatic bass; internationally famous singer

ROY, Gabrielle, literary arts. St Boniface, Man., 1909–83. Popular novelist. *The Tin Flute*

RUBES, Jan, performing arts. Czech, 1920. Singer; actor; operatic bass; TV host; film actor

RUBINEK, Saul, performing arts. Toronto, Ont., 1948. Versatile character player. "The Quarrel"

RUSSELL, Loris, science. USA, 1904. Paleontologist; suggested dinosaurs might be warm-blooded

RUTHERFORD, Ernest, science. NZ, 1871–1937. Physicist; much of his seminal work done at McGill Univ.

RYAN, Tommy, business. Guelph, Ont., 1882–1961. Entrepreneur; invented 5-pin bowling (1909)

RYBCZYNSKI, Witold, literary arts/visual arts. Scot., 1943. Architect; critic; writer. "Paper heroes"

RYERSON, Egerton, politics. Norfolk County, UC, 1803–1882. Leading figure in 19th century politics and education

SAFDIE, Moshe, visual arts. Israel, 1938. Architect; Habitat, National Gallery of Canada

SAFER, Morley, media. Toronto, Ont., 1931. Broadcaster; co-host, "60 Minutes" since 1971

SAHL, Mort, performing arts. Montreal, Que., 1926. Comedian; delivered political satirist in monologues

SAINTE-MARIE, Buffy, performing arts. Craven, Sask., 1941. Native singer. "Soldier Blue"

SALABERRY, Charles de, military. Beauport, Que., 1778–1829. Soldier; repelled American force in Battle of Chateaugay (1813)

SARRAZIN, Michael, performing arts. Quebec, Que., 1940. Leading man. *They Shoot Horses, Don't They?*

SAUNDERS, Sir Charles, science. London, Ont., 1867–1937. Agriculturalist; introduced Marquis wheat to W Canada

SAUVE, Jeanne, politics. Prud'homme, Sask., 1922. Governor general, 1984–89

SAWCHUCK, Terry, sports. Winnipeg, Man., 1929–70. Hockey goaltender; all-time shutouts leader (103)

SCHREYER, Edward, politics. Beausejour, Man., 1935. NDP premier of Man., 1969-77; governor general of Canada, 1979–84

SCOTT, Barbara Ann, sports. Ottawa, Ont., 1928. Figure skater; women's world champion, 1947–48; Olympic gold medal, 1948

SCOTT, Duncan Campbell, literary arts. Ottawa, Ont., 1862–1947. Poet. "New World Lyrics and Ballads"

SCOTT, Frank Raymond, literary arts. Quebec, Que., 1899–1985. Poet. "Collected Poems"

SCOTT, Jack, literary arts. Windsor, Ont., 1936. Singer; 1950s rockabilly star. "My True Love"

SCRIVEN, Joseph, religion. Ire., 1919–86. Hymn writer; wrote "What a Friend We Have in Jesus"

SECORD, Laura, military. USA, 1775–1868. Heroine; warned British of American attack (1813)

SELKIRK, George, sports. Huntsville, Ont., 1899–1987. Baseball player; outfielder on several NY Yankee champions; replaced Babe Ruth in 1934.

SELKIRK, Thomas Douglas, Earl of, exploration & discovery. Scot., 1771–1820. Colonizer; established Red River settlement in Manitoba

SELYE, Hans, medicine. Austria, 1907–1982. Endocrinologist; author; pioneer in stress research. *The Stress of Life*

SENNETT, Mack, visual arts. Danville, Que., 1880–1960. Producer; silent comedy pioneer; *Keystone Kops*

SERVICE, Robert, literary arts. Eng., 1874–1958. Poet of the Yukon. "Songs of a Sourdough"

SETON, Ernest Thompson, literary arts. Eng., 1860–1946. Naturalist; writer. "Wild Animals I Have Known"

SHATNER, William, performing arts. Montreal, Que., 1931. Actor; Capt. Kirk on TV/movies "Star Trek"

SHEARER, Norma, performing arts. Edmonton, Alta., 1900–83. Actress; Hollywood star. *Romeo and Juliet*

SHIELDS, Carol, literary arts. USA, 1935. Writer; won 1993 Booker Prize for *The Stone Diaries*

SHORE, Eddie, sports. Ft Qu'Apelle, Sask., 1902–1985. Hockey player; Boston defenseman; four-time Hart Trophy winner

SHORT, Martin, performing arts. Toronto, Ont., 1951. Comedian; TV/film star; SCTV's Ed Grimley. *3 Amigos*

SHULMAN, Dr Morton, business/medicine. Toronto, Ont., 1925. Investor; physician; author; stock promoter; introduced anti-Parkinson's disease drug into Canada

SHUSTER, Frank, performing arts. Toronto, Ont., 1918. Comedian; straighter half of Wayne & Shuster team

SHUSTER, Joe, visual arts. Toronto, Ont., 1914–92. Cartoonist; co-creator of Superman

SIFTON, Sir Clifford, politics. Arva, Canada W, 1861–1929. Promoted immigration to settle western Canada

SILVERHEELS, Jay, performing arts. Six Nations Reserve, Ont., 1919–1980. Actor; played Tonto in "Lone Ranger"

SIMCOE, John Graves, politics. Eng., 1752–1806. Upper Canada's first lieutenant-governor, 1792–96

SIMPSON, Sir George, business. Scot., 1787–1860. Financier; gov, Hudson's Bay Co., 1820–60

SINCLAIR, Gordon, media. Toronto, Ont., 1900–1984. Journalist; feisty commentator; long-time "Front Page Challenge" panelist

SKOVERCKY, Joseph, literary arts. Czech, 1924. Intellectual writer; novelist; critic. *The Engineer of Human Souls*

SLOCUM, Joshua, literary arts. Wilmot Twsp, NS, 1844–1909. Sailor; wrote classic *Sailing Alone Around the World*

SMALLWOOD, Joseph "Joey," politics. Gambo, Nfld. 1900–92. Led Newfoundland into Confederation, 1949; premier 1949–72

SMART, Elizabeth, literary arts. Ottawa, Ont., 1913–1986. Novelist. *By Grand Central Station I Sat Down and Wept*

SMELLIE, Elizabeth, medicine. Port Arthur, Ont., 1884–1968. Nurse; builder, Victorian Order of Nurses

SMITH, Sir Donald, Baron Strathcona, politics. Scot., 1820–1914. Politician, businessman, diplomat; drove the Last Spike

SMITH, Graham, sports. Edmonton, Alta, 1958. Swimmer; six gold medals, 1978 Commonwealth Games

SMITH, Lois, performing arts. Vancouver, BC, 1929. National Ballet's first prima ballerina

SMITH, Michael, science. Eng., 1932. Biochemist; 1993 Nobel Prize winner in chemistry

SMITH, Michael, sports. Kenora, Ont., 1967. Decathlete; silver medal, 1991 world championships

SMYTH, Conn, sports. Toronto, Ont., 1895–1980. Hockey executive; owner of Toronto Maple Leafs, 1930–61

SNIDERMAN, Sam, business. Toronto, Ont., 1920. Retailer; established Sam the Record Man; 130 stores

SNOW, Hank, performing arts. Liverpool, NS, 1914. Country music singer. "I'm Movin' On"

SNOW, Michael, visual arts. Toronto, Ont., 1929. Painter; sculptor; film-maker; photographer

SOBEY, Frank, business. Lyons Brook, NS, 1902–1985. Industrialist; turned family grocery business into a major industry

SOMERS, Harry, performing arts. Toronto, Ont., 1925. Composer; wrote opera "Louis Riel"

SOPINKA John, justice/sports. Broderick, Sask., 1933. Supreme Ct justice; former CFL player

SOUSTER, Raymond, literary arts. Toronto, Ont, 1921. Poet; editor. "The Colour of the Times"

SOUTHAM, William, media. Montreal, Que., 1843–1932. Publisher; founded Southam newspaper dynasty

SPICER, Keith, media. Toronto, Ont., 1934. Civil servant; chairman, Canadian Radio-Television and Communications Commission

SPOHR, Arnold, performing arts. Rhein, Sask., 1927. Ballet teacher; led Royal Winnipeg Ballet to world fame

STANFIELD, Robert, politics. Truro, NS, 1914. PC premier of NNS, 1956–67; as federal PC leader, lost three elections to Trudeau

STARYK, Steven, performing arts. Toronto, Ont., 1932. Violinist; virtuoso performer and teacher

STEACIE, Edgar, science. Montreal, Que., 1900–62. Chemist; authority on free radical kinetics

STEELE, Sir Sam, justice. Purbrook, Canada W, 1849–1919. NWMP and WWI officer

STEFANSSON, Vilhjalmur, exploration & discovery. Arnes, Man., 1879–1962. Controversial arctic explorer

STEINBERG, David, performing arts. St Boniface, Man., 1942. Stand-up comic; talk show host

STEINBERG, Sam, business. Hungary, 1905–78. Retailer; turned family grocery into supermarket empire

STEPHENSON, Sir William, military. Winnipeg, Man., 1896–1989. Spy; "Intrepid," head of British counter-espionage during WWII; invented wirephotos

STEWART STREIT, Marlene, sports. Cereal, Alta, 1934. Golfer; won many international titles.

STOWE, Emily, medicine. Norwich, UC, 1831–1903. Physician; first Canadian woman to practice medicine; had to obtain degree in US

STOJKO, Elvis, sports. Newmarket, Ont., 1972. Figure skater; silver medal, 1994 Olympics

STRACHAN, John, religion. Scot., 1778–1867. Anglican bishop; strove to keep Upper Canada British

STRATAS, Teresa, performing arts. Toronto, Ont., 1938. Opera soprano; Diva with strong stage presence

STRONACH, Frank, business. Austria, 1954. Industrialist; chairman, Magna Intl; built machine company into global enterprise

SULLIVAN, Kevin, media. Toronto, Ont., 1955. Producer; made "Anne of Green Gables;" launched popular "Road to Avonlea" TV series

SUNG, Alfred, business. Toronto, Ont., 1948. Fashion designer; top designer of the 1980s

SURIN, Bruny, sports. Haiti, 1967. Sprinter; world 100 m outdoor champion, 1993

SUTHERLAND, Donald, performing arts. St John, NB, 1934. Actor; Canada's best-known star. "Don't Look Now"

SUZUKI, David, media/science. Vancouver, BC, 1936. Geneticist; promoter of environmental causes; columnist; host of CBC's "Quirks and Quarks"

SWAN, Anna, performing arts. Mill Brook, NS, 1846–88. Giantess; at 7'6, 352 lbs; was P.T. Barnum star

SZNAJDER, Andrew, sports. Toronto, Ont., 1968. Four-time Canadian singles tennis champ

TALON, Jean, politics. France, 1625–94. Governor; as intendant, sought to diversify economy of New France with minerals, timber, farming

TANNER, Elaine, sports. Vancouver, BC, 1951. Canada's best woman swimmer by age 15; world records in individual medley and butterfly

TASCHEREAU, Louis-Alexandre, politics. Quebec, Que., 1867–1952. Liberal premier of Quebec, 1920–36; anti-nationalist leader

TAYLOR, E.P., business. Ottawa, Ont., 1901–1989. Industrialist; founded Argus Corp; notable horseman

TAYLOR, Fred "Cyclone," sports. Tara, Ont., 1883–1979. Hockey's first great star

TAYLOR, Kenneth, politics. Calgary, Alta, 1934. Diplomat; engineering freedom for six US hostages in Iran made him an instant celebrity in 1980

TAYLOR, Richard, science. Medicine Hat, Alta, 1929. Physicist; nuclear accelerator pioneer

TAYLOR, Ronald, medicine/sports. Toronto, Ont., 1937. Major league relief pitcher (1962–72) and sports medicine pioneer

TENNANT, Veronica, performing arts. Eng., 1947. Prima ballerina, National Ballet of Canada

TEWKSBURY, Mark, sports. Calgary, Alta, 1968. Swimmer; gold medal, 100 m backstroke, 1992 Olympics

THOM, Linda, sports. Hamilton, Ont., 1943. Shooter; gold medal, women's sports pistol, 1984 Olympics

THOM, Ron, visual arts. Penticton, BC, 1923. Architect; Shaw Festival Theatre, Toronto Zoo

THOMSON, Ken, business/media. Toronto, Ont., 1923. Businessman; art collector; chairman, Thomson Newspapers Ltd

THOMSON, Roy (Lord Thomson of Fleet), media. Toronto, Ont., 1894–1976. Publisher; owned major newspapers in English-speaking world

THOMPSON, David, exploration & discovery. Eng., 1770–1857. Charted Columbia River

THOMPSON, Sir John, politics. Halifax, NS, 1845–1894. Canada's fourth prime minister; largely responsible for establishment of the criminal code

THOMPSON, Tom, visual arts. Claremont, Ont., 1877–1917. Influential painter. "Autumn Foliage"

THORBURN, Cliff, sports. Victoria, BC, 1948. Snooker player; world champion, 1980

TIMMINS, Noah, business. Mattawa, Ont., 1867–1936. Mining operator; developed N America's largest gold mine; town named for him

TORY, Henry, educator. Pt Shoreham, NS, 1864–1947. University founder: UBC, Carleton, etc.

TOWN, Harold, visual arts. Toronto, Ont., 1924–90. Influential painter, sculptor, writer

TRACY, Paul, sports. Scarborough, Ont., 1968. Auto racer; winner of three Indy titles in 1993

TRAILL, Catherine Parr, literary arts. Eng., 1802–1899. Writer. *The Backwoods of Canada*

TREBEK, Alex, media. Sudbury, Ont., 1940. TV host of "Jeopardy" quiz show

TREMBLAY, Michel, literary arts. Montreal, Que., 1942. Playwright; novelist. *Le Vrai Monde*

TRUDEAU, Pierre, politics. Montreal, Que., 1919. Prime minister of Canada 1968–1979

TSUI, Dr Lap-Chee, medicine. China, 1950. Geneticist; identified gene carryinng cystic fibrosis

TUPPER, Sir Charles, politics. Amherst, NS, 1821–1915. Appointed as Canada's sixth prime minister

TURCOTTE, Ron, sports. Drummond, NB, 1941. Jockey; long-time leading jockey rode Secretariat to Triple Crown (1973)

TURNER, John, politics. Eng., 1929. Prime minister of Canada June 1984–July 1984, 1988–1989

TYRRELL, Joseph, science. Weston, Canada W, 1858–1957. Geologist; discovered S Alberta dinosaur beds

TYSON, Ian, performing arts. Victoria, BC, 1933. Singer/songwriter; half of Ian & Sylvia. "Four Strong Winds"

TYSON, Sylvia, performing arts. Chatham, Ont., 1940. Singer; half of Ian & Sylvia. "You Were on My Mind"

UNDERHILL, Barbara, sports. Pembroke, Ont., 1963. Figure skater; world pairs champion (with Paul Martini), 1984

UNGER, Jim, visual arts. Eng., 1937. Cartoonist; creator of popular "Herman" cartoon strip

VAILLANCOURT, Armand, visual arts. Black L., Que., 1932. Sculpts in aid of social activism

VANCOUVER, George, exploration & discovery. Eng., 1757–98. Navigator; surveyor of BC coastline

VANDERBERG, Helen, sports. Calgary, Alta, 1959. Synchronized swimmer; dominated sport in 1979

VANELLI, Gino, performing arts. Montreal, Que., 1954. Pop singer. *Brother to Brother, Nightwalker*

VAN HORNE, Sir William, business. USA, 1843–1915. Driving force behind Canadian Pacific Railroad

VANIER, Georges, politics. Montreal, Que., 1888–1967. Governor general, 1959–67

VANIER, Jean, religion. Switz, 1928. Spiritual leader; man of great moral conviction established homes for handicapped around the world

VAN VOGT, A.E., literary arts. Winnipeg, Man., 1912. Writer; science fiction standout. *Slan*

VARLEY, Frederick, visual arts. Eng., 1881–1969. Member, Group of Seven. "Vera"

VEREGIN, Peter, religion. Russia, 1859–1924. Charismatic Doukhobor leader

VERNON, John, performing arts. Montreal, Que., 1931. TV and film actor. "Wojeck"

VEZINA, Georges, sports. Chicoutimi, Que., 1887–1926. Hockey goalie; NHL trophy named for him

VICKERS, Jon, performing arts. Prince Albert, Sask., 1926. Tenor; operatic star; Wagner specialist

VILLENEUVE, Gilles, sports. St Jean, Que., 1950–1982. Auto racer; won six Grand Prix titles

WAGNER, Barbara, sports. Toronto, Ont., 1938. Figure skater; with Robert Paul, won four pairs titles and 1960 Olympic gold

WALDO, Carolyn, sports. Montreal, Que., 1964. Synchronized swimmer; two gold medals, 1988 Olympics

WALKER, Larry, sports. Maple Ridge, BC, 1966. Baseball player; star Montreal Expos outfielder

WALTERS, Angus, exploration & discovery. Lunenburg, NS, 1882–1968. Bluenose captain; skipper of celebrated schooner

WARD, Max, business. Edmonton, Alta, 1921. Capitalist; charter flights pioneer; founded Wardair

WATKINS, Melville, business. Toronto, Ont., 1932. Economist; founded left-wing Waffle Movement

WATSON, Homer, visual arts. Doon, Canada W, 1855–1936. Landscape painter. "The Pioneer Mill"

WATSON, John, literary arts. Scot., 1847–1939. Philosopher; metaphysician. "Kant and His English Critics"

WATSON, Ken, sports. Minnedosa, Man., 1904–86. Curler; three-time Brier winner; curling teacher

WATSON, Patrick, media. Toronto, Ont., 1929. TV host; actor; writer; producer

WATSON, William "Whipper Billy," sports. Toronto, Ont., 1917–1990. Wrestler; twice world pro champion

WAXMAN, Al, performing arts. Toronto, Ont., 1935. Movie and TV performer. "King of Kensington"

WAYNE, Johnny, performing arts. Toronto, Ont., 1918–1990. Comedian; wilder half of Wayne & Shuster comedy team

WEINZWEIG, John, performing arts. Toronto, Ont., 1913. Influential composer using 12-tone technique. "Red Ear of Corn"

WELLS, Clyde, politics. Buchans Junction, Nfld, 1937. Newfoundland premier since 1989

WESTON, Galen, business. Eng., 1940. Industrialist; Canadian head for George Weston Ltd

WESTON, W. Garfield, business. Toronto, Ont., 1893–1978. Industrialist; pioneer in food retailing

WHEELER, Anne, visual arts. Edmonton, Alta, 1946. Filmmaker. "A Change of Heart"

WHEELER, Lucille, sports. Montreal, Que., 1935. Skier; first N American to win world title, downhill and slalom (1958)

WHITE, Bob, business. Ire., 1935. Labour leader; first head of Canadian Auto Workers' Union

WHITTON, Charlotte, politics. Renfrew, Ont., 1896–1975. Reformer; outspoken Ottawa mayor

WIEBE, Rudy, literary arts. Speedwell, Sask., 1934. Mennonite novelist. *Temptations of Big Bear*

WILLIAMS, Percy, sports. Vancouver, BC, 1908–82. Sprinter; Olympic gold in 100 m and 200 m, 1928

WILSON, Bertha, justice. Scot., 1923. First woman named to Supreme Court of Canada (1982)

WILSON, Sir Daniel, educator. Scot., 1816–92. Darwinian opposed idea of natural selection; energetic administrator, author, scholar

WILSON, Ethel, literary arts. S Africa, 1888–1980. BC novelist. *Swamp Angel*

WILSON, J. Tuzo, science. Ottawa, Ont., 1908–1993. Geophysicist; pioneered plate techtonics theory

WISEMAN, Joseph, performing arts. Montreal, Que., 1918. Actor; title role in James Bond movie, *Dr. No*

WOLFE, James, military. Eng., 1727–59. Soldier; took Quebec for British; died on Plains of Abraham

WOODCOCK, George, literary arts. Winnipeg, Man., 1912. Historian; journalist; activist. *Anarchism*

WOODSWORTH, James S., politics. Etobicoke, Ont., 1874–1942. Founder, Cooperative Commonwealth Federation (later NDP)

WRAY, Fay, performing arts. Medicine Hat, Alta, 1910. Famous as screaming heroine in *King Kong*

WRIGHT, Michelle, performing arts. Merlin, Ont., 1960. Sultry country songstress. "Now and Then"

Y

YANOVSKY, Zal, performing arts. Toronto, Ont., 1944. Singer; member of folk-rock group, Lovin' Spoonful

YOUNG, Neil, performing arts. Toronto, Ont., 1945. Singer/songwriter; seminal rocker. *After the Gold Rush*

YOUVILLE, Marguerite de, religion. Varennes, Que., 1701–71. First Canadian to be beatified by Pope; founded Grey Nuns

ZNAIMER, Moses, media. Toronto, Ont., 1942. TV executive; founder of CITY-TV, Much Music

ZUCKERMAN, Mortimer, business. Montreal, Que., 1937. Financier; developer, magazine publisher

A Canadian Sports Chronology, 1994

January 1—September 30, 1994

■ January

Jan 4: Canada captures its fifth world junior hockey team title in seven years with a 6-4 win over Sweden in Ostrava, Czech Republic.

Jan 6: Edi Podivinsky of Edmonton and Cary Mullen of Banff finish 1-2 in a World Cup downhill race in Saalbach, Austria, the first such achievement by Canadians since 1978.

Jan 8: Dino Ciccarelli of the Detroit Red Wings becomes the 19th NHL player to score 500 career goals in a 6-3 win over the Los Angeles Kings.

Jan 9: Chris Lori of Windsor leads his four-man bobsled team to victory in the Canadian championships at Calgary, defeating Pierre Lueders of Edmonton, who had recently won two world cup races. The luge titles are won by Bob Gaspar of Calgary and Clay Ives of Bancroft, Alta in men doubles; Harrington Telford of Calgary in men's singles; and Deb Begeson of Calgary in women's singles.

Jan 14: Defenceman Paul Coffey of the Detroit Red Wings becomes the sixth NHL player to reach 900 assists with four helpers in a 9-3 rout of the Dallas Stars.

—Sprinter Bruny Surin of Montreal loses his first indoor race in nearly two years, finishing second to Henry Neal of the US in a meet at Hamilton.

—World pairs figure skating champions Isabelle Brasseur of St-Jean-sur-Richelieu, Que and Lloyd Eisler of Seaforth, Ont win their fourth consecutive Canadian title and fifth in six years, at Edmonton. Matthew Smith of Edmonton and Jennifer Robinson of Windsor take the men's and women's junior titles.

Jan 15: Elvis Stojko of Richmond Hill, Ont completes eight triple jumps to wrestle the Canadian men's figure skating title from world champion Kurt Browning. Ice dancing winners are Shae-Lynn Bourne of Chatham, Ont and Victor Kraatz of Vancouver.

Jan 16: Josée Chouinard, skating out of Toronto, wins her third national women's figure skating title. Edmonton's Susan Humphreys upsets Karen Preston of Mississauga, Ont for the other Olympic berth.

—Philippe LaRoche of Lac-Beauport, Que sets a World Cup record in freestyle ski aerials with 243.03 points in a meet at Breckenridge, Colo.

Jan 19: Montreal Expos and Toronto Blue Jays are placed in the eastern divisions of the National and American Leagues as major league baseball re-aligns divisions and expands the playoffs to four teams from each league.

Jan 22: The East beats the West, 9-8, in the NHL's annual all-star shootout in New York. Beleaguered goalies face 102 shots.

—Staying Together, the world's fastest harness racer in 1993, is Canada's Horse of the year. The four-year-old set several world records in winning 21 of 26 races and more than $1.1 million in purses.

Jan 27: Pierre Lueders of Edmonton teams with Dave MacEachern of Charlottetown to become the first Canadians to win the world two-man bobsled title, at St Moritz, Switzerland. Three days later, Lueders finishes sixth in the four-man event, but captures the overall combined World Cup.

—Wally Buono of the Calgary Stampeders, which set a franchise record 15-3 long before losing the Western final to the Edmonton Eskimos, is CFL Coach of the Year, edging Winnipeg's Cal Murphy.

Jan 29: Susan Auch of Winnipeg is second to Bonnie Blair of the US in the women's 500 metres at the world speed skating championships in Calgary. A day later, Kevin Scott of Sault Ste Marie wins the men's 1000 metres, in 1 min., 12.69 secs.

■ February

Feb 2: Scotty Bowman, the winningest coach in NHL history, chalks up win number 1000 (including playoffs) as the Detroit Red Wings beat Tampa Bay 3-1.

Feb 6: Dawn Coe-Jones of Lake Cowichan, BC wins her second LPGA tournament, the Palm Beach Classic at Lake Worth, Fla, with a 15-under par 201 for three rounds. Lisa Walters of Prince Rupert, BC finishes fourth.

Feb 9: Ontario and the NBA settle a dispute over betting which had threatened the Toronto franchise. The league's demand that its games be pulled from a sports lottery is met by Ontario premier Bob Rae. The BC government of Mike Harcourt makes a similar commitment, clearing the way for Vancouver's entry into the NBA. Both teams begin play in 1995.

Feb 12: Skater Kurt Browning carries Canada's flag at the opening ceremonies of the Winter Olympics in Lillehammer, Norway.

Feb 13: Edmonton's Edi Podivinsky earns Canada's first medal of the 1994 Olympics with a bronze in men's downhill skiing. Tommy Moe (US) wins gold.

Feb 15: Isabelle Brasseur and Lloyd Eisler, despite the presence of two pairs of Russian professionals, a rib injury to Brasseur, and some questionable judging, win their second straight Olympic bronze medal in pairs skating with a brilliant performance. Gold medallists are Sergei Grinkov and Ekaterina Gordeeva.

Feb 16: Jean-Luc Brassard of Grande Ile, Que, wins Canada's first gold at the Winter Olympics, capturing the moguls ski event.

Feb 18: Myriam Bedard wins Canada's second Olympic gold medal in the 15K biathlon, an event combining skiing and shooting. Bedard, of Loretteville, Que, won bronze at Albertville two years earlier.

Feb 19: A superior free skating performance earns Elvis Stojko Olympic silver. Despite a far more demanding program than Russia's Alexei Urmanov, Stojko's non-classical style seems to alienate some judges. Kurt Browning rallies to finish fifth.

—Winnipeg's Susan Auch also wins silver, finishing behind Bonnie Blair of the US in the women's 500-metre speed skating final.

Feb 20: Toronto Blue Jays pitchers Dave Stewart and Todd Stottlemyre are arrested for allegedly assaulting police officers outside a Tampa, Fla night club.

Feb 22: Olympic short track speed skating lives up to its wild image after a confused night of bodies strewn all over the ice, and protests over unfair tactics. Canada wins two

medals: four Quebec women—Sylvie Daigle, Isabelle Charest, Christine-Isabel Boudrias, and world champion Nathalie Lambert—take silver in the 3000-metre relay; Marc Gagnon of Chicoutimi wins bronze in the men's 1000 metres.

Feb 23: Myriam Bedard becomes the first Canadian woman to win two Winter Olympic golds when she stages a late rally to win the women's 7.5K biathlon.

Feb 24: Philippe LaRoche and Lloyd Langlois of Magog, Que win silver and bronze medals in the men's freestyle skiing aerials.

Feb 26: Nathalie Lambert salvages some pride for Canada's short-track speed skating team, finishing second in the women's 1000 metres. Five-time world champion Sylvie Daigle is disqualified after judges, the source of much controversy and anger all week, rule her responsible for a collision that knocks two skaters out of contention.

—Kate Pace of North Bay, Ont, disappointed at finishing out of the Olympic downhill skiing medals, wins her first Canadian downhill title at Kananaskis, Alta. Ralf Sacher of Vancouver is men's champion.

Feb 27: Canada completes its best Winter Olympic showing ever as Team Canada wins a silver medal in hockey to raise the count to 13 medals, including three gold and six silver. Canada loses to Sweden 3-2 in a shootout when the game is tied 2-2 after 70 minutes of play.

■ March

March 2: Four-time world figure skating champion Kurt Browning retires from amateur competition.

—The Winnipeg Jets end a 19-game winless streak, defeating Dallas 4-2.

—Melanie Turgeon of Quebec City wins the Europa Cup of alpine skiing at Abetone, Italy.

March 4: Alan Eagleson, former hockey czar and architect of the Canada Cup, is indicted by a US federal grand jury in Boston on 32 counts of racketeering, fraud and embezzlement.

March 5: Saskatchewan's Sandra Peterson repeats as Canadian women's curling champion, beating two-time winner Connie Laliberte of Manitoba, 5-3 at Waterloo.

—Cary Mullen of Banff wins his first world

cup downhill race at Aspen, Col.

—The University of Winnipeg women's basketball team sets a new record for consecutive victories by a North American women's college team. The Wesmen's 70th in a row, 74-62 over provincial rivals University of Manitoba, breaks the record of the 1988-90 University of Calgary Dinosaurs.

March 6: The Laval Rouge et Or defeat the University of Manitoba Bisons 17-15, 15-11, 15-12 to win the Canadian university men's volleyball title in Halifax. In the women's final at Winnipeg, Calgary beats Winnipeg, 15-2, 15-10, 15-12.

—In the Commonwealth Games trials at Victoria, Nancy Sweetnam of Laurentian University sets a long-course record in the women's 400-metre individual medley of 4 min., 46.89 secs.

March 7: Cam Neeley of the Boston Bruins ties Mario Lemieux for the second-fastest 50 goals, in his 44th game, a 6-3 win over the Washington Capitals.

March 10: Forward Duane Dennis of Acadia Axemen wins the Sullivan Trophy as Canada's best collegiate hockey player. Dennis had 35 goals and 39 assists in 26 games.

March 13: Rick Folk of BC beats Ontario's Russ Howard 8-5 at Red Deer, Alta to become the first skip to win men's curling titles for two provinces. Folk won the Canadian and world titles for Saskatchewan in 1980.

—Guard Sandra Carroll scores 37 points as the University of Winnipeg Wesmen capture the CIAU women's basketball title, 90-76 over the University of Toronto Blues, at Calgary. The Wesmen's record winning string hits 73 games.

—The Lethbridge Pronghorns hockey team win their first University Cup with a 5-2 win over the Guelph Gryphons at Toronto.

—Philippe LaRoche retires from aerial skiing after winning the World Cup. It's a clean sweep for the Quebec Air Force as teammates Lloyd Langlois and Nicholas Fontaine, both of Magog, Que, are second and third.

—Melanie Turgeon wins the women's giant slalom at the world junior ski championships at Lake Placid, NY. It is her third medal of the competition.

—Toronto speed skater Pat Kelly, 31, wins the over-all silver medal at the Golden Skate competition in Inzell, Germany. Kelly is the son of former hockey great Red Kelly.

March 16: Kate Pace is second in the final downhill race at Vail, Col, finishing second in World Cup standings behind Germany's Katja Seizinger.

March 20: Wayne Gretzky ties Gordie Howe's record of 801 NHL goals; his second goal of the game puts the LA Kings into a 6-6 tie with the San Jose Sharks.

—The Alberta Golden Bears beat the McMaster Marauders 73-66 for their first university men's basketball title.

March 23: Wayne Gretzky scores his record 802nd goal in a 6-3 LA Kings loss to Vancouver Canucks. Gretzky now holds virtually every important career and single-season record.

—Despite Isabelle Brasseur's cracked rib, she and partner Lloyd Eisler end their amateur careers with a silver medal at the world figure skating championships in Chiba, Japan.

March 24: Elvis Stojko's brilliant free skating performance, including a 6.0 from one judge, gives him the world men's championship at Chiba, Japan.

March 26: Thomas Grandi of Banff wins the giant slalom at the US alpine ski championships in Winter Park, Col.

March 27: Marianne Limpert of Fredericton, NB wins the 100-metre individual medley in the world short course swimming championships at Paris.

March 29: Canadian Rick Fox scores a career high 33 points as the Boston Celtics beat the Milwaukee Bucks, 119-107 in overtime.

■ April

Apr 2: In the short track speed skating championships at Guildford, England, Nathalie Lambert of Montreal retires as world champion for the third time in four years, winning the 1000- and 3000-metre events. Marc Gagnon of Chicoutimi defends his world title, winning the 1000 metres. Frederic Blackburn of Chicoutimi wins the 500-metre and the women's 3000-metre relay team takes its eighth straight title.

Apr 3: Canada wins both men's and women's titles in a junior swim meet at Cadiz, Spain. In women's, Nicole Davey of Markham, Ont wins the 100M butterfly and Katie Brambley of Victoria the 200M freestyle. The men's team wins both the 4x100M medley and freestyle.

Apr 4: Toronto Blue Jays open defence of their back-to-back World Series titles with a 7-3 win over the Chicago White Sox as rookie Carlos Delgado hits a long home run. The Montreal Expos, expected to contend in the National League, fall 6-5 in 12 innings to the Houston Astros.

Apr 6: Goodwin "Goody" Rosen, who hit .325 for the Dodgers in 1945 and was the National League's all-star centre fielder, dies in Toronto at age 81.

Apr 9: Canada sweeps the world junior curling championships at Sofia, Bulgaria. The Toronto rink of Kim Gellard, Corie Beveridge, Lisa Savage and Sandy Graham beats the US 10-7 while the Edmonton quartet of Colin Davison, Kelly Mittelstadt, Scott Pfeifer and Sean Morris downs Germany 6-2.

Apr 13: The CBC wins broadcast rights for the 1996 Atlanta Summer Olympics with a bid of $20.75 million (US).

—The NHL regular season ends with the Detroit Red Wings, Calgary Flames, Pittsburgh Penguins and New York Rangers as division winners. The Rangers' 112 points leads the league. Winnipeg, Edmonton, Quebec and Ottawa all miss the playoffs. Wayne Gretzky wins his 10th scoring title with 130 points, while Vancouver's Pavel Bure leads with 60 goals.

Apr 17: Canada scores its second curling sweep in two weekends at the world championships in Oberstdorf, Germany. The Regina foursome of skip Sandra Peterson, Jan Betker, Joan McCusker and Marcia Gudereit sweeps by Scotland 5-3 while BC's Rick Folk guides his rink of Pat Ryan, Bert Gretzinger and Gerry Richard to a last rock 3-2 win over Sweden.

—The Canadian women's hockey team beats the US 6-3 for its third straight world championship at Lake Placid, NY.

Apr 28: In an NHL playoff series reminiscent of old-time hockey, Toronto Maple Leafs defeat the Chicago Black Hawks 1-0 to take the series in six games, three of them by 1-0 scores. The previous night, Buffalo and New Jersey played the sixth longest game ever, with the Sabres winning 1-0 at 5:43 of the fourth overtime.

Apr 29: Los Angeles Kings owner Bruce McNall, his financial empire crumbling, resigns as chairman of the NHL board of governors. McNall, with co-owners John Candy and Wayne Gretzky, had temporarily revived the Toronto Argonauts, which he will sell to The Sports Network on May 5.

◼ May

May 1: Makato Sasaki of Tokyo, a 22-year-old in his first marathon, wins the Vancouver Marathon in a record 2 hours, 17 mins, 24 secs.

—Golfer Barb Bunkowsky of Burlington, Ont is third in the $1.2 million Sprint Championship at Daytona Beach, Fla. It's a payday of $81,519.

May 2: Toronto's Joe Carter, who set a major league record with 31 RBIs in April, is named American League Player of the Month.

May 6: Lennox Lewis, who won a heavyweight boxing gold medal for Canada at the 1988 Olympics, retains his World Boxing Council Heavyweight title, knocking out Phil Jackson of Miami in the eighth round at Atlantic City.

May 8: Canada wins the world hockey title for the first time since 1961, defeating Finland in a shootout after the teams finish regulation and a 10-minute overtime in a 1-1 tie at Milan. Luc Robitaille scores the winning goal.

May 14: Jacques Villeneuve of St Jean, Que sets a record for fastest qualifying rookie at the Indianapolis 500, a four-lap average of 226.259MPH.

May 15: Taking its cue from the popular movie Jurassic Park, the new Toronto NBA franchise is dubbed The Raptors. The name refers to a voracious dinosaur, but is now confined to a class of birds of prey.

—Peter Maher of Thornhill, Ont wins the Toronto Marathon in 2 hours, 16 mins, 7 secs. Women's winner is Carole Rouillard of Beauport, Que in 2:32:49.

May 19: Hockey Canada suspends its investigation of Allan Eagleson due to mounting legal costs and the absence of documents from the 1987 Canada Cup.

May 22: The Kamloops Blazers defeat the Laval Titan 5-3 to win the Memorial Cup at Laval, Que. It is the second title in three years for Kamloops, which hosts next year's Cup.

May 24: The Vancouver Canucks reach the NHL finals for the first time since 1982, beating the Toronto Maple Leafs 4-3 in double overtime at Vancouver to take the series 4-1.

—Houston Rockets centre Hakeem Olajuwon

is the NBA's most valuable player, nosing out San Antonio's David Robinson and Chicago's Scottie Pippen.

—Former Detroit Pistons star guard Isiah Thomas is named general manager of the new Toronto Raptors NBA franchise.

May 26: Canada's Sports Hall of Fame names six new members: skater Kurt Browning, hockey star Bernard "Boom Boom" Geoffrion, swimmer Anne Ottenbrite, 19th century baseball star James "Tip" O'Neill, skier Karen Percy and broadcaster Rene Lecavalier, French voice of the Montreal Canadiens for four decades.

May 29: Jacques Villeneuve finishes second to Al Unser Jr in his first Indianapolis 500, averaging 160.749MPH. Canadians Paul Tracy and Scott Goodyear finish 23rd and 30th.

■ June

June 1: In the first of five exhibition matches against teams bound for soccer's World Cup, Canada ties Morocco 1-1 at Montreal.

June 4: Canada's rugby team, developing a reputation for upsets, stuns touted France 18-16 in a match at Nepean, Ont.

June 5: Canada shocks Brazil, holding soccer's top-rated team to a 1-1 draw at Edmonton.

—Sonya Jeyaseelan of Vancouver reaches the finals of the French Open junior women's event, losing 6-3, 6-1 to Switzerland's Martina Hingis. Sergi Bruguera and Arantxa Sanchez Vicario, both of Spain, take the men's and women's titles.

June 8: Canada suffers its first exhibition loss to a World Cup-bound soccer team, losing 2-0 to Germany at Toronto.

June 9: Johnny Huang of Toronto wins bronze at the world table tennis championships in Beijing, losing to China's Ma Wenge in the semi-final 21-16, 16-21, 21-17, 14-21, 21-11.

June 10: Spain beats Canada 2-0 in a World Cup tune-up in Montreal.

—In a Paris regatta, Canada finishes opening day with six gold medals, three silvers and a bronze. Former 500M K-1 champion Renn Crichlow of Nepean, Ont leads the way with two golds.

—Mark McCoy, who won a gold medal medal in the 110M hurdles for Canada at the 1992 Olympics, applies for Austrian citizenship.

June 12: Paul Tracy takes his first IndyCar race of the season, winning the ITT Automotive Detroit Grand Prix, edging Emerson Fittipaldi. The same day, Michael Schumacher of Germany wins the Canadian Grand Prix race in Montreal.

—The Netherlands World Cup squad whips a tired Canadian side 3-0 in a match at Toronto.

—Thilo Giese and Scott Davis of Vancouver sail to victory in the 470 Class at the US nationals yachting championships in, of all places, Wichita, Kansas.

—At the Canadian rowing championships in Victoria, winners are—women's: Marnie McBean, Toronto, single sculls; Julie Jesperson, Sidney BC, and Kelly Mahon, Victoria, coxed pairs; Wendy Wiebe, St Catharines, lightweight single sculls. Mens winners: Derek Porter, Victoria, single sculls; Darren Barber, Victoria, and Phil Graham, Corner Brook, Nfld, coxed pairs; Brian Peaker, London, lightweight single sculls; Gavin Hassett and Bryn Thompson, Victoria, lightweight coxed pairs.

—Led by two gold medals by Steve Giles of Lake Echo, NS, Canadian paddlers win 15 medals—six gold, five silver, four bronze—in 15 events at the Paris canoe-kayak regatta.

June 13: Jeff Fassero of the Montreal Expos loses a no-hit bid with two out in the ninth inning and two strikes on batter Carlos Garcia, who glances an infield single off Fassero's glove.

June 14: The New York Rangers end a 54-year drought, defeating the Vancouver Canucks 3-2 in the seventh game to capture the Stanley Cup. Rangers defenceman Brian Leetch wins the Conn Smythe Trophy as playoff MVP.

June 16: Sergei Fedorov, the Detroit Red Wings centre, wins the Hart Trophy as the NHL's most valuable player as well as the Selke Award as best defensive forward. Boston's Ray Bourque wins his fifth Norris Trophy as top defenceman. Other winners; Buffalo Sabres' Dominik Hasek, Vezina Trophy as best goalie; New Jersey Devils' goalie Martin Brodeur, Calder Trophy for top rookie; Jacques Lemaire of New Jersey, Jack Adams Award as best coach.

June 17: Soccer's World Cup opens in the US as a full house at Chicago's Soldier Field and a worldwide audience of 1 billion watch defending champion Germany top Bolivia

1-0. Spain and South Korea draw 2-2 in the other opener.

Jun 19: Dawn Coe-Jones of Lake Cowichan, BC is second in the LPGA Rochester International at 274, one shot behind Lisa Kiggens.

June 20: Greg Rusedski of Pt Claire, Que becomes the highest-rank Canadian men's tennis player ever, 41st in the world, as he defeats Sweden's Nicklas Kulti 6-3, 6-4, 6-2 in the opening round at Wimbledon.

June 26: In her first competition since overcoming a broken leg to win a bronze medal at the Barcelona Olympics in 1992, rower Silken Laumann of Mississauga, Ont wins the women's 2000M single sculls at an Amsterdam regatta.

June 28: In a daring draft day move, Toronto Maple Leafs trade heart and soul winger Wendel Clark to the Quebec Nordiques for centre Mats Sundin.

■ July

July 2: For the second straight year, the men's doubles team of Vancouver's Grant Connell and Patrick Martin of the US is defeated in the Wimbledon final by Australians Todd Woodbridge and Mark Woodforde, this time 7-6 (7-3), 6-3, 6-1. Martina Navratilova misses her 10th title, losing in the final to Spain's Conchita Martinez 6-4, 3-6, 6-3.

July 3: Toronto's Marnie McBean defeats Kathrin Borin of Germany by four boat lengths in the 2000-metre single sculls final at the Royal Henley Regatta in Henley, England.

July 6: A radically revamped Canadian Football League begins play with 12 teams, four of them American and three new. The hometown Ottawa Roughriders beat the Shreveport (La) Pirates 40-10.

—Leroy Burrell of the US runs the 100 metres in 9.85 seconds at a meet in Lausanne, Switzerland, breaking Carl Lewis's record of 9.86. Mark McCoy of Toronto and Austria wins the 110M hurdles in 13.19.

July 7: Baltimore's still-nameless new CFL entry opens play by defeating the Toronto Argonauts 28-20 in Toronto before a paltry 13,101 spectators.

July 8: The Las Vegas Posse make a successful CFL debut, defeating the Sacramento Gold Miners 32-26 in Sacramento.

July 10: Basqueian, ridden by Jack Lauzon and owned by business tycoon Frank Stronach, outruns favourite Bruce's Mill by seven lengths to capture the 135th Queen's Plate in Toronto.

—Sebastien Lareau of Boucherville, Que beats Patrice Boies 7-6 (7-3), 4-6, 6-3 to win the men's singles title at the SunLife Nationals in Toronto. Women's winner is Jana Nejedly of Richmond, BC, over Rene Simpson-Alter 4-6, 6-4, 6-2.

—The Montreal Expos enter baseball's all-star break in first place in the National League's Eastern Division, defeating San Diego Padres 8-2 while the Atlanta Braves fall 6-1 to the St Louis Cardinals. The Expos 54-33 record is baseball's best. Meanwhile, the Toronto Blue Jays languish in last place in the American League east at 38-48.

—Canada beats Germany 93-89 to finish undefeated in the Supercup basketball tourney in Berlin. The underdog Canadians also beat Italy and Russia.

July 12: The National League ends a six-game all-star losing streak, beating the AL 8-7 in 10 innings as Montreal's Moises Alou doubles in the winning run. It is the ninth extra-inning all-star game, all of them won by the NL. Five Expos and four Blue Jays take part in the Pittsburgh extravaganza.

July 14: The Canadian Amateur Hockey Association and Hockey Canada merge to form the Canadian Hockey Association.

—Winnipeg quarterback Matt Dunigan sets a CFL single-game passing record, throwing for 713 yards as the Bombers beat Edmonton 50-35 in Winnipeg. Dunigan shatters the mark of 601, set last season by Danny Barrett of the BC Lions.

July 16: The Shreveport Pirates, Baltimore CFL Colts and Las Vegas Posse all play their first CFL home games. Baltimore draws 39,247 while losing 42-16 to Calgary; Shreveport falls 35-34 to the Toronto Argonauts in front of 20,634 fans; and the Posse defeat Saskatchewan 32-22 before 12,213 spectators.

—The CFL Hall of Fame inducts four new members: quarterback Tom Clements and linemen Gene Gaines and Bill Baker, as well as builder Donald McNaughton.

July 17: Brazil becomes the first nation to capture four soccer World Cups, defeating Italy 3-2 in a shootout at Pasadena, Cal, after 90 minutes of play and 30 minutes of overtime failed to produce a goal. Brazilian strik-er Romario is named the tournament's top player.

—Silken Laumann defeats team-mate Marnie McBean in the single sculls final of the Rotsee Regatta in Switzerland, earning a spot in the world championships.

—Michael Andretti wins his fourth Molson Indy car race in Toronto. Canada's Paul Tracy finishes fifth.

July 22: Saskatchewan's Ray Elgaard becomes the CFL's all-time leading pass receiver, passing Rocky DiPietro's 706 in the Roughrider's 35-24 win over the Toronto Argos.

July 24: Grant Connell of Vancouver and US partner Patrick Galbraith win the doubles title at the Mason Tennis Classic in Washngton, DC.

—Canada's national student team wins the Commonwealth basketball championship over defending champion England 64-50 in Kuala Lumpur, Malaysia.

—Mississauga's Tomas Buday, 18, wins two gold medals at the world junior canoe and kayak championships in Harkstede, Netherlands, winning the C-1 1000- and 5000-metre races, as well as a silver in the C-500. Buday's father, Tamas Sr, won two bronze medals for Hungary at the 1976 Montreal Olympics.

July 28: The Supreme Court of Canada rules in favour of hockey old-timers in a $50-mil-lion plus pension lawsuit against the NHL for misappropriating funds from 700 to 800 retired players.

July 29: Canada wins the bronze medal at the world lacrosse championships at Bury, England, defeating England 25-10. The US wins gold, 21-7 over Australia.

July 30: The University of Calgary women's relay swim team sets a 4x100M freestyle record (3:51.09) at the Canadian championships in Toronto.

—Canada's Vincent Godbout captures the first degree title in the Taekwondo world championships in Kuala Lumpur, Malaysia.

July 31: Winnipeg is awarded the 1999 Pan American Games. The city also staged the Games in 1967.

—Scott Goodyear of Newmarket, Ont earns his second IndyCar victory, both in the Michigan 500 at Brooklyn, Mich.

—Karen Snelgrove of Kitchener, Ont pitches a perfect game to run Canada's record to 3-0 in a 17-0 win over the Czech Republic at the world women's softball championships in St John's.

—South Africa's Roger Wessels wins the first Canadian Masters golf championship, at Alberton, Ont, firing a 12-under 272 to beat Canada's Ray Stewart by one stroke.

—Bruce's Mill, ridden by Craig Perret, defeats Queen's Plate winner Basqueian by 4 1/2 lengths in the Prince of Wales Stakes at Fort Erie.

—Andre Agassi of the US wins the Canadian Open tennis tournament in Toronto, beating Australian Jason Stoltenberg 6-4, 6-4.

—Jon Cleveland wins his 28th Canadian swim title, leading the University of Calgary to the team crown at the Canadian champi-onships.

—BC and Ontario win the Canadian junior basketball championships at Waterloo. The BC men beat Ontario 85-71; Ontario women return the favour, 75-62.

■ August

Aug 1: Toronto's Joe Carter hits the 300th home run of his career as the Jays beat Boston 6-2.

—Canadians win 49 medals, including 20 gold, at the disabled games in Berlin.

Aug 4: The World Basketball Championships get underway in Toronto. Canada defeats Angola 83-52 in its first game.

Aug 5: Canada earns a place in the medal round at the World Basketball Championships with a 91-73 win over Argentina.

Aug 7: Toronto driver David Empringham wins the Atlantic Championship Grand Prix in Trois Rivieres, Que.

—The 112th Henley Regatta, North America's largest club rowing event, ends in St Catharines with more than 2300 rowers competing. The men's eight of dominant University of Victoria win the Ned Hanlan Memorial Trophy, while Tracey Black of the Toronto Argonaut R.C. wins three gold medals.

Aug 10: Canada's medal hopes end at the World Basketball Championships in Toronto with a 92-61 thumping at the hands of Croatia.

Aug 11: Vancouver's National Basketball Assocation franchise, to begin play in 1995-96, will be known as the Grizzlies.

Aug 12: Baseball parks are closed as the eighth work stoppage in 22 years begins. The Montreal Expos lose their final game 4-0 to Pittsburgh, but maintain baseball's best record at 74-40. The disappointing Toronto Blue Jays, 55-60, win their finale, 8-7 over the Yankees in 13 innings.

Aug 13: Glace Bay, NS wins its fourth Canadian Little League championship, beating Toronto's High Park Braves 4-0 in Calgary.

—Toronto driver Ron Fellows wins the SCAA Trans-Am race at Watkins Glen, NY, his third of the season.

Aug 14: The US Dream Team II thrashes Russia 137-91 to win the World Basketball Championship before 32,616 spectators in Toronto. Canada finishes seventh with a 104-76 win over China.

—Canada wins the women's wheelchair basketball title, 45-34 over the US in Aylesbury, England.

Aug 18: The fifteenth Commonwealth Games open in Victoria, BC. South Africa makes its first appearance since 1958. Angela Chalmers, the runner from Brandon, Man and Victoria carries Canada's flag.

Aug 19: Canada wins the first gold medal of the Commonwealth Games as Wayne Sorensen of Calgary and Jean-Francois Senecal of Laval, Que win the men's pairs air rifle event.

—Canada's women's soccer team qualifies for next year's World Cup in Sweden, defeating Trinidad and Tobago 5-0 in the regional tournament at Montreal.

Aug 20: Warren Sye of Brampton, Ont wins the 89th Canadian Amateur Golf title over Guelph's Bryan DeCorso on the first play-off hole in Ancaster, Ont.

Aug 21: Canada dominates the wrestling mat at the Commonwealth Games, winning nine of ten gold medals and a silver.

—Spain's Arantxa Sanchez Vicario defeats number one-ranked Steffi Graf 7-5, 1-6, 7-6 (7-4) in Montreal to win her second Canadian Open tennis title.

—Stella Umeh of Mississauga, Ont wins the women's all-around gymnastics gold medal at the Commonwealth Games. Umeh will win four more medals, including a gold in the vault.

—Defending champion Toronto Gators lose 5-4 to the Green Bay (Wis) Roadrunners in the world softball championship final at Summerside, PEI.

—Queen's Plate winner Basqueian, with Jack Lauzon aboard, captures the Breeders Stakes, the third leg of the Canadian Triple Crown, at Ft. Erie in 2:47 4/5.

Aug 23: Angela Chalmers defends her Commonwealth games 3000-metre title in Canadian and games record time of eight minutes, 32.17 seconds. Olympic champion Linford Christie of England wins the glamorous 100 metres in a games record 9.91 seconds.

—Canada is eliminated from contention at the Little League World Series in Williamsport, PA, losing 6-3 to a Saudi Arabian team made up of expatriate Americans. A team from Venezuela wins, defeating Northridge, Cal 4-3.

Aug 24: After a sluggish start, Michael Smith of Kenora, Ont and Toronto, defends his Commonwealth Games decathlon title.

Aug 26: Tanya Dubnicoff of Winnipeg, who had failed to defend her world sprint bicycling championship just a week earlier, wins the match sprint gold medal at the Commonwealth Games.

Aug 27: Four Canadian boxers win Commonwealth Games gold medals: featherweight Casey Patton of London, Ont, lightweight Mike Strange of Niagara Falls, middleweight Rowan Donaldson of Montreal and light heavyweight Dale Brown of Calgary.

Aug 28: On the last day of the Commonwealth Games, Canada's men's 4x100-metre relay team— Bruny Surin of Montreal, Donovan Bailey of Toronto, Glenroy Gilbert of Ottawa, Carlton Chambers of Brampton, Ont—wins the Commonwealth Games gold medal in a record 38.39 seconds. Canada finishes a distant second to Australia with 128 medals, 40 gold. The Aussies win 182, 87 of them gold.

—Martha Nause of Sheboygan, Wis wins the du Maurier Classic in Ottawa with an eight-under-par 279, one shot ahead of Michelle McGann.

Aug 31: Canadians fare well in the Commonwealth rowing championships at London, Ont, winning six women's events and four men's, with four second place finishes. Women's winners include Marnie McBean of London in single sculls, Michelle Darville of Mississauga in lightweight sculls, and the fours and eights teams. Among men's winners: Derek Porter of Victoria in single sculls and Tim Prince of St Catharines in lightweight sculls.

September

Sept 2: A 50 to 1 long shot, Rover Hanover, wins the $531,000 Metro Pace race at Toronto's Woodbine.

Sept 3: Angela Chalmers bests a strong field to win the IAAF Grand Prix 1500 meter race in Paris in a time of 4:01.61.

—David Empringham of Willowdale, Ont wins his second Players Ltd/Toyota Atlantic Championship car race of the season in Vancouver.

Sept 4: Al Unser Jr wins the Vancouver IndyCar race, his eighth win in 13 events.

—Commonwealth games gold medallist Annie Pelletier is the first Canadian to win a diving medal at the world aquatic championships in Rome, taking the bronze medal behind two Chinese divers.

Sept 8: Greg Streppel of Victoria wins the gold medal in the 25-kilometer race at the world aquatic championships, Canada's first world championship since the late Victor Davis won the 100-metre breaststroke in 1986. Streppel covers the grueling course in five hours, 35 minutes, 26.56 seconds.

Sept 10: Arantxa Sanchez Vicario of Spain wins the US Open women's tennis crown over number one seed Steffi Graf 1-6, 7-6, 6-4 at Flushing Meadow, NY.

Sept 11: Nick Price wins his sixth PGA tourney of the year and second Canadian Open with a score of 275.

—Jacques Villeneuve of Berthierville, Que wins his first IndyCar race at the Road America track in Elkhart Lake, Wis. He is the third Canadian winner this season, after Scott Goodyear of Toronto and Paul Tracey of Scarborough, Ont.

Sept 12: The Big Train, the late Lionel Conacher, voted Canada's athlete of the half-century by Canadian Press, is named to the Hockey Hall of Fame. He is joined by Harry Watson, a stalwart left winger with the Maple Leafs and Brian O'Neill, former NHL executive vice-president.

Sept 14: The major league baseball season is declared dead as players and managers remain at an impasse. For the first time since 1904, there will be no World Series.

—Six Nations Chiefs capture the Mann Cup, emblematic of Canadian lacrosse supremacy, with an 8-6 win over the New Westminster Salmonbellies to win their series 4-2.

Sept 17: Wendy Wiebe of St Catharines and Colleen Miller of Winnipeg defend their lightweight double sculls title at the world rowing championships in Indianapolis. It's the only victory for the once powerful Canadian team, which had taken four golds at each of the past two world championships and at the 1992 Olympics. Marnie McBean of London and Kathleen Heddle of Vancouver win silver in double sculls, but Silken Laumann, in a bid to regain her 1991 title, false starts twice and is disqualified in the single sculls final.

—Winnipeg sophomore running back Blaise Bryant sets a team record, running for 249 yards in the Bombers' 38-21 win over the Hamilton Tiger-Cats.

—Alison Sydor of North Vancouver wins the world's cross-country world bicycling championship at Vail, Colo in two hours, 12 minutes, seven seconds, more than three minutes ahead of the runner-up.

Sept 18: Paul Tracy wins his second IndyCar race of the season, at Nazareth, Pa, to move into third place in overall standings

—Poland's Marek Adamski wins his third straight Montreal Marathon in 2:16:03.

Sept 24: Marlene Stewart Streit, 60, of Stouffville, Ont, probably Canada's greatest woman golfer, wins the US Senior Women's Amateur Championship at St. Simons Island, Ga by two strokes in an 18-hole playoff with American Nancy Fitzgerald.

Sept 26: In an effort to fend of the loss of a storied by financially beleaguered CFL franchise, the Hamilton Tiger-Cats, averaging on 12, 000 fans per game, cut ticket prices by 33%. Unless the team boots attendance significantly and gains corporate support, it will be moved before the 1995 season.

Sept 30: Final talks collapse between players and owners as the scheduled Oct 1 start of the NHL season is officially postponed until at least Oct 15. Owners reject a proposal from players to create a pool of money for small-market teams. The decision leaves sports fans without major league baseball and hockey, and with the threat of a basketball lockout looming as well.

OLYMPICS

Summary Olympics

Year	Location	Date of competition	Competitors		Nations Repre-sented	Unofficial Winners
			Men	Women		
1896	Athens, Greece	Apr. 6–15	311	0	13	United States
1900	Paris, France	May 20–Oct. 28	1 319	11	22	United States
1904	St. Louis, United States	July 1–Nov. 23	681	6	12	United States
1906[1]	Athens, Greece	Apr. 22–May 2	877	7	20	United States
1908	London, England	Apr. 27–Oct. 31	1 999	36	23	United States
1912	Stockholm, Sweden	May 5–July 22	2 490	57	28	United States
1916	Cancelled because of World War I					
1920	Antwerp, Belgium	Apr. 20–Sept. 12	2 543	64	29	United States
1924	Paris, France	May 4–July 27	2 956	136	44	United States
1928	Amsterdam, Netherlands	May 17–Aug. 12	2 724	290	46	United States
1932	Los Angeles, United States	July 30–Aug. 14	1 281	127	37	United States
1936	Berlin, Germany	Aug. 1–16	3 738	328	49	Germany
1940	Cancelled because of World War II					
1944	Cancelled because of World War II					
1948	London, England	July 29–Aug. 14	3 714	385	59	United States
1952	Helsinki, Finland	July 19–Aug.3	4 407	518	69	United States
1956	Melbourne, Australia[2]	Nov. 22–Dec. 8	2 958	384	67	USSR
1960	Rome, Italy	Aug. 25–Sept. 11	4 738	610	83	USSR
1964	Tokyo, Japan	Oct. 10–24	4 457	683	93	United States
1968	Mexico City, Mexico	Oct. 12–27	4 750	781	112	United States
1972	Munich, West Germany	Aug. 26–Sept. 10	5 848	1 299	122	USSR
1976	Montreal, Canada	July 17–Aug. 1	4 834	1 251	92[3]	USSR
1980	Moscow, USSR	July 19–Aug. 3	4 265	1 088	81	USSR
1984	Los Angeles, United States	July 28–Aug. 12	5 458	1 620	141	United States
1988	Seoul, South Korea	Sept. 17–Oct. 2	7 105	2 476	160	USSR
1992	Barcelona, Spain	July 25–Aug. 9	7 555	3 008	172	Unified Team
1996	Atlanta, United States	July 19–Aug. 4				
2000	Sydney, Australia					

(1) 1906 Games were not recognized by the International Olympic Committee. (2) The equestrian events were held in Stockholm, Sweden, June 10–17, 1956. (3) Most sources list this figure as 88. Cameroon, Egypt, Morocco and Tunisia all boycotted the 1976 Olympics; however, their athletes had already competed before the boycott was officially announced. (n.a.) not available.

Final Medal Standings of the Summer Olympics, 1992

(Barcelona, Spain, July 25–Aug. 9, 1992)

Country	Gold	Silver	Bronze	Total	Country	Gold	Silver	Bronze	Total
Unified Team	45	38	29	112	Bulgaria	3	7	6	16
United States	37	34	37	108	Netherlands	2	6	7	15
Germany	33	21	28	82	Sweden	1	7	4	12
China	16	22	16	54	New Zealand	1	4	5	10
Cuba	14	6	11	31	North Korea	4	0	5	9
Hungary	11	12	7	30	Kenya	2	4	2	8
South Korea	12	5	12	29	Czechoslovakia	4	2	1	7
France	8	5	16	29	Norway	2	4	1	7
Australia	7	9	11	27	Turkey	2	2	2	6
Spain	13	7	2	22	Denmark	1	1	4	6
Japan	3	8	11	22	Indonesia	2	2	1	5
Britain	5	3	12	20	Finland	1	2	2	5
Italy	6	5	8	19	Jamaica	0	3	1	4
Poland	3	6	10	19	Nigeria	0	3	1	4
Canada	7	4	7	18	Brazil	2	1	0	3
Romania	4	6	8	18	Morocco	1	1	1	3

Country	Gold	Silver	Bronze	Total
Ethiopia	1	0	2	3
Latvia	0	2	1	3
Belgium	0	1	2	3
Croatia	0	1	2	3
Iran	0	1	2	3
Independent [1]	0	1	2	3
Greece	2	0	0	2
Ireland	1	1	0	2
Algeria	1	0	1	2
Estonia	1	0	1	2
Lithuania	1	0	1	2
Austria	0	2	0	2
Namibia	0	2	0	2
South Africa	0	2	0	2
Israel	0	1	1	2
Mongolia	0	0	2	2

Country	Gold	Silver	Bronze	Total
Slovenia	0	0	2	2
Switzerland	1	0	0	1
Mexico	0	1	0	1
Peru	0	1	0	1
Taiwan	0	1	0	1
Argentina	0	0	1	1
Bahamas	0	0	1	1
Colombia	0	0	1	1
Ghana	0	0	1	1
Malaysia	0	0	1	1
Pakistan	0	0	1	1
Philippines	0	0	1	1
Puerto Rico	0	0	1	1
Qatar	0	0	1	1
Suriname	0	0	1	1
Thailand	0	0	1	1

(1) Yugoslavians competed as individual athletes.

Canada's Olympic Gold Medalists, 1900–94

■ Winter Olympic Games

1920 Winnipeg Falcons, Ice Hockey (Although the Olympic Winter Games did not begin until 1924, ice hockey was an official event at the 1920 Olympic Games.)

1924 Toronto Granites, Ice Hockey

1928 University of Toronto Graduates, Ice Hockey

1932 Winnipeg Hockey Team, Ice Hockey

1948 Barbara Ann **Scott,** Women's Figure Skating; **RCAF Flyers,** Ice Hockey

1952 Edmonton Mercurys, Ice Hockey

1960 Anne **Heggtveit,** Alpine Skiing, Women's Slalom; Barbara **Wagner** & Robert **Paul,** Pairs Figure Skating

1964 Vic **Emery,** John **Emery,** Douglas **Anakin** & Peter **Kirby,** Four-Man Bobsled

1968 Nancy **Greene,** Alpine Skiing, Women's Giant Slalom

1976 Kathy **Kreiner,** Alpine Skiing, Women's Giant Slalom

1984 Gaetan **Boucher,** Speed Skating, Men's 1 000 m; Gaetan **Boucher,** Speed Skating, Men's 1 500 m

1992 Kerrin **Lee-Gartner,** Alpine Skiing, Women's Downhill; Sylvie **Daigle,** Nathalie **Lambert,** Annie **Perreault,** Angela **Cutrone,** Speed Skating, Women's Short Track Relay; Philippe **Laroche,** Freestyle Skiing, Men's Aerials (demonstration)

1994 Jean-Luc **Brassard,** Freestyle Skiing, Men's Alpine; Myriam **Bedard,** Biathlon, Women's 7.5 km Sprint; Myriam **Bedard,** Biathlon, Women's 15 km

■ Summer Olympic Games

1900 George **Orton,** 2 500 Steeplechase (Although a Canadian citizen, he represented the University of Pennsylvania; Canada did not officially appear at the Olympics until 1904.)

1904 Étienne **Desmarteau,** 56-pound Weight Throw; George **Lyon,** Golf; **The Galt Association Football Club,** Football (Soccer); **The Winnipeg Shamrocks Lacrosse Club,** Lacrosse 190; William **Sherring,** Marathon (The 1906 Games are not officially recognized by the I.O.C.)

1908 Walter **Ewing,** Trapshooting; Robert **Kerr,** Men's 200 m Run; **The All Canadas,** Lacrosse

1912 George **Goulding,** 10 000 m Walk; George **Hodgson,** Swimming, Men's 400 m Freestyle; George **Hodgson,** Swimming, Men's 1 500 m Freestyle

1920 Albert **Schneider,** Boxing, Welterweight; Earl **Thomson,** Men's 110 m Hurdles

1928 Ethel **Catherwood,** Women's High Jump; Percy **Williams,** Men's 100 m Run; Percy **Williams,** Men's 200 m Run; Women's Relay Team (Fanny **Rosenfeld,** Ethel **Smith,** Florence **Bell** & Myrtle **Cook),** Women's 4 x 100 m Relay

1932 Horace **Gwynne,** Boxing, Bantamweight; Duncan **McNaughton,** Men's High Jump

1936 Francis **Amyot,** Canoeing, Canadian Singles 1 000 m

1952 George **Genereux,** Trapshooting

1956 Gerald **Ouellette,** Small-Bore Rifle (Prone); University of British Columbia Team (Archibald **McKinnon,** Lorne **Loomer,** Walter **D'Hondt** & ▶

▶ Donald **Arnold,** Rowing, Four-Oared Shell without Coxswain

1964 George **Hungerford** & Roger **Jackson,** Rowing, Pair-Oared Shell without Coxswain

1968 Equestrian Team (James **Elder,** James **Day** & Thomas **Gayford**), Grand Prix (Jumping)

1984 Alex **Baumann,** Swimming, Men's 200 m Individual Medley; Alex **Baumann,** Swimming, Men's 400 m Individual Medley; Sylvie **Bernier,** Women's Spring-board Diving; Larry **Cain,** Canoeing, Canadian Singles 500 m; Victor **Davis,** Swimming, 200 m Breaststroke; Hugh **Fisher** & Alwyn **Morris,** Canoeing, Kayak Pairs 1 000 m; Lori **Fung,** Rhythmic Gymnastics, All-Around; Anne **Otten-brite,** Swimming, Women's 200 m Breast-stroke; Linda **Thom,** Women's Sport Pistol; National Team (Patrick **Turner,** Kevin **Neufeld,** Mark **Evans,** Grant **Main,** Paul **Steele,** J. Michael **Evans,** Dean **Crawford,** Blair **Horn** & Brian **McMahon**), Eight-Oared Shell with Coxswain

1988 Lennox **Lewis,** Boxing, Super heavyweight; Carolyn **Waldo,** Synchronized Swimming, Solo; Carolyn **Waldo** & Michelle **Cameron,** Synchronized Swimming, Duet

1992 Marnie **McBean** and Kathleen **Heddle,** Rowing, Women's Pairs; Mark **McKoy,** Track, Men's 110 m Hurdles; Mark **Tewksbury,** Swimming, Men's 100 m Backstroke; Women's Fours, Rowing (Kirsten **Barnes,** Brenda **Taylor,** Jessica **Monroe,** Kay **Worthington**); Men's Eights, Rowing (John **Wallace,** Bruce **Robertson,** Michael **Forgeron,** Darren **Barber,** Robert **Marland,** Michael **Rascher,** Andy **Crosby,** Derek **Porter,** Terry **Paul**); Women's Eights, Rowing (Kirsten **Barnes,** Brenda **Taylor,** Megan **Delehanty,** Shannon **Crawford,** Marnie **McBean,** Kay **Worthington,** Jessica **Monroe,** Kathleen **Heddle,** Lesley **Thompson**); Sylvie **Frechette,** synchronized swimming

---

Canada's 1992 Summer Olympic Medal Winners

■ Gold

Rowing, Women's Pairs Marnie McBean, Toronto, Ont., and Kathleen Heddle, Vancouver, B.C.

Rowing, Women's Fours Kirsten Barnes, Victoria, B.C.; Brenda Taylor, Sidney, B.C.; Jessica Monroe, North Vancouver, B.C.; Kay Worthington, Toronto, Ont.

Rowing, Women's Eights with Coxswain Kirsten Barnes, Victoria, B.C.; Brenda Taylor, Sidney, B.C.; Megan Delehanty, Vancouver, B.C.; Shannon Crawford, Toronto, Ont.; Marnie McBean, Toronto, Ont.; Kay Worthington, Toronto, Ont.; Jessica Monroe, North Vancouver, B.C.; Kathleen Heddle, Vancouver, B.C.; Lesley Thompson, London, Ont.

Rowing, Men's Eights with Coxswain John Wallace, Burlington, Ont.; Bruce Robertson, Victoria, B.C.; Michael Forgeron, West Vancouver, B.C.; Darren Barber, Victoria, B.C.; Robert Marland, Mississauga, Ont.; Michael Rascher, Fernie, B.C.; Andy Crosby, Hamilton, Ont.; Derek Porter, Victoria, B.C.; Terry Paul, Victoria, B.C.

Swimming, Men's 100 m Backstroke Mark Tewksbury, Calgary, Alta.

Synchronized Swimming, Solo Sylvie Frechette, Montreal, Que. (Awarded in 1993, correcting a judge's error.)

Track and Field, Men's 110 m Hurdles Mark McKoy, Toronto, Ont.

■ Silver

Boxing, Light Welterweight Mark Leduc, Toronto, Ont.

Synchronized Swimming, Duet Penny and Vicky Vilagos, Montreal, Que.

Taekwondo (demonstration sport) Marcia King, London, Ont.

Track and Field, 20 km Racewalk Guillaume Leblanc, Rimouski, Que.

Wrestling, Super Heavyweight Jeff Thue, Port Moody, B.C.

■ Bronze

Boxing, Middleweight Chris Johnson, Kitchener, Ont.

Cycling, Individual Sprint Curt Harnett, Thunder Bay, Ont.

Judo, Middleweight Nicolas Gill, Montreal, Que.

Rowing, Women's Single Sculls Silken Laumann, Mississauga, Ont.

Swimming, Men's 4 x 100-Metre Medley Relay Mark Tewksbury, Calgary, Alta.; Jon Cleveland, Calgary, Alta.; Marcel Gery, Toronto, Ont.; Stephen Clarke, Brampton, Ont.

Track and Field, 3 000 m Angela Chambers, Victoria, B.C.

Yachting, Star Ross MacDonald, Vancouver, B.C. and Eric Jesperson, Sidney, B.C.

Summer Olympic Games Champions, 1896–1992

(*indicates Olympic record; **indicates Olympic and world record)

■ Men's Track and Field Events

100-Metre Run

1896	Thomas Burke, U.S.	12.0
1900	Francis Jarvis, U.S.	11.0
1904	Archie Hanh, U.S.	11.0
1908	Reginald Walker, South Africa	10.8
1912	Raph Craig, U.S.	10.8
1920	Charles Paddock, U.S.	10.8
1924	Harold Abrahams, Great Britain	10.6
1928	**Percy Williams, Canada**	10.8
1932	Eddie Tolan, U.S.	10.3
1936	Jesse Owens, U.S.	10.3
1948	Harrison Dillard, U.S.	10.3
1952	Lindy Remigino, U.S.	10.4
1956	Bobby Morrow, U.S.	10.5
1960	Armin Hary, Germany	10.2
1964	Bob Hayes, U.S.	10.0
1968	Jim Hines, U.S.	9.95
1972	Valery Borzov, USSR	10.14
1976	Hasely Crawford, Trinidad	10.06
1980	Allan Wells, Great Britain	10.25
1984	Carl Lewis, U.S.	9.99
1988	Carl Lewis, U.S.	9.92*
1992	Linford Christie, Great Britain	9.96

200-Metre Run

1900	John Tewksbury, U.S.	22.2
1904	Archie Hahn, U.S.	21.6
1908	**Robert Kerr, Canada**	22.6
1912	Ralph Craig, U.S.	21.7
1920	Allen Woodring, U.S.	22.0
1924	Jackson Scholz, U.S.	21.6
1928	**Percy Williams, Canada**	21.8
1932	Eddie Tolan, U.S.	21.2
1936	Jesse Owens, U.S.	20.7
1948	Melvin Patton, U.S.	21.1
1952	Andrew Stanfield, U.S.	20.7
1956	Bobby Morrow, U.S.	20.6
1960	Livio Berruti, Italy	20.5
1964	Henry Carr, U.S.	20.3
1968	Tommie Smith, U.S.	19.83
1972	Valery Borzov, USSR	20.00
1976	Donald Quarrie, Jamaica	20.23
1980	Pietro Mennea, Italy	20.19
1984	Carl Lewis, U.S.	19.80
1988	Joe Deloach, U.S.	19.75
1992	Mike Marsh, U.S.	20.01*

(set Olympic record of 19.73 in semi-finals)

400-Metre Run

1896	Thomas Burke, U.S.	54.2
1900	Maxey Long, U.S.	49.4
1904	Harry Hillman, U.S.	49.2
1908	Wyndham Halswelle, Great Britain	50.0
1912	Charles Reidpath, U.S.	48.2
1920	Bevil Rudd, South Africa	49.6
1924	Eric Liddell, Great Britain	47.6
1928	Ray Barbuti, U.S.	47.8
1932	William Carr, U.S.	46.2
1936	Archie Williams, U.S.	46.5
1948	Arthur Wint, Jamaica	46.2
1952	George Rhoden, Jamaica	45.9
1956	Charles Jenkins, U.S.	46.7
1960	Otis Davis, U.S.	44.9
1964	Michael Larrabee, U.S.	45.1
1968	Lee Evans, U.S.	43.86*
1972	Vincent Matthews, U.S.	44.66
1976	Alberto Juantorena, Cuba	44.26
1980	Viktor Markin, USSR	44.60
1984	Alonzo Babers, U.S.	44.27
1988	Steven Lewis, U.S.	43.87
1992	Quincy Watts, U.S.	43.50*

800-Metre Run

1896	Edwin Flack, Australia.	2:11.0
1900	Alfred Tysoe, Great Britain	2:01.2
1904	James Lightbody, U.S.	1:56.0
1908	Mel Sheppard, U.S.	1:52.8
1912	Ted Meredith, U.S.	1:51.9
1920	Albert Hill, Great Britain	1:53.4
1924	Douglas Lowe, Great Britain	1:52.4
1928	Douglas Lowe, Great Britain	1:51.8
1932	Thomas Hampson, Great Britain	1:49.7
1936	John Woodruff, U.S.	1:52.9
1948	Mal Whitfield, U.S.	1:49.2
1952	Mal Whitfield, U.S.	1:49.2
1956	Thomas Courtney, U.S.	1:47.7
1960	Peter Snell, New Zealand	1:46.3
1964	Peter Snell, New Zealand	1:45.1
1968	Ralph Doubell, Australia	1:44.3
1972	Dave Wottle, U.S.	1:45.9
1976	Alberto Juantorena, Cuba	1:43.5
1980	Steve Ovett, Great Britain	1:45.4
1984	Joaquim Cruz, Brazil	1:43.0*
1988	Paul Ereng, Kenya	1:43.45
1992	William Tanui, Kenya	1:43.66

1 500-Metre Run

1896	Edwin Flack, Australia	4:33.2
1900	Charles Bennett, Great Britain	4:06.2
1904	James Lightbody, U.S.	4:05.4
1908	Mel Sheppard, U.S.	4:03.4
1912	Arnold Jackson, Great Britain	3:56.8
1920	Albert Hill, Great Britain	4:01.8
1924	Paavo Nurmi, Finland	3:53.6
1928	Harry Larva, Finland	3:53.2
1932	Luigi Beccali, Italy	3:51.2
1936	Jack Lovelock, New Zealand	3:47.8
1948	Henry Eriksson, Sweden	3:49.8
1952	Josef (Josy) Barthel, Luxembourg	3:45.1
1956	Ron Delany, Ireland	3:41.2
1960	Herb Elliott, Australia	3:35.6
1964	Peter Snell, New Zealand	3:38.1
1968	Kipchoge Keino, Kenya	3:34.9

1972	Pekka Vasala, Finland	3:36.3
1976	John Walker, New Zealand	3:39.17
1980	Sebastian Coe, Great Britain	3:38.4
1984	Sebastian Coe, Great Britain	3:32.53*
1988	Peter Rono, Kenya	3:35.96
1992	Fermin Cacho Ruiz, Spain	3:40.12

3 000-Metre Steeplechase

1920	Percy Hodge, Great Britain	10:00.4
1924	Ville Ritola, Finland	9:33.6
1928	Toivo Loukola, Finland	9:21.8
1932	Volmari Iso-Hollo, Finland	10:33.4
	(About 3 460 m extra lap by error)	
1936	Volmari Iso-Hollo, Finland	9:03.8
1948	Thore Sjöstrand, Sweden	9:04.6
1952	Horace Ashenfelter, U.S.	8:45.4
1956	Chris Brasher, Great Britain	8:41.2
1960	Zdzislaw Krzyszkowiak, Poland	8:34.2
1964	Gaston Roelants, Belgium	8:30.8
1968	Amos Biwott, Kenya	8:51.0
1972	Kipchoge Keino, Kenya	8:23.6
1976	Anders Gärderud, Sweden	8:08.2
1980	Bronislaw Malinowski, Poland	8:09.7
1984	Julius Korir, Kenya	8:11.80
1988	Julius Kariuki, Kenya	8:05.51*
1992	Matthew Birir, Kenya	8:08:84

5 000-Metre Run

1912	Johannes Kolehmainen, Finland	14:36.6
1920	Joseph Guillemot, France	14:55.6
1924	Paavo Nurmi, Finland	14:31.2
1928	Ville Ritola, Finland	14:38.0
1932	Lauri Lehtinen, Finland	14:30.0
1936	Gunnar Höckert, Finland	14:22.2
1948	Gaston Reiff, Belgium	14:17.6
1952	Emil Zátopek, Czechoslovakia	14:06.6
1956	Vladimir Kuts, USSR	13:39.6
1960	Murray Halberg, New Zealand	13:43.4
1964	Bob Schul, U.S.	13:48.8
1968	Mohamed Gammoudi, Tunisia	14:05.0
1972	Lasse Viren, Finland	13:26.4
1976	Lasse Viren, Finland	13:24.76
1980	Miruts Yifter, Ethiopia	13:21.0
1984	Said Aouita, Morocco	13:05.59*
1988	John Ngugi, Kenya	13:11.70
1992	Dieter Baumann, Germany	13:12.52

10 000-Metre Run

1912	Johannes Kolehmainen, Finland	31:20.8
1920	Paavo Nurmi, Finland	31:45.8
1924	Ville Ritola, Finland	30:23.2
1928	Paavo Nurmi, Finland	30:18.8
1932	Janusz Kusocinski, Poland	30:11.4
1936	Ilmari Salminen, Finland	30:15.4
1948	Emil Zátopek, Czechoslovakia	29:59.6
1952	Emil Zátopek, Czechoslovakia	29:17.0
1956	Vladimir Kuts, USSR	28:45.6
1960	Ptyor Bolotnikov, USSR	28:32.2
1964	Billy Mills, U.S.	28:24.4
1968	Naftali Temu, Kenya	29:27.4
1972	Lasse Viren, Finland	27:38.4
1976	Lasse Viren, Finland	27:40.38

1980	Miruts Yifter, Ethiopia	27:42.7
1984	Alberto Cova, Italy	27:47.54
1988	M. Brahim Boutaib, Morocco	27:21.46*
1992	Khalid Skah, Morocco	27:46.7

Marathon

1896	Spiridon Louis, Greece	2:58:50
1900	Michel Théato, France	2:59:45
1904	Thomas Hicks, U.S.	3:28:63
1908	John Hayes, U.S.	2:55:18.4
1912	Kenneth McArthur, South Africa	2:36:54.8
1920	Johannes Kolehmainen, Finland	2:32:35.8
1924	Albin Stenroos, Finland	2:41:22.6
1928	Boughèra El Ouafi, France	2:32:57.0
1932	Juan Zabala, Argentina	2:31:36.0
1936	Kee-Chung Sohn (Kitei Son), Japan/Korea	2:29:19.2
1948	Delfo Cabrera, Argentina	2:34:51.6
1952	Emil Zátopek, Czechoslovakia	2:23:03.2
1956	Alain Mimoun, France	2:25:00.0
1960	Abebe Bikila, Ethiopia	2:15:16.2
1964	Abebe Bikila, Ethiopia	2:12:11.2
1968	Mamo Wolde, Ethiopia	2:20:26.4
1972	Frank Shorter, U.S.	2:12:19.8
1976	Waldemar Cierpinski, E. Germany	2:09:55.0
1980	Waldemar Cierpinski, E. Germany	2:11:03.0
1984	Carlos Lopes, Portugal	2:09:21.0*
1988	Gelindo Bordin, Italy	2:10.32
1992	Hwang Young-cho, S. Korea	2:13:23.0

20-Kilometre Walk

1956	Leonid Spirin, USSR	1:31:27.4
1960	Vladimir Golubnichiy, USSR	1:34:07.2
1964	Kenneth Mathews, Great Britain	1:29:34.0
1968	Vladimir Golubnichiy, USSR	1:33:58.4
1972	Peter Frenkel, E. Germany	1:26:42.4
1976	Daniel Bautista, Mexico	1:24:40.6
1980	Maurizio Damilano, Italy	1:23:35.5
1984	Ernesto Canto, Mexico	1:23:13.0
1988	Jozef Pribilinec, Czechoslovakia	1:19:57.0*
1992	Daniel Plaza, Spain	1:21:45.0

50-Kilometre Walk

1932	Thomas Green, Great Britain	4:50:10
1936	Harold Whitlock, Great Britain	4:30:41.4
1948	John Ljunggren, Sweden	4:41.52
1952	Giuseppe Dordoni, Italy	4:28:07.8
1956	Norman Read, New Zealand	4:30:42.8
1960	Donald Thompson, Great Britain	4:25:30.0
1964	Abdon Pamich, Italy	4:11:12.4
1968	Christoph Höhne, E. Germany	4:20:13.6
1972	Bernd Kannenberg, W. Germany	3:56:11.6
1980	Hartwig Gauder, E. Germany	3:49:24.0
1984	Raúl González, Mexico	3:47:26.0
1988	Viacheslav Ivanenko, USSR	3:38:29.0
1992	Andrei Perlov, Unified Team	3:50:13.0

110-Metre Hurdles

1896	Thomas Curtis, U.S.	17.6
1900	Alvin Kraenzlein, U.S.	15.4
1904	Frederick Schule, U.S.	16.0
1908	Forrest Smithson, U.S.	15.0

1912	Frederick Kelly, U.S.	15.1
1920	**Earl Thomson, Canada**	14.8
1924	Daniel Kinsey, U.S.	15.0
1928	Sydney Atkinson, South Africa	14.8
1932	George Saling, U.S.	14.6
1936	Forrest Towns, U.S.	14.2
1948	William Porter, U.S.	13.9
1952	Harrison Dillard, U.S.	13.7
1956	Lee Calhoun, U.S.	13.5
1960	Lee Calhoun, U.S.	13.8
1964	Hayes Jones, U.S.	13.6
1968	Willie Davenport, U.S.	13.3
1972	Rod Milburn, U.S.	13.24
1976	Guy Drut, France	13.30
1980	Thomas Munkelt, E. Germany	13.39
1984	Roger Kingdom, U.S.	13.20
1988	Roger Kingdom, U.S.	12.98*
1992	**Mark McKoy, Canada**	13.12

400-Metre Hurdles

1900	John Tewksbury, U.S.	57.6
1904	Harry Hillman, U.S.	53.0
1908	Charles Bacon, U.S.	55.0
1920	Frank Loomis, U.S.	54.0
1924	F. Morgan Taylor, U.S.	52.6
1928	Lord David Burghley, Great Britain	53.4
1932	Robert Tisdall, Ireland	51.7
1936	Glenn Hardin, U.S.	52.4
1948	Roy Cochran, U.S.	51.1
1952	Charles Moore, U.S.	50.8
1956	Glenn Davis, U.S.	50.1
1960	Glenn Davis, U.S.	49.3
1964	Rex Cawley, U.S.	49.6
1968	David Hemery, Great Britain	48.12
1972	John Akii-Bua, Uganda	47.82
1976	Edwin Moses, U.S.	47.64
1980	Volker Beck, E. Germany	48.70
1984	Edwin Moses, U.S.	47.75
1988	Andre Phillips, U.S.	47.19
1992	Kevin Young, U.S.	46.78**

High Jump

1896	Ellery Clark, U.S.	1.81 m
1904	Samuel Jones, U.S.	1.90 m
1908	Harry Porter, U.S.	1.80 m
1912	Alma Richards, U.S.	1.90 m
1920	Richmond Landon, U.S.	1.93 m
1924	Harold Osborn, U.S.	1.93 m
1928	Robert King, U.S.	1.94 m
1932	**Duncan McNaughton, Canada**	1.97 m
1936	Cornelius Johnson, U.S.	2.03 m
1948	John Winter, Australia	1.98 m
1952	Walter Davis, U.S.	2.04 m
1956	Charles Dumas, U.S.	2.12 m
1960	Robert Shavlakadze, USSR	2.16 m
1964	Valery Brumel, USSR	2.18 m
1968	Dick Fosbury, U.S.	2.24 m
1972	Yuri Tarmak, USSR	2.23 m
1976	Jacek Wszola, Poland	2.25 m
1980	Gerd Wessig, E. Germany	2.36 m
1984	Dietmar Mögenburg, W. Germany	2.35 m

1988	Guennadi Avdeenko, USSR	2.38 m*
1992	Javier Soto-Mayor, Cuba	2.34 m

Long Jump

1896	Ellery Clark, U.S.	6.35 m
1900	Alvin Kraenzlein, U.S.	7.18 m
1904	Meyer Prinstein, U.S.	7.34 m
1908	Frank Irons, U.S.	7.48 m
1912	Albert Gutterson, U.S.	7.60 m
1920	William Petersson, Sweden	7.15 m
1924	William De Hart Hubbard, U.S.	7.44 m
1928	Edward Hamm, U.S.	7.73 m
1932	Edward Gordon, U.S.	7.64 m
1936	Jesse Owens, U.S.	8.06 m
1948	Willie Steele, U.S.	7.82 m
1952	Jerome Biffle, U.S.	7.57 m
1956	Gregory Bell, U.S.	7.83 m
1960	Ralph Boston, U.S.	8.12 m
1964	Lynn Davies, Great Britain	8.07 m
1968	Bob Beamon, U.S.	8.90 m*
1972	Randy Williams, U.S.	8.24 m
1976	Arnie Robinson, U.S.	8.35 m
1980	Lutz Dombrowski, E. Germany	8.54 m
1984	Carl Lewis, U.S.	8.54 m
1988	Carl Lewis, U.S.	8.72 m
1992	Carl Lewis, U.S.	8.67 m

4 x 100-Metre Relay

1912	Great Britain	42.4
1920	United States	42.2
1924	United States	41.0
1928	United States	41.0
1932	United States	40.0
1936	United States	39.8
1948	United States	40.6
1952	United States	40.1
1956	United States	39.5
1960	Germany	39.5
1964	United States	39.0
1968	United States	38.2
1972	United States	38.19
1976	United States	38.33
1980	USSR	38.26
1984	United States	37.83
1988	USSR	38.19
1992	United States	37.40**

4 x 400-Metre Relay

1908	United States (medley relay)	3:29.4
1912	United States	3:16.6
1920	Great Britain	3:22.2
1924	United States	3:16.0
1928	United States	3:14.2
1932	United States	3:08.2
1936	Great Britain	3:09.0
1948	United States	3:10.4
1952	Jamaica	3:03.9
1956	United States	3:04.8
1960	United States	3:02.2
1964	United States	3:00.7
1968	United States	2:56.16*
1972	Kenya	2:59.8

1976	United States	2:58.65
1980	USSR	3:01.1
1984	United States	2:57.91
1988	United States	2:56.16
1992	United States	2:55.74**

Pole Vault

1896	William Hoyt, U.S.	3.30 m
1900	Irving Baxter, U.S.	3.30 m
1904	Charles Dvorak, U.S.	3.50 m
1908	Alfred Gilbert, U.S.	
	Edward Cooke, U.S.	3.71 m
1912	Harry Babcock, U.S.	3.95 m
1920	Frank Foss, U.S.	4.09 m
1924	Lee Barnes, U.S.	3.95 m
1928	Sabin Carr, U.S.	4.20 m
1932	William Miller, U.S.	4.31 m
1936	Earle Meadows, U.S.	4.35 m
1948	Guinn Smith, U.S.	4.30 m
1952	Robert Richards, U.S.	4.55 m
1956	Robert Richards, U.S.	4.56 m
1960	Don Bragg, U.S.	4.70 m
1964	Fred Hansen, U.S.	5.10 m
1968	Bob Seagren, U.S.	5.40 m
1972	Wolfgang Nordwig, E. Germany	5.50 m
1976	Tadeusz Slusarski, Poland	5.50 m
1980	Wladyslaw Kozakiewicz, Poland	5.78 m
1984	Pierre Quinon, France	5.75 m
1988	Sergey Bubka, USSR	5.90 m*
1992	Maxim Tarassov, Unified Team	5.80 m

Hammer Throw

1900	John Flanagan, U.S.	49.73 m
1904	John Flanagan, U.S.	51.23 m
1908	John Flanagan, U.S.	51.92 m
1912	Matt McGrath, U.S.	54.74 m
1920	Pat Ryan, U.S.	52.87 m
1924	Fred Tootell, U.S.	53.295 m
1928	Patrick O'Callaghan, Ireland	51.39 m
1932	Patrick O'Callaghan, Ireland	53.92 m
1936	Karl Hein, Germany	56.49 m
1948	Imre Németh, Hungary	56.07 m
1952	József Csérmák, Hungary	60.34 m
1956	Harold Connolly, U.S.	63.19 m
1960	Vasily Rudenkov, USSR	67.10 m
1964	Romuald Klim, USSR	69.74 m
1968	Gyula Zsivótsky, Hungary	73.36 m
1972	Anatoly Bondarchuk, USSR	75.50 m
1976	Yuri Sedykh, USSR	77.52 m
1980	Yuri Sedykh, USSR	81.80 m
1984	Juha Tiainen, Finland	78.08 m
1988	Serguei Litvinov, USSR	84.80 m*
1992	Andrey Abduvaliyev, Unified Team	82.54 m

Discus Throw

1896	Robert Garrett, U.S.	29.15 m
1900	Rudolf (Rezsö) Bauer, Hungary	36.04 m
1904	Martin Sheridan, U.S.	39.28 m
1908	Martin Sheridan, U.S.	40.89 m
1912	Armas Taipale, Finland	45.21 m
1920	Elmer Niklander, Finland	44.685 m
1924	Clarence "Bud" Houser, U.S.	46.15 m

1928	Clarence "Bud" Houser, U.S.	47.32 m
1932	John Anderson, U.S.	49.49 m
1936	Ken Carpenter, U.S.	50.48 m
1948	Adolfo Consolini, Italy	52.78 m
1952	Sim Iness, U.S.	55.03 m
1956	Al Oerter, U.S.	56.36 m
1960	Al Oerter, U.S.	59.18 m
1964	Al Oerter, U.S.	61.00 m
1968	Al Oerter, U.S.	64.78 m
1972	Ludvik Danek, Czechoslovakia	64.40 m
1976	Mac Wilkins, U.S.	67.50 m
1980	Viktor Rashchupkin, USSR	66.64 m
1984	Rolf Dannenberg, W. Germany	66.60 m
1988	Jurgen Schult, E. Germany	68.82 m*
1992	Romas Ubartas, Lithuania	65.12 m

Triple Jump

1896	James Connolly, U.S.	13.71 m
1900	Meyer Prinstein, U.S.	14.47 m
1904	Meyer Prinstein, U.S.	14.35 m
1908	Timothy Ahearne, Great Britain/Ireland	14.92 m
1912	Gustaf Lindblom, Sweden	14.76 m
1920	Vilho Tuulos, Finland	14.50 m
1924	Anthony Winter, Australia	15.52 m
1928	Mikio Oda, Japan	15.21 m
1932	Chuhei Nambu, Japan	15.72 m
1936	Naoto Tajima, Japan	16.00 m
1948	Arne A"hman, Sweden	15.40 m
1952	Adhemar Ferriera da Silva, Brazil	16.22 m
1956	Adhemar Ferriera da Silva, Brazil	16.35 m
1960	József Schmidt, Poland	16.81 m
1964	József Schmidt, Poland	16.85 m
1968	Viktor Saneyev, USSR	17.39 m
1972	Viktor Saneyev, USSR	17.35 m
1976	Viktor Saneyev, USSR	17.29 m
1980	Jaak Uudmaë, USSR	17.35 m
1984	Al Joyner, U.S.	17.26 m
1988	Hristo Markov, Bulgaria	17.61 m
1992	Mike Conley, U.S.	18.17 m

(wind-aided; earlier set Olympic record 17.63 m)

16 lb Shot Put

1896	Robert Garrett, U.S.	11.22 m
1900	Richard Sheldon, U.S.	14.10 m
1904	Ralph Rose, U.S.	14.81 m
1908	Ralph Rose, U.S.	14.21 m
1912	Pat McDonald, U.S.	15.34 m
1920	Ville Pörhölä, Finland	14.81 m
1924	Clarence "Bud" Houser, U.S.	14.99 m
1928	John Kuck, U.S.	15.87 m
1932	Leo Sexton, U.S.	16.00 m
1936	Hans Woellke, Germany	16.20 m
1948	Wilbur Thompson, U.S.	17.12 m
1952	Parry O'Brien, U.S.	17.41 m
1956	Parry O'Brien, U.S.	18.57 m
1960	William Nieder, U.S.	19.68 m
1964	Dallas Long, U.S.	20.33 m
1968	Randy Matson, U.S.	20.54 m
1972	Wladyslaw Komar, Poland	21.18 m
1976	Udo Beyer, E. Germany	21.05 m
1980	Vladimir Kiselyov, USSR	21.35 m
1984	Alessandro Andrei, Italy	21.26 m

1988 Ulf Timmermann, E. Germany .... 22.47 m*
1992 Mike Stulce, U.S. .... 21.70 m

Javelin

1908 Erik Lemming, Sweden .... 54.82 m
1912 Erik Lemming, Sweden .... 60.64 m
1920 Jonni Myyrä, Finland .... 65.78 m
1924 Jonni Myyrä, Finland .... 62.96 m
1928 Eric Lundkvist, Sweden .... 66.60 m
1932 Matti Järvinen, Finland .... 72.71 m
1936 Gerhard Stöck, Germany .... 71.84 m
1948 Kai Rautavaara, Finland .... 69.77 m
1952 Cy Young, U.S. .... 73.78 m
1956 Egil Danielson, Norway .... 85.71 m
1960 Viktor Tsibulenko, USSR .... 84.64 m
1964 Pauli Nevala, Finland .... 82.66 m
1968 Janis Losis, USSR .... 90.10 m
1972 Klaus Wolfermann, W. Germany ..... 90.48 m
1976 Miklos Németh, Hungary .... 94.58 m*
1980 Dainis Kula, USSR .... 91.20 m
1984 Arto Härkönen, Finland .... 86.76 m
1988 Tapio Korjus, Finland .... 84.28 m
1992 Jan Zelezny, Czechoslovakia .... 89.66 m

Decathlon

		Points
1904	Thomas Kiely, Ireland	6 036[1]
1908	not held	
1912	Hugo Wieslander, Sweden	7 724[2]
1920	Helge Lövland, Norway	6 803
1924	Harold Osborn, U.S.	7 711
1928	Paavo Yrjölä, Finland	8 053
1932	James Bausch, U.S.	8 462
1936	Glenn Morris, U.S.	7 900
1948	Robert Mathias, U.S.	7 139
1952	Robert Mathias, U.S.	7 887
1956	Milton Campbell, U.S.	7 937
1960	Rafer Johnson, U.S.	8 392
1964	Willi Holdorf, Germany	7 887
1968	Bill Toomey, U.S.	8 193
1972	Nikolai Avilov, USSR	8 454
1976	Bruce Jenner, U.S.	8 617
1980	Daley Thompson, Great Britain	8 495
1984	Daley Thompson, Great Britain	8 798[*3]
1988	Christian Schenk, E. Germany	8 488
1992	Robert Zmelik, Czechoslovakia	8 611

Former point systems used prior to 1964.

(1) All 10 events held on same day. (2) Jim Thorpe of the U.S. won the 1912 Decathlon with 8 412 pts. but was disqualified and had to return his medals because he had played professional baseball prior to the Olympic games. The medals were restored posthumously in 1982. (3) Scoring change effective Apr., 1985.

■ Women's Track and Field Events

100-Metre Run

1928 Elizabeth Robinson, U.S.............. 12.2
1932 Stella Walsh (Stanislawa Walasiewicz), Poland . 11.9
1936 Helen Stephens, U.S.............. 11.5
1948 Francina "Fanny" Blankers-Koen, Netherlands . 11.9
1952 Marjorie Jackson, Australia 11.5
1956 Betty Cuthbert, Australia 11.5

1960 Wilma Rudolph, U.S. 11.0
1964 Wyomia Tyus, U.S. 11.4
1968 Wyomia Tyus, U.S. 11.0
1972 Renate Stecher, E. Germany 11.07
1976 Annegret Richter, W. Germany 11.08
1980 Lyudmila Kondratyeva, USSR 11.06
1984 Evelyn Ashford, U.S. 10.97
1988 Florence Griffith-Joyner, U.S. 10.54
1992 Gail Devers, U.S. 10.82

200-Metre Run

1948 Francina "Fanny" Blankers-Koen, Netherlands . 24.4
1952 Marjorie Jackson, Australia 23.7
1956 Betty Cuthbert, Australia 23.4
1960 Wilma Rudolph, U.S. 24.0
1964 Edith McGuire, U.S. 23.0
1968 Irena Szewinska, Poland 22.5
1972 Renate Stecher, E. Germany 22.40
1976 Bärbel Eckert, E. Germany 22.37
1980 Bärbel Wockel (Eckert), E. Germany 22.03
1984 Valerie Brisco-Hooks, U.S. 21.81
1988 Florence Griffith-Joyner, U.S. 21.34*
1992 Gwen Torrence, U.S. 21.81

400-Metre Run

1964 Betty Cuthbert, Australia 52.0
1968 Colette Besson, France 52.0
1972 Monika Zehrt, E. Germany 51.08
1976 Irena Szewinska, Poland 49.29
1980 Marita Koch, E. Germany 48.88
1984 Valerie Brisco-Hooks, U.S. 48.83
1988 Olga Bryzguina, USSR 48.65*
1992 Marie-Jose Perec, France 48.83

800-Metre Run

1928 Lina Radke, Germany 2:16.8
1960 Lyudmila Shevtsova, USSR 2:04.3
1964 Ann Packer, Great Britain 2:01.1
1968 Madeline Manning, U.S. 2:00.9
1972 Hildegard Falck, W. Germany 1:58.55
1976 Tatyana Kazankina, USSR 1:54.94
1980 Nadezhda Olizarenko, USSR 1:53.42*
1984 Doina Melinte, Romania 1:57.6
1988 Sigrun Wodars, E. Germany 1:56.10
1992 Ellen Van Langen, Netherlands 1:55.54

1 500-Metre Run

1972 Lyudmila Bragina, USSR 4:01.4
1976 Tatyana Kazankina, USSR 4:05.48
1980 Tatyana Kazankina, USSR 3:56.6
1984 Gabriella Dorio, Italy 4:03.25
1988 Paula Ivan, Romania 3:53.96*
1992 Hassiba Boulmerka, Algeria 3:55.30

3 000-Metre Run

1984 Maricica Puica, Romania 8:35.96
1988 Tatiana Samolenko, USSR 8:26.53*
1992 Elena Romanova, Unified Team 8:46.04

10 000-Metre Run

1988 Olga Bondarenko, USSR 31:05.21*
1992 Derartu Tulu, Ethiopia 31:06.02

4 x 100-Metre Relay

1928	Canada	48.4
1932	United States	46.9
1936	United States	46.9
1948	Netherlands	47.5
1952	United States	45.9
1956	Australia	44.5
1960	United States	44.5
1964	Poland	43.6
1968	United States	42.8
1972	West Germany	42.81
1976	East Germany	42.55
1980	East Germany	41.60*
1984	United States	41.65
1988	United States	41.98
1992	United States	42.11

4 x 400-Metre Relay

1972	East Germany	3:23.0
1976	East Germany	3:19.23
1980	USSR	3:20.2
1984	United States	3:18.29
1988	USSR	3:15.18*
1992	Unified Team	3:20.20

80-Metre Hurdles

1932	Mildred "Babe" Didriksen, U.S.	11.7
1936	Trebisonda Valla, Italy	11.7
1948	Francina "Fanny" Blankers-Koen, Netherlands	11.2
1952	Shirley Strickland, Australia	10.9
1956	Shirley Strickland, Australia	10.7
1960	Irina Press, USSR	10.8
1964	Karin Balzer, E. Germany	10.5
1968	Maureen Caird, Australia	10.3*

100-Metre Hurdles

1972	Annelie Ehrhardt, E. Germany	12.59
1976	Johanna Schaller, E. Germany	12.77
1980	Vera Komisova, USSR	12.56
1984	Benita Brown-Fitzgerald, U.S.	12.84
1988	Jordanka Donkova, Bulgaria	12.38*
1992	Paraskevi Patoulidou, Greece	12.64

400-Metre Hurdles

1984	Nawal El Moutawakel, Morocco	54.61
1988	Debra Flintoff-King, Australia	53.17*
1992	Sally Gunnell, Great Britain	53.23

High Jump

1928	Ethel Catherwood, Canada	1.59 m
1932	Jean Shiley, U.S.	1.657 m
1936	Ibolya Csák, Hungary	1.60 m
1948	Alice Coachman, U.S.	1.68 m
1952	Esther Brand, South Africa	1.67 m
1956	Mildred McDaniel, U.S.	1.76 m
1960	Iolanda Balas, Romania	1.85 m
1964	Iolanda Balas, Romania	1.90 m
1968	Miloslava Rezková, Czechoslovakia	1.82 m
1972	Ulrike Meyfarth, W. Germany	1.92 m
1976	Rosemarie Ackermann, E. Germany	1.93 m
1980	Sara Simeoni, Italy	1.97 m
1984	Ulrike Meyfarth, W. Germany	2.02 m
1988	Louise Ritter, U.S.	2.03 m*
1992	Heike Henkel, Germany	2.02 m

Discus Throw

1928	Halina Konopacka, Poland	39.62 m
1932	Lillian Copeland, U.S.	40.58 m
1936	Gisela Mauermayer, Germany	47.63 m
1948	Micheline Ostermeyer, France	41.92 m
1952	Nina Romashkova, USSR	51.42 m
1956	Olga Fikotová, Czechoslovakia	53.69 m
1960	Nina Ponomaryeva, USSR	55.10 m
1964	Tamara Press, USSR	57.27 m
1968	Lia Manoliu, Romania	58.28 m
1972	Faina Melnik, USSR	66.62 m
1976	Evelin Schlaak, E. Germany	69.00 m
1980	Evelin Jahl (Schlaak), E. Germany	69.96 m
1984	Ria Stalman, Netherlands	65.36 m
1988	Martina Hellman, E. Germany	72.30 m*
1992	Maritza Marten Garcia, Cuba	70.06 m

Javelin Throw

1932	Mildred "Babe" Didriksen, U.S.	43.68 m
1936	Tilly Fleischer, Germany	45.57 m
1952	Dana Zátopková, Czechoslovakia	50.47 m
1956	Inese Jaunzeme, USSR	53.86 m
1960	Elvira Ozolina, USSR	55.98 m
1964	Mihaela Penes, Romania	60.54 m
1968	Angéla Németh, Hungary	60.36 m
1972	Ruth Fuchs, E. Germany	63.88 m
1976	Ruth Fuchs, E. Germany	65.94 m
1980	Maria Colon Rueñes, Cuba	68.40 m
1984	Tessa Sanderson, Great Britain	69.54 m
1988	Petra Felke, E. Germany	74.68 m*
1992	Silke Renk, Germany	68.34 m

Shot Put (4 kg)

1948	Micheline Ostermeyer, France	13.75 m
1952	Galina Zybina, USSR	15.28 m
1956	Tamara Tishkevich, US.	16.59 m
1960	Tamara Press, USSR	17.32 m
1964	Tamara Press, USSR	18.14 m
1968	Margitta Gummel, E. Germany	19.61 m
1972	Nadezhda Chizhova, USSR	21.03 m
1976	Ivanka Hristova, Bulgaria	21.16 m
1980	Ilona Slupianek, E. Germany	22.41 m*
1984	Claudia Losch, W. Germany	20.47 m
1988	Natalia Lisovskaya, USSR	22.24 m
1992	Svetlana Kriveleva, Unified Team	21.06m

Long Jump

1948	Olga Gyarmati, Hungary	5.695 m
1952	Yvette Williams, New Zealand	6.24 m
1956	Elzbieta Krzeskinska, Poland	6.35 m
1960	Vyera Krepkina, USSR	6.37 m
1964	Mary Rand, Great Britain	6.76 m
1968	Viorica Viscopoleanu, Romania	6.82 m
1972	Heidemarie Rosendahl, W. Germany	6.78 m
1976	Angela Voigt, E. Germany	6.72 m
1980	Tatiana Kolpakova, USSR	7.06 m
1984	Anisoara-cusmir-Stanciu, Romania	6.96 m
1988	Jackie Joyner-Kersee, U.S.	7.40 m*
1992	Heike Drechsler, Germany	7.14 m

Pentathlon

		Points
1964	Irina Press, USSR	5 246
1968	Ingrid Becker, W. Germany	5 098
1972	Mary Peters, England	4 801
1976	Sigrun Siegl, E. Germany	4 745
1980	Nadezhda Tkachenko, USSR	5 083*

Heptathlon

		Points
1984	Glynis Nunn, Australia	6 390
1988	Jackie Joyner-Kersee, U.S.	7 291*
1992	Jackie Joyner-Kersee, U.S.	7 044

Marathon

1984	Joan Benoit, U.S.	2:24:52*
1988	Rosa Mota, Portugal	2:25.40
1992	Valentina Yegorova, Unified Team	2:32.41

10-kilometre Walk

1992	Chen Yueling, China	44:32

Former point system, 1964–68

■ Men's Swimming

50-Metre Freestyle

1904	Zoltán Halmay, Hungary	28.0
1988	Matt Biondi, U.S.	22.14
1992	Alexander Popov, Unified Team	21.91*

100-Metre Freestyle

1896	Alfréd Hajós, Hungary	1:22.2
1904	Zoltán Halmay, Hungary (100 yards)	1:02.8
1906	Charles Daniels, U.S.	1:13.4
1908	Charles Daniels, U.S.	1:05.6
1912	Duke Paoa Kahanamoku, U.S.	1:03.4
1920	Duke Paoa Kahanamoku, U.S.	1:01.4
1924	Johnny Weissmuller, U.S.	59.0
1928	Johnny Weissmuller, U.S.	58.6
1932	Yasuji Miyazaki, Japan	58.2
1936	Ferenc Csik, Hungary	57.6
1948	Wally Ris, U.S.	57.3
1952	Clarke Scholes, U.S.	57.4
1956	Jon Henricks, Australia	55.4
1960	John Devitt, Australia	55.2
1964	Don Schollander, U.S.	53.4
1968	Michael Wenden, Australia	52.2
1972	Mark Spitz, U.S.	51.22
1976	Jim Montgomery, U.S.	49.99
1980	Jörg Woithe, E. Germany	50.40
1984	Rowdy Gaines, U.S.	49.80
1988	Matt Biondi, U.S.	48.63*
1992	Alexander Popov, Unified Team	49.02

200-Metre Freestyle

1900	Frederick Lane, Australia (220 yd.)	2:25.2
1904	Charles Daniels, U.S. (220 yd.)	2:44.2
1906-64		not held
1968	Michael Wenden, Australia	1:55.2
1972	Mark Spitz, U.S.	1:52.78
1976	Bruce Furniss, U.S.	1:50.29

1980	Sergei Kopliakov, USSR	1:49.81
1984	Michael Gross, W. Germany	1:47.44
1988	Duncan Armstrong, Australia	1:47.25
1992	Evgueni Sadovyi, Unified Team	1:46.70*

400-Metre Freestyle

1896	Paul Neumann, Austria (500 m)	8:12.6
1904	Charles Daniels, U.S. (440 yards)	6:16.2
1908	Henry Taylor, Great Britain	5:36.8
1912	**George Hodgson, Canada**	5:24.4
1920	Norman Ross, U.S.	5:26.8
1924	Johnny Weissmuller, U.S.	5:04.2
1928	Albert Zorilla, Argentina	5:01.6
1932	Clarence "Buster" Crabbe, U.S.	4:48.4
1936	Jack Medica, U.S.	4:44.5
1948	William Smith, U.S.	4:41.0
1952	Jean Boiteux, France	4:30.7
1956	Murray Rose, Australia	4:27.3
1960	Murray Rose, Australia	4:18.3
1964	Don Schollander, U.S.	4:12.2
1968	Mike Burton, U.S.	4:09.0
1972	Brad Cooper, Australia	4:00.27
1976	Brian Goodell, U.S.	3:51.93
1980	Vladimir Salnikov, USSR	3:51.31
1984	George DiCarlo, U.S.	3:51.23
1988	Uwe Dassler, E. Germany	3:46.95
1992	Evgueni Sadovyi, Unified Team	3:45.00**

1 500-Metre Freestyle

1896	Alfred Hajós, Hungary (1 200 m)	18:22.2
1900	John Arthur Jarvis, Great Britain (1 000 m)	13:40.2
1904	Emil Rausch, Germany (1 mile)	27:18.2
1908	Henry Taylor, Great Britain	22:48.4
1912	**George Hodgson, Canada**	22:00.0
1920	Norman Ross, U.S.	22:23.2
1924	Andrew "Boy" Charlton, Australia	20:06.6
1928	Arne Borg, Sweden	19:51.8
1932	Kusuo Kitamura, Japan	19:12.4
1936	Noboru Terada, Japan	19:13.7
1948	James McLane, U.S.	19:18.5
1952	Ford Konno, U.S.	18:30.3
1956	Murray Rose, Australia	17:58.9
1960	Jon Konrads, Australia	17:19.6
1964	Robert Windle, Australia	17:01.7
1968	Mike Burton, U.S.	16:38.9
1972	Mike Burton, U.S.	15:52.58
1976	Brian Goodell, U.S.	15:02.40
1980	Vladimir Salnikov, USSR	14:58.27*
1984	Michael O'Brien, U.S.	15:05.20
1988	Vladimir Salnikov, USSR	15:00.40
1992	Kieren Perkins, Australia	14:43.48**

4 x 100-Metre Medley Relay

1960	United States	4:05.4
1964	United States	3:58.4
1968	United States	3:54.9
1972	United States	3:48.16
1976	United States	3:42.22
1980	Australia	3:45.70
1984	United States	3:39.30
1988	United States	3:36.93*
1992	United States	3:36.93*

4 x 100-Metre Freestyle Relay

1964	United States	3:33.2
1968	United States	3:31.7
1972	United States	3:26.42
1976-80		not held
1984	United States	3:19.03
1988	United States	3:16.53*
1992	United States	3:16.74**

4 x 200-Metre Freestyle Relay

1908	Great Britain	10:55.6
1912	Australia/New Zealand	10:11.6
1920	United States	10:04.4
1924	United States	9:53.4
1928	United States	9:36.2
1932	Japan	8:58.4
1936	Japan	8:51.5
1948	United States	8:46.0
1952	United States	8:31.1
1956	Australia	8:23.6
1960	United States	8:10.2
1964	United States	7:52.1
1968	United States	7:52.33
1972	United States	7:35.78
1976	United States	7:23.22
1980	USSR	7:23.50
1984	United States	7:15.69
1988	United States	7:12.51
1992	Unifed Team	7:11.95**

100-Metre Backstroke

1904	Walter Brack, Germany (100 yds.)	1:16.8
1908	Arno Bieberstein, Germany	1:24.6
1912	Harry Hebner, U.S.	1:21.2
1920	Warren Paoa Kealoha, U.S.	1:15.2
1924	Warren Paoa Kealoha, U.S.	1:13.2
1928	George Kojac, U.S.	1:08.2
1932	Masaji Kiyokawa, Japan	1:08.6
1936	Adolf Kiefer, U.S.	1:05.9
1948	Allen Stack, U.S.	1:06.4
1952	Yoshinobu Oyakawa, U.S.	1:05.4
1956	David Thiele, Australia	1:02.2
1960	David Thiele, Australia	1:01.9
1964		not held
1968	Roland Matthes, E. Germany	58.7
1972	Roland Matthes, E. Germany	56.58
1976	John Naber, U.S.	55.49
1980	Bengt Baron, Sweden	56.33
1984	Rick Carey, U.S.	55.79
1988	Daichi Suzuki, Japan	55.05
1992	**Mark Tewksbury, Canada**	53.98*

200-Metre Backstroke

1900	Ernst Hoppenberg, Germany	2:47.0
1904-60		not held
1964	Jed Graef, U.S.	2:10.3
1968	Roland Matthes, E. Germany	2:09.6
1976	John Naber, U.S.	1:59.19
1980	Sándor Wladár, Hungary	2:01.93
1984	Rick Carey, U.S.	2:00.23
1988	Igor Polianski, USSR	1:59.37

1992	Martin Lopez-Zubera, Spain	1:58.47*

100-Metre Breaststroke

1968	Donald McKenzie, U.S.	1:07.7
1972	Nobutaka Taguchi, Japan	1:04.94
1976	John Hencken, U.S.	1:03.11
1980	Duncan Goodhew, Great Britain	1:03.44
1984	Steve Lundquist, U.S.	1:01.65
1988	Adrian Moorhouse, Great Britain	1:02.04
1992	Nelson Diebel, U.S.	1:01.50*

200-Metre Breaststroke

1908	Frederick Holman, Great Britain	3:09.2
1912	Walter Bathe, Germany	3:01.8
1920	Håken Malmroth, Sweden	3:04.4
1924	Robert Skelton, U.S.	2:56.6
1928	Yoshiyuki Tsuruta, Japan	2:48.8
1932	Yoshiyuki Tsuruta, Japan	2:45.4
1936	Tetsuo Hamuro, Japan	2:41.5
1948	Joseph Verdeur, U.S.	2:39.3
1952	John Davies, Australia	2:34.4
1956	Masaru Furukawa, Japan	2:34.7
1960	William Mulliken, U.S.	2:37.4
1964	Ian O'Brien, Australia	2:27.8
1968	Felipe Muñoz, Mexico	2:28.7
1972	John Hencken, U.S.	2:21.55
1976	David Wilkie, Great Britain	2:15.11
1980	Robertas Zhulpa, USSR	2:15.85
1984	**Victor Davis, Canada**	2:13.34
1988	Jozsef Szabo, Hungary	2:13.52
1992	Mike Barrowman, U.S.	2:10.16**

100-Metre Butterfly

1968	Doug Russell, U.S.	55.90
1972	Mark Spitz, U.S.	54.27
1976	Matt Vogel, U.S.	54.35
1980	Pär Arvidsson, Sweden	54.92
1984	Michael Gross, W. Germany	53.08
1988	Anthony Nesty, Suriname	53.00*
1992	Pablo Morales, U.S.	53.32

200-Metre Butterfly

1956	William Yorzyk, U.S.	2:19.3
1960	Michael Troy, U.S.	2:12.8
1964	Kevin Berry, Australia	2:06.6
1968	Carl Robie, U.S.	2:08.7
1972	Mark Spitz, U.S.	2:00.70
1976	Mike Bruner, U.S.	1:59.23
1980	Sergei Fesenko, USSR	1:59.76
1984	Jon Sieben, Australia	1:57.04
1988	Michael Gross, W. Germany	1:56.94
1992	Mel Stewart, U.S.	1:56.26*

200-Metre Individual Medley

1968	Charles Hickcox, U.S.	2:12.0
1972	Gunnar Larsson, Sweden	2:07.17
1976-80		not held
1984	**Alex Baumann, Canada**	2:01.42
1988	Tamas Darnyi, Hungary	2:00.17*
1992	Tamas Darnyi, Hungary	2:00.76

400-Metre Individual Medley

1964	Dick Roth, U.S.	4:45.4
1968	Charles Hickcox, U.S.	4:48.4
1972	Gunnar Larsson, Sweden	4:31.98
1976	Rod Strachan, U.S.	4:23.68
1980	Aleksandr Sidorenko, USSR	4:22.89
1984	**Alex Baumann, Canada**	4:17.41
1988	Tamas Darnyi, Hungary	4:14.75
1992	Tamas Darnyi, Hungary	4:14.23*

Springboard Diving

		Points
1908	Albert Zürner, Germany	85.5
1912	Paul Günther, Germany	79.23
1920	Louis Kuehn, U.S.	675.40
1924	Albert White, U.S.	696.40
1928	Pete Desjardins, U.S.	185.04
1932	Michael Galitzen (Mickey Riley), U.S.	161.38
1936	Richard Degener, U.S.	163.57
1948	Bruce Harlan, U.S.	163.64
1952	David Browning, U.S.	205.29
1956	Robert Clotworthy, U.S.	159.56
1960	Gary Tobian, U.S.	170.00
1964	Kenneth Sitzberger, U.S.	159.90
1968	Bernie Wrightson, U.S.	170.15
1972	Vladimir Vasin, USSR	594.09
1976	Phillip Boggs, U.S.	619.05
1980	Aleksandr Portnov, USSR	905.025
1984	Greg Louganis, U.S.	754.41
1988	Greg Louganis, U.S.	730.80
1992	Mark Lenzi, U.S.	676.53

Platform Diving

		Points
1904	George Sheldon, U.S.	12.66
1908	Hjalmar Johansson, Sweden	83.75
1912	Erik Adlerz, Sweden	73.94
1920	Clarence Pinkston, U.S.	100.67
1924	Albert White, U.S.	97.46
1928	Pete Desjardins, U.S.	98.74
1932	Harold Smith, U.S.	124.80
1936	Marshall Wayne, U.S.	113.58
1948	Sam Lee, U.S.	130.05
1952	Sam Lee, U.S.	156.28
1956	Joaquin Capilla, Mexico	152.44
1960	Robert Webster, U.S.	165.56
1964	Robert Webster, U.S.	148.58
1968	Klaus Dibiasi, Italy	164.18
1972	Klaus Dibiasi, Italy	504.12
1976	Klaus Dibiasi, Italy	600.51
1980	Falk Hoffmann, E. Germany	835.650
1984	Greg Louganis, U.S.	710.91
1988	Greg Louganis, U.S.	638.61
1992	Sun Shu-wei, China	677.31

■ Women's Swimming

50-Metre Freestyle

1988	Kristin Otto, E. Germany	25.49
1992	Yang Wenyi, China	24.79*

100-Metre Freestyle

1912	Fanny Durack, Australia	1:22.2
1920	Ethelda Bleibtrey, U.S.	1:13.6
1924	Ethel Lackie, U.S.	1:12.4
1928	Albina Osipowich, U.S.	1:11.0
1932	Helene Madison, U.S.	1:06.8
1936	Hendrika "Rie" Mastenbroek, Netherlands	1:05.9
1948	Greta Andersen, Denmark	1:06.3
1952	Katalin Szöke, Hungary	1:06.8
1956	Dawn Fraser, Australia	1:02.0
1960	Dawn Fraser, Australia	1:01.2
1964	Dawn Fraser, Australia	59.5
1968	Jan Henne, U.S.	1:00.0
1972	Sandra Neilson, U.S.	58.59
1976	Kornelia Ender, E. Germany	55.65
1980	Barbara Krause, E. Germany	54.79
1984	(tie) Carie Steinseifer, U.S.	55.92
	Nancy Hogshead, U.S.	55.92
1988	Kristin Otto, E. Germany	54.93
1992	Zhuang Yong, China	54.64*

200-Metre Freestyle

1968	Debbie Meyer, U.S.	2:10.5
1972	Shane Gould, Australia	2:03.56
1976	Kornelia Ender, E. Germany	1:59.26
1980	Barbara Krause, E. Germany	1:58.33
1984	Mary Wayte, U.S.	1:59.23
1988	Heike Friedrich, E. Germany	1:57.65*
1992	Nicole Haslett, U.S.	1:57.90

400-Metre Freestyle

1920	Ethelda Bleibtrey (300 m)	4:34.0
1924	Martha Norelius, U.S.	6:02.2
1928	Martha Norelius, U.S.	5:42.8
1932	Helene Madison, U.S.	5:28.5
1936	Hendrika "Rie" Mastenbroek, Netherlands	5:26.4
1948	Ann Curtis, U.S.	5:17.8
1952	Valéria Gyenge, Hungary	5:12.1
1956	Lorraine Crapp, Australia	4:54.6
1960	S. Christine von Saltza, U.S.	4:50.6
1964	Virginia Duenkel, U.S.	4:43.3
1968	Debbie Meyer, U.S.	4:31.8
1972	Shane Gould, Australia	4:19.44
1976	Petra Thümer, E. Germany	4:09.89
1980	Ines Diers, E. Germany	4:08.76
1984	Tiffany Cohen, U.S.	4:07.10
1988	Janet Evans, U.S.	4:03.85*
1992	Dagmar Hase, Germany	4:07.18

800-Metre Freestyle

1968	Debbie Meyer, U.S.	9:24.0
1972	Keena Rothhammer, U.S.	8:53.68
1976	Petra Thümer, E. Germany	8:37.14
1980	Michelle Ford, Australia	8:28.90
1984	Tiffany Cohen, U.S.	8:24.95
1988	Janet Evans, U.S.	8:20.20*
1992	Janet Evans, U.S.	8:25.52

100-Metre Backstroke

1924	Sybil Bauer, U.S.	1:23.2
1928	Maria Braun, Netherlands	1:22.0

1932	Eleanor Holm, U.S.	1:19.4
1936	Dina Senff, Netherlands	1:18.9
1948	Karen Margrete Harup, Denmark	1:14.4
1952	Joan Harrison, South Africa	1:14.3
1956	Judith Grinham, Great Britain	1:12.9
1960	Lynn Burke, U.S.	1:09.3
1964	Cathy Ferguson, U.S.	1:07.7
1968	Kaye Hall, U.S.	1:06.2
1972	Melissa Belote, U.S.	1:05.78
1976	Ulrike Richter, E. Germany	1:01.83
1980	Rica Reinisch, E. Germany	1:00.86
1984	Theresa Andrews, U.S.	1:02.55
1988	Kristin Otto, E. Germany	1:00.89
1992	Krisztina Egerszegi, Hungary	1:00.68*

200-Metre Backstroke

1968	Lillian "Pokey" Watson, U.S.	2:24.8
1972	Melissa Belote, U.S.	2:19.19
1976	Ulrike Richter, E. Germany	2:13.43
1980	Rica Reinisch, E. Germany	2:11.77
1984	Jolanda de Rover, Netherlands	2:12.38
1988	Krisztina Egerszegi, Hungary	2:09.29
1992	Krisztina Egerszegi, Hungary	2:07.06*

100-Metre Breaststroke

1968	Djurdjica Bjedov, Yugoslavia	1:15.8
1972	Catherine Carr, U.S.	1:13.58
1976	Hannelore Anke, E. Germany	1:11.16
1980	Ute Geweniger, E. Germany	1:10.22
1984	Petra van Staveren, Netherlands	1:09.88
1988	Tania Dangalakova, Bulgaria	1:07.95*
1992	Elena Rudkovskaya, Unified Team	1:08.00

200-Metre Breaststroke

1924	Lucy Morton, Great Britain	3:33.2
1928	Hildegard Schrader, Germany	3:12.6
1932	Clare Dennis, Australia	3:06.3
1936	Hideko Maehata, Japan	3:03.6
1948	Petronella van Vliet, Netherlands	2:57.2
1952	Eva Székely, Hungary	2:51.7
1956	Ursula Happe, Germany	2:53.1
1960	Anita Lonsbrough, Great Britain	2:49.5
1964	Galina Prozumenshikova, USSR	2:46.4
1968	Sharon Wichman, U.S.	2:44.4
1972	Beverly Whitfield, Australia	2:41.71
1976	Marina Koshevaia, USSR	2:33.35
1980	Lina Kaciusyté, USSR	2:29.54
1984	**Anne Ottenbrite, Canada**	2:30.38
1988	Silke Hörner, E. Germany	2:26.71
1992	Kyoko Iwasaki, Japan	2:26.65*

200-Metre Individual Medley

1968	Claudia Kolb, U.S.	2:24.7
1972	Shane Gould, Australia	2:23.07
1984	Tracy Caulkins, U.S.	2:12.64
1988	Daniela Hunger, E. Germany	2:12.59
1992	Lin Li, China	2:11.65**

400-Metre Individual Medley

1964	Donna De Varona, U.S.	5:18.7
1968	Claudia Kolb, U.S.	5:08.5
1972	Gail Neall, Australia	5:02.97

1976	Ulrike Tauber, E. Germany	4:42.77
1980	Petra Schneider, E. Germany	4:36.29*
1984	Tracy Caulkins, U.S.	4:39.24
1988	Janet Evans, U.S.	4:37.76
1992	Krisztina Egerszegi, Hungary	4:36.54

100-Metre Butterfly

1956	Shelley Mann, U.S.	1:11.0
1960	Carolyn Schuler, U.S.	1:09.5
1964	Sharon Stouder, U.S.	1:04.7
1968	Lyn McClements, Australia	1:05.5
1972	Mayumi Aoki, Japan	1:03.34
1976	Kornelia Ender, E. Germany	1:00.13
1980	Caren Metschuck, E. Germany	1:00.42
1984	Mary T. Meagher, U.S.	59.26
1988	Kristin Otto, E. Germany	59.00
1992	Qian Hong, China	59.34

200-Metre Butterfly

1968	Ada Kok, Netherlands	2:24.7
1972	Karen Moe, U.S.	2:15.57
1976	Andrea Pollack, E. Germany	2:11.41
1980	Ines Geissler, E. Germany	2:10.44
1988	Kathleen Nord, E. Germany	2:09.51
1992	Summer Sanders, U.S.	2:08.67

100-Metre Medley Relay

1960	United States	4:41.1
1964	United States	4:33.9
1968	United States	4:28.3
1972	United States	4:20.75
1976	East Germany	4:07.95
1980	East Germany	4:06.67
1984	United States	4:08.34
1988	East Germany	4:03.74
1992	United States	4:02.54**

100-Metre Freestyle Relay

1912	Great Britain	5:52.8
1920	United States	5:11.6
1924	United States	4:58.8
1928	United States	4:47.6
1932	United States	4:38.0
1936	Netherlands	4:36.0
1948	United States	4:29.2
1952	Hungary	4:24.4
1956	Australia	4:17.1
1960	United States	4:08.9
1964	United States	4:03.8
1968	United States	4:02.5
1972	United States	3:55.19
1976	United States	3:44.82
1980	East Germany	3:42.71
1984	United States	3:43.43
1988	East Germany	3:40.63
1992	United States	3:39.46**

Springboard Diving

		Points
1920	Aileen Riggin, U.S.	539.9
1924	Elizabeth Becker, U.S.	474.5
1928	Helen Meany, U.S.	78.62

1932	Georgia Coleman, U.S.	87.52
1936	Marjorie Gestring, U.S.	89.27
1948	Victoria M. Draves, U.S.	108.74
1952	Patricia McCormick, U.S.	147.30
1956	Patricia McCormick, U.S.	142.36
1960	Ingrid Krämer, E. Germany	155.81
1964	Ingrid Engel-Krämer, E. Germany	145.00
1968	Sue Gossick, U.S.	150.77
1972	Micki King, U.S.	450.03
1976	Jennifer Chandler, U.S.	506.19
1980	Irina Kalinina, USSR	725.91
1984	**Sylvie Bernier, Canada**	530.70
1988	Gao Min, China	580.23
1992	Gao Min, China	572.40

Platform Diving

		Points
1912	Greta Johansson, Sweden	39.90
1920	Stefani Fryland-Clausen, Denmark	34.60
1924	Caroline Smith, U.S.	33.20
1928	Elizabeth Becker Pinkston, U.S.	31.60
1932	Dorothy Poynton, U.S.	40.26
1936	Dorothy Poynton Hill, U.S.	33.93
1948	Victoria Draves, U.S.	68.87
1952	Patricia McCormick, U.S.	79.37
1956	Patricia McCormick, U.S.	84.85
1960	Ingrid Krämer, Germany	91.28
1964	Lesley Bush, U.S.	99.80
1968	Milena Duchková, Czechoslovakia	109.59
1972	Ulrika Knape, Sweden	390.00
1976	Elena Vaytsekhovskaya, USSR	406.59
1980	Martina Jäschke, E. Germany	596.25
1984	Zhou Jihong, China	435.51
1988	Yanmei Xu, China	445.20
1992	Fu Mingxia, China	461.43

■ Men's Basketball

1936	United States	1972	USSR
1948	United States	1976	United States
1952	United States	1980	Yugoslavia
1956	United States	1984	United States
1960	United States	1988	USSR
1964	United States	1992	United States
1968	United States		

■ Women's Basketball

1976	USSR
1980	USSR
1984	United States
1988	United States
1992	Unified Team

■ Boxing

Light Flyweight

1968	Francisco Rodrigues, Venezuela
1972	Georgy Gedo, Hungary
1976	Jorge Hernandez, Cuba
1980	Shamil Sabyrov, USSR
1984	Paul Gonzales, U.S.
1988	Ivalio Hristov, Bulgaria
1992	Rogelio Marcelo Garcia, Cuba

Flyweight

1904	George Finnegan, U.S.
1920	Frank Di Gennara, U.S.
1924	Fidel LaBarba, U.S.
1928	Antal Kocsis, Hungary
1932	Istva Enekes, Hungary
1936	Willi Kaiser, Germany
1948	Pascual Rerez, Argentina
1952	Nathan Brooks, U.S.
1956	Terence Spinks, Great Britain
1960	Gyula Torok, Hungary
1964	Fernando Atzori, Italy
1968	Ricardo Delgado, Mexico
1972	Georgi Kostadinov, Bulgaria
1976	Leo Randolph, U.S.
1980	Peter Lessov, Bulgaria
1984	Steve McCrory, U.S.
1988	Kim Kwang-Sun, South Korea
1992	Su Choi-choi, North Korea

Bantamweight

1904	Kirk Oliver, U.S.
1908	A. Henry Tomas, Great Britain
1920	Clarence Walker, South Africa
1924	William Smith, South Africa
1928	Vittorio Tamagnini, Italy
1936	Ulderico Sergo, Italy
1948	Tibor Csik, Hungary
1952	Pentti Hamalainen, Finland
1956	Wolfgang Behrendt, E. Germany
1960	Oleg Grigoryev, USSR
1964	Takao Sakurai
1968	Valery Sokolov, USSR
1972	Orlando Martinez, Cuba
1976	Yong-jo Gu, China
1980	Juan Hernandez, Cuba
1984	Maurizio Stecca, Italy
1988	Kennedy McKinney, U.S.
1992	Joel Casamayor, Cuba

Featherweight

1904	Oliver Kirk, U.S.
1908	Richard Gunn, Great Britain
1920	Paul Fritsch, France
1924	John Fields, U.S.
1928	Lambertus van Klaveren, Holland
1932	Carmelo Robledo, Argentina
1936	Arthur Casanovas, Argentina
1948	Ernesto Formenti, Italy
1952	John Zachara, Czechoslovakia
1956	Vladimir Safronov, USSR
1960	Francesco Musso, Italy
1964	Stanislav Stepashkin, USSR
1968	Antonio Roldan, Mexico
1972	Boris Kousnetsov, USSR
1976	Angel Herrera, Cuba
1980	Rudi Fink, E. Germany
1984	Meldrick Taylor, U.S.

| 1988 | Giovanni Parisi, Italy |
| 1992 | Andreas Tews, Germany |

Lightweight

1904	Harry Spanger, U.S.
1908	Frederick Grace, Great Britain
1920	Samuel Mosberg, U.S.
1924	Hans Nielsen, Denmark
1928	Carli Orlando, Italy
1932	Lawrence Stevens, South Africa
1936	Imre Harangi, Hungary
1948	Gerald Dreyer, South Africa
1952	Aureliano Bolognesi, Italy
1956	Richard McTaggart, Great Britain
1960	Kazimierz Pazdzior, Poland
1964	Jozef Grudzien, Poland
1968	Ronald Harris, U.S.
1972	Jan Szczepanski, Poland
1976	Howard Davis, U.S.
1980	Angel Herrera, Cuba
1984	Pernell Whitaker, U.S.
1988	Andreas Zvelow, East Germany
1992	Oscar De La Hoya, U.S.

Light-Welterweight

1952	Charles Adkins, U.S.
1956	Vladimir Yengibaryan, USSR
1960	Bohumil Nemecek, Czechoslovakia
1964	Jerzy Kulej, Poland
1968	Jerzy Kulej, Poland
1972	Ray Seales, U.S.
1976	Ray Leonard, U.S.
1980	Patrizio Oliva, Italy
1984	Jerry Page, U.S.
1988	Viatcheslav Janovski, USSR
1992	Hector Vinent, Cuba

Welterweight

1904	Albert Young, U.S.
1920	**Albert Schneider, Canada**
1924	Jean DeLarge, Belgium
1928	Edward Morgan, New Zealand
1932	Edward Flynn, U.S.
1936	Sten Suvio, Finland
1948	Julius Torma, Czechoslovakia
1952	Zygmunt Chychla, Poland
1956	Bucikae Kubcam Rinabua
1960	Giovanni Benvenuti, Italy
1964	Marian Kasprzyk, Poland
1968	Manfred Wolke, Great Britain
1972	Emilio Correa, Cuba
1976	Jochen Bachfeld, Great Britain
1980	Andres Aldama, Cuba
1984	Mark Breland, U.S.
1988	Robert Wangila, Kenya
1992	Michael Carruth, Ireland

Light-Middleweight

1952	Laszlo Papp, Hungary
1956	Laszlo Papp, Hungary
1960	Wilbert McClure, U.S.
1964	Boris Lagutin, USSR

1968	Boris Lagutin, USSR
1972	Dieter Kottysch, Germany
1976	Jerzy Rybicki, Poland
1980	Armando Martines, Cuba
1984	Frank Tate, U.S.
1988	Park Si-Hun, South Korea
1992	Juan Lemus, Cuba

Middleweight

1904	Charles Mayer, U.S.
1908	John Douglas, Great Britain
1920	Harry Mallin, Great Britain
1924	Harry Mallin, Great Britain
1928	Piero Toscani, Italy
1932	Carmen Barth, U.S.
1936	Jean Despeaux, France
1948	Laszlo Papp, Hungary
1952	Floyd Patterson, U.S.
1956	Gennady Schatkov, USSR
1960	Edward Crook, U.S.
1964	Valery Papenchenko, USSR
1968	Christopher Finnegan, Great Britain
1972	Vyacheslav Lemechev, USSR
1976	Michael Spinks, U.S.
1980	Jose Gomez, Cuba
1984	Joun-sup Shin, China
1988	Henry Maske, East Germany
1992	Ariel Hernandez Ascuy, Cuba

Light-Heavyweight

1920	Edward Egan, U.S.
1924	Harry Mitchell, Great Britain
1928	Victor Avendan, Argentina
1932	David Carstens, South Africa
1956	James Boyd, U.S.
1976	Leon Spinks, U.S.
1980	Slobodan Cacar, Yugoslavia
1984	Anton Josipovic, Yugoslavia
1988	Andrew Maynard, U.S.
1992	Torsten May, Germany

Heavyweight

1984	Herny Tillman, U.S.
1988	Ray Mercer, U.S.
1992	Felix Savon, Cuba

Super Heavyweight

1904	Samuel Berger, U.S.
1908	A.L. Oldham, Great Britain
1928	Arturo R. Jurado, Argentina
1956	Peter Rademacher, U.S.
1960	Franco De Piccoli, Italy
1964	Joseph Frazier, U.S.
1968	George Foreman, U.S.
1972	Teofilo Stevenson, Cuba
1976	Teofilo Stevenson, Cuba
1988	**Lennox Lewis, Canada**
1992	Roberto Balado, Cuba

Soccer

| 1900 | Great Britain |
| 1904 | **Canada** |

1908	Great Britain
1912	Great Britain
1920	Belgium
1924	Uruguay
1928	Uruguay
1932	not held
1936	Italy
1948	Sweden
1952	Hungary
1956	USSR
1960	Yugoslavia
1964	Hungary
1968	Hungary
1972	Poland
1976	E. Germany
1980	Czechoslovakia
1984	France
1988	USSR
1992	Spain

■ Men's Volleyball

1964	USSR
1968	USSR
1972	Japan
1976	Poland
1980	USSR
1988	United States
1992	Brazil

■ Women's Volleyball

1964	Japan
1968	USSR
1972	USSR
1976	Japan
1980	USSR
1984	China
1988	USSR
1992	Cuba

Winter Olympics

Year	Location	Date of Competition	Competitors Men	Competitors Women	Nations Represented	Unofficial Winners
1924	Chamonix, France	Jan. 25–Feb. 4	281	13	16	Norway
1928	St. Moritz, Switzerland	Feb. 11–19	468	27	25	Norway
1932	Lake Placid, United States	Feb. 4–15	274	32	17	United States
1936	Garmisch-Partenkirchen, Germany	Feb. 6–16	675	80	28	Norway
1940	Cancelled because of World War II					
1944	Cancelled because of World War II					
1948	St. Moritz, Switzerland	Jan. 30–Feb. 8	636	77	28	Sweden
1952	Oslo, Norway	Feb. 14–25	623	109	30	Norway
1956	Cortina d'Ampezzo, Italy	Jan. 26–Feb. 5	686	132	32	U.S.S.R.
1960	Squaw Valley, United States	Feb. 18–28	521	144	30	U.S.S.R.
1964	Innsbruck, Austria	Jan. 29–Feb. 9	986	200	36	U.S.S.R.
1968	Grenoble, France	Feb. 6–18	1 081	212	37	Norway
1972	Sapporo, Japan	Feb. 3–13	1 015	217	35	U.S.S.R.
1976	Innsbruck, Austria	Feb. 4–15	900	228	37	U.S.S.R.
1980	Lake Placid, United States	Feb. 14–23	833	234	37	East Germany
1984	Sarajevo, Yugoslavia	Feb. 7–19	1 180	409	49	U.S.S.R.
1988	Calgary, Canada[1]	Feb. 13–28	1 128	317	57	U.S.S.R.
1992	Albertville, France	Feb. 8–23	1 545	602	64	Germany
1994 [2]	Lillehammer, Norway	Feb. 12–27	1216	521	67	Norway
1998	Nagano, Japan					

(1) Including demonstration sports a total of 1 759 athletes competed in Calgary. (2) Beginning with 1994, the summer and winter games will be held 2 years apart, instead of in the same year.

Final Medal Standings of the Winter Olympics, 1994

(Lillehammer, Norway, Feb. 12–27, 1994)

Country	Gold	Silver	Bronze	Total	Country	Gold	Silver	Bronze	Total
Norway	10	11	5	26	France	0	1	4	5
Germany	9	7	8	24	Netherlands	0	1	3	4
Russia	11	8	4	23	Sweden	2	1	0	3
Italy	7	5	8	20	Slovenia	0	0	3	3
United States	6	5	2	13	China	0	1	2	3
Canada	3	6	4	13	Kazakhstan	1	2	0	3
Switzerland	3	4	2	9	Ukraine	1	0	1	2
Austria	2	3	4	9	Belarus	0	2	0	2
South Korea	4	1	1	6	Britain	0	0	2	2
Finland	0	1	5	6	Uzbekistan	1	0	0	1
Japan	1	2	2	5	Australia	0	0	1	1

Canada's 1994 Winter Olympic Medal Winners

■ Gold

Freestyle Skiing, Men's Moguls: Jean-Luc Brassard
Biathlon, Women's 7.5 km Sprint and 15 km: Myriam Bedard

Short Track Speed Skating, Women's 3000 m Relay: Canada
Ice Hockey: Canada

■ Silver

Freestyle Skiing, Men's Aerials: Phillipe Laroche
Figure Skating, Men's: Elvis Stojko
Speed Skating, Women's 500 m: Susan Auch
Short Track Speed Skating, Women's 1000 m: Nathalie Lambert

■ Bronze

Alpine Skiing, Men's Downhill: Edi Podivinsky
Freestyle Skiing, Men's Aerials: Lloyd Langlois
Figure Skating, Pairs: Isabelle Brasseur & Lloyd Eisler
Short Track Speed Skating, Men's 1000 m: Marc Gagnon

Medal Winners, 1994 Winter Olympics

(Lillehammer, Norway)

■ Alpine Skiing

Downhill, Men			Downhill, Women		
T. Moe	US	1:45.75	K. Seizinger	Ger	1:35.93
K. A. Aamodt	Nor	1:45.79	P. Street	US	1:36.59
E. Podivinsky	**Can**	**1:45.87**	I. Kostner	Ita	1:36.85
Super-G, Men			**Super-G, Women**		
M. Wasmeier	Ger	1:32.53	D. Roffe	US	1:22.15
T. Moe	US	1:32.61	S. Gladischeva	Rus	1:22.44
K. A. Aamodt	Nor	1:32.93	I. Kostner	Ita	1:22.45
Giant Slalom, Men			**Giant Slalom, Women**		
M. Wasmeier	Ger	2:52.46	D. Compagnoni	Ita	2:30.97
U. Kaelin	Switz	2:52.48	M. Ertl	Ger	2:32.19
C. Mayer,	Aut	2:52.58	V. Schneider	Switz	2:32.97
Combined Competition, Men			**Combined Competition, Women**		
L. Kjus	Nor	3:17.53	P. Wiberg	Swe	3:05.16
K. A. Aamodt	Nor	3:18.55	V. Schneider	Switz	3:05.29
H. Nilsen	Nor	3:19.14	A. Dovzan	Slo	3:06.64
Slalom, Men			**Slalom, Women**		
T. Stangassinger	Aut	2:02.02	V. Schneider	Switz	1:56.01
A. Tomba	Italy	2:02.17	E. Eder	Aut	1:56.35
J. Kosir	Slo	2:02.53	K. Koren	Slo	1:56.61

◼ Freestyle Skiing

Moguls, Men			Moguls, Women		
J. Brassard	**Can**	**27.24**	S. Hattestad	Nor	25.97
S. Shoupletsov	Rus	26.90	E. McIntyre	US	25.89
E. Grospiron	Fra	26.64	E. Kojevnikova	Rus	25.81
Aerials, Men			**Aerials, Women**		
A. Schoenbaechler	Switz	234.76	L. Tcherjazova	Uzbek	166.84
P. Laroche	**Can**	**228.63**	M. Lindgren	Swe	165.88
L. Langlois	**Can**	**222.44**	H. Lid	Nor	164.13

◼ Nordic Skiing

10 km Classic Technique, Men			5 km Classic Technique, Women		
B. Daehlie	Nor	24:20.1	L. Egorova	Rus	14:08.8
V. Smirnov	Kazak	24:38.3	M. Di Centa	Ita	14:28.3
M. Albarello	Ita	24:42.3	M. L. Kirvesniemi	Fin	14:36.0
10 km + 15 km Pursuit, Men			**5 km + 10 km Pursuit, Women**		
B. Daehlie	Nor	1:00:08.8	L. Egorova	Rus	41:38.1
V. Smirnov	Kazak	1:00:38.0	M. Di Centa	Ita	41:46.4
Silvio Fauner	Ita	1:01:48.6	S. Belmondo	Ita	42:21.1
30 km Free Technique, Men			**15 km Free Technique, Women**		
T. Alsgaard	Nor	1:12:26.4	M. Di Centa	Ita	39:44.5
B. Daehlie	Nor	1:13:13.6	L. Egorova	Rus	41:03.0
M. Myllylae	Fin	1:14:14.5	N. Gavriluk	Rus	41:10.04
10 km Sprint, Men			**30 km Classic Technique, Women**		
S. Tchepikov	Rus	28:07.0	M. Di Centa	Ita	1:25:41.6
R. Gross	Ger	28:13.0	M. Wold	Nor	1:25:57.8
S. Tarasov	Rus	28:27.4	M. L. Kirvesniemi	Fin	1:26:13.6
50 km Classic Technique, Men			**4x5 km Relay, Women**		
V. Smirnov	Kazak	2:07:20.3		Rus	57:12.5
M. Myllylae	Fin	2:08:41.9		Nor	57:42.6
S. Sivertsen	Nor	2:08:49.0		Ita	58:42.6
4x10 km Relay, Men					
	Ita	1:41:15.0			
	Nor	1:41:15.4			
	Fin	1:42:15.6			

◼ Nordic Combined (ski jump + cross-country)

Individual		Team	
F. Lundberg	Nor	Jap	
T. Kono	Jap	Nor	
B. E. Vik	Nor	Swit	

◼ Ski Jumping

90 k			Team, 120 k	
E. Bredesen	Nor	282.0	Ger	970.1
L.Ottesen	Nor	268.0	Jap	956.9
D. Thoma	Ger	260.5	Austria	918.9
120 k				
J. Weissflog	Ger	274.5		
E. Bredesen	Nor	266.5		
A. Goldberger	Aut	255.0		

◼ Biathlon

20 km, Men			7.5 km Sprint, Women		
S. Tarasov s	Rus	57:25.3	**M. Bedard**	**Can**	**26:08.8**
F. Luck	Ger	57:28.7	S. Paramygina	Bel	26:09.9
S. Fischer	Ger	57:41.9	V. Tserbe	Ukr	26:10.0

Relay, 4x7.5 km, Men

	Ger	1:30:22.1
	Rus	1:31:23.6
	Fra	1:32:31.3

15 km, Women

M. Bedard	Can	**52:06.6**
A. Briand	Fra	52:53.3
U. Disl	Ger	53:15.3

4x7.5 km Relay, Women

	Rus	1:47:19.5
	Ger	1:51:16.5
	Fra	1:52:28.3

■ Bobsled

Two-Man

G. Weder, D. Acklin	Switz	3:30.81
R. Goetschi, G. Acklin	Switz	3:30.86
G. Huber, S. Ticci	Ita	3:31.01

Four-Man

	Ger 2	3:27.78
	Switz 1	3:27.84
	Ger 1	3:28.01

■ Luge

Single, Men

G. Hackl	Ger	3:21.57
M. Prock	Aut	3:21.58
A. Zoeggeler	Ita	3:21.83

Double, Men

K. Brugger, W. Huber	Ita	1:36.72
H., Raffl, N. Huber	Ita	1:36.77
S. Krausse, J. Behrendt	Ger	1:36.95

■ Figure Skating

Men		pts.
A. Urmanov	Rus	1.5
E. Stojko	**Can**	**3.0**
P. Candeloro	Fra	6.5

Women		pts.
O. Baiul	Ukr	2.0
N. Kerrigan	US	2.5
L. Chen	China	5.0

Pairs		
E. Gordeeva & S. Grinkov	Rus	1.5
N. Mishkutenok & A. Dmitriev	Rus	3.0
I. Brasseur & L. Eisler	**Can**	**4.5**

Ice Dance		
O. Grichtchuk & Y. Platov	Rus	3.4
M. Usova & A. Zhulin	Rus	3.8
J. Torvill & C. Dean	G Br	4.8

■ Speed Skating

500 M, Men		
A. Golubev	Rus	36.33*
S. Klevchenya	Rus	36.39
M. Horii	Jap	36.53

1000 M, Men		
D. Jansen	US	1:12.43**
I. Zhelezovsky	Bel	1:12.72
S. Clevchenya	Rus	1:12.85

1500 M, Men		
J. Koss	Nor	1:51.29**
R. Ritsma	Neth	1:51.99
F. Zandstra	Neth	1:52.38

5000 M, Men		
J. Koss	Nor	6:34.96**
K. Storelid	Nor	6:42.68
R. Ritsma	Neth	6:43.94

10,000 M, Men		
J. Koss	Nor	13:30.55**
S. Storelid	Nor	13:49.25
B. Veldkamp	Neth	13:56.73

500 M, Women		
B. Blair	US	39.25
S. Auch	**Can**	39.61
F. Schenk	Ger	39.70

1000 M, Women		
B. Blair	US	1:18.74
A. Baier	Ger	1:20.12
Q. Ye	Chn	1:20.22

1500 M, Women		
E. Hunyady	Aut	2:02.19
S. Fedotkina	Rus	2:02.69
G. Niemann	Ger	2:03.41

3000 M, Women		
S. Bazhanova	Rus	4:17.43
E. Hunyady	Aut	4:18.14
C. Pechstein	Ger	4:18.34

5000 M, Women		
C. Pechstein	Ger	7:14.37
G. Niemann	Ger	7:14.88
H. Yamamoto	Jap	7:19.68

■ Short Track Speed Skating

500 M, Men			500 M, Women		
J. Chae	Kor	43.45*	C. Turner	US	45.98*
M. Vuillermin	Ita	43.47	Y. Zhang	Chn	46.44
N.Gooch	G Br	43.68	A. Peterson	US	46.76
1000 M, Men			**1000 M, Women**		
K. Kim	Kor	1;34.57	L. K. Chun	Kor	1:36.87*
J.H. Chae	Kor	1:34.92	**N. Lambert**	**Can**	**1:36.97**
M. Gagnon	**Can**	**1:35.03**	S. H. Kim	Kor	1:37.09
5000 M Relay, Men			**3000 M Relay, Women**		
	Ita	7:11.74		Kor	4:26.64*
	USA	7:13.37		**Can**	**4:32.04**
	Australia	7:13.68		USA	n.a.

■ Ice Hockey

Sweden
Canada
Finland

Source: *Canadian Olympic Association*   * Olympic Record ** World Record

COMMONWEALTH GAMES

Final Medal Standings of the 15th Commonwealth Games

(Victoria, BC, August 18-28, 1994)

Country	Gold	Silver	Bronze	Total	Country	Gold	Silver	Bronze	Total
Australia	87	52	43	182	Nauru	3	0	0	3
Canada	40	42	46	128	Sri Lanka	1	2	0	3
England	31	45	49	125	Pakistan	0	0	3	3
New Zealand	5	16	20	41	Namibia	1	0	1	2
Nigeria	11	13	13	37	Trinidad-Tobago	0	0	2	2
India	6	11	7	24	Uganda	0	0	2	2
Scotland	6	3	11	20	Papua New Guinea	0	1	0	1
Kenya	7	4	8	19	Western Samoa	0	1	0	1
Wales	5	8	6	19	Bermuda	0	0	1	1
South Africa	2	4	5	11	Botswana	0	0	1	1
Northern Ireland	5	2	3	10	Ghana	0	0	1	1
Jamaica	2	4	2	8	Guernsey	0	0	1	1
Malaysia	2	3	2	7	Norfolk Island	0	0	1	1
Zimbabwe	0	3	3	6	Seychelles	0	0	1	1
Cyprus	2	1	2	5	Tanzania	0	0	1	1
Zambia	1	1	2	4	Tonga	0	0	1	1
Hong Kong	0	0	4	4					

Note: No silver or bronze awarded in some events. Disabled medals count in overall total.

15th Commonwealth Games

*(Victoria, BC, August 18-28, 1994, *Games Record)*

■ Men's Swimming

50-Metre Freestyle

1. Mark Foster, Eng 23.12
2. Darren Lange, Aus 23.13
3. Peter Williams, S Afr 23.16

100 Freestyle

1. Stephen Clarke, Brampton, Ont **50.21**
2. Christopher Fydler, Aus 50.51
3. Andrew Baildon, Aus 50.71

200 Freestyle

1. Kieren Perkins, Aus 1:49.31*

2. Trent Bray, NZ 1:49.47
3. Danyon Loader, NZ 1:49.54

400 Freestyle

1. Kieren Perkins, Aus 3:45.77*
2. Danyon Loader, NZ 3:49.65
3. Danile Kowalski, Aus 3:50.41

1500 Freestyle

1. Kieren Perkins, Aus 14:41.66**
2. Daniel Kowalski, Aus 14:53.61
3. Glen Houseman, Aus 15:02.59
** world record

100 Breaststroke

1. Philip Rogers, Aus 1:02.62
2. Nick Gillingham, Eng 1:02.65
3. Jon Cleveland, Calgary 1:03.20

200 Breaststroke

1. Nick Gillingham, Eng 2:12.54*
2. Philip Rogers, Aus 2:13.56
3. Jon Cleveland, Calgary 2:14.91

100 Backstroke

1. Martin Harris, Eng 55.77*
2. Steven Dewick, Aus 56.09
3. Adam Ruckwood, Eng 56.52

200 Backstroke

1. Adam Ruckwood, Eng 2:00.79*
2. **Kevin Draxinger, Richmond, BC 2:02.19**
3. Scott Miller, Aus 2:02.43

100 Butterfly

1. Scott Miller, Aus 54.39
2. **Stephen Clarke, Brampton, Ont 54.45**
3. Adam Pine, Aus 54.76

200 Butterfly

1. Danyon Loader, NZ 1:59.54
2. Scott Miller, Aus 1:59.70
3. James Hickman, Eng 2:00.87

200 Individual Medley

1. Matthew Dunn, Aus 2:02.28
2. **Curtis Myden, Calgary, Alta 2:03.47**
3. Fraser Walker, Scot 2:04.28

400 Individual Medley

1. Matthew Dunn, Aus 4:17.01*
2. **Curtis Myden, Calgary, Alta 4:17.73**
3. Philip Bryant, Aus 4:21.34

4x100 Freestyle

1. Australia 3:20.89
2. New Zealand 3:21.79
3. England 3:22.61

4x200 Freestyle

1. Australia 7:20.80*

2. New Zealand 7:21.67
3. England 7:26.19

4x100 Medley

1. Australia 3:40.41*
2. **Canada 3:43.25**
3. England 3:43.72

Disabled 100 Freestyle

1. **Andrew Haley, Dartmouth, NS 1:03.07**
2. Brendan Burkett, Aus 1:03.75
3. Sean Tretheway, NZ, ... 1:05.30

■ Women's Swimming

50 Freestyle

1. Karen Van Wirdum, Aus 25.90
2. **Andrea Nugent, Calgary, Alta 26.24**
3. **Shannon Shakespeare, Winnipeg, Man . . 26.27**

100 Freestyle

1. Karen Pickering, Eng 56.20*
2. Karen Van Wirdum, Aus 56.42
3. **Marianne Limpert, Fredericton, NB 56.54**

200 Freestyle

1. Susan O'Neill, Aus 2:00.86
2. Nicole Stevenson, Aus 2:01.34
3. Karen Pickering, Eng 2:01.50

400 Freestyle

1. Hayley Lewis, Aus 4:12.56
2. Stacey Gartrell, Aus 4:13.06
3, Sarah Hardcastle, Eng 4:13.29

100 Breaststroke

1. Samantha Riley, Aus 1:08.02*
2. Rebecca Brown, Aus 1:09.40
3. Penelope Heyns, S Afr 1:09.86

200 Breaststroke

1. Samantha Riley, Aus 2:25.53*
2. Rebecca Brown, Aus 2:30.24
3. **Lisa Flood, Pickering, Ont 2:31.85**

100 Backstroke

1. Nicole Stevenson, Aus 1:02.68
2. Ellie Overton, Aus 1:02.90
3. Katharine Osher, Eng 1:03.27

200 Backstroke

1. Nicole Stevenson, Aus 2:12.73
2. Anna Simcic, NZ 2:13.94
3. Ellie Overton, Aus 2:14.96

100 Butterfly

1. Petria Thomas, Aus 1:00.21*
2. Susan O'Neill, Aus 1:00.24
3. Ellie Overton, Aus 1:00.88

200 Butterfly

1. Susan O'Neill, Aus 2:09.96*
2. Hayley Lewis, Aus 2:12.21
3. Julie Majer, Aus 2:12.43

200 Individual Medley

1. Ellie Overton, Aus 2:15.59*
2. **Marianne Limpert, Fredericton, NB** . . **2:15.97**
3. **Nancy Sweetnam, Lindsay, Ont** **2:16.67**

400 Individual Medley

1. Elinora Overton, Aus 4:44.01
2. **Nancy Sweetnam, Lindsay, Ont** **4:46.20**
3. Hayley Lewis, Aus 4:46.62

4x200 Freestyle

1. Australia 8:08.06*
2. England 8:09.62
3. **Canada** **8:14.97**

4x100 Medley

1. Australia 4:07.89*
2. England 4:12.83
3. **Canada** **4:14.04**

Disabled 100 Freestyle

1. Melissa Carlton, Aus 1:09.61
2. Claire Bishop, Eng 1:11.00
3. Kelly Barnes, Aus 1:11.03

■ Synchronized Swimming

Solo

	Points
1. **Lisa Alexander, Mississauga, Ont**	**189.4835**
2. Kerry Shcklock, Eng	183.9717
3. Celeste Ferraris, Aus	172.6626

Duet

1. **Lisa Alexander, Mississauga,Ont,**
Erin Woodley, Toronto, Ont **188.0894**
2. Kerry Shacklock, Laila Vakil, Eng 182.6803
3. Celeste Ferraris, Monique Downs, Aus 167.1646

■ Women's Diving

10-metre Platform

	Points
1. **Anne Montminy, Pt-Claire, Que**	**428.58**
2. **Paige Gordon, W Vancouver BC**	**414.36**
3. **Myriam Boileau, Blainville, Que**	**411.21**

One-metre Springboard

1. **Annie Pelletier, Montreal, Que** **279.66**
2. Jodie Rogers, Aus 252.72
3. **Mary DiPiero, Thunder Bay, Ont** **245.34**

Three-metre Springboard

1. **Annie Pelletier, Montreal, Que** **529.86**
2. **Paige Gordon, West Vancouver, BC** **529.08**
3. Jodie Rogers, Aus 474.81

■ Men's Diving

One-metre Springboard

	Points
1. **Jason Napper, Thunder Bay, Ont**	**364.08**
2. Michael Murphy, Aus	363.18
3. Evan Stewart, Zim	357.78

Three-metre Springboard

1. Michael Murphy, Aus 671.76
2. Evan Stewart, Zim 625.86
3. **Jason Napper, Thunder Bay, Ont** **621.03**

10-metre Platform

1. Michael Murphy, Aus 614.70
2. Robert Morgan, Wales 585.96
3. **Claude Villeneuve, Jonquiere, Que** **581.22**

■ Men's Athletics

100 Metres

1. Linford Christie, Eng 9.91*
2. Michael Green, Jam 10.05
3. Frankie Fredericks, Nam 10.06

200 Metres

1. Frankie Fredericks, Nam 19.97*
2. John Regis, Eng 20.25
3. Daniel Effiong, Nig 20.40

400 Metres

1. Charles Gotnga, Ken 45.00
2. Duaine Ladejo, Eng 45.11
3. Sunday Bada, Nig 45.45

800 Metres

1. Patrick Konchellah, Ken 1:45.18
2. Hezekiel Sepeng, S Afr 1:45.76
3. Svaieri Ngidhi, Zimb 1:46.06

1500 Metres

1. Reuben Chesang, Ken 3:36.70
2. **Kevin Sullivan, Brantford, Ont** **3:36.79**
3. John Mayock, Eng 3:37.22

5000 Metres

1. Robert Denmark, Eng 13:23.00
2. Philemon Hanneck, Zim 13:23.20
3. John Nuttall, Eng 13:23.54

10,000 Metres

1. Lameck Agutu, Ken 28:38.22
2. Tendai Chimusasa, Zimb 28:47.72
3. Fackson Nkandu, Zamb 28:51.72

4x100 Relay

1. **Canada** **38.39***
2. Australia 38.88
3. England 39.39

4x400 Relay

1. England 3:02.14*
2. Jamaica 3:02.32
3. Trinidad & Tobago 3:02.78

110-Metre Hurdles

1. Colin Jackson, Wales 13.08*
2. Anthony Jarrett, Eng 13.22
3. Paul Gray, Wales 13.54

400-Metre Hurdles

1. Samuel Mtete, Zambia 48.67*
2. Gidoen Biwait, Ken 49.43
3. Barnabas Kenyor, Ken 49.50

3000 Metre Steeplechase

1. Johnstone Kipkoech, Ken 8:14.72*
2. Geodion Chirchir, Ken 8:15.25
3. **Graeme Fell, Vancouver , BC** **8:23.28**

30-km Race Walk

1. Nicholas A'Hern, Aus 2:07:53
2. **Tim Berrett, Edmonton , Alta** **2:08:22**
3. Scott Nelson, NZ 2:09:10

Marathon

1. Stephen Moneghetti, Aus 2:11:49
2. Sean Quilty, Aus 2:14:57
3. Mark Hudspith, Eng 2:15:11

Wheelchair Marathon

1. Paul Wiggins, Aus 1:37:33
2. Ivan Newman, Eng 1:41:55
3. Benjamin Lucas, NZ 1:42:19

800-Metre Wheelchair

1. **Jeff Adams, Brampton, Ont** **1:44.94**
2. David Holding, Eng 1:45:13
3. Paul Wiggins, Aus 1:45.40

High Jump

1. Tim Forsyth, Aus 2.32
2. Stephen Smith, Eng 2.32
3. Geoffrey Parsons, Scot 2.31

Long Jump

1. Obinna Eregbu, Nig 8.05
2. David Culbert, Aus 8.00
3. **Ian James, Georgetown, Ont** **7.93**

Triple Jump

1. Julian Golley, Eng 17.03*
2. Jonathan Edwards, Eng 17.00
3. Brian Wellman, Bermuda 17.00

Pole Vault

1. Neil Winter, Wales 5.40*
2. **Curtis Heywood, Penticton, BC** **5.30**
3. James Miller, Aus 5.30

Javelin

1. Steve Backley, Eng 82.74
2. Michael Hill, Eng 81.84
3. Gavin Lovegrove, NZ 80.42

Discus

1. Werner Reiterer, Aus 62.78
2. Adewale Olukoju, Nig 62.46
3. Robert Weir, Eng 60.86

Hammer

1. Sean Carlin, Aus . . . . 73.48 m
2. Peter Vivian, Eng . . . . 69.80 m
3. Micheal Jones, Eng . . . . 68.42 m

Shot Put

1. Matthew Simson, Eng 19.49
2. Courtney Ireland NZ 19.38
3. Chima Ugwu, Nig 19.26

Decathlon

	Points
1. **Michael Smith, Toronto, Ont**	**8326**
2. Peter Winter, Aus	8074
3. Simon Shirley, Eng	7980

■ Women's Athletics

100 Metres

1. Mary Onyali, Nig 11.06
2. C. Opara-Thompson, Nig 11.22
3. Paula Thomas, Eng 11.23

200 Metres

1. Catherine Freeman, Aus 22.25*
2. Mary Onyali, Nig 22.35
3. Melinda Gainsford, Aus 22.68

400 Metres

1. Catherine Freeman, Aus 50.38*
2. Fatima Yusuf, Nig 50.53
3. Sandie Richards, Jam 50.59

800 Metres

1. Inez Turner, Jam 2:01.74
2. **Charmaine Crooks, N Vancouver , BC** **2:02.35**
3. Gladys Warnuyu, Ken 2:03.12

1500 Metres

1. Kelly Holmes, Eng 4:08.86
2. **Paula Schnurr Burlington, Ont** **4:09.65**
3. Gwen Griffiths, S Afr 4:10.16

3000 Metres

1. Angela Chalmers, Victoria 8:32.17*
2. **Robyn Meagher, Mulgrave, NS** **8:45.59**
3. Alison Wyeth, Eng 8:47.9

10,000 Metres

1. Yvonne Murray, Scot 31:56.97
2. Elana Meyer, S Afr 32:06.02
3. Jane Omora, Ken 32:13.01

4x100 Relay

1. Nigeria 42.99*
2. Australia 43.43
3. England 43.46

4x400 Relay

1. England 3:27.06*
2. Jamaica 3:27.63
3. **Canada** **3:32.52**

100-Metre Hurdle

1. Michelle Freeman, Jam 13.12
2. Jacqueline Agyepong, Eng 13.14
3. S. Farquharson, Eng 13.38

400-Metre Hurdles

1. Sally Gunnell, Eng 54.51*
2. Deon Hemmings, Jam 55.11
3. Debbie-Ann Parris, Jam 55.25

10-km Race Walk

1. Kerry Saxby-Junna, Aus 44:25*
2. Anne Manning, Aus 44:37
3. **Janice McCaffrey, Calgary, Alta** **44:54**

Marathon

1. **Carol Rouillard, Montreal, Que** **2:30:41**
2. **Lizanne Bussieres, Frelighsburg, Que** **2:31:07**
3. Yvonne Danson, Eng 2:32:24

High Jump

1. Alison Inverarity, Aus 1.94*
2. Charmaine Weavers, S Afr 1.94
3. Debora Marti, Eng 1.91

Long Jump

1. Nicole Boegman, Aus 6.82
2. Oluyinka Idowu Nig 6.73
3. C. Opara-Thompson, Nig 6.72

Javelin

1. Louise McPaul, Aus 63.76
2. Kirsten Hellier, NZ 60.40
3. Sharon Gibson, Eng 58.20

Discus

1. Daniela Castian, Aus 63.72*
2. Beatrice Faumunia, ... NZ 57.12
3. Maria Etzebeth, S Afr 55.74

Shot Put

1. Judy Oakes, Eng 18.16
2. Myrtle Augee, Eng 17.64
3. Lisa Vizaniari, Aus 16.61

Heptathlon

	Points
1. Denise Lewis, Eng	6325
2. Jane Flemming, Aus	6317
3. **Catherine Bond-Mills, Woodstock, Ont**	**6193**

■ Women's Cycling

50K Time Trial

1. Australia 1:04:03.20
2. **Canada** **1:04:18.92**
3. England 1:05:32.85

93-6-km Road Race

1. Kathryn Watt, Aus 2:48:04
2. **Linda Jackson, Ottawa, Ont** **2:48:34**
3. **Alison Sydor, N Vancouver, BC** **2:50:17**

3000-Metre Individual Pursuit

1. Kathryn Watt, Aus 3:48.522*
2. Sarah Ulmer, NZ 3:50.953
3. Jacqueline nelson, NZ 3:55.241

25-km Points Race

1. Yvonne McGregor, Eng
2. Jacqueline Nelson, NZ
3. Sally Hodge, Wales

Sprint

1. Tanya Dubnicoff, Winnipeg, Man
2. Michelle ferris, NZ
3. Donna Wynd, NZ

■ Men's Cycling

100K Time Trial

1. Australia 1:53:19.13
2. England 1:56:40.76
3. New Zealand 1:56:52.82

181.9-km Road Race

1. Mark Rendell, NZ 4:46:07
2. Brian Fowler, NZ 4:48:09
3. W. Englebrecht, S Af 4:48:10

1000-metre Time Trial

1. Shane Key, Aus 1:05.386*
2. Darryl Hill, Aus 1:05.632
3. Tim O'Shannessy, Aus 1:06.789

4000-metre Individual Pursuit

1. Bradley McGee, Aus
2. Shaun Wallace, Eng
3. Stuart O'Grady, Aus

10 Miles

1. Stuart O'GRady, Aus 18:50.52*
2. Glenn McLeay, NZ
3. **Brian Walton, Delta, BC**

Sprint

1. Gary Niewand, Aus
2. **Curt Harnett, Thunder bay, Ont**
3. Darryn Hill, Aus

40K Points Race

1. Brett Aitken, Aus
2. Stuart O'Grady, Aus
3. Dean Woods, Aus

4000 Team Pursuit

1. Australia
2. England

■ Women's Gymnastics

	Points
Team	
1. England	114.225
2. **Canada**	**113.650**
3. Australia	113.625
Individual All-around	
1. **Stella Umeh, Mississauga, Ont**	**38.400**
2. Rebecca Stoyel, Aus	38.037
3. Zita Lusack, Eng	37.725
Vault	
1. **Stella Umeh, Mississauga, Ont**	**9.556**
2. Sonia Lawrence, Wales	9.543
3. **Lisa Simes, Regina, Sask**	**9.506**
Uneven Bars	
1. Rebecca Stoyel, Aus	9.525
2. **Stella Umeh, Mississauaga, Ont**	**9.450**
3. Sarah Thompson, NZ	9.337
Floor	
1. Annika Reeder, Eng	9.750
2. Jacqueline Brady, Eng	9.662
3. **Lisa Simes, Regina, Sask**	**9.550**
Balance Beam	
1. Sally Wills, Aus	9.075
2. Zita Lusack, Eng	8.987
3. Ruth Moniz, Aus	8.900

■ Men's Gymnastics

	Points
Team	
1. **Canada**	**164.700**
2. Australia	164.500
3. England	162.375

Individual All-around

1. Neil Thomas, Eng 55.950
2. Brennon Dowrick, Aus 55.525
3. Peter Hogan, Aus 54.950

Floor

1. Neil Thomas, Eng 9.662
2. Kris Burley, Truro, NS 9.437
3. **Alan Nolet, Brampton, Ont** **9.150**

Pommel Horse

1. Brennon Dowrick, Aus 9.425
2. Nathan Kingston, Aus 9.400
3. **Richard Ikeda, Abbotsford, BC** **9.225**

Rings

1. Lee McDermott, Eng 9.475
2. Peter Hogan, Aus 9.275
3. **Richard Ikeda, Abbotsford, BC** **9.150**
   Brennon Dowrick Aus 9.150

Vault

1. Bret Hudson, Aus 9.375
2. Kris Burley, Truro 9.312
3. Neil Thomas, Eng 9.306

Parallel Bars

1. Peter Hogan, Aus 9.400
2. Kris Burley, Truro 9.350
3. Brennon Dowrick, Aus 9.250

Horizontal Bar

1. **Alan Nolet, Brampton, Ont** **9.512**
2. **Richard Ikeda, Abbotsford, BC** **9.500**
3. Nathan Kingston, Aus 9.325

■ Rhythmic Gymnastics

	Points
Team	
1. **Canada**	**106.9**
2. Australia	105.3
3. England	103.3
Individual All-around	
1. Kasumi Takahashi, Aus	36.85
2. **Camille Martens, Vernon, BC**	**36.60**
3. Debbie Southwick, Eng	36.35
Hoop	
1. Kasumi Takahashi, Aus	9.30
2. **Lindsay Richards, Brampton, Ont**	**9.05**
3. Aicha McKenzie, Eng	8.90
Joanne Walker, Scot	8.90
Ball	
1. Kasumi Takahashi, Aus	9.20
2. **Camille Martens, Vernon, BC**	**9.00**
3. **Gretchen McLennan, Delta, BC**	**8.80**
Aicha McKenzie, Eng	8.80

Clubs

1. Kasumi Takahashi, Aus 9.40
2. **Camille Martens, Vernon, BC** **9.15**
3. Leigh Marning, Aus 9.00

Ribbon

1. Kasumi Takahashi, Aus 9.20
2. **Camille Martens, Vernon, BC** **9.05**
3. Gretchen McLennan, Delta, BC **9.00**

■ Men's Shooting

Points

Pairs Air Rifle

1. **J-F Senecal, Laval,**
Wayne Sorensen, Calgary, Alta **1166***
2. Christopher Hector, Nigel Wallace, Eng 1161
3. David Rattray, Robert Law, Scot 1145

Pairs Free Pistol

1. Philip Adams, Bengt Sandstrom, Aus 1074
2. Julian Lawton, Greg Yelavich, NZ 1094
3. Michael Gault, Paul Leatherdale, Eng 1082

Pairs Smallbore Rifle Prone

1. Stephen Petterson, Lindsay Arthur, NZ, ... 1181
2. D.H. Chandasiri, L. Rajasingh, Sri Lanka 1177
3. David Clifton, Dean Turley, Aus 1176

Pairs Rapid Fire Pistol

1. Patrick Murray, Robert Dowling, Aus 1148
2. Richard Craven, Michael Jay, Wales, ... 1142
3. Adrian Breton, G. Le Maitre, Guernsey 1131

Pairs Trap

1. Thomas Hewitt, Samuel Allen, N Ire 188
2. **Ron Bonotto, Toronto,**
George Leary, Newmarket, Ont **187**
3. Robert Borsley, John Grice, Eng 186

Pairs Running Target

1. **Mark & Matthew Bedlington,**
Bridgenorth, Ont **1088**
(only gold awarded)

Pairs Centre-fire Pistol

1. Jaspal Rana, Ashok Pandit, Ind 1168
2. Philip Adams, Kelvin Vickers, Aus 1140
3. **John Rochon, Elliot Lake, Ont,**
Stanley Wills, Lethbridge, Alta **1148**

Pairs Fullbore Rifle

1. Albert Bowden, Geoffrey Grenfell, Aus 593
2. Glyn Barnett, Tony Ringer, Eng 588
3. David Calvert, Martin Milar, N Ire 584

Pairs Air Pistol

1. M. Gisutiniano, B. Sandstrom, Aus 1137
2. **Jean-Pierre Huot, Pondbriand, Que,**
John Rochon, Elliot Lake, Ont **1135**

3. Jaspal Rana, Vivek Singh, Ind 1133

Pairs Smallbore Rifle, 3-position

1. **Michel Dion, Pt-Rouge, Que,**
Wayne Soresen, Calgary, Alta **2300**
2. Alister Allan, William Murray, Scot 2271
3. Chris Hector, Trevor Langridge, Eng 2259

Open Pairs Skeet

1. Antonis Andreou, Kristos Kourtellas, Cyprus . . 189
2. Brian Thompson, Geoffrey Jukes, NZ 186
3. Michael Thompson, Ian Marsden, Eng 186

Air Rifle

1. Chris Hector, Eng 685.9*
2. **J-F Senecal, Laval, Que** **683.0**
3. Nigel Wallace, Eng 680.0

Smallbore Rifle Prone

1. Stephen Petterson, NZ 698.4*
2. James Cornish, Eng 696.9
3. Michel Dion, Pont Rouge 694.6

Running Target

1. Brian Wilson, Aus 657.9*
2. **Mark Bedlington, Bridgenorth, Ont** **656.0**
3. Paul Carmine, NZ 650.7

Open Trap

1. Mansher Singh, Ind 141
2. **George Leary, Newmarket, Ont** **140**
3. Andreas Anglou, Cyprus 137

Rapid Fire Pistol

1. Michael jay, Wales 670.2*
2. Robert Dowling, Aus 668.4
3. Pat Murray, Aus 668.1

Fullbore Rifle

1. David Calvert, N Ire 398*
2. Geoffrey Smith, NZ 398
3. Glyn Barnett, Eng 397

C-Fire Pistol

1. Jaspal Rana, Ind 581
2. Michael Gault, Eng 581
3. Gregory Yelavich, NZ 575

Smallbore Rifle, 3-position

1. **Michel Dion, Pont-Rouge, Que** **1234.2***
2. **Wayne Sorensen, Calgary, Alta** **1228.7**
3. Alister Allan, Scot 1224.8

Air Pistol

1. Jean-Pierre Huot, Pondbriand 672.4*
2. Jaspal Rana, Ind 670.7
3. Gregory Yelavich, NZ 668.5

Skeet

1. Ian Hale, Aus 144
2. Christos Kourtellas, Cyp 143
3. Andrew Austin, Eng 143

■ Women's Shooting

Points

Pair Sports Pistol

1. Christine Trefry, Annette Woodward, Aus . . . 1,134
2. **Sharon Cozzarin, Fergus, Ont,
Helen Smith, London, Ont** **1,132**
3. Margaret Thomas, Carol Page, Eng 1,129

Pairs Smallbore Rifle Prone

1. Kim Frazer, Sylvia Purdie, Aus 1,160
2. Shirley McIntosh, P. Littlechild, Scot 1,158
3. **Christina Ashcroft, Waterloo, Ont,
Lydia Szuiga, Pt-Claire, Que** **1,158**

Pairs Smallbore Rifle, 3-position

1. **Sharon Bowes, Pt-Claire, Que,
Christina Ashcroft, Waterloo, Ont** **1143**
2. Karen Morton, Lindsay Volpin, Eng 1132
3. Roopa Unikrishnan, Kuhel Gangulee, India . . 1110

Pairs Air Pistol

1. Annette Woodward, Christine Trefry, Aus 747
2. Gerd Barkman, Jocelyn Lees, NZ 745
3. Carol Page, Margaret Thomas, Eng 743

Sport Pistol

1. Christine Trefry, Aus 679.4
2. Margarte Thomas, Eng 675.0
3. Annette Woodward, Aus, ... 674.0

Smallbore Rifle Prone

1. Shirley McIntosh, Scot 586
2. Sylvia Purdie, Aus 585
3. P. Littlechild, Scot 585

Air Rifle

1. Fani Theofanous, Cyprus 101.7
2. Mali Wickremasingh, Sri Lanka 103.5
3. **Sharon Bowes, Pt-Claire , Que** **97.4**

Air Pistol

1. **Helen Smith, London, Ont** **474.2**
2. Annette Woodward, Aus 466.1
3. Sharon Cozzarin, Fergus 465.8

Smallbore Rifle, 3-position

1. **Sharon Bowes, Pt-Claire, Que** **666.4**
2. Roopa Unikrishnan 662.5
3. **Christina Ashcroft, Courtenay, BC** **661.6**

■ Badminton

Team Final

England 4, Malaysia 2

Men's Singles

Rashid Sidek, Malaysia def, Ewe Hock Ong, Malaysia
15-6, 15-4

Men's Doubles

Soan Kit Cheah and Beng Kiang Soo, Malaysia def. Siumon
SArcher and Christopehr Hunt, Eng 15-10, 15-9

Women's Singles

Lisa Campbell, Aus def. Si-an Deng, Richmond, BC 11-2, 11-5

Women's Doubles

Joanne Muggeride and Joanne Wright, Eng def. Gillian Clark
and Julie Bradbury, Eng 15-9, 15-11

Mixed Doubles

Christopher Hunt and Gillian Clark, Eng def Simon Archer and
Julie Brabdury, Eng 15-11, 15-4

■ Men's Lawn Bowling

Singles

Scotland 25 England 20

Pairs

Australia 18 Wales 14

Fours

South Africa 21 Australia 18

■ Women's Lawn Bowling

Singles

Northern Ireland 25 Wales 17

Pairs

Scotland 32 South Africa 18

Fours

South Africa 24 Papua New Guinea 17

■ Visually Impaired Lawn Bowling

Men's Singles

Scotland 21 Australia 18

Women's Singles

New Zealand 21, Wales 6

■ Wrestling

Light Flyweight (48kg)

1. Jacob Isaac, Nig
2. **Paul Ragusa, Kingston, Ont**
3. Ramesh Kumar, Ind

Flyweight (52kg)

1. **Selwyn Tam, Vancouver, BC**
2. Andrew Hutchinson, Eng
3. Kirpa Shankar, Ind

Bantamweight (57kg)

1. **Robert Dawson, Windsor, Ont**
2. Ashok Kumar, Ind
3. Cory O'Brien, Aus

Featherweight (62kg)

1. **Marty Calder, St Catharines, Ont**
2. John Melling, Eng
3. A. Barseguian, Cyprus

Lightweight (68kg)

1. **Chris Wilson, Winnipeg, Man**
2. Ibo Oziti, Nig
3. Muhammed Umar, Pak

Welterweight (74kg)

1. **David Hohl, Winnipeg, Man**
2. Reinold Ozoline, Aus
3. Calum McNeil, Scot

Middleweight (82kg)

1. **Justin Abdou, Moose Jaw, Sask**
2. Randir Singh, Ind
3. M. Bhala Bhola, Pak

Light Heavyweight (90kg)

1. **Scott Bianco, Kamloops, BC**
2. Kodel Victor, Nigeria
3. Graeme English, Scot

Heavyweight (100kg)

1. **Greg Edgelow, Vernon, BC**
2. Noel Loban, Eng
3. Subhash Verma, Ind

Super Heavyweight (130kg)

1. **Andrew Borodow, Montreal, Que**
2. Bidei Jackson, Nig
3. Amerjit Singh, Eng

■ Weightlifting

	Kilos

54 kg Snatch

1. Murgeson Virasamy, Ind 105
2. Badathala Adisekhar, Ind 105
3. **Francois Lagace, St-Hyacinthe, Que** . . . **105**

54 kg Clean and Jerk

1. B. Adisekhar, Ind 132.5
2. Matin Gunthali, Mal 130
3. M. Veerasamy, Ind 127.5

54 kg Total

1. B. Adisekhar, Ind 237.5
2. M. Veerasamy, Ind 232.5
3. **Francois Lagace, St-Hyacinthe, Que** . . . **227.5**

64 kg Snatch

1. Najite Ogbodu, Nig N.A.
2. Sevdalin Marinov, Aus N.A.
3. Oliver Toby, Nig N.A.

64 kg Clean and Jerk

1. Oliver Toby, Nig N.A.
2. Sevdalin Marinov, Aus N.A.
3. Najite Ogbodu, Nig N.A.

64 kg Total

1. Sevdalin Marinov, Aus 277.5
2. Najite Ogbodu, Nig 275.0
3. Oliver Toby, Nig N.A.

76 kg Snatch

1. David Morgan, Wales 147.5*
2. **Serge Tremblay, Dolbeau, Que** **145.0**
3. Damian Brown, Aus 142.5

76 kg Clean and Jerk

1. Damian Brown, Aus 182.5
2. David Morgan, Wales 180.0
3. Serge Tremblay, Dolbeau 172.5

76 kg Total

1. David Morgan, Wales 327.5
2. Damian Brown, Aus 325.0
3. Serge Tremblay, Dolbeau 317.5

83 kg Snatch

1. Kiril Kounev, Aus 152.5
2. Stephen Ward, Eng 147.5
3. **Yvan Darsigny, St-Hyacinthe, Que** . . . . . **142.5#**

83 kg Clean and Jerk

1. Kiril Kounev, Aus 200.0
2. Stephen Ward, Eng 187.5
3. **Yvan Darsigny, St-Hyacinthe, Que** . . . . . **175.0#**

83 kg Total

1; Kiril Kounev, Aus 352.5
2. Stephen Ward, Eng 335.0
3. **Yvan Darsigny, St-Hyacinthe, Que** . . . . . **317.5#**

Darsigny awarded all bronze medals when Jim Dan Corbett of new Waterford, NS tested positive for banned stimulants

91 kg Snatch

1. Harvey Goodman, Aus 162.5
2. Peter May, Eng 155.0
3. Collins Okath, Ken 120.0

91 kg Clean and Jerk

1. Harvey Goodman, Aus 200.0
2. Peter May, Eng 190.0
3. Collins Okath, Ken 120.0

91 kg Total

1. Harvey Goodman, Aus 362.5
2. Peter May, Eng 345.0
3. Collins Okath, Ken 240.0

99 kg Snatch

1. Chris Onyezie, Nig 155.0
2. Andrew Saxtoon, Aus 155.0
3. Phillip Christou, Aus 152.5

99 kg Clean and Jerk

1. Andrew Callard, Eng 197.5
2. Andrew Saxton, Aus 192.5
3. Chris Onyezie, Nig 190.0

99 kg Total

1. Andrew Callard, Eng 347.5
2. Andrew Saxton, Aus 347.5
3. Chris Onyezie, Nig 345.0

108 kg Snatch

1. Nicu Vlad, Aus 185
2. Innocent Chika, Nig 160
3. Gareth Hives, Wales 130

108 kg Clean and Jerk

1. Nicu Vlad, Aus 220
2. Innocent Chika, Nig 200
3. Gareth Hives, Wales 160

108 kg Total

1. Nicu Vlad, Aus 405
2. Innocent Chika, Nig 360
3. Gareth Hives, Wales 290

108 plus kg Snatch

1. Steven Kettner, Aus 165.0
2. Stefan Botev, Aus 160.0
3. Victor Edem, Aus 155.0

108 plus kg Clean and Jerk

1. Stefan Botev, Aus 200
2. Steven Kettner, Aus 195
3. Victor Edem, Nig 190

108 plus kg Total

1. Stefan Botev, Aus 360
2. Steven Kettner, Aus 360
3. Victor Edem, Nig 345

■ Boxing

Light Flyweight (48kg)

1. Haman Ramadhani, Ken
2. Victor Kasote, Zamb

Flyweight (51kg)

1. Paul Shepherd, Scot
2. Dancan Karanja, Ken

Bantamweight (54kg)

1. Robert Peden, Aus
2. Spencer Oliver, Eng

Featherwieght (57kg)

1. Casey Patton, London, Ont
2. Jason Cook, Wales

Lightweight (60kg)

1. Mike Strange, Niagara falls, Ont
2. Martin Renaghan, N Ire

Light Welterweight (63.5 kg)

1. Peter Richardson, Eng
2. Mark Winters, N Ire

Welterweight (67kg)

1. Neil Sinclair, N Ire
2. Albert Eromosele, Nig

Light Middleweight (71kg)

1. James Webb, N Ire
2. Bob Gasia, Western Samoa

Middleweight (75kg)

1. Rowan Donaldson, Montreal, Que
2. Rasmus Ojemaye, Nig

Light Heavyweight (81kg)

1. Dale Brown, Calgary, Atla
2. John Wilson, Scot

Heavywright (91kg)

1. Omsaar Ahmed, Ken
2. Stephen Gallinger, St Catharines, Ont

Super Heavyweight (plus 91kg)

1. Duncan Dakiwari, Nig
2. Miriambo Anyim, Ken

National Hockey League, 1993–94

Final Standings

Eastern Conference

■ Northeast Division

	W	L	T	GF	GA	Pts
Pittsburgh	44	27	13	299	285	101
Boston	42	29	13	289	252	97
Montreal	41	29	14	283	248	96
Buffalo	43	32	9	282	218	95
Quebec	34	42	8	277	292	76
Hartford	27	48	9	227	288	63
Ottawa	14	61	9	201	397	37

■ Atlantic Division

	W	L	T	GF	GA	Pts
NY Rangers	52	24	8	299	231	112
New Jersey	47	25	12	306	220	106
Washington	39	35	10	277	263	88
NY Islanders	36	36	12	282	264	84
Florida	33	34	17	233	233	83
Philadelphia	35	39	10	294	314	80
Tampa Bay	30	43	11	224	251	71

Western Conference

■ Central Division

	W	L	T	GF	GA	Pts
Detroit	46	30	8	356	275	100
Toronto	43	29	12	280	243	98
Dallas	42	29	13	286	265	97
St Louis	40	33	11	270	283	91
Chicago	39	36	9	254	240	87
Winnipeg	24	51	9	245	344	57

■ Pacific Division

	W	L	T	GF	GA	Pts
Calgary	42	29	13	302	256	97
Vancouver	41	40	3	279	276	85
San Jose	33	35	16	252	265	82
Anaheim	33	46	5	229	251	71
Los Angeles	27	45	12	294	322	66
Edmonton	25	45	14	261	305	64

*Until 1993-94, the Eastern Conference was the Prince of Wales Conference, the Western Conference was the Clarence Campbell Conference

NHL Playoff Results, 1994

■ Eastern Conference

Teams, Result

NY Islanders	0	at	NY Rangers	6
NY Islanders	0	at	NY Rangers	6
NY Rangers	5	at	Ny Islanders	1
NY Rangers	5	at	Ny Islanders	2

NY Rangers won series 4–0

Washington	5	at	Pittsburgh	3
Washington	1	at	Pittsburgh	2
Pittsburgh	0	at	Washington	2
Pittsburgh	1	at	Washington	4
Washington	2	at	Pittsburgh	3
Pittsburgh	3	at	Washington	6

Washington won series 4–2

Buffalo	2	at	New Jersey	0
Buffalo	1	at	New Jersey	2
New Jersey	2	at	Buffalo	1
New Jersey	3	at	Buffalo	5
Buffalo	3	at	New Jersey	5
New Jersey	0	at	Buffalo	1
Buffalo	1	at	New Jersey	2

New Jersey won series 4–3

Montreal	2	at	Boston	3
Montreal	3	at	Boston	2
Boston	6	at	Montreal	3
Boston	2	at	Montreal	5
Montreal	2	at	Boston	1
Boston	3	at	Montreal	2
Montreal	3	at	Boston	5

Boston won series 4–3

▶

■ Western Conference

Teams, Result

San Jose	5	at	Detroit	4
San Jose	0	at	Detroit	4
Detroit	3	at	San Jose	2
Detroit	3	at	San Jose	4
Detroit	4	at	San Jose	6
San Jose	1	at	Detroit	7
San Jose	3	at	Detroit	2

San Jose won series 4–3

Vancouver	5	at	Calgary	0
Vancouver	5	at	Calgary	7
Calgary	4	at	Vancouver	2
Calgary	3	at	Vancouver	2
Vancouver	2	at	Calgary	1
Calgary	2	at	Vancouver	3
Vancouver	4	at	Calgary	3

Vancouver won series 4–3

Chicago	1	at	Toronto	5
Chicago	0	at	Toronto	1
Toronto	4	at	Chicago	5
Toronto	3	at	Chicago	4
Chicago	0	at	Toronto	1
Toronto	1	at	Chicago	0

Toronto won series 4–2

St Louis	3	at	Dallas	5
St Louis	2	at	Dallas	4
Dallas	5	at	St Louis	4
Dallas	2	at	St Louis	1

Dallas won series 4–0

■ Eastern Conference Semifinals

Teams, Result

Washington	3	at	NY Rangers	6
Washington	2	at	NY Rangers	6
NY Rangers	3	at	Washington	0
NY Rangers	2	at	Washington	4
Washington	3	at	NY Rangers	4

NY Rangers won series 4–1

Boston	2	at	New Jersey	1
Boston	6	at	New Jersey	5
New Jersey	4	at	Boston	2
New Jersey	5	at	Boston	4
Boston	0	at	New Jersey	2
New Jersey	5	at	Boston	3

New Jersey won series 4–2

■ Eastern Conference Finals

Teams, Result

New Jersey	4	at	NY Rangers	3
New Jersey	0	at	NY Rangers	4
NY Rangers	3	at	New Jersey	2
NY Rangers	1	at	New Jersey	3
New Jersey	4	at	NY Rangers	1
NY Rangers	4	at	New Jersey	2
New Jersey	1	at	NY Rangers	2

NY Rangers won series 4–3

■ Western Conference Semifinals

Teams, Result

San Jose	3	at	Toronto	2
San Jose	1	at	Toronto	5
Toronto	2	at	San Jose	5
Toronto	8	at	San Jose	3
Toronto	2	at	San Jose	5
San Jose	2	at	Toronto	3
San Jose	2	at	Toronto	4

Toronto won series 4–3

Vancouver	6	at	Dallas	4
Vancouver	3	at	Dallas	0
Dallas	4	at	Vancouver	3
Dallas	1	at	Vancouver	2
Dallas	2	at	Vancouver	4

Vancouver won series 4–1

■ Western Conference Finals

Teams, Result

Vancouver	2	at	Toronto	3
Vancouver	4	at	Toronto	3
Toronto	0	at	Vancouver	4
Toronto	0	at	Vancouver	2
Toronto	3	at	Vancouver	4

Vancouver won series 4–1

■ Stanley Cup Finals

Teams, Result

Vancouver	3	at	NY Rangers	2
Vancouver	1	at	NY Rangers	3
NY Rangers	5	at	Vancouver	1
NY Rangers	4	at	Vancouver	2
Vancouver	6	at	NY Rangers	3
NY Rangers	1	at	Vancouver	4
Vancouver	2	at	NY Rangers	3

NY Rangers won series 4–3

Major League Arenas and Stadiums in Canada

■ Hockey

Name, Location	Seating Capacity
Le Collisée, Quebec	15 399
Maple Leaf Gardens, Toronto	15 642
Montreal Forum	16 197
Northlands Coliseum, Edmonton	17 313
Olympic Saddledome, Calgary	20 133
Pacific Coliseum, Vancouver	16 123
Winnipeg Arena	15 393

■ Football/Baseball

Name, Location	Seating Capacity
B.C. Place, Vancouver	59 478b
Commonwealth Stadium, Edmonton	60 081
Ivor Wynne Stadium, Hamilton	29 123
Frank Clair Stadium, Ottawa	30 927
McMahon Stadium, Calgary	37 317
Olympic Stadium, Montreal	43 739
Taylor Field, Regina	27 637
Winnipeg Stadium	32 648
SkyDome, Toronto	50 377a

(a) Baseball capacity is approx. 51 000, including restaurant and box seating. (b) Regular season capacity 40,800)

Stanley Cup Champions, 1918–94

The Stanley Cup, the oldest trophy competed for by professional athletes in North America, was donated by Frederick Arthur, Lord Stanley of Preston, in 1893. Originally presented to the amateur hockey champions of Canada, it has been awarded to the top professional team since 1910 and, since 1926, has been competed for only by NHL teams.

Year	Champion	Final Opponent	Series Result	Winning Coach	Winning Manager
1918	Toronto Arenas	Vancouver	3-2	Dick Carroll	Charlie Querrie
1919[1]	No decision				
1920	Ottawa Senators	Seattle	3-2	Pete Green	Tommy Gorman
1921	Ottawa Senators	Vancouver	3-2	Pete Green	Tommy Gorman
1922	Toronto St. Pats	Vancouver	3-2	Eddie Powers	Charlie Querrie
1923[2]	Ottawa Senators	Vancouver; Edm.	3-1; 2-0	Pete Green	Tommy Gorman
1924[3]	Montreal Canadiens	Vancouver; Calgary	2-0; 2-0	Leo Dandurand	Leo Dandurand
1925	Victoria Cougars	Montreal	3-1	Lester Patrick	Lester Patrick
1926	Montreal Maroons	Victoria	3-1	Eddie Gerard	Eddie Gerard
1927	Ottawa Senators	Boston	2-0	Dave Gill	Dave Gill
1928	New York Rangers	Montreal	3-2	Lester Patrick	Lester Patrick
1929	Boston Bruins	New York	2-0	Cy Denneny	Art Ross
1930	Montreal Canadiens	Boston	2-0	Cecil Hart	Cecil Hart
1931	Montreal Canadiens	Chicago	3-2	Cecil Hart	Cecil Hart
1932	Toronto Maple Leafs	New York	3-0	Dick Irvin	Conn Smythe
1933	New York Rangers	Toronto	3-1	Lester Patrick	Lester Patrick
1934	Chicago Black Hawks	Detroit	3-1	Tommy Gorman	Tommy Gorman
1935	Montreal Maroons	Toronto	3-0	Tommy Gorman	Tommy Gorman
1936	Detroit Red Wings	Toronto	4-0	Jack Adams	Jack Adams
1937	Detroit Red Wings	New York	3-2	Jack Adams	Jack Adams
1938	Chicago Black Hawks	Toronto	4-1	Bill Stewart	Bill Stewart
1939	Boston Bruins	Toronto	4-1	Art Ross	Art Ross
1940	New York Rangers	Toronto	4-2	Frank Boucher	Lester Patrick
1941	Boston Bruins	Detroit	4-0	Cooney Weiland	Art Ross
1942	Toronto Maple Leafs	Detroit	4-3	Hap Day	Conn Smythe
1943	Detroit Red Wings	Boston	4-0	Jack Adams	Jack Adams
1944	Montreal Canadiens	Chicago	4-0	Dick Irvin	Tommy Gorman
1945	Toronto Maple Leafs	Detroit	4-3	Hap Day	Conn Smythe
1946	Montreal Canadiens	Boston	4-1	Dick Irvin	Tommy Gorman
1947	Toronto Maple Leafs	Montreal	4-2	Hap Day	Conn Smythe
1948	Toronto Maple Leafs	Detroit	4-0	Hap Day	Conn Smythe
1949	Toronto Maple Leafs	Detroit	4-0	Hap Day	Conn Smythe
1950	Detroit Red Wings	New York	4-3	Tommy Ivan	Jack Adams
1951	Toronto Maple Leafs	Montreal	4-1	Joe Primeau	Conn Smythe

▶

▶ 1952	Detroit Red Wings	Montreal	4-0	Tommy Ivan	Jack Adams
1953	Montreal Canadiens	Boston	4-1	Dick Irvin	Frank Selke
1954	Detroit Red Wings	Montreal	4-3	Tommy Ivan	Jack Adams
1955	Detroit Red Wings	Montreal	4-3	Jimmy Skinner	Jack Adams
1956	Montreal Canadiens	Detroit	4-1	Toe Blake	Frank Selke
1957	Montreal Canadiens	Boston	4-1	Toe Blake	Frank Selke
1958	Montreal Canadiens	Boston	4-2	Toe Blake	Frank Selke
1959	Montreal Canadiens	Toronto	4-1	Toe Blake	Frank Selke
1960	Montreal Canadiens	Toronto	4-0	Toe Blake	Frank Selke
1961	Chicago Black Hawks	Detroit	4-2	Rudy Pilous	Tommy Ivan
1962	Toronto Maple Leafs	Chicago	4-2	Punch Imlach	Punch Imlach
1963	Toronto Maple Leafs	Detroit	4-1	Punch Imlach	Punch Imlach
1964	Toronto Maple Leafs	Detroit	4-3	Punch Imlach	Punch Imlach
1965	Montreal Canadiens	Chicago	4-3	Toe Blake	Sam Pollock
1966	Montreal Canadiens	Detroit	4-2	Toe Blake	Sam Pollock
1967	Toronto Maple Leafs	Montreal	4-2	Punch Imlach	Punch Imlach
1968	Montreal Canadiens	St. Louis	4-0	Toe Blake	Sam Pollock
1969	Montreal Canadiens	St. Louis	4-0	Claude Ruel	Sam Pollock
1970	Boston Bruins	St. Louis	4-0	Harry Sinden	Milt Schmidt
1971	Montreal Canadiens	Chicago	4-3	Al MacNeil	Sam Pollock
1972	Boston Bruins	New York	4-2	Tom Johnson	Milt Schmidt
1973	Montreal Canadiens	Chicago	4-2	Scotty Bowman	Sam Pollock
1974	Philadelphia Flyers	Boston	4-2	Fred Shero	Keith Allen
1975	Philadelphia Flyers	Buffalo	4-2	Fred Shero	Keith Allen
1976	Montreal Canadiens	Philadelphia	4-0	Scotty Bowman	Sam Pollock
1977	Montreal Canadiens	Boston	4-0	Scotty Bowman	Sam Pollock
1978	Montreal Canadiens	Boston	4-2	Scotty Bowman	Sam Pollock
1979	Montreal Canadiens	New York	4-1	Scotty Bowman	Irving Grundman
1980	N.Y. Islanders	Philadelphia	4-2	Al Arbour	Bill Torrey
1981	N.Y. Islanders	Minnesota	4-1	Al Arbour	Bill Torrey
1982	N.Y. Islanders	Vancouver	4-0	Al Arbour	Bill Torrey
1983	N.Y. Islanders	Edmonton	4-0	Al Arbour	Bill Torrey
1984	Edmonton Oilers	New York	4-1	Glen Sather	Glen Sather
1985	Edmonton Oilers	Philadelphia	4-1	Glen Sather	Glen Sather
1986	Montreal Canadiens	Calgary	4-1	Jean Perron	Serge Savard
1987	Edmonton Oilers	Philadelphia	4-3	Glen Sather	Glen Sather
1988	Edmonton Oilers	Boston	4-0	Glen Sather	Glen Sather
1989	Calgary Flames	Montreal	4-2	Terry Crisp	Cliff Fletcher
1990	Edmonton Oilers	Boston	4-1	John Muckler	Glen Sather
1991	Pittsburgh Penguins	Minnesota	4-2	Bob Johnson	Craig Patrick
1992	Pittsburgh Penguins	Chicago	4-0	Scotty Bowman	Craig Patrick
1993	Montreal Canadiens	Los Angeles	4-1	Jacques Demers	Serge Savard
1994	New York Rangers	Vancouver	4-3	Mike Keenan	Neil Smith

Source: *National Hockey League*

(1) The series between Montreal Canadiens and Seattle Metropolitans was halted by Spanish influenza epidemic with the series tied at 2 wins each. (2) Ottawa also met and defeated Edmonton Eskimos, champions of the WCHL. (3) Because of an agreement between the NHL and the 2 western leagues (WCHL and PCHA), Canadiens had to play the champions of each league.

Directory of Selected Hockey Organizations

Hockey Hall
of Fame
30 Yonge St
Toronto, Ont.
M5E 1X8
Tel: (416)360-7735
Fax: (416)360-1316

National
Hockey League
1155 Metcalfe St, Suite 960
Montreal, Que.
H3B 2W2
Tel: (514)871-9220

National Hockey League
Players' Association
1 Dundas St West, Suite 2406
Toronto, Ont.
M5G 1Z3
Tel: (416)408-4040

NHL Scoring Leaders, 1993–94

Player	GP	G	A	Pts	+/-	PIM	PP	SH	S	Pct
Wayne Gretzkey, LA	81	38	92	130	-25	20	14	4	233	16.3
Sergei Fedorov, Det.	82	56	64	120	48	34	13	4	337	16.6
Adam Oates, Bos	77	32	80	112	10	45	16	2	197	16.2
Doug Gilmour, Tor.	83	27	84	111	25	105	10	1	167	16.2
Pavel Bure, Van..	76	60	47	107	1	86	25	4	374	16.0
Jeremy Roenick, Chi.	84	46	61	107	21	125	24	5	281	16.4
Mark Recchi, Phil.	84	40	67	107	-2	46	11	0	217	18.4
Brendan Shanahan, St. L.	81	52	50	102	-9	211	15	7	397	13.1
Jaromie Jagr, Pit.	80	32	67	99	15	61	9	0	298	10.7
Dave Andreychuk, Tor.	83	53	45	98	22	98	21	5	333	15.9
Brett Hull, St. L.	81	57	40	97	-3	38	25	3	392	14.5
Eric Lindros, Phil.	65	44	53	97	16	103	13	2	197	22.3
Rod BrinD'Amour, Phil.	84	35	62	97	-9	85	14	1	230	15.2
Pierre Turgeon, NYI	69	38	56	94	14	18	10	4	254	15.0
Ray Sheppard, Det.	82	52	41	93	13	26	19	0	260	20.0
Mike Modano, Dal.	76	50	43	93	-8	54	18	0	281	17.8
Robert Reichel, Cal.	84	40	53	93	20	58	14	0	249	16.1
Ron Francis, Pit.	82	27	66	93	-3	62	8	0	216	12.5
Joe Sakic, Que.	84	28	64	92	-8	18	10	1	279	10.0
Vincent Damphousse, Mtl	84	40	51	91	0	75	13	0	274	14.6
Raymond Bourque, Bos.	72	20	71	91	26	58	10	3	386	5.2

GP = Games played; G = Goals; A = Assists; Pts = Points; +/- = Plus/minus statistic, which shows the number of even-strength and shorthanded goals scored by a player's team, minus those scored against it, while he is on the ice; PIM = Penalties in minutes; PP = Power play goals; SH = Shorthanded goals; S = Shots on goal; Pct = Percentage of shots that score goals.

NHL Playoff Scoring Leaders, 1993–94

Player	GP	G	A	Pts	+/-	PIM	PP	SH	S	Pct
Brian Leetch, NYR	23	11	23	34	19	6	4	0	88	12.5
Pavel Bure, Van..	24	16	15	31	8	40	3	0	101	15.8
Mark Messier, NYR	23	12	18	30	14	33	2	1	75	16.0
Doug Gilmour, Tor.	18	6	22	28	3	42	5	0	31	19.4
Trevor Linden, Van.	24	12	13	25	3	18	5	1	67	17.9
Alexei Kovalev, NYR.	23	9	12	21	5	18	5	0	71	12.7
Geoff Courtnall, Van.	24	9	10	19	10	51	0	1	77	11.7
Sergei Zubov, NYR.	22	5	14	19	10	0	2	0	60	8.3
Claude Lemieux, NJ.	20	7	11	18	4	44	0	0	50	14.0
Igor Larionov, SJ	14	5	13	18	-1	10	0	0	27	18.5
Dave Ellett, Tor.	18	3	15	18	1	31	3	0	33	9.1
Adam Graves, NYR	23	10	7	17	12	24	3	0	93	10.8
Wendel Clark, Tor.	18	9	7	16	0	24	2	0	72	12.5
Steve Larmer, NYR.	23	9	7	16	8	14	3	0	54	16.7
John MacLean, NJ.	20	6	10	16	-2	22	2	0	65	9.2

NHL Individual Records

(up to the end of the 1992–93 season)

Most seasons	**26, Gordie Howe,** Det, 1946/47 through 1970/71; Htfd, 1979/80
Most games	**1 767, Gordie Howe,** Det, 1946/47 through 1970/71; Htfd, 1979/80
Most goals	**803, Wayne Gretzky,** Edm, LA, in 15 seasons, 1 125 games
Most assists	**1 655, Wayne Gretzky,** Edm, LA, in 15 seasons, 1 125 games
Most points	**2 328, Wayne Gretzky,** Edm, LA, in 14 seasons, 1 044 games (765 goals, 1 563 assists)
Most penalty minutes	**3 966, Dave Williams,** Tor, Vcr, Det, LA, Htfd, in 14 seasons, 962 games
Most consecutive games	**964, Doug Jarvis,** Mtl, Wash, Htfd from Oct. 8, 1975 through Oct. 10, 1987
Most games appeared in by a goaltender, career	**971, Terry Sawchuk,** Det, Bos, Tor, LA, NYR (1949–70)
Most consecutive complete games by a goaltender	**502, Glenn Hall,** Det, Chi.

Played 502 games from beginning of 1955/56 season through first 12 games of 1962/63. In his 503rd straight game, Nov. 7, 1962, at Chicago, Hall was removed from the game against Boston with a back injury in the first period.

Most shutouts by a goaltender, career	**103, Terry Sawchuk,** Det, Bos, Tor, LA, NYR, in 20 seasons
Most 50-or-more goal seasons	**9, Mike Bossy,** NYI; **Wayne Gretzky,** Edm, LA
Most goals, one season	**92, Wayne Gretzky,** Edm, 1981/82 (80 games)
Most assists, one season	**163, Wayne Gretzky,** Edm, 1985/86 (80 games)
Most goals, one season, by a defenceman	**48, Paul Coffey,** Edm, 1985/86 (79 games)
Most goals, one season, by a centre	**92, Wayne Gretzky,** Edm, 1981/82 (80 games)
Most goals, one season, by a right winger	**86, Brett Hull,** StL, 1990/91 (80 games)
Most goals, one season, by a left winger	**63, Luc Robitaille,** LA, 1992/93 (84 games)
Most goals, one season, by a rookie	**76, Teemu Selanne,** Win, 1992/93 (84 games)
Most points, one season, by a defenceman	**139, Bobby Orr,** Bos, 1970/71 (78 games)
Most points, one season by a centre	**215, Wayne Gretzky,** Edm, 1985/86 (80 games)
Most points, one season, by a right winger	**147, Mike Bossy,** NYI, 1981/82 (80 games)
Most points, one season, by a left winger	**125, Luc Robitaille,** LA, 1992/93 (84 games)
Most points, one season, by a rookie	**132, Teemu Selanne,** Win, 1992/93 (84 games)
Most power-play goals, one season	**34, Tim Kerr,** Phi, 1985/86 (76 games)
Most penalty minutes, one season	**472, Dave Schultz ,** Ph, 1974/75 (80 games)
Most shutouts, one season	**22, George Hainsworth,** Mtl, 1928/29 (44 games)

Regular Season NHL Scoring Champions, 1917–94

Season	Player, Team	GP	G	A	Pts	Season	Player, Team	GP	G	A	Pts
1917–18[1]	Joe Malone, Mtl	20	44	—	44	1937–38	Gordie Drillon, Tor	48	26	26	52
1918–19	Newsy Lalonde, Mtl	17	23	9	32	1938–39	Toe Blake, Mtl	48	24	23	47
1919–20	Joe Malone, Que	24	39	6	45	1939–40	Milt Schmidt, Bos	48	22	30	52
1920–21	Newsy Lalonde, Mtl	24	33	8	41	1940–41	Bill Cowley, Bos	46	17	45	62
1921–22	Punch Broadbent, Ott	24	32	14	46	1941–42	Bryan Hextall, NYR	48	24	32	56
1922–23	Babe Dye, Tor	22	26	11	37	1942–43	Doug Bentley, Chi	50	33	40	73
1923–24	Cy Denneny, Ott	21	22	1	23	1943–44	Herbie Cain, Bos	48	36	46	82
1924–25	Babe Dye, Tor	29	38	6	44	1944–45	Elmer Lach, Mtl	50	26	54	80
1925–26	Nels Stewart, Mtl Maroons	36	34	8	42	1945–46	Max Bentley, Chi	47	31	30	61
1926–27	Bill Cook, NYR	44	33	4	37	1946–47	Max Bentley, Chi	60	29	43	72
1927–28	Howie Morenz, Mtl	43	33	18	51	1947–48	Elmer Lach, Mtl	60	30	31	61
1928–29	Ace Bailey, Tor	44	22	10	32	1948–49	Roy Conacher, Chi	60	26	42	68
1929–30	Cooney Weiland, Bos	44	43	30	73	1949–50	Ted Lindsay, Det	69	23	55	78
1930–31	Howie Morenz, Mtl	39	28	23	51	1950–51	Gordie Howe, Det	70	43	43	86
1931–32	Harvey Jackson, Tor	48	28	25	53	1951–52	Gordie Howe, Det	70	47	39	86
1932–33	Bill Cook, NYR	48	28	22	50	1952–53	Gordie Howe, Det	70	49	46	95
1933–34	Charlie Conacher, Tor	42	32	20	52	1953–54	Gordie Howe, Det	70	33	48	81
1934–35	Charlie Conacher, Tor	48	36	21	57	1954–55	Bernie Geoffrion, Mtl	70	38	37	75
1935–36	Dave Schriner, NY Americans	48	19	26	45	1955–56	Jean Béliveau, Mtl	70	47	41	88
1936–37	Dave Schriner, NY Americans	48	21	25	46	1956–57	Gordie Howe, Det	70	44	45	89
						1957–58	Dickie Moore, Mtl	70	36	48	84
						1958–59	Dickie Moore, Mt l	70	41	55	96
						1959–60	Bobby Hull, Chi	70	39	42	81 ▶

Season	Player, Team	GP	G	A	Pts	Season	Player, Team	GP	G	A	Pts
1960–61	Bernie Geoffrion, Mtl	64	50	45	95	**1977–78**	Guy Lafleur, Mtl	78	60	72	132
1961–62	Bobby Hull, Chi	70	50	34	84	**1978–79**	Bryan Trottier, NYI	76	47	87	134
1962–63	Gordie Howe, Det	70	38	48	86	**1979–80**	Marcel Dionne, LA	80	53	84	137
1963–64	Stan Mikita, Chi	70	39	50	89	**1980–81**	Wayne Gretzky, Edm	80	55	109	164
1964–65	Stan Mikita, Chi	70	28	59	87	**1981–82**	Wayne Gretzky, Edm	80	92	120	212
1965–66	Bobby Hull, Chi	65	54	43	97	**1982–83**	Wayne Gretzky, Edm	80	71	125	196
1966–67	Stan Mikita, Chi	70	35	62	97	**1983–84**	Wayne Gretzky, Edm	74	87	118	205
1967–68	Stan Mikita, Chi	72	40	47	87	**1984–85**	Wayne Gretzky, Edm	80	73	135	208
1968–69	Phil Esposito, Bos	74	49	77	126	**1985–86**	Wayne Gretzky, Edm	80	52	163	215
1969–70	Bobby Orr, Bos	76	33	87	120	**1986–87**	Wayne Gretzky, Edm	79	62	121	183
1970–71	Phil Esposito, Bos	78	76	76	152	**1987–88**	Mario Lemieux, Pit	77	70	98	168
1971–72	Phil Esposito, Bos	76	66	67	133	**1988–89**	Mario Lemieux, Pit	76	85	114	199
1972–73	Phil Esposito, Bos	78	55	75	130	**1989–90**	Wayne Gretzky, LA	73	40	102	142
1973–74	Phil Esposito, Bos	78	68	77	145	**1990–91**	Wayne Gretzky, LA	78	41	122	163
1974–75	Bobby Orr, Bos	80	46	89	135	**1991–92**	Mario Lemieux, Pit	64	44	87	131
1975–76	Guy Lafleur, Mtl	80	56	69	125	**1992–93**	Mario Lemieux, Pit	60	69	91	160
1976–77	Guy Lafleur, Mtl	80	56	80	136	**1993–94**	Wayne Gretzky, LA	81	38	92	130

Source: *National Hockey League*

(a) Number of assists not recorded.

Top 25 All-Time NHL Point-Scoring Leaders

(to the end of the 1993/94 season; active players in bold type)

Player/Teams	Seasons	Games	Goals	Assists	Points	Points/Game
Wayne Gretzky, Edm/LA	15	1 125	803	1 655	2 458	2.185
Gordie Howe, Det/Htfd	26	1 767	801	1 049	1 850	1.047
Marcel Dionne, Det/LA/NYR	18	1 348	731	1 040	1 771	1.314
Phil Esposito, Chi/Bos/NYR	18	1 282	717	873	1 590	1.240
Stan Mikita, Chi	22	1 394	541	926	1 467	1.052
Bryan Trottier, NYI/Pit	17	1 238	520	890	1 410	1.139
John Bucyk, Det/Bos	23	1 540	556	813	1 369	.889
Guy Lafleur, Mtl/NYR/Que	17	1 126	560	793	1 353	1.202
Gilbert Perreault, Buf	17	1 191	512	814	1 326	1.113
Mark Messier, Edm/NYR	15	1 081	478	838	1 316	1.217
Dale Hawerchuk, Wpg, Buf	13	1 032	484	814	1 298	1.258
Alex Delvecchio, Det	24	1 549	456	825	1 281	.827
Paul Coffey, Edm/Pit/Det	14	1 033	344	934	1 278	1.237
Jean Ratelle, NYR/Bos	21	1 281	491	776	1 267	.989
Jari Kurri, Edm/LA	13	990	555	712	1 267	1.280
Denis Savard, Chi/Mtl/tB	14	1 020	441	797	1 238	1.214
Peter Stastny, Que/NJ	14	971	449	778	1 237	1.274
Norm Ullman, Det/Tor	20	1 410	490	739	1 229	.872
Jean Béliveau, Mtl	20	1 125	507	712	1 219	1.084
Mario Lemieux, Pit	10	599	494	717	1 211	2.022
Bobby Clarke, Phi	15	1 144	358	852	1 210	1.058
Raymond Bourque, Bos	15	1 100	311	877	1 188	1.080
Mike Gartner, Wash/Minn/NYR/Tor	15	1 170	617	554	1 171	1.001
Bobby Hull, Chi/Wpg/Htfd	16	1 063	610	560	1 170	1.101
Michel Goulet, Que, Chi	14	1 033	532	590	1 122	1.086

Source: *National Hockey League*

Top Ten NHL Draft Selections, 1989–94

(Teams selected by in parentheses)

	1989	1990	1991
1.	Matt Sundin, Que	Owen Nolan, Que	Eric Lindros, Que
2.	Dave Chyzowski, NYI	Petr Nedved, Vcr	Pat Falloon, SJ
3.	Scott Thornton, Tor	Keith Primeau, Det	Scott Niedermayer, NJ
4.	Stu Barnes, Wpg	Mike Ricci, Phi	Scott Lachance, NYI
5.	Bill Guerin, NJ	Jaromir Jag, Pit	Aaron Ward, Wpg
6.	Adam Bennett, Chi	Scott Scissons, NYI	Peter Forsber, Phi
7.	Doug Zmolek, Min	Darryl Sydor, LA	Alex Stojanov, Vcr
8.	Jason Herter, Vcr	Derian Hatcher, Min	Richard Matvichuk, Min
9.	Jason Marshall, StL	John Slaney, Wash	Patrick Poulin, Htfd
10.	Robert Holik, Htfd	Drake Berehowsky, Tor	Martin Lapointe, Det

	1992	1993	1994
1.	Roman Hamrlik, TB	Alexander Daigle, Ott	Ed Javanovski, Fla
2.	Alexei Yashin, Ott	Chris Pronger, Htfd	Oleg Tverdovsky, Ana
3.	Mike Rathje, SJ	Chris Gratton,TB	Radek Bonk, Ott
4.	Todd Warriner, Que	Paul Kariya, Ana	Jason Bonsignore, Edm
5.	Darius Kasparaitis, NYI	Rob Neidermayer, Fla	Jeff O'Neill, Htfd
6.	Cory Stillman, Cal	Viktor Kozlovi, SJ	Ryan Smith, Edm
7.	Ryan Sittler, Phi	Jason Arnott, Edm	Jamie Storr, LA
8.	Brandon Convery, Tor	Niklas Sundstrom, NYR	Jason Weimer, TB
9.	Robert Petrovicky, Htfd	Todd Harvey, Dal	Brett Lindros, NYI
10.	Andrei Mazarov, Min	Jocelyn Thibault, Que	Nolan Saumgartner, Wash

NHL All-Star Teams, 1989–94[1]

First Team	Second Team	First Team	Second Team
1989		**1990**	
Patrick Roy, Mtl, g	Mike Vernon, Cal, g	Patrick Roy, Mtl, g	Daren Puppa, Buf, g
Chris Chelios, Mtl, dl	Al MacInnis, Cal, d	Raymond Bourque, Bos, d	Paul Coffey, Pit, d
Paul Coffey, Pit, d	Raymond Bourque, Bos, d	Al MacInnis, Cal, d	Doug Wilson, Chi, d
Mario Lemieux, Pit, c	Wayne Gretzky, LA, c	Mark Messier, Edm, c	Wayne Gretzky, LA, c
Joe Mullen, Cal, rw	Jari Kurri, Edm, rw	Brett Hull, StL, rw	Cam Neely, Bos, rw
Luc Robitaille, LA, lw	Gerald Gallant, Det, lw	Luc Robitaille, LA, lw	Brian Bellows, Min, lw
1991		**1992**	
Ed Belfour, Chi, g	Patrick Roy, Mtl g	Patrick Roy, Mtl, g	Kirk McLean, Vcr, g
Raymond Bourque, Bos, d	Chris Chelios, Chi, d	Brian Leetch, NYR, d	Phil Housley, Wpg, d
Al MacInnis, Cal, d	Brian Leetch, NYR, d	Raymond Bourque, Bos, d	Scott Stevens, NJ, d
Wayne Gretzky, LA, c	Adam Oates, StL, c	Mark Messier, NYR, c	Mario Lemieux, Pit, c
Brett Hull, StL, rw	Cam Neely, Bos, rw	Brett Hull, StL, rw	Mark Recchi, Pit/Phi, rw
Luc Robitaille, LA, lw	Kevin Sevens, Pit, lw	Kevin Stevens, Pit, lw	Luc Robitaille, LA, lw
1993		**1994**	
Ed Belfour, Chi, g	Tom Barasso, Pit, g	Dominik Hasek, Buf, g	John Vanbiesbrovek, Fla, g
Chris Chelios, Chi, d	Larry Murphy, Pit, d	Raymond Bourque, Bos, d	Al MacInnis, Cal, d
Raymond Bourque, Bos, d	Al Iafrate, Wash, d	Scott Stevens, NJ, d	Brian Leetch, NYR, d
Mario Lemieux, Pit, c	Pat LaFontaine, Buf, c	Sergei Federov, Det, c	Wayne Gretzky, Bos, rw
Teemu Selanne, Win, rw	Alexander Mogilny, Buf, rw	Pavel Bure, Van, rw	Cam Neely, Bos, rw
Luc Robitaille, LA, lw	Kevin Stevens, Pit, lw	Brendan Shanahan, SH, lw	Adam Graves, NYR, lw

(1) As selected by members of the Professional Hockey Writers' Association at the end of the season.

NHL Individual Award Winners, 1950–94

Hart Trophy (Most Valuable Player)[1]

1950 Charlie Rayner, NYR	1965 Bobby Hull, Chi	1980 Wayne Gretzky, Edm
1951 Milt Schmidt, Bos	1966 Bobby Hull, Chi	1981 Wayne Gretzky, Edm
1952 Gordie Howe, Det	1967 Stan Mikita, Chi	1982 Wayne Gretzky, Edm
1953 Gordie Howe, Det	1968 Stan Mikita, Chi	1983 Wayne Gretzky, Edm
1954 Al Rollins, Chi	1969 Phil Esposito, Bos	1984 Wayne Gretzky, Edm
1955 Ted Kennedy, Tor	1970 Bobby Orr, Bo	1985 Wayne Gretzky, Edm
1956 Jean Béliveau, Mtl	1971 Bobby Orr, Bos	1986 Wayne Gretzky, Edm
1957 Gordie Howe, Det	1972 Bobby Orr, Bos	1987 Wayne Gretzky, Edm
1958 Gordie Howe, Det	1973 Bobby Clarke, Phi	1988 Mario Lemieux, Pit
1959 Andy Bathgate, NYR	1974 Phil Esposito, Bos	1989 Wayne Gretzky, LA
1960 Gordie Howe, Det	1975 Bobby Clarke, Phi	1990 Mark Messier, Edm
1961 Bernie Geoffrion, Mtl	1976 Bobby Clarke, Phi	1991 Brett Hull, StL
1962 Jacques Plante, Mtl	1977 Guy Lafleur, Mtl	1992 Mark Messier, NYR
1963 Gordie Howe, Det	1978 Guy Lafleur, Mtl	1993 Mario Lemieux, Pit
1964 Jean Béliveau, Mtl	1979 Bryan Trottier, NYI	1994 Sergei Fedorov, Det

Calder Trophy (Best Rookie)[1]

1950 Jack Gelineau, Bos	1965 Roger Crozier, Det	1980 Raymond Bourque, Bos
1951 Terry Sawchuk, Det	1966 Brit Selby, Tor	1981 Peter Stastny, Que
1952 Bernie Geoffrion, Mtl	1967 Bobby Orr, Bos	1982 Dale Hawerchuk, Wpg
1953 Lorne Worsley, NYR	1968 Derek Sanderson, Bos	1983 Steve Larmer, Chi
1954 Camille Henry, NYR	1969 Danny Grant, Min	1984 Tom Barrasso, Buf
1955 Ed Litzenberger, Chi	1970 Tony Esposito, Chi	1985 Mario Lemieux, Pit
1956 Glenn Hall, Det	1971 Gilbert Perreault, Buf	1986 Gary Suter, Cal
1957 Larry Regan, Bos	1972 Ken Dryden, Mtl	1987 Luc Robitaille, LA
1958 Frank Mahovlich, Tor	1973 Steve Vickers, NYR	1988 Joe Nieuwendyk, Cal
1959 Ralph Backstrom, Mtl	1974 Denis Potvin, NYI	1989 Brian Leetch, NYR
1960 Bill Hay, Chi	1975 Eric Vail, Atlanta	1990 Sergei Makarov, Cal
1961 Dave Keon, Tor	1976 Bryan Trottier, NYI	1991 Ed Belfour, Chi
1962 Bobby Rousseau, Mtl	1977 Willi Plett, Atl	1992 Pavel Bure, Vcr
1963 Kent Douglas, Tor	1978 Mike Bossy, NYI	1993 Teemu Selanne, Wpg
1964 Jacques Laperrière, Mtl	1979 Bobby Smith, Min	1994 Martin Brodeur, NJ

James Norris Trophy (Best Defenceman)[1]

1954 Red Kelly, Det	1968 Bobby Orr, Bos	1982 Doug Wilson, Chi
1955 Doug Harvey, Mtl	1969 Bobby Orr, Bos	1983 Rod Langway, Wash
1956 Doug Harvey, Mtl	1970 Bobby Orr, Bos	1984 Rod Langway, Wash
1957 Doug Harvey, Mtl	1971 Bobby Orr, Bos	1985 Paul Coffey, Edm
1958 Doug Harvey, Mtl	1972 Bobby Orr, Bos	1986 Paul Coffey, Edm
1959 Tom Johnson, Mtl	1973 Bobby Orr, Bos	1987 Raymond Bourque, Bos
1960 Doug Harvey, Mtl	1974 Bobby Orr, Bos	1988 Raymond Bourque, Bos
1961 Doug Harvey, Mtl	1975 Bobby Orr, Bos	1989 Chris Chelios, Mtl
1962 Doug Harvey, NYR	1976 Denis Potvin, NYI	1990 Raymond Bourque, Bos
1963 Pierre Pilote, Chi	1977 Larry Robinson, Mtl	1991 Raymond Bourque, Bos
1964 Pierre Pilote, Chi	1978 Denis Potvin, NYI	1992 Brian Leetch, NYR
1965 Pierre Pilote, Chi	1979 Denis Potvin, NYI	1993 Chris Chelios, Chi
1966 Jacques Laperrière, Mtl	1980 Larry Robinson, Mtl	1994 Raymond Bourque, Bos
1967 Harry Howell, NYR	1981 Randy Carlyle, Pittsburgh	▶

Vezina Trophy (Best Goalkeeper)[2]

1950 Bill Durnan, Mtl	1967 Glenn Hall, Chi	1979 Ken Dryden, Mtl
1951 Al Rollins, Tor	Denis Dejordy, Chi	Michel Larocque, Mtl
1952 Terry Sawchuk, Det	1968 Lorne Worsley, Mtl	1980 Bob Suavé, Buf
1953 Terry Sawchuk, Det	Rogie Vachon, Mtl	Don Edwards, Buf
1954 Harry Lumley, Tor	1969 Jacques Plante, StL	1981 Richard Sevigny, Mtl
1955 Terry Sawchuk, Det	Glenn Hall, StL	Denis Herron, Mtl
1956 Jacques Plante, Mtl	1970 Tony Esposito, Chi	Michel Larocque, Mtl
1957 Jacques Plante, Mtl	1971 Ed Giacomin, NYR	1982 Bill Smith, NYI
1958 Jacques Plante, Mtl	Gilles Villemure, NYR	1983 Pete Peeters, Bos
1959 Jacques Plante, Mtl	1972 Tony Esposito, Chi	1984 Tom Barrasso, Buf
1960 Jacques Plante, Mtl	Gary Smith, Chi	1985 Pelle Lindbergh, Phi
1961 Johnny Bower, Tor	1973 Ken Dryden, Mtl	1986 John Vanbiesbrouck, NYR
1962 Jacques Plante, Mtl	1974 Bernie Parent, Phi	1987 Ron Hextall, Phi
1963 Glenn Hall, Chi	Tony Esposito, Chi	1988 Grant Fuhr, Edm
1964 Charlie Hodge, Mtl	1975 Bernie Parent, Phi	1989 Patrick Roy, Mtl
1965 Terry Sawchuk, Tor	1976 Ken Dryden, Mtl	1990 Patrick Roy, Mtl
Johnny Bower, Tor	1977 Ken Dryden, Mtl	1991 Ed Belfour, Chi
1966 Lorne Worsley, Mtl	Michel Larocque, Mtl	1992 Patrick Roy, Mtl
Charlie Hodge, Mtl	1978 Ken Dryden, Mtl	1993 Ed Belfour, Chi
	Michel Larocque, Mtl	1994 Dominic Hasek, Buf

Lady Byng Trophy (Most Sportsmanlike)[1]

1950 Edgar Laprade, NYR	1965 Bobby Hull, Chi	1980 Wayne Gretzky, Edm
1951 Red Kelly, Det	1966 Alex Delvecchio, Det	1981 Rick Kehoe, Pit
1952 Sid Smith, Tor	1967 Stan Mikita, Chi	1982 Rick Middleton, Bos
1953 Red Kelly, Det	1968 Stan Mikita, Chi	1983 Mike Bossy, NYI
1954 Red Kelly, Det	1969 Alex Delvecchio, Det	1984 Mike Bossy, NYI
1955 Sid Smith, Tor	1970 Phil Goyette, StL	1985 Jari Kurri, Edm
1956 Earl Reibel, Det	1971 John Bucyk, Bos	1986 Mike Bossy, NYI
1957 Andy Hebenton, NYR	1972 Jean Ratelle, NYR	1987 Joe Mullen, Cal
1958 Camille Henry, NYR	1973 Gilbert Perreault, Buf	1988 Mats Naslund, Mtl
1959 Alex Delvecchio, Det	1974 John Bucyk, Bos	1989 Joe Mullen, Cal
1960 Don McKenney, Bos	1975 Marcel Dionne, Det	1990 Brett Hull, StL
1961 Red Kelly, Tor	1976 Jean Ratelle, NYR/Bos	1991 Wayne Gretzky, LA
1962 Dave Keon, Tor	1977 Marcel Dionne, LA	1992 Wayne Gretzky, LA
1963 Dave Keon, Tor	1978 Butch Goring, LA	1993 Pierre Turgeon, NYI
1964 Ken Wharram, Chi	1979 Bob MacMillan, Atl	1994 Wayne Gretzky, LA

Conn Smythe Trophy (Most Valuable in Playoffs) [3]

1965 Jean Béliveau, Mtl	1975 Bernie Parent, Phi	1985 Wayne Gretzky, Edm
1966 Roger Crozier, Det	1976 Reggie Leach, Phi	1986 Patrick Roy, Mtl
1967 Dave Keon, Tor	1977 Guy Lafleur, Mtl	1987 Ron Hextall, Phi
1968 Glenn Hall, StL	1978 Larry Robinson, Mtl	1988 Wayne Gretzky, Edm
1969 Serge Savard, Mtl	1979 Bob Gainey, Mtl	1989 Al MacInnis, Cal
1970 Bobby Orr, Bos	1980 Bryan Trottier, NYI	1990 Bill Ranford, Edm
1971 Ken Dryden, Mtl	1981 Butch Goring, NYI	1991 Mario Lemieux, Pit
1972 Bobby Orr, Bos	1982 Mike Bossy, NYI	1992 Mario Lemieux, Pit
1973 Yvan Cournoyer, Mtl	1983 Bill Smith, NYI	1993 Patrick Roy, Mtl
1974 Bernie Parent, Phi	1984 Mark Messier, Edm	1994 Brian Leetch, NYR

Frank J. Selke Trophy (Best Defensive Forward)[1]

1978	Bob Gainey, Mtl	**1984**	Doug Jarvis, Wash	**1990**	Rick Meagher, StL
1979	Bob Gainey, Mtl	**1985**	Craig Ramsay, Buf	**1991**	Dirk Graham, Chi
1980	Bob Gainey, Mtl	**1986**	Troy Murray, Chi	**1992**	Guy Carbonneau, Mtl
1981	Bob Gainey, Mtl	**1987**	Dave Poulin, Phi	**1993**	Doug Gilmour, Tor
1982	Steve Kasper, Bos	**1988**	Guy Carbonneau, Mtl	**1994**	Sergei Fedorov, Det
1983	Bobby Clarke, Phi	**1989**	Guy Carbonneau, Mtl		

(1) As selected at the end of the regular season by members of the Professional Hockey Writers' Association in the 21 NHL cities. (2) Since the 1981–82 season, Vezina Trophy winners have been selected by general managers of the 21 NHL clubs. In earlier seasons the trophy was awarded to the goalkeeper(s) of the team allowing the fewest goals during the regular season. (3) As selected by members of the Professional Hockey Writers' Association at the end of the last game of the Stanley Cup finals.

Men's World Hockey Championships, 1994

(Milan, Italy)

Team	W	L	T	GF	GA	Team	W	L	T	GF	GA
Canada	5	0	0	24	7	Finland	4	0	1	29	11
Russia	4	1	0	30	7	Sweden	3	1	1	22	11
Italy	3	2	0	17	16	USA	3	2	0	21	19
Austria	1	3	1	15	15	Czech Rep.	1	2	2	15	17
Germany	1	3	1	10	14	France	1	4	0	8	25
Britain	0	5	0	7	44	Norway	0	3	2	9	21

Quarter finals: Canada 3, Czech Rep. 2; Finland 10, Austria 0; Sweden 7, Italy 2; US 3, Russia 6 **Semi-finals:** Canada 6, Sweden 0; Finland 8, US 0 **Gold Medal:** Canada 2, Finland 1 (shoot-out) **Bronze Medal:** Sweden 7, US 2

World Junior Hockey Tournament

(Prague, Czech Republic)

Team	W	L	T	F	A	Pts	Team	W	L	T	F	A	Pts
Canada	6	0	1	39	24	13	Czech Rep.	3	4	0	30	29	6
Sweden	6	1	0	35	16	12	US	1	5	1	20	32	3
Russia	5	1	1	23	17	11	Germany	1	6	0	10	26	2
Finland	4	3	0	27	24	8	Switzerland	0	6	1	10	30	1

Gold: Canada 6, Sweden 4 **Bronze:** Russia 5, Finland 4.

World Junior All-Stars

First Team		**First Team**	
Evgeni Riabchitcov, Russia	G	David Vybomy, Czech Rep.	C
Kimmo Timonen, Finland	D	Valery Bure, Russia	RW
Kenny Jonsson, Sweden	D	Niklas Sunelstrom, Sweden	LW

* repeat winner

Previous winners

▶ 1993 . . . . Canada
1992 . . . . C.I.S. (fomer Soviet Union)
1991 . . . . Canada
1990 . . . . Canada
1989 . . . . Soviet Union
1988 . . . . Canada
1987 . . . . Finland
1986 . . . . Soviet Union
1985 . . . . Canada

1984 . . . . Soviet Union
1983 . . . . Soviet Union
1982 . . . . Canada
1981 . . . . Sweden
1980 . . . . Soviet Union
1979 . . . . Soviet Union
1978 . . . . Soviet Union
1977 . . . . Soviet Union

Memorial Cup Winners, 1919–94

(Canadian Junior Hockey Champions)

1919 University of Toronto Schools	1957 Flin Flon Bombers
1920 Toronto Canoe Club	1958 Ottawa-Hull Canadiens
1921 Winnipeg Falcons	1959 Winnipeg Braves
1922 Fort William War Veterans	1960 St. Catharines Tee Pees
1923 University of Manitoba—Winnipeg	1961 St. Michael's Majors
1924 Owen Sound Greys	1962 Hamilton Red Wings
1925 Regina Pats	1963 Edmonton Oil Kings
1926 Calgary Canadians	1964 Toronto Marlboros
1927 Owen Sound	1965 Niagara Falls Flyers
1928 Regina Monarchs	1966 Edmonton Oil Kings
1929 Toronto Marlboros	1967 Toronto Marlboros
1930 Regina Pats	1968 Niagara Falls Flyers
1931 Winnipeg Elmwoods	1969 Montreal Jr. Canadiens
1932 Sudbury	1970 Montreal Jr. Canadiens
1933 Newmarket	1971 Quebec Remparts
1934 Toronto St. Michael's	1972 Cornwall Royals
1935 Winnipeg Monarchs	1973 Toronto Marlboros
1936 West Toronto Redmen	1974 Regina Pats
1937 Winnipeg Monarchs	1975 Toronto Marlboros
1938 St. Boniface Seals	1976 Hamilton Fincups
1939 Oshawa Generals	1977 New Westminster Bruins
1940 Oshawa Generals	1978 New Westminster Bruins
1941 Winnipeg Rangers	1979 Peterborough Petes
1942 Portage La Prairie	1980 Cornwall Royals
1943 Winnipeg Rangers	1981 Cornwall Royals
1944 Oshawa Generals	1982 Kitchener Rangers
1945 Toronto St. Michael's	1983 Portland Winter Hawks
1946 Winnipeg Monarchs	1984 Ottawa 67's
1947 Toronto St. Michael's	1985 Prince Albert Raiders
1948 Port Arthur West End Bruins	1986 Guelph Platers
1949 Montreal Royals	1987 Medicine Hat Tigers
1950 Montreal Canadiens	1988 Medicine Hat Tigers
1951 Barrie Flyers	1989 Swift Current Broncos
1952 Guelph Biltmores	1990 Oshawa Generals
1953 Barrie Flyers	1991 Spokane Chiefs
1954 St. Catharines Tee Pees	1992 Kamloops Blazers
1955 Toronto Marlboros	1993 Sault Ste. Marie Greyhounds
1956 Toronto Marlboros	1994 Kamloops Blazers

Source: *Canadian Amateur Hockey Association*

Team Canada in International Hockey Competition

The 1972 Series
(an 8–game series)

Goal: Ken Dryden, Tony Esposito; **Defence:** Don Awrey, Gary Bergman, Guy Lapointe, Brad Park, Serge Savard, Rod Seiling, Pat Stapleton, Bill White; **Forwards:** Red Berenson, Wayne Cashman, Bobby Clarke, Yvan Cournoyer, Ron Ellis, Phil Esposito, Rod Gilbert, Bill Goldsworthy, Vic Hadfield, Paul Henderson, Dennis Hull, Frank Mahovlich, Peter Mahovlich, Stan Mikita, Jean-Paul Parise, Gilbert Perreault, Jean Ratelle

Date	Location	Score	Date	Location	Score
Sept. 2	Montreal	Soviets 7, Team Canada 3	Sept. 22	Moscow	Soviets 5, Team Canada 4
Sept. 4	Toronto	Team Canada 4, Soviets 1	Sept. 24	Moscow	Team Canada 3, Soviets 2
Sept. 6	Winnipeg	Soviets 4, Team Canada 4	Sept. 26	Moscow	Team Canada 4, Soviets 3
Sept. 8	Vancouver	Soviets 5, Team Canada 3	Sept. 28	Moscow	Team Canada 6, Soviets 5

Canada won the series 4 games to 3, with 1 game tied.

The Canada Cup, 1976

Final-Round Results
Canada 6, Czechoslovakia 0
Canada 5, Czechoslovakia 4*
Canada won best 2-out-of-3 final series 2 games to 0.

*overtime

The Canada Cup, 1981

Semi-Final Results
Soviet Union 4, Czechoslovakia 1
Canada 4, United States 1
Final Game Score
Soviet Union 8, Canada 1
The Soviet Union won the series.

The Canada Cup, 1984

Playoff Results
Canada 3, Soviet Union 2, Sweden 9, United States 2
Final Results
Canada 5, Sweden 2
Canada 6, Sweden 5
Canada won best-2-out-of-3 series 2 games to 0.

The Canada Cup, 1987

Semi-Final Results
Canada 5, Czechoslovakia 3
Soviet Union 4, Sweden 2
Final Results
Soviet Union 6, Canada 5*
Canada 6, Soviet Union 5*
Canada 6, Soviet Union 5*
Canada won the best-2-out-of-3 series 2 games to 1.

*overtime

The Canada Cup, 1991

Goal: Ed Belfour, Sean Burke, Bill Ranford; **Defence:** Paul Coffey, Eric Desjardins, Al MacInnis, Jamie Macoun, Larry Murphy, Steve Smith, Scott Stevens; **Forwards:** Shayne Corson, Russ Courtnall, Theoren Fleury, Dirk Graham, Wayne Gretzky, Dale Hawerchuk, Steve Larmer, Eric Lindros, Mark Messier, Luc Robitaille, Brendan Shanahan, Brent Sutter, Rick Tocchet.

Semi-Final Results
United States 7, Finland 3
Canada 4, Sweden 0
Final Results
Canada 4, United States 1
Canada 4, United States 2
Canada won the best-2-out-of-3 series 2 games to 0.

Amateur Hockey Organizations

Canadian Amateur Hockey Association
1600 James Naismith Dr.
Gloucester, Ont. K1B 5N4
Tel: (613)748-5613
Fax: (613)748-5709

Canadian Olympic Association
2380 Pierre Dupuy
Montreal H3C 3R4
Tel: (514)861-3371
Fax: (514)861-2896

The Hockey Hall of Fame and Museum

(Toronto, Ont.)
(year of election to the Hall indicated in brackets)

Abel, Sid (1969)
Adams, Jack (1959)
Apps, Syl (1961)
Armstrong, George (1975)
Bailey, Ace (1975)
Bain, Dan (1945)
Baker, Hobey (1945)
Barber, Bill (1990)
Barry, Marty (1965)
Bathgate, Andy (1978)
Béliveau, Jean (1972)
Benedict, Clinton (1965)
Bentley, Doug (1964)
Bentley, Max (1966)
Blake, Toe (1966)
Boivin, Leo (1986)
Boon, Dickie (1952)
Bossy, Mike (1991)
Bouchard, Butch (1966)
Boucher, Frank (1958
Boucher, Buck (1960)
Bower, Johnny (1976)
Bowie, Russell (1945)
Brimsek, Frank (1966)
Broadbent, Punch (1962)
Broda, Turk (1967)
Bucyk, Johnny (1981)
Burch, Billy (1974)
Cameron, Harry (1962)
Cheevers, Gerry (1985)
Clancy, King (1958)
Clapper, Dit (1945)
Clarke, Bob (1987)
Cleghorn, Sprague (1958)
Colville, Neil (1967)
Conacher, Charlie (1961)
Conucher, Lionel (1994)
Connell, Alex (1958)
Cook, Bill (1952)
Coulter, Art (1974)
Cournoyer, Yvan (1982)
Cowley, William (1968)
Crawford, Rusty (1962)
Darragh, Jack (1962)
Davidson, Scotty (1950)
Day, Hap (1961)
Delvecchio, Alex (1977)
Denneny, Cy (1959)
Dionne, Marcel (1992)
Drillon, Gordie (1975)
Drinkwater, Charles (1950)
Dryden, Ken (1983)
Dumart, Woody (1992) **Dunderdale,**
Thomas (1974)
Durnan, Bill (1964)
Dutton, Red (1958)

Dye, Babe (1970)
Esposito, Phil (1984)
Esposito, Tony (1988)
Farrell, Arthur (1965)
Flaman, Fern (1990)
Foyston, Frank (1958)
Frederickson, Frank (1958)
Gadsby, Bill (1970)
Gainey, Bob (1992)
Gardiner, Chuck (1945)
Gardiner, Herb (1958)
Gardner, Jimmy (1962)
Geoffrion, Boom Boom (1972)
Gerard, Eddie (1945)
Giacomin, Ed (1987)
Gilbert, Rod (1982)
Gilmour, Billy (1962)
Goheen, Moose (1952)
Goodfellow, Ebbie (1963)
Grant, Mike (1950)
Green, Shorty (1962)
Griffis, Si (1950)
Hainsworth, George (1961)
Hall, Glenn (1975)
Hall, Joe (1961)
Harvey, Doug (1973)
Hay, George (1958)
Hern, Riley (1962)
Hextall, Bryan (1969)
Holmes, Hap (1972)
Hooper, Tom (1962)
Horner, Red (1965)
Horton, Tim (1977)
Howe, Gordie (1972)
Howell, Syd (1965)
Howell, Harry (1979)
Hull, Bobby (1983)
Hutton, Bouse (1962)
Hyland, Harry (1962)
Irvin, Dick (1958)
Jackson, Busher (1971)
Johnson, Moose (1952)
Johnson, Ching (1958)
Johnson, Tom (1970)
Joliat, Aurel (1947)
Keats, Duke (1958)
Kelly, Red (1969)
Kennedy, Teeder (1966)
Keon, Dave (1986)
Lach, Elmer (1966)
Lafleur, Guy (1988)
Lalonde, Newsy (1950)
Laperrière, Jacques (1987)
Lapointe, Guy (1993)
Laprate, Edgar (1993)
Laviolette, Jack (1962)

Lehman, Hugh (1958)
Lemaire, Jacques (1984)
LeSueur, Percy (1961)
Lewis, Herbie (1989)
Lindsay, Ted (1966)
Lumley, Harry (1980)
Mackay, Mickey (1952)
Mahovlich, Frank (1981
Malone, Joe (1950)
Mantha, Sylvio (1960)
Marshall, Jack (1965)
Maxwell, Steamer (1962)
McDonald, Lanny (1992)
McGee, Frank (1945)
McGimsie, Billy (1962)
McNamara, George (1958)
Mikita, Stan (1983)
Moore, Dickie (1974)
Moran, Paddy (1958)
Morenz, Howie (1945)
Mosienko, Bill (1965)
Nighbor, Frank (1947)
Noble, Reg (1962)
O'Connor, Buddy (1988)
*****O'Neill,** Brian (1994)
Oliver, Harry (1967)
Olmstead, Bert (1985)
Orr, Bobby (1979)
Parent, Bernie (1984)
Park, Brad (1988)
Patrick, Lynn (1980)
Patrick, Lester (1947)
Perreault, Gilbert (1990)
Phillips, Tommy (1945)
Pilote, Pierre (1975)
Pitre, Didier "Pit" (1962)
Plante, Jacques (1978)
Potvin, Denis (1991)
Pratt, Babe (1966)
Primeau, Joe (1963)
Pronovost, Marcel (1978)
Pulford, Bob (1991)
Pulford, Harvey (1945)
Quackenbush, Bill (1976)
Rankin, Frank (1961)
Ratelle, Jean (1985)
Rayner, Chuck (1973)
Reardon, Ken (1966)
Richard, Henri (1979)
Richard, Maurice "Rocket" (1961)
Richardson, George (1950)
Roberts, Gordon (1971)
Ross, Art (1945)
Russel, Blair (1965)
Russell, Ernest (1965)
Ruttan, Jack (1962)

▶

Savard, Serge (1986)
Sawchuk, Terry (1971)
Scanlan, Fred (1965)
Schmidt, Milt (1961)
Schriner, Sweeney (1962)
Seibert, Earl (1963)
Seibert, Oliver (1961)
Shore, Eddie (1947)
Shutt, Steve (1993)
Siebert, Babe (1964)
Simpson, Bullet Joe (1962)
Sittler, Darryl (1989)
Smith, Alfred (1962)

Smith, Bill (1993)
Smith, Clint (1991)
Smith, Hooley (1972)
Smith, Thomas (1973)
Stanley, Allan (1981)
Stanley, Barney (1962)
Stewart, Black Jack (1964)
Stewart, Nels (1962)
Stuart, Bruce (1961)
Stuart, Hod (1945)
Taylor, Cyclone (1947)
Thompson, Tiny (1959)
Tretiak, Vladislav (1989)

Trihey, Harry (1950)
Ullman, Norm (1982)
Vezina, Georges (1945)
Walker, Jack (1960)
Walsh, Marty (1962)
*Watson, Harry (1994)
Watson, Moose (1962)
Weiland, Cooney (1971)
Westwick, Harry (1962)
Whitcroft, Fred (1962)
Wilson, Phat (1962)
Worsley, Lorne "Gump" (1980)
Worters, Roy (1969)

* New inductees

BASEBALL

American League Final Standings, 1994

Eastern Division					Central Division					Western Division				
Club	W	L	Pct	GB	Club	W	L	Pct	GB	Club	W	L	Pct	GB
New York	70	43	.619	—	Chicago	67	46	.593	—	Texas	52	62	.456	—
Baltimore	63	49	.563	6.5	Cleveland	66	47	.584	1	Oakland	51	63	.447	1
Toronto	55	60	.478	16	Kansas City	64	51	.557	4	Seattle	49	63	.438	2
Boston	54	61	.470	17	Minnesota	53	60	.469	14	California	47	68	.409	5.5
Detroit	53	62	.461	18	Milwaukee	53	62	.461	15					

Note: Major league players went on strike Aug. 12, 1994 and the owners suspended the season Sept. 15, 1994.

American League Leaders, 1993

Batting

Batting Average

Paul O'Neill, NY, 359
Albert Belle, Cle., 357
Frank Thomas, Chi., 353
Ken Lofton, Cle., 349
Wade Boggs, NY., 342

Runs

Frank Thomas, Chi., 106
Kenny Lofton, Cle., 105
Ken Griffey, Sea., 94
Tony Phillips, Det., 91
Albert Belle Cle., 90
Cal Ripken, Bal., 140

Hits

Kenny Lofton, Cle., 160
Paul Molitor, Tor...155
Albert Belle, Cle., 147
Frank Thomas, Chi., 141
Ken Griffey, Sea., 140

Runs Batted In

Kirby Puckett, Minn., 112
Joe Carter, Tor., 103
Albert Belle, Cle., 101
Frank Thomas, Chi., 101
Julio Franco, Chi., 98

Doubles

Chuck Knoblauch, Minn., 45
Albert Belle, Cle., 35
Travis Frymman, Det., 34
Frank Thomas, Chi., 34
4 tied with 32

Triples

Lance Johnson, Chi., 14
Vince Coleman, KC., 12
Kenny Lofton, Cle., 9
Alex Diaz, Mil., 7
3 tied with 6

Home Runs

Ken Griffey, Sea., 40
Frank Thomas, Chi., 38
Albert Belle, Cle., 6
Jose Canseco, Tex., 31
Cecil Fielder, Det., 28

Slugging Average

Frank Thomas, Chi., 729
Albert Belle, Cle., 714
Ken Griffey, Sea., 674
Paul O'Neil, NY., 603
Bob Hamelin, KC, 599

On-Base Pct.

Frank Thomas, Chi., 487
Paul O'Neil, NY, 60
Albert Belle,Cle., 438
Wade Boggs, NY, 433
Will Clark, Tex., 431

▶

Stolen Bases

Kenny Lofton, Cle., 60
Vince Coleman, KC., 50
Otis Nixon, Bos., 42
Chuck Knoblauch, Minn., 35
Brady Anderson, Balt., 31

Walks

Frank Thomas, Chi., 109
Mickey Tettleton, Det., 97
Tony Phillips, Det., 95
Rickey Henderson, Oak., 72
Paul O'Neill,NY, 72

Strikeouts

Travis Fryman, Det., 128
Jose Canseco, Tex., 114
Mo Vaughn, Bos., 112
Danny Tartabull,NY, 111
Cecil Fielder, Det., 110

Pitching

Wins

Jimmy Key, NY, 17
David Cone, KC, 16
Mike Mussina, Balt., 16
Ben McDonald, Balt., 14
Pat Hentgen, Tor., 13
Randy Johnson, Sea., 13

Earned Run Average

Steve Ontiveros, Oak., 2.65
Roger Clemens, Bos., 2.85
David Cone, KC, 2.94
Mike Mussina, Balt., 3.06
Randy Johnson, Sea., 3.19

Strikeouts

Randy Johnson, Sea., 204
Roger Clemens,Bos., 168
Chuck Finley, Cal., 148
Pat Hentgen, Tor., 147
Kevin Appier, KC, 145

Saves

Lee Smith, Balt., 33
Jeff Montgomery, KC, 27
Rick Aguilera, Minn., 23
Dennis Eckersley, Oak., 19
Bobby Ayala, Sea., 18

Shutouts

Randy Johnson, Sea., 4
Alex Fernandez, Chi., 3
David Cone, KC., 3
Dennis Martinze, Cle., 3
Pat Hentgen,Tor., 3
Bobby Witt, Oak., 3

Innings Pitched

Chuck Finley, Cal., 183.1
Jack McDowell, Chi., 181.0
Cal Eldred, Mil., 179.0
Dennis Martinez, Cle., 176.2
Mike Mussina, Balt., 176.1

Games

Bob Wickman, NY, 53
Jose Mesa, Cle., 51
Billy Brewer, KC, 50
Mark Guthrie, Minn., 50
Carl Willis, Minn., 49

Bases on Balls

Mike Moore, Det., 89
Tod Van Poppel, Oak., 89
Tom Gordon, KC, 87
Cal Eldred, Mil., 84
Jason Bere, Chi., 80

Complete Games

Randy Johnson, Sea., 9
Chuck Finley, Cal., 7
Dennis Martinez, Cle., 7
4 with 6

National League Final Standings, 1994

Eastern Division Club	W	L	Pct	GB	Central Division Club	W	L	Pct	GB	Western Division Club	W	L	Pct	GB
Montreal	74	40	.649	—	Cincinnati	66	48	.579	—	Los Angeles	58	56	.509	—
Atlanta	68	46	.596	6	Houston	66	49	.574	.5	San Francisco	55	60	.478	3.5
New York	55	58	.487	18.5	Pittsburgh	53	61	.465	13	Colorado	53	64	.453	6.5
Philadelphia	54	61	.470	20.5	St Louis	53	61	.465	13	San Diego	47	70	.402	12.5
Florida	51	64	.443	23.5	Chicago	49	64	.434	16.5					

Note: Major league players went on strike Aug. 12, 1994 and the owners suspended the season Sept. 15, 1994.

National League Leaders, 1994

Batting

Batting Average

Tony Gwynn, SD, 394
Jeff Bagwell, Hou., 368
Moises Alou, Mon., 339
Hal Morris, Cin., 335
Kevin Mitchell, Cin., 326

Runs

Jeff Bagwell, Hou., 104
Marquis Grissom, Mon., 96
Barry Bonds, SF, 89
Ray Lankford, Stl, 89
Craig Biggio, Hou., 88

Hits

Tony Gwynn, SD, 165
Jeff Bagwell, Hou., 147
Dante Bichette,Col., 147
Hal Morris, Cin., 146
Jeff Conine, Fla, 144

Runs Batted In	Doubles	Triples
Jeff Bagwell, Hou., 116	Larry Walker, Mon., 44	Darren Lewis, SF, 9
Matt Williams, SF, 96	Craig Biggio, Hou., 44	Brett Butler, LA, 9
Dante Bichette, Col., 95	Jay Bell, Pitt., 35	Mike Kingery, Col., 8
Fred McGriff, Atl., 94	Tony Gwynn, SD, 35	Raul Modesi, LA, 8
Mike Piazza, LA, 92	Dante Bichette, Col., 33	Reggis Sanders, Cin., 8

Home Runs	Slugging Average	On-Base Pct.
Matt Williams, SF, 43	Jeff Bagwell, Hou., 750	Tony Gwynn, SD, 454
Jeff Bagwell, Hou., 39	Kevin Mitchell, Cin., 681	Jeff Bagwell, Hou., 451
Barry Bonds, SF, 37	Barry Bonds, SF, 647	Kevin Mitchell, Cin., 429
Fred McGriff, Atl., 34	Fred McGriff, Atl., 623	Dave Justice, Atl., 427
Andres Gallaraga, Col., 31	Matt Williams, SF, 607	Barry Bonds, SF, 426

Stolen Bases	Walks	Strikeouts
Craig Biggio, Hou., 39	Barry Bonds, SF, 74	Reggie Sanders, Cin., 114
Deion Sanders, Atl/Cin., 38	Dave Justice, Atl., 69	Ray Lankford, Stl, 113
Marquis Grissom, Mon., 36	Brett Butler, LA, 68	Bobby Bonilla, NY, 101
Chuck Carr, Fla, 32	Lenny Dykstra, Phi., 68	Kurt Abbott, Fla, 98
Darren Lewis, SF, 30	Jeff Bagwell, Hou., 65	Ryan Thompson, NY, 94

Pitching

Wins/Losses	Earned Run Average	Strikeouts
Ken Hill, Mon., 16	Greg Maddux, Atl., 1.56	Andy Benes, SD, 189
Greg Maddux, Atl., 16	Bret Saberhagen, NY, 2.74	Jose Rijo, Cin., 171
Danny Jackson, Phi., 14	Doug Drabek, Hou., 2.84	Greg Maddux, Atl., 156
Bret Saberhagen, NY, 14	Jeff Fassero, Mon., 2.99	Bret Saberhagen, NY, 143
Tom Glavine, Atl., 13	Shane Reynolds, Hou., 3.05	Pedro Martinez, Mon., 142

Saves	Shutouts	Innings Pitched
John Franco, NY, 30	Greg Maddux, Atl., 3	Greg Maddux, Atl., 202.0
Rod Beck, SF, 28	Ramon Martinez, LA, 3	Danny Jackson, Phi., 179.1
Doug Jones, Phi., 27	Andy Benes, SD, 2	Bret Saberhagen, NY, 177.1
John Wetteland, Mon., 25	Doug Drabek, Hou., 2	Andy Benes, SD, 172.1
Greg McMichael, Atl., 21		Jose Rijo, Cin., 172.1
Randy Myers, Chi., 21		

Games	Bases on Balls	Complete Games
Steve Reed, Col., 61	Daryl Kile, Hou., 82	Greg Maddux, Atl., 10
Mel Rojas, Mon., 58	Tom Glavine, Atl., 70	Doug Drabek, Hou., 6
Jose Bautista, Chi., 58	Pat Rapp, Fla, 69	Tom Candiotti, LA, 5
Dave Burba, SF, 57	David Weathers, Fla, 59	5 with 4
Mike Munoz, Col., 57	3 with 56	

Directory of Selected Baseball Organizations in Canada

Canadian Federation of Amateur Baseball
1600 James Naismith Dr.
Gloucester, Ont.
K1B 5N4
Tel: (613)748-5606
Fax: (613)748-5706

Major League Baseball
350 Park Ave
New York, NY 10022
Tel: (212)339-7800

Montreal Expos Baseball Club
PO Box 500,
Station M
Montreal, Que
H1V 3P2
Tel: (514)253-3434
Fax: (514)253-8282

Toronto Blue Jays
The Skydome
300 The Esplanade
West, Suite 3200
Toronto, Ont.
M5V 3B3
Tel: (416)341-1000

Major League Pennant Winners, 1901–93

National League

Year	Winner	Won	Lost	Pct.
1901	Pittsburgh	90	49	.647
1902	Pittsburgh	103	36	.741
1903	Pittsburgh	91	49	.650
1904	New York	106	47	.693
1905	New York	105	48	.686
1906	Chicago	116	36	.763
1907	Chicago	107	45	.704
1908	Chicago	99	55	.643
1909	Pittsburgh	110	42	.724
1910	Chicago	104	50	.675
1911	New York	99	54	.647
1912	New York	103	48	.682
1913	New York	101	51	.664
1914	Boston	94	59	.614
1915	Philadelphia	90	62	.592
1916	Brooklyn	94	60	.610
1917	New York	98	56	.636
1918	Chicago	84	45	.651
1919	Cincinnati	96	44	.686
1920	Brooklyn	93	61	.604
1921	New York	94	59	.614
1922	New York	93	61	.604
1923	New York	95	58	.621
1924	New York	93	60	.608
1925	Pittsburgh	95	58	.621
1926	St. Louis	89	65	.578
1927	Pittsburgh	94	60	.610
1928	St. Louis	95	59	.617
1929	Chicago	98	54	.645
1930	St. Louis	92	62	.597
1931	St. Louis	101	53	.656
1932	Chicago	90	64	.584
1933	New York	91	61	.599
1934	St. Louis	95	58	.621
1935	Chicago	100	54	.649
1936	New York	92	62	.597
1937	New York	95	57	.625
1938	Chicago	89	63	.586
1939	Cincinnati	97	57	.630
1940	Cincinnati	100	53	.654
1941	Brooklyn	100	54	.649
1942	St. Louis	106	48	.688
1943	St. Louis	105	49	.682
1944	St. Louis	105	49	.682
1945	Chicago	98	56	.636
1946	St. Louis	98	58	.628
1947	Brooklyn	94	60	.610

American League

Year	Winner	Won	Lost	Pct.
1901	Chicago	83	53	.610
1902	Philadelphia	83	53	.610
1903	Boston	91	47	.659
1904	Boston	95	59	.617
1905	Philadelphia	92	56	.622
1906	Chicago	93	58	.616
1907	Detroit	92	58	.613
1908	Detroit	90	63	.588
1909	Detroit	98	54	.645
1910	Philadelphia	102	48	.680
1911	Philadelphia	101	50	.669
1912	Boston	105	47	.691
1913	Philadelphia	96	57	.627
1914	Philadelphia	99	53	.651
1915	Boston	101	50	.669
1916	Boston	91	63	.591
1917	Chicago	100	54	.649
1918	Boston	75	51	.595
1919	Chicago	88	52	.629
1920	Cleveland	98	56	.636
1921	New York	98	55	.641
1922	New York	94	60	.610
1923	New York	98	54	.645
1924	Washington	92	62	.597
1925	Washington	96	55	.636
1926	New York	91	63	.591
1927	New York	110	44	.714
1928	New York	101	53	.656
1929	Philadelphia	104	46	.693
1930	Philadelphia	102	52	.662
1931	Philadelphia	107	45	.704
1932	New York	107	47	.695
1933	Washington	99	53	.651
1934	Detroit	101	53	.656
1935	Detroit	93	58	.616
1936	New York	102	51	.667
1937	New York	102	52	.662
1938	New York	99	53	.651
1939	New York	106	45	.702
1940	Detroit	90	64	.584
1941	New York	101	53	.656
1942	New York	103	51	.669
1943	New York	98	56	.636
1944	St. Louis	89	65	.578
1945	Detroit	88	65	.575
1946	Boston	104	50	.675
1947	New York	97	57	.630

National League

Year	Winner	Won	Lost	Pct.
1948	Boston	91	62	.595
1949	Brooklyn	97	57	.630
1950	Philadelphia	91	63	.591
1951	New York	98	59	.624
1952	Brooklyn	96	57	.627
1953	Brooklyn	105	49	.682
1954	New York	97	57	.630
1955	Brooklyn	98	55	.641
1956	Brooklyn	93	61	.604
1957	Milwaukee	95	59	.617
1958	Milwaukee	92	62	.597
1959	Los Angeles	88	68	.564
1960	Pittsburgh	95	59	.617
1961	Cincinnati	93	61	.604
1962	San Francisco	103	62	.624
1963	Los Angeles	99	63	.611
1964	St. Louis	93	69	.574
1965	Los Angeles	97	65	.599
1966	Los Angeles	95	67	.586
1967	St. Louis	101	60	.627
1968	St. Louis	97	65	.599
1969	New York	100	62	.617
1970	Cincinnati	102	60	.630
1971	Pittsburgh	97	65	.599
1972	Cincinnati	95	59	.617
1973	New York	82	79	.509
1974	Los Angeles	102	60	.630
1975	Cincinnati	108	54	.667
1976	Cincinnati	102	60	.630
1977	Los Angeles	98	64	.605
1978	Los Angeles	95	67	.586
1979	Pittsburgh	98	64	.605
1980	Philadelphia	91	71	.562
1981	Los Angeles	63	47	.573
1982	St. Louis	92	70	.568
1983	Philadelphia	90	72	.556
1984	San Diego	92	70	.568
1985	St. Louis	101	61	.623
1986	New York	108	54	.667
1987	St. Louis	95	67	.586
1988	Los Angeles	94	67	.584
1989	San Francisco	92	70	.568
1990	Cincinnati	91	71	.562
1991	Atlanta	94	68	.580
1992	Atlanta	98	64	.605
1993	Philadelphia	97	65	.599
*1994 no winner				

American League

Year	Winner	Won	Lost	Pct.
1948	Cleveland	97	58	.626
1949	New York	97	57	.630
1950	New York	98	56	.636
1951	New York	98	56	.636
1952	New York	95	59	.617
1953	New York	99	52	.656
1954	Cleveland	111	43	.721
1955	New York	96	58	.623
1956	New York	97	57	.630
1957	New York	98	56	.636
1958	New York	92	62	.597
1959	Chicago	94	60	.610
1960	New York	97	57	.630
1961	New York	109	53	.673
1962	New York	96	66	.593
1963	New York	104	57	.646
1964	New York	99	63	.611
1965	Minnesota	102	60	.630
1966	Baltimore	97	63	.606
1967	Boston	92	70	.568
1968	Detroit	103	59	.636
1969	Baltimore	109	53	.673
1970	Baltimore	108	54	.667
1971	Baltimore	101	57	.639
1972	Oakland	93	62	.600
1973	Oakland	94	68	.580
1974	Oakland	90	72	.556
1975	Boston	95	65	.594
1976	New York	97	62	.610
1977	New York	100	62	.617
1978	New York	100	63	.613
1979	Baltimore	102	57	.642
1980	Kansas City	97	65	.599
1981	New York	59	48	.551
1982	Milwaukee	95	67	.586
1983	Baltimore	98	64	.605
1984	Detroit	104	58	.642
1985	Kansas City	91	71	.562
1986	Boston	95	66	.590
1987	Minnesota	85	77	.525
1988	Oakland	104	58	.642
1989	Oakland	99	63	.611
1990	Oakland	103	59	.636
1991	Minnesota	95	67	.586
1992	**Toronto**	**96**	**66**	**.593**
1993	**Toronto**	**95**	**67**	**.586**
*1994 no winner				

* Players strike Aug. 12, 1994; owners suspended season, Sept. 14, 1994

World Series Results, 1903–93

Year	Champion	Final Opponent	Series Result
1903	Boston Red Sox, AL	Pittsburgh Pirates, NL	5-3
1904	No series		
1905	New York Giants, NL	Philadelphia Athletics, AL	4-1
1906	Chicago White Sox, AL	Chicago Cubs, NL	4-2
1907	Chicago Cubs, NL	Detroit Tigers, AL	4-0; 1 tie
1908	Chicago Cubs, NL	Detroit Tigers, AL	4-1
1909	Pittsburgh Pirates, NL	Detroit Tigers, AL	4-3
1910	Philadelphia Athletics, AL	Chicago Cubs, NL	4-1
1911	Philadelphia Athletics, AL	New York Giants, NL	4-2
1912	Boston Red Sox, AL	New York Giants, NL	4-3; 1 tie
1913	Philadelphia Athletics, AL	New York Giants, NL	4-1
1914	Boston Braves, NL	Philadelphia Athletics, AL	4-0
1915	Boston Red Sox, AL	Philadelphia Phillies, NL	4-1
1916	Boston Red Sox, AL	Brooklyn Dodgers, NL	4-1
1917	Chicago White Sox, AL	New York Giants, NL	4-2
1918	Boston Red Sox, AL	Chicago Cubs, NL	4-2
1919	Cincinnati Reds, NL	Chicago White Sox, AL	5-3
1920	Cleveland Indians, AL	Brooklyn Dodgers, NL	5-2
1921	New York Giants, NL	New York Yankees, AL	5-3
1922	New York Giants, NL	New York Yankees, AL	4-0; 1 tie
1923	New York Yankees, AL	New York Giants, NL	4-2
1924	Washington Senators, AL	New York Giants, NL	4-3
1925	Pittsburgh Pirates, NL	Washington Senators, AL	4-3
1926	St. Louis Cardinals, NL	New York Yankees, AL	4-3
1927	New York Yankees, AL	Pittsburgh Pirates, NL	4-0
1928	New York Yankees, AL	St. Louis Cardinals, NL	4-0
1929	Philadelphia Athletics, AL	Chicago Cubs, NL	4-1
1930	Philadelphia Athletics, AL	St. Louis Cardinals, NL	4-2
1931	St. Louis Cardinals, NL	Philadelphia Athletics, AL	4-3
1932	New York Yankees, AL	Chicago Cubs, NL	4-0
1933	New York Giants, NL	Washington Senators, AL	4-1
1934	St. Louis Cardinals, NL	Detroit Tigers, AL	4-3
1935	Detroit Tigers, AL	Chicago Cubs, NL	4-2
1936	New York Yankees, AL	New York Giants, NL	4-2
1937	New York Yankees, AL	New York Giants, NL	4-1
1938	New York Yankees, AL	Chicago Cubs, NL	4-0
1939	New York Yankees, AL	Cincinnati Reds, NL	4-0
1940	Cincinnati Reds, NL	Detroit Tigers, AL	4-3
1941	New York Yankees, AL	Brooklyn Dodgers, NL	4-1
1942	St. Louis Cardinals, NL	New York Yankees, AL	4-1
1943	New York Yankees, AL	St. Louis Cardinals, NL	4-1
1944	St. Louis Cardinals, NL	St. Louis Browns, AL	4-2
1945	Detroit Tigers, AL	Chicago Cubs, NL	4-3
1946	St. Louis Cardinals, NL	Boston Red Sox, AL	4-3
1947	New York Yankees, AL	Brooklyn Dodgers, NL	4-3
1948	Cleveland Indians, AL	Boston Braves, NL	4-2
1949	New York Yankees, AL	Brooklyn Dodgers, NL	4-1
1950	New York Yankees, AL	Philadelphia Phillies, NL	4-0
1951	New York Yankees, AL	New York Giants, NL	4-2
1952	New York Yankees, AL	Brooklyn Dodgers, NL	4-3
1953	New York Yankees, AL	Brooklyn Dodgers, NL	4-2
1954	New York Giants, NL	Cleveland Indians, AL	4-0
1955	Brooklyn Dodgers, NL	New York Yankees, AL	4-3
1956	New York Yankees, AL	Brooklyn Dodgers, NL	4-3
1957	Milwaukee Braves, NL	New York Yankees, AL	4-3
1958	New York Yankees, AL	Milwaukee Braves, NL	4-3
1959	Los Angeles Dodgers, NL	Chicago White Sox, AL	4-2
1960	Pittsburgh Pirates, NL	New York Yankees, AL	4-3
1961	New York Yankees, AL	Cincinnati Reds, NL	4-1

1962	New York Yankees, AL	San Francisco Giants, NL	4-3
1963	Los Angeles Dodgers, NL	New York Yankees, AL	4-0
1964	St. Louis Cardinals, NL	New York Yankees, AL	4-3
1965	Los Angeles Dodgers, NL	Minnesota Twins, AL	4-3
1966	Baltimore Orioles, AL	Los Angeles Dodgers, NL	4-0
1967	St. Louis Cardinals, NL	Boston Red Sox, AL	4-3
1968	Detroit Tigers, AL	St. Louis Cardinals, NL	4-3
1969	New York Mets, NL	Baltimore Orioles, AL	4-1
1970	Baltimore Orioles, AL	Cincinnati Reds, NL	4-1
1971	Pittsburgh Pirates, NL	Baltimore Orioles, AL	4-3
1972	Oakland Athletics, AL	Cincinnati Reds, NL	4-3
1973	Oakland Athletics, AL	New York Mets, NL	4-3
1974	Oakland Athletics, AL	Los Angeles Dodgers, NL	4-1
1975	Cincinnati Reds, NL	Boston Red Sox, AL	4-3
1976	Cincinnati Reds, NL	New York Yankees, AL	4-0
1977	New York Yankees, AL	Los Angeles Dodgers, NL	4-2
1978	New York Yankees, AL	Los Angeles Dodgers, NL	4-2
1979	Pittsburgh Pirates, NL	Baltimore Orioles, AL	4-3
1980	Philadelphia Phillies, NL	Kansas City Royals, AL	4-2
1981	Los Angeles Dodgers, NL	New York Yankees, AL	4-2
1982	St. Louis Cardinals, NL	Milwaukee Brewers, AL	4-3
1983	Baltimore Orioles, AL	Philadelphia Phillies, NL	4-1
1984	Detroit Tigers, AL	San Diego Padres, NL	4-1
1985	Kansas City Royals, AL	St. Louis Cardinals, NL	4-3
1986	New York Mets, NL	Boston Red Sox, AL	4-3
1987	Minnesota Twins, AL	St. Louis Cardinals, NL	4-3
1988	Los Angeles Dodgers, AL	Oakland Athletics, AL	4-1
1989	Oakland Athletics, AL	San Francisco Giants, NL	4-0
1990	Cincinnati Reds, NL	Oakland Athletics, AL	4-0
1991	Minnesota Twins, AL	Atlanta Braves, NL	4-3
1992	**Toronto Blue Jays,** AL	Atlanta Braves, NL	4-2
1993	**Toronto Blue Jays,** AL	Philadelphia Phillies, NL	4-2
1994	No World Series: season suspended Sept. 15, 1994		

World Series MVPs

1955	Johnny Podres, Bklyn	1969	Donn Clendenon, NY (NL)	1981	Steve Yeager, LA
1956	Don Larsen, New York (AL)	1970	Brooks Robinson, Bal	1982	Darrell Porter, StL
1957	Lew Burdette, Mil	1971	Roberto Clemente, Pgh	1983	Rick Dempsey, Bal
1958	Bob Turley, NY (AL)	1972	Gene Tenace, Oak	1984	Alan Trammell, Det
1959	Larry Sherry, LA	1973	Reggie Jackson, Oak	1985	Bret Saberhagen, KC
1960	Bobby Richardson, NY (AL)	1974	Rollie Fingers, Oak	1986	Ray Knight, NY (NL)
1961	Whitey Ford, NY (AL)	1975	Pete Rose, Cin	1987	Frank Viola, Min
1962	Ralph Terry, NY (AL)	1976	Johnny Bench, Cin	1988	Orel Hershiser, LA
1963	Sandy Koufax, LA	1977	Reggie Jackson, NY (AL)	1989	Dave Stewart, Oak
1964	Bob Gibson, StL	1978	Bucky Dent, NY (AL)	1990	Jose Rijo, Cin
1965	Sandy Koufax, LA	1979	Willie Stargell, Pgh	1991	Jack Morris, Min
1966	Frank Robinson, Bal	1980	Mike Schmidt, Pha	1992	**Pat Borders, Tor**
1967	Bob Gibson, StL	1981	Ron Cey, LA	1993	**Paul Molitor, Tor**
1968	Mickey Lolich, Det	1981	Pedro Guerrero, LA	1994	No award

Cy Young Award Winners, 1956–93[1]

Year	Player, club	Year	Player, club
1956[1]	Don Newcombe, Brooklyn Dodgers	1963[1]	Sandy Koufax, Los Angeles Dodgers
1957[1]	Warren Spahn, Milwaukee Braves	1964[1]	Dean Chance, California Angels
1958[1]	Bob Turley, New York Yankees	1965[1]	Sandy Koufax, Los Angeles Dodgers
1959[1]	Early Wynn, Chicago White Sox	1966[1]	Sandy Koufax, Los Angeles Dodgers
1960[1]	Vernon Law, Pittsburgh Pirates	1967 (NL)	Mike McCormick, San Francisco Giants
1961[1]	Whitey Ford, New York Yankees	(AL)	Jim Lonborg, Boston Red Sox
1962[1]	Don Drysdale, Los Angeles Dodgers	1968 (NL)	Bob Gibson, St. Louis Cardinals

▶

▶ (AL) Dennis McLain, Detroit Tigers
1969 (NL) Tom Seaver, New York Mets
(AL) Dennis McLain, Detroit Tigers
(AL) Mike Cuellar, Baltimore Orioles
1970 (NL) Bob Gibson, St. Louis Cardinals
(AL) Jim Perry, Minnesota Twins
1971 (NL) Ferguson Jenkins, Chicago Cubs
(AL) Vida Blue, Oakland A's
1972 (NL) Steve Carlton, Philadelphia Phillies
(AL) Gaylord Perry, Cleveland Indians
1973 (NL) Tom Seaver, New York Mets
(AL) Jim Palmer, Baltimore Orioles
1974 (NL) Mike Marshall, Los Angeles Dodgers
(AL) Jim (Catfish) Hunter, Oakland A's
1975 (NL) Tom Seaver, New York Mets
(AL) Jim Palmer, Baltimore Orioles
1976 (NL) Randy Jones, San Diego Padres
(AL) Jim Palmer, Baltimore Orioles
1977 (NL) Steve Carlton, Philadelphia Phillies
(AL) Sparky Lyle, New York Yankees
1978 (NL) Gaylord Perry, San Diego Padres
(AL) Ron Guidry, New York Yankees
1979 (NL) Bruce Sutter, Chicago Cubs
(AL) Mike Flanagan, Baltimore Orioles
1980 (NL) Steve Carlton, Philadelphia Phillies
(AL) Steve Stone, Baltimore Orioles

1981 (NL) Fernando Valenzuela, Los Angeles Dodgers
(AL) Rollie Fingers, Milwaukee Brewers
1982 (NL) Steve Carlton, Philadelphia Phillies
(AL) Pete Vuckovich, Milwaukee Brewers
1983 (NL) John Denny, Philadelphia Phillies
(AL) LaMarr Hoyt, Chicago White Sox
1984 (NL) Rick Sutcliffe, Chicago Cubs
(AL) Willie Hernandez, Detroit Tigers
1985 (NL) Dwight Gooden, New York Mets
(AL) Bret Saberhagen, Kansas City Royals
1986 (NL) Mike Scott, Houston Astros
(AL) Roger Clemens, Boston Red Sox
1987 (NL) Steve Bedrosian, Philadelphia Phillies
(AL) Roger Clemens, Boston Red Sox
1988 (NL) Orel Hershiser, Los Angeles Dodgers
(AL) Frank Viola, Minnesota Twins
1989 (NL) Mark Davis, San Diego Padres
(AL) Bret Saberhagen, Kansas City Royals
1990 (NL) Doug Drabek, Pittsburgh Pirates
(AL) Bob Welch, Oakland A's
1991 (NL) Tom Glavine, Atlanta Braves
(AL) Roger Clemens, Boston Red Sox
1992 (NL) Greg Maddux, Chicago Cubs
(AL) Dennis Eckersley, Oakland A's
1993 (NL) Greg Maddux, Atlanta Braves
(AL) Jack McDowell, Chicago White Sox

(1) One award, 1956–66

Most Valuable Player, 1931–93[1]

National League	American League
1931[1] Frank Frisch, St. Louis Cardinals	Lefty Grove, Philadelphia Athletics
1932 Chuck Klein, Philadelphia Phillies	Jimmie Foxx, Philadelphia Athletics
1933 Carl Hubbell, New York Giants	Jimmie Foxx, Philadelphia Athletics
1934 Dizzy Dean, St. Louis Cardinals	Mickey Cochrane, Detroit Tigers
1935 Gabby Hartnett, Chicago Cubs	Hank Greenberg, Detroit Tigers
1936 Carl Hubbell, New York Giants	Lou Gehrig, New York Yankees
1937 Joe Medwick, St. Louis Cardinals	Charley Gehringer, Detroit Tigers
1938 Ernie Lombardi, Cincinnati Reds	Jimmie Foxx, Boston Red Sox
1939 Bucky Walters, Cincinnati Reds	Joe DiMaggio, New York Yankees
1940 Frank McCormick, Cincinnati Reds	Hank Greenberg, Detroit Tigers
1941 Dolph Camilli, Brooklyn Dodgers	Joe DiMaggio, New York Yankees
1942 Mort Cooper, St. Louis Cardinals	Joe Gordon, New York Yankees
1943 Stan Musial, St. Louis Cardinals	Spud Chandler, New York Yankees
1944 Marty Marion, St. Louis Cardinals	Hal Newhouser, Detroit Tigers
1945 Phil Cavarretta, Chicago Cubs	Hal Newhouser, Detroit Tigers
1946 Stan Musial, St. Louis Cardinals	Ted Williams, Boston Red Sox
1947 Bob Elliott, Boston Braves	Joe DiMaggio, New York Yankees
1948 Stan Musial, St. Louis Cardinals	Lou Boudreau, Cleveland Indians
1949 Jackie Robinson, Brooklyn Dodgers	Ted Williams, Boston Red Sox
1950 Jim Konstanty, Philadelphia Phillies	Phil Rizzuto, New York Yankees
1951 Roy Campanella, Brooklyn Dodgers	Yogi Berra, New York Yankees
1952 Hank Sauer, Chicago Cubs	Bobby Shantz, Philadelphia Athletics
1953 Roy Campanella, Brooklyn Dodgers	Al Rosen, Cleveland Indians
1954 Willie Mays, New York Giants	Yogi Berra, New York Yankees
1955 Roy Campanella, Brooklyn Dodgers	Yogi Berra, New York Yankees
1956 Don Newcombe, Brooklyn Dodgers	Mickey Mantle, New York Yankees
1958 Ernie Banks, Chicago Cubs	Jackie Jensen, Boston Red Sox
1959 Ernie Banks, Chicago Cubs	Nelson Fox, Chicago White Sox
1960 Dick Groat, Pittsburgh Pirates	Roger Maris, New York Yankees
1961 Frank Robinson, Cincinnati Reds	Roger Maris, New York Yankees
1962 Maury Wills, Los Angeles Dodgers	Mickey Mantle, New York Yankees
1963 Sandy Koufax, Los Angeles Dodgers	Elston Howard, New York Yankees

National League	American League
1964 Ken Boyer, St. Louis Cardinals	Brooks Robinson, Baltimore Orioles
1965 Willie Mays, San Francisco Giants	Zoilo Versalles, Minnesota Twins
1966 Roberto Clemente, Pittsburgh Pirates	Frank Robinson, Baltimore Orioles
1967 Orlando Cepeda, St. Louis Cardinals	Carl Yastrzemski, Boston Red Sox
1968 Bob Gibson, St. Louis Cardinals	Denny McLain, Detroit Tigers
1969 Willie McCovey, San Francisco Giants	Harmon Killebrew, Minnesota Twins
1971 Joe Torre, St. Louis Cardinals	Vida Blue, Oakland Athletics
1972 Johnny Bench, Cincinnati Reds	Dick Allen, Chicago White Sox
1975 Joe Morgan, Cincinnati Reds	Fred Lynn, Boston Red Sox
1976 Joe Morgan, Cincinnati Reds	Thurman Munson, New York Yankees
1979 Keith Hernandez, St. Louis Cardinals;	Don Baylor, California Angels
Willie Stargell, Pittsburgh Pirates	
1980 Mike Schmidt, Philadelphia Phillies	George Brett, Kansas City Royals
1981 Mike Schmidt, Philadelphia Phillies	Rollie Fingers, Milwaukee Brewers
1982 Dale Murphy, Atlanta Braves	Robin Yount, Milwaukee Brewers
1983 Dale Murphy, Atlanta Braves	Cal Ripken, Jr., Baltimore Orioles
1984 Ryne Sandberg, Chicago Cubs	Willie Hernandez, Detroit Tigers
1985 Willie McGee, St. Louis Cardinals	Don Mattingly, New York Yankees
1986 Mike Schmidt, Philadelphia Phillies	Roger Clemens, Boston Red Sox
1987 André Dawson, Chicago Cubs	**George Bell, Toronto Blue Jays**
1988 Kirk Gibson, Los Angeles Dodgers	Jose Canseco, Oakland Athletics
1989 Kevin Mitchell, San Francisco Giants	Robin Yount, Milwaukee Brewers
1990 Barry Bonds, Pittsburgh Pirates	Rickey Henderson, Oakland Athletics
1991 Terry Pendleton, Atlanta Braves	Cal Ripken, Jr., Baltimore Orioles
1992 Barry Bonds, Pittsburgh Pirates	Dennis Eckersley, Oakland A's
1993 Barry Bonds, San Francisco Giants	Frank Thomas, Chicago White Sox

(1) 1931: First year award voted by Baseball Writers of America.

Batting Champions, 1924–94

	National League			American League	
Year	Player/Club	Pct	Year	Player/Club	Pct
1924	Rogers Hornsby, St. Louis	.424	1924	Babe Ruth, New York	.378
1925	Rogers Hornsby, St. Louis	.403	1925	Harry Heilmann, Detroit	.393
1926	Eugene Hargrave, Cincinnati	.353	1926	Heinie Manush, Detroit	.377
1927	Paul Waner, Pittsburgh	.380	1927	Harry Heilmann, Detroit	.398
1928	Rogers Hornsby, Boston	.387	1928	Goose Goslin, Washington	.379
1929	Lefty O'Doul, Philadelphia	.398	1929	Lew Fonseca, Cleveland	.369
1930	Bill Terry, New York	.401	1930	Al Simmons, Philadelphia	.381
1931	Chick Hafey, St. Louis	.349	1931	Al Simmons, Philadelphia	.390
1932	Lefty O'Doul, Brooklyn	.368	1932	Dale Alexander, Detroit-Boston	.367
1933	Charles Klein, Philadelphia	.368	1933	Jimmie Foxx, Philadelphia	.356
1934	Paul Waner, Pittsburgh	.362	1934	Lou Gehrig, New York	.363
1935	Arky Vaughan, Pittsburgh	.385	1935	Buddy Myer, Washington	.349
1936	Paul Waner, Pittsburgh	.373	1936	Luke Appling, Chicago	.388
1937	Joe Medwick, St. Louis	.374	1937	Charlie Gehringer, Detroit	.371
1938	Ernie Lombardi, Cincinnati	.342	1938	Jimmie Foxx, Boston	.349
1939	John Mize, St. Louis	.349	1939	Joe DiMaggio, New York	.381
1940	Debs Garms, Pittsburgh	.355	1940	Joe DiMaggio, New York	.352
1941	Pete Reiser, Brooklyn	.343	1941	Ted Williams, Boston	.406
1942	Ernie Lombardi, Boston	.330	1942	Ted Williams, Boston	.356
1943	Stan Musial, St. Louis	.357	1943	Luke Appling, Chicago	.328
1944	Dixie Walker, Brooklyn	.357	1944	Lou Boudreau, Cleveland	.327
1945	Phil Cavarretta, Chicago	.355	1945	George Stirnweiss, New York	.309
1946	Stan Musial, St. Louis	.365	1946	Mickey Vernon, Washington	.352
1947	Harry Walker, Philadelphia	.363	1947	Ted Williams, Boston	.343
1948	Stan Musial, St. Louis	.376	1948	Ted Williams, Boston	.369
1949	Jackie Robinson, Brooklyn	.342	1949	George Kell, Detroit	.343
1950	Stan Musial, St. Louis	.346	1950	Billy Goodman, Boston	.354
1951	Stan Musial, St. Louis	.355	1951	Ferris Fain, Philadelphia	.344 ▶

Year	Player/Team	AVG	Year	Player/Team	AVG
▶ 1952	Stan Musial, St. Louis	.336	1952	Ferris Fain, Philadelphia	.327
1953	Carl Furillo, Brooklyn	.344	1953	Mickey Vernon, Washington	.337
1954	Willie Mays, New York	.345	1954	Roberto Avila, Cleveland	.341
1955	Richie Ashburn, Philadelphia	.338	1955	Al Kaline, Detroit	.340
1956	Hank Aaron, Milwaukee	.328	1956	Mickey Mantle, New York	.353
1957	Stan Musial, St. Louis	.351	1957	Ted Williams, Boston	.388
1958	Richie Ashburn, Philadelphia	.350	1958	Ted Williams, Boston	.328
1959	Hank Aaron, Milwaukee	.355	1959	Harvey Kuenn, Detroit	.353
1960	Dick Groat, Pittsburgh	.325	1960	Pete Runnels, Boston	.320
1961	Roberto Clemente, Pittsburgh	.351	1961	Norm Cash, Detroit	.361
1962	Tommy Davis, Los Angeles	.346	1962	Pete Runnels, Boston	.326
1963	Tommy Davis, Los Angeles	.326	1963	Carl Yastrzemski, Boston	.321
1964	Roberto Clemente, Pittsburgh	.339	1964	Tony Oliva, Minnesota	.323
1965	Roberto Clemente, Pittsburgh	.329	1965	Tony Oliva, Minnesota	.321
1966	Matty Alou, Pittsburgh	.342	1966	Frank Robinson, Baltimore	.316
1967	Roberto Clemente, Pittsburgh	.357	1967	Carl Yastrzemski, Boston	.326
1968	Pete Rose, Cincinnati	.335	1968	Carl Yastrzemski, Boston	.301
1969	Pete Rose, Cincinnati	.348	1969	Rod Carew, Minnesota	.332
1970	Rico Carty, Atlanta	.366	1970	Alex Johnson, California	.329
1971	Joe Torre, St. Louis	.363	1971	Tony Oliva, Minnesota	.337
1972	Billy Williams, Chicago	.333	1972	Rod Carew, Minnesota	.318
1973	Pete Rose, Cincinnati	.338	1973	Rod Carew, Minnesota	.350
1974	Ralph Garr, Atlanta	.353	1974	Rod Carew, Minnesota	.364
1975	Bill Madlock, Chicago	.354	1975	Rod Carew, Minnesota	.359
1976	Bill Madlock, Chicago	.339	1976	George Brett, Kansas City	.333
1977	Dave Parker, Pittsburgh	.338	1977	Rod Carew, Minnesota	.388
1978	Dave Parker, Pittsburgh	.334	1978	Rod Carew, Minnesota	.333
1979	Keith Hernandez, St. Louis	.344	1979	Fred Lynn, Boston	.333
1980	Bill Buckner, Chicago	.324	1980	George Brett, Kansas City	.390
1981	Bill Madlock, Pittsburgh*	.341	1981	Carney Lansford, Boston	.336
1982	**Al Oliver, Montreal**	.331	1982	Willie Wilson, Kansas City	.332
1983	Bill Madlock, Pittsburgh	.323	1983	Wade Boggs, Boston	.361
1984	Tony Gwynn, San Diego	.351	1984	Don Mattingly, New York	.343
1985	Willie McGee, St. Louis	.353	1985	Wade Boggs, Boston	.368
1986	**Tim Raines, Montreal**	.334	1986	Wade Boggs, Boston	.357
1987	Tony Gwynn, San Diego	.370	1987	Wade Boggs, Boston	.363
1988	Tony Gwynn, San Diego	.313	1988	Wade Boggs, Boston	.366
1989	Tony Gwynn, San Diego	.336	1989	Kirby Puckett, Minnesota	.339
1990	Willie McGee, St. Louis	.335	1990	George Brett, Kansas City	.329
1991	Terry Pendleton, Atlanta	.319	1991	Julio Franco, Texas	.341
1992	Gary Sheffield, San Diego	.330	1992	Edgar Martinez, Seattle	.343
1993	Andres Galarraga, Colorado	.370	**1993**	**John Olerud, Toronto**	.363
1994	Tony Gwynn, San Diego*	.394	1994	Paul O'Neill, New York*	.359

* strike abbreviated season

Individual Earned Run Average Leaders, 1901–94

National League

Year	Player/Team	ERA	Year	Player/Team	ERA	Year	Player/Team	ERA
1901	Jesse Tannehill, Pgh	2.18	1913	Christy Mathewson, NY	2.06	1925	Dolf Luque, Cin	2.63
1902	Jack Taylor, Chi	1.33	1914	Bill Doak, StL	1.72	1926	Ray Kremer, Pgh	2.61
1903	Sam Leever, Pgh	2.06	1915	Grover Alexander, Pha	1.22	1927	Ray Kremer, Pgh	2.47
1904	Joe McGinnity, NY	1.61	1916	Grover Alexander, Pha	1.55	1928	Dazzy Vance, Brooklyn	2.09
1905	Christy Mathewson, NY	1.27	1917	Grover Alexander, Pha	1.86	1929	Bill Walker, NY	3.09
1906	Three Finger Brown, Chi	1.04	1918	Hippo Vaughn, Chi	1.74	1930	Dazzy Vance, Brooklyn	2.61
1907	Jack Pfiester, Chi	1.15	1919	Grover Alexander, Chi	1.72	1931	Bill Walker, NY	2.26
1908	Christy Mathewson, NY	1.43	1920	Grover Alexander, Chi	1.91	1932	Lon Warneke, Chi	2.37
1909	Christy Mathewson, NY	1.14	1921	Bill Doak, StL	2.59	1933	Carl Hubbell, NY	1.66
1910	George McQuillan, Pha	1.60	1922	Rosy Ryan, NY	3.01	1934	Carl Hubbell, NY	2.30
1911	Christy Mathewson, NY	1.99	1923	Dolf Luque, Cin	1.93	1935	Cy Blanton, Pgh	2.58
1912	Jeff Tesreau, NY	1.96	1924	Dazzy Vance, Brooklyn	2.16	1936	Carl Hubbell, NY	2.31

Year	Player/Team	ERA
1937	Jim Turner, Bos	2.38
1938	Bill Lee, Chi	2.66
1939	Bucky Walters, Cin	2.29
1940	Bucky Walters, Cin	2.48
1941	Elmer Riddle, Cin	2.24
1942	Mort Cooper, StL	1.78
1943	Howie Pollet, StL	1.75
1944	Ed Heusser, Cin	2.38
1945	Hank Borowy, Chi	2.13
1946	Howie Pollet, StL	2.10
1947	Warren Spahn, Bos	2.33
1948	Harry Brecheen, StL	2.24
1949	Dave Koslo, NY	2.50
1950	Jim Hearn, StL/NY	2.49
1951	Chet Nichols, Bos	2.88
1952	Hoyt Wilhelm, NY	2.43
1953	Warren Spahn, Mil	2.10
1954	Johnny Antonelli, NY	2.30
1955	Bob Friend, Pgh	2.83
1956	Lew Burdette, Mil	2.70

Year	Player/Team	ERA
1957	Johnny Podres, Brooklyn	2.66
1958	Stu Miller, SF	2.47
1959	Sam Jones, SF	2.83
1960	Mike McCormick, SF	2.70
1961	Warren Spahn, Mil	3.02
1962	Sandy Koufax, LA	2.54
1963	Sandy Koufax, LA	1.88
1964	Sandy Koufax, LA	1.74
1965	Sandy Koufax, LA	2.04
1966	Sandy Koufax, LA	1.73
1967	Phil Niekro, Atl	1.87
1968	Bob Gibson, StL	1.12
1969	Juan Marichal, SF	2.10
1970	Tom Seaver, NY	2.81
1971	Tom Seaver, NY	1.76
1972	Steve Carlton, Pha	1.97
1973	Tom Seaver, NY	2.08
1974	Buzz Capra, Atl	2.28
1975	Randy Jones, SD	2.24
1976	John Denny, StL	2.52

Year	Player/Team	ERA
1977	John Candelaria, Pgh	2.34
1978	Craig Swan, NY	2.43
1979	J.R. Richard, Hou	2.71
1980	Don Sutton, LA	2.21
1981	Nolan Ryan, Hou	1.69*
1982	**Steve Rogers, Mtl**	**2.40**
1983	Atlee Hammaker, SF	2.25
1984	Alejandro Pena, LA	2.48
1985	Dwight Gooden, NY	1.53
1986	Mike Scott, Hou	2.22
1987	Nolan Ryan, Hou	2.76
1988	Joe Magrane, StL	2.18
1989	Scott Garrelts, SF	2.28
1990	Danny Darwin, Hou	2.21
1991	**Dennis Martinez, Mtl**	**2.39**
1992	Bill Swift, S	2.08
1993	Greg Maddux, Atl.	2.36
1994	Greg Maddux, Atl.	1.56*

* strike abbreviated season

American League

Year	Player/Team	ERA
1901	Cy Young, Bos	1.62
1902	Ed Siever, Det	1.91
1903	Earl Moor, Cle	1.77
1904	Addie Joss, Cle	1.59
1905	Rube Waddell, Pha	1.48
1906	Doc White, Chi	1.52
1907	Ed Walsh, Chi	1.60
1908	Addie Joss, Cle	1.16
1909	Harry Krause, Pha	1.39
1910	Ed Walsh, Chi	1.27
1911	Vean Gregg, Cle	1.81
1912	Walter Johnson, Wash	1.39
1913	Walter Johnson, Wash	1.09
1914	Dutch Leonard, Bos	1.01
1915	Smoky Joe Wood, Bos	1.49
1916	Babe Ruth, Bos	1.75
1917	Eddie Cicotte, Chi	1.53
1918	Walter Johnson, Wash	1.27
1919	Walter Johnson, Wash	1.49
1920	Bob Shawkey, NY	2.45
1921	Red Faber, Chi	2.48
1922	Red Faber, Chi	2.80
1923	Stan Coveleski, Cle	2.76
1924	Walter Johnson, Wash	2.72
1925	Stan Coveleski, Wash	2.84
1926	Lefty Grove, Pha	2.51
1927	Wilcy Moore, NY	2.28
1928	Garland Braxton, Wash	2.51
1929	Lefty Grove, Pha	2.81
1930	Lefty Grove, Pha	2.54
1931	Lefty Grove, Pha	2.06
1932	Lefty Grove, Pha	2.84

Year	Player/Team	ERA
1933	Monte Pearson, Cle	2.33
1934	Lefty Gomez, NY	2.33
1935	Lefty Grove, Bos	2.70
1936	Lefty Grove, Bos	2.81
1937	Lefty Gomez, NY	2.33
1938	Lefty Grove, Bos	3.08
1939	Lefty Grove, Bos	2.54
1940	Bob Feller, Cle	2.61
1941	Thornton Lee, Chi	2.37
1942	Ted Lyons, Chi	2.10
1943	Spud Chandler, NY	1.64
1944	Dizzy Trout, Det	2.12
1945	Al Newhouser, Det	1.81
1946	Al Newhouser, Det	1.94
1947	Spud Chandler, NY	2.46
1948	Gene Bearden, Cle	2.43
1949	Mel Parnell, Bos	2.77
1950	Early Wynn, Cle	3.20
1951	Saul Rogovin, Det/Chi	2.78
1952	Allie Reynolds, NY	2.06
1953	Ed Lopat, NY	2.42
1954	Mike Garcia, Cle	2.64
1955	Billy Pierce, Chi	1.97
1956	Whitey Ford, NY	2.47
1957	Bobby Shantz, NY	2.45
1958	Whitey Ford, NY	2.01
1959	Hoyt Wilhelm, Bal	2.19
1960	Frank Baumann, Chi	2.67
1961	Dick Donovan, Wash	2.40
1962	Hank Aguirre, Det	2.21
1963	Gary Peters, Chi	2.33
1964	Dean Chance, LA	1.65

Year	Player/Team	ERA
1965	Sam McDowell, Cle	2.18
1966	Gary Peters, Chi	1.98
1967	Joel Horlen, Chi	2.06
1968	Luis Tiant, Cle	1.60
1969	Dick Bosman, Wash	2.19
1970	Diego Segui, Oak	2.56
1971	Vida Blue, Oak	1.82
1972	Luis Tiant, Bos	1.91
1973	Jim Palmer, Bal	2.40
1974	Catfish Hunter, Oak	2.49
1975	Jim Palmer, Bal	2.09
1976	Mark Fidrych, Det	2.34
1977	Frank Tanana, Cal	2.54
1978	Ron Guidry, NY	1.74
1979	Ron Guidry, NY	2.78
1980	Rudy May, NY	2.47
1981	Steve McCatty, Oak	2.32*
1982	Rick Sutcliffe, Cle	2.96
1983	Rick Honeycutt, Tex	2.42
1984	Mike Boddicker, Bal	2.79
1985	**Dave Stieb, Tor**	**2.48**
1986	Roger Clemens, Bos	2.48
1987	**Jimmy Key, Tor**	**2.76**
1988	Allan Anderson, Min	2.45
1989	Bret Saberhagen, KC	2.16
1990	Roger Clemens, Bos	1.93
1991	Roger Clemens, Bos	2.62
1992	Roger Clemens, Bos	2.41
1993	Kevin Appier, KC	2.56
1994	Steve Ontiveras, Oak	2.65*

Source: *The Baseball Encyclopedia*

* strike abbreviated season

Montreal Expos Year-By-Year Record

Year	Won	Lost	Pct.	Pos.	GB	Home Attendance	Manager
1969	52	110	.321	6th	48	1 212 608	Gene Mauch
1970	73	89	.451	6th	16	1 424 683	Gene Mauch
1971	71	90	.441	5th	25¹/2	1 290 963	Gene Mauch
1972	70	86	.449	5th	26¹/2	1 142 145	Gene Mauch
1973	79	83	.488	4th	3¹/2	1 246 863	Gene Mauch
1974	79	82	.491	4th	8¹/2	1 019 134	Gene Mauch
1975	75	87	.463	5th	17¹/2	908 292	Gene Mauch
1976	55	107	.340	6th	46	646 704	K. Kuehl/C. Fox
1977	75	87	.463	5th	26	1 433 757	Dick Williams
1978	76	86	.469	4th	14	1 427 007	Dick Williams
1979	95	65	.594	2nd	8	2 102 173	Dick Williams
1980	90	72	.556	2nd	1	2 208 175	Dick Williams
1981	60	48	.556	—	—	1 534 564	Dick Williams/Jim Fanning
1st half	30	25	.545	3rd	4	—	
2nd half	30	23	.566	1st	+¹/2	—	
1982	86	76	.531	3rd	6	2 318 292	Jim Fanning
1983	82	80	.506	3rd	8	2 320 651	Bill Virdon
1984	78	83	.484	5th	18	1 606 531	BillVirdon/Jim Fanning
1985	84	77	.522	3rd	16¹/2	1 502 494	Buck Rodgers
1986	78	83	.484	4th	29¹/2	1 128 981	Buck Rodgers
1987	91	71	.562	3rd	4	1 850 324	Buck Rodgers
1988	81	81	.500	3rd	20	1 478 659	Buck Rodgers
1989	81	81	.500	4th	12	1 783 533	Buck Rodgers
1990	85	77	.525	3rd	10	1 421 388	Buck Rodgers
1991	70	91	.441	6th	26¹/2	978 045	Buck Rodgers/Tom Runnells
1992	87	75	.537	2nd	9	1 731 566	Tom Runnells/Felipe Alou
1993	94	68	.580	2nd	3	1 641 437	Felipe Alou
1994	74	40	.649	1st(a)	6	1 276 250	Felipe Alou

(a) Eastern Division: first year with three divisions

Montreal Expos Individual Statistics, 1994

	Avg	OBA	AB	R	H	2B	3B	HR	RBI	BB	SO	SB	CS	E
				Batters										
Alou	339	.397	422	81	143	31	5	22	78	42	63	7	6	3
Walker	322	.394	395	76	127	44	2	19	86	47	74	15	5	9
Cordero	294	.363	415	65	122	30	3	15	63	41	62	16	3	22
Grissom	288	.344	475	96	137	25	4	11	45	41	66	36	6	5
Floyd	281	.332	334	43	94	19	4	4	41	24	63	10	3	6
Bell	278	.372	97	12	27	4	0	2	10	15	21	4	0	2
R. White	278	.358	97	16	27	10	1	2	13	9	18	1	1	2
Berry	278	.347	320	43	89	19	2	11	41	32	50	14	0	14
Webster	273	.370	143	13	39	10	0	5	23	16	24	0	0	1
Frazier	271	.358	140	25	38	3	1	0	14	18	23	20	4	1
Lansing	266	.328	394	44	105	21	2	5	35	30	37	12	8	10
Fletcher	260	.314	285	28	74	18	0	10	57	25	23	0	0	2
Spehr	250	.325	36	8	9	3	1	0	5	4	11	2	0	0
Milligan	232	.337	82	10	19	2	0	2	12	14	21	0	0	4
Gardner	219	.286	32	4	7	0	0	0	1	3	5	0	0	2
Benavides	188	.222	85	8	16	5	1	0	6	3	15	0	0	2
Team Totals	278	.343	4000	585	1111	246	30	108	542	379	669	137	36	94

AVG = batting average; OBA = on base average; AB = times at bat; R = runs; H = hits; 2B = doubles; 3B = triples; HR = home runs; RBI = runs batted in; BB = walks; SO = strikeouts; SB = stolen bases; CS = caught stealing; E = errors.

Pitchers

	W	L	ERA	G	GS	SV	IP	H	R	ER	HR	BB	SO
Haynes	0	0	0.00	4	0	0	3.2	3	1	0	0	3	1
Henry	8	3	2.43	24	15	1	107.1	97	30	29	10	20	70
Scott	5	2	2.70	40	0	1	53.1	51	17	16	0	18	37
Wetteland	4	6	2.83	52	0	25	63.2	46	22	20	5	21	68
Fassero	8	6	2.99	21	21	0	138.2	119	54	46	13	40	119
Hill	16	5	3.32	23	23	0	154.2	145	61	57	12	44	85
Rojas	3	2	3.32	58	0	16	84.0	71	35	31	11	21	84
Martinez	11	5	3.42	24	23	1	144.2	115	58	55	11	45	142
Heredia	6	3	3.46	39	3	0	75.1	85	34	29	7	13	62
Shaw	5	2	3.88	46	0	1	67.1	67	32	29	8	15	47
Rueter	7	3	5.17	20	20	0	92.1	106	60	53	11	23	50
G. White	1	1	6.08	7	5	1	23.2	24	16	16	24	11	17
Boucher	0	1	6.75	10	2	0	18.2	24	16	14	6	7	17
Henderson	0	1	9.45	3	2	0	6.2	9	9	7	1	7	3
Looney	0	0	22.50	1	0	0	2.0	4	5	5	1	0	2
Eischen	0	0	54.00	1	0	0	0.2	4	4	4	0	0	1
Team Totals	**74**	**40**	**3.56**	**114**	**114**	**46**	**1036.2**	**970**	**454**	**410**	**120**	**288**	**805**

W = games won; L = games lost; ERA = earned run average; G = games played in; GS = games started; SV = saves; IP = innings pitched; H = hits allowed; R = runs allowed; ER = earned runs; HR = home runs allowed; BB = walks allowed; SO = strikeouts.

Montreal Expos Team Records

Batting

Single Season

Batting Average: Tim Raines, 1986, .334; Moises Alou, 1994, .339 (106g)
At Bats: Warren Cromartie, 1979, 659
Games: Rusty Staub, 1971, 162; Ken Singleton, 1973, 162; Warren Cromartie, 1980, 162
Hits: Al Oliver, 1982, 204
Runs: Tim Raines, 1983, 133
Singles: Tim Raines, 1986, 140
Doubles: Warren Cromartie, 1979, 46
Triples: Rodney Scott, 1980, 13; Tim Raines, 1985, 13; Mitch Webster, 1986, 13
Home Runs: Andre Dawson, 1983, 32
Runs Batted In: Tim Wallach, 1987, 123
Total Bases: Andre Dawson, 1983, 340
Slugging Average: Moises Alou, 1994, .592 (106g); Andre Dawson, 1981, .553
On-Base Average: Tim Raines, 1987, .431
Stolen Bases: Ron LeFlore, 1980, 97
Strikeouts: Andres Galarraga, 1990, 169
Walks: Ken Singleton, 1973, 123
Hit By Pitch: Ron Hunt, 1971, 50
Hitting Streak: Delino Deshields, 1993, 21
Pinch Hits: Jose Morales, 1976, 25

Career Leaders

Batting Average: Al Oliver, .315
At Bats: Tim Wallach, 6 529
Games: Tim Wallach, 1 767
Hits: Tim Wallach, 1 694
Runs: Tim Raines, 934
Singles: Tim Raines, 1,148
Doubles: Tim Wallach, 360
Triples: Tim Raines, 81
Home Runs: Andre Dawson, 225
Runs Batted In: Tim Wallach, 905
Total Bases: Tim Wallach, 2 728

Stolen Bases: Tim Raines, 634

Walks: Tim Raines, 775

Pitching

Single Season

Games: Mike Marshall, 1973, 92
Games Started: Steve Rogers, 1977, 40
Complete Games: Bill Stoneman, 1971, 20
Innings Pitched: Steve Rogers, 1977, 302
Wins: Ross Grimsley, 1978, 20
Losses: Steve Rogers, 1974, 22
Saves: John Wetteland, 1993, 43
Earned Run Average: Mark Langston, 1989, 2.39; Dennis Martinez, 1991, 2.39

Career Leaders

Games: Tim Burke, 425
Games Started: Steve Rogers, 393
Complete Games: Steve Rogers, 129
Innings Pitched: Steve Rogers, 2 839
Wins: Steve Rogers, 158
Losses: Steve Rogers, 152
Saves: Jeff Reardon, 152
Earned Run Average: Dennis Martinez, 2.93

▶

▶ **Earned Run Average (Relief Pitcher):** Dale Murray, 1974, 1.03
Shutouts: Bill Stoneman, 1969, 5; Steve Rogers, 1979, 5;
   Steve Rogers, 1983, 5; Dennis Martinez, 1991, 5
Strikeouts: Bill Stoneman, 1971, 251
Walks: Bill Stoneman, 1971, 146
Home Runs Allowed: Carl Morton, 1970, 27; Steve Renko, 1970, 27;
   Bill Gullickson, 1984, 27
Hit Batsmen: Bill Stoneman, 1970, 14

Shutouts: Steve Rogers, 37

Strikeouts: Steve Rogers, 1 621
Walks: Steve Rogers, 876

Source: *Montreal Expos*

Montreal Expos Player of the Year

1969 Rusty Staub	**1976** Woodie Fryman	**1983** Andre Dawson;	**1989** Tim Wallach
1970 Carl Morton	**1977** Gary Carter	Tim Raines (tie)	**1990** Tim Wallach
1971 Ron Hunt	**1978** Ross Grimsley	**1984** Gary Carter	**1991** Dennis Martinez
1972 Mike Marshall	**1979** Larry Parrish	**1985** Tim Raines	**1992** Larry Walker
1973 Mike Marshall	**1980** Gary Carter	**1986** Tim Raines	**1993** Marquis Grissom
1974 Willie Davis	**1981** Andre Dawson	**1987** Tim Wallach	
1975 Gary Carter	**1982** Al Oliver	**1988** Andres Galarraga	

Directory of Sports Organizations

A number of Canadian amateur sports organizations can be reached at 1600 James Naismith Drive, Gloucester, Ontario K1B 5N4. These include:

Other sports organizations include:

Basketball Canada
(613)748-5607

Canadian Amateur Boxing Assn
Tel: (613)748-5611
Fax: (613)748-5740

Canadian Amateur Diving Assn
Tel: (613)748-5631

Canadian Amateur Hockey Association
Tel: (613)748-5613
Fax: (613)748-5709

Canadian Curling Association
Tel: (613)748-5628
Fax: (613)748-5713

Canadian Cycling Assn
Tel: (613)748-5629
Fax: (613)748-5692

Canadian Federation of Amateur Baseball
Tel: (613)748-5606
Fax: (613)748-5706

Canadian Figure Skating Association
Tel: (613)748-5635
Fax: (613)748-5718

Canadian Interuniversity Athletic Union
Tel: (613)748-5619
Fax: (613)748-5764

Canadian Soccer Association
Tel: (613)748-5667
Fax: (613)745-1938

Canadian Track and Field Assn
Tel: (613)748-5678
Fax: (613)748-5645

Canadian Volleyball Assn
Tel: (613)748-5681

Football Canada
Tel: (613)748-5636
Fax: (613)748-5702

National Alpine Ski Team
Tel: (613)748-5661
Fax: (613)748-5704

Rowing Canada
Tel: (613)748-5656
Fax: (613)748-5712

Softball Canada
Tel: (613)748-5668

Swimming Canada
Tel: (613)748-5715
Fax: (613)748-5673

Canadian Automobile Sports Clubs
693 Petrolia Rd
Downsview, Ont.
M3J 2N6
Tel: (905)667-9500
Fax: (905)667-9555

Canadian Trotting Assn
2150 Meadowvale Blvd
Mississauga, Ont.
L5N 6R6
Tel: (905)858-3060
Fax: (905)858-3111

Royal Canadian Golf Association
1333 Dorval Dr.
Oakville, Ont.
L6J 4Z3
Tel: (416)849-9700
Fax: (416)845-7040

Toronto Blue Jays Year-By-Year Record

Year	Won	Lost	Pct.	Pos.	GB	Home Attendance	Manager
1977 54	107	.335	7th	45½	1 701 052	Roy Hartsfield
1978 59	102	.366	7th	50	1 562 585	Roy Hartsfield
1979 53	109	.327	7th	50½	1 431 651	Roy Hartsfield
1980 67	95	.414	7th	36	1 400 327	Bob Mattick
1981 37	69	.349	—	—	755 083	Bob Mattick
1st half 16	42	.276	7th	19	—	
2nd half ... 21	27	.438	7th	7½	—	
1982 78	84	.481	6th[1]	17	1 275 978	Bobby Cox
1983 89	73	.549	4th	9	1 930 415	Bobby Cox
1984 89	73	.549	2nd	15	2 110 009	Bobby Cox
1985 99	62	.615	1st	+2	2 468 925	Bobby Cox
1986 86	76	.531	4th	9½	2 455 477	Jimy Williams
1987 96	66	.593	2nd	2	2 778 459	Jimy Williams
1988 87	75	.537	3rd	2	2 595 175	Jimy Williams
1989 89	73	.549	1st	+2	3 375 573	Williams/Cito Gaston
1990 86	76	.531	2nd	2	3 885 284	Cito Gaston
1991 91	71	.562	1st	+7	4 001 526	Cito Gaston
1992 96	66	.593	1st	+4	4 028 318	Cito Gaston
1993 95	67	.586	1st	+7	4 057 947	Cito Gaston
1994 55	60	.476	3rd[2]	16	2 907 933	Cito Gaston

(1) Tied. (2) Eastern Division: first year with three divisions

Toronto Blue Jays Individual Statistics, 1994

Batters

	AVG	OBA	AB	R	H	2B	3B	HR	RBI	BB	SO	SB	CS	E
Molitor	341	.410	454	86	155	30	4	14	75	55	48	20	0	0
Alomar	306	.386	392	78	120	25	4	8	38	51	41	19	8	4
Huff	304	.392	207	31	63	15	3	3	25	27	27	2	1	1
Olerud	297	.393	384	47	114	29	2	12	67	61	53	1	2	6
Carter	271	.317	435	70	118	25	2	27	103	33	64	11	0	2
White	270	.313	403	67	109	24	6	13	49	21	80	11	3	6
Schofield	255	.332	325	38	83	14	1	4	32	34	62	7	7	11
Borders	247	.284	295	24	73	13	1	3	26	15	50	1	1	8
Knorr	242	.301	124	20	30	2	0	7	19	10	35	0	0	2
Sprague	240	.296	405	38	97	18	1	11	44	23	95	1	0	14
Delgado	215	.325	130	17	28	2	0	9	24	25	46	1	1	2
Coles	210	.263	143	15	30	6	1	4	15	10	25	0	0	4
Cedeno	196	.261	97	14	19	2	3	0	10	10	31	1	2	8
Butler	176	.250	74	13	13	0	1	0	5	7	8	0	1	1
Gonzalez	151	.224	53	7	8	3	1	0	1	4	17	3	0	6
Perez	125	.125	8	0	1	0	0	0	0	0	1	0	0	0
Green	091	.118	33	1	3	1	0	0	1	1	8	1	0	0
Team Totals	**269**	**.336**	**3 962**	**566**	**1 064**	**210**	**30**	**115**	**534**	**387**	**691**	**79**	**26**	**81**

AVG = batting average; OBA = on base average; AB = times at bat; R = runs; H = hits; 2B = doubles; 3B = triples; HR = home runs; RBI = runs batted in; BB = walks; SO = strikeouts; SB = stolen bases; CS = caught stealing; E = errors.

Pitchers

	W	L	ERA	G	GS	SV	IP	H	R	ER	HR	BB	SO
Cox.	1	1	1.45	10	0	3	18.2	7	3	3	0	7	14
Castillo	5	2	2.51	41	0	1	63.0	66	22	19	7	28	43
Hentgen	13	8	3.40	24	24	0	174.2	158	74	66	21	59	147
Hall.	2	3	3.41	30	0	17	31.2	26	12	12	3	14	28
Williams.	1	3	3.64	38	0	0	59.1	44	24	24	5	33	56
Stottlemyre	7	7	4.22	26	19	1	140.2	149	67	66	19	48	105
Leiter.	6	7	5.08	20	20	0	11.2	125	68	63	6	65	100
Timlin	0	1	5.18	34	0	2	40.0	41	25	23	5	20	38
Guzman	12	11	5.68	25	25	0	147.1	165	102	93	20	76	124
Stewart	7	8	5.87	22	22	0	133.1	151	89	87	26	62	111
Brow.	0	3	5.90	18	0	2	29.0	34	27	19	4	19	15
Cornett	1	3	6.68	9	4	0	31.0	40	25	23	1	11	22
Small	0	0	9.00	1	0	0	2.0	5	2	2	1	2	0
St. Claire	0	0	9.00	2	0	0	2.0	4	4	2	0	2	2
Flighetti	0	1	10.18	20	0	0	20.1	22	23	23	5	19	14
Spoljaric	0	1	38.57	2	1	0	2.1	5	10	10	3	9	2
Team Totals	**55**	**60**	**4.70**	**115**	**115**	**28**	**1 025.0**	**1 053**	**579**	**535**	**126**	**482**	**832**

W = games won; L = games lost; ERA = earned run average; G = games played in; GS = games started; SV = saves; IP = innings pitched; H = hits allowed; R = runs allowed; ER = earned runs; HR = home runs allowed; BB = walks allowed; SO = strikeouts.

Toronto Blue Jays Team Records

Batting

Single Season

Batting Average: John Olerud, 1993, .363

At Bats: Tony Fernandez, 1986, 687

Games: Tony Fernandez, 1986, 163

Hits: Tony Fernandez, 1986, 213

Runs: Paul Molitor, 1993, 121

Singles: Tony Fernandez, 1986, 161

Doubles: John Olerud, 1993, 54

Triples: Tony Fernandez, 1990, 17

Home Runs: George Bell, 1987, 47

Runs Batted In: George Bell, 1987, 134

Total Bases: George Bell, 1987, 369

Slugging Average: George Bell, 1987, .605

On-Base Average: John Olerud, 1993, .473

Stolen Bases: Dave Collins, 1984, 60

Strikeouts: Fred McGriff, 1988, 149

Walks: Fred McGriff, 1989, 119

Hit By Pitch: Joe Carter, 1992, 11

Hitting Streak: John Olerud, 1993, 26

Career Leaders

Batting Average: Roberto Alomar, .310

At Bats: Lloyd Moseby, 5,124

Games: Lloyd Moseby, 1,392

Hits: Lloyd Moseby, 1,319

Runs: Lloyd Moseby, 768

Singles: Lloyd Moseby, 868

Doubles: Lloyd Moseby, 242

Triples: Tony Fernandez, 70

Home Runs: George Bell, 202

Runs Batted In: George Bell, 740

Total Bases: George Bell, 2,201

Slugging Average: Fred McGriff, .530

On-Base Average: Fred McGriff, .391

Stolen Bases: Lloyd Moseby, 255

Strikeouts: Lloyd Moseby, 1,015

Walks: Lloyd Moseby, 547

Hit By Pitch: Lloyd Moseby, 50

Pitching

Single Season	Career Leaders
Games: Mark Eichhorn, 1987, 89	**Games:** Tom Henke, 446
Games Started: Jim Clancy, 1982, 40	**Games Started:** Dave Stieb, 405
Complete Games: Dave Stieb, 1982, 19	**Complete Games:** Dave Stieb, 103
Innings Pitched: Dave Stieb, 1982, 288.1	**Innings Pitched:** Dave Stieb, 2 822.2
Wins: Jack Morris, 1992, 21	**Wins:** Dave Stieb, 174
Losses: Jerry Garvin, 1977, 18; Phil Huffman, 1979, 18	**Losses:** Jim Clancy, 140
Saves: Duane Ward, 1993, 45	**Saves:** Tom Henke, 217
Earned Run Average: Dave Stieb, 1985, 2.48	**Earned Run Average:** Tom Henke, 2.48
Shutouts: Dave Stieb, 1982, 5	**Shutouts:** Dave Stieb, 30
Strikeouts: Dave Stieb, 1984, 198	**Strikeouts:** Dave Stieb, 1 631
Walks: Jim Clancy, 1980, 128	**Walks:** Dave Stieb, 1 003
Home Runs Allowed: Jerry Garvin, 1977, 33	**Home Runs Allowed:** Jim Clancy, 219
Hit Batsmen: Dave Stieb, 1986, 15	**Hit Batsmen:** Dave Stieb, 124

Source: *Toronto Blue Jays*

Toronto Blue Jays Player of the Year

1977	Bob Bailor	1983	Lloyd Moseby	1989	George Bell
1978	Bob Bailor	1984	Dave Collins	1990	Kelly Gruber
1979	Alfredo Griffin	1985	Jesse Barfield	1991	Roberto Alomar
1980	John Mayberry	1986	Jesse Barfield	1992	Roberto Alomar
1981	Dave Stieb	1987	George Bell	1993	Paul Molitor
1982	Damaso Garcia	1988	Fred McGriff		

Canadian Players in Major League Baseball, 1994

Player	G	AB	R	H	2B	3B	HR	RBI	BA	OBA	SA
Larry Walker											
1994 Montreal	103	395	76	127	44	2	19	86	.322	.394	.587
Career	674	2366	368	666	147	16	99	384	.281	.359	.483
Rob Ducey											
1994 Texas	10	29	1	5	1	0	0	1	.172	.226	.207
Career	251	493	70	118	27	6	4	42	.239	.312	.343
Rob Butler											
1994 Toronto	32	74	13	13	0	1	0	5	.176	.280	.203
Career	49	122	21	26	4	1	0	7	.213	.333	.262

Pitcher	W	L	Pct.	G	ShO	Sv	IP	H	BB	SO	ERA
Real Cormier											
1994 St. Louis	3	2	.600	77	0	0	39.2	40	7	26	5.45
Career	24	23	.511	67	0	0	438.2	471	74	256	4.12
Kirk McCaskill											
1994 Chicago (AL)......	1	4	.200	40	0	3	52.2	21	22	37	3.42
Career	95	99	.489	296	11	5	1596.1	1579	601	925	4.08
Mike Gardiner											
1994 Detroit..........	2	2	.500	38	0	5	58.2	53	23	31	4.14
Career	17	27	.386	127	0	5	381.1	393	159	232	4.91 ▶

► Paul Spoljaric

1994 Toronto	0	1	.000	2	0	0	2.1	5	9	2	38.57

Paul Quantrill

1994 Philadelphia	2	2	.500	18	0	1	30.0	39	10	13	6.00
Career	10	17	.370	94	0	3	217.1	245	69	103	3.81

Denis Boucher

1994 Montreal	0	1	.000	10	0	0	18.2	24	7	17	6.75
Career	5	11	.313	35	0	0	146.0	170	54	77	5.42
Vince Horsman...1994 Oakland	0	1	.000	33	0	0	29.1	29	11	20	4.91
Career	4	2	.667	135	0	1	101.2	95	50	57	3.81

(1) First year in 1993.

Career Records of Some Canadian Major League Players of the Past

Player	G	AB	R	H	2B	3B	HR	RBI	BA	OBA	SA
Jeff Heath, 1936–49	1 383	4 937	777	1 447	279	102	194	887	.293	.370	.509
Terry Puhl, 1977–90	1 531	4 855	676	1 361	226	56	62	435	.280	.350	.388
George Gibson, 1905–18 . .	1 213	3 776	295	893	142	49	15	335	.236	.294	.312
Tip O'Neill, 1883–92 . .	1 054	4 255	880	1 386	222	92	52	435	.326	.392	.458
Pete Ward, 1962–70	973	3 060	345	776	136	17	98	427	.254	.342	.405
George Selkirk 1934–42	846	2 790	503	810	131	41	108	576	.290	.400	.483
Jack Graney 1908–22	1 402	4 705	706	1 178	219	79	18	420	.250	.354	.342
Frank O'Rourke 1917–31 . . .	1 131	4 069	547	1 032	196	42	15	430	.254	.315	.333

Pitcher	W	L	Pct.	G	ShO	Sv	IP	H	BB	SO	ERA
Ferguson Jenkins, 1965–83 . .	284	226	.557	664	49	7	4 498	4 142	997	3 192	3.34
Reggie Cleveland, 1969–81 . .	105	106	.498	203	12	25	1 809	1813	543	930	4.01
Russ Ford, 1909–15	99	71	.582	199	15	9	1 487	1 318	376	710	2.59
Phil Marchildon, 1942–50[1] .	68	75	.476	185	6	2	1 214	1084	684	4 81	3.93
Oscar Judd, 1941–48	40	51	.440	161	4	7	770	744	397	304	3.90
John Hiller 1965–80	87	76	.534	545	6	125	1 242	1040	535	1 036	2.83
Dick Fowler 1941–52.	66	79	.455	221	11	4	1 303	1367	578	382	4.11
Ron Taylor 1962–72	45	43	.511	491	0	72	800	794	209	464	3.93

G: Games played. **AB:** At bats. **R:** Runs. **H:** Hits. **2B:** Doubles. **3B:** Triples. **HR:** Home runs. **RBI:** Runs batted in. **BA:** Batting average. **OBA:** On-base percentage. **SA:** Slugging average.

W: Wins. **L:** Losses. **Pct.:** Percentage. **G:** Games pitched. **ShO:** Shutouts. **Sv:** Saves. **IP:** Innings pitched. **H:** Hits allowed. **BB:** Walks. **K:** Strikeouts. **ERA:** Earned run average.

(1) Marchildon was in Canadian Armed Forces in 1943–44

FOOTBALL

Canadian Football League

(1993 Standings)

	W	L	T	F	A	Pts		W	L	T	F	A	Pts
Calgary	15	3	0	646	418	30	Winnipeg	14	4	0	146	421	28
Edmonton	12	6	0	507	372	24	Hamilton	6	12	0	316	567	12
Saskatchewan. . . .	11	7	0	511	495	22	Ottawa	4	14	0	387	517	8
BC	10	8	0	574	583	20	Toronto	3	15	0	390	593	6
Sacramento	6	12	0	498	509	12							

Semi-final: Edmonton 51, Saskatchewan 13, Calgary 17, BC 9
Final: Edmonton 29, Calgary 15

Semi-final: Hamilton 21, Ottawa 10
Final: Winnipeg 20, Hamilton 19

Grey Cup: Edmonton 33, Winnipeg 23

The Grey Cup

The Grey Cup was donated in 1909 by Governor General Earl Grey for the "Rugby Football Championship of Canada." Since 1954, only teams in the Canadian Foot-ball League have challenged for the trophy, with the winners of the East and West divisions meeting in the championship game.

1909 . . . . . U. of Toronto 26, Parkdale 6
1910 . . . . . U. of Toronto 16, Ham. Tigers 7
1911 . . . . . U. of Toronto 14, Toronto 7
1912 . . . . . Ham. Alerts 11, Toronto 4
1913 . . . . . Ham. Tigers 44, Parkdale 2
1914 . . . . . Toronto 14, U. of Toronto 2
1915 . . . . . Ham. Tigers 13, Tor. R.A.A. 7
1916–19 . . No games held.
1920 . . . . . U. of Toronto 16, Toronto 3
1921 . . . . . Toronto 23, Edmonton 0
1922 . . . . . Queen's U. 13, Edmonton 1
1923 . . . . . Queen's U. 54, Regina 0
1924 . . . . . Queen's U. 11, Balmy Beach 3
1925 . . . . . Ott. Senators 24, Winnipeg 1
1926 . . . . . Ott. Senators 10, U. of Toronto 7
1927 . . . . . Balmy Beach 9, Ham. Tigers 6
1928 . . . . . Ham. Tigers 30, Regina 0
1929 . . . . . Ham. Tigers 14, Regina 3
1930 . . . . . Balmy Beach 11, Regina 6
1931 . . . . . Mtl. A.A.A. 22, Regina 0
1932 . . . . . Ham. Tigers 25, Regina 6
1933 . . . . . Toronto 4, Sarnia 3
1934 . . . . . Sarnia 20, Regina 12
1935 . . . . . Winnipeg 18, Ham. Tigers 12
1936 . . . . . Sarnia 26, Ott. R.R. 20
1937 . . . . . Toronto 4, Winnipeg 3
1938 . . . . . Toronto 30, Winnipeg 7
1939 . . . . . Winnipeg 8, Ottawa 7
1940[1] . . . . Ottawa 12, Balmy Beach 5
Ottawa 8, Balmy Beach 2
1941 . . . . . Winnipeg 18, Ottawa 16
1942 . . . . . Tor. R.C.A.F. 8, Win. R.C.A.F. 5
1943 . . . . . Ham. F. Wild 23, Win. R.C.A.F. 14
1944 . . . . . Mtl. St. H.D. Navy 7, Ham. F. Wild 6
1945 . . . . . Toronto 35, Winnipeg 0
1946 . . . . . Toronto 28, Winnipeg 6
1947 . . . . . Toronto 10, Winnipeg 9
1948 . . . . . Calgary 12, Ottawa 7
1949 . . . . . Mtl. Als. 28, Calgary 15
1950 . . . . . Toronto 13, Winnipeg 0
1951 . . . . . Ottawa 21, Saskatchewan 14

1952 . . . . . Toronto 21, Edmonton 11
1953 . . . . . Hamilton 12, Winnipeg 6
1954 . . . . . Edmonton 26, Montreal 25
1955 . . . . . Edmonton 34, Montreal 19
1956 . . . . . Edmonton 50, Montreal 27
1957 . . . . . Hamilton 32, Winnipeg 7
1958 . . . . . Winnipeg 35, Hamilton 28
1959 . . . . . Winnipeg 21, Hamilton 7
1960 . . . . . Ottawa 16, Edmonton 6
1961 . . . . . Winnipeg 21, Hamilton 14
1962 . . . . . Winnipeg 28, Hamilton 27
1963 . . . . . Hamilton 21, British Columbia 10
1964 . . . . . British Columbia 34, Hamilton 24
1965 . . . . . Hamilton 22, Winnipeg 16
1966 . . . . . Saskatchewan 29, Ottawa 14
1967 . . . . . Hamilton 24, Saskatchewan 1
1968 . . . . . Ottawa 24, Calgary 21
1969 . . . . . Ottawa 29, Saskatchewan 11
1970 . . . . . Montreal 23, Calgary 10
1971 . . . . . Calgary 14, Toronto 11
1972 . . . . . Hamilton 13, Saskatchewan 10
1973 . . . . . Ottawa 22, Edmonton 18
1974 . . . . . Montreal 20, Edmonton 7
1975 . . . . . Edmonton 9, Montreal 8
1976 . . . . . Ottawa 23, Saskatchewan 20
1977 . . . . . Montreal 41, Edmonton 6
1978 . . . . . Edmonton 20, Montreal 13
1979 . . . . . Edmonton 17, Montreal 9
1980 . . . . . Edmonton 48, Hamilton 10
1981 . . . . . Edmonton 26, Ottawa 23
1982 . . . . . Edmonton 32, Toronto 16
1983 . . . . . Toronto 18, B.C. 17
1984 . . . . . Winnipeg 47, Hamilton 17
1985 . . . . . B.C. 37, Hamilton 24
1986 . . . . . Hamilton 39, Edmonton 15
1987 . . . . . Edmonton 38, Toronto 36
1988 . . . . . Winnipeg 22, B.C. 21
1989 . . . . . Saskatchewan 43, Hamilton 40
1990 . . . . . Winnipeg 50, Edmonton 11
1991 . . . . . Toronto 36, Calgary 21
1992 . . . . . Calgary 24, Winnipeg 10
1993 . . . . . Edmonton 33, Winnipeg 23

(1) A 2-game total point series.

CFL Individual Player Records

(up to the end of the 1993 season)

Most games played:	**288, Ron Lancaster,** Ott/Sask (1960–78)
Most career points:	**2 829, Lui Passaglia,** BC (1976–93)
Most points one season:	**236, Lance Chomyc,** Tor, 1991
Most points one game:	**36, Bob McNamara,** Wpg, Wpg at BC, Oct. 13, 1956
Most touchdowns one season:	**20, Pat Abbruzzi,** Mtl, 1956; **Darrell K. Smith,** Tor, 1990; **Blake Marshall,** Edm, 1991; **Jon Volpe,** BC, 1991
Most touchdowns one game:	**6, Bob McNamara,** Wpg, Wpg at BC, Oct. 13, 1956
Most touchdown passes one season:	**44, Doug Flutie,** Cal, 1993
Most touchdown passes one game:	**8, Joe Zuger,** Ham, Sask at Ham, Oct. 15, 1962
Most touchdowns scored rushing one season:	**18, Gerry James,** Wpg, 1957; **Jim Germany,** Edm, 1981
Most touchdowns scored rushing one game:	**5, Earl Lunsford,** Cal, Edm at Cal, Sept. 3, 1962
Most touchdowns on pass receptions one season:	**20 , Darrell K. Smith,** Tor, 1990
Most touchdowns on pass receptions one game:	**5, Ernie Pitts,** Wpg, Wpg at Sask, Aug. 29, 1959
Most passes thrown one season:	**770, Kent Austin,** Sask, 1992
Most passes thrown one game:	**65, Kent Austin,** Sask, Edm at Sask, Sept. 15, 1991
Most passes completed one season:	**466, Doug Flutie,** BC, 1991
Most passes completed one game:	**41, Dieter Brock,** Wpg, Wpg at Ott, Oct. 3, 1981
Most yards passed one season:	**6 619, Doug Flutie,** BC, 1991
*Most yards passed one game:	**601, Davey Barrett,** BC, Tor at BC, Aug. 12, 1993
Most consecutive pass completions:	**18, Joe Paopao,** BC, Tor at BC, Sept. 22, 1979
Longest pass:	**109 yds, Sam Etcheverry to Hal Patterson,** Mtl, Ham at Mtl, Sept. 22, 1956; **Jerry Keeling to Terry Evanshen,** Cal, Cal at Wpg, Sept. 27, 1966
Most yards rushing one season:	**1 896, Willie Burden,** Cal, 1975
Most yards rushing one game:	**287, Ron Stewart,** Ott, Ott at Mtl, Oct. 10, 1960
Longest rushing plays:	**109 yds, George Dixon,** Mtl, Ott at Mtl, Sept. 2, 1963; **Willie Fleming,** BC, BC at Edm, Oct. 17, 1964
Most carries one season:	**332, Willie Burden,** Cal, 1975
Most carries one game:	**37, Doyle Orange,** Tor, Ham at Tor, Aug. 13, 1975
Most pass reception yardage one season:	**2 003, Terry Greer,** Tor, 1983
Most pass reception yardage one game:	**338, Hal Patterson,** Mtl, Mtl at Ham, Sept. 29, 1956
Most pass receptions one season:	**118, Allen Pitts,** Cal, 1991
Most pass receptions one game:	**16, Terry Greer,** Tor, Tor at Ott, Aug. 19, 1983
Most combined yards one game:	**401, Raghib Ismail,** Tor, Tor at Ott, July 9, 1992
Most field goals one season:	**59, Dave Ridgway,** Sask, 1990
Most field goals one game:	**8, Dave Ridgway,** Sask, 1984 and 1988
Longest field goal:	**60 yds, Dave Ridgway,** Sask, Wpg at Sask, Sept. 6, 1987
Longest punt:	**108 yds, Zenon Andrusyshyn,** Tor, Tor at Edm, Oct. 23, 1977
Best punting average one season:	**50.2, Lui Passaglia,** BC, 1983
Most interceptions one game:	**5, Rod Hill,** Wpg, Ham at Wpg, Sept 9, 1990
Most interceptions one season:	**15, Al Brenner,** Ham, 1972
Most quarterback sacks one season:	**26.5, James Parker,** BC, 1984

Source: *Canadian Football League*

* 1994, Winnipeg's Matt Dunigan threw for 713 yards, Edmonton at Winnipeg, July 14, 1994

Leading CFL Quarterbacks, by Year

(by number of yards)

Year	Eastern Division	Yards	Western Division	Yards
1954	Sam Etcheverry, Mtl	3 610	Frank Tripucka, Sask	2 003
1955	Sam Etcheverry, Mtl	3 657	Don Klosterman, Cal	2 405
1956	Sam Etcheverry, Mtl	4 723	Frank Tripucka, Sask	3 274
1957	Sam Etcheverry, Mtl	3 341	Frank Tripucka, Sask	2 589
1958	Sam Etcheverry, Mtl	3 548	Frank Tripucka, Sask	2 766
1959	Sam Etcheverry, Mtl	3 133	Joe Kapp, Cal	2 990
1960	Tobin Rote, Tor	4 247	Joe Kapp, Cal	3 060
1961	Tobin Rote, Tor	3 093	Eagle Day, Cal	1 800
1962	Tobin Rote, Tor	2 532	Joe Kapp, BC	3 279
1963	Russ Jackson, Ott.	2 910	Joe Kapp, BC	3 126
1964	Russ Jackson, Ott	2 156	Joe Kapp, BC	2 816
1965	Russ Jackson, Ott	2 303	Joe Kapp, BC	2 961
1966	Russ Jackson, Ott	2 400	Ron Lancaster, Sask	2 976
1967	Russ Jackson, Ott	3 332	Peter Liske, Cal	4 479
1968	Wally Gabler, Tor	3 242	Peter Liske, Cal	4 333
1969	Russ Jackson, Ott	3 641	Jerry Keeling, Cal	3 179
1970	Gary Wood, Ott	2 759	Ron Lancaster, Sask	2 779
1971	Joe Theismann, Tor	2 440	Don Jonas, Wpg	4 036
1972	Chuck Ealey, Ham	2 573	Don Jonas, Wpg	3 583
1973	Joe Theismann, Tor	2 496	Ron Lancaster, Sask	3 767
1974	Mike Rae, Tor	2 501	Peter Liske, Cal/BC	3 259
1975	Tom Clements, Ott	2 013	Ron Lancaster, Sask	3 545
1976	Tom Clements, Ott	2 856	Ron Lancaster, Sask	3 869
1977	Tom Clements, Ott	2 804	Ron Lancaster, Sask	3 072
1978	Jimmy Jones, Ham	2 060	Dieter Brock, Wpg	3 755
1979	Tony Adams, Tor	2 692	Dieter Brock, Wpg	2 383
1980	Mark Jackson, Tor	3 041	Dieter Brock, Wpg	4 252
1981	Tom Clements, Ham	4 536	Dieter Brock, Wpg	4 796
1982	Tom Clements, Ham	4 706	Warren Moon, Edm	5 000
1983	Conredge Holloway, Tor	3 184	Warren Moon, Edm	5 648
1984	Dieter Brock, Ham	3 966	Tom Clements, Wpg	3 845
1984	Joe Barnes, Mtl	3 432	Roy Dewalt, BC	4 237
1986	Brian Ransom, Mtl	3 204	Rick Johnson, Cal	4 379
1987	Tom Clements, Wpg	4 686	Roy Dewalt, BC	3 855
1988	Gilbert Renfroe, Tor	4 113	Matt Dunigan, BC	3 776
1989	Sean Salisbury, Wpg	4 049	Matt Dunigan, BC	4 509
1990	Tom Burgess, Wpg	3 958	Kent Austin, Sask	4 604
1991	Damon Allen, Ott	4 275	Doug Flutie, BC	6 619
1992	Tom Burgess, Ott.	4 026	Kent Austin, Sask.	6 225
1993	Tom Burgess, Ott.	5 063	Doug Flutie, Cal	6 092

Source: *Canadian Football League*

Leading CFL Pass Receivers, by Year

	Eastern Division	Receptions	Western Division	Receptions
1954	Al Pfeifer, Tor	68	Bud Grant, Wpg	49
1955	Red O'Quinn, Mtl	78	Willie Roberts, Cal	59
1956	Hal Patterson, Mtl	88	Bud Grant, Wpg	63
1957	Red O'Quinn, Mtl	61	Jack Gotta, Cal	39
1958	Red O'Quinn, Mtl	65	Jack Hill, Sask	60
1959	Red O'Quinn, Mtl	53	Ernie Pitts, Wpg	68
1960	Dave Mann, Tor	61	Gene Filipski, Cal	47
	Hal Patterson, Mtl	61		
1961	Dave Mann, Tor	53	Farrell Funston, Wpg	47
1962	Dick Shatto, Tor	47	Tommy Joe Coffey, Edm	65
1963	Dick Shatto, Tor	67	Bobby Taylor, Cal	74
1964	Dick Shatto, Tor	53	Tommy Joe Coffey, Edm	81
1965	Terry Evanshen, Mtl	37	Tommy Joe Coffey, Edm	81
1966	Bobby Taylor, Tor	56	Terry Evanshen, Cal	67
1967	Bobby Taylor, Tor	53	Terry Evanshen, Cal	96
1968	Bobby Taylor, Tor	56	Ken Nielsen, Wpg	68
1969	Tommy Joe Coffey, Ham	71	Herman Harrison, Cal	68
1970	Dave Fleming, Ham	56	Herman Harrison, Cal	70
1971	Terry Evanshen, Mtl	50	Herman Harrison, Cal	70
			Jim Thorpe, Wpg	70
1972	Eric Allen, Tor	53	Jim Thorpe, Wpg	70
1973	Johnny Rodgers, Mtl	41	George McGowan, Edm	81
1974	Tony Gabriel, Ham	61	Rudy Linterman, Cal	64
1975	Tony Gabriel, Ott	65	George McGowan, Edm	98
1976	Tony Gabriel, Ott	72	Rhett Dawson, Sask	65
1977	Tony Gabriel, Ott	65	Molly McGee, Sask	68
1978	Tony Gabriel, Ott	67	Joe Poplawski, Wpg	75
1979	Leif Pettersen, Ham	56	Waddell Smith, Edm	74
1980	Bob Gaddis, Tor	68	Mike Holmes, Wpg	79
1981	James Scott, Mtl	81	Eugene Goodlow, Wpg	100
1982	Nick Arakgi, Mtl	89	Joey Walters, Sask	102
1983	Terry Greer, Tor	113	Brian Kelly, Edm	104
1984	Rocky DiPietro, Ham	71	Craig Ellis, Sask	91
	Paul Pearson, Tor	71		
1985	Terry Greer, Tor	78	Craig Ellis, Sask	102
1986	James Hood, Mtl	95	James Murphy, Wpg	116
1987	Marc Lewis, Ott	94	Jim Sandusky, BC	80
1988	James Murphy, Wpg	76	David Williams, BC	83
1989	Tony Champion, Ham	95	Donald Narcisse, Sask	81
1990	Darrell K. Smith, Tor	93	Craig Ellis, Edm	106
1991	Darrell K. Smith, Tor	73	Allen Pitts, Cal	118
1992	Stephen Jones, Ott	75	Allen Pitts, Cal	103
1993	David Williams, Wpg	84	David Sapunjis, Cal	103

Source: *Canadian Football League*

Leading CFL Rushers, by Year

	Eastern Division	Yards	Western Division	Yards
1954	Alex Webster, Mtl.	984	Howard Waugh, Cal	1 043
1955	Pat Abbruzzi, Mtl.	1 248	Normie Kwong, Edm	1 250
1956	Pat Abbruzzi, Mtl.	1 062	Normie Kwong, Edm	1 437
1957	Gerry McDougall, Ham	1 053	Johnny Bright, Edm	1 679
1958	Gerry McDougall, Ham	1 109	Johnny Bright, Edm	1 722
1959	Dave Thelen, Ott	1 339	Johnny Bright, Edm	1 340
1960	Dave Thelen, Ott	1 407	Earl Lunsford, Cal	1 343
1961	Don Clark, Mtl	1 143	Earl Lunsford, Cal	1 794
1962	George Dixon, Mtl	1 520	Nub Beamer, BC	1 161
1963	George Dixon, Mtl	1 270	Lovell Coleman, Cal	1 343
1964	Ron Stewart, Ott	867	Lovell Coleman, Cal	1 629
1965	Dave Thelen, Ott	801	George Reed, Sask	1 768
1966	Don Lisbon, Mtl	1 007	George Reed, Sask	1 409
1967	Bo Scott, Ott	762	George Reed, Sask	1 471
1968	Bill Symons, Tor	1 107	George Reed, Sask	1 222
1969	Dennis Duncan, Mtl	1 037	George Reed, Sask	1 353
1970	Bill Symons, Tor	908	Hugh McKinnis, Cal	1 135
1971	Leon McQuay, Tor	977	Jim Evenson, BC	1 237
1972	Dave Buchanan, Ham	1 163	Mack Herron, Wpg	1 527
1973	Andy Hopkins, Ham	1 223	Roy Bell, Edm	1 455
1974	Steve Ferrughelli, Mtl	1 134	George Reed, Sask	1 447
1975	Art Green, Ott	1 188	Willie Burden, Cal	1 896
1976	Art Green, Ott	1 257	Jim Washington, Wpg	1 277
1977	Jimmy Edwards, Ham	1 581	Jim Washington, Wpg	1 262
1978	Jimmy Edwards, Ham	840	Mike Strickland, Sask	1 306
1979	David Green, Mtl	1 678	Jim Germany, Edm	1 324
1980	Richard Crump, Ott	1 074	Jimmy Sykes, Cal	1 263
1981	David Overstreet, Mtl	952	Jimmy Sykes, Cal	1 107
1982	Alvin (Skip) Walker, Ott	1 141	William Miller, Wpg	1 076
1983	Alvin (Skip) Walker, Ott	1 431	Willard Reaves, Wpg	898
1984	Dwaine Wilson, Mtl	1 083	Willard Reaves, Wpg	1 733
1985	Ken Hobart, Ham	928	Willard Reaves, Wpg	1 323
1986	Walter Bender, Ham	618	Gary Allen, Cal	1 153
1987	Willard Reaves, Wpg	1 471	Gary Allen, Cal	857
1988	Orville Lee, Ott	1 075	Tony Cherry, BC	889
1989	Gill Fenerty, Tor	1 247	Reggie Taylor, Edm	1 503
1990	Robert Mimbs, Wpg	1 341	Tracy Ham, Edm	1 096
1991	Robert Mimbs, Wpg	1 769	Jon Volpe, BC	1 395
1992	Michael Richardson, Wpg	1 153	Jon Volpe, BC	941
1993	Michael Richardson, Wpg	925	Damon Allen, Edm	920

Source: *Canadian Football League*

All-Time Leading CFL Players

(up to the end of the 1993 season)

Touchdowns

	TD	Seasons		TD	Seasons
George Reed, Sask	137	13	(1963–75)		
Brian Kelly, Edm	97	9	(1979–87)		
Dick Shatto, Tor	91	12	(1954–65)		
Tom Scott, Wpg/Edm/Cal	91	11	(1974–84)		
Jackie Parker, Edm/Tor/BC	88	13	(1954–68)		
Craig Ellis, Wpg/Cal/Sask/Tor/Edm	88	9	(1982–92)		
Willie Fleming, BC	86	8	(1959–68)		
Normie Kwong, Cal/Edm	83	13	(1948–60)		
Terry Evanshen, Mtl/Cal/Ham/Tor	80	14	(1965–78)		
Virgil Wagner, Mtl.	79	9	(1946–54)		
Leo Lewis, Wpg	79	12	(1955–66)		
Hal Patterson, Mtl/Ham	79	14	(1954–67)		
Tony Gabriel, Ham/Ott	72	11	(1971–81)		

	TD	Seasons
Johnny Bright, Cal/Edm	71	13	(1952–64)
Jim Germany, Edm	71	7	(1977–83)
Bob Simpson, Ott	70	13	(1950–62)
Jeff Boyd, Wpg/Tor	70	9	(1983–91)
Jim Young, BC	68	13	(1967–79)
Ron Stewart, Ott	67	12	(1959–70)
Tommy Joe Coffey, Edm/Ham/Tor	65	14	(1959–73)
Gerry James, Wpg/Sask	63	11	(1952–64)
Milson Jones, Wpg/Edm/Sask	63	11	(1982–92)
James Murphy, Wpg	62	8	(1983–90)
Lovell Coleman, Cal/Ott/BC	62	10	(1960–70)
Tom Forzani, Cal	62	11	(1973–83)

Points

	Points	TD	Con	FG	Sing		Seasons
Lui Passaglia, BC	2 824	1	744	609	252	18	(1976–93)
Dave Cutler, Edm	2 237	0	627	464	218	16	(1969–84)
Dave Ridgway, Sask	2 058	0	475	501	100	12	(1982–93)
Trevor Kennerd, Wpg	1 840	0	509	394	149	12	(1980–91)
Bernie Ruoff, Wpg/Ham	1 772	0	401	384	219	14	(1975–88)
Lance Chomyc, Tor	1 498	0	412	337	75	9	(1985–93)
Gerry Organ, Ott	1 462	2	391	318	105	12	(1971–83)
John T. Hay, Ott/Cal	1 411	0	363	308	124	11	(1978–88)
Don Sweet, Mtl/Ham	1 342	0	327	314	73	14	(1972–85)
Paul Osbaldiston, BC/Wpg/Ham	1 310	0	290	295	135	8	(1986–93)
Dean Dorsey, Tor/Ott	951	0	244	219	50	8	(1982–91)
Larry Robinson, Cal	1 030	9	362	171	101	14	(1961–74)
Zenon Andrusyshyn, Tor/Ham/Edm/Mtl	1 010	0	222	21	143	12	(1971–86)
Tommy Joe Coffey, Edm/Ham/Tor	971	65	204	108	53	14	(1959–73)
Mark McLoughlin, Cal	1 139	0	299	254	78	6	(1988–93)
Jack Abendschan, Sask	863	0	312	59	74	11	(1965–75)
George Reed, Sask	823	137	0	0	1	13	(1963–75)
Jackie Parker, Edm/Tor/BC	750	88	103	40	19	13	(1954–68)
Don Sutherin, Ham/Ott/Tor	714	4	270	114	78	12	(1958–70)
Gerry James, Wpg/Sask	645	63	143	40	21	11	(1952–64)
Ian Sunter, Ham/Tor	626	0	155	135	66	6	(1972–79)
Brian Kelly, Edm	586	97	2	0	0	9	(1979–87)
Cyril McFall, Cal	578	0	131	134	45	5	(1974–78)
Jerry Kauric, Edm	577	0	170	122	65	4	(1987–91)
Bob Macoritti, Wpg/Sask	576	0	145	122	65	6	(1975–80)

Rushing

	Yards	Carries	Avg	Long	TD		Seasons
George Reed, Sask	16 116	3 243	5.0	71	134	13	(1963–75)
Johnny Bright, Cal/Edm	10 909	1 969	5.5	90	69	13	(1952–64)
Normie Kwong, Cal/Edm	9 022	1 745	5.2	60	78	13	(1948–60)
Leo Lewis, Wpg	8 861	1 351	6.5	92	48	11	(1955–66)
Dave Thelen, Ott/Tor	8 463	1 530	5.5	77	47	9	(1958–66)
Jim Evenson, BC/Ott	7 060	1 460	4.8	68	37	7	(1968–74)
Earl Lunsford, Cal	6 994	1 199	5.8	85	55	6	(1956–63) ▶

	Yards	Carries	Avg	Long	TD	Seasons
Dick Shatto, Tor	6 958	1 322	5.3	67	39	12 (1954–65)
Lovell Coleman, Cal/Ott/BC	6 566	1 135	5.8	85	42	10 (1960–70)
Willie Burden, Cal	6 234	1 242	5.0	71	32	8 (1974–81)

Passing
(ranked by total yards)

	Attempts	Comp	Yards	Pct	Avg[1]	Int	TD	Seasons
Ron Lancaster, Ott/Sask	6 233	3 384	50 535	54.3	14.9	396	333	19 (1960–78)
Tom Clements, Ott/Sask/Ham/Wpg	4 657	2 807	39 041	60.3	13.9	214	252	12 (1975–87)
Dieter Brock, Wpg/Ham	4 535	2 602	34 830	57.4	13.4	158	210	11 (1974–84)
Matt Dunigan, Edm/BC/Tor/Wpg	4 191	2 329	33 256	55.6	14.3	275	226	11 (1983–93)
Sam Etcheverry, Mtl	2 829	1 630	25 582	57.6	15.7	163	174	7 (1953–60)
Condredge Holloway, Ott/Tor/BC	3 013	1 710	25 193	56.8	14.7	94	155	13 (1975–87)
Russ Jackson, Ott	2 530	1 356	24 592	53.6	18.1	125	185	12 (1958–69)
Bernie Faloney, Edm/Ham/Mtl/BC	2 876	1 493	24 264	51.9	16.3	201	151	12 (1954–66)
Roy Dewalt, BC/Wpg/Ott	3 130	1 803	24 147	57.6	13.4	96	132	9 (1980–88)
Joe Kapp, Cal/BC	2 709	1 476	22 725	54.5	15.4	130	136	8 (1959–67)
Tom Wilkinson, Tor/BC/Edm	2 662	1 613	22 579	60.6	14.0	126	154	15 (1967–81)
Joe Paopao, BC/Sask/Ott[b]	3 008	1 721	22 474	57.2	13.1	157	117	11 (1976–87)
John Hufnagel, Cal/Sask/Wpg	2 665	1 495	21 594	55.5	14.6	131	127	12 (1976–87)
Peter Liske, Tor/Cal/BC	2 571	1 449	21 266	56.4	14.7	133	130	7 (1 965–75)
Warren Moon, Edm	2 382	1 369	21 228	57.5	15.5	77	144	6 (1978–83)

(1) Yards per pass completed. (2) Did not play in 1988 or 1989.

Pass Receiving

	Rec	Yards	Avg	TD	Seasons
*Rocky DiPietro, Ham	706	9 762	13.8	45	14 (1978–91)
Ray Elgaard, Sask	694	11 253	16.2	69	11 (1983–93)
Tommy Joe Coffey, Edm/Ham/Tor	650	10 320	15.9	63	14 (1959–73)
Tom Scott, Wpg/Edm/Cal	649	10 837	16.7	88	11 (1974–84)
Tony Gabriel, Ham/Ott	614	9 832	16.0	69	11 (1971–81)
Terry Evanshen, Mtl/Cal/Ham/Tor	600	9 697	16.2	80	14 (1965–78)
Craig Ellis, Wpg/Cal/Sask/Tor/Edm	578	7 706	13.3	58	9 (1982–92)
Brian Kelly, Edm	575	11 169	19.4	97	9 (1979–87)
James Murphy, Wpg	573	9 036	15.8	61	8 (1983–90)
Tom Forzani, Cal	553	8 285	15.0	62	11 (1973–83)
Joe Poplawski, Wpg	549	8 341	15.2	48	9 (1978–86)
Jim Young, BC	522	9 248	17.7	65	13 (1967–79)
Rick House, Wpg/Edm	522	8 139	15.6	55	13 (1979–91)

Source: *Canadian Football League*

* Elgaard passed DiPietro early in the 1994 season.

CFL Outstanding Player Awards[1]

Outstanding player

1953	Billy Vessels, Edm	1961	Bernie Faloney, Ham	1969	Russ Jackson, Ott
1954	Sam Etcheverry, Mtl	1962	George Dixon, Mtl	1970	Ron Lancaster, Sask
1955	Pat Abbruzzi, Mtl	1963	Russ Jackson, Ott	1971	Don Jonas, Wpg
1956	Hal Patterson, Mtl	1964	Lovell Coleman, Cal	1972	Garney Henley, Ham
1957	Jackie Parker, Edm	1965	George Reed, Sask	1973	George McGowan, Edm
1958	Jackie Parker, Edm	1966	Russ Jackson, Ott	1974	Tom Wilkinson, Edm
1959	Johnny Bright, Edm	1967	Peter Liske, Cal	1975	Willie Burden, Cal
1960	Jackie Parker, Edm	1968	Bill Symons, Tor	1976	Ron Lancaster, Sask

▶ **1977**	Jimmy Edwards, Ham	**1983**	Warren Moon, Edm	**1989**	Tracy Ham, Edm
1978	Tony Gabriel, Ott	**1984**	Willard Reaves, Wpg	**1990**	Mike Clemons, Tor
1979	David Green, Mtl	**1985**	Mervyn Fernandez, BC	**1991**	Doug Flutie, BC
1980	Deiter Brock, Wpg	**1986**	James Murphy, Wpg	**1992**	Doug Flutie, Cal
1981	Deiter Brock, Wpg	**1987**	Tom Clements, Wpg	**1993**	Doug Flutie, Cal
1982	Condredge Holloway, Tor	**1988**	David Williams, BC		

Outstanding Canadian

1954	Gerry James, Wpg	**1968**	Ken Nielson, Wpg	**1982**	Rocky DiPietro, Ham
1955	Normie Kwong, Edm	**1969**	Russ Jackson, Ott	**1983**	Paul Bennett, Wpg
1956	Normie Kwong, Edm	**1970**	Jim Young, BC	**1984**	Nick Arakgi, Mtl
1957	Gerry James, Wpg	**1971**	Terry Evanshen, Mtl	**1985**	Paul Bennett, Ham
1958	Ron Howell, Ham	**1972**	Jim Young, BC	**1986**	Joe Poplawski, Wpg
1959	Russ Jackson, Ott	**1973**	Gerry Organ, Ott	**1987**	Scott Flagel, Wpg
1960	Ron Stewart, Ott	**1974**	Tony Gabriel, Ham	**1988**	Ray Elgaard, Sask
1961	Tony Pajaczkowski, Cal	**1975**	Jim Foley, Ott	**1989**	Rocky DiPietro, Ham
1962	Harvey Wylie, Cal	**1976**	Tony Gabriel, Ott	**1990**	Ray Elgaard, Sask
1963	Russ Jackson, Ott	**1977**	Tony Gabriel, Ott	**1991**	Blake Marshall, Edm
1964	Tommy Grant, Ham	**1978**	Tony Gabriel, Ott	**1992**	Ray Elgaard, Sask
1965	Zeno Karcz, Ham	**1979**	Dave Fennell, Edm	**1993**	Dave Sapunjis, Cal
1966	Russ Jackson, Ott	**1980**	Gerry Dattilio, Mtl		
1967	Terry Evanshen, Cal	**1981**	Joe Poplawski, Wpg		

Outstanding defensive player

1955	Tex Coulter, Mtl	**1968**	Ken Lehmann, Ott	**1981**	Dan Kepley, Edm
1956	Kaye Vaughan, Ott	**1969**	John LaGrone, Edm	**1982**	James Parker, Edm
1957	Kaye Vaughan, Ott	**1970**	Wayne Harris, Cal	**1983**	Greg Marshall, Ott
1958	Don Luzzi, Cal	**1971**	Wayne Harris, Cal	**1984**	James Parker, BC
1959	Roger Nelson, Edm	**1972**	John Helton, Cal	**1985**	Tyrone Jones, Wpg
1960	Herb Gray, Wpg	**1973**	Ray Nettles, BC	**1986**	James Parker, BC
1961	Frank Rigney, Wpg	**1974**	John Helton, Cal	**1987**	Gregg Stumon, BC
1962	John Barrow, Ham	**1975**	Jim Corrigall, Tor	**1988**	Grover Covington, Ham
1963	Tom Brown, BC	**1976**	Bill Baker, BC	**1989**	Danny Bass, Edm
1964	Tom Brown, BC	**1977**	Dan Kepley, Edm	**1990**	Greg Battle, Wpg
1965	Wayne Harris, Cal	**1978**	Dave Fennell, Edm	**1991**	Greg Battle, Wpg
1966	Wayne Harris, Cal	**1979**	Ben Zambiasi, Ham	**1992**	Willie Pless, Edm
1967	Ed McQuarters, Sask	**1980**	Dan Kepley, Edm	**1993**	Jearld Baylis, Sask

Outstanding offensive lineman

1974	Ed George, Mtl	**1981**	Larry Butler, Wpg	**1988**	Roger Aldag, Sask
1975	Charlie Turner, Edm	**1982**	Rudy Phillips, Ott	**1989**	Rod Connop, Edm
1976	Dan Yochum, Mtl	**1983**	Rudy Phillips, Ott	**1990**	Jim Mills, BC
1977	Al Wilson, BC	**1984**	John Bonk, Wpg	**1991**	Jim Mills, BC
1978	Jim Coode, Ott	**1985**	Nick Bastaja, Wpg	**1992**	Rob Smith, Ott
1979	Mike Wilson, Edm	**1986**	Roger Aldag, Sask	**1993**	Chris Walby, Wpg
1980	Mike Wilson, Edm	**1987**	Chris Walby, Wpg		

Outstanding rookie

1972	Chuck Ealey, Ham	**1980**	William Miller, Wpg	**1988**	Orville Lee, Ott
1973	Johnny Rodgers, Mtl	**1981**	Vince Goldsmith, Sask	**1989**	Stephen Jordan, Ham
1974	Sam Cvijanovich, Tor	**1982**	Chris Isaac, Ott	**1990**	Reggie Barnes, Ott
1975	Tom Clements, Ott	**1983**	Johnny Shepherd, Ham	**1991**	Jon Volpe, BC
1976	John Sciarra, BC	**1984**	Dwaine Wilson, Mtl	**1992**	Mike Richardson, Wpg
1977	Leon Bright, BC	**1985**	Michael Gray, BC	**1993**	Michael O'Shea, Ham
1978	Joe Poplawski, Wpg	**1986**	Harold Hallman, Cal		
1979	Brian Kelly, Edm	**1987**	Gill Fenerty, Tor		

Source: *Canadian Football League*

(1) Winners are chosen by a vote of the Football Reporters of Canada; prior to 1989 they were known as the Schenley Awards.

Canadian Football League All-Stars, 1993

(voted by Football Reporters of Canada)

Offence

Quarterback: Doug Flutie, Cal*
Fullback: Sean Millington, BC
Running Back: Michael Richardson, Wpg*
Slotback: Ray Elgaard, Sask*
Slotback: Dave Sapunjis, Cal
Wide Receiver: David Williams, Wpg
Wide Receiver: Rod Harris, Sask
Centre: Rod Connop, Edm*
Guard: David Black, Wpg
Guard: Rob Smith, BC
Tackle: Bruce Covernton, Cal
Tackle: Chris Walby, Wpg
Punter: Bob Cameron, Wpg
Kicker: David Ridgway, Sask
Specialty Teams: Henry Williams, Edm*

Defence

Tackle: Harold Hasselbach, Cal
Tackle: Jearld Baylis, Sask*
End: Will Johnson, Cal*
End: Tim Cofield, Ham
Linebacker: Willie Press, Edm*
Linebacker: Elfrid Payton, Wpg
Linebacker: John Motton, Ham*
Cornerback: Karl Anthony, Cal
Cornerback: Barry Wilburn, Sask
Halfback: Don Wilson, Edm
Halfback: Darryl Sampson, Wpg
Safety: Glen Suitor, Sask*

Source: *Canadian Football League. (*) Also All-Stars in 1993*

Canadian Football League Attendance, 1993

Team	1992 Ave.	1993 Ave.	Team	1992 Ave.	1993 Ave.
BC Lions	25 318	28 433	Sacramento Gold Miners	NA	16 979
Calgary Stampeders	25 440	28 169	Saskatchewan Roughriders	21 704	23 851
Edmonton Eskimos	28 309	30 537	Toronto Argonauts	32 053	25 324
Hamilton Tigercats	19 357	17 540	Winnipeg Blue Bombers	26 083	25 101
Ottawa Rough Riders	24 345	22 027	**Average**	**25 376**	**24 218**

Canadian Football Hall of Fame[1]

(only players listed, not builders)

Player / Year Elected / Team(s)

Atchison, Ron, (1978) Sask
Bailey, Byron (1975) BC
Baker, Bitt (1994) Sask/BC
Barrow, John (1976) Ham
Batstone, Harry (1963) Tor/Queen's
Beach, Ormond (1963) Sarnia
Box, Ab (1965) Balmy Beach/Tor
Breen, Joseph (1963) U of Toronto/Tor
Bright, Johnny (1970) Edm/Cal
Brown, Tom (1984) BC
Casey, Tom (1964) Wpg
Charlton, Ken (1992) Ott/Sask
Clements, Tom (1994) Ott/Sask/Ham/Wpg
Coffey, Tommy Joe (1977) Edm/Cal
Conacher, Lionel (1963) Tor
Copeland, Royal (1988) Tor
Corrigal, Jim (1990) Tor
Cox, Ernest (1963) Ham
Craig, Ross (1964) Ham
Cronin, Carl (1967) Wpg
Cutler, Wes (1968) Tor
Dalla Riva, Peter (1993) Mtl

Player / Year Elected / Team(s)

Dixon, George (1974) Mtl
Eliowitz, Abe (1969) Ott/Mtl
Emerson, Eddie (1963) Ott
Etcheverry, Sam (1969) Mtl
Evanshen, Terry (1984) Mtl/Cal/Ham/Tor
Faloney, Bernie (1974) Edm/Ham
Fear, Cap (1967) Tor/Mtl/Ham
Fennell, Dave (1990) Edm
Ferraro, John (196)6 Ham/Mtl
Fieldgate, Norm (1979) BC
Fleming, Willie (1982) BC
Gabriel, Tony (1984) Ham/Ott
Gaines, Geve (1994) Mtl/Ott
Gall, Hugh (1963) U of Toronto
Golab, Tony (1964) Ott
Gray, Herb (1983) Wpg
Griffing, Dean (1965) Sask/Cal
Hanson, Fritz (1963) Wpg
Harris, Wayne (1976) Cal
Harrison, Herman (1993) Cal
Helton, John (1985) Cal/Wpg
Henley, Garney (1979) Ham

▶

▶ **Hinton,** Tom (1991) BC
Huffman, Dick (1987) Wpg/Cal
Isbiste,r Bob (1965) Ham
Jackson, Russ (1973) Ott
Jacobs, Jack (1963) Wpg
James, Eddie (1963) Wpg/Reg
James, Gerry (1981) Wpg
Kabat, Greg (1966) Wpg
Kapp, Joe (1984) Cal/BC
Keeling, Jerry (1989) Cal/Ott/Ham
Kelly, Brian (1991) Edm
Kelly, Ellison (1992) Edm/Ham
Krol, Joe (1963) Tor/Ham
Kwong, Normie (1969) Cal/Edm
Lawson, Smirle (1963) U. of Toronto
Leadlay, Frank (1963) Queen's/Ham
Lear, Les (1974) Wpg/Cal
Lewis, Leo (1973) Wpg
Lunsford, Earl (1983) Cal
Luster, Marv (1990) Mtl/Tor
Luzzi, Don (1985) Cal
McCance, Chester (1976) Wpg/Mtl
McGill, Frank (1965) Mtl
McQuarters, Ed (1988) Sask
Miles, Rollie (1980) Edm
Morris, Frank (1983) Tor/Edm
Morris, Ted (1964) Tor
Mosca, Angelo (1987) Ham
Nelson, Roger (1985) Edm
Neumann, Peter (1979) Ham
O'Quinn, Red (1981) Mtl
Pajaczkowski, Tony (1988) Cal/Mtl
Parker Jackie (1971) Edm/Tor/BC
Patterson, Hal (1971) Mtl/Ham
Perry, Gordon (1970) Mtl

Perry, Norman (1963) Sarnia
Ploen, Ken (1975) Wpg
Quilty, Silver (1966) U. of Ottawa
Rebholz, Russ (1963) Wpg
Reed, George (1979) Sask
Reeve, Ted (1963) Tor
Rigney, Frank (1984) Wpg
Rodden, Michael (1964) Queen's/Tor
Rowe, Paul (1964) Cal
Ruby, Martin (1974) Sask
Russel, Jeff (1963) Ott
Scott, Vince (1982) Ham
Shatto, Dick (1975) Tor
Simpson, Benjamin (1963) Ham
Simpson, Bob (1976) Ott
Sprague, David (1963) Ham/Ott
Stevenson, Art (1969) Wpg
Stewart, Ron (1977) Ott
Stirling, Bummer (1966) Sarnia
Sutherin, Don (1992) Ham/Ott
Thelen, Dave (1989) Ott/Tor
Timmis, Brian (1963) Ham/Ott
Tinsley, Buddy (1982) Wpg
Tommy, Andrew (1989) Ott/Tor
Trawick, Herb (1975) Mtl
Tubman, Joe (1968) Ott
Tucker, Whit (1993) Ott
Urness, Ted (1989) Sask
Vaughn, Kaye (1978) Ott
Wagner, Virgil (1980) Mtl
Welch, Huck (1964) Ham/Mtl
Wilkinson, Tom (1987) Edm
Wylie, Harvey (1980) Cal
Young, Jim (1991) BC
Zock, William (1984) Tor/Edm

Source: *Canadian Football League*

NFL Final Standings, 1993

National Conference

■ Eastern Division

	W	L	T	Pct	Pts	OP
Dallas*	12	4	0	.750	346	229
NY Giants #	11	5	0	.688	288	205
Philadelphia	8	8	0	.500	293	315
Phoenix	7	9	0	.438	326	269
Washington	4	12	0	.250	230	345

■ Central Division

	W	L	T	Pct	Pts	OP
Detroit *	10	6	0	.625	298	292
Minnesota #	9	7	0	.563	277	290
Green Bay #	9	7	0	.563	340	282
Chicago	7	9	0	.438	234	230
Tampa Bay	5	11	0	.313	237	376

■ Western Division

	W	L	T	Pct	Pts	OP
San Francisco*	10	6	0	.625	473	295
New Orleans#	8	8	0	.500	317	343
Atlanta	6	10	0	.375	316	385
LA Rams	5	11	0	.312	221	367

American Conference

■ Eastern Division

	W	L	T	Pct	Pts	OP
Buffalo	2	4	0	.250	29	42
Miami	9	7	0	.563	49	351
NY Jets	8	8	0	.500	270	247
New England	5	11	0	.313	38	286
Indainapolis	4	12	0	.250	189	378

■ Central Division

	W	L	T	Pct	Pts	OP
Houston*	12	4	0	.750	368	238
Pittsburgh #	9	7	0	.563	308	281
Cleveland	7	9	0	.458	304	307
Cincinnati	3	13	0	.188	187	319

■ Western Division

	W	L	T	Pct	Pts	OP
Kansas City*	11	5	0	.688	328	291
LA Raiders#	10	6	0	.625	306	326
Denver	9	7	0	.563	373	284
San Diego	8	8	0	.500	322	290
Seattle	6	10	0	.375	280	314

*Division Champion #Wild Card Team Minnesota finished ahead of Green Bay based on a head-to-head sweep (2-0). ▶

Playoffs

■ Wild Card
NFC: Green Bay 28, Detroit 24
NY Giants 17, Minnesota 10
AFC: LA Raiders 42, Denver 24
Kansas City 27, Pittsburgh 24 (OT)

■ Divisional Playoffs
NFC: San Francisco 44, NY Giants 3
Dallas 27, Green Bay 17
AFC: Buffalo 29, LA Raiders 23
Kansas City 28, Houston 20

■ Championships
NFC : Dallas 38, San Francisco 21
AFC: Buffalo 30, Kansas City 13

■ Super Bowl XXVIII
(at Georgia Dome Atlanta)
Dallas 30, Buffalo 13

■ AFC-NFC Pro Bowl/(at Aloha Stadium, Honolulu, Hawaii)
NFC 17, AFC 3

Source: *National Football League*

All-Time Pro Football Records

(all conferences; up to the start of the 1994 season)

Leading Lifetime Scorers

	Yrs	TD	PAT	FG	Total		Yrs	TD	PAT	FG	Total
George Blanda	26	9	943	335	2 002	Jim Breech	14	0	517	243	1 246
Jan Stenerud	19	0	580	373	1 699	Gary Anderson	12	0	384	285	1 239
Nick Lowery	15	0	486	329	1 473	Chris Bahr	14	0	490	241	1 213
Pat Leahy	18	0	558	304	1 470	Matt Bahr	15	0	459	250	1 209
Jim Turner	16	1	521	304	1 439	Morlen Anderson	12	0	380	274	1 202
Mark Moseley	16	0	482	300	1 382	Gino Cappelletti	11	42	350	176	1 130
Jim Bakken	17	0	534	282	1 380	Ray Wersching	15	0	456	222	1 122
Fred Cox	15	0	519	282	1 365	Norm Johnson	12	0	444	222	1 110
Lou Groza	17	1	641	234	1 349	Don Cockroft	13	0	432	216	1 080
Eddie Murray	16	0	437	277	1 263	Garo Yepremian	14	0	444	210	1 074

Most points, one season .... **176, Paul Hornung,** GB, 1960 (15 TD, 41 PAT, 15 FG)
Most points, one game .... **40, Ernie Nevers,** Chi Cardinals vs. Chi Bears, Nov. 28, 1929 (6 TD, 4 PAT)
Most touchdowns, career .... **126, Jim Brown,** Cleve., 1957–65
Most touchdowns, one season .... **24, John Riggins,** Wash, 1984 (24 rushing)
Most touchdowns, one game .... **6, Ernie Nevers,** Chi Cardinals vs. Chi Bears, Nov. 28, 1929 (6 rushing)
Dub Jones, Clev vs. Chi Bears, Nov. 25, 1951 (4 rushing, 2 pass receptions)
Gale Sayers, Chi Bears vs. SF, Dec. 12, 1965 (4 rushing, 1 pass reception, 1 punt return)
Most points after touchdown, one season .... **66, Uwe von Schamann,** Mia, 1984
Most points after touchdown, career .... **943, George Blanda,** 4 teams, 1949–75
Most consecutive points after touchdown .... **234, Tommy Davis,** SF, 1959–69
Most field goals, one game .... **7, Jim Bakken,** StL vs. Pitt, Sept. 24, 1967
Rich Karlis, Minn vs. LA Rams, Nov. 5, 1989
Most field goals, one season .... **35, Ali Haji-Sheikh,** NY Giants, 1983
Most field goals, career .... **373, Jan Stenerud,** 3 teams, 1967–85
Most consecutive field goals .... **29, John Carneg,** SD, 1992–93
Longest field goal .... **63 yds, Tom Dempsey,** NO vs. Det, Nov. 8, 1970

Pass Interceptions

Most passes had intercepted, one game .... **8, Jim Hardy,** Chi Cardinals vs. Phil, Sept. 24, 1950 (39 attempts)
Most passes had intercepted, one season .... **42, George Blanda,** Hou, 1962
Most passes had intercepted, career .... **277, George Blanda,** Chi Bears, 1949–58;
Balt, 1950; Hou, 1960–66; Oak, 1967–75
Most consecutive passes attempted without interception .... **308, Bernie Kosar,** Clev, 1990–91
Most interceptions by, one season .... **14, Dick (Night Train) Lane,** LAs Rams, 1952
Most interceptions by, career .... **81, Paul Krause,** Wash, 1964–67; Minn, 1968–79 ▶

Punting

Most punts, one game .... 15, **John Teltschick,** Phil vs. N. Giants, Dec. 6, 1987 (OT)
Most punts, career .... 1 154, **Dave Jennings,** NY Giants, 1974–84; N.Y. Jets, 1985–87
Most punts, season .... 114, **Bob Parsons,** Chi Bears, 1981
Highest punting average, season (20 punts) .... 51.40, **Sam Baugh,** Wash., 1940 (35 punts)
Longest punt .... 98 yds, **Steve O'Neal,** NY Jets vs. Den, Sept. 21, 1969

Miscellaneous Records

Most fumbles, one season .... 18, **Dave Krieg,** Sea, 1989; **Warren Moon,** Hou, 1990
Most fumbles, one game .... 7, **Len Dawson,** KC vs. SD, Nov. 15, 1964
Most sacks, career .... 121.5, **Lawrence Taylor,** NY Giants, 1982–91
Most sacks, season .... 22, **Mark Gastineau,** NY Jets, 1984
Most seasons, active player .... 26, **George Blanda,** Chi Bears, 1949–58; Balt, 1950; Hou, 1960–66; Oak, 1967–75
Most consecutive games played, career .... 282, **Jim Marshall,** Cle, 1960; Minn, 1961–79
Highest punt return average, season .... 23.00 yards, **Herb Rich,** Baltimore, 1950
Highest punt return average, career .... 12.78 yards, **George McAfee,** Chicago, 1940–41, 1945–50
Highest kickoff return average, season .... 41.06 yards, **Travis Williams,** Green Bay, 1967
Highest kickoff return average, career .... 30.56 yards, **Gale Sayers,** Chicago, 1965–71
Most consecutive games played, career .... **282, Jim Marshall,** Cle, 1960; Minn, 1961–79

Leading Lifetime Rushers

	Yrs	Att	Yards	Avg		Yrs	Att	Yards	Avg
Walter Payton	13	3 838	16 726	4.4	Jim Taylor	10	1 941	8 597	4.4
Eric Dickerson	11	2 996	13 259	4.4	Joe Perry	14	1 737	8 378	4.8
Tony Dorsett	12	2 936	12 739	4.3	Roger Craig		1 991	8 189	4.1
Jim Brown	9	2 359	12 312	5.2	Gerald Riggs	10	1 989	8 188	4.1
Franco Harris	13	2 949	12 120	4.1	Larry Csonka	11	1 891	8 081	4.3
John Riggins	14	2 916	11 352	3.9	Freeman McNeil	12	1 798	8 074	4.5
O.J. Simpson	11	2 404	11 236	4.7	James Brooks	12	1 685	7 962	4.7
O.J. Anderson	14	2 562	10 273	4.0	Thurman Thomas	6	1 731	7 631	4.4
Earl Campbell	8	2 187	9 407	4.3	Herschel Walker	8	1 794	7 468	4.2
Marcus Allen	12	2 296	9 309	4.1	Mike Pruitt	11	1 844	7 378	4.0

Most yards gained, one season .... 2 105, **Eric Dickerson,** LAs Rams, 1984
Most yards gained, one game .... 275, **Walter Payton,** Chi Bears vs. Minn, Nov. 20, 1977
Most touchdowns rushing, career .... 110, **Walter Payton,** Chi Bears, 1975–87
Most touchdowns rushing, one season .... 24, **John Riggins,** Wash, 1983
Most touchdowns rushing, one game .... 6, **Ernie Nevers,** Chi Cardinals vs. Chi Bears, Nov. 8, 1929
Most rushing attempts, one season .... 407, **James Wilder,** Tam, 1984
Most rushing attempts, one game .... 45, **Jamie Morris,** Wash vs. Cin, Dec. 17, 1988
Longest run .... 99 yds, **Tony Dorsett,** Dal vs. Minn, Jan. 3, 1983

Leading Lifetime Receivers

	Yrs	No.	Yards	Avg		Yrs	No.	Yards	Avg
Art Monk	14	888	12 026	13.5	Gary Clark	9	612	9 580	15.6
Steve Largent	14	819	13 089	16.0	Henry Ellard	11	593	9 761	16.5
James Lofton	16	764	14 804	18.3	Harold Carmichael	14	590	8 985	15.2
Charlie Joiner	18	750	12 146	16.2	Fred Biletnikoff	14	589	8 974	15.2
Jerry Rice	9	708	11 776	16.6	Andre Reed	9	586	8 233	14.0
Ozzie Newsome	13	662	7 980	12.1	Mark Clayton	11	582	8 974	15.4
Charley Taylor	13	649	9 110	14.0	Harold Jackson	16	579	10 372	17.9
Drew Hill	14	634	9 831	13.5	Lionel Taylor	10	567	7 195	12.7
Don Maynard	15	633	11 834	18.7	Wes Chandler	11	559	8 966	16.0
Raymond Berry	13	631	9 275	14.7	Roy Green	14	559	8 965	16.0 ▶

▶ Most yards gained, one season .... **1 746, Charley Hennigan**, Hou, 1961
Most yards gained, one game .... **336, Willie Anderson**, LA Rams vs. NO, Nov. 26, 1989
Most pass receptions, one season .... **112, Sterling Sharpe**, Green Bay, 1993
Most pass receptions, one game .... **18, Tom Fears**, LA Rams vs. GB, Dec. 3, 1950 (189 yds)
Most consecutive games, pass receptions .... **177, Steve Largent**, Sea, 1976–89
Most touchdown passes, career .... **118, Jerry Rice**, SF, 1985–93
Most touchdown passes, one season .... **22, Jerry Rice**, SF, 1987
Most touchdown passes, one game .... **5, Bob Shaw**, Chi Cardinals vs. Balt, Oct. 2, 1950; **Kellen Winslow**,
SD vs. Oak, Nov. 22, 1981; **Jerry Rice**, SF vs. Atl, Oct. 14, 1990

Leading Lifetime Passers
(Minimum 1 500 attempts)

	Rtg1	Yrs	Att	Comp	Yards		Rtg1	Yrs	Att	Comp	Yards
Joe Montana	93.1	14	4 898	3 110	37 268	Ken Anderson	81.9	16	4 475	2 654	32 838
Steve Young	93.0	9	1 968	1 222	15 900	Bernie Kosar	81.9	9	3 213	1 889	22 314
Dan Marino	88.1	11	5 434	3 219	40 720	Danny White	81.7	13	2 950	1 761	21 959
Jim Kelly	86.0	8	3 494	2 112	26 413	Troy Aikman	81.0	5	1 920	1 191	13 627
Roger Staubach	83.4	11	2 958	1 685	22 700	Bart Starr	80.5	16	3 149	1 808	24 718
Neil Lomax	82.7	8	3 153	1 817	22 771	Ken O'Brien	80.4	10	3 602	2 110	25 094
Sonny Jurgensen	82.6	18	4 262	2 433	32 224	Warren Moon	80.4	10	4 546	2 632	33 685
Len Dawson	82.6	19	3 741	2 136	28 711	Fran Tarkenton	80.4	18	6 467	3 686	47 003
Boomer Esiason	82.1	10	3 851	2 185	29 092	R. Cunningham	80.3	9	2 751	1 540	19 043
Dave Krieg	82.0	14	4 178	2 431	30 485	Dan Fouts	80.2	15	5 604	3 297	43 040

Most yards gained, one season .... **5 084, Dan Marino**, Mia, 1984
Most yards gained, one game .... **554, Norm Van Brocklin**, LA Rams vs. NY Giants, Sept. 28, 1951
(27 completions in 41 attempts)
Most touchdowns passing, career .... **342, Fran Tarkenton**, Minn, 1961–66; NY Giants, 1967–71; Vikings, 1972–78
Most touchdowns passing, one season .... **48, Dan Marino**, Mia, 1984
Most touchdowns passing, one game ...... **7, Sid Luckman**, Chi Bears vs. NY Giants, Nov. 14, 1943; **Adrian Burk,** Phil vs.
Wash, Oct. 17, 1954; **George Blanda**, Hou vs. NY Titans, Nov. 19, 1961;
Y.A. Tittle, NY Giants vs. Wash, Oct. 28, 1962; **Joe Kapp**, Minn vs. Balt, Sept. 28, 1969
Most passing attempts, one season .... **655, Warren Moon**, Hou, 1991
Most passing attempts, one game .... **68, George Blanda**, Hou vs. Buff, Nov. 1, 1964 (37 completions)
Most passes completed, one season .... **404, Warren Moon**, Hou, 1991
Most passes completed, one game .... **42, Richard Todd**, NY Jets vs. SF 49ers, Sept. 21, 1980

Source: *National Football League*

(1) Rating based on performance standards for completion percentage, interception percentage, touchdown percentage and average gains.

Canadian Junior Football Champions, 1908–93

1908	Parkdale Canoe Club 18, Montreal III, 1
1909	Toronto St. Michaels College 7, Hamilton Alerts 2
1910	Hamilton Alerts III 4, St. Lambert 3
1911	Petrolia 27, Kingston Royal Military College 20
1912	Hamilton Alerts III 13, Ontario Agro College (Guelph) 7
1913	Ottawa Capitals 17, Montreal Westmounts 2
1914	Univ. of Western Ontario (London) 23, Ontario Agric College (Guelph) 9
1915–20	No series
1921	Toronto St. Aldens 18, Queen's University 8
1922	Montreal A.A.A.
1923	Loyola College (Montreal) 9, Toronto Canoe Club 3
1924	Toronto Canoe Club 7, Ottawa Rideaus 1
1925	Montreal A.A.A. 6, Regina Pats 4
1926	Montreal A.A.A. 16, St. Thomas Tigers 5
1927	Montreal A.A.A. 4, Toronto Varsity 2

1928	Regina Pats 9, St. Thomas Tigers 6
1929	St. Thomas Tigers 14, Moose Jaw Maroons 0
1930	Toronto Argos 7, Winnipeg Native Sons 1
1931	Woodstock Grads 14, Moose Jaw Maroons 13
1932	Toronto Varsity 8, Moose Jaw Maroon 6
1933	Toronto Argos 14, Montreal Westwards 6 Calgary Altonas 11, Winnipeg Deer Lodge 6 Toronto Argos received trophy.
1934–35	No series
1936	No final
1937	Hamilton Italo Canadians 27, Regina Dales 2
1938	Regina Dales 4, Montreal Westmounts 3
1939–45	No series
1946	No final
1947	Vancouver Blue Bombers 19, Hamilton Tigers 8 (2-game total-point series)
1948	Hamilton Wildcats 23, Saskatoon Hilltops 10

▶

▶ 1949 Hamilton Wildcats 14, Vancouver Blue Bombers 11
1950 Hamilton Tigercats 14, Vancouver Blue Bombers, 5
1951 Hamilton Tiger Cats 22, Edmonton Maple Leafs 1
1952 Windsor A.K.O. 15, Edmonton Wildcats 12
1953 Saskatoon Hilltops 34, Windsor A.K.O. 6
1954 Windsor A.K.O. 13, Winnipeg Rods 9
1955 Winnipeg Rods 19, Windsor A.K.O. 13
1956 Winnipeg Rods 21, Toronto Parkdale Lions 10
1957 Toronto Parkdale Lions 20, Winnipeg Rods 13
1958 Saskatoon Hilltops 18, Montreal N.D.G. 14
1959 Saskatoon Hilltops 46, Toronto North York Knights 7
1960 Montreal Rosemount Bombers 22, Saskatoon Hilltops, 20
1961 Winnipeg Rods 16, Montreal Rosemount Bombers 13
1962 Edmonton Huskies 7, Montreal N.D.G. 3
1963 Edmonton Huskies 47, Montreal N.D.G. 27
1964 Edmonton Huskies 48, Montreal N.D.G. 27
1965 Montreal N.D.G. 2, Edmonton Huskies 1
1966 Regina Rams 29, Montreal N.D.G. 14
1967 Edmonton Wildcats 29, Burlington Braves 6
1968 Saskatoon Hilltops 27, Ottawa Sooners 7
1969 Saskatoon Hilltops 28, Ottawa Sooners 7

1970 Regina Rams 39, Burlington Braves 8
1971 Regina Rams 42, Burlington Braves 13
1972 Hamilton Hurricanes 33, Regina Rams 8
1973 Regina Rams 9, Ottawa Sooners 0
1974 Ottawa Sooners 17, Vancouver Meralomas 4
1975 Regina Rams 38, Hamilton Hurricanes 19
1976 Regina Rams 45, Hamilton Hurricanes 23
1977 Edmonton Wildcats 23, Hamilton Hurricanes 0
1978 Saskatoon Hilltops 24, Ottawa Sooners 4
1979 Ottawa Sooners 13, Regina Rams 9
1980 Regina Rams 26, Hamilton Hurricanes 24
1981 Regina Rams 46, Hamilton Hurricanes 24
1982 Renfrew Trojans 46, Montreal Junior Concordes 0
1983 Edmonton Wildcats 30, Ottawa Sooners 11
1984 Ottawa Sooners 46, Richmond Raiders 23
1985 Saskatoon Hilltops 29, Ottawa Sooners 11
1986 Regina Rams 53, Ottawa Sooners 12
1987 Regina Rams 31, St. Vital Mustangs 23
1988 Okanagan Sun 50, Burlington Jr. Tiger-Cats 0
1989 Calgary Colts 23, Burlington Jr. Tiger-Cats 6
1990 Calgary Colts 50, Windsor A.K.O. Fratmen 15
1991 Saskatoon Hilltops 48, Ottawa Sooners 7
1992 Ottawa Sooners 35, Surry Rams 18

Source: Football Canada

Note: Canadian Rugby Union, 1908–46; Canadian Amateur Football Association, 1947–74; Leader Post Trophy to winner. Canadian Junior Football League, 1975– ; Armadale Cup 1975–88; Canadian Bowl 1989– .

Major Bowl Games, 1993

Bowl	Site	Result
Cotton	Dallas, TX	Notre Dame 24, Texas A&M 21
Fiesta	Tempe, AZ	Arizona 29, Miami 0
Rose	Pasadena, CA	Wisconsin 21, UCLA 16
Orange	Miami, FL	Florida State 18, Nebraska 16
Sugar	New Orleans, LA	Florida 41, West Virginia 7

U.S. College Football Top 20, 1993

	Record	Pts		Record	Pts
1. Florida	12-1-0	1 532	11. Ohio St	10-1-1	970
2. Notre Dame	11-1-0	1 478	12. Tennessee	9-2-1	870
3. Nebraska	11-1-0	1 418	13. Boston College	9-3-1	817
4. Auburn	11-0-1	1 375	14. Alabama	9-3-1	685
5. Florida	9-0-3	1 307	15. Miami	9-3-0	611
6. Wisconsin	10-2-0	1 228	16. Colorado	8-3-1	574
7. West Virginia	12-1-0	1 090	17. Oklahoma	9-3-1	521
8. Penn St.	10-2-0	1 074	18. UCLA	8-4-0	460
9. Texas A & M	10-3-0	992	19. North Carolina	10-3-0	447
10. Arizona	9-4-0	992	20. Kansas	9-2-1	444

Source: Associated Press

BASKETBALL

National Basketball Association, 1992–94

Final Standings

Eastern Conference

■ Atlantic Division

	W	L	Pct	GB
New York	57	25	.695	—
Orlando	50	32	.610	7
New Jersey	45	37	.549	12
Miami	42	40	.312	15
Boston	32	50	.390	25
Philadelphia	25	57	.305	32
Washington	24	58	.293	33

■ Central Division

	W	L	Pct	GB
Atlanta	57	25	.695	—
Chicago	55	27	.671	2
Cleveland	47	35	.573	10
Indiana	47	35	.573	10
Charlotte	41	41	.500	16
Detroit	20	62	.244	37
Milwaukee	20	62	.244	37

Western Conference

■ Midwest Division

	W	L	Pct	GB
Houston	58	24	.707	—
San Antonio	55	27	.671	3
Utah	53	29	.646	5
Denver	42	40	.512	16
Minnesota	20	62	.244	38
Dallas	13	69	.159	45

■ Pacific Division

	W	L	Pct	GB
Seattle	63	19	.768	—
Phoenix	56	26	.683	7
Golden State	50	32	.610	13
Portland	47	35	.573	16
Los Angeles Lakers	33	49	.402	30
Sacramento	28	54	.341	35
Los Angeles Clippers	27	55	.329	36

NBA Playoff Results, 1993–94

Eastern Conference

First Round (best-of-5)
Chicago defeated Cleveland 3–0
Atlanta defeated Miami 3–2
Indiana defeated Orlando 3–0
New York defeated New Jersey 3–1
Semifinals (best-of-7)
New York defeated Indiana 4–3

Western Conference

First Round (best-of-5)
Houston defeated Portalnd 3–1
Denver defeated Seattle 3–2
Phoenix defeated Golden State 3–0
Utah defeated San Antonio 3–1
Finals (best-of-7)
Houston defeated Utah 4–1

Championship (best-of-7)
Houston defeated New York 4-3

Source: *NBA News*

NBA Individual Highs, 1993–94

Minutes played, season	**3533, Latrell Sprewell**, G.S.
Minutes played, game	**56, Karl Malone**, Utah vs. SA Feb. 23 (2 OT)
Points, game	**71, David Robinson**, SA vs. LAC Apr. 24
Field goals, game	**26, David Robinson**, SA vs.LAC Apr. 24
Field goal attempts, game	**41, David Robinson**, SA vs. LAC Apr. 24
3-point field goals, game	**8, Dan Majerle**, Phoe. vs. LAC Nov. 9 **8, Mitch Richmond**, Sac. vs. LAC Feb. 25
3-point field goal attempts, game	**16, Nick Van Exel**, LAL vs. Utah Apr. 24
Free throws, game	**20 Kenny Anderson**, NJ vs. Det. Apr. 15 (OT) **18 David Robinson**, SA vs. LAC Apr. 24
Free throw attempts, game	**25, David Robinson**, SA vs. LAC Apr. 24
Rebounds, game	**32, Dennis Rodman**, SA vs. Dall. Jan. 22
Offensive rebounds, game	**14, Shaquille O'Neal**, Orl. vs. Bos. Feb. 15 **14, Olden Polynice**, Sac. vs. Milw. Mar. 11 ▶

▶ Defensive rebounds, game . . . . **23, Dennis Rodman,** SA vs. Dall. Jan. 22
Offensive rebounds, season . . . . **453, Dennis Rodman,** SA
Defensive rebounds, season . . . . **914, Dennis Rodman,** SA
Assists, game. . . . . **25, Kevin Johnson,** Phoe. vs. SA Apr. 6
Blocked shots, game. . . . . **15, Shaquille O'Neal,** Orl. vs. NJ Nov. 20
Steals, game . . . . **10, Kevin Johnson,** Phoe. vs. Wash. Dec. 9
Personal fouls, season . . . . **312, Sean Kemp,** Sea.
Games disqualified, season . . . . **11, Sean Kemp,** Sea. **11, Smits,** Ind.

Source: *National Basketball Association*

NBA Statistical Leaders, 1993–94

■ Scoring

	FG	Pts	Avg
Robinson, SA	840	2383	29.8
O'Neal, Orl.	953	2377	29.3
Olajuwon, Hou.	894	2184	27.3
Wilkins, Atl. LA-C	698	1923	26.0
K. Malone, Utah	772	2063	25.2
Ewing, NY	745	1939	24.5
Richmond, Sac.	635	1823	23.4
Pippen, Chi.	627	1587	22.0
Barkley, Pho.	518	1402	21.6
Rice, Mia.	663	1708	21.1
Sprewell, GS	613	1720	21.0
Manning, LA-C, Atl.	586	1403	20.6
Dumars, Det.	505	1410	20.4
Coleman, NJ	541	1559	20.2
Harper, LA-C	569	1508	20.1
C. Robinson, Por.	641	1647	20.1
Miller, Ind.	524	1574	19.9
Jackson, Dal.	637	1576	19.2
Mashburn, Dal.	561	1513	19.2
Willis, Atl.	627	1531	19.1

■ Rebounds

	Def	Total	Avg
Rodman, SA	914	1367	17.3
O'Neal, Orl.	688	1072	13.2
Willis, Atl.	628	963	12.0
Olajuwon, Hou.	726	955	11.9
Polynice, Det., Sac.	510	809	11.9
Mutombo, Den.	685	971	11.8
Oakley, NY	616	965	11.8
K. Malone, Utah	705	940	11.5
Coleman, NJ	608	870	11.3
Ewing, NJ	666	885	11.2

■ Field Goal Percentage

	FG	FGA	Pct
O'Neal, Orl.	953	1591	.599
Mutombo, Den.	365	642	.569
Thorpe, Hou.	449	801	.561
Webber, GS	572	1037	.522
Kemp, Sea.	533	990	.538
Vaught, LA-C	373	695	.537
Ceballos, Pho.	425	795	.535
Smits, Ind.	493	923	.534
D. Davis, Ind.	308	582	.529
Olajuwon, Hou.	894	1694	.528
Stockton, Utah.	458	868	.528

■ Free Throw Percentage

	FT	FTA	Pct
Abdul-Rauf, Den.	219	229	.956
Miller, Ind.	403	444	.908
Pierce, Sea.	189	211	.896
Threatt, LA-L.	138	155	.890
Price, Cle.	238	268	.888
Rice, Mia.	250	284	.880
Hornacek, Phi., Utah	260	296	.878
Skiles, Orl.	195	222	.878
Porter, Por.	204	234	.872
Smith, Hou.	135	155	.871

■ Assists

	G	Ast	Avg
Stockton, Utah	82	1031	12.6
Bogues, Cha.	77	780	10.1
Blaylock, Atl.	81	789	9.7
K. Anderson, NJ	82	784	9.6
K. Johnson, Pho.	67	637	9.5
Strickland, Por.	82	740	9.0
Douglas, Bos.	78	683	8.8
Jackson, LA-C	79	678	8.6
Price, Cle.	76	589	7.8
M. Williams, Min.	71	512	7.2

■ 3-Point Field Goal Percentage

	3FG	3FGA	Pct
Murray, Por.	50	109	.459
Armstrong, Chi.	60	135	.444
Miller, Ind.	123	292	.421
Kerr, Chi.	52	124	.419
Skiles, Orl.	68	165	.412
Murdock, Mil.	69	168	.411
Richmond, Sac.	127	312	.407
Smith, Hou.	89	220	.405
Curry, Cha.	152	378	.402
Davis, NY	53	132	.402 ▶

▶ ■ **Steals**

	G	Steals	Avg
McMillan, Sea.	73	216	2.96
Pippen, Chi.	72	211	2.93
Blaylock, Atl.	81	212	2.62
Stockton, Utah	82	199	2.43
Murdock, Mil.	82	197	2.40
Hardaway, Orl.	82	190	2.32
Playton, Sea.	82	188	2.29
Gugliotta, Wash.	78	172	2.21
Sprewell, GS	82	180	2.20
Brown, Bos.	77	156	2.03

■ **Blocked Shots**

	G	Blocks	Avg
Mutombo, Den.	82	336	4.10
Olajuwon, Hou.	80	297	3.71
Robinson, SA	80	265	3.31
Mourning, Cha.	60	188	3.13
Bradley, Phi.	49	147	3.00
O'Neal, Orl.	81	231	2.85
Ewing, NY	79	217	2.75
Miller, Pho.	69	156	2.26
Webber, GS	76	164	2.16
Kemp, Sea.	79	166	2.10

All-Time NBA Statistical Leaders

(as of the end of the 1993–94 season)

Scoring Average

(400 games or 10 000 points minimum)

	G	FGM	FTM	Points	Avg
Michael Jordan	667	8 079	5 096	21 541	32.3
Wilt Chamberlain	1 045	12 681	6 057	31 419	30.1
Elgin Baylor	846	8 693	5 763	23 149	27.4
Jerry West	932	9 016	7 160	25 192	27.0
Dominique Wilkins*	907	9 020	5 455	24 009	26.5
Bob Pettit	792	7 349	6 182	20 880	26.4
George Gervin	791	8 045	4 541	20 708	26.2
Karl Malone*	652	6 230	4 236	16 833	25.8
Oscar Robertson	1 040	9 508	7 694	26 710	25.7
Kareem Abdul-Jabbar	1 560	15 837	6 712	38 387	24.6

Source: *National Basketball Association*

*active player

Canada's Basketball Squad

(Canadian basketball team roster, 1994 world championships, Aug 4-14, 1994, Toronto)

Rick Fox, guard/forward, Toronto, Ont

Kory Hallas, forward, Almonte, Ont

J.D. Jackson, guard, Vancouver, BC

Martin Keane, forward, Toronto, Ont

Spencer McKay, forward, Oliver, BC

Ronn McMahon, guard, Magrath, Alta

Steve Nash, guard, Victoria, BC

Will Njoku, forward, Halifax, NS

Mike Smrek, centre, Port Robinson, Ont

Joey Vickery, guard, Winnipeg, Man

Dwight Walton, forward, Montreal, Que

Greg Wiltjer, centre, Sidney, BC

Coach: Ken Shields

Assistant coaches: Gerry Hemmings, Mike Katz, Doc Ryan ▶

World Basketball Championships

(Toronto, Aug. 4-14, 1994)

■ **First Round**

Pool A

	W	L
United States	3	0
China	2	1
Spain	1	2
Brazil	0	3

US 115, Spain 100
China 97, Brazil 93 (OT)
US 132, China 77
Spain 73, Brazil 67
US 105, Brazil 82
China 78, Spain 76

Pool B

	W	L
Croatia	3	0
Australia	2	1
Cuba	1	2
South Korea	0	3

Croatia 85, Cuba 65
Australia 87, S Korea 85
Croatia 104, S Korea 53
Australia 93, Cuba 87
Croatia 83, Australia 69
Cuba 92, S Korea 79

Pool C

	W	L
Russia	3	0
Canada	2	1
Argentina	1	2
Angola	0	3

Canada 83, Angola 52
Russia 84, Argentina 64
Canada 91, Argentina 73
Russia 94, Angola 57
Russia 73, Canada 66
Argentina 67, Angola 59

Pool D*

	W	L
Greece	2	1
Puerto Rico	2	1
Germany	2	1
Egypt	0	3

Greece 68, Germany 58
Puerto Rico 102, Egypt 74
Greece 69, Egypt 53
Germany 81, Puerto Rico 74
Puerto rico 72, Greece 64
Germany 78, Egypt 56

■ **Medal Round**

Pool W

	W	L
U.S.	3	0
Russia	2	1
Australia	1	2
Puerto Rico	0	3

US 130, Australia 74
Russia 101, PR 85
US 134, PR 83
Russia 103, Australia 76
Australia 94, PR 81
US 111, Russia 94

Pool X

	W	L
Croatia	3	0
Greece	2	1
Canada	1	2
China	0	3

Greece 74, Canada 71
Croatia 105, China 73
Croatia 92, Canada 61
Greece 77, China 61
Canada 90, China 58
Croatia 81, Greece 55

■ **Semi-finals**

US 97, Greece 58
Russia 66, Croatia 64

■ **Consolation semi-finals**

Puerto Rico 85, Canada 82
Australia 95, China 57

Gold Medal: US 137, Russia 91
Bronze Medal: Croatia 78, Greece, 60
Fifth Place: Australia 96, Puerto Rico 83
Seventh Place: Canada 104, China 76

* Greece and Puerto Rico advance based on point differential.

Canadian Curling Champions

Men

Year	Skip, Province	Year	Skip, Province	Year	Skip, Province
1927	Murray Macneill, N.S.	1952	Billy Walsh, Man.	1974	Hector Gervais, Alta.
1928	Gordon Hudson, Man.	1953	Ab Gowanlock, Man.	1975	Bill Tetley, N. Ont.
1929	Gordon Hudson, Man.	1954	Matt Baldwin, Alta.	1976	Jack MacDuff, Nfld.
1930	Howard Wood, Man.	1955	Garnet Campbell, Sask.	1977	Jim Ursel, Que.
1931	Bob Gourley, Man.	1956	Billy Walsh, Man.	1978	Ed Lukowich, Alta.
1932	Jim Congalton, Man.	1957	Matt Baldwin, Alta.	1979	Barry Fry, Man.
1933	Cliff Manahan, Alta.	1958	Matt Baldwin, Alta.	1980	Rick Folk, Sask.
1934	Leo Johnson, Man.	1959	Ernie Richardson, Sask.	1981	Kerry Burtnyk, Man.
1935	Gordon Campbell, Ont.	1960	Ernie Richardson, Sask.	1982	Al Hackner, N. Ont.
1936	Ken Watson, Man.	1961	Hec Gervais, Alta.	1983	Ed Werenich, Ont.
1937	Cliff Manahan, Alta.	1962	Ernie Richardson, Sask.	1984	Mike Riley, Man.
1938	Ab Gowanlock, Man.	1963	Ernie Richardson, Sask.	1985	Al Hackner, N. Ont.
1939	Bert Hall, Ont.	1964	Lyall Dagg, B.C.	1986	Ed Lukowich, Alta.
1940	Howard Wood, Man.	1965	Terry Braunstein, Man.	1987	Russ Howard, Ont.
1941	Howard Palmer, Alta.	1966	Ron Northcott, Alta.	1988	Pat Ryan, Alta.
1942	Ken Watson, Man.	1967	Alf Phillips, Jr., Ont.	1989	Pat Ryan, Alta.
1946	Billy Rose, Alta.	1968	Ron Northcott, Alta.	1990	Ed Werenich, Ont.
1947	Jimmy Welsh, Man.	1969	Ron Northcott, Alta.	1991	Kevin Martin, Alta.
1948	Frenchy D'Amour, B.C.	1970	Don Duguid, Man.	1992	Vic Peters, Man.
1949	Ken Watson, Man.	1971	Don Duguid, Man.	1993	Russ Howard, Ont.
1950	Tom Ramsay, N. Ont.	1972	Orest Meleschuk, Man.	1994	Rick Folk, BC
1951	Don Oyler, N.S.	1973	Harvey Mazinke, Sask.		

Women

Year	Skip, Province	Year	Skip, Province	Year	Skip, Province
1961	Joyce McKee, Sask.	1973	Vera Pezer, Sask.	1984	Connie Laliberte, Man.
1962	Ina Hansen, B.C.	1974	Emily Farnham, Sask.	1985	Linda Moore, B.C.
1963	Mabel DeWare, N.B.	1975	Lee Tobin, Que.	1986	Marilyn Darte, Ont.
1964	Ina Hansen, B.C.	1976	Lindsay Davie, B.C.	1987	Pat Sanders, B.C.
1965	Peggy Casselman, Man.	1977	Myrna McQuarrie, Alta.	1988	Heather Houston, Ont.
1966	Gail Lee, Alta.	1978	Cathy Pidzarko, Man.	1989	Heather Houston, Ont.
1967	Betty Duguid, Man.	1979	Lindsay Sparkes, B.C.	1990	Alison Goring, Ont.
1968	Hazel Jamieson, Alta.	1980	Marj Mitchell, Sask.	1991	Julie Sutton, B.C.
1969	Joyce McKee, Sask.	1981	Susan Seitz, Alta.	1992	Connie Laliberte, Man.
1970	Dorenda Schoenhais, Sask.	1982	Colleen Jones, N.S.	1993	Sandra Peterson, Sask.
1971	Vera Pezer, Sask.	1983	Penny LaRocque, N.S.	1994	Sandra Peterson, Sask
1972	Vera Pezer, Sask.				

The World Cup

Soccer's World Cup, a month-long tournament held every four years, is widely regarded as the world's biggest sporting event. More than 100 countries spend two years competing in qualifying rounds to determine which nations earn the distinction of competing in the 24-team final round. Canada has only qualified for the final once, in 1986.

The final 24 teams are divided into six groups of four, with each team playing once against each of the others in its group. The two top teams in each group, plus the four with the next best records, advance to an elimination round leading to the final.

The 1990 final began in Milan June 8 and finished in Rome a month later. On July 8, an estimated one billion world-wide television viewers watched West Germany defeat defending champion Argentina in a 1-0 contest. It was the lowest-scoring final in the 60-year history of the event. Argentina managed only one shot on goal the entire game; West Germany got its only goal on a controversial penalty kick with only six minutes remaining in regulation time.

The 1998 World Cup will be hosted by France.

Year	Host nation	Final Game	Third Place	Tournament's Top scorer
1930	Uruguay	**Uruguay** 4, Argentina 2	—	Stabile, Argentina (8)
1934	Italy	**Italy** 2, Czechoslovakia 1	Germany 3, Austria 2	Several (4)
1938	France	**Italy** 4, Hungary 2	Brazil 4, Sweden 2	Leonadis, Brazil (8)
1942–46		Tournament not held because of Second World War		
1950	Brazil	**Uruguay** 2, Brazil 1	Sweden[1]	Ademir, Brazil (8)
1954	Switzerland	**W. Germany** 3, Hungary 2	Austria 3, Uruguay 1	Kocsis, Hungary (11)
1958	Sweden	**Brazil** 5, Sweden 2	France 6, W. Germany 3	Fontaine, France (13)
1962	Chile	**Brazil** 3, Czechoslovakia 1	Chile 1, Yugoslavia 0	Jerkovic, Yugoslavia (5)
1966	England	**England** 4, W. Germany 2	Portugal 2, Russia 1	Eusebio, Portugal (9)
1970	Mexico	**Brazil** 4, Italy 1	W. Germany 1, Uruguay 0	Muller, W. Germany (10)
1974	W. Germany	**W. Germany** 2, Holland 1	Poland 1, Brazil 0	Lato, Poland (7)
1978	Argentina	**Argentina** 3, Holland 1	Brazil 2, Italy 1	Kempes, Argentina (6)
1982	Spain	**Italy** 3, W. Germany 1	Poland 3, France 2	Rossi, Italy (6)
1986	Mexico	**Argentina** 3, W. Germany 2	France 4, Belgium 2	Lineker, England (6)
1990	Italy	**W. Germany** 1, Argentina 0	Italy 2, England 1	Schillaci, Italy (6)
1994	USA	**Brazil** 0, Italy 0*	Sweden 4, Bulgaria 0	Salenko, Russia (6)

(1) Based on point system.

World Cup All-Stars

Goalkeeper:	Michel Prud'homme, Belgium
Defenders:	Jorghino, Brazil
	Marcio Santos, Brazil
	Paolo Maldini, Italy
Midfielders:	Dunga, Brazil
	Gheorghe Hagi, Romania
	Tomas Brolin, Sweden
	Krassimir balakov, Bulgaria
Forwards:	Romario, Brazil
	Roberto Baggio, Italy
	Hristo Stoichkov, Bulgaria

World Cup , 1994 Finals

■ **Quarterfinals**

Sweden 3, Romania 2
Brazil 3, Netherlands 2
Italy 2, Spain 1
Bulgaria 2, Germany 1

■ **Semifinals**

Brazil 1, Sweden 0
Italy 2, Bulgaria 1

■ **Third place**

Sweden 4, Bulgaria 0

■ **Final**

Brazil 0, Italy 0
(Brazil wins shoot-out 3-2)

Canadian Interuniversity Athletic Union Champions

Men

	Basketball	Football	Ice Hockey	Soccer	Swimming	Volleyball	Track & Field
1975/76	Manitoba	Ottawa	Toronto	Alberta	Toronto	B.C.	—
1976/77	Acadia	Western	Toronto	Concordia	Waterloo	Winnipeg	—
1977/78	St. Mary's	Western	Alberta	York	Waterloo	Manitoba	—
1978/79	St. Mary's	Queen's	Alberta	Manitoba	Waterloo	Saskatchewan	—
1979/80	Victoria	Acadia	Alberta	Alberta	Toronto	Manitoba	—
1980/81	Victoria	Alberta	Moncton	New Brunswick	Toronto	Alberta	Toronto
1981/82	Victoria	Acadia	Moncton	McGill	Calgary	Calgary	Toronto
1982/83	Victoria	B.C.	Saskatchewan	McGill	Calgary	B.C.	York
1983/84	Victoria	Calgary	Toronto	Laurentian	Calgary	Manitoba	York
1984/85	Victoria	Guelph	York	B.C.	Calgary	Manitoba	Toronto
1985/86	Victoria	Calgary	Alberta	B.C.	Toronto	Winnipeg	Toronto
1986/87	Brandon	B.C.	Trois-Rivières	B.C.	Calgary	Winnipeg	Saskatchewan
1987/88	Brandon	McGill	York	Victoria	Calgary	Manitoba	Manitoba
1988/89	Brandon	Calgary	York	Toronto	Calgary	Calgary	Manitoba
1989/90	Concordia	Western	Moncton	B.C.	Calgary	Laval	Manitoba/Toronto
1990/91	Western	Saskatchewan	Trois-Rivières	B.C.	Calgary	Manitoba	Windsor
1991/92	Brock	Wilfrid Laurier	Alberta	B.C.	Toronto	Laval	Manitoba
1992/93	St. Francis Xavier	Queen's	Acadia	B.C.	Toronto	Calgary	Windsor
1993/94	McMaster	Toronto	Lethbridge	Sherbrooke	Toronto	Laval	Manitoba

Women

	Basketball	Field Hockey	Swimming & Diving	Track & Field	Volleyball
1975/76	Laurentian	Toronto	—	—	Western
1976/77	Laurentian	Dalhousie	Acadia	—	B.C.
1977/78	Laurentian	Toronto	Acadia	—	B.C.
1978/79	Laurentian	B.C.	Toronto	—	Saskatchewan
1979/80	Victoria	Toronto	Toronto	—	Saskatchewan
1980/81	Victoria	B.C.	Toronto	Western	Saskatchewan
1981/82	Victoria	Toronto	Toronto	Western	Dalhousie
1982/83	Bishop's	B.C.	Toronto	Western	Winnipeg
1983/84	Bishop's	B.C.	Toronto	York	Winnipeg
1984/85	Victoria	Victoria	B.C.	Alta. & Sask.	Winnipeg
1985/86	Toronto	Toronto	B.C.	Saskatchewan	Winnipeg
1986/87	Victoria	Toronto	Toronto	Calgary	Winnipeg
1987/88	Manitoba	Victoria	Toronto	York	Winnipeg
1988/89	Calgary	Toronto	Toronto	Toronto	Calgary
1989/90	Laurentian	Victoria	Toronto	York	Manitoba
1990/91	Laurentian	B.C.	Toronto	Calgary	Manitoba
1991/92	Victoria	Victoria	Toronto	Windsor	Manitoba
1992/93	Winnipeg	Victoria	Toronto	Windsor	Winnipeg
1993/94	Winnipeg	Toronto	BC	Windsor	Calgary

Source: *Canadian Interuniversity Athletic Union.*

Canadian Tennis Champions, 1970–94

Men's Singles

1970	Mike Belkin	1979	Dale Power	1987	Andrew Sznajder
1971	Peter Burwash	1980	Greg Halder	1988	Andrew Sznajder
1972	Mike Belkin	1981	Glenn Michibata	1989	Andrew Sznajder
1973	Keith Carpenter	1982	Glenn Michibata	1990	Brian Gyetko
1974	Pierre Lamarche	1983	Derek Segal	1991	Grant Connell
1975	Tony Bardsley	1984	Stephane Bonneau	1992	Andrew Sznajder
1976	Jim Boyce	1985	Stephane Bonneau	1993	Andrew Sznajder
1977	Harry Fritz	1986	Andrew Sznajder	1994	Sebastian Lareau
1978	Harry Fritz				

Women's Singles

1970	Andree Martin	1979	Marjorie Blackwood	1987	Helen Kelesi
1971	Vicki Berner	1980	Wendy Barlow	1988	Helen Kelesi
1972	Janice Tindle	1981	Nina Bland	1989	Helen Kelesi
1973	Janice Tindle	1982	Carling Bassett	1990	Helen Kelesi
1974	Susan Stone	1983	Carling Bassett	1991	Patricia Hy
1975	Susan Stone	1984	Marianne Groat	1992	René Simpson-Alter
1976	Susan Stone	1985	Jane Young	1993	Patricia Hy
1977	Marjorie Blackwood	1986	Carling Bassett	1994	Jana Nejedly
1978	Marjorie Blackwood				

Source: *Tennis Canada*

Canadian Swimming Records

(as of August 21, 1994)

Women

Event	Time	Swimmer	Site	Date
Freestyle				
50 m	26.01	Andrea Nugent	Montreal	Mar., 1987
	26.01	Kristin Topham	Havana	Aug. 18, 1991
100 m	56.29	Marianne Limpert	Buffalo	July 14, 1993
200 m	2:00.61	Patricia Noall	Toronto	Aug. 17, 1988
400 m	4:12.83	Julie Daigneault	Montreal	July 29, 1983
800 m	8:36.24	Debbie Wurzburger	Seoul	Sept. 23, 1988
1 500 m	16:40.60	Elissa Purvis	Los Altos, Cal.	July, 1986
Backstroke				
100 m	1:03.28	Nancy Garapick	Montreal	July 21, 1976
200 m	2:14.23	Cheryl Gibson	Berlin	Aug. 24, 1978
Breaststroke				
100 m	1:08.86	Allison Higson	Seoul	Sept. 23, 1988
200 m	2:27.27	Allison Higson	Montreal	May 29, 1988
Butterfly				
100 m	1:01.18	Kristin Topham	Vancouver	Aug. 31, 1991
200 m	2:11.48	Jill Horstead	Montreal	July 31, 1985

▶

Event	Time	Swimmer	Site	Date
I.M.				
200 m	2:15.15	Marianne Limpert	Montreal.	May 17, 1992
400 m	4:45.58	Nancy Sweetnam	Montreal.	May 13, 1992
Relays				
Freestyle				
100 m	3:45.89	1994 National Team	Rome	Sept. 7, 1994
		Marianne Limpert, Shannon Shakespeare,		
		Jessica Amey, Joanne Malar		
200 m	8:10.65	1993 Canadian National Team	Kobe	Aug. 13, 1993
		Kathy Bald, Patricia Noall,		
		Andrea Nugent, Jane Kerr		
Medley				
100 m	4:09.26	1992 Olympic Team	Barcelona	July 14, 1992
		Nikki Dryden, Guylaine Cloutier,		
		Kristin Topham, Andrea Nugent		

Men

Event	Time	Swimmer	Site	Date
Freestyle				
50 m	22.81	Mark Andrews	Indianapolis.	Apr. 10, 1988
100 m	50.18	Stephen Clarke	Rome	Sept. 7, 1994
200 m	1:49.71	Turlough O'Hare	Perth.	Jan. 7, 199
400 m	3:50.49	Peter Szmidt	Etobicoke	July 16, 1980
800 m	8:00.22	Chris Bowie	Etobicoke.	Aug. 3, 1990
1 500 m	15:12.63	Harry Taylor	Auckland, N.Z.	Jan. 30, 1990
Backstroke				
100 m	53.98[1]	Mark Tewksbury.	Barcelona	July 30, 1992
200 m	2:00.54	Kevin Draxinger	Edmonton.	Aug. 24, 1991
Breaststroke				
100 m	1:01.99	Victor Davis	Los Angeles.	July 29, 1984
200 m	2:13.34	Victor Davis	Los Angeles	Aug. 2, 1984
Butterfly				
100 m	53.73	Marcel Gery	Gothenburg	Feb. 14, 1990
200 m	1:58.14	Tom Ponting	Montreal.	May 31, 1988
Individual Medley				
200 m	2:01.42	Alex Baumann	Los Angeles	Aug. 4, 1984
400 m	4:17.41	Alex Baumann	Los Angeles.	July 30, 1984
Relays				
Freestyle				
100 m	3:21.74	1987 Canadian National Team	Brisbane	Aug., 1987
		Vlastimil Cerny, Sandy Goss,		
		Blair Hicken, Marcel Gery		
200 m	7:22.74	1991 World Championships Team.	Perth	Jan. 8, 1991
		Eddie Parenti, Paul Szekula,		
		Darren Ward, Turlough O'Hare		
Medley				
100 m	3:39.28	1988 Olympic Team	Seoul	Sept. 25, 1988
		Mark Tewksbury, Victor Davis,		
		Tom Ponting, Sandy Goss		

Source: *Swim Magazine*   (1) Olympic record

Canadian Alpine Skiing Champions, 1979–94

Men

	Downhill	Slalom	Giant Slalom	Super Giant Slalom
1979	Ken Read	Raymond Pratte	Peter Monod	—
1980	Ken Read	Peter Monod	Peter Monod	—
1981	Robin McLeish	Peter Monod	Peter Monod	—
1982	Urs Raeber (SUI)	Peter Monod	Jim Read	—
1983	Steve Podborski	Francois Jodoin	Mike Tommy	—
1984	Steve Podborski	Mike Tommy	Jim Read	Jim Read
1985	Steven Lee (AUS)	Gordon Perry	Jim Read	Mike Brown (USA)
1986	Don Stevens	Jim Read	Jim Read	Derek Trussler
1987	Brian Stemmle	Alain Villiard	Alain Villiard	Jim Read
1988	Steven Lee (AUS)	Jack Miller (USA)	Tiger Shaw (USA)	Leonard Stock (AUT)
1989	Mike Carney	Alain Villiard	Alain Villiard	Felix Belczyk
1990	Felix Belczyk	Rob Crossan	Robbie Parisien	David Duchesne
1991	Edi Podivinsky	Eric Villiard	Eric Villiard	Rob Boyd
1992	Reggie Crist (USA)	Rob Crossan	Thomas Grandi	Reggie Crist (USA)
1993	John Mealey	Rob Crossan	Thomas Grandi	Eric Villiard
1994	Ralf Socher	Stanley Hayer	Christopher Pickett (US)	Ralf Socher

Women

	Downhill	Slalom	Giant Slalom	Super Giant Slalom
1979	Lani Kletl	Kathy Kreiner	Judy Richardson	—
1980	Laurie Graham	Lynn Lacasse	Ann Blackburn	—
1981	Gerry Sorensen	Josée Lacasse	Diana Haight	—
1982	Dianne Lehodey	Lynn Lacasse	Lynn Lacasse	—
1983	Gerry Sorensen	Lynn Lacasse	Liisa Savijarvi	—
1984	Diana Haight	Andréa Bedard	Liisa Savijarvi	Laurie Graham
1985	Laurie Graham	Andréa Bedard	Liisa Savijarvi	Karen Percy
1986	Karen Percy	Josée Lacasse	Josée Lacasse	Karen Percy
1987	Liisa Savijarvi	Julie Klotz	Josée Lacasse	Karen Percy
1988	Laurie Graham	Josée Lacasse	Karen Percy	Karen Percy
1989	Lucie LaRoche	Sonja Rusch	Karen Percy	Kendra Kobelka
1990	Lucie LaRoche	Josée Lacasse	Josée Lacasse	Nancy Gee
1991	Kerrin Lee-Gartner	Sonja Rusch	Annie Laurendeau	Michelle McKendry
1992	Kerrin Lee-Gartner	Annie Laurendeau	Michelle McKendry	Michelle McKendry
1993	Kerrin Lee-Gartner	Nanci Gee	Melanie Turgeon	Michelle Ruthven*
1994	Kate Pace	Katarina Tichy (Czech)	Edith Rozsa	Michelle Ruthven

Source: *Alpine Canada*

*Michelle McKendry's married name is Ruthven

Figure Skating Champions, 1952–94

	Canadian Champions		World Champions	
	Men	**Women**	**Men**	**Women**
1952	Peter Firstbrook	Marlene Smith	Richard Button, U.S.	Jacqueline du Bief, France
1953	Peter Firstbrook	Barbara Gratton	Hayes Jenkins, U.S.	Tenley Albright, U.S.
1954	Charles Snelling	Barbara Gratton	Hayes Jenkins, U.S.	Gundi Busch, W. Germany
1955	Charles Snelling	Carole Jane Pachl	Hayes Jenkins, U.S.	Tenley Albright, U.S.
1956	Charles Snelling	Carole Jane Pachl	Hayes Jenkins, U.S.	Carol Heiss, U.S.
1957	Charles Snelling	Carole Jane Pachl	Dave Jenkins, U.S.	Carol Heiss, U.S.
1958	Charles Snelling	Margaret Crosland	Dave Jenkins, U.S.	Carol Heiss, U.S.
1959	Donald Jackson	Margaret Crosland	Dave Jenkins, U.S.	Carol Heiss, U.S.
1960	Donald Jackson	Wendy Griner	Alain Giletti, France	Carol Heiss, U.S.
1961	Donald Jackson	Wendy Griner	none[1]	none[1]
1962	Donald Jackson	Wendy Griner	Don Jackson, Canada	Sjoukje Dijkstra, Neth.
1963	Donald McPherson	Wendy Griner	Don McPherson, Canada	Sjoukje Dijkstra, Neth.
1964	Charles Snelling	Petra Burka	Manfred Schnelldorfer, W. Germany	Sjoukje Dijkstra, Neth.
1965	Donald Knight	Petra Burka	Alain Calmat, France	Petra Burka, Canada
1966	Donald Knight	Petra Burka	Emmerich Danzer, Austria	Peggy Fleming, U.S.
1967	Donald Knight	Valerie Jones	Emmerich Danzer, Austria	Peggy Fleming, U.S.
1968	Jay Humphry	Karen Magnussen	Emmerich Danzer, Austria	Peggy Fleming, U.S.
1969	Jay Humphry	Linda Carbonetto	Tim Wood, U.S.	Gabriele Seyfert, E. Germany
1970	David McGillivray	Karen Magnussen	Tim Wood, U.S.	Gabriele Seyfert, E. Germany
1971	Toller Cranston	Karen Magnussen	Ondrej Nepela, Czech.	Beatrix Schuba, Austria
1972	Toller Cranston	Karen Magnussen	Ondrej Nepela, Czech.	Beatrix Schuba, Austria
1973	Toller Cranston	Karen Magnussen	Ondrej Nepela, Czech.	Karen Magnussen, Canada
1974	Toller Cranston	Lynn Nightingale	Jan Hoffman, E. Germany	Christine Errath, E. Germany
1975	Toller Cranston	Lynn Nightingale	Sergei Volkov, USSR	Dianne de Leeuw, Neth.-U.S.
1976	Toller Cranston	Lynn Nightingale	John Curry, Gr. Brit.	Dorothy Hamill, U.S.
1977	Ron Shaver	Lynn Nightingale	Vladimir Kovalev, USSR	Linda Fratianne, U.S.
1978	Brian Pockar	Heather Kemkaran	Charles Tickner, U.S.	Anett Poetzsch, E. Germany
1979	Brian Pockar	Janet Morrisey	Vladimir Kovalev, USSR	Linda Fratianne, U.S.
1980	Brian Pockar	Heather Kemkaran	Jan Hoffmann, E. Germany	Anett Poetzsch, E. Germany
1981	Brian Orser	Tracey Wainman	Scott Hamilton, U.S.	Denise Biellmann, Switzerland
1982	Brian Orser	Kay Thomson	Scott Hamilton, U.S.	Elaine Zayak, U.S.
1983	Brian Orser	Kay Thomson	Scott Hamilton, U.S.	Rosalyn Sumners, U.S.
1984	Brian Orser	Kay Thomson	Scott Hamilton, U.S.	Katarina Witt, E. Germany
1985	Brian Orser	Elizabeth Manley	Alexandre Fadeev, USSR	Katarina Witt, E. Germany
1986	Brian Orser	Tracey Wainman	Brian Boitano, U.S.	Debi Thomas, U.S.
1987	Brian Orser	Elizabeth Manley	Brian Orser, Canada	Katarina Witt, E. Germany
1988	Brian Orser	Elizabeth Manley	Brian Boitano, U.S.	Katarina Witt, E. Germany
1989	Kurt Browning	Karen Preston	Kurt Browning, Canada	Midori Ito, Japan
1990	Kurt Browning	Lisa Sargeant	Kurt Browning, Canada	Jill Trenary, U.S.
1991	Kurt Browning	Josée Chouinard	Kurt Browning, Canada	Kristi Yamaguchi, U.S.
1992	Michael Slipchuk	Karen Preston	Victor Petrenko, Russia	Kristi Yamaguchi, U.S.
1993	Kurt Browning	Josée Chouinard	Kurt Browning, Canada	Oksana Baiul, Ukraine
1994	Elvis Stojko	Josée Chouinard	Elvis Stojko, Canada	Yuka Sato, Japan

Source: *Canadian Figure Skating Association*

(1) The 1961 world championships were cancelled after an air crash killed the entire U.S. team travelling to the competition.

Canadian Open Golf Tournament, 1904–94

	Winner	Score		Winner	Score
1904	J.H. Oke	156	**1952**	John Palmer	263
1905	George Cumming	146	**1953**	Dave Douglas	273
1906	Charles Murray	170	**1954**	Pat Fletcher[1]	280
1907	Percy Barrett	306	**1955**	Arnold Palmer	265
1908	Albert Murray	300	**1956**	Doug Sanders	273
1909	Karl Keffer	309	**1957**	George Bayer	271
1910	Daniel Kenny	303	**1958**	Wesley Ellis Jr.	267
1911	Charles Murray	314	**1959**	Doug Ford	276
1912	George Sargent	299	**1960**	Art Wall Jr.	269
1913	Albert Murray	295	**1961**	Jacky Cupit	270
1914	Karl Keffer	300	**1962**	Ted Kroll	278
1915–1918	No Tournament		**1963**	Doug Ford	280
1919	J. Douglas Edgar	278	**1964**	Kel Nagle	277
1920	J. Douglas Edgar	298	**1965**	Gene Littler	273
1921	W.H. Trovinger	293	**1966**	Don Massengale	280
1922	Al Watrous	303	**1967**	Bill Casper	279
1923	C.W. Hackney	295	**1968**	Bob Charles	274
1924	Leo Diegel	285	**1969**	Tommy Aaron	275
1925	Leo Diegel	295	**1970**	Kermit Zarley	279
1926	Macdonald Smith	283	**1971**	Lee Trevino	275
1927	T.D. Armour	288	**1972**	Gay Brewer	275
1928	Leo Diegel	282	**1973**	Tom Weiskopf	278
1929	Leo Diegel	274	**1974**	Bobby Nichols	270
1930	T.D. Armour	277	**1975**	Tom Weiskopf	274
1931	Walter Hagen	292	**1976**	Jerry Pate	267
1932	Harry Cooper	290	**1977**	Lee Trevino	280
1933	Joe Kirkwood	282	**1978**	Bruce Lietzke	283
1934	T.D. Armour	287	**1979**	Lee Trevino	281
1935	Gene Kunes	280	**1980**	Bob Gilder	274
1936	Lawson Little	271	**1981**	Peter Oosterhuis	280
1937	Harry Cooper	285	**1982**	Bruce Lietzke	277
1938	Sam Snead	277	**1983**	John Cook	277
1939	Harold McSpaden	282	**1984**	Greg Norman	278
1940	Sam Snead	281	**1985**	Curtis Strange	279
1941	Sam Snead	274	**1986**	Bob Murphy	280
1942	Craig Wood	275	**1987**	Curtis Strange	276
1943–1944	No Tournament		**1988**	Ken Green	275
1945	Byron Nelson	280	**1989**	Steve Jones	271
1946	George Fazio	278	**1990**	Wayne Levi	278
1947	Robert Locke	268	**1991**	Nick Price	273
1948	C.W. Congdon	280	**1992**	Greg Norman	280
1949	E.J. Dutch Harrison	271	**1993**	David Frost	279
1950	Jim Ferrier	271	**1994**	Nick Price	275
1951	Jim Ferrier	273			

Source: *Royal Canadian Golf Association*

(1) Last Canadian winner.

Du Maurier Ltd. Women's Golf Classic, 1973–94

Winner	Score	Winner	Score
1973[1] Jocelyne Bourassa	214	1984 Juli Inkster	274
1974[1] Carol Jo Skala	208	1985 Pat Bradley	278
1975[1] JoAnne Carner	214	1986 Pat Bradley	276
1976[1] Donna Caponi Young	212	1987 Jodi Rosenthal	272
1977[1] Judy T. Rankin	212	1988 Sally Little	279
1978 JoAnne Carner	278	1989 Tammie Green	279
1979 Amy Alcott	285	1990 Cathy Johnston	276
1980 Pat Bradley	277	1991 Nancy Scranton	279
1981 Jan Stephenson	278	1992 Sherri Steinhauer	277
1982 Sandra Haynie	280	1993 Brandie Burton[2]	277
1983 Hollis Stacy	277	1994 Martha Nause	279

(1) Three rounds only. (2) Won on first playoff hole vs. Betsy King.

The Queen's Plate, 1920–94

The Queen's Plate, first run in 1860, is North America's oldest annual sports event. The race for 3-year-olds foaled in Canada, is run at Toronto's Woodbine Race Track in late June or July.

	Winner	Jockey	Time[1]		Winner	Jockey	Time[1]
1920	St. Paul	Roxy Romanelli	2:09	1958	Calendon Beau	Al Coy	2:04.1
1921	Herendesy	Jimmy Butwell	2:10	1959	New Providence	Robert Ussery	2:04.4
1922	South Shore	Kenny Parrington	2:12	1960	Victoria Park	Avelino Gomez	2:02
1923	Flowerful	Terry Wilson	2:11	1961	Blue Light	Hugo Dittfach	2:05
1924	Maternal Pride	George Walls	1:57.3	1962	Flaming Page	Jim Fitzsimmons	2:04.3
1925	Fairbank	Chick Lang	1:56.2	1963	Canebora	Manuel Ycaza	2:04
1926	Haplite	Henry Erickson	1:59.3	1964	Northern Dancer	Bill Hartack	2:02.1
1927	Troutlet	Francis Horn	1:55.4	1965	Whistling Sea	Tak Inouye	2:03.4
1928	Young Kitty	Lester Pichon	1:57	1966	Titled Hero	Avelino Gomez	2:03.3
1929	Shorelint	Jaydee Mooney	1:57.3	1967	Jammed Lovely	Jim Fitzsimmons	2:03
1930	Aymond	Henry Little	1:57.1	1968	Merger	Wayne Harris	2:05.2
1931	Froth Blower	Frank Mann	1:59.1	1969	Jumpin Joseph	Avelino Gomez	2:04.1
1932	Queensway	Frank Mann	1:55.1	1970	Almoner	Sandy Hawley	2:04.4
1933	King O'Connor	Eddie Legere	1:56.2	1971	Kennedy Road	Sandy Hawley	2:03
1934	Horometer	Frank Mann	1:54.1	1972	Victoria Song	Robin Platts	2:03.1
1935	Sally Fuller	Herb Lindberg	1:55.1	1973	Royal Chocolate	Ted Colangelo	2:08
1936	Monsweep	Danny Brammer	1:55	1974	Amber Herod	Robin Platts	2:09.1
1937	Goldlure	Sterling Young	1:55.2	1975	L'Enjoleur	Sandy Hawley	2:02.3
1938	Bunty Lawless	John Bailey	1:54.2	1976	Norcliffe	Jeffrey Fell	2:05
1939	Archworth	Sydney D. Birley	1:54.2	1977	Sound Reason	Robin Platts	2:06.3
1940	Willie the Kid	Ronnie Nash	1:55.4	1978	Regal Embrace	Sandy Hawley	2:02
1941	Budpath	Bobby Watson	1:56.4	1979	Steady Growth	Brian Swatuk	2:06.3
1942	Ten to Ace	Charlie Smith	1:57.4	1980	Driving Home	Bill Parsons	2:04.1
1943	Paolita	Pat Remillard	2:02.3	1981	Fiddle Dancer Boy	David Clark	2:04.4
1944	Acara	Bobby Watson	1:54.4	1982	Son of Briartic	John-Paul Souter	2:04.3
1945	Uttermost	Bobby Watson	1:53.4	1983	Bompago	Larry Attard	2:04.1
1946	Kingarvie	Johnny Dewhurst	1:55.3	1984	Key to the Moon	Robin Platts	2:03.4
1947	Moldy	Colin McDonald	1:54.1	1985	La Lorgnette	David Clark	2:04.3
1948	Last Mark	Howard Bailey	1:52	1986	Golden Choice	Vince Bracciale	2:07.1
1949	Epic	Chris Rogers	1:52.1	1987	Market Control	Ken Skinner	2:03.2
1950	McGill	Chris Rogers	1:52.2	1988	Regal Intention	Jack Lauzon	2:06.1
1951	Major Factor	Alf Bavington	1:53	1989	With Approval	Don Seymour	2:03
1952	Epigram	Gil Robillard	1:58.3	1990	Izvestia	Don Seymour	2:01.4
1953	Canadiana	Eddie Arcaro	1:52.1	1991	Dance Smartly	Pal Day	2:03.2
1954	Collisteo	Chris Rogers	1:52	1992	Alydeed	Craig Perret	2:04.6
1955	Ace Marine	George Walker	1:52.2	1993	Peteski	Craig Perret	2:04.2
1956	Canadian Champ	Dave Stevenson	1:55	1994	Basquean	Jack Laron	2:03.4
1957	Lyford Cay	Avelino Gomez	2:02.3				

Source: *Ontario Jockey Club*

(1) Fractions of a second are in fifths.

1994 U.S. Triple Crown Winners

Race	Winner	Jockey
Kentucky Derby	Go for Gin	Chris McCarron
Preakness	Tabasco Cat	Pat Day
Belmont Stakes	Tabasco Cat	Pat Day

Prince of Wales Stakes, 1960–94

	Winner	Jockey	Time[1]		Winner	Jockey	Time[1]
1960	Bulpamiru	Hugo Dittfach	2:19.4	1978	Overskate	Robin Platts	2:34.2
1961	Song of Even	Jim Fitzsimmons	2:29.0	1979	Mass Rally	George Ho Sang	2:33.2
1962	King Gorm	Hugo Dittfach	2:21.1	1980	Allan Blue	Joe Belowus	2:34.4
1963	Canebora	Hugo Dittfach	2:30.3	1981	Cadet Corps	Robin Platts	2:34.4
1964	Canadillis	Avelino Gomez	2:35.0	1982	Runaway Groom	Robin Platts	2:38.2
1965	Good Old Mort	S. McComb	2:22.4	1983	Archdeacon	Vince Bracciale	2:32.0
1966	He's A Smoothie	Hugo Dittfach	2:19.0	1984	Val Dansant	John LeBlanc	2:48.3
1967	Battling	Hugo Dittfach	2:21.0	1985	Imperial Choice	Irwin Driedger	2:34.3
1968	Rouletabille	Richard Grubb	2:18.3	1986	Golden Choice	Vince Bracciale	2:44.2
1969	Sharp-Eyed Quillo	H. Gustines	2:16.3	1987	Coryphee	Brian Swatuk	2:39.3
1970	Almoner	Sandy Hawley	2:19.4	1988	Regal Classic	Sandy Hawley	2:00.1
1971	New Pro	Jim Kelly	2:15.1	1989	With Approval	Don Seymour	1:56.4
1972	Presidial	John LeBlanc	2:16.3	1990	Izvestia	Don Seymour	1:56.2
1973	Tara Road	Sandy Hawley	2:16.4	1991	Dance Smartly	Pal Day	1:56.3
1974	Rushton's Corsair	Jim Kelly	2:23.2	1992	Benburb	Larry Attard	1:57.2
1975	L'Enjoleur	Sandy Hawley	2:32.2	1993	Peteski	Dave Penna[2]	1:34.4
1976	Norcliffe	Jeff Fell	2:30.1	1994	Bruce's Mill	Craig Perret	1:53.4
1977	Dance in Time	Gary Stahlbaum	2:31.4				

Source: *Ontario Jockey Club*

(1) Fractions of a second are in fifths. (2) Peteski's regular jockey, Craig Perret, was serving a 15-day suspension.

Breeders Stakes, 1960–93

Year	Winner	Jockey	Time[1]	Year	Winner	Jockey	Time[1]
1960	Hidden Treasure	Al Coy	2:34.2	1971	Belle Geste	Noel Turcotte	2:28
1961	Song of Even	Jim Fitzsimmons	2:31.3	1972	Nice Dancer	Sandy Hawley	2:35.4
1962	Crafty Lace	Ron Turcotte	2:52	1973	Come In Dad	Wayne Green	2:33.3
1963	Canebora	Manuel Ycaza	2:32.1	1974	Haymaker's Jig	Robin Platts	2:30.4
1964	Artic Hills	R. Armstrong	2:33.3	1975	Momigi	Gary Melanson	2:38.1
1965	Good Old Mort	P. Kallai	2:43	1976	Tiny Tinker	Sandy Hawley	2:31.1
1966	Titled Hero	Avelino Gomez	2:31.2	1977	Dance in Time	Gary Stahlbaum	3:01.3
1967	Pine Point	Avelino Gomez	2:32.1	1978	Overskate	Robin Platts	2:29.2
1968	No Parando	John LeBlanc	2:30	1979	Bridle Path	Sandy Hawley	2:29.3
1969	Grey Whiz	John LeBlanc	2:29	1980	Ben Fab	Gary Stahlbaum	2:31.3
1970	Mary of Scotland	Richard Grubb	2:38.2	1981	Social Wizard	George Ho Sang	2:48.4

Year	Winner	Jockey	Time[1]	Year	Winner	Jockey	Time[1]
1982	Runaway Groom	Robin Platts	2:32.1	1989	With Approval	Don Seymour	2:29
1983	Kingsbridge	Robin Platts	2:32.2	1990	Izvestia	Don Seymour	2:33.2
1984	Bounding Away	David Clark	2:32.3	1991	Dance Smartly	Pal Day	2:31.2
1985	Crowning Honors	Brian Swatuk	2:50	1992	Blitzer	Don Seymour	2:35.3
1986	Carotene	Richard Dos Ramos	2:32.3	1993	Peteski	Craig Perret	2:30.4
1987	Hangin On a Star	Dave Penna	2:30	1994	Basqueian	Jack Lauzon	2:47.4
1988	King's Deputy	Sandy Hawley	2:30.3				

Source: *Ontario Jockey Club*   (1) Fractions of a second are in fifths.

World Track and Field Records

(as of Sept. 1994)

Men

Event	Record	Holder/Country	Date	Where Made
■ Running				
100 m	9.85	Leroy Burrell, U.S.	July 6, 1994	Lausanne, Switz
200 m	19.72	Pietro Mennea, Italy	Sept. 12, 1979	Mexico City
400 m	43.29	Harry Reynolds, U.S.	Aug. 17, 1988	Zurich
800 m	1:41.7	Sebastian Coe, Gr. Britain	June 10, 1981	Florence
1 000 m	2:12.181	Sebastian Coe, Gr. Britain	July 11, 1981	Oslo
1 500 m	3:28.86	Nourredine Morceli, Algeria	Sept. 6, 1992	Rieti, Italy
1 mile	3:44.39	Nourredine Morceli, Algeria	Sept. 4, 1993	Rieti, Italy
2 000 m	4:50.81	Said Aouita, Morocco	July 16, 1987	Paris
3 000 m	7:25.11	Nourredine Morceli, Algeria	Aug. 2, 1994	Monte Carlo
5 000 m	12:58.39	Said Aouita, Morocco	July 22, 1987	Rome
10 000 m	26:52.23	William Segei, Kenya	July 22, 1994	Oslo
20 000 m	56:55.60	Arturo Barrios, Mexico	Mar. 30, 1991	La Fleche
25 000 m	1.13:55.80	Toshihiko Seko, Japan	Mar. 22 1981	Christchurch, N.Z.
30 000 m	1.29:18.80	Toshihiko Seko, Japan	Mar. 22, 1981	Christchurch, N.Z.
3 000 m steeplechase	8:05.35	Peter Koech, Kenya	July 3, 1989	Stockholm
Marathon	2.06:06.50	Belayneh Dinsamo, Ethiopia	Apr. 17, 1988	Rotterdam
■ Hurdles				
110 m	12.91	Colin Jackson, Gr. Britain	Aug. 20 1993	Stuttgart
400 m	46.78	Kevin Young, U.S.	Aug. 6, 1992	Barcelona
■ Relay Races				
100 m	37.40	(Marsh, Burrell, Mitchell, Lewis), U.S.	Aug. 8, 1992	Barcelona
	37.40	(Drummond, Cason, Mitchell, Burrell), U.S.	Aug. 21, 1993	
800 m	7:03.89	(Elliott, Cook, Cram, Coe), Gr. Britain	Aug. 30, 1982	London
■ Field Events				
High jump	2.44 m	Javier Sotomayor, Cuba	July 27, 1993	Salamanca, Spain
Long jump	8.95 m	Mike Powell, U.S.	Aug. 30, 1991	Tokyo
Triple jump	17.97 m	Willie Banks, U.S.	June 16, 1985	Indianapolis
Pole vault	6.14 m	Sergey Bubka, Ukraine	Aug. 30, 1992	Tokyo
7.26 kg shot put	23.12 m	Randolph Barnes, U.S.	May 20, 1990	Los Angeles
Discus throw	74.08 m	Jurgen Schult, E. Germany	June 6, 1986	E. Germany
Javelin throw	91.46 m	Steve Backley, Gr. Britain	Jan. 25, 1992	Auckland, N.Z.
7.26 kg hammer throw	86.74 m	Yuri Sedykh, USSR	Aug. 30, 1986	Stuttgart
Decathlon	8 847 pts.	Daley Thompson, Gr. Britain	Aug. 8–9, 1984	Los Angeles

▶

▶ ■ **Walking**

30 km	2.03:56.51	Thierry Toutain, France	Mar. 24, 1991	Hericourt
50 km	3.37:00.41	Andrey Perlov, USSR	Aug. 5, 1989	Leningrad

Women

Event	Record	Holder/Country	Date	Where Made
■ Running				
100 m	10.49	Florence Griffith-Joyner, U.S.	July 16, 1988	Indianapolis
200 m	21.34	Florence Griffith-Joyner, U.S.	Sept. 29, 1988	Seoul
400 m	47.60	Marita Koch, E. Germany	Oct. 6, 1985	Canberra
800 m	1:53.28	Jarmila Kratochvilova, Czech.	July 26, 1983	Munich
1 500 m	3:50.46	Qu Yunxia, China	Sept. 11, 1993	Beijing
1 mile	4:15.61	Paula Ivan, Romania	July 10, 1989	Nice
2 000 m	5:28.69	Maricica Puica, Romania	July 11, 1986	London
3 000 m	8:06.11	Wang Junxia, China	Sept. 13, 1993	Beijing
5 000 m	14:37.33	Ingrid Kristiansen, Norway	Aug. 5, 1986	Stockholm
10 000 m	29:31.78	Wang Junxia, China	Sept. 8, 1993	Beijing
30 000 m	1:47:05.6	Karolina Szabo, Hungary	Apr. 22, 1988	Budapest
Marathon	2:21:06.00	Ingrid Kristiansen, Norway	Apr. 21, 1985	London
■ Hurdles				
100 m	12.21	Yordanka Donkova, Bulgaria	Aug. 20, 1988	Stara Zagora
400 m	52.74	Sally Gunnell, Gr. Britain	Aug. 19, 1993	Stuttgart
■ Field Events				
High jump	2.09 m	Stefka Kostadinova, Bulgaria	Aug. 8, 1987	Rome
Shot put	22.63 m	Natalya Lisovskaya, USSR	June 7, 1987	Moscow
Long jump	7.52 m	Galina Christyakova, USSR	June 11, 1988	Leningrad
Discus throw	76.80	Gabriele Reinsch, E. Germany	July 9, 1988	Neubrandenburg
Javelin	80.00 m	Petra Felke, E. Germany	Sept. 9, 1988	Potsdam
Heptathlon	7 291 pts.	Jackie Joyner-Kersee, U.S.	Sept. 24, 1988	Seoul
Triple jump	15.09 m	Ana Biryukova, Russia	Aug. 21, 1993	Stuttgart
Hammer throw	64.44 m	Alla Fyodorova, USSR	Feb. 26, 1991	Adler, USSR
■ Relay Races				
100m	41.37	National team, E. Germany	Oct. 6, 1985	Canberra
200m	1:28.15	National team, E. Germany	Aug. 9, 1980	Jena, E. Germany
400m	3:15.17	National team, USSR	Oct. 1, 1988	Seoul
800m	7:50.17	National team, USSR	Aug. 5, 1984	Moscow
■ Walking				
5 000 m	20:17.19	Kerry Saxby, Australia	Jan. 14, 1990	Sydney
10 000 m	41:56.23	Nadezhda Ryashkina, USSR	July 24, 1990	Seattle

Source: *Canadian Track and Field Association*   (1) Record set at high altitude. (*) Pending ratification.

Auto Racing

Molson Indy

Toronto

1986: Bobby Rahal
1987: Emerson Fittipaldi
1988: Al Unser Jr.
1989: Michael Andretti
1990: Al Unser Jr.
1991: Michael Andretti
1992: Michael Andretti
1993: Paul Tracy*
1994: Michael Adretti

Vancouver

1990: Al Unser Jr.
1991: Michael Andretti
1992: Michael Andretti
1993: Al Unser Jr.
1994: Al Unser Jr.

* Canadian

The America's Cup

Competition for the America's Cup grew out of the first contest to establish a world yachting championship, one of the carnival features of the London Exposition of 1851. The race, open to all classes of yachts from all over the world, covered a 60-mile course around the Isle of Wight; the prize was a cup worth about $500, donated by the Royal Yacht Squadron of England, known as the "America's Cup" because it was first won by the United States yacht *America*. Successive efforts of British and Australian yachtsmen had failed to win the famous trophy until 1983 when the Australian yacht *Australia II* defeated the US entry *Liberty*.

Winners of the America's Cup

1851 America
1870 Magic defeated Cambria, England (1-0)
1871 Columbia (first three races) and Sappho (last two races) defeated Livonia, England (4-1)
1876 Madeline defeated **Countess of Dufferin, Canada** (2-0)
1881 Mischief defeated **Atalanta, Canada** (2-0)
1885 Puritan defeated Genesta, England (2-0)
1886 Mayflower defeated Galatea, England (2-0)
1887 Volunteer defeated Thistle, Scotland (2-0)
1893 Vigilant defeated Valkyrie II, England (3-0)
1895 Defender defeated Valkyrie III, England (3-0)
1899 Columbia defeated Shamrock, England (3-0)
1901 Columbia defeated Shamrock II, England (3-0)
1903 Reliance defeated Shamrock III, England (3-0)
1920 Resolute defeated Shamrock IV, England (3-2)
1930 Enterprise defeated Shamrock V, England (4-0)

1934 Rainbow defeated Endeavour, England (4-2)
1937 Ranger defeated Endeavour II, England (4-0)
1958 Columbia defeated Sceptre, England (4-0)
1962 Weatherly defeated Gretel, Australia (4-1)
1964 Constellation defeated Sovereign, England (4-0)
1967 Intrepid defeated Dame Pattie, Australia (4-0)
1970 Intrepid defeated Gretel II, Australia (4-1)
1974 Courageous defeated Southern Cross, Australia (4-0)
1977 Courageous defeated Australia, Australia (4-0)
1980 Freedom defeated Australia, Australia (4-1)
1983 Australia II, Australia defeated Liberty, (4-3)
1987 Stars & Stripes defeated Kookaburra III, Australia (4-0)
1988 Stars & Stripes defeated New Zealand, New Zealand (2-0) (New Zealand awarded forfeit)
1992 America 3 defeated Il Moro de Venezia, Italy (4-1)

Canadian Sports Hall of Fame

(living members as of Sept. 1994)

Anakin, Douglas, bobsled
Apps, Syl, hockey
Arnold, Don, rowing
Athans, George, Jr., water skiing
Balding, Al, golf
Baldwin, Matt, curling
Baumann, Alex, swimming
Béliveau, Jean, hockey
Bell, Florence, track relay
Bell, Marilyn, marathon swimming
Bernier, Sylvie, diving
Bionda, Jack, lacrosse
Blake, Hector (Toe), hockey builder
Boldt, Arnie, field high jump
Boucher, Gaetan, speed skating
Box, Ab, football
Boys, Bev, diving
Brooks, Lela, speed skating
Brouillard, Lou, boxing
*****Browning,** Kurt, figure skating
Burka, Petra, figure skating
Burka, Sylvia, speed skating
Callura, Jackie, boxing
Cameron, Michelle, synchro swimming
Chuvalo, George, boxing
Cliff, Leslie, swimming
Clifford, Betsy, skiing

Coleman, Jim, sports journalism
Côté, Gérard, marathon swimming
Cowan, Gary, golf
Cranston, Toller, figure skating
Crothers, Bill, track mid-distance
D'hondt, Walter, rowing
Dafoe, Frances, figure skating
Day, James, equestrian
Dexter, Glen, yachting
Drake, Clare, hockey builder
Drayton, Jerome, marathon running
Dryden, Ken, hockey
Duguid, Don, curling
Dunnell, Milt, all-around builder
Durrelle, Yvon, boxing
Eagleson, Alan, hockey builder
Elder, James, equestrian
Emery, Dr. John, bobsled
Emery, Victor, bobsled
Esaw, Johnny, all-around builder
Esposito, Phil, hockey
Filion, Hervé, harness racing
Fogh, Hans, yachting
Fortier, Sylvie, synchro swimming
Gabriel, Tony, football
Galbraith, Sheldon, figure sk. builder
Gate, George, swimming builder

▶ **Gaudaur**, Jake, Jr., football builder
Gayford, Tom, equestrian
***Geoffrion**, Bernard "Boom Boom," hockey
Golab, Tony, football
Graham, Laurie, skiing
Greene, Nancy, skiing
Grenier, Jean, speed skating builder
Gwynne, Horace, boxing
Hall, Glenn, hockey
Hanson, Fritz, football
Hartman, Barney, skeet shooting
Heggtveit, Anne, skiing
Hepburn, Doug, weightlifting
Hildebrand, Ike, lacrosse
Howe, Gordie, hockey
Hull, Bobby, hockey
Hungerford, George W., rowing
Huot, Jules, golf
Hutton, Ralph, swimming
Jackson, Donald, figure skating
Jackson, Dr. Roger, rowing
Jackson, Russ, football
Jelinek, Maria, figure skating
Jelinek, Otto, figure skating
Jenkins, Ferguson, baseball
Josenhans, Andreas, yachting
Juckes, Gordon, hockey builder
Kelly, Leonard (Red), hockey
Kidd, Bruce, track mid-distance
Kirby, Kirby, bobsled
Kreiner, Kathy, skiing
Krol, Joe, football
Kwong, Norm, football
Lancaster, Ron, football
***Le cavelier**, Rene, broadcasting
Leonard, Stan, golf
Lessard, Lucille, archery
Lévesque, Jean-Louis, equestrian
Lidstone, Dorothy, archery
Loney, Don, football builder
Longden, Johnny, horse racing
Loomer, Lorne, rowing
Lovell, Jocelyn, cycling
Luftspring, Sammy, boxing
MacDonald, Irene, diving
MacDonald, Noel, basketball
McKinnon, Archie, rowing
MacKinnon, Lt. Col. Dan, harness racing builder
McLarnin, Jimmy, boxing
MacMillan, Sandy, yachting
McNaughton, Duncan, field high jump
McPherson, Donald, figure skating
Magnussen, Karen, figure skating
Mahovlich, Frank, hockey
Marchildon, Phil, baseball
Martini, Paul, figure skating
Miles, John C., marathon swimming
Mitchell, Ray, bowling
Nattrass, Susan, trap shooting
Nicholas, Cindy, marathon swimming
Northcott, Ron, curling
O'Donnell, Bill, harness racing
***O'Neill**, James "Tip", baseball

Orr, Robert (Bobby), hockey
Orser, Brian, figure skating
***Ottenbrite**, Anne, swimming
***Parker**, Jackie, football
Paul, Robert, figure skating
Peden, Doug, multi-sport
***Percy**, Karen, skiing
Perry, Gordon, football
Podborski, Steve, skiing
Pollock, Sam, hockey builder
Porter, R.A. (Bobby), multi-sport
Post, Sandra, golf
Presley, Gerald, bobsled
Primrose, John, trap shooting
Ramage, Pat, skiing builder
Read, Ken, skiing
Reed, George, football
Richard, Henri, hockey
Richard, Maurice (Rocket), hockey
Richardson, Arnold, curling
Richardson, Ernie, curling
Richardson, Garnet, curling
Richardson, Wes, curling
Robertson, Bruce, swimming
Robinson, Graydon, bowling
Rogers, Doug, judo
Saunders, Claude, rowing builder
Schmidt, Milt, hockey
Schneider, Bert, boxing
Scott, Barbara Ann, figure skating
Seller, Peggy, synchro swimming
Shedd, Marjory, badminton
Smith, Graham, swimming
Sorensen, Gerry, skiing
Steen, Dave, decathlon
Stewart, Marlene, golf
Stewart, Nels, hockey
Stewart, Ron, football
Stirling, Hugh, football
Storey, R.A. (Red), all-around
Stukus, Annis, football builder
Sullivan, Jack, sports journalism
Tanner, Elaine, swimming
Taylor, Ron, baseball
Thom, Linda, shooting
Thompson, James, speedboating builder
Townsend, Cathy, bowling
Trifunov, James, wrestling
Turcotte, Ron, horse racing
Underhill, Barbara, figure skating
Vanderburg, Helen, synchro swimming
Wagner, Barbara, figure skating
Waldo, Carolyn, synchro swimming
Waples, Keith, harness racing
Watson, Ken J., curling
Weslock, Nick, golf
Wheeler, Lucille, skiing
Whitaker, Brig. Gen. Denis, equestrian builder
Wilson, Harold A., speed boating
Worrall, Jim, builder
Wright, Harold, builder
Young, Michael, bobsled

Source: *Canadian Sports Hall of Fame*

* New members in 1994

Canadian Press Athlete of the Year

	Male (Lionel Conacher Award)	Female
1932	**Somerville**, Sandy, golf	No award
1933	**Komonen**, Dave, track and field	**Mackenzie**, Ada, golf
1934	**Webster**, Harold, track and field	**Dewar**, Phyllis, swimming
1935	**Rankine**, Robert (Scotty), track and field	**Meagher**, Aileen, track and field
1936	**Edwards**, Phil, track and field	**Taylor**, Betty, track and field
1937	**Apps**, Syl, hockey	**Higgins**, Robina, track and field
1938	**Stirling**, Hugh (Bummer), football	**Macdonald**, Noel, basketball
1939	**Hanson**, Fritz, football	**Thacker**, Mary Rose, figure skating
1940	**Cote**, Gerard, track and field	**Walton**, Dorothy, badminton
1941	**Golab**, Tony, football	**Thacker**, Mary Rose, figure skating
1946	**Krol**, Joe, football	**Scott**, Barbara Ann, figure skating
1947	**Krol**, Joe, football	**Scott**, Barbara Ann, figure skating
1948	**O'Connor**, Buddy, hockey	**Scott**, Barbara Ann, figure skating
1949	**Filchock**, Frank, football	**Strong**, Irene, swimming
1950	**Conacher**, Lionel named athlete of the half century (no athlete of the year)	**Rosenfeld**, Bobbie, track and field, named athlete of the half century (no athlete of the year)
1952	**Richard**, Maurice, hockey	**Stewart**, Marlene, golf
1953	**Hepburn**, Doug, weightlifting	**Stewart**, Marlene, golf
1954	**Ferguson**, Rich, track and field	**Bell**, Marilyn, swimming
1955	**Kwong**, Normie, football	**Bell**, Marilyn, swimming
1956	**Beliveau**, Jean, hockey	**Stewart**, Marlene, golf
1957	**Richard**, Maurice, hockey	**Stewart**, Marlene, golf
1958	**Richard**, Maurice, hockey	**Wheeler**, Lucile, skiing
1959	**Jackson**, Russ, football	**Heggtveit**, Anne, skiing
1960	**Stewart**, Ron, football	**Heggtveit**, Anne, skiing
1961	**Kidd**, Bruce, track and field	**Stewart**, Mary, swimming
1962	**Kidd**, Bruce, track and field	**Stewart**, Mary, swimming
1963	**Howe**, Gordie, hockey	**Stewart Streit**, Marlene, golf
1964	**Crothers**, Bill, track and field	**Burka**, Petra, figure skating
1965	**Hull**, Bobby, hockey	**Burka**, Petra, figure skating
1966	**Hull**, Bobby, hockey	**Tanner**, Elaine, swimming
1967	**Jenkins**, Ferguson, baseball	**Greene**, Nancy, skiing
1968	**Jenkins**, Ferguson, baseball	**Greene**, Nancy, skiing
1969	**Jackson**, Russ, football	**Boys**, Beverley, diving
1970	**Orr**, Bobby, hockey	**Boys**, Beverley, diving
1971	**Jenkins**, Ferguson, baseball	**Van Kiekebelt**, Debbie, track and field; **Brill**, Debbie, track and field (tie)
1972	**Esposito**, Phil, hockey	**Bourassa**, Jocelyn, golf
1973	**Esposito**, Phil, hockey	**Magnussen**, Karen, figure skating
1974	**Jenkins**, Ferguson, baseball	**Cook**, Wendy, swimming
1975	**Clarke**, Bobby, hockey	**Garapick**, Nancy, swimming
1976	**Joy**, Greg, track and field	**Kreiner**, Kathy, skiing
1977	**Lafleur**, Guy, hockey	**Nicholas**, Cindy, swimming
1978	**Smith**, Graham, swimming	**Jones-Konihowski**, Diane, track and field
1979	**Villeneuve**, Gilles, auto racing	**Post**, Sandra, golf
1980	**Gretzky**, Wayne, hockey	**Post**, Sandra, golf
1981	**Gretzky**, Wayne, hockey	**Wainman**, Tracey, figure skating
1982	**Gretzky**, Wayne, hockey	**Sorensen**, Gerry, skiing
1983	**Gretzky**, Wayne, hockey	**Bassett**, Carling, tennis
1984	**Baumann**, Alex, swimming	**Bernier**, Sylvie, diving
1985	**Gretzky**, Wayne, hockey	**Bassett**, Carling, tennis
1986	**Johnson**, Ben, track and field	**Graham**, Laurie, skiing
1987	**Johnson**, Ben, track and field	**Waldo**, Carolyn, synchronized swimming
1988	**Lemieux**, Mario, hockey	**Waldo**, Carolyn, synchronized swimming
1989	**Gretzky**, Wayne, hockey	**Kelesi**, Helen, tennis
1990	**Browning**, Kurt, figure skating	**Kelesi**, Helen, tennis
1991	**Browning**, Kurt, figure skating	**Laumann**, Silken, rowing
1992	**Tewksbury**, Mark, swimming	**Laumann**, Silken, rowing
1993	**Lemieux**, Mario, hockey	**Pace**, Kate, skiing

Source: *Canadian Press*

QUICK REFERENCE

Canadian Imperial Measures

Name	Abbrev.	Equivalent in Related Units	Metric Equivalent
■ Length			
inch	in.	—	2.54 cm
foot	ft.	12 in.	30.48 cm
yard	yd.	3 ft.; 36 in.	0.91 m
mile	mi.	1 760 yd.; 5 280 ft.	1.609 km
■ Mass (Weight)			
grain	gr.	—	0.06 g
dram	dr.	27.343 gr.	1.77 g
ounce	oz.	16 dr.	28.35 g
pound	lb.	16 oz.	0.453 kg
hundredweight			
(short)	cwt.	100 lb.	45.36 kg
(long)	cwt.	112 lb.	50.80 kg
ton (short)	—	2 000 lb.	0.907 t
ton (long)	—	2 240 lb.	1.016 t
■ Volume and Capacity			
fluid dram	fl. dr.	0.22 cu. in.	3.55 cm^3
fluid ounce	fl. oz.	8 fl. dr.; 1.7 cu. in.	28.41 cm^3
pint	pt.	20 fl. oz.; 34.7 cu. in.	568.3 cm^3
quart	qt.	2 pt.; 69.4 cu. in.	1.14 dm^3
gallon	gal.	4 qt.; 277 cu. in.	4.55 dm^3
peck	pk.	2 gal.; 555 cu. in.	9.09 dm^3
bushel	bu.	4 pk.; 2 219 cu. in.	36.37 dm^3
barrel (oil)	bbl	35 gal.	0.159 m^3
cubic foot	ft.^{3}	1 728 in.^{3}	0.028 m^3
cubic yard	yd.^{3}	27 ft.^{3}	0.765 m^3
■ Area			
square foot	ft.^{2}	144 sq. in.	0.09 m^2
square yard	yd.^{2}	9 sq. ft.	0.836 m^2
acre	—	4 840 sq. yd.	4 047 m^2
square mile	sq. mi.	640 acres	2.590 km^2

Source: *Gage Canadian Dictionary*

Conversion Chart

(approximations)

FROM METRIC:

Symbol	When you know:	Multiply by:	To find:	Symbol
		Length		
mm	millimetres	0.04	inches	in.
cm	centimetres	0.4	inches	in.
m	metres	3.3	feet	ft.
m	metres	1.1	yards	yd.
km	kilometres	0.6	miles	m.

748

Symbol	When you know:	Multiply by:	To find:	Symbol
		Area		
cm²	square centimetres	0.16	square inches	in.²
m²	square metres	1.2	square yards	yd.²
km²	square kilometres	0.4	square miles	mi.²
ha	hectares (10 000m²)	2.5	acres	
		Mass (Weight)		
g	grams	0.035	ounce	oz.
kg	kilograms	2.2	pounds	lb.
t	tonnes (1 000kg)	1.1	short tons	
		Volume		
mL	millilitres	0.03	fluid ounces	fl.oz.
L	litres	2.1	pints	pt.
L	litres	1.06	quarts	qt.
L	litres	0.26	gallons (US)	gal. (US)
L	litres	0.22	gallons (Imp.)	gal. (Imp.)
m³	cubic metres	35	cubic feet	ft.³
m³	cubic metres	1.3	cubic yards	yd.³
		Temperature (Exact)		
°C	Celsius	9/5 (+32)	Fahrenheit	°F

TO METRIC:

Symbol	When you know:	Multiply by:	To find:	Symbol
		Length		
in.	inches	2.54 (exactly)	centimetres	cm
ft.	feet	30	centimetres	cm
yd.	yards	0.9	metres	m
m.	miles	1.6	kilometres	km
		Area		
in.²	square inches	6.5	square centimetres	cm²
ft.²	square feet	0.09	square metres	m²
yd.²	square yards	0.8	square metres	m²
mi.²	square miles	2.6	square kilometres	km²
	acres	0.4	hectares	ha
		Mass (Weight)		
oz.	ounces	28	grams	g
lb.	pounds	0.45	kilograms	kg
	short tons (2 000 lb.)	0.9	tonnes	t
		Volume		
tsp.	teaspoons	5	millilitres	mL
tbsp.	tablespoons	15	millilitres	mL
f.l oz.	fluid ounces	30	millilitres	mL
c.	cups	0.24	litres	L
pt.	pints	0.47	litres	L
qt.	quarts	0.95	litres	L
gal.	gallons (US)	3.8	litres	L
gal.	gallons (Imp.)	4.5	litres	L
ft.³	cubic feet	0.03	cubic metres	m³
yd.³	cubic yards	0.76	cubic metres	m³
		Temperature (Exact)		
°F	Fahrenheit temp.	(-32) 5/9	Celsius temp.	°C

Temperature Equivalents

(Celsius and Fahrenheit)

°C	°F	°C	°F	°C	°F	°C	°F	°C	°F
-50	-58	-30	-22	-10	14	10	50	30	86
-49	-56.2	-29	-20.2	-9	15.8	11	51.8	31	87.8
-48	-54.4	-28	-18.4	-8	17.6	12	53.6	32	89.6
-47	-52.6	-27	-16.6	-7	19.4	13	55.4	33	91.4
-46	-50.8	-26	-14.8	-6	21.2	14	57.2	34	93.2
-45	-49	-25	-13	-5	23	15	59	35	95
-44	-47.2	-24	-11.2	-4	24.8	16	60.8	36	96.8
-43	-45.4	-23	-9.4	-3	26.6	17	62.6	37	98.6
-42	-43.6	-22	-7.6	-2	28.4	18	64.4	38	100.4
-41	-41.8	-21	-5.8	-1	30.2	19	66.2	39	102.2
-40	-40	-20	-4	0	32	20	68	40	104
-39	-38.2	-19	-2.2	1	33.8	21	69.8	41	105.8
-38	-36.4	-18	-0.4	2	35.6	22	71.6	42	107.6
-37	-34.6	-17	1.4	3	37.4	23	73.4	43	109.4
-36	-32.8	-16	3.2	4	39.2	24	75.2	44	111.2
-35	-31	-15	5	5	41	25	77	45	113
-34	-29.2	-14	6.8	6	42.8	26	78.8	50	122
-33	-27.4	-13	8.6	7	44.6	27	80.6	100	212
-32	-25.6	-12	10.4	8	46.4	28	82.4	150	302
-31	-23.8	-11	12.2	9	48.2	29	84.2	200	392

Large Numbers

1 thousand	= 1 000
1 million	= 1 000 000 or 10^6
1 milliard: used in Europe, USSR, former French possessions	= 1 000 000 000 or 10^9
1 billion:	= 1 000 000 000 000 or 10^{12}
Canada, the United States and France	= 1 000 000 000 or 10^9
1 trillion:	= 1 000 000 000 000 000 000 or 10^{18}
Canada and the United States	= 1 000 000 000 000 or 10^{12}

Source: *World Weights and Measures*

Roman Numerals

I	1	VII	7	XX	20	C	100	$\overline{V}$	5 000
II	2	VIII	8	XXX	30	CC	200	$\overline{X}$	10 000
III	3	IX	9	XL	40	CD	400	$\overline{L}$	50 000
IV	4	X	10	L	50	D	500	$\overline{C}$	100 000
V	5	XI	11	LX	60	CM	900	$\overline{D}$	500 000
VI	6	XIX	19	XC	90	M	1 000	$\overline{M}$	1 000 000

The International System of Units (SI)

Name	Symbol	Quantity
■ SI Base Units		
metre	m	length
kilogram	kg	mass
second	s	time
ampere	A	electric current
kelvin	K	thermodynamic temperature
mole	mol	amount of substance
candela	cd	luminous intensity
■ SI Supplementary Units		
radian	rad	plane angle
steradian	sr	solid angle
■ Common SI Derived Units With Special Names		
hertz	Hz	frequency
pascal	Pa	pressure, stress
watt	W	power, radiant flux
volt	V	electric potential, electromotive force
newton	N	force
joule	J	energy, work
coulomb	C	electric charge
ohm	Ω	electric resistance
farad	F	electric capacitance
■ Common Units Used With the SI		
litre	L	volume or capacity (= 1 dm^3)
degree Celsius	°C	temperature (= 1 K; 0°C = 273.2 K)

Name	Symbol	Quantity
hectare	ha	area (= 10 000 m^2)
tonne	t	mass (= 1000 kg)
electronvolt	eV	energy (= 0.160 aJ)
nautical mile	M	distance (navigation) (= 1852 m)
knot	kn	speed (navigation) (= 1 M/h)
standard atmosphere	atm	atmospheric pressure (= 101.3 kPa)

■ SI Prefixes

Name	Symbol	Multiplying Factor*
exa-	E	10^{18}
peta-	P	10^{15}
tera-	T	10^{12}
giga-	G	10^9
mega-	M	10^6
kilo-	k	10^3
hecto-	h	10^2
deca-	da	10
deci-	d	10^{-1}
centi-	c	10^{-2}
milli-	m	10^{-3}
micro-	μ	10^{-6}
nano-	n	10^{-9}
pico-	p	10^{-12}
femto-	f	10^{-15}
atto-	a	10^{-18}

*10^2 = 100; 10^3 = 1 000; 10^{-1} = 0.1; 10^{-2} = 0.01; Thus, 2 km = 2 x 1 000 = 2 000 m ; 3 cm = 3 x 0.01 = 0.03 m

Source: *Gage Canadian Dictionary*

Birthstones

Month	Stone	Month	Stone	Month	Stone	Month	Stone
January	Garnet	April	Diamond	July	Ruby	October	Opal or tourmaline
February	Amethyst	May	Emerald	August	Sardonyx or peridot	November	Topaz
March	Aquamarine or bloodstone	June	Pearl, moonstone or alexandrite	September	Sapphire	December	Turquoise, zircon or lapis lazuli

Special Birthday and Anniversary Greetings

- ■ *Greetings from the **Prime Minister** are sent on the occasion of a 25th wedding anniversary or a 70th birthday.*
- ■ *Greetings from the **Governor General** are sent on the occasion of a 50th wedding anniversary or a 90th or 95th birthday.*
- ■ *Greetings from **Her Majesty the Queen** are sent on the occasion of a 60th wedding anniversary or a 100th birthday.*

Contact the office of your local Member of Parliament (federal) to arrange for the greetings to be sent. Allow at least 6 weeks notice.

Canada's Food Guide To Healthy Eating[1]

Canada's Food Guide, revised in November of 1992, recognizes that the amount of food each Canadian needs every day from the four food groups and other foods depends on age, body size, activity level, whether the individual is male or female, and if the individual is pregnant or breast-feeding. That's why the Food Guide gives a range of possible servings for each food group—young children can choose the lower number of recommended servings from a particular group, while male teenagers can go to the higher number. Most other people can choose servings somewhere in between.

Canada's Food Guide recommends, every day:

■ 5 to 12 servings from the grain products group. An example of one serving would be one slice of bread; 30 g of cold cereal or 175 mL of hot cereal. Two servings would be a bagel, pita or bun; or 250 mL of rice or pasta.

■ 5 to 10 servings of vegetables and fruit.

One serving would be one medium size vegetable or fruit; 125 mL of fresh, frozen or canned vegetables or fruit; 250 mL of salad; or 125 mL of juice.

■ 2 to 3 servings of meat or alternatives. One serving would be 50-100 g of meat, poultry or fish; 1-2 eggs; 125-250 mL of beans; 100 g of tofu; or 30 mL of peanut butter.

■ Recommended servings of milk products vary according to age: 2-3 servings for children aged 4-9; 3-4 servings for young people aged 10-16; 2-4 servings for adults; and 3-4 servings for pregnant or breast-feeding women. Examples of one serving would be 250 mL of milk, 50 g of cheese or 175 g of yogurt.

Taste and enjoyment can also come from other foods and beverages that are not part of the four food groups. Some of these foods are higher in fat or calories, so it is recommended that these foods be used in moderation. The important things to remember are: enjoy a variety of foods from each group every day and choose lower-fat foods more often.

Source: Health and Welfare Canada

(1) For people four years and over.

Functions of Nutrients

Calcium aids in the formation and maintenance of strong bones and teeth; promotes healthy nerve function and normal blood clotting.

Carbohydrate supplies energy; assists in the utilization of fats.

Fat supplies energy; aids in the absorption of fat-soluble vitamins.

Fibre provides undigestible bulk, which encourages the normal elimination of body wastes.

Folacin (folic acid) aids red blood cell formation.

Iodine aids in function of the thyroid gland.

Iron combines with protein to form hemoglobin, the red blood cell constituent that transports oxygen and carbon dioxide.

Magnesium aids in formation and maintenance of strong bones and teeth; aids in energy metabolism and tissue formation.

Phosphorus aids in formation and maintenance of strong bones and teeth.

Protein builds and repairs body tissues; builds antibodies, the blood components that fight infection.

Riboflavin (vitamin B_2) maintains healthy skin and eyes; maintains a normal nervous system; releases energy to body cells during metabolism.

Thiamin (vitamin B_1) releases energy from carbohydrate; aids normal growth and appetite.

Vitamin A aids normal bone and tooth development; promotes good night vision; maintains the health of skin and membranes.

Vitamin B_{12} (cobalamin) aids in red blood cell formation; maintains healthy nerve and gastrointestinal tissues.

Vitamin C (ascorbic acid) maintains healthy teeth and gums; maintains strong vessel walls.

Vitamin E (tocopherol)protects the fat in body tissues from oxidation.

Zinc aids in energy and metabolism and tissue formation.

Source: *Canada's Food Guide Handbook*

Laundry Care Symbols

The Canadian Care Labelling Program is a voluntary one that provides consumer information on the care of textiles, usually clothing. It uses five basic symbols, illustrated in the conventional "traffic light" colours. The program takes into consideration the fabric's colourfastness (i.e. whether the dye will bleed into the water and other clothing); whether it will shrink or stretch; how bleach will affect the garment; and how it may be ironed safely.

This labelling program does not apply to upholstered furniture, mattresses, carpets, leather, fur, or yarn.

The basic symbols represent washing, bleaching, drying, ironing and drycleaning, and the colours represent stop/do not (red), be careful (yellow), and go ahead (green). The red/crossed out symbol is only used when the procedure would damage the article.

Symbol	Red	Yellow	Green
	Stop	**Be careful**	**Go ahead**
Washing	Do not wash	Hand wash in cool water / Machine wash in cool water at a gentle setting—reduced agitation (30°C) / Machine wash in lukewarm water at a gentle setting—reduced agitation (40°C) / Machine wash in warm water at a gentle setting—reduced agitation (50°C)	Machine wash in warm water at a normal setting (50°C) / Machine wash in hot water at a normal setting (70°C)
Bleaching	Do not use chlorine bleach	Use chlorine bleach with care	
Drying		Dry flat / Tumble dry at low temperature	Tumble dry at medium to high temperature / Hang to dry / Drip dry
Ironing	Do not iron	Iron at low setting (110°C) / Iron at medium setting (150°C)	Iron at high setting (200°C)
Dry Cleaning	Do not dry clean	Dry clean—with caution	Dry clean

Source: *Industry Canada*

How to Poison-Proof Your Home

The average household contains as many as 250 poisons and each year in Canada hundreds of fatalities are caused by poisoning. There are two key steps to poison-proofing your home: identification and storage.

Common Household Poisons:

- Cleaners and bleaches: including detergents, ammonia, naphtha, oven cleaner and bleach.
- Solvents: including paint remover, kerosene and turpentine.
- Polishes and waxes: including paint, car and furniture wax, silver polish.
- Herbicides, insecticides and insect repellents.
- Mercury (from a thermometer).
- Cosmetics and toiletries: including aftershave, bubble bath, nail polish, hair lotions.
- Drugs and medicines: including both prescription and non-prescription drugs such as vitamins, ASA, cough medicines and cold medications.
- House plants, ornamental plants and flower and vegetable garden plants.

How to Store Them:

- Keep products in clearly labelled original containers.
- Store prescription drugs out of the reach of children and in containers with safety lids.
- Store household cleaners on high shelves, not underneath the sink.
- Return medication or cleaning products to a safe place after using them.
- Keep all poisonous liquids and solids out of the reach of children; if possible, install child-proof locking cabinets.
- Never call medicine "candy"; it gives children a distorted idea.
- Warn children at an early age not to eat household plants or wild plants and berries.
- Never keep food and household cleaners next to each other.
- Don't continue to store old products around the house.
- Don't leave a purse or handbag where a child can reach it because there are often prescription drugs inside.
- If poisoning occurs, identify the suspected poison and immediately seek medical help. Many areas have poison information centres. Never attempt to induce vomiting without medical advice.

Wedding Anniversary Gifts

Year	Traditional	Modern	Year	Traditional	Modern
1st	Paper	Clocks	15th	Crystal or watches	Watches
2nd	Cotton	China	20th	China	Platinum
3rd	Leather	Glass or crystal	25th	Silver	Silver plate or sterling silver
4th	Fruit & flowers	Small electric appliances			
5th	Wood	Silverware	30th	Pearl	Pearl
6th	Sugar & candy	Iron or Wood	35th	Coral	Jade
7th	Wool or pottery	Copper or pen/pencil sets	40th	Ruby	Ruby
8th	Bronze	Linen	45th	Sapphire	Sapphire
9th	Pottery or willow	Pottery	50th	Gold	Gold
10th	Tin	Aluminum	55th	Emerald	Emerald
11th	Steel	Fashion jewellery	60th	Diamond	Diamond (from 60th anniversary on)
12th	Silk or linen	Pearls			
13th	Lace or fur	Textiles	75th	Diamond	
14th	Ivory	Gold jewellery			

OBITUARIES

October 1, 1993–September 30, 1994

AMECHE, Don, 85. US actor who won an Academy Award in 1985 for his role in *Cocoon*. December 6, 1993.

ANDREW, Arthur, 78. Served as assistant undersecretary of state and Canada's chief representative in Greece, Israel, Sweden, and Cyprus. May 31, 1994.

ANTALL, Jozsef, 61. Prime minister of Hungary. December 12, 1993.

ARCEL, Ray, 94. Boxing trainer who worked with several champions including Alfonso (Peppermint) Frazer, Abe Goldstein, and Benny Leonard. March 7, 1994.

BICH, Marcel, 79. Founder of the manufacturer of disposable pens, razors and lighters that are marketed under the Bic name. May 30, 1994.

BIXBY, Bill, 59. US TV actor who starred in such popular series as "My Favorite Martian", "The Courtship of Eddie's Father" and "The Incredible Hulk". November 21, 1993.

BOULLE, Pierre, 81. French author best known for his books *The Bridge on the River Kwai* and *Planet of the Apes*. January 30, 1994.

BROWN SIMPSON, Nicole, 35. Ex-wife of former US football star O.J. Simpson, who was later charged with her murder and that of a companion, Ronald Goldman. June 12, 1994.

BURGESS, Anthony, 76. Writer and composer, best known for his novel *A Clockwork Orange*. November 22, 1993.

CANDY, John, 43. Comic actor and former alumnus of SCTV, best known for his film roles in *Uncle Buck* and *Planes, Trains and Automobiles*. March 4, 1994.

CLAVELL, James, 69. Best-selling author, film-maker and poet whose works included *Shogun*, *The Fly* and *King Rat*. September 7, 1994.

COBAIN, Kurt, 27. Lead singer of grunge rock band Nirvana. April 8, 1994.

COLOSIO, Luis Donaldo, 44. PRI presidential candidate in Mexican elections. Killed by an assassin. March 23, 1994.

COMFORT, Charles, 93. Painter and former director of the National Gallery of Canada. July 5, 1994.

CONRAD, William, 78. US TV actor who starred in the series *Cannon* and *Jake and the Fat Man*. February 11, 1994.

COTTEN, Joseph, 88. Film actor who debuted in *Citizen Kane* and went on to star in over 60 films. February 6, 1994.

CURRY, John, 44. British born Olympic champion ice skater and ice dancer. April 15, 1994.

CUSHING, Peter, 81. US film actor best known for his role in *The Curse of Frankenstein*. August 1994.

DE MILLE, Agnes, 84. Choreographer. Best known for her work in the Broadway musical *Oklahoma!* October 7, 1993.

DOISNEAU, Robert, 81. French photographer best known for his images of postwar Paris. April 1, 1994.

ELLISON, Ralph, 80. US author best known for his book *The Invisible Man*. April 16, 1994.

ENDICOTT, Rev. James, 94. Outspoken missionary and peace activist. November 27, 1993.

ERIKSON, Erik, 91. World-renowned psychoanalyst and writer who coined the phrase "identity crisis." May 12, 1994.

ESCOBAR, Pablo, 44. Head of the Medellin cocaine cartel, escaped from prison July 1992. Gunned down by Colombian police and soldiers after more than a year on the run. December 2, 1993.

FELLINI, Federico, 73. Italian film director whose films, characterised by the combination of autobiographical elements and fantasy, include *La strada, 8 1/2, Roma*, and *Amarcord*. October 31, 1993.

FULLER, Thomas, 85. Founder of one of Canada's most successful construction firms. May 9, 1994.

FURNESS, Betty, 78. Consumer advocate who began her career as an actress and pitchwoman for Westinghouse appliances and went on to become a consumer affairs adviser to US president Johnson and a reporter for NBC's "Today" show. April 2, 1994.

GACY, John Wayne, 52. Executed after being convicted of the murder of 33 young men and boys in 1980. May 10, 1994.

GERULAITIS, Vitas, 40. Former tennis star. September 17, 1994.

GREGOIRE, Paul Cardinal, 82. Former Roman Catholic archbishop of Montreal. October 30, 1993.

GRIFFITHS, Frank, 77. Owner of the Vancouver Canucks and broadcast entrepreneur. April 7, 1994.

HABYARIMANA, Juvenal. President of Rwanda. His death in a plane crash, which also killed his counterpart in Burundi, touched off a murderous civil war between Tutsi and Hutu citizens in his country. April 6, 1994.

HALDEMAN, Harry Robbins (H.R. or Bob), 67. Former chief of staff for US president Richard Nixon, jailed for his role in the Watergate cover up. November 12, 1993.

HALL, Louis, 77. Controversial Mohawk writer who interpreted the Great Law of the Peace and claimed natives had the right to carry and use weapons. December 10, 1993.

HARTMAN, Grace, 75. Labour leader who served as president of the Canadian Union of Public Employees, the first woman to hold such a post. December 18, 1993.

HAYES, Elliot, 37. Playwright best known for his work *Homeward Bound*, which opened the 1991 Stratford Festival. February 28, 1994.

HEAD, Wilson, 79. Activist, teacher and founder of both the Urban Alliance on Race Relations and the later National Black Coalition. October 9, 1994.

HINDMARSH, Ruth Atkinson, 101. Director of *The Toronto Star* and daughter of Joseph Atkinson, one of the paper's dynamic presidents. March 27, 1994.

HOLST, Johan Joergen, 56. Norway's foreign minister, credited with bringing Israel and the PLO together and keeping Middle East peace talks moving. January 13, 1994.

HONECKER, Erich, 81. Leader of East Germany from 1971 until 1989 when the Berlin Wall fell. May 29, 1994.

HOUPHEOUET-BOIGNY, Felix, 88. President of the Ivory Coast since its independence in 1960. December 7, 1993.

IONESCO, Eugene, 84. Playwright best known for his works *The Bald Soprano* and *The Lesson*. March 28, 1994.

KELLEY, Virginia, 70. Mother of US president Bill Clinton. January 6, 1994.

KENNEDY ONASSIS, Jacqueline Bouvier, 65. Widow of assassinated US president John F. Kennedy. May 19, 1994.

LAHN, Mervyn, 60. Former head of Canada Trust and a leading figure in the financial services industry. January 21, 1994.

LANTZ, Walter, 93. Creator of the popular cartoon character Woody Woodpecker. March 22, 1994.

LEVESQUE, Gerard, 67. Longest-serving member of the Quebec provincial legislature. November 18, 1993.

LIGGIO, Luciano, 68. Mafia leader credited with transforming the Corleone clan into Sicily's most vicious criminal organization. November 15, 1993.

LOY, Myrna, 88. US movie star best known for her role as Nora Charles in the *Thin Man* series. December 14, 1993.

LYNCH, Charles, 74. Veteran political columnist and writer. His newspaper and broadcast careers spanned ten prime ministers. July 21, 1994.

MANCINI, Henry, 79. Composer best known for his songs "Moon River" and "The Days of Wine and Roses". June 14, 1994.

MATTHEY, Jeannette, 37. CBC radio journalist who covered the Soviet Union during its last days. October 7, 1993.

MATTUS, Reuben, 81. Named Haagen-Daz ice-cream and created a multi-million dollar product. January 27, 1994.

MERCOURI, Melina, 68. Actor best known for her role in the film *Never on Sunday* who went on to a career in Greek politics and served as minister of culture in two governments. March 6, 1994.

MILLAR, Margaret, 79. Award-winning mystery writer. March 26, 1994.

MOORE, Garry, 78. US TV pioneer who starred in variety and quiz shows. November 28, 1993.

MOSIENKO, Bill, 72. Scored hockey's fastest hat trick, three goals in 21 seconds for the Chicago Black Hawks in 1952. July 9, 1994.

NILSSON, Harry, 52. Grammy-award winning musician won his first Grammy for the theme song to the movie *Midnight Cowboy*. January 15, 1994.

NIXON, Richard, M., 81. US president from 1969 to 1974, forced to resign from office during the Watergate scandal. April 22, 1994.

O'NEILL, Thomas (Tip), 81. Longtime US politician who served as Speaker of the House of Representatives from 1977 to 1986. January 5, 1994.

OCHOA, Severo, 88. Spanish biochemist whose work in the chemistry of nucleic acids—he synthesized RNA—laid foundation for modern molecular biology. Co-winner of the 1959 Nobel Prize for Medicine. November 1, 1993.

OSBORNE, Gregory, 39. Principal dancer with National Ballet of Canada until 1990; also danced with the American Ballet Theatre. January 8, 1994.

PAPROSKI, Steve, 65. Former Tory MP for Edmonton North and former lineman for Edmonton Eskimos. December 3, 1993.

PAULING, Linus, 93. US scientist and two-time winner of Nobel Prizes (chemistry, 1954; peace, 1962); Best known for his promotion of vitamin C as a cure-all. August 19, 1994.

PEALE, Norman Vincent, 95. US author best known for his book *The Power of Positive Thinking*. December 24, 1994.

PELLER, Andrew, 90. Founder of Andres wines and a pioneer in the Canadian wine industry. April 5, 1994.

PEPPARD, George, 65. Stage and screen actor best known for his role in the TV series *The A-Team*. May 8, 1994.

PHOENIX, River, 23. US film actor hailed as "the next James Dean"; best known for his roles in *My Own Private Idaho* and *Stand By Me*. October 31, 1993.

POTTER, Dennis, 59. British novelist and playwright best known for his screenplays for *Pennies from Heaven* and the television series "The Singing Detective." June 7, 1994.

POULTON, Ron, 77. Journalist who wrote the history of the *Toronto Sun* entitled *Life in a Word Factory*. November 15, 1993.

PRICE, Vincent, 82. Film actor who starred in classic horror films such as *The Fly*, and later was host of the Mystery series of public television. October 25, 1993.

RADDALL, Thomas, 90. Historical novelist and three-time winner of Governor General's Awards for literature. April 1, 1994.

REY, Fernando, 76. Actor best known for his role in *The French Connection*. March 9, 1994.

REYNOLDS, R.J. III, 60. Heir to the tobacco-company that bears his name, he died of emphysema and heart failure. June 28, 1994.

RODRIGUEZ, Sue, 43. Crippled by ALS, she fought for physician-assisted suicide and brought the issues of quality of life and the right to die to the attention of Canadians. February 12, 1994.

ROMERO, Cesar, 86. US film actor. January 1, 1994.

SAFTAWI, Assad, 58. Leading intermediary amongst PLO, Israel and Egypt in the negotiations for Palestinian autonomy. Killed by assassin. October 21, 1993.

SARGENT, Dick, 64. TV actor best known for his role in "Bewitched." July 8, 1994.

SAVALAS, Telly, 70. American TV actor best known for his role as Kojak in the series of the same name. January 22, 1994.

SCARRY, Richard, 74. Best-selling author and illustrator of children's books. April 30, 1994.

SENNA, Ayrton, 34. Brazilian Formula One race driver and three-time World Champion. May 1, 1994.

SEXTON, Tommy, 36. Comic actor and founding member of CODCO. December 13, 1993.

SHERRIN, Muriel, 60. A versatile arts administrator associated with CBC, the Canada Council, the National Arts Centre, and the Stratford Festival. July 8, 1994.

SHILTS, Randy, 42. US AIDS activist and author of *And the Band Played On*. February 17, 1994.

SHIRER, William, 89. US author best known for his book *The Rise and Fall of the Third Reich*. December 28, 1993.

SHORE, Dinah, 76. Star from the golden age of television in the 1950s and 60s. February 24, 1994.

SMITH, John, 55. British Labour Party leader who was considered to be the front runner for the prime minister's job in the next British election. May 11, 1994.

STYNE, Jule, 88. American composer of over 1 500 songs, best known for musicals such as *Gypsy* and *Funny Girl*. September 20, 1994.

SUNG, Kim Il, 82. Ruler of North Korea since 1948. July 9, 1994.

SWINTON, William, 93. Paleontologist wrote one of the first textbooks on dinosaurs, taught zoology at the University of Toronto, served as head of the Royal Ontario Museum and helped set up the Ontario Science Centre. June 12, 1994.

TAFT, Sammy, 81. Toronto business man who gave hockey the term "hat trick" after striking a deal with Chicago Black Hawks rookie Alex Kaleta. If the young player scored three goals in one game against the Maple Leafs, Taft would give him a hat. January 2, 1994.

TARNOPOLSKY, Walter, 61. Ontario Court of Appeal judge and international human rights scholar. September 15, 1993.

TATA, J.R.D., 89. Former head of India's largest business entity; credited with building $64 million family business into a $5 billion conglomerate. November 29, 1993.

THOMAS, Caitlin, 80. Widow of Welsh poet Dylan Thomas. August, 1994.

TRAVERS, Bill, 72. Animal conservationist and actor. Best known for his role in the film *Born Free*. March 29, 1994.

ZAPPA, Frank, 52. Rock and roll star who led the band Mothers of Invention in the 1960s and went on to a solo career. December 4, 1993.

ZETTERLING, Mai, 68. Swedish film actress and director. March 15, 1994.

NEWS EVENTS OF 1993–94

October 1, 1993 to September 30, 1994

October

INTERNATIONAL

Bosnia: As the peace plan proposed by Britain's Lord Owen continued to be stalled the US began to canvass for support to lift the arms embargo on the country's Muslims. **Burundi:** Army paratroopers staged an abortive coup and killed Hutu Pres. Ndadaye and six ministers on Oct. 21; by Oct. 28 Prime Min. Kinigi announced she had regained control of the government. **Georgia:** Forces loyal to ousted Pres. Gamsakhurdia seized the province of Mingrelia in the west and moved the country closer to a full-blown ethnic civil war. By the end of the month, Russian troops were deployed at the request of former Soviet Foreign Min. Shevardnadze who faced separatists in the northern province Abkhazia as well as Gamsakhurdia's forces in the west. Troops loyal to Shevardnadze managed to drive the rebels back and regain the lost territory. **Germany:** The constitutional court of Germany ruled the Maastricht Treaty did not violate that country's constitution and that the necessary ratification documents could be filed in Rome by the Nov. 1 deadline; as the last country to do so, the move ensured that the European Community was ready to take the next step toward the European Union. **Greece:** Voters returned Andreas Papandreou to the prime minister's chair after a four-year break; the Socialist prime minister's first move was to cancel plans to privatize much of the Greek economy, as proposed by his Conservative predecessor. **Haiti:** Hopes for a civilian-run police force were ended when the chief negotiator, the Justice Minister, was executed; a ship carrying US and Canadian troops deployed to help restore exiled Pres. Aristide was prevented from docking, prompting the UN Security Council to vote to reinstate an oil and arms embargo. **India:** The final death toll in the Sept. 1993 earthquake was set at 9 748; it was initially feared that close to 28 000 had died, however there were charges of undercounting to reduce government compensation claims. **Libya:** Western

diplomats heard reports that a handful of army units had mutinied against their ruler, Col. Gadafi, over unpaid wages. **Mozambique:** UN Sec. Gen. Boutros Boutros-Ghali announced a breakthrough in peace negotiations aimed at ending the civil war. **Pakistan:** On Oct. 19, Benazir Bhutto was sworn in as prime minister; the elections left no party with a clear majority in parliament and Bhutto had to build a coalition to obtain the necessary votes. **Peru:** In a nationwide referendum on Oct. 31, 55.3% of voters affirmed Pres. Fujimori's new constitution. **Philippines:** The 25th typhoon of the year flooded central Luzon, killing nearly 100 and forcing over a million from their homes; an estimated $100 million damage was done to crops and nearly 3 000 villages were submerged; in the worst year for typhoons since 1964, it was estimated that there could be seven more by year-end. **Russia:** In Moscow, the standoff begun on Sept. 24 continued with armed clashes around the Russian parliamentary buildings on Oct. 3; the rebels barricaded inside the "White House" surrendered on Oct. 4 after Pres. Yeltsin's forces used tanks and invaded the buildings. **Somalia:** A US negotiator secured the release of a captured US pilot and a Nigerian peace keeper after talks with Gen. Aidid; after the release the Americans indicated that Aidid's faction would be included in any negotiations to settle the civil war and that the manhunt for the Somali leader would end; later in the month, rival clans were again staging shoot-outs, raising the spectre of renewed civil war rather than a negotiated peace. **South Africa:** On Oct. 8 the UN officially lifted economic sanctions. **Sweden:** The Nobel Prize committee announced that the 1993 Peace Prize would be shared jointly between Nelson Mandela and F.W. de Klerk for their work to end apartheid peacefully in South Africa. Other prizes went to Richard Roberts (UK) and Phillip Sharp (US) for Medicine; and Kary B. Mullis (US) and Michael Smith (Can) for Chemistry. **United States:** Brush fires in California devastated over 75 000 hectares of the state and six counties were declared disaster areas. The Sec. of State announced an agreement with Ukraine to help pay for the dismantling of all nuclear weapons in their territory.

CANADA

TV leadership debates leading up to the Oct. 25 federal election were inconclusive, but the Tory release of two television ads characterizing Lib. leader Jean Chrétien as unfit to lead the country ignited a storm of protest and negative publicity for the Conservative party. On Oct. 8, Nova Scotia premier John Savage ran into stiff opposition to his provincial budget, which, contrary to election promises, included tax increases. Despite the tough measures Moody Inv. Services downgraded the province's rating from A2 to A3. Financial agreements for the building of the bridge from PEI to the mainland were finalized on Oct. 8; the bridge is to be completed by May 1997. On Oct. 14, 44 environmentalists were jailed for protests at Clayoquot Sound held in defiance of court injunctions banning such activities. On Oct. 16 Canadian forces pulled out of Haiti; two Canadian destroyers and a supply ship joined the international blockade to try and force the government to resign. CN announced plans to get rid of half of its track in Eastern and Central Canada by 1995. Candy manufacturer Neilsen's announced a major business deal that will give the company access to the potentially huge market in Mexico. The Toronto Blue Jays won their second consecutive World Series title with a 9th-inning home run in the 6th game on Oct. 23. The Oct. 25 federal election radically changed the face of Canada's parliament: the Liberals took 178 seats, the Bloc Québécois became the Official Opposition with 54, the Reform Party took 52 seats, the NDP 8 and the ruling Conservatives were cut down to 2 seats, with 1 Independent. The new parliament will have an unprecedented number of rookie MPs (201), more women (54) than ever before and a new presence for members of Canada's visible minorities. A year after the explosion in the Giant gold mine in Yellowknife, a miner was arrested and charged in connection with the 9 deaths that resulted from the bomb blast.

November

INTERNATIONAL

Algeria: Muslim extremists issued an ultimatum giving foreign residents until Dec. 1 to leave the country or face execution. Muslim militants have been battling the government since Jan. 1992 when early election results indicating a majority win for Muslim candidates, prompted the government to cancel the remaining voting. **Argentina:** Pres. Carlos Menem and the leader of the opposition party agreed on a constitutional measure to end the ban on successive presidential terms, paving the way for Menem to run again in mid-1995. **Bosnia:** Croatian gunners destroyed a 16th century bridge in the town of Mostar, shattering one of the finest examples of Ottoman architecture; shelling in Sarajevo was on the increase and at month end Serbian forces temporarily blocked UN aid convoys, despite a week-old ceasefire that had guaranteed the roads would be open. **Germany:** Prosecutors revealed that a German company, UB Plasma, was under investigation for failing to screen blood products for the AIDS virus before releasing them for distribution in Germany and other European countries. Later in the month a second company was also charged with improper testing and shut down. At Volkswagen AG staff agreed to a four-day, 28.8 hour work week that would preserve jobs, but result in a 10% reduction in pay. **Israel:** Palestinians and Jewish settlers unhappy with the peace agreement continued to skirmish; in an unprecedented move PLO chairman Yasser Arafat criticized members of his own faction for killing a Jewish settler and called for an end to the violence. Nevertheless it continued on both sides throughout the month. **Jordan:** Voters cut the number of parliamentary seats held by Islamic fundamentalists nearly in half (from 32 to 18) in the lower house and gave King Hussein a large majority in support of his pro-peace policies; they also elected their first female parliamentarian. **Korea, North:** The UN Gen. Assembly was informed that North Korea was preventing the International Atomic Energy Agency from inspecting that country's nuclear sites. **Nigeria:** Just three months after Ernest Shonekan assumed office as the first civilian head of state, the defence minister forced him to resign and reasserted direct military rule, banning the major political parties and dismantling local civilian governments. **Somalia:** The UN released eight of Somali warlord Aidid's aides and called off their search for him; Aidid emerged from hiding to celebrate with thousands of supporters. **South Africa:** The white minority government, together with black political leaders approved a constitution that guaranteed freedom of speech, movement and political activity for all citizens, effectively ending apartheid; the document also provided for a transitional all-race body that would oversee national elections called for Apr. 1994. **Sri Lanka:** Tamil rebels renewed the 10-year struggle for independence by overrunning one military base and laying siege to another; estimates of casualties on both sides totaled over 400. **Sweden:** Art thieves hid on the roof of the Museum of Modern Art and then sawed a hole and entered without triggering an alarm; five paintings by Picasso plus one of his sculptures and two paintings by Georges Braque were stolen. **Turkey:** Militant Kurds campaigning for a separate state staged attacks on Turkish consulates, banks and other business enterprises in Germany, Britain, Switzerland, Austria and Denmark, causing extensive property damages, one death and many injuries. **United States:** NAFTA passed in the house of Representatives by a comfortable 234-200 tally; citizens of Puerto Rico narrowly voted to remain a commonwealth of the US instead of pursuing state status thereby preserving some tax advantages and retaining the right to field its own Olympic teams. Fires continued to rage in California as six years of drought, stiff winds and recurrent arson spawned new fires in Malibu and elsewhere in the state.

CANADA

High school students in three schools in Calgary and Edmonton staged demonstrations to protest their provincial government's cutbacks in education spending. An increase in home construction (3.9%) indicated that the modest economic recovery was continuing. CN announced the sale of its US subsidiary Central Vermont Railway as the first step in cutting its rail network east of Winnipeg in half. The US tabloid TV show "A Current Affair" aired a segment on the Teale-Homolka case and many Canadian viewers were able to watch the show, despite the publication ban on details in effect. A rock burst at the Macassa mine in Kirkland Lake, Ont. left two miners trapped underground and rescuers were unable to reach them. Ontario's credit rating was cut from double A to a dou-

ble A minus, down from triple A in 1990. Grace McCarthy was elected as leader of BC's faltering Social Credit party on Nov. 6. Rev. Victoria Matthews was elected the first female Anglican bishop. The incoming Liberal government scrapped the controversial EH101 helicopter deal as promised during the election campaign. The Edmonton Eskimos won the Grey cup, beating the Winnipeg Blue Bombers 33-23.

December

INTERNATIONAL

Bosnia: Muslims rejected a peace plan that proposed a Croat-Serbian partition of the territory. At month end a 15 bus convoy was allowed to leave Sarajevo under UN escort, carrying 700 people out of the besieged capital. **Brazil:** A political scandal that continued to confound even the most jaded citizens took a more tragic turn when the former budget director, already implicated in a fraud and corruption scandal, was charged with arranging for the murder of his wife. **Colombia:** Drug trafficker Pablo Escobar was shot and killed in Medellin on Dec. 2, 16 months after he escaped from his custom-built prison near his home. **Egypt:** A six-month lull in a campaign of violence that used foreign tourists as targets in a battle to overthrow the government ended with a firebomb attack on a sightseeing bus. The campaign has badly damaged the tourist industry, a mainstay of the Egyptian economy. **Germany:** Much of Western Europe, including Germany, France and Belgium reeled under amounts of snow, sleet and torrential rain not seen since the 18th century; major rivers overflowed and thousands were left without fuel or electricity. **Greece:** The Athens government expressed outrage over the decision of many Western governments to recognize the former Yugoslav republic of Macedonia, fearing that it could spark a surge for independence in their own province of the same name. **Israel:** Violence continued to plague the occupied territories as extremists on both sides attempted to derail the peace plan; Israel responded by moving soldiers to the West Bank and Gaza Strip, warning that the deadline for withdrawing from both areas would likely be missed. **Italy:** Municipal elections in many of Italy's largest cities—including Genoa, Rome,

Trieste and Venice—saw the return of alliances supported by former communists. **Korea, North:** A war of words erupted over the N. Koreans' refusal to allow inspection of its nuclear sites; Washington warned that if the state ever used the weapon it was suspected of developing that the response would destroy their country. North Korea responded by announcing that any attempt to impose sanctions would be viewed as an "act of war." The N. Korean government eventually offered to allow partial inspection; the proposal was rejected by American officials. **Russia:** The Hammer and Sickle—the images on the seal of the former communist Soviet regime—were abolished and replaced by the two-headed eagle that served as the royal emblem for five centuries before the communist takeover. Voters in a national election and referendum on a new constitution gave Pres. Boris Yeltsin broad new powers, however at the same time they gave the majority of their support to a highly reactionary Liberal Democratic party led by Vladimir Zhirinovsky. **Serbia:** Pres. Milosevic, leader of the Serbian war of expansion into neighbouring Bosnia, increased his party's control of the Serbian government after voters gave his party 123 seats in the 250-seat legislature. **South Africa:** The multi-party congress recommended that the black homelands of Bophuthatswana, Ciskei, Transkei and Venda be dissolved and returned to South African sovereignty; by mid-month, a multiracial, multi-party Transitional Executive Council had been inaugurated to oversee the country until the national elections in April 1995. The last act of the white-controlled parliament was approval of a constitution that granted equal rights, including the right to vote in elections, to all citizens. **Sweden:** Police made two arrests in connection with the theft of Picassos at the Stockholm Museum of Modern Art and recovered three of the six Picassos. **Switzerland:** The Uruguay Round of the GATT talks finally ended with an agreement among 117 countries to lower trade barriers and establish a mechanism for resolving disputes. **United Kingdom:** Prim. Min. John Major revealed that secret talks had begun the previous March between the IRA and London, aimed at ending the violence in Northern Ireland and bringing the IRA into the peace process; on Dec. 15 the Irish and British governments outlined a peace plan

that would include a referendum in Northern Ireland to decide its fate. The last mine in the historic Durham coal field in northeast England closed down, reducing a one-mighty industry that counted 170 mines as recently as the 1980s to just 22 working pits. **United States:** New York's Long Island Rail Road was the scene of a shooting that left five dead and 18 wounded and reopened the debate on gun control laws. Astronauts aboard the US shuttle *Endeavour* made the world's most expensive repair call when they visited the crippled Hubble telescope and replaced malfunctioning solar panels and gyroscopes and installed corrective lenses.

CANADA

The Alberta government continued its campaign to eliminate its deficit by 1997 by cutting public sector wages and benefits by 5% and announcing wages would stay at that level for two years. In Ontario, delegates to the annual meeting of the Ontario Federation of Labour voted to cut all ties with the governing NDP party to protest the enactment of that government's social contract legislation, which froze wages and instituted days of unpaid leave. In the Maritimes, the Fisheries Resource Conservation Council announced that the ban on cod fishing, imposed in the summer of 1992, had not halted the decline of fish stocks, and recommended that the ban be extended to include the Gulf of St. Lawrence area and last until the end of the decade; the federal government did just that on Dec. 20. Striking union members at the Giant gold mine in Yellowknife returned to their jobs after a labour board imposed a back-to-work protocol, ending the 19-month dispute. After some last-minute discussions, the new Liberal government agreed to proclaim NAFTA, the trade agreement with the US and Mexico, by Jan. 1. The new Liberal government also announced that the controversial deal to privatize Pearson International Airport would be cancelled, citing an "inadequate contract" and a "flawed process" in arriving at the deal. Former prime minister Kim Campbell announced her resignation as Conservative leader on Dec. 13 and Jean Charest became the party's interim leader. In Quebec, Daniel Johnson was acclaimed as leader of the Liberal party on Dec. 15, to replace retiring Robert Bourassa as premier of the province. Quebec and Ontario ended a trade dispute when Quebec removed barriers to out-of-province companies bidding on provincial government contracts. On Dec. 22, 11 Canadian peace keepers were taken captive by drunken Bosnian Serb militiamen in the eighth such incident since July. On Dec. 29, Canadian forces made their 1 000th humanitarian relief flight into Sarajevo. Bank of Canada governor John Crow withdrew his candidacy for a second term in the post and senior deputy governor Gordon Thiessen was named as his successor. The provincial premiers held their first meeting since the federal election and agreed to work to eliminate interprovincial trade barriers by June 1. In the community of Davis Inlet, a protest over court sentences that were deemed to be too harsh prompted the federal Indian affairs minister to cancel a planned visit to the Labrador community.

January

INTERNATIONAL

Afghanistan: Rivals in the mujhedin, who successfully drove the Soviets out of the country, once again fractured into battling factions that left 500 dead and 3 000 wounded before another uneasy ceasefire was negotiated. **Algeria:** Violence continued to escalate as foreigners were targeted by the terrorists, as well as intellectuals, officials and police; nearly 3 500 have died since the skirmishes began. **Australia:** The northern part of the state of New South Wales was devastated by fires that threatened 25% of the state and numbered 150 by mid-January; Sydney was surrounded on all sides by fires fanned by dry weather and wind. **Bosnia:** The city of Sarajevo continued to suffer as Serbians stepped up their shelling, bombarding the city with over 1 000 shells per day. Although NATO members repeated their threats of air strikes, UN officials cautioned that ground support would also be required if the effort was to yield results. **Guatemala:** 84% of the voters in a constitutional referendum either boycotted the vote or destroyed their ballots in a protest over the continued corruption in the political system; the proposed reforms passed with 69% of the votes cast. **Korea, North:** The government continued its dispute with the International Atomic Energy Agency over inspection of nuclear

sites, refusing to acknowledge the existence of two sites and hampering the IAEA's plans for inspecting the remaining ones. **Mexico:** Rebels in the southern state of Chiapas seized four towns in fighting that left 100 dead on New Year's Day; the rebels, calling themselves the Zapatista Army of National Liberation, declared war on the Mexican government, demanding immediate improvements in housing, health care, education, democracy and justice. Archaeologists announced the discovery of a large ruined city on the Gulf coast of Mexico; the city reportedly flourished over 1 500 years ago and could have had as many as 20 000 citizens. **Romania:** The former Soviet bloc country became the first to join NATO's Partnership for Peace, able to take part in joint military exercises but excluded from complete political equality and security guarantees. **Russia:** In the aftermath of Dec.'s elections Pres. Yeltsin and his prime minister announced a new cabinet made up of conservatives widely expected to slow down, if not reverse, the program of economic reform that had led to chaos in the marketplace. The move sparked resignations from a top-level economic advisor, as well as the Finance Minister. The World Bank and the IMF also expressed dismay over the possible slowdown of economic reform. **Rwanda:** On Jan. 5 Juvenal Habyarimana was sworn in as president to head an interim government slated to serve for 22 months; multi-party elections were scheduled for Oct. 1995. Appointment of a broadly based government was again delayed amid accusations of presidential interference with the selection of ministers. **Somalia:** Local warlords returned to factional fighting as US troops scaled down their intervention efforts and the UN Security Council voted to do the same in an effort to pressure the Somalis to make peace. **Syria:** Pres. Assad announced his intention to seek "normal, peaceful" relations with Israel, provided Israel returns the Golan Heights. **United Kingdom:** US-born author Joan Brady became the first woman to win the Whitbread Book of the Year award, for her novel *Theory of War*. **United States:** The US Justice Department subpoenaed files belonging to Pres. Clinton and his wife concerning their dealings with the Whitewater Development Corp. in Arkansas. The US figure skating championships were disrupted by an attack on one of the main competitors, Nancy Kerrigan, which forced her to withdraw from the competition. Los Angeles was hit by a major earthquake measuring 6.6 on the Richter scale, with the epicentre just northwest of the city; early estimates of damage were between $15 and $30 billion. In a controversial court case, Lorena Bobbit was acquitted on charges of maiming her husband despite the fact that she had cut off his penis. At month end the US announced an end to the 30-year trade embargo on Vietnam, giving US businesses the go-ahead to begin operations there. **Venezuela:** A prison riot lasting four hours left 123 inmates dead; order was restored by the National Guard after the jail was filled with tear gas. The violence was blamed on an ethnic feud between Guajiro Indian and non-Indian inmates.

CANADA

Liberal leader Daniel Johnson was sworn in as premier of Quebec, replacing Robert Bourassa on Jan. 11. Canadian softwood lumber producers became eligible for refunds of about $500 million in cash deposits they were required to pay under a US duty that was imposed in 1992; dismissing the US claim that Canadian softwood lumber producers were unfairly subsidized, a binational trade panel ruled that the duty had to be eliminated. The BC government announced a new 575 000 acre wilderness park for the southwestern corner of the province; the province's sixth largest park will ban logging and mining within its boundaries. Alberta continued its war on the provincial deficit; Prem. Klein announced $1.5 billion in spending cuts to education and health and social services. Ontario officially recognized midwifery as a profession, paving the way for increased midwife participation in routine childbirths. Most of the country west of the Rockies went into the deep freeze in January and stayed there for much of the month, either challenging or breaking low temperature records set in the 1950s. The government asked members of parliament for opinions on Canada's role in Bosnia, which was due for review in April; the question of when the safety of the peace keepers outweighed the importance of the mission was not settled. Immigration Canada announced that refugee claimants would be allowed to seek work in an effort to curb rising costs of welfare.

Telesat Canada's two satellites, Anik E-1 and Anik E-2, were knocked out of service on Jan. 20 by a solar storm; E-1's back-up system allowed service to be restored to its customers. By month end officials had begun work on building a new tracking system that would allow them to regain control of Anik E-2 and return it to service.

February

INTERNATIONAL

Afghanistan: The latest truce in the war amongst the allies was broken as more than 70 rockets fell on the capital city. **Algeria:** That country's battle between the military government and fundamentalist groups took to the streets of Algiers as security forces gunned down one of the opposition's leaders and nine of his supporters. A state journalist and a local educator were killed in retaliation. **Bosnia:** A mortar attack on a crowded marketplace in downtown Sarajevo killed at least 66 and injured 200, prompting renewed calls for lifting the siege. After months of fence-sitting, NATO issued a blunt warning to the Bosnian Serbs: if they did not withdraw their guns from Sarajevo, they would be bombed. The guns over Sarajevo finally fell silent after repeated threats of NATO air strikes and pressure not only from the US but from Russia. The withdrawal of guns began amid reports of savage fighting in other parts of the country. By month end, attacks were reduced to sniper fire and elsewhere in the country Croats and Muslims had agreed to end their war; NATO fighters shot down 4 Serb jets violating a "no-fly" zone over Bosnia. **European Union:** Agreements were reached with Austria, Sweden and Finland concerning possible membership; talks with Norway continued. Each country must hold a referendum to have its citizens ratify the decision to join. **Ghana:** 5 000 died in the first two weeks of a civil conflict between ethnic Nanumba and the Konkomva, settlers from neighbouring Togo. **Hong Kong:** Gov. Patton pushed the first phase of his democratic reform package through the colony's Legislative Council, despite the assertion by China that the council and any other local bodies would be abolished when the colony reverts to Chinese control in 1997. **Indonesia:** An earthquake measuring 7.2 on the Richter scale hit the island of

Sumatra, killing over 200 and leaving 3 000 injured. **Israel:** A heavily-armed Jewish settler entered a mosque in Hebron on the West Bank and opened fire on Muslim worshippers as they knelt in prayer; 40 Palestinians died and more than 250 were wounded in the riots that followed. The gunman was killed by angry worshippers. Israeli Prim. Min. Rabin denounced the massacre and vowed that it would not stop the peace process. **Italy:** Undercover police recovered a 16th century painting by Raphael that had been missing since the early 1800s; five Italian businessmen and art dealers were detained. **Korea, North:** After a stalemate that lasted 11 months the North Korean government agreed to allow international inspectors at 7 nuclear sites; two other sites not acknowledged by the North Koreans were not included in the arrangement. **Mexico:** The government opened negotiations with the Zapatista rebels, insisting that only local matters be discussed, but vowing to work to ease the poverty in some of the poorer regions; proposals included the redistribution of land and a public works program for the region of Chiapas. **Norway:** Just as the XVII Winter Olympics got underway in Lillehammer thieves broke into the Norwegian National Gallery and stole the world famous painting *The Scream* by Edvard Munch. **Poland:** 30 000 citizens protested their declining living standards by marching on Warsaw in the biggest demonstration since the fall of communism. **Russia:** Russia's lower house gave the hard-liners who had led the Dec. seizure of the White House amnesty; the leaders of the 1991 coup against Pres. Gorbachev were also freed. The leaders of the Dec. uprising included some of Pres. Yeltsin's strongest rivals. **Rwanda:** A Hutu-born cabinet minister was killed in the capital of Kigali and a mob killed a Tutsi politician in retaliation. Ethnic rioting followed. **South Africa:** All race national elections were formally called for Apr. 26-28. The success of the elections was immediately placed in jeopardy when several parties on both ends of the political spectrum announced a boycott of the vote. The African National Congress was registered as a participant by leader Nelson Mandela, but the leader of Zulu's Inkatha Freedom Party continued to resist efforts to draw his party into the coming elections, despite concessions from the ANC. It was feared that the planned boycott would

seriously disrupt the vote, however the party was eventually registered provisionally. **Sudan:** Sudanese, already suffering from a civil war that has dragged on for over 10 years, faced drought as well as renewed fighting as Christian rebels from the south battled Islamic fundamentalist government forces from the north; the increased fighting forced foreign aid workers to withdraw from the area. **United States:** Continuing a process begun by the Europeans, the US government extended official recognition to the former Yugoslav republic of Macedonia, despite continued protests from the Greek government. The US government stepped up its trade dispute with Japan, raising the spectre of sanctions if the disagreement over market access was not resolved. As US figure skaters moved to Norway for the Olympics the public continued to be fascinated by the Tonya Harding vs. Nancy Kerrigan case. A mid-level officer in the CIA, Aldrich Ames, and his Colombian-born wife were arrested and charged with spying for Moscow as early as the mid-1980s; on Feb. 21 Ames pleaded guilty to the charges. **Venezuela:** The banking scandal surrounding Banco Latino, the second largest bank in the country, continued to widen as 83 bankers and businessmen were charged with fraud; the government vowed to prop up the troubled bank rather than let it collapse.

CANADA

After a parliamentary discussion on the issue, the Liberal cabinet approved the extension of the agreement allowing the US to test cruise missiles over parts of Canada, allowing two upcoming tests over the Arctic. The ban on cod fishing in Newfoundland was extended to personal use as the fisheries minister banned the traditional practice of jigging for cod. The Liberal government announced that federal taxes on cigarettes would be cut by $5 per carton and invited provincial governments to follow suit. Quebec and New Brunswick did so immediately, Ontario joined the group on Feb. 21 and other provincial governments considered the move, which will cost millions in lost revenues, but curb the flourishing black market in smuggled cigarettes. A report recommending that the Canadian Red Cross Society's role in the collection and distribution of blood products be severely curtailed received approval from provincial health ministers. On Feb. 12, Sue Rodriguez of BC, who was terminally ill with ALS, ended her life with the assistance of a physician, in defiance of a Supreme Court decision that denied her that right. On Feb. 16, parliament passed legislation amending the original agreement that brought PEI into Confederation, changing the obligation to provide ferry service to accommodate the proposed bridge and paving the way for the $840 million project. Finance Minister Paul Martin introduced his first budget, cutting defence spending, UI benefits, tax deductions and foreign aid, and freezing transfer payments and public sector salaries. The Treasury Board announced that MP's salaries would also be frozen until at least 1997.

March

INTERNATIONAL

Algeria: Armed Islamists attacked a high-security prison and up to 1 000 prisoners escaped; by mid-month 24 of them had been killed and over 100 recaptured. The fundamentalists stepped up their campaign by killing three high schools girls who appeared in public without veils. **Bosnia:** Heavy weapons around the city of Mostar were removed by Croat forces; after nine months of shelling every structure in the Muslim eastern quarter had been heavily damaged. In Sarajevo, that city's battered trolley system made its first run in several months and residents could walk about more or less freely, although they remained cut off from the outside world. By mid-month an agreement between Bosnian Serbs and the Muslim government provided for the opening of Sarajevo to the outside world, although no military or commercial traffic was permitted. Bosnian Serbs continued to reject peace plans for a Muslim-Croat federation, preferring to connect their territory to a Serbian federation. **Burundi:** In a continuing ethnic conflict, Hutus murdered dozens of Tutsis to avenge the killing of 200 Hutus in the capital. **Cambodia:** The guerrilla headquarters of the Khmer Rouge was overrun by government troops; the victory drove 20 000 civilians and fighters into neighbouring Thailand to seek shelter. **El Salvador:** The country's first elections since the 12-year civil war resulted in victory for the Nationalist Republican

Alliance, a right-wing party. **Israel:** The aftermath of the Feb. massacre in Hebron continued as negotiations aimed at finalizing the peace agreement faltered and violence between Palestinians and Jewish settlers escalated. **Italy:** A engineer based at the University of Turin rescued the leaning Tower of Pisa from collapse by installing 600 tons of lead counterweights on the opposite side; although the bell tower will never be upright, the leaning process has been reversed. A right-wing coalition won a majority in national parliamentary elections with billionaire Silvio Berlusconi leading the three-party Freedom Alliance to victory. **Japan:** A poor rice harvest in 1993 forced the government to open Japanese markets to foreign rice; it was announced that the rice available would be a blend of foreign and domestic, prompting a run on the remaining "pure" stocks of the domestic crop. **Korea, North:** Despite months of negotiations the international monitoring group sent in to inspect North Korea's nuclear sites was denied full access to one of its facilities. South Korea broke off talks in protest and the US threatened to reschedule joint military exercises with its southern allies. North Korea responded by promising to turn Seoul into a "sea of fire." **Liberia:** The three main rival factions began to disarm as UN peacekeeping troops made up of members from eight African nations moved in to supervise the process. **Mexico:** A billionaire bank president was kidnapped by six gunman and held for ransom; in the last five years nearly 2 000 Mexican businessmen have been held. On Mar. 23, the leading PRI candidate in the fall election, Luis Colosio, was gunned down during a campaign stop in Tijuana. The party chose Ernest Zedillo Ponce de León as his replacement. **Russia:** As Moldova became the 12th former member of the Warsaw Pact to join NATO's Partnership for Peace, Russia indicated that it was also prepared to join, but expected a special role. **Somalia:** US forces pulled out just as two of the most powerful warlords signed a peace agreement in Nairobi and UN peace keepers took over the supervisory mission. Gen. Aidid and his rivals signed a peace agreement repudiating violence. A cholera outbreak reported in Feb. grew to epidemic proportions in March as more than 1 700 cases were reported. **South Africa:** The South African government moved to take over the territory known as the independent homeland of Bophuthatswana after residents rioted when their president announced they would be prevented from taking part in the country's first all-race elections. A last stand by right wing members of both black and white supremacist groups resulted in a handful of deaths and ended their stand in the homeland. The takeover led to the collapse of the Freedom Party's resistance to the election and fears of serious disruptions were sharply reduced. A report from a judicial inquiry shocked the country with revelations that a special branch of the police trained hit squads, gave arms to the Inkatha enemies of the ANC and instigated massacres. The Ciskei homeland was the next to be taken over by the South African government as the date of the national elections neared. Inkatha supporters marched past ANC headquarters in Johannesburg, sparking the worst riot in the city's history. By month-end the government in Pretoria moved to declare a state of emergency in the Zulu-dominated province of Natal and sent in troops. **Switzerland:** A UN conference on toxic waste reached an agreement, signed by all industrialized nations except the US, that endorsed an end to the dumping of such materials in third world countries. **Turkey:** Local elections were won by a centrist party, however Islamic fundamentalists won the mayor's seat in 22 cities. In general, the Islamic party, characterized as anti-Israel and anti-western, came in third in a very strong showing. **United Kingdom:** The General Synod of the Church of England ordained its first women priests, ending a male monopoly that has lasted for 460 years. London's Heaththrow airport was the target of mortar fire for two days in a row; there were no injuries and little damage, however operations were delayed; the IRA claimed responsibility. **United States:** The question of renewal of China's trading status as a "most favoured nation" with the US was used to try to pressure China to improve their human rights record; as negotiations proceeded however, the Chinese government was unmoved. **Venezuela:** The scandal caused by the January collapse of Banco Latino widened to threaten the country's fragile democracy as well as its economy. The collapse jeopardized military pensions and many small towns and businesses shut down due to lack of funds as six other banks affected were near insolvency.

CANADA

Canada's peacekeeping mission in Bosnia was extended for another six months. The RCMP announced it had seized over five tons of cocaine from a fishing vessel docked in Shelburne, NS. Rogers Communications Inc. signed a $3.1 billion deal to take over Maclean Hunter Ltd., giving that company a very large stake in Canada's communications industry. Pte E.K. Brown was the first to be convicted in the beating death of a Somalian civilian in March of 1993; at the time, he was serving with Canada's peacekeeping forces in Somalia. The Social Credit party in BC suffered yet another setback when three of its six elected MLAs left the party to join a newly created BC Reform party. A private consortium purchased Toronto's SkyDome from the Ontario government for about half of what it cost to build the stadium. The Heritage Minister announced a new parks policy that focusses on protecting the eco-system rather than tourism and development; recreation facilities will be permitted only if they do no damage to wilderness areas, sport fishing will be restricted and hunting will be banned. On Mar. 27, a British engineer was the victim of a drive-by shooting in Ottawa.

April

INTERNATIONAL

Bosnia: Serbian forces turned their attention to the Muslim enclave of Gorazde, formerly a UN-designated "safe area"; by mid-month the city was close to collapse and tensions escalated when Serb forces shot down a British Sea Harrier jet. NATO forces responded by bombing Serb targets, but the attacks did nothing to stop Serb artillery. After three weeks NATO threatened to increase their own bombing raids if the Serbs did not pull back and by month end troops and heavy weapons had been moved away. **Cambodia:** Government troops, which had seized a stronghold of the Khmer Rouge in March, had it taken from them in a surprise attack by 3 000 fighters. The Cambodian government renewed accusations that neighbouring Thailand was harbouring and bankrolling its enemies. **El Salvador:** The first elected president since the end of the 12-year civil war, Armando Calderon Sol of the right-wing ARENA party, won the presidential runoff election. **India:** 150 000 demonstrators in New Delhi protested the government's decision to sign the GATT agreement. The protest became violent as 2 000 police became the target of bricks and stones; police retaliated with water cannons, rubber bullets and tear gas. **Iraq:** US fighter planes shot down two helicopters in a "no-fly" zone, killing 5 Kurds and 15 Americans who were part of UN forces; flight crews claimed that the downed aircraft had failed to identify themselves as friendly. **Israel:** Violence continued throughout Israel and the occupied territories as Islamic fundamentalists claimed responsibility for the suicide bombing of a bus and Israeli soldiers clashed with Palestinians in a demonstration outside the Hebron mosque. Meetings continued to hammer out a final agreement on self-rule for Jericho and the Gaza Strip, as Prime Min. Rabin began to suggest talks with Syria and indicated that the control of the Golan Heights was negotiable. **Japan:** After less than a year in office, Prime Min. Morihiro Hosokawa was forced to resign amid charges of corruption; when elected Hosokawa had pledged to end the scandals that had plagued Japanese politics. Foreign Min. Tsutomu Hata was named as his successor. **Mexico:** Selected violence continued as a second wealthy executive was kidnapped and the police chief of Tijuana was gunned down near the site of the murder of presidential candidate Luis Colosio. **Morocco:** Representatives from 117 nations gathered in Marrakech on Apr. 15 to sign the GATT treaty, ending the long and contentious Uruguay round of talks and paving the way for the creation of the World Trade Organization. **Rwanda:** The Hutu-born presidents of Rwanda and Burundi died in a plane crash and Rwandan soldiers subsequently went on a rampage, targeting the rival Tutsis, killing thousands in Kigali, and prompting the evacuation of foreigners from the country. After two weeks, the death toll was estimated in the tens of thousands and the UN began the evacuation of its forces. The killing continued without a pause throughout the month; hundreds of thousands fled to neighbouring countries to escape the violence while Tutsi-led rebel forces mounted a drive to contain the carnage. **South Africa:** Zulu leaders continued to insist they would boycott the national elections, demanding independence for their territory; as the election date neared violence

in the province of Natal also escalated. A week before the vote the Zulu chief agreed to drop the boycott in exchange for continuation of the Zulu monarchy. The first ever all race elections were held from the 26th to the 28th after months of tension; the election was generally peaceful and foreign observers cited no serious problems as thousands of voters lined up to cast their ballots; voting was extended an extra day to accommodate them. Nelson Mandela was declared the country's new president. **Ukraine:** Two alarms at the Chernobyl nuclear plant, triggered by minor problems, prompted new calls for a complete shutdown of the reactor, which has two units still running. **United Kingdom:** Police conducted raids in England, Ireland and Northern Ireland in an effort to cut off funds for the IRA; cash, drugs and evidence of money laundering were seized in the sweep. **United States:** House of Rep. passed a crime bill to expand federal use of the death penalty and put those convicted of felonies or drug offenses three times behind bars for life. **Vatican:** Notice was sent to bishops around the world that girls may be acolytes at Mass, formalizing a practice that has become prevalent in recent years. **Yemen:** Fighting erupted between soldiers from the conservative north and the formerly Marxist areas of the south; an Egyptian mediator opened negotiations aimed at settling the dispute.

CANADA

Revenue Canada announced in a ruling that the US and 10 other countries had dumped (i.e. sold the goods for less than it cost to produce them) galvanized sheet steel in Canada, and imposed tariffs of up to 166% on their products. A midtown Toronto restaurant robbery turned into a murder when the intruders shot and killed one of the patrons; the latest killing sparked more calls for gun control. Statistics Canada announced that the net debt of all levels of government stood at $23 065 for each Canadian at the end of March; in 1982, the debt was $4 339 per person. It was also announced that the national unemployment rate dropped to 10.6%, down from 11.1% in February. On Apr. 15, 16 Canadian peace keepers were detained in an ongoing campaign of harassment of UN forces in Bosnia. Canadian Airlines announced a deal with American Airlines, selling that company a 1/3 interest in Canadian in an effort to solve its financial difficulties. The Nova Scotia government announced a cut in tobacco taxes, citing the flood of cheap cigarettes from those provinces that had already made the cut (Quebec, Ontario, New Brunswick and PEI). NDP leader Audrey McLaughlin announced on April 18 that she would step down as leader of the federal party as soon as a successor was chosen. For the first time in 28 years, the Canada Pension Plan posted a deficit and dipped into its accumulated surplus to cover its obligations. On Apr. 29, the Nova Scotia legislature was disrupted by a demonstration by angry construction workers; the group invaded the legislature and the Speaker cancelled the session as MLAs were escorted from the building. The workers were angry over a recent provincial decision to allow nonunion workers on union construction sites.

May

INTERNATIONAL

Antarctica: Scientists announced the discovery of dinosaur remains dating from the Jurassic era. **Bosnia:** After weeks of ineffectual pressure toward a peace settlement, France threatened to withdraw its soldiers if no progress was made. The Bosnian Federation of Muslims and Croats, created in March, held its first meeting on May 30th. The organization decided that any settlement would have to award them at least 58% of the territory in Bosnia-Hercegovina. Serb forces refused to leave the exclusion zone around Gorazde, despite UN demands. **Indonesia:** An earthquake in eastern Java generated 6 m tidal waves that flowed 500 m inland, sweeping away 680 homes and killing 200. **Israel:** The accord that inaugurated Palestinian self-rule in the Gaza Strip and the West Bank town of Jericho was signed by Yasser Arafat and Ytzhak Rabin on May 4th. Palestinians welcomed the first members of their own police force to the territory and the PLO began the process of creating a government structure. Israel forces pulled out of the Gaza Strip area by mid-month. **Italy:** Brazilian Formula One racing star Ayrton Senna da Silva was killed during the San Marino Grand Prix; many drivers complained that the governing body's decision to ban high-tech electronics from the cars had made the sport more dangerous. **Korea, North:** The nuclear standoff with the US continued as the government began removing fuel rods from a nuclear reactor without the participation of the Atomic Energy Agency. Neighbouring governments and the US sought to impose sanctions amid rising fears that the North Korean government had the atomic bomb; North Korea issued more statements denouncing any sanctions and promising devastating consequences if any were imposed. **Norway:** Police in Oslo recovered Edvard Munch's *The Scream* three months after it was stolen. **Pakistan:** Anti-government demonstrators were fired upon by police during a peaceful demonstration and the riots that followed left 27 dead and 150 injured. **Rwanda:** Ethnic warfare between the Hutu and Tutsi tribes continued to escalate as a UN relief plane was fired on at Kigali airport and humanitarian flights were suspended. As rebel forces led by Tutsis began to win territory, hundreds of thousands more fled to refugee camps in neighbouring countries. **Singapore:** US teen Michael Fay received four strokes of the cane for vandalism despite American diplomatic protests. **South Africa:** Nelson Mandela was sworn in as president with F.W. de Clerk and Thabo Mbeki as Deputy Presidents. **United States:** Physicists working at the Fermi National Accelerator Lab near Chicago announced success in the hunt for the final building blocks of matter—subatomic particles known as "top" quarks. Bill Clinton's presidency came under attack from yet another quarter when Paula Jones, a former clerk at an Arkansas state agency, charged him with sexual harassment. Former First Lady Jacqueline Kennedy Onassis died of cancer at 64. US policy on Haiti continued to waver as Pres. Clinton pressed for tougher sanctions, threatened invasion and returned Haitian refugees to their home. By month-end Clinton had promised to end the practice of forced repatriation. **Vatican:** In an apostolic letter sent to bishops around the world on May 30th, Pope John Paul II reconfirmed that the Catholic church would not ordain women as priests. **Yemen:** The conflict begun in April was stepped up as foreigners fled the capital and southerners were expelled from the government. As the forces from the north made in-roads into southern territory, southerners mounted stiff resistance.

CANADA

Court martials over the beating death of a

Somali civilian by Canadian peace keepers continued as a second member of the Airborne regiment pleaded guilty and it was revealed that another soldier involved was not fit to stand trial after a failed suicide attempt. The city of Vancouver won an NBA basketball franchise, joining Toronto on the circuit in the 1995-96 season. On May 8, Canada won the World Hockey Championship for the first time since 1961. Teachers in Newfoundland walked off the job on May 16 after negotiations failed to reach an acceptable settlement. The Federal Court of appeal announced a ruling on the tax status of single parents, decreeing that those receiving child-support payments should be exempt from paying income tax on the money; Ottawa launched an appeal of the decision. Quebec and Ontario signed deals that ended the Quebec practice of barring Ontario workers and firms and recognized each province's guidelines for accrediting workers. In Alberta, the province's doctors reached an agreement with the government that would bar out-of-province doctors from practicing in Alberta; the move followed restrictions in Ontario and BC on the number of doctors allowed to practice and was intended to stem any flood of new physicians arriving from those provinces. In BC, the Social Credit party suffered another blow when leader Grace McCarthy resigned on May 3 after she failed to win a seat in the legislature in a by-election, leaving the party with just two MLAs. Ontario's first casino opened in Windsor, joining Quebec and Manitoba in the gambling business.

June

INTERNATIONAL

Afghanistan: Pres. Rabbani forced Prime Min. Hakmatyar out of the capital, Kabul, by bombarding the city; the Prime Min. retaliated by ordering the bombing the city of Herat. **Bosnia:** The pattern of broken truces and ceasefires continued as Bosnian Serbs and the coalition of Bosnian Muslims and Croats agreed to a one-month ceasefire that was violated almost immediately. The US House of Rep. called for an end to the arms embargo on the Bosnian Muslims. Evidence supporting tales of torture, pogroms against ethnic groups and murder in prison camps was gathered by outside experts hoping to eventually bring

war criminals to justice. **Brazil:** The worst frost in 20 years hit the country's coffee plantations, killing as much as one-third of the crop. **China:** An underground nuclear test was conducted, despite protests from Japan, the US and other governments. **Colombia:** An earthquake that measured 6.4 triggered a massive avalanche that killed hundreds of people in a mountainous region southwest of Bogota. **France:** Dignitaries and veterans from around the world gathered in Normandy to mark the 50th anniversary of the D-day invasion. In Paris, the International Earth Rotation Service gave the final minute of the last day in June an extra second in order to coordinate the precise atomic clocks with the turns of the planet; the 19th such extra second since 1972. **Haiti:** Efforts to restore the democratic government there were stepped up as the US banned all commercial flights to the island and stopped most banking transactions. Thousands of Haitians fled the island in an effort to escape the ravages of the blockade and the possible invasion. **Iraq:** Turkey received permission to pump oil from a pipeline in Iraq's oil fields; US officials termed the deal unique and not an end of the embargo imposed during the Gulf War period. **Israel:** The Vatican and Israel established full diplomatic ties. Yasser Arafat visited the newly autonomous Gaza Strip after an absence of 27 years. **Japan:** The two-month old government of Prime Min. Tsuomu Hata lost a no-confidence vote and resigned, once again throwing the Japanese Diet (parliament) into a turmoil as various parties tried to form a stable government. The conservative Liberal Democrats eventually formed a coalition with the Socialist Party, and Socialist leader Tomiichi Murayama became the new Prime Min. **Korea, North:** The government's war of words with the rest of the world escalated again as it declared it "will never allow inspections" of two of its nuclear dumping facilities and reiterated that sanctions would lead to war. However after a visit by former US Pres. Jimmy Carter, the North Koreans agreed to a meeting with their southern counterparts and decided not to expel international nuclear inspectors. They also agreed to a freeze on their nuclear program and a three-day summit with their South Korean counterparts was set for July 25. **Mexico:** The family of a banker kidnapped in March agreed to pay a ransom of close to $30 million to obtain his release. **Nigeria:** Military leaders clamped down on the apparent winner of last year's presidential election after he threatened to establish a government despite the government cancellation of the election; Moshood Abiola was then declared a fugitive with a $1 600 price on his head; he was later arrested and jailed. **Russia:** Pres. Boris Yeltsin announced new measures to fight the crime wave sweeping his country. **Rwanda:** Tutsi rebels made further territorial gains against government troops, pushing the mainly Hutu group into the western part of the country and thousands of Hutus fled for fear of reprisals. France dispatched troops to help protect civilians as the massacres continued, amid fears that, given France's colonial activity in the region, the troops would not be neutral. **South Africa:** After 24 years the UN General Assembly once again granted full membership to South Africa. **Vatican:** The Pontifical Academy of Sciences released a paper suggesting that couples should have no more than two children, a direct contradiction of papal policy on birth control. **United Arab Emirate:** 12 former executives of the failed Bank of Credit & Commerce International were convicted on charges of fraud and mismanagement in one of the largest financial scandals in the world. **United States:** TV viewers watched a freeway chase involving Los Angeles police and former football star O.J. Simpson, who later gave himself up and was charged with the murder of his ex-wife and a companion. Action in the 52-match World Cup series opened in Chicago and continued throughout the month at various venues in the US. The US dollar went into a record-breaking dive, and the Fed. Reserve had to intervene to prop it up as it dropped to a post-war low against the Japanese yen.

CANADA

A landmark in downtown Halifax, the 194-year-old St. George's Anglican Church, was destroyed by fire; the church had recently been designated as a historic site and was believed to be the only wooden church of its type in North America. Members of the Royal Canadian Legion sparked a nationwide debate when they voted to maintain the ban on head coverings on Legion premises at their national convention. A report on academic integrity at Concordia University concluded that charges of irregularity made by former teacher Valery Fabrikant had some validity and recommended changes that would be applicable at all Canadian universities; Fabrikant shot and killed four colleagues at Concordia in August 1992 during a dispute over tenure and credit for research. Newfoundland teachers returned to work on June 13th. After an acrimonious debate, the Ontario NDP government's bill to authorize equal rights for spousal and other benefits for same-sex couples was defeated 68-59. In response to charges that Alaska fishermen were over fishing northern BC salmon stocks, the federal fisheries department announced that US commercial fishing vessels would have to purchase a licence if they wished to move into BC waters. Efforts to rescue Telesat Canada's broadcast satellite Anik E-2 were successful on June 21; the satellite was expected to resume broadcasting in July after some fine-tuning of the new system. The Vancouver Canucks lost the Stanley Cup final series to the New York Rangers and fans took to the streets in what turned into a six-hour riot that did millions of dollars worth of damage. Statistics Canada reported that inflation in May had dropped to -0.2%, or deflation, for the first time since August of 1955.

July

INTERNATIONAL

Algeria: Seven Italian sailors sleeping aboard their cargo ship had their throats slashed by suspected Islamic extremists targetting foreigners. **Argentina:** A bomb blast in the capital destroyed the offices of two Jewish groups, killing 49 and injuring over 150; a radical Islamic group claimed responsibility. **Bosnia:** The Bosnian Serb leader rejected a peace plan that would cut their territory back to 49%, but still allow them to keep much of what they had captured. The supply road to Sarajevo was closed later in the month as UN troops were attacked and one British soldier was killed. **Brazil:** In an effort to curb inflation and bring price stability to its citizens, the Brazilian government scrapped its existing currency, the cruzeiro, and replaced it with a new one, the real. Severe budget cuts also took effect. **China:** The country's APT Satellite Co. launched its first satellite on July 21, without consultation with international bodies who monitor satellites to make sure they do not interfere with each other. China's launch raised concerns that the two satellites closest to the Apstar-1, Japan's Sakura-3A and Tonga's Rimsat-1, would have their operations disrupted by static from the new satellite and that the satellite itself would not be fully functional either. **Germany:** The post Cold War military pullout continued as US troops began to leave Berlin and prepared to hand facilities over to the German government. Germany's highest court ruled that the armed forces could take part in international missions provided that the move was sanctioned by a parliamentary majority. **Haiti:** As boatloads of refugees continued to leave the country, the US announced that they would be sent to other Caribbean nations rather than allowed entry into the US. Preparations for a possible invasion continued, in an effort to step up the pressure on the military rulers. **Israel:** Jordan and Israel signed a peace agreement in Washington that set the stage for friendlier and more open relations between the two. **Jupiter:** A string of comet fragments known as Shoemaker-Levy 9 collided with the giant planet between July 16 and 22nd, causing massive explosions in the planet's atmosphere that were recorded by satellites and observatories around the world. **Korea, North:** Ruler Kim Il Sung died of a heart attack just as discussions over the country's nuclear program were resuming. He was succeeded by his son Kim Jong Il, although the two-day postponement of the funeral gave rise to speculation that the younger Kim's hold on power was not secure. **Pakistan:** The most destructive monsoon in 17 years left 40 dead and the city of Karachi without power for nearly a week, sparking riots in protest over the slow repair. **Russia:** An investment firm offering 2000% interest annually collapsed, leaving thousands with worthless stocks and wiping out the savings of many. **Rwanda:** Rebels in the mainly Tutsi Rwandan Patriotic Front captured Kigali and Butare, two of the largest cities and a cease-fire was declared by mid-month. The flood of refugees into neighbouring countries such as Zaire continued as the defeated Hutus spread rumours of reprisal killings and by month end the camps themselves became death traps as cholera and starvation killed victims already weakened by their flight. **Spain:** The heat and drought conditions in Spain brought on the worst season of wildfires in 50 years; more than 160 000 hectares were burned with 20 dead and tens of thousands forced from their homes. Basques separatists exploded a powerful car bomb in Madrid, leaving 130 families homeless and killing 3. **Turkey:** Officials announced they had seized 10 kg of high-grade uranium suspected to have been smuggled out of facilities in the former Soviet Union. **United States:** In televised preliminary hearings, a California judge declared there was sufficient evidence to order a trial for O.J. Simpson on charges of murder. On the eve of the World Cup final, the three tenors (Pavarotti, Domingo and Carrerras) gave a reprise of their phenomenally successful concert of four years earlier; the next day Brazil won the month-long tournament. An anti-abortion activist shot and killed a doctor and his associate outside a Florida clinic. **Yemen:** Government troops captured Aden, the base for southern secessionists, and separatist leaders fled the country.

CANADA

Scientists studying east coast fish stocks reported that, despite the moratoriums on fishing, cod stocks continued to decline and were now at just 3% of their 1990 level. The Krever inquiry into Canada's blood supply heard testimony in the Maritimes that indicated that the NB Red Cross had knowingly distributed unsafe blood products. Members of Saskatchewan Wheat Pool, formed in 1924, voted to transform the organization from a member-owned cooperative to a public company, citing the need for more capital to fund diversification. The Canada-US wheat war continued as the US International Trade Commission ruled that Canadian wheat exports were hurting US farmers and asked for tariffs and quotas on the commodity; Canadian officials vowed that if the measures were put in place, retaliatory steps would be taken. On July 18 the prime minister and provincial premiers signed an internal trade agreement to end trade barriers among provinces. On July 25, Canada sent a 200-member field hospital unit to the Rwanda-Zaire border area; 400 communications specialists and security forces were sent earlier to join UN forces commanded by Cdn. General Roméo Dallaire. The Innuit of Quebec signed a self-government deal with Quebec on July 21, setting up a framework to create an elected assembly for the region that would take on existing powers as well as policing, wildlife management, education and social services. Winnipeg was awarded the 1999 Pan-American Games.

August

INTERNATIONAL

Algeria: Islamic militants killed five French nationals inside a foreign compound and left behind a car bomb that was defused shortly before it was set to explode. Later in the month an earthquake registering 5.6 on the Richter scale hit the northwestern part of the country before dawn, leaving 171 dead and over 10 000 homeless. **Belgium:** Brussels' police recovered a Picasso stolen in Nov. from the Stockholm Modern Art Museum; three Swedes were arrested. **Bosnia:** Bosnian Serbs broke into a UN compound and stole heavy weapons the day after Serbia cut off economic and political ties in response to the Bosnians rejection of a peace plan; NATO responded to the move by bombing Bosnian Serb positions. The Muslim-led Bosnian army won an important victory in the northwest as US Pres. Clinton renewed calls to lift the arms embargo against them. **Cambodia:** 50 000 villagers were left homeless and eight died after torrential rains flooded five provinces. **Cuba:** Four ferries on Havana Bay were highjacked to Florida in three weeks as an increasing number of Cubans sought to leave the country; leader Fidel Castro threatened to open the gates to allow unlimited emigration to the US and accused the US of encouraging the flow. **France:** French magistrates, inspired by their Italian counterparts, began investigations into high-level business and government corruption, charging a number of ministers, mayors and party leaders with bribery and fraud. In response to the killing of French nationals in Algeria, France began to round up and expel suspected Islamic extremists. **Germany:** Officials announced the fourth seizure of smuggled plutonium that was traced to the former Soviet Union. **Greece:** The Greek government protested the trial of five Greeks in Albania on espionage charges by expelling 17 500 illegal Albanian immigrants. A Greek airforce plane dropped thousands of leaflets urging the overthrow of the government in south Albania and the

Albanian government recalled its Greek ambassador in its own protest. **Haiti:** The UN Security Council unanimously authorized the US to restore democracy by any means necessary, including invasion. The US marshalled its forces, but continued to try and make a deal that would allow the military leaders to leave peacefully. **Israel:** A border crossing between Jordan and Israel was opened for tourists and telephone links were established on the heels of a Jordan-Israel peace agreement. Palestinian self-rule continued to take hold as the school system was handed over to the new authorities. **Japan:** A heat wave begun in early July continued as record high temperatures scorched many parts of the country; in early August Tokyo recorded an all-time high of 39.1°C. **Korea, North:** The government agreed to continue to freeze its nuclear program and stay on as a member of the nuclear non-proliferation treaty in return for US assistance in changing to safer nuclear technology. Later in the month it rejected a South Korean request that its nuclear program be opened to full inspection by international authorities. **Lesotho:** King Letsie III dissolved the cabinet of the first democratically election government and installed a six-person provisional council to govern for the next year; thousands of protesters marched on the royal palace. **Mexico:** 77% of the electorate turned out for Mexico's national elections, won by the incumbent Institutional Revolutionary Party led by Ernesto Zedillo; foreign observers reported that the election was fair. **Nigeria:** Five million members of the National Labor Congress joined in a two-day strike initiated by the oil workers to try to bring down the military government; five people died during the strike and crackdown that followed while dozens were arrested as the government tried to break the strike, which dragged on for more than six weeks. **Pakistan:** A former prime minister announced during a political rally that the country did indeed possess the atom bomb, touching off a flurry of denial from government officials and a storm of protest from neighbouring countries. **Rwanda:** Refugees anxious to return home from crowded and squalid camps in neighbouring countries were warned by Hutu propaganda that the victorious Tutsi rebels would institute revenge killings; many chose to remain despite the hazards of the camps themselves. French soldiers, who arrived in June, to try to install some order on the country handed their mission over to UN forces and left the country. **Sudan:** The world's most-wanted terrorist, known as Carlos the Jackal, was arrested in Sudan and flown to France where he faced trial on charges related to a 1982 bombing in Paris and the murder of two French counter-intelligence officers in 1975. **United States:** Baseball players and owners failed to come to an agreement over salary issues and a strike began on Aug. 12. The 25th anniversary of Woodstock was celebrated with a concert in nearby Saugerties, New York. As the flow of Cuban refugees grew to hundreds per day, the Clinton administration announced an end to free admittance of Cuban refugees and began to apply standard regulations to the would-be immigrants.

CANADA

On Aug. 2 the government announced a one-year truce in the wheat war with the US, tariffs will be imposed on Canadian exports over 1.5 million tons in the 1994-95 crop year; 2.5 million tons of durum wheat went south of the border in the 1993-94 crop year, mostly to satisfy the demand for high-quality wheat for pasta. Scientists in Saskatchewan continued to excavate a 65-million-year-old dinosaur skeleton identified as a Tyrannosaurus rex, hoping to find a complete skeleton. Statistics Canada reported that unemployment dropped in July and the number of bankruptcies was also down slightly. On Aug. 5 the Nova Scotia government announced that the Westray mine would never reopen and the remains of the 11 miners who died in the explosion would not be recovered. Ontario's OPP instituted photo radar as their latest weapon against speeding drivers, despite objections from civil libertarians; the system is already in effect in Alberta. An aide to the former Tory solicitor general leaked government documents alleging that the country's largest neo-Nazi group was founded by a paid informant of CSIS. The XV Commonwealth Games opened in Victoria on Aug. 18, with 3 300 participants from 64 nations taking part. A wildfire near Penticton, BC burned out of control, destroying 13 500 acres and 18 homes; a teenager was arrested and charged with arson. The remaining 30 Canadian troops left the CFB Lahr, officially ending 27 years of Canadian service for NATO in Europe. Canada's fifth-largest life insurer, Confederation Life, was taken over by federal regulators on Aug. 11 after talks aimed at bailing out the financially troubled institution failed. Nova Scotia tuna fishermen blockaded out-of-province boats at the government wharf in Shelburne to protest inroads into the bluefin tuna fishery. A fire at Vancouver's grain terminal dock burned for 24 hours before firefighters managed to put out the blaze; visitors to the Pacific National Exhibition were evacuated from the grounds. The Algonquins of Golden Lake Ontario and the government signed an agreement on Aug. 26 to begin negotiating a land claim to 8.5 million acres in southern Canada, including Parliament Hill, Algonquin Park and a large part of the Ottawa region.

September

INTERNATIONAL

Australia: Australians were shocked by the assassination of a politician—only the second in the country's 206-year history; a Labor party state legislator known for his campaign against Asian crime and gangs was gunned down in his driveway. **Baltic States:** 54 years of Russian occupation of Latvia and Estonia ended with the departure of the last Russian soldiers. **Bosnia:** 90% of the voters in a referendum held in Bosnian Serb territory rejected an international peace plan and stepped up their ethnic cleansing program in northern Bosnia. Pope John Paul II cancelled a planned visit to the besieged city of Sarajevo, citing threats to the safety of the crowds that would turn out to see him; he later visited Zagreb. **Cuba:** As the flood of refugees continued to head for the coast of Florida, Washington attempted to set new guidelines for Cuban immigrants and encourage the Cuban government to deter would-be immigrants from taking to sea. **Egypt:** The UN International conference on population was held in Cairo. Representatives from 180 nations debated global population control and reached consensus on a 113-page program for action, which included calls for more than tripling spending on population control by the year 2000. **Finland:** A car ferry en route from Estonia capsized and sank in rough seas, killing over 900 passengers and crew. **Germany:** After a ceremony in Berlin attended by Russian Pres. Boris Yeltsin, Russian troops left Germany after 49 years of occupation. **India:** An outbreak of pneumonic plague in the city of Surat sparked panic among its residents. Many fled the area, raising the spectre of the plague travelling with them and spreading to other major cities. **Israel:** Prime Min. Rabin gave details of a plan for a limited withdrawal from the Golan Heights and a 3-year trial period of the withdrawal in exchange for peace with Syria. **Japan:** The government offered to spend $1 billion during the next 10 years to fund projects such as cultural exchanges and research into wartime activities in an effort to atone for wartime atrocities. **Mexico:** The head of the country's fifth largest banking group was accused of siphoning up to $700 million from the bank for his own private use. **Nigeria:** Oil workers ended their protest strike over the arrest of the opposition leader widely believed to have won last year's election and the next day the country's military leader declared that he had absolute power. The military government placed itself above the nation's courts, giving itself the right to detain people for up to three months without charges. **Korea, North:** Preliminary talks were held with US officials, aimed at opening diplomatic channels; leader Kim Jong Il invited former US Pres. Carter to act as mediator in the dispute over North Korea's nuclear program. **Northern Ireland:** The political wing of the Irish Republican Army announced a "complete cessation of military operations," paving the way for participation in talks aimed at creating peace in the country. **Philippines:** An explosion in a coal mine south of Manila killed at least 81 miners and left 68 injured, the country's worst ever mining accident. **Russia:** A summit meeting between Pres. Boris Yeltsin and Chinese Pres. Jiang Zemin finalized agreements on outstanding border disputes, relative troop strength along their mutual borders and paved the way for increased trade. Three Russian cosmonauts managed to dock with their supply ship on the third try; the mission is to continue in orbit and perform joint missions with the European Space Agency and NASA. **Serbia:** Western diplomats reached agreement with the Serbian government to monitor the Serbian embargo against Bosnian Serbs, suggesting that if the embargo held, the UN might consider lifting some of the sanctions on Serbia. **Sri Lanka:** Tamil rebels and government troops clashed north of the capital and 35 rebels were killed; the battle came only days after the rebels had agreed to sit down to peace talks with the government. **United States:** Official ties with Taiwan were expanded but fell short of recognizing it as a country separate from China; the move aroused mild hostility in China and did not go far enough to please the Taiwanese. On Sept. 8, a Boeing 737 crashed just outside of Pittsburgh killing all 132 passengers. The US issued a blunt ultimatum to the military junta in Haiti and sent a delegation to conduct last ditch talks aimed at persuading the government to step aside without violence; US troops landed on Sept. 19, after a deal was cut. In baseball, owners announced that due to the lengthy strike the remainder of the season and the World Series would be cancelled.

CANADA

A fierce takeover battle for Lac Minerals ended when Royal Oak Mines withdrew its offer for the company, leaving the victory to American Barrick Resources Corp. of Toronto. A report from Statistics Canada showed that the economy had its strongest growth since 1987 in the second quarter of 1994. The Innu of Davis Inlet continued their battles with the Newfoundland justice system as they refused access to their community to the provincial court system. As expected, the Parti Québécois won the Quebec provincial election, but split in the popular vote (44.7% for the PQ and 44.3% for the Liberals) was closer than expected and the outcome was not interpreted as a vote for separation. 1 800 workers at the Saskatchewan Wheat Pool went on strike, the first in the co-operative's 70-year history. The Krever inquiry into Canada's blood supply system continued to hear revelations of mishandling of tainted blood during the 1980s that led to nearly 1 000 Canadians receiving blood product containing the HIV virus. Southam Inc. announced that it was selling its 258-store Coles chain to rival Smithbooks, creating a chain with $350 million in sales. NHL president Gary Bettman made good his threat to lock out players if they failed to settle their contract dispute with owners before the start of the season and the hockey season, like baseball, was halted by the work stoppage.

Index

1994

JANUARY
S	M	T	W	T	F	S
					[1]	
2	3	4	5	6	7	8
9	10	11	12	13	14	15
16	17	18	19	20	21	22
23	24	25	26	27	28	29
30	31					

FEBRUARY
S	M	T	W	T	F	S
		1	2	3	4	5
6	7	8	9	10	11	12
13	14	15	16	17	18	19
20	21	22	23	24	25	26
27	28					

MARCH
S	M	T	W	T	F	S
		1	2	3	4	5
6	7	8	9	10	11	12
13	14	15	16	17	18	19
20	21	22	23	24	25	26
27	28	29	30	31		

APRIL
S	M	T	W	T	F	S
					[1]	2
3	4	5	6	7	8	9
10	11	12	13	14	15	16
17	18	19	20	21	22	23
24	25	26	27	28	29	30

MAY
S	M	T	W	T	F	S
1	2	3	4	5	6	7
8	9	10	11	12	13	14
15	16	17	18	19	20	21
22	[23]	24	25	26	27	28
29	30	31				

JUNE
S	M	T	W	T	F	S
			1	2	3	4
5	6	7	8	9	10	11
12	13	14	15	16	17	18
19	20	21	22	23	24	25
26	27	28	29	30		

JULY
S	M	T	W	T	F	S
					[1]	2
3	4	5	6	7	8	9
10	11	12	13	14	15	16
17	18	19	20	21	22	23
24	25	26	27	28	29	30
31						

AUGUST
S	M	T	W	T	F	S
	1	2	3	4	5	6
7	8	9	10	11	12	13
14	15	16	17	18	19	20
21	22	23	24	25	26	27
28	29	30	31			

SEPTEMBER
S	M	T	W	T	F	S
				1	2	3
4	[5]	6	7	8	9	10
11	12	13	14	15	16	17
18	19	20	21	22	23	24
25	26	27	28	29	30	

OCTOBER
S	M	T	W	T	F	S
						1
2	3	4	5	6	7	8
9	[10]	11	12	13	14	15
16	17	18	19	20	21	22
23	24	25	26	27	28	29
30	31					

NOVEMBER
S	M	T	W	T	F	S
		1	2	3	4	5
6	7	8	9	10	11	12
13	14	15	16	17	18	19
20	21	22	23	24	25	26
27	28	29	30			

DECEMBER
S	M	T	W	T	F	S
				1	2	3
4	5	6	7	8	9	10
11	12	13	14	15	16	17
18	19	20	21	22	23	24
[25]	[26]	27	28	29	30	31

1996

JANUARY
S	M	T	W	T	F	S
	[1]	2	3	4	5	6
7	8	9	10	11	12	13
14	15	16	17	18	19	20
21	22	23	24	25	26	27
28	29	30	31			

FEBRUARY
S	M	T	W	T	F	S
				1	2	3
4	5	6	7	8	9	10
11	12	13	14	15	16	17
18	19	20	21	22	23	24
25	26	27	28	29		

MARCH
S	M	T	W	T	F	S
					1	2
3	4	5	6	7	8	9
10	11	12	13	14	15	16
17	18	19	20	21	22	23
24	25	26	27	28	29	30
31						

APRIL
S	M	T	W	T	F	S
	1	2	3	4	[5]	6
7	8	9	10	11	12	13
14	15	16	17	18	19	20
21	22	23	24	25	26	27
28	29	30				

MAY
S	M	T	W	T	F	S
			1	2	3	4
5	6	7	8	9	10	11
12	13	14	15	16	17	18
19	[20]	21	22	23	24	25
26	27	28	29	30	31	

JUNE
S	M	T	W	T	F	S
						1
2	3	4	5	6	7	8
9	10	11	12	13	14	15
16	17	18	19	20	21	22
23	24	25	26	27	28	29
30						

JULY
S	M	T	W	T	F	S
	[1]	2	3	4	5	6
7	8	9	10	11	12	13
14	15	16	17	18	19	20
21	22	23	24	25	26	27
28	29	30	31			

AUGUST
S	M	T	W	T	F	S
				1	2	3
4	5	6	7	8	9	10
11	12	13	14	15	16	17
18	19	20	21	22	23	24
25	26	27	28	29	30	31

SEPTEMBER
S	M	T	W	T	F	S
1	[2]	3	4	5	6	7
8	9	10	11	12	13	14
15	16	17	18	19	20	21
22	23	24	25	26	27	28
29	30					

OCTOBER
S	M	T	W	T	F	S
		1	2	3	4	5
6	7	8	9	10	11	12
13	[14]	15	16	17	18	19
20	21	22	23	24	25	26
27	28	29	30	31		

NOVEMBER
S	M	T	W	T	F	S
					1	2
3	4	5	6	7	8	9
10	11	12	13	14	15	16
17	18	19	20	21	22	23
24	25	26	27	28	29	30

DECEMBER
S	M	T	W	T	F	S
1	2	3	4	5	6	7
8	9	10	11	12	13	14
15	16	17	18	19	20	21
22	23	24	[25]	[26]	27	28
29	30	31				

1995 CALENDAR AND HOLIDAYS

JANUARY

S	M	T	W	T	F	S
1	2	3	4	5	6	7
8	9	10	11	12	13	14
15	16	17	18	19	20	21
22	23	24	25	26	27	28
29	30	31				

FEBRUARY

S	M	T	W	T	F	S
			1	2	3	4
5	6	7	8	9	10	11
12	13	14	15	16	17	18
19	20	21	22	23	24	25
26	27	28				

MARCH

S	M	T	W	T	F	S
			1	2	3	4
5	6	7	8	9	10	11
12	13	14	15	16	17	18
19	20	21	22	23	24	25
26	27	28	29	30	31	

APRIL

S	M	T	W	T	F	S
						1
2	3	4	5	6	7	8
9	10	11	12	13	14	15
16	17	18	19	20	21	22
23	24	25	26	27	28	29
30						

MAY

S	M	T	W	T	F	S
	1	2	3	4	5	6
7	8	9	10	11	12	13
14	15	16	17	18	19	20
21	22	23	24	25	26	27
28	29	30	31			

JUNE

S	M	T	W	T	F	S
				1	2	3
4	5	6	7	8	9	10
11	12	13	14	15	16	17
18	19	20	21	22	23	24
25	26	27	28	29	30	

JULY

S	M	T	W	T	F	S
						1
2	3	4	5	6	7	8
9	10	11	12	13	14	15
16	17	18	19	20	21	22
23	24	25	26	27	28	29
30	31					

AUGUST

S	M	T	W	T	F	S
		1	2	3	4	5
6	7	8	9	10	11	12
13	14	15	16	17	18	19
20	21	22	23	24	25	26
27	28	29	30	31		

SEPTEMBER

S	M	T	W	T	F	S
					1	2
3	4	5	6	7	8	9
10	11	12	13	14	15	16
17	18	19	20	21	22	23
24	25	26	27	28	29	30

OCTOBER

S	M	T	W	T	F	S
1	2	3	4	5	6	7
8	9	10	11	12	13	14
15	16	17	18	19	20	21
22	23	24	25	26	27	28
29	30	31				

NOVEMBER

S	M	T	W	T	F	S
			1	2	3	4
5	6	7	8	9	10	11
12	13	14	15	16	17	18
19	20	21	22	23	24	25
26	27	28	29	30		

DECEMBER

S	M	T	W	T	F	S
					1	2
3	4	5	6	7	8	9
10	11	12	13	14	15	16
17	18	19	20	21	22	23
24	25	26	27	28	29	30
31						

New Year's Day (January 1), Good Friday (April 14), Victoria Day (May 22), Canada Day (July 1), Labour Day (September 4), Thanksgiving (October 9), Christmas Day (December 25) and Boxing Day (December 26)

Other Holidays and Holy Days

Jewish Holy Days: Purim—March 6; Passover—April 15; Shavouth—June 4; Rosh Hashanah—September 25; Yom Kippur—October 4; Sukkoth—October 9; Simhat Torah—October 17; Hanukkah—December 18.
Muslim Holy Days: Ramadam—February 1; Id al-Fitr—March 3; Id al-Adha—May 10; New Year's Day—May 31; Ashura Day—June 9. (dates subject to confirmation by moon (crescent sighting))
St. Jean Baptiste Day (Quebec)—June 24.
Newfoundland Holidays (government and some collective agreements): St. Patrick's Day—March 20; St. George's Day—April 24; Discovery Day—June 26; Orangeman's Day—July 10.
Government and bank holidays: April 17 (Easter Monday), November 11 (Remembrance Day).